PLANT GROUPS

H Mukherjee

Formerly Head of the Department of Botany
City College, Rammohan College and
Anandamohan College, Kolkata, West Bengal

To be had of

New Central Book Agency (P) Ltd

LONDON
HYDERABAD ERNAKULAM BHUBANESWAR
NEW DELHI KOLKATA PUNE GUWAHATI

NCBA

REGD OFFICE
8/1 Chintamoni Das Lane, Kolkata 700 009, India
email: ncbapvtltd@eth.net

OVERSEAS
NCBA (UK) Ltd, 149 Park Avenue North, Northampton, NN3 2HY, UK
email: ncbauk@yahoo.com

EXPORT
NCBA Exports Pvt. Ltd, 212 Shahpur Jat, New Delhi 110 049
email: ncbaexports@ncbapvtltd.com

BRANCHES

2/27 Ansari Road, 1st Floor
Daryaganj, New Delhi 110 002
email: ncbadel@ncbapvtltd.com

House No. 3-1-315, 1st Floor
Nimboliadda, Kachiguda, **Hyderabad** 500 027
email: ncbahydb@ncbapvtltd.com

Shop Nos. 3 & 4, Vinayak Towers
681/B Budhwar Peth, Appa Balwant Chowk
Pune 411 002
email: ncbapune@ncbapvtltd.com

GSS Shopping Complex, 1st Floor
Opposite College Post Office, Convent Road
Ernakulam 682 035
0484-4021054 / 53

Shop No. 15, Bharati Towers, Ground Floor
Forest Park
Bhubaneswar 751 001
email: ncbabub@ncbapvtltd.com

Radhamayee Complex (Second Floor)
Opp. SBI, Panbazar, Jaswanta Road
Guwahati 781 001
email: ncbaguwahati@ncbapvtltd.com

PLANT GROUPS • H. Mukherjee

Ninth Edition: 1981

Reprinted: 1990, 1995, 1997, 1999, 2003, 2005, 2011, 2013, 2016

PUBLISHER
Central Educational Enterprises (P) Ltd
54B Patuatola Lane, Kolkata 700 009

PRINTER
New Central Book Agency (P) Ltd
Web-Offset Division, Dhulagarh, Sankrail, Howrah

ISBN: 978 81 7381 094 7

Price ₹ 650.00

PREFACE TO THE FIRST EDITION

PART I

The want of a text-book dealing with the life-histories of different plant groups was very keenly felt by the students and teachers alike for a considerable length of time. The present volume, it is hoped, will remove that difficulty as it covers the entire syllabus for B.A. & B.Sc. Pass course in Botany of all Indian Universities.

Authorities differ in regard to the classifications of plant groups, specially of the lower plants, but it would be out of place to discuss them here. I have simply endeavoured to arrange the materials under Thallophyta (Algae, Fungi, Bacteria and Lichens), Bryophyta (Liverworts, Anthocerotes and Mosses), Pteridophyta (Lycopods, Equisetums and Ferns) and Spermatophyta (Gymnosperms and Angiosperms) and the life-histories of these groups and the progress from the lower to higher forms form the principal features of this volume. The families of Angiosperms, however, have been treated separately in the Vol. II of this book.

I have freely consulted the books of Strasburger, Small, Smith, Holman & Robbins, Hill, Overholts & Popp, Smith, Gilbert, Evans *et al*, Coulter, Barnes & Cowles, Chamberlain, Coulter & Chamberlain, Pearson, Rendle, Campbell, Bower, Eames, Buller, Gwynne-Vaughan & Barnes, Bessey and others to all of whom I owe my deep sense of gratitude.

I am also indebted to my esteemed friend and old colleague Sri S. N. Banerji of the University College of Science & Technology, C. U., for his invaluable help and guidance in the preparation of this book. Lastly, it is my pleasant duty to owe acknowledgment to Sri A. K. Ganguli, once my pupil and now my colleague, for his constant help in the preparation of the manuscript, for proof-reading and valuable suggestions.

Any criticism or suggestion for improvement will be thankfully received.

PART II

The present volume is an outcome of the author's experience of teaching Systematic Botany for the last twenty-seven years. There

are several good Text-Books of Systematic Botany in the market, but, unfortunately, as all of them are written either by English or American authors, none of them is found suitable for the students of our Universities. Neither are our students familiar with the common English or American names, e.g., Buttercup, Foxglove, etc., nor is the flora of India in any way similar to that of Europe or America.

With this end in view, an attempt was made to write a Text-Book of Systematic Botany, which may be of some real help to our students, and the present volume is the result of that attempt. The book is intended for the students of Degree course. Outline classification of the systems of Linnaeus, Bentham and Hooker, and Engler have been dealt with and the latest phylogenetic system of Hutchinson has also been discussed. But the system of Bentham and Hooker has mainly been followed here as the great herbaria at the Kew Gardens, England and at the Royal Botanic Garden, Sibpur, Howrah, are kept according to this system. The families, which are prescribed for the B.Sc. (Pass) syllabus of the Calcutta University are marked with asterisks.

The outstanding feature of the book is that a key to genera has been given to each family so that students can readily identify common plants to their genera. The scientific as well as vernacular names of the plants have also been given. The use of scientific names cannot be dispensed with in a popular text-book as some of the vernacular names and even English names are often misleading and also a source of trouble and confusion. As for examples, one "Khet-papra" (*Mollugo stricta*) belongs to Focoideae and another "Khet-papra" (*Oldenlandia corymbosa*) belongs to Rubiaceae. Similarly, the names Chagalbati, Kalojira, Dudhilata, Brahmi, Sialkanta, Himsagar, Jhau, Debdaru, Madar, etc., are applicable to two or more different plants. The vernacular name of a plant may differ not only from district to district, but also from village to village, in the same province. Lilies embrace a large number of plants of Amaryllidaceae and Liliaceae. *Casuarina equisetifolia* is known by several English names—Swamp-oak, She-oak, Beef-wood tree and Whip tree. The so-called "Crotons" of our gardens and not Crotons at all. Some of them belong to another genus of Euphorbiaceae and others to Labiatae. In short, no pains have been spared to make it helpful to those for whom it is meant.

Last, but not the least of all, it is the author's pleasant duty to owe his deep sense to gratitu'e to his revered teacher Prof. Anutosh Das Gupta, M.A., Head of the Department of Botany, Bangabasi College, Calcutta, for his much esteemed help rendered in the preparation of the text. He is also grateful to his colleague Prof. Promothanath Goswami, M.Sc., for his advice, helpful criticism and preparing the manuscript.

City College, H. M.

Dated the 12th Feb, 1950.

PREFACE TO THE NINTH EDITION

At the outset, I apologise to my readers for not being able to bring out the book earlier, due to my indisposition for several months and also owing to a bereavement.

The present volume has been divided into *eleven sections* dealing with the different aspects of plants. The salient features are the incorporation of Plant Pathology and Palaeobotany, the inclusion of Bacteria and Viruses under Plant Pathology, and the substitution of the term Taxonomy for Systematic Botany.

I am thankful to Prof. A. K. Ghosh (C. U.), Dr. R. P. Purkayastha (C. U.), Dr. N. M. Datta (City College), Prof. A. K. Banerji (City College), Prof. N. C. Banerji (Rammohan College) and Prof. D. Gupta (Vidyasagar College) and also to Shri Biswanath Chakravarty, M.Sc., for active help and their valuable suggestions in the preparation of the book.

Lastly, I shall be failing in my duty if I do not convey my thanks to Shri J. N. Sen of New Central Book Agency who has encouraged me, in my present state of health, to revise the book.

DOLE PURNIMA

Calcutta, dated the 9th of March, 1982. H. M.

CONTENTS

SECTION I

ALGAE

INTRODUCTION

General consideration

Algae and Fungi represent the oldest and the most primitive type of plants characterized by the simplicity of structure of their vegetative bodies and of reproductive method. In size, Algae and Fungi range from microscopic forms to macroscopic ones, often attaining a length of about 25-30 metres. Algae and Fungi are further characterized by the lack of differentiation of plant body into roots, stems and leaves ; such an undifferentiated plant body is called a **thallus.** The thallus in the simplest case consists of a single cell, whereas the more complex forms are multicellular, which are either all alike or may show considerable differentiation of tissues. Some Algae and Fungi develop stem-like, leaf-like and root-like organs, but their structures are very simple as compared to those in higher plants. Other characters which separate Algae and Fungi from their allied groups are : (1) unicellular sex organs in the majority of cases, but when multicellular, all the cells form the gametes, *i.e.* there is no jacket of sterile cells surrounding the gametes, as in the case of bryophytes and pteridophytes ; (2) one-celled sporangia, but these are not so in the case of higher plants ; and (3) the zygote never forms a multicellular embryo while still enclosed within the female sex organ.

Algae and Fungi reproduce in a variety of ways. The unicellular forms usually reproduce by the method of cell division, giving rise to two daughter cells, each of which is complete by itself and represents a distinct individual. When multicellular, specialized cells are often delimited for the purpose of reproduction. These specialized cells are, in general, known as **spores,** each of which is capable of giving rise to a new plant. The spores are produced within sacs to which the general term **sporangia** is applied. But these methods of reproduction are *asexual* in nature. They also reproduce *sexually*. The sexual reproductive units are known as **gametes,** which are naked protoplasts formed within specialized cells known as **gametangia.** When the gametes fuse, they give rise to bodies known as **zygotes** which develop into new plants. The gametic union may be an union of two gametes of equal size (**isogamy**), or by the union of two motile gametes of unequal sizes (**anisogamy**), or by the union of a small motile and flagellate male gamete (**antherozoid** or **spermatozoid**) with a large, non-flagellate, passive female gamete (**oosphere** or **ovum**), the phenomenon being termed as **oogamy.** When the reproduction is oogamous, the gametangia are differentiated into **antheridium** (male) producing the antherozoids, and **oogonium** (female) giving rise to oosphere or ovum or, egg. The phenomenon of 'alternation of generations' has been definitely established in the thallophytes, though not well marked in all cases.

Differences between Algae and Fungi

(1) Algae possess the green colouring matter known as **chlorophyll** ; Fungi, on the other hand, never possess chlorophyll. (2) Algae are **autophytes,** *i.e.* they can prepare their own food from simple inorganic materials with the help of chlorophyll ; Fungi are **heterophytes,** *i.e.* they cannot prepare their own food, hence they must secure their food either directly or indirectly from other organisms and as such live as parasites or saprophytes. (3) Algae cannot live in darkness, as light is absolutely necessary for the preparation of their food ; Fungi can live in light as well as in darkness (4) The vegetative body of Algae is composed of parenchyma tissue ; whereas the body of Fungi is composed of plectenchyma made up of fungal tissue. (5) The cellwalls of Algae are mainly composed of cellulose, but those of Fungi mostly of chitin or fungus cellulose.

The algae constitute an important group of thallophytes. They all possess chlorophyll and are, therefore, capable of manufacturing their own food. The chlorophyll, though invariably present, is not always pure green in colour, because the green colour is sometimes masked by the presence of other pigments, such as blue, golden-brown, red, etc., and on this colour depends the classification of the group. The habitats of the algae are very diverse ; some live in freshwater, some in brackish water, some are marine, some of them grow on rocks and walls or on barks of trees, while others live as **endophytes** within the tissues of certain higher plants. In a few cases, as in Lichens, the algae live in symbiotic association with fungi. The cellwall is usually composed of cellulose, and the reserve food materials are starch, oil and various other substances.

Origin of Algae and evolution among them

The origin of the various groups of present-day algae is supposed to have taken place from some unicellular non-flagellate aquatic protista. From this hypothetical ancestor there appeared the diverse groups polyphylectically. The oldest-known fossil records of algae that could have been traced so far, disclose the presence of some members of the Myxophyceae on the Proterozoic rocks. Cytologically also, excepting the bacteria, the class Myxophyceae, represents the most primitive group of living organisms, as no one member of this group possesses a well-organized nucleus, nor is there any trace of any other mode of reproduction other than the vegetative. With these facts in view, the Myxophyceae may be considered to have come first of all the algal lines. Some workers like Fritsch (1935), however, regard the Myxophyceae as the most reduced and consequently, the most advanced group among the algae.

Whatever might be the most primitive algal member, the class Chlorophyceae appears to have been derived from some *Chlamydomonas*-like flagellate unicellular ancestor. Each class of algae is characterized by the constancy in position of its flagella* in zoospores or gametes. From this hypothetical ancestral stock a progressive evolution took place in four different directions. One of these lines of development terminated in plants like *Volvox* having a motile colony. In another direction the colonies were non-motile, as in *Hydrodictyon* and *Pediastrum*. The third series gave rise to plant bodies with tubular or siphonaceous thalli, as may be found in *Vaucheria*. As a result of evolution in the last direction, there appeared multicellular filamentous forms, which were at first unbranched, as in *Ulothrix, Spirogyra, Zygnema*, and *Oedogonium*, and subsequently the branched ones, as in *Cladophora, Chaetophora, Draparnaldia, Draparnaldiopsis, Stigeoclonium, Bryopsis,* and others. It is believed that from some members of this filamentous line of Chlorophyceae the bryophytes originated.

Because of the fact that the Phaeophyceae possess motile reproductive cells, it is thought that the group has arisen from some flagellate unicellular brown algae, in a line parallel with the Chlorophyceae. It is of interest to note, however, that though the class has attained a very high degree of specialization in the body organization, it has not apparently been able to give rise to any higher category of plants.

The class Rhodophyceae is rather unique among the algae in several respects, and resembles no other algal class excepting the Myxophyceae. Members of both these two classes lack any type of motile flagellate cells. Further, the nature of pigments is also allied in them, for *phycocyanin* which is universally present in the Myxophyceae, is also found in some Rhodophyceae, and the phycoerythrin-like red pigment is also present in some blue-green algae. The red algae also represent a very ancient algal line, and its fossil records can be traced as far back as to the Ordovician. This group appears to have originated independently from some non-flagellate

* There are two types of flagella generally met with in the different groups of algae : one is known as the *tinsel type,* while the other is referred to as the *whiplash type*. In the former case, the flagellum is provided with two rows of cilia or *mastigonenes,* while the latter one is without any such mastegonene.

unicellular form. Some workers believe that the Ascomycetes, among the fungi, have originated from the Rhodophyceae.

Range of structure

The vegetative bodies in Algae in different classes show a gradual progression from simple to more complex forms and the whole range of structure may be grouped under the following heads :

(*a*) **Motile unicellular type.** The thallus is unicellular, more or less spherical or pear-shaped in form and flagellate. The flagella, two in number, are attached to the narrowed anterior end of the plant body. The nucleus occupies the middle region of the protoplast and the chromatophores, when present, either lie along the sides or occupy the posterior region of the cell. In certain cases, special rigid envelope with an aperture for the emergence of the flagella and separated from the cell proper by space can be seen. These forms are called *encapsuled* forms, (e.g. *Chrysococcus*). Sometimes the thalli are colourless due to absence of chromatophores.

(*b*) **Motile colonial type.** In this group are to be found those forms in which the individual flagellate cells become aggregated together within a mucous envelope to form a spherical grouping or colony. The cells are all alike in form, complete in themselves and retain their motile character in the vegetative condition. The movement of the entire colony is brought about by the simultaneous activity of their flagella, (e.g. *Volvox*).

(*c*) **Palmelloid type.** In this type, during the vegetative phase, the individual cells are without flagella so that the motility disappears and the daughter cells produced by vegetative divisions remain embedded within a common gelatinous envelope, formed by gelatinization of the parent cellwall. This **'Palmelloid stage'** may be temporary, since sooner or later, the cells may develop flagella and resume active movement, (e.g. *Chlamydomonas*). It may also be of a permanent nature characterized by the loss of motility during the vegetative phase. In this case the reproductive cells are flagellate and motile, (*e.g. Tetraspora*).

(*d*) **Dendroid type.** This type of thallus is similar to that of the palmelloid type but the mucilage is produced locally, usually at the base of the cell, (e.g. *Prasinocladus*).

(*e*) **Coccoid type.** In this group the thalli are characterized by motionless unicellular individuals which become motile only during reproduction, (e.g. *Chlorococcus*). The power of dividing vegetatively is lost in this case and the reproduction takes place by the formation of zoospores.

(*f*) **Filamentous type.** The thalli are characterized by the type of cell division, called **vegetative division.** During the process, a parent protoplast ordinarily divides within the original cellwall and the two units of the protoplast are simply separated by the formation of a strip of membrane (septum) which is jointed laterally to the cellwall of the parent cell. Repeated vegetative division in one plane results in a filamentous thallus, (e.g. *Ulothrix*, *Spirogyra*, *Oedogonium*, etc.). If the septa are formed along two planes and at right angles to one another, a flattened leaf-like thallus develops, (e.g. *Ulva*). The branching habit in a filamentous thallus is obtained due to formation of lateral outgrowths of more or less numerous cells and in which septa-formation takes place in transverse plane as in the main axis, (e.g. *Cladaphora* and many other Chlorophyceae).

(*g*) **Heterotrichous type.** This type represents the most highly evolved filamentous plant body. The thallus is characterized by having two distinct well-differentiated parts, namely, (*i*) a prostrate creeping system of the branching filaments which are attached to the sub-stratum, and (*ii*) an erect system consisting of one or more branched filaments that trail out in water, (e.g. *Chaetophora*, *Draparnaldiopsis*, *Bryopsis*, *Batrachospermum*, etc.).

(*h*) **Siphonaceous type.** This group is characterized by considerable extense of the thalli without any septation. Thus, a large multinucleate **coenocytic** structure originate, (e.g. *Vaucheria*, *Botrydium*, etc.).

(*i*) **Complex type.** In this group the thalli range from more or less compact pseudo-parenchymatous bodies to true parenchymatous bodies of well-differentiated macroscopic forms as evidenced in Phaeophyceae and Rhodophyceae.

Evolutionary tendencies. Assuming flagellated origin of algae, it is conceivable that motile unicellular organisation is most primitive in nature. By aggregation of numerous unicells in a common envelop, motile colonial type has been originated. In another line of evolution by loss of motility, palmelloid type and coccoid type develop which gave rise to dendroid type by basal gelatinous encapsulation. In another line from the unicellular form nuclear division without the formation of cellwall originated the siphonaceous form. From the unicellular type following nuclear division and formation of septa the filamentous form has been originated. On the basis of distribution of labour heterotrichous form with prostrate and projecting system appeared which ultimately led to the more complex thallus organisation.

Reproduction

The various methods of reproduction in Algae can be grouped under the following categories :

Vegetative. In unicellular forms, it takes place by cell divisions and the daughter cells, thus produced, function as new individuals. In colonial forms, two individual colonies may arise by mere splitting of the mature colony, (e.g. Volvocales). In filamentous types, vegetative reproduction takes place by fragmentation of the threads and each broken part gives rise to a new individual. Vegetative reproduction is found in various classes of Algae and is the characteristic feature of the Myxophyceae* where complex specialized structures are to be found.

Asexual. This is the commonest method of reproduction in which spores, one (e.g. *Oedogonium*) to several hundred, (e.g. *Cladophora*), are formed within specialized cells, called **sporangia** which may not be morphologically different from the vegetative cells. The spores may be naked, motile and with two to four flagella (**zoospores**), or may be non-motile (**aplanospores**). The aplanospores are modified zoospores which have lost their power of movement and each is surrounded by a definite wall which is distinct from the parent cellwall. An aplanospore with greatly thickened wall is a **hypnospore.** The zoospores resemble morphologically the unicellular members of the Volvocales and from the standpoint of phylogeny they show reversion to primitive ancestral flagellate condition.

Sexual. This type of reproduction is characterized by the fusion of two gametes and its different methods are as follows :

(*a*) **Isogamy.** In this case two gametes of the same morphological identity, flagellate or non-flagellate, fuse to form **zygote.** Majority of isogamous Algae are dioecious, since the fusing gametes come from different individuals of opposite strains.

(*b*) **Anisogamy.** It is a case of modified isogamy and the fusing flagellate gametes show slight difference in their behaviour, one being more passive than the other, (e.g. Chlamydomonadaceae). In some cases the fusing gametes are unequal in size. This is known as **heterogamy.**

(*c*) **Oogamy.** This type of reproduction represents the highest stage in the series. Here, a large motionless, non-flagellate female gamete, called **oosphere** or **egg,** is fertilized by a much smaller flagellate, active male gamete, called **antherozoid** (e.g. Volvocales, Ectocarpales). Both types of gametes may be produced on the same (*monoecism*) or different individuals (*dioecism*). Usually, the oosphere or egg is retained within the female sex organ, the **oogonium,** where it receives the male gamete. It is, therefore, a receiving cell. The male gametes, produced within the male sex organ, the **antheri-**

* Discussed in detail under **Myxophyceae.**

dium, are ultimately discharged and one or more of them enter the oogonium, through an aperture on its wall. In Rhodophyceae the oogamous reproduction is of a specialized type. The male gametes are non-flagellate, therefore, non-motile and passively carried to the female sex organ by current.

Life cycles

The type of life cycles in algae can be conveniently grouped into two broad categories, namely, (1) an alternation of haploid generations in which a diploid generation is absent, and (2) an alternation of distinct haploid and diploid generations.

Those forms in which regular alternating haploid and diploid generations are absent can be divided into two groups : (*a*) the oogonium is haploid and (*b*) the oogonium is diploid. In the former case, the vegetative body of the plant is a gametophyte. The diploid phase, resulting from the sexual union, is restricted only to the zygote. The diploid nucleus of the zygote, at the time of germination, undergoes meiosis producing four haploid nuclei, from which usually four asexual reproductive units are formed, each of which is capable of producing a new haploid plant. This type of life cycle may be found in the majority of Chlorophyceae and possibly in all Xanthophyceae and Chrysophyceae. In case, where the oogonium is diploid, the vegetative body of the alga is a sporophyte and is evidently in the diploid condition. Meiosis takes place during the formation of gametes which represent only the haploid phase. These gametes soon fuse in pairs to form diploid zygotes, each of which is capable of giving rise to a new diploid plant. This type of life cycle can be met with in some members of Siphonales and all Bacillariophyceae.

The cases where an alternation of haploid and diploid generations takes place can be grouped under the following categories :

(*a*) **Isomorphic alternation.** This type is characterized by the presence of two individuals which are morphologically identical, but one of them is haploid (gametophyte) producing gametes and the other is diploid (sporophyte) producing spores. Meiosis takes place in the diploid generation, during the formation of spores, and each of the spores on germination produces a haploid generation. Gametes, formed from this haploid generation, unite and give rise to the diploid generation, as found in some Chlorophyceae (e.g. Cladophorales, Ulvaceae), Phaeophyceae (e.g. Dictyotales, Cutleriales) and a number of Rhodophyceae. Some members of the Rhodophyceae are very peculiar in that they are **diplobiontic,** in which diploid generations alternate with a haploid one.

(*b*) **Heteromorphic alternation.** This type of life cycle is characterized by an alternation of haploid and diploid generations which are morphologically dissimilar. Usually, the diploid plant (sporophyte) is much larger than the small, few-celled, haploid individual (gametophyte), as can be found in some members of Ectocarpales, Laminariales, etc. This type of alternation is quite similar to that found in higher cryptogamic plants (e.g. ferns and their allies).

CLASSIFICATION OF ALGAE

A. Fritsch's Classification

The algae have broadly been divided by F. F. Fritsch in 1935 into eleven *Classes* according to their colour.

I. **Chlorophyceae** or green algae. e.g. *Chlamydomonas*, *Volvox*, *Oedogonium*, *Spirogyra*, *Vaucheria*, *Chara*, etc.

II. **Xanthophyceae** or yellow—green algae e.g. *Botrydium.*

*III. **Chrysophyceae.**

IV. **Bacillariophyceae** or golden-brown algae e.g. Diatom.

*V. **Cryptophyceae.**

*VI. **Dinophyceae.**

*VII. **Chloromonadineae.**

*VIII. **Eugleninae.**

*IX. **Phaeophyceae** or brown algae, e.g. *Fctocarpus*, *Laninaria*, *Dictyota*, *Fucus*, etc.

X. **Rhodophyceae** or red algae e.g. *Batrachospermun*, *Polysiphonia*, etc.

XI. **Myxophyceae** or *blue-green* algae, e.g. *Oscillatonia*, *Nostoc*, etc.

B. Smith's Classification

In 1955 G. M. Smith has classified algae into seven *Divisions*, each of which contains one or more *Classes*. A brief account of this classification is given below :

I. **Cyanophyta** or blue green algae-inhabitants of moist soil and rocks, fresh water or saline water ; unicellular or colonial ; plastids not well-defined ; presence of nucleoplasm in the centre of the cell and chromoplasm in the periphery ; nucleus is primitive ; *phycocyanin* is the chief pigment but sometimes *phycoerythrin* may be present ; sexual reproduction and flagellated cells are always absent ; reproduction is vegetative or asexual by resting spores ; glycogen is the reserve food. Examples : *Oscillatoria*, *Nostoc*, *Gleocapsa*, etc.

* It is not dealt in the present volume.

II. **Chlorophyta** or green algae—found in fresh water or saline water ; unicellular, multicellular or colonial ; cells flagellated or non-flagellated ; reproduction is asexual or sexual ; presence of chlorophyll, carotin and xanthophyll like higher plants ; reserve food is starch. Examples : *Spirogyra*, *Oedogonium*, *Ulothrix*, *Vaucheria*, *Chara*, etc.

* III. **Euglenophyta**—found in fresh water or stagnant water or on moist soil ; cells flagellated or naked ; coloured plastids prominent ; cell divisions longitudinal ; reserve food is *paramyleum* (a kind of carbohydrate). Example : *Euglena*.

* IV. **Pyrophyta**—chiefly marine ; unicellular ; presence of two unequal flagella ; yellowish green or yellowish brown pigments present ; sexual reproduction is rare ; reserve food is starch or oil.

V. **Chrysophyta**—Chiefly consists of Diatoms ; terrestrial, fresh water or saline water ; flagellated or non-flagellated ; unicellular or multicellular, colonial or filamentous ; cellwall made of pectin with deposition of silica particles on the surface ; of the pigments *carotin* and *Xanthophyll* are present in abundance ; special method of sexual reproduction ; oil and *leucosin* (a complex carbohydrate) are reserve food.

The Division consists of three classes, of which **Bacillariophyceae** is the main ; plants consisting of this class are known as **Diatoms** or golden brown algae ; the yellow pigment *diatomin* is always present with chlorophyll.

VI. **Phaeophyta** or brown algae—chiefly marine ; plant body large and complicated by the presence of pigment like *fucoxanthin* and *phycophene* ; both sexual and asexual reproduction take place ; sexual reproduction is isogamous and oogamous carbohydrate and oil are reserve food. Examples : *Ectocarpus*, *Fucus*, etc.

VII. **Rhodophyta** or red algae-chiefly marine ; plant body is very complex ; main pigment is *phycoerythrin* ; sexual reproduction is oogamous ; male gametes known as *spermatia*, are non-flagellated ; reserve food is *Florideam starch*. Examples ; *Batrachospermum*, *Polysiphonia*, etc.

N. B. Fritch's classification of algae has been followed in this book.

* It is not dealt in the present volume.

CHAPTER I

CHLOROPHYCEAE

Salient features

The Chlorophyceae. or the green algae, are characterized in having grassgreen-coloured chloroplasts containing the photosynthetic pigments, chlorophyll *a*, chlorophyll *b*, carotenes and xanthophylls, of which the first two predominate over the others. There are several xanthophylls in the chloroplasts which are not found in other algae, and of these, *lutin* is found in abundance. Food reserves are stored in the form of starch, whose formation is intimately associated with pyrenoids. Motile reproductive bodies, zoospores and gametes, are usually associated with two or four whip-like flagella of equal length.

General characters

The members of this group are found both in fresh and salt waters. The majority of them occur as submerged, freshwater plants being attached to submerged rocks, wood-pieces and similar other objects, but may also float on the surface of stagnant water forming green scums. Quite a large number of species grow on moist soil, rocks and cliffs, damp wood-work, barks of trees and even on snow and ice. A few species are internal parasites on land plants, or may occur as epiphytes upon land animals.

In general, the members of Chlorophyceae show great variations in form and structure of their vegetative body, ranging from simple unicellular types to typical multicellular filaments through intermediate colonial forms. When multicellular, the number of cells may be definite or indefinite. But when indefinite, the cells of the thallus may be arranged in irregular masses, in filaments, in sheets, or in solid or hollow cylinders. The unicellular forms may be non-motile or motile by flagella. Typically, the plant body is filamentous and it occupies a prominent place among most of the Orders of the green algae.

With the exception of a few primitive unicellular genera, the protoplast of Chlorophyceae is surrounded by a distinct cellwall which often becomes considerably thick. The cellwall consists of at least two concentric portions : (*a*) an inner homogeneous or concentrically stratified layer, mostly or wholly made up of cellulose, and (*b*) an outer pectose layer which in some genera may be chitinized or impregnated with lime.

The protoplast is well-differentiated into cytoplasm, nuclei and chloroplasts. It mostly occurs as the primordial utricle surrounding a conspicuous central vacuole. But, in some cases, several vacuoles may be present instead. When the cells are flagellate, as in the unicellular and some of the colonial forms, there are usually two small **contractile vacuoles** near the base of the flagella. They expand and contract alternately and are regarded as excretory organs. In some cases, the sap of the vacuole becomes coloured due to anthocyanin. There may be one or more nuclei in each protoplast, and these are found either in the primordial utricle or are suspended in a mass of cytoplasm at the centre of the vacuole by means of cytoplasmic threads. The nucleus possesses a distinct nuclear membrane, one or more nucleoli and a characteristic chromatin reticulum. The nuclear division is mitotic. The chloroplasts are most characteristic and are of various forms. They may be cup-shaped, laminate, entire or perforate, disciform, peripheral in position, and are mostly with one or more pyrenoids. Each pyrenoid has a central proteinaceous portion which is surrounded by plates of starch. The food reserves are usually in the form of starch, but fats and oils are found in some cases.

Within the chloroplasts the photosynthetic (chlorophll *a* and chlorophyll *b*) and other pigments (carotenes : α-carotene and β-carotene ; xanthophylls : lutin, zeaxanthine, viola-xanthine and neoxanthine) become associated together, but the chlorophylls predominate over the others. The amount of the pigment also varies from species to species, and according to their proportions, typically grass-green to almost light-green Chlorophyceae are found in nature. In some genera, the vegetative cells and the zygotes also contain a red pigment, **haematochrome,** which masks other pigments. Haematochrome is a carotenoid pigment. Sometimes the colour of the cells in certain species is modified by the presence of **anthocyanin** pigments of the cell sap.

The motile vegetative and reproductive cells are provided with flagella inserted at the anterior end of the cell. They are usually of equal length. Located near the insertion of the flagella there is an orange-red to reddish-brown circular or oval spot, called the **eye-spot** or **stigma,** which is regarded as a photo-receptive organelle and is supposed to control the directive movement of the flagella.

Reproduction

The methods of reproduction in green algae are well-advanced and show great variations. All the three principal methods of reproduction, as detailed below, are found in this group.

Vegetative reproduction takes place usually by the process of fragmentation. Among filamentous forms, fragmentation is either due to accidental breaking of a filament or certain cells of the filament may produce spores or gametes, so that short sections of the filament become ultimately separated from one another resulting in the increase of the number of filaments. The colonial genera reproduce vegetatively by accidental fragmentation of the colony. Among unicellular forms, vegetative reproduction always takes place by cell division, which, in multicellular forms, becomes a method for the growth of the thallus.

Asexual reproduction usually takes place by the production of spores within metamorphozed vegetative cells. The spores may vary in number, from one to many in each cell and may be either naked and motile or provided with a distinct wall. The motile spores are known as **zoospores,** which are provided with two, four or more flagella of equal length at the anterior end. The liberation of zoospores usually takes place by the formation of a pore in the wall of the mother cell, or by the breaking or gelatinization of the sporangial wall. The non-motile spores are known as **aplanospores,** whose walls are quite distinct from the wall of the mother cell. These are in reality modified zoospores which have secreted wall around them prior to the liberation from the mother cell. The aplanospores are liberated by the rupture or decay of the wall of the mother cell. The mother cell producing these spores is termed a **sporangium,** which, in most cases, is not morphologically different from the vegetative cells. Sometimes, the wall of the aplanospore becomes greatly thickened and forms a **hypnospore.** Asexual reproduction also takes place by the formation of **akinetes.** (Fig. 1). In such cases, a sin-

Fig. 1. Formation of akinete in Chlorophyceae.

gle non-motile spore is formed within the sporangium whose wall is not distinct from that of the spore. But, the vegetative cells often become very much thick-walled containing abundant food reserve to form akinete-like structures for tiding the alga over unfavourable periods.

The sexual reproduction in Chlorophyceae ranges in complexity from the simplest to the most complex sex structures. The methods of gametic union may be arranged in an evolutionary series, and are noticeable from the most primitive to the most highly advanced forms with specialized and differentiated sex structures.

In the simplest case, sexual union is by **isogamy,** *i.e.* gametic union takes place between morphologically identical flagellate or non-flagellate gametes. *Ulothrix* is a familiar example in which there is a fusion of a flagellate gamete with another gamete of identical size and structure. This is known as **planogamic union.** Sometimes (as in *Spirogyra*, *Zygnema*, etc.) there is union of gametes without flagella, and this type of isogamy is known as **aplanogamy.** In some cases, the plant reproduces by **anisogamy,** in which gametic union is effected between two flagellate gametes of unequal sizes, as in *Caulerpa*. The most advanced method of reproduction is **oogamy.** In this case, gametic union takes place between a small flagellate, motile, active male gamete and a large non-flagellate, non-motile, passive female gamete as in *Vaucheria*, *Oedogonium*, etc. The male gametangium producing the antherozoids is known as the **antheridium,** and is usually a distinct structure easily recognizable from the vegetative cells. Each antheridium produces one or more antherozoids. In most cases the oosphere or egg is produced singly within the female gametangium, known as the **oogonium,** which differs morphologically from the vegetative cells. The **zygote** formed as a result of sexual union, usually after a period of rest, gives rise to one or more new plants. Many species of Chlorophyceae are **homothallic,** *i.e.* **monoecious.** In such cases, gametes derived from a single parent plant unite in pairs. Other species are **heterothallic,** *i.e.* **dioecious.** Here gametes of different parentage fuse in pairs.

There are various instances in which **parthenospores** (or **azygospores** or **aboospores** or **azygotes**) are formed directly from the gametes in the absence of sexual union.

Classification

The Chlorophyceae are divided into nine Orders (Fritsch, 1935*) which may be distinguished as follows.

1. **Volvocales :**—Unicellular or colonial ; motile throughout life or form sedentary colonies which readily revert to a motile condition ; reproduce asexually as well as sexually ; mainly freshwater. Examples—*Chlamydomonas, Sphaerella, Pandorina, Eudorina, Volvox*, etc.

2. **Chlorococcales :**—Unicellular or colonial ; non-motile in the vegetative condition ; reproduced by zoospores or aplanospores ; almost exclusively freshwater. Examples—*Hydrodictyon*, *Pediastrum*, etc.

3. **Ulotrichales :**—Filamentous, simple and unbranched or cellular expanse with small cells ; chloroplasts parietal, axial or stellate ; sometimes filaments simple and with large multinucleate

* Fritsch, F. E. (1935), The Structure and Reproduction of Algae.

cell ; mostly isogamous ; most species freshwater, some are marine. Examples—*Ulothrix*, *Ulva*, etc.

4. **Cladophorales** :—Simple or branched, filamentous with cells containing two to many nuclei and usually with elaborate large chloroplasts ; mostly isogamous ; freshwater and marine.—Example—*Cladophora*.

5. **Chaetophorales** :—Filamentous and sharply differentiated into prostrate and erect portions (**heterotrichous**) ; erect portion often reduced and the prostrate portion often forming discoid expanse ; hairs of diverse type are often present ; mostly isogamous and freshwater. Examples—*Chaetophora*, *Enteromorpha*, *Draparnaldiopsis*, *Trentepohlia*, *Coleophaete*, *Protococcus*, etc.

6. **Oedogoniales** :—Simple or branched, filamentous ; zoospores multiflagellate ; oogamous ; cell divisions characterized by intercalation of strips of membrane between two parts of the mother cell ; entirely freshwater. Example—*Oedogonium*.

7. **Conjugales** :—Unicellular or colonial (generally filamentous) with elaborate chloroplasts ; motile gametes unknown ; reproduction by vegetative cell division or by conjugation of amoeboid gametes ; exclusively freshwater. Examples—*Spirogyra*, *Zygnema*, *Cosmarium*, *Closterium*, etc.

8. **Siphonales** :—Filamentous ; without septa or elaborately differentiated ; all parts coenocytic ; chloroplasts numerous and discoid ; sexual reproduction mainly isogamous, sometimes oogamous, unknown in many cases ; mostly marine. Examples—*Vaucheria*, *Caulerpa*, *Bryopsis*, etc.

9. **Charales** :—Thallus well-differentiated into nodes and internodes ; internodes sometimes corticated ; branches of limited growth in whorls ; chloroplasts numerous and discoid ; cells usually uninucleate ; reproduction vegetative and sexual with elaborate oogonia and antheridia ; germination of zygote indirect ; freshwater and brackish water. Examples—*Chara*, *Nitella*, etc.

Alternation of generations

Some Chlorophyceae show regular alternation of similar haploid and diploid generations, but in great majority the plant body is haploid with the zygote representing the only diploid phase. In the simplest case, as illustrated by *Chlamydomonas*, the life cycle consists of alternation of unicellular haploid and diploid phases. This alternation is, however, not obligatory in the sense that the haploid phase will always give rise to the diploid phase, because there may be a formation of haploid individuals in succession before the formation of a diploid phase. On the contrary, it is obligatory in the sense that the diploid phase always gives rise to a haploid one. This represents, therefore, the most primitive type of life cycle. Starting from this primitive condition, one finds an evolution of multicellular thalli in either phases (haploid, as in *Spirogyra*, *Oedogonium*, etc., or diploid, as in *Codium*) of the life cycle. In such cases, there is an alternation of a multicellular haploid generation with an unicellular diploid phase, or a multicellular diploid generation with an unicellular haploid phase. Lastly, there may be an alternation between multicellular haploid and diploid generations (as in Cladophoraceae, Ulvaceae, Chaetophoraceae). The two generations may be quite identical (**isomorphic**) with each other, or they are morphologically different (**heteromorphic**).

ORDER 1. **VOLVOCALES**

Unicellular or colonial ; motile throughout life or form sedentary colonies which readily revert to a motile condition ; reproduce asexually as well as sexually ; mainly freshwater.

CHLAMYDOMONAS

(Fam. CHLAMYDOMONADACEAE)

Chlamydomonas is a widely distributed free-swimming, green alga which inhabits stagnant water or damp soils.

The common Indian species of *Chlamydomonas* are *C. atactogama*, *C. gloesgamia*, *C. intermedia* and *C. reinpardi*.

Vegetative body (Fig. 2)

The plant body is unicellular and the cells are either spherical, ellipsoidal or pyriform (pear-shaped). The protoplast is surrounded by a definite layer of cellulose wall, and in some cases an additional external gelatinous sheath may be present. Each cell is provided with two **flagella,** which are inserted at its anterior end and are very close to each other. In some cases, the cellwall is provided with a distinct papilla at the anterior end. The major portion of the protoplast is usually occupied by a single, massive, cup-shaped chloroplast. There is a single nucleus which is, in most cases, embedded in a colourless cytoplasm filling the cup. Sometimes the chloroplast may be star-shaped or laminate in form. Usually, a single pyrenoid is present in each

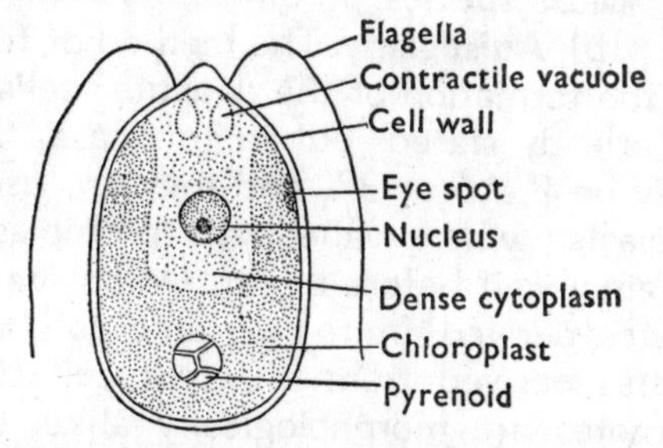

Fig. 2. *Chlamydomonas*, A vegetative cell.

chloroplast, but in some cases two or more pyrenoids may be present, or they may be totally absent. Typically, there are two **contractile vacuoles** at the anterior end of the protoplast occupying the bases of the flagella, but the number and position of these vacuoles may vary in different species. There is a photo-receptive organ, the **'eyespot'**, which lies at the anterior end and is supposed to be concerned in directing the movement of the flagella.

Reproduction

Chlamydomonas reproduces by three methods :

(a) **Isogamy.** During asexual reproduction the protoplast of each vegetative cell divides longitudinally into two protoplasts, which again divide and re-divide forming 4 or 8 daughter protoplasts. Each daughter protoplast then secretes a wall around it and develops a pair of flagella at its anterior end. The ceilwall of the parent cell ruptures or undergoes gelatinization and thereby the daughter cells are liberated.

Very rarely the protoplast of a vegetative cell contracts, rounds up and forms an **aplanospore** after secreting a wall of its own.

When *Chlamydomonas* grows on damp soil, the daughter cells formed by the successive divisions of the protoplast do not develop their flagella but remain embedded in a common gelatinous matrix, formed by the gelatinization of the cellwall of the parent cell. This is usually followed by division and re-division of the daughter cells by the subsequent gelatinization of their walls forming colonies consisting of hundreds of cells embedded in a common matrix. This is known as the **'palmella stage'** (Fig. 3B) resembling the genus *Palmella*, a green alga forming amorphous colonies. If these colonies be flooded with water, each daughter cell may develop its flagella and may swim away from the colony. Sometimes these daughter cells may develop into resting spores, called **akinetes.**

Most species of *Chlamydomonas* reproduce sexually.

(b) **Anisogamy.** The method of formation of gametes is similar to the formation of the daughter cells from a vegetative protoplast as arleady stated. But in this case, the number of daughter cells may be 8, 16 or 32, and they are usually naked, biflagellate protoplasts ; when walled, the protoplast of each gamete leaves its original wall before union. Union may take place between the gametes derived from the same cell (**homothallic**), or between gametes derived from different cells (**heterothallic**). Where fuisng gametes are morphologically alike (**isogametes**), the process is called isogamy.

During the process, two isogametes meet each other and they are entangled with their flagella. Then the gametes fuse end to end or side to side and a quadriflagellate structure is formed. Then the cytoplasm and nuclei fuse to form a zygote. **Isogamy** is found in *Chlamydomonas moewusii*.

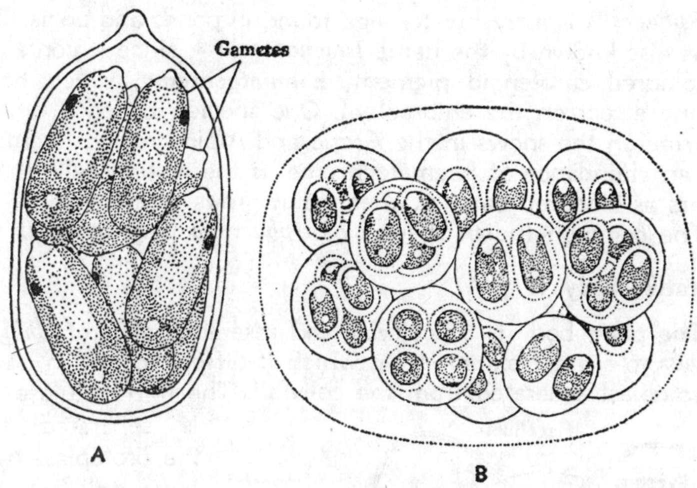

Fig. 3. *Chlamydomonas.*
A, Formation of gametes within the parent cell ;
B, Palmella stage.

Anisogamy is evident in *Chlamydomonas braunii*, where the smaller gamete or microgamete is more active than the macrogamete—the larger gamete. The two gametes unite by their anterior side. Then their flagella disappear. The fusion of cytoplasm along with nucleus takes place and zygote is formed.

(c) **Oogamy.** *Chlamydomonas coccifera* shows oogamous type of sexual reproduction. In this case, the female gamete or macrogamete is larger. During its formation, the vegetative cell enlarges and its flagella disappear. The male gametes or spermatoziods are smaller and elongated. Each of them bear two flagella. The male gamate fuses with the female gamete to form zygote.

The **zygote** after its formation, it comes to rest and secretes a wall around it. The wall of the zygote is thick and shows surface reticulations, or may bear spiny projections. Before germination the diploid nucleus of the zygote undergoes reduction division, typically forming four haploid nuclei. By cleavage process uninucleate protoplasts are formed following reduction division and each protoplast is metamorphozed into a biflagellate daughter cell. These four cells are finally liberated by the rupture of the zygote wall.

SPHAERELIA

(Fam. CHLAMYDOMONADACEAE)

Sphaerella is a freshwater alga found in ponds and pools. This alga is also known by the name *Haematococcus*, since it contains a red-coloured carotenoid pigment, **haematochrome,** which has a masking effect on the chlorophyll. One species, called *S. nivalis*, occurring on the snows in the Arctic and Alpine regions, contains such an abundance of haematochrome in the resting cells that it appears as bloodred patches wherever it grows.

The common Indian species of *Sphaerella* is *S. lacustris*.

Vegetative body (Fig. 4)

The plant body is unicellular and resembles that of *Chlamydomonas* to a great extent, from which it differs mainly in having its protoplast separated from the cellwall. The thin cellulose wall is separated from the protoplast by an inner wall, which is thick and mucilagenous, and pierced by a number of delicate cytoplasmic strands (**pseudopodia**). The large hemispherical, hollow solitary chloroplast lies embedded in the cytoplasm. The nucleus lies in the central region of the colourless cytoplasm. There are a number of pyrenoids, numerous, irregularly scattered contractile vacuoles, and an eyespot. The haematochrome granules are also numerous, on whose relative proportion depends the colour of a par-

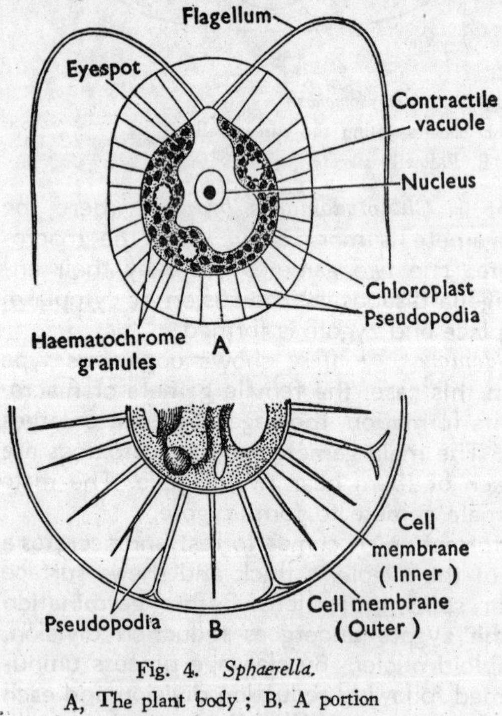

Fig. 4. *Sphaerella.*
A, The plant body ; B, A portion of the same (magnified).

ticular cell. At the anterior end there are two long flagella. By withdrawing these flagella the alga generally forms a **cyst**, and in this encysted condition it is commonly found.

Reproduction

Sphaerella reproduces both asexually and sexually.

During asexual reproduction longitudinal division of the protoplast of the motile cell takes place, but typical, zoospores are not formed. These blocks of protoplast finally come out of the mother cell, and each one develops into a new *Sphaerella* plant.

The protoplasmic contents of an encysted cell sometimes undergo repeated divisions thereby giving rise to the *palmella stage*. These resting cells produce minute, motile gametes, which unite in pairs to give rise to the zygote. As in *Chlamydomonas*, by the reduction division of the zygote nucleus and subsequent cleavages, uninucleate protoplasts are formed. These blocks are ultimately converted into biflagellate cells, which finally get liberated by the rupture of the zygote wall.

PANDORINA

(Fam. CHLAMYDOMONADACEAE)

Pandorina is a widely distributed freshwater alga.

The common Indian species of *Pandorina* is *P. morum*.

Vegetative body (Fig. 5)

The plant body is a free-swimming **coenobium**, *i.e.* a colony of a definite number of cells, arranged in a specific manner. The hollow, spherical coenobium is made up of four to thirty-two biflagellate cells, lying closely fitted together and embedded within a mucilagenous matrix of homogeneous consistency. In some cases, an additional watery outer sheath may be present. The cells in

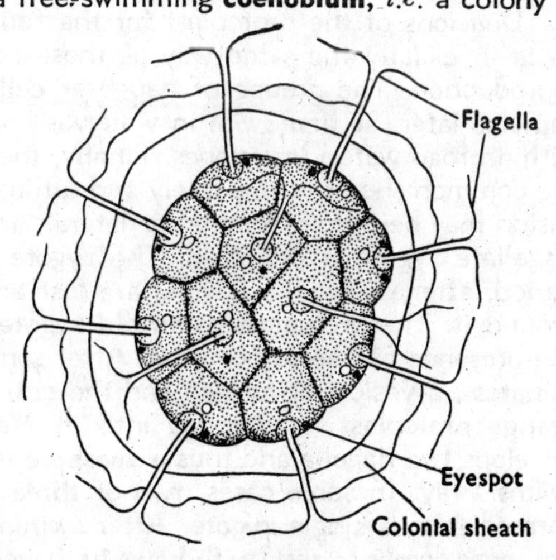

Fig. 5. *Pandorina*.

a colony are generally so closely pressed that they become laterally flattened exception being found in one species. A vegetative cell is usually pear-shaped with a prominent, cup-shaped chloroplast containing one to several pyrenoids and a single nucleus. At the anterior end of the cell there is a prominent eyespot and two flagella. At the base of the flagella two contractile vacuoles are always present.

Reproduction

Pandorina reproduces both asexually and sexually.

Before asexual reproduction a colony stops its movement, becomes inactive, and sinks to the bottom of water. Its sheath becomes more watery in nature and swells up considerably. Each individual cell of the coenobium undergoes simultaneous longitudinal division to form a daughter coenobium of sixteen or thirty two cells. After the first three divisions, the cells are cruciately disposed, and a typical eight-celled curved plate or **plakea** is formed. Further division stops either at the sixteen-celled or thirty-two-celled stage. Though not recorded properly, yet it is generally presumed that inversion takes place in a developing young coenobium. These daughter colonies then come out of the envelope of the parent colony and swim away.

The sexual reproduction is anisogamous, in which two biflagellate gametes of unequal sizes unite together. The larger of the two is the female gamete, which is usually less active than the smaller one, the male gamete.

Divisions of the protoplast for the formation of gametes take place in exactly the same way as those occurring during asexual reproduction. The groups of daughter cells, which are to act as gametes later, at first swim in water as colony-like units enclosed within broad watery envelopes. Finally, the gametes escape out of the common sheath, swim freely and ultimately unite in pairs. The fusion may be either terminal or lateral, and as a result, a quadriflagellate zygote is produced. The zygote swims for a very short period, after which the flagella are lost and a wall is secreted all around it. The protoplast of an old zygote is red-coloured due to the presence of haematochrome. After some time, the zygote germinates ; a vesicle is formed and the entire irregularly green and orange protoplast is extruded into it. Very soon the protoplast develops two flagella and thus a **zoospore** is developed, which then swims away. In some cases, two or three such zoospores may be formed from a single zygote. After swimming for some time, the zoospore comes to rest, withdraws its flagella, secretes a gelatinous sheath, and undergoes several divisions giving rise to a typical *Pandorina* colony.

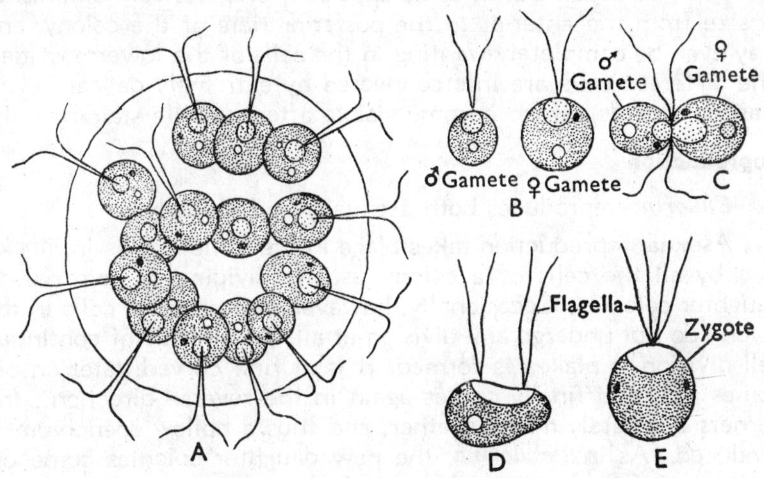

Fig. 6. *Pandorina.*
A, A female colony ; B, The two types of gametes ; C, Union of gametes ; D—E, Zygotes in different stages of development.

EUDORINA

(Fam. CHLAMYDOMONADACEAE)

Eudorina is widely distributed in freshwater lakes, ponds and ditches as well as in small puddles. It is found as a plankton, particularly in the autumn.

The common Indian species of *Eudorina* are *E. elegans*, *E. indica* and *E. illinoisensis*.

Vegetative body (Fig. 7)

The vegetative body of *Eudorina* is a globose, or obovoid, or ellipsoid coenobium of sixteen to sixty-four cells. The latter types of coenobia usually have several lamillate projections, developed at their posterior pole. The colony, however, is usually made up of thirty-two cells, arranged in five distinct transverse tiers ; each of the anterior and posterior tiers contains four cells, while in each of the three medium ones there are eight cells present. The colonial envelope is homogeneous. Each individual cell is globose, and is of the usual *Chlamydomonas* structure, but the number of pyrenoids varies from one to several, according to the species. The eyespot is solitary as usual, but in some species it progressively diminishes in size from the anterior to the posterior tiers of the colony, and may even be completely wanting in the cells of the lowermost tier. The different cells are interconnected by extremely delicate cytoplasmic strands, which become visible after suitable staining only.

Reproduction

Eudorina reproduces both asexually and sexually.

Asexual reproduction takes place in the same way as in *Pandorina* by all the cells of a colony usually dividing to give rise to daughter colonies. Occasionally, however, one or a few cells in the colony do not undergo any division at all. As a result of continued cell division, a plakea is formed. It is at first curved, later on becomes flat, and finally curves again in the reverse direction ; the corners ultimately meet together, and thus a hollow coenobium is produced. As in *Pandorina*, the new daughter colonies come directly out of the parent colony, and swim away.

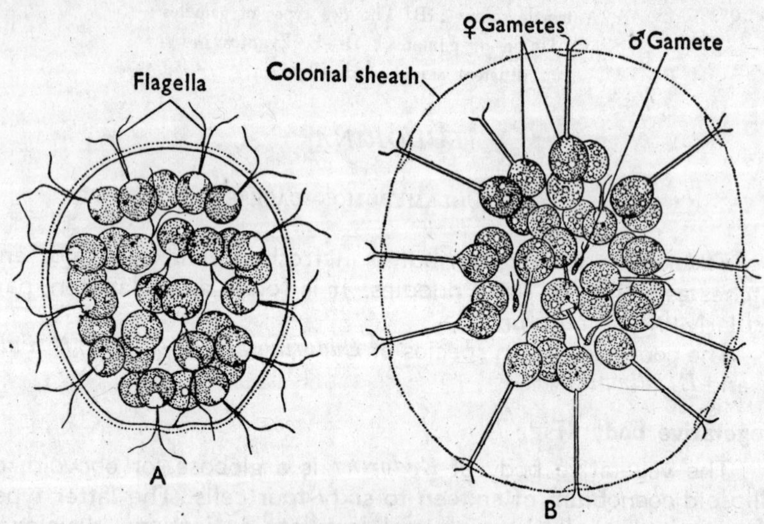

Fig. 7. *Eudorina*.
A, A colony ; B, Two types of gametes enclosed within the colonial sheath.

On account of gradual desiccation, a *palmella stage* may be developed from a vegetative colony. But as soon as sufficient water is available, the palmelloid cells once again develop flagella, and come out as independent **zoospores,** each of which may give rise to a typical *Eudorina* colony in course of a few hours only. Sometimes the cells of a colony lose their flagella, and are converted into akinetes.

The sexual reproduction in *Eudorina*, though of the anisogamous type, is of a very advanced nature, and is almost oogamous. The gametes are very much dissimilar as regards their shape and size. Further, the female gametes are never free-swimming and get fertilized *in situ.* The colonies are homothallic or heterothallic. In the former, usually the four anterior cells give rise to the male gametes, and the rest behaving as the female ones. The cells producing the male gametes divide in the same manner as in the case of asexual reproduction. Each cell finally produces a curved plakea of sixty-four fusiform, biflagellate male gametes. In heterothallic species, the male gametes escape from the old envelope in bunches, and swim as individual units. When a bunch comes in the neighbourhood of a female colony, the individual gametes are set free. In both homothallic and heterothallic species the ordinary vegetative cells are directly converted into female gametes without any considerable change. The swimming male gametes enter straight through the enveloping matrix of a female colony, and ultimately coming in contact with the female gametes fuse with them. A zygote, produced as a result of such a fusion, is smooth-walled and its protoplast is deeply red-coloured due to presence of haematochrome. It remains confined inside the female colony till liberation by disintegration of the colonial sheath. At the time of germination, a vesiclelike structure is formed on one side of the wall, which is somewhat swollen by this time. Inside the vesicle there usually lies one red-coloured zoospore and two or three minute colourless bodies, which may be the disintegrating zoospores. Finally, the zoospore escapes from the vesicle, swims for some time in water, and ultimately undergoes several divisions to produce a new colony.

VOLVOX

(Fam. VOLVOCACEAE)

Volvox is a freshwater green alga which occurs abundantly in tanks, pools, etc.

The common Indian species of *Volvox* are *V. globator, V. aureus, V. africanus, V. prolificus,* etc.

Vegetative body (Fig. 8)

The plant is a free-swimming coenobium. The coenobium is hollow, spherical or ovoid, appears in nature as large as a pinhead, and is composed of thousands of cells arranged in a layer joined to one another by a mucous sheath. Each cell has got a cellulose wall and a thick mucous sheath. It is more or less oval in shape, and has (1) a central nucleus, (2) one cup-shaped or stellate chloroplast with one or more pyrenoids, at the posterior end, (3) two equal flagella at the anterior end, directed towards the surface of the coenobium, (4) 2-6, often scattered, contractile vacuoles, and (5) an eyespot, in the form of a reddish or brownish dot at the anterior end. The eyespot is a photo-receptive organ, intimately concerned with directing the movement of the flagella. Contractile vacuoles alternately expand and contract, and probably serve as excretory organs. It is due to the movement of these flagella of all the cells that the colony moves in water.

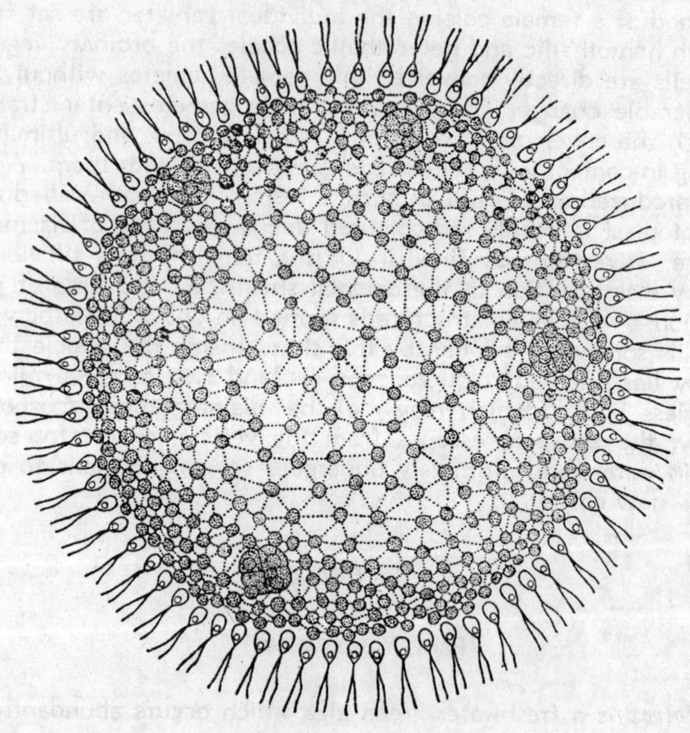

Fig. 8. ***Volvox.***
A mature colony with young colonies inside.

Reproduction

Reproduction is asexual at the beginning of the growing season, but sexual at the end.

A colony develops usually from 4-10 asexual reproductive cells, called **gonidia,** which become many times larger than the ordinary cells, lose their flagella and lie within the globular mucilage sac that projects towards the interior of the colony. Each of them, by repeated divisions, gives rise to a spherical group of cells and forms a daughter colony, which swims about in the cavity of the parent colony. The daughter colonies are ultimately liberated due to rupture or decay of the mother colony.

During the formation of daughter colonies, the plakea undergoes an inversion just as in *Eudorina*.

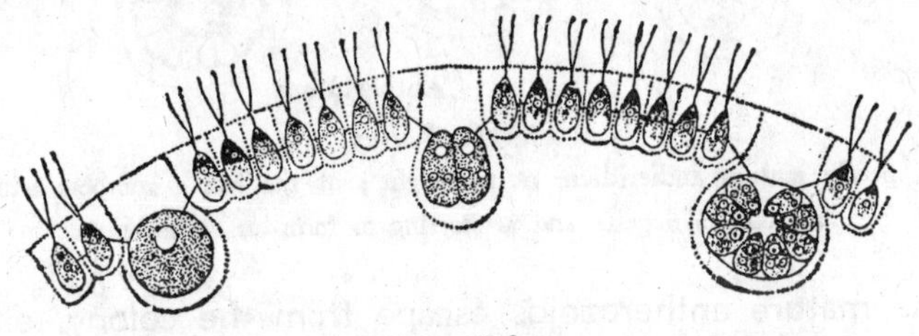

Fig. 9. *Volvox.*
Formation of daughter colony in the rim of mature colony which has lost its flagella and started to form a new colony.

The sexual reproduction is **oogamous** due to the fusion of a motile antherozoid with a non-motile egg. Though the gametes may be formed in any cell of the colony, the gamete-formation is usual-

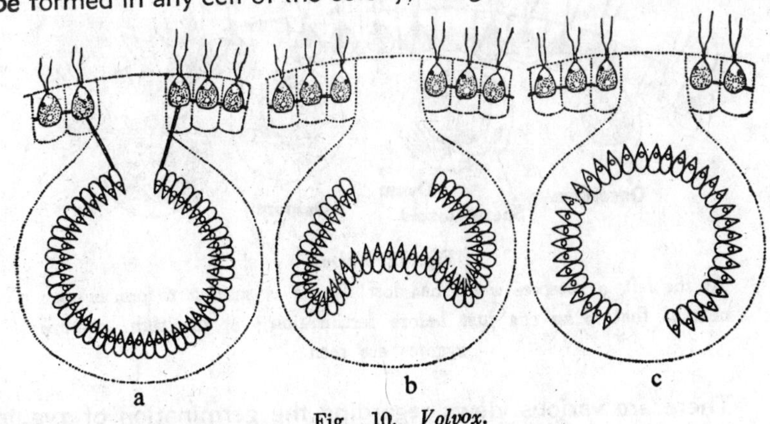

Fig. 10. *Volvox.*
a—c, Stages in the plakeal inversion.

ly restricted to certain cells only. Oogonia and antheridia are highly enlarged cells within a mucous sheath. The oogonium contains a single spherical egg. The antheridium divides repeatedly and forms a bundle of 16, 32, 64, 128 or more, small, fusiform, yellowish, biflagellate bodies, the **antherozoids.**

The colony may be monoecious, or dioecious, and the same individual may or may not form gonidia.

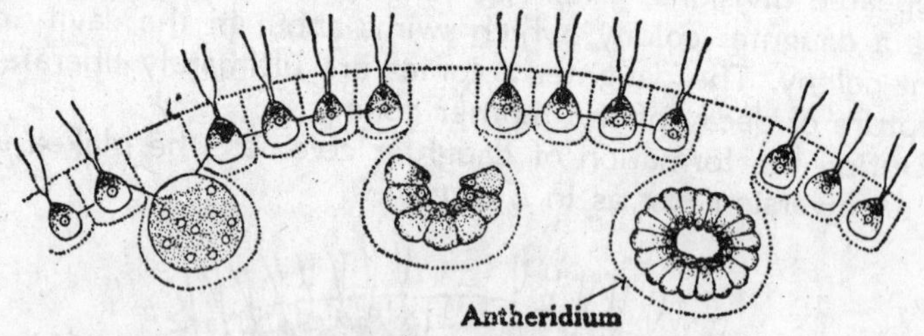

Fig. 11. *Volvox*.
A nearly mature antheridium at the right ; at the left a zoospore which has lost its flagella and is starting to form an antheridium.

The mature antherozoids escape from the colony, either as free-swimming individuals, or as a free-swimming colony that dissociates into individual male gametes later on. The antherozoids, attracted by an egg, make their way through the gelatinous envelope, which surrounds the egg, but only one of them finally unites with the egg and forms the zygote (oospore).

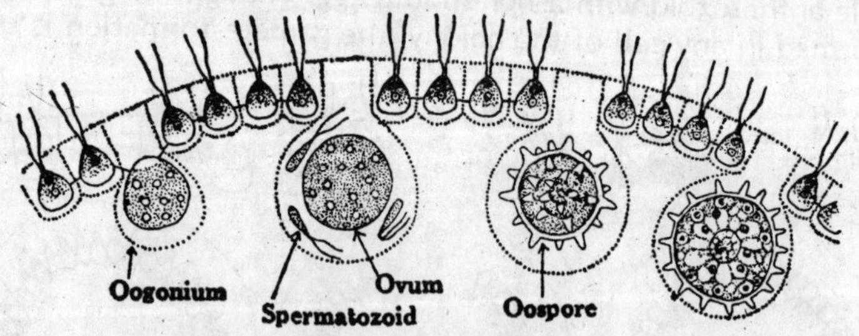

Fig. 12. *Volvox*.
At the left, a zoospore which has lost flagella is starting to form an egg ; next to that is an egg just before fertilization ; at the right, mature zygotes are seen.

There are various views regarding the germination of zygote. According to the opinion of Pocock, the diploid nucleus of the zygote divides into a number of daughter nuclei, the first one being reductional and gives rise to biflagellate zoospores, of which only one survives. The protoplast of this swimming zoospore now divides repeatedly giving rise to a new daughter colony.

The zygote develops a thick wall and is retained within the colony until its decay. Then it falls to the bottom of the pool and undergoes a period of rest. Finally, the wall of the zygote breaks and the protoplast comes out. It divides and soon forms a free-swimming colony of the *Volvox* plant.

ORDER 2. **CHLOROCOCCALES**

Unicellular or colonial ; non-motile in the vegetative condition ; reproduce by zoospores or aplanospores ; almost exclusively freshwater.

HYDRODICTYON

(Fam. HYDRODICTYACEAE)

Hydrodictyon, commonly known as the 'water-net', is a somewhat rare alga. It occurs, often in considerable quantity, in stagnant water of permanent pools or other bodies.

Of the known species, *H. reticulatum* is the most common and is comparatively widely distributed. *H. indicum*, a new species from Madras, has been described by Iyenger.

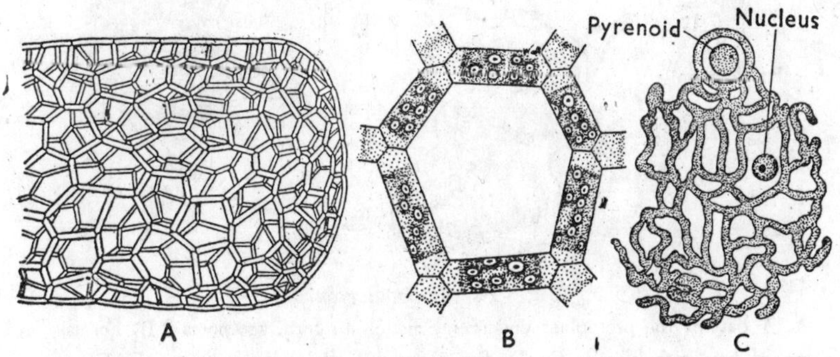

Fig. 13. *Hydrodictyon.*

A, A portion of the thallus showing the network ; B, A group of cells ; C, Part of the chloroplast showisg the pyrenoid and a nucleus.

Vegetative body (Fig. 10).

All species of *Hydrodictyon* form colonies of a definite number of cylindrical or ovoid cells (coenobia) which are united to form a free-floating, hollow, cylindrical network. usually closed at either ends and reaching a length as much as 15-30 cm. The meshes of the reticulum are formed by the union of elongated cells. Each mature cell is multi-nucleate and the nuclei lie in the peripheral layer or cytoplasm internal to the cellwall and surrounding a large central vacuole. The chloroplast is peripheral, reticulate and possesses numerous pyrenoids.

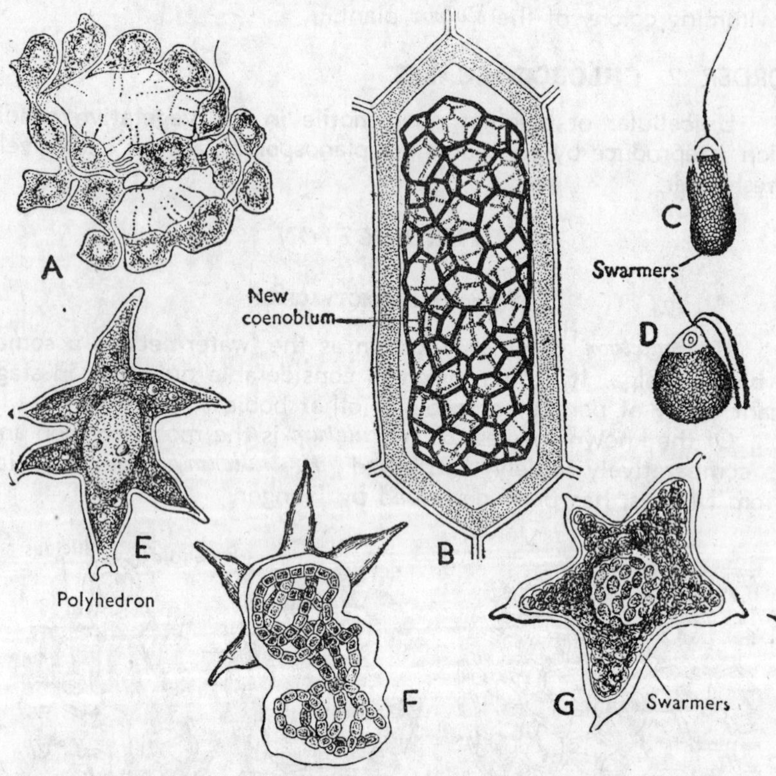

Fig. 14. *Hydrodictyon.*

A, A part of the protoplast undergoing fission to form zoospores ; B, Formation of new coenobium ; C—D, Swarmers ; E, Polyhedron stage : F. Formation of a net within the polyhedron ; G, Formation of swarmers within the polyhedron.

Reproduction

Hydrodictyon reproduces both asexually and sexually.

Any cell of the coenobium may form zoospores, but the adjacent cells may or may not show any sign of zoospore-formation. Thousands of uninucleate, biflagellate zoospores are produced from the protoplast of the mature coenocytic cells by progressive cleavages. They do not escape from the mother cell, but remain confined within the wall of the parent coenocyte and exhibit a somewhat restricted movement. The necessary space for the movement of the zoospores is provided by the extension of the longitudinal cellwalls and by the diminution in size of the vacuole. They finally come to rest, arrange themselves in straight rows in three directions and touching one another withdraw their flagella, secrete membranes and form a new coenobium by the elongation of these cells. The young coenobium at first remains enclosed within the mother cellwall, which later on gelatinizes and liberates the new coenobium.

Hydrodictyon is a monoecious and the **isogametes** formed from the same coenobium may conjugate in pairs. The gametes are produced in the same way as the zoospores but they are much smaller in size. Further, they are liberated from a parent cell through a hole in the cellwall. After fusion of two gametes, their flagella are withdrawn immediately and a spherical zygote with a thin cellwall results. This zygote gradually increases in size, appears red in colour due to formation of haematochrome and accumulates oil as reserve food. After a period of rest, this zygote nucleus undergoes reduction division and the protoplast is divided into four large, biflagellate **zoospores.** Each zoospore contains numerous discoid chloroplasts without pyrenoids. They are finally liberated by the rupture of the wall of the zygote and swim for some time. After the period of swimming, a zoospore comes to rest and develops to form a polyhedral cell resembling some species of *Tetraedron*. This may be regarded as an **aplanospore.** This polyhedral cell greatly increases in size forming zoospores in the usual way, and these again unite to form a new coenobium, which is liberated by the rupture of the cellwall.

PEDIASTRUM

(Fam. HYDRODICTYACEAE)

Pediastrum occurs as a freshwater free-floating organism, commonly in ponds, ditches and lakes. Occasionally, however, it also occurs in permanent or semi-permanent ponds and ditches.

The common Indian species of *Pediastrum* are *P. simplex*, *P. clathratum*, *P. duplex*, *P. tetras*, etc.

Vegetative body (Fig. 15)

The body of *Pediastrum* is usually a single-layered coenobium consisting of a few to several cells (some multiple of 2) and are commonly arranged in distinct rings around the central cell. The cells fit closely together with their plane faces or their walls may be lobed so that small spaces of variable size are found between

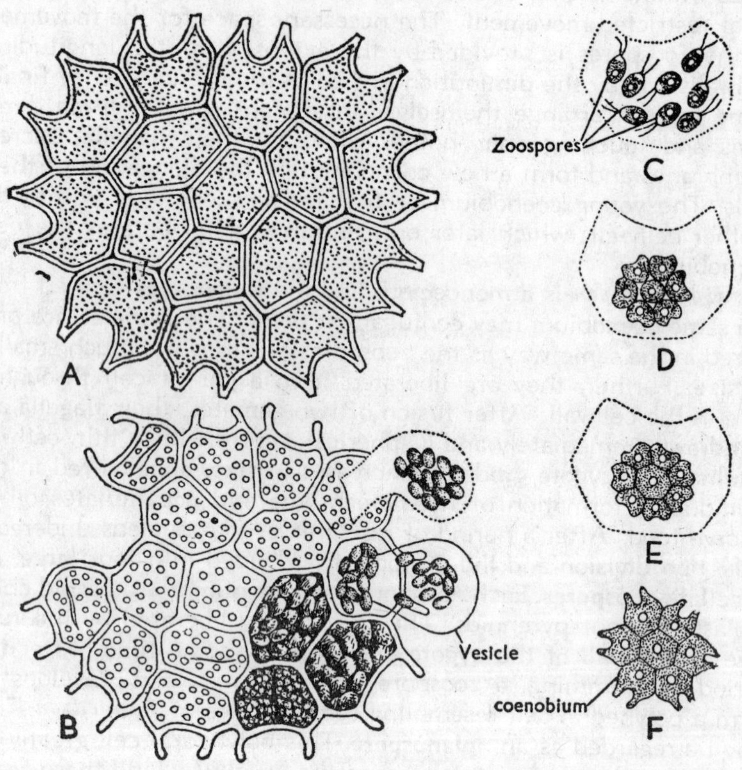

Fig. 15. *Pediastrum.*
A, A colony ; B, Liberation of zoospores ; C, Zoospores enclosed within a vesicle ; D—F, Stages in the formation of a daughter colony.

them. The peripheral cells produce, on their outer faces, diverging processes, one or two from each, and they differ in shape from the internal cells. Each adult cell is multinucleate (2-8) with a single parietal plate-like chloroplast containing one to four pyrenoids. The chloroplasts sometimes show definite perforations.

Reproduction

Pediastrum reproduces both by asexual and sexual methods.

Asexual reproduction takes place by the formation of biflagellate zoospores. Every cell of the coenobium is capable of forming zoospores. The protoplast of a cell, following successive nuclear divisions and progressive cleavages, forms **zoospores.** These are

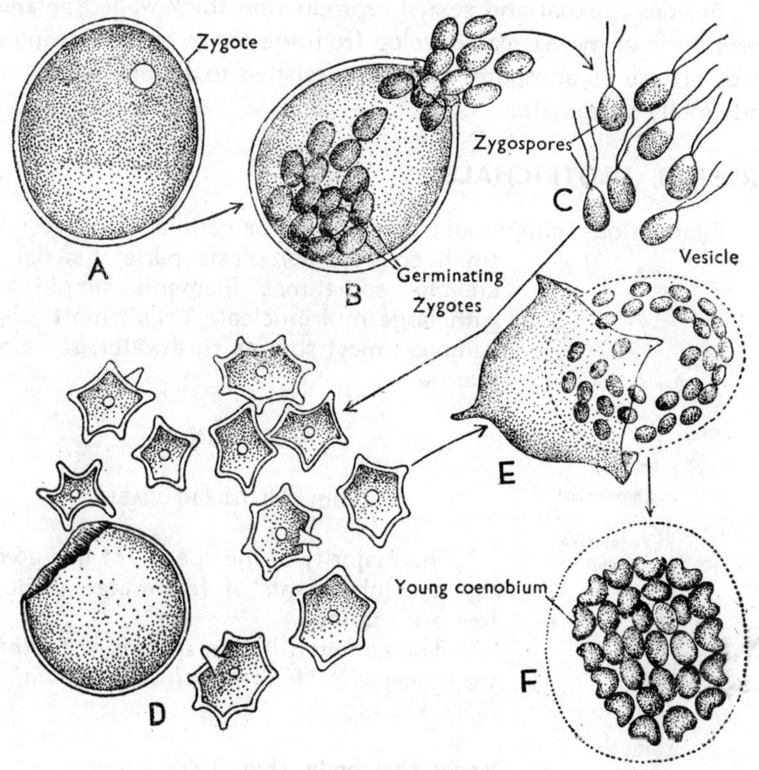

Fig. 16. *Pediastrum*.
A, A zygote ; B, A germinating zygote ; C, Zoospores produced on germination of a zygote ; D, An empty zygote and angular cells developed from zoospores ; E—F, Germination of an angular cell to form a new coenobium.

suddenly liberated due to rupture of the cellwall into a newly-formed vesicle within which they move about actively, but finally arrange themselves in one plane to form a new coenobium before liberation.

Sexual reproduction in *Pediastrum* has been reported in some species in which it takes place by the formation of biflagellate gametes that unite to form a spherical zygote. Details of germination of the zygote are not known, but the presence of *Tetraedron stage* like that of *Hydrodictyon* has been observed in some cases.

This suggests that germination of the zygote probably takes place as in *Hydrodictyon*.

Besides asexual and sexual reproduction thick-walled **aplanospores** (one or more) may develop from the entire protoplast in rare cases. These aplanospores are very resistive to adverse conditions and finally germinate.

ORDER 3. ULOTRICHALES

Filamentous, simple and unbranched or cellular expanse with small cells ; chloroplasts parietal, axial or stellate ; sometimes filaments simple and with large multinucleate cells ; mostly isogamous ; most species freshwater, some are marine.

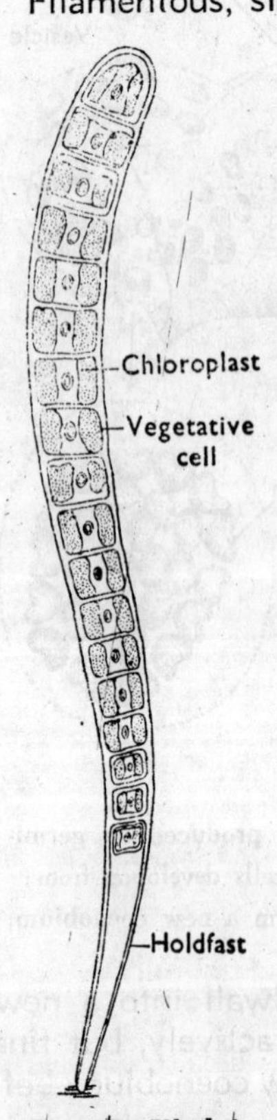

Fig. 17. *Ulothrix.* Holdfast and the vegetative cells.

ULOTHRIX

(Fam. ULOTRICHACEAF)

The majority of the species of this green alga are inhabitants of freshwater, while a few are marine.

The common Indian species of *Ulothrix* are *U. aequalis*, *U. pectinalis*, *U. zonata*, *U. variabilis*, etc.

Vegetative body (Fig. 17)

The vegetative body is a thallus which is an unbranched filament of indefinite length, consisting of a single row of short, cylindrical cells joined end on end. The filament is differentiated into base and apex, since its basal cell is colourless, elongated and gradually narrowed to form a **holdfast,** which helps in its attachment to the substratum. Each cell possesses either a thick or a thin cellwall, which often becomes stratified. The protoplast of each cell is always uninucleate and contains a single girdle-shaped chloroplast, which encircles it partially or completely. The chloroplast contains one to several pyrenoids.

Reproduction

Ulothrix reproduces in a variety of ways mentioned below :

Vegetative reproduction takes place usually by the accidental breaking of the filament into many fragments with a few cells in each.

Asexual reproduction takes place by the formation of zoospores, which develop from the protoplasts of ordinary vegetative cells excepting the holdfast. According to species, the number of zoospores produced from each protoplast may be 1, 2, 4, 8, 16, or 32. In any case, during the formation of zoospores there is a slight contraction of the protoplast followed by nuclear division and subsequent cleavage of the cytoplasm forming two daughter protoplasts, and this process may continue until 32 daughter protoplasts are formed. Each daughter protoplast is then usually metamorphozed into a **quadriflagellate zoospore.** When a single zoospore is formed the protoplast of the entire vegetative cell is directly metamorphozed into it. Each zoospore is pyriform in shape with a stellate chloroplast at the posterior end and a prominent eyespot and is either (*a*) large, 4-flagellate, with an anterior eyespot, called **macrozoospore,** or (*b*) small, 4- or 2-flagellate, with a median eyespot, called **microzoospore.** The zoospores are liberated through a pore on the lateral wall of the parent cell. They swim actively in water from one to several days, but ultimately cease their movement and attach themselves to some objects in water by the flagellate end. Finally, the flagella disappear, a wall is secreted around each and by elongation of the cell and subsequent divisions a new plant is formed.

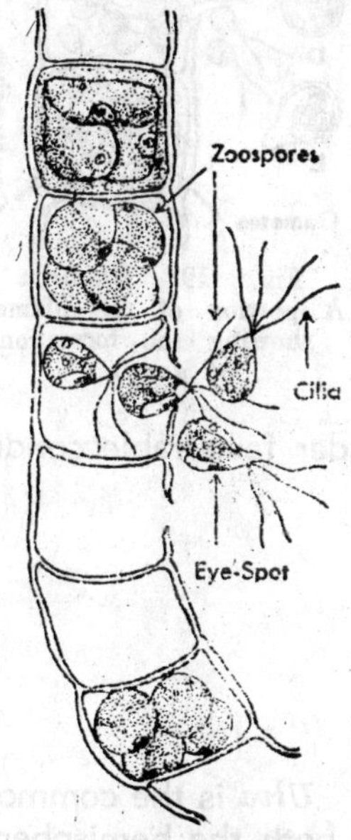

Fig. 18. *Ulothrix*, A portion of the filament showing the formation of zoospores.

When zoospores are not liberated from the parent cells, each of them secretes a cellwall around it and forms a thin-walled **aplanospore.** The aplanospores may germinate even before liberation from the parent cell. In some cases, the protoplast of a vegetative cell may be directly metamorphozed into a single thick-walled aplanospore which ultimately germinates into a new plant.

The sexual reproduction is **isogamous,** which takes place by the union of two flagellate gametes of equal size. But the fusing gametes come from different plants. Hence, the plant is dioecious (heterothallic).

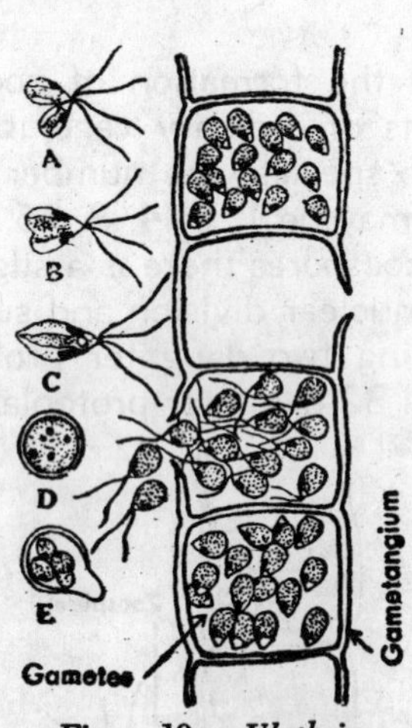

Fig. 19. *Ulothrix.* A portion of the filament showing the formation of gametes.

The formation of gametes, as well as their mode of liberation from the parent cell, takes place in the same manner as the zoospores. The number of gametes produced may be 8, 16, 32, or 64. Each gamete is **biflagellate,** pyriform, with a conspicuous eyespot and smaller in size than a zoospore. After gametic union a quadriflagellate zygote is formed, which remains motile for a time but ultimately comes to rest, secretes a thick wall around it and after accumulation of considerable amount of food-reserve passes into a resting period. At the end of the resting period, the *zygote nucleus undergoes reduction division* and forms 4 to 16 daughter nuclei, from which either zoospores or aplanospores are produced. The zoospores or aplanospores under favourable conditions develop into new plants.

ULVA

(Fam. ULVACEAE)

Ulva is the common 'sea lettuce' of the mid-tidal zone of seas of both the hemispheres. Some of the marine species are also to be found growing in brackish waters. It also grows luxuriantly in the sewage-polluted water. It is an edible alga.

The common Indian species of *Ulva* are *U. fasciata, U. oxycocca, U. lobata,* etc.

Vegetative body (Fig. 20)

The vegetative body is an expanded thalloid sheet of two-celled thickness. From the lower end of the thallus some cells give rise to rhizoidal outgrowths, which help to fix the plant to the substratum. These outgrowths finally become closely attached to one

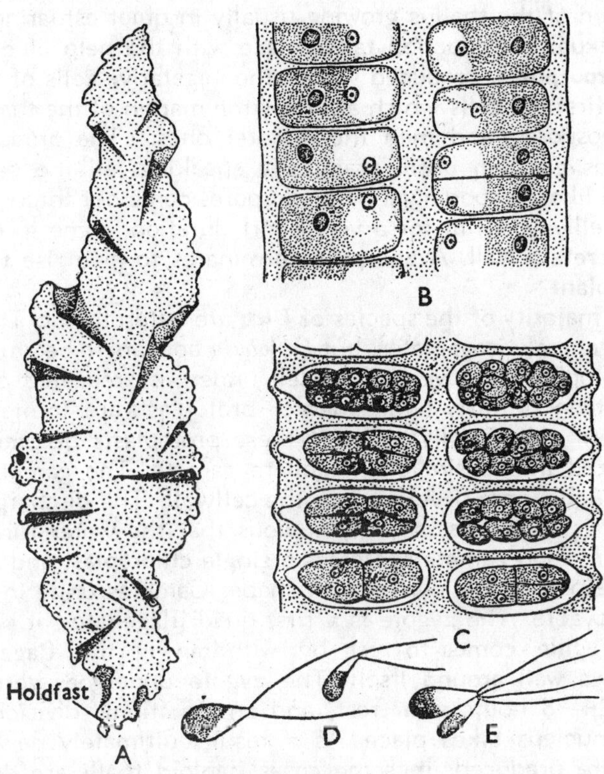

Fig. 20. *Ulva,*
A, The plant body ; B, A portion of the thallus showing cell arrangement ; C, Formation of gametes ; D, Gametes ; E, Union of gametes.

another, and give rise to a pseudo-parenchymatous holdfast, which is perennial in nature and bears new **blades** every year during the spring. In cross-sectional view, the cells of the thallus are more or less isodiametric or somewhat vertically elongated to the surface of the thallus, and their walls are somewhat fused with one another forming a matrix, which is rather thick and gelatinous in consistency. Each cell contains towards its inner face a solitary nucleus, and towards its outer face there is a single laminate to cup-shaped chloroplast with one pyrenoid only. New cells are formed by divisions of pre-existing cells in perpendicular directions to the surface of the thallus.

Reproduction

Ulva reproduces vegetatively, asexually as well as sexually.

Vegetative reproduction in *Ulva* takes place by accidental fragmentation of the thallus growing usually in quiet estuarine waters.

Asexual reproduction takes place with the help of **quadriflagellate zoospores,** produced within the vegetative cells of the thallus. At first the cells which are near the margin of the thallus produce zoospores, and then the remoter ones. The production of zoospores goes on until, practically speaking, all the cells have behaved like zoosporangia. The zoospores come out through a pore in the cellwall, swim for a very short duration, come to rest, and then secrete a wall. A zoospore germinates to give rise to a new sexual plant.

The majority of the species of *Ulva* are heterothallic. The gametes are generaly isogametes, but *U. lobata* appears to be anisogamic. The protoplast of a vegetative cell undergoes repeated cleavages until sixteen or thirty-two daughter protoplasts are formed within the parent cell. Finally, each of these protoplasts becomes metamorphozed into a single biflagellate gamete. The gametes come out through a pore developed on the cellwall. The discharge of the gametes is sometimes so very copious that the water turns green in colour. Each gamete possesses a single chloroplast and a prominent eyespot, and is pyriform in shape. Gametes unite in pairs to form a zygote. The zygote is a first quadriflagellate ; it swims for a short while, comes to rest by withdrawing the flagella, and secretes a wall around itself. The zygote undergoes germination within 24-48 hours after rest, and an equational division of the zygote nucleus takes place. As a result, ultimately new diploid plants are produced. In some cases haploid thalli are developed parthenogenetically from the gametes.

It is of interest to note that in the life-history cycle of *Ulva* an isomorphic alternation of generations can be traced. Morphologically the two types of plants, the sporophyte and the gametophyte, are identical. The sporophytic thallus produces the haploid zoospores, which develop into gametophytes. The zygotes, produced by the union of gametes developed on these gametophytes, give rise to new diploid thalli.

ENTEROMORPHA

(Fam. ULVACEAE)

Enteromorpha grows in saline habitat. There are a few species under the genus, of which *E. intestinalis* is widely distributed. The other common Indian species of *Enteromorpha* are *E. prolifera*, *E. compressa*, etc.

Vegetative body (Fig. 21)

At the very beginning the thallus is an uniseriate filament ; very soon it becomes multiseriate and tube-like in appearance. The thallus is branched at intervals and exhibits some diversities of form. In a large number of species the thallus is attached to the substratum by means of **rhizoids,** while others, particularly those inhabiting salt marshes, remain free-floating, either throughout their life or at least a part of it ; one species (*E. nana*) possesses a basal prostrate region. The branching depends upon two major external factors,—the degree of salinity in the substratum and temperature. It has further been recorded that the thallus has got some power of regeneration. If any injury takes place near about the apex, papillate outgrowths appear from the injured cells, whereas if the basal region is subjected to an injury rhizoids are developed. The cells of the thallus are somewhat tubular, much longer than broad, and contain a number of chromatophores, with pyrenoids.

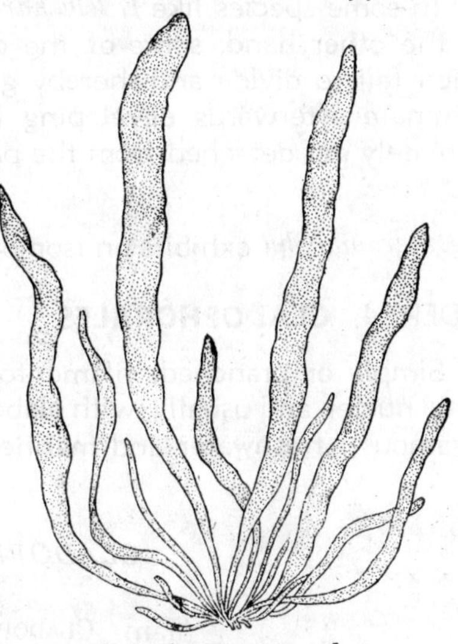

Fig. 21. *Enteromorpha*, Plant body.

Reproduction

Enteromorpha reproduces both asexually and sexually.

The asexual reproduction takes place by means of **zoospores,** as in *Ulva*. Each zoospore on germination gives rise to a new haploid plant. In the species (*E. nana* and *E. procera*) diploid zoospores are produced, and these are termed as **neutrospores,** or neutral spores.

Enteromorpha is heterothallic and the mode of sexual reproduction is usually isogamous. An anisogamous type of reproduction is, however, found in *E. intestinalis*, where the smaller gamete with a rudimentary pyrenoid is regarded as a male one. As a result of fusion between two motile gametes a zygote is formed, which also remains motile for about an hour. After this period the flagella are withdrawn and the motility ceases, but the division of the zygote does not commence before several days.

In some species like *E. clatharta* there is no union of gametes. On the other hand, some of the cells of the gametangial region, which fail to divide and thereby give rise to gametes (**rest cells**) germinate afterwards developing into new haploid plants. These ultimately get detached from the parent plant and live as independent ones.

Enteromorpha exhibits an isomorphic alternation of generations.

ORDER 4. **CLADOPHORALES**

Simple or branched, filamentous with cells containing two to many nuclei and usually with elaborate large chloroplasts ; mostly isogamous ; freshwater and marine.

CLADOPHORA

(Fam. CLADOPHORACEAE)

Cladophora is one of the largest genera of green algae. It occurs both in the freshwater as well as in the sea, and is widely distributed throughout the world. In many lakes it sometimes spreads to their bottom and extends up to a depth of 24 metres. In some species the different thalli are held together by interlacing branches, often forming compact cushions attached mainly to some substratum, or loose hollow balls as big as human head.

The common Indian species of *Cladophora* are *C. bengalensis, C. glomerata, C. crispata, C. incurvata, C. codioia, C. scitula,* etc.

Vegetative body (Fig. 22)

The vegetative body is a much-branched thallus which remains attached to the substratum by long rhizoidal branches, many of which develop adventitiously from several cells near the base of the thallus. Each branch is made up of a row of elongated cylindrical cells joined end to end. A branch always arises as a lateral outgrowth from the upper end of a cell situated towards the apical portion of the filament.

Each cell consists of a stratified cellwall made up of an inner cellulose layer, a middle pectic zone and an outer chitinous layer.

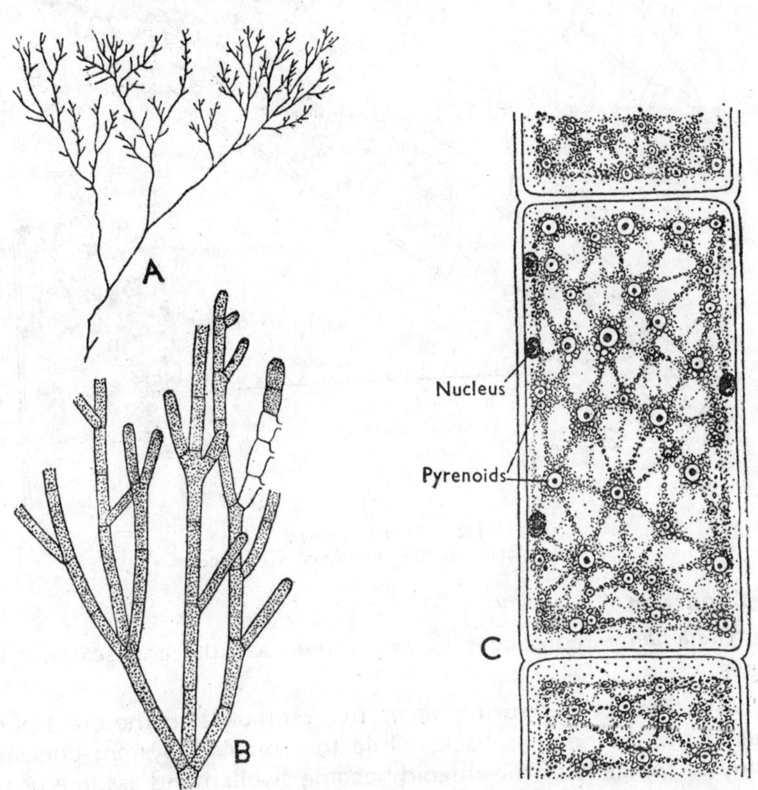

Fig. 22. *Cladophora,*
A, General habit of the plant ; B, A portion of the thallus (magnified) ; C, A part of B magnified to show the cell structure.

The protoplast is, in most cases, multinucleate and the cytoplasm appears in the form of a primordial utricle surrounding a central vacuole. As regards the nature of the chloroplast, there is still much difference of opinion among the algologists. Possibly, the chloroplast is fundamentally a parietal reticulate structure with inward processes and numerous scattered pyrenoids. According to the most recent view, however, the mature chloroplast is regarded to be composed of numerous discoid chloroplasts with pyrenoids.

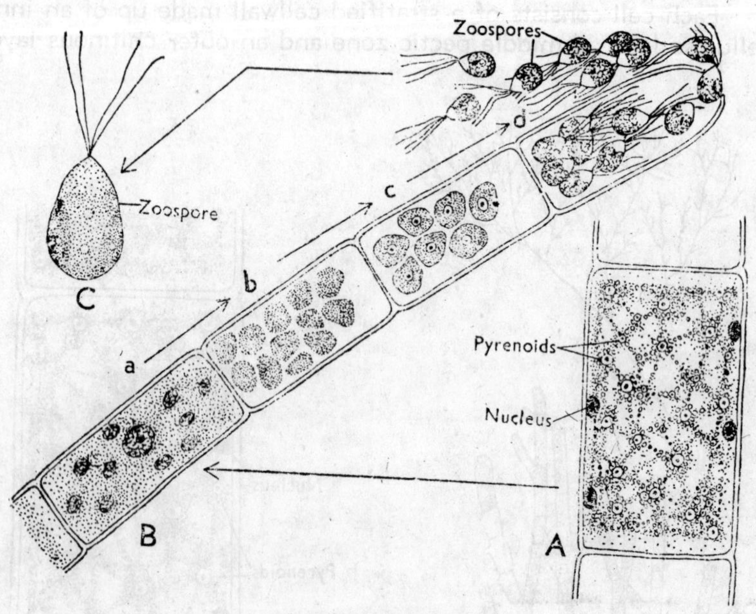

Fig. 23. *Cladophora*.
A—C, Stages in the formation of zoospores.

Reproduction

Cladophora reproduces by vegetative, asexual and sexual methods.

In some species during vegetative reproduction the erect portion of the thallus dies back, while the rhizoidal system persists. Many of the cells of the rhizoid become swollen and assume pear-shaped form. These thick-walled cells usually develop from unbranched rhizoidal branches. After a period of dormancy and under favourable conditions, these cells give rise to new erect filaments. This is an instance of akinete-formation without dissociation of the branches. In some cases, cells of the rhizoids get dissociated and each cell can give rise to a new thallus.

Asexual reproduction takes place by means of **biflagellate** or **quadriflagellate zoospores** formed by the cleavage of the protoplasts of vegetative cells of the younger apical filaments in basepetal succession. Before the formation of zoospores, the nuclei multiply by divisions and in some species it has been recorded that meiosis takes place at this stage. At the distal end of the mother cell a pore is formed through which zoospores escape singly. Each zoospore ultimately develops into a **germling,** which develops into two branches, one of which gives rise to the erect portion, the other to the rhizoidal system.

Sexual reproduction takes place by means of **biflagellate gametes.** The modes of formation and liberation of gametes are much the same as those of the zoospores. Certain species are definitely heterothallic and the fusing gametes belong to different thalli. Reproduction is isogamous. After fusion a **zygote** is formed, which directly develops into a diploid plant.

In some species, when conjugation fails, **parthenospores** are produced directly from the gametes. Each parthenospore is haploid, and, on germination, gives rise to the thallus of the same generation.

In some species of *Cladophora* there is an alternation of diploid asexual generation with a haploid sexual generation, which are morphologically alike.

ORDER 5. CHAETOPHORALES

Filamentous and sharply differentiated into prostrate and erect portions (**heterotrichous**) ; erect portion often reduced and the prostrate portion often forming discoid expanse ; hairs of diverse types are often present ; mostly isogamous and freshwater.

CHAETOPHORA

(Fam. CHAETOPHORACEAE)

Chaetophora is abundantly found as an epiphyte on submerged water plants. It also occurs in stagnant water being attached to stone and woodwork.

The common Indian species of *Chaetophora* are *C. chlorotica, C. pisiformis, C. elegans, C. incrassata,* etc.

Vegetative body (Fig. 24)

The vegetative body is of definite macroscopic form. It is exceedingly tough and is made up of globular, irregularly tuberculate or elongated thallus ; when globular, the thallus is differentiated into a palmelloid base and radiating branches showing different degrees of branching. Each branch is surrounded by a tough gelatinous sheath, which may or may not be fused with the sheaths of other branches. The palmelloid portion of the thallus is usually impregnated with calcium carbonate. The elongated thallus, on the other hand, has an axial strand made up of intertwined filaments which bear branches throughout its entire length. In both cases, however, the apices of the branches are prolonged into multicellular, hyaline hairs, which gradually become attenuated into a fine point.

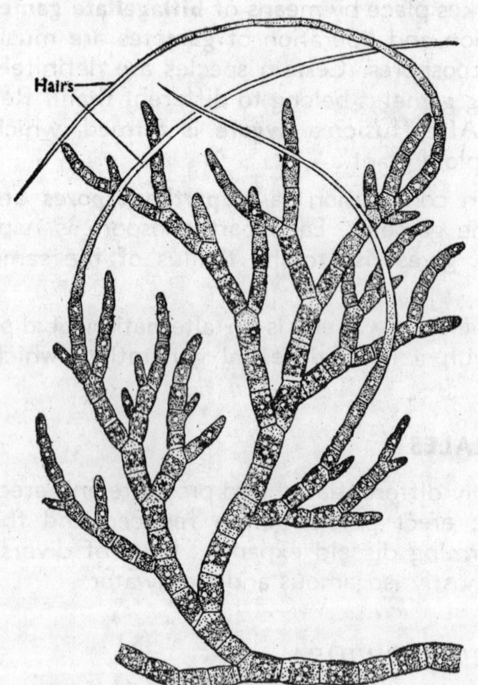

Fig. 24. *Chaetophora*. A portion of the thallus body.

The mature cells are somewhat cylindrical to barrel-shaped containing a protoplast having a transverse zonate band of chloroplast with many pyrenoids. In young cells, the chloroplast is peripheral in position ; it covers the entire sidewalls and is provided with a single pyrenoid. The cells are uninucleate.

Reproduction

Chaetophora reproduces both asexually and sexually. Vegetative reproduction by fragmentation is very rare due to tough nature of the thallus. Two types of swarmers are recognized, viz. (*a*) **quadriflagellate macrozoospores** and (*b*) **biflagellate microzoospores.** Both types of zoospores are developed from the protoplasts of mature vegetative cells by the usual cleavage process. These are liberated through an opening formed on the cellwall of the mother cell. The macrozoospores develop directly into new thalli. The microzoospores, on the other hand, seem to be gametic in nature, as they usually fuse in pairs forming zygotes. Sometimes, they form **resting spores** without fusion, or in rare cases grow out into new plants. Occasionally, **akinetes** are formed either from any part of the vegetative filament or only from the cells of the ultimate branches.

DRAPARNALDIOPSIS

(Fam. CHAETOPHORACEAE)

Of the two species of *Draparnaldiopsis*, *D. indica** was first reported to occur at Banaras, India, in a shallow water of a pond forming pale green, thin, gelatinous covering on leaves of grasses and sedges.

Vegetative body (Fig. 25)

The thallus has a main axis, which is differentiated into cylindrical, elongated and somewhat barrel-shaped internodal cells, which alternate with one another in a very regular fashion. The internodal cells are about two to three times longer than the nodal cells. The axis is attenuated towards the apex and the base. The lowest of the basal cells forms a rhizoid, while a few other cells

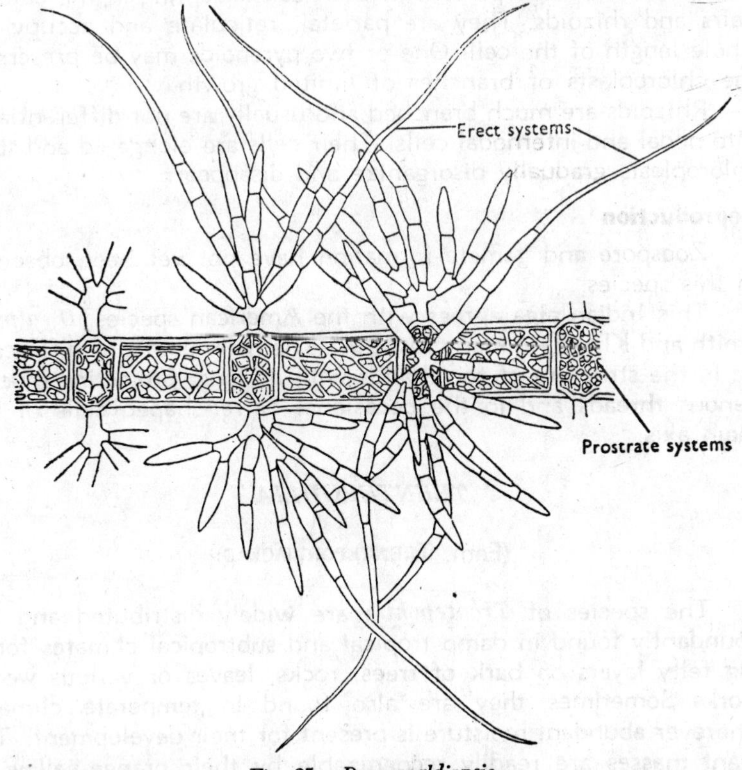

Fig. 25. ***Draparnaldiopsis*, A portion of the thallus body.**

* Bharadwaja, Y. (1933), *New Phytologist* **32,** 165-74.

situated above develop rhizoidal branches forming a dense cortex around the base of the main axis.

The main axis usually bears a number of lateral branches of **unlimited growth.** They arise from some of the nodal cells. Short branches of **limited growth** also arise from the nodal cells as opposite pairs in whorls of four. They may develop also on the branches of unlimited growth. Some of the nodal cells may bear both branches of limited and unlimited growth.

The branches of limited growth form more or less orbicular clusters due to their spreading character. Each branch is subulate and is terminated in a long, hyaline hair at the distal end. In this species, there is a great tendency for the transformation of branches of limited growth into rhizoid-like structures, particularly at the points where branches of unlimited growth arise. The entire thallus is enveloped by mucilage.

Chloroplasts are present in each cell excepting in the cells of hairs and rhizoids. They are parietal, reticulate and occupy the whole length of the cell. One or two pyrenoids may be present in the chloroplasts of branches of limited growth.

Rhizoids are much branched and usually are not differentiated into nodal and internodal cells. Their cells are elongated and their chloroplasts gradually disorganize and disappear.

Reproduction

Zoospore and gamete-formation have not yet been observed in this species.

This Indian alga agrees with the American species, *D. alpinia* Smith and Klyver, in many respects. The main points of difference lie in the structure of the thallus with its long, projecting mucilagenous threads and in the occasional barrel-shaped cells of the main axis.

TRENTEPOHLIA

(Fam. TRENTEPOHLIACEAE)

The species of *Trentepohlia* are widely distributed and are abundantly found in damp tropical and subtropical climates forming felty layers on bark of trees, rocks, leaves or various woodworks. Sometimes they are also found in temperate climates wherever abundant moisture is present for their development. The plant masses are readily recognizable by their orange-yellow or brownish-red coloured cushions, but sometimes they may form fine crusts.

The common Indian species of *Trentepohlia* are *T. abietina, T. calamicola, T. gracilis, T. odorata, T. torulosa, T. polycarpa, T. tenuis,* etc.

Vegetative body (Fig. 26)

In great majority of the species the thallus is differentiated into prostrate and erect filaments. In some cases, the erect filaments are often very little developed or may be entirely absent. In the latter case, the prostrate portion forms an almost pseudo-parenchymatous structure. The erect filaments are well branched. The branches are either alternate, opposite or unilateral and arise

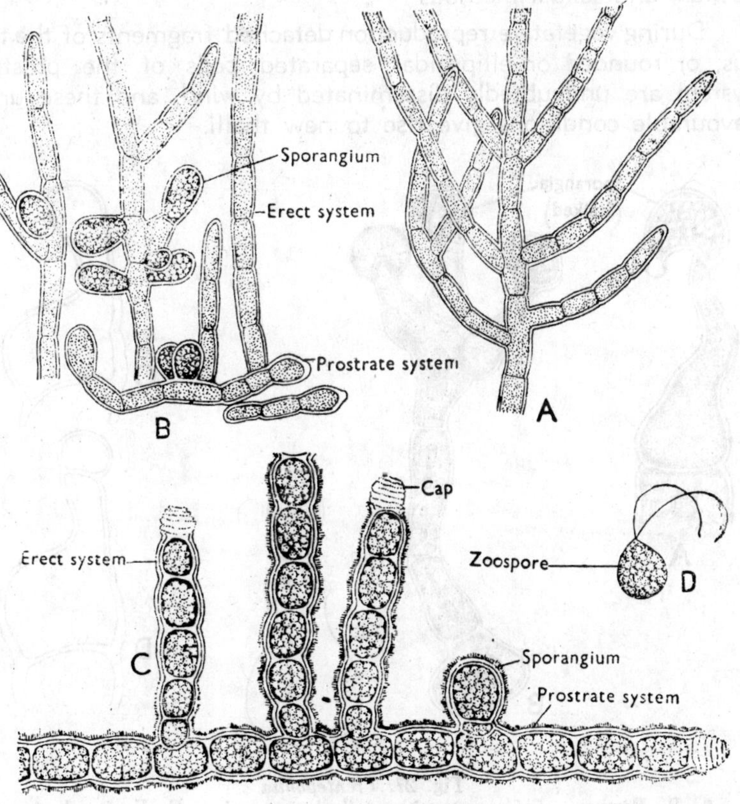

Fig. 26. *Trentepohlia,*
A, A portion of the erect system of the thallus ; B, Part of the thallus with two systems of filaments and sporangia ; C, Part of B magnified ; D, A zoospore.

usually from the distal end or from the middle of the parent cells. The cells are cylindrical or barrel-shaped with thick, stratified cellulose walls. There is usually a cap of pectose at the apex of each branch. The protoplast of each cell is uninucleate when young, but usually becomes multinucleate when old. There are always a number of discoid or band-shaped parietal chloroplasts, the former type being often arranged in bands. They are often obscured by the presence of orange-red haematochrome dissolved in fat globules, which are found around the chloroplasts making the green colour of the latter.

Reproduction

Reproduction in *Trentepohlia* takes place by a vegetative, asexual and sexual methods.

During vegetative reproduction detached fragments of the thallus, or rounded or ellipsoidal separated cells of the prostrate system are undoubtedly disseminated by wind, and these under favourable conditions give rise to new thalli.

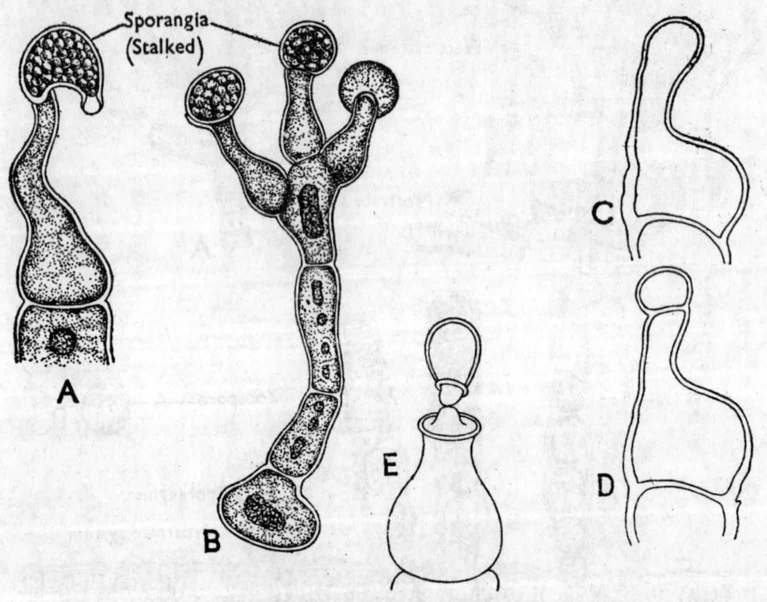

Fig. 27. *Trentepohlia.*
A—B, Portions of filament with stalked sporangia ; C—E, Development and detachment of the stalked sporangium.

During the wet season the plant reproduces asexually by means of **zoospores,** formed within special ellipsoidal or oval sporangia, mainly of two types : (*i*) **sessile,** and (*ii*) **stalked.** The sessile sporangia are formed by enlargement of cells, which may be terminal, lateral, intercalary or axillary in position. They liberate zoospores without themselves being detached from the filaments. The stalked sporangia, on the other hand, develop as terminal or lateral appendages from an enlarged supporting cell. A tubular outgrowth from the supporting cell becomes separated by the formation of a wall and later a sporangium is cut off at its apex, and it is somewhat bent in a knee-shaped manner. The sporangia finally get detached from the stalks and produce **biflagellate zoospores,** while those produced by the sessile sporangia may be **quadriflagellate.** The zoospores ultimately give rise to new thalli again.

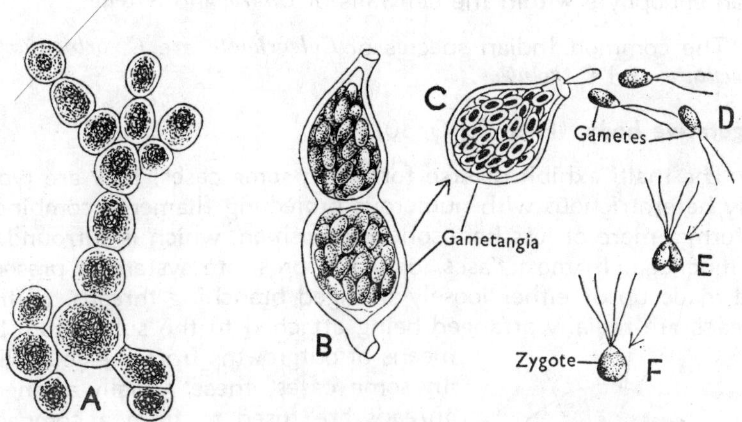

Fig: 28. *Trentepohlia.*
A, Fragment of the prostrate system of the thallus ; B—F, Stages in the formation of the gametes and the development of the zygote.

Under certain conditions, the sporangia form thick-walled **aplanospores** instead of zoospores. **Akinetes** are also formed from several successive cells of the prostrate system which germinate directly and produce new thalli.

It has been stated by several investigators that sexual reproduction takes place in some species by the fusion of isogametes, which are identical in structure with the biflagellate zoospores. The gametangia, from which they are produced, are also similar to the sessile sporangia. It may be, therefore, justified in assuming that the sessile sporangia are gametangial in nature. The failure of biflagellate zoospores, produced by the same individual, to fuse in pairs may possibly be due to the heterothallic nature of some species of *Trentepohlia.* In some cases both types of reproductive structures occur on the same individual, while in others they are

4

found on two distinct plants, which fact possibly suggests an alternation of generations.

COLEOCHAETE

(Fam. COLEOCHAETACEAE)

Coleochaete occurs abundantly in freshwater as an epiphyte on submerged plants or submerged portions of higher plants and on some green algae, e.g. *Vaucheria*, *Oedogonium*, etc. It also occurs as an endophyte within the cellwalls of *Chara* and *Nitella*.

The common Indian species of *Coleochaete* are *C. orbicularis*, *C. scutata* and *C. soluta*.

Vegetative body (Figs. 29 & 30)

The thalli exhibit diverse forms. In some cases, they are typically heterotrichous with numerous projecting filaments combined to form a more or less hemispherical cushion, which is surrounded by mucilage. In most cases, only the prostrate system is present and made up of either loosely-arranged branching threads, or the threads are radially arranged being attached to the substratum by means of outgrowths from the cellwalls. In some cases, these radially-arranged threads are fused to form a compact, more or less discoid, one- to many-layered structures. Branching of the filaments is lateral or it is effected by dichotomy of the apical cell.

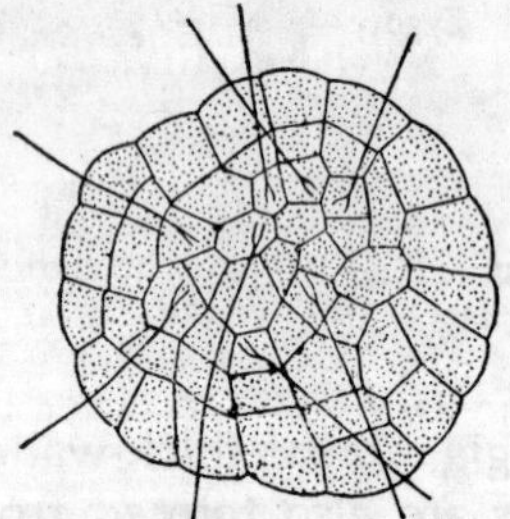

Fig. 29. *Coleochaete*, Discoid form.

The cells of the filaments are uninucleate with the large, irregular, parietal chloroplast having one or two pyrenoids ; usually most of the cells bear characteristic unbranched cytoplasmic bristles, each being ensheathed at its base by a cylinder of gelatinous material.

Reproduction

Coleochaete reproduces both asexually and sexually.

Asexual reproduction takes place by means of large, ovoid, **biflagellate zoospores** which are formed singly within an ordinary cell. Each zoospore is often provided with a chloroplast. The zoospore escapes through a circular opening, formed at the apex of a short papilla developed on the cellwall. It swims for an hour or so, comes to rest, secretes a wall around it, and begins to germinate. During germination it at first divides into two cells and later forms its characteristic thallus. In some cases thick-walled **aplanospores** may develop singly within a vegetative cell.

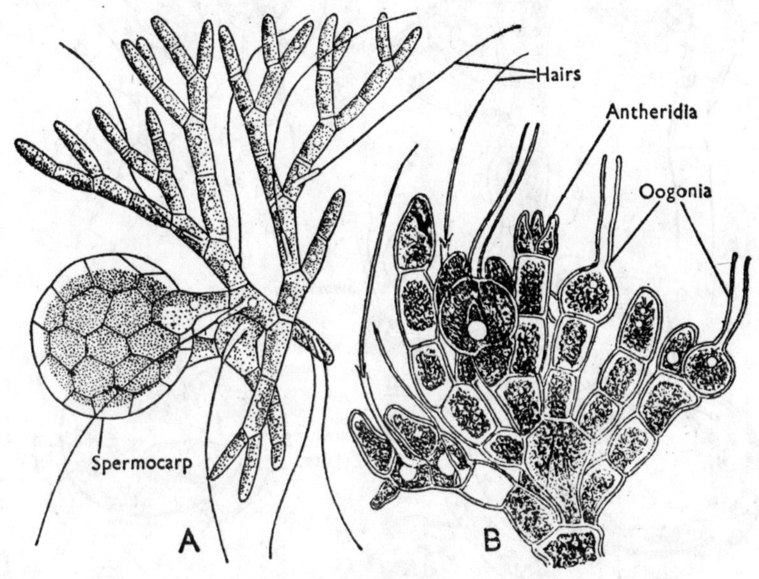

Fig. 30. *Coleochaete.*
A, A portion of the thallus bearing a spermocarp ; B, Part of the thallus showing antheridia and oogonia.

Sexual reproduction takes place by **oogamy.** *Coleochaete* may be both homothallic or heterothallic.

The **oogonia** are borne terminally on short lateral branches of the projecting threads. They eventually occupy a lateral position due to the development of a branch arising from a basal cell. The oogonium is flask-shaped with a basal swollen portion and an upper elongated long neck (**trichogyne**) and contains protoplast with chloroplasts. When it attains maturity, the apical portion of the neck disintegrates, thereby exuding some amount of cytoplasm and the remaining portion of the protoplast within the oogonium forms the **ovum** or **egg.** In discoid forms the oogonia appear as hemispherical structures with short papillae.

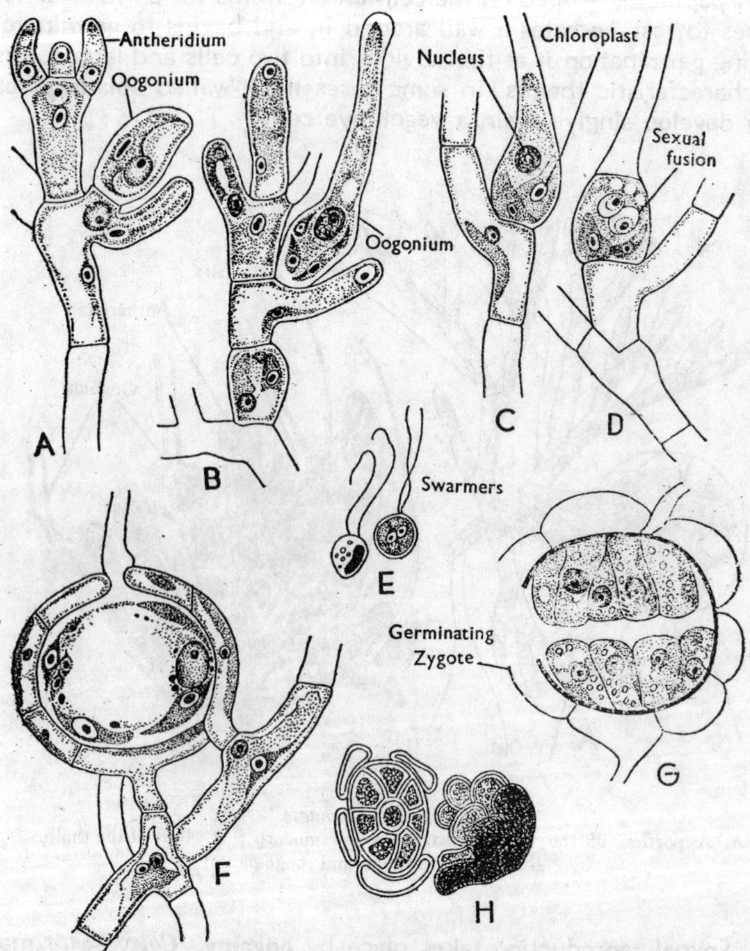

Fig. 31. *Coleochaete.*
A—G, Successive stages in the development and germination of zygote ; H, Development of swarmers within two mature zygotes.

The **antheridia** are also borne terminally in clusters on the branches of the projecting systems. In homothallic species, the same branch often bears the oogonium. They arise as small, colourless outgrowths which are separated from the mother cells by the formation of septa. In discoid forms, they usually develop from the marginal cells. Each antheridium produces a single, colourless, spherical or oval **spermatozoid** with two apical flagella. The spermatozoids are set free by the dissolution of the wall of the antheridium at the apex.

After fertilization, an oospore is formed inside the oogonium as usual. The basal portion of the oogonium is then cut off from the neck by the formation of a transverse septum. Meanwhile, numerous filaments develop from the underlying cells and overgrow the oogonium. These are finally fused to form a more or less pseudoparenchymatous sheath and appear reddish-brown in colour ; the entire structure is termed a **spermocarp.** In discoid forms, these are formed only at one side away from the substratum, and a thick-walled oospore is eventually formed, whose wall is partly made up of the oogonial wall and partly of the inner walls of the investing threads. The cells of the investment finally die down and the oospore perennates for some time in this condition. During germination the oospore produces several **swarmers** or **biflagellate zoospores** that are liberated by the breaking down of its wall. These zoospores are quite different in shape from those formed during asexual reproduction. After a period of swarming they come to rest and develop directly into new thalli. It has been demonstrated that reduction division of the zygote nucleus takes place during germination.

PROTOCOCCUS (=PLEUROCOCCUS)

(Fam. PROTOCOCCACEAE)

Protococcus is the commonest green alga in the world, being very prevalent in the temperate regions of both hemispheres excluding those parts which are very dry. It forms a thin green coating on various substrata, such as exposed rocky surfaces, fence posts, trunks and branches of trees, etc., being generally restricted to the most shaded and moist sides. The cells of *Protococcus* are remarkably resistant to drought and can readily absorb moisture from the atmosphere, when the conditions are favourable.

The common Indian species of *Protococcus* are *P. cohaerens, P. viridis, P. greville,* etc.

Vegetative body (Fig. 32A)

The vegetative body may be unicellular, or in groups of 2, 3, 4, or rarely more cells. Each cell is spherical to ellipsoidal in form with a thick wall, devoid of any gelatinous sheath. The multicellular condition arises only due to successive divisions of the solitary cell. When growing under conditions of excessive moisture, cell divisions may continue to form colonies of 50 or more cells, and there may be a development of profusely and irregularly branched condition (**Pseudo-pleurococcus stage**). The protoplast of each cell contains a definite nuclear membrane, and a large parietal, laminate and marginally lobed chloroplast, usually without pyrenoids.

Reproduction (Fig. 32B—D)

Protococcus reproduces only vegetatively by means of cell division. The two or more daughter cells, thus formed, may remain

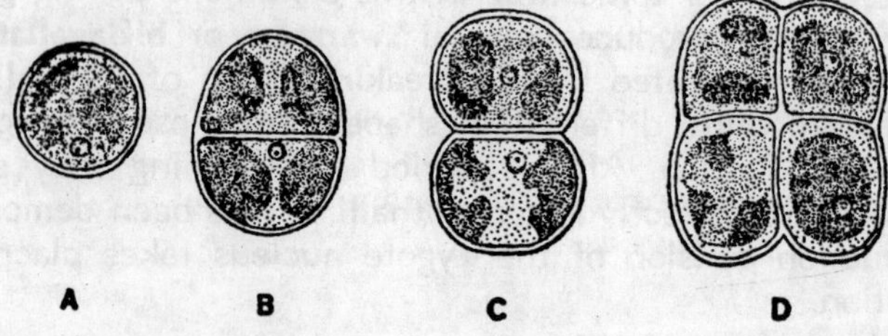

Fig. 32. *Protococcus.*
A, A vegetative cell ; B—D, Vegetative reproduction and formation of daughter cells.

attached with one another for some time, or they may ultimately separate and assume a spherical shape.

ORDER 6. OEDOGONIALES

Simple or branched, filamentous ; zoospores multiflagellate ; oogamous ; cell divisions characterized by intercalation of strips of membrane between two parts of the mother cell ; entirely freshwater.

OEDOGONIUM

(Fam. OEDOGONIACEAE)

Oedogonium is a freshwater, submerged, filamentous, green alga. It occurs in permanent or semipermanent pools or ponds. All species, at the beginning, are sessile, *i.e.* attached to some substratum. Some remain in this condition throughout their entire length of life, while in others, filaments get detached from the substratum and float on the surface of water forming densely interwoven masses. Some are epiphytic and grow on stems and leaves of submerged aquatic vascular plants or on larger green algae.

The common Indian species of *Oedogonium* are *O. acmandrium*, *O. areolatum*, *O. armigerum*, *O. aster*, *O. elegans*, *O. calvum*, *O. glabrum*, *O. inerme*, etc.

Vegetative body (Fig. 33)

The thallus is an unbranched filament consisting of a single row of cylindrical cells joined end on end. The filament shows distinction into base and apex. The basal cell becomes modified and forms a **holdfast** by means of which the thallus fixes itself to the substratum. The apical cell is usually convex, but may be pointed.

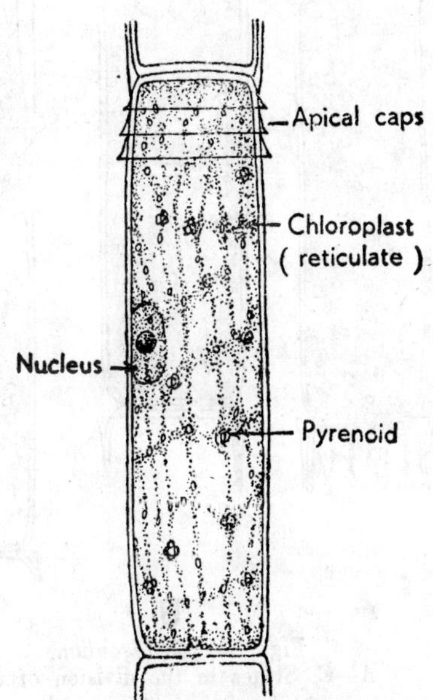

Fig. 33. *Oedogonium.* A vegetative cell.

The cellwall, though appears to be homogeneous, consists of three concentric portions : (1) an innermost cellulose layer lying in contact with the protoplast, (2) a median pectose layer, and (3) an outermost layer chiefly made up of chitin. In the basal cell this outermost chitinous layer is absent. The transverse wall of each cell towards the distal end is provided with transverse striations which constitute the **apical cap.** Thus, the intercalary cells also show distinction into base and apex.

The protoplast, in an adult cell, lies next to the cellwall containing a single nucleus. The nucleus is large, biscuit-shaped, with one or more prominent nucleoli and a distinct nuclear reticulum. It lies midway between the two poles of a cell and is located in the peripheral layer of cytoplasm. The chloroplast is very characteristic. It is in the form of a hollow cylindrical net extending from pole to pole and is lodged on the peripheral layer of cytoplasm, external to the nucleus. There are numerous pyrenoids at the crossings of the reticulum, each being surrounded by a plate of starch. The starch grains, as they are formed, may move away from the pyrenoids and accumulate in the connecting strands of the chloroplast, thereby finally obscuring the nature of it. This is known as **stroma starch.**

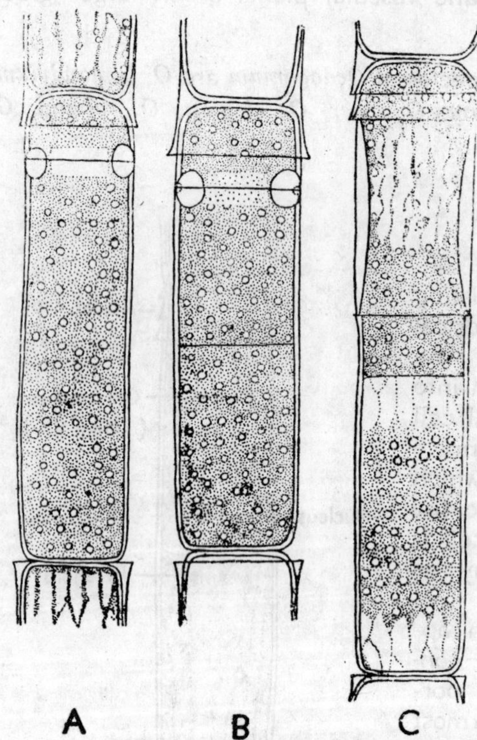

Fig. 34. *Oedogonium.* A—C, Stages in the division of cell and formation of cap cells.

The filament elongates by division of any cell but the basal one. During cell division, a transverse ring of thickening appears at the upper end of the cell just beneath the septum. The cellwall breaks across transversely at this point and the ring gradually extends to form a membrane across the rent. The mitotic nuclear division is followed by cytokinesis (transverse) and elongation of daughter cells to about the same length as the mother cell. The lower one elongates until its upper end is at about the level of the ring and its lateral wall is the lateral wall of the mother cell. The upper one elongates meanwhile, and its lateral wall is formed by a stretching of the ring except for the persistent projecting portion of the ruptured mother cellwall, the apical cap. These cap cells usually divide repeatedly showing as many caps as there are divisions.

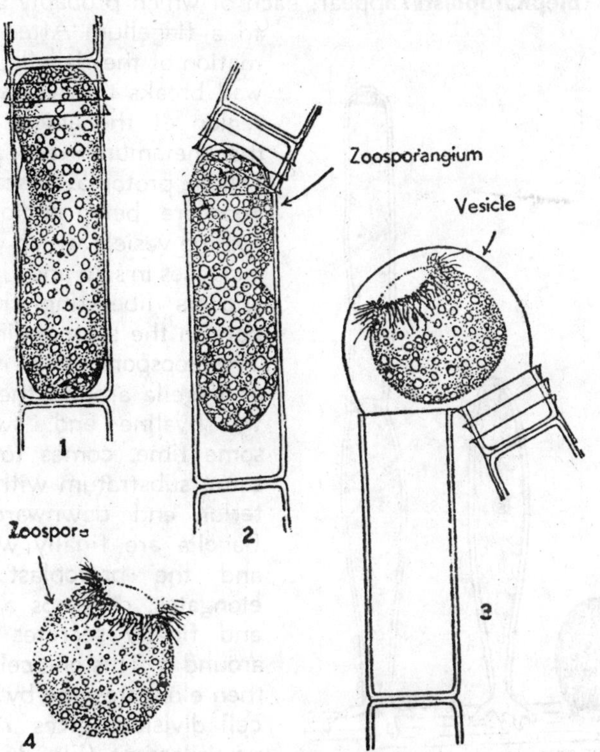

Fig. 35. *Oedogonium.*
1—3, Formation and liberation of the zoospore ; 4, A mature zoospore.

Reproduction

Oedogonium reproduces by vegetative, asexual and sexual methods.

When reproduction takes place vegetatively, it is chiefly by the accidental breaking of the filaments, and in submerged aquatic species it is by the process of fragmentation.

Most species of *Oedogonium* reproduce asexually by the production of **multiflagellate zoospores** formed within zoosporangia (Fig. 35). Any intercalary vegetative cell, rich in accumulated oil-reserve, may become a zoosporangium and form a zoospore. During its formation, the nucleus slightly recedes inwards, and a hyaline region appears in the cytoplasm between the cellwall and the nucleus. Around the margin of this hyaline region numerous granules (**blepharoplasts**) appear, each of which probably gives rise to a flagellum. After the formation of the flagella, the cell-wall breaks transversely at the region of the apical cap and the metamorphozed multiflagellate protoplast escapes as a zoospore, being enclosed by a hyaline vesicle which gradually increases in size and finally disappears liberating the zoospore in the surrounding water. The zoospore, with its crown of flagella around the base of the hyaline end, swims for some time, comes to rest on some substratum with the anterior end downwards. The flagella are finally withdrawn and the protoplast slightly elongates, develops a holdfast and finally secretes a wall around it. This one-celled plant then elongates and by repeated cell divisions gives rise to a new filament (Fig. 36).

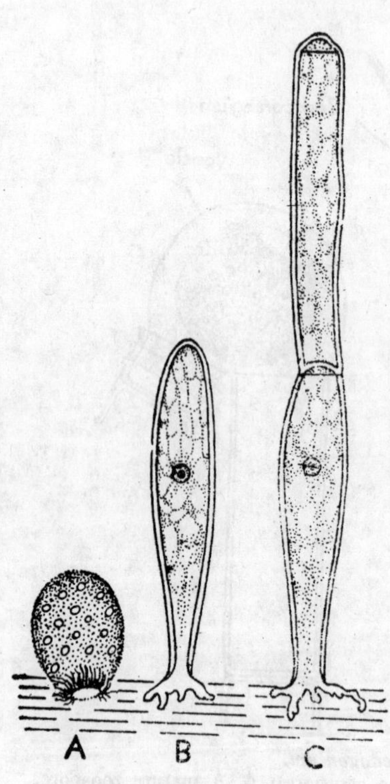

Fig. 36. *Oedogonium.* Germination of a zoospore and formation of a young plant.

Sometimes *Oedogonium* may form **akinetes** in chains of 10-40, within the vegetative cells. The akinetes contain sufficient amount of reserve starch and red-coloured oil. Under favourable conditions an akinete germinates into a new plant.

Sexual reproduction in *Oedogonium* is of an oogamous type, in which a gametic union takes place by the fusion of a small motile spermatozoid with a large, non-motile egg. The sexual organs, antheridia and oogonia, may be produced on the filaments of normal size (**macrandrous species**), or the oogonia are borne on normal filament, the antheridia being produced on special **dwarf male filament** or **nannandrium** (**nannandrous species**) consisting of a few cells.

Macrandrous species may be homothallic or heterothallic. Any vegetative cell excepting the basal one may act as an antheridium mother cell. The position of the antheridium may be terminal or intercalary. The antheridium mother cell divides into two daughter cells of unequal sizes, the short terminal cell being transformed into an antheridium. The lower much longer sister cell may, in turn, act as an antheridium mother cell, and divides repeatedly in a similar manner forming a row of 8-40 antheridia. The protoplast of each antheridium is metamorphozed into a single spermatozoid, or it divides into two daughter protoplasts and forms two spermatozoids. The spermatozoids look like zoospores, but are much smaller in size and with fewer flagella. The mode of liberation of the spermatozoids is similar to that of zoospores, and there is the usual formation of a vesicle at the time of liberation.

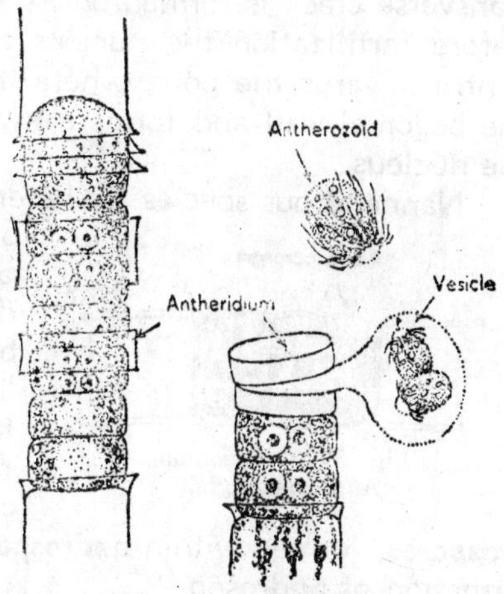

Fig. 37. *Oedogonium*. Formation of antheridia and liberation of spermatozoids.

Similarly, the terminal or any intercalary vegetative cell may act as an oogonium mother cell. The oogonium mother cell, as before, divides into two daughter cells of unequal sizes, the shorter cell at the distal end forms the oogonium and is always provided with one or more caps at the upper end. The lower larger sister cell is

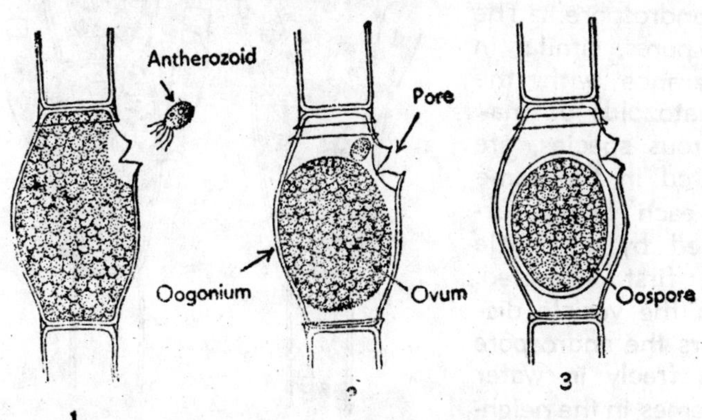

Fig. 38. *Oedogonium*.
1, An oogonium ready for fertilization ; 2, The same just at the time of fertilization ; 3, An oogonium with a zygote (oospore).

called the **suffultory cell.** This cell either remains as such or acts as another oogonium mother cell, which divides and re-divides forming two or more intercalary oogonia in a chain. The oogonium swells up and becomes more or less spherical with a diameter greater than that of any vegetative cell. The protoplast of the oogonium is gradually metamorphozed into a uninucleate oosphere or ovum. As the oogonium approaches maturity, a small pore or transverse crack is formed on its wall towards the upper end. Just before fertilization the nucleus of the ovum migrates from the centre towards the pore, where the ovum slightly contracts from the oogonial wall and forms a hyaline receptive spot just outside the nucleus.

Nannandrous species are heterothallic. The structure and mode of development of the oogonia are similar to those in macrandrous species, and these are borne on filaments of normal size. The dwarf male filaments bearing antheridia are produced as a result of germination of the special type of zoospores, called **androspores,** formed within **androsporangia** (Fig. 39). The mode of formation of androsporangia is similar to that of the antheridia. The protoplast of an androsporangium is metamorphozed into only one androspore. The androspores, similar in apprearance with the spermatozoids of macrandrous species, are liberated in the same way, each being surrounded by a vesicle when first liberated. When the vesicle disappears the androspore swims freely in water and comes in the neighbourhood of an oogonium or an oogonium

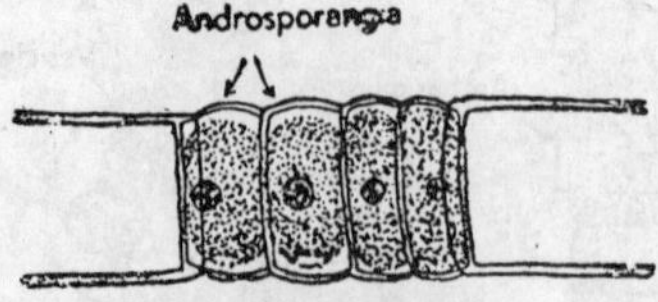

Fig. 39. *Oedogonium* Androsporangia.

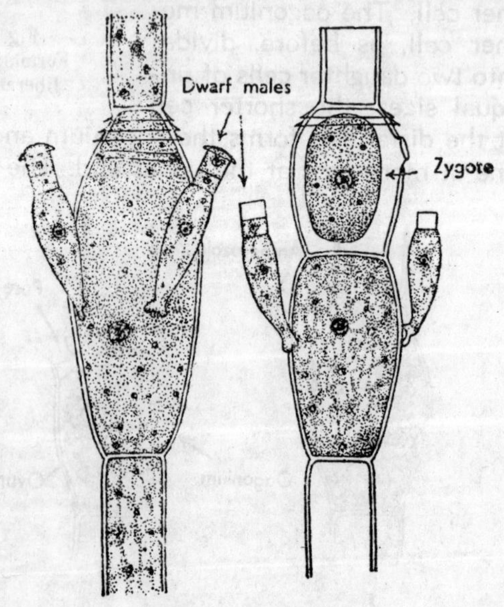

Fig. 40. *Oedogonium* Sexual reproduction in a nannandrous species.

mother cell. In the former case, the androspore attaches itself, with its hyaline end downwards, to the oogonial wall or to the wall of the suffultory cell and forms the dwarf male filament there. In the later case, when it affixes itself to the wall of the oogonium mother cell, it has been found to form the dwarf male filament always on the suffultory cell after the division and formation of oogonium. When an androspore affixes itself to the wall, it develops a holdfast, surrounds itself with a delicate wall and forms a one-celled plant (**germling**). This cell acts as an antheridium mother cell and cuts off one or more antheridia at its apex. The protoplast of each antheridium divides into two parts and forms two spermatozoids.

Nannandrous species of *Oedogonium* may bear both oogonia and androsporangia on the same filament (**gynandrosporous**), or they are borne on different filaments of normal sizes (**idioandrosporous**).

In both macrandrous and nannandrous species, fertilization of the ovum takes place by the entry of a spermatozoid through the pore at the hyaline receptive spot. The zygote (oospore) slightly retracts from the oogonial wall and soon forms a wall of two or three concentric layers around it. The middle layer may often show pits or reticulations. At maturity, the oospore becomes reddish brown in colour due to the accumulation of oil. Finally, the oogonial wall disintegrates, the oospore falls to the bottom of the pond, where it undergoes a period of rest for a year or more. Prior to germination the diploid nucleus of the protoplast undergoes reduction division forming four haploid nuclei. Subsequently, the cytoplasm divides and collects around each of the four nuclei forming four **zoospores.** At the time of germination the wall of the oospore bursts and zoospores escape being surrounded by the vesicle. Finally, the vesicle disappears, and the zoospores swim freely in water. Subsequent development of the zoospore and the formation of the vegetative filament take place in the usual way.

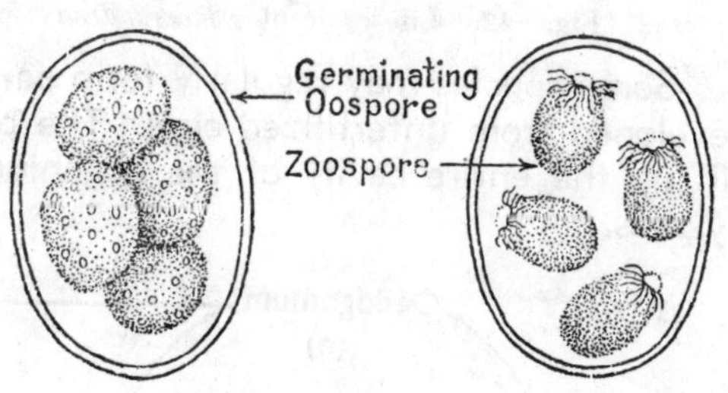

Fig. 41. *Oedogonium*
Germinating oospore.

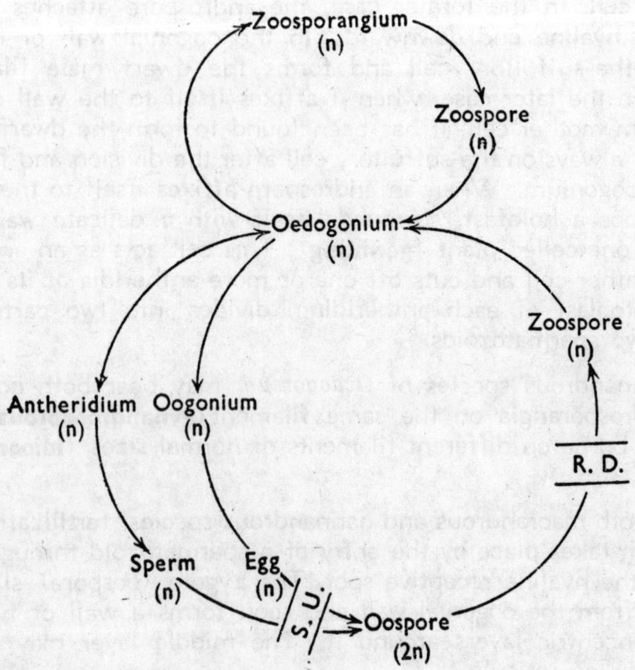

Fig. 42. Life cycle of a *macrandrous* species of *Oedogonium.*

Some species may regularly form **parthenospores (aboospores)** developed from unfertilized eggs. The parthenospores completely fill up the entire cavity of the oogonium and possess walls like zygotes.

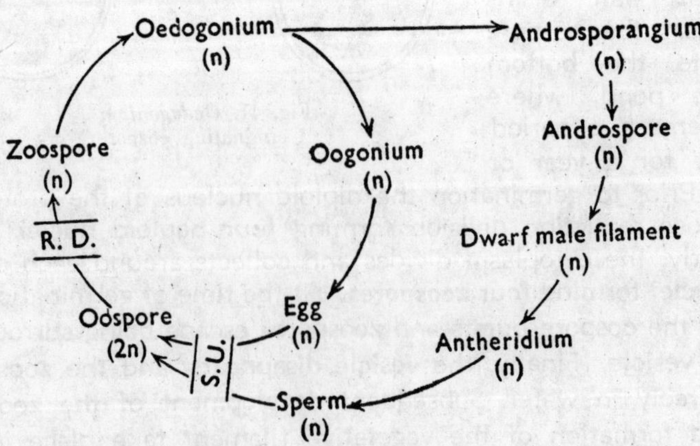

Fig. 43. Life cycle of a *nannandrous* species of *Oedogonium,*

ORDER 7. CONJUGALES

Unicellular or colonial (generally filamentous) with elaborate chloroplasts ; motile gametes unknown ; reproduction by vegetative cell division or by conjugation of amoeboid gametes ; exclusively freshwater.

SPIROGYRA

(Fam. ZYGNEMATACEAE)

Spirogyra represents one of the commonest freshwater green algae. It is usually found as a free-floating inhabitant of the stagnant water of ponds, tanks, ditches, etc., forming a green slippery mass. Occasionally, it is found in running streams and springs, where it attaches itself to rocks or other objects by means of holdfasts or haptera. These develop as much-branched outgrowths of the lateral walls of the vegetative cells.

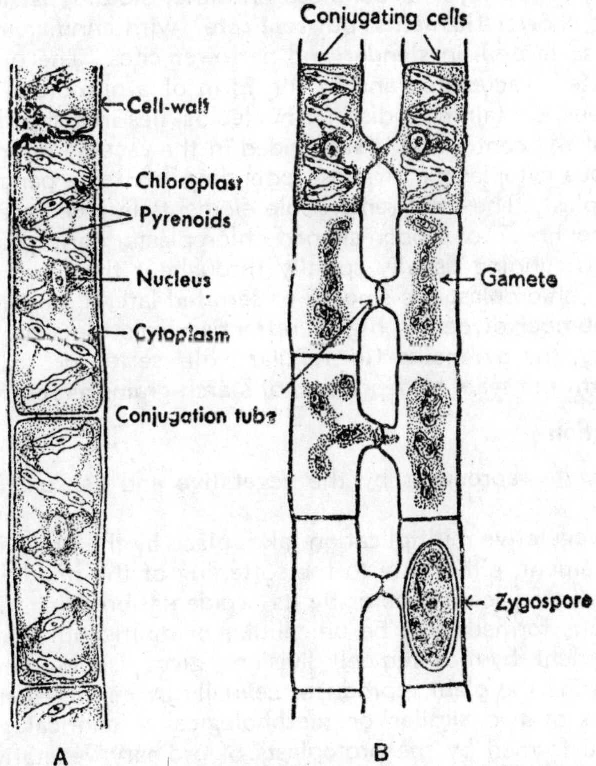

Fig. 44. *Spirogyra.*
A, Portion of the filament showing vegetative cells ; B, Successive stages in scalariform conjugation.

The common Indian species of *Spirogyra* are *S. adnata*, *S. affinis*, *S. biformis*, *S. crassa*, *S. elongata*, *S. exilis*, *S. inflata*, *S. neglecta*, etc.

Vegetative body (Fig. 44A)

The vegetative body of the plant consists of an unbranched filament, a number of which are intermingled with one another into a mass, commonly called the **pond scum.** A filament is composed of a single row of cylindrical cells joined end on end, usually in the case of free-floating species, without any distinction into base and apex. The filament increases in length by ordinary cell division and by subsequent growth of individual cells, each of which is equally capable of further divisions. The lateral walls of the cells are three-layered, the inner two of cellulose and the outermost one of pectose of variable thickness. The middle lamella (cross wall) is made up of pectose with a layer of cellulose on either side. It is simple in dwarf and shorter filaments, but **replicate** (with annular ingrowth of cellulose layers) in slender and narrower ones. The protoplast is granulated, vacuolated and in the form of a primordial utricle. The nucleus, containing a distinct nucleolus, lies in a sheath of cytoplasm at the centre and is suspended in the vacuole by means of conspicuous cytoplasmic strands, extending from the periphery of the protoplast. The most remarkable elements in a cell are a varying number (1—7) of ribbon-shaped chloroplasts, peripheral in location and running usually spirally throughout the length of the cell. Each chloroplast has smooth or serrated lateral margins and a varying number of dense, highly refractive, colourless proteinaceous bodies, the **pyrenoids** (in regular axile series or scattered), which form the seats of deposition of starch grains as reserve food.

Reproduction

Spirogyra reproduces by the vegetative and sexual methods only.

The vegetative multiplication takes place by the breaking down of the filament, either due to the softening of the middle lamella between two adjacent cells or by its accidental breaking. The filaments, thus formed, may be unicellular or multicellular and each such fragment, by repeated cell divisions, gives rise to a new plant.

In spring the plant reproduces sexually by **conjugation,** *i.e.* by the union of two similar or morphologically identical gametes, which are formed by the protoplasts of ordinary vegetative cells. Each of these vegetative cells is called a **gametangium,** and its undifferentiated, uninucleate protoplast is called a **gamete.**

In heterothallic species, conjugation takes place between the cells of two different filaments. At first the two filaments lie in close proximity with each other throughout their entire lengths, and there is a secretion of a common gelatinous envelope around them. In this position short transverse papillae are developed in opposite directions from the walls of cells of the adjacent filaments. These papillae come in contact with corresponding pairs and grow further, thus pushing the original filaments apart. Finally, the endwalls of these outgrowths are dissolved and the cells are connected by an open tube (**conjugation tube**). By this time the protoplasts (gametes of the two conjugating cells) have begun to contract, and after the for-

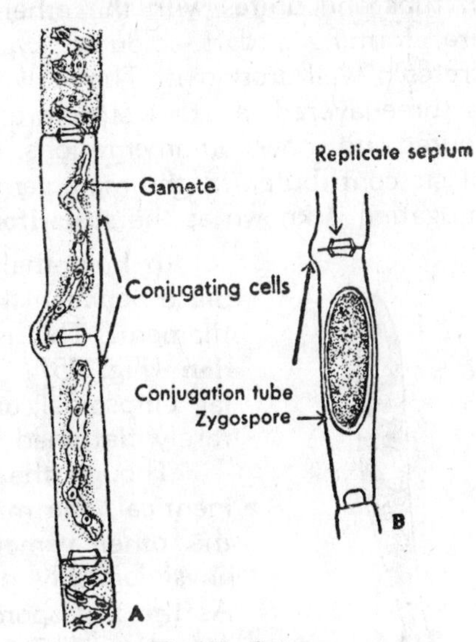

Fig. 45. *Spirogyra.*
A—B, Stages in lateral conjugation.

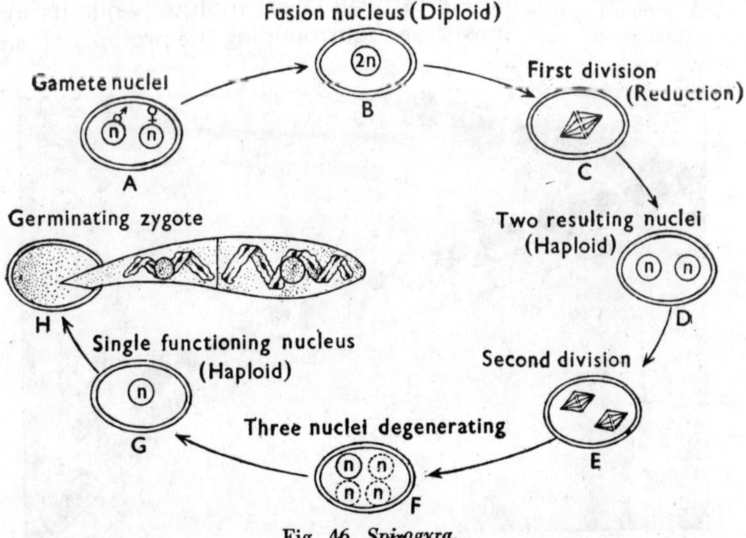

Fig. 46. *Spirogyra.*
Nuclear changes of the zygospore (diagrammatic).

mation of the conjugation tube, the protoplast (male gamete), which began its contraction earlier, migrates through the conjugation tube and unites with the other protoplast (female gamete) there, forming a dark-coloured zygote, called **zygospore,** which secretes a wall around it. The wall formed around the zygospore is a three-layered resistant structure, of which the middle layer is coloured and shows ornamentations. In exceptional cases the chloroplasts contributed by the male gamete disintegrate. This type of conjugation is known as the **scalariform conjugation** (Fig. 44).

Fig. 47. *Spirogyra.* A germinating zygospore.

In homothallic species conjugation takes place between the adjoining cells of the same filament. This is termed the **lateral conjugation** (Fig. 45). The zygospore may be globular, ellipsoidal, or cylindrical with obtuse ends, rarely flattened and discoid in shape.

Though the gametes are morphologically identical, the migration of one of them into the other gametangium proves them to be physiologically or biologically differentiated. As the zygospore attains maturity, there is a reduction division of its fusion nucleus forming four haploid nuclei, of which three undergo disintegration. After a considerable period of rest the zygospore germinates, its two outermost wall layers rupture, while its innermost layer (surrounding the protoplast) emer-

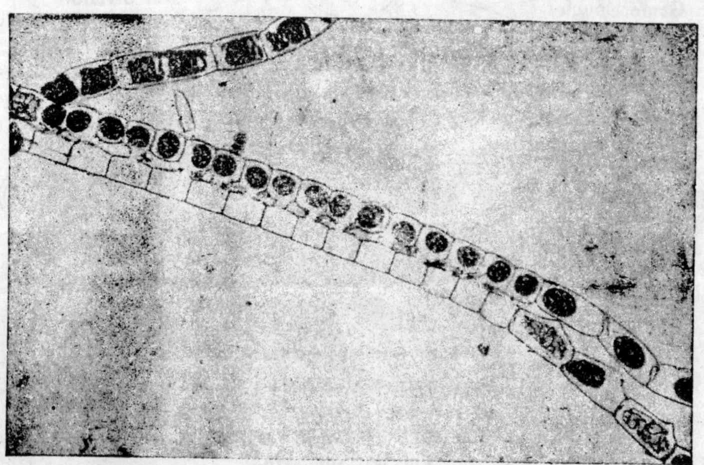
Fig. 48. Photomicrograph of *Spirogyra* showing scalariform conjugation.

ges in the form of a tubular outgrowth. By the formation of a transverse septum a cell is formed at the distal end, which by successive new divisions, gives rise to a *Spirogyra* filament.

It has been observed that during scalariform conjugation usually all the cells of the filament may produce gametes of one sex, so that after conjugation there is migration of all gametes of one filament (may be regarded as the male) to the cells of other filament (female) forming zygotes there. But, it may so happen that each filament may contain both male and female gametes so that cross conjugation may occur forming zygotes in both the filaments. It should be noted that all the cells of a filament may be fertile or there may be regular alternation of fertile and sterile ones.

When conjugation fails, the gamete surrounds itself with a thick wall and forms a **parthenospore** or **azygospore,** which after a period of rest germinates into a new plant.

ZYGNEMA

(Fam. ZYGNEMATACEAE)

Zygnema is another widely distributed, freshwater, green alga which occurs in much the same type of habitats as does *Spirogyra.*

The common Indian species of *Zygnema* are *Z. amplum, Z. gangeticum, Z. giganteum, Z. gorakhporense, Z. indica, Z. iyengari, Z. melanosporum, Z. sphaerica,* etc.

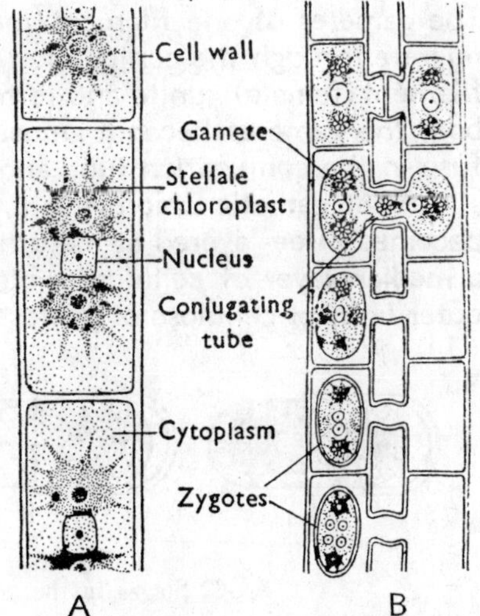

Fig. 49. *Zygnema.*
Part of a filament (on the left); Successive stages in conjugation and formation of zygospores (on the right).

Vegetative body (Fig. 49A)

The thallus, the *Spirogyra,* is an unbranched filament without any distinction into base and apex. A filament consists of a single row of similar cylindrical cells, usually having lengths slightly greater than breadths ; occasionally, the cell may be 2-5 times as long as broad. Holdfasts or haptera are rarely formed. The wall structure is much the same as that in *Spirogyra*, but the outermost pectose layer rarely becomes thick. The transverse walls are never replicated. The protoplast is uninucleate, and the nucleus is embedded in a broad strand of cytoplasm connecting two chloroplasts on either side : this band occupies the longitudinal axis of the cell. Each chloroplast is stellate or starshaped with a prominent pyrenoid at its centre, and it may have numerous delicate strands extending towards the periphery of the cytoplasm. The filament increases in length by cell divisions and subsequent growth of the individual cells. Prior to the cell division, the nucleus divides mitotically into two, so that after cytokinesis, each daughter cell receives one daughter nucleus and a chloroplast of the parent cell, the former lying lateral to the latter. Subsequently, the chloroplast with its pyrenoid divides into two and the nucleus migrates and occupies a position midway between the two daughter chloroplasts.

Reproduction

Zygnema reproduces by vegetative and sexual methods.

The vegetative reproduction usually takes place by the accidental breaking of the filament and never due to the softening of the cross wall of the adjacent cells.

Most species of *Zygnema* reproduce sexually, in the spring, by the process of **conjugation** (Fig. 49B). Conjugation is usually scalariform, but lateral conjugation is not of rare occurrence. The process of scalariform conjugation is much the same as that in *Spirogyra*. The gametes of one filament (male) become active, amoeboid and migrate through the conjugation tubes to the gametes of the other filamént (female), unite and form zygospores. But in some species both the gametes become amoeboid, migrate towards each other, fuse in the conjugation tube and form a zygospore there.

After gametic union, the zygote is invested by a wall, which becomes three-layered at maturity (a thin inner layer of cellulose, a median layer of cellulose which is often chitinized, and a thin outer layer of cellulose or pectose). The colouration and ornamen-

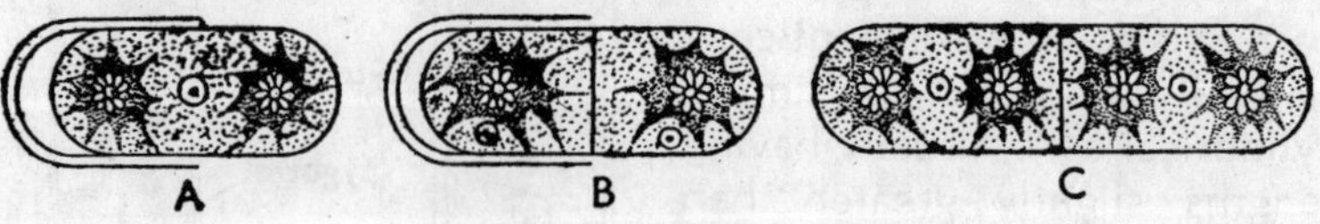

Fig. 50. *Zygnema*.
A—C, Stages in the germination of the zygote.

tation are restricted to the middle layer, as in *Spirogyra*. The zygotes, at maturity, are finally liberated by the disintegration of the gametangial wall or of the wall of the conjugation tube, and usually undergo a period of rest for several months. With the advent of the following spring the zygote germinates, and prior to this germination there is a reduction division of the zygote nucleus forming four haploid nuclei, of which three disintegrate. During germination the two outer walls of the zygote rupture and the protoplast being still enclosed by the innermost wall-layer may partially or wholly escape from the ruptured walls. This protoplast by repeated divisions gives rise to a new filament.

When conjugation fails, a gamete may form azygospore or parthenospore. But these are not produced in abundance in the genus.

COSMARIUM

(Fam. DESMIDIACEAE)

Cosmarium and other members of the Family Desmidiaceae are commonly known as "desmids". They are all inhabitants of freshwater and are found sparingly intermingled with other free-floating algae everywhere.

The common Indian species of *Cosmarium* are *C. abruptum*, *C. aequale*, *C. americanum*, *C. apertum*, *C. aversum*, *C. bengalense*, *C. barrackporeanum*, *C. biobeonicum*, *C. coloratum*, *C. deacuminatum*, *C. dubium*, *C. ellipsoidale*, *C. exile*, *C. forceps*, *C. lacustre*, etc.

Vegetative body (Fig. 51)

Cosmarium is a unicellular genus which may be easily recognized in having small compressed cells, each being divided by a conspicuous median constriction (**sinus**) into two distinct symmetrical halves (**semi-cells**), united together by a comparatively narrow connecting zone (**isthmus**). Its species are distinguished partly from such characters as cell shape, ornamentation of the wall, etc. Each cell should be examined in front, side and vertical views. In front view the semi-cells may be circular, elliptical, reniform or sub-quadrangular in shape, whereas in vertical view they are usually elliptical in outline. In side view the semi-cells, in most cases, appear more or less circular in outline.

The cellwall in *Cosmarium* is never spiny, and it consists of three concentric layers : (1) an innermost thin cellulose layer, (2) a somewhat thicker median layer consisting of cellulose and pectic compounds, and (3) an outer thick or thin layer of gelatinous sheath made up of pectose. Excepting at the isthmus region the inner two layers are perforated by vertical pores, being usually arranged in a definite pattern and are distributed all over the semi-cells, or may be localized. The outer wall is usually smooth, but may sometimes appear somewhat granular.

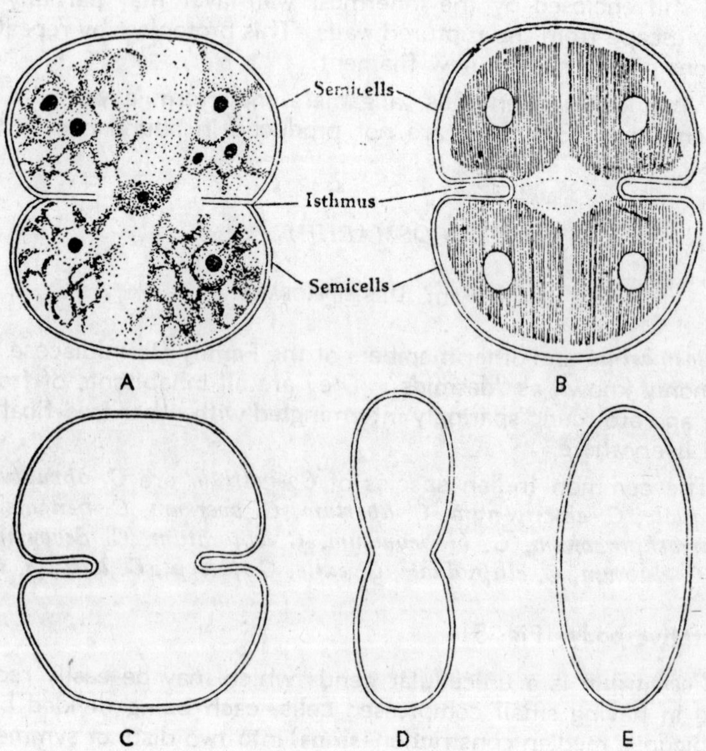

Fig. 51. *Cosmarium.*
A, A vegetative cell in section ; B, Diagrammatic representation of the vegetative cell ; C—E, Front side and vertical views of the vegetative cell (*Diagrammatic*).

The protoplast contains a single nucleus which always lies at the isthmus and is sometimes connected with the string-like projections of the chloroplast. Each nucleus contains a conspicuous nucleolus and well-defined nuclear reticulum.

Usually, there is only one chloroplast in each semi-cell, but sometimes two or four chloroplasts may be present. Each chloroplast contains a single pyrenoid and is provided with four to several radiating plate-like extensions.

The cells of *Cosmarium* exhibit movement which consists in a series of jerks. This is due to the secretion of gelatinous material through the vertical pores.

Reproduction (Figs. 52 & 53)

Cosmarium reproduces both by vegetative and sexual methods.

The vegetative method of reproduction takes place by the method of cell division and two daughter cells are formed from the

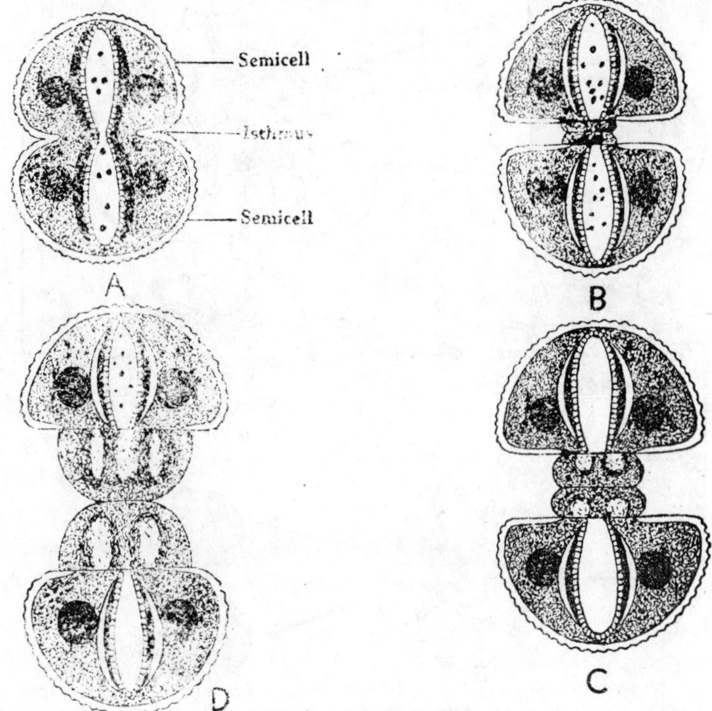

Fig. 52. *Cosmarium.*
A, A vegetative cell ; B—D, Vegetative reproduction showing formation of daughter cells.

parent cell. During the process the nucleus first divides into two daughter nuclei and the isthmus slightly elongates. A transverse wall is formed across the isthmus in such a way that each semi-cell receives one daughter nucleus. The portion of the isthmus, attached to each semi-cell, now enlarges and forms a new semi-cell, and in this way two daughter cells are formed. The daughter cells remain attached to each other for some time but finally separate. Thus, it is evident that of the two semi-cells, one semi-cell is younger than the other, which belongs to the parent cell. The newly formed semi-cell receives a chloroplast with a pyrenoid by the division of thd pre-existing one of the other semi-cell. Sometimes pyrenoid may be formed *de novo* in the newly formed chloroplasts.

Sexual reproduction is **isogamous** and consists in the union of two identical gametes, produced usually by two mature individuals.

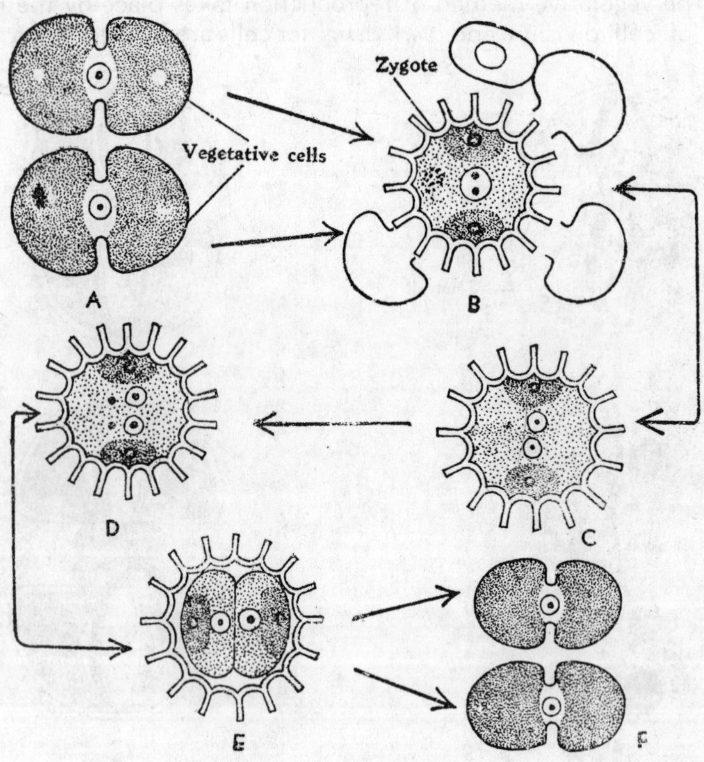

Fig. 53. *Cosmarium.*
A—F, Stages in sexual reproduction, and formation and germination of the zygote.

Conjugation may also take place between two newly formed sister cells. During conjugation, usually two mature cells come to lie in contact with each other and become surrounded by a common gelatinous sheath secreted for the purpose. The protoplast of each cell functions as a gamete. Each cell then breaks at the isthmus and the gamete escapes. The two gametes, thereupon, fuse outside and after secreting a thick wall around it form a somewhat globose or angular **zygospore.** Its wall may be smooth, papillate or spiny. The zygospore, after a considerable period of rest, germinates. The fusion nucleus undergoes a reduction division forming four haploid nuclei, of which two degenerate and the remaining two are functional. The protoplast then divides into two equal halves, each receiving one functional nucleus and a chloroplast. Each daughter protoplast finally develops into a vegetative cell, which is liberated by the rupture of the zygote wall.

When conjugation fails, **azygospores** or **parthenospores** may be formed. The parthenospore, during germination, contains three degenerating nuclei and one functional nucleus, which, by division, gives rise to the nuclei of the two resulting vegetative cells.

CLOSTERIUM

(Fam. DESMIDIACEAE)

Closterium is one of the largest genera of planktonic desmids. It is widely distributed throughout the world being altogether restricted to freshwater of small ponds, margins of rocky lakes and other bodies of water which are not alkaline.

The common Indian species of *Closterium* are *C. abruptum*, *C. anastomosum*, ***C. costatum***, *C. exiguum*, *C. intermedium*, *C. legumen*, *C. khasianum*, *C. manipurense*, *C. striatum*, etc.

Vegetative body (Fig. 54)

The body of *Closterium* is strictly unicellular, which is elongated or somewhat lunate without any median constriction, and attenuated at both ends. The cellwall is provided with delicate pores and in most cases with longitudinal striations. It is mainly made up of cellulose and often appears yellowish-brown in colour due to impregnation with iron compounds. The cellwall consists of two halves, one belonging to the older generation and the other to the younger one. They fit so closely and firmly that they are not easily recognizable in living conditions but become separated after death or during conjugation. The protoplast contains two chloroplasts, one within each half of the cellwall and usually with a few pyrenoids. The chloroplasts are either entire or they are provided with radiating longitudinal

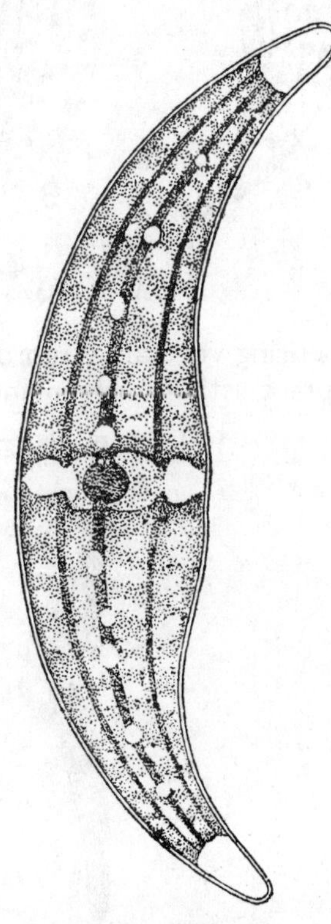

Fig. 54. *Closterium.* An entire plant.

ridges. The nucleus lies embedded in a mass of cytoplasm and is connected with the two chloroplasts by means of thin cytoplasmic strands. At the attenuated ends (**poles**) of each cell there is a conspicuous vacuole in which are embedded one or more cystals of gypsum salts.

Reproduction

Closterium reproduces vegetatively as well as by the sexual method.

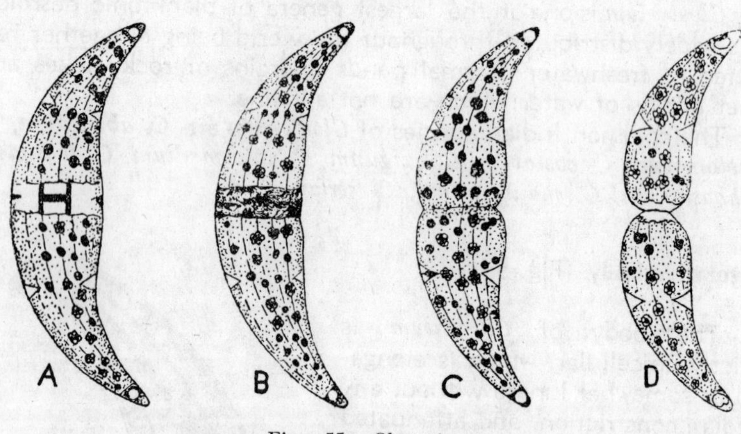

Fig. 55. *Closterium*.
A—D, Stages in vegetative reproduction.

During vegetative reproduction there is a transverse division of the pre-existing nucleus and the two chloroplasts. It is very pecu-

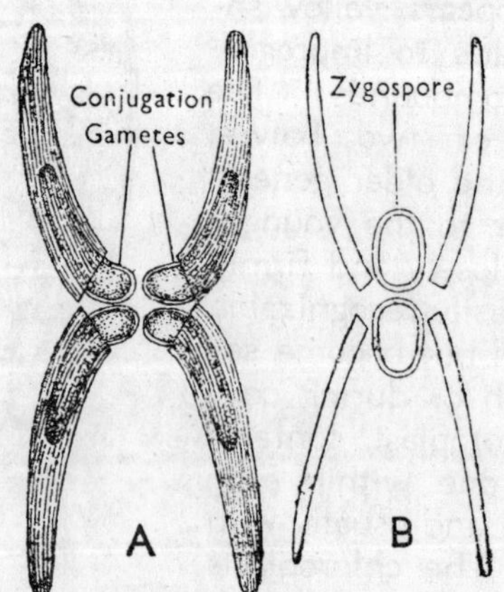

Fig. 56. *Closterium*.
A—B, Stages in sexual reproduction.

liar that in this case the dividing wall is not formed in the middle of the cell but a little away from the centre and within the younger half wall of the cell.

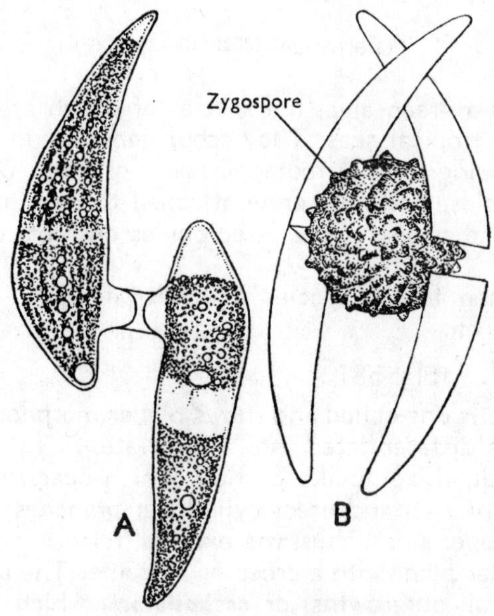

Fig. 57. *Closterium.*
A—B, Stages in formation of zygospore.

Sexual reproduction takes place by **conjugation** of amoeboid gametes from two conjugating cells. In some cases, a rudimentary conjugation tube may be formed between them ; in others, sister cells probably conjugate. In most cases, the cellwall breaks in the middle region (isthmus) and its protoplast escapes as an amoeboid gamete, which, on finding its mate, unites with it and forms a spherical, ovoid or quadrangular zygote (zygospore) with thick or ornamented walls. After the resting period the zygote germinates, its nucleus divides reductionally forming four daughter nuclei, of which two degenerate. This is followed by the division of the protoplast, each of which contains a single chloroplast, a functional and a disintegrating nucleus. The daughter protoplast sooner or later surrounds itself with a cellwall and assumes the shape characteristic of the genus.

ORDER 8. **SIPHONALES**

Filamentous ; without septa or elaborately differentiated ; all parts coenocytic ; chloroplasts numerous and discoid ; sexual reproduction mainly isogamous, sometimes oogamous, unknown in many cases ; mostly marine.

CAULERPA

(Fam. CAULERPACEAE)

Caulerpa is a green alga, the species of which are mostly distributed in the tropical seas. They occur generally in shallow and calm waters, being usually rooted in sand or mud. Quite a large number of species, however, grow attached to rock or coral reefs and may sometimes also occur as epiphytes on roots of mangrove plants.

The common Indian species of *Caulerpa* are *C. clavifera*, *C. scalpeldiformis*, etc.

Vegetative body (Fig. 58)

The thallus is one-celled and shows higher morphological differentiation. It is differentiated into a prostrate, more or less branched, cylindrical, rhizome-like portion, which bears on its underside root-like rhizoids and erect cylindrical branches or the **leafy shoots** on its upper side. Thus, the external form is comparable to that of a vascular plant with a creeping rhizome. The upright branches bear lateral outgrowths or **assimilators,** which are usually flattened, but the forms of the shoots may vary from species to

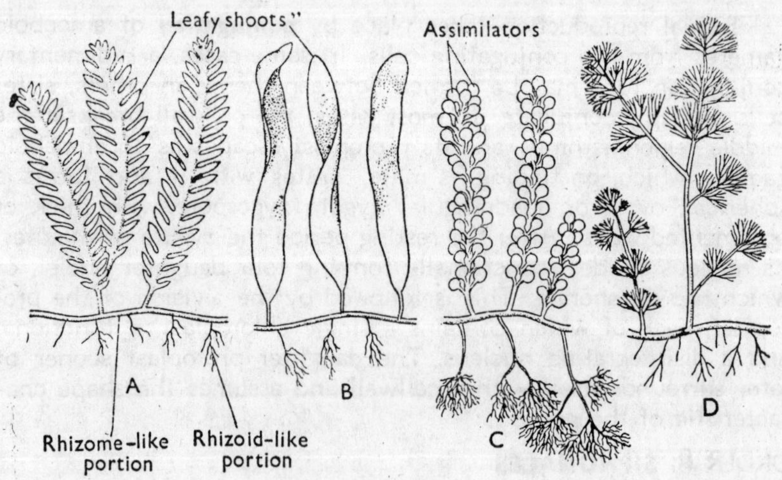

Fig. 58. *Caulerpa.*
A—D, Portions of the vegetative bodies of different Indian species of the same.

species, often resembling the cacti, the mosses or the lycopods. The entire unicellular body is a branched coenocyte without transverse septa. The cytoplasm is continuous lying internal to the cell-wall, and contains numerous nuclei and disciform chloroplasts without pyrenoids. There is a single central vacuole which runs throughout the entire length of the plant.

The cellwall is comparatively thick and is provided with numerous transverse and longitudinal skeletal strands or **trabeculae** traversing the central cavity of the thallus. These trabeculae are most strongly developed in the rhizomatous portion, but becoming fewer and fewer in the assimilators and may be poorly developed in the rhizoids or altogether absent. As the thallus gradually becomes older due to the deposition of successive strata of wall materials, the lateral wall as well as the trabeculae become distinctly stratified in appearance. The wall is composed of callose, pectin, pectic acids and pentose, cellulose being entirely absent. The rigidity of the plant is maintained due to the turgidity of the thallus and thickness of the cellwall.

Reproduction

Caulerpa reproduces the vegetative, asexual and sexual methods.

During vegetative reproduction the older parts of the rhizome gradually die away, thereby separating the erect shoots. These detached shoots are dispersed by the waves and possess the remarkable power of producing new plants when affixed to any suitable substratum. In this way rapid multiplication of the plant is effected.

Several species of *Caulerpa* reproduce asexually by the produc-

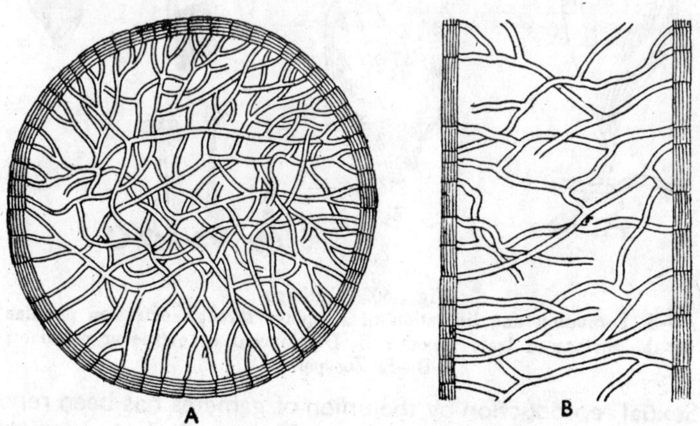

Fig. 59. *Caulerpa.*
A, Trabeculae in rhizomatous portion ; B, The same in an assimilator.

tion of **zoospores,** but the details of the zoospore-formation and their behaviour are very little known. Zoospores may be produced from any portion of the leafy shoots or rarely from the rhizome. After their formation, the zoospores appear to remain in reticulate masses within the cell and numerous papillate outgrowths are developed on the surface of the thallus. These papillae are known as **extrusion papillae,** through which zoospores are liberated in a mass of mucilagenous matter in such an enormous quantity that the water surrounding the thallus appears green for the time being. Each zoospore is biflagellate, pyriform in shape and possesses a single curved chloroplast without any pyrenoid. In many species it disorganizes after liberation.

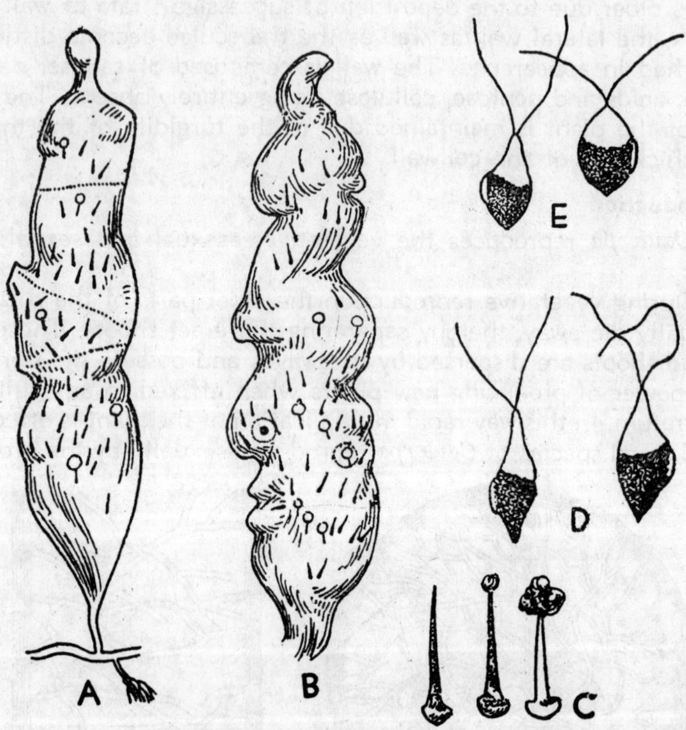

Fig. 60. *Caulerpa.*
A—B, Formation and liberation of zoospores through extrusion papillae on the surface of leafy shoots ; C, Developcent of extrusion papillae ; D—E, Zoospores.

Sexual reproduction by the union of gametes has been reported in several oriental species. In one of them, *Caulerpa clavifera*, a heterothallic plant, reproduction has been shown to be **anisogamous.**

VAUCHERIA

(Fam. VAUCHERIACEAE)

Vaucheria is an inhabitant of freshwater, though a few marine species are not uncommon. Some are terrestrial and may grow on bare moist soil or in ploughed fields forming extensive interwoven felty sheets.

The common Indian species of *Vaucheria* are *V. aversa*, *V. clavata*, *V. orientalis*, *V. ornithocephala*, *V. submarina*, *V. uncinata*, *V. sessiles*, etc.

Vegetative body (Fig. 61)

The thallus consists of a sparingly branched tubular, coenocytic filament having no cross-walls excepting at the reproductive regions. They are attached to the substratum by means of rhizoid-like branches.

The growth of the thallus is restricted to the apices of the branches. The coenocytic thallus, when injured, may develop transverse septa blocking the injured portion. The cellwall is thin and consists of an inner layer of cellulose and a pectose layer external to it. Just within the cellwall there is a thin layer of cytoplasm surrounding a large central vacuole which runs, without interruption, throughout the entire length of the thallus. Embedded in the peripheral layer of cytoplasm are numerous nuclei and chloroplasts, the former lying towards the inner face and the latter towards the outer face of the cytoplasm. The chloroplasts are without pyrenoids and are either circular or elliptical

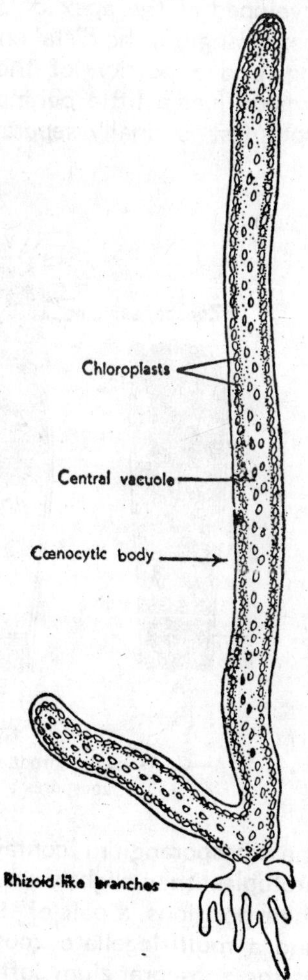

Fig. 61. *Vaucheria*. An entire plant.

in outline. Food reserves are stored as oil under natural condition, but when continuously illuminated, starch may be formed instead.

Reproduction

Vaucheria reproduces both asexually and sexually.

There are various methods of asexual reproduction. Typically, the method is by means of large **multiflagellate zoospores** (Fig. 62), each being formed singly within a club-shaped zoosporangium developed at the apex of a branch. During the development of a zoosporangium the distal end of a branch forms a club-shaped swelling, and a portion of the protoplast is cut off by its transverse division just a little behind the branch apex. This portion of the protoplast is finally separated by a transverse septum and forms

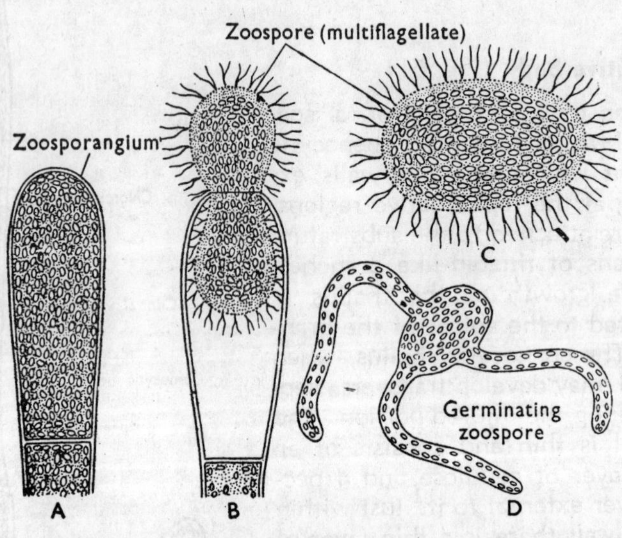

Fig. 62. *Vaucheria.*
A—C, Asexual reproduction showing formation and liberation of zoospores ; D, A germinating zoospore.

the zoosporangium containing a multinucleate protoplast. This protoplast then slightly contracts, the nuclei and chloroplasts change their positions, a pair of flagella develops external to each nucleus and a multiflagellate zoospore is formed. At maturity, the apex of the zoosporangium softens forming a small pore through which the zoospore squeezes its way and finally swims freely but slowly in water. After a short period of activity, the zoospore comes to rest, withdraws its flagella, and secretes a wall around it. The germination starts immediately by the formation of one or more tubular outgrowths which finally develop into a new thallus.

In species of *Vaucheria*, growing on damp soil in greenhouses, the entire protoplast of the sporangium, instead of producing a zoospore, may develop into a thin-walled **aplanospore** or a thin-walled

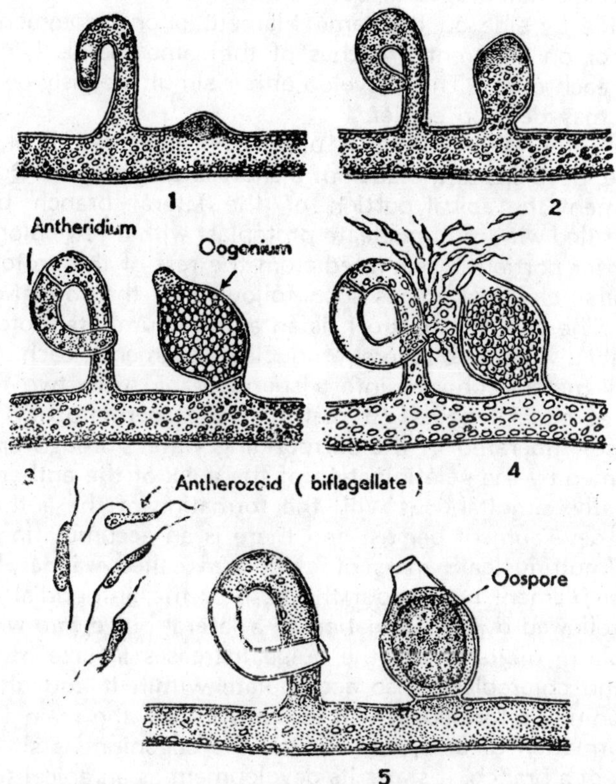

Fig. 63. *Vaucheria.*
1—5, Development of sex organs and progress of sexual reproduction.

akinete. This aplanospore is liberated by the rupture of the sporangial wall, and on germination, gives rise to a thallus. The akinete becomes separated from the thallus or germinates *in situ*. Sometimes due to scarcity of water, the entire protoplast of *Vaucheria* undergoes transverse divisions into short segments, around each of which a thick wall is secreted. These are thick-walled aplanospores (**hypnospores**), which either germinate directly or the protoplast of each divides into a number of thin-walled **cysts.** At maturity, the protoplast of each cyst escapes in an amoeboid fashion and eventually comes to rest, rounds up, secretes a wall around it, and germinates into a new thallus.

All species of *Vaucheria* reproduce sexually and are oogamous. They are mostly homothallic, but a few marine species are heterothallic.

In homothallic species both antheridia and oogonia develop, either side by side on the same filament, or on a common lateral branch, or on different branches of the same thallus lying quite close to each other. They develop either simultaneously or the antheridia may develop earlier.

The antheridium, which is usually an elongated, hook-shaped structure, develops at the apex of a short lateral branch. During its development the apical portion of the lateral branch becomes densely filled with multinucleate protoplast with a few chloroplasts. This denser portion is separated from the rest of the protoplast by a transverse cleavage and is soon followed by the formation of a septum. The cell, thus cut off, is an antheridium. Its protoplast is eventually divided into several uninucleate segments, each of which is finally metamorphozed into a spermatozoid with two terminal flagella of equal lengths. At maturity, the spermatozoids are, in most cases, liberated in the surrounding water through an apical pore formed by the gelatinization of the apex of the antheridium.

Usually, simultaneous with the formation of the antheridium oogonial development begins, and there is an accumulation of colourless multinucleate mass of cytoplasm (called **wanderplasm**) in the main filament near about the base of the antheridial branch. This is followed by the formation of a lateral bulge into which the wanderplasm migrates. As the bulge increases in size, numerous nuclei and chloroplasts also accumulate within it and ultimately the oogonium is formed, which is cut off from the main filament by the formation of a septum. When the oogonium is situated at the apex of a branch, it starts its development as an apical swelling, which is finally cut off from the rest of the branch by the formation of a transverse septum. A mature oogonium contains a uninucleate egg. There is a great diversity of opinion as to the formation of the uninucleate egg. According to some, the uninucleate condition is obtained by the degeneration of all the nuclei excepting one ; others hold that all the nuclei, but one, migrate out of the oogonium before the formation of the transverse septum. There are still others who hold that the differentiation of the ovum and fertilization take place prior to the formation of the transverse wall. At maturity, a **beak** is formed at the end of the oogonium and it undergoes gelatinization, forming an apical pore through which a droplet of gelatinous material excudes.

The spermatozoids, liberated from the neighbouring antheridia, swim towards the oogonium and accumulate round the droplet. Usually, several spermatozoids enter through the apical pore of the oogonium, but only one fertilizes the ovum. The nuclei of the two gametes, following union, soon after fuse near about the apical pore, but the fusion nucleus finally migrates towards the centre of the zygote. Following fertilization the zygote secretes a thick wall, often consisting of 3—7 layers, around itself and its protoplast becomes rich in oil reserves. This zygote, after a period of rest for several months, germinates into a new filament. It has been held by the algologists that the division of the zygote nucleus, prior to its germination, is probably reductional.

Systematic position

The systematic position of *Vaucheria* is a much debated point. Workers like Fritsch and others have placed it with all the other oogamous siphonaceous green-coloured algae under the Class Chlorophyceae. Chadefaud was the first to question this position of *Vaucheria*, and formally placed it in the Order Heterosiphonales belonging to the Class Xanthophyceae. It was so placed because of the absence of starch in *Vaucheria* and the special colour of its chomatophore. Since then, additional proofs have been forthcoming from the works of Strain (1948), Koch (1951) and other workers to show that *Vaucheria* decidedly belongs to the Xanthophyceae. These include the following points mainly : (*a*) the pigments in the chromatophores of *Vaucheria* are those typically found in the Xanthophyceae, (*b*) the two xanthophylls, which are found only in the Siphonales, are lacking in *Vaucheria*, and (*c*) of the two equal-sized flagella borne anteriorly by an antherozoid, one is of the tinsel type and the other of the whiplash type.

Comparison of Spirogyra, Oedogonium and Vaucheria

Spirogyra	*Oedogonium*	*Vaucheria*
(*a*) *Structure*		
1. Plant body is an unbranched filament consisting of a row of cylindrical cells attached end on end, usually free-floating in mass embedded in mucilage.	1. Same as *Spirogyra*, but the cells are provided with apical caps and is attached to the substratum by holdfast.	1. Plant body is sparingly branched coenocytic filament with a long central vacuole, and is attached to the substratum by root-like process.

Comparison of Spirogyra, Oedogonium and Vaucheria (*Contd.*)

Spirogyra	*Oedogonium*	*Vaucheria*
2. Cellwall is three layered : the outermost layer is made up of pectose and the inner two layers of cellulose.	2. Cellwall is three layered : the outermost layer is made up of chitin, the middle layer of pectose, and the innermost layer of cellulose.	2. Cellwall is two layer ed : the outer layer is made up of pectose and the inner layer of cellulose.
3. Nucleus lies suspended in the vacuole by cytoplasmic threads.	3. Nucleus is large and biscuit-shaped and lies towards the cellwall in the middle of the cell.	3. Numerous nuclei lie towards the vacuole.
4. Chloroplast (1—7) are ribbon-shaped and spirally arranged and bear pyrenoids on their surface.	4. Chloroplast is reticulate and bears pyrenoids at the crossings of thread.	4. Chloroplasts are spherical or ellipsoidal and lie towards the cellwall.
(*b*) *Reproduction*		
5. No asexual reproduction.	5. Asexual reproduction takes place by zoospores which are provided with crown of flagella round the colourless ends.	5. Asexual reproduction takes place by zoospores, which are provided with flagella all round their body.
6. Sexual reproduction is isogamous and takes place by conjugation. A conjugation tube is formed between the cells of two filaments or between the adjacent cells of the same filament. Gamete of the cell passes through the tubes to the other cell and fuses with the gamete therein forming zygospore.	6. Sexual reproduction is oogamous and takes places by fertilization. In macrandrous sp. antheridia and oogonia are produced on normal filaments, whereas in nannandrous sp. oogonia are produced on normal filaments but the antheridia on dwarf male filaments. One of the sperms set free from the antheridium enters into an oogonium through the pore on its wall and fuses with the egg forming oospore.	6. Same as *Oedogonium.* Antheridia and oogonia are produced as outgrowths from the same or different filaments. Antheridium is a curved tubular structure which produces numerous biflagellate sperms, while the oogonium is a globular body containing an egg. One of the sperms enters into the oogonium through its beak and fuses with the egg forming an oospore.
7. Zygospore on germination gives rise to a new filament.	7. Oospore on germination produces four zoospores, each of which gives rise to a new filament.	7. Oospore on germination gives rise to a filament directly.

BRYOPSIS

(Fam. BRYOPSIDACEAE)

Bryopsis is a marine alga, mainly distributed in the warm tropical seas, but a few of them may be found in cold water also during spring and early summer.

Vegetative body (Fig. 64)

The vegetative body of *Bryopsis* is a coenocytic thallus, which can be differentiated into several parts. There is a sparsely branched, horizontally growing rhizome-like portion, remaining attached to the substratum by rhizoids. This portion is supposed to be perennial. From this rhizomatous body there appear some erect axes or branches, which are pinnately branched, and the pinnules

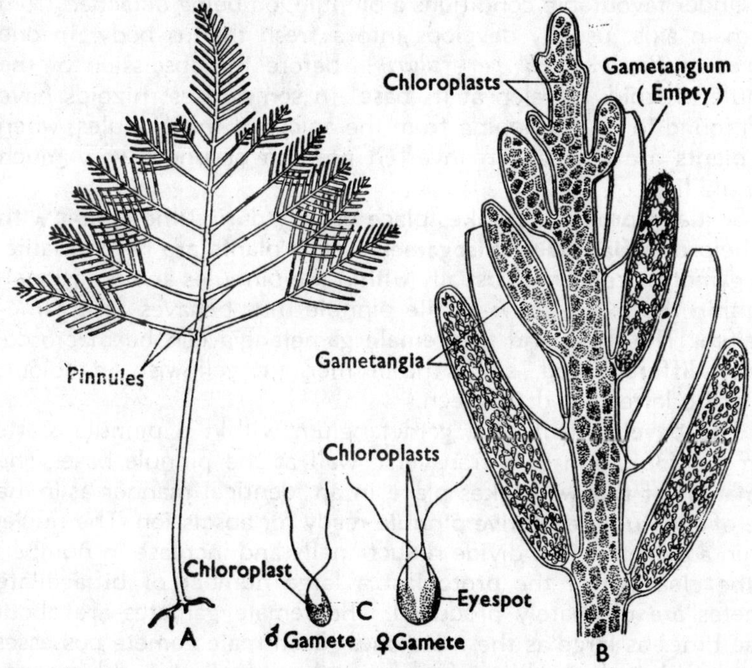

Fig. 64. ***Bryopsis.***
A, The plant body ; B, A portion of the plant body (magnified) showing gametangia ; C, The two types of gametes.

in their turn may again be similarly branched. It is not definitely known whether these erect branches are perennial or annual. In the majority of species the pinnules are arranged on the erect axis in two vertical rows, but in some cases these are developed on all sides of the axes. The fully mature pinnules continually fall off, and consequently, the lower half of the axis is usually free from any appendage. The pinnules are arranged in an acropetal order, and each one is provided with a constriction at the base at the point of its attachment with the main axis. The solitary cell of the plant body possesses a large continuous central vacuole. Lining this vacuole there runs a layer of cytoplasm containing numerous nuclei and many minute disc- to spindle-shaped chloroplasts. Usually each chloroplast contains a single pyrenoid. Though there is no septation within the body of the plant at an early stage, a cross-wall is distinctly laid down at the time of abscission of an old pinnule.

Reproduction

Bryopsis reproduces vegetatively as well as sexually.

Under favourable conditions a pinnule, on being detached from the main axis, usually develops into a fresh thallus body. In one species of *Bryopsis* (*B. corticularis*), before the abscission of the pinnule, rhizoids develop at its base. In some cases rhizoids have been found to be developing from the apices of the pinnules, when the plants are kept in an inverted position or under very much diffused light.

Sexual reproduction takes place usually during the spring with the help of **biflagellate anisogametes.** The plants are heterothallic. The gametes are formed usually within the pinnules and occasionally within the axis also. A fertile pinnule thus behaves as a gametangium. The male and the female gametangia can be macroscopically differentiated, since the former are yellowish in colour, while the latter are dark-green.

The development of a gametangium within a pinnule starts with the formation of a transverse wall at the pinnule base. The formation of this wall takes place in an identical manner as in the case of a mature vegetative pinnule ready for abscission. The nuclei within a gametangium divide reductionally and increase in number. By the cleavage of the protoplast a large number of biflagellate gametes are ultimately produced. The female gametes are about three times as large as the male ones. Each male gamete possesses a single chloroplast, while a female one has usually two chloroplasts and a very prominent eye-spot. The gametes escape either through one or more minute apertures developed on the wall of the gametangium, or by the gelatinization of the apex. On liberation, the gametes swim vigorously for a few hours, and then unite and give rise to a zygote, which, in some cases, has been found to be quadriflagellate for some time. Later on, it gets rounded off and enclosed by a wall. The zygote germinates directly, and very quickly gives rise to a new diploid plant. It is to be noted that the zygote nucleus does not divide reductionally, but equationally.

ORDER 9. CHARALES

Thallus well-differentiated into nodes and internodes ; internodes sometimes corticated ; branches of limited growth in whorls ; chloroplasts numerous and discoid ; cells usually uninucleate ; reproduction vegetative and sexual with elaborate oogonia and antheridia ; germination of zygote indirect ; freshwater and brackish water.

CHARA

(Fam. CHARACEAE)

Chara, or 'stonewort', is a submerged green alga which usually grows in freshwater ponds and lakes being attached to a muddy or sandy bottom, often forming an extensive sub-aquatic vegetation below the surface of water. Several species become incrustated with calcium carbonate.

The common Indian species of *Chara* are *C. zeylanica*, *C. fragilis*, *C. brachypus*, etc.

Vegetative body (Fig. 65)

The thallus consists of an erect branched axis being attached to the substratum by means of rhizoids. The rhizoids are branched filaments which may or may not have nodes and internodes. The erect axis is distinctly differentiated into nodes and internodes. At each node there is a whorl of **branches of limited growth**, the **leaves.** The so-called leaf usually possesses 3—8 internodes. One or more **branches of unlimited growth** may also develop in the axils of these leaves. In some species, each internode consists of a single elongated cell which is many times longer than broad, but in most cases the internodal cell is

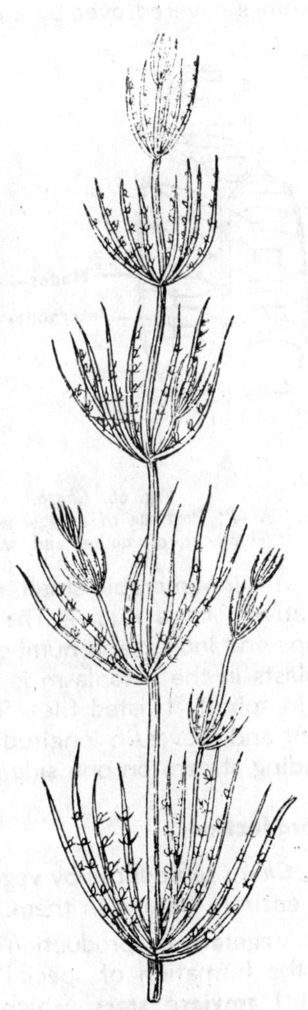

Fig. 65. *Chara*. A portion of the vegetative body.

corticated, *i.e.* surrounded by a single layer of much smaller, vertically elongated cells. The axes grow by means of apical cells from which segments are cut off successively by transverse walls. Each of these segments divides transversely into two cells, the lower one of which enlarges to form a long internodal cell, and the upper one, by successive divisions, gives rise to the layer of nodal cells, to the lateral branches or to the rhizoids. The long internodal cell becomes covered over by a cortical layer consisting of longitudinal rows of cells formed by division of the basal cells of the leaves of the upper and lower nodes, the basal node of each leaf producing one **ascending initial** and one **descending initial.**

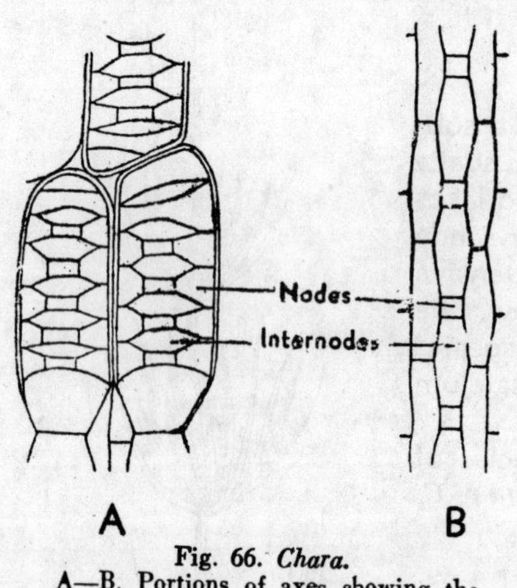

Fig. 66. *Chara.*
A—B, Portions of axes showing the development of nodes and internodes.

The cells in the terminal portion of a branch are always uninucleate and always without prominent vacuoles. But in the mature regions a large central vacuole is always present. In the latter case, the cytoplasm is in the form of a primordial utricle with innumerable small, ellipsoidal chloroplasts and a few comparatively large nuclei. The nuclei are more or less irregular in shape and increase in number by amitosis. The disposition of chloroplasts in the cytoplasm is vertically parallel, and they appear to be in spirally twisted files. The cytoplasm shows streaming movement and moves in longitudinal direction, so that, there is an ascending stream on one side and a descending one on the other.

Reproduction

Chara reproduces by vegetative and sexual methods. Zoospores are entirely lacking in them.

Vegetative reproduction is quite common and may be effected by the formation of special vegetative reproductive bodies, such as (*a*) **amylase stars,** which are star-shaped aggregates of cells densely filled with starch grains and developed in the lower internodes, (*b*) **bulbils** formed on the rhizoids, and (*c*) **protonema-like outgrowths** developed from the nodes.

Sexual reproduction takes place by oogamy. The male reproductive structure is called a **globule** and the female one, a **nucule,** though they are sometimes loosely called antheridium and oogonium respectively. They are always produced at the nodes of the so-called leaves and occupy the sides facing the main axis. Most of the species are homothallic, though heterothallic species are not uncommon. The nucule and the globule have definite orientations with respect to each other, the former being placed above the latter, and they may develop either simultaneously or the globule develops earlier.

Fig. 67. *Chara.* A portion of a 'leaf' bearing nucule and globule.

A superficial nodal cell of the so-called leaf facing towards the main axis forms an apical cell that cuts off two cells, the upper one elongates and forms the internodal cell that acts as the **pedicel** of the future globule, and the lower cell divides and re-divides to form a node. The apical cell enlarges, becomes spherical and divides by two vertical planes to form four cells which re-divide transversely to form an octant. Each of these octants divides into two cells by wall parallel to the surface (periclinal division) forming two daughter cells, of which the outer one divides again in a similar manner so that a row of three cells is formed. Of these, the outer cell is a **shield cell,** the middle one is a **handle cell** or **manubrium,** and the innermost one is a **primary capitulum.** The shield cells, as they attain maturity, enlarge and expand laterally so that a cavity gradually develops within the globule. With the gradual development of the cavity, the handle cells or the manubria also elongate radially and there is an ingrowth of the pedicel cell within the cavity, the primary capitula remaining in close contact with one another. The outer wall of a mature shield cell develops radial inward projections (anticlinal walls), thus incompletely dividing the cell into several compartments. Each primary capitulum divides and forms six **secondary capitula,** which may or may not divide any further. The secondary capitula cut off cells which form branched or unbranched filaments. These filaments may also be produced from the primary or tertiary capitula. Each **antheridial filament** may contain about 5—150 cells, each of which when fully developed becomes an antheridium, whose protoplast is metamorphozed into a biflagellate, spirally coiled **antherozoid.** At maturity, the globule appears bright yellow or red in colour and the shield cells separate from one another, thus exposing the mature antheridial filaments which are attached to the capitula on the handle cells or manubria. The liberation of antherozoids in the surrounding water then takes place in the morning through a small pore on the antheridial wall.

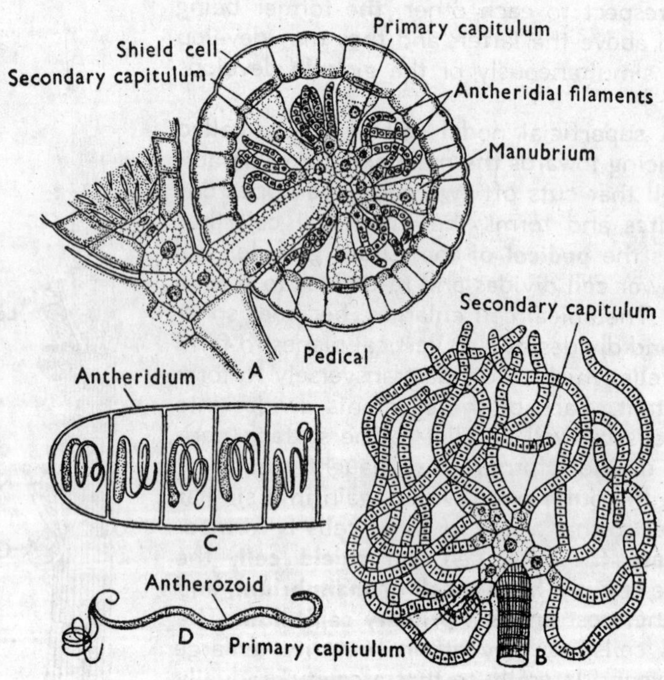

Fig. 68. *Chara.*
A, Section through a globule showing its different parts ; B, The handle cell with antheridial filaments on secondary capitulum ; C, A portion of antheridial filament ; D, An antherozoid.

A cell of the basal node of the nucule, facing towards, the main axis, divides to form a row of three cells. The lowermost cell does not divide at all, but simply enlarges and becomes the **pedicel cell** supporting the developing nucule. The uppermost cell acts as the mother cell of the oogonium. This cell elongates and divides unequally by a transverse wall into a short **basal cell** or **stalk cell** and an upper elongated **oogonium.** The protoplast of the oogonium is gradually metamorphozed into a uninucleate **oosphere** or **ovum** or **egg,** which becomes densely filled with large starch grains prior to fertilization. During the development of the oogonial mother cell the median cell of the original axial row divides and re-divides by vertical walls into five lateral cells surrounding a central one. These lateral cells then grow upwards forming a protective covering or sheath of the oogonial mother cell. Each of these cells then divides transversely, so that two tiers of five cells each are formed. The cells of the lower tier, called the **tube cells,** elongate spirally several times surrounding the enlarging oogonium and bear the upper tier of five cells which mature into the **corona** at the top of the nucule. At maturity, the cells of the sheath slightly separate just below the corona forming five angular openings.

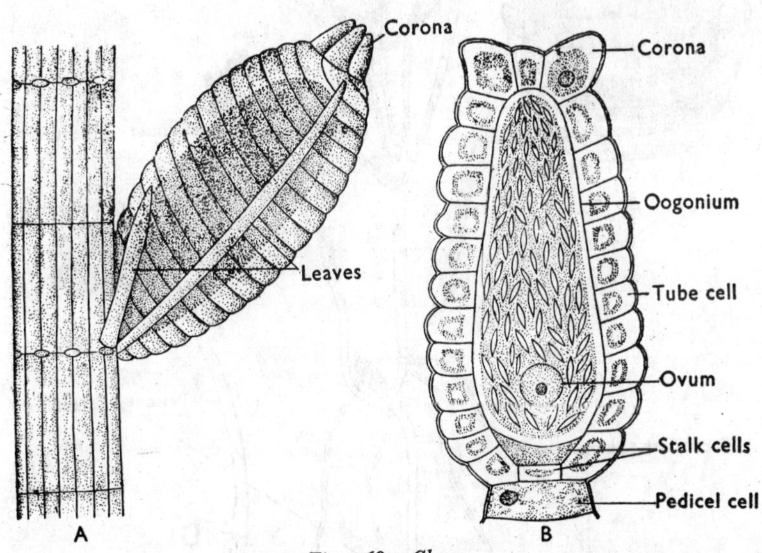

Fig. 69. *Chara.*
A, A mature nucule ; B, Vertical section through the same.

Fertilization then follows in which the free-swimming antherozoids enter the nucule through the angular openings, one ultimately penetrates the oogonium through its gelatinized wall and finally unites with the ovum there. The fertilized ovum then secretes a thick wall and forms an oospore. As the oospore matures the inner tangential walls of the tube cells also thicken forming an additional protective covering round it, while the unthickened portions of the sheath become disorganized. This oospore, surrounded by the thickened sheath, falls to the bottom of the pool and germinates after a resting period of several weeks.

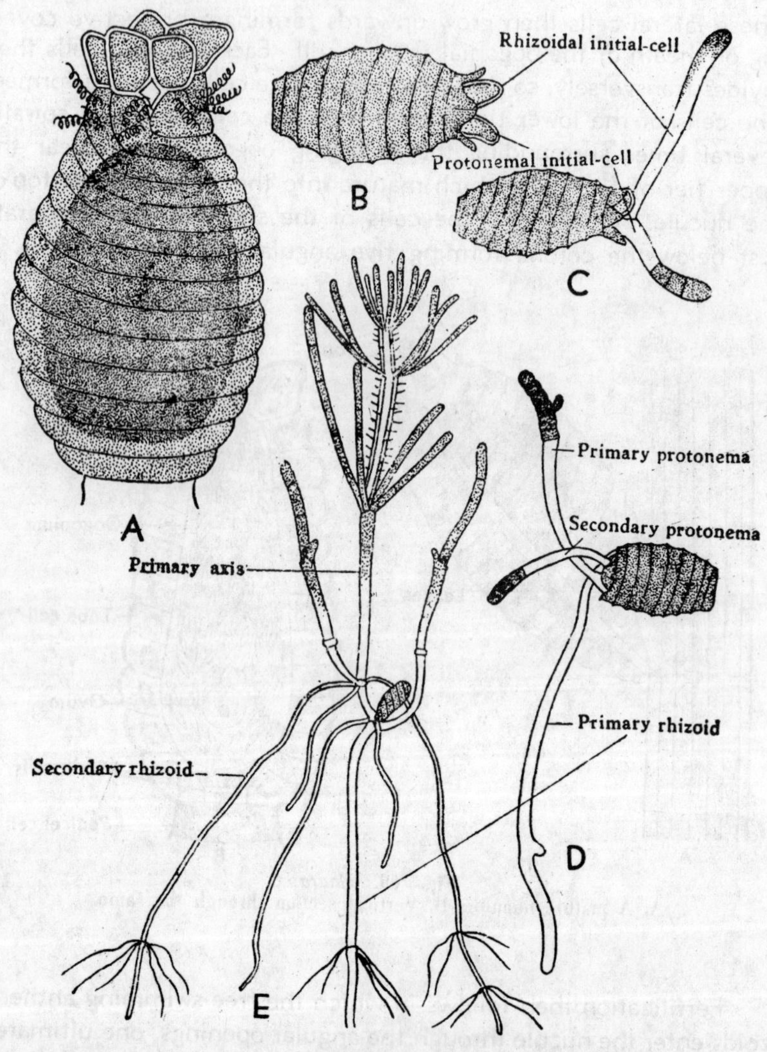

Fig. 70. *Chara.*
A, Entry of antherozoids through the angular slits just below the corona ; B—E, Germinating zygotes and development of the young plant.

During germination, the zygote-nucleus travels towards the apex of the zygote and divides by reduction division into four haploid nuclei. This is followed by the division of the zygote into two asymmetrical cells, of which the distal one is uninucleate and the basal, trinucleate. The distal cell is then exposed by the rupture of the zygote wall and undergoes division into two cells by a vertical wall. Of these two cells, one becomes the **rhizoidal initial cell** and the other, **protonemal initial cell.** The nuclei of the basal cell eventually disintegrate. The rhizoidal initial cell forms a colourless rhizoid with nodes and internodes. From its nodes **secondary rhizoids** also develop. The protonemal initial cell also elongates and forms a green filamentous **primary protonema,** differentiated into nodes and internodes. The lowermost node of this primary protonema may bear **rhizoidal** or **secondary protonemal appendages.**

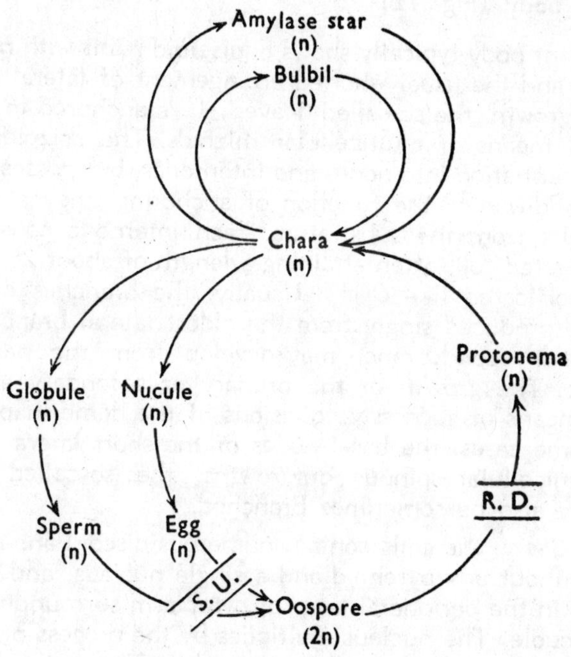

Fig. 71. Life cycle of *Chara.*

The next upper node also bears a whorl of appendages, of which all but one are simple green filaments. The remaining one elongates into a typical axis of the new *Chara* plant.

In the life history of *Chara*, the plant body represents only the gametophytic generation, and the nucleus of the zygote represents the sporophytic stage in the entire life cycle.

NITELLA

(Fam. CHARACEAE)

Nitella is allied to *Chara* and is usually widely distributed in freshwater forming extensive sub-aquatic meadows, but growing deeper than *Chara*. Most species are often incrustated with abundant calcium carbonate and these eventually form considerable calcareous deposits at the bottom of water in which they live.

The common Indian species of *Nitella* are *N. mirabilis, N. acuminata, N. flagellifera, N. mucronata, N. hyalina,* etc.

Vegetative body (Fig. 72)

The plant body typically shows equisetoid habit with nodes and internodes and the usual whorled arrangement of lateral branches of limited growth, the so-called 'leaves'. It is anchored to the substratum by means of multicellular rhizoids. The rhizoids do not show differentiation into nodes and internodes, but possess oblique septa. In addition to the function of anchoring, they also absorb mineral salts from the substratum. Each internode consists of a single elongated cell, often attaining a length of about 25 cm., and is never corticated like *Chara*. Usually, the branches of limited growth are produced singly from the oldest lateral branch, but in some cases a second branch may develop from the next oldest lateral one. The growth of the primary or secondary axis takes place by means of successive divisions of the dome-shaped apical cell. In some cases, the basal nodes of the short lateral branches produce unicellular spinous outgrowths, the so-called **stipules,** which may also be sometimes branched.

As in *Chara*, the cells contain numerous discoid and oval chloroplasts without any pyrenoid and a single nucleus, and these are embedded in the peripheral layer of cytoplasm surrounding a large central vacuole. The nucleus multiplies by the process of amitosis. Protoplasmic streaming is also noticeable. The cellwall mainly consists of cellulose. The superficial layer is of an unknown composition and is more or less gelatinous in texture in which deposition of calcium carbonate takes place.

Reproduction

Nitella reproduces by vegetative and sexual methods.

Vegetative reproduction occurs at all stages in the life cycle of *Nitella*. It takes place by the formation of secondary protonemat

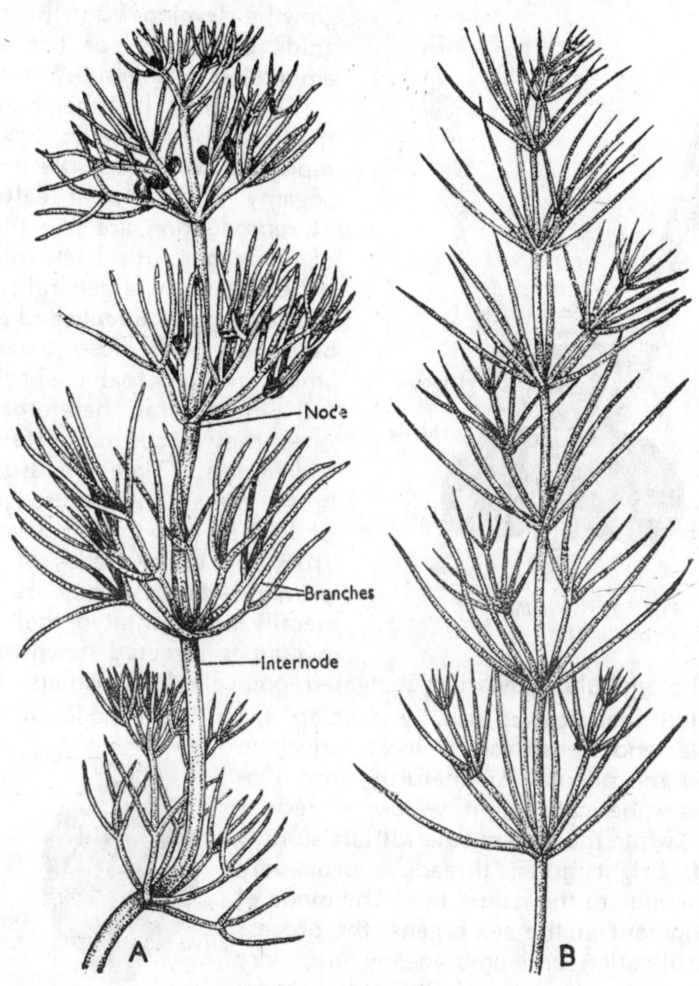

Fig. 72. *Nitella*.
A, Reproductive shoot ; B, Vegetative shoot.

originating from the basal node of the primary rhizoid or the rhizoidal node of protonema. Secondary protonemata sometimes develop from the dormant apical portion of the surviving nodes of an older plant after a period of perennation. A fragment of the plant with a node, when placed under favourable conditions, may give rise to secondary protonemata. Occasionally, tuber-like out-growths develop from the rhizoids or portion of the axis embedded in the substratum.

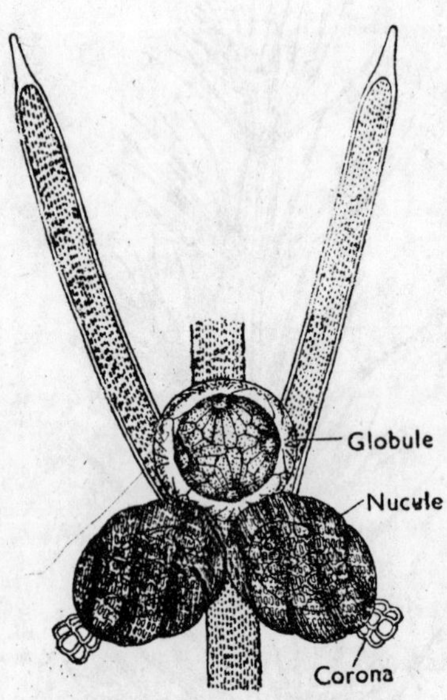

Fig. 73. *Nitella.* Sex organs.

The plant is either homothallic or heterothallic. Sexual reproduction takes place by oogamy. The essential features of reproduction are like those of *Chara* but with a few minor differences. As a general rule, the sex organs, **nucule** and **globule,** develop in close juxtaposition in homothallic species, but in several heterothallic ones they occur on different individuals. They are usually borne on secondary branches of limited growth and develop from the upper nodes of the primary laterals. They are generally so orientated that the nucule is directed downwards and the globule, upwards. Elongated one-celled branchlets, the so-called **brancteoles,** usually develop from basal node of the globule and constitute a loose envelope around the nucule. At maturity, the globule is spherical, bright yellow or red in colour, while the oval nucule with its spirally coiled, bright green threads appear very conspicuous to the naked eye. The mode of development of the sex organs, the process of fertilization and embryogeny are more or less similar to those of *Chara*. It is to be noted, however, that the corona is made up of two tiers of cells.

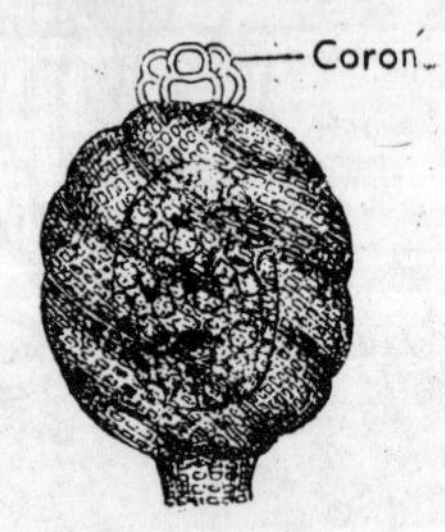

Fig. 74. *Nitella*, A mature nucule.

Systematic position and affinities of Charales

The Charales occupy rather an uncertain and ill-defined position in the plant kingdom. Though they are green in colour, they differ markedly from all other members of the Chlorophyceae by their vegetative body, sex organs and antherozoids. On account of these characters a large number of algologists consider this group is quite separate from any other groups of algae while some would even recommend its removal from the Thallophyta.

Strasburger placed the Charales in a separate Class. According to him the Characeae or Charophyta represent a group of highly specialized green-coloured thallophytes, whose origin might be traced back to the Chlorophyceae. But they cannot be directly connected with the other oogamous Chlorophyceae on account of the peculiar structure of their sex organs. On the other hand, they show some approach towards the Phaeophyceae in certain characters, but differ from them mainly in having pure green-coloured chromatophores.

Sachs considered that the Charales are so very different from other groups of thallophytic organisms that they should form a special group by themselves co-ordinate in rank with Thallophyta Mussinae, which they resemble in the form of antherozoids but from which they differ also in the structures of their vegetative and reproductive organs. The distinctive characters of the nucule and the globule afford no indication or clue to any affinity of this group with other existing groups of plants.

Fritsch is of opinion that the Charales should be regarded as an Order under the Chlorophyceae, because the tendencies characterizing them are found in other Orders of Chlorophyceae as well. Further, if it would have been possible to obtain detailed fossil records, probably all intermediate transitional forms to the complexities of the Charales could be noted. He also suggests that the complex vegetative body and reproductive organs are not restricted to the Charales alone as parallel cases of complexities can be found in other groups of algae also, as in the Ectocarpales of the Phaeophyceae.

In all probability, the Charales may be regarded as a remnant of many probable evolutionary lines of algae trying for colonization on the land. In course of such an attempt, they have advanced to some extent and some of their characters towards the higher land plants, while in others they still retain some of the characteristics of Chlorophyceae.

CHAPTER 11

CLASS : XANTHOPHYCEAE

Salient features

The members of this Class contain yellow-green chloroplasts owing to the preponderance of the yellow pigment **xanthophyll.** Starch gains are never formed as product of photosynthesis and pyrenoids are mostly wanting. Oil is stored as a reserve food.

General characters

The most advanced members of this Class possess simple filamentous bodies, and they are distributed more widely in freshwater than in the sea. The cellwall is rich with pectic compounds, and is made up of two equal or unequal pieces, overlapping each other by their edges. There are usually several chloroplasts in each cell, and they are discoid in form. Motile reproductive cells are generally provided anteriorly with two flagella (sometimes only one). Sexual reproduction is usually isogamous or may be rarely oogamous.

BOTRYDIUM

(Fam. BOTRYDIACEAE)

Botrydium is a terrestrial alga. It is usually found on damp soil, particularly on the drying muddy banks of streams, forming abundant granular patches covering the substratum.

The common Indian species of *Botrydium* are *B. divisum*, *B. granulatum*, *B. tuberosum*, etc.

Vegetative body (Fig. 75A)

The thallus is unicellular and is differentiated into an upper subaerial part and a branched rhizoidal part, which penetrates the soil. The subaerial part is globose, pear-shaped or elongated, cylindrical in form, depending on the environmental conditions, and about 1-2 mm. in diameter. It is surrounded by a tough wall, within which is a peripheral layer of protoplasm surrounding a central vacuole. The protoplasm contains many nuclei and discoid chromatophores with pyrenoid-like bodies, but oil instead of starch is formed as food-reserve. The rhizoidal portion shows various degrees of branching and is colourless due to the absence of chloroplasts. Numerous nuclei are found distributed in the vacuolated cytoplasm. It is evident that within the body of the unicellular alga the protoplasm is continuous throughout, and is characteristic of a coenocyte.

Reproduction

Botrydium usually reproduces asexually, but sexual repro-

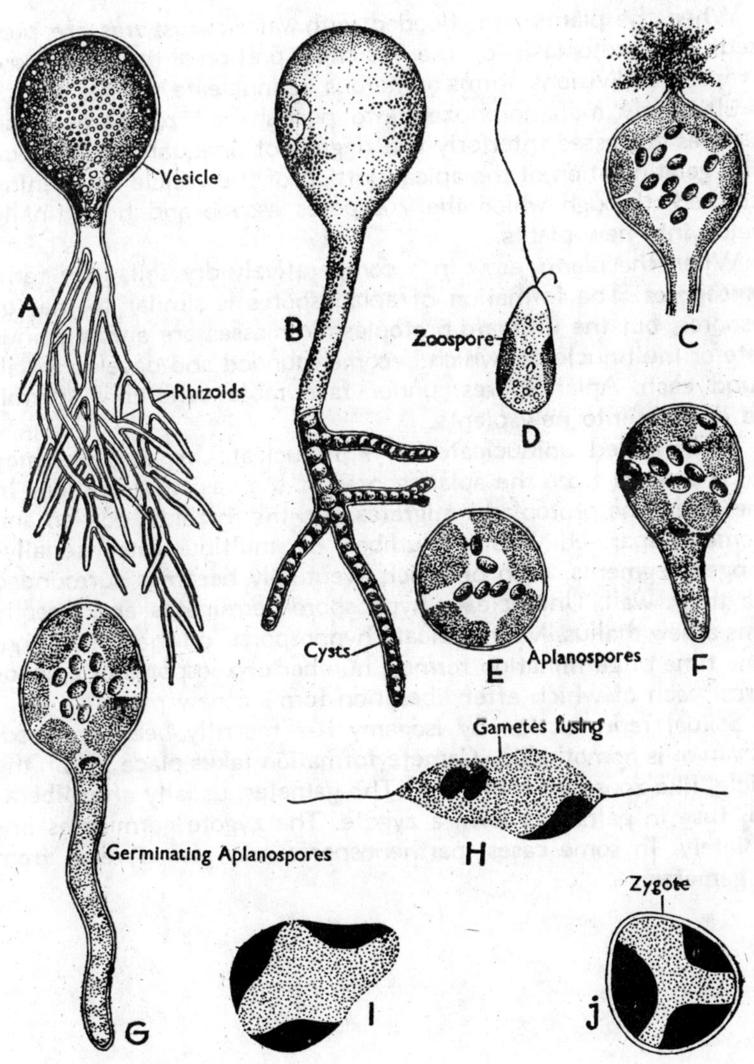

Fig. 75. *Botrydium.*

A, An entire plant ; B, Showing the formation of cysts ; C. Liberation of zoospores ; D, A zoospore ; E—G, Stages in the germination of aplanospore ; H—J, Stages in the formation of zygote.

duction has also been reported in some cases. It is incapable of any vegetative reproduction.

Asexual reproduction takes place by means of zoospores, aplanospores or hypnospores.

When the plants are flooded with water, **zoospores** are produced. The protoplasm of the vesicular portion of the plant body, by repeated divisions, forms numerous uninucleate masses which are ultimately metamorphozed into pear-shaped zoospores. Each zoospores possesses anteriorly two flagella of unequal lengths. Due to the gelatinization of the apical portion of the vesicle an opening is formed, through which the zoospores escape and these finally develop into new plants.

When the plants grow in a comparatively dry soil, they form **aplanospores.** The formation of aplanospores is similar to that of zoospores, but the ultimate protoplasmic masses are either uninucleate or multinucleate, which become rounded and develop a wall around each. Aplanospores, under favourable conditions, germinate directly into new plants.

Thick-walled uninucleate or multinucleate **hypnospores** may also be formed from the aplanospores of the vesicular portion. In some cases, the protoplasm migrates into the rhizoidal portion and becomes separated into a number of multinucleate, serially-arranged segments, each of which eventually becomes surrounded by a thick wall. Uninucleate hypnospore germinates and directly forms a new thallus. Multinucleate hypnospores, on the other hand, at the time of germination forms a number of zoospores or aplanospores, each of which after liberation forms a new plant.

Sexual reproduction by isogamy has recently been reported. *Botrydium* is homothallic. Gamete-formation takes place within the vesicle, like zoospore-formation. The gametes, usually after liberation, fuse in pairs and form a zygote. The zygote germinates immediately. In some cases, parthenospores may also develop from the gametes.

CHAPTER III

CLASS : BACILLARIOPHYCEAE (DIATOMS)

Salient features

The members of this class are either unicellular or form colonies, All are characterized by the presence of golden-brown chromatophores which, besides the usual pigments, contain some brown pigments of obscure nature. The cellwall is made up of both pectic substances and silica, and usually consists of two halves with rich ornamentations on their surface. The cells are either radially or bilaterally symmetrical. The members of Pennales show special type of sexual union between protoplasts of vegetative cells. They are probably all diploid. Diatoms are widely distributed both in fresh and salt water of all kinds. Some are also terrestrial.

General characters

The Bacillariophyceae, popularly known as **diatoms,** constitute a very large assemblage of unicellular algae. Owing to the colour of their chromatophores they appear to be brown algae, but they are usually considered as a separate and distinct group. They are readily distinguished from other algae by the following salient features : (*a*) the plant is usually unicellular and always non-flagellate, the silicified wall consisting of two overlapping halves ; (*b*) the photosynthetic reserve materials are fats and volutin but never starch ; (*c*) the photosynthetic pigments of the chromatophores are masked by the presence of a golden-brown pigment known as **diatomin** ; (*d*) special type of large rejuvenescent cells (**auxospores**) are formed, either directly from the vegetative protoplast or as a result of sexual union, a feature not found in other groups of algae.

Occurrence and distribution

Diatoms are inhabitants of both fresh and salt water, being usually associated together in great abundance. Some diatoms are either strictly marine or strictly freshwater. Both freshwater and marine diatoms may be sessile in habit or free-floating (plankton) ; when sessile, they are attached to other types of algae or affixed to rocks or other solid inanimate objects under water.

After the death of individual cells, the silicified wall of a diatom remains unaltered and great numbers of these walls are deposited at the bottom of ponds, lakes or any other body of water in which diatoms thrive. If the conditions are favourable, deposition goes on unimpeded for ages, and as a result, accumulation may attain a considerable thickness. Deposits of such fossil diatoms are known as the **diatomaceous earth,** which are found distributed all over the world.

Vegetative body (Fig. 76)

Diatoms are usually unicellular and display a great diversity of forms, but sometimes cells are united together to form simple fi-

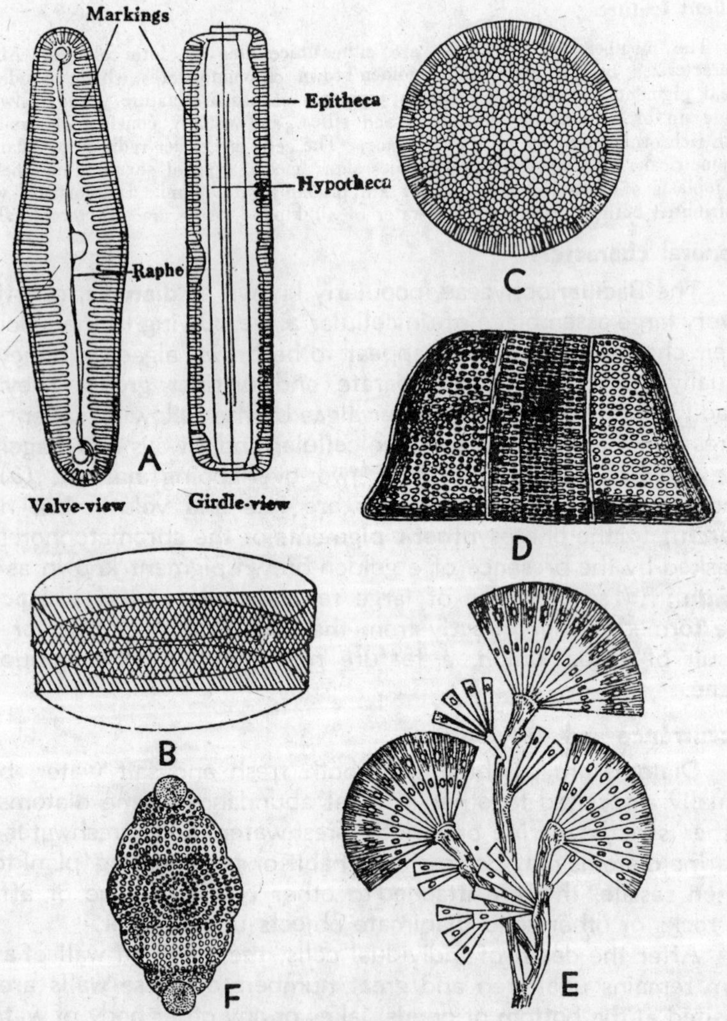

Fig. 76. *Diatoms,*
A—E, Different types of Diatoms ; F, Diagrammatic representation of the epitheca and hypotheca in a diatomaceous cell.

lamentous or branched colonies. Each cell of a living diatom or its wall alone is called a **frustule,** which consists of two overlapping halves or **valves** that fit together like a pair of Petri dishes. The outer valve is called **epitheca** and the inner, **hypotheca.** Each frustule thus presents two different views, namely **girdle view** and **valve view,** according to the position in which it is observed.

Both the valves of a frustule have their outer walls strongly silicified and made up of an organic matrix chiefly consisting of pectin, there being no microchemical reaction for cellulose. The siliceous deposit on a valve is not uniform but in the form of numerous fine transverse markings or ribs and also as small protuberances and **areolae.** The areolae may consist of minute vertical pores as incomplete canals which do not perforate the wall completely. They are seldom perforated by minute pores through which mucilagenous secretion comes out. The ornamentation is either radially symmetrical with reference to a central point (**Centric diatoms**), or bilaterally symmetrical or asymmetrical with respect to a long axis (**Pennate diatoms**).

Lying internal to the cellwall there is a thick layer of cytoplasm as a primordial utricle surrounding a conspicuous central vacuole and containing one or more chromatophores, with or without one to several pyrenoids. There is only one spherical to ovoid nucleus of the normal type embedded in the peripheral layer of cytoplasm, or it is suspended in a mass of cytoplasm at the centre of the vacuole and is connected to the peripheral layer by means of broad cytoplasmic strands.

The chromatophores are mostly rich golden brown in colour and vary in shape and number from species to species. This particular colour of the chromatophores is due to the presence of a special pigment, known as **diatomin,** which masks the photosynthetic pigments, chlorophyll and the associated carotenoids. Food reserves are in the form of fatty oil accumulated as droplets of variable size in the cytoplasm or in the chromatophores.

Many planktonic unicellular diatoms exhibit spontaneous movements, either as a series of jerks directed along the long axis of the cell or as forward and backward progression and retrogression, and these are also seen in some of the colonial forms.

The common Indian species of Centric diatoms are *Melosira varians, M. jurgensii, Coscinopiscus radiatus*, etc., while those of Pennate ones are *Synedra ulna, S. acus, Navicula stauroptera, N. viridis, Gomphonema acuminatum, Rhopalodia gibba, Asterionella formosa,* etc.

Reproduction

Diatoms reproduce vegetatively by cell division. During the process the protoplast of the mother cell swells up and the valves are slightly pushed apart. The nucleus now divides by mitosis into two daughter nuclei. Cytoplasm undergoes cleavage in such a way that each valve receives a daughter nucleus and a portion of cytoplasm. Then a new valve is secreted outside the daughter protoplast within each old valve. In this way two daughter cells are formed. These two daughter cells are unequal in size and one of the valves belongs to the parent cell and the other is newly formed. In the subsequent cell divisions, the sizes of the daughter cells successively become smaller and smaller. When a certain definite minimum size is reached, a special mode of reproduction takes place by the formation of a special large rejuvenation takes place by the formation of a special large rejuvenating cell called **auxospore** such that the original size of the cell is regained.

In *Centric diatoms*, the protoplast becomes about three times

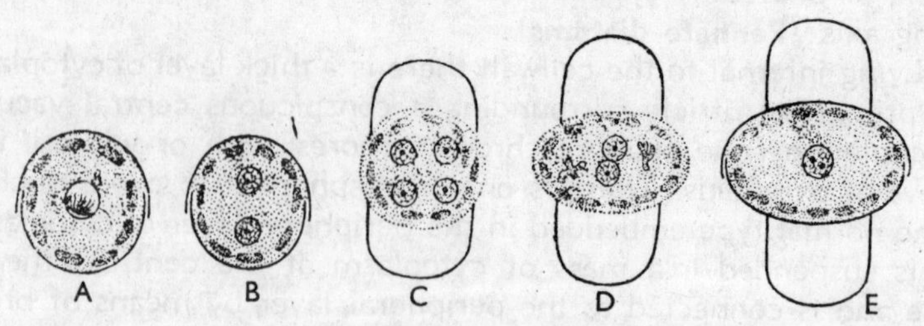

Fig. 77. *Diatoms*,
Diagrammatic representation of stages in the formation of an auxospore in a Centric diatom.

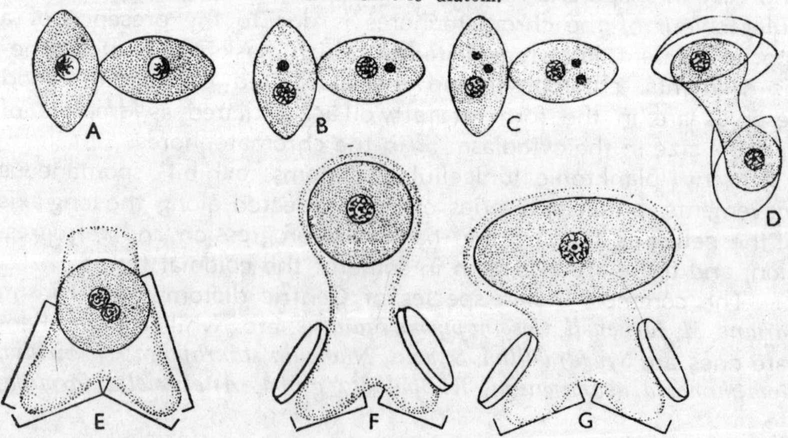

Fig. 78. *Diatoms*,
Diagrammatic representation of stages in the formation of an auxospore by the conjugating cells of a Pennate diatom.

bulky by the absorption of water and the valves are widely pushed apart. This increased bulk of protoplast now secretes two overlapping valves and the entire structure thus formed is known as an **auxospore.** The auxospore divides vegetatively and gives rise to vegetative cells.

In *Pennate diatoms*, the auxospore is formed from the zygote which is the product of fusion of gametes produced by a single or two vegetative cells.

Two conjugating diatoms come to lie close together and become enveloped by a common mucilagenous sheath. The diploid nucleus of each now divides by meiosis to form four haploid nuclei of which a single or two haploid daughter nuclei persist in each vegetative cell. Cytoplasm now collects around each of these daughter nuclei and in this way each vegetative cell gives rise to a

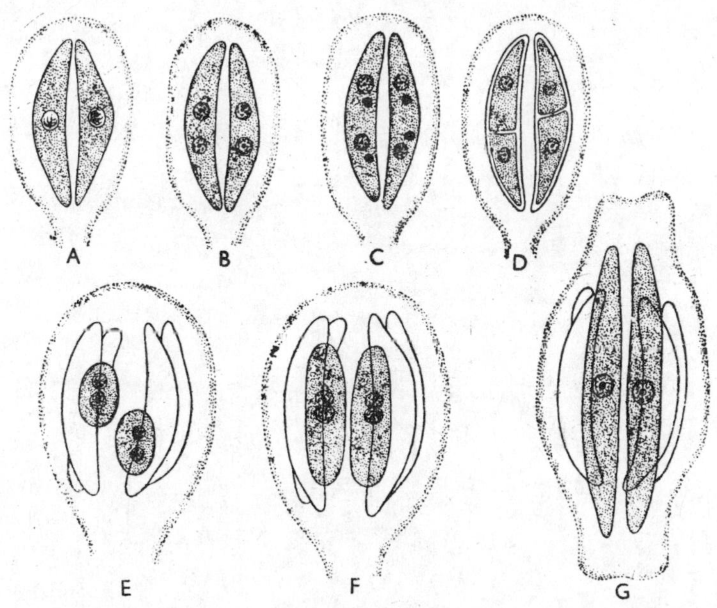

Fig. 79. *Diatoms,*
Diagrammatic representation of stages in the formation of two auxospores by two conjugating cells of a pennate diatom.

single or two gametes. The gametes fuse sexually and give rise to a single or two zygotes and function as auxospores. Sometimes, two gametes are produced from a single vegetative cell, which fuse together to form zygote and auxospore.

In some rare cases, two cells come in contact, but no conjugation takes place, and ultimately they give rise to a pair of auxospores by parthenogenesis.

Economic importance

The uses of the diatomaceous earth are very varied, viz. as a filtering material, as a substance used in insulation of boilers, blast furnaces, etc., as a cementing material, as a mild abrasive in metal polishes and toothpastes, as an absorbent for liquid nitroglycerine (the explosive material of the dynamite), and as a material for painting the ship to protect it against the attack of sea barnacles.

CHAPTER IV

CLASS : PHAEOPHYCEAE

Salient features

The Phaeophyceae, or the brown algae, represents a group of marine algae having wide range of distribution and includes forms varying from plants of microscopic size and simple structure to the largest and most highly differentiated bodies of macroscopic forms among the thallophytes. Its members are characterized in having : (1) cells with definite nuclei and plastids with all the photosynthetic pigments, chlorophyll *a*, chlorophyll *b*, carotene and xanthophyll and an accessory golden brown pigment, called **fuco-xanthin,** which usually masks entirely the green colour of the chlorophyll ; (2) thalli which are always multicellular and in most cases possessing a definite macroscopic form ; and (3) flagellate reproductive cells, zoospores of gametes, which are pyriform in shape with two laterally inserted flagella of unequal lengths. The two latter characters separate this group from both the green and red algae.

General characters

With the exception of two or three freshwater species, nearly all the brown algae are marine, and these forms attain their greatest development in the cool ocean waters of the temperate and frigid (arctic and antarctic) zones than those which are inhabitants of warm tropical seas. Most of the marine species grow attached to rocks or similar other objects along the shores up to a depth of about 17 metres under the water. Some of the giant 'kelps' (e.g. *Laminaria* and others) grow along the Pacific coasts of America on rocks at a depth, even beyond 20 metres, below the surface of water. Others may grow as epiphytes in association with other algae or within their tissues as endophytes.

The Phaeophyceae show great diversity in form and structure of the plant body among its various members and in a great majority of cases possessing regular alternation of generations between free-living multicellular gametophytes and sporophytes. Both the generations may be indentical in form and structure, or the sporophyte is larger than the gametophyte, or *vice versa*. Both these generations may be annual or perennial, or the gametophyte is annual and the sporophyte, perennial. The range of thalli varies from genus to genus, all the way beginning from single, few-celled gametophytes or sporophytes of microscopic size to definite macroscopic forms attaining a length of 27—33 metres or more, without having any relationship between the size and longevity of the plants concerned. The gametophyte or the sporophyte of a plant, possessing a definite form, is differentiated into a holdfast supporting an upright simple or branched portion, which is either solid or hollow and tubular, but may also be spherical or compressed. Great complexity in form is encountered among the 'kelps', where the thallus is differentiated into a **root-like holdfast,** a simple or branched stem (**stipe**) and one or more **leaf-like blades.**

The cell of brown algae has a distinct cellwall, which is differentiated into an inner firm cellulose portion and an outer gelatinous portion made up of a pectic compound, known as '**algin**'. The protoplast is vacuolated and generally contains a single nucleus of normal form and structure. The division of protoplast takes place by mitosis. During the division, centrosomes become evident near the poles, and these appear to be a constant feature in the dividing cells of the various members of the Phaeophyceae. There is usually more than one plastids in each cell and they are always without pyrenoids. They are usually flattened or discoid in shape and may have irregular outlines. The plastids, in addition to the four photosynthetic pigments, contain a golden brown carotinoid pigment, **fuco-xanthin,** which is supposed to be a mixture of two pigments, **fuco-xanthin a** and **fuco-xanthin b.** Food reserves are in the form of carbohydrates which are found in a dissolved state in the vacuoles and in the cytoplasm. Of these, sugar is present in small quantity. A dextrin-like carbohydrate (polysaccharide) known as '**laminarin**' is always present. Another widely distributed carbohydrate is **mannitol.** Fats and oils are also found in some species.

Reproduction

The methods of reproduction in Phaeophyceae are very diverse and a brief summary of the principal methods has been given below :

Many brown algae reproduce by vegetative method by the process of fragmentation of the young or adult thallus. Fragments of the thallus, thus produced, may become detached from the parent plant and float away to form new individuals, or they remain united with one another forming an aggregation of individuals, being attached to the substratum by the common holdfast. In some cases, special reproductive branches (**propagula**) are formed and these are separated from the parent plant, ultimately developing into new individuals.

All brown algae, excepting the *Fucus* and a few allied genera, reproduce asexually by the production of zoospores or aplanospores. The zoospores are produced within both **unilocular** (or unicellular) and **plurilocular** (or multicellular) **sporangia** and are *always borne on the diploid thallus* (sporophyte). The unilocular sporangium is a true sporangium, because reduction division of the uninucleate pro toplast takes place prior to the formation of the haploid zoospores. The nucleus of the protoplast first divides reductionally into two nuclei, which subsequently divide and re-divide mitotically into 32, 64 or 128 nuclei. This is followed by the cleavage of the protoplast forming uninucleate masses, each of which is finally metamorphozed into a biflagellate zoospore. Each of these zoospores, after liberation, produces a haploid thallus (gametophyte). On the other hand, the zoospores produced by the plurilocular sporangium are diploid, each of which on germination gives rise to a diploid thallus, similar to the thallus from which it is derived. These zoospores are, therefore, termed **neutral zoospores** and the sporangium, **neutral sporangium.** During the formation of neutral zoospores, the uninucleate protoplast of each cell of the plurilocular sporangium (neutral sporangium), without undergoing reduction division, is directly metamorphozed into a neutral zoospores with two flagella. Thus, by the neutral zoospores the same generation is reduplicated. Sometimes the unilocular sporangium, instead of producing the zoospores, may produce 4-8 large, non-flagellate aplanospores.

Sexual reproduction in the brown algae may be a case of (i) isogamy, *i.e.* by the union of two motile morphologically identical gametes, (ii) anisogamy, *i.e.* by the union of two motile gametes of unequal size, and (iii) oogamy, *i.e.* by the union of a motile, flagellate antherozoid with a non-motile, non-flagellate, passive egg. The iso- and aniso-gametes are produced within multicellular gametangia, which are similar in appearance with the neutral sporangia but these are *always produced on the gametophyte*, which is either homothallic or heterothallic. The zygotes, thus produced, develop into new sporophytes. Several members of the Phaeophyceae are oogamous and heterothallic. The male sex organ, the antheridium, may be unicellular or multicellular, and the entire protoplast of each cell is directly metamorphozed into a single antherozoid with two flagella. The female sex organ, the oogonium, is always unicellular containing within it 1-8 oospheres or eggs. In some cases, the egg is extruded from the oogonium or even discharged from it, so that fertilization takes place outside the body of the oogonium.

When sexual union fails, the gametes either degenerate or the unsuccessful gametes may develop into **parthenospores.**

Alternation of generations

Previously it was thought that the Phaeophyceae do not possess any alternation of generations. But, it is well known at present that all the members of this Class, excepting the Order Fucales, have a typical alternation of generations, which may be isomorphic (e.g.

Ectocarpales, Dictyotales, etc.) or heteromorphic (e.g. Laminariales, Desmarestiales, etc.). These alternations have been studied chiefly under laboratory conditions, and for this purpose cultures should be examined starting both from the zoospores as well as the zygotes.

The Laminariales and the Dictyotales have a gametophyte regularly alternating with a sporophyte and *vice versa* ; furthermore, this alternation is obligatory. On the other hand, there is a large number of brown algae where the alternation of the two generations is not only well marked, but also further complicated by a reduplicating of the sporophytic and as well as gametophytic generation.

The first method of reduplication of sporophyte is by fragmentation. Secondly, vegetative multiplication may also be due to the formation and abscission of special reproductive branches—The **propagula.** Thirdly the sporophyte may be reduplicated by means of **neutral zoospores.** These neutral zoospores are formed inside the *neutral sporangium*. It develops from a single cell which divides and redivides to form an elongated multicellular structure composed of many blocks of cells. This is known as **pleurilocular** or **multilocular sporangium.** It produces diploid neutral zoospores with two laterally inserted unequal flagella. Zoospores on germination give rise to new sporophyte.

The life cycle may be complicated by the formation of *sporophytic displonema*, the reproduction by which is always vegetative. The gametophyte may also be reduplicated either by vegetative multiplication, by fragmentation or by the formation of **vegetative protonema.**

Other Phaeophyceae produce dwarf stages, which are called **plethysmothalli.** This plethysmothallic form may be reduplicated itself or may develop into adult sporophyte. In some cases this form may bear neutral sporangium to produce neutral zoospores which give rise to new sporophytes. Neutral zoospores in turn may produce plethysmothalli or adult sporophyte.

Unilocular sporongia may be developed directly from the sporophyte. Its development begins with an enlargement of an uninucleate cell and division and redivision of the nucleus into 32, 64 or 128 daughter nuclei. The first division of the diploid nucleus is meiotic. There is then cleavages into uninucleate protoplasts and metamorphosis of each protoplast into biflagellate haploid zoospore. These haploid zoospores give rise to gametophytic plants. The gametophyte may be alike morphologically with the sporophyte, as in **isogeneratae** or may be dissimilar with that of sporophyte, as in **heterogeneratae.** The gametophyte then produces either iso- or aniso gametes or antherozoid and egg. The fusion of the gametes results into zygote which again gives rise to new sporophytic plant.

A plethysmothallus may also produce haploid zoospores from unilocular zoosporangium. This zoospores germinates to from gametophyte. From this gametophyte by sexual reproduction plethysmothallus or typical sporophyte may be formed. Gamete produced by gametophyte may also germinate perthenogenitically to repeat the gametophytic generation.

The Fucales, however, present a very naughty problem, because here a many-celled diploid generation alternates with a one-celled haploid stage. Strasburger regards the *Fucus* plant itself as a sporophyte and antheridia and oogonia as micro- and mega-sporangia respectively, the gametophytic stages being restricted to the sperms and eggs only. Yamanouchi and Lloyd Williams also hold the same view. Church, however, challenges this idea seriously and considers that *Fucus* is a gametophyte and is a very much advanced plant, which may be compared to an animal, because there is no other method of reproduction in the entire life history cycle, excepting that taking place by means of sperms and eggs only.

Classification

The Phaeophyceae has been divided (Fritsch, 1935) into the following *nine* Orders :

Order 1. Ectocarpales. Plants filamentous, pseudo-parenchymatous or truly parenchymatous in form ; asexual reproduction by zoospores produced from unilocular and plurilocular zoosporangia ; sexual reproduction is usually oogamous, rarely anisogamous. Examples—*Ectocarpus*, *Punctaria*, *Castagnea*, etc.

***Order 2. Tilopteridales.** Plants filamentous ; asexual reproduction by monospores or by zoospores produced from unilocular sporangia ; sexual reproduction perhaps anisogamous. Examples—*Tilopteris*, *Haplospora*, etc.

* **Order 3. Cutleriales.** Plant body generally composed of thread-like structures ; asexual reproduction by zoospores produced in unilocular sporangia ; sexual reproduction anisogamous. Examples—*Cutleria*, *Zonardinia*, etc.

* **Order 4. Sporochnales.** Thallus bulky and complex ; asexual reproduction by zoospores formed within unilocular sporangia ; sexual reproduction possibly oogamous. Examples—*Sporochnus*, *Carpomitra*, etc.

*Not treated in this book.

* **Order 5. Desmarestiales.** Thallus uniaxial in construction with complex cortication ; asexual reproduction by zoospores formed within unilocular sporangia ; sexual reproduction oogamous. Examples—*Desmarestio*, *Arthrocladia*, etc.

Order 6. Laminariales. Plant bulky, body truly parenchymatous ; asexual reproduction by zoospores formed within unilocular sporangia ; sexual reproduction distinctly oogamous. Examples—*Laminaria*, *Macrocystis*, *Postelsia*, etc.

* **Order 7. Sphacelariales.** Plant small, parenchymatous, heterotrichous ; asexual reproduction by zoospores formed within unilocular sporangia ; sexual reproduction isogamous. Examples—*Sphacelaria*, *Halopteris*, etc.

Order 8. Dictyotales. Plants with frequent dichotomous branching and slightly differentiated parenchymatous forms ; asexual reproduction by non-motile tetraspores formed within unilocular sporangia ; sexual reproduction oogamous. Examples—*Dictyota*, *Padina*, etc.

Order 9. Fucales. Plants with parenchymatous forms and complex external and internal differentiations ; asexual reproduction unknown ; sexual reproduction oogamous. Examples—*Fucus*, *Sargassum*, etc.

ORDER 1. ECTOCARPALES

Plants filamentous, pseudo-parenchymatous or truly parenchymatous in form ; asexual reproduction by zoospores produced from unilocular and plurilocular zoosporangia ; sexual reproduction is usually oogamous, rarely anisogamous.

ECTOCARPUS

(Fam. ECTOCARPACEAE)

Ectocarpus is a brown alga, all species of which are marine and widely distributed. It has a life cycle in which there is an alternation of a free-living multicellular sporophytic generation with a free-living multicellular gametophytic generation, which are identical in vegetative structure.

Vegetative body (Fig. 80)

The thallus is differentiated into a prostrate, irregularly and more or less profusely-branched portion by means of which it remains attached to the substratum, and an erect portion made up of tufts of branched filaments, whose cells are joined end to end in a single series and are generally narrowed towards the apices of the branches. In some species, the older portions of the main branches are corticated by the development of a sheath formed by the descending rhizoidal branches. The protoplast of each cell is uninucleate and contains either many disc-shaped chloroplasts or a few band-shaped ones with irregular margins.

Reproduction

Ectocarpus reproduces both asexually and sexually.

The asexual reproduction takes place by the formation of biflagellate zoospores produced within unilocular or multilocular zoosporangium borne by the sporophytic plant, usually terminally and singly on lateral branchlets.

The terminal cell of a branchlet enlarges considerably, becomes more or less ellipsoidal in shape and forms a unilocular sporangium.

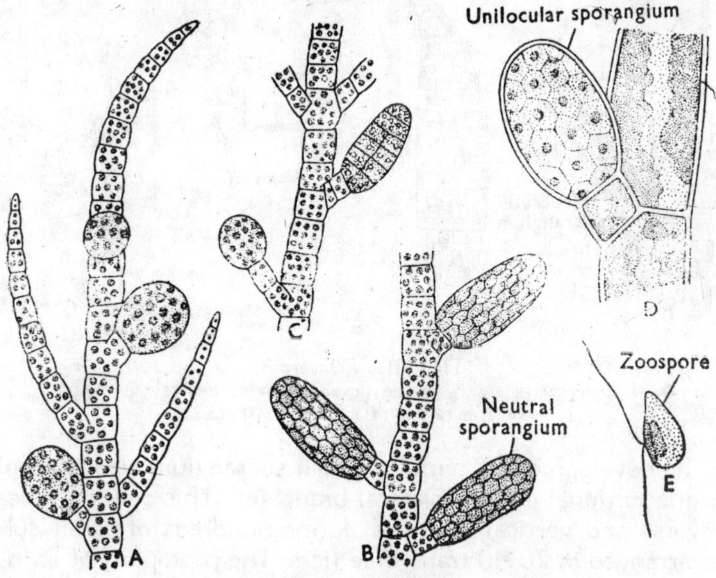

Fig. 80. *Ectocarpus.*
A, A portion of the thallus with unilocular sporangia ; B, The same with neutral sporangia ; C, The same with both unilocular and neutral sporangia ; D, An unilocular sporangium showing division of its protoplasts ; E, A zoospore.

As it increases in size, the number of chloroplasts also increases considerably. The nucleus first divides by reduction division and is subsequently followed by several mitoses into 32-64 daughter nuclei. Then, there follows a progressive cleavage of the entire protoplast forming several uninucleate daughter protoplasts, each with a single chloroplast. Each daughter protoplast is finally metamorphosed into a zoospore with two laterally inserted flagella of unequal lengths. The whole mass of zoospores, thus formed, is extruded through a small opening at the apex of the zoosporangium, and they begin to swim freely in water in all directions. Each zoospore, after a period of activity, comes to rest and develops into a new gametophytic plant.

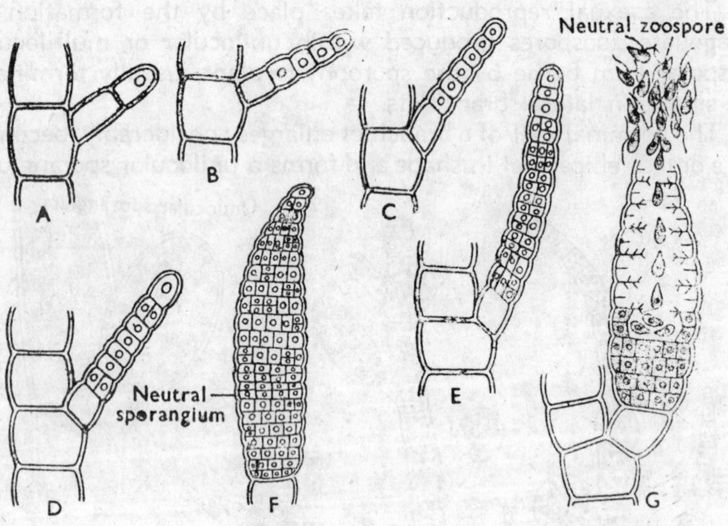

Fig. 81. *Ectocarpus.*
A—F, Successive stages in the development of neutral sporangia ; G, Liberation of neutral zoospores.

The development of a multicellular sporangium also takes place from the terminal cell of a lateral branchlet. This cell, by repeated transverse and vertical divisions, forms hundreds of small cubical cells, arranged in 20-40 transverse tiers. The protoplast of each cell is then metamorphossed directly into a single biflagellate zoospore. These zoospores are liberated through a small pore, either terminal or lateral, on the wall. Each zoospore, after a period of activity, comes to rest and gives rise to a sporophytic plant, *i.e.* a plant of the same generation from which it has developed.

It is to be noted that the unilocular sporangia are sporangial in nature in which reduction division takes place prior to the formation of haploid zoospores, and these are borne on the sporophytic plant (diploid). The multilocular sporangia borne by the sporophyte are also diploid. The zoospores produced by these structures are diploid, since there is no reduction division preceding their formation. In order to differentiate the multilocular sporangia from the multilocular gametangia, which are morphologically alike but are borne on the gametophytic plant, these have been designated as **neutral sporangia** and the zoospores, **neutral zoospores,** as they give rise to the same generation (sporophyte) instead of the alternate generation (gametophyte).

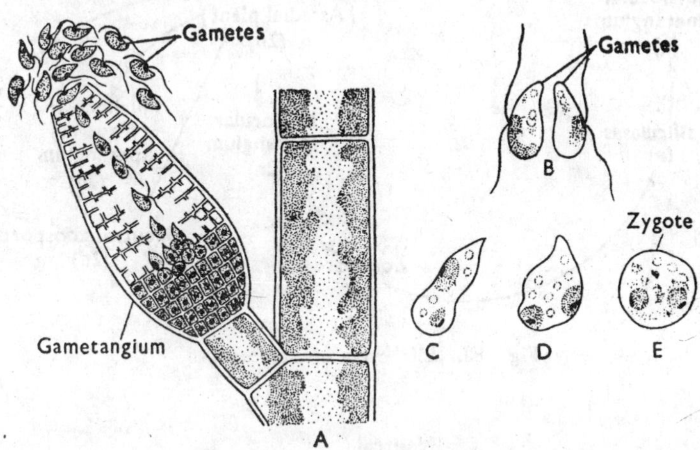

Fig. 82. *Ectocarpus.*
A, A gametangium liberating gametes ; B—D, Stages in the union of gametes ; E, A zygote.

Sexual reproduction takes place by the fusion of physiologically different isogametes produced within multilocular gametangia borne by the gametophytes.

The structure and mode of development of these gametangia are similar to those of the neutral sporangia borne by the sporophytic plant. Each protoplast of a gametangium develops into a biflagellate gamete. The gametes are similar to zoospores* and fusion occurs only between the gametes from separate gametophytic plants (heterothallic), which are often interpreted as sexually distinct. The diploid zygote, thus formed as a result of union of gametes, germinates and forms the sporophytic plant (diploid).

In the life cycle of an *Ectocarpus* there is an alternation of a distinct haploid generation of sexual plants bearing male and female gametes respectively and a generation of diploid asexual plant producing the zoospores.

* In *E. secundus* two types of gametangia—micro- and mega-gametangia are produced liberating gametes of unequal sizes.

Sometimes the gametes may develop parthenospores which give rise to new gametophytes.

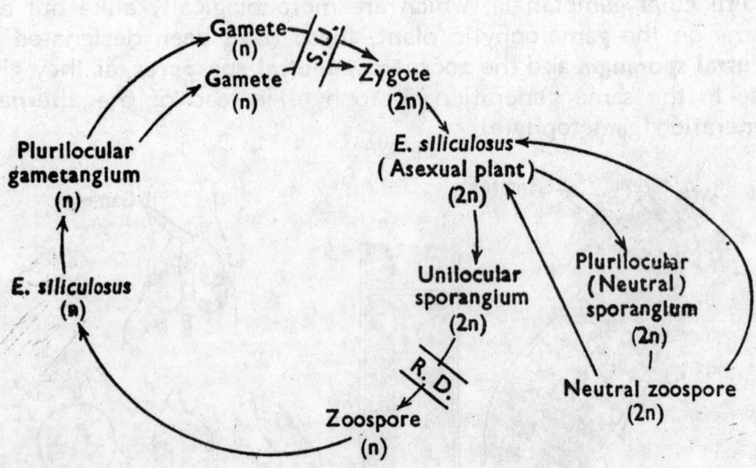

Fig. 83. Life cycle of *Ectocarpus*.

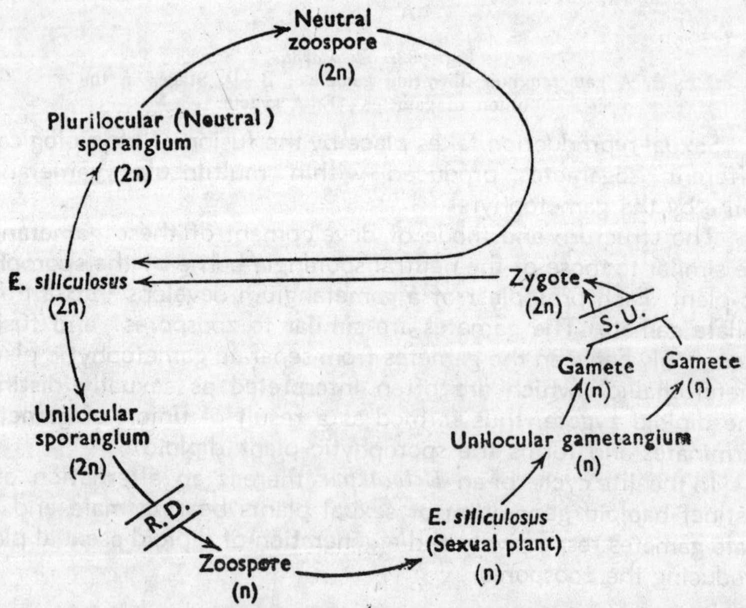

Fig. 84. Another type of life cycle of *Ectocarpus*.

ORDER 6. **LAMINARIALES**

Plants bulky, body truly parenchymatous ; asexual reproduction by zoospores formed within unilocular sporangia ; sexual reproduction distinctly oogamous.

LAMINARIA

(Fam. LAMINARIACEAE)

Laminaria grows along the coasts of Europe, America, Africa, China, Japan and Russia, usually in the subtropical regions. Majo-

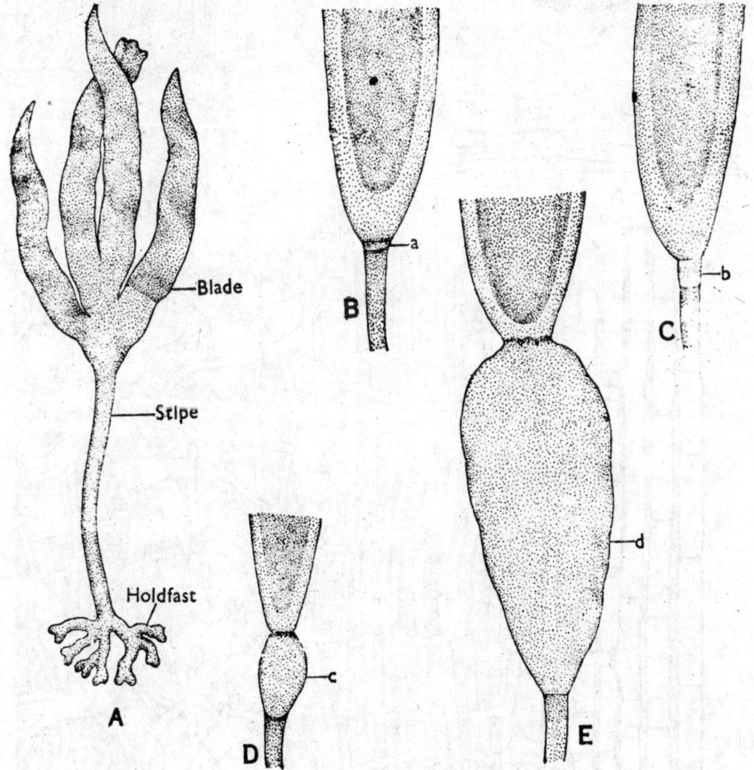

Fig. 85. ***Laminaria.***
A, A sporophytic plant ; B—E, Stages in the development of a new blade.

rity of the species are perennial lithophytes (having their blades annual), generally forming a dense belt slightly below the low-tide limit in quieter water.

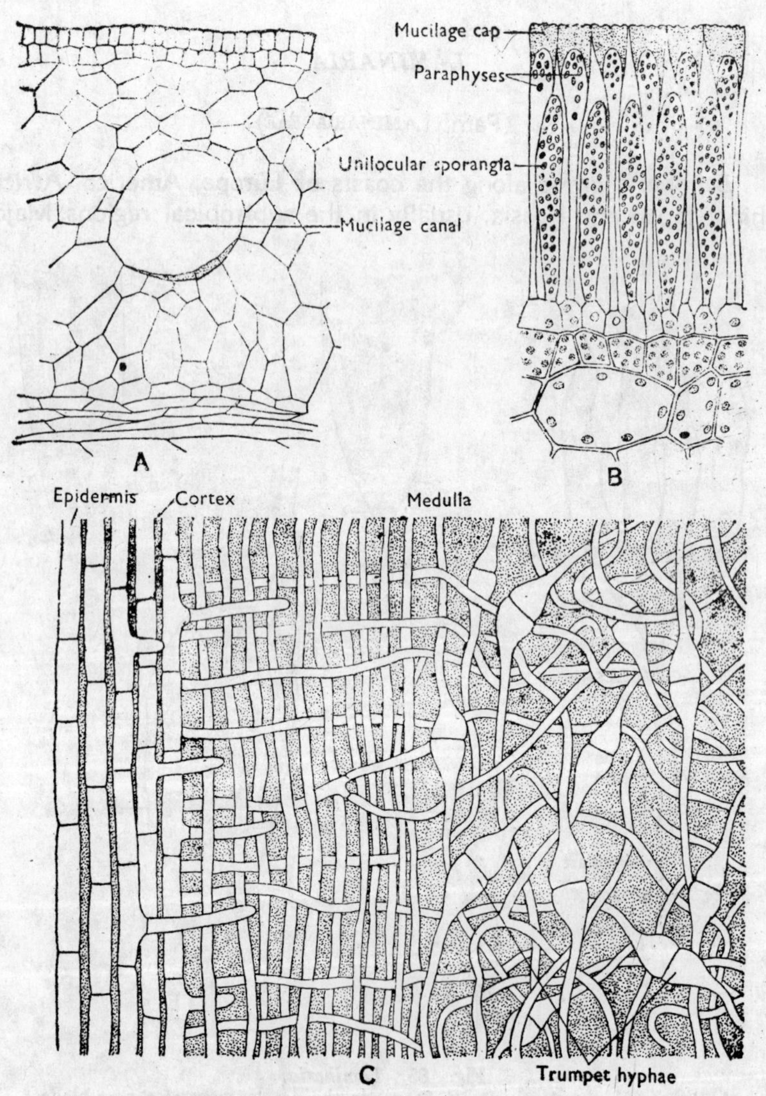

Fig. 86. *Laminaria.*
A, T.s. of a blade (in part); B, T.s. through a sorus (in part); C, L.s. through a part of the medulla of the stipe.

Vegetative body (Fig. 85A)

The sporophytic plant body is differentiated into (*a*) a simple, or incised, smooth and flat or highly convoluted, leathery **blade** about 2-4 metre in length, (*b*) an unbranched and usually cylindrical **stipe,** and (*c*) a **holdfast** ; the holdfast is usually an elaborate structure and is composed of a number of branched root-like bodies, called **haptera.** The growth of the sporophyte takes place with the help of an intercalary meristem situated at the junction between the blade and the stipe. This meristem not only helps both the blade and the stipe to grow in length, but also gives rise to a new blade to replace that of the last season. The newly formed blade at first appears as a small widening at the top of the stipe, separated from the previous year's blade by a prominent constriction. This new blade then goes on enlarging by a prominent constriction. Then the new blade goes on enlarging and the older one undergoes decay, remains attached to its apex as a mere appendage for some time, and finally breaks off from it.

Internally, the blade and the stipe are alike in structure. In each case, three distinct zones, the **epidermis,** the **cortex** and the **medulla,** can be differentiated (Fig. 86) although these tissues are more clearly marked off in the stipe than in the blade. The epidermal zone (the epidermis as well as the outermost cortical cells) is assimilatory in function. The cells of the medulla are highly modified, particularly in respect of certain cells which stop dividing early and are drawn out into long attenuating filaments, which maintain their original breadth near the transverse walls. These are known as the **trumpet hyphae** and are comparable to the sieve tubes of the higher plants. They also possess some spiral bands of thickening matters of cellulose on their walls. The real function of these trumpet hyphae is yet unknown. A system of anastomosing **mucilage canals** is noted in the cortex.

Reproduction

Laminaria reproduces both by asexual and sexual methods.

Asexual reproduction takes place by unilocular sporangia which are borne in widely extended **sori** on both the surfaces of a blade and, as a rule, formed at a specific season, either during the summer or in the early autumn. The sporangia lie in between the unicellular, club-shaped **paraphyses,** which form a palisade-like layer ; at the top of each paraphysis there is a prominent **mucilagenous cap,** and the caps of all the paraphyses in a sorus remain attached together keeping the sorus firm. The single nucleus of the sporangium, dividing meiotically gives rise to 32-64 nuclei, each of which along with a little amount of cytoplasm is ultimately metamorphosed into a pear-shaped, biflagellate zoospore. The zoospores are liberated through the apex of the sporangium enclosed in a sheath, which persists for a very short time and finally dissolves away leaving the zoospores swimming freely. After swimming for some time, each zoospore comes to rest, rounds up, secretes a wall around it and very quickly puts forth a germ tube. About half of the total number of zoospores develop into male plants and the other half, into female ones.

Both the gametophytic plants are filamentous in nature and are composed of a number of cells, which are rather smaller in size in case of the males than in the females.

The sex organs are produced on the lateral branches of the thallus. The antheridium is a small, somewhat spherical, single cell

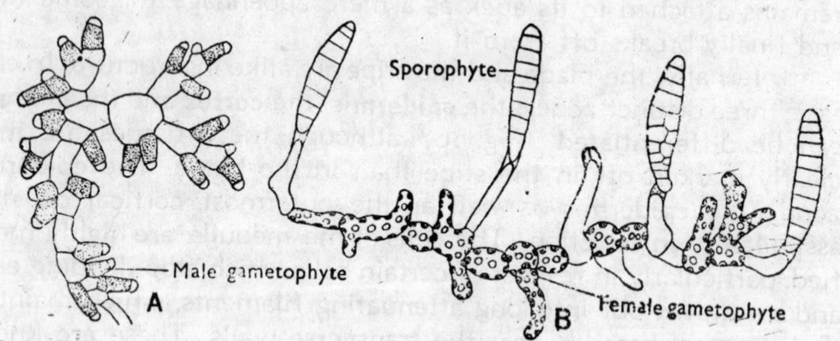

Fig. 87. ***Laminaria.***
A—B, The two types of gametophytes,

whose protoplast is metamorphosed into a single antherozoid provided with two long, unequal, laterally inserted flagella. The oogonium gives rise to a single egg, which on maturity is extruded out through the apical pore of the oogonium but remains attached to it. Fertilization takes place in the usual way by the union of the two gametes, and thus an oospore is formed. An oospore on germination gives rise to a new sporophyte. An egg which fails to get fertilized may develop into a sporophyte parthenogenetically.

The life cycle of *Laminaria* exhibits heteromorphic alternation of two generations.

Economic importance

Laminaria is a good source of the polysaccharide 'laminarin' Formerly, the plant was extensively used for the production of iodine. It is also used as a diet under the name 'Kombu' by the Japanese. The Chinese as well as the Russians also use it as a food.

ORDER 8. **DICTYOTALES**

Plants with frequent dichotomous branching and slightly differentiated parenchymatous forms ; asexual reproduction by non-motile tetraspores formed within unilocular sporangia ; sexual reproduction oogamous.

DICTYOTA

(Fam. DICTYOTACEAE)

Dictyota, a cosmopolitan species, is widely distributed in the tropical seas. It grows along the shores in the intertidal zones, usually attached to the rocky substratum by a disc-shaped holdfast. The most common species, *D. dichotoma*, is an annual.

Vegetative body (Fig. 88A)

The plant body is a regularly, dichotomously branched, flat, membraneous, frond-like thallus, which spreads out in a more or less fan-shaped fashion from a comparatively narrow, cylindrical base with a holdfast ; the holdfast remains attached to the substratum with the help of rhizoids. The entire plant grows by means of a single apical cell.

Internally, a thallus consists of three layers, a central one (**medulla**) composed of large-sized cells, and an upper and a lower **epidermal layers,** which are made up of smaller cells containing chromatophores ; groups of mucilage hairs arise from these epidermal layers.

Reproduction

Dictyota reproduced by vegetative, asexual and sexual methods.

Vegetative reproduction may take place by the decay of the older parts of the thallus, followed by subsequent fragmentation. In some cases, specially modified structures, called **gemmae or brood buds,** are developed on the body of the thallus for the purpose.

Asexual reproduction takes place with the help of large, non-motile spores, called **tetraspores.** The tetraspores are produced

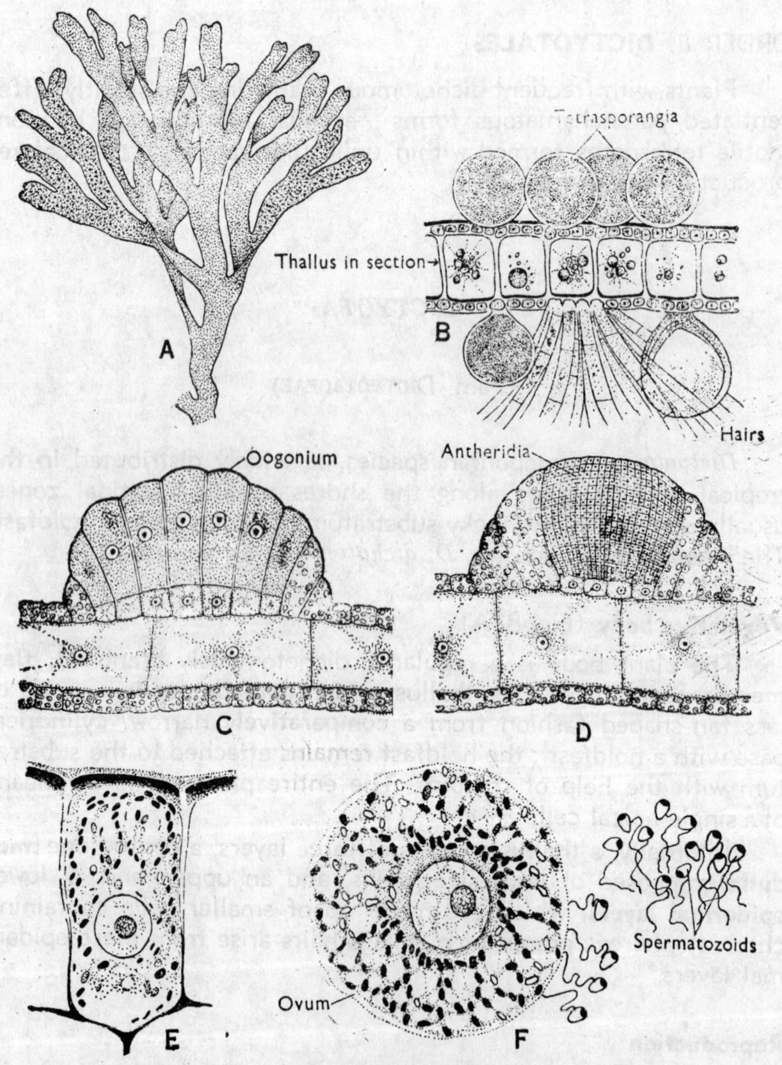

Fig. 88. ***Dictyota.***
A, An entire plant ; B, Section of the thallus showing tetrasporangia ; C, V.s. through oogonial sorus ; D, V.s. through antheridial sorus ; E, Rudiment of an young oogonium ; F, An egg during fertilization.

inside **tetrasporangia,** which are usually grouped together forming ill-defined **sori** on both the sides of the thallus. The tetrasporangia are without any involucral covering and are produced on diploid asexual plants only. The solitary nucleus of a tetrasporangium undergoes a reduction division and gives rise to four, slightly elongated, naked tetraspores, each having a haploid set of chromosomes. On maturity, the tetraspores come out through an apical opening on the tetrasporangial wall and germinate directly giving rise to male and female sexual plants in equal proportions, which are morphologically alike with the asexual plants. In some cases, a tetrasporangium may fail to produce tetraspores, and then it germinates quickly and reduplicates the same diploid generation.

Sexual reproduction is oogamous. The gametophytes are normally heterothallic. The sex organs are differentiated in groups of sori on the male plants, each sorus being enclosed by a well-defined involucre (a sterile jacket layer of cells). Each white and glistening antheridial sorus consists of about 100-200 antheridia, and each antheridium forms about 1500 uniflagellate sperms. The oogonial sori are deep brown in colour and are also invested by individual rudimentary involucre. Each oogonial sorus contains about 25-50 oogonia, each producing a single egg. On maturity, the apex of the oogonium becomes gelatinized and dehisces, thereby liberating the egg. There is a marked periodicity, usually correlated with the fortnightly sequence of spring and neap tides of the lunar month, in the development of sex organs and gametes. When sperms and eggs are discharged in sea-water, the latter secrete a substance which attracts the sperms and fertilization is effected very soon (often in course of half an hour's time). The fertilized egg or oospore readily germinates into a diploid asexual plant. In rare cases, an unfertilized egg secretes a wall around it and germinates parthenogenetically.

It is to be noted that *Dictyota* possesses an isomorphic alternation of generations.

ORDER 9. **FUCALES**

Plants with parenchymatous forms and complex external and internal differentiations ; asexual reproduction unknown ; sexual reproduction oogamous.

FUCUS

(Fam. FUCACEAE)

***Fucus*, the best-known brown alga, is widely distributed and is an inhabitant of salt-water along the coasts of the oceans of the**

temperate and colder zones. Most of the species grow permanently attached to rocks between the high and low tide levels, and are

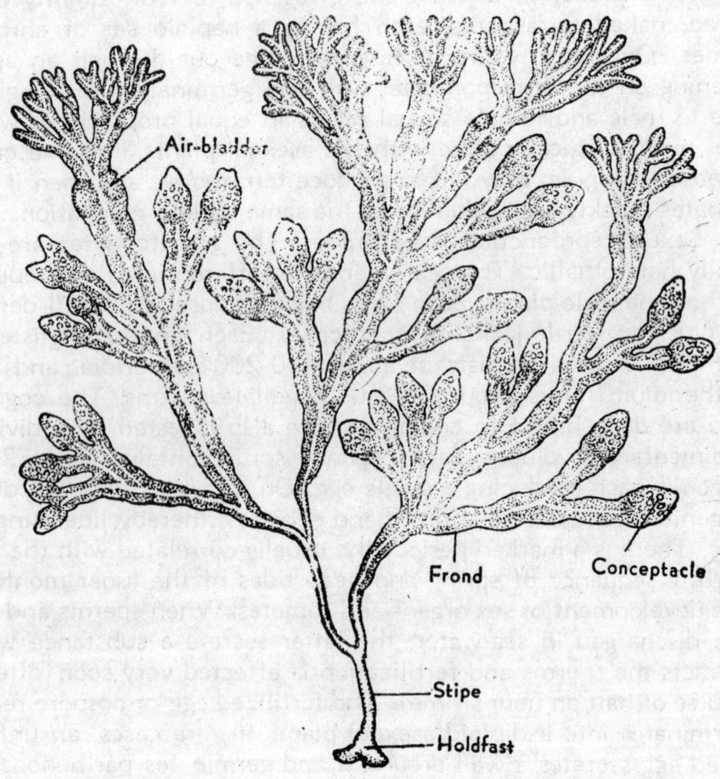

Fig. 89. *Fucus vesiculosus.*
A mature thallus with swollen ends of the branches containing conceptacles, in which sex organs are formed.

often torn loose by storms and carried hundreds of miles away into the sea.

Vegetative body (Fig. 89)

The thallus, which is a sporophyte, shows the greatest complexity of form with an external differentiation comparable to that of a vascular plant. It has a disc-like **holdfast** from which arises a stem-like **stipe,** that bears a broad leaf-like flattened portion, the **frond.** The plant as a whole is about 35-70 centimetre long, and the leafy portion of the thallus shows regular dichotomous branching. As the plant grows the fronds may fork repeatedly.

The thalli of some species of *Fucus* (e.g. *F. vesiculosus*) contain, a little behind the apices of the branches, **air-bladders,** which are formed due to the accumulation of gas in large intercellular spaces, and these help the plants to keep erect when they are submerged under water.

A cross-section of the thallus shows that it is internally differentiated into two distinct tissues : (1) the central **medulla** composed of loose mass of colourless elongated cells, and (2) the surrounding **cortex** forming a compact dark-brown outer region, made up of more or less isodiametric cells, which contain chromatophores towards the periphery. The protoplast of the vegetative cell is vacuolated and usually contains a single nucleus having a nuclear membrane, a nucleolus and a chromatin network. There are usually more than one chromatophores without any pyrenoid.

Reproduction

Fucus always reproduces by the sexual method, and the gametic union is of an oogamous type. Though a sporophyte, it bears gametangia, antheridia and oogonia, within spherical chambers, called **conceptacles.** At maturity, the tips of the branches become swollen in which these conceptacles are embedded, and these appear as warty elevations on the surface even when viewed without a lens. A mature conceptacle is globose and opens at the surface by a small pore, the **ostiole.** Numerous slender multicellular unbranched hairs, called **paraphyses,** grow out from the inner surface of the conceptacle ; these are usually directed towards the ostiole. Some unbranched hairs may grow out through the ostiole forming cottony tufts, and are then known as **periphyses.**

The common eastern species, *Fucus vesiculosus*, is heterothallic, since some plants have conceptacles containing only antheridia, while other plants contain only oogonia, But in some species, the antheridia and oogonia may be produced within the same conceptacle.

The antheridia, at the beginning, are ovoid cells, which are produced on much-branched hairs and are associated with the paraphyses within the antheridial or mixed conceptacles. Each of these ovoid cells, which is destined to develop into an antheridium, is uninucleate, and this nucleus divides and re-divides until 64 nuclei are produced, the first nuclear division being reductional*. Ulti-

* It is to be noted that the development of the antherozoids is similar to that of the zoospores within the unilocular sporangia produced on the sporophyte of *Ectocarpus,* and that in this case the spores produced by the unilocular sporangia function as gametes.

mately, each nucleus, with some amount of cytoplasm becomes more or less pear-shaped antherozoid with two laterally attached flagella of unequal lengths and an eyespot. At maturity, the wall of the antheridium ruptures, and the whole mass of antherozoids

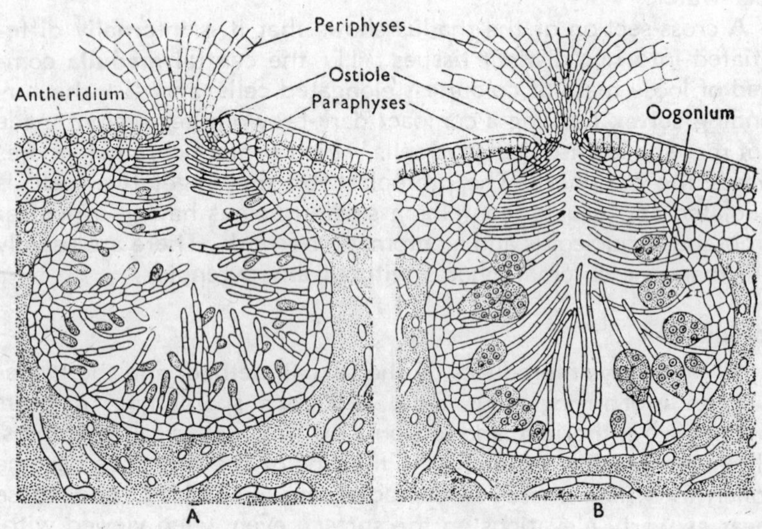

Fig. 90. *Fucus vesiculosus.*
A, Part of cross-section of the thallus through a male conceptacle containing antheridia ; B, The same through a female conceptacle containing oogonia.

within it escapes and is lodged in a considerable amount of mucilage secreted by the paraphyses for the purpose. The *Fucus* plant, when exposed to air during low tide, undergoes shrinkage, and as a result, the mass of gametes, embedded in the mucilage, is extruded through the ostiole. At high tide these are washed off and the antherozoids are set free for fertilization.

The oogonia are also produced among the paraphyses within the oogonial or mixed conceptacles. During the development of an oogonium, a short outgrowth develops from the layer of cells forming the wall of the conceptacle. This outgrowth divides transversely into two cells, the distal one becomes the oogonium while the basal one is called the **stalk cell.** The oogonial cell, densely filled with cytoplasm, is uninucleate, and as it enlarges the nucleus divides by three successive divisions forming eight daughter nuclei, the first division being always reductional. This is followed by the division of the cytoplasm into eight uninucleate masses, each of which becomes rounded and forms an egg. The oogonial wall becomes differentiated into two relatively firm layers, separated from each other by a softer gelatinous layer. When the eggs become mature, the outer wall ruptures. The eight eggs escape from the outer wall of the oogonium being still enclosed by the two inner

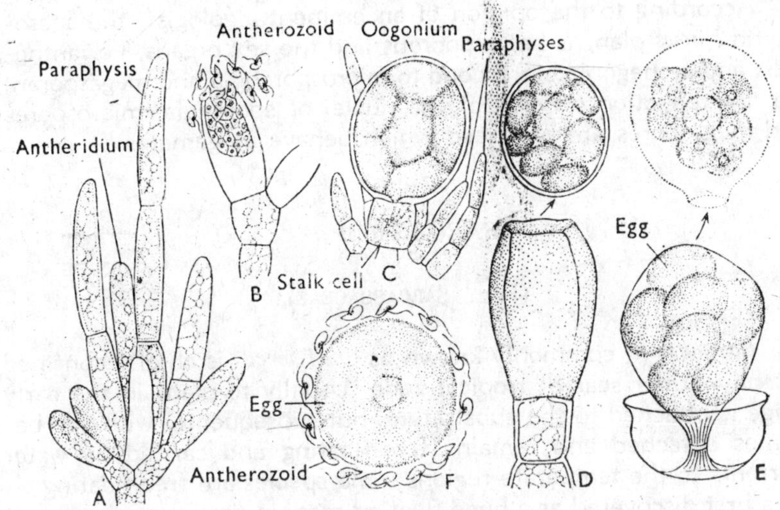

Fig. 91. *Fucus vesiculosus.*
A, An antheridial branch with antheridia ; B, Liberation of antherozoids ; C, The oogonium ; D, Oogonium from which a group of eight eggs still enclosed within the inner oogonial walls is escaping ; E, Later stages of the same ; F, An egg surrounded by numerous antherozoids.

walls, and are pushed outwards and finally through the ostiole. These two inner layers also rupture in succession, and the egg are finally extruded into the sea where fertilization takes place.

The fertilization of the eggs outside the body of the plant is made possible by reason of the great number and motility of the antherozoids, as well as, due to the characteristic smell of a substance secreted by the egg by which the antherozoids are attracted. Each fertilized egg then secretes a thin cellulose wall around it forming a zygote, and this does not become a resting spore. It soon germinates and grows into a new plant.

Alternation of generations

The life-history of *Fucus* reveals that there are no regular alternation of generations. The plant body is a sporophyte and it is diploid although it bears sex organs, i.e. antheridia and oogonia. The diploid nucleus of the sex organs divides reductionally and gives rise to the gametes, i.e. sperm and egg. These gametes represent only the gametophytic generation as they soon undergo sexual fusion forming diploid zygote, which germinates into the sporophytic plant.

According to the opinion of an eminent algologist, the sporophytic *Fucus* plant is heterosporous and the sex organs, i.e. antheridia and archegonia correspond to microsporangia and megasporangia. By reduction division of the nuclei of sporangia, microspores and megaspores are produced which behave as gametes.

SARGASSUM

(Fam. SARGASSACEAE)

Sargassum, commonly known as '*gulf weed*' is chiefly confined to the warmer seas of tropical zone. Usually to plant in the early stage is attached to the substratum, but subsequently with age becomes detached and remains free-floating and carried by water currents to the temperate regions some species are free-floating. It was first discovered as a huge floating mass in the Sargasso sea, off the coast of North Africa, from which the name of the plant has been derived. It is found in Australia, Japan, Indonesia, Ceylon and other places. In India it grows along the western and eastern coasts, being attached to rocks below low-tide level. There are 7 species of Indian *Sargassum*, viz., *S. tennarimum, S. cenerlum, S. plagiaphylla, S. illicifolium, S. wightii, S. myriocystium* and *S. crytifolium*. Some species (e.g. *S. energive*) are edible.

Vegetative body (Fig. 92A)

The plant resembles a bushy seed-plants. The structure of the plant body is very complicated, both morphologically and anatomically. It consists of a main axis, lateral branches and rhyzoids. The main axis, commonly known as the *stem*, is much-branched producing lateral branches, both secondly and tertiary ones, attractively. The secondary branches bear short leaf-like structures, so-called "leaves", with or without midrib and sometimes with serrated margins. Moreover, these branches are sterile and the upper cells at their bases are modified into round, golden-brown, stalked *air-bladders*, which enable them to float on water. The tertiary branches are fertile and much-dissected forming finger-like structures, commonly known as *receptacles*. The flask-shaped *conceptacles* bearing the sex organs are embedded in the receptacles. The main axis is fixed to the substratum by means of stout rhizoids produced from its base.

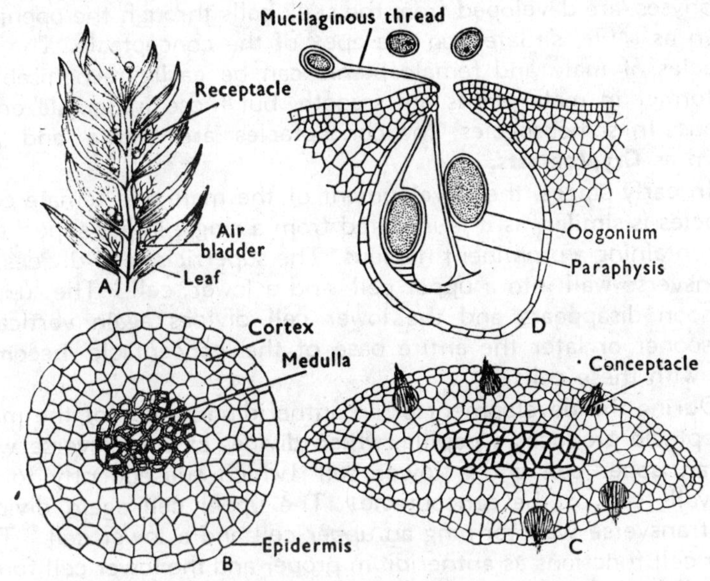

Fig. 92. *Sargassum.*
A, Portion of the plant body, B, T.s. of stem. C, Portion of t,s, of receptacle ; D, Female conceptacle containing oogonium.

A cross-section of the main stem shows three distinct regions (Fig. 92B) :

1. *Epidermis.* It consists of a single layer of cells containing plastids, and with or without any cuticle, but is meristematic. Hence, it is called *meristoderm.*

2. *Cortex.* It is composed of many layers of parenchyma cells.

3. *Medulla.* It is the central core and its cells contain scalariform thickenings. It is probably assent for the conduction of food.

Reproduction

Sargassum reproduces by vegetative and sexual methods.

Vegetative reproduction takes place by fragmentation of the plant into many pieces, each of which produces a new plant by division and growth.

Sexual reproduction is oogamous. The sex organs, antheridia and oogonia, are produced within the flask-shaped conceptacles. The same conceptacle may contain both antheridia and oogonia, or only antheridia or oogonia, but in dioecious species the conceptacles contain either antheridia or oogonia on different plants. The branches bearing antheridia or oogonia as well as the sterile paraphyses, are developed from the stalk cells through the opening, known as *ostile*, situated on the apex of the conceptacle. The receptacles of male and female plants can be easily recognisable ; the former in male plants are smooth, but those in female ones, spinous. In some species, the conceptacles are sterile and are known as **Cryptoblasts.**

In early stages, the development of the male and female conceptacles is similar, as it is initiated from a single larger superficial cell containing a prominent nucleus. The superficial cell divides by a transverse wall into a upper cell and a lower cell. The upper cell soon disappears and the lower cell divides again vertically and sooner or later the entire base of the conceptacle becomes lined with these cells.

During the development of an antheridium, a cell of the male conceptacle produces a papilla, which divides by a transverse wall into an upper cell and a lower cell (which subsequently forms the wall—cell of the conceptacle). The upper cell again divides by a transverse wall forming an upper cell and a lower cell. The upper cell functions as antheridium proper and the lower cell forms the stalk cell, from which the paraphyses are developed. A number of antheridia is formed inside the male conceptacle. In the young stage, the antheridium possesses a single diploid nucleus. During maturity, it divides reductionally and is subsequently followed by a number of mitotic divisions, giving rise to 64 nuclei. Now cleavage of the cytoplasm takes place forming 64 pear-shaped, biflagellate antherozoids. The mature antheridium is a small ovoid body provided with a thick mucilagenous wall. Now the antheridium is detached from the stalk cell by strong water current, comes out of the conceptacle and floats on the surface of water. A mass of an antherozoids is liberated by the rupture of the antheridium mall.

The cell of the inner lining of the female conceptacle gives rise to oogonial initial. It soon divides by a transverse wall forming an upper cell and a lower cell. The lower cell forms the stalk and the upper cell functions as oogonium proper. The number of oogonia is less than that of antheridia. When young, the oogonium has a single diploid nucleus and is provided with a wall of three layers. During maturity, the nucleus undergoes three divisions, one of which is reductional, forming eight daughter nuclei. Out of these nuclei, one is functional and other seven degenerate. Recent investigations show that this nuclear division takes place when the oogonium comes out of the conceptacle, and that all the eight nuclei are potential eggs and as soon as one becomes fertilized, seven others degenerate. When the oogonium matures, the outermost wall ruptures, the second one forms the wall of the oogonium. When the oogonium comes out of the female conceptacle, through the ostiole, it at first remains attached to its apex by the mucilagenous thread, but afterwards set free and floats on the surface of sea-water (Fig. 92D).

Fertilization takes place in the usual way. The egg becomes surrounded by a number of antherozoids, one which enters into the egg and fuses with it forming oospore. The oospore finally develops into a new plant.

The life cycle of *Sargassum*, as in *Fucus*, does not show any alternation of generations.

CHAPTER V

CLASS RHODOPHYCEAE

Salient features

The Rhodophyceae, or the red algae, are readily distinguished from other algae by the following salient characters: (*a*) presence of chromatophores with a red pigment, **phycoerythrin**, in addition to the usual photosynthetic pigments and rarely with a blue pigment, **phycocyanin**; the presence of phycoerythrin in a large quantity often gives the plant a distinctive red colour, though green, olive-green and golden-brown red algae are not uncommon; (*b*) total lack of flagellate asexual spores; (*c*) transportation of non-flagellate male gamete to the female sex organ, the **carpogonium**, and deposition against it at the time of sexual reproduction; (*d*) indirect formation of spores mostly takes place from the zygote, but in some cases the zygote directly divides to form spores.

General characters

A great majority of red algae are strictly marine, but freshwater species are not uncommon. The former are found in all oceans including the Arctic and Antarctic oceans where the number of species is very few. They usually occupy the intertidal or littoral zones, but there are some which grow at levels never exposed by tides. These latter species usually grow in association with Chlorophyceae and Phaeophyceae. The greatest depth at which Rhodophyceae occur has been reported to be 200 metre. The majority of the marine Rhodophyceae are normally sessile, and grow upon rocks or some other inanimate substratum. Some species grow upon other Chlorophyceae, Phaeophyceae and Rhodophyceae, either as epiphytes or as true parasites, being mostly restricted to a single host. The sessile species, when become detached and free-floating, soon die.

In great majority of cases, there is a single, large vacuole in each cell, and the protoplasm usually forms a thin lining layer just internal to the cellwall. The cellwall is made up of cellulose and various other pectic compounds. In most cases a pore-like opening is found in the wall between adjacent cells, through which broad cytoplasmic strands connect the two protoplasts. The vegetative cells are mostly uninucleate, but in some multinucleate ones the number of nuclei may go up to three to four thousands in each cell. Each resting nucleus possesses a well-defined nuclear membrane, a conspicuous nucleolus, and an intervening hyaline zone. In each vegetative cell of the primitive red algae there is a single, centrally located, star-shaped chromatophore with a central pyrenoid without any starch sheath. In more advanced species, they are disciform without pyrenoids, and are usually more than one in each cell. Carbohydrate food reserves are found in the form of small grains, known as **floridean starch,** distributed in the general mass of cytoplasm outside the chromatophores. The floridean starch is an intermediate product between starch and dextrin, and when treated with iodine solution, becomes light brown or wine-red in colour. Besides a soluble sugar, **floridoside,** often accumulates.

The chromatophores of red algae contain the same photosynthetic pigments (chlorophyll *a*, chlorophyll *b*, carotene and xanthophyll), but the relative proportion is different from that in the higher plants. In addition to these, a water-soluble red pigment, **phycoerythrin,** is always present. Besides, in some species a blue pigment is also present, and this pigment resembles the phycocyanin of Myxophyceae.

A high light intensity increases the rhodophycean phycocyanin (*r*-phycocyanin) formation, and retards the development of phycoerythrin. The function of *r*-phycocyanin is not yet known, while that of phycoerythrin also remains a debatable point. It is generally believed that phycoerythrin functions as a photosynthetic pigment in blue light, and thus enables the deep water Rhodophyceae to carry on with their photosynthesis. Some workers are of opinion that the deep red colours of some members of this group are due to the absence of *r*-phycocyanin with a corresponding presence of a high percentage of phycoerythrin, and other shades of colour are due to an increasing proportion of *r*-phycocyanin. The great diversity of shapes and colours in Rhodophyceae is obviously due to the variation in the component ratio of these pigments.

With the exception of two genera, the thallus of Rhodophyceae is multicellular. This multicellular thallus may be a simple, branched filament made up of a row of cells, or it may assume a complex body of definite macroscopic form. The complex types usually attain a height of 10 cm., but may be more than a metre in a few cases.

Reproduction

Red algae seldom reproduce vegetatively. Vegetative reproduction may take place by the fragmentation of the thallus.

Asexual reproduction takes place by one or more types of non-flagellate asexual spores.

In the sexual reproduction, the male sex organ (**spermatangium**), and the female sex organ (**procarp** or **carpogonium**) are produced, either on the same plant or on different plants. The male gamete (**spermatium**) is produced from the spermatangium, and its nucleus fuses with the carpogonial nucleus to give rise to the zygote nucleus.

Alternation of generations

In the Subclass Bangioideae, there is no definite alternation of generations. On the other hand, the Subclass Florideae is characterized by having a regular alternation of generations in which the sexual plant—the gametophyte alternates with the parasitic asexual plant, i.e. carposporophyte. Others are **triphasic,** i.e. gametophyte, diploid carposporophyte and diploid tetrasporophyte successively follows one another. The Subclass Florideae also differ from other plants in that alternation of generations, is not always accompanied by an alternation in number of chromosomes.

Three types of life cycles may be recognised among Florideae :

(a) A biphasic alternation of gametophyte with haploid carposporophyte.

(b) A biphasic alternation of gametophyte with diploid carposporophyte.

(c) A triphasic alternation of gametophyte with diploid carposporophyte and diploid tetrasporophyte.

A biphasic alternation of gametophyte with a haploid carposporophyte has been found in *Batrachospermum*. The gametophyte may be reduplicated by means of monospores produced singly in the monosporangium.

The gametophyte may be homothallic or heterothallic. The male sex organs is called spermatangium which develops terminally on a specialised cell. Its protoplast called the **spermatium,** escapes by the rupture of the spermatangial wall. The female sex organ—the **carpogonium** develops terminally on a few celled, short secondary lateral branch, called carpogonial filament. Carpogonium has a swollen base with a prominent nucleus and a prolonged distal portion—the **trichogyne.**

The spermatia after liberation lodged on the wall of trichogyne and at the point of contact the intervening walls dissolve. The spermatial nucleus migrates into the trichogyne and ultimately fuses with the egg in the carpogonial base and the zygote is formed. After fertilization in case of haploid carposporophyte the zygote undergoes immediate reduction division and forms haploid daughter nuclei. Then the haploid **gonimoblast filaments** grow out of the carpogonial base and ultimately haploid carposporophyte is formed.

Carposporangia and **carpospores** are formed at the terminal portion of the gonimoblast filaments. Carpospore on germination gives rise to gametophytic plant.

A biphasic alternation of gametophyte with diploid carposporophyte is found in *Liagora tetrasporifera*. In this case carposporangium contains diploid nucleus which undergoes reduction division and ultimately four carpospores are produced. From this haploid carpospore gametophyte plant is developed.

Polysiphonia shows triphasic alternation of generations where the gametophyte alternates with diploid carposporophyte and diploid tetrasporophyte. The gametophyte which produces male and female sex organs, may be homothallic or heterothallic. The process of fertilization is as usual. After fertilization the zygote does not divide meiotically but it migraets to the **auxiliary cell.** The diploid gonimoblast filaments are produced from the auxiliary cell. The auxiliary cell is daughter cell of the **supporting cell.** The terminal cell of the gonimoblast filament develop into carposporangium. Single carpospore is produced in each carposporangium. The carpospore gives rise to free living diploid **tetrasporophytic plant** which is identical in morphological structure with that of gametophyte. The tetrasporophyte then produces **tetraspores** in the tetrasporangium. Prior to the formation of tetraspore there is meiosis and ultimately four tetraspores are produced. Tetraspore on germination gives rise to gametophytic plant.

Classification

The Rhodophyceae has been divided (Fritsch, 1935) primarily into two Subclasses, one having only *one* Order under it, while the other possesses *six* Orders. A brief outline of the classification is given below :

I. Subclass Bangioideae

Plants simple, filaments never aggregated ; no pit-connections between the cells ; very little specialization of sex organs ; direct division of the zygote gives rise to carposporangia ; terrestrial, freshwater, and marine.

Order Bangiales. Plants ranging from unicellular to parenchymatous form ; accessory reproduction by means of monospores ; life cycle haplobiontic. Examples—*Compsopogon*, *Porphyra*, etc.

II Subclass Florideae

Plants usually filamentous with aggregation of filaments forming pseudo-parenchymatous thalli ; cells with pit-connections ;

sex organs clearly differentiated ; gonimoblast filaments bearing carposporangia formed directly or indirectly from zygote ; mainly marine.

Order 1. Nemalionales. Plants filamentous ; construction of thallus uniaxial or multiaxial ; accessory reproduction with the help of monospores or tetraspores ; life cycle haplobiontic ; some forms freshwater. Examples—*Nemalion*, *Batrachospermum*, etc.

* **Order 2. Gelidiales.** Plants filamentous ; uniaxial ; generally with cruciate tetrasporangia ; life cycle probably diplobiontic. Example—*Gelidium*.

* **Order 3. Cryptonemiales.** Plants filamentous ; uniaxial or multiaxial ; tetraspores zonate or cruciate ; some special fertile areas (conceptacles, nemathecia) noted in some cases ; life cycle diplobiontic. Examples—*Cryptosiphonia*, *Corallina*, *Lithothamnion* etc.

Order 4. Gigartinales. Plants filamentous ; uniaxial or multiaxial ; tetraspores zonate or cruciate ; life cycle diplobiontic. Examples—*Agardhiella*, *Iridea*, etc.

***Order 5. Rhodymeniales.** Plants filamentous ; multiaxial ; tetraspores tetrahedral or cruciate ; life cycle diplobiontic. Examples—*Rhodymenia*, *Gastrodonium*, *Champea*, etc.

Order 6. Ceramiales. Plants filamentous ; uniaxial ; tetraspores generally tetrahedral ; carpogonial branch 4-celled ; life cycle diplobiontic. Examples—*Ceramium*, *Callithamnion*, *Polysiphonia*, etc.

SUBCLASS I. BANGIOIDEAE

Plants simple, filaments never aggregated ; not pit-connections between the cells ; very little specialization of sex organs ; direct division of the zygote gives rise to carposporangia ; terrestrial, freshwater, and marine.

ORDER BANGIALES

Plants ranging from unicellular to parenchmatous forms ; accessory reproduction by means of monospores ; life cycle haplobiontic.

*COMPSOPOGON***

Compsopogon is a freshwater alga, commonly occurring in bunches in tropical and subtropical streams, and occasionally along

* Not treated in this book.

** *Compsopogon* is a number of doubtful systematic position. Fritsch does not include it either under the Family Bangiaceae nor under the Family Porphyridiaceae. Smith, however, places it under the Family Erythrotrichiaceae.

the embankments of ponds, attached either to some submerged parts of acquatic plants, or to the mud beolw the water level.

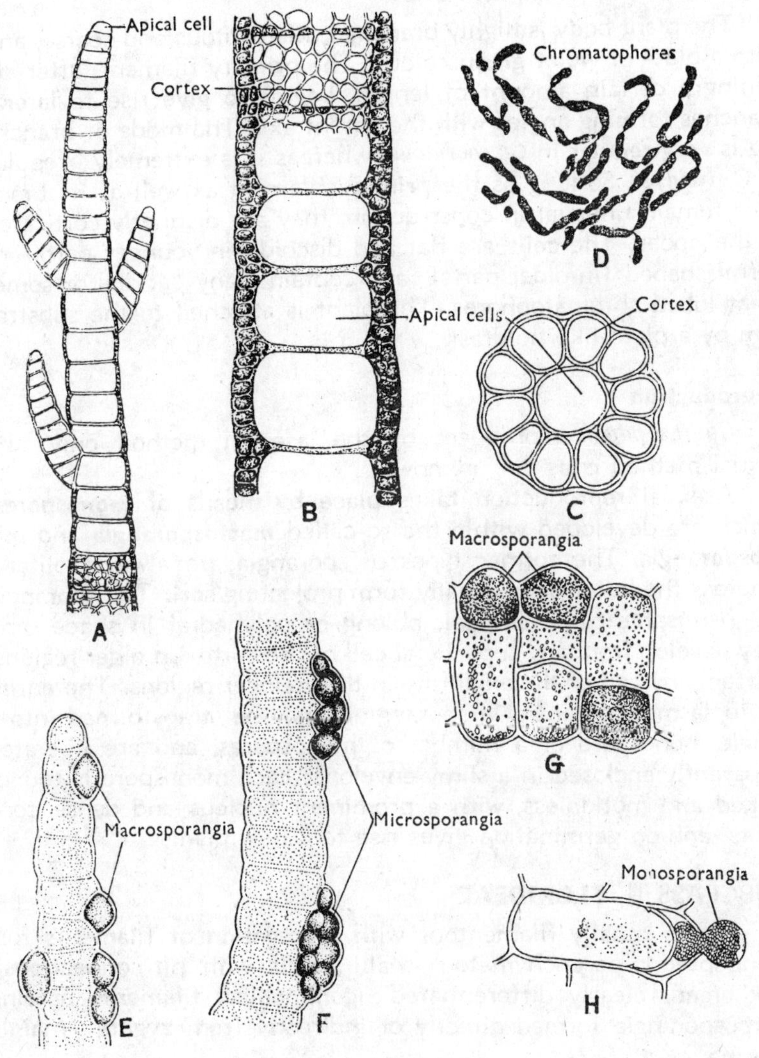

Fig. 93. *Compsopogon.*
A, A portion of the plant body ; B, A portion of an old filament showing the cortex and the apical cell ; C, T.s, of the same ; D, Chromatophores ; E, A portion of the filament with macrosporangia ; F, A portion of the filament with microsporangia ; G, A portion of E highly magnified ; H, A portion of the filament showing monosporangia.

The common Indian species of *Compsopogon* are *C. coeruleus* and *C. lividus.*

Vegetative body (Fig. 93A & B)

The plant body is highly branched, filamentous and coarse, and with a blue- or violet-green colour. The primary filament, after attaining a certain amount of length, begins to give rise to lateral branches forming angles with the parent axis. The mode of branching is very regular in *C. coeruleus*, whereas it is extremely irregular in *C. lividus*. So long as the primary filament as well as its branches remain uniaxial in construction, they are distinctly corticated at the nodes. The cells are flat and discoid (in younger parts) or barrel-shaped (in older parts), and contain many parietal or somewhat lobed chromatophores. The plant is attached to the substratum by a plate-like holdfast.

Reproduction

Compsopogon reproduces by the asexual method only, the sexual method is as yet unknown.

Asexual reproduction takes place by means of **monospores,** which are developed within the so-called **macrosporangia** and **microsporangia.** The former types of sporangia are always solitary, whereas the latter ones usually form projecting **sori.** The sporangia are hemispherical, spherical, oblong or polyhedral in shape, and may develop from any superficial cell of the cortex in older regions, or from any cell of the axial row in the younger regions. The entire protoplasmic content of a sporangium may be transformed into a single monospore or a number of monospores, and are liberated apparently enclosed in a slimy envelope. Each monospore is round, naked and motionless, with a prominent nucleus and dense contents, and on germination gives rise to a new plant.

SUBCLASS II. **FLORIDEAE**

Plants usually filamentous with aggregation of filaments forming pseudo-parenchymatous thalli ; cells with pit-connections ; sex organs clearly differentiated ; gonimoblast filaments bearing carposporangia formed directly or indirectly from zygote ; mainly marine.

ORDER 1. **NEMALIONALES**

Plants filamentous ; construction of thallus uniaxial or multiaxial ; accessory reproduction with the help of monospores or tetraspores ; life cycle haplobiontic ; some forms freshwater.

BATRACHOSPERMUM

(Fam. BATRACHOSPERMACEAE)

Batrachospermum, a simple red alga, grows generally in temperate and tropical climates in rapidly flowing streams or in cold springs, being attached to the stones, pebbles or woodwork during spring and summer. Sometimes it also occurs in lakes up to a depth of 50 metres.

The most common Indian species of *Batrachospermum* is *B. vagum*.

Vegetative body (Fig. 94)

The plant is characterized by having a thallus body of delicate, freely-branched, filiform filaments, varying in size from a few to several centimetres in length. The branches are usually moniliform,

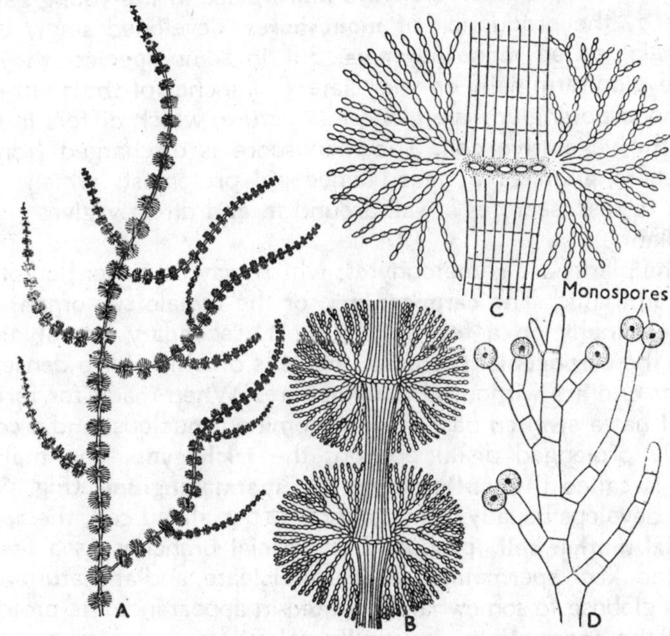

Fig. 94. *Batrachospermum.*
A, A portion of the thallus showing the general habit ;
B, Three nodes of the thallus enlarged ; C, A single node highly magnified ;
D, Lateral branches bearing monospores.

and have a gelatinous consistency. Its colour varies from bluish-green to olive-green, but may be of violet or reddish tint when it grows in deep water under shady places. The older portions of the thallus are made up of large cells arranged in an axial row bearing numerous vertical branches, which are either simple or divided in a forked manner, and the lateral branches are repeatedly forked. The lateral branches usually occur in the form of globose clusters at the nodes imparting to the plant its characteristic beaded appearance, and these may lie quite close to or a little distance apart from one another. From the basal cell of the lateral branches threads also grow downwards covering the external surface of the large axial row of cells, ultimately forming a complete cortex-like sheath. The protoplast of each cell is uninucleate, and contains several discoid or elongated chromatophores, each with a pyrenoid.

Reproduction

Batrachospermum reproduces both asexually and sexually.

Asexual reproduction always takes place in the young gametophytes by the production of **monospores,** developed singly within sporangia, called **monosporangia.** But in some species, they may also develop terminally on short lateral branches of the adult plant. The monosporangium is a globose structure, which differs in shape from the vegetative cell. The monospore is discharged from the monosporangium as a naked amoeboid protoplast, which finally comes to rest, secretes a wall around it, and directly gives rise to a new plant.

The plants are gametophytes, which may be either homothallic or heterothallic. The **carpogonium,** or the female sex organ, develops terminally on a few-celled, short, secondary lateral branch, called the **carpogonial filament,** the cells of which have denser protoplasts and are without chromatophores. When ready for fertilization, it has a swollen base with a prominent nucleus, and a conspicuously prolonged distal portion, the **trichogyne.** The male sex organ is called the **antheridium** or **spermatangium** (Fig. 95A), which develops usually terminally on a specialized cell, the **spermatogonial mother cell,** produced on special branches as a terminal member. Each spermatangium is uninucleate, and at maturity it becomes globose to somewhat elongated in appearance. Its protoplast, called the **spermatium,** is usually colourless, but may sometimes contain a chromatophore. The spermatium ultimately escapes by the rupture of the spermatangial wall, being still enveloped by another delicate wall whose morphological nature is doubtful.

The spermatia, after liberation, are carried away by the currents of water, and are finally lodged on the wall of the trichogyne. At the point of contact the intervening walls dissolve, and the nucleus of the spermatium migrates into the trichogyne, and finds its way into the base of the carpogonium, where fusion takes place between it and the carpogonial nucleus. In some cases, it has been

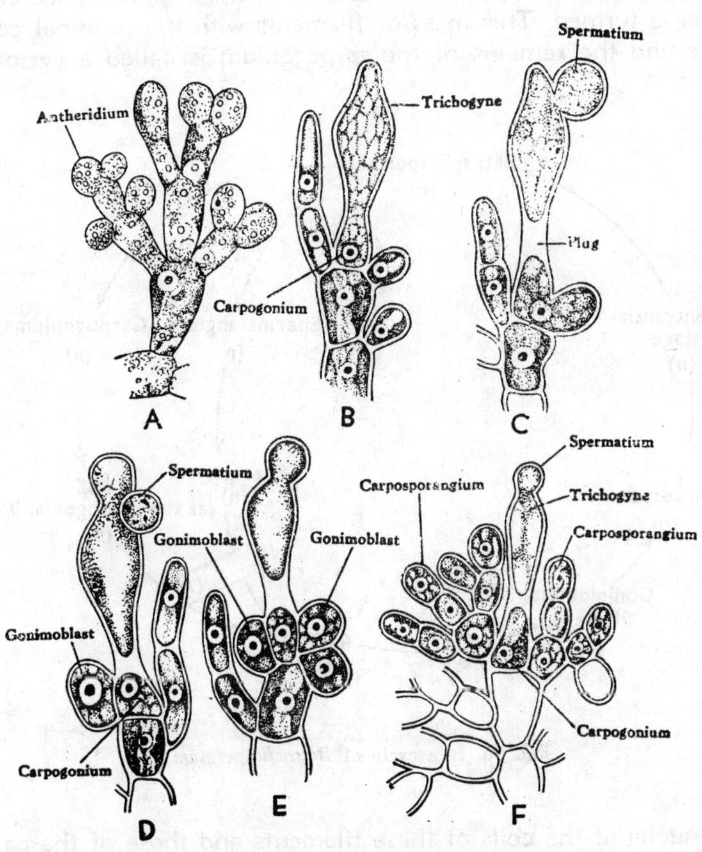

Fig. 95. *Batrachospermum.*
A, A group of antheridia ; B, A mature carpogonium ; C—D, Early and E, Later stages of gonimoblast development ; F, Mature gonimoblast with carposporangia.

observed that the spermatial nucleus may divide into two nuclei during its passage into the trichogyne, and one of them fuses with the carpogonial nucleus. After fusion, the basal portion of the carpogonium becomes separated from the trichogyne by the formation of a cross wall. This is followed by an immediate reduction division of the zygote nucleus, and two daughter nuclei are formed, one of which migrates into a lateral protrusion on the wall of the old zygote, and is ultimately cut off by the formation of a wall. The remaining nucleus may divide again and repeat the same process. From these cells a mass of filaments (**gonimoblast filaments**) is produced. At the distal end of each filament a spore, called **carpospore,** is formed. This mass of filaments with the terminal carpospore and the remains of the carpogonium is called a **cystocarp.**

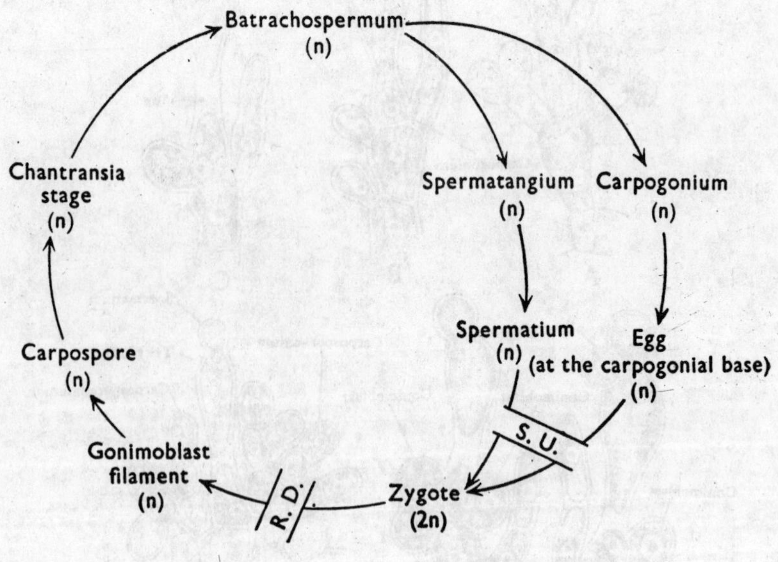

Fig. 96. Life cycle of *Batrachospermum.*

The nuclei of the cells of these filaments and those of the carpospores are, threfore, all haploid structures. When the carpospore matures the cellwall burts, the protoplast floats away, comes to rest, secretes a wall around it, and germinates into a simple, filamentous plant (**Chantransia stage**) from whose branches ultimately adult gametophytic plants are derived. It is to be noted that in the entire life history the zygote only represents the diploid structure, and the life cycle is biphasic.

ORDER 6. **CERAMIALES**

Plants filamentous ; uniaxial ; tetraspores generally tetrahedral ; carpogonial branch 4-celled ; life cycle diplobiontic.

CERAMIUM

(Fam. CERAMIACEAE)

Ceramium occurs in abundance both in deep waters as well as between tidal levels, and is mainly marine. One or two species may be found in the rivers, particularly in the estuaries.

The common Indian species of *Ceramium* is *C. gracillimum*.

Vegetative body (Fig. 97)

The plants grow in tufts varying from 2 to 30 cm. in length and remain attached to rocky substrata by means of multicellular

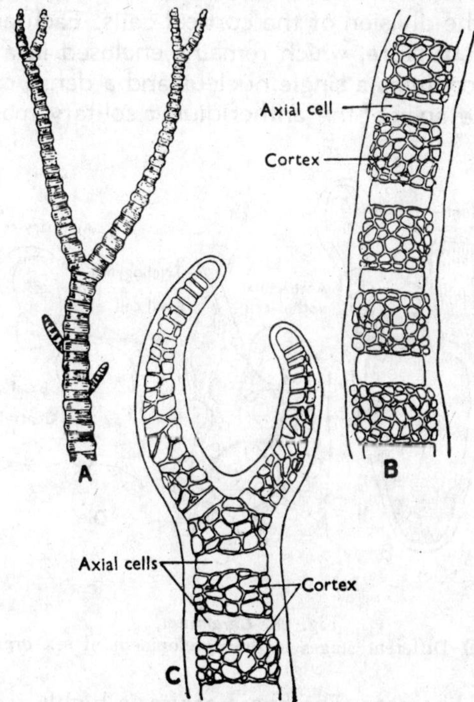

Fig. 97. *Ceramium*.
A, A portion of the plant body ; B, A part of the mature thallus showing cortex and axial cell ; C, The same showing dichotomous branching.

rhizoids, which form the holdfast. The thallus is irregularly, dichotomously branched with the apices of filaments incurved. In deep waters *Ceramium* appears red in colour, while in shallow tidal waters it exhibits a yellowish green or reddish brown colour. Each filament consists of a central siphon and can be differentiated into nodes and internodes. In some species, in mature condition, the nodes cannot be clearly marked out owing to the presence of continuous cortical cells around them, while in others the nodal band of cortical cells becomes separated from one another by the axial cells. In some cases, spines may be developed from the primary cortical cells at the nodes. There is no apparent morphological differentiation between the sexual and asexual plants.

Reproduction

Ceramium reproduces both by sexual and asexual methods.

The plants are heterothallic. The **antheridia** or **spermatangia** are scattered over the entire surface of the thallus forming patches. They arise by the division of the cortical cells. Each antheridium is a single-celled structure, which remains enclosed in a thick gelatinous wall and contains a single nucleus and a dense cytoplasm. By a rupture at the apex of the antheridium a solitary male gamete or

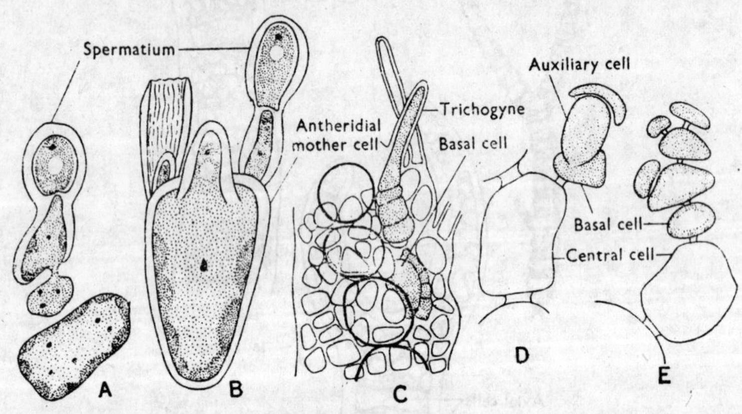

Fig. 98. *Ceramium*,
A—E, Different stages in the development of sex organs.

spermatium is liberated. The spermatium is highly vacuolated and contains a solitary nucleus. The female sex organs (**carpogonia** or **procarps**) are produced terminally on short lateral branches. Each procarp branch is normally 4-celled and produced from the basal cell. The terminal cell of the carpogonium elongates at its tip forming a tubular **trichogyne.** Fertilization is effected by the union of the spermatial nucleus with the carpogonial nucleus. After fertilization, the basal cell gives rise to a large **auxiliary cell,** on the side opposite to the procarp branch, into which passes the zygote nucleus. The auxiliary cell then by divisions gives rise to a number of **gonimoblast filaments.** From the tips of these filaments **carpospores** are produced, each of which on germination gives rise to the diploid **tetrasporic plant.** No well-developed cystocarp is produced, but the carpospores are partially protected by a number of short, lateral, upwardly projecting branches.

The asexual plant bears **tetrasporangia,** which arise in the cortical cells at the nodal regions. The nucleus of each tetraspore mother cell divides meiotically giving rise to four haploid **tetraspores,** which may be arranged cruciately or tetrahedrally. Each tetraspore, on liberation, reaches a suitable substratum and forms a new gametophytic plant by division.

The life history cycle in *Ceramium*, thus, exhibits a triphasic alternation of generations.

In some species, some specialized spores, called **paraspores,** are formed on the tetrasporic (diploid) plants, but their germination has not been studied.

CALLITHAMNION

(Fam. CERAMIACEAE)

The species of *Callithamnion* are usually perennials inhabiting mud-covered rocky substrate near low water-mark levels in the tropical seas. Some are epiphytes with deeply penetrating rhizoids.

Vegetative body (Fig. 99A & B)

The plant body is richly branched with an usual height of 2-5 cm. The branches are alternate and are arranged in definite spiral order (polystichous or distichous). Sometimes some of the lateral branches may exhibit pseudo-dichotomy. The central axis is composed of broad, thick-walled cells and generally the older parts remain enveloped by means of delicate, multicellular, corticating filaments. The cells are uninucleate or multinucleate, and generally possess ribbon-shaped chromatophores. The outer cells of the corticating filamentous envelope may also contain chromatophores. The plant remains anchored to the substratum by means of multicellular rhizoidal filaments, coming out from the cortex as well as from the basal cells of the lower branches ; these filaments sometimes unite to form a definite disc-shaped holdfast.

10

Reproduction

Callithamnion reproduces both by sexual and asexual methods. The plant is heterothallic. The male plants are usually smaller

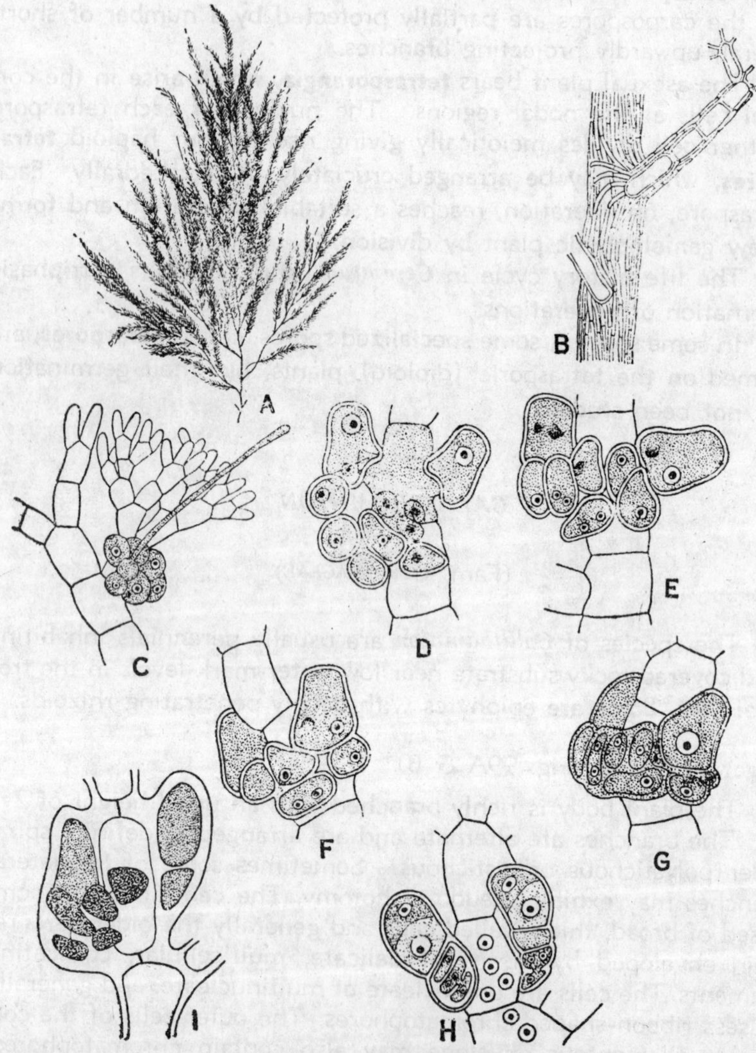

Fig. 99. *Callithamnion.*
A, The plant body ; B, A portion of the same magnified to show cortication ; C—I, Stages in the formation and development of sex organs.

than the female ones. The **antheridia** or **spermatangia** occur in spherical or cushion-like groups forming **sori** on the lateral branches. Each of these sori remains enclosed within a common gelatinous sheath and is composed of a mass of small-celled filaments, from whose tips the mother cells appear ; the mother cells ultimately give rise to antheridia. The entire protoplasmic contents of an antheridium, on maturity, is liberated as a **spermatium.** The **procarp** generally has two mother cells (**pericentrals**), only one of which bears the curved, 4-celled **carpogonial branch.** The position of the **carpogonium** is approximately midway between the two mother cells and it consists of a dilated basal region containing the egg nucleus inside, and a distally tapering **trichogyne.** A liberated spermatium, while floating on water, lodges against the trichogyne. A dissolution takes place at the point of contact and the spermatial nucleus passes down through the opening and unites with the egg nucleus. After fertilization, each of the two mother cells, lying on the two sides of the carpogonium, cuts off an **auxiliary cell.** The carpogonium, at this stage, becomes broader and divides longitudinally forming two cells. Each of these cells, in its turn, cuts off a small **connecting cell,** which joins up with the minute protuberance developed from the adjacent auxiliary cell. The haploid nucleus of the auxiliary cell sinks to the bottom along with one of the two diploid nuclei, while the other diploid nucleus migrates to the apical region of the auxiliary cell. The basal region of the auxiliary cell, containing degenerating auxiliary as well as the diploid nuclei, is cut off from the apical portion by means of a septum. The apical region of the auxiliary cell then produces the **gonimoblast filaments** which bear **carposporangia.** The naked, usually spherical masses of carposporangia remain enclosed in a common gelatinous sheath. Each carposporangium liberates a single **carpospore,** which on germination gives rise to a diploid plant, called the **tetrasporophyte.** No definite cystocarp is formed.

The tetrasporophyte bears **tetrasporangia** developed from the fertile pericentral cells, only one pericentral cell of a transverse tier giving rise to a sporangium. The single nucleus of the tetrasporangium undergoes meiotic divisions and four tetrahedrally arranged **tetraspores** are ultimately formed. On liberation the tetraspores develop into the gametophytes.

There is, thus present in the life cycle of *Callithamnion*, a definite triphasic type of alternation of generations.

In some species, there occur **polysporangia** in the position of the tetrasporangia which develop **polyspores** within. It is believed that the polyspores are mere derivatives of the tetraspores.

POLYSIPHONIA

(Fam. RHODOMELACEAE)

Polysiphonia, the most thoroughly studied red alga, is well known and the details of its life history illustrate certain principal features of Rhodophyceae in general. It chiefly occurs in shallow water along the coasts of the Atlantic and Pacific oceans ; some species may also grow as epiphytes on certain members of the family Fucaceae.

The common Indian species of *Polysiphonia* is *P. angustissimum.*

Vegetative body (Fig. 100)

The thalli in general are small, being a few to several centimetres in length. Each thallus is made up of several united filaments or siphons, from which the name '*Polysiphonia*' is derived. It bears at its basal end an elongated, unseptate rhizoid, whose apical portion expands to form an irregularly lobed holdfast. Secondary rhizoids may also develop from the lower portion of the thallus for additional anchorage of the plant. The thallus, as it grows lengthwise, produces along its length in a spiral succession dichotomously-branched, gradually tapering multicellular filaments, the **trichoblasts,** made up of a single row of cells (uniseriate). In some species, the older portion of the '*polysiphonous*' thallus may become ensheathed (corticated) by the formation of a peripheral layer of small cells. The characteristic protoplasmic connections are evident between the vegetative cells of the thallus. The uninucleate protoplast of a trichoblast cell is usually colourless, or it may contain a faintly coloured chromatophore.

Reproduction

Polysiphonia reproduces both by sexual and asexual methods.

Most species of *Polysiphonia* are heterothallic. The male sex organs, the **spermatangia** (Fig. 101B), are produced from superficial **spermatangial mother cells** in very dense clusters upon the branches of the fertile trichoblasts, situated near the growing apex of the male thallus. A spermatangial mother cell produces 2-4 spermatangia, each of which is a simple, single cell structure producing a **spermatium.** At maturity, the wall of the spermatangium ruptures and the spermatium escapes as a single-walled cell, leaving the empty wall of the spermatangium attached to the filament. It floats in water and is finally carried to the carpogonium.

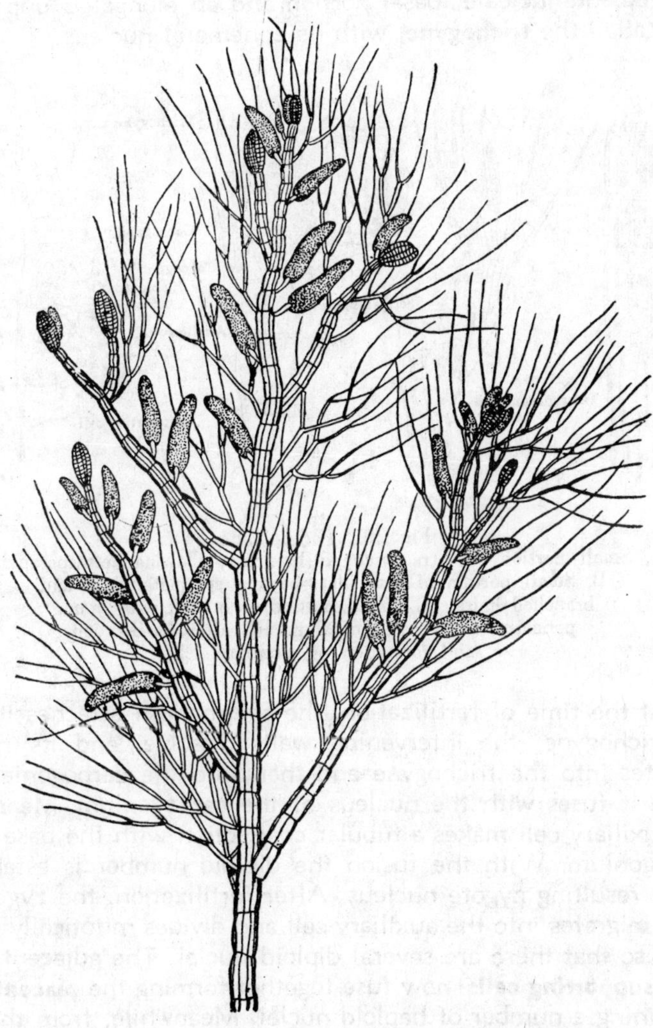

Fig. 100. *Polysiphonia.*
A portion of the thallus showing the general habit.

The female sex organ, the **carpogonium,** is produced upon a greatly reduced fertile trichoblast of a female gametophyte. The branch bearing the carpogonium is called the **carpogonial branch**

(Fig. 101D), which is a curved, 4 celled filament, whose terminal cell is metamorphozed into a carpogonium. One of the adjacent cells is known as the **auxiliary cell.** The carpogonium consists of an enlarged, uninucleate, basal portion and an elongated upper portion, called the **trichogyne,** with its ephemeral nucleus.

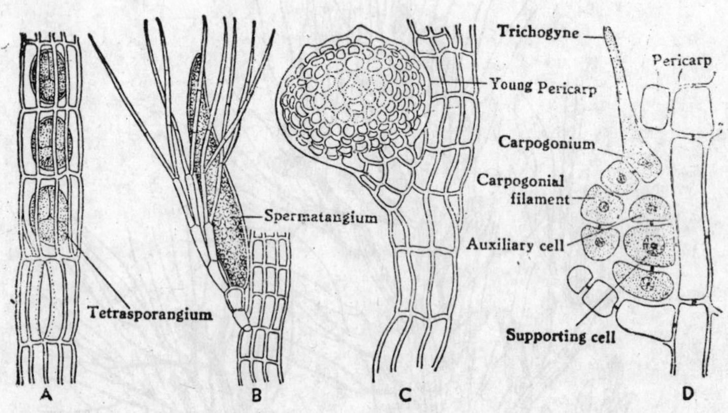

Fig. 101. *Polysiphonia.*
A, Small portion of tetrasporangial branchlet showing tetrasporangia; B, Small portion of branchlet showing spermatangium and branched hairs; C, Small portion of branch with young pericarp; D, A carpogonial branch after fertilization and formation of auxiliary cell,

At the time of fertilization, the spermatium attaches itself to the trichogyne, the intervening walls dissolve, and its nucleus migrates into the trichogyne and then into the carpogonial base, where it fuses with the nucleus of the carpogonium. Meanwhile, the auxiliary cell makes a tubular connection with the base of the carpogonium. With the fusion the diploid number is established in the resulting zygote nucleus. After fertilization, the zygote nucleus migrates into the auxiliary cell and divides mitotically several times so that there are several diploid nuclei. The adjacent sterile cells (**supporting cells**) now fuse together forming the **placental cell,** containing a number of haploid nuclei. Meanwhile, from the auxiliary cell numerous short multicellular filaments (**gonimoblast filaments**) begin to develop into which the diploid nuclei migrate. At the distal end of each filament a spore, called the **carpospore,** is formed within an unicellular carposporangium. The carpospore evidently contains a nucleus with the double number of chromosomes. Along with the development of the carpospores, the placental cell also gives rise to some haploid filaments, which grow up and cover the mass of filaments bearing the carpospores. This resulting enveloping structure is haploid and urn-shaped containing within it the diploid carpospores, and the whole structure is called the **cystocarp.** When the carpospores attain maturity, they are liberated from the cystocarp and each on germination produces the asexual or sporophytic plant (**tetrasporic plant** or **tetrasporophyte**). The plant, thus produced from the diploid carpospore, is, therefore, a diploid structure.

The tetrasporic plants are strictly asexual in nature and produce sporangia on short stalk cells, derived from the central region of the axis of the plant in course of development. Each sporangium

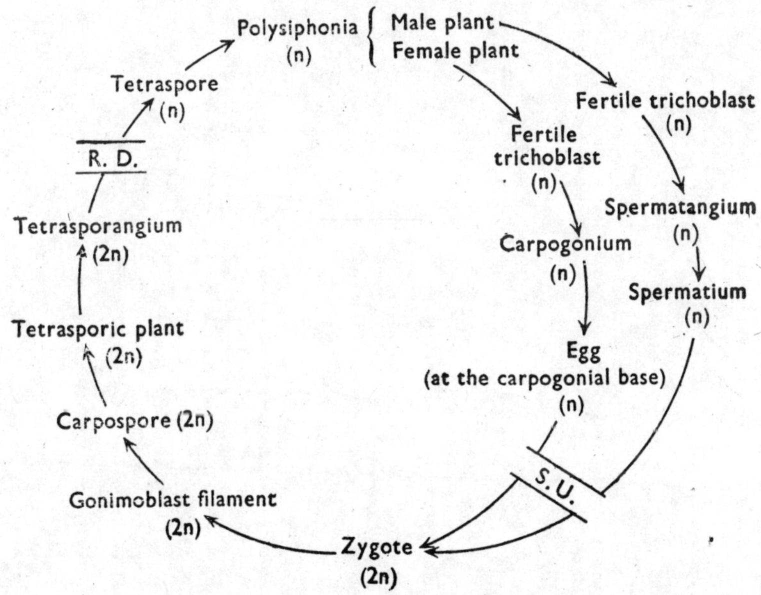

Fig. 102. Life cycle of *Polysiphonia.*

is a **tetrasporangium,** since its nucleus during development undergoes reduction division forming four haploid nuclei, around which a group of four spores, called **tetraspores,** is formed during the maturation. The tetraspores, at maturity, are liberated by rupture of the sporangial wall. Half of the tetraspores on germination produces the male gametophytes, the other half, the female gametophytes.

Thus, in the life history of *Polysiphonia* there are plants of three kinds : (1) **male plant** bearing spermatangia, (2) **female plant** bearing carpogonia and ultimately forming cystocarp as a result of fertilization, and (3) **tetrasporic plant** developed from carpospore and producing spores in groups of four, called tetraspores. Half of the tetraspores on germination produce the male plants and the other half, the female plants. Thus, in the life cycle, the male and the female plants represent the sexual or gametophytic generation, while the tetrasporic plant, which never produces gametes but always produces tetraspores, represents the asexual or sporophytic generation. These sexual and asexual plants not only differ in their functions, but they reproduce each other in succession showing an alternation of generations.

CHAPTER VI

CLASS MYXOPHYCEAE (CYANOPHYCEAE)

Salient features

The chief characteristics of Myxophyceae are: (1) a primitive and simple type of cell structure, (2) the presence of a blue pigment called **c-phycocyanin** and a red pigment (**c-phycoerythrin**) in addition to the usual photosynthetic pigments (chlorophyll *a*, carotenes and xanthophylls) and these are not localized in the chromatophores but are distributed in the peripheral portion of the protoplast, known as **chromoplasm,** and (3) the presence of a primitive type of nucleus, called **central body,** which lacks a nucleolus and a nuclear membrane. Other prominent features which are not restricted to them alone are: (1) the presence of an outer gelatinous cellwall surrounding the protoplast, (2) production of photosynthetic reserves, mainly in the form of glycogen but not starch, (3) total absence of sexual reproduction by gametic union, and (4) the lack of formatio of any flagellate asexual reproductive unit.

General characters

This group of blue-green algae consists of a small assemblage of primitive thallophytic plants, not apparently closely related to other subdivisions of algae. They are inhabitants of damp terrestrial places or are entirely aquatic in nature. Among aquatic forms a great majority are freshwater species as free-floating organisms (**plankton**). Some species are marine and may occur as epiphytes on other marine algae, or are found within their tissues as endophytes.

The vegetative body may remain strictly unicellular. This is due to immediate separation of daughter cells following cell divisions. In great majority of species, however, the daughter cells following cell divisions remain united with one another forming a multicellular filamentous or non-filamentous thallus. The non-filamentous colonies arise due to the union of gelatinous walls surrounding individual cells. This union may be so complete that the existence of individual gelatinous envelopes disappear completely, (e.g. *Microcystis*), or it may be incomplete, so that a more or less recognizable sheath is evident around each cell, (e.g. *Gleocapsa, Chroococcus*). The form of a non-filamentous colony depends upon the planes in which its cells divide. Thus, division in two planes results in a layer of cells which may be either a flat plate, (e.g. *Merismopedia*) or a hollow sphere, (e.g. *Coelosparium*). If the divisions are regular and in three planes, a cubical colony results, (e.g. *Eucapsis*) or the arrangement of cells in the colony may be quite irregular, (e.g. *Microcystis*). If the divisions take place repeatedly in a single plane, a filamentous colony is formed, (e.g. *Oscillatoria, Nostoc, Anabaena, Rivularia, Gleotrichia*).

In a filamentous colony, the cells either remain united together by the common walls of the adjacent cells or a single row of cells remains enclosed within a gelatinous sheath. A single row of cells is termed a **trichome.** A trichome with its surrounding sheath is called a **filament.** Within a filament there may be a single, (e.g. *Nostoc*, *Porphyrosiphon*) or several trichomes, (e.g. *Microcoleus*). The trichome may either be of uniform diameter, (e.g. *Porphyrosiphon*) or it is gradually narrowed towards the distal end, (e.g. *Rivularia*, *Gleotrichia*). The trichomes are generally unbranched, but in a few cases they may be branched, (e.g. *Nostocopsis*).

In unicellular forms, the cellwall surrounding each protoplast consists of two concentric portions : (*a*) an inner thin and firm layer, chiefly made up of cellulose, and (*b*) an outer gelatinous portion, often called the **sheath.** This sheath may be thick or thin, hyaline or coloured, and may often be stratified in appearance. On the other hand, in filamentous colonies this gelatinous layer is restricted only to the free and outer faces of the cell.

The protoplast of Myxophyceae presents an extremely interesting but difficult problem. All investigators recognize that the protoplast consists of an outer pigmented portion, called the **chromoplasm,** which surrounds a clear central portion, the so-called **central body** (Fig. 103). These parts have been variously interpreted from time to time. The central region of the cell is almost colourless and forms the central body. Most of the investigators are of opinion that it is nuclear in nature as it gives staining reactions like those of nucleus. There are other workers who do not recognize the nuclear nature of the central body due to the fact that it lacks nuclear membrane, nucleoli and definite chromosomes. Moreover, unlike the true nucleus the central body cannot undergo meiotic division. An electron microscopic study of the nature of the central body reveals that the chromosomes are dispersed throughout the protoplast and these are not localised into the central body. Recent investigators, like R. N. Singh (1961) and Patrick Echlin (1966), have

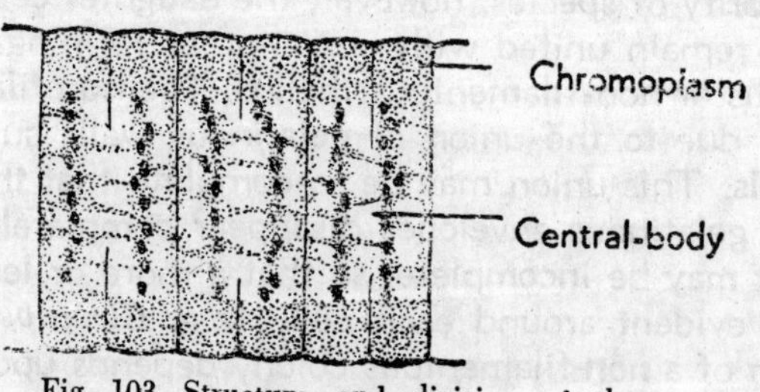

Fig. 103. Structure and division of the cells in Myxophyceae.

made a detailed study of the nature of the central body under an electron microscope and detected the presence of riboses, nucleoplasm D.N.A. fibrils, lipoid granules, food reserve, etc.

From the study of the nature of the central body as stated above, it may be concluded that it is a somewhat nuclear in nature although its meiotic division may be lacking. It is interpreted as a primitive or incipient nucleus from which nuclei of higher plants have been evolved. The peripheral portion has been recognized to be the cytoplasm corresponding to the cytoplasm of higher plants. Recently an electron microscopic study of the chromoplasm reveals the presence of photosynthetic lamellae which according to R. N. Singh are formed as a result of collapse of vesicle also present in the chromoplasm.

The chromoplasm of a myxophycean cell may contain a green pigment (**chlorophyll a**), yellowish pigments, *carotenes* (**b-carotene** and **flavicin**), and xanthophylls (**myxoxanthophyll**), a blue pigment (**c-phycocyanin**) and a red pigment (**c-phycoerythrin**). Of these, chlorophyll *a*, *b*-carotene and *c*-phycocyanin predominate. All these pigments are neither always present in the protoplast nor are present in equal amounts.

Reserve food, mostly in the form of granules, is present in the pigmented portion of the protoplast. Some think that these granules are glycogen, while according to others, these are glycoproteins. Besides these, there are also true protein granules and minute droplets of oil, but no starch.

Many freshwater planktonic species of Myxophyceae show the presence of **pseudo-vacuoles** in their protoplasts. These appear as black bodies under low magnification of a microscope and are distributed throughout the protoplasts. Under high magnification they appear somewhat reddish in colour, which is probably a refraction phenomenon. At first these pseudo-vacuoles were thought to be gasfilled vacuoles, since by pressure or in a partial vacuum they disappear and gas bubbles appear near the surface of the cell. Others believe them to be cavities filled with a viscous substance. They probably give greater buoyancy to planktonic species and act as light-screens against intense illumination.

Some filamentous species of Myxophyceae have the ability to move spontaneously. The locomotion may be due to the forward or backward gliding of the filament, spiral progression or retrogression, or a slow waving of the terminal portion of the filament. This is remarkably affected by various external factors, such as temperature, light, etc. Increased illumination and gradual rise of temperature from 0°—30°C accelerate movement.

The members of the Myxophyceae are very successful in terrestrial and subaerial habitats, and can tolerate a wide range of external conditions. The presence of a mucilagenous sheath around the cell or the trichome increases the water-absorbing and water-retaining capacity of the plant. The cells do not readily plasmolyze due to the absence of large vacuoles and elasticity of the cellwalls. This helps them to tide over prolonged drought with little change. The power of adjustment to lights of different intensities and due to colour variation many species are able to utilize the different qualities (colour) of available light, and thus can grow in diverse habitats. The so-called pseudo-vacuoles or gas-vacuoles give them a greater buoyancy for planktonic existence or serve as light-screens allowing only optimum light.

Reproduction

The methods of reproduction are extremely simple and are entirely asexual in nature, there being no production of flagellate gametes. Formation of thick-walled **resting spores** or **akinetes** or **heterocysts** also help the plants to tide over unfavourable conditions. Asexual reproduction may take place by the following methods :

Cell division. In unicellular types, multiplication takes place by cell division and the two daughter cells, thus formed, remain united by a common gelatinous sheath. Repeated cell divisions, in this way, give rise to a non-filamentous colony. But in case of multicellular forms, this process of cell division becomes a method of growth and not a means of multiplication.

Fragmentation. In filamentous forms, thalli capable of indefinite growth, usually break up under certain conditions into smaller portions, consisting of 2, 3 or more cells called **hormogones.** Each hormogone, by cell division, gives rise to a new filamentous colony and possesses great capacity for locomotion. This breaking up of the filament is either due to animal beings, or death of certain cells of the filament, or weaker union between certain cells of the filament.

Spore formation. In most filamentous forms, certain vegetative cells of the filament form some kind of resting cells, called **akinetes.** During the formation of an akinete, a vegetative cell enlarges, accumulates reserve food within it and the entire protoplast becomes invested by the appreciably thickened original cellwall forming the spore coat, which is often differentiated into an outer **exospore** and an inner **endospore.** The spores remain either singly or in groups and may either occur anywhere in the filament or have a fixed position (next to the heterocyst). They are resistive to unfavourable external conditions, can tide over unfavourable periods and germinate during the rainy season giving rise to new individuals.

In some marine forms, the protoplast of certain vegetative cells may divide to form a number of small, spherical or angular spores, called **endospores,** filling the original cell cavity.

Heterocyst formation. All filamentous Myxophyceae, excepting the members of the Family Oscillatoriaceae, form spore-like bodies which differ structurally from ordinary vegetative cells and spores. They occur singly or in pairs, and are either terminal or intercalary in position. During development, a very young vegetative cell expands, its protoplasm becomes transparent, homogeneous and viscous, and a wall, internal to the original cellwall, is secreted round the protoplast. If the heterocyst occupies the terminal portion of the filament, there is a pore on its wall through which cytoplasmic connection between it and its adjacent vegetative cell can be observed. On the other hand, if it be intercalary, there are two such pores, and these pores are closed at maturity by button-like thickenings, called **polar nodules.** Heterocysts are generally functionless, but they may germinate in exceptional cases.

Classification

The Myxophyceae is divided into *five* Orders (Fritsch, 1942) as follows :

(a) Hormogones absent

Order 1. Chroococcales :—Thallus unicellular or colonial ; reproduction by cell division and by the formation of endospores ; mostly freshwater, some lithophytes. Examples—*Chroococcus, Gleocapsa, Aphanotheca, Aphanocapsa,* etc.

* **Order 2. Chamaesiphonales :**—Thallus unicellular or colonial ; reproduction by endospores or exospores ; epiphytes or lithophytes, marine or freshwater. Examples—*Chamaesiphon, Darmocarpa,* etc.

* **Order 3. Pleurocapsales :**—Thallus filamentous heterotrichous and without heterocysts ; reproduction by the formation o endospores ; generally marine lithophytes, also in lakes and in rapid streams while a few are marine epiphytes. Examples—*Pleurocapsa, Radaisia,* etc.

---

* Not treated in this book.

(b) Hormogones present

Order 4. Nostocales :—Thallus filamentous, non-heterotrichous, commonly with heterocysts and often showing false (rarely true) branching ; reproduction by hormogones, heterocysts and akinetes ; large majority occur in freshwater as hydrophytes or lithophytes. Examples—*Nostoc, Oscillatoria, Lyngbia, Anabaena, Rivularia, Gleotrichia, Scytonema*, etc.

* **Order 5. Stigonemales :**—Thallus filamentous, heterotrichous with true branching and mostly with heterocysts ; reproduction by hormogones and heterocysts but rarely by akinetes ; mostly as lithophytes or freshwater hydrophytes. Examples—*Stigonema, Nostocopsis*, etc.

ORDER 1. CHROOCOCCALES

Thallus unicellular or colonial ; reproduction by cell division and by the formation of endospores ; mostly freshwater, some lithophytes.

GLEOCAPSA

(Fam. CHROOCOCCACEAE)

Gleocapsa is a genus of unicellular form, chiefly found in subaerial rather than aquatic habitats. They are very common in green

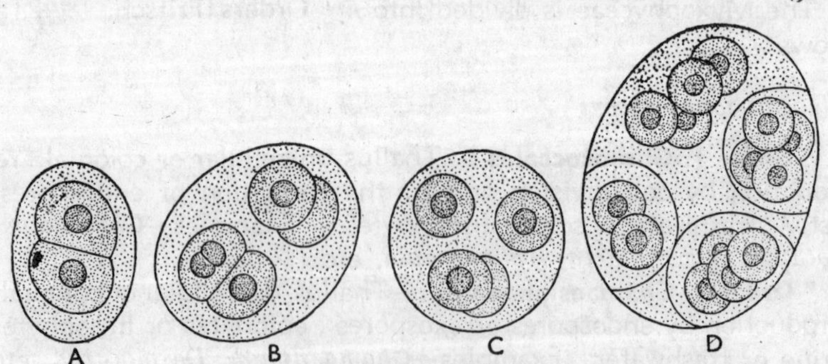

Fig. 104. ***Gleocapsa.***
A—D, Various stages of cell division, the daughter cells being embedded in the gelatinous matrix produced by their walls.

houses and sometimes found on flower pots which are constantly kept moist. They often form a gelatinous coating on rocks or on

* Not treated in this book.

moist stone walls forming olive-coloured, purplish brown, reddish or violet-coloured plant masses.

The common Indian species of *Gleocapsa* are *G. atrata, G. gelatinosa, G. punctata, G. rupestris, G. montana, G. aeruginosa, G. luteofusca*, etc.

Vegetative body (Fig. 104A)

The thallus is unicellular, but frequently two to several daughter cells remain aggregated together within the sheath of the parent cell, forming a more or less persistent gelatinous colony of no definite shape. In such cases the cellwalls of individual cells are quite distinct from one another, but are more or less confluent forming the colony. Each cell is more or less spherical in shape at maturity, and its protoplast is surrounded by a thick homogeneous or stratified, hyaline or coloured gelatinous cellwall (**sheath**) enclosing an inner firm cellulose layer. The protoplast has much the same structure and range of colour as are found among other Myxophyceae.

Reproduction

Gleocapsa reproduces asexually only by the process of cell division. During the process a cell somewhat elongates, its 'central body' divides into masses and cytokinesis takes place by the process of constriction. Each daughter protoplast then secretes its own gelatinous sheath.

ORDER 4. **NOSTOCALES**

Thallus filamentous, non-heterotrichous, commonly with heterocysts and often showing false (rarely true) branching ; reproduction by hormogones, heterocysts and akinetes ; large majority occur in freshwater as hydrophytes or lithophytes.

OSCILLATORIA

(Fam. OSCILLATORIACEAE)

The majority of the species of this blue-green alga are inhabitants of freshwater, while others are marine. They may occur singly, or interwoven with one another, forming extensive sheets usually on terrestrial substrata. They are found in all possible habitats, viz. moist rocky cliffs, damp soil, muddy banks of streams and ponds ; they may often grow luxuriantly in pools of stagnant water and are found as a free-floating organism intermingled with other algae.

The common Indian species of *Oscillatoria* are *O. acuminata, O. agardhii, O. animalis, O. amphibia, O. articulata, O. calcuttensis, O. chilkensis, O. chlorina, O. homogenea, O. cruenta, O. limosa, O. nigra, O. nigroviridis, O. princeps, O. rubescens, O. splendida, O. tenuis, O. versicolor,* etc.

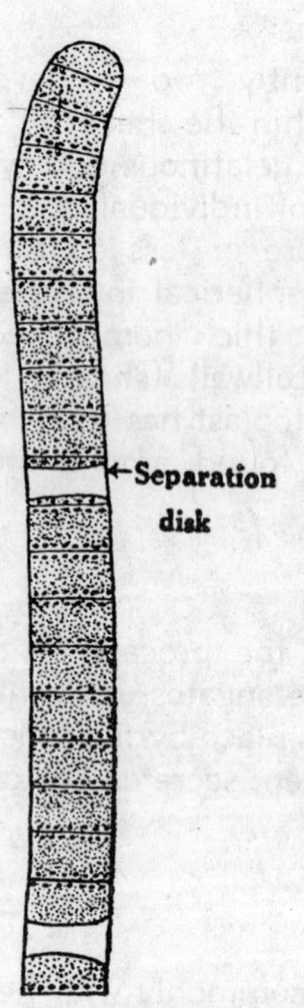

Fig. 105. *Oscillatoria.* A portion of the filament.

Vegetative boy (Fig. 105)

The thallus is an unbranched, cylindrical, narrow or broad filament, entirely without or with barely perceptible watery, hyaline and mucilagenous sheath. Each filament consists of a single row of cells in the form of short cylinders, which may even be shorter than they are wide. The terminal cell is usually convex or rounded at its free end, but in some cases it may taper to a point. In some species, the free outer wall of the apical cell may be thickened to form a definite calyptra. The cell structure is more or less similar to those of other Myxophyceae.

Reproduction

Oscillatoria reproduces only by the vegetative method. Reproduction by the formation of zoospores or by gametes is unknown. Each filament does not grow indefinitely in length, but regularly breaks up into short fragments, called **hormogones,** each containing 2, 3 or several cells. Before separation, the hormogones are delimited in the filament by the formation of double concave disks (**separation disks**) of gelatinous consistency between the hormogones. Each hormogone may develop into a new filament by divisions.

The most characteristic feature of *Oscillatoria* is the fact that the filaments, particularly the hormogones, are capable of swaying or oscillating movements to which the plant owes its name.

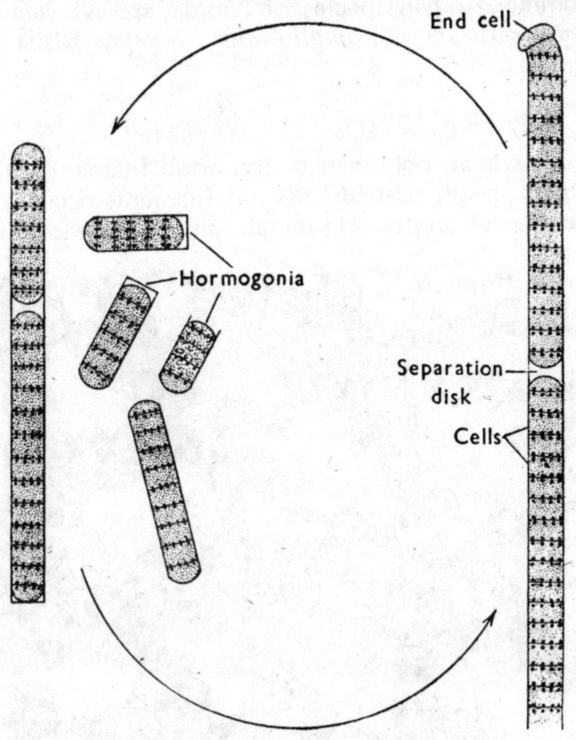

Fig. 106. Life cycle of *Oscillatoria*.

NOSTOC

(Fam. NOSTOCACEAE)

Nostoc occurs in nature as a free-floating blue-green alga forming lump of jelly-like masses (colonies) in which numerous filaments are embedded. When young, these are of microscopic size, more or less spherical in shape and solid. As the colony increases and becomes macroscopically visible in size, it remains solid or may become hollow and has a smooth or somewhat convoluted surface. The hollow colony may rupture and form expanded sheets with irregular margins. They live either immersed in water but sometimes prefer moist terrestrial habitats being attached to the substratum. Some species occur as endophytes within other plants, such as *Anthoceros*, *Cycas*, *Lemna*, etc. Some species are edible and are used as food in various parts of the world.

The common Indian species of *Nostoc* are *N. commune*, *N. gregarium*, *N. carneum*, *N. amplissimum*, *N. sphaericum*, *N. paludosum*, etc.

Vegetative body (Fig. 107)

The thallus is an unbranched, contorted filament with a definite-gelatinous sheath. Usually, several filaments occur in densely inter-woven masses and always remain embedded within a film of

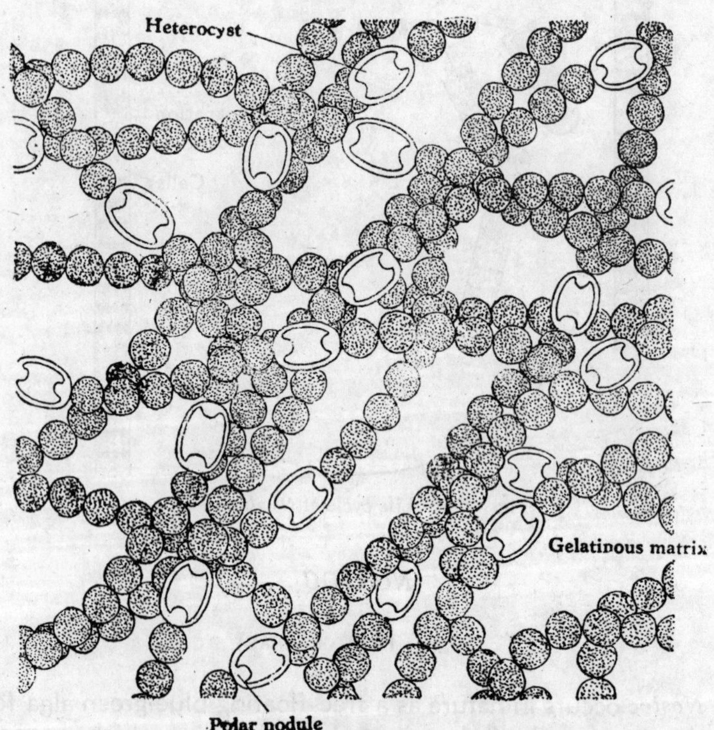

Fig. 107. *Nostoc.*
Filamentous colonies within the gelatinous matrix ; several heterocysts shown, dividing the filaments into hormogones.

gelatinous envelope. Each cell of the filament is spherical, barrel-shaped, or more or less cylindrical in shape. The cells of the filament increase in number by cell divisions in parallel planes. During divisions, they nearly separate, round off and become tangent to one another giving rise to a filament resembling a string of beads.

The cell structure is more or less similar to those of other Myxophyceae. The characteristic feature of each filament is the presence of **heterocysts,** which are usually intercalary but may be terminal in position.

Reproduction

Nostoc reproduces asexually either by fragmentation, or by the formation of akinetes. A filament seems to break off easily, next to the heterocyst, forming short filaments called **hormogones.**

ANABAENA

(Fam. NOSTOCACEAE)

Anabaena occurs in nature, either singly or in colonies, forming free-floating floccose masses. Sometimes it forms a delicate mucous layer on the surface of the soil. It is primarily an aquatic alga and is found in abundance in semi-permanent pools. Many species occur as planktons in lakes and ponds forming water-blooms. *Anabaena azollae* is found within the leaves of *Azolla*, and *A. cycadeae* occurs as an intercellular parasite in the cortical tissues of the coralloid roots of *Cycas*.

The common Indian species of *Anabaena* are *A. ballyganji, A. circinalis, A. ambigua, A. orientalis, A. mollis, A. variabilis, A. fertilissima*, etc.

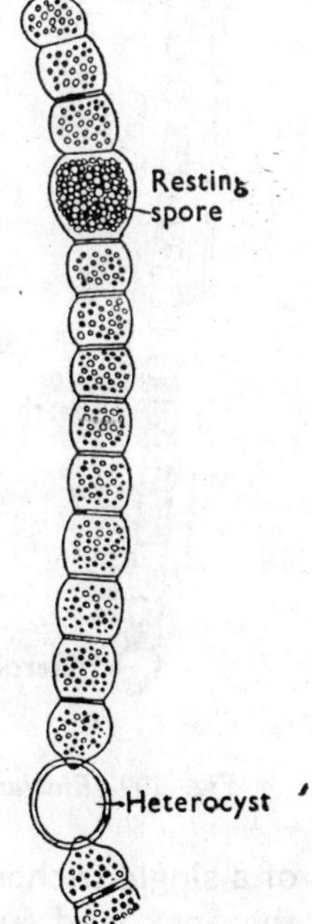

Fig. 108. *Anabaena.*

Vegetative body (Fig. 108)

The thallus is an unbranched, straight, circinate or irregularly contorted filament of uniform thickness throughout its entire length or slightly narrowed at the ends. Each filament consists of a trichome which is enveloped by a watery, hyaline sheath of variable thickness. The cells of the filament are usually spherical or barrel-shaped and contain protoplasts, which are either homogeneous or granulose and filled with numerous pseudovacuoles. The colour of the filament is variable, but usually it is grey or blue-green. There are always several intercalary **heterocysts,** which occur usually singly and are approximately of the same shape as the vegetative cells.

Reproduction

Anabaena, like *Nostoc*, reproduces asexually, either by the formation of hormogones or by means of akinetes. These akinetes develop singly or in chains, either next to the heterocysts or remote from them or in both positions. They are larger than the vegetative cells and are more or less cylindrical in shape with rounded ends.

Both *Anabaena* and *Nostoc* resemble each other so closely that it becomes very difficult to distinguish between the two. *Anabaena* never forms colonies of definite form in which the trichomes are usually not contorted. Besides, the sheath around the trichome is extremely hyaline and gelatinous. *Nostoc*, on the other hand, possesses a colony with a firm envelope, and within the colony the trichomes are very much contorted.

RIVULARIA

(Fam. RIVULARIACEAE)

Rivularia usually grows on submerged substrata, such a stones, woodworks and stems of water plants. Occasionally it is found on rocky cliffs. It forms hemispherical thalli of united filaments of exceedingly firm consistency and often heavily incrustated with lime.

The common Indian species of *Rivularia* are *R. globiceps*, *R. lens*, *R. natans*, etc.

Fig. 109. *Rivularia.*

Vegetative body (Fig. 109)

Each filament is whip-like and consists of a single trichome, which is gradually attenuated from the base to the apex, and surrounded by a distinct sheath. There is always a **heterocyst** at the base of each trichome. The sheath, either homogeneous or stratified, is usually distinct towards the lower portion of the trichome. The sheaths of several such filaments become partially or wholly fused forming hemispherical, globose or expanded masses of macroscopic size. Within such a mass, the filaments are somewhat radiately arranged, and this is due to repeated false branchings towards the basal portion of the thallus. But these branches are so much displaced that it becomes difficult for observation in a mature thallus.

Reproduction

Reproduction takes place by the formation of **hormogones**, which are normally developed towards the distal end of each filament. Akinetes are not found in this alga.

GLEOTRICHIA

(Fam. RIVULARIACEAE)

Species of *Gleotrichia* are always aquatic. They form spherical or hemispherical masses, which are either free-floating or attached to some submerged substrata throughout their entire surface. In some species, the thalli at first remain attached to the substratum but eventually become free-floating.

The common Indian species of *Gleotrichia* are *G. atra*, *G. natas*, *G. raciborskii*, *G. pisum*, etc.

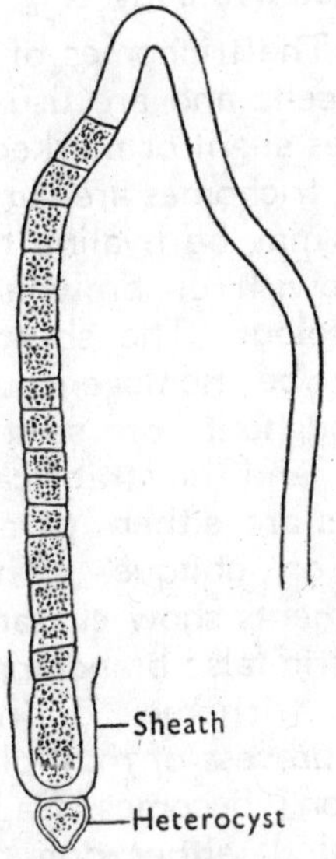

Sheath

Heterocyst

Fig. 110. *Gleotrichia.*

Vegetative body (Fig. 110)

The filament of *Gleotrichia* is more or less similar in structure with that of *Rivularia*, having trichomes gradually attenuated from base to apex with enclosing gelatinous sheaths, which are wholly confluent with one another forming globose or hemispherical masses. There occurs the same basal **heterocyst,** but in addition intercalary ones are also found. The filaments always possess **akinetes,** either singly, next to heterocysts, or in short series separated from one another by two or three vegetative cells.

Reproduction

Reproduction takes place by formation of **hormogones** formed towards the distal ends of the filaments, and by means of akinetes.

SCYTONEMA

(Fam. SCYTONEMACEAE)

Scytonema usually occurs in subaerial habitats, such as damp soil, dripping faces of rocks, etc., forming felty masses of interwoven filaments, but may also occur in hot springs.

The common Indian species of *Scytonema* are *S. amplum*, *S. aureum*, *S. javanicum*, *S. caldarium*, *S. tomentosum*, *S. varium*, *S. simplex*, *S. pascheri*, etc.

Vegetative body (Fig. 111)

The trichomes of *Scytonema* consists of more or less cylindrical cells and are usually of uniform diameter throughout. Sometimes slight or marked constrictions appear at the transverse walls. The trichomes are surrounded by sheaths of extremely fine texture and may be hyaline or yellowish or brownish in colour. The sheath may be homogeneous throughout or stratified, and the stratifications are either parallel or oblique. The filaments show characteristic false branching. The trichome, during the process of multiplication, becomes fragmented, either due to disintegration of the intercalary cells or due to formation of separating disks or heterocysts. These fragments are immobile and begin to grow within the original sheath. The branching results due to interruption of such newly formed trichomes at certain points. As a result, portions of one or both the trichomes perforate the firm sheath and grow out as laterals, which secrete a distinct sheath of their own. These false branches usually appear in pairs and occupy approximately the middle portion between two heterocysts. The **heterocysts,** intercalary in origin, occur singly or in series of twos or threes. They are more or less of the same size as the vegetative cells.

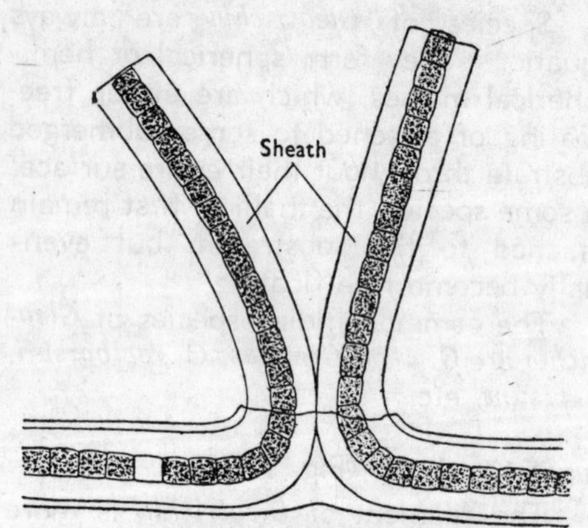

Fig. 111. *Scytonema*.

Reproduction

Reproduction by means of **hormogones** is usually the only method of multiplication. Akinetes are rarely formed in this alga.

Origin and evolution of sex in algae

The starting point in the origin of sexuality is denoted by the formation of gametes. The different types of sexual reproduction in algae range from isogamy to oogamy, the culminating point.

Ulothrix, in which modes of formation of gametes and zoospores are identical, has often been taken to illustrate the possibility of the origin of gametes from zoospores, consequently, the origin of sex. Two types of zoospores, large and small, are produced in *Ulothrix* depending on the number of successive nuclear divisions, and the smaller zoospores are morphologically alike with gametes and also in the method of production. The difference between the gametes and the zoospores depends mainly, therefore, on the number of nuclear divisions occurring during their development. When the number of divisions is less, the zoospores are formed, but when it is long continued, gametes develop. It has been suggested that possibly due to accidental fusion of the small zoospores in pairs sexual reproduction has originated. The larger zoospores on germination can only give rise to strong individuals, but the smaller ones on germination can produce only weaklings. But, if these smaller zoospores combine in pairs, zygotes are produced, and the resources of the two fusing cells are brought together forming a new identity full of increased vitality and vigour. This act of union of two naked protoplasts is a sexual act, and the two fusing cells are, therefore, regarded as sexual cells or gametes. The sexual reproduction originates when zoospores behave as gametes. It is believed that sexual reproduction in plants takes place in response to unfavourable environmental conditions for vegetative activity. When the conditions are most favourable, the plant usually reproduces vegetatively. When these conditions are on the decline, the plant reproduces sexually and the gametes are produced. These gametes, by fusing in pairs, produce zygotes, which usually pass into a state of dormancy or resting period, and in this condition the plant perennates. Thus, the formation of zygote is more in response to unfavourable growing conditions for the protection against extermination of the individual than a method for the multiplication of the plant.

The origin of sex in algae is associated with the gradual differentiation of sex. By differentiation of sex is meant the morphological differentiation, *i.e.*, difference in appearance, which involves in the difference in size and activity of the motile organs associated with it. This differentiation of sex leads to such differentiation of gametes that they can be easily recognized as male and female ones. Morphological similarity of pairing gametes is called **isogamy,** while morphological dissimilarity of the pairing gametes is called **heterogamy.** In isogamous plants the terms 'male' and 'female' are not used, but in heterogamous ones they are commonly applied. The type of isogametes which gradually gives rise to heterogametes is clearly of the active swimming zoospore type, the two copulating gametes being similar in size and activity. Beginning with this type of gamete, a series of algae can be arranged in which there are increasing differences, step by step, in the pairing gametes and culminating with gametes, morphologically so different in appearance that they can be easily recognized as male and female, and do not suggest identical origin. It is the gradual appearance of differences that makes the two sexes recognizable and not due to gradual differentiation of maleness and femaleness. In the series of differentiation of sex among algae beginning with isogamy there are types in which one of the pairing flagellate gametes becomes recognizably larger than the other (**anisogamy**) to the types in which this relative difference in size gradually increases until finally one of the pairing gametes becomes non-flagellate, non-motile, passive and many times larger than that of its small, active and flagellate (**oogamy**).

The following cases may be chosen to illustrate the gradual differentiaton of sex among algae :

Chlamydomonas, *Ulothrix*, *Ectocarpus*, etc., illustrate isogamy, in which the pairing gametes are zoospore-like bodies which are flagellate and motile. *Spirogyra* is also isogamous, and the fusing gametes are non-flagellate but are ordinary protoplasts of vegetative cells. Of the two fusing gametes, one remains passive and the other moves through the conjugation tube and fuses with it. This difference in motility is a feature of sperm and egg, therefore, the two pairing protoplasts of *Spirogyra* may be regarded as male and female, although they do not differ in size. *Zygnema*, a relative of *Spirogyra*, has both of its fusing gametes motile at the time of union. Therefore, the advance to the condition of *Spirogyra* is the entire loss of motility of one gamete and its retention by the other.

The next step in the evolution of sex is anisogamy, which may be illustrated by forms like some species of *Chlamydomonas*, *Pandorina*, *Caulerpa*, etc., where the fusing gametes, differing only in size, are both flagellate. In *Pandorina* both the gametes are motile, but the larger one may be more sluggish than its mate. In a few species of *Chlamydomonas* and in *Eudorina*, a relative of *Pandorina* and *Volvox*, one may be motile, the other immobile, and hence, they show a very close approach to oogamy in that the larger gametes are not free-swimming and in that the gametes are dissimilar in size and shape.

The maximum differentiation of sex is found among oogamous forms like *Volvox*, *Oedogonium*, *Vaucheria*, *Chara*, *Fucus*, etc., in which the gametes are not only differentiated into male and female by their differences in size, but also due to the fact that the larger female gamete becomes a completely passive cell so far as motility is concerned, due to the final disappearances of its swimming appendages (flagella). On the other hand, the male gamete becomes less bulky than its mate and develops swimming mechanism as a secondary feature.

The mode of sexual reproduction in Rhodophyceae, though oogamous, is of a highly specialized nature and illustrates further essential feature of the gametes. In this group distinct male and female organs are present, but the sperms resembling ordinary protoplasts are not even detached from the cellwalls. In some cases, they are discharged but without any swimming appendages, and sometimes they are not discharged. Within the female sex organ no egg is recognizable as different from the ordinary protoplast. It does not separate from the wall of the sex organ and rounds off, so that it is not a typical egg. It is simply the protoplast functioning as the female gamete, because the sperm or its nucleus fuses with it. Thus, in this group, the sexuality is of a distinctive type, there being no eggs and sperms in the ordinary sense, their role being played by two protoplasts not different in appearance from vegetative protoplasts.

Life Cycles in Algae

There are 4 types of life cycles in algae :

(a) Haplontic or monogenetic type

The algae are always haploid (n) and gametophytes as they are produced sexually by gametes. After gametic union zygote is produced which is ($2n$). The zygote nucleus undergoes reduction division and gives rise to 4 haploid nuclei, of which three are disintegrated. From the single functioning nucleus a haploid plant is produced. Examples : *Spirogyra*, *Zygnema*, etc.

In the case of *Oedogonium*, *Ulothrix*, etc., the diploid zygote nucleus, by meiosis, gives rise to four zoospores, which germinate into four haploid plants. Thus, it is seen that in both the cases the haploid gametophytic generation is predominant, but the diploid

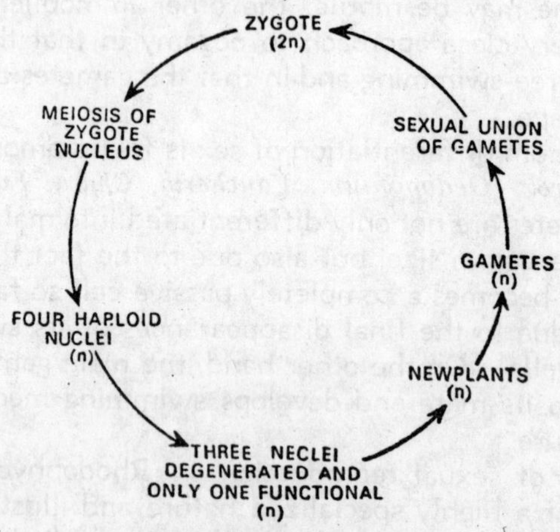

Fig. 112. Haplontic type of cycles in *Spirogyra*.

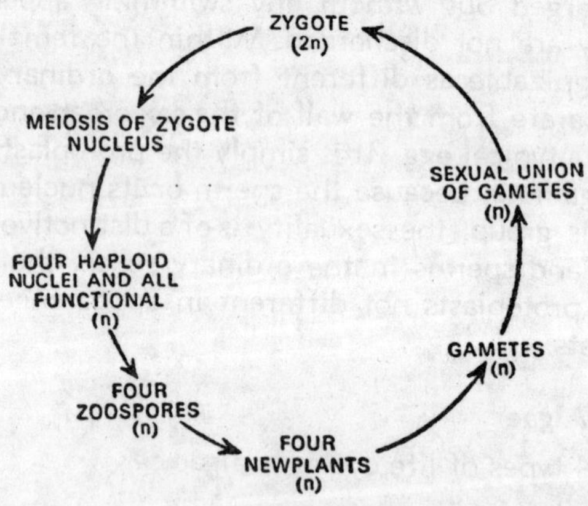

Fig. 113. Haplontic types of life cycle in *Ulothrix*.

or sporophytic generation is represented only by the zygote. No true alternation of generations is found in this case.

(b) Diplontic type

The plant is always diploid (*2n*). The nuclei in the gametangia divide by meiosis and form haploid gametes. The zygote formed after gametic union is diploid (2n), which gives rise to a diploid plant. Thus, it is seen that in such cases the diploid generation is

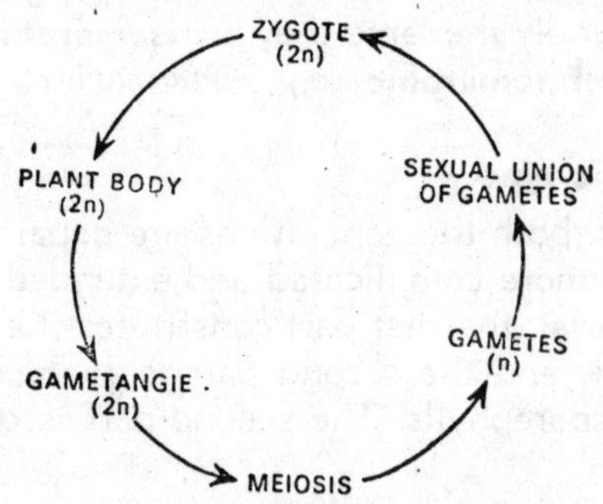

Fig. 114. Diplontic types of cycle in Algae.

predominant and it is multicellular. The haploid generation is represented only by the gametes. Examples : *Fucus*, *Sargassum*, etc.

(c) Haplodiplontic or digenetic type

In such cases, the diploid zygote instead of germinating into a new plant gives rise to a new sporophytic generation. It bears sporangium and its nucleus undergoes reduction division and gives

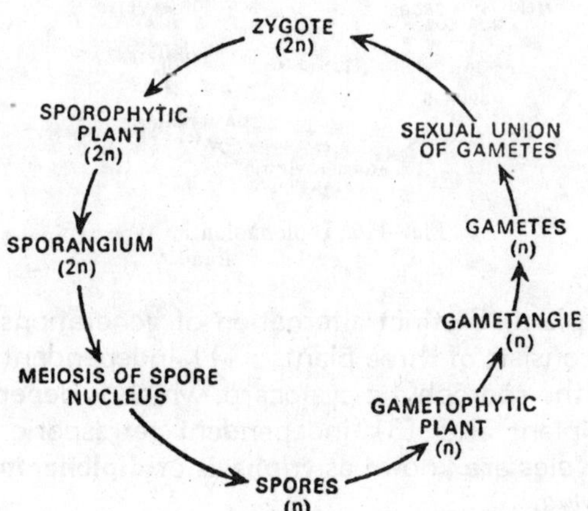

Fig. 115. Haplodiplontic type of life cycle in Algae.

rise to spores. The spores germinate into new haploid gametophytic plants. Thus, it is seen that in such cases, the two generations are equally prominent and multicellular. The sporophyte bears spores and the gametophytes gametes. Distinct alternation of generations is not seen in such cases. If the plants belonging to both the generations are structurally the same they are **isomorphic** (e.g., *Dictyota*) but if different, **heteromorphic** (e.g., *Laminaria*).

(d) Diplohaplontic type

In such cases, both the generations are equally prominent, but the sporophyte is more complicated and extended. The sporophyte consists of two parts : the first part constitutes the **independent heteromorphic plant,** and the second part is **cyctocorp,** which bears the diploid carposporephylls. The second part is dependent on the

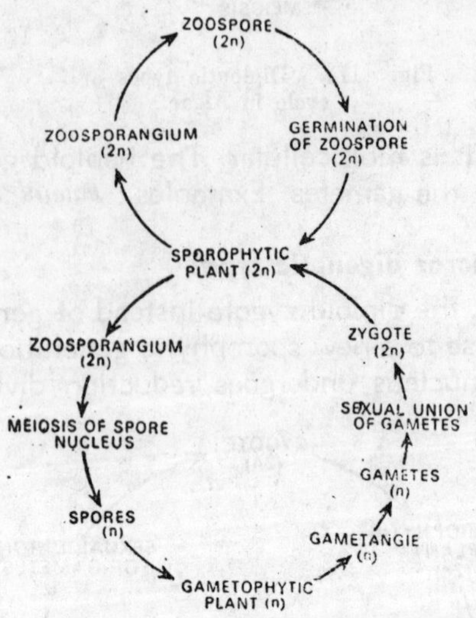

Fig. 116. Diplohaplontic type of cycle of algae.

gametophytic plant. Distinct alternation of generations is seen and the life cycle consists of three plants : (1) independent gametophytic plant, (2) the sporophytic cystocarp, which is dependent on the gametophytic plant and (3) independent tetrasporic plant. Such types of life cycles are known as **triphasis** or **diplohaplontic.** Example : *Polysiphonia*.

Economic importance of Algae

The economic importance of algae is very diverse. Some of the algae are used as food and fodder, in agriculture, industry, medicine, purification of water, aviation and as a source of petroleum and natural gas. A brief account of the uses of algae is given below :

(a) Algae used as food.

The red, brown and green algae, growing along the coasts of the Pacific Ocean, are now extensively used as food. *Ulva*, a green alga, commonly known as 'sea lettuce', is taken by man as a vegetable. Caulerpa racemosa, another green alga, is cultivated by the Philippinase for food. Chlorella, a green alga, contains vitamins A and B, which has food value equivalent to lemon juice. The Japanese take chlorella powder along with green tea. Some of the brown algae, like *Laminaria*, *Sargassum*, *Fucus*, etc., are taken as food by man, particularly by the Chinese and by the Japanese. Americans are fond of "seatron", which is a preparation made from the bladders and stalks of *Nereocystis*, a brown algae. The red algae, like *Porphyra*, *Chondrus*, *crispus*, etc., are used in the preparation of soups, desserts and puddings.

The people of the Western Europe, particularly of France and Denmark, like to take "blankmanges" delicious food, which is prepared by boiling an alga, like *Chondrous*, with milk and then mixed with fruit's juice and scented with vanilla. *Rhodymenia*, another red alga, is also taken by man. It has been observed that about 25% of marine algae are included within the food menu by the Japanese.

(b) Algae used as fodder.

The blue green algae as well as green algae and a few red algae form the food for various fishes and aquatic animals. Some of the marine algae are used as fodder for Cattle by the Americans, French and Danish people. The people living in the American Pacific coasts use pieces of sea weeds from which kelp is prepared for poultry. For this purpose small industries for cultivation of *Archophyllum*, *Fucus*, *Laminaria*, etc., have been raised. *Pelvetia*, a brown sea weed, increases the milk-content of the cattle and sometimes its butter and fat. A few red algae, like *Rhodymenia*, are taken by the cattle. *Sargassum* is a good cattle food.

(c) Algae used in agriculture.

Some blue green algae, like *Nostoc*, *Anabaena*, etc., increases the fertility of soil by nitrogen fixation, thus thereby helping the production of crops. The people of France, Ceylon, etc., use a few marine algae as fertilisers. *Chlorella* is used to purify the soil. It liberates oxygen by photosynthesis which decomposes the rotten substances. The brown algae, like *Pelargophycus*, *Macracystis*, *Nereocystis*, etc. furnish us with potash, which is used as a manure.

(d) Algae used in industry.

The algae are used in various kinds of industries. These are as follows :

(1) *Agar industry.* Agar is a transparent substance obtained from the red algae, like *Gelidium*, *Gracillaria*, etc. It is solid at normal temperature but becomes liquid above 95°C. Agar has diverse uses. Agar is used for the preparation of culture media for fungi and bacteria in the laboratory as well as a sizing material in the textile industry, as a laxative, and as a solidifying agent in the preparation of desserts.

(2) *Algin industry.* Algin is a gelatinous or jelley like substance obtained from the cell-wall of some red algae. It is used in different commercial purposes, like the preparation of shampoos, cosmetics, hair dressings, shaving creams and other articles of toilet, shoe polishes, lubricating jellies, ice-creams and desserts. It is also used in paints and rubber industry.

(3) *Kelp industry.* The ash left behind, after burning the brown algae, like *Laminaria*, *Sargassum*, etc., is known as kelp. It chiefly contains potassium and iodine. Formerly, these algae were used for the production of the ingredients but it has been discarded at present.

(4) *Diatomaceous earth industry.* The diatomaceous earth is a kind of earth deposited at the bottom of the sea, after the death and decay of Diatoms. The largest diatomaceous earth deposit has been discovered in Santamaria oil-fields in California. The uses of diatomaceous earth are much varied, viz., as a filtering material, as a substance used in insulation of boilers, blast furnaces, etc., as a cementing material, as a mild abrassive in metal polishes and tooth-pastes, as an absorbent for liquid nitroglycerine (the explosive material of the dynamite), as a material for painting the ship to protect it against the attack of sea-barnacles.

(e) Algae used in medicine.

A large number of medicines is obtained from algae. The brown algae, like *Laminaria*, *Sargassum*, etc., are good sources of iodine. These algae also yield medicines for treatment of goitre and gland diseases. Antibiotics are also prepared from some of these algae. Chloranthus, an antibiotic is obtained from *Chlorella*. The red algae, like *Gelidium*, *Gracillaria*, etc., yield agar, which is a laxative and used in the preparation of medicinal pills and ointments.

(f) Algae used in the purification of water.

The green algae play an important role in the purification of water in which they grow. They utilise the carbon dioxide released by the various animals during their respiration and give off oxygen during photosynthesis and thus the water is purified.

(g) Algae used in aviation.

The aviator prior to their flight store lumps of algae, such as *Chlorella*, in the craft along with Oxygen-cylinders. The oxygen of the cylinders are utilised by the aviators when the plane rises to high altitude where the air is much rarefied. In case, there be a shortage or stoppage of oxygen supply from the cylinders the algae give off necessary oxygen for carrying on respiration.

(h) Algae as a source of petroleum and gas.

The minute marine algae about the solar energy store it up as a potential energy inside their body. When these algae are taken by the marine animals it gets in their body and is stored up as such. After the death of these animals their dead bodies are deposited in heaps at the bottom of the sea. Subsequently the dead bodies are decomposed by bacteria in absence of oxygen and being subjected to a great hydrostatic pressure of sea water. Their organic substances containing the energy are gradually converted into oil and gas. These are utilised by man for various purposes.

SECTION II

FUNGI

INTRODUCTION

General consideration

This great group of thallophytes is readily distinguished from other groups by the total lack of the photosynthetic pigment, chlorophyll, reseulting in the disability of manufacturing their own food. Hence, they are compelled to live either as parasites, or as saprophytes. But, sometimes they live in close association with algae, as in the case of lichens ; such a mode of life is known as **symbiosis,** in which the associates derive mutual benefit from each other. They also live in close association with the roots of certain higher plants, particularly forest trees. This combination of the fungus and the host is known as **mycorrhiza.** This symbiotic relationship does not seem to be distinctly harmful to the tree, yet it is often thought to be a mild form of parasitism. The habitats of fungi are extremely diverse. They not only occur as parasites forming **haustoria** (Fig. 117) within the host cells, and saprophytes, but are often found as epiphytes and may even be subterranean.

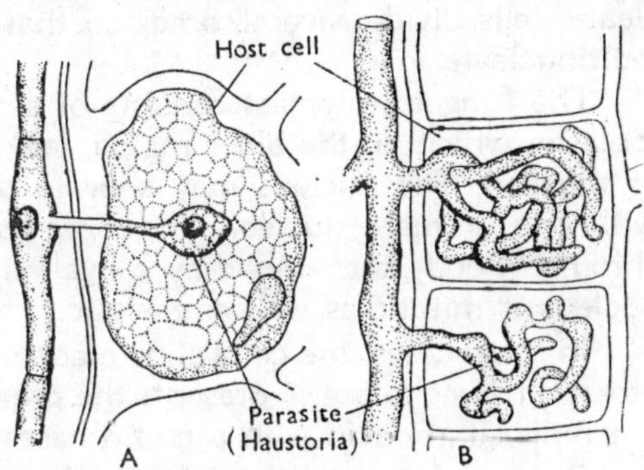

Fig. 117. Different types of haustoria. A, Formation of apresorium within the host cell ; B, Formation of finger-like processes within the host cell.

Most fungi have a life history which consists of two phases : (*a*) **vegetative phase,** in which the fungus grows through the host or substratum and constructs its vegetative body, and (*b*) **reproductive phase,** in which the fungus produces spores or other reproductive structures by means of which it perpetuates itself.

The vegetative body, with the exception of the unicellular forms, consists of a more or less extensive, much-branched, filamentous, colourless or coloured structure, called the **mycelium,** in which a single filamentous branch is called a **hypha.** This mycelium originates as a result of germination of a **spore**, which, in the simplest case, is unicellular and uninucleate and may or may not be motile. A spore germinates, by pushing out from any point or from a thin place (**germ pore**) on its wall, in a tube-like or a filament-like process, called the **germ tube.** Rapid elongation and branching follow and a mycelium is formed, the growth of the hypha being restricted at the tip.

The mycelium may be septate or aseptate. When aseptate, the protoplast is continuous throughout and contains numerous minute nuclei and vacuoles within it ; such a mycelium is known as a **coenocyte.** The septate mycelium contains many hyphal cells, and each cell contains a uninucleate, binucleate, or multinucleate protoplast.

Among higher fungi the life cycle consists of two phases : (*a*) **monokaryon phase,** in which the mycelium consists of hyphal cells which are regularly uninucleate, and (*b*) **dikaryon phase,** with binucleate cells. In some cases, the nuclei of uninucleate and binucleate cells divide several times so that the hyphal cells become multinucleate.

The fungal protoplast consists of a granular or reticulated cytoplasm, which, in the older region, leaves a vacuole in the middle of the cell. The nucleus may show a delicate nuclear reticulum with one or more nucleoli, its contents contracted into a dense chromatin body surrounded by a hyaline area. The division of the nucleus is mitotic as well as meiotic.

In some cases, the cellwall is made up of pure cellulose, but in others little cellulose is present, the greater part of the wall being a complex fatty acid with a chitin base.

Owing to the absence of the photosynthetic pigments, fungi accumulate carbohydrate reserves, such as sugars and glycogen instead of starch. Oils and proteins are also found as reserve materials. The fungal protoplast also secretes various types of enzymes during its activity, and these not only help the fungus to deal with reserve materials but also assist the parasitic fungi to enter or break down the tissues of the host.

In many cases the hyphae grow together, intertwine, adhere and form a thick tissue, called the **plectenchyma** (Fig. 118). It is of two types : (*a*) **prosoplectenchyma** or **prosenchyma,** when in a tissue the single hyphal elements are recognizable, and (*b*) **paraplectenchyma** or **pseudoparenchyma,** in which the hyphal individuality is entirely lost, so that it appears more or less isodiametric in section, resembling a parenchyma.

When the plectenchyma becomes tuberiform in appearance

with a pseudoparenchymatic outer rind and a prosenchymatic central core, it is called a **sclerotium.** A sclerotium is a resting body, with abundant food reserves, which carries the fungus over unfavourable conditions of growth, and on the return of normal conditions either directly develops into a mycelium or gives rise to a fructification. Sometimes plectenchyma is formed chiefly from parallel hyphae forming root-like strands, called **rhizomorphs,** which under suitable conditions give rise to the mycelium.

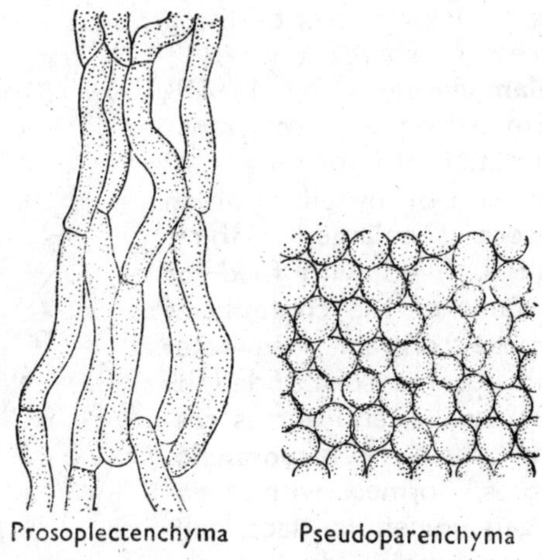

Prosoplectenchyma Pseudoparenchyma

Fig. 118. Types of plectenchyma.

Reproduction

Most fungi reproduce by vegetative, asexual and sexual methods.

The fungi may reproduce vegetatively by the fragmentation of the whole thallus or of considerable portions of it. Vegetative cells of some yeasts and also the ascospores and the basidiospores in some higher fungi may give rise to lateral outgrowths, which cut off **buds,** and this process of cell multiplication is known as **budding.**

Asexual reproduction takes place by the production of one or more types of asexual reproductive bodies, called **spores.** Some of these tpyes are formed by the sporophyte at a specific time in the life cycles of higher fungi (Ascomycetes and Basidiomycetes) immediately following reduction division of the spore mother cells. When formed within (endogenous) the mother cells, they are called **ascospores,** and the mother cell, an **ascus ;** when the mother cell produces spores externally (exogenous), the spores are termed **basidiospores,** and the mother cell, a **basidium.** These two types of spores actually correspond to the spores of vascular plants. Other types of spores are also formed for accessory methods of multiplication, but do not possess any relation to a sexual process and do not take part in the alternation of generations. They are purely vegetative in nature and produce mycelia, identical with those producing them.

These are devices for rapid increase and dissemination of the organisms, and are either produced by the sporophyte (e.g. rusts and a few other Basidiomycetes) or by the gametophyte (e.g. most of the Phycomycetes and Ascomycetes). Some of the principal types of these accessory spores are : (1) **chlamydospores** (Fig. 119B), formed by the direct transformation of hyphal cells, or segments of mycelium which become enlarged, thick walled, filled with food, or portions of the contents of hyphae contract, lose water and become surrounded by thick walls, and act as resting spores ; (2) **sporangiospores,** formed within enlarged unicellular sacs, called **sporangia**, due to the successive cleavage of their protoplasts ; these spores may be either naked and amoeboid, or are provided with flagella forming free-swimming cells, and are known as **zoospores,** and the sporangia, **zoosporangia.** When the spores, thus formed, become distinctly walled and non-motile, they are termed **aplanospores** or simply **spores** ; (3) **conidia,** when cut off externally from the tip of a hypha, fall off and are disseminated by the wind ; and (4) **oidia** (Fig. 119A), which are another kind of vegetatively formed cells arising directly from the breaking up of a hypha.

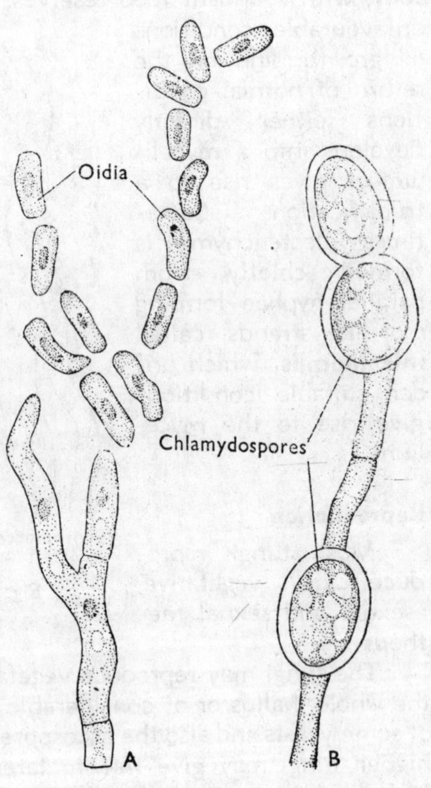

Fig. 119. Oidia and chlamydospores.

Sexual reproduction in fungi is extremely diverse when considered in detail, but when taken as a whole, it shows some evolutionary sequence. Among lower Phycomycetes **isogamy** is represented by the union of two morphologically indentical cells, called **gametes,** which fuse in pairs to form a zygote. A somewhat advanced condition is also noticed among Phycomycetes where there is a union of two flagellate gametes of unequal size (**aniso-**

gamy), of which the larger one is regarded as the female cell. The next higher step in the sexual process, when considered in evolutionary sequence, is **oogamy.** In this case, the female gamete (**oosphere** or **ovum**) is a large, non-flagellate, non-motile and passive cell, and the male gamete (**spermatozoid** or **antherozoid**) is a small, flagellate, motile and active cell, as in a few Phycomycetes. Besides these normal processes, there are cases where variations occur. For instance, in some Ascomycetes the male gamete is set free as a naked or very thin-walled, non-motile sperm, which becomes attached to the wall of the oogonium or to a tube-like extension of the oogonium, called the **trichogyne.** Among higher Phycomycetes distinct sperm cells are not produced but only male nuclei are introduced into the oogonium. Sometimes fusion takes place between two gametangia, distinguishable or indistinguishable, whereby the multinucleate protoplasts of the two eventually unite. Among Basidiomycetes, with the exception of rust fungi, sex organs are entirely absent, but the mycelium may exist in two or more sexually differentiated strains. In such cases, any cell of a plant of one sexual phase may unite with any cell of the plant of the opposite sexual phase, as a result of which a sporophytic or diploid (dikaryon) mycelium is produced.

The product of union of gametes is a **zygote** (**zygospore** or **oospore**), depending on the nature of the uniting gametes. Such spores are known as **sexual spores,** which are diploid, and they also take part in the alternation of generations.

Origin of Fungi

As regards the origin of the true fungi, there are two opposite schools of view. Workers like DeBary (1881), von Tavel (1892), Bessey (1942), and Gaumann (1949) belonging to one school believe that they have come from the algae, while Dangeard (1886, 1903), Fischer (1892), Atkinson (1909), Cavers (1915), Scherffel (1925), and Cook (1928) favour their derivation from the protozoa.

The proponents of the algal origin of the fungi suggest that some algae, which somehow had lost their chlorophyll and thereby had to change their mode of nutrition from an autotrophic to a heterotrophic one, had given rise to the true fungi, and this had taken place in diverse lines. According to them, the Phycomycetes have come from one class of algae, and the Ascomycetes from another, while the Basidiomycetes have been evolved from the Ascomycetes.

A good deal of controversy centres around the hypothetical

algal ancestor of the Phycomycetes. Some suggest that the probable ancestor was a siphonaceous green alga, while others regard it to be an oogamous Xanthophyceae, or one of its unicellular coccoid members. The question which still remains unsolved in whether the Zygomycetes came first or the Oomycetes. Depending on the similarities in the structure of reproductive organs as well as in the gonimoblast filaments and ascogenous hyphae in the Rhodophyceae and the Ascomycetes, the latter are also thought by some, to have been derived from the former.

Those who favour a protozoan origin of fungi suggest that at first the chytrids appeared, and they, in turn, gave rise later on to the other Phycomycetes with an extensive hyphal system, and this origin had been polyphyletic. Believers in this idea are of opinion that the Oomycetes have originated from the Zygomycetes.

Evolution among Fungi

Though unquestionable fossil records of the Phycomycetes have been found even as far back as the Devonian, they are not of much help in clarifying the problem of evolution among the true fungi.

Whatever, might have been the ancestral form of the fungi, the non-mycelial chytrids are almost unanimously regarded as the most primitive among the Phycomycetes. From these chytrids there appeared two distinct series,—one with uniflagellate swarmers and the other with biflagellate ones. In both these directions evolution has taken place from isogamy to oogamy, and most probably the Zygomycetes are reduced forms evolved from the Oomycetes.

If the phycomycetous origin of the Ascomycetes is accepted, then those Ascomycetes, which possess a single ascus produced by the fusion of two cells (Plectomycetes) are to be considered as the most primitive, from which the other types have arisen. Most probably some higher Ascomycetes, in which the dikaryotic hypha produced the ascus, underwent modifications in the ascus, and the basidium of the Basidiomycetes came into existence. Based on this hypothesis, the Basidiomycetes possessing an aseptate basidium are the most primitive, from which the bi-directional evolution has taken place. The basidium, in one line of development, is typically vertically septate, while in the other, it is always transversely septate.

Classification of Fungi

The fungi are more or less universally divided into *four* Classes as follows :

A. The vegetative body is usually a *coenocytic mycelium* which may sometimes be absent or rudimentary — **Phycomycetes** (e.g. *Synchytrium Saprolegnia, Pythium. Phytophthora, Peronospora, Albugo, Mucor, Rhizopus, Pilobolus,* etc.).

B. A well-developed *septate mycelium* is always present :

(*a*) Characteristic asexual spores, the *ascospores* are formed *endogenously* within specialized spore mother cells, called *asci* — **Ascomycetes** (e.g. *Saccharomyces, Eurotium, Penicillium, Peziza, Ascobolus, Erysiphe, Claviceps, Pyronema, Humaria, Morchella, Sphaerotheca,* etc.).

(*b*) Characteristic asexual spores, the *basidiospores,* are formed *exogenously* on specialized spore mother cells, known as *basidia* .. — **Basidiomycetes** (e.g. *Ustilago, Tilletia, Puccinia, Polyporus, Agaricus, Phallus, Lycoperdon, Cyathus,* etc.).

(*c*) Both ascospores and basidiospores are not produced but the fungi reproduce mostly by means of *conidia* .. .. — **Deuteromycetes** or **Fungi imperfecti** (e.g. *Fusarium, Cercospora, Curvularia, Alternaria, Helminthosporium. Colletotrichum.* etc.).

CHAPTER I

CLASS PHYCOMYCETES

The Class Phycomycetes is also termed as 'algal fungi', because it resembles certain green algae as regards the structure of their filamentous vegetative body and their modes of reproduction. It includes such common fungi as bread mould (*Rhizopus*), water mould (*Saprolegnia*), 'white rust' of mustards (*Albugo*), and the 'downy mildews' (*Peronospora*). The lower forms are mostly aquatic and may live either as parasites on plants and animals, or as saprophytes on submerged organic materials A great majority of them are parasites on terrestrial phanerogamic plants, or they live as saprophytes on various decomposed organic materials. Others are amphibious, occurring as parasites on living organisms, or as saprophytes on damp soil. The vegetative body, when present, is a much-branched coenocytic mycelium but its older portions may sometimes become septate. Asexual reproductive spores, both zoospores and sporangiospores, are produced within unicellular sacs, known as **sporangia,** which are cut off from the tips of hyphae. Some of them may produce conidia and gonidiospores. Sexual reproduction may be isogamous, anisogamous or oogamous, and the plants may be homothallic or heterothallic. When an entire thallus is capable of producing gametes, it is said to be **holocarpic.** But when the gamete-production is restricted to the gametangia only, it is referred to as a **eucarpic** thallus. Besides, among some higher forms union between gametangia takes place whereby their undifferentiated, multinucleate protoplasts unite to form a zygote. The zygote, produced as a result of sexual union, forms a thick wall and passes through a period of rest prior to germination.

CLASSIFICATION

The class Phycomycetes has been divided into *three* subclasses :

Subclass I. Archimycetes. Characterized in having rounded or lobed non-mycelial thallus formed by the enlargement of zoospores, sometimes possessing rhizoids ; higher forms may be develop a rudimentary mycelium.

It includes *three* orders :

Order 1. *Chytridiales.* Thallus is variable in form, mostly holocarpic, producing one or more sporangia or gametangia ; zoospores uniflagellate or biflagellate, zoogametes uniflagellate. Common genera are *Synchritium*, *Olpidium*, etc.

* *Order* 2. *Ancylistales*.

* *Order* 3. *Protomycetales*.

Subclass II. Oomycetes. Characterized in having well-developed coenocytic mycelium, often become septate ; characteristic mode of sexual reproduction is **oogamy** and the zygote always an **oospore ;** accessory spores are mostly motile zoospores formed in most of them.

It includes *five* orders :

* *Order* 1. *Blastocladiales*.

Order 2. *Monoblepharidales*. Aquatic saprophytes ; cytoplasm foamy ; zoospores uniflagellate ; resting spores bear warts : union of a motile male gamete with an oosphere contained in an oogonium.

* *Order* 3. *Leptomitales*.

* *Order* 4. *Saprolegniales*. Mostly aquatic sometimes terrestrial, parasitic on animals and plants ; mycelium aseptate and branched, hyphae not constricted at intervals ; sporangia at the tips of hyphae ; zoospores biflagellate, usually exhibit diplanatisue ; sexual reproduction oogamous, oogonium contains one to several oospheres without periplasm. Common genera are *Saprolegnia*, *Achlya*, etc.

Order 5. *Peronosporales*. Mostly parasitic on land plants, some being saprophytic ; biflagellate zoospores are liberated from zoosporangia, which often function as conidia depending on external conditions ; sexual reproduction is oogamous ; oogonium contains solitary oosphere with well-defined perlplasm. Common genera are *Peronospora*, *Pythium*, *Phytophthora*, *Albugo*, etc.

Subclass III. Zygomycetes. Characterized in having a well-developed mycelium, often becoming septate ; characteristic mode of sexual reproduction is by conjugation of two gametangia, where undifferentiated contents fuse to form a zygote known as *zygospore* ; accessory spores are non-motile aplanospores, known as sporangiospores, formed within an unicellular sac called sporangium.

In includes *two* orders :

Order 1. *Mucorales*. Mostly saprophytes on various substrata, rarely parasitic ; mycelium coenocytic, at first aseptate and very regular, but irregular and septate with age ; sporangiospores formed inside globose or ovoid sporangia ; sexual reproduction by union of multinucleate, morphologically alike, gametangia, mostly

* Orders marked with asterisks are not treated in this book.

heterothallic, may be homothallic also. Common genera are *Mucor*, *Rhizopus*, *Pilobolus*, etc.

* *Order 2. Entomophthorales.*

ORDER **CHYTRIDIALES**

Thallus is variable in form, mostly holocarpic, producing one or more sporangia or gametangia ; zoospores uniflagellate or biflagellate ; zoogametes uniflagellate. Common genera are *Synchritium*, *Olpidium*, etc.

SYNCHYTRIUM

(Fam. SYNCHYTRIACEAE)

There are about 50 species under the genus, of which *Synchytrium endobioticum* is described below. This species is responsible for causing the **wart disease** of potatoes. Usually, this parasite attacks the potato tuber at the ground level in spring, and consequently, some gall-like swellings appear on the tubers.

Vegetative body

The thallus is unicellular, endobiotic and holocarpic. The walls are usually composed of chitin.

Reproduction

Synchytrium reproduces both asexually and sexually.

Asexual reproduction takes place by means of uniflagellate

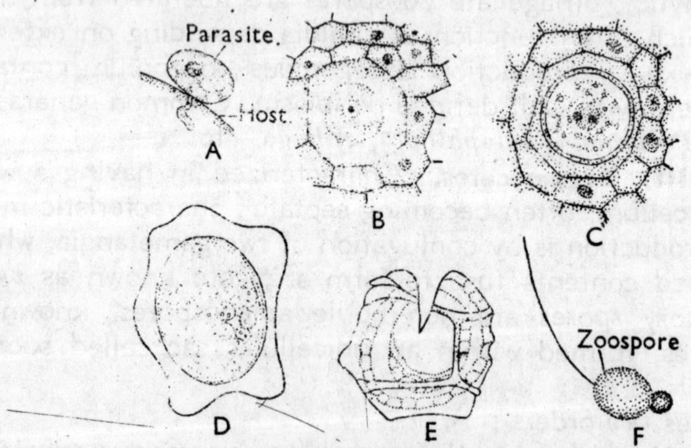

Fig 120, *Synchytrium*.
A, Infection of the host by the zygote ; B—E, Stages in the development of the zoosporangium ; F, A zoospore.

zoospores. The zoospore, under suitable conditions, enters into the epidermal cell of the host leaving its flagellum outside the host cell.

* Orders marked with asterisks are not treated in this book.

This spore then settles at the bottom of the cell and enlarges in size by absorbing food from the surrounding protoplasts. It secretes an outer thick and inner thin, cellwall. This structure is known as the **summer spore.** Meanwhile, the surrounding host cells are stimulated by the local infection, and consequently, the cells divide and enlarge in size forming tumours or gall-like outgrowths. The summer spore then germinates inside the host cell, its outer wall ruptures and the protoplast with the inner thin wall pushes out into the upper portion of the host cell. Its nucleus divides repeatedly forming 32 nuclei, and this multinucleate structure is known as the **prosorus.** Subsequently, the prosorus is divided into four to nine multinucleate segments by cleavages. The individual segment is known as the **sporangium** or **gametangium,** depending on the environmental conditions. When the moisture content is very high, then each segment of the prosorus acts as a **zoosporangium** or **summer sporangium.** The nucleus of the sporangium divides forming two hundred to three hundred nuclei, and the entire protoplast of the sporangium becomes segmented into a number of smaller

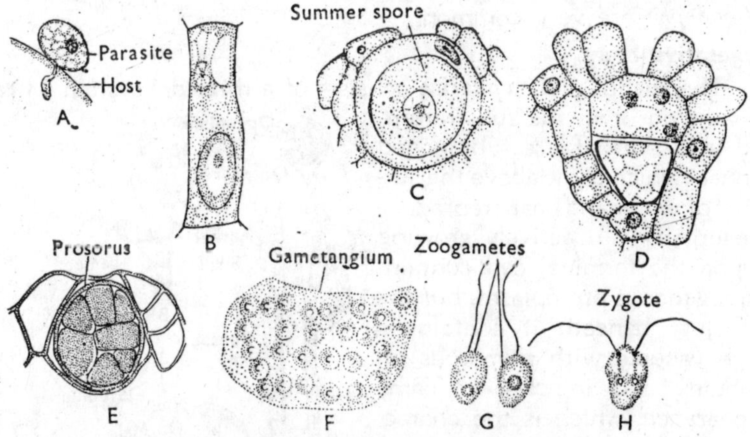

Fig. 121, *Synchytrium.*
A, Infection of the host by a zoospore ; B, Zoospore within the host cell ; C—F, Stages in the formation of the gametangium ; G, Zoogametes ; H, A zygote.

blocks. Each block, consisting of a nucleus with the surrounding cytoplasm, develops into a uniflagellate **zoospore.** When the zoospores attain maturity, the sporangium comes out of the prosorus, and the zoospores are discharged through the papilla in presence of a film of water and initiate new infections.

When moisture is lacking, the segment of the prosorus acts as a gametangium and the gametes, which are produced inside the gametangium, are known as **zoogametes.** The zoogametes of different gametangia may unite to form a biflagellate zygote. The zygote then retracts its flagella and secretes a thin wall. This zygote may infect the host plant like a zoospore. The zygote again forms a thick wall round it within the host cell and acts as the resting sporangium. Its protoplasts divide in the next spring and form zoospores, which ultimately escape and infect another plant.

ORDER **MONOBLEPHARIDALES**

Aquatic saprophytes ; cytoplasm foamy ; zoospores uniflagellate ; resting spores bear warts ; union of a motile male gamete with an oosphere contained in an oogonium.

MONOBLEPHARIS

(Fam. MONOBLEPHARIDACEAE)

The species of *Monoblepharis* are saprophytes occurring on vegetable material in water. When observed with the naked eye it appears as small whitish brush-like tufts or as loose brownish mass. There are 8 pecies of *Monoblepharis*, of which *M. spherica* and *M. polymorpha* are very common.

Vegetative body

The thallus of *M. spherica* consists of a rhizoidal system which remains on or in the substratum, and a cluster of erect branched hyphae which come above the surface of water and bear reproductive organs. In actively growing hypha, the terminal cell contains homogeneous protoplasm, but the cell just beneath it contains a large vacuole with numerous oil globules and imports a foamy appearance, which is the characteristic of the genus.

Reproduction (Fig. 122)

Monoblepharis reproduces both asexually and sexually.

Asexual reproduction takes place by means of *uniflagellate zoospores* produced within narrow cylindrical *zoosporangia*. Since the zoosporangium is narrow the zoospores are arrang-

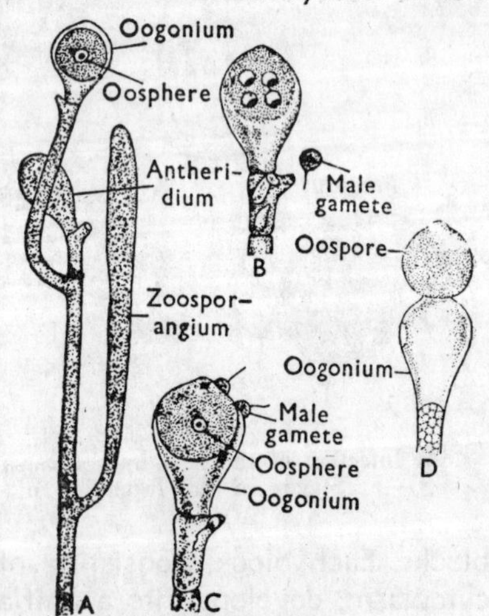

Fig. 122. *Monoblepharis.* A, Portion of a plant with sex organs ; B, Discharge of sperms ; C, Crawling of two sperms on the oogonism ; D, Escape of oospore from the oogonium.

ed uniseriately. During the formation of a zoosporangium, cytoplasm with many nucli accumulate in the end of a lateral hypha and is then cut off by a basal septum separating it from the rest of hypha. Subsequently, each nucleus is organised into a posteriorly uniflagellate zoospore. At maturity, the zoospores are liberated through a pore formed on the tip of the zoosporangium. They swim in water for some time, settle on a suitable substratum in well aerated water and then germinates producing two germ tubes, one of which gives rise to the rhizoidal system and the other to be branched hyphae.

Sexual reproduction is oogamous. The sex organs, *oogonia* and *antheridia*, are produced on the same thallus. The oogonium is a swollen structure which is developed at the tip of an erect hypha, while the antheridium is usually developed just beneath the swollen oogonium. During the formation of an oogonium, some amount of cytoplasm and a nucleus accumulate in the rudiment of the oogonium and then is cut off by a basal septum. The nucleus is organised into a single *oosphere*, the female gamete. The antheridium contains 5—6 nuclei, each of which is organised into an *antherozoid* or *male gamete*. At maturity, a small lateral beak-like outgrowth is formed from the antheridium, the tip of which subsequently opens to liberate the posteriorly uniflagellate male gametes. These gametes resemble the zoospores, but are smaller in size.

When the oogonium attains maturity, a pore is formed at its tip, which secretes a substance for attracting the male gametes. They reach the oogonium by swimming and then slight on it. Now after crawling on the oogonium for some time in an amoeboid manner, one of them enters into the oogonium through its pore and fuses with the oosphere forming oosphore. After fusion, the oospore moves with the help of flagellum derived from the male gamete. Usually it goes towards the base of the oogonium and then towards the pore and sometimes emerges through it. It exhibits amoeboid movement, becomes rounded and provided with a thin wall which gradually becomes thickened and warty and undergoes rest. If fusion fails to take place the oosphere is surrounded by a membrane and develop parthenogenetically to a thick-walled resting spore. The germination of oospore has not yet been observed in *Monoblepharis spherica* but in another species, after a period of rest the wall ruptures and a stout germ tube is produced. Meiosis takes place during the germination of the oospore.

M. polymorpha is similar to *M. spherica* in general characters with the following exceptions : the male gamete nerves crawls over the oogonium but enters into it directly through the pore ; the oosphore does not exhibit any perceptible amoeboid movement; the oospore usually comes out of the oogonium and matures outside it remaining attached to the edge of the pore.

ORDER **SAPROLEGNIALES**

Mostly aquatic, sometimes terrestrial, parasitic on animals and plants; mycelium aseptate and branched, hyphae not constricted at intervals; sporangia at the tips of hyphae; zoospores biflagellate, usually exhibit diplanatism; sexual reproduction oogamous, oogonium contains one to several oospheres without periplasm. Common genera are *Saprolegnia*, *Achlya*, etc.

SAPROLEGNIA

(Fam. SAPROLEGNIACEAE)

Saprolegnia and its allies are often known as 'water moulds', because they are commonly found growing in water saprophytically upon dead bodies of insects, or upon other animals, or plant remains. They can also grow on surface soils, and some of them are active parasities on angiosperms.

Vegetative body

The mycelium is typically coenocytic, consisting of much-branched hyphae, which contain multinucleate, granulated and vacuolated protoplasm. The hyphae are usually long, but some of them, which penetrate the substratum, are short and function like rhizoids.

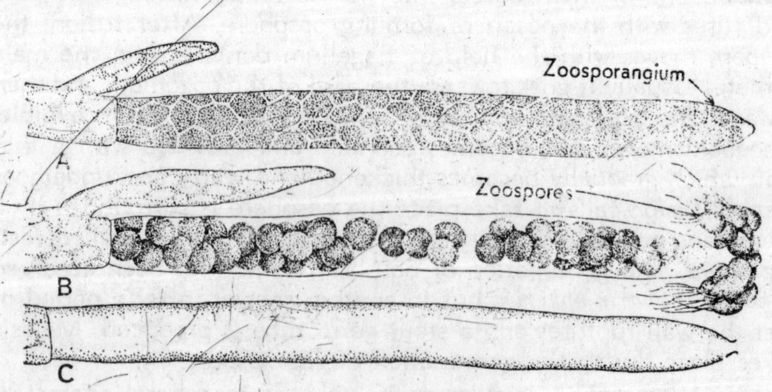

Fig. 123. *Saprolegnia*.
A, A zoosporangium; B, The same liberating zoospores; C, An empty zoosporangium after the liberation of its contents.

Reproduction

Saprolegnia reproduces both asexually and sexually.

Asexual reproduction takes place by the formation of zoospores, within zoosporangia, formed at the apices of the hyphae. During the development of a zoosporangium, the apical portion of a hypha slightly enlarges, and there is an accumulation of cytoplasm and nuclei within it. It is then cut off from the rest of the hypha by the formation of a transverse wall. Its multinucleate protoplast by progressive cleavage is divided into uninucleate zoospores. Each zoospore is pear-shaped with two flagella at the narrow anterior end. Finally, the zoospores escape through an exit pore, formed at the apex of the sporangium, and begin to swim in water. After a period of activity, each zoospore comes to rest ; its flagella disappear, rounds up, secretes a wall around it and passes into a resting period. This resting period is of a very short duration, and

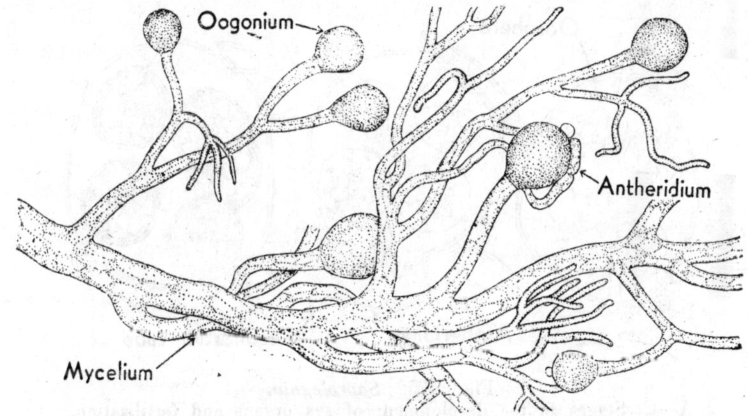

Fig. 124. *Saprolegnia.*
A portion of the mycelium young sex organs.

when the period is over, its protoplast comes out as a zoospore through a pore in the wall and starts swimming again, but in another form. This time it is kidney-shaped with two lateral flagella attached to its concave side. This phenomenon is known as **diplanetism.** The kidney-shaped zoospore, after swimming for a short period, comes to rest, rounds up, secretes a wall around it and directly germinates to form a germ tube, which ultimately ramifies and forms a new mycelium.

After the zoospores have escaped from a sporangium, its base may proliferate inside the empty sporangium forming a new sporangium which again gives rise to zoospores. This process may be repeated a few times. As a result, the sporangia, which are formed in succession, lie enclosed one within the other, and this is referred to as the **sporangial proliferation.**

Some species of *Saprolegnia* regularly form **chlamydospores** in a chain at the apices of the hyphae and germinate directly into new mycelia.

In some cases, a hypha undergoes direct division forming spore-like bodies, called **gemmae,** which are usually produced terminally in a alternate series but may also be intercalary in position.

Sexual reproduction is oogamous. All the species of *Saprolegnia*, so far investigated, have been noted to be homothallic. Sex organs, antheridia and oogonia, are borne terminally at the apices of the hyphae. During the development of an oogonium the apical portion of a hypha swells up and forms a globular structure into which some amount of cytoplasm and many nuclei flow. This is

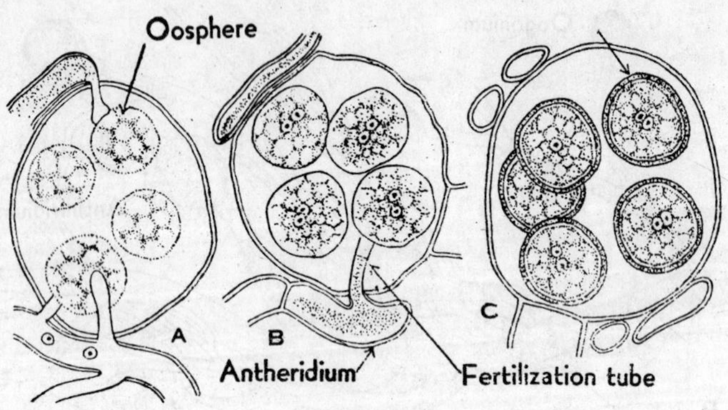

Fig. 125. *Saprolegnia.*
A—C, Stages in the development of sex organs and fertilization.

then cut off from the rest of the hypha by the formation of a transverse wall. Oogonia may be formed either at the apex of the main strand of hypha or at the apices of its branches. Soon there appears a central vacuole in the protoplast of the oogonium, and as it enlarges it presses the peripheral protoplasm against the wall of the oogonium. The nuclei divide in the peripheral region and some of these degenerate. By progressive cleavage this protoplasm is cut into uninucleate blocks, which round up and form several oospheres or eggs (1-20). The oospheres lie free in the oogonium, and there is no residual cytoplasm within it.

Similarly, antheridia also develop at the apices of the hyphal branches, usually located nearby. Such species are called **diclinous.** In other cases, they are **androgynous,** because antheridial branches develop from the stalk of the oogonium. This shows that the species are homothallic, although there is the possibility for a few species to be heterothallic also. Antheridial development begins with the enlargement of the terminal portion of an antheridial branch, and this portion is cut off by the formation of a transverse wall. Its protoplasm contains several male nuclei.

A contact between the antheridium and the oogonium is brought about by the curvature of the antheridial hypha, so that the antheridium is applied to the wall of the oogonium. Sometimes the

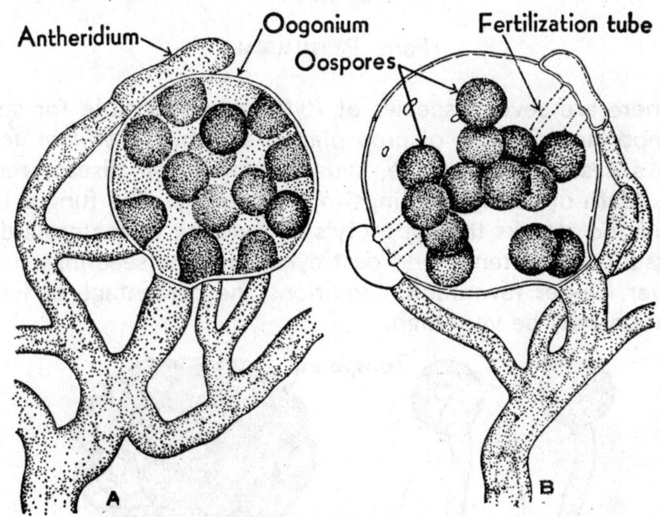

Fig. 126. *Saprolegnia.*
A, Mature sex organs ; B, Formation of oospores after fertilization.

antheridial hypha branches, and each branch forms a separate antheridium, so that several antheridia come in contact with the oogonial wall. A fertilization tube from each antheridium penetrates the wall of the oogonium, reaches an oosphere and emits its protoplasmic contents. Only one male nucleus fertilizes the oosphere which rounds up, secretes a thick wall around it and forms an oospore. Similarly, male nuclei from other antheridia fertilize other oospheres forming oospores. Each oospore has a thick **epispore** and a thinner **endospore** and contains brown or yellowish fat materials as reserve food. The mature oospore germinates after a period of rest ; its epispore ruptures and the endospore elongates to form a long germ tube, which either directly invades the substratum, or with or without branching becomes terminated by a zoosporangium. It is assumed that the zygote nucleus probably divides reductionally at the time of germination.

ORDER **PERONOSPORALES**

Mostly parasitic on land plants, some being saprophytic ; biflagellate zoospores are liberated from zoosporangia, which often function as conidia depending on external conditions ; sexual reproduction is oogamous ; oogonium contains solitary oosphere with well-defined periplasm. Common genera are *Peronospora*, *Pythium*, *Phytophthora*, *Albugo*, etc.

PYTHIUM

(Fam. PYTHIACEAE)

There are several species of *Pythium* responsible for some of the important diseases of crop plants, of which *Pythium de Baryanum*, a destructive parasite, causes *damping off* disease resulting in the death of young seedlings in our country. The fungus lives in the soil and attacks the hypocotyls of seedling at the ground level, the tissues are softened and destroyed, and the seedlings suddenly fall over. Under favourable conditions the percentage of loss in a plantation may be very high.

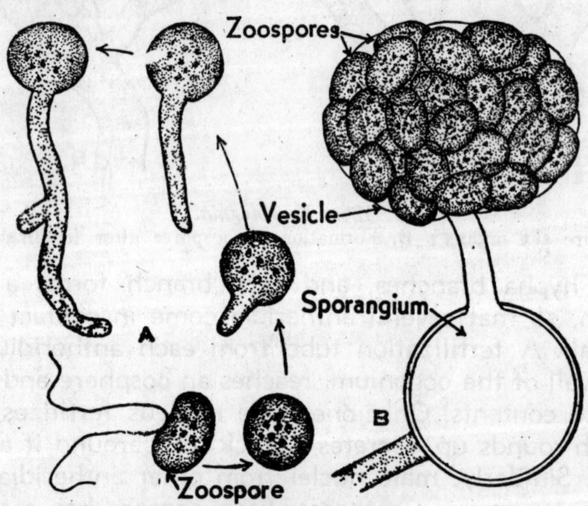

Fig. 127. *Pythium.*
A—B, Formation and germination of zoospores.

Vegetative body

The fungus produces a much-branched, hyaline, coenocytic mycelium with hyphae evenly attenuated towards their apices. When the mycelium becomes old, septa do appear even in the coenocytic mycelium, particularly during the formation of the reproductive bodies. Within the tissues of the host the mycelium ramifies in all directions through the intercellular spaces, but intracellular hyphae are not uncommon.

Reproduction

The fungus reproduces both asexually, by the formation of conidia and zoospores, and sexually by the union of heterogametes to form oospores.

At the time of asexual reproduction, some of the hyphae, projecting from the substratum, bear globular sporangia, which are cut off from the supporting hyphae by transverse walls. When these structures grow in the air, they germinate *directly* by putting forth germ tubes and thus behave as **conidia.** The germ tubes ramify and

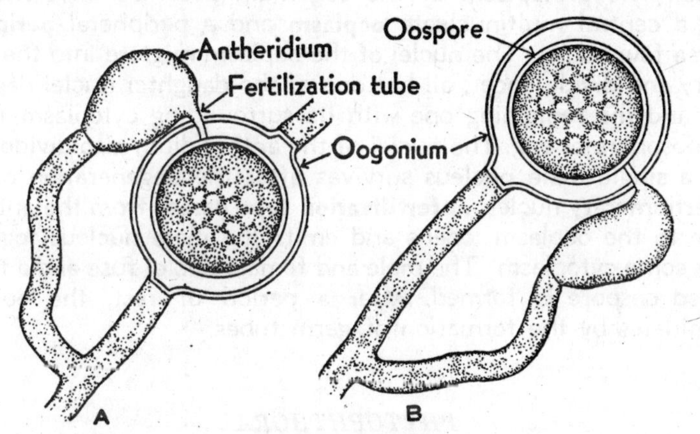

Fig. 128. *Pythium.*
A—B, Stages in the process of fertilization and formation of oospore.

form new mycelia. If, on the other hand, they grow in wet conditions, such as on substrata in shallow water, their *indirect* germination by the formation of zoospores takes place, and then they behave as **sporangia.** The contents of each sporangium undergo cleavage to form zoospores. During the formation of zoospores, the sporangium puts forth a lateral tube, whose apical portion swells considerably to form a vesicle, and the contents of the sporangium pass into it. Within the vesicle the organization of the zoospores is completed. Eventually, the vesicle bursts and several kidney-shaped zoospores, each with two lateral flagella, are liberated. After a period of activity, each zoospore comes to rest, rounds up, secretes a wall around it, germinates by putting forth a germ tube and brings about infection of a new host.

The fungus reproduces sexually when it lives as a saprophyte after killing its host. It is oogamous and both antheridia and oogonia are produced on the same thallus (homothallic). The oogonium is a globular structure, which develops terminally on a lateral branch, and is cut off from the latter by the formation of a transverse septum. From the stalk of the oogonium a branch develops, at whose apex an unicellular antheridium is cut off. Due to the curvature of the antheridial stalk, the tip of the antheridium becomes applied to the side of the oogonium, and the antheridium is said to be **paragynous.**

Both oogonia and antheridia contain dense cytoplasm and many nuclei. The protoplasm of the oogonium becomes differentiated into a central multinucleate **ooplasm** and a peripheral **periplasm** with a few nuclei. The nuclei of the ooplasm migrate into the periphery and divide once ; all but one of the daughter nuclei degenerate and the remaining one with its surrounding cytoplasm forms the oosphere or egg. The nuclei of the antheridium also divide once and a single male nucleus survives after the degeneration of the supernumerary nuclei. A **fertilization tube** passes from the antheridium to the ooplasm, opens and emits the male nucleus together with some cytoplasm. The male and female nuclei fuse and a thick-walled oospore is formed. After a period of rest, the oospore germinates by the formation of germ tubes.

PHYTOPHTHORA

(Fam. PYTHIACEAE)

The species of *Phytophthora* usually occur as parasites on terrestrial flowering plants, but also live as saprophytes. Of these species, *P. infestans* causes a disease known as *late blight* and *rot* of the potato, the most serious of all potato diseases. The aerial parts of plants, particularly the leaves, are attacked and as a result these are gradually killed and dried up causing a blight, but sometimes the tubers are also invaded making soft or dry rots.

Vegetative body

The vegetative body or the mycelium of *P. infestans* is a coenocyte, which lives in the intercellular spaces of the host tissue.

It draws nourishment from the adjacent living cells by short specialized hyphal branches, known as **haustoria,** which penetrate them.

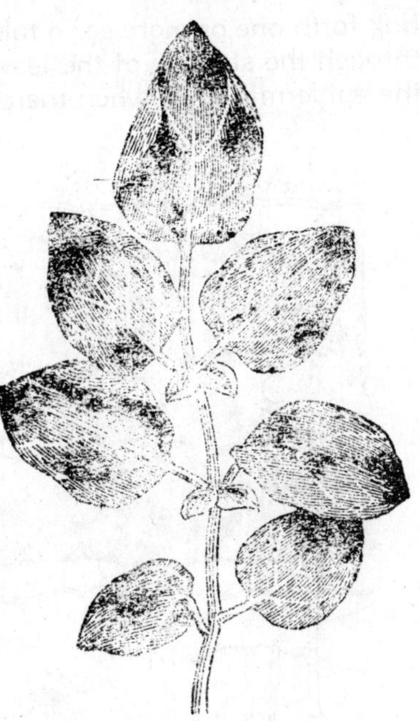

Fig. 129. *Phytophthora infestans.* Leaves of potato showing terminal and marginal infections of 'late blight'.

Reproduction

P. infestans reproduces both asexually and sexually.

At the time of asexual reproduction slender aerial septate hyphae come out through the stomata in groups from the internal mycelium. These are known as **conidiophores.** The conidiophore is sympodially branched and bears conidia at the tips of its branches. Each **conidium** is ovoid or lemon-shaped and thick-walled, and has a thin-walled, hyaline, apical papilla. It contains multinucleate and granulated protoplasm with several vacuoles and oil drops as food-reserves. At maturity, the conidium germinates in two ways, and the type of germination is influenced by the conditions of temperature, moisture and substratum.

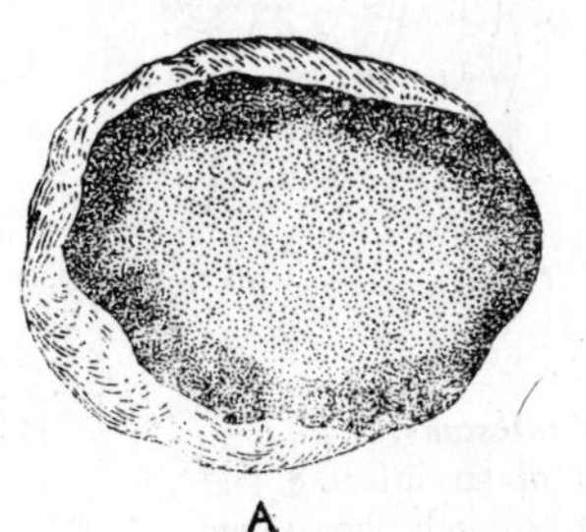

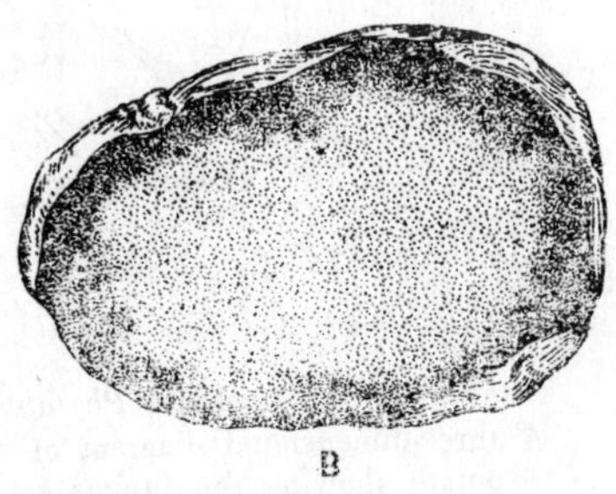

A B

Fig. 130. *Phytophthora infestans.*
A—B, Sections through potato tubers affected with 'late blight' rot.

When the temperature condition is comparatively high and there is less of moisture, the conidium germinates directly by putting forth one or more germ tubes, which penetrate the host tissues through the stomata of the leaves or stems, or by breaking through the epidermis. But, when there is excessive moisture and the tem-

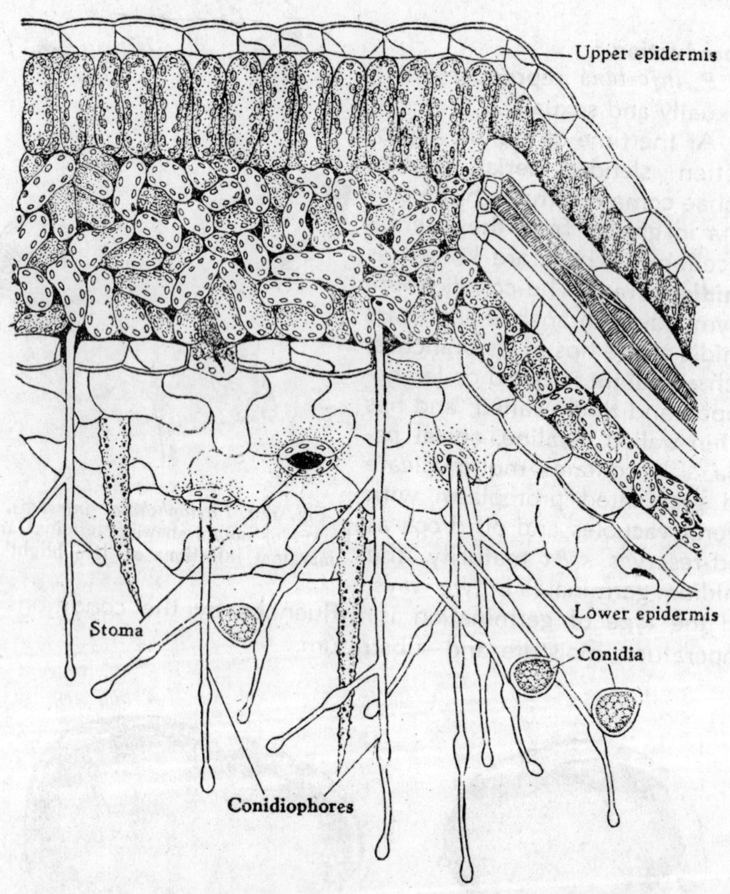

Fig. 131. *Phytophthora infestans.*
A three-dimensional diagram of a part of an infected leaf of potato showing the fungus emerging through the stomata and successive stages in the development of conidiophores and conidia.

perature condition is low, the conidium behaves like a **zoosporangium.** Its multinucleate protoplast, by progressive cleavage, forms biflagellate zoospores. At maturity, the apical papilla of the zoosporangium dissolves and the zoospores come out through the terminal pore. Each zoospore, after a period of activity, settles down, rounds up and puts forth a germ tube, which brings about infection of the host plant as stated before. The infection of the tubers probably takes place directly through the lenticels.

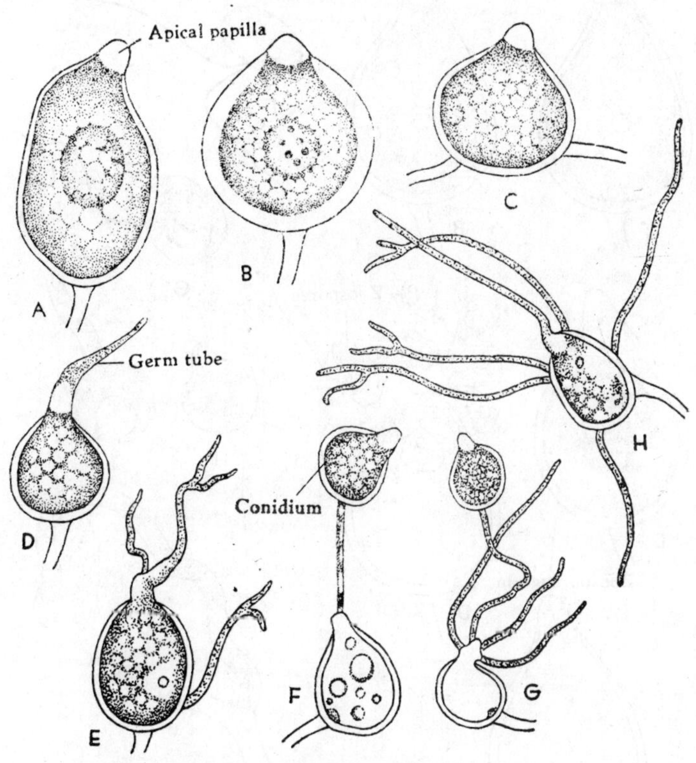

Fig, 132. *Phytophthora,*
A—C, Different types of conidia ; D—E and H, Stages in germination of a conidium ; F—G, Conidia germinating and producing secondary conidia in artificial culture,.

When this fungus is grown artificially on culture media, the mycelium often forms thick-walled **chlamydospores.** Each chlamydospore is more or less spherical, terminal or intercalary, with numerous oil drops as food-reserves. On germination a chlamydospore produces either an extensive mycelium or one or more simple or branched hyphae on which conidia or zoosporangia are borne.

P. infestans is homothallic and oogamous. Normally sex organs do not appear to form in the host, but they have been obtained in abundance in artificial culture.

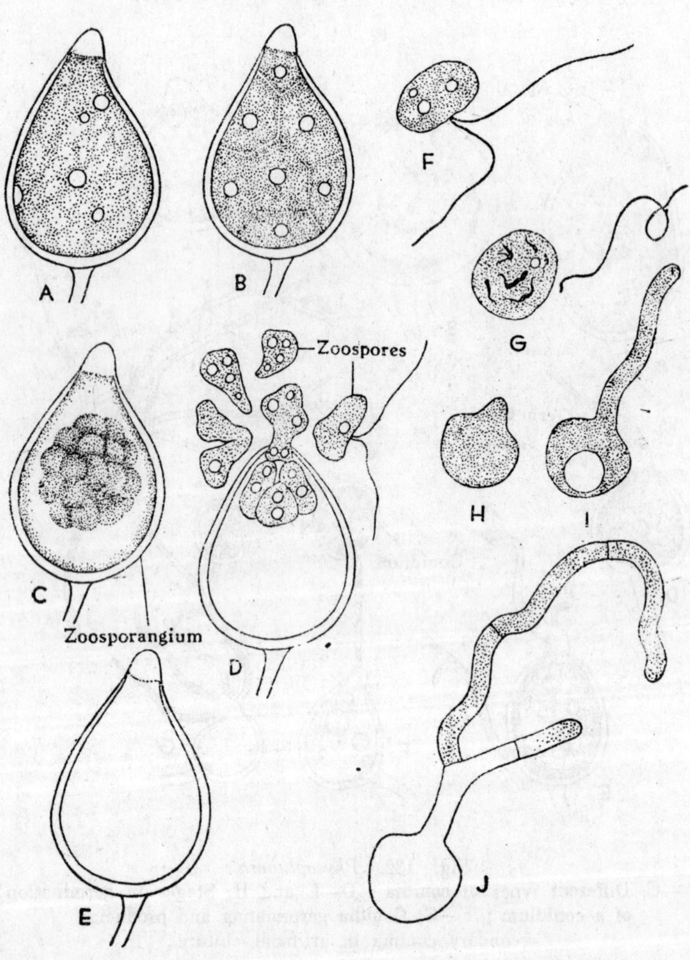

Fig, 133. *Phytophthora,*
A—E, Stages in the germination of zoosporangium and formation of zoospores ; F, A zoospore ; G—J, Germination of a zoospore to form infection threads.

The sex organs, antheridium and oogonium, are borne at the tips of specialized hyphal branches, which, when very young, cannot be readily distinguished from each other. However, the two branches grow towards each other, and the tip of the female branch penetrates the apex of the male branch. The apical portion of the male branch, with its densely accumulated protoplasm, is cut off by the formation of one or two transverse septa forming an antheridium. Meanwhile, the tip of the oogonial branch grows through the antheridium and comes out on its other side forming a

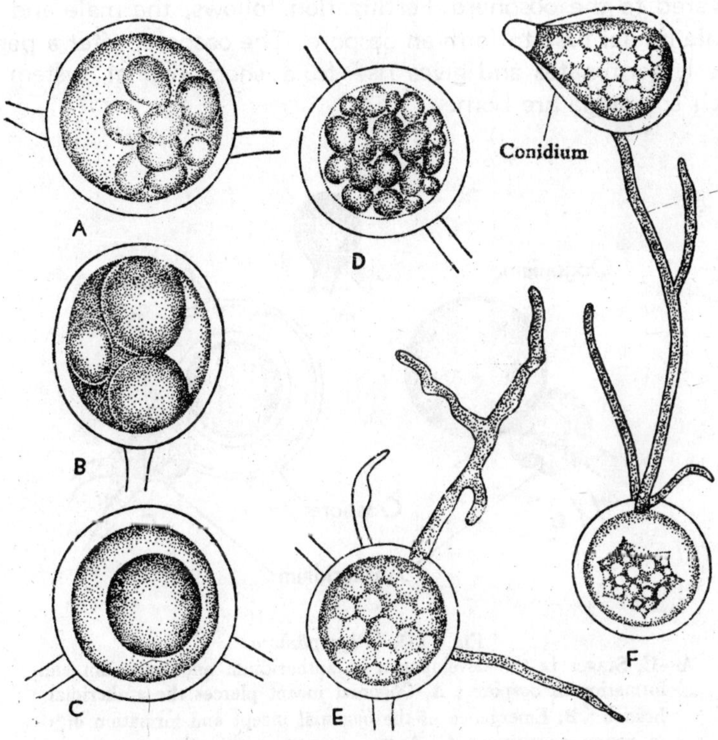

Fig, 134. *Phytophthora.*
A—D, Kinds of chlamydospores ; E—F, A germinating chlamydospore producing a secondary conidium in artificial culture.

rounded swelling. This is the young oogonium, which contains granulated cytoplasm and many nuclei. The base of the oogonium is funnel-shaped and it lies within the antheridium. This type of antheridium is known as **amphigynous.** The oogonium is separated from the rest of the hypha by the formation of an irregular **plug** at its base.

Most of the nuclei of the oogonium degenerate and the remaining ones divide, undergo further disintegration with the exception of one nucleus, around which cytoplasm collects and an oosphere is formed. A peripheral layer of cytoplasm surrounding the oosphere is also recognizable, and is known as the **periplasm.** Similarly, the antheridial nuclei also divide and then all but one disintegrate. Soon there follows the formation of a fertilization tube through which the male nucleus and some cytoplasm are delivered to the oösphere. Fertilization follows, the male and the female nuclei fuse to form an oospore. The oospore, after a period of rest, germinates and gives rise to a short hyphal system on which sporangia are borne.

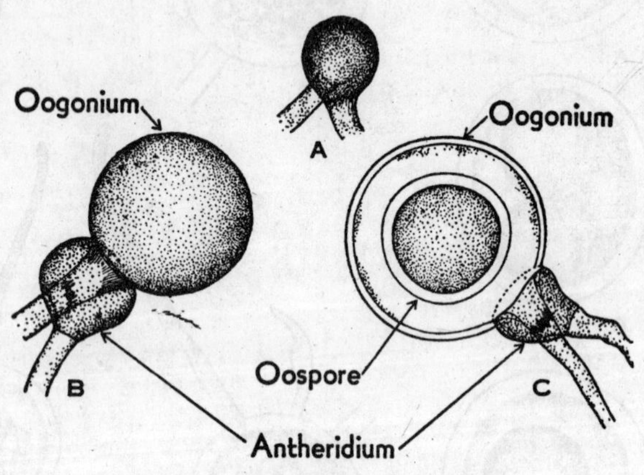

Fig, 135. *Phytophthora.*
A—C, Stages in the development of antheridium and oogonium and formation of oospore ; A, Oogonial incept pierces the antheridial branch ; B, Emergence of the oogonial incept and formation of a young oogonium ; C, A ripe oospore within the oogonium with the empty antheridium attached to its base.

PERONOSPORA

(Fam. PERONOSPORACEAE)

The genus *Peronospora* includes about 75 species. Almost all the species are obligate parasites. They are responsible for a common plant disease, generally known as *downy mildews*. The appearance of thin and greyish-white downy patches on the under surface of the leaf justifies the name of the disease. The other symptoms as localized yellow or brown spots, are also noticeable on the dorsal surface of the leaf. Of various mildews, *downy mildew* of crucifers caused by *Peronospora parasitica* is described below. This is widely distributed in Europe, America and also in India, particularly on cabbage, cauliflower, radish and turnip. All these host plants usually remains stunted when they are attacked with mildew.

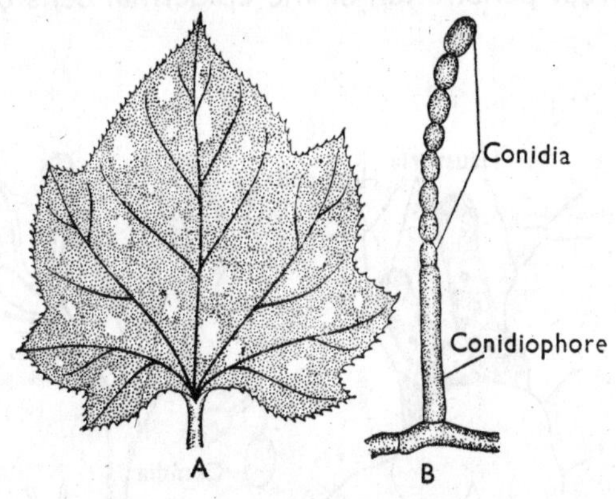

Fig. 136. *Peronospora*.
A, A cucurbit leaf infected with the pathogen ;
B, Formation of conidia in chains on a conidiophore

Vegetative body

The mycelium is typically coenocytic, consisting of much-branched hyphae. These hyphae usually ramify in the intercellular spaces of the host cells. It draws nourishment from the adjacent living cells by means of haustoria.

Reproduction

Peronospora reproduces both asexually and sexually.

At the time of asexual reproduction several **conidiophores**, developed from the intercellular mycelium, emerge through the stomata on the ventral surface of the leaves. Subsequently, they elongate considerably and bifurcate 6—8 times at the apex and the ultimate branches bear **conidia** at their tips. The conidia are usually oval, sometimes spherical, hyaline and uninucleate. Eventually, these conidia are disseminated by the wind, and when fall on suitable host, they germinate under favourable conditions and give rise to germ tubes from indeterminate points on the sides of the conidia. The germ tubes usually enter into the host through the stomata, or direct penetration of the epidermal cells of the host plants.

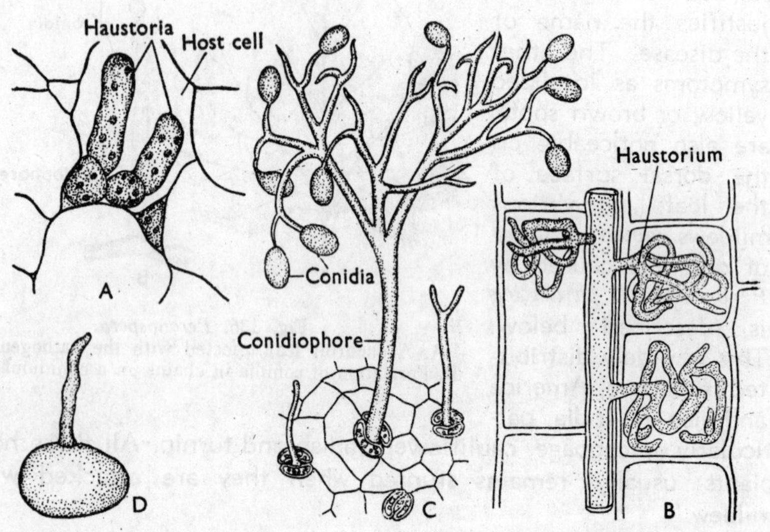

Fig. 137. *Peronospora.*
A, Haustoria within the host cell ; B, Ramification of haustoria into finger-like processes within host cells ; C, Emergence of conidiophores through the stomata, and the formation of conidia ; D, A germinating conidium.

Sexual reproduction is oogamous. In this case well differentiated antheridia and oogonia are developed from the nearby hyphae. The antheridium is multinucleate in the beginning, but gradually all the nuclei except one degenerate. The remaining nucleus acts as the male nucleus. On the other hand, the oogonium is also multinucleate at the early stage but with further development, it becomes differentiated into central uninucleate **oosphere** and peripheral multinucleate **periplasm.** During gametangial contact, a fertilization tube is formed by the antheridium which penetrates the periplasm and finally discharges the male nucleus into the oosphere. The male nucleus then fuses with the female nucleus and consequentlp, a zygote is formed. After fertilization, the zygote develops a thick wall and after a period of rest inside the host or in the soil, it germinates by producing germ tubes under favourable conditions, and initiates fresh infection. Possibly, the first nuclear division is reductional inside the zygote.

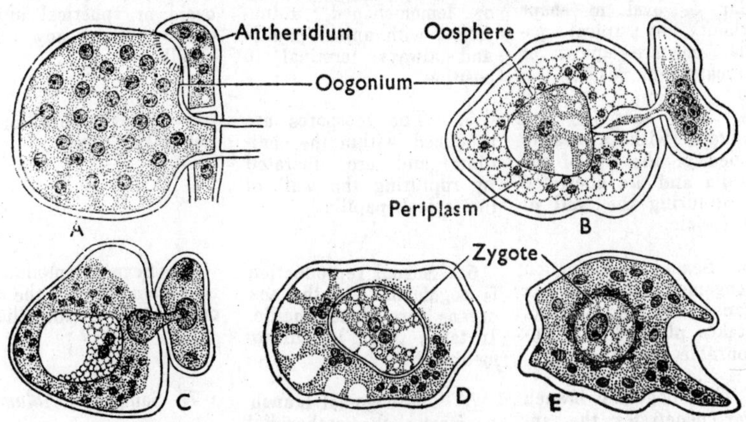

Fig. 138. *Peronospora.*
A—E, Stages in the formation of the zygote.

Control measures

The disease may be partially controlled by spraying with chloranil (spergon) and zinc sulphate, and crowding of plants should be avoided.

Comparison of Pythium, Phytophthora and Peronospora

Pythium	*Phytophthora*	*Peronospora*
1. It is a parasite which infects the hypocostyl of the seedlings of crop plants causing 'damping off' disease a few species are saprophytes or aquatic in nature.	1. It is a parasite which infects the potato plants causing 'late blight' disease ; a few species are saprophytes.	1. It is an obligate parasite which infects mustard, cucurbits, etc., causing 'downy mildew' disease.
2. The mycelium is a much-branched coenocyte, intercellular or intracellular is position of the host tissues, but never produce any haustoria.	2. The mycelium is a coenocyte which grows within the intercellular spaces of the host and gives rise to haustoria which penetrate the host tissue for drawing nutrition.	2. Same as *Phytophthora.*
3. The conidia are borne on some distinct aerial somatic, hyphae forming conidiophores.	3. The conidia are borne on aerial sympodially branched conidiophores, which are quite distinct, from the somatic hyphae.	3. Same as Phytophthora, but the *conidiophore* is never sympodially branched.

Pythium	*Phytophthora*	*Peronospora*
4. The conidia are globular or oval in shape without any apical papilla, and are apical or intercalary in position.	4. The conidia are oval or lemon-shaped, uninucleate, with apical papilla and always terminal in position.	4. The conidia are ovoid or spherical uninucleate, without any apical papilla.
5. The zoospores are produced with a vesicle formed at the tip of the conidia and are aberrated by rupturing the wall of the vesicle.	5. The zoospores are produced within the conidium and are liberated by rupturing the wall of the apical papilla.	5. No zoospore formation takes place.
6. Sexual reproduction is oogamous and the sex organs are homothallic. It takes place during unfavourable condition.	6. Sexual reproduction is oogamous and the sex organs are heterothallic. It takes place in culture medium.	6. Sexual reproduction is oogamous and the sex organs are heterothallic.
7. The oogonial branch never penetrates the antheridiate branch. The antheridium is of amphigynous type.	7. The oogonial branch penetrates the antheridial branch and then branches swell at their tips forming the antheridium and oogonium. The antheridium lies completely within the large oogonium and the . funnel-shaped base giving rise to an amphigynous type.	7. Same as *Pythium*.

ALBUGO

(Fam. ALBUGINACEAE)

Albugo candida, formerly known as *Cystopus candidus*, is a most common species causing *white rust* of cruciferous plants throughout the world. It is an obligate parasite, which forms white shining patches on stems and leaves, and causes much deformation of the inflorescences and fruits.

Vegetative body (Fig. 139)

It is a much-branched, intercellular, coenocytic mycelium with rather coarse hyphae, which bear numerous small, rounded, intercellular haustoria within the neighbouring cells.

Reproduction

Albugo reproduces both asexually and sexually.

During asexual reproduction, hyphae collect beneath the epidermis and form closely-packed groups of simple or branched, club-shaped structures (**conidiophores** or **sporangiophores**) forming

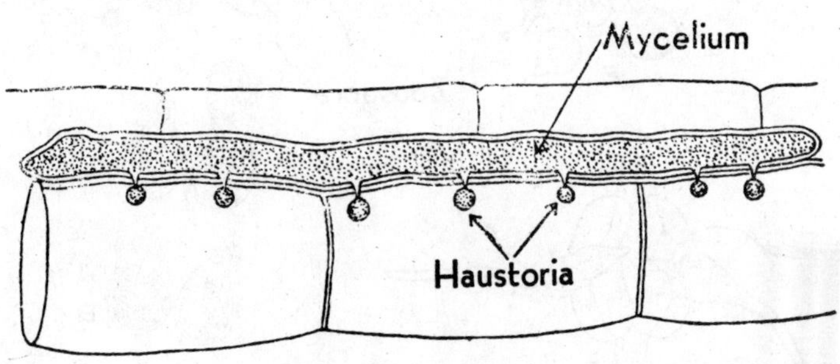

Fig. 139. *Albugo.*
Part of the mycelium bearing haustoria.

a palisade-like layer, which pushes the epidermis outwards to form whitish blister-like areas, called **sori.** Each club-shaped structure

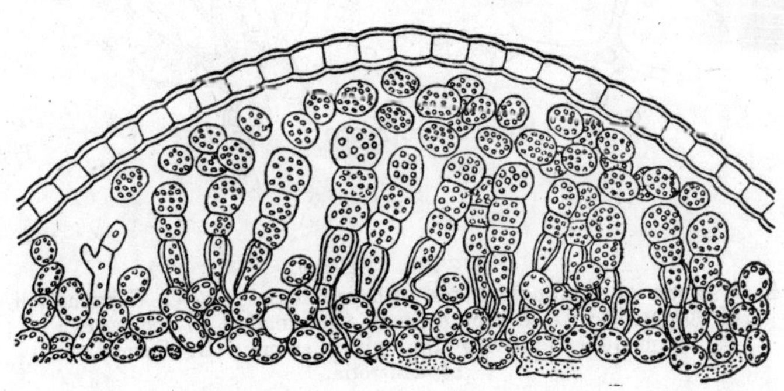

Fig. 140. *Albugo.*
Development of conidia (sporangia).

cuts off successively from its apex, a chain of globular bodies (**conidia** or **sporangia**), each with five to six nuclei. They are separated from one another by short neck-like projections of some gelatinous material. As the chains elongate, they press the epidermis above and ultimately it becomes ruptured. The globular structures successively break off and are easily disseminated by the wind.

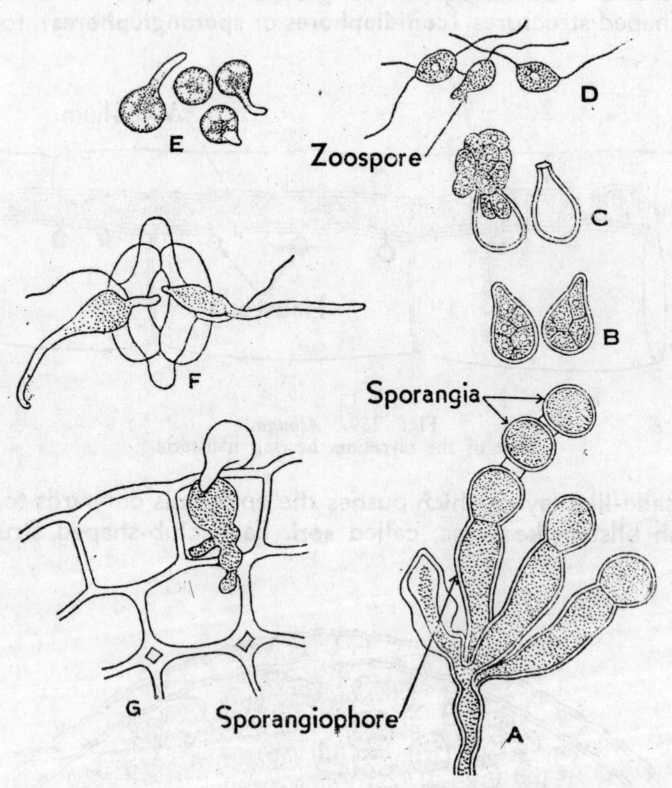

Fig. 141. *Albugo.*
A, A group of sporangiophores with sporangia ; B—C, Germination of sporangia ; D, Zoosporest ; E, Germination of zoospores ; F, Germ tubes entering through a stoma ; G, Formation of haustoria.

Each globular body, under favourable conditions, germinates directly by the production of germ tubes and behaves as a conidium, or indirectly by the production of zoospores and functions as a sporangium. In presence of water and a low temperature, the zoospores are produced, but in a relatively dry condition the germ tubes are formed. In the latter case, the germ tube may enter into various parts of plants and bring about infections.

When germination takes place indirectly, the contents of a sporangium, by the process of cleavage, form 4-8 **zoospores,** which either escape, one by one, through a pore formed on the wall of the sporangium, or an adherent mass of zoospores is discharged into a vesicle formed by the sporangium itself. The vesicle eventually disappears and the zoospores are set free. The zoospores are ovate to slightly kidney-shaped in form and each bears two unequal flagella.

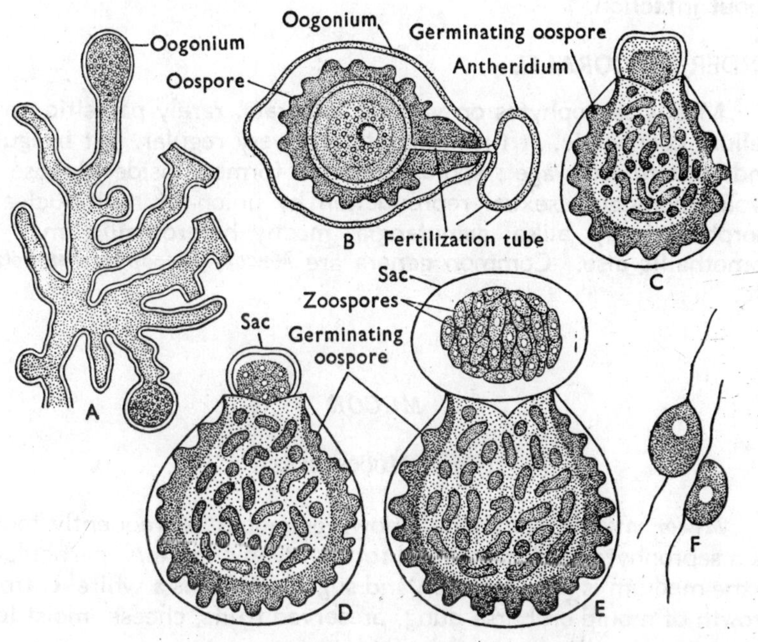

Fig. 142. *Albugo.*
A, Young oogonium ; B, Formation of oospore ; C—E, Germination of oospore ; F, Zoospores.

After a period of swimming, a zoospore comes to rest, its flagella disappear and a wall is secreted around the protoplast. It then germinates directly by forming a germ tube, which usually enters through a stoma and brings about infection.

Sexual reproduction takes place by oogamy. Both antheridia and oogonia develop within the host tissues, particularly in those of the flowers and axes of the inflorescences. The sexual process is essentially similar to that of *Pythium de Baryanum* but differing in detail. In this case, more periplasm is formed and the female nucleus lies in a deeply-stainable mass of cytoplasm at the centre of the ooplasm. After fertilization when the zygote is formed, the zygote nucleus divides, soon after its formation, into about 32 nuclei so that the resting oospore is multinucleate. There is evidence that the reduction division takes place during the division of the zygote nucleus. Under favourable conditions when the oospore germinates, its outer wall ruptures partly exposing an internal transparent sac-like structure containing zoospores. This sac finally ruptures and biflagellate zoospores are set free, which may eventually bring about infection.

ORDER **MUCORALES**

Mostly saprophytes on various substrata, rarely parasitic ; mycelium coenocytic, at first aseptate and very regular, but irregular and septate with age ; sporangiospores formed inside globose or ovoid sporangia ; sexual reproduction by union of multinucleate, morphologically alike gametangia, mostly heterothallic, may be homothallic also. Common genera are *Mucor*, *Rhizopus*, *Pilobolus*, etc.

MUCOR

(Fam. MUCORACEAE)

Mucor mucedo, commonly known as mould, is frequently found as a saprophyte on decayed and rotten organic matters, particularly if the medium is rich in starch and sugars. It forms a white, cottony growth of mould on horse dung, preserved fruits, cheese, moist leather, etc., usually during the rainy season.

Vegetative body (Fig. 143)

The vegetative body of the fungus, which is a filamentous and much-branched thallus, is known as the mycelium, and the filaments of which the mycelium is made up are called the hyphae. Some of these hyphae penetrate the substratum, serve as anchors for the superficial mycelium and draw nourishment therefrom. The mycelium is normally non-septate and contains abundant granular cytoplasm, numerous minute nuclei and small vacuoles ; it is, therefore, a coenocyte. While non-septate condition is characteristic of the young vigorously growing mycelium, cross walls are frequently found in the older hyphae, and the reproductive parts are generally separated from the vegetative ones by septa.

Reproduction

Mucor reproduces both asexually and sexually.

When conditions are favourable, the plant reproduces asexually by the formation of **spores** (or **gonidia**). During the process some aerial hyphae bear at their tips some spherical **sporangia** (or **gonidangia**), and each simple aerial branch bearing a sporangium is called a **sporangiophore** (or **gonidangiophore**). The formation of a sporangium takes place in the following way :

An aerial hypha gradually elongates, and after it has elongated to a certain height, its tip begins to enlarge into a sporangium. Into this enlargement a certain amount of cytoplasm with many nuclei

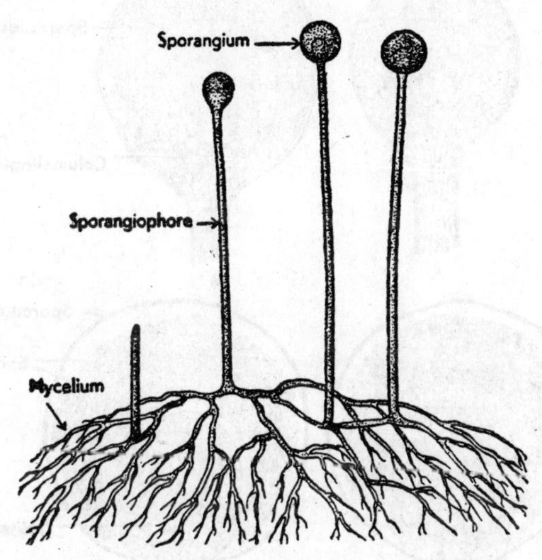

Fig. 143. *Mucor.*
Mycelium and sporangiophores bearing sporangia.

and a considerable amount of reserve food flow from the adjoining region. Then, a dome-shaped area of vacuoles appears within the cytoplasm towards the base of the sporangial wall. This region of cytoplasm is known as the **columellaplasm,** which is surrounded by a peripheral layer of nucleated cytoplasm, known as the **sporeplasm.** The vacuoles then flatten, fuse end to end into one continuous cavity, around which gradually a wall is laid down forming the so-called **columella.** Then, there follows a progressive cleavage of the sporangial cytoplasm from the periphery to the centre and *vice versa*, with the result that the cytoplasm becomes gradually **cut** off into smaller and smaller polyhedral blocks, eventually resulting into small multinucleate or rarely uninucleate units. These ultimate units take on a definite wall and become the **spores** without any further nuclear division. When mature, the spores are thin-walled and ovate in shape, hyaline or dully coloured in mass. The wall breaks up and ultimately disappears on coming in contact with water. In some species, where the sporangial wall is thin, a liquid droplet appears at the junction of the sporangiophore and sporangium on one side. This droplet then gradually increases in size and

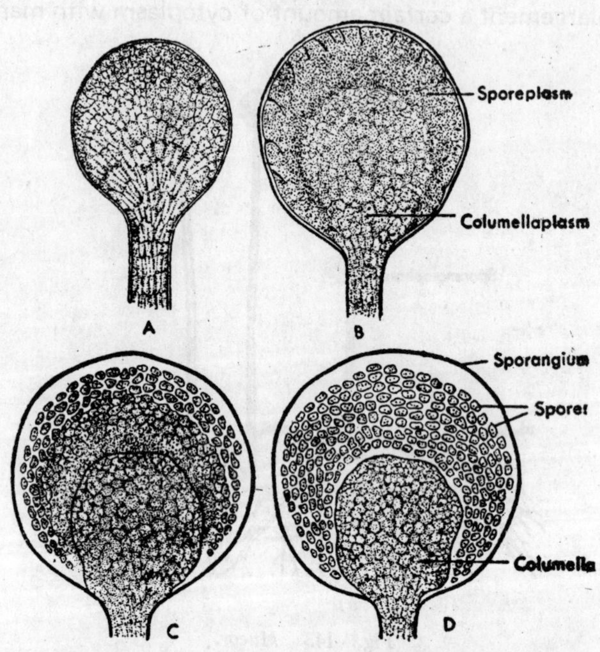

Fig. 144. *Mucor.*
A—D, Successive stages in the development of sporangium. columella and spores (as seen in longitudinal section).

envelops the entire sporangium. After some time, the sporangial wall disintegrates, and the droplet forms a conspicuous **sporangial drop** holding the spores in suspension. The sporangiophore on losing turgidity then collapses, usually brings the drop against a solid surface, and it spreads out rapidly owing to surface tension. Ultimately on drying, the spore masses remain firmly adherent together with mucilage, which, however, is readily dissolved and the spores are later on separated in water. Each spore, under favourable conditions, puts forth one or more germ tubes, which ultimately ramifying develop into a new mycelium.

Under certain conditions, especially when the food supply of the mycelium is exhausted, the plant reproduces sexually and the organs of sexual reproduction are formed. The reproduction is isogamous, which consists in the conjugation of two like gametes. During the process, two club-shaped hyphae (**progametangia**) of

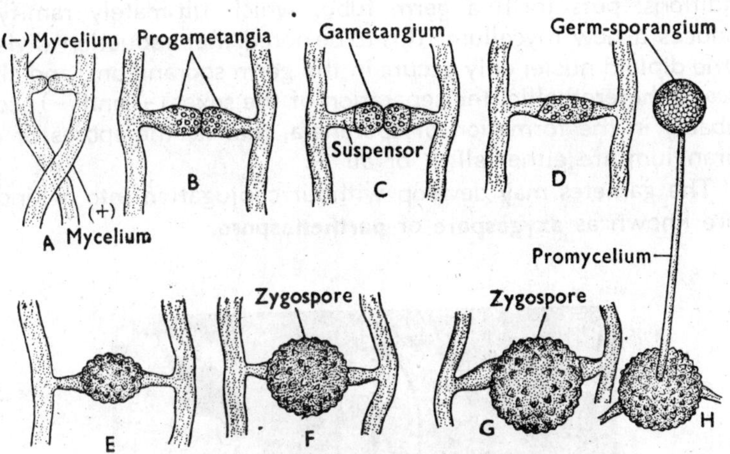

Fig. 145. *Mucor hiemalis.*
A — B, Contact of (+) and (—) mycelia and formation of progametangia ; C, Progametangia divided to form gametangia and suspensors ; D, Conjugation ; E—G, Formation and development of zygospore ; H, Germination of zygospore and formation of germ sporangium.

different sexes* (**plus** and **minus strains**) approach, come in contact end on end with each other, and a conjugate cell is cut off at the apex of each progametangium by the formation of a transverse wall. The two conjugating cells are the two **gametangia,** and their undifferentiated protoplasmic contents form the **gametes.** The remainder of the special branch bearing a gametangium is known as a **suspensor.** The walls between the gametangia generally break down, the two multinucleate gametes thereupon coalesce, cytoplasm with cytoplasm but the nuclei fuse in pairs and a **zygospore** is formed.

* In 1904 Blakeslee demonstrated the presence of two sexually different strains in *Mucor* which he termed as (+) or female, and (—) or male. Zygospore-formation is only possible by the union of these two sexually different strains of mycelia. Although the mycelia are morphologically similar, the *plus* or *minus* strains are physiologically different.

Those nuclei which do not fuse ultimately degenerate. The resulting zygospore increases in size and forms a heavy, dark and often spiny or otherwise roughened wall. After a considerable period of rest, the zygospore increases in size and then germinates, its outer wall (**exospore**) bursts and the inner wall (**endospore**) puts forth a long germ tube, known as **promycelium,** which ultimately becomes terminated by a germ **sporangium.** Each of the spores contained therein, on being set free germinates under suitable conditions, puts forth a germ tube, which ultimately ramifying produces a new mycelium. It is to be noted that reduction division of the diploid nuclei only occurs in the germ sporangium, and since *Mucor* is heterothallic, the separation of the sexes (+ and −) occurs probably in the formation of sporangia, that is, the spores of one sporangium are either all + or all −.

The gametes may develop without conjugation into a kind of spore known as **azygospore** or **parthenospore.**

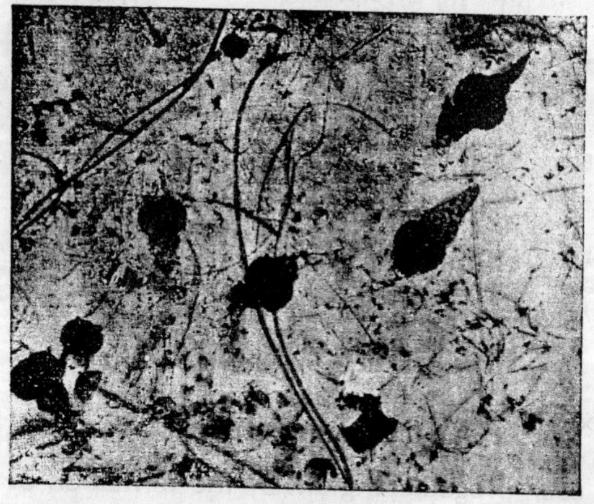

Fig, 146, Photomicrograph showing formation of zygospore in *Mucor*.

Torula state or yeast condition of Mucor

If a portion of the mycelium of *Mucor* be placed in a sugar solution, it becomes divided by transverse walls into thin-walled cells, known as **oidia.** These cells go on budding like the yeast and can excite alcoholic fermentation in the sugar solution producing alcohol and carbon dioxide.

Physiological control of Sexual reactions in *Mucor mucedo.* **Plempel and his associates (1957, 1960, 1963) made extensive** studies on the regulation of sexual reactions between + and − strains of *Mucor mucedo*. He discovered a system which could explain the physiological control of sexual reactions in *M. mucedo.* This system is shown in the following diagram.

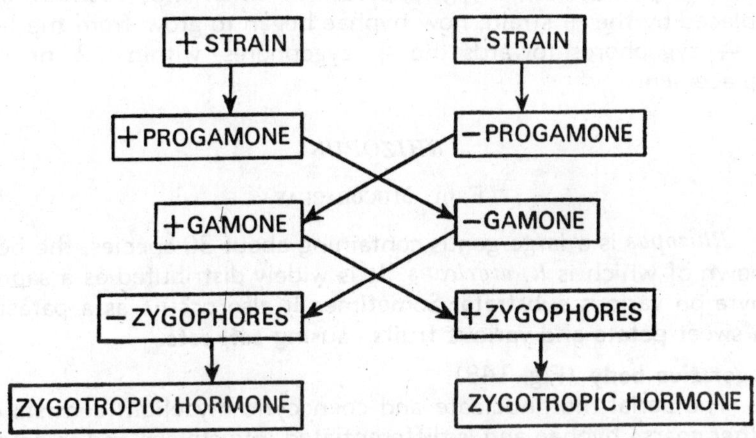

Fig, 147, Diagram shows the induction of progamone, gamone and zygotropic hormones by interaction of + and − strains of *M. mucedo.*

According to Plempel, each strain + or — if grown separately in liquid culture produced a substance known as progamone, i.e. a + strain produced a + progamone and a − strain a — progamone. When fungus free culture filtrates from either of the two were applied to mycelia of the opposite strain, synthesis of another substance called gamone was induced. In other words, culture filtrate containing a + progamone applied to — mycelia induced the formation of — gamone and *vice versa*. The gamones in turn induced zygophores (i.e. swollen hyphae which would develop into gametangia in normal circumstances) in the opposite strains and this was highly specific, i.e. — gamone was ineffective in a − strain, but could form zygophores only in a + strain and not in a — one. The zygophores of the two opposite strains grew towards each other and showed zygotropic curvature due to the production of two zygotropic hormones. Plempel also demonstrated that when two agar blocks containing zygophores of two opposite strains + and — were placed at a distance of 2.5 mm from each other and separated by a mica membrane having a hole (3.5 mm diameter), the — zygophores began to grow towards the hole in the mica membrane after 6—8 hr. After 14 hr., the — zygophores were in contact with the + ones. If the two agar blocks were separated by a greater distance, the zygophores just opposite the hold enlongated more than those away from the hole. When the + strain was replaced by — strain, the two opposing zygophores were of the similar — strains so instead of growing towards each other original — zygophores produced sporangiophores. But when the – strain was replaced by the + strain, now hyphae began to grow from the lips of — zygophores towards the + zygophores within 12 hr. of replacement.

RHIZOPUS

(Fam. MUCORACEAE)

Rhizopus is a large genus containing about 30 species, the best known of which is *R. nigricans*. It is widely distributed as a saprophyte on various substrata. Sometimes it also occurs as a parasite on sweet potato and various fruits causing **soft rots.**

Vegetative body (Fig. 148)

The aerial multinucleate and coenocytic mycelium consists of rather coarse hyphae and is differentiated into stolons and rhizoids.

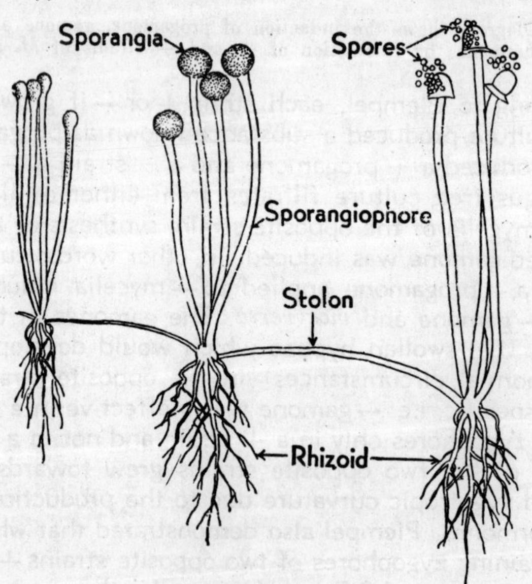

Fig. 148. *Rhizopus.*
Portion of a mycelium showing the vegetative and asexual reproductive structures.

The stolon is an aerial hypha that grows more or less horizontally above the substratum for some distance, and then bends down to the substratum forming a tuft of repeatedly branched, dark-coloured rhizoids. Just exactly opposite the point of origin of the rhizoids, there arise from the stolon a tuft of vertically erect and unbranched sporangiophores bearing globose sporangia containing dark-coloured spores.

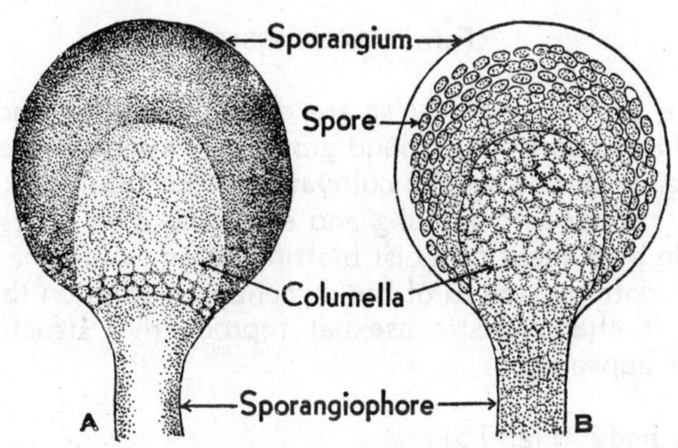

Fig. 149. *Rhizopus.*
A—B, Stages in the development of the sporangium.

Reproduction

Rhizopus nigricans reproduces both asexually and sexually and

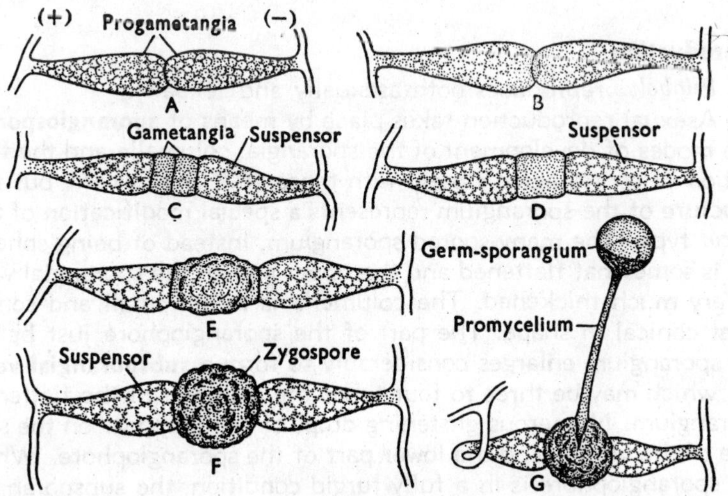

Fig. 150. *Rhizopus.*
A—F, Stages in the formation of zygospore ; G, Germination of zygospore.

the modes of reproduction agree with those of *Mucor mucedo* in essential details. Furthermore, the fungus is also heterothallic, and the formation of the zygospore is dependent on hyphae of two different sexes coming in contact with each other.

PILOBOLUS

(Fam. PILOBOLACEAE)

All the species of *Pilobolus* are dung-inhabiting, and of these *P. crystallinus* is commonly found growing as a saprophyte on moist horse dung. It can be readily cultivated in the laboratory by bringing freshly dropped horse dung and enclosing it in a large bell jar lined inside by a sheet of moist blotting paper. Within a couple of days white, cottony growth of the mycelium appears on the surface, and from it characteristic asexual reproductive structures soon make their appearance.

Vegetative body (Fig. 151)

Like *Mucor mucedo*, its vegetative body is a much-branched coenocytic mycelium consisting of rather coarser white hyphae and containing multinucleate, granulated and vacuolated protoplasm. Some of the hyphae penetrate the substratum and draw nourishment therefrom.

Reproduction

Pilobolus reproduces both asexually and sexually.

Asexual reproduction takes place by means of **sporangiospores.** The modes of development of the sporangia, columella and the formation of spores agree closely with those of *Mucor mucedo*, but the structure of the sporangium represents a special modification of the *Mucor* type. The many-spored sporangium, instead of being spherical, is somewhat flattened and the upper half of the sporangial wall is very much thickened. The columella is rather small and somewhat conical in shape. The part of the sporangiophore just below the sporangium enlarges considerably to form a **subsporangial vesicle,** which may be three to four times the diameter of the flattened sporangium. Numerous glistening drops of water appear on the surface of the vesicle and the lower part of the sporangiophore. When the sporangiophore is in a fully turgid condition, the subsporangial vesicle has been found to be sensitive to the directive influence of light. This stimulus causes curvature of the lower part of the sporangiophore, and the sporangium is directed towards the source of light. The neck, *i.e.* the constricted portion between the sporangium and the sub-sporangial vesicle, undergoes softening and

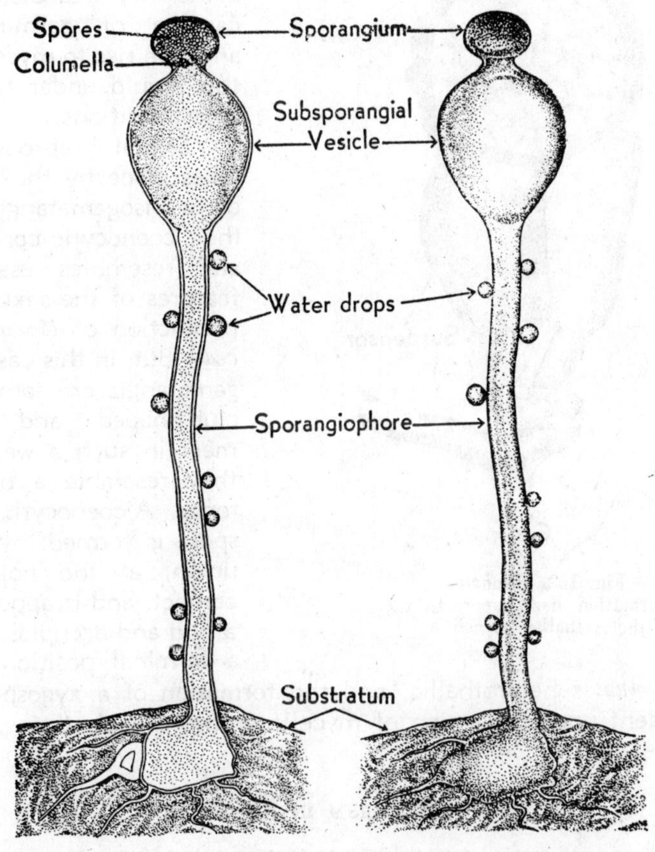

Fig. 151. *Pilobolus*,
General structure of the fungus with the sporangium ; the left hand figure denotes an optical longitudinal section of the right hand one.

stretching and finally the turgidity of the vesicle reaches to such a degree that the neck ruptures and the entire sporangium, with mature spores, is blown off along with the watery contents of the vesicle towards the source of light, without much scattering of aim, to a distance of several centimetres. Hence, it is known as **Pilobolus**

gun. The sporangia finally descend on the vegetation, adhere to it and are taken up by animals. The spores, only after passing out of their alimentary canals, are capable of germination and give rise to mycelia of this mould under favourable conditions.

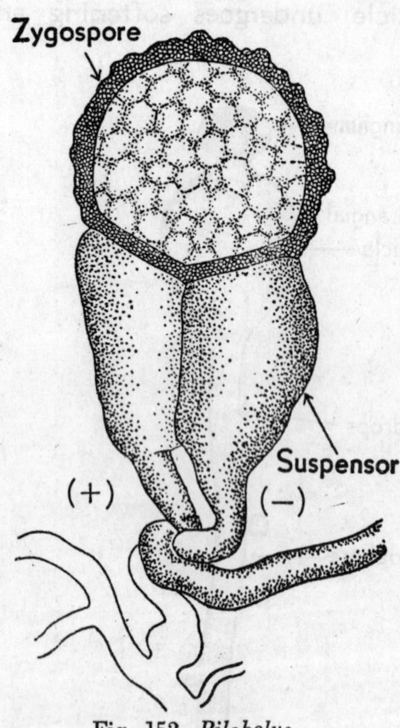

Fig. 152. *Pilobolus.* Formation of zygospore by the heterothallic mycelium.

Sexual reproduction takes place by the union of two isogametangia and their coenocytic contents, and resembles essential features of the sexual reproduction of *Mucor mucedo*. But, in this case, the gametangia are somewhat club-shaped and they meet in such a way that they resemble a pair of tongs. A coenocytic zygospore is formed, by their union, at the point of contact, and it appears as a bud and occupies, as if, a terminal position. ***P. crystallinus*** is heterothallic, and the formation of a zygospore is dependent upon the union of mycelia of two sexual strains, (+) and (–).

Heterothallism in Mucorales

The species in which conjugation depends on the interaction of two thalli of different sexes are said to be **heterothallic** and the phenomenon is known as **heterothallism.** While those give rise to zygote in mycelium and form a single sporangiospore and therefore consist of one kind of thalli or strains are known as *homothallic* and the phenomenon is known as *homothallism*.

Heterothallism was first discovered by Blakeslee (1904). He found that the zygospore formation in certain Mucorales depends on the hyphae of two different strains coming into contact. These strains are morphologically similar but physiologically different. These physiologically different strains were termed by Blakeslee as + or — strains. Only when these two strains come in contact sexual reproduction is possible.

Prior to this work a number of theories were put forward by different mycologists. According to some, zygospore formation depends on the factors, like nature of the medium, humidity of atmosphere and respiration.

In some species, there are visible differences between the two strains, one being more luxuriant in growth than the other. To the relatively well-developed strain the term + was given, to the weaker, – term was applied.

But, as there are some species in which there is one morphological difference in the strains and they are also termed + and –, according to their physiological differences.

Recently Blakeslee and his co-workers have attempted to establish physiological differences between these two strains or sexes along the biochemical lines. Satina and Blakeslee have made chemical tests on the two sexual strains of several species and found different reactions. Blakeslee (1920) and others have observed that the sexual differences show different degrees of intensity. A plant that is very strongly male will conjugate with plants of all degrees of femaleness and *vice versa*. On the contrary, a plant weakly male will not conjugate with one weakly female.

Instances of heterothallism in different species of Mucorales

The different conditions found in Mucorales in connection with heterothallism can be summarized as follows :

(*a*) *Sporodinia grandis*

In this species zygospores are obtained from a single spore-culture and therefore they are homothallic. Zygospore on germination gives rise to the germ sporangium, the spores of which on germination give rise to homothallic mycelium.

(*b*) *Mucor mucedo*

In this species all the spores in the sporangium are of the same strain. The spores from the sporangium on germination produce only one kind of mycelia, either + or – strain, since meiosis takes place in the zygospore before its germination, there should be two types of nuclei (+ and –) segregating from each zygote nucleus. We would expect, therefore, some of the sporangiospores in the sporangium would contain + nuclei and the rest contain – nuclei, but such is not in this case ; one or the other type of nuclei either disintegrate or at any rate do not seem to be included in the sporangiospore. Hence, this species is heterothallic.

(*c*) *Phycomyces nitens*

In this case, + and − spores as well as ± spores are formed which have not yet been differentiated into + and − and which on germination produce homothallic mycelia. This is explained by the fact that segregation of sexes occur before the formation of spores. The sexual character of the homothallic mycelia produced from the undifferentiated spores are unstable and after a few generations, the homothallic condition disappears.

It is interesting to note that there is apparently no numerical ratio between + and − spores and it sometimes happens that all the spores are of one strain. Sometimes conjugation does not occur in heterothallic forms when the appropriate strains are brought together. Because, poor nutrition and unfavourable temperature may prevent the formation and union of gametangia.

In *Mucor mucedo* and other species, prolonged cultivation under unfavourable conditions may cause the loss of conjugation, so that neutral races are formed, which are unable to respond either to + or − strains.

CHAPTER II

CLASS ASCOMYCETES

The Class Ascomycetes, commonly known as **sac fungi** include such forms as the 'brewer's yeasts' (*Saccharomyces*), the black mould (*Aspergillus niger*), the blue moulds of oranges (*Penicillium expansum*), the powdery mildews of cultivated crops (*Erysiphe*), the cup fungi (*Peziza, Ascobolus*), the common edible morel (*Morchella*), the ergot (*Claviceps*), and other fungi of considerable economic importance. A great number of them are parasites on higher plants but most of the species are saprophytes.

The Ascomycetes are characterized by the production of specialized asexual reproductive cells, known as **ascospores,** produced

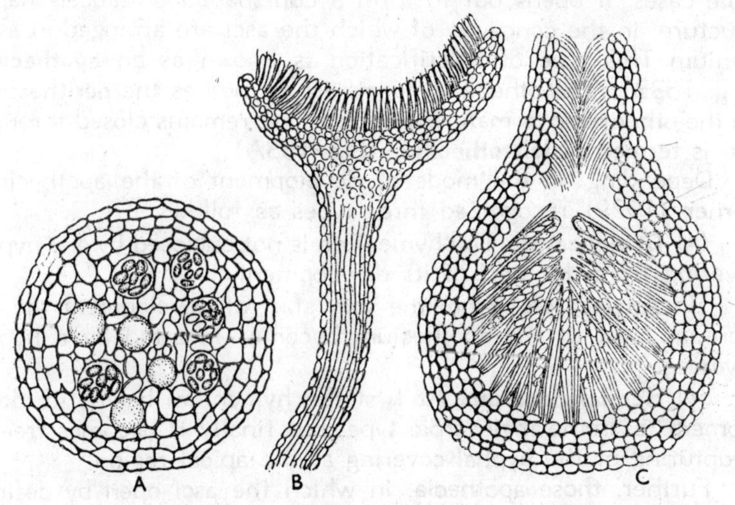

Fig. 153.
A, Cleistothecium ; B, Apothecium ; C, Perithecium.

(usually eight in number) within a mother cell, called an **ascus** (spore sac), which are typically club-shaped or cylindrical, but may also be globose or pyriform in shape. The asci are often arranged side by side in a definite layer forming a **hymenium,** but sometimes they occur singly or are arranged irregularly, so that no definite hymenium is formed. Intermingled with the asci of a well-developed hymenium there also occur sterile haploid branches, usually slightly exceeding the asci in length, known as **paraphyses.** An ascus develops as a dikaryon cell in which the nuclei fuse and then divide reductionally into eight nuclei, which with some adjacent cytoplasm, are cut off by walls (free cell formation) forming ascospores. Among the simpler Ascomycetes, as the yeasts, the entire vegetative body (a cell) is directly transformed into an ascus. In addition to ascospores, multiplication may also take place by means of conidia and chlamydospores.

In most Ascomycetes the asci usually arise in groups and remain protected by a common wall of hyphal tissue, known as the **peridium,** and a definite structure, thus formed, is a fructification, called the **ascocarp.** When young, the ascocarp is somewhat globose in form and remains completely closed. At maturity, it may become flask-shaped in outline opening only by a terminal pore, called the **ostiole** ; such a fructification is called a **perithecium**. In some cases, it opens out to form a cup-shaped or saucer-shaped structure, in the concavity of which the asci are arranged in a hymenium. This type of fructification is known as an **apothecium** (Fig. 153B). The other two forms are termed as the **perithecium.** On the other hand, a mature ascocarp, if it remains closed throughout, is termed a **cleistothecium** (Fig. 153A).

Depending on the mode of development of the apothecium, Corner (1929) recognized three types as follows :

(*a*) **Gymnocarpic.** The hymenium is not enclosed by any hyphal covering from the start of its development.

(*b*) **Angiocarpic.** From the very start of development the hymenium layer of the apothecium becomes invested by a hyphal covering.

(*c*) **Hemiangiocarpic.** At first the hymenium begins its development, as in the angiocarpic type, but finally it becomes free by a rupturing of the hyphal covering at the apical region.

Further, those apothecia, in which the asci open by definite apical pores, are known as the **operculate** apothecia, while those in which the asci have no such regular pores but get irregularly ruptured at their tips, are termed as the **inoperculate** apothecia.

The vegetative body of Ascomycetes, with the exception of unicellular yeasts, consists of a mycelium which is much-branched and septate, and contains uninucleate or multinucleate cells. The mycelium usually develops within the substratum, but in a few cases part of it may be superficial. In saprophytic forms it is quite extensive, but in many parasitic forms the mycelium is localized at the region of infection. The parasitic mycelium may be entirely intracellular, or it lives in the intercellular spaces of the host tissue and frequently develops special hyphal branches, which penetrate the living cells and function as absorbing organs, called **haustoria.**

The problem of sexual reproduction in Ascomycetes is very variable and has received considérable attention during recent years. In general, it may be summarized that a gradual decline in sexuality can be traced in the group and the range includes from a well-developed oogamy, in which both antheridia and oogonia are present and functional, to complete suppression of sex organs, although perhaps there always remains a fusion of nuclei at a certain stage in the life cycle, representing the essentials of sexual reproduction. In between these two extremes, there are intermediate forms in which the oogonia are always present but the antheridia are either absent or when present entirely functionless. The sex organs may be uninucleate or multinucleate.

The Ascomycetes may also be homothallic or heterothallic. In the former case, two mycelia are necessary for sexual union and the formation of ascus and ascospores, while in the latter, only single mycelium is required for the same purpose. In the majority of homothallic species, all the ascospore nuclei of a single ascus are genetically the same, so far as the sex factors are concerned ; this phenomenon is referred to as the **primary homothallism.** On the other hand, the ascospores may be genetically dissimilar with respect to the sex factors. Still the mycelia produced from these ascospores will be homothallic, and such a phenomenon is termed as the **secondary homothallism.** Heterothallism also may be of two types : morphological and physiological. In the morphologically heterothallic species, the mycelia belong to two different categories : (*a*) the male mycelium producing antheridia or spermatia, and (*b*) the female one bearing the ascogonia only. A physiologically heterothallic mycelium, however, gives rise to both the male and female elements, but itself suffers from self-sterility. It can, nevertheless, unite sexually with some other compatible mycelia belonging to the same species.

Formation of ascus and ascospores

In the lower Ascomycetes (e.g. *Eremascus*, *Dipodascus*, *Saccharomyces*, etc.) the ascus is developed either directly from a zygote, or parthenogenetically from a gametangium. Usually the two nuclei of opposite sexes fuse inside the young zygote, which is now regarded as the developing ascus. The ascus then enlarges considerably, and the fusion nucleus undergoes reduction division forming usually 4—8 haploid daughter nuclei. From these nuclei, ultimately, 4—8 ascospores are produced.

In the higher Ascomycetes (e.g. *Pyronema*, *Peziza*, *Ascobolus*, etc.), however, the ascogonium never develops directly into an ascus after fertilization. From the ascogonium, on the contrary, one to several unbranched or profusely branched, aseptate or septate, filiform **ascogenous hyphae** are produced. In an ascogenous hypha either all the cells or only a few cells at its apical portion are binucleate, the two nuclei being of different sexualities. Usually, the terminal cell (of the ascogenous hypha) becomes curved like a hook, and is often termed as a **crozier.** The two nuclei in the crozier divide conjugately, and the daughter nuclei get themselves oriented in such a fashion, that the arch of the crozier receives one pair of them (of opposite sexes), the extreme tip of the crozier having only one, while the other solitary daughter nucleus is situated in the region below the crozier arch. Following this, two partition walls are laid down resulting in the formation of three cells. Of these, the ultimate cell is uninucleate, the penultimate one is binucleate, and the antepenultimate one is also uninucleate. From the binucleate cell, finally an ascus is developed. The two uninucleate ultimate and antepenultimate cells generally unite together to form another binucleate cell. This type of ascus development* is commonly found in *Pyronema confluens*.

The binucleate cell developing into an ascus becomes greatly enlarged and somewhat clavate. Meanwhile, the two nuclei fuse together forming a diploid nucleus. This diploid nucleus then undergoes a complete meiotic division followed by a mitotic one, resulting in the formation of eight haploid nuclei. Nuclear division, as a rule, stops at this stage, but cases of formation of 32—1,024 nuclei have also been recorded. Around each of these eight nuclei, some amount of cytoplasm collects, and finally eight ascospores are delimited. The remaining cytoplasm, which is left inside the ascus, after the formation of ascospores, is known as **epiplasm.**

It was considered previously that the gamete nuclei fused in pairs inside the ascogonium, and consequently, each of the two nuclei in the cells of an ascogenous hypha was diploid. So, when two such nuclei fused in the developing ascus, a tetraploid nucleus was formed. Subsequently, this tetraploid nucleus had to undergo a double reduction in the number of chromosomes in order to give rise to the haploid ascospore nuclei. This phenomenon was known as **brachymeiosis,** and was regarded as a unique feature of the ascomycetous fungi. Recent investigators, however, do not support this idea. They suggest that the gamete nuclei do not fuse, but lie in pairs in very proximity. In this paired condition, the nuclei migrate

* Dangeard terms it as the **curvascous type.**

into the ascogenous hyphae, and the fusion nucleus in the ascus is, therefore, only diploid, and not tetraploid. Consequently, there can be only one reduction in the number of chromosomes.

Besides the normal crozier or hook type, other types of ascus development are also found in the higher Ascomycetes. A brief account of these is given below :

In *Geopyxis catinus* (*Peziza catinus*), the tip cell of an ascogenous hypha is uninucleate just like the ultimate cell of the crozier in *Pyronema confluens*, while the cell behind it is binucleate. This binucleate subterminal cell finally pushes out in a lateral direction and grows out into an ascus.

The next type of ascus development, called the **Plicaria (Galactinia) type,** is exemplified by *Plicaria succosa* (*Galactinia succosa*) and *Acetabula leucomelas* (*Peziza leucomelas*). In this case, a number of cells towards the tip of an ascogenous hypha possess a dikaryon each. The two nuclei in the terminal cell fuse and this cell ultimately develops into an ascus.

In *Pustularia vesiculosa* (*Peziza vesiculosa*) the terminal cell of an ascogenous hypha may form a crozier as in *Pyronema confluens*. The binucleate penultimate cell, however, grows out into another hypha with several binucleate cells, the terminal one of which forms an ascus following the *Plicaria* type of formation.

A fourth type of ascus formation, termed the **rectascous type** by Dangeard, has been found in the lower plectascales. In this case, the cell is binucleate, as in the *Plicaria* type. Here, however, a number of asci are formed in a chain lying one behind the other ; but this has not been properly examined from cytological standpoint.

In the last type, which can be referred to as the **Laboulbenia type**, true ascogenous hyphae are lacking entirely. Instead, after fertilization, a cell complex appears from the ascogonium, and these cells give rise to asci.

CLASSIFICATION

The class Ascomycetes has been divided into *two* subclasses :

Subclass I. Protoascomycetes or Hemiascomycetes. Characterized by the formation of naked asci directly from the zygote, either singly or in loose clusters ; ascogenous hyphae and ascocarp absent.

Subclass II. Euascomycetes. Characterized by the formation of asci from the ascogonium produced by the ascogenous hyphae, in dense clusters within the ascocarps.

Euascomycetes has been subdivided into *three* series :

Series A. Plectomycetes. Characterized in having a closed ascocarp without any definite opening, the *cleistothecium*, within which the asci either arise from the floor and stand parallel to one another, or they are irregularly arranged ; in some cases a definite fructification is wanting.

It includes *three* orders :

Order 1. *Plectascales*. Simple types without apothecium or perithecium asci are produced either single, one from an ascogonium and without any covering, or a number of asci irregularly arranged within a protective covering of thick-walled hyphae forming the cleistothecium. Common genera are *Saccharomyces*, *Eurotium* (*Aspergillus*), *Penicillium*, etc.

Order 2. *Erysiphales.* Superficially growing parasites ; aerial mycelia colourless or dark-coloured ; mostly having a single layer of cylindrical asci, arranged parallel to one another within a cleistothecium with prominent appendages. Common genera are *Erysiphae*, *Sperotheca*, etc.

**Order* 3. *Exoascales*

Series B. Discomycetes. Characterized in having a fruit body, an *apothecium*, which becomes more or less cup-shaped at maturity ; the asci intermingled with paraphyses stand in parallel series forming a hymenium which occupies the concavity of the cup.

It includes *five* orders :

Order 1. *Pezizales*. Saprophytes with well-developed mycelia ; ascocarp is usually fleshy, but sometimes leathery, apothecium (usually cup-shaped) ; usually bounded by a peridium which is closed at first, but later on pushed open exposing the hymenium. Ascus contains usually 8 (sometimes more or less) ascospores and opening by the shedding of an operculum. Common genera are *Peziza*, *Ascobolus*, *Pyronema*, *Humaria*, etc.

Order 2. *Helvellales*. Saprophytes, ascocarp mostly large, fleshy and stalked ; and is often convoluted ; fertile region distinct from the sterile stalk ; spreads over the upper surface ; ascus opening by an operculum. Common genera are *Helvella*, *Morchella*, etc.

**Order* 3. *Tuberales.*

**Order* 4. *Phasidiales.*

**Order* 5. *Hysteriales.*

Series C. Pyrenomycetes. Characterized in having a flask-shaped fructification, the *perithecium*, opening at the top by an ostiole, and containing within it asci in parallel series.

It includes *four* orders :

Order 1. *Hypocreales*. Parasites or saprophytes ; mycelium

* Orders marked with asterisks are not treated in this book.

usually forms a *stroma* (parenchymatous mass) in which the perithecia are partially or entirely embedded ; the perithecial-wall and stroma, when present, are distinct and soft in texture, colourless or light coloured ; asci are formed within the perithecium ; peridium absent. Common genera are *Claviceps*, *Nectria*, etc.

**Order* 2. *Sphaeriales.*
**Order* 3. *Dothidiales.*
**Order* 4. *Laboulbeniales.*

ORDER **PLECTASCALES**

Simple types without apothecium or perithecium ; asci are produced either singly, one from an ascogonium and without any covering, or a number of asci irregularly arranged within a protective covering of thick-walled hyphae forming the cleistothecium. Common genera are *Saccharomyces*, *Eurotium* (*Aspergillus*), *Penicillium*, etc.

SACCHAROMYCES

(Fam. SACCHAROMYCETACEAE)

Saccharomyces are unicellular fungi, which are commonly known as yeasts. They were first discovered by Leeuwenhock, a Dutchman, in 1860. Most yeasts are saprophytes.

Distribution and occurrence

There are about 40 species of yeasts which are widely distributed in nature. They are commonly found on organic substances rich in sugar. Such as fruit juices, nectaries of flowers, exudates of plant tissues and on the soils of vineyards. Some are distinctly parasitic on plants and animals including man.

Vegetative body (Fig. 154)

Yeast is unicellular, spherical or oval in shape. The cell is so minute that its composition of cellwall is a matter of dispute. However, with the introduction of electron microscope and by X-ray diffraction and chemical analysis it reveals that the cell wall consists of protein, lipid, polysaccharides, chitin and various other substances. The budding regions of the cellwall are found to be slightly elevated forming **bud scars.** A number of such bud scars, may be found on the cellwall. Just below the cellwall,

* Orders marked with asterisks are not treated in this book,

cytoplasmic membrane, invaginated at certain places, is found. It contains within it *endoplasmic reticulum*, *mitochondria*, *glycogen* and *fats* as reserved food. The central portion of the cell contains a large *vacuole* which is also enclosed by a membrane. The vacuole consists of a few granular as well as some denser substances. There denser substances sometimes unite together to form a reticulum. The *nucleus* is situated near the vacuoles and it is bounded by a porous membrane made of two layers. Yeast cells are haploid or diploid and the diploid chromosome number is generally eight.

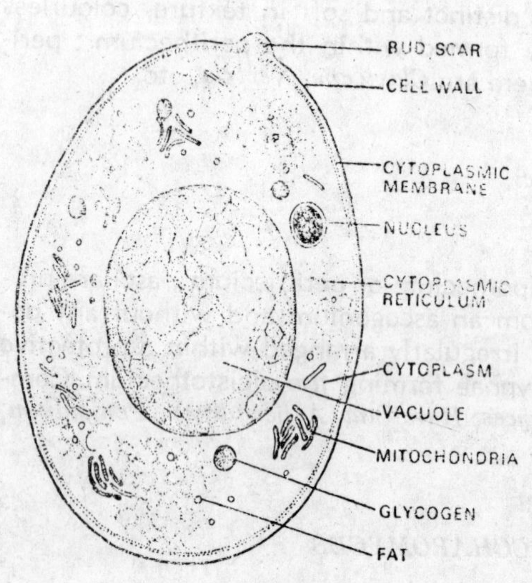

Fig. 154. Structure of Yeast cell. (Diagrammatic)

Reproduction

Saccharomyces reproduces by vegetative, asexual and several methods.

Vegetative reproduction takes place by *fission* and budding under normal conditions, when yeasts grow in a solution containing abundant sugar.

(*a*) **Fission** (Fig. 155). During the process of fission an yeast cell elongates and its nucleus divides into two daughter nuclei,

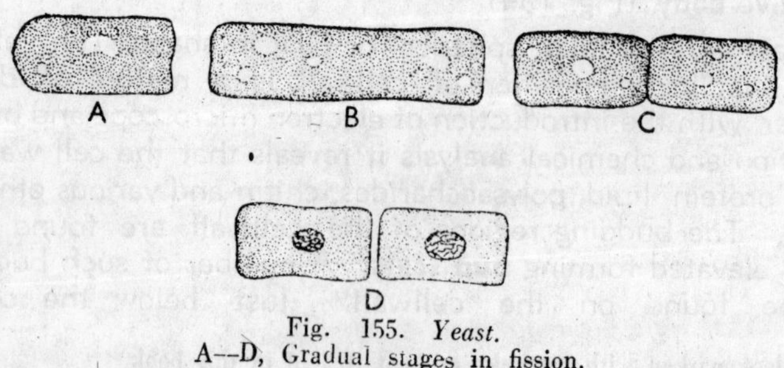

Fig. 155. *Yeast.*
A--D, Gradual stages in fission.

which soon separate from each other. Gradually a partition wall is laid down in the middle of matter cell so that two uninucleate daugther cells of equal size are formed. The daughter cells either remain attached together for sometime or they soon separate and begin to divide.

(*b*) **Budding** (Fig. 156). At the time of budding a portion of the cellwall near one end of an yeast cell softens by the action of an enzyme secreted by the cytoplasm. A small amount of cytoplasm of

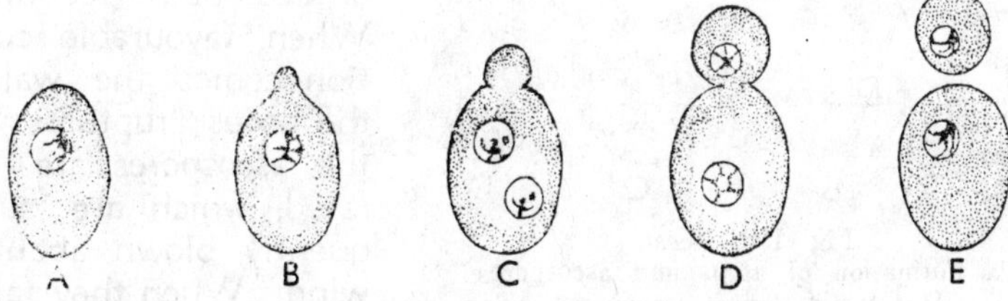

Fig. 156. *Yeast.*
A—E, Gradual stages in budding.

the mother cell, covered by a thin plasm membrane, bulges out through the softened region into a bud-like structure, which subsequently develops into a daughter cell. Meanwhile the nucleus of the mother cell divides mitotically forming two daughter nuclei, one of which migrates into the enlarging bud. A gradual constriction of the plasma membrane at the point of origin of the bud leads to the formation of two daughter cells of unequal sizes. The small daughter cell enlarges and buds in its turn and is ultimately detached from the mother cell. Sometimes budding is so very rapid that the successive daughter cells remain attached to one another forming one or more chains, which is sometimes called *pseudomycelium* (Fig. 157). The attachment of the cells in the chains is not firm as they separate into individual cells with the slightest disturbance.

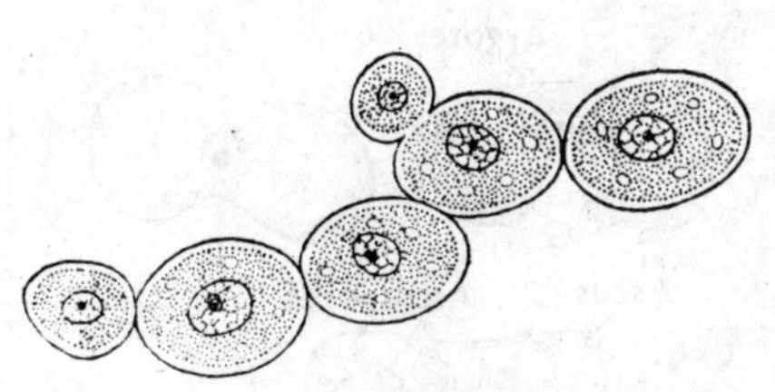

Fig. 157. *Yeast.*
Pseudomycelium.

Asexual reproduction (Fig. 158) takes place under unfavourable conditions, particularly when the amount of sugar is scanty or almost exhausted. During the process the yeast cell becomes larger and behaves like a sporangium. It is then called an *ascus*.

In presence of sufficient oxygen the nucleus divides mitotically into four (sometimes two or eight) daughter nuclei. Now cytoplasm collects round each daughter nucleus and ultimately a thick wall is secreted, and thus four *ascospores* are formed. The ascospores are resting spores and can withstand unfavourable condition. When favourable condition comes the wall of the ascus ruptures and the ascospores are liberated, which are subsequently blown about by wind. When they fall on suitable substratum germinate and reproduce by the process of budding.

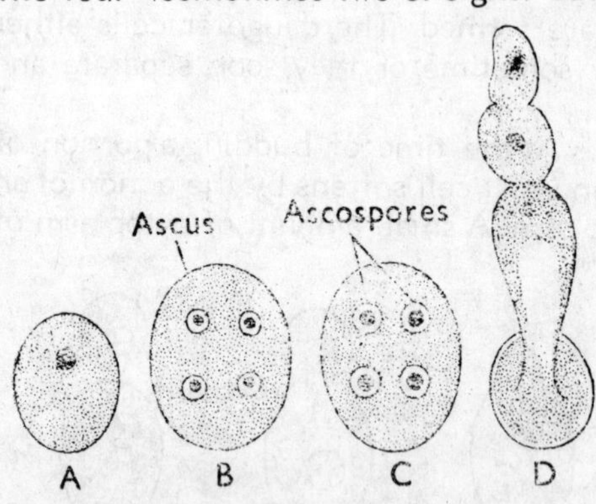

Fig. 158. *Yeast.*
A, Formation of ascus and ascospores
D, Germination of ascospores.

Vegetative reproduction takes place by **budding.** At the time of budding a small outgrowth, a **bud,** is formed at one pole of the mother cell. The nucleus divides into two daughter nuclei.

The species of **Saccharomyces** were previously thought to be wholly parthenogenetic, but recent researches of Dr. Winge (1935)

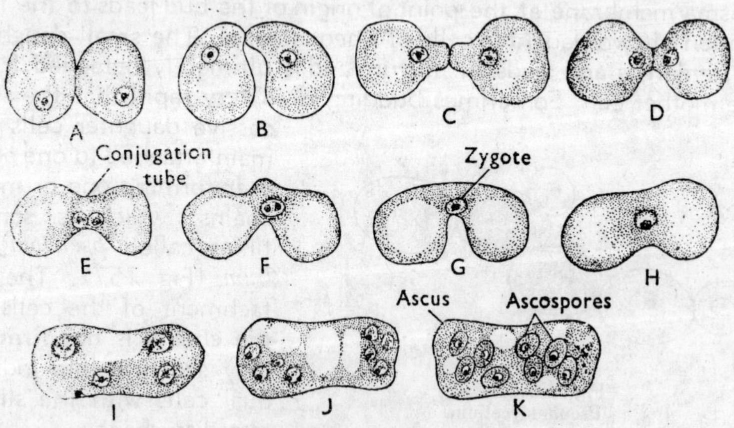

Fig. 159 *Saccharomyces.*
A—K, Gradual stages in the formation of ascus with ascospores.

have shown that it is not so. Sexual reproduction also occurs and it is isogamous. It is accomplished either by the union of two haploid vegetative cells (**plasmogamy**) or of two ascospores (**Karyogamy**). These may be either homothallic or heterothallic. The ascospores usually function as gametangia.

According to Guilliermond (1940) yeasts exhibit three types of ilfe-cycles which are as follows :

1. Haplobiontic type of life-cycle. This type of life-cycle is exhibited by **Schizo saccharomyces octospores.** In this case, there is conjugation between two haploid vegetative cells. Each of the two conjugating cells produces a short protuberance, and two such protuberances ultimately unite to form a **conjugation tube.** The two nuclei of the two conjugating cells migrate into the conjugation tube, finally fuse and form a diploid nucleus. The conjugation

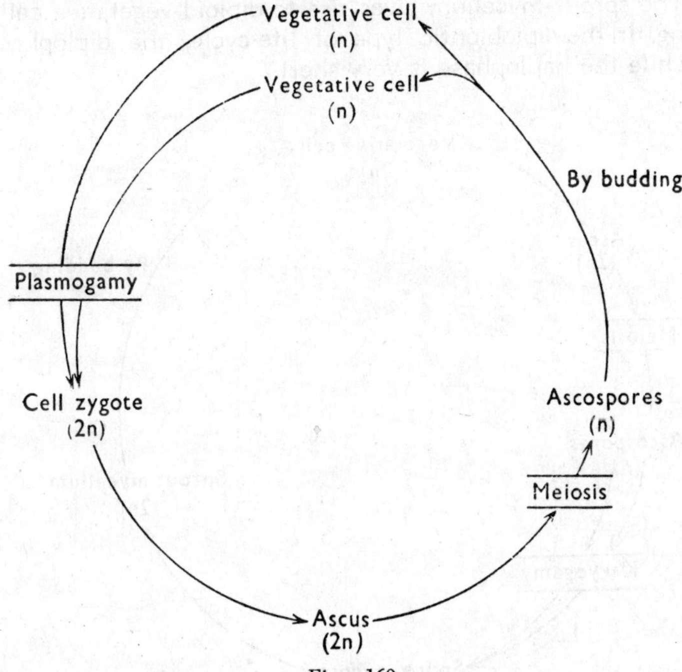

Fig. 160.
Life-cycle of *Schizosaccharomyces octosporus.*

tube then gradually broadens and form a more or less dumbbell-shaped zygote (**cell zygote**). The diploid nucleus of the zygote undergoes three successive division forming eight haploid daughter nuclei. Around each of three nuclei eight **ascospores** are delimited within the mother cell (**zygote**) called as **ascus** (Fig. 159). At maturing the ascus wall bursts, the ascospores are liberated and these under favourable conditions multiply by budding and behave like somatic cells. Thus, it will be observed that in the haplobiontic type of life-cycle the haploid stage (haplophase) is long and the diploid stage (diplophase) is very short. Diplophase is represented by the cell zygote only.

II. Diplobiontic type of life-cycle. This type of life-cycle is exhibited by **Saccharomycodes ludwigii.** In this case the diploid vegetative cells function as **asci.** The nucleus of each ascus divides micotically forming four haploid daughter nuclei around which four **ascospores** are delimited. The ascospores fuse in pairs enclosed within the ascus, forming two diploid zygote (**spore zygote**) .At the time of germination each zygote puts forth a germ-tube, known as **sprout-mycelium,** which comes out of the ascus after piercing its wall. The sprout-mycelium gives rise to diploid vegetative cells by budding. In the diplobiontic type of life-cycle, the diplophase is long while the haplophase is very short.

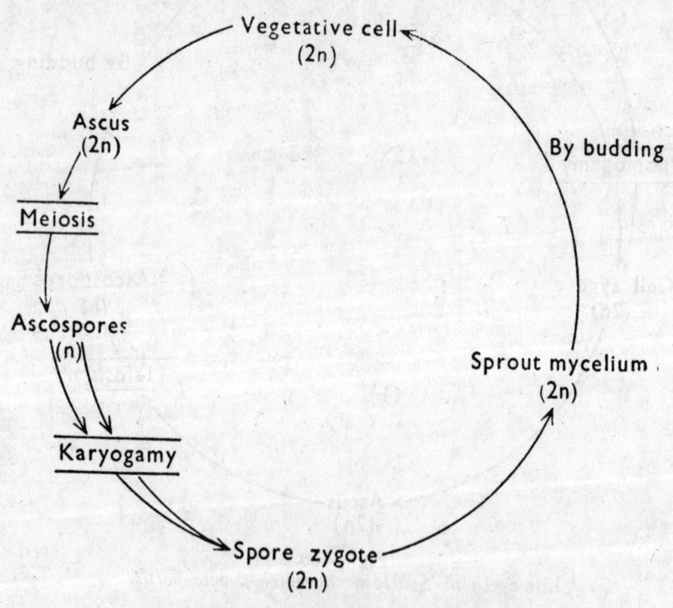

Fig. 161.
Life-cycle of *Saccharomycodes ludwigii.*

III. Haplo-diplobiontic type of life-cycle. This type of life-cycle is exhibited by **Saccharomycervisiae.** Two haploid vegetative cells bearing composite strains conjugate to form a diploid cell (**cell**

zygote). This diploid zygote function as a **vegetative cell** and multiplies by budding subsequently, each diploid cell function as an **ascus.** Each ascus, like the diplobiontic type, produces four haploid **ascospores.** The ascospores on being liberated from the ascus multiplies by the budding producing haploid vegetative cells. In the haplo-diplobiontic type of life-cycle, the haplophase and diplophase are equally well-developed and it clearly indicates that there is a definite alternation of generations in the life-cycle.

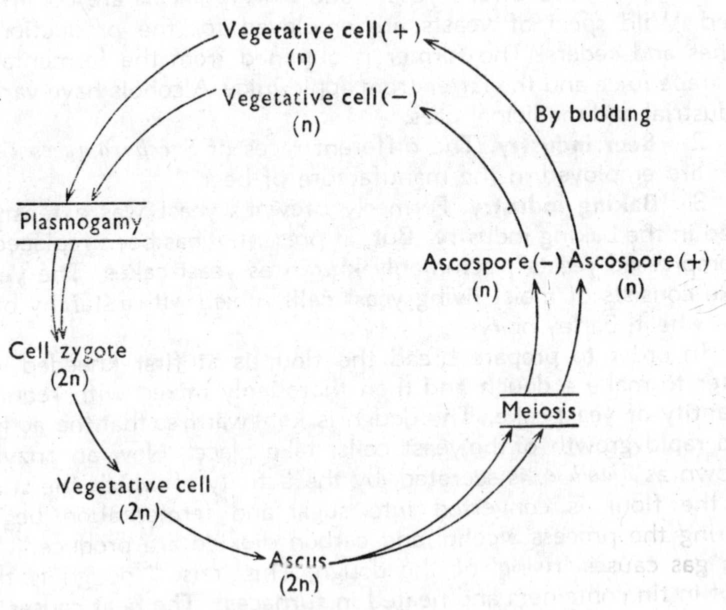

Fig. 162.
Life-cycle of *Saccharomyces cervisiae.*

Economic importance

Yeasts are economically important, both for their harmful as well as beneficial effects. If we consider both these effects, they will be found to be more helpful than harmful.

I. *Harmful yeasts*

1. **Food spoilage.** Our foodstuffs, like tomato products, soft cheese, etc., are spoilt by yeasts, evolving foul 'yeasty' odour.

2. **Diseases.** Some yeasts came diseases of man. *Cryptococcus neoformans* attacks the nervous system causing mental disorder. *Candida albicans* attacks mucous membrane, lungs, skin and nails. *Yeast vaginites* produces female disease.

II. *Beneficial yeasts*

1. **Production of alcohols.** Alcohols are produced by fermentation of sugar by yeasts. Sugar is decomposed by the enzyme (*zymase*) into alcohol and carbon dioxide. The gas is given off in streams of bubbles forming froth, whereas the alcohol remains in the solution. If the supply of oxygen be in excess little alcohol is formed, but when the supply of oxygen is least more alcohol is formed. In fermentation industry two species of yeasts, *Saccharomyces cervisiae* (Brewer's yeast) and *S. ellipsoidens* are commonly used. Wild speci of yeasts are employed for the production of wines and ceders. The former is obtained from the fermentation of grape juice and the latter from apple juice. Alcohols have various industrial and medicinal uses.

2. **Beer industry.** The different races of *Saccharomyces cervisiae* are employed in the manufacture of beer.

3. **Baking industry.** Formerly Brewer's yeast was extensively used in the baking industry. But, at present, it has been replaced by "compressed yeasts", commonly known as yeast-cakes. The yeast-cake consists of moist living yeast cells mixed with a starchy base, like wheat, barley or rye.

In order to prepare bread the flour is at first kneeded with water to make a dough and then thoroughly mixed with requisite quantity of yeast-cake. The dough is kept warm so that the activity and rapid growth of the yeast cells, take place. Now an enzyme, known as *diastase*, is secreted, by the activity of which the starch of the flour is converted into sugar and fermentation begins. During the process alcohol and carbon dioxide are produced, and the gas causes 'rising' of the dough. This 'raised' dough is then kept in tin containers and heated in furnaces. The heat causes the bubbles of the gas to expand and then burst, making the bread porous. Meanwhile, alcohol is vapourised by the heat of the furnace and thus bread is produced.

4. **Medicine.** At present yeasts are extensively used in medicine for treatment of certain skin diseases. Yeast contain antineuratic vitamin, vitamin B, and pellagra preventive vitamins B_2 and G.

EUROTIUM

(Fam. ASPERGILLACEAE)

Most of the species of *Eurotium* are saprophytes and occur on a wide variety of organic substrata. A few species are parasites and cause diseases of the skin, ear and respiratory organs of higher animals including man. They are commonly found as filamentous mouldy growth on the surface of damp fruits and vegetables, preserved fruits, moist breads, jams and various conserves, and also on imperfectly dried herbarium specimens. Many species are commercially important on account of their hydrolysing powers on starch and sugars and cause fermentation to citric and oxalic acids, and rarely to alcohol.

The generic name *Aspergillus* was given to the conidial stage of the fungus long before its ascospores were found, and this name still survives in the name of the family.

Vegetative body (Fig. 163)

The vegetative body is a much-branched mycelium consisting of usually colourless, septate hyphae. It ramifies in or on the surface of the substratum, or through the intercellular spaces of the host tissue. Each hyphal cell contains granulated, vacuolated and multinucleate protoplasm with oil globules as food reserves.

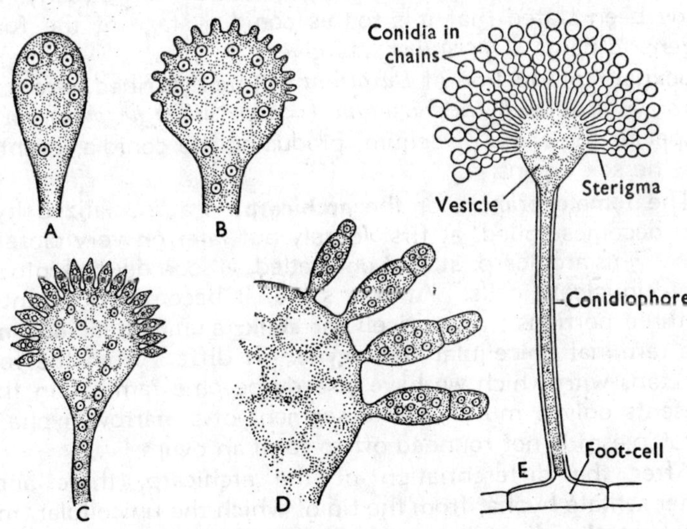

Fig. 163. *Eurotium* (*Aspergillus* stage).
A—D, Successive stages in the development of conidiophore and formation of conidia on sterigmata ; E, A conidiophore with sterigmata bearing conidia in chains (sectional).

Reproduction

Eurotium reproduces both asexually and sexually.

During asexual reproduction numerous straight, thick-walled, aseptate and upright hyphae shoot up in the air. These are called **conidiophores.** The free end of each conidiophore swells up and usually becomes spherical forming a vesicle. This vesicle buds out a large number of peg-like outgrowths, called **sterigmata.** From the tip of each sterigma spherical or nearly spherical, smooth or roughened **conidia** are cut off in basepetal succession, *i.e.* the youngest conidia remain in contact with the sterigmata, while the oldest ones are farthest away from them. The cytoplasm and nuclei stream up the conidiophore into the sterigmata and finally into the developing conidia. The number of nuclei in each conidium is variable and it varies from species to species. Usually, it is multinucleate, but in some rare cases there may be one nucleus in each conidium. The conidia, as they are formed, are not separated from one another for the time being, but they remain in rows or chains on the sterigmata till they become ripe. They are produced in enormous quantities and at maturity become deciduous, and are readily carried away by the wind. Each conidium, under favourable conditions, germinates on a suitable substratum and produces a mycelium directly. It has already been stated that it is to this conidial stage of the fungus, the generic name *Aspergillus* was given.

Sexual reproduction of *Eurotium* will be described here for the bestknown species *E. herbariorum* (=*Aspergillus herbariorum*). In the species the same mycelium, producing the conidia, eventually bears the sex organs.

The female branch, or the **archicarp,** is a specialized hypha, which becomes coiled, at first loosely but later on very closely, in a helix. This archicarp, at first one-celled, is soon divided into several multinucleate cells. At this stage, it becomes differentiated into three portions : a multicellular **stalk,** a unicellular **oogonium,** and a terminal unicellular **trichogyne.** It differs from the female sex organs with which we have already become familiar in that it represents only a multinucleate segment of a narrow hypha, and its protoplasm is not rounded off to form an ovum.

After the differentiation of the archicarp, there appears another septate hypha, from the tip of which the unicellular, multinucleate **antheridium** is cut off. The antheridium develops either independently of the archicarp on another hypha, or is formed on slender branches arising from beneath the archicarp. After its formation, the antheridium appears to climb up the side of the coiled archicarp. The union between the antheridium and the archicarp has not been observed in any case and possibly does not take place. The antheridium appears to be rudimentary and its nuclei usually degenerate before it attains the full size. The growth of the antheridium may even be checked, or the antheridium may not develop at all.

However, the oogonium soon becomes septate and forms binucleate cells. From these binucleate cells small outgrowths develop, which grow and form branched hyphae, the **ascogenous hyphae.** From the terminal or subterminal cell of an ascogenous hypha an

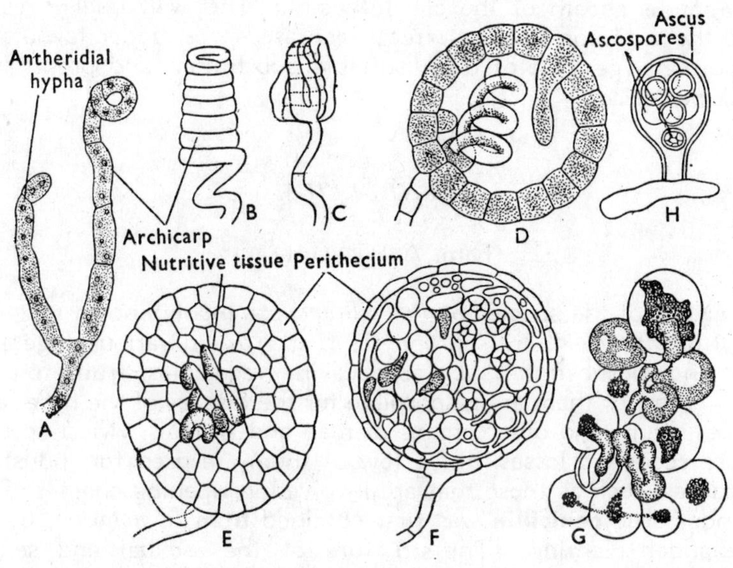

Fig. 164. *Aspergillus herbariorum.*
A—F, Successive stages in the development of a perithecium (cleistothecium) ; G, Group of young asci ; H, A mature ascus with ascospores.

ascus develops. When young, each ascus is binucleate. The two nuclei fuse to form a fusion nucleus. It undergoes three divisions, in one of which reduction in chromosome number takes place, forming eight daughter nuclei, around which **ascospores** are delimited. The cytoplasm, which is not used up in the formation of ascospores, constitutes the **epiplasm** containing food substances, especially glycogen. Each ascospore has a sculptured spore wall (**epispore**) and is of characteristic form, and when seen laterally, somewhat resembles a pulley wheel or a butcher's tray.

A little before the septation of the oogonium some vegetative hyphae grow up and cover the sex organs. The hyphae by interweaving and septation form a thick outer wall of small-celled pseudoparenchyma which completely encloses the sex organs. Some of the hyphae grow inwards and form a nutritive tissue around the sex organs. The entire structure, thus formed, is the fructification of *Eurotium* and is termed a **cleistothecium.** The wall of the cleistothecium becomes invested with a brittle-yellow substance. At maturity, the ascogenous hyphae, the cells of the nutritive tissue and the walls of the asci disintegrate and are ultimately absorbed, so that the ascospores lie free within the outer brittle pseudoparenchymatous sheath of the cleistothecium. This wall finally decays and the ascospores are set free. Each ascospore, under favourable conditions, germinates on a suitable substratum and produces a new mycelium.

PENICILLIUM

(Fam. ASPERGILLACEAE)

Most of the species of *Penicillium*, commonly known as *green mold* or *blue mold*, are saprophytes that grow on various vegetable and animal substrata, such as decaying vegetables, fruits, meats, etc. A few of them are responsible for the diseaes of the nose, ear, throat, lungs and other organs of man and animals. Most species cause economic losses, but a few of them are used for industrial purposes, such as those that are involved in ripening cheeses. The wonder drug **penicillin** was first obtained from *P. notatum*, by Sir Alexander Fleming. The structure of the asexual and sexual reproductive organs vary from species to species. *P. vermiculatum* is one of the species whose life-history has been fairly worked out and a brief description of the fungus is given in the following paragraphs.

Vegetative body

The mycelium consists of much-branched, septate and anastomosing hyphae that creep over the surface of the substratum and produce very fine rhizoids, which penetrate the substratum and draw nourishment therefrom. The hyphal cells are constantly uninucleate. When the fungus grows on potato, the mycelium is at first colourless, then slowly becomes sulphur-yellow and eventually reddish with age.

Reproduction

Penicillium reproduces both asexually and sexually.

Asexual reproduction takes place by means of **conidia**, which are cut off from the apices of the **conidiophores** (Fig. 165). Aerial slender branches, consisting of 2-3 cells, grow upwards from the mycelium and form the conidiophores. Each conidiophore produces a whorl of symmetrical branches at its tip, and each of these branches, in its turn, produces a number of closely-packed branches in a whorl. These ultimate branches are known as **sterigmata,** and the branches bearing the sterigmata are called **metulae.** The whole branching system constitutes the **penicillus,** meaning a brush or broom, which is the characteristic of the genus *Penicillium.* Each sterigma is a slender tube, narrowed at its apex to a long acuminate point, from which elliptical, thick-walled, minutely spiny and uninucleate conidia are successively cut off in a chain. The conidia are deciduous and are usually disseminated by the wind. Each conidium, under favourable conditions, puts forth a germ tube, which ramifying produces a new mycelium.

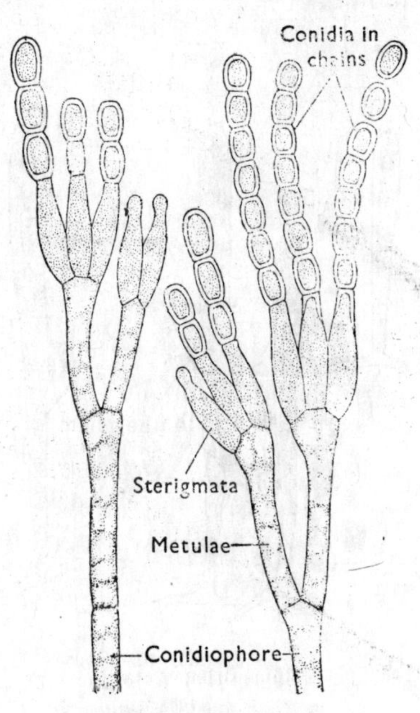

Fig. 165. *Penicillium.* Conidiophores bearing sterigmata and conidia in chains.

Sexual reproduction is oogamous. The **ascogonium** develops from erect unicellular hyphal branches. When young, it is uninucleate. As it elongates, the nucleus divides and re-divides to form 32-64 nuclei, which are distributed in the general mass of the cytoplasm of the ascogonium. Meanwhile, another uninucleate branch develops from a neighbouring hypha and cuts off a uninucleate terminal cell, the **antheridium.** This antheridial branch, during its development, forms several spirals around the ascogonium. The tip of the antheridium becomes applied to the ascogonium, and at the point of their mutual contact a pore is formed by the dissolution of the intervening walls. The actual fusion between the male and female nuclei has not, however, been observed so far, but owing to the heterothallic nature of the fungus, it can be assumed that gametic union possibly takes place. In any case, the multinucleate ascogonium undergoes septation to form a row of binucleate cells, and from these cells one or more **ascogenous hyphae** of binucleate cells grow out. Meanwhile, sterile entangled vegetative hyphae grow up around the sex organs and form a loosely-felted outer region of a mature **ascocarp** (**cleistothecium**). Further details of the ascus development are unknown, but mature asci have been found to lie irregularly distributed within a mature

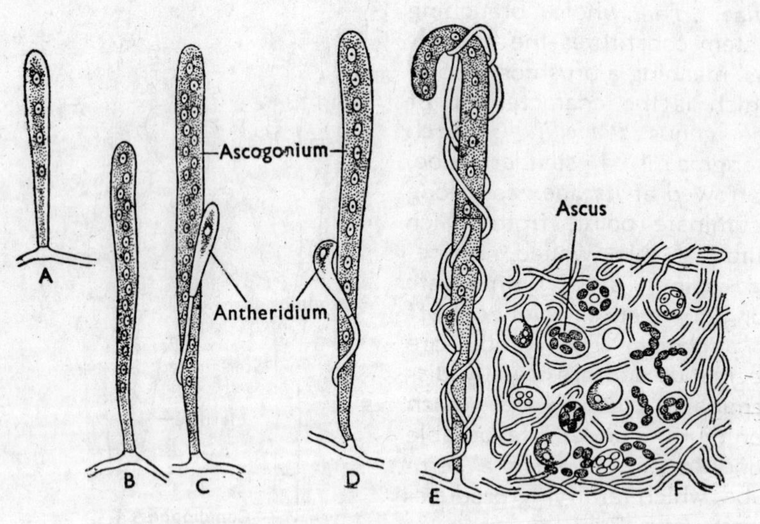

Fig. 166. *Penicillium.*
A—B, Young ascogonia ; C—D, Ascogonium after development of antheridium ; E, Ascogonium surrounded with sterile hyphae ; F, T.S. of an ascocarp showing asci, sterile hyphae, etc.

ascocarp. Each **ascus** is somewhat globose in shape and contains 4 to 6 elliptical **ascospores** with minutely spiny outer wall. Since the fungus is heterothallic, the ascospores are of two sexes. On germination, they give rise to different types of mycelia consisting of uninucleate hyphal cells.

ORDER **ERYSIPHALES**

Superficially growing parasites ; aerial mycelia colourless or dark-coloured ; mostly having a single layer of cylindrical asci arranged parallel to one another within a cleistothecium with prominent appendages. Common genera are *Erysiphae*, *Spherovheca*, etc.

ERYSIPHE

(Fam. ERYSIPHACEAE)

Several species of *Erysiphe* cause a type of plant disease, generally known as the *powdery mildew* or *blight*. They are so called, because the large number of conidia, produced by the causal agent on the surface of the host, appear as white powdery patches. The disease is widely distributed throughout the world. Some of the species cause serious damage to a number of vegetables and ornamental plants. About 10 species have been reported on a wide variety of hosts, of which *Erysiphe polygoni* is described in the following paragraphs. This species is responsible for the disease known as '*powdery mildew of peas*'. Every year, particularly by the end of January or in February, the recognizable symptoms of the powdery mildew appear on the pea plants. At first white powdery spots become visible on the upper surface of the leaves, but gradually these extend to the lower surface as well. Eventually, the leaves turn yellowish and fall off. Sometimes the leaves become reduced in size and the infected pods get dried and shrivelled.

Vegetative body

The mycelium consisting of short uninucleate cells is entirely superficial. It is attached to the leaves and draws nourishment by means of haustorial branches that pierce the walls of the living cells of the host.

Reproduction

Erysiphe polygoni reproduces both asexually and sexually.

At the time of **asexual reproduction** somatic hyphae produce a large number of erect **conidiophores,** which bear several **conidia** in chains at their tips. The conidia are usually hyaline, elliptical. sometimes barrel-shaped or cylindrical. When these conidia fall on a suitable host, they germinate under favourable conditions and produce mycelia. It has been recorded by Brodie (1945) that a considerable percentage of conidia may germinate in air entirely devoid of moisture.

During **sexual reproduction,** usually **male** and **female gametangia** come in cantact. At first their intervening walls dissolve, and then nuclear migration takes place. There is a considerable difference of opinion regarding the nuclear fusion. Possibly after nuclear fusion, the female gametangium, the **oogonium,** elongates and divides to form a row of cells. The penultimate cell of the newly formed row gives rise to **ascogenous hyphae,** from the cells of which **asci** are developed. During the development of asci, the sex organs are surrounded by the nearby hyphae forming the outer

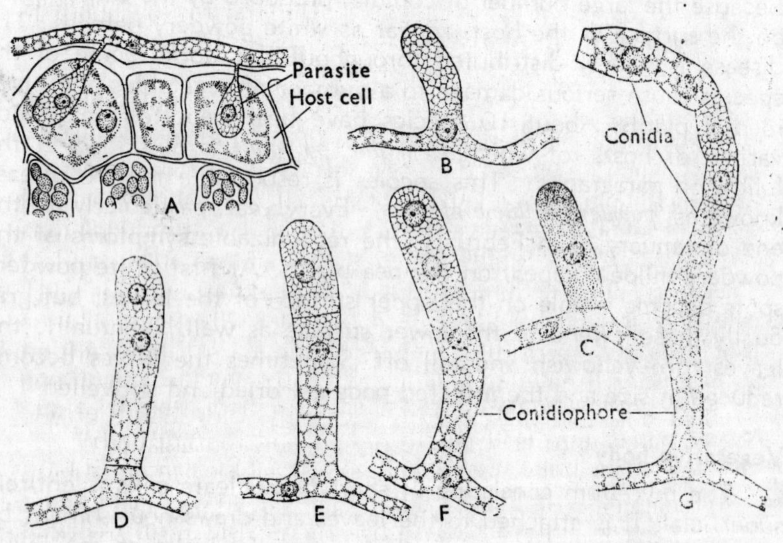

Fig. 167. *Erysiphe.*
A, Parasitic haustoria within epidermal cells of the host ; B—G, Stages in the development of conidia on the conidiophore.

layer of the **cleistothecium.** This cleistothecium is spherical to subglobose and composed of polygonal cells. They are covered by long, unbranched, interwoven or free appendages. Generally 2 to 8 asci are found within the cleistothecium. Each ascus is ovate and usually contains 4 **ascospores.** These are hyaline, elliptical and one-celled. When the ascospores mature, they are discharged from the ascus and also from the cleistothecium, fall on the suitable host and germinate under favourable conditions giving rise to new mycelia.

Control measures

The disease may be controlled by treating the seeds with water at 50°C for 10 minutes, or dusting the plants with sulphur as well as by selecting the resistant varieties.

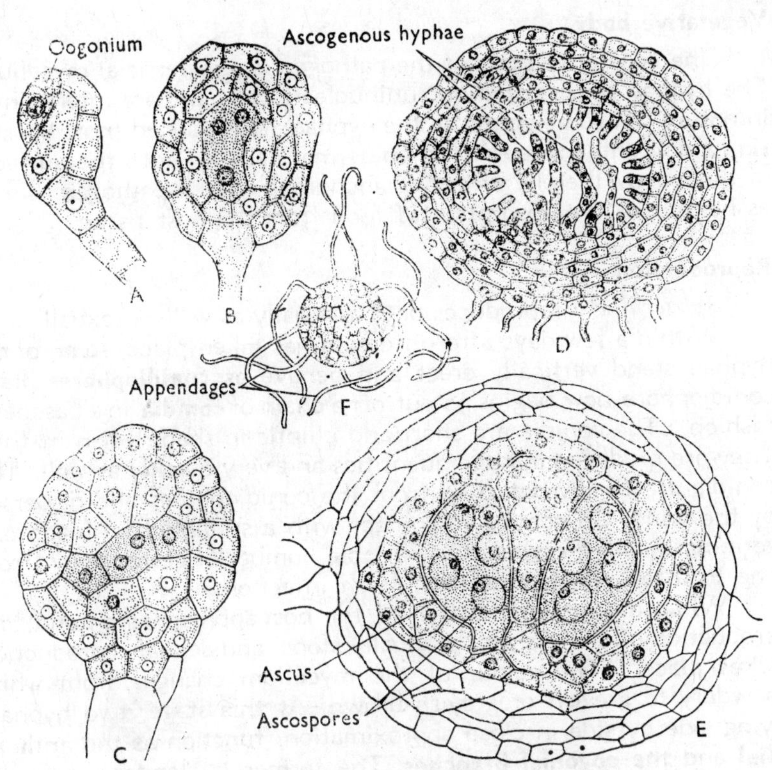

Fig. 168. *Erysiphe.*
A—E, Gradual stages in the formation of sex organs and subsequent development of ascus and ascospores ; F, A cleistothecium.

SPHAEROTHECA

(Fam. ERYSIPHACEAE)

Sphaerotheca is a common parasitic fungus. It occurs every year during the later part of the winter season in the Indo-Gangetic plain, while in the hills it grows in summer as well. Some of the species are important from the economic standpoint, as they cause damage to several cultivated crop plants, such as rose, hops, strawberry, gooseberry, raspberry and various cucurbits.

The disease first makes its appearance as patches of white powdery masses on the leaves, stems and sometimes even on the flowers of the host plants. Very quickly these patches extend and completely cover up the surfaces on which they are growing. The popular name of the disease is the *powdery mildew.*

Vegetative body

The vegetative body of the pathogen is a superficial mycelium. The hyphae consist of short, uninucleate cells and are intertwining in nature. At some points on the hyphae are produced short **haustoria,** which enter through the epidermal cells on both the surfaces of the leaves, thereby effecting anchorage for the pathogen as well as helping in the absorption of food from the host tissue.

Reproduction

Sphaerotheca reproduces both asexually as well as sexually.

Within a few days after infection has taken place, some of the hyphae stand vertically erect and behave as **conidiophores.** Each conidiophore now begins to cut off a chain of **conidia** in a basepetal fashion. The conidia are short and elliptic in shape when mature. They are produced in huge quantities and very quickly as well. The conidia are finally detached from the conidiophores and dispersed by the wind. On coming in contact with a suitable host, each one germinates and gives rise to a variable number of germ tubes (from one to three) which then start fresh infections.

When the growing season of the host approaches an end, the production of conidia also gradually stops, and sexual reproduction takes place. The colour of the mycelium changes from white powdery to greyish or greyish-brown. At this stage, two hyphae, lying side by side in close approximation, function as the **antheridial** and the **oogonial branches.** The former is slender, while the latter is somewhat stouter and round. A partition wall is laid down in the antheridial branch, thereby forming a terminal, uninucleate **antheridium** on a uninucleate stalk cell. The oogonial branch may remain unicellular and uninucleate, or may be divided to give rise to a minute stalk cell and the large, terminal, uninucleate cell, which is the **oogonium** proper or the **ascogonium.** The antheridium comes in contact with the ascogonium, dissolution takes place at the point of contact, and the antheridial nucleus passes down into the ascogonium. According to some workers, like Harpar and others, these two nuclei fuse in the ascogonium, while Claussen, Bergemann and others consider that they do not undergo any fusion within the ascogonium. Subsequent to this, the ascogonium elongates and becomes partitioned into three to five cells. Of this row of cells, the penultimate one is binucleate, while the rest are all uninucleate. Inside the penultimate cell the two nuclei undergo fusion, and thus this cell is regarded as the **ascus mother cell.** The ascus mother cell enlarges to some extent forming the **ascus,** and by three successive nuclear divisions eight **ascospores** are formed within it. Each ascospore is a haploid body, and on being forcibly liberated from the ascus and coming in contact with a suitable host, germinates and starts the infection afresh.

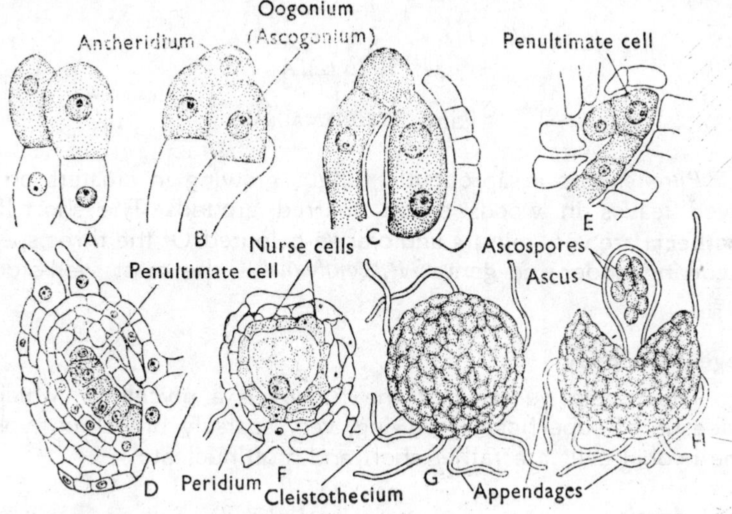

Fig. 169. *Sphaerotheca.*
A—E, Stages in the development of sex organs ; F, The young ascus mother cell surrounded by a layer of 'nurse cells' ; G, A mature cleistothecium ; H, The same bursting out to liberate the ascus.

While the ascus is developing, some of the hyphae from beneath the ascogonium, rapidly grow up and enclose it completely by forming the **peridium.** As a result, a **cleistothecium** is produced. The innermost layer of the peridium, which is two to three layers thick, supplies nourishment to the developing ascus ; the cells of this layer are termed the **nurse cells** by Hein (1927). From some of the cells of the outer protective layer of the peridium filamentous mycelоid appendages come out. The cleistothecia are minute and round in shape, which are more or less white when young, turning black with age. Each cleistothecium contains a solitary ascus. This ascus swells up by absorbing moisture, cracks open the cleistothecium and emerges out. Finally, the tip of the ascus dehisces and the ascospores are liberated.

ORDER **PEZIZALES**

Saprophytes with well-developed mycelia ; ascocarp usually fleshy but sometimes leathery apothecium (usually cup-shaped) usually bounded by a peridium, which is closed at first but later on pushed open exposing the hymenium ; ascus contains usually 8 (sometimes more or less) ascospores, and opening by the shedding of an operculum. Common genera are *Peziza*, *Ascobolus*, *Humaria*, *Pyronema*, etc.

PYRONEMA

(Fam. PYRONEMACEAE)

Pyronema is a saprophytic fungus growing in clusters on decayed leaves in woods or on charred grounds. The short-lived **apothecia** are very minute and orange-coloured. Of the three species occurring under the genus, *P. confluens* is the most well-studied one.

Vegetative body

The vegetative body of the fungus is a mycelium, which is made up of superficially growing, very sparsely branched hyphae. The hyphal cells are rather short and multinucleate.

Reproduction

Pyronema reproduces both asexually and sexually.

During asexual reproduction some of the hyphae from the vegetative body stand erect and cut off chains of **conidia** from their tips. Each conidium is capable of giving rise to a new mycelium on germination.

Pyronema is a homothallic fungus with well-developed sex organs. Though the vegetative hyphae are rarely branched, some of them which bear the sex organs, become forked at one or more points. From these forkings lateral branches develop in upward directions forming tufts. These hyphae then branch repeatedly in a dichotomous fashion, and the ultimate cells of each pair become converted into an **antheridium** or an **ascogonium.** The antheridium is clavate in form and is borne upon one or two stalk cells. The stalk cells are uninucleate, while the antheridium is multinucleate. In the female branch, similarly, the baloon-shaped swollen, multinucleate ascogonium is borne on one or two stalk cells. From the distal end of the unicellular ascogonium a curved, tubular, unicellular but multinucleate structure, the **trichogyne,** is produced. As the sex organs mature, the nuclei in both the antheridium as well as the ascogonium enlarge in size ; those in the trichogyne, however, remain minute and do not increase in size, and finally disintegrate.

The trichogyne comes in contact with the antheridium and dissolution of walls at the point of union takes place. Meanwhile, the nuclei of the trichogyne are degenerated, and the antheridial nuclei

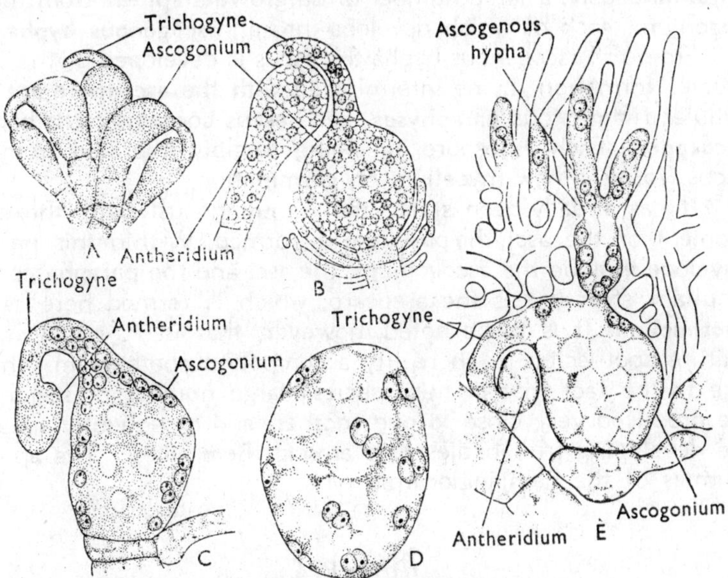

Fig. 170. *Pyronema.*
A—B, Sex organs ; C, Union of sex organs and the passage of antheridial nuclei into the ascogonium ; D, Union of nuclei inside the ascogonium ; E, Dikaryotic ascogenous hypha.

with some amount of cytoplasm migrate into the trichogyne. Now the common wall in between the trichogyne and the ascogonium also undergoes disorganization*, and the ascogonial nuclei move towards the centre of the ascogonium. From the trichogyne the antheridial nuclei with the cytoplasm then migrate into the ascogonium and lie in close association with the ascogonial nuclei. Though plasmogamy takes place immediately, the actual fusion of the male and female nuclei in pairs remains a very much debatable point. Some workers consider that karyogamy occurs within the ascogonium, and as a result the nuclei become diploid, while others are of opinion that the male and female nuclei simply lie in pairs or in small groups in very close proximity but do not fuse. The present-day wokers favour the latter view.

* According to some workers (Buller, 1933 ; Wilson, 1952) a pore is formed in the common wall separating the trichogyne from the ascogonium through which the antheridial nuclei migrate downwards. After the migration is over, this pore is blocked by the **pore plug,** a granular body.

Within a few hours of the aforesaid process the ascogonium becomes invested by a **peridium,** which is an envelope formed by the vegetative hyphae originating from the lower cells of the tuft. Simultaneously, a large number of outgrowths appear from the ascogonium, each of which develops into an **ascogenous hypha.**

From the ascogenous hypha the ascus is developed by the usual crozier formation. Lying intermingled with the asci there are unicellular filamentous **paraphyses.** Each ascus contains eight haploid **ascospores.** Each ascospore, on being forcibly liberated from the ascus, forms a new mycelium on germination.

It has already been stated that simultaneously with the development of the asci, the peridium is formed. Within this peridial envelope thus lie the ascogonium, the asci and the paraphyses. The resultant structure is the ascocarp, which is termed here as the **apothecium.** It is to be noted, however, that in *P. confluens* the mature apothecium is in reality a compound apothecium. This is due to the fact that in this species a large number of sex organs are produced very close to one another, and cosequently some of the developing fruit bodies fuse among themselves. The apothecium is of the hemiangiocarpic type.

HUMARIA

(Fam. PEZIZACEAE)

All the members of the genus *Humaria* are saprophytes. Two common species of the genus are *H. granulata* and *H. rutians*. The former grows on cowdung and the latter, on soil rich in humus or among the mosses.

Vegetative body

The vegetative body is a much-branched mycelium. The hyphae are septate and the hyphal cells contain comparatively large nuclei and granular contents.

Reproduction

Humaria reproduces both sexually and asexually. Sexual reproduction is very variable as there is a great reduction of sex organs.

In *H. granulata* (Fig. 171) the female sex organ, the ascogonium, is only developed, while the antheridium is totally absent. The *archicarp*, or the female branch, arises as a lateral branch from the vegetative hypha. It consists of a long multicellular stalk and a terminal, spherical or oval, multinucleate cell, known as the *ascogonium* or *oogonium*, but the trichogyne is lacking. The nuclei of two vegetative hyphae bearing opposite strains fuse, and the fusion nuclei migrate into the ascogonium and arrange themselves in pairs

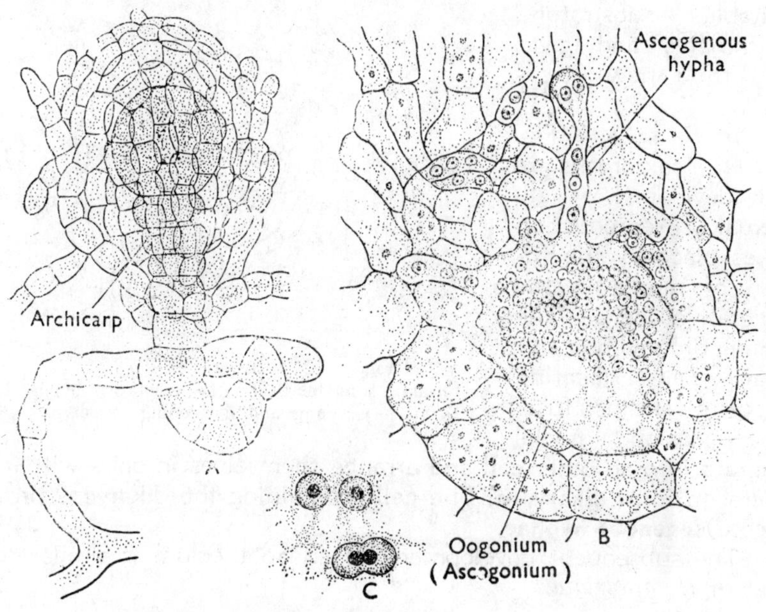

Fig. 171. *Humaria granulata.*
A, A young archicarp ; B, An ascogenous hypha being produced from the ascogonium ; C, Fusion of nuclei in pairs taking place inside the ascogenous hypha.

with its nuclei. These pairs of nuclei are called *dikaryons*. There is difference of opinion whether complete fusion of the dikaryons takes place or not. However, the dikaryons pass into the **ascogenous hyphae,** produced from the ascogonium. The entire structure is now becomes surrounded by a protective covering formed by a number of intertwining vegetative hyphae. Now nuclear fusion takes place resulting in the formation of dull red or orange coloured **apothecium.** The apothecia are small just like the size of pin heads.

A vertical section through the apothecium shows that the concave surface of the cup is lined by the **hymenium,** consisting of long cylindrical **asci** intermingled with the septate hyphae, the **para-**

physes. The asci do not extend beyond the level of the hymenium. Each ascus contains 8 **ascospores,** arranged uniseriately. Each ascospore on being liberated and falling on suitable substratum, germinates and gives rise to a new mycelium.

In *H. rutilans* (Fig. 172) the sex organs are not developed at all. Sexual reproduction takes place by the fusion of nuclei in the vegetative cells. The nuclei of any two hyphal cells bearing opposite strains fuse. The fusion nuclei migrate into an other cell and arrange themselves in pairs with its nuclei to form **dikaryons.** The cells containing the dikaryons produce **ascogenous hyphae.**

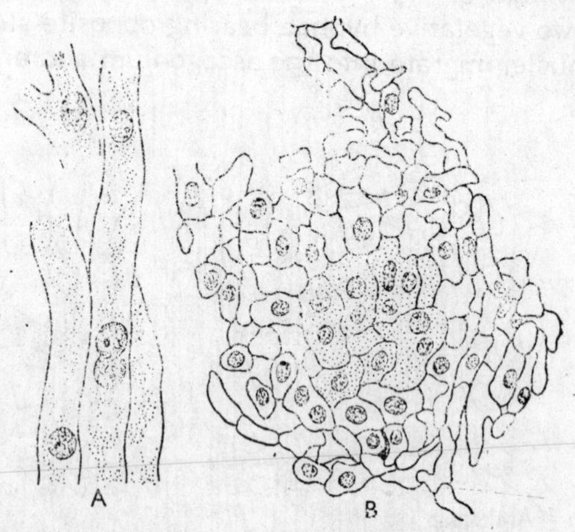

Fig. 172. *Humaria rutilans.*
A, Fusion of nuclei inside the vegetative hypha ;
B, A very young and developing ascocarp.

The subsequent development of an apothecium is similar to that of *H. granulata.*

PEZIZA

(Fam. PEZIZACEAE)

Most species of *Peziza* are saprophytic on ground, on dead wood or on dung.

Vegetative body

The mycelium generally grows in soils rich in organic matter, or in decaying wood. The mycelial filaments are divided by septa into multinucleate cells and the branching is extensive.

Reproduction

Peziza reproduces both asexually and sexually. Excepting the formation of ascospores, asexual reproduction is rare, and takes place by means of conidia.

At the time of sexual reproduction, there arises from the mycelium a conspicuous fruit body known as the **apothecium.** Usually,

Fig. 173. A few fruit bodies of *Peziza* growing on ground.

the apothecium is a fleshy, sessile or sub-sessile cup or saucer-shaped body, regular in form, often brightly coloured, 2 to 40 cm. in diameter, and without any hair. A vertical section through the apothecium shows that the upper surface constitues the **hymenium,**

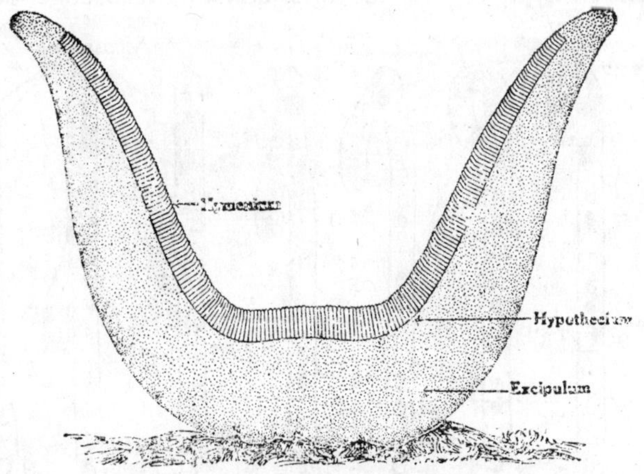

Fig. 174. *Peziza.*
Vertical section through the apothecium.

a layer of elongated cells standing at right angles to the surface like a palisade. It consists of **asci** intermingled with supporting and protective filamentous hyphae, the **paraphyses.** Immediately below the hymenium is a layer, thin or fairly thick, the **hypothecium,** consisting mainly of light-coloured hyphae and running parallel to the surface of the hymenium. The basal portion of the cup is known as the **excipulum.**

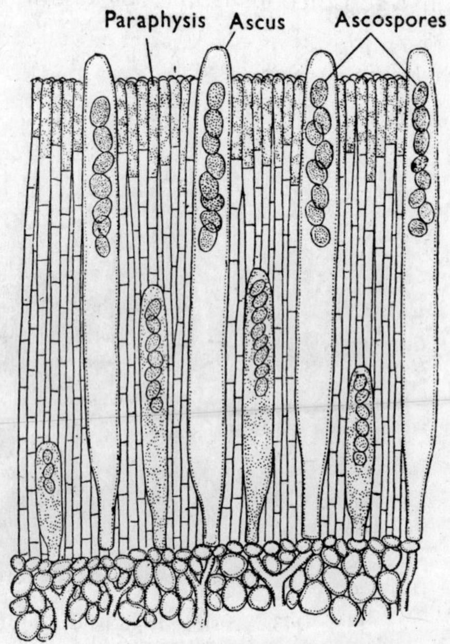

Fig. 175. *Peziza.*
Part of a section through the hymenium showing asci with ascospores and paraphyses.

The sex organs are entirely absent in *Peziza*, but somatic copulation occurs between certain vegetative cells at the time of reproduction. Consequently, the nucleus of one cell migrates into the other and thus a binucleate cell is formed. Such binucleate cells give rise to a number of **ascogenous hyphae.** The terminal cell of the ascogenous hypha

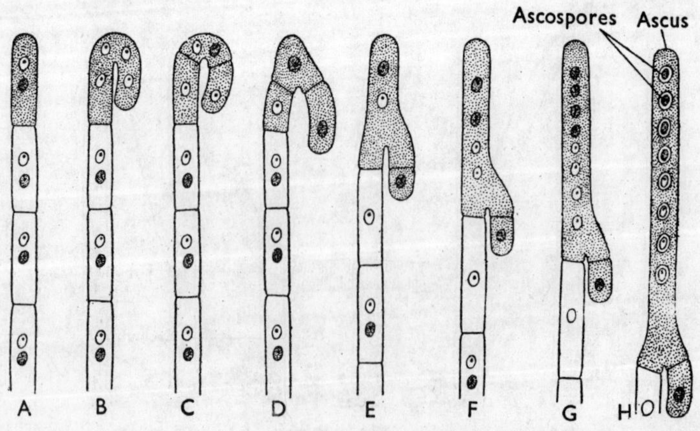

Fig. 176. *Peziza.*
A—H, Successive stages in the development of ascus.

elongates and bends over forming a crozier, and the **ascus** is developed in the usual way. Eight haploid **ascospores** are produced within each ascus. The fully formed ascospores are oval, unicellular and hyaline. When they become mature, each ascus opens explosively by a lid and the spores are shot out in a jet of liquid. Each spore, under favourable conditions, germinates and forms a new mycelium.

ASCOBOLUS

(Fam. ASCOBOLACEAE)

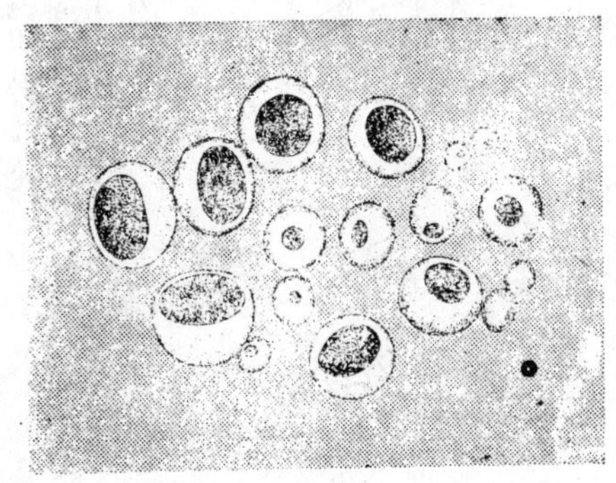

Fig. 177. A few fruit bodies of *Ascobolus* growing on ground.

The members of the genus *Ascobolus* are generally found growing saprophytically on cow-dung, horse-dung and on the excreta of other animals ; sometimes they are also found on the soil rich in organic matters. Of the various species of the genus, the life-history of *A. magnificus* is described below.

Vegetative body (Fig. 178)

The mycelium of the fungus consists of much-branched, septate, hyphal cells with protoplasm, and a considerable amount of oil drops as reserve foods.

Reproduction

A. magnificus reproduces both sexually and asexually.

Though the fungus is morphologically homothallic and bears both types of sex organs, **antheridia** and **ascogonia**, yet it is self-sterile, because union does not take place between the sex organs of the same mycelium ; only the sex organs of two complementary mycelia unite with each other. In this sense, the fungus is physiologically heterothalic and cross-fertile. As a result of this union, the fruit body, the **apothecium**, is formed. The male sex organs, the **antheridia**, and the female sex organs, the **ascogonia**, may develop from the hyphae of both the complementary strains. The antheridium is multinucleate, and more or less clavate or cylindrical in form. The ascogonium, on the other hand, is also multinucleate, and a globose structure with a terminal septate portion, the **trichogyne.** When the antheridium and the ascogonium of the complementary strains meet, the trichogyne first twists round the

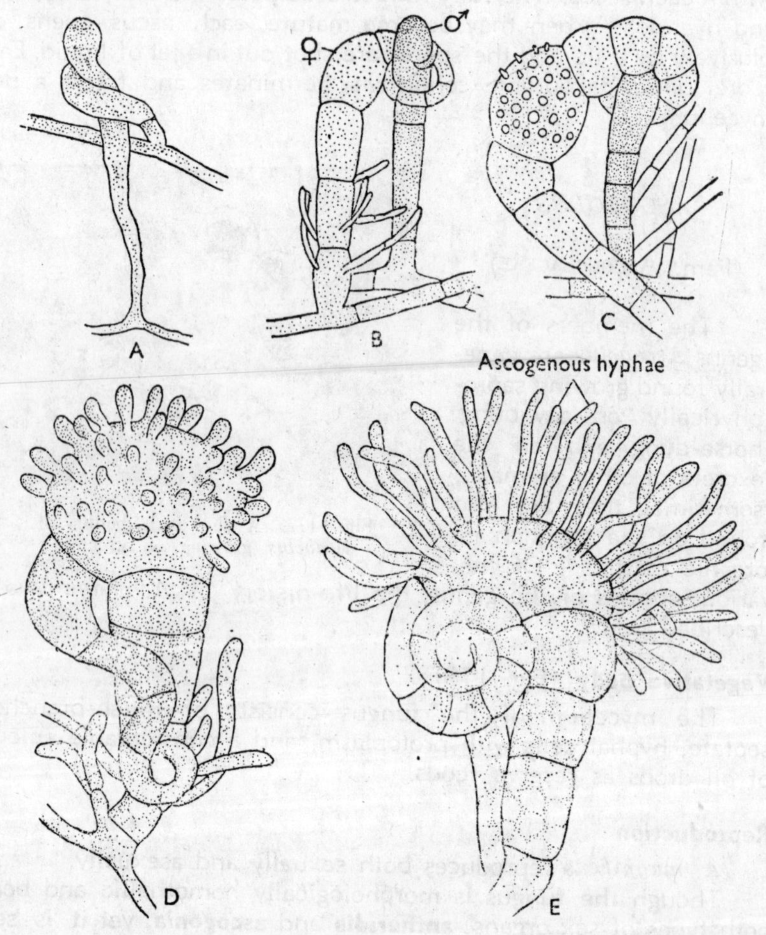

Fig. 178. *Ascobolus.*
A—E, Successive stages in the development of sex organs and the subsequent formation of ascogenous hyphae.

antheridium, and a passage is established in between the antheridium and the terminal cell of the trichogyne. The male nuclei then travel through the trichogyne, and fuse in pairs with the female nuclei in the ascogonium.

After fertilization, numerous **ascogenous hyphae** begin to develop from the ascogonium, and a number of paired nuclei enter into them. As the ascogenous hyphae elongate, they undergo septation. The **ascus** develops from the binucleate penultimate

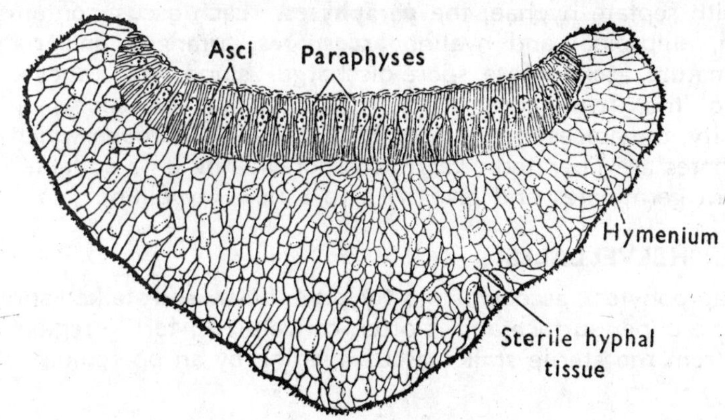

Fig. 179. ***Ascobolus.***
V. S. of apothecium.

cell of each ascogenous hypha by the usual crozier formation method. The eight **ascospores** of each ascus are ultimately discharged, and they germinate under favourable conditions to form new mycelia. During the sexual union, several vegetative hyphae grow up surrounding the sex organs, unite, and there finally arises a fleshy, cup- or saucer-shaped fruit body, known as the **apothecium.** Common genera are *Helvella*, *Morchella*, etc.

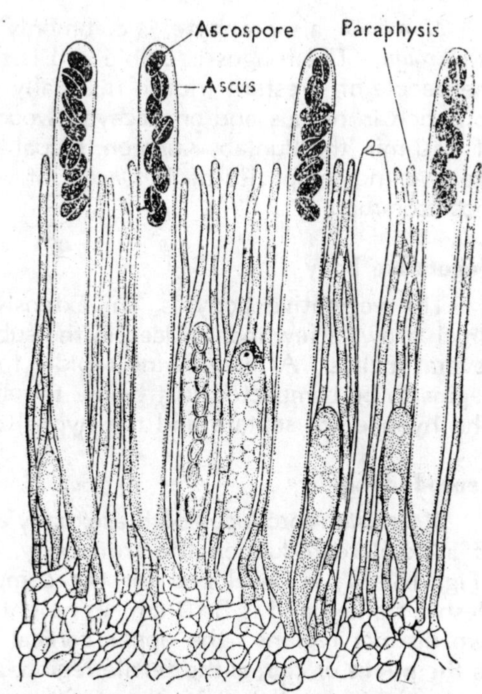

Fig. 180. *Ascobolus.*
Part of a vertical section through the hymenium showing asci with ascospores and paraphyses.

A vertical section through an apothecium shows that the concave surface of the cup is lined by **hymenium** and the basal portion is composed of a mass of sterile hyphal tissue

(Fig. 180). The hymenium consists of cylindrical **asci** intermingled with septate hyphae, the **paraphyses.** Each ascus contains 8 brown, ellipsoidal and hyaline **ascospores**, arranged uniseriately. The mature asci, before spore-discharge, stand well above the level of the hymenium (Fig. 180). When the spores attain maturity, the apices of asci usually open by lids, through which the ascospores are liberated. Each ascospore falling on a suitable substratum germinates and gives rise to a new mycelium.

ORDER **HELVELLALES**

Saprophytes ; ascocarps mostly large, fleshy and stalked spreads over the upper surface and is often convoluted ; fertile region distinct from the sterile stalk ; ascus opening by an operculum.

MORCHELLA

(Fam. HELVELLACEAE)

Morchella, a saprophyte, is commonly known as *morel* or *sponge mushroom.* The fungus is edible and is taken with great relish by the people of Western India. It usually grows in cluster on moist soils rich in humus and on decayed wood in the deciduous forests of Kashmir, the Punjab, Kumaon, Nepal and Uttar Pradesh. There are five Indian species of *Morchella*, of which *M. esenlenta* is the most common.

Vegetative body (Fig. 181)

The vegetative body is an extensively branched mycelium which grows a few inches deep in the substratum and extends over several inches. After growing rapidly for sometime mycelial mat begins to be compacted just below the surface of the substratum. The hyphae are septate and the hyphal cells are multinucleate.

Reproduction

Morchella reproduces both asexually and sexually. At the time of asexual reproduction the fruit body, known as the **ascocarp** (Fig. 181A), is developed for the compacted hyphal mat. It is fleshy, stalked and is 8-10 cm. in height. A mature ascocarp has two distinct regions : the upper conical spongy structure, known as the **pileus** or **cap,** is the fertile region, and the stalk (also known as **stipe)** bearing the cap is the sterile region. When the archicarp emerges from the soil, the cap is at first smooth but later on due to irregular growth ridges and furrows are formed and it becomes more or less convoluted in appearance. The stipe as well as the ridges are cream-coloured, but the furrows are brown in colour.

A vertical section through the ascocarp (Fig. 181C) shows

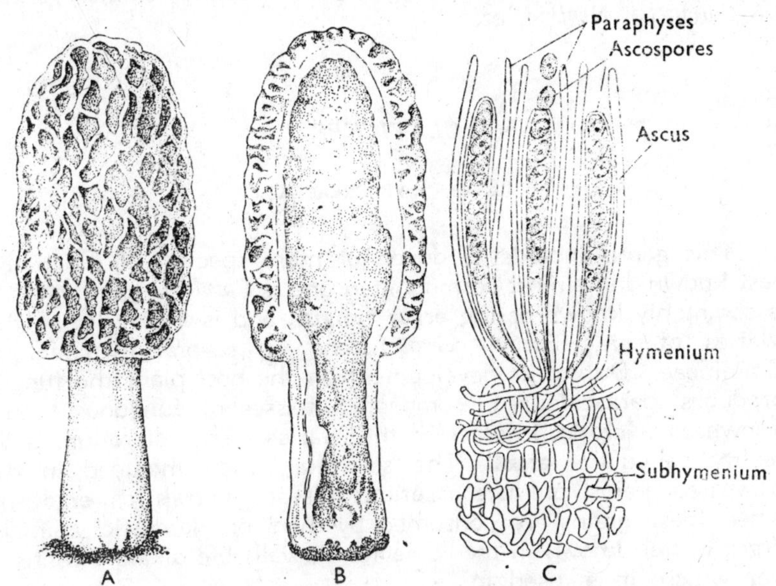

Fig. 181. *Morchella.*
A, A fruit body (ascocarp) ; B, V.S. of the same ; C, Part of a section through the hymenial region.

that the stipe is composed of pseudoparenchyma cells, and the furrows are lined with the **hymenium,** or the fertile layer. The hymenium consists of long cylindrical **asci** intermingled with **paraphyses.** In between the cells of the stipe and the hymenium layer, just below the latter, a group of multinucleate cells occur, forming the **sub-hymenium.** Each ascus contains 8 oval hyaline **ascospores,** arranged uniseriately.

When the ascospores attain maturity, the ascocarp withers and the epices of asci open by lids through which the ascospores are liberated. Each ascospore falling on a suitable substratum germinates and gives rise to a new mycelium.

In *Morchella* sex organs have not yet been discovered. Sexual reproduction takes place by the fusion of nuclei in the vegetative cells.

ORDER **HYPOCREALES**

Parasites or saprophytes ; mycelium usually forms a stroma (parenchymatous mass) in which the perithecia are partially or entirely embedded ; the perithecia ; wall and stroma, when present, are distinct, soft in texture, colourless or light-coloured ; asci are formed within the perithecium ; peridium absent. Common genera are *Claviceps*, *Nectria*, etc.

CLAVICEPS

(Fam. HYPOCREACEAE)

This genus includes a dozen or more species of which the best known and almost cosmopolitan one is *Claviceps purpurea*. It is commonly known as the **ergot fungus,** and is a parasite on the ovaries of rye (*Secale cereale*) and on several members of Gramineae. During its development on the host plant the fungus produces dark-coloured, compacted masses of funguous tissue, known as **sclerotia,** in place of the ovaries. The sclerotium is, in reality, called the **ergot.** The sclerotia, when included in the harvested grains, produce a serious disease known as **ergotism,** when these grains are consumed by man or domestic animals. Ergot is well known in medicine for its valuable alkaloid-contents for which it is used in small doses for stopping haemorrhage after child-birth, as well as in larger doses for causing profuse blood discharge.

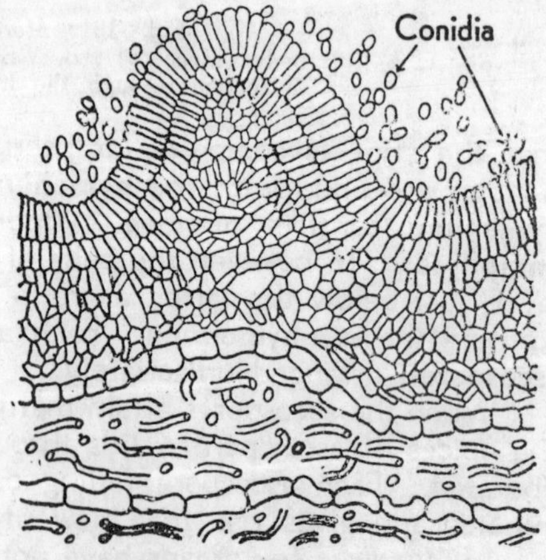

Fig. 182. *Claviceps*. Formation of conidia showing 'sphacelia stage'.

During the flowering season of the host plants, ascospores, being carried away by the wind, reach the ovaries, ultimately germinate there and bring about infection. The germ tube, produced on germination of an ascospore, penetrates the wall of the ovary, ramifies and produces a much-branched mycelium of septate hyphae within it. Finally, the ovary is destroyed and is replaced by a soft mycelial mass having the same shape of the ovary. From the surface of this mycelial mass numerous minute, ovoid, uninucleate **conidia** are cut off from the free ends of the hyphae, which constitute the **conidiophores.** This stage of the fungus is known as the **sphacelial stage.** As the conidia are cut off they accumulate in a sweetish liquid excreted from the infected spikelet. This liquid, commonly known as 'honey dew', attracts insects, which carry the conidia with them to other flowers, where they germinate and produce infection. In this way, the disease is disseminated rapidly during the flowering season of the host plants. Eventually, the hyphal mass ceases to form conidia and develops into a densely compacted, hard and dark-brown or bluish-black coloured structure, known as the **sclerotium.** In this way the sphacelial stage is replaced by the **sclerotial stage.** A mature sclerotium is considerably longer and broader than the normal grains of the host plant.

When the sclerotia ripen, they either fall on the ground and remain there, or become mixed with the grains at the time of harvesting and thrashing. These may return to the field again in the next growing season of the host plant. The sclerotia are resting

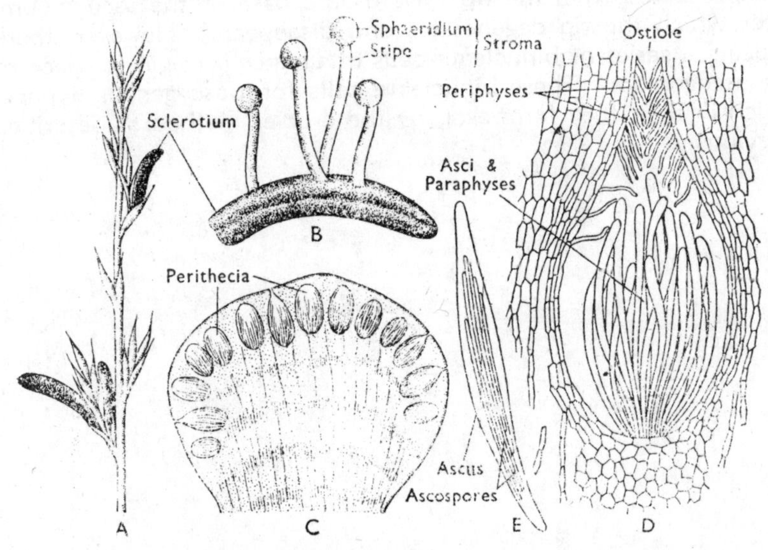

Fig. 183. *Claviceps.*
A, Part of an infected rye plant with sclerotia ; B, A germinating sclerotium ; C, V.S. through a sphaeridium ; D, A perithecium (enlarged) ; E, An ascus with ascospores.

bodies and serve as a means of tiding over unfavourable seasons. In the next season, *i.e.* in the next spring, these sclerotia germinate. Each sclerotium, on germination, produces half a dozen or more small capitate structures, called the **stromata**, constituting the

ascogenous stage of the fungus. The capitate portion of each storma, the **sphaeridium,** bears numerous flask-shaped **perithecia.** The perithecia are entirely immersed within the tissue of the stroma. Each perithecium opens at the surface of the capitate portion of the stroma by means of a pore called the **ostiole.** Within the basal portion of the perithecium there are numerous elongated **asci,** each containing eight needle-shaped **ascospores.** The ascospores are forcibly discharged from the ascus, come out through the ostioles and are carried away by the wind. As this happens during the flowering season of the host plant, the ascospores on reaching the spikelets bring about new infection and in this way the life cycle of the fungus is completed.

So far very little is known about the development and formation of the sex organs and also of the ascogenous hyphae. During the formation of a perithecium coenocytic antheridium and oogonium have been reported to be developed from a common hyphal branch and undergone fusion. Migration of nuclei has been observed from the tip towards the base of the ascogonium, after which the tip degenerates and disappears. However, there appears a series of binucleate cells of unknown origin in place of the ascogonium. These binucleate cells form ascogenous hyphae, which in their turn form asci, by the crozier method as described previously.

CHAPTER III

CLASS BASIDIOMYCETES

The Class Basidiomycetes includes such forms as the mushrooms, toadstools, bracket fungi and their allies (*Hymenomycetales*), the puff balls, bird's nest fungi and their allies (*Gasteromycetales*), the smuts (*Ustilaginales*), and the rusts (*Uredinales*). The smut and the rust fungi are obligate parasites on higher plants for at least a portion of their life cycle, while others are usually saprophytes.

The Basidiomycetes is a heterogeneous group, but all the members are characterized by the production of specialized, asexual reproductive units, called the **basidiospores,** which are produced externally on a mother cell, called the **basidium.** In most cases, the basidium develops directly by the elongation of the terminal cell of a dikaryon hypha (as in *Agaricus*), but it may also develop as a result of germination of a specialized binucleate spore, called **teliospore** (as in smuts and rusts). Usually, the basidia are club-shaped and unicellular, but they vary considerably in structure, some being transversely 4-celled, while others are longitudinally so. The basidia are mostly arranged side by side in a palisade-like layer forming the **hymenium,** which may either be exposed to the external atmosphere, either directly or indirectly (e.g. *Hymenomycetes*), or may form the lining of completely closed chambers (e.g. *Gasteromycetes*). The hymenia are produced upon or within fructifications, which usually attain great complexity in structure, form and size. These are the familiar structures which are ordinarily referred to as the 'fungus', but are in reality fruit bodies only, the vegetative body or the mycelium producing these fructifications remaining hidden within the substratum. The basidiospores are typically borne on horn-like projections, the **sterigmata,** developed usually from the top of the basidium. The spores, produced from the basidium, are generally 4 in number, but sometimes may be 2, 6 or more. A basidiospore is always unicellular and uninucleate, thin-walled or thick-walled, and may be hyaline or coloured. Besides basidiospores, conidia and chlamydospores are formed in some species, but they play minor parts in reproduction.

The basidiospore, on germination, usually produces an extensive, much-branched, septate mycelium which may be **primary** (**monokaryon**) or **secondary** (**dikaryon**). The primary mycelium consists of uninucleate hyphal cells and represents the haplophase, whereas the secondary mycelium with constantly binucleate cells represents the diplophase in the entire life cycle. The diplophase ends with the basidial development, and the formation of basidiospores marks the beginning of the haplophase. These two phases are either represented in different mycelia or combined in the same mycelium.

Formation of basidia and basidiospores

Excepting the rusts and the smuts, the basidia are generally developed from the terminal cell of a diplophasic secondary mycelium. Such a developing basidium does not only bear two nuclei of opposite sexuality, but also is characterized in the majority of the species by the presence of a clamp-connexion at its base.

Clamp-connexions indicate the dikaryotic nature of the mycelium. It is generally formed during the division of binucleate cells.

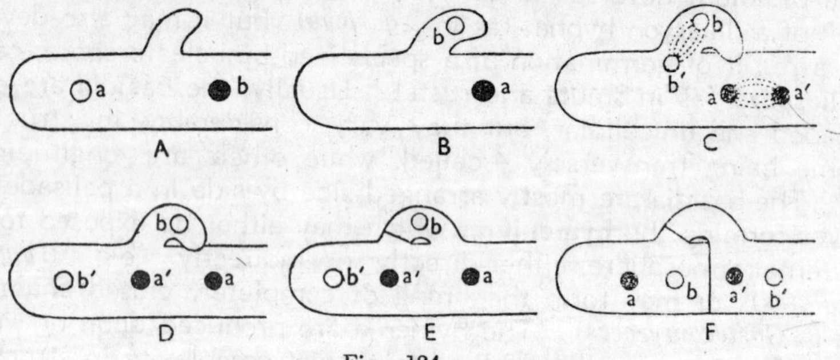

Fig. 184.

A—F, Successive stages in the formation of clamp-connexion.

When the dikaryon is ready to divide, a lateral outgrowth is first formed between the two nuclei, and begins to form a curve. The nuclei divide conjugately, and the lower nucleus of the upper pair passes into the curve. This curved outgrowth, the **clamp,** with a single nucleus is cut off from the main cell by a septum, and at the same time another septum is also formed between the two nuclei of the lower pair. Subsequently, the outgrowth fuses with the lower cell and its nucleus passes into the latter. This curved outgrowth, which acts as a by-pass, is known as the **clamp-connexion** (Fig. 184).

The basidium gradually increases in size, becomes more or less clavate, and the two nuclei within it undergo fusion. The fusion nucleus then migrates towards the basidium apex, where it divides meiotically forming four haploid nuclei. Subsequently, four slender projections, the **sterigmata,** are developed at the apical region of the basidium. The tip of each sterigma becomes somewhat swollen, into which a nucleus passes out of the basidium. By the formation of a partition wall at the base of the swelling, a **basidiospore** is now formed. Each basidiospore is more or less uniform and is provided with a small, eccentrically placed, spine-like projection at its basal end, where it remains attached with the sterigma ; this projection is called the **hilum.** Of the four basidiospores thus produced, two are of one sex and the other two of another.

Sexuality in Basidiomycetes

In the life history of a large number of basidiomycetous fungi two distinct sexual phases have been noted, one of which is the **monokaryotic** or **primary mycelium,** the other being the **dikaryotic** or **secondary mycelium.** The process by means of which a monokaryotic mycelium is converted into a dikaryotic one, is known as **diploidization** or **dikaryotization** and the mycelium is said to be **diploidized.** The diploidization may take place in different ways, as follows :

(*a*) An oidium of one sexual phase can diploidize a monokaryotic mycelium of opposite sex.

(*b*) Two monokaryotic hyphae of opposite sex may unite and produce a dikaryotic hypha.

(*c*) An oidium, produced by a monokaryotic hypha, develops into a new typical hypha representing the parent one, which can either diploidize or itself becomes diploidized on coming in contact with another monokaryotic hypha of opposite sexual phase.

Besides these usual processes of diploidization, a monokaryotic mycelium may become diploidized by a dikaryotic one. This was first discovered by Prof. Buller and is referred to as the **Buller phenomenon.** In this case, at the time of diploidization one nucleus from a binucleate cell of the dikaryotic mycelium passes into a cell of the monokaryotic mycelium. This introduced nucleus then divides mitotically and one of the daughter nuclei passes through a pore in the septum into the adjoining cell, thus making it also binucleate. This daughter nucleus, in its turn, again undergoes another mitotic division, and the process is continued until all the cells of the monokaryotic mycelium possess two nuclei each. If the sex factors present in the original nucleus of the cell in the monokaryotic mycelium do not become by any means duplicated by the sex factors present in the introduced (*i.e.* the dikaryotizing) nucleus, it is said to be a case of **legitimate combination ;** such a combination gives rise to a dikaryotic mycelium which is capable of producing basidia and basidiospores. On the other hand, if any of these sex factors be duplicated, it is called an **illegitimate combination**, and the dikaryotic mycelium produced as a result of this can never give rise to basidia or basidiospores.

A basidium of the higher Basidiomycetes gives rise to 4 basidiospores. Each of these spores on germination produces a primary mycelium. It has been observed that in about 90 per cent of the species studied, the primary mycelia are heterothallic, while the same in the rest are homothallic. The heterothallic species, in their turn, fall under two categories : **bipolar species** and **tetrapolar species.**

In bipolar species, the nucleus in each cell of a primary mycelium bears a single sex factor, which is directly opposite in nature (allelomorphic) to that present in the nucleus of a cell of another compatible primary mycelium. These sex factors are borne on homologous chromosomes, and are usually designated as A and B. As a result of diploidization a secondary mycelium is produced, each of whose cells contains two nuclei, one bearing A factor and the other B factor. During the formation of the basidium from such a mycelium, karyogamy takes place in the young basidium resulting in the formation of a diploid nucleus having a factor content AB. At the time of basidiospore formation, this fusion nucleus undergoes meiotic division, and of the four spores produced two bear the factor A, and the other two, the factor B. Each one of the primary mycelia developed from the spores containing the factor A is compatible with either of the mycelia containing the factor B or *vice versa*.

On the other hand, two allelomorphic sex factors, borne on separate pairs of chromosomes are responsible for making a species tetrapolar. In such cases, if the sex factors in the nucleus of a cell of a primary mycelium be designated by the factors A and B, then those in the nucleus of its compatible partner are usually referred to as a and b factors. Therefore, the fusion nucleus in a young basidium has the factor content AaBb. This fusion nucleus undergoes meiosis and as a result four haploid nuclei are formed which eventually migrate to the developing basidiospores. If both the chromosome pairs bearing the different sex factors in the fusion nucleus undergo disjunction in the first division of meiosis, the two daughter nuclei thus produced may bear Ab and aB factors or AB and ab factors, as the chances permit. However, if they undergo disjunction in the second division of meiosis, the chromosomes split up and four haploid nuclei are thereby produced ; two each of these will, therefore, contain the factors Ab and aB or AB and ab, respectively. If, on the other hand, both the chromosome pairs do not undergo any disjunction in the first division of meiosis, then the two daughter nuclei, produced after the first division, will each have the factor content AaBb as the parent one. When disjunction takes place subsequently in the second division of meiosis two conditions may happen : the four resultant nuclei may all be different, or for each of the two nuclei the factor contents will be Ab and aB or AB and ab as before. On the other hand, if disjunction takes place in one chromosome pair at the division of meiosis and in another pair at the second one, the four resultant nuclei will be all different bearing the factor contents Ab, aB, AB and ab. In cases where each of the two basidiospores bear the sex factors Ab and aB or AB and ab, the primary mycelia produced from them, behave in the same fashion as in the case of a bipolar species. But, when all the four spores are different, the species exhibits a rigid tetrapolar sexuality.

It has already been stated that all the heterothallic species exhibit either a bipolar or a tetrapolar sexuality. It is interesting, however, to note that in a number of cases a primary mycelium developed from a basidiospore, borne on the basidium of a fructification, is compatible with all the four primary mycelia developed from the basidiospores produced by a basidium of another fructification of the same species. Such fructifications were thought to be of different **geographical races,** as this phenomenon of such complete interfertility was first recorded in fructifications collected from widely separated regions on the globe. But, it has now been established that these so-called 'races' may occur not only in quite nearby localities but also on the same lump of dung, log of wood or similar other substrata. The cause of this may be attributed to the presence of multiple allelomorphs in the sex factors of the primary mycelia.

There is never any development of typical sex organs in Basidiomycetes, but nevertheless, a change in the nuclear condition from the haplophase to the diplophase takes place in the life cycle, as stated before, and the mycelium may exist in two or more sexually different strains. In such cases, any cell of a mycelium of one sexual phase may unite with any cell of the mycelium of opposite sexual phase, as a result of which a sporophytic or diplophasic mycelium is produced.

CLASSIFICATION

The class Basidiomycetes has been divided into *three* subclasses :

Subclass I. Hemibasidiomycetes. Characterized by the fact that more than 4 basidiospores are produced on the basidium which is either aseptate or divided transversely into 4 cells.

It includes only *one* order.

Order Ustilaginales. Obligate parasites causing diseases of different crop plants mainly ; chlamydospores (taleutospores) produced from intercalary binucleate cells of mycelium give rise to aseptate or transversely septate epibasidium ; number of basidiospores more than 4 ; sterigmata absent. Common genera are *Ustilago*, *Tilletia*, etc.

Subclass II. Protobasidiomycetes. Characterized by the production of regularly septate (transverse, longitudinal or oblique) basidium which always bears a definite number of basidiospores, usually 4

It includes *three* orders :

Order 1. Uredinales. Obligate parasites growing chiefly on angiosperms or gymnosperms and sometimes on ferns ; teleutospores produced from the terminal binucleate cells of mycelium give rise to transversely septate basidium ; number of basidiospores is usually 4 ; sterigmata present ; macrocyclic or microcyclic, autocious or heterocious. Common genera are *Puccinia Melampsora*, etc.

***Order 2. Auriculariales.**

***Order 3. Tremellales.**

Subclass III. Autobasidiomycetes. Characterized by having unicellular basidium, which produces definite number of basidiospores, usually 4 but may be 2, 6 or more ; basidia are always arranged in a hymenium which may either be exposed to the external atmosphere directly or indirectly (*Hymenomycetes*) or may form the lining of completely closed chambers (*Gasteromycetes*).

It includes *two* orders :

Order 1. Hymenomycetales. Chiefly saprophytic and often with prominent subaerial fructification ; hymenium variously disposed but always exposed (at least at maturity) ; basidium never septate. Common genera are *Agaricus*, *Polyporus*, *Clavaria*, *Coprinus*, *Lentinus*, etc.

Order 2. Gasteromycetales. As in the order Hymenomycetes but with fructifications either subterranean or subaerial ; hymenium remains closed within the peridium until the spores have attained maturity ; basidium never aseptate. Common genera are *Phallus*, *Lycoperdon*, *Cyathus*, etc.

* Orders marked with asterisks are not treated in this book.

ORDER **USTILAGINALES**

Obligate parasites causing diseases of different crop plants mainly ; chlanydospores (teleutospores) produced from intercalary binucleate cells of mycelium give rise to aseptate or transversely septate epibasidium ; number of basidiospores more than 4 ; sterigmata absent. Common genera are *Ustilago*, *Tilletia*, etc.

USTILAGO

(Fam. USTILAGINACEAE)

The species of *Ustilago*, commonly known as 'smut fungi', belong to a group of obligate parasitic basidiomycetes, which are responsible for the **smut diseases.** They are so called because of their black soot-like spore-masses formed externally on the host plant. The spores are known as **smut spores** (also **chlamydospores, brand spores, resting spores** or **teleutospores**). A mature chlamydospore contains a single diploid nucleus and is surrounded by a thin endospore and a thick, smooth or sculptured exospore. Smut spores are formed, either as separate individual units, or in compacted aggregations of several spores, giving rise to the **spore balls.** At maturity, these smut spore-masses either break up into fine dust-like powder and are readily carried away by the wind **(loose smut)**, or they remain firm, compacted together and more or less covered **(covered** or **kernel smut)**.

Smut fungi are of considerable economic importance, since they attack most of our cultivated cereals and a few wild and cultivated grasses. The most affected parts of plants are the grains or the entire inflorescences, thus reducing the yield of the cereal grains by 25 to 50 per cent. Most species of *Ustilago* grow parasitically upon a selective host species.

Smuts of our cultivated crops may be grouped into three kinds, on the basis of the time of germination of the smut spores and also the type of infection as follows : (*a*) **shoot infection** or **general infection type,** e.g. corn smut (*Ustilago maydis* = *U. zeae*), (*b*) **blossom infection type,** e.g. loose smut of wheat (*U. tritici*), and (*c*) **seedling infection type,** e.g. loose smut of oat (*U. avenae*).

Corn smut (*Ustilago maydis* = *U. zeae*)

The corn smut infects the Indian corn plant during its growing period. Usually, the ears and the tassels of the plant are attacked, but sometimes various other aerial parts, such as stems, leaves or aerial roots, are also infected. The infection is localized and does not pervade the whole system of the plant. The chlamydospores, formed during the last growing season of the host plant usually lie dormant on the dried stems, in the soil or in other favourable

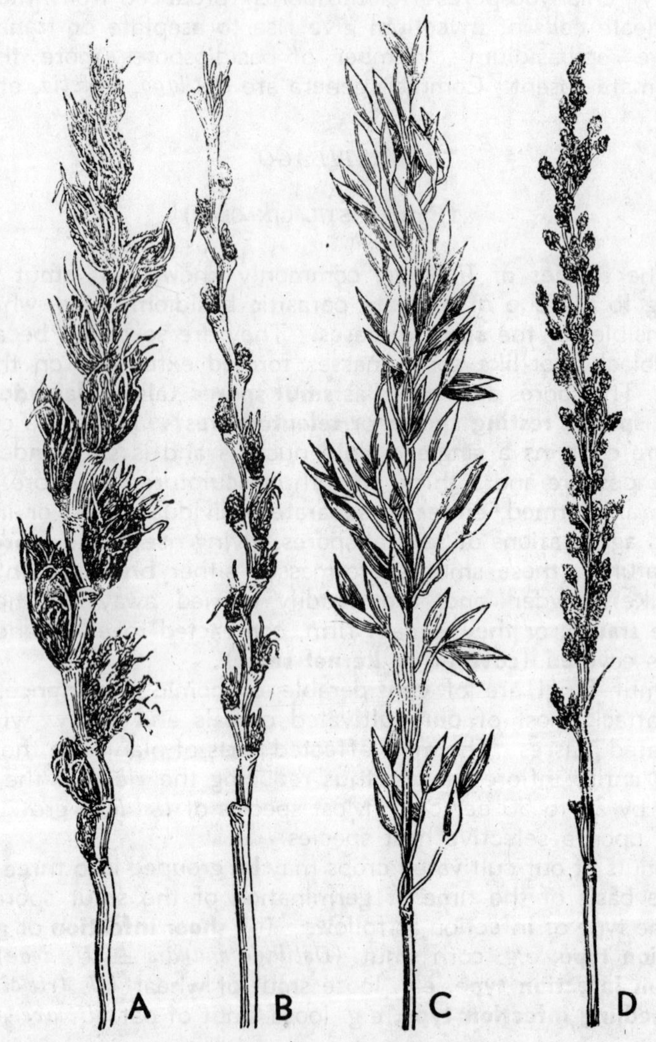

Fig. 185. Smutted inflorescences of wheat (A—B), and of oat (C—D). A—B, *Ustilago tritici* ; C—D, *Ustilago avenae*.

places. With the advent of the spring or the following summer they germinate in abundance. Each chlamydospore containing a diploid nucleus, on germination, produces a small tubular outgrowth, called the **epibasidium.** Its nucleus divides reductionally into four haploid nuclei, all of which either remain within the elongated epibasidium or only three of them migrate into the epibasidium, while the fourth one remains within its old spore wall. The epibasidium is then divided by transverse walls into four uninucleate cells. The nucleus of each cell divides into two daughter nuclei, of which one migrates into a basidiospore, which buds off from any point on the cellwall, and the other remains within the mother cell. This process may be repeated so that a few more basidiospores may be produced from a single cell. The corn smut is heterothallic, and out of the four cells formed in the epibasidium, two cells contain nuclei of one sex and the other two of opposite sex. Thus, the basidiospores derived from these cells are of two sexes. Each basidiospore, before or after detachment from the epibasidium, may sometimes bud off conidia of the same sex.

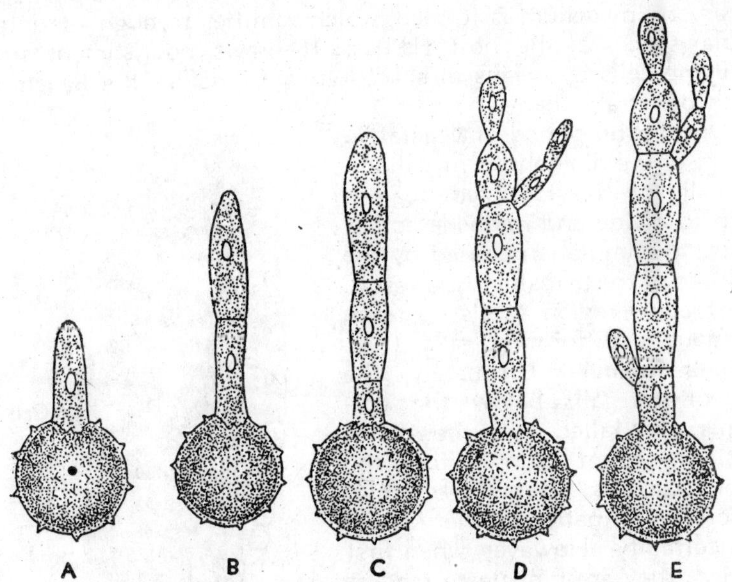

Fig. 186. *Ustilago zeae.*
A—E, Germinating chlamydospores showing the stages in the formation of basidia and the production of conidia by the budding of the basidiospores.

The **basidiospores** or **conidia** are disseminated by the wind, and when they reach the host plant, bring about infection. Typical infection is only possible if the host plant is infected with the basidiospores or the conidia of both sexes. A basidiospore or conidium germinates on any part of the host plant and sends out a **germ tube**, which soon penetrates the epidermis of the host, enters the intercellular spaces and grows more or less horizontally, forming a haplophasic (monokaryon) mycelium of a few uninucleate cells. Soon union follows between cells of two haplophasic mycelia of opposite sexes. In some cases this union may take place early, just after the penetration of the germ tubes resulting from the basidiospores or conidia of opposite sexes. During union, a cell of a haplophasic mycelium of one sex fuses with a cell of a haplophasic mycelium of opposite sex and the nucleus of one is introduced into the other, so that a binucleate condition (diplophasic or dikaryon) is established. This cell, usually a terminal one, now elongates, its two unfused nuclei divide simultaneously forming four daughter nuclei and a cross wall is formed containing a pair of nuclei of opposite sexes. The process is repeated several times, as a result of which a considerable amount of diplophasic (dikaryon) mycelium is formed, which ramifies through the intercellular spaces of the host tissues. It draws nourishment from the living cells by means of short hyphal branches, the **haustoria**, which penetrate them.

During the period of vegetative activity of the diplophasic mycelium, the cells of the localized regions begin to divide and re-divide actively due to stimulation caused by the presence of the parasite. As a result, the infected region swells up to an enormous size forming **galls** (Fig. 187) or **tumours**. Ultimately, the cells of the galls below the epidermis are killed and the diplophasic mycelium begins to form the chlamydospores. Details of chlamydospore formation are not known with certainty. However, when first formed, they are binucleate, and as they attain maturity the two nuclei of each chlamydospore fuse to form a diploid nucleus, and its protoplast becomes surrounded by a thick wall. At this stage the gall consists of the epidermis surrounding the masses of chlamydospores, a few sterile hyphae, and the remains of the host cells. Ultimately, the epidermis

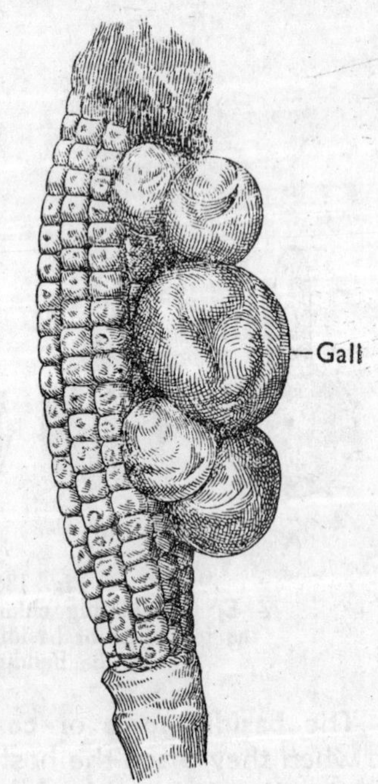

Fig. 187, *Ustilago zeae*. An ear of corn infected with corn smut forming galls.

ruptures and the powdery mass of chlamydospores are blown away by the wind. The chlamydospores are resting spores and usually do not germinate until the following spring or early summer, the growing season of the host plant.

Loose smut of wheat (*Ustilagotritici*)

Loose smut of wheat infects the healthy wheat plants at the time of flowering. Just when the wheat plants head out, the **chlamydospores** of *U. tritici* are blown about by the wind and numerous spores are lodged between the glumes, where they germinate on reaching the feathery stigmas. Each spore, on germination, produces a germ tube, which grows down the style and enters the ovary. It then pierces the integuments of the ovule, passes through the nucellus, endosperm and scutellum, and finally enters the axis of the embryo. Here, the fungus continues to grow within the embryo without doing any injury to it,

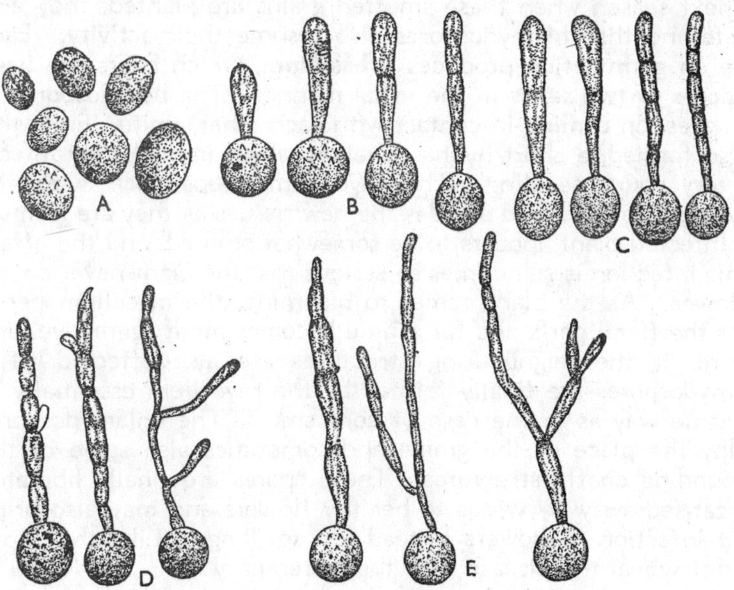

Fig. 188, *Ustilago tritici.*
A, Chlamydospores ; B—E, Various stages of germination of chlamydospores in water.

and as the seed matures, it passes into the stage of dormancy along with the seed. These seeds, though infected with the fungal mycelium, appear perfectly healthy. In the following spring, when these seeds are planted, the internal dormant mycelium resumes its activity and grows as an internal parasite keeping pace with the growth of the developing seedling. When the plant attains maturity and at the time of flowering, the fungus makes a vigorous development and destroys the spikelets of the flowering heads, which are finally transformed into black powdery masses of chlamydospores. In most cases, the spikelets are completely destroyed, and when the chlamydospores are blown about by the wind or washed away by rain, only the bare structure of the central axis of the head is left behind. The disease is systemic and not localized as in the case of corn smut, since the mycelium pervades the whole system of the plant body.

Loose smut of oat (*Ustilago avenae*)

The infection of an oat plant chiefly takes place in very young seedlings. The **chlamydospores,** produced on the smutted inflorescences of oat plants, are usually lodged on the surface of healthy grains. These spores can retain their vitality at least for a year. In the next season when these smutted grains are planted, they germinate and the chlamydospores also resume their activity. Each spore on germination produces a **basidium,** which bears the **basidiospores** of two sexes in the usual manner. The basidiospores of two sexes, on coming in contact with each other, unite. From this cell so formed, a short hypha develops which immediately infects the very young seedling. The mycelium keeps pace with the growth of the plant and invades the new tissues as they are formed. The infected plant appears to be somewhat stunted, and the effect of this infection is sometimes so serious that the plant never comes to flower. As the plant comes to blooming, the mycelium penetrates the floral parts and for a time becomes more aggressive, and as a result, the neighbouring structures are also affected. The chlamydospores are finally formed by the mycelium essentially in the same way as in the case of corn smut. The chlamydospores occupy the place of the grains and sometimes also some of the surrounding chaffy structures. These spores are finally liberated and carried away by winds to healthy flowers and may also bring about infection in flowers instead of seedlings. Like the loose smut of wheat the disease is of the systemic type.

Control measures

(*a*) *Corn smut.* Since the infection is localized and restricted to the aerial parts of plants only, spraying of healthy corn plants with Bordeaux mixtures can prevent the spread of the disease. There are also other recommended methods : (1) rotation of crops, *i.e.* corn plants are not cultivated on the same field for at least three years ; (2) destruction of the infected parts, such as inflorescences and stalks, before the spores are disseminated, and (3) use of manure free from smut spores.

(*b*) *Loose smut of wheat.* Infection due to loose smut can be effectively controlled by treating the infected seeds with hot water in such a way that the internal mycelium is killed without killing the embryo. This is done by immersing the seeds for a period of ten minutes in hot water bath, maintained at a temperature of 125°F. to 129°F. Great care should be taken during treatment, since, any rise of temperature above 131°F. will kill the embryo and a temperature below 125.5°F. will not kill the fungus at all.

(*c*) *Loose smut of oat.* The loss due to this disease is prevented by treating the seeds with fungicides that kill the spores lodged on the surface of the grains without affecting the vitality of the seeds. For this purpose, an equal part of commercial formaldehyde and water when sprayed or sprinkled on oats give effective results.

TILLETIA

(Fam. TILLETIACEAE)

There are two species of *Tilletia* which attack wheat in India causing a disease, known as **bunt** or **stinking smut.** It is so called, because the infected heads of wheat emit a strong smell resembling that of decaying fish, and this is given out by the **brand spores** or **chlamydospores** of the organism. Of the two species, *Tilletia tritici* is characterized by having chlamydospores whose epispore is reticulated.

Fig. 189. *Tilletia.* An infected inflorescence of wheat.

Infection by *T. tritici* takes place by means of binucleate conidia during the seedling stage of the host plant. A germinating **conidium** sends out a hypha, which directly penetrates the host by pushing between the epidermal cells and a much-branched mycelium of dikaryotic cells is produced within the tissue. Certain cells of the dikaryotic mycelium may become multinucleate by subsequent division of the nuclei. At this stage, the seedling does not exhibit any external symptom of the disease. The mycelium develops within the seedling, keeping pace with the development of the host tissue. Subsequently, when the host begins to flower, there is a vigorous development of the mycelium within the floral organs. The infected flowers have abortive stamens and enlarged ovaries, which are about twice the normal size than those of the uninfected ones. At this time, when the normal grains begin to grow on the infected plants, the ovules are destroyed by the mycelium, and from this mycelium binucleate chlamydospores are produced, replacing the ovules within the infected ovary. At maturity, the two nuclei of each chlamydospore fuse to form a single diploid nucleus. The ovary matures just as in the normal grain, but it contains a mass of chlamydospores or **smut balls** in place of the kernel. The wall of the infected grains containing the smut balls remain intact until the following growing season of the host. The wall eventually breaks, and the chlamydospores from the broken infected grains lodge upon normal grains and return to the field at the time of plantation.

The chlamydospore, on germination, produces a **promycelium** or **basidium**, into which the fusion nucleus passes and divides meiotically into four haploid nuclei. Subsequent division or divisions of

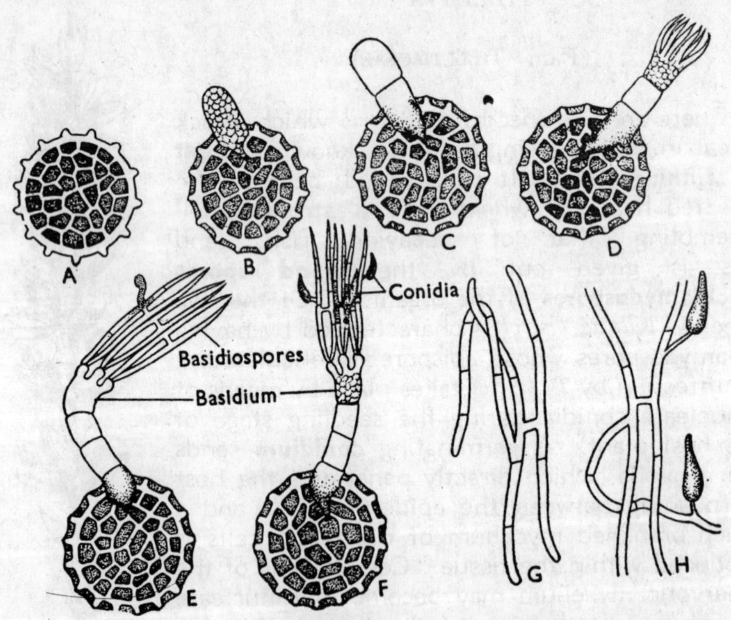

Fig. 190. *Tilletia.*
A, A chlamydospore ; B—D, Chlamydospore germinating and forming basidium ; E—F, Conjugation of basidiospores and formation of conidia ; G, Development of mycelium from a conjugated pair of basidiospores ; H, Formation of secondary conidia.

the nuclei increase the number to eight or more. As the basidium elongates, its protoplasm becomes restricted to the growing tip and at its evacuated basal portion a few transverse septa are laid down in succession. At the apex of the basidium eight, but occasionally a large number of acicular **basidiospores** are budded off and each receives a single nucleus. As the fungus is heterothallic, half of these spores are of one sex and half of the other sex, segregation taking place during meiosis. Short conjugation tubes connect the neighbouring basidiospores in pairs, usually before they are shed, and the nucleus of one passes into the other. In this way the binucleate condition is established.

After migration, the basidiospores become septate and under damp conditions, filaments of binucleate cells develop from the segments containing two nuclei. From the binucleate cells of these filaments binucleate sickle-shaped **conidia** are budded off, and from these mycelia of dikaryotic cells may further be produced. When the atmosphere is comparatively dry, similar conidia may be formed directly from the binucleate segments of the basidiospores while they are still attached to the basidium.

The conidia, whether primary or secondary, are discharged forcibly from the basidium in the same way as that of the basidiospores of *Agaricus*, to be described subsequently, and under favourable conditions they germinate and infect seedlings of the hosts.

ORDER **UREDINALES**

Obligate parasites growing chiefly on angiosperms or gymnosperms and sometimes on ferns ; teleutospores produced from the terminal binucleate cells of mycelium give rise to transversely septate basidium ; number of basidiospores is usually 4 ; sterigmata present ; macrocyclic or microcyclic, autoecious or heteroecious. Common genera are *Puccinia*, *Melampsora*, etc.

PUCCINIA

(Fam. PUCCINIACEAE)

Puccinia includes a group of parasitic basidiomycetes, which live upon a few ferns but in the main on various species of seed-plants (Gymnosperms and Angiosperms). They are commonly known as **rust fungi** owing to the fact that they cause brown or rusty spots or streaks on living plants, particularly on the leaves. All are obligate parasites and most of them grow on particular host plants or on a small group of closely related hosts. The ravages made by them are well known wherever plants are cultivated, as they cause damage to various cereals worth thousands of rupees every year. They produce at least two distinct types of spores, other have three, four or even five different kinds of spore-forms in a complete life cycle. A rust is said to be **polymorphic,** when several spore-forms occur in its complete life cycle. When a rust

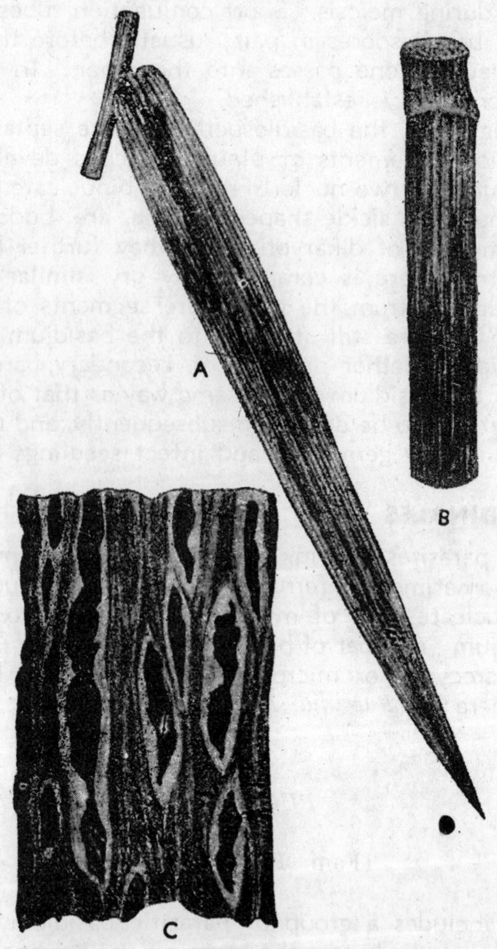

Fig. 191. *Puccinia graminis var. tritici*, A—B, Leaf and stem of wheat infected with 'black stem-rust' bearing uredosori and teleutosori respectively ; C, Part of the infected stem showing highly magnified teleutosori.

produces all the spore-forms in the life cycle on a particular host plant or on closely related hosts, it is called **autoecious.** A large number of species, however, produce their different spore-forms on distantly related hosts, and they are said to be **heteroecious.**

The best-known species of rust fungi is *Puccinia graminis var. tritici*, commonly known as the **black stem rust of wheat,** which causes greater economic loss and is responsible for one of the most important plant-diseases known. It is polymorphic, since it exhibits a total of five different spore-forms in its complete life cycle, and these are : (*a*) **uredospores (urediniospores**), (*b*) **teliospores (teleutospores)**, (*c*) **basidiospores (sporidia)**, (*d*) **pycniospores (spermatia)**, and (*e*) **aeciospores (aecidiospores)**. Besides the basidiospores and pycniospores which are uninucleate, all other spore-forms are always binucleate. *P. graminis* is, therefore, a **macrocylic rust,** since it produces, besides the teleutospores, two

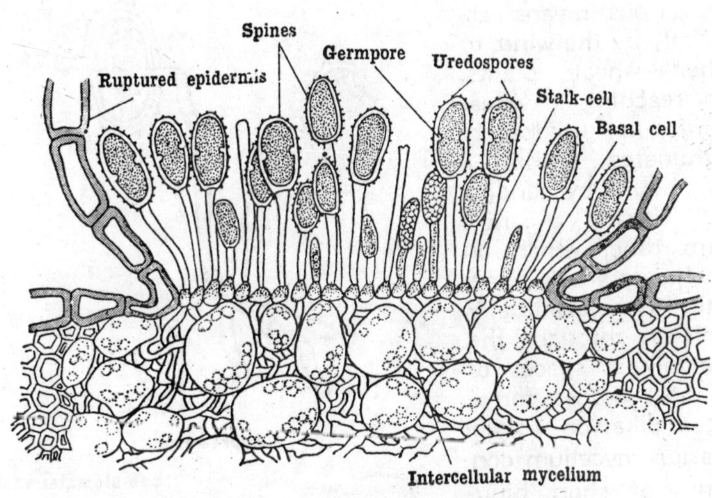

Fig. 192. *Puccinia graminis var. tritici,* Section through a uredosorus showing uredospores in various stages of development.

other additional types of binucleate spores. This rust is a heteroecious species producing certain of its spore-forms on wheat plants and others on the leaves of barberry plant. Besides the wheat plant it may also attack oat, rye, barley and many other grasses during the growing season of these plants. Based on this behaviour of the fungus, a large number of strains or physiological races have been established within the species *P. graminis*. These races are sometimes also referred to as subspecies. Of these, the one which infects the wheat plant (*Triticum aestivum= T. vulgare*) is known as *P. graminis var tritici*.

The life-history of *P. graminis* can be divided into five different stages as follows :

Uredinial or red rust stage (Fig. 192). In late spring there appear, on the stems and leaves of wheat plants, vertically elongated reddish-brown pustules (sori) or blisters called **uredosori (uredinia)**, each of which at maturity contains a powdery mass of innumerable small orange-red spores called **uredospores (urediniospores, or summer spores, or red rust spores)**. A uredospore is somewhat ovoid in form, binucleate, always unicellular, minutely spiny and with a constant number of germ pores. At maturity, the epidermis of the blister ruptures and the uredospores of a uredosorus are freely exposed and disseminated by various means, especially by the wind, to other wheat plants. On reaching a wheat plant, a uredospore germinates within a few hours by sending out usually a single germ tube, which on reaching a stoma penetrates it, and eventually ramifies through the intercellular spaces of the host tissues forming a dikaryon (diplophasic) mycelium consisting of short binucleate cells. The mycelium derives its nourishment from the neighbouring cells by means of short haustorial hyphal branches. The growth of the mycelium is localized and does not grow deep into the tissues of the host. Beneath the epidermis of the host the hyphal branches become more numerous, and within 5-6 days

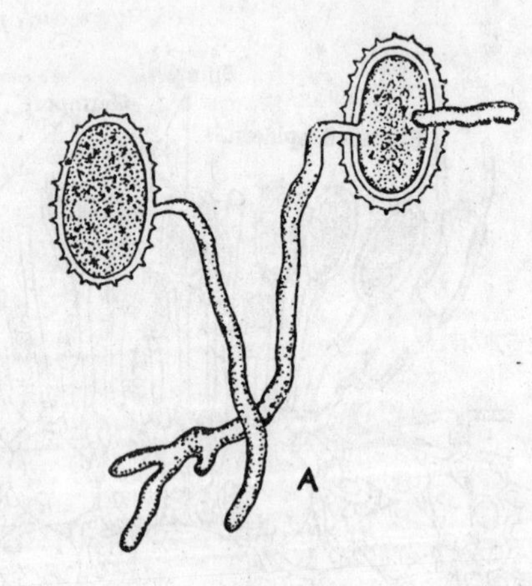

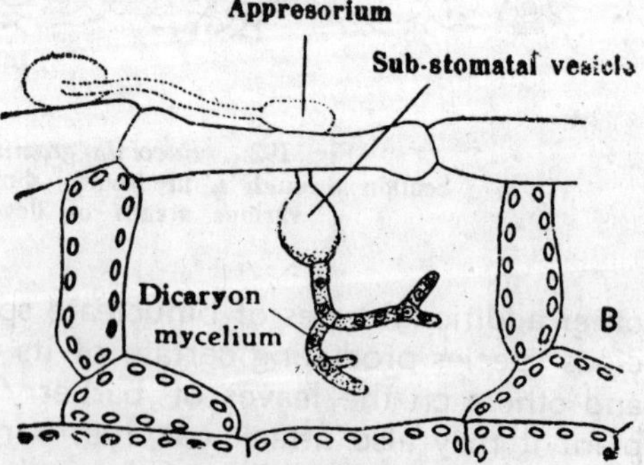

Fig. 193. *Puccinia graminis var, tritici.* A, A germinating uredospore ; B, Infection of wheat plant by the growth of the infection hypha of a germinating uredospore through a stoma.

after infection, begins to form uredosori with uredospores. When very young, a uredosorus consists of a layer of parallel binucleate **basal cells,** which are pressed directly against the inner walls of the epidermis. Each of these cells elongates vertically and divides transversely ; the lower daughter cell, thus formed, remains undivided and is called a **foot cell.** The upper daughter cell divides again to form two cells, the terminal one matures into a **uredospore** and the lower one into a **stalk cell.** Like the cells of the mycelium the foot cell, the stalk cell and the uredospore are

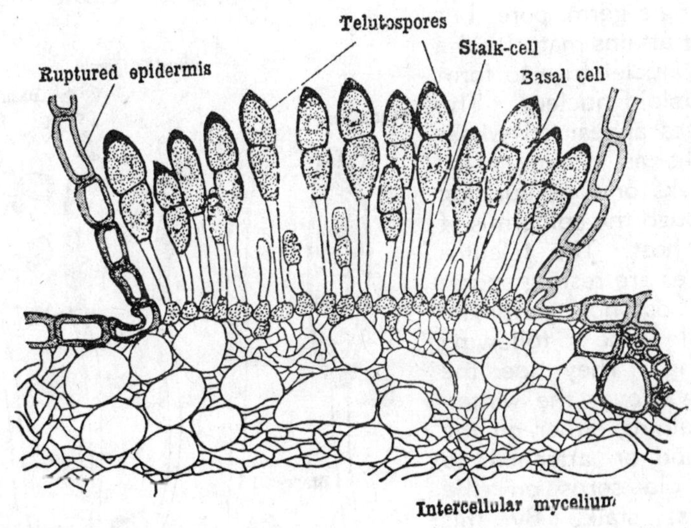

Fig. 194. *Puccinia graminis var. tritici*, Section through a teleutosorus showing teleutospores in various stages of development.

all binucleate. The maturation of the uredospores is followed by rupturing of the overlying epidermis of the host plant, resulting in their final dissemination. Other wheat plants become gradually infected by these uredospores, and within 10-12 days a new crop of uredospores is produced on the newly infected plants, and these may repeat the same stage. It is for this reason the uredospores are often spoken of as **repeating spores.** In this way the uredospores are blown about from one field to a neighbouring one and the disease spreads like a wild fire within a very short time.

Telial (teleuto) or black rust stage (Fig. 194). Towards the end of summer, as the wheat plants attain maturity, the mycelium, which up to this time bore uredospores, begins to produce another type of spores, called **teleutospores** (**teliospores, or winter spores, or black rust spores**) within the **teleutosori** (**telia**). At first the teleutospores are produced in a sorus containing uredospores, but later on new teleutosori containing teleutospores only develop on the host plant. The development of a teleutospore is similar to that of a uredospore excepting that the upper sister cell of the stalk cell, instead of directly developing into a teleutospore, divides into binucleate cells, which mature into a two-celled, thick-walled teleutospore. The teleutospores are dark-brown but in mass black in colour. Each spore, when young, is binucleate and with a single germ pore, but as it attains maturity the two nuclei fuse to form a diploid nucleus. The spores appear on wheat stalks as narrow black streaks or sori, bursting through the epidermis of the host. The teleutospores are resting spores and do not germinate until the following spring. They tide the fungus over the winter, remaining either on the ground or attached to the old sorus on the wheat stalk. By this time the wheat crop matures fully, and further growth of the fungus is stopped.

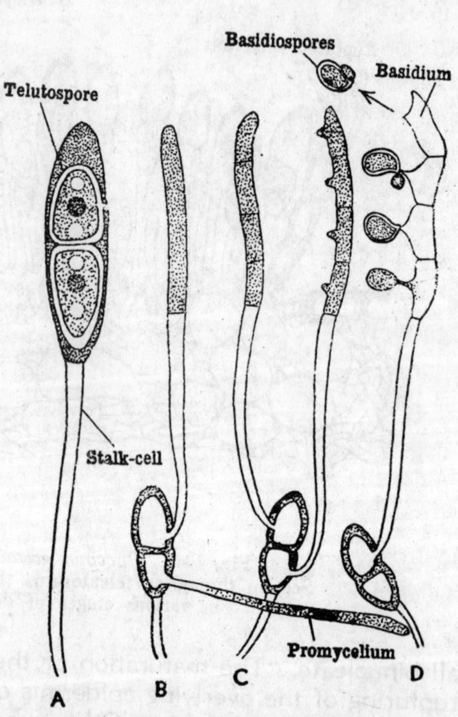

Fig, 195, *Puccinia graminis var, tritici,* A, A mature teleutospore ; B—D, Stages in the germination of a teleutospore showing the successive stages of development of the basidium and the basidiospores.

Basidial stage (Fig. 195). Under suitable conditions of temperature and moisture, a teleutospore germinates and from each of its cells a tubular outgrowth is formed. This tubular outgrowth elongates at its apex and becomes curved at its free end. The fusion nucleus migrates into this curved terminal portion, divides reductionally into four daughter nuclei, after which transverse walls are laid down forming four uninucleate cells, more or less equal in size. This is the **basidium (promycelium).** Each cell develops a small lateral projection, the **sterigma**, through which pass the nucleus and most of the cytoplasm. The swollen apex of the sterigma containing the nucleus becomes separated as a **basidiospore (sporidium).** A spore forms a small projection, at one side of it, called the **hilum**, where it joins a sterigma. At maturity, all the four spores are attached to the sterigmata somewhat obliquely and are soon shot away in succession to the air from the sterigmata with considerable force. Just before spore discharge a small drop of water is excreted at the spore-hilum. This water drop gradually increases in volume and the spore along with the drop is violently shot away from its sterigma. *P. graminis tritici* is heterothallic. The basidiospores, thus formed, are, therefore, of different sexes (+ and —), two are of one sex and the other two of the opposite sex. The basidiospores are incapable of infecting the wheat plants, but can germinate only when they come in contact with the alternate host, the barberry.

Pycnial or spermogonial stage (Fig. 196). The basidiospores are carried away in all directions by the wind, and when they reach a barberry plant they begin to germinate. A basidiospore (+ or —), on falling on a leaf, twig or fruit of barberry, puts forth a germ tube, which penetrates directly through the epidermal cells and branches through the intercellular spaces of the host tissue forming a branched haplophasic (monokaryon) mycelium consisting of uninucleate cells. The infected areas soon become swollen and yellowish in colour.

Within 4-5 days, after infection, there appear between the upper epidermis and the palisade tissue, isolated hyphal mats, which at maturity become flask-shaped and each develops a pore-like opening, the **ostiole.** These ostioles appear as minute dark spots on the upper surface of discoloured areas on the leaves of barberry. These are known as **pycnia (spermogonia).** Inwardly projecting hyphae, lining the cavity of each spermogonium, cut off from their tips, a succession of small uninucleate spore-like cells, called **pycniospores (spermatia)**, which gradually accumulate inside the spermogonial cavity. The pycniospores have gelatinous wall and these are extruded in a drop of nectar exuded through the ostiole. Besides the pycniospores, each pycnium sends out through the ostiole numerous straight, pointed, red hairs, the **periphyses,** and a small number of simple or branched **flexuous hyphae** projecting beyond the cloud of spores into the nectar. The haplophasic mycelium, the pycnia and the pycniospores are all haploid structures and may be either of the + or of the — sexual strain, depending on the nature of the basidiospore from which they develop. Individually, each pycniospore cannot re-infect the barberry plant, and was previously thought to be a spore that has become functionless. But it has been proved that they are essential structures, which are responsible for the initiation of the diplophase. This initiation of diplophase is rendered possible by the transference of pycniospores from a pycnium of one sex to another of the opposite sex usually with the

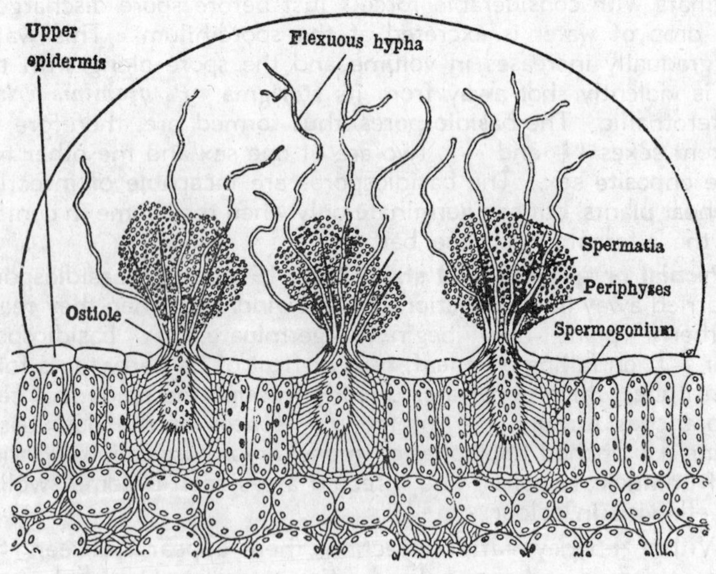

Fig. 196. *Puccinia graminis var. tritici*, Semi-diagrammatic representation of a part of a section through the upper surface of a leaf of barberry showing spermogonia covered by a big drop of nectar in which spermatia are being exuded, (*Redrawn after Buller*).

help of insects. The fragrance and sugary contents of the nectar are attractive to the insects and induce them to crawl from one pycnium to another, thereby mixing the pycnial exudates of the two opposite sexes. A pycniospore of one sex usually fuses with the tip of a flexuous hypha of the opposite sex, and its protoplasmic contents finally enter into the latter ; this is the initiation of the diplophase. The spermatization of the flexuous hypha may also take place by compatible pycniospores, which come in contact with these hyphae while floating freely in a big nectar drop, produced by the coalescence of a number of smaller drops exuded through the ostioles of several pycnia. How the entire haplophasic mycelium becomes diplophasic is not known with certainty.

Aecial (Aecidial) or cluster-cup stage (Fig. 197). While the pycnia are being formed towards the upper infected regions of the barberry leaf, masses of hyphae accumulate at various points just within the lower epidermis of the infected areas. These are the rudiments of aecia (**proto-aecidia** of Buller), and are haploid structures. Presumably, after diploidization, the nuclei migrate through the hypha to an aecial initial, and as a result it is stimu-

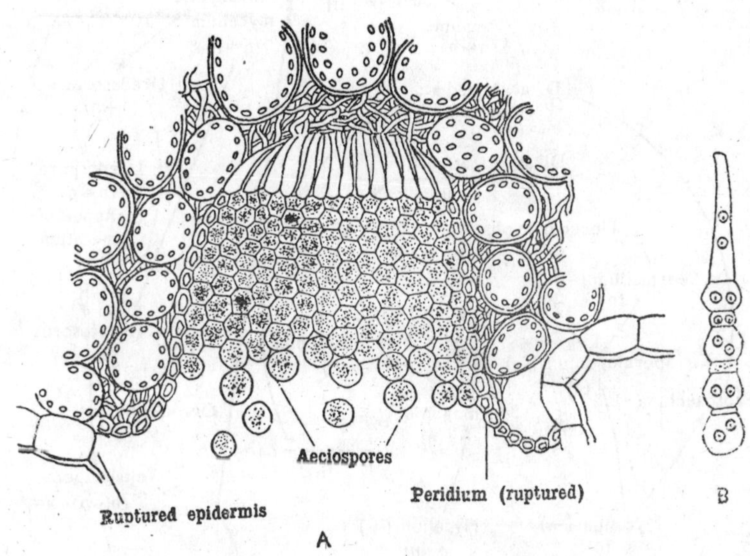

Fig. 197. *Puccinia graminis var. tritici.*
A, A section through an aecium showing aeciospores in various stages of development ; B, Formation of aeciospores.

lated to further development. Some cells of the aecial initial become binucleate, and a layer of binucleate basal cells is formed in a manner similar to that produced in a sorus. Each basal cell, by nuclear and cell divisions, produces a chain of alternately large and small binucleate cells. The large cells mature into **aeciospores,** and the smaller ones disintegrate. These chains of spores are surrounded by a continuous protective layer of fungal tissue, known as the **peridium,** in which the radial and outer tangential walls are greatly thickened. The entire structure is known as the **aecium (aecidium or cluster-cup).** At maturity, the peridium ruptures, the entire aecium becomes distinctly cup-shaped and the binucleate aeciospores are liberated. The aeciospores are always unicellular, orange or yellow in colour and with minutely warty hyaline walls.

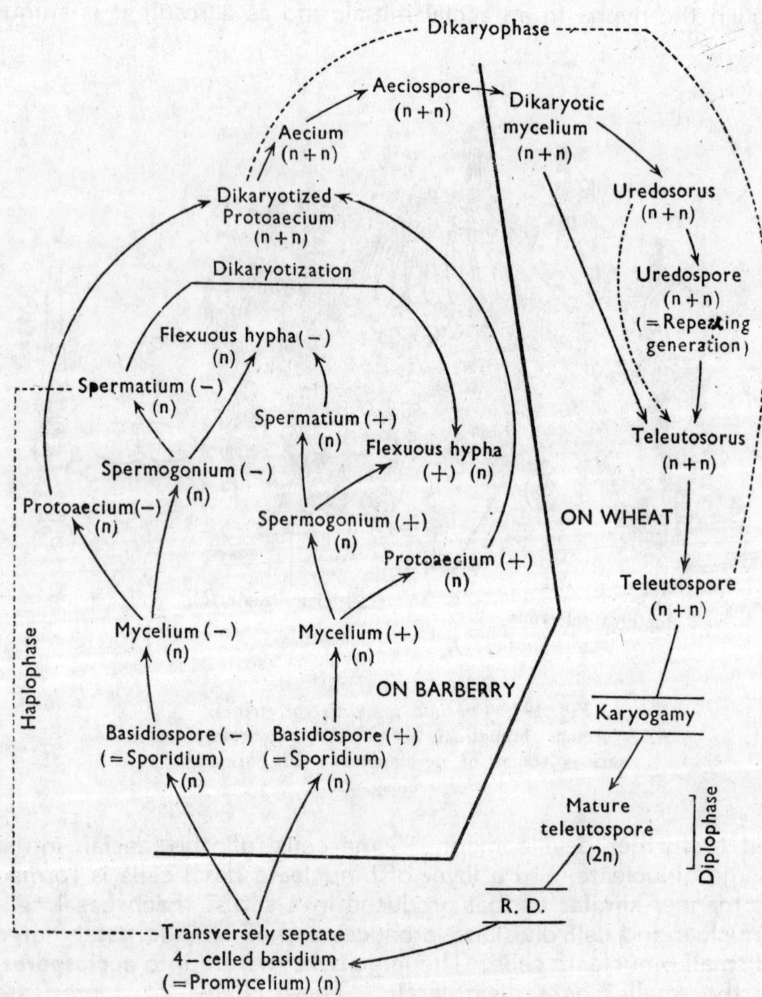

Fig. 198. Life history cycle of *Puccinia graminis var, tritici,*

In late spring when these aeciospores are liberated, they are disseminated by wind. They cannot re-infect the barberry, but if a spore reaches a wheat plant, it germinates, puts forth a germ tube, which penetrates a stoma, and ultimately ramifies through the intercellular spaces of the host and again forms a diplophasic mycelium, which within 10-12 days begins to form the first crop of uredospores. Thus, in typical cases, the first infection of the wheat plant is brought about by the aeciospores.

The annual recurrence of *P. graminis* var. *tritici* in the plains of India is still a highly intricating problem. Once it was thought that the eradication of barberry would be absolutely effective in controlling the disease. In fact, countries like U.S.A., Canada and some others in Europe have been able to do so. But, in our country, the majority of the wheat crop is cultivated in the plains, and not even a single barberry plant is found to be growing in the neighbourhood of these wheat-growing areas. Still the black rust of wheat every year causes great damages to the crop.

Unlike the western countries situated in the temperate zone, the first appearance of this rust is noted on the stems and leaves of wheat in late February in our country ; these are the uredosori. As the climate continues to become drier and hotter, teleutosori are formed. So, in India teleutospores are really the summer spores. But the teleutospores are not expected to survive the very high temperature (about 47°C. in some cases) lasting for a few days at a stretch. Furthermore, as has already been pointed out, barberries are entirely absent in the plains ; consequently, the question of aeciospore-formation can be completely ruled out. So, the focus of infection in the plains must lie somewhere else, and in fact, the hills of India can be considered as such foci. In the hills the uredospores usually over-summer on some self-grown wheat and some graminaceous weeds and cause an infection of the early sown crop in winter. The over-wintering of the rust necessarily takes place on wheat at comparative lower altitudes where the winter is not so severe. From these infected sources the disease gradually spreads downwards into the plains through the agency of wind.

Besides *P. graminis* var. *tritici*, the black rust, there are two other rusts found commonly attacking the wheat plants,—*P. glumarum*, the yellow rust, and *P. triticina*, the brown rust. A brief account of some of the macroscopic features of these three rusts is given in the following table by means of which they can be identified in the field :

P. graminis var, *tritici* (Black or stem rust)	*P. glumarum* (Yellow or striped rust)	*P. triticina* (Brown or orange rust)
1. Attacks chiefly the stems ; ears, leaves and leaf-sheaths are also infected but to a lesser degree,	1. Attacks mainly the leaves, also the ears, leaves and leaf-sheaths to some extent.	1. Attacks practically the leaves only ; in rare cases infections may be found on the leaf-sheaths and still more rarely on stems.
2. Uredosori large and elongated, brown in colour, coalescent and maturing early and causing conspicuous breakage or rupture of the epidermis of the host.	2. Uredosori somewhat smaller in size and oval in shape, lemon-yellow in colour and not coalescing but arranged in rows or stripes, maturing late and the epidermis of the host is slightly displaced by the rupture of the sori.	2. Uredosori usually smaller than those of *P. graminis* but longer than those of *P. glumarum*, orange-coloured when young but turning brown on maturity, scattered irregularly and not coalescing, maturing rather early, and the broken epidermis of the host remains as a fringe around a ruptured uredosorus.
3. Teleutosori almost like uredosori but black or dark-coloured, cause heavy rupture of the epidermis of the host ; found practically speaking on all aerial green parts.	3. Teleutosori like uredosori but dull black in colour and often coalescing, not causing any rupture of the epidermis of the host ; found mainly on the lower surfaces of leaves, but occasionally on the aerial green parts.	3. Teleutosori generally absent otherwise like uredosori but somewhat flat and dark in colour, not causing any rupture of the epidermis of the host ; found almost exclusively on the lower surfaces of leaves.

Control measures

From the discussions above, it is evident that eradication of barberry plant will not be effective in controlling the black rust in India. This was the well-considered opinion of late Principal Mehta, the pioneer worker and authority on cereal rusts in India. Practically speaking, the only effective control measure for combating the disease lies in cultivation of resistant varieties of wheat, and for this purpose crossings of our wheats with Kenya wheats have yielded some satisfactory results.

ORDER **HYMENOMYCETALES**

Chiefly saprophytic and often with prominent subaerial fructifications ; hymenium variously disposed but always exposed (at least at maturity ; basidium never septate. Common genera are *Agaricus*, *Polyporus*, *Clavaria*, *Coprinus*, *Lentinus*, etc.

POLYPORUS

(Fam. POLYPORACEAE)

Of the various species of the genus *Polyporus* so far described from Bengal, *Polyporus ostreiformis* is a common saprophyte, which grows singly or in groups during the rainy season on logs and

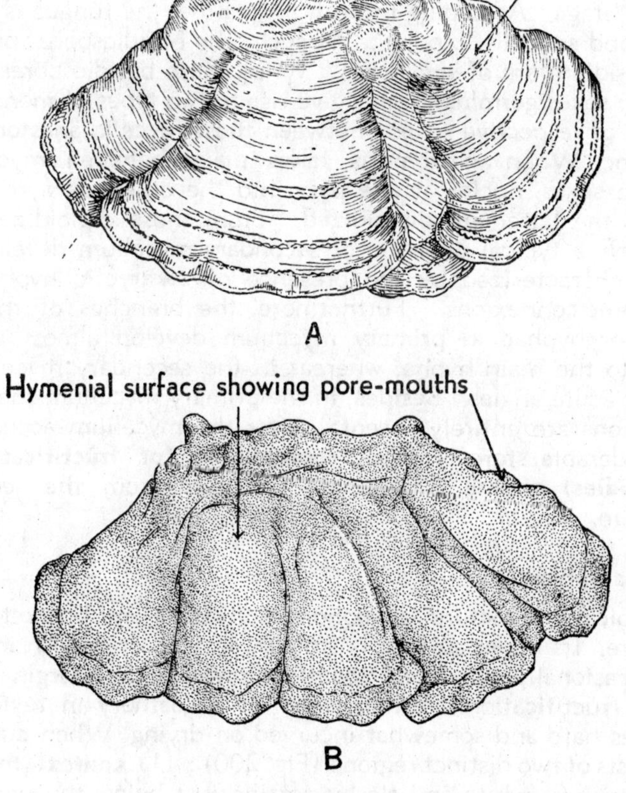

Fig. 199, *Polyporus.*
A, Dorsal view of a sporophore ; B, Ventral view of the same.

stumps of various trees, ultimately causing their decay. It is a **white rot** fungus, because it can attack both cellulose and lignin constituents of the cell walls. It has also been reported as a parasite causing a disease of Areca palm in Malayasia.

Vegetative body

The mycelium, which lives within the woody tissues, is both inter- and intra-cellular and consists of much-branched, septate and white hyphae, by means of which the plant not only vegetates but also draws nourishment from the substratum. There are two phases in the development of the mycelium, *viz.*, (1) **monokaryon phase**, consisting of uninucleate hyphal cells, and (2) **dikaryon phase**, in which the hyphal cells are constantly binucleate. Since it is a basidiomycetous fungus the mycelium derived from the germination of a basidiospore is always in the monokaryon or primary stage. According to Prof. S. R. Bose, the fungus is heterothallic and sexually 'bipolar'. As such, the basidiospores produced by a basidium are of two sexes. When these basidiospores of two opposite sexes germinate, they give rise to two types of monokaryon mycelia of respective sexes. Between these mycelia anastomosis is common. When anastomosis takes place between mycelia of opposite sexes, nuclei of one pass into the other, as a result the cells of the latter are diploidized. From these diploidized cells, ultimately a typical dikaryon or secondary mycelium develops and this is characterized by the presence of dikaryotic hyphal cells and clamp-connexions. Furthermore, the branches of the main strand or hyphae in primary mycelium develop almost at right angles to the main hypha, whereas in the secondary mycelia they grow at acute angles. Besides, in the primary mycelium the clamp-connexions are entirely absent. After the mycelium accumulates a considerable store of food, **sporophores (or fructifications or fruit bodies)** of the fungus are produced from the secondary mycelium.

The sporophore

Typically, a mature sporophore is a sessile and bracket-shaped structure. Its upper surface is smooth, whitish or greyish in colour and occasionally with faint zonations towards the margin or edge of the fructification. When moist, it is leathery in texture but becomes hard and somewhat incurved on drying. When cut across it consists of two distinct regions (Fig. 200) : (1) **context**, the thick, homogeneous, white and fleshy portion just below the upper surface, and (2) **pore-tubes,** consisting of comparatively long tubes which form a single layer below the context. These pore-tubes occur at the lower or hymenial surface. The pore-mouths on the hymenial surface are regular and more or less circular in cross-section. The hymenial surface is also smooth, whitish, or greyish in colour, and with a shining lustre. Sections through the pore-tubes reveal the presence of **basidia** forming a **hymenium,** which lines the inner surface of each pore-tube. The basidia are club-shaped and each bears four **sterigmata** with four **basidiospores.** The basidiospores are hyaline, more or less oblong in shape and flattened at one side. At maturity, the basidiospores are discharged by 'water-drop

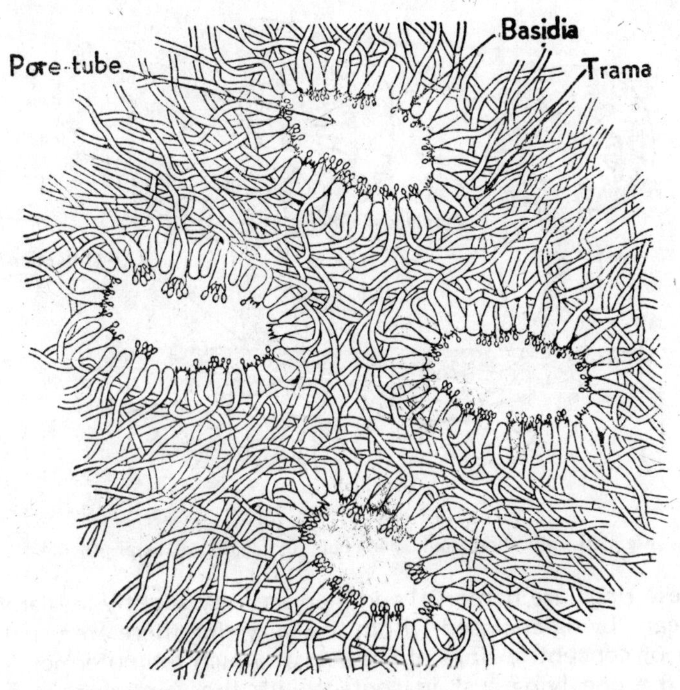

Fig. 200. *Polyporus.*
T. S. of a mature sporophore showing basidia, basidiospores, etc.

mechanism'. The basidia always develop from the terminal cell of the dikaryotic hyphae that project into the cavity of each pore-tube.

After the basidiospores are shed, they germinate under favourable conditions by putting forth germ tubes, from which primary mycelia of different sexes are derived.

AGARICUS (=*PSALLIOTA*)

(Fam. AGARICACEAE)

Agaricus campestris (=*Psalliota campestris*), a common edible gilled mushroom, is the species that is sold in the market. It is a saprophyte which grows, singly or in groups, during the rainy season in pastures, grassy places, richly manured unploughed fields, but never in thick woods. In open field, sometimes the fruit-bodies of the fungus come up forming small or large rings, the so-called **fairy rings.**

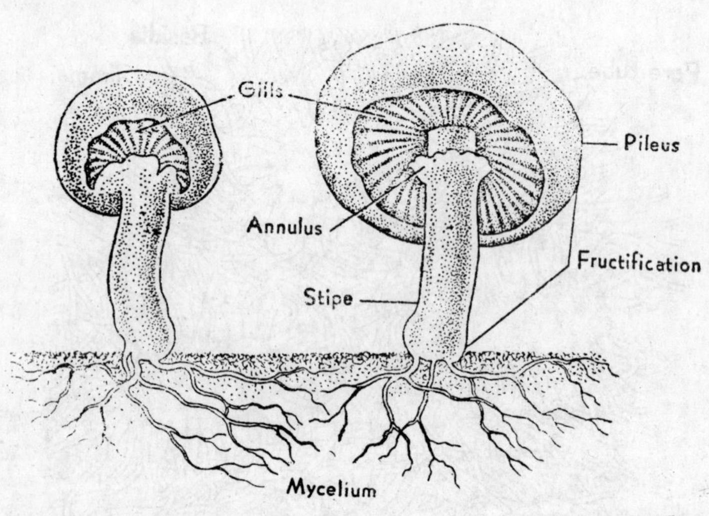

Fig. 201. Mycelium and sporophore of *Agaricus campestris*.

These rings are perennial and increase very slightly in diameter every year. Lying enclosed within the fairy ring there are usually a number of concentric rings of grasses, of which the outermost one, that is the one lying just in contact with the fairy ring, is quite healthy and luxuriant, as also in the innermost one. On the contrary, the intermediate ring of grass is extremely depressed in growth or may even be completely dead. The luxuriance in growth in the outermost ring is most probably due to the action of vigorously growing and centrifugally radiating mycelia on the various proteins and other organic materials present in the soil, thereby liberating a good deal of ammonia. The nitrifying soil bacteria convert this into nitrate which is ultimately utilized by the grasses as their food. On the other hand, the depression of growth in the intermediate grass ring can be explained by the fact that the water relations of the soil are unbalanced to a great extent by the fungal mycelia ramifying within the soil, consequently causing a drought during the dry season, and hence, causing damage to the zone.

The body of the fungus consists of two parts (Fig. 202), namely : the vegetative portion or the **mycelium,** and the **sporophore** (or **fructification** or **fruiting body**), concerned with the reproduction of the plant.

Vegetative body (Fig. 201)

The mycelium, which is perennial and subterranean, consists of extensively branched strands of septate, white hyphae, by means of which the plant not only vegetates but also draws nourishment from the substratum. The hyphal cells contain granulated, vacuolated and multinucleated (in most cases with twelve or more nuclei) protoplasm containing droplets of oil as reserve food. Hyphae of a centrifugally developing mycelium may be free from one another or may unite to form small rope-like strands, called **rhizomorphs.** When reproduction becomes necessary and after the mycelium has accumulated considerable stores of food, sporophores or the reproductive bodies of plants are produced on the rhizomorphic portion of the mycelium.

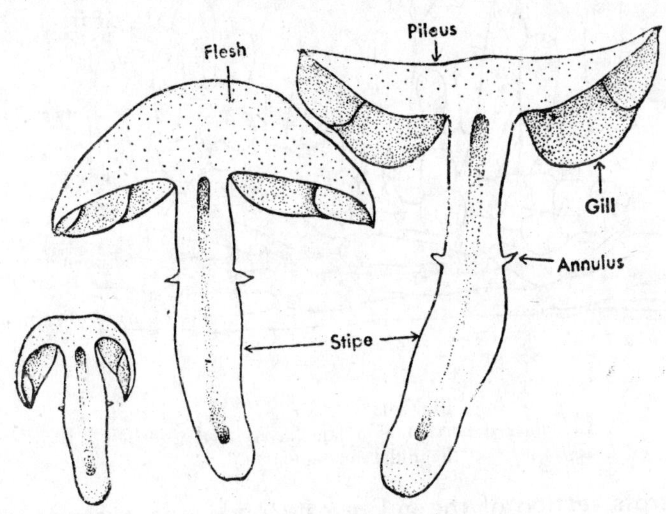

Fig. 202 *Agaricus*, Median longitudinal section through the sporophores showing different parts.

The sporophore (Fig. 202)

Typically, a mature sporophore consists of two parts : The **stipe** (about 5 to 8 cm. long, and 0.8 to 1.8 cm. in diameter) is the stalk-like portion which is composed of united aerial hyphae. It is at first solid and bulbous, but later on cylindrical and tapering below, and whitish in colour. In the stalk a broad, thin, white, fragile ring or **annulus** is also present. The stipe bears at its top an umbrella-like structure, known as the **pileus** (4 to 9.5 cm. in diameter), which is at first more or less convex, thin, flat, dry, smooth, soft, usually satiny white in colour, sometimes with minute brownish scales (triangular) and with a thin, wavy, white and delicate margin. The upper thick and white part of the pileus is known as the **flesh,** on the underside of which some delicate white to pink or flesh-coloured, thin, plate-like structures are seen. These are called the **gills** or **lamellae** (0.6 to 1.6 cm. broad in the middle and with 300 to 600 gills per pileus). The gills, which are free from the stipe ultimately become purple-brown to chocolate-brown to almost black with age, and they radiate outwards from the stalk towards the margins of the pileus.

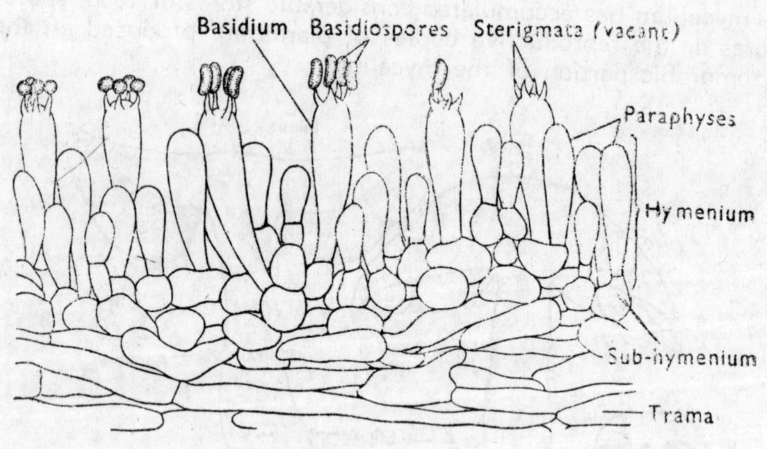

Fig. 203. *Agaricus*.
An enlarged portion of a lamella in section showing the different regions.

A cross section of the gill reveals, under the microscope, the following regions (Fig. 203) : (*a*) a central portion, the **trama**, consists of elongated multinucleate hyphal cells, which terminate both ways, right and left, to (*b*) **subhymenial** layers consisting of more or less circular hyphal cells (innermost cells multinucleate, outer ones binucleate) which end in (*c*) the **hymenium,** mainly composed of closely-packed, club-shaped cells known as **basidia.** Thus, each surface of the gill is covered with a layer of hymenium, the cells of which grow at right angles to its surface.

The basidia are really the spore-mother cells. Each basidium is binucleate at its first formation. These nuclei fuse to form a diploid nucleus which soon undergoes reduction division. After reduction division, four haploid daughter nuclei are formed, which furnish the nuclei of the basidiospores. Each basidium produces four **sterigmata,** through each of which a nucleus passes out to form a purple-brown or violet-brown, slightly kidney-shaped, thick-walled, uninucleate **basidiospore** (usually with a highly refractive oil-globule) at the tip, so that four basidiospores are produced on each basidium. Each spore, when separated, is provided with a small, eccentrically placed spine-like projection at the basal end, the former point of attachment of the sterigma.

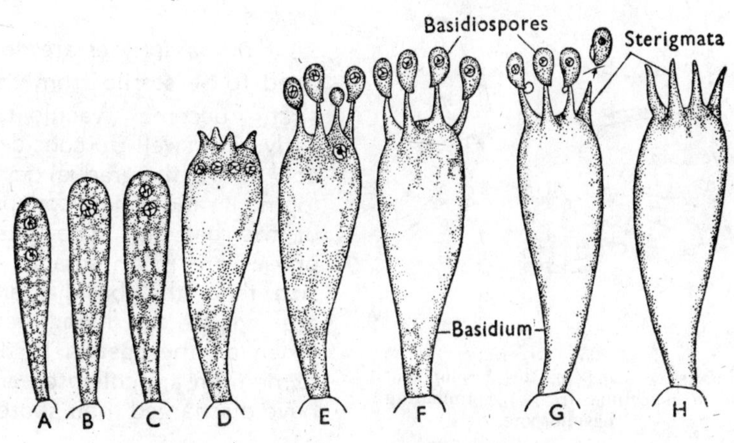

Fig. 204. *Agaricus.*
A—H. Diagrams showing successive stages in the development of the basidium and basidiospores, etc,

At maturity, just before spore discharge, a drop of water appears at the **spore hilum.** When the water drop attains full size, the spore is shot off which considerable violence.* The spores fall to the ground and under suitable conditions begin to germinate. Each spore, at the time of germination, becomes multinucleate and contains oil globules. On germination, it puts forth one, two, or even three, spherical or irregularly shaped germ tubes from any point, which ramifying profusely produce a new mycelium.

There are irregular ways of basidial development in a hymenium of *Agaricus*, which consists of five types of elements, according to Buller, viz. (1) basidia of past generation that have already discharged their spores, (2) basidia of present genera-

* "A single spore (1) takes 30 to 40 minutes to grow from a tiny rudiment to a full size, (2) remains colourless for the next 2 hours, (3) gradually becomes pigmented during the next 2 hours, (4) remains in the fully pigmented condition on the end of its sterigma for further 3 hours and about 10 minutes, and (5) is then discharged."—Buller, 1942.

tion with mature spores ready for discharge, (3) basidia of succeeding generation with developing sterigmata and immature spores, (4) basidia of future generation (erroneously called **paraphyses**) which have not yet formed sterigmata and spores, and (5) paraphyses.

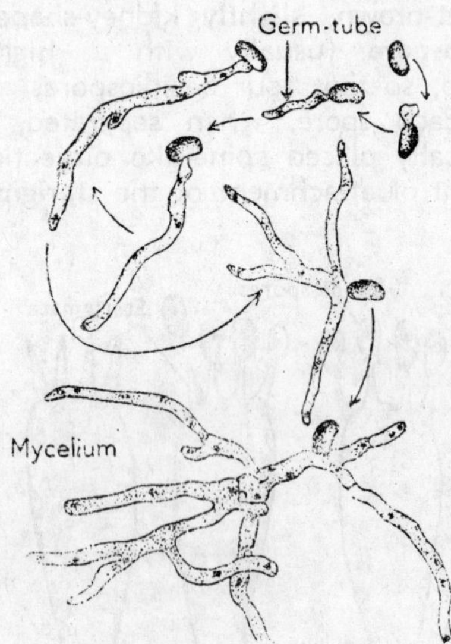

Fig. 205. *Agaricus*. Successive stages in the development of a mycelium from a germinating basidiospore.

The paraphyses are destined to be sterile from the first, become vaculoated early. and swell up considerably during the gradual development and final collapse of the basidia. The paraphyses are much smaller in size than the basidia and are visible as living cells when all the basidia in the hymenium are collapsed and have discharged their spores.

CULTIVATION OF EDIBLE MUSHROOM

Mushroom has been a popular food to a section of people since ancient times. Paddy straw mushroom is one of the most popular edible species in South-East Asia. Probably its cultivation started somewhere in China about 200 years ago according to Shu-Ting Chang (1977). Subsequently, some other South-East Asian countries also started its cultivation.

Possibilities of mushroom industry in India by cultivation was pointed out by S. R. Bose, in 1921. However, the cultivation of paddy straw mushroom was first attempted in this country by K. M. Thomas, (1943) at Coimbatore.

Method of cultivation

Fresh, uncrumpled and not more than one year old, paddy straw is usually used for cultivation of *Volvariella*. Leafy material is first removed from the straw before making bundles. Each bundle weighing $\frac{1}{2}$-1 kg is tied at both ends. Unequal parts are cut off and then immersed in clean water in a tank for 18—24 hours. Later, excess water is drained off and then 4 water soaked straw bundles are placed side by side on a bamboo or wooden frame (approximately 1 sq. metre). Another set of 4 bundles is placed opposite to the first layer. These 8 bundles constitute the first layer. This layer is spawned by broadcasting. The edge of the bed (about 4-6″ from the margin) is kept unspawned. After spawning, gram or pigeon pea (arhar dal) powder is dusted over the spawn. Then a 2nd layer of 8 bundles is placed across the first layer and this layer is again spawned like the first one. Similarly, a 3rd layer of 8 straw bundles is placed across the 2nd layer and spawned. In the first 3 layers, powdered gram or pigeon pea (arhar dal) is applied by dusting but the 4th layer (two layer) is left as such. The fourth layer of straw bundles is placed across the 3rd layer and is slightly pressed and tied with a rope. The bed is covered with a polythene or plastic sheet in such a way that it does not touch the straw. Usually one bottle of spawn and about 300g of gram or arhar dal powder are used for each bed.

The beds are watered once or twice daily depending upon the local environmental conditions. High temperature (35-40°C) and moisture are favourable for the production of paddy straw mushroom.

Precautions taken during cultivation

(a) Appropriate moisture content of the substrate must be maintained. (b) BHC Linden or Gammexane powder may be used against flies and insects. (c) *Coprinus*, a common weed fungus of mushroom beds should not be allowed to grow on the beds. This can be partially controlled by spraying beds with captan and zineb (0.2%). (d) During picking of mushrooms very young buttons should not be touched.

Picking of mushroom

Small buttons of mushroom usually start appearing 10-14 days after spawning. Picking can be done once or twice a day before the buttons open or the volva has just ruptured. Mushroom continues to appear at least for a period of 2 weeks, but maximum yield is obtained at the first flush.

Preservation of mushroom

This paddy straw mushroom is very delicate and should be consumed fresh. It can be stored in a refrigerator for 1 or 2 days. If the mushrooms are immersed in 10% salt solution and are dried in air, they can be stored for a longer period. Paddy straw mushrooms can be easily dried in the sun or in shade.

ORDER GASTEROMYCETALES

As in the Order Hymenomycetales but with fructifications either subterranean or subaerial ; hymenium remains closed within the peridium until the spores have attained maturity ; basidium never aseptate. Common genera are *Phallus*, *Lycoperdon*, *Cyathus*, etc.

PHALLUS

(Fam. PHALLACEAE)

Phallus impudicus, one of the well-known 'stink horn' fungi, is commonly found as saprophytes that grow in humus soil as well as on decaying wood and sawdust piles around the timber yards during the rainy season.

Vegetative body (Fig. 206)

The mycelium is subterranean and consists of irregularly-branched, white and septate hyphae which are often organized into smooth, string-like **rhizomorph.** The rhizomorph has a central prosenchymatous core and a pseudoparenchymatous cortical sheath. The hyphal cells are mostly dikaryotic and show typical clamp-connexions, but nothing is known about the existence of the monokaryon phase of the mycelium or about the manner in which the dikaryon mycelium is formed. Occasionally, a rhizomorph develops into an irregularly shaped **sclerotium.**

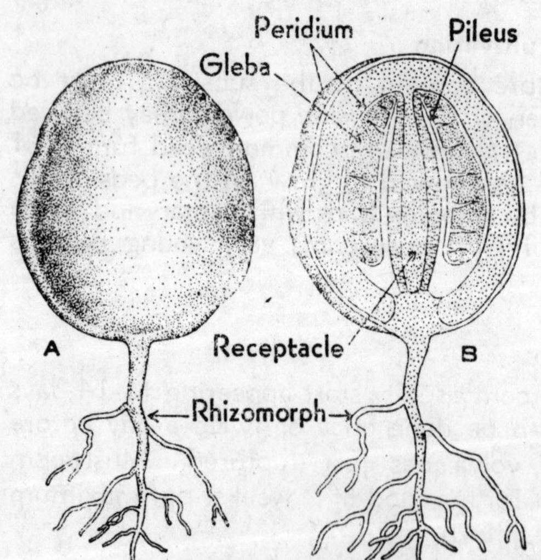

Fig. 206. *Phallus*,
A. A developing sporophore ; B, Median longitudinal section of the same,

The sporophore (Fig. 207)

When reproduction becomes necessary the mycelium bears, from its rhizomorphic portion, one to several **fructifications** or **sporophores,** the reproductive structures of the fungus. The fundament of a sporophore develops at the apex of a rhizomorph and during its development it remains hidden under the humus. The young sporophore soon increases in diameter and attains the size and shape of a hen's egg. At this stage, it consists of a wall, called the **peridium,** which is differentiated into an outer (**exoperidium**) and an inner (**endoperidium**) layers. The peridium encloses an internal fertile tissue, known as the **gleba.** Between exo- and endo-peridia there develops, at an early stage, a gelatinous layer, which is formed due to the disintegration of some of the hyphae. The exoperidium is continuous at the base of the fruit-body with a sterile column, or **receptacle,** running up the middle of the gleba. The gleba originates from the peripheral region of the internal tissue just within the endoperidium. It is differentiated into a number of closed chambers, each being lined internally by the hymenium. Very little is known about the development of **basidia**, but it is known that the young basidia are binucleate and formed early. Mature basidia are club-shaped, and each bears eight **basidiospores** on sterigmata at the apex. The tissue of the upper portion of the receptacle, lying just within the gleba, develops into a sterile **pileus,** while its basal portion forms a hollow **stipe,** subsequently developing into a mature sporophore of the 'stink horn'.

When the spores become ripe a mucilagenous, viscous matrix replaces the gleba, and this is formed by the disintegration of the basidia and the sterile glebal tissues. In this sticky matrix the spores remain embedded.

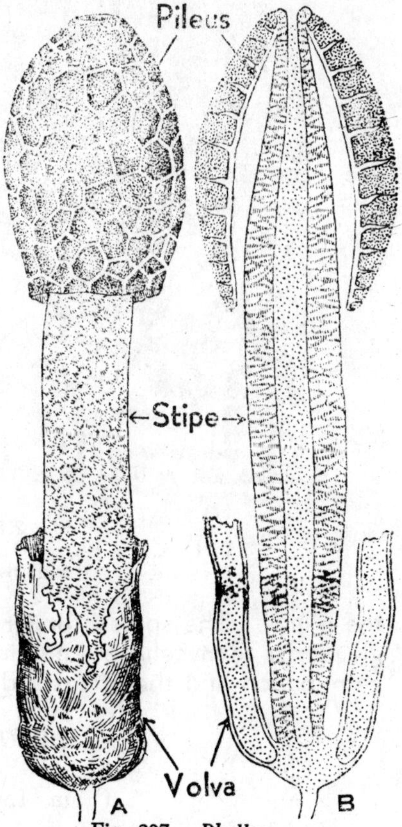

Fig. 207, *Phallus.*
A, A mature sporophore ; B, The same in median longitudinal section.

The unopened sporophores, commonly known as the 'eggs', may remain in this condition for a considerable time, but at any time with the approach of favourable conditions the elongation of the stipe begins, the peridium is ruptured, and the pileus with the sticky and gelatinous spore-mass is carried up into the air. Full development of the fructification takes place within half an hour or more, after the rupture of the peridium. When fully formed, the sporophore consists of an apical pileus covered by the viscous spore-mass and a hollow, chambered stipe filled internally with mucilage. The ruptured peridium forms a cup-like structure, known as the **volva,** at the base of the stipe. The sporophore emits foetid smell, characteristic of the fungus, and also a sweetish taste of the disintegrated gleba attracts various types of flies, which act as the major agency for spore-dispersal. Spores may also be discharged due to rains which wash down the basidiospores from

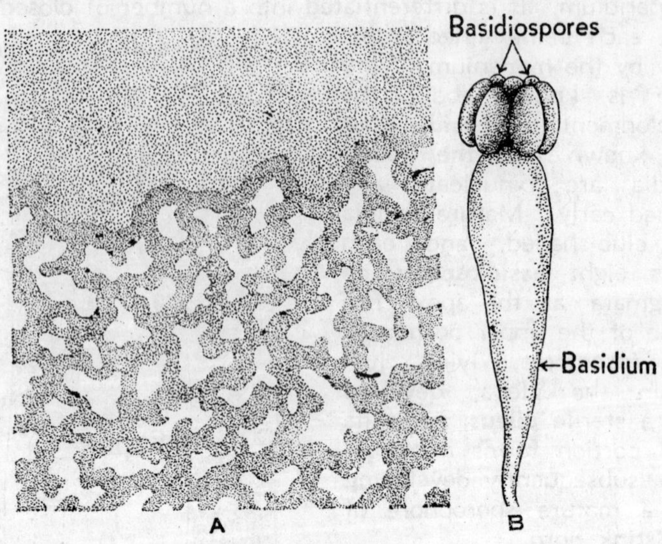

Fig, 208. *Phallus,*
A, T. S, of a part of the sporophore ; B, A basidium with basidiospores,

the pileus. The spores, under favourable conditions, germinate giving rise to mycelia, but nothing so far is known concerning spore-germination and the origin and nature of the mycelium.

LYCOPERDON

(Fam. LYCOPERDACEAE)

The members of the genus *Lycoperdon* are commonly known as *puff balls*. They are usually found to grow singly or in clusters on the ground in the woods, sometimes on grassy lands or in open fields. Almost all the species are edible at their young stage. The fruit-bodies are more or less pear-shaped with a thick, sterile stalk and they are variable in size.

Vegetative body

The primary mycelium is much-branched consisting of short uninucleate cells. The secondary mycelium, developed from the primary mycelium, may form several **rhizomorphs.** Each rhizomorph is a complex structure, usually composed of an outer cortical layer of loose hyphae, a subcortical layer of compact hyphae, and a central core of parallel hyphae.

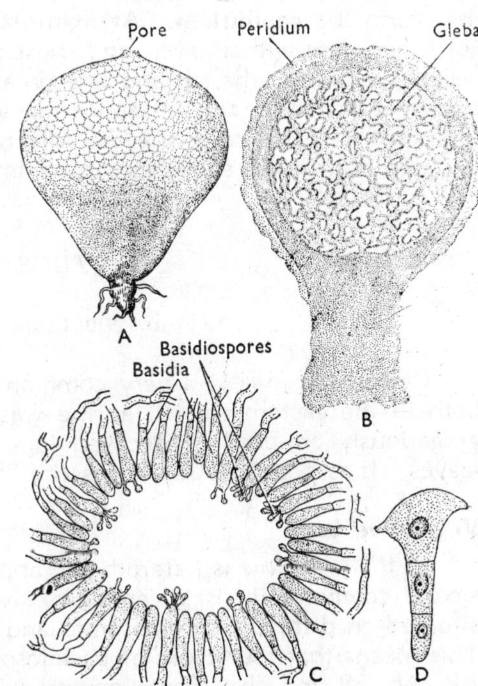

Fig. 209. *Lycoperdon*.
A, A mature sporophore ; B, V, S, through a young sporophore ; C, Section through the gleba showing the hymenial layer and the glebal cavity ; D, A germinating basidiospore.

The sporophore (Fig. 209)

At the time of reproduction, small hyphal knots develop at the tips of the rhizomorphs. These are the primordia of the **fruit-bodies** or **basidiocarps.** In early stage, the young primordium is a homogeneous structure, usually about 5 mm. in diameter but gradually, with age, they are differentiated into a sterile outer layer, the **peridium,** and an inner fertile region, the **gleba.** The peridium is also differentiated into two portions, the outer pseudoparenchymatous layer, the **exoperidium,** and the inner palisade-like layer, the **endoperidium.** As the basidiocarp increases in size, numerous, small, irregular cavities are distinguished inside the gleba, and these cavities are usually lined with loose interwoven hyphae. From these hyphae, eventually, the young **basidia** are developed. This type of gleba is known as the **lacunose gleba.**

Each young basidium at first contains two nuclei, but after karyogamy one fusion nucleus is formed. This fusion nucleus divides reductionally and gives rise to four nuclei. Meanwhile, four sterigmata are usually developed on each basidium and each of the sterigmata finally bears one **basidiospore.** The 4 nuclei of the basidium then migrate to the four basidiospores through sterigmata. When the spores attain maturity, they are collected inside the cavities. These spores with other glebal contents together form the **capillitium.** At maturity of the basidiocarp, the outer peridium withers away and subsequently, the inner peridium develops a pore at the top and as soon as the basidiocarp is pressed by any external force, the spore masses are discharged through the pores. In this case, the pressure may be exerted by wind or by large rain drops, sometimes by animals as well.

CYATHUS

(Fam. NIDULARIACEAE)

Cyathus striatus is a very common saprophytic species found both in the eastern as well as the western hemispheres, growing gregariously on dead or decayed logs of wood bark, twigs and leaves. It is popularly known as the "birds' nest fungus".

Vegetative body

Cyathus striatus is heterothallic and sexually tetrapolar, *i.e.* its sexual compatibility is governed by two pairs of factors AaBb situated on different chromosomes and segregating independently. This means that four types of basidiospores are produced, namely, AB, Ab, aB and ab. These spores on germination produce four types of primary monokaryophasic mycelia with different diploidizing possibilities. Deploidization is effected in the two mycelia of the combinations (AB) $\times$ (ab) and (Ab) $\times$ (aB) in which there are no factors in common, but not in the two mycelia in the combinations (AB) $\times$ (Ab), (AB) $\times$ (aB), (ab) $\times$ (Ab) and (ab) $\times$ (aB) in which one factor is common. Thus, in *Cyathus striatus* the combination (AB) $\times$ (ab) produces the dikaryophasic mycelium (AB) + (ab) and the combination (Ab) $\times$ (aB), the dikaryophasic mycelium (Ab) + (aB).

Each primary mycelium consists of short, uninucleate hyphal cells and is much branched. The dikaryophasic secondary mycelium is also much branched, whitish or brownish in colour with distinct simple clamp-connexions but with binucleate hyphal cells. It is this dikaryophasic mycelium that gives rise to the fructification (**basidiocarp** or **sporophore**) at the time of reproduction.

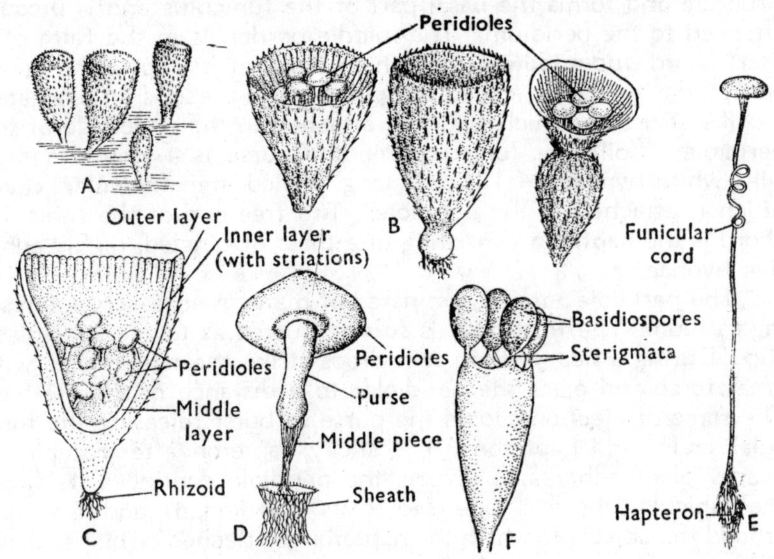

Fig. 210. *Cyathus striatus*.
A, A group of fructifications ; B, Three fructifications (in magnified view), two of them showing peridioles ; C, V. S, through a fruit-body ; D, A mature peridiole with its associated parts ; E, A disseminated peridiole ; F, Basidium with basidiospores.

The sporophore

A mature sporophore is vase-shaped or inverted bell-shaped structure, 5-9 mm. wide at the apex and 8-13 mm. high. The basal portion is solid and is known as the **stipe,** which arises from a reddish-brown mycelial mat. The wall of the fruit-body is called **peridium,** which consists of three layers. The outer layer is yellowish-brown or greyish-brown in colour and covered with coarse, shaggy and matted hairs which become worn off with age. The middle layer is fibrous, and the inner layer is greyish-brown, membranous and striate. Within the cavity of the sporophore there are several lentil-shaped dark grey or black **peridioles.** Each peridiole, about 2 mm. in diameter, is attached to the inner layer of the peridium by means of a slender connection, the **funiculus.** The peridiole is a capsule within which basidiospores are developed. It is bounded externally by a thin **tunica** which often flakes off. Within the tunica is a **cortex** of hard tissue. Basidiospores are produced by basidia which line the cavity in the centre of the peridiole. Externally, the funiculus shows three component parts—the **sheath,** the **middle piece** and the **purse.** The sheath is a tubular structure and forms the basal part of the funiculus and is broadly attached to the peridium. The middle portion is in the form of a short chord, the **middle piece,** which flares at its top to the upper part of the funiculus, called the **purse.** The purse is an elongated sac-like structure which is firmly attached to the underside of the peridiole. Coiled or folded within the purse is a long strand of silky-white hyphae, 4-12 cm. long, called the **funicular chord** which is attached to the peridiole. The free end of the funicular chord is the **hapteron** consisting of a mass of tangled, highly adhesive hyphae.

The peridioles are disseminated at maturity in a very interesting fashion. The fruit-body is so constructed as to act as a splash cup. During a heavy storm rain drops strike the fruit-bodies with great force and eject the peridioles to a distance of 3 to 4 feet. The force of ejection causes the purse to burst releasing the funicular chord and hapteron. The sticky hapteron after reaching a nearby plant adheres to it. As the peridiole continues its flight the funicular chord is extended to its full length and is coiled around the objects to which the hapteron is attached. The peridiole, by germinating as a whole, can propagate the fungus and spreads it locally. The mycelium, thus produced, is dikaryophasic and generally identical with the parent sporophore. There appears to be no evidence that the basidiospores locked within a peridiole can germinate. The basidiospores are hyaline, thick-walled, smooth, ovoid to elliptical and $6\text{-}12 \times 12\text{-}22\,\mu m$ in dimension.

CHAPTER IV

CLASS DEUTEROMYCETES (FUNGI IMPERFECTI)

The Deuteromycetes include those fungi, in which the 'perfect stage' is unknown. The term perfect stage means the stage in the life cycle in which the ultimate sex structures, like oospores, zygospores, asci, basidia, and teleutospores, etc., are formed. The vegetative body of these fungi are always septate mycelia, hyaline or coloured, much-branched and having hyphal cells usually with variable number of nuclei. Most of them reproduce by means of accessory spores, the **conidia,** which are characteristically different in form, colour, and septation from species to species. In many cases **chlamydospores** are produced in artificial cultures. Sometimes the vegetative bodies develop **sclerotia,** from which, under suitable conditions new mycelia are produced. They live either saprophytically or parasitically, and many of them are responsible for causing important diseases of the various crop plants.

Deuteromycetes are usually divided into *four* Orders, which are characterized as follows :

Conidia borne on superficial conidiophores, simple or branched, single or united into bundles, or conidiophores developed from a stromatic structure made up of matted hyphae	**Moniliales** (e.g. *Helminthosporium, Curvularia, Alternaria, Fusarium,* etc.)
Conidia produced within a flask-shaped or globose structure made up of plectenchyma, opening by means of an apical pore or ostiole, and embedded in a substratum ..	**Sphaeropsidales** (e.g. *Phyllosticta, Dendrophoma,* etc.)
Conidia produced in acervuli, which are saucer-shaped stromatic structures formed within the hosts, bearing conidiophores on their surfaces, and finally exposing the spores by the rupture of the overlying tissues ..	**Melanconiales** (e.g. *Colletotrichum, Pestalotia,* etc.)
Conidia unknown	**Mycelia sterilia** (e.g. *Rhizoctonia*)

ORDER MONILIALES

Conidia borne on superficial conidiophores, simple or branched, single or united into bundles, or conidiophores developed from a stromatic structure made up of matted hyphae.

HELMINTHOSPORIUM

(Fam. DEMATIACEAE)

The genus *Helminthosporium* is of considerable economic importance, because several species of this genus are responsible for bringing about a colossal devastation by their pathogenic action on the cereal crops of our country. As a result of the severe infection of the fungus, the yield of the cereal grains is abnormally decreased, and at the same time the quality of the grains become very poor. Sometimes the seedlings are seriously attacked, and they ultimately succumb to the disease. Among the various species, *H. oryzae* causes the most common **leaf spot** disease of rice, and in Bengal particularly, it occurs as a parasite on both the rabi and kharif crops. It has been observed that the infection caused by the pathogen may not necessarily be a systemic one only but also a localized one as well. It may also be noted that certain external agencies, e.g. continuous rainy days, cloudy weather, and irrigated field, etc., also add incentive towards the spread of this disease.

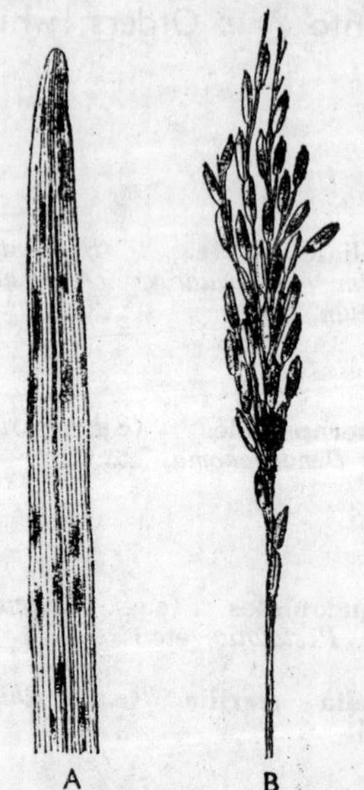

Fig. 211, *Helminthosporium*, A, Infected leaf ; B, Infected ear.

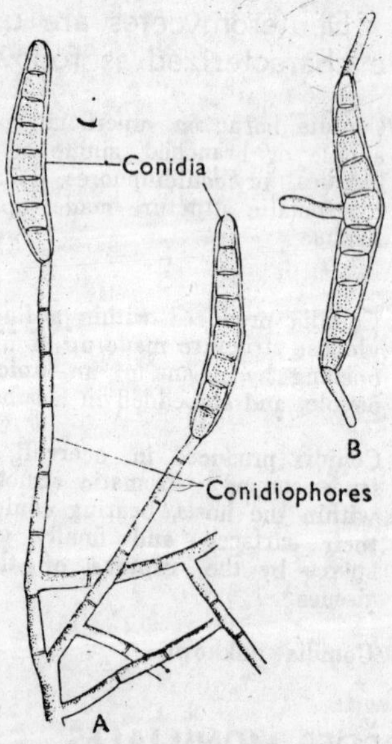

Fig. 212. *Helminthosporium*. A, Conidiophores with conidia ; B, A germinating conidium.

At first small brown spots are usually observed on both the surfaces of the leaves, intensity being greater specially on the lower surface. With age, the colour gradually changes from brown to dark-brown with a yellowish tinge at the margin of the spots. As the number of spots increases, they finally unite to form irregular areas, and the colour of the leaves changes to greyish-yellow. When the infection is intense, the colour of culms also turns to yellow, and eventually becomes dark-brown. Lesions appear on or near the lower joints of the rachis, and the glumes are first attacked at the junction of the outer and the inner ones. Owing to severe infection of the fungus, the ears may be sterile and the grain formation may be totally stopped.

Vegetative body

The vegetative body of the fungus is a branched mycelium, consisting of septate hyphae, which are generally found in intra- and intercellular regions of the host.

Reproduction

Sometimes branched or unbranched, erect, and septate **conidiophores** arise from the mycelium through the stomata, and rarely through the ruptured epidermis. The conidiophores bear terminally, and sometimes laterally, a more or less cylindrical or obclavate, multiseptate (generally 5-10 septa) and brown **conidia.** The conidia are ultimately discharged from the conidiophores, germinate under suitable conditions and infect other plants.

Control measures

Regarding the control of the disease, no successful measures have yet been precisely known. Since the seeds are infected both externally and internally, the familiar methods of control do not provide any fruitful result, the only way out being to select the 'immune' varieties.

ALTERNARIA

(Fam. DEMATIACEAE)

Alternaria is a pathogenic fungus causing diseases in a number of crop plants. Of the different species, *A. solani* is the one, which has been investigated in detail.

A. solani causes a disease in potatoes which is known as the **early blight.** The disease occurs widely in India and abroad. In the plains of India, however, it is the most ravaging disease of potatoes caused by any fungus.

The potato plant may be infected by the pathogen almost during any stage of its development. It has been noted, however, that the plant is usually attacked vigorously only when it has tided over its period of maximum growth.

The outward symptom of the 'early blight' disease appears as a few irregularly scattered, small, isolated, and pale-brown coloured spots appearing on the leaf surface. At first there may be a few spots only, but under favourable conditions, they increase in number. In case of virulent attack spots appear on petioles and even on stems. The infected leaves gradually begin to wither from base upwards leaving only a few near about the apex. After the leaf is dead, the spots begin to increase in size with their growth, they appear to be irregularly circular with a number of concentric ridges, and often provided with a spreading out, narrow and faded peripheral zone.

Vegetative body

The vegetative body of *A. solani* is a mycelium, which is composed of sparsely branched, septate hyphae. These hyphae

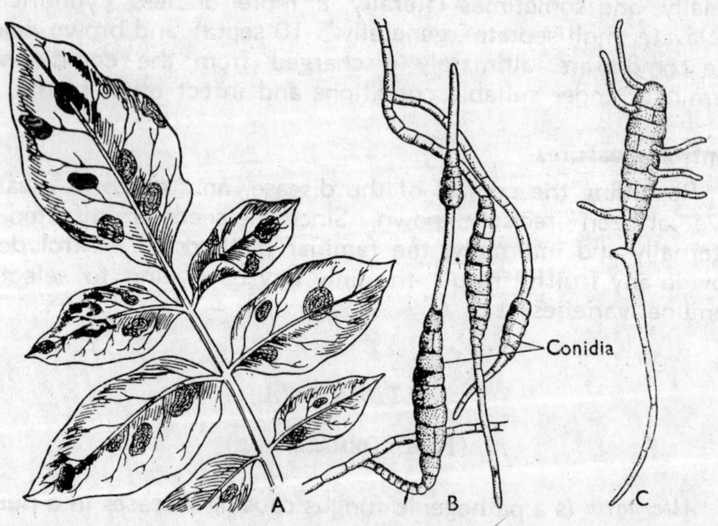

Fig. 213. *Alternaria.*
A, Leaflets of potato infected with the pathogen ; B, Conidia ; C, A germinating conidium.

are narrow, light-brown coloured, radiating and ramifying within the intercellular spaces of the invaded host tissue ; they also penetrate into the cells. So, the fungus is intercellular as well as intracellular in nature. On maturity, the mycelium becomes rather irregular and closely branched.

Reproduction

Reproduction in *A. solani* takes place only with the help of **conidia.** From the spots the **conidiophores** come out through the stomata bearing conidia. The conidia are usually five-to-ten-septate, and generally obclavate in shape ; occasional longitudinal septa are also frequently noted. Each of them is borne singly on the conidiophore and ends in a long, septate, tapering beak, which is sometimes branched. If the weather is moist a conidium readily germinates, and puts forth five to ten germ tubes. These germ tubes usually enter a fresh host through the stomata, but in rare cases a direct penetration has been recorded, where a germ tube pierces straight through the wall of the epidermis.

Control measures

The disease becomes very widespread when there is plenty of moisture and a corresponding high temperature unsuitable for the host plant. On the other hand, it is checked as a result of continued drought. The primary infection from the soil can be controlled by practising crop rotation. A proper spraying of Bordeaux mixture is also very much helpful in controlling the disease.

FUSARIUM

(Fam. TUBERCULARIACEAE)

Fusarium, like *Alternaria*, occurs on a number of crop plants. *F. udum* in an economically important species, since it causes the most serious type of damage to the pigeon peas (***Cajanus cajan***) by causing the **wilt disease.** The disease is particularly destructive in Bihar, Madhya Pradesh, Uttar Pradesh, and some parts of Maharashtra.

The pathogen enters the host through the delicate branch roots and possibly the root hairs, but never through any subaerial part. The first visible symptoms of the disease appear when the plant is only about one and a half month's old. The leaves of the infected plant become prematurely yellow and then wither ; finally, the whole plant becomes dried up, and dies very quickly. Wilting, in some cases, may be partial, when only the attacked parts become dry. The vascular tissues of the root and stem of an infected plant reveal on examination the appearance of thin or thick black streaks, depending on the stage of the disease.

Vegetative body

The vegetative body of the fungus is a hyaline mycelium, which is both intracellular as well as intercellular in nature, being restricted, as a rule, to the vascular tissues. The hyphae are branched and septate, which grow profusely within the tracheal lumens and subsequently become matted and coiled, thus clogging the lumens. The pathogen also exerts toxic influences on the adjoining living cells by secreting harmful substances.

Reproduction

The reproduction in *Fusarium* takes place by means of **conidia** and **chlamydospores** produced within the host tissues. The chlamydospores are thick-walled, and may occur either singly or in chains,

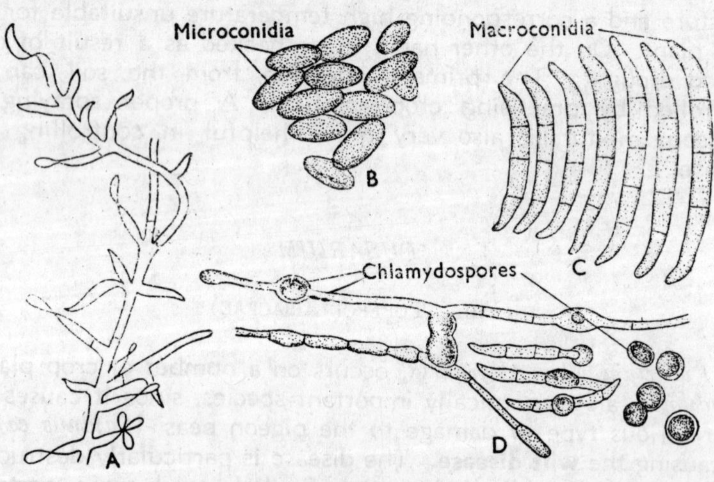

Fig, 214. *Fusarium.*
A, Formation of microconidia on conidiophores ; B, Microconidia ; C, Macroconidia ; D, Different forms of chlamydospores.

either terminally or in an intercalary fashion. They are more durable and viable than the conidia. The conidia are of two types : **macroconidia** and **microconidia.** Both these types of conidia are formed on **conidiophores.** The former are long, somewhat curved and pointed at both the ends, and are generally provided with a number of septa. On the other hand, the latter are small, curved or elliptical bodies, either unicellular or provided with one or two septa only.

These conidia and chlamydospores remain viable for a considerable length of period in the soil. When the crop is sown in such a soil, it gets readily attacked by the germinating spores.

Another important species of *Fusarium* is *F. vasinfectum* causing the 'wilt disease' of cotton. The disease can be found in different parts of India, but particularly in Madhya Pradesh and Maharashtra, as it is restricted to black cotton soils. The pathogen enters into the body of the host, when it is only one to three weeks old. The symptoms and etiology of the disease are like those caused by *F. udum* in pigeon peas.

Control measures

The wilt disease cannot be controlled effectively by any direct treatment. The intensity of the disease can, however, be minimized by the rotation of crops. The best method for controlling the disease is the cultivation of suitable resistant varieties.

ORDER **MELANCONIALES**

Conidia produced in acervuli, which are saucer-shaped stromatic structures formed within the hosts, bearing conidiophores on their surfaces, and finally exposing the spores by the rupture of the overlying tissues.

COLLETOTRICHUM

(Fam. MELANCONIACEAE)

Colletotrichum causes diseases on several crop plants in India and abroad. Of the different species, the one that attacks the sugarcane, is very important from the economic standpoint of view. The most destructive fungal disease of the sugarcane is the **red rot** due to *C. falcatum*. Practically, it can be found in any country wherever the sugarcane is commercially cultivated. In India it occurs in almost all the States.

All the subaerial parts of the sugarcane plant, particularly the stems and midribs of leaves, are prone to the attacks of *C. falcatum*. In the leaves the infection starts as a dark-red patch on the midrib. This patch elongates quickly and gives rise to blood-red lesions, provided with dark-coloured margins. In mature lesions, the central region becomes pale-yellow or straw-coloured. In the stems external symptoms are usually not visible until the disease has spread far internally. When the internal rotting of the stem is complete, the bright colour of the rind is lost, and shrinkage takes place at the nodes. The upper leaves of the infected plant become pale and droop down a little. At about this time their tips begin to wither. Subsequently, this withering begins to travel in a downward direction along both the margins, the central portion remaining unaffected and green. On splitting open an internally rotted stem, one or a few of the internodes, usually the basal ones, are noted to be red-coloured in longitudinal directions. Characteristically and crosswisely developed white patches interrupt these red striations. This red colouration is extremely deep in the region of the vascular bundles. In the case of a serious attack the colour is found to be extending through a large number of internodes, and the entire crop withers and droops.

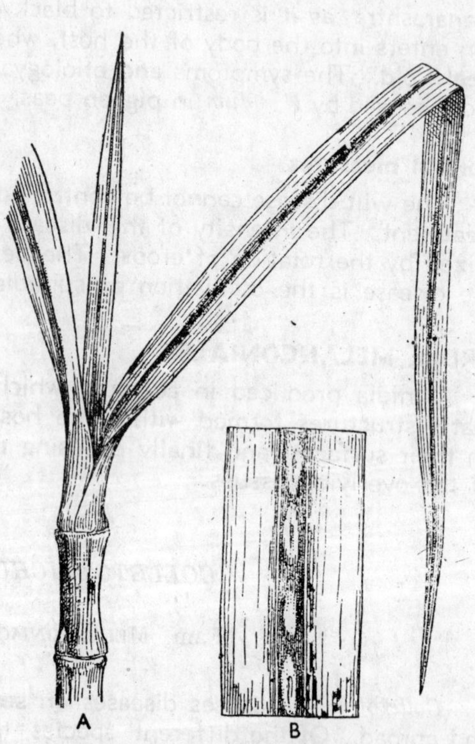

Fig. 215. *Colletotrichum.*
A, Part of a sugarcane plant infected with the pathogen ; B, A portion of an infected leaf (magnified).

Though it is usually believed that the pathogen cannot persist in the soil, recently it has been investigated in India that it can do so up to a period of six months. Satisfactory evidences to prove it, however, are still lacking. At any rate, it has been observed that if sugarcane trash from infected plants be put in the soil, the fresh crop becomes largely infected.

Vegetative body

The vegetative body of the pathogen is a mycelium, which is found mainly in the pith cells as well as in their intercellular spaces. The hyphae constituting the mycelium are septate, narrow, hyaline and extensively branched. The cells contain oil droplets.

Reproduction

C. falcatum reproduces by means of **conidia.** In the United States of America, however, the **perfect** or **ascigerous stage** has recently been discovered, both in the laboratory as well as in the field. This perfect stage is *Physalospora* sp. belonging to the Order Sphaeriales under the Ascomycetes.

In the shrunken up stems, in depressions or ridges just above or below the nodes, the **acervuli** appear on the rind as clusters of minute, velvety, dark-coloured bodies. These acervuli consist of long septate **setae** and a number of smaller-sized unseptate **conidiophores** bearing **conidia** singly near about the tips. The conidia are single-celled, hyaline but densely granular, usually falcate or sickle-shaped and guttulate. In some cases the setae develop forming a fringe around an acervulus. Occasionally, intercalary or terminal **chlamydospores** are found, which are greenish-black in colour. A conidium, on germination, either develops directly into a mycelium or gives rise to an **apresorium.** The conidia usually remain enclosed within the sheaths of the leaf-bases, where moisture is also retained. This helps in the germination of the conidia and when the leaves are torn off, innumerable scars are left behind at the nodes, through which the pathogen enters the host.

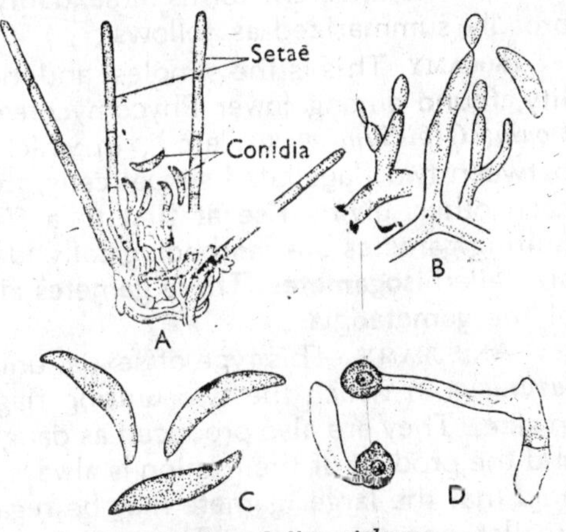

Fig. 216. *Colletotrichum.* A, Part of an acervulus ; B, Conidia being formed on conidiophores ; C, Conidia ; D, Germinating conidia forming appresoria.

Control measures

The use of healthy seeds, destruction of diseased plants and trash, improved cultural methods, and rotation of crops help in controlling the disease. The cultivation of red-rot resistant varieties is, however, the most effective method in checking the disease.

Evolution and Degeneration of Sexuality in Fungi

It is the usual practice with the botanists to consider plants having definite sex organs and sexual reproductive units (gametes) as primitive ones and placed low in the scale of evolution than those which do not possess any apparent sex organs or gametes. The mode of sexual reproduction in fungi, in this respect, affords a very good example of gradual reduction and final obliteration of any trace of the sex organs or gametes. If one gradually advances from the Phycomycetes to the Basidiomycetes through the Ascomycetes, one can never fail to notice it, though occasional types may be found, which shows a tendency towards the primitive forms. The different forms of sexuality found among fungi may be broadly summarized as follows :

Isogamy. This is the simplest and most primitive form of sexuality, found among lower Phycomycetes (e.g. *Synchytrium endobioticum*, *Olpidium viciae*, etc.), in which sexual union takes place between two flagellated sexual cells, that are not closely related to each other, giving rise at first to a flagellated zygote. Since, the uniting gametes are morphologically identical with each other, they are called **isogametes.** These gametes always arise as daughter cells of the gametangia.

Anisogamy. This type of sexual union is exhibited by *Allomyces javanicus* in which the two uniting flagellated gametes differ only in size. They are also produced as daughter cells of the gametangia and the product of their union is always a zygote. Some mycologists hold that the larger gamete may be regarded as the female and the smaller one the male. The gametangium that gives rise to the female gamete is usually larger than the gametangium producing the male gamete.

Oogamy. In this type of sexuality the gametes not only arise as daughter cells of the gametangia but they are sexually differentiated into male and female gametes. Typical oogamous reproduction is found in *Monoblepharis* where sexual union takes place between a flagellated small, motile male gamete or spermatozoid and a large, non-motile, non-flagellated female gamete or oosphere or ovum. The product of the union is always an oospore (zygote). The sex organs are also differentiated into antheridium (male gametangium) and oogonium (female gametangium). In other cases, as in *Saprolegnia*, *Phytophthora*, *Pythium*, *Albugo*, etc., though the antheridia and oogonia become more marked and well-developed, the antheridium never gives rise to motile spermatozoids, which are represented by the male gamete nuclei. In such cases the male nuclei from the antheridium pass into the oogonium through the fertilization-tube and are discharged near the oosphere. Only one male nucleus then unites with the female nucleus of the ovum, and an oospore is formed. In *Saprolegnia* there are several oospheres within the oogonium. In this case, several antheridia are formed and from these different fertilization-tubes penetrate the wall of the oogonium and discharge the sperm nuclei to the individual oospheres and fertilization takes place. As a result of union several oospores are produced within the single oogonium. The type of sexual reproduction in which oospores are produced is known as **oomycetous,** and the group of fungi producing it is known as **Oomycetes.**

GAMETANGIAL COPULATION. This type of sexuality represents the first step towards the gradual reduction of sex in fungi. In this case the gamete formation is suppressed and union takes place between gametangia instead of gametes. The role of gametes is taken over by the gametangia, and as a result of gametangial fusion their multinucleate contents fuse to form a strong coenocytic zygote, known as the zygospore. Sexual reproduction resulting in zygospore formation is known as the **zygomycetous** type and the fungi forming zygospores are known as **Zygomycetes.** This type of sexuality is commonly found in *Mucor*, *Rhizopus*, *Phycomyces*, *Pilobolus*, etc. The species may be homothallic or heterothallic. In heterothallic forms the thalli as well as the gametangia produced by them are designated as (+) or female, and (—) or male.

SELF-FERTILIZATION. This type of sexuality represents the next higher step towards reduction of sex in fungi and is found among the members of Ascomycetes. In this case only a functional oogonium is present, and an antheridium is either abortive or entirely absent. As a result, union cannot take place between two sex organs. There are two ways by which the sexual act is performed. In *Ascobolus citrinus* the female sexual organ is multicellular and union takes place between two cells of the female sexual organs (**parthenogamy**). In *Humaria granulata*, on the other hand, the oogonium is multinucleate and fusion takes place between the sexual nuclei in pairs within the oogonium and not by cell fusion (**autogamy**).

PSEUDO-FERTILIZATION. In this case the degeneration is sexuality has gone a step further. The sex organs have completely disappeared and sexual union takes place between two vegetative cells. In many heterothallic Basidiomycetes (e.g. *Peniophora sambauci*, *Polyporus ostreiformis*, *Polystictus sanguineus*, *Polystictus hirsutus*, *Stereum fuscum*, *Lentinus subnudus*, etc.) fusion between the vegetative cells of mycelia bearing opposite sexual strains takes place and the nuclei of complementary strains become associated together. In this case plasmogamy occurs and karyogamy is delayed till the formation of the basidium in which the two nuclei fuse to form a zygote nucleus. In some yeats (e.g. *Saccharomyces*, *Zygosaccharomyces*, etc.) union takes place between two vegetative cells, the nuclei fuse and a zygote is formed. The uniting cells may be entirely unrelated or may be mother and daughter cells.

Parthenogenesis and Apogamy. These processes represent the last step in the reduction of sexuality in which reproduction takes place vegetatively without cell- or nuclear-fusion. In parthenogenesis new individuals are produced from haploid sexual cells, while in apogamy the individuals arise from diploid sexual cells without meiosis.

Economic importance of Fungi

The fungi are of great economic importance on account of their both harmful as well as beneficial effects. A large number of fungi cause destructive havoc to our valuable crop and timber plants, various kinds of food and food products. They also attack the live-stock as well as human beings. Some serious diseases of the skin, eye, ear, nose and throat as well as intestinal and bronchial disorders are also caused by the various groups of fungi. But, all of them are not harmful to the mankind, as most of the species bring about decomposition of dead bodies of plants and animals as well as of animal dung ; thus the organic debris is removed from the surface of the earth and the fertility of the soil is enriched. Further, some species are edible and quite a good number of them produce various kinds of vitamins, organic acids, drugs, enzymes, alcohols and other medicinally and industrially important substances.

The Phycomycetes usually cause damage to different crop plants. For example, *Pythium de Baryanum* causes the 'damping off' disease resulting in the death of young seedlings. *Phytophthora infestans* is responsible for the serious 'late blight' and 'rot' of potato. *Albugo candida* brings about much deformation of the inflorescences and fruits of cruciferous plants throughout the world. *Peronospora parasitica* is the pathogen causing the 'downy mildew' of crucifers. *Saprolegnia parasitica* causes serious damage to the fishing industry. The various species of *Mucor* and *Rhizopus* spoil the preserved fruits, pickles, jams and jellies, bread, butter, cheese, leather and various other consumable articles. A few members of the Order Mucorales, however, can produce some organic acids.

Of the different ascomycetous fungi, the three medicinally most important ones are the yeasts, penicillia and ergot fungi. Various species of *Saccharomyces* are very good sources of vitamin B. *Penicillium notatum* and *P. chrysogenum* yield the wonder drug 'penicillin'. *Claviceps purpurea* produces the 'ergot', which is extensively used for stopping haemorrhage after child birth. The different types of yeasts are employed for the preparation of various kinds of alcoholic drinks as well as in baking breads. Some species of *Aspergillus* are used in the preparation of diastase and organic acids, while some costly cheeses are prepared with the help of a few species of *Penicillium*. *Morchella esculenta*, the common morel, is an edible fungus.

The polypores among the Basidiomycetes are the chief agents in causing serious damages to the timber trees, lumbers, railway sleepers, telegraph and fencing posts, and wooden buildings and furniture. It is interesting to note that some of them, however, are taken as food by man, such as *Daedalea flavida*. Besides various mushrooms, puff balls also form table delicacies. Some of them are, however, deadly poisonous to the human system, and may even cause death. The members of the orders Uredinales and Ustilaginales are highly destructive to the various important crop plants, like wheat, maize, oat, barley and others. Researches are going on for the discovery of antibiotics from some polypores. *Auricularia auricula* is locally used in some parts of India for curing car sores.

Many of the Deuteromycetes not only cause diseases of some higher plants but also are responsible for the athletes foot, ringworm and other skin diseases in man.

SECTION III

MYXOMYCETES

MYXOMYCETES

GENERAL CONSIDERATION

The Myxomycetes or slime moulds occupy a dubious systematic position. As they show marked affinities with the Protozoa, some botanists favour their exclusion from the plant kingdom, while others consider that they occupy a position among the plants equal in status with the true fungi. They resemble the true fungi in the absence of chlorophyll as well as in the nature of reserve food materials, but they differ from them in having a single, large, naked, multinucleate amoeboïd protoplast (**plasmodium** or **pseudoplasmodium**).

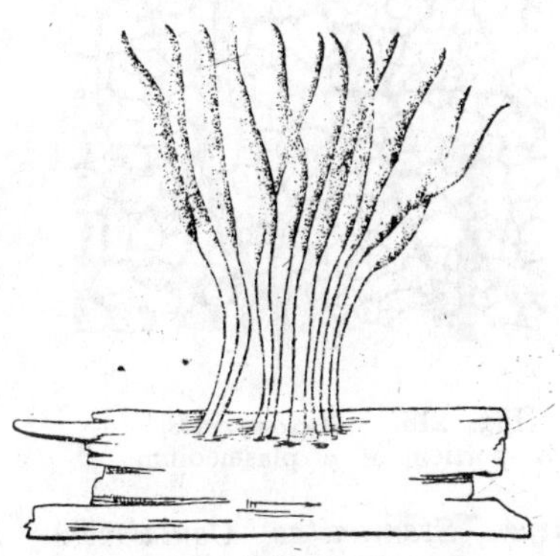

Fig. 217. *Myxomycetes.* Vegetative body of a plant.

The Myxomycetes are mainly terrestrial organisms, commonly found on fallen leaves, decaying wood, humus soil, etc. They are cosmopolitan in their distribution.

The free-living plasmodia of slime moulds look like gigantic amoeba and may be several centimetres in diameter. A plasmodium is capable of a creeping motion with the help of **pseudopodia,** which are finger-like protrusions developed from the body, and are alternately pushed out and withdrawn in succession. The vegetative body is multinucleate and cytoplasmic movements may be noted within it. Like amoeba it can also ingest solid food, such as spores, small remains of plant or animal bodies, bacteria and other microscopic organisms.

At the time of reproduction an entire plasmodium comes out of the substratum, forms a heap and gives rise to one or a few stalked or sessile **sporangia.** The sporangia are variously shaped. There is usually found a network of tube-like structures called the **capillitium,** within a sporangium, and numerous small **spores,** each surrounded by a wall of its own, are found in the meshes of the capillitium. On maturity, the sporangial wall ruptures and the spores are dispersed. Each spore, on germination, gives rise to 1-4 uniflagellate-like bodies, which may fuse in pairs immediately or undergo vegetative multiplication. If the swarmers unite in pairs, an amoeboid zygote is produced, which ultimately develops into a multinucleate plasmodium.

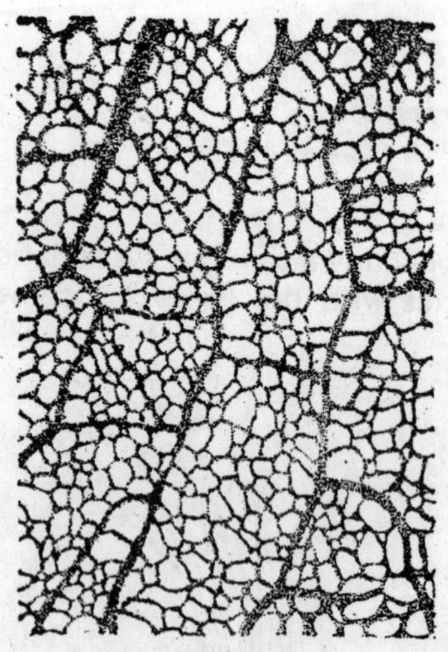

Fig. 218. *Myxomycetes*. A portion of a plasmodium,

The Myxomycetes include about 50 genera and 400 species and are generally divided into two subclasses : (1) **Endosporeae,** where the spores are produced within the sporangium, and (2) **Exosporeae,** where the spores are borne externally on branched pillar-like structures. The former subclass consists of the following genera which are found in India : *Physarum*, *Physarella*, *Trichemphara*, *Craterium*, *Diderma*, *Diachea*, *Didymium*, *Stemonites*, *Comatricha*, *Lamproderma*, *Cribraria*, *Lycogala*,

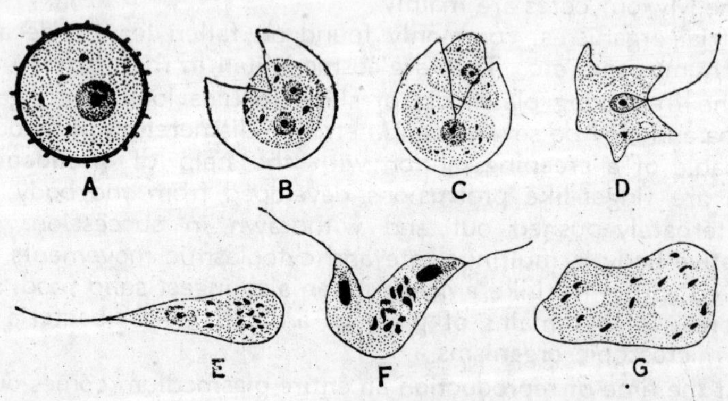

Fig. 219, *Myxomycetes*.
A, A mature spore ; B—E, Germination of the spore and development of a swarmer ; F, Two swarmers uniting ; G, An amoeboid zygote.

Trichia, *Hemitrichia*, *Cornuvia*, *Arcyria*, *Perichaena*, while the latter one is represented in India by the only genus *Ceratiomyxa*.

ORDER **PLASMODIOPHORALES**

PLASMODIOPHORA

(Fam. PLASMODIOPHORACEAE)

Plasmodiophora attacks a number of cultivated cruciferous plants. The best-known species is *P. brassicae*, which causes the **clubrot** or **finged-and-toe** diseases of the cabbage.

The host may be attacked at any time during its active growth, but infection usually takes place at the seedling stage. The amount of moisture present in the soil is an important factor in the occurrence of the disease. The infection takes place when the soil contains about 60 per cent. moisture or above, but not when the percentage falls to 45 per cent. or below. Light soils and moorlands are also the favourite dwelling places of this pathogen than loamy and clayey soils. As the popular name suggests, the infection essentially takes place in the roots. A uniflagellate **swarmspore*** comes in contact with the cell-wall of the root hair, loses its flagellum and then enters into the root hair in an amoeboid fashion. It may also directly penetrate into the older regions of the root cortex. The affected part begins to grow remarkably, and in the long run becomes abnormally swollen. When the disease is considerably advanced so as to cause a disturbance in the continuity of the vascular system, the leaves turn yellow, wilt and fall off, and the plant becomes stunted in growth.

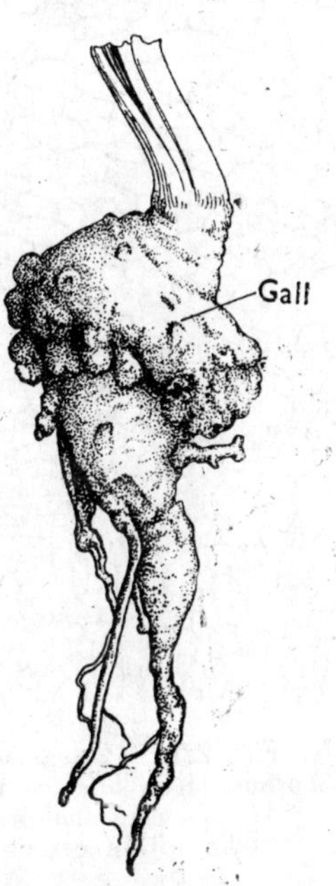

Fig. 220. *Plasmodiophora*. Formation of the gall on tap root due to infection.

Vegetative body

The vegetative body is an intracellular multinucleate **plasmodium.**

Reproduction

Plasmodiophora reproduces both asexually and sexually.

Chupp (1917), and Cook and Schwartz (1930) are of the

* Butler and Jones (1949) consider that the swarmspore is unequally biflagellate.

opinion that the swarmspore, which causes the primary infection of the root, is a haploid body. The nucleus of the amoeboid cell, after it has entered into the root hair, divides repeatedly, and ultimately a multinucleate plasmodium is formed. Later on, the plasmodium breaks up into a number of uninucleate masses, each surrounded by a wall of its own.

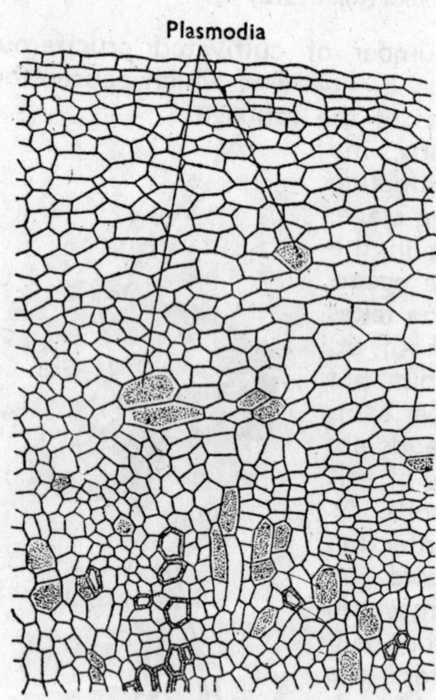

Fig. 221. *Plasmodiophora,* A portion of an infected root in transverse section showing the presence of plasmodia within certain cells.

During sexual reproduction each of these uninucleate cells, produced asexually, may develop into a **gametangium.** The gametangial nucleus again undergoes divisions forming four or eight nuclei. The cytoplasm is again cleaved, and each uninucleate mass is finally metamorphozed into a tiny, uniflagellate **zoogamete.** The zoogametes unite in pairs, either within the root hair itself, or after they have migrated into the neighbouring cortical cells. The product of fusion is an amoeboid zygote with one diploid nucleus. This zygote is known as the **myxamoeba.**

The myxamoeba then increases in size and its nucleus undergoes a few divisions, thus forming a diploid plasmodium. This plasmodium begins to migrate from one cell to another within the host tissue and even comes inside the cambial cell. Vertical upward or downward migrating movements of the plasmodia through the cambium have been noted. Finally, when a plasmodium, after its outward migration, reaches a food-laden cortical cell it lodges within it, and increases considerably in size. Thus the swelling in the root is formed. Along with the increase in size of the plasmodium, its nuclei divide repeatedly, the last two series of divisions being meiotic (Lutman, 1913 ; Cook and Schwartz ; Cook. 1933). When the nuclear divisions are complete, innumerable vacuoles of various sizes appear within the cytoplasm. Ultimately, the plasmodium is fragmented into many minute, uninucleate bits, each of which becomes a distinct **spore.** When the host undergoes

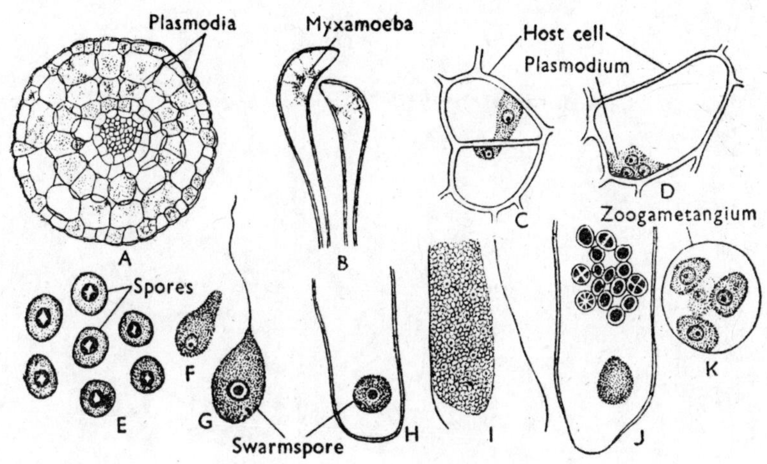

Fig. 222. *Plasmodiophora.*
A. T. S. of an infected root showing plasmodia ; B, Myxamoebae within root hairs ; C-D, Host cells with plasmodia ; E, spores ; F, A germinating spore ; G, A swarmspore ; H, A swarmspore (inside a root hair) with its flagellum withdrawn ; I—J, Stages in the formation of zoogametangia:; K, A zoogametangium containing developing zoogametes.

degeneration, the spores are liberated as **swarmspores,** and fresh infections occur in the soil.

SECTION IV

PLANT PATHOLOGY

INTRODUCTION

Plant Pathology deals with the various diseases of plants and their remedy as well. By the term 'disease' is meant the disorders in plants. These diseases are caused by organisms, known as **pathogens.** which are carried to health plants through the agency of air, water, insects, etc.

The Plant diseases are broadly divided into two types: **systemic** and **localised.** Systemic disease is plants disease in the entire plant which is affected by the diseases while in the localised disease only certain parts or parts of organs suffer from the disease. For instance, in a parasite or virus disease the plant as a whole or its major portion becomes affected by the pathogen and thereby causing derangement in the normal life process of the plant is a disease of the systemic type. Besides the very commonly observed the yellowing of plants is also a disease of this type. On the other hand, diseases like leaf spot, fruit rots, localised killing of roots flowers, fruits, etc., causing disturbances in the affected organs only are of the localised type.

Plant diseases may also be of three types : **endemic, epiphylotic** or **epidemic** and **sporadic**—according to the period of recurrence. **Edemic diseases** are those which occur more or less constantly every year, either in a moderate or virulent form. **Epiphytotic or epidemic diseases** occur periodically but cause widespread destruction in a community or communities of plants. **Sporadic diseases** are also epidemic diseases which break out in relating few cases as well as in different localities and that also at irregular intervals.

CLASSIFICATION OF PLANT DISEASES

Plant diseases have been classified into three categories based on *causes*.

(a) Diseases of plants caused by parasites or **parasitic diseases**

These diseases include all the attacks on a living plant caused by another living organism, which is a parasite. The majority of parasitic diseases are caused firstly by the fungi, both higher and lower, and secondly by the bacteria. A few seed plants like Mistletoes, Dodders and a few others also act as parasites. Similarly, a few parasitic species of algae as well as a number of animals, particularly the nematodes or round worms, bring about these types of disease The affected plant is usually referred to as the *host*.

(b) Diseases of plants caused by many parasitic or **Non-parastic diseases**

A large number of diseases belong to this group, but comparatively a few only have been properly studied. Such diseases include many departures from the normal healthy state of the plant caused by unfavourable conditions, which may be nutritional disturbances, undesirable or adverse environmental conditions, as well as harmful mechanical causes.

(c) Diseases of plants caused by viruses or **Virus diseases**

These diseases are of the systemic type and are caused by the transmission, of an active principle, the **virus,** which acts as an infection, spreading the disease from infected to healthy plants. The transmission of the infectious principle may take place by contact only or by budding or grafting as well as by inoculation of healthy plants with the juice from the infected ones. The majority of the virus diseases are, however, transmitted naturally by the insect visitors, usually termed as *vectors*, who cause punctures on the plant body during their feeding and thus transmit the disease, which they have already carried from some diseased plant sources.

CHAPTER I

TERMS AND DEFINITIONS

The following terms and definitions are commonly used in Plant Pathology.

1. **Causal complex**

A combination of a number of environmental and other factors facilitate an attack by a parasitic organism, this combination of factors, along with the parasite itself, constitutes a causal complex. A parasite is usually referred to as the cause of a disease. But this is a loose statement. A parasite should, strictly speaking, be termed as the incitent or **causal organism.**

2. **Pathogenicity**

It is the capacity of an organism by means of which it may become a part of the causal complex and thereby can produce a disease. An organism which causes a disease is called a **pathogen.**

3. **Suscept and susceptibility**

When a parasite utilizes an entire living organism or a part of it as its substratum, the living substratum so utilised by the parasite is called the **suscept** or host.

The sum of the qualities of the parasite causing the growth and development of the suscept and also of the qualities of the suscept is called **susceptibility.**

4. **Resistance and immunity**

It is the sum total of the qualities of a host and a causal organism that resists the growth and development of the causal agent. Resistance is mainly specific for a particular pathogenic organism, although the resistance of a plant to more than one pathogens is by no means rare. It should also be remembered in this connection that a plant which is resistant to a particular pathogen may not be so at all to another ; even one part of a particular plant may not be resistant to the same degree as another. The nature of the resistance of a suscept to a pathogen may be either purely mechanical or physiological.

(a) **Mechanical resistance**—A parasite usually depends upon an artificial or a natural opening through which it may enter into the body of a plant. Where there is no such opening, the parasite cannot infect the suscept, and the plant, under such conditions, is considered to be resistant. Similarly, a thick, waxy or hairy coating present in some varieties of a particular plant make them more resistant than their less fortunate sister varieties which have no such coating. Thus, the stomatal size and shape of a plant also, in certain cases, plays important parts in offering resistance to pathogens. In some cases, even when the parasite has entered the suscept, the suscept forms a mechanical barrier of layers of cork cells. These layers prevent any further spreading of the parasite through the healthy suscept tissue.

(b) **Physiological resistance**—Such resistances are offered by the protoplasm of the cells themselves. The cells of the suscept in these cases may contain inhibitory chemical substances. They may also be very poor in respect of specific substances required by a parasite as its food. The growth of the pathogen will, in either case, be prevented.

Immunity is that condition of an organism in which a zero relationship exists between it and an attacking pathogen, and the organism is then termed **immune.** In other words, an immune organism is hundred per cent resistant to a disease. Such an immunity is, however, only relative. Absolute immunity is rather rare in plants.

Immunity may be of two types, natural and acquired. Only the former is found in a few cases in the plant kingdom. Recent researches, however, show that these may be some degree of acquired immunity in some plants. For example, a tobacco plant, after a recovery from an attack of the ring-spot disease, becomes practically immune to another attack though it may harbour the virus within its body. A variety of a plant is regarded as naturally immune, when it is genetically related to the suscept of a particular pathogenic organism, but is not susceptible to its attack.

5. Primary and secondary inocula

When a pathogen becomes a part of the causal complex, at first it is found to be overwintering (or oversummering) in various forms on some sort of suscept or substrate. This suscept or subtrate is known as the source of a primary inoculum, and may directly act as an agent in bringing about an infection. This substrate thus acts as a primary inoculum. In some cases, a crop of spores is produced by the infection source, and these then act as the primary inoculum. When, after the primary infection stage, the suscept has become diseased, the pathogen gives rise to another crop of spores. These spores collectively constitute the secondary inoculum, which causes the secondary infection.

6. **Penetration and infection**

By the term **penetration** is meant the initial attack made on a suscept by a pathogen by its entrance into the former's body. In many cases, however, for lack of susceptibility in the suscept, the invading pathogen soon dies. In cases where it can establish itself within the suscept after penetration, it is said to cause an infection. When this organism is capable of being transmitted from a diseased, suscept plant to a healthy one and can also incite the disease, it is called an infectious organism.

It should, however, be noted that one or more environmental factors make a suscept liable to the attack of a pathogen. The effect of environmental factors is called predisposition.

7. **Symptoms and disease cycle**

As a result of an infection, some external manifestations become evident on the body of the suscept plant. These manifestations are known as **symptoms,** and the events taking place in between the time of infection and the external expression of symptoms are collectively referred to as disease development. The chain of events in disease development constitute the **disease cycle** and the process by means of which disease development takes place is called **pathogenesis.**

8. **Parasitism**

Parasitism is a complex phenomenon. There are indeed a number of pathogens which are not in a position to complete their life cycles, until they come in contact with their respective specific suscepts. Such pathogens are known as **obligate parasites.** A large number of fungi belong to this category. On the other hand, there exists another group of organisms called **facultative parasities.** A large number of organisms which cause the damping-off diseases are ordinarily saprophytes. But they may indeed behave as parasites under certain conditions of life.

Various levels of parasitism have been found to exist among the parasitic micro-organisms. The parasitism may be either mild or severe. In extreme cases of parasitism the suscept ultimately dies. A parasite may also perish from starvation. In milder cases, however, both the suscept and the parasite remain alive for a considerable length of time. Another case of a mild kind of parasitism is usually designated as **symbiosis.** In a case of symbiosis two organisms playing their part together are known as **symbionts.**

Here, the two organisms are, practically speaking, parasitic upon each other. For example, there is the classical instance of lichens where an alga and a fungus lie in close partnership with each other. Another example which is often cited is the case of the relation existing between the root-nodule bacteria and their respective suscepts which are invariably members of the papilionaceous group.

9. Saprophytism

There exist micro-organisms of another group deriving their nourishment from inorganic sources or dead and decayed organic tissue. These are the **saprophytes,** and the behaviour exhibited by them is known as **saprophytism.** The saprophytes also may be broadly divided into **obligate** and **facultative saprophytes.** The former are those which are in no way connected with any living cell. The latter, however, remain attached to a living suscept for a part of their life-cycle. The life of a facultative saprophyte is similar to that of an obligate saprophyte. But it should be noted that no sharp line of demarcation can be drawn between facultative parasites and facultative saprophytes.

10. Koch's Postulates

In order to study the pathogenicity of an organism, Robert Koch (1976) made some observations from his studies on the anthrax-causing bacterium (bacillus anthrecis). These are known as **Koch's Postulates.** These postulates are invariably employed in determining the relationship between the causal agent and the suscept. The postulates are as follows :

(a) The pathogenic organism, which is, as a rule, found constantly associated with a particular diseased condition of a suscept, should be isolated and grown in a pure culture.

(b) This culture should thus be inoculated into the body of a sound and healthy, disease-free suscept.

(c) The particular type of disease should thus be reproduced in the body of the healthy suscept.

(d) The pathogen should, finally, be re-isolated from the second suscept, cultured again in a pure form and compared with the original culture.

CHAPTER 11

DISSEMINATION OF PATHOGENS

Among the various agencies involved in dispersal of plant pathogens air, water, insects, animals and man are important.

1. Dispersal by Air

Horizontal air movement is one of the most important factors in dispersal of plant pathogens. Wind direction and speed are important contributory factors too. Air movements may be regular or irregular. The former include a steady wind, blowing fairly strongly—carrying spores in the horizontal direction without causing them to rise. Irregular air movements include slight breezes and irregular air currents blowing in all directions so that the air movements are random and haphazard.

Spores of pathogens have also been located at very high altitudes. Those of *Alternaria*, *Cladosporium*, *Aspergillus*, yeasts and bacteria have been found at altitudes as high as 18,240 m—27,360 m while uredospores of rusts (*Puccinia graminis*) are known to rise several thousand meters above infected wheat growing areas. The spores which rise very high by air currents must come down to the infecting surfaces by various means. Rain is probably the most important factor which brings down spores from high altitudes. Down draughts also help them to come down but these redistribute the spores rather than help them to settle on host surfaces. Pathogens can also be carried away by air currents over great distances, e.g., sporangia of *Phytophthora infestans* travel 72 km in 2½ hours. But this in turn depends upon the viability and longevity of the spores. Uredospores of *Puccinia graminis* remain viable for 70 hours at 10°C while Sclerotia of *Corticium rolfseii*—remain viable for more than 1 year. The main factors involved in the survival of air borne spores are temperature, humidity and radiation.

A number of factors are involved in the deposition of spores, one of which is spore size. The larger the size, the greater are the chances for them to be deposited by impact. Thus foliage pathogens such as *Helminthosporium*, *Alternaria* rusts, powdery mildews etc. produce larger spores than those of *Penicillium* or *Aspergillus*. The former tend to deposit their spores on plant surfaces, the latter seem to miss them. The nature of the plant surface is important in this respect. Wet, rough, hairy or sticky surfaces favour deposition whereas smooth dry ones are unfavourable.

2. Dispersal by Water

Water is not as important a factor as wind for the dispersal of pathogens. It includes water in the form of rain or overhead irrigation. Large water droplets are more efficient than small ones because the latter may evaporate quickly and the spores become air borne. Large water droplets do not travel very far but due to their larger size they do not evaporate quickly and are likely to spread on the surfaces of plants, particularly on those of leaves and thus keep them moist. When a second splash occurs, the spores on the humid surfaces are not as easily washed off as those on dry surfaces. Furthermore, the larger droplets are also important because they supply moisture for spore germination. Spores which are very rough and adhere strongly to each other or to plant surfaces are broken up by water drops. They float singly to the surface of the water drop and are dispersed later by rain. This is well exemplified by the uredospores of *Hemileia vastatrix,* which are dispersed according to the method described above. Spores of *Septoria*, *Colletotrichum* and *Fusarium* are dispersed by water droplets and air-currents combined together, but very little is known about this method of dispersal which has been named as the "splash method". True water dispersal is found only in cases of aquatic and soil-inhabiting pathogen. These include *Xanthomonas malvacearum* inciting bacterial blight of cotton and *Plasmodiophora brassicae* (Clubroot of brassicas).

3. Dispersal by Insects

Insect dispersal in some ways is less wasteful than transmission either by air or water, since it is not a random process like the other two. Besides, it has the disadvantage that spread will be reduced if the appropriate insects are absent or have a rather limited flight range.

Sometimes the insect is partially or completely dependent upon the fungus for food or it may be that the fungus secretes some digestive agents which will react on the food and soften it so that the insect can easily digest it. In this way the insect will disperse the spores of the fungus. This is a symbiotic association. Other associations may be *semiparasitic* and in which the fungus has an adverse effect on the insect and may even multiply within them. The insects may or may not colonize specific plants and in doing so may spread the spores of the fungus, which may act as pathogen of the plant. In this case the insect acts as an alternate host.

Dispersal may be purely mechanical without damaging the plant. The insect transports pathogens from plant to plant ; for example the conidia of *Claviceps*. In *Ceratostomella ulmi* causing Dutch elm disease, the spores are dispersed by bark beetles, accompanied by mechanical injury. The insect may directly inject the plant during feeding, thereby enabling the pathogen to enter into it or cause talls which the fungus invades. Insects may have pouches or bristles which bear the pathogens. Bacterial wilt of maize caused by *Xanthomonas stewarli* is chiefly spread by flea beetles. Spores of fungi such as those of *Ustilago violacea* (Anther smut of Caryophyllaceae) are carried from the anther of one flower to the stigma of another flower. Sporangia of *Phytophthora infestans* stick to the legs of bristles and bodies of aphids. Many insects attack the fruits of plants such as certain fruit flies and beetles which feed on rotten-figs, disperse the spores of *Aspergillus niger* (causing "smut" of fig fruits). Insects may also weaken the body of the plant and make it vulnerable to fungal attack.

Mites and nematodes are also known to be agents of transport. Examples are afforded by spores of *Sporotrichum* carried by mites and inciting carnation bud rot, "Cotton wilt" caused by *Fusarium oxysporum. Vasinfectum* sp. is associated with root knot nematodes.

4. Dispersal by Other Animals

Conidia of *Mycosphaerella linorum* which infect flax leaves are spread in the field by spiders, frogs, mice, birds and dogs. Furs of animals and feathers of birds also carry plant pathogens. For example *Endothia parasitica*, spores are carried by downny woodpecker which infect chestnuts. Migrating birds also spread pathogens over long distances.

5. Dispersal by Man

Man has been responsible for the spread of many plant pathogens over short or long distances, particularly for the latter. Plant pathogens may be spread over short distances by being attached to clothes, implements and farm animals or in soil adhering to shoes etc. Examples are seen in case of wilt (*Verticillium albo-atrum*) in hop gardens ; bacterial canker (caused by *Corynebacterium michiganense*) is spread in tomato plants by pruning.

Long distance spread by man is caused in several ways : (1) When moving from one area to another (intracontinental or intercontinental). He has taken with him plant material or edible parts of plants, which may carry pathogens either on or within their surfaces. So that unknowingly he may have been instrumental in introducing new diseases. (2) Spores and other propagules with long viability may be carried on the clothings of travellers ; (3) trading of plants at the international level may have dangerous consequences and complex laws of legislation must be reinforced to inhibit the spread of new pathogens. (4) Introduction of pathogens deliberately during war time into enemy areas.

However, not every new pathogen introduced is able to establish itself in its new environment, because this depends on the interplay of a number of factors, such as the climatic conditions of its new environment which may not be suitable for it. Therefore plants growing in the new areas may be resistant to the new pathogen.

CHAPTER III

PHYTOALEXINS

Marshall Ward (1905) in England and Noel Bernard (1911) in France first pointed out that a plants' response to an invading fungal pathogen could be partially related to the restricted growth of the pathogen in resistant plant tissues. This idea was further developed some 30 years later by Müller and Borger (1940) who postulated the Phytoalexin Theory of Disease Resistance. Müller (1958) defined **phytoalexins** as "antibiotics which are produced as a result of the interaction of two metabolic systems, host and parasite and which inhibit the growth of micro-organisms pathogenic to plants". Several other authors later redefined the term phytoalexin. In 1973 Ingham stated that phytoalexins are "post-infectional metabolites whose formation involves either gene de-repression or activation of a latent enzyme system". Recently Cruickshank defined phytoalexins as fungal-elicited host-metabolites with antifungal activity formed in hypersensitive tissues which play a significant role in the inhibition of fungal growth *in vivo*. This, however, does not limit the formation of phytoalexins to hypersensitive tissues only, but does put the emphasis on their occurrence in host tissues which are resistant to fungal diseases. A number of phytoalexins have been identified and characterized in a variety of host-pathogen interactions. The structures of some phytoalexins and names of hosts and parasites are given in Table 1 and figure 223.

It was originally believed that phytoalexin could be host specific. But this can no longer be substantiated. Because in several instances, same compound (phytoalexin) has been isolated from different host genera infected with fungi. For instance, medicarpin has been isolated from *Vicia faba* (infected with *Botrytis cinerea*), *Medicago sativa* (infested with *Stemphylium botryosum*) as well as from *Vigna unguiculata* (infected with *Colletotrichum lindemuthianum*). On the contrary, more than one phytoalexin may also be obtained from one host species. For example, Medicarpin and Wyerone acid have been isolated from *Vicia faba* while phaseollin, kievitone and 6a- Hydroxyphaseollin have been extracted from *Phaseollus vulgaris*.

Table—1 : *Names of hosts and parasites producing phytoalexins*

Sl. No.	Compound	Name of host	Name of Pathogen	Disease reaction
1.	Glyceollin	*Glycine max* (L.) Merrill	*Phytophthora megasperma* var. *sojae* (races)	I and C
2.	6a-Hydroxy-phaseollin	*Phaseolus vulgaris* L.	*Colletotrichum lindemuthianum*	C
3.	Phaseollin	*Phaseolus vulgaris* L.	*Monilinia fructicola* (wint) Honey *C. lindemuthianum* (races)	I I and C
4.	Kievitone	*Phaseolus vulgaris* L. *Vigna unguiculata* (L.) Walp. Stat	*Rhizoctonia solani* Kühn. *Phytophthora vignae Purss*	C I and C
5.	Wyerone	*Vicia faba* L.	*Botrytis fabae* Sard, *Botrytis cinerea* Fr. *Phytophthora megasperma* Drechs. var, *Sojae* A. A. Hilds	C I I
6.	Wyerone acid	*Vicia faba* L.	*Botrytis fabae* Sard. *Botrytis cinerea* Fr.	C I
7.	Medicarpin	*Vicia faba* L. *Vigna unguiculata* (L.) Walp, S. lat *Carnavalia ensiformis* (L,) DC. *Medicago sativa* L. *Trifolium pratense* L.	*Botrytis cinerea* Fr. *C. lindemuthianum* (races) *P. megasperma* var. sojae *Stemphylium botryosum* Wallr. *Helminthosporium turcicum* *H. turcicum*	I C I C I I

Table 1 (Contd.)

Sl. No.	Compound	Name of host	Name of Pathogen	Disease reaction
8.	Vignofuran	*Vigna unguiculata* (L.) Walp	*C. lindemuthianum*	C
9.	Pisatin	*Pisum sativum* L.	*Ascochyta pisi* Lib, *Monilinia fructicola*	C I
10,	Maackiain	*Pisum sativum* L. *Trifolium pratense* L.	*M. fructicola* *H. turcicum*	I I
11.	Lubimin	*Datura stramonium* L. *Solanum tuberosum* L.	*M. fructicola* *Phytophthora infestans*	I I and C
12	Capsidiol	*Datura stramonium* L. *Capsicum frutescens*	*M. fructicola* *M. fructicola* *F. oxysporum* f. sp, *vasinfectum*	I I C
13.	Ipomeamarone	*Lycopersicum esculentum* *Ipomea batatus* L.	*Ceratocystis fimbriata*	I and C
14,	Rishitin	Mill *Solanum tuberosum* L.	*Phytophthora infestans* *P. infestans*	I I and C

I = Incompatible host-pathogen interaction (resistant)
C = Compatible host-pathogen interaction (susceptible)

Several workers believe that host-pathogen specificity is associated with the production of phytoalexin elicitors or inducers. These are sometimes found in culture filtrates and cell walls of fungal pathogens. Many fungal metabolites and host nutrients have been considered as phytoalexin inducers. Metlitskii *et al.* (1974) have postulated that elicitors (inducers) of phytoalexins are

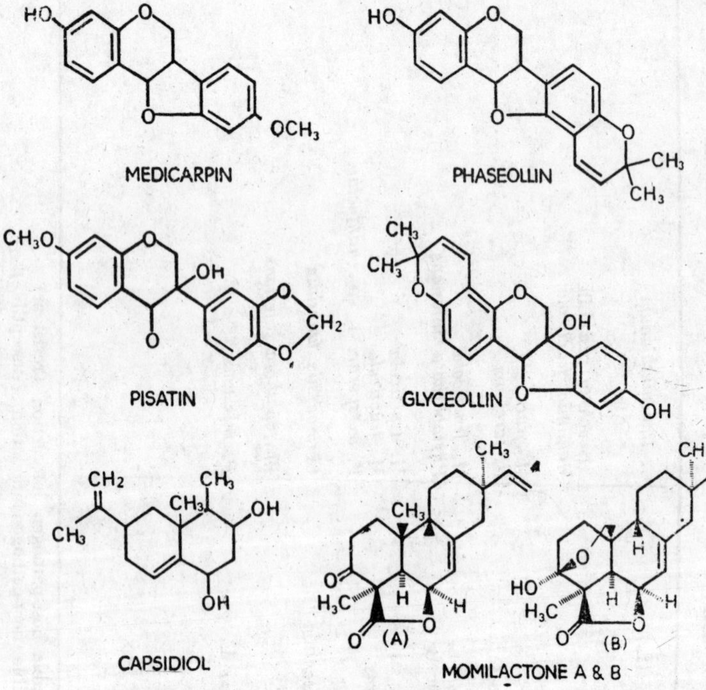

Fig. 223. Chemical structures of Phytoalexins.

released by a pathogen when it comes in contact with cells of a resistant host. On the other hand, contact with cells of a susceptible culture does not release the elicitors (inducers) or they are released in smaller amounts. In some cases, cell wall polysaccharides have been found to act as elicitors of phytoalexin.

Induction of Phytoalexin

There is evidence that phytoalexin production in plants could be induced or enhanced by auxins, antiauxins, polyphenols, chlorides, ethylene, ribonuclease or by certain antibiotics. Consequently the disease resistance of plants could be altered to a considerable extent. Phytoalexin production could also be altered by amino acids or antagonists of nucleic acids and protein synthesis.

Degradation of Phytoalexin

Evidences have indicated *in vitro* studies that a number of pathogens are capable of degrading the phytoalexin produced by their particular host. Thus *Stemphylium botryosum* degrades the alfa-alfa (*Medicago sativa* L.) phytoalexin, medicarpin, both *in vitro* and in leaf diffusates. This fungus has also been shown to alter and possibly degrade, two other phytoalexins, namely, pisatin and phaseollin, found in non-host plants. The first conversion product formed from pisatin or phaseollin is as inhibitory to fungal growth as the parent phytoalexin but later it is further broken down during incubation of mycelial cultures. A compound formed from phaseollin was identified as phaseollinisoflavin. Wilson (1963) showed that *Botrytis cinerea* and *B. fabae* could metabolise Rishitin, a phytoalexin produced by them.

Studies on plant disease resistance have shown that phytoalexins play a significant role in the defence mechanisms of plants, although no chemical similarity exists between the two. It is, however, likely that phytoalexin synthesis depends on the combination of host-parasite proteins or specific antigens. Many explanation have been put forward.

Role of Phytoalexins in Defence Mechanism

Phytoalexins have been implicated in disease resistant reactions in many plant species. Formation of phytoalexins is probably associated with necrobiosis of the affected host cells in parasitic diseases. Although both infected susceptible and resistant cultivars produce phytoalexin, latter one produces phytoalexin more quickly and possibly in larger quantities. These phytoalexins discourage infection by reducing spore germination and growth of pathogens. Susceptibility of plants, on the other hand, could be related to failure of the pathogen to stimulate phytoalexin production, or to its low tolerance to phytoalexin produced, or its capacity to degrade phytoalexin. However, the role of phytoalexins in disease resistance of crop plants has already been established by several research workers.

CHAPTER IV

AFLATOXIN

Through centuries of food-gathering, man has learnt to distinguish between edible and poisonous mushrooms. He has also become cautious that some fungi associated with foodstuffs could be toxic, and he usually takes care that his food should be free from contaminating micro-organisms. He takes less care, however, about the food he provides for his domestic animals. Fungi growing on plant material used for animal food may escape the attention of workers. This has led in the past to delay in recognizing the source of particular toxins that cause poisoning of farm animals. The fungal toxins are known as **mycotoxins.** The number of confirmed mycotoxins for which the responsible fungi have been identified, and their toxins characterised are very small. Mycotoxicology deals with diseases in man and animals caused by or resulting from ingestion of foods made toxic by metabolic products of fungi. Aflatoxin is one of the numerous mycotoxins.

Aspergillus flavus or *A. flavus-oryzae* is a "group" species that contains 11 species, so that this name is used both for the group and for a separate species within the group which produces aflatoxin. Another species in the group, *A. parasiticus* Speare, appears to be more potent producer of aflatoxin than is *A. flavus* Link.

Conditions that favour growth of A. flavus and Production of Aflatoxin

The ecology of aflatoxin production by *A. flavus* has been worked out thoroughly. The minimum moisture content for growth of *A. flavus* is that in equilibrium with a relative humidity of 85%. In the starchy cereal grains such as maize, sorghum, wheat, oats, barley and rice, the moisture content is 18.0-18.5% on a wet weight basis ; in peanut and sunflower seeds with a high oil content, the moisture content is 9-10%. The minimum, optimum and maximum temperatures for aflatoxin production are 12°, 27° and 42°C. respectively. Under optimum conditions for aflatoxin production in pure culture in the laboratory, some aflatoxins will be produced within 24 hours and a maximum amount will be reached within 10 days or less after which the amount produced may decrease sharply. Later it may increase again. Mixed cultures, common in grains and seeds undergoing deterioration in nature also influence aflatoxin formation but this has not been thoroughly studied. According to available evidence (Christensen *et al.* 1973), when a mixture of fungi is present, little or no aflatoxin is produced even when the moist grain is inoculated with a known aflatoxin-producing strain of *A. flavus* and held under conditions favourable for its growth.

There is enough evidence summarized by Christensen & Kaufmann (1969) to indicate that seeds of wheat, barley, oats, rice, maize, sorghum or milo, soybeans, peas, and common beans are not invaded properly by storage fungi, including *A. flavus*, before harvest.

Some materials are much more likely than others to contain appreciable amounts of aflatoxin. In part, this may be due to the inherent nature of the material—some substrates are more favourable than others for aflatoxin production, even though the fungus may grow equally well on both groups—and in part it may be due to a more favourable environment. A combination of a favourable substrate in a favourable environment naturally makes for a much higher aflatoxin risk than does an unfavourable substrate in an unfavourable environment. Among the high aflatoxin-risk materials are peanuts, brazil nuts and probably other kinds of nuts grown in warm and humid regions as well as cotton seeds, copra and fishmeal.

In 86.5% of 52 samples of peanut products tested, aflatoxin is present. Seeds of cereal crops and of soybeans are, in general, of low aflatoxin risk.

In some cases the workers have been able to identify the food contaminated with aflatoxin. For example, rice that has been cooked and stored for future consumption, without refrigeration, carries a very high risk of aflatoxin contamination, especially in the warm and humid tropics.

Effects of Aflatoxins on Animals

Animals differ greatly in sensitivity to injury caused by aflatoxin. A small proportion of the aflatoxin consumed by dairy cattle is excreted in the milk in a slightly changed but still toxic form called M_1. Brewington *et al.* (1970) tested many hundreds of samples of fluid milk from different marketing areas in the United States and from farms, and many samples of dried milk, and found no aflatoxin in any of them.

Aflatoxin Derivatives

The most commonly encountered aflatoxins are B_1, G_1, B_2 and G_2. These toxins may occur together and their concentrations and occurrence may also vary. Some isolates produce all four principal aflatoxins, but the ratio of one to the other may differ. M_1 is another aflatoxin and a product of metabolism of the animals and usually occurs in milk and urine, but is also produced in cultures of *A. parasiticus* and *A. flavus*. Its activity is almost equal to that of B_1 ; it occurs in the milk of lactating humans and animals who have ingested B_1 and is carcinogenic. The incidence of B_1 in meat is rare. M_2 is similar to M_1 but varies only with the unsaturation in the terminal furane ring. The chemical structures of M_1 and M_2 were determined by Holzapfel *et al.* (1966) ; Masvi *et al.* (1967) and Buchi & Weinreb (1969). The intensity of fluorescence of M_1 and M_2 is approximately 3 times that of B_1.

Two other closely related derivatives are B_{2a} and G_{2a} which have a hydroxyl group in the 2 position of the furane ring. Hydroxylation in this position is important because such derivatives are virtually non-toxic and might be a detoxification mechanism of the host.

Fig. 224. Chemical structure of Aflatoxin.

Derivatives	R_1	R_2	R_3	R_4	R_5	X	
B_1	H	H	H	CH_3	O	H_2	
G_1	H	H	H	CH_3	O	$-OCH_2$	(lactone)
B_2	H_2	H_2	H	CH_3	O	H_2	
G_2	H_2	H_2	H	CH_3	O	$-OCH_2$	(lactone)
B 2*a*	OH	H_2	H	CH_3	O	H_2	
G ₂*a*	OH	H_2	H	CH_3	O	$-OCH_2$	(lactone)
M_1	H	H	OH	CH_3	O	H_2	
M_2	H_2	H_2	OH	CH_3	O	H_2	

Both synthetic and naturally occurring aflatoxins suppress precursor incorporation into liver RNA and cause similar fine structure changes in liver cells. A higher dose of the synthetic toxins is necessary to incite a response equal to that of the natural toxins.

CHAPTER V

DISEASES OF A FEW CROP PLANTS

* [The diseases of a few crop plants and their control measures are stated below :]

1. BROWN SPOT OF RICE

This disease is caused by the pathogen *Helminthosporium Oryzae* under the Class Deuteromycetes. It is a very common disease of rice, occurring practically in all the rice-growing areas of the world, and is known as Brown spot or Leaf spot or *Helminthosporium disease.* In India, it is widely found in Kerala, Andhra, Carnatak and West Bengal. In West Bengal it occurs both on rabi and kharif crops. As a result of the severe infection the yield of the cereal grain is abnormally reduced and at the same time the quality of the grain becomes very poor. Besides India, the disease is also severe in countries like Japan, Philippines, Bangla Desh, Sree Lanka and in the countries of South East Asia and Southern Parts of America.

Symptoms

At first small brown spots are usually observed on both the surfaces of the leaves, intensity being greater especially on the lower surface. With age, the colour gradually changes from brown to dark brown with a yellowish tinge at the margins of the spot. As the number of spots increases, they finally unite to form irregular areas and the colour of the leaves changes to grayish yellow. When the infection is intense, the colour of the culms also turns yellow, and eventually becomes dark brown. Lesion appears on or near the lower joints of the rachis, and the glumes are first attacked at the junction of the outer and the inner ones. Owing to severe infection of the pathogen, the ears may be sterile and the grain-formation may be totally stopped.

All parts of the host including the grains are affected, there might be brown discolouration of the kernel. The seeds may even fail to germinate. Sometimes the seedlings are seriously attacked, and they ultimately succumb to the disease.

The Causal Dragonism

The pathogen is a fungal parasite which grows both intercellularly and intracellularly in the mesophyll tissue of the leaves. The vegetative body consists of much branched, septate mycelium. It reproduces by *conidia* borne on stout and erect *conidiophores*, arising in tufts through the stomata or any other opening on the leaf surface. When the atmosphere is humid *mycelial mats* develop superficially on the spots and the conidiophores are also given cut from these mats. Conidiophores are septate, branched only at the bases, darker at the base and paler above. Conidia are borne singly from a growing point. Conidia are somewhat curved and transversely septate, 5 to 10 times. They are brown in colour, more or less cylindrical or obovate and quite variable in size and septation. The conidia are carried by the wind and under suitable conditions bring about new infection.

From cultural studies the perfect stage of the pathogen has been known as *Cochleobolus miyabeanus*.

Disease Cycle

Conidia on the surface of the seeds and mycelia within the seed may serve as the primary inoculum. Commonly the pathogen perrenates in this condition. Rice field weeds may also help perrenation. Continuous rain helps the process. From the germination of infected seeds the pathogen may become active and

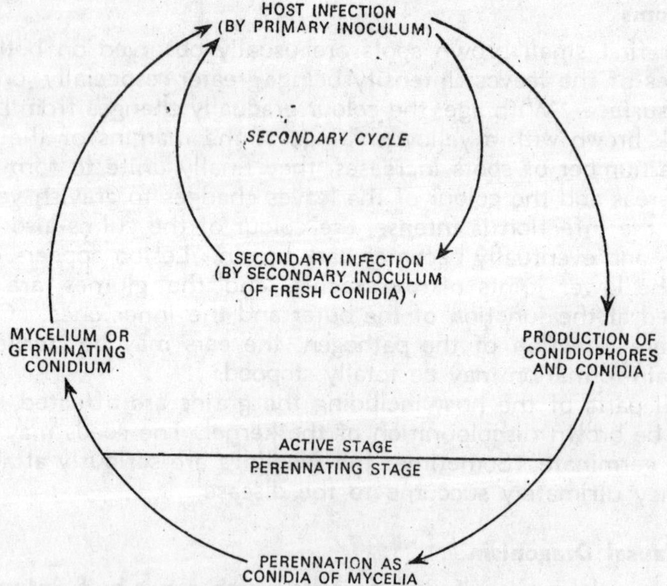

Fig. 225. Disease Cycle of Brown Spot of Rice.

re-infect seedlings. The host tissue may be infected by conidia which are disseminated by wind and rain. After development in the host tissue, the hyphae produce conidiophore through the stomata. Conidia, produced by the conidiophores, are disseminated and bring about new infection of other plants in the field, thus causing secondary infection.

Control measures

Regarding the control of the disease, no measure has been known to be very much successful. Since the seeds are infected both externally and internally, the familiar methods of control do not provide any fruitful result.

As the disease is seed-borne, hot water treatment of seeds may be useful. Secondly, infection may be controlled by the spraying of fungicides, like Bordeaux mixture. The most successful way of controlling the disease, however, is the use of resistant varieties.

2. BLACK STEM RUST OF WHEAT

This disease is caused by the pathogen *Puccinia graminis* var. *tritici* under the Class Bastero mycetes. It is also known as black rust or stem rust. The rusts occur in all the wheat-growing countries of the world. The damage made by them to the crops is very heavy so that a large sum of money is wasted every year. The disease has been reported from very ancient times.

Symptoms

In late spring there appear, on the stems and leaves of wheat plants, vertically enlongated reddish brown pustules (*sori*) or blisters called *uredosori*, each of which at maturity contains a powdery mass of innumerable small orange-red spores called *uredospores* (summer spore or red rust spores) (Fig. 194). *This is the red rust stage*. The disease may spread to the leaf sheaths and inflorescence and the adjacent uredosori may from long powdery streaks. Towards the end of summer, as the wheat plant's attain maturity, the mycelium which upto this time bore uredospore's begin to produce another type of spores, called *teleutospores* (winter spores or black rust spores) within the *teleutosori* (telia) (Fig. 195). At first the teleutospores are produced in a sorus containing uredospores, but later on new teleutosori containing teleutospores only develop on the host plant. The teleutospores are dark-brown but in mass black in colour. The pustules developed by the teleutosori are similar to those of uredosori except that they are black in colour. *This is the black rust stage.*

As the pathogen is a heterocious rust, its alternate host is the barberry plant, where two other stages of its life appear. On the upper surface of barberry leaf small yellowish spots appear, representing the pycniral or spermogonial stage. The spots bear within them flask-shaped spermogonia or pycnia containing *spermatia* or *pycniospores*, flexuous hyphae, and periphyses. On the lower surface of the same leaf, orange-yellow coloured inverted cup-like structures appear, representing the *aecial or cluster cup stage* of the pathogen. These cups contain orange-yellow coloured *aeciospores*.

The Causal Organism

The pathogen is a heterocious rust fungus growing alternately on wheat and barberry. As it produces as many as five kinds of spore-forms, the rust is *polymorphic*. It is also a *macrocyclic rust*, since it produces, besides the teleutospores, two other additional types of binucleate spores.

Inside the wheat host the vegetative mycelium of the pathogen is septate, branched and dicaryotic. The mycelium grows in the intercellular spaces producing branched haustoria which penetrate inside the host cells. The uredospores, borne in the uredosorus, are unicellular, stalked, golden-brown and dicaryotic. The uredospores may repeatedly attack the wheat plants but ultimately teleutosorus bearing teleutospores appear. The teleutospores are two-celled, stalked, dark-brown and initially dicaryotic. The teleutospores are resting spores and do not germinate until the following spring, and remain either on the ground or attached to the old sorus on the wheat stalk. With maturity as the teleutospores become dark-brown, the pair of nuclei in each of its cell fuse, producing a diploid nucleus in each cell. It now represents the diploid phase in the life cycle of the pathogen.

Under suitable conditions, teleutospore germinates and from each of its cells a tubular, somewhat curved outgrowth is formed. The fusion nucleus migrates into it and divides reductionally into four haploid daughter nuclei, after which transverse walls are laid down forming four uninucleate cells. This is the *basidium or promycelium* (Fig. 192). Each cell produces, through a sterigma, one uninucleate basidiospore or *sporidia*. As the pathogen is sexually heterothallic the four basidiospores, thus formed, are, therefore, of different sexes (+and—), two are of one sex and the other two of the opposite sex.

The basidiospores are incapable of infecting the wheat plants. They are carried away by the wind and as soon as they reach the leaves of the alternate host, the barberry, they begin to germinate and infection takes place. The germ tubes penetrate through the epidermal cells and branch through the intercellular spaces of the host tissue forming a branched haplophatic (monocaryotic) mycelium. Within 4-5 days, after infection, there appear between the upper apidermis and the yalisade tissue, flosk a shaped **spermogonia (pycnia)**, which open out by an ostiole at the epidermis. The spermatia, flexuous hypha and the .periphyses borne by a spermogonium may be either of the + or of the — sexual strain, depending on the nature of the basidiospores from which they develop. Being transferred by the insects visiting the honey dew exuded by the spermogonia, spermatia from a spermogonium of one sex usually fuses with the tip of a flexuous hypha of the opposite sex, and the protoplasmic content of the spermatium enter into the cell of the flexous hypha (Fig. 220); *this is the initiation of the dicaryotic phase.* While the spermogonia are formed towards the upper infected regions of the barberry leaf, **aecia** appear on its lower surface. Presumably, after dicaryotisation the nuclei migrate through the hypha to an aecial initial, and as a result it is stimulated to further development. When young, the aeclum is covered by a **peridium,** which ruptures at maturity. An aeclum is distinctly cup-shaped and bears **aeciospores** in chains (Fig. 221). The aeciospores are unicellular, orange-yellow in colour and with minutely warty hyaline walls.

In late spring, when the aeciospores are liberated, they are disseminated by wind. They cannot re-infect the barberry, but if a spore reaches a wheat plant, it germinates, puts forth a **germ tube**, which penetrates a stoma, and ultimately ramifies through the intercellular spaces of the host and again forms a dicaryophasic mycelium, which within 10-12 days begins to form the first crop of uredospores. Thus in typical cases, the primary infection of the wheat plant is brought about by the aeciospores.

Disease Cycle

The resting spores or teleutospores are the perennating structures of the pathogen, which remain either on the ground or attached to the old sorus on the wheat stalk and tide the pathogen over the winter. The teleutospores, on germination, produce promycelium which bears the basidiospores, and these are carried away by the wind to the leaves of the alternate host, the barberry. Due to the infection by the basidiospores, spermogonia appear towards the upper surface of the barberry leaf. By the transference of complimentary spermatia to the flexuous hypae, dicaryotic condition is established. This initiates the development of aecia and aeciospores towards the lower surface of the leaf. On liberation, the aeciospores are carried by the wind. As soon as they reach the wheat plants, they serve as the primary inoculum for the infection of the wheat plant. As stated before the aeciospores, germinate on the surface, enter through the stomata and develop vegetative mycelia in the intercellular spaces ; ultimately the uredosorus appears on the surfaces. Uredospores liberated from the uredosorus, are disseminated throughout the field and fresh secondary infection to the host plant takes place. As the wheat begins to ripen, the formation of uredosorus gradually stops and teleutosorus begins to appear.

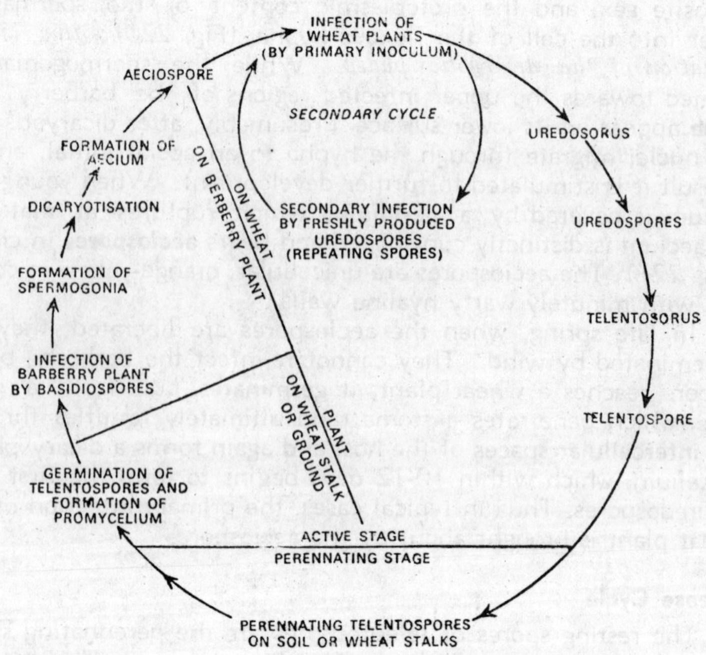

Fig. 226. Disease cycle of Black Stem rust of Wheat.

Control measures

The most effective control measure for combating the rust disease lies in cultivation of resistant varieties of wheat, and for this purpose crossing of our wheats with kenyan wheats have yielded some satisfactory results. Several disease resistant varieties have been suggested for cultivation in India by the research workers.

Unlike the western countries eradication of the alternate host, barberry, will not be effective in controlling the black rust of wheat in India. The preventive measures which have been suggested are as follows : Wheat cultivation in the hills (where the alternate host is available) should be discontinued. Eradication of the substitute grasses, where the pathogen may, harbour in absence of wheat, has been suggested along with admissible changes at the time of cultivation of wheat. The growing wheat plants should be treated with appropriate fungicides at intervals so that the spores falling on them become ineffective. Some of the recommended fungicides are sulphur dusts, Diathane Z-78, Diathane M-22, etc.,

3. Stem rot of Jute

Jute is one of the cheapest and most important of all the textile fibres next to cotton. It is used extensively in the manufacture of different types of packaging materials for various agricultural and industrial products. From seedling stage, the jute crop is liable to be attacked by various diseases, mostly caused by fungal pathogens. All parts of the plant body are subject to attack and the yield as well as the quality of fibres are also affected.

Stem rot of jute is caused by the pathogen *Macrophomina phaseolina* under Deuteromycetes is a serious disease of the crop in Assam, Bengal, Bihar, Orissa and other jute growing areas. Plants in all stages of growth are attacked and when mortality rate is high large gaps occur in the field. Usually jute seeds are sown thickly in order to minimize branching of the plants. The plants, therefore, develop tall, supple stems, yielding fibre of excellent quality. But gaps induce branching, rendering the plants unsuitable for fibre production.

Symptoms

On the seedlings, the first symptoms appear on the hypocotyls and cotyledons in the form of blackish-brown streaks. When the seedlings are attacked, necrotic lesions are formed on the hypocotyl as well as on the cotyledonary leaves. Under wet conditions, such seedlings show seedling blight symptoms. In mature plants necrotic lesions occur mainly along the apex and margin of the leaf ultimately covering the whole of it. Necrosis often extends to the petiole. The organism after damaging the petiole enters the node where it starts stem-rot. Lesions are common on the stems as blackish-brown depressions which increase in size and finally coalesce and girdle the stem. Sometimes streaks run along the length of the stems without girdling them and in that case the cortex becomes shredded, exposing the fibrous tissue. In advanced stage of disease, **pycnidia** develop on the attacked leaves and **pycnidiospores** from such leaves are dispersed by wind. These are responsible for the secondary spread of the disease. The infection usually spreads from the leaves of axillary branches to the infloresceence and then to the fruit. Direct infection of the fruits by the pycnidiospores is not uncommon. Infected mature capsules often split and shed seeds covered with pycnidia. The extent of capsule infection usually depends upon rain. The infected seeds can be distinguished by their dull, often shrunken appearance. The healthy seeds are usually smooth and glossy brown.

The mycelium penetrates all the tissues of the stem, the epidermis and cortex being most affected. Pycnidia are embedded in the epidermis but the sclerotia are restricted to ray cells and softer tissues of the phloem and xylem. The sclerotia are black, spherical, and vary in diameter from 40 to 85 μm. Pycnospores measure 16-27 μm in length and 6-10 μm in breadth.

Usually there are two phases of the disease. During the first phase, the fungus kills a large number of seedlings and young plants in the first two months. The second phase starts when the plants become four to five months old.

Control measures

The disease is both soil and seed-borne but primary infection occurs due to infected seeds, Seed borne infection is more important in initiating the disease than soil contamination. But disease cannot be prevented by sowing disease free seeds in infested soil. It is found that hot water seed treatment at 55°-60°C destroys the pathogen causing serious deterioration of seed viability although deep seated sclerotia can survive even at 70°C. New improved cereson, flit 40 or agrosan G and nomensan prove to be effective fungicides as seed treatment.

The primary infection could be controlled by dry seed treatment with commercial dusts. Proper drying at least for 4 days, followed by treatment with Organo-mercuric compounds (viz. Agrosan 'G', Agrosan 'GN', Ceresan, Nomensan etc.) is recommended before storage. Granosan M, Ceresol, Granosan M200, 6334 and 6335 have also brought adequate control of seeds-borne disease of jute. Under field conditions, lime sulphur (0.2%), Perenox (0.5%) and Bordeaux mixture (5 : 5 : 40) give complete protection from leaf infection. Captan (5g/kg of seed), thiram powder (3g) and various slurry mixtures, bisdithane (2g), dithane M-45 (2.5g) ; Voronit (3g) and Orthocide 75 (0.95g) are as effective as Agrosan 'GN' at 5g/kg against *M. phaseolina*. Timely weeding and proper thinning have been found to reduce leaf infection and mortality. Jute stubbles are an important source of secondary infection since sclerotial stage of the fungus is found in the stubbles. Therefore, removal of jute stubbles minimizes chances of *Macrophomina* infection.

4. Late blight of Potato

This disease is caused by the pathogen *Phytophthora infestans* under the Class Phycomycetes. Of all the potato diseases of the world, the late blight is the most serious. It occurs more abundantly in the temperate zones of the world. Perhaps the disease appeared in its native-area—South America first and gradually spread to North America, Canada, Europe and ultimately to other parts of the world.

Symptoms

The aerial parts of plants, particularly the leaves are attacked and as a result these are gradually killed and dried up causing a blight, but sometimes the tubers are also invaded making for dry rots.

The first symptom appears as brownish to purplish-black lesions on leaves and stems which gradually enlarge under favourable condition. If the weather is warm and humid the colour gradually changes to black. The entire aerial parts may be affected and ultimately shrivelled on drying. A smell of decaying vegetable matter is given off from the lesions.

In the affected tubers a brownish dry rot extends a little below the surface, while a brown or purple discoloration takes place on the skin. Due to a secondary infection wet rot may also develop. (Fig. 130).

The Causal Organism

Coenocytic mycelium of *P. infestans* lives mainly in the intercellular spaces of the host tissue. It draws nourishment from the adjacent living cells by short specialised hyphal branches, known as **haustoria**, which penetrate them. During asexual reproduction slender aerial hyphae come out through the stomata, in groups, from the internal mycelia. From the tubers hyphal branches come out mainly through the lenticels. These are known as **conidiophores** (Fig. 131), which are sympodially branched and bears **conidia** at the tips of the branches. Each conidium is ovoid or lemon-shaped and thick walled and has a thin walled, hyaline apical papilla. It contains multinucleate and granulated protoplasm with several vacuoles and oil drops as food reserves.

When the temperature condition is comparatively high and there is less moisture, the conidium germinates directly by putting forth, one or more **germ tubes,** which penetrate the host tissues through the stomata or directly through the epidermal cells. But when there is excessive moisture and temperature condition is low, the conidium behaves like a **zoosporangium.** Its multinucleate protoplast, by progressive cleavage, forms biflagelate **zoospores.** At maturity, the apical papilla of the zoosporangium dissolves and the zoospores come out through the terminal pore. Each zoospore, after a period of activity settles down, rounds up and puts forth a germ tube, which brings about infection of the host plant as stated before. The infection of the tubers probably takes places directly through the lenticels.

The pathogen reproduces sexually by oogamous method. Though the sex organs are obtained in artificial culture in abundance, they rarely occur on host tissues. Oospores have been reported to occur on diseased tubers. Barrett (1948) has reported the heterothallic nature of the pathogen.

Disease Cycle

Most likely the primary inoculum of the disease comes from the infected tubers, either over-wintering in the soil or freshly

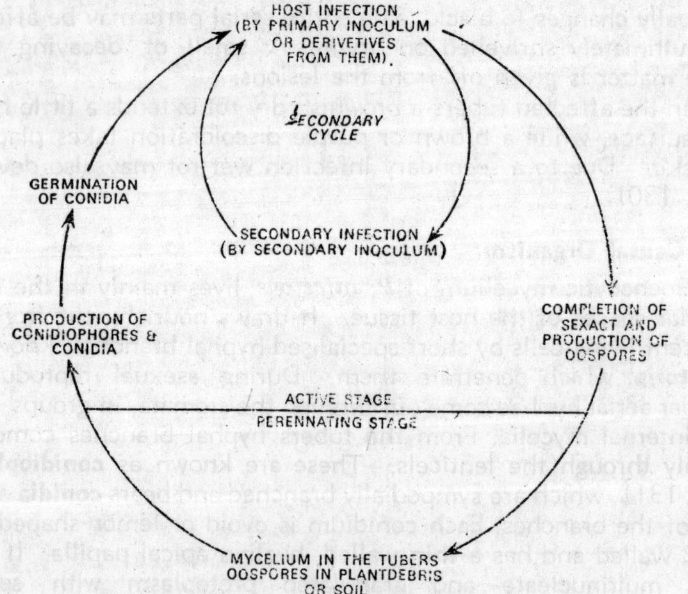

Fig. 227. Disease Cycle of Late blight of Potato.

planted. The pathogen may also over-winter in the soil as a saprophyte in the form of oospores. The oospores or the enclosed mycelium in the tubers renews active growth and spreads to the subaerial parts, chiefly between the cells of the cortex. The pathogen can establish itself more easily in the tissues of the young sprouts. Very soon hyphal branches come through the stomata to form the conidiophores which bear conidia at the tips. The conidia, thus produced or the zoospores derived from them, depending on environmental conditions, constitute the secondary inocula. The secondary inocula infects the host and causes the secondary cycles.

Control measures

The disease can be effectively controlled by spraying or dusting with a fungicide, thus directly attacking the pathogen. Firstly, care should be taken to destroy the previous year's plant debris. At the very first appearance of the disease, the sprayings of Bordeaux mixtures (copper sulphate, lime and water in varying proportions), or dusting with copper lime dust (dehydrated copper sulphate, hydrated lime and calcium arsenate) have given increased yields, better control of pathogen and insects, and lessened the physiological defects.

Besides these, there are other methods, such as, selection of healthy seeds at the time of sowing, or by storing the tubers at low temperatures (at or below b0°F), which can prevent the spread of the disease. By growing resistant varieties the disease can be effectively prevented.

5. Canker of Citrus

It is a very common disease of *Citrus* and met with in almost all the countries of the world wherever *Citrus* is cultivated. Besides India, the disease is reported from Bangladesh, Pakistan, Australlia, Newzealand, South Africa, China, Japan, United States and many other countries of the world. Not only citrus but grape fruits are also liable to attack of the disease.

The Causal Organism

The causal organism is a bacterial pathogen known as *Xanthomonas citri*. The organism is very minute and rod shaped with a single flagellum at the distal end. The bacterium is aerobic and surrounded by a mucilagenous capsule. It it also provided with a yellow and water soluble pigment. Humid weather and temperature ranging between 20°C to 35°C are the favourable conditions for spreading of the disease.

Symptoms

All the aerial parts of the plant, specially the leaves, stems and fruits an susceptible to the disease. In case of leaves, small transluscent dark green pustules appear on the ventral surface. The central region of the pustule is slightly raised giving rise to a convex appearance. The pustule gradually turn slight brown and are somewhat spongy in nature. These mature spots are ultimately brownish or pinkish in colour and give rise to cankerous

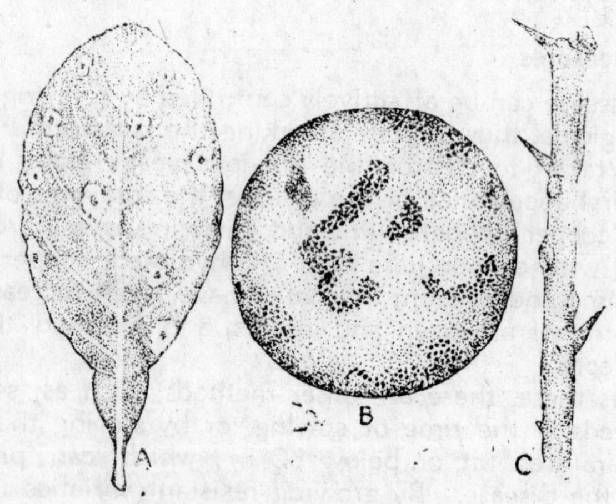

Fig. 228. Citrus Canker
A, on leave ; B, on fruits ; C. on twig.

apptarances. The cankerous lesions of the twigs and fruist are similar to those of the leaves. In case of fruits, the lesions gradually coalesce together forming irregular conspicuous patches (Fig. 228).

Control measures

The following control measures are usually adopted for checking the infection :

1. *Eradication*—Complete eradication of the infected citrus plants proves most effective. If it is not possible, at least the infected portions such as leaves and branches should be pruned. This should be done during the dry season of the year.

2. *Use of fungicides*—Spraying of Bordeaux mixture and sulphur lime on infected fruits during their first three months of development is effective in controlling the disease.

3. *Use of disease resistant varieties*—Cultivation of disease resistant varieties of citrus plants sometimes glives better results

Disease Cycle

The bacteria find their way into the host tissue through stomata, lenticel or any injured portion where they remain dormant for some time. During favourable condition, the inoculum is

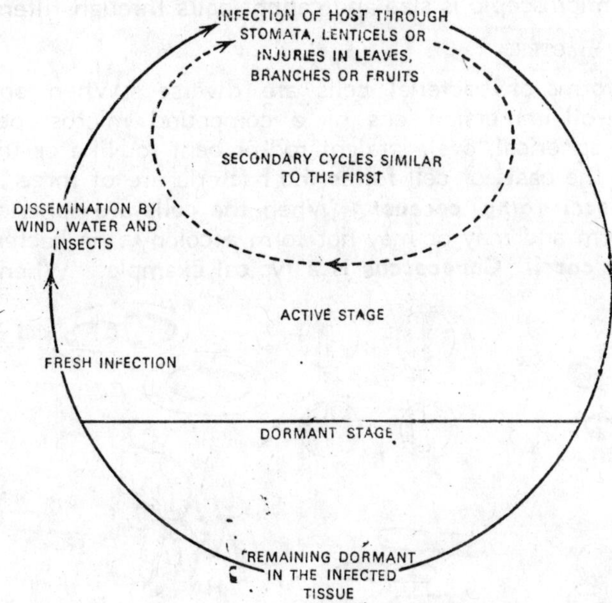

Fig. 229. Disease Cycle of Citrus Canker.

disseminated by wind, rains or insects and induces fresh infection. The disease cycle is shown herewith.

CHAPTER VI

BACTERIA AND VIRUS

BACTERIA

Bacteria, are small organisus which are found in every place. They are microscopic is size and cannot pairs through filters.

FORMS OF BACTERIA

The forms of bacterial cells are diverse. When observed under the oil immersion lens of a compound microscope they appear as spherical, oval, straight rod or bent rod-like or filamentous. On the basis of cell forms the bacteria are of three kinds :

1. **Cocci** (*Sing.* **coccus**). When the cells are spherical are oval in form and may or may not form a colony, the bacteria are said to be **cocci. Gonococcus** is a typical example. When **cocci**

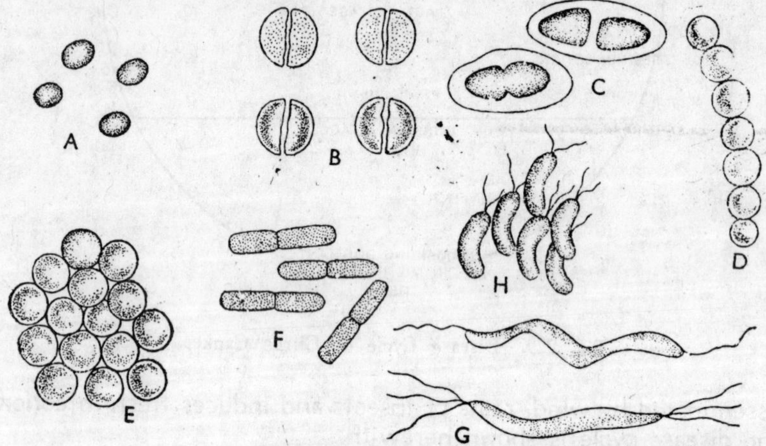

Fig. 230. *Bacteria,*
Different forms : A, Micrococcus ; B, Diplococcus ; C, Encapsulated diplococcus ; D, Streptococcus ; E, Staphylococcus ; F, Bacilli ; G, Spililla ; H, Commas.

occur singly they are known as **micrococcus ;** when they occur in pairs they are known as diplococci *Sing* **diplococcus**) but if they are enclosed in a common covering, **encapsulated diplococcus.** When cocci form chains, the term used is **streptococcus.** When they are arranged in sheet-like colonies, **staphylococcus** is the term used. Cocci may also occur in cubical colonies of 8 and this type of coccal form is called **sarcina.**

2. **Bacilli** (*Sing.* **bacillus**). The cells in the form of straight rods are found in bacteria ; these are said to be **bacilli.** The common

examples are tuberculosis bacteria (*Mycobacterium tuberculosis*), typhoid bacteria (*Salmonella typhi*), diptheria bacteria (*Corynebacterium diphtheriae*), tetanus bacteria (*Clostridium tetani*), etc. When the cells are in the form of bent rods and appear as commas, that is having a single curve they are said to be **comma bacillus** or **vibrio.** Cholera bacilli (*Vibrio cholerae*) is a familiar example. The bacilli are provided with one or two whip-like structures, known as **flagella,** at one or both ends. They are able to move from one place to another with the help of these flagella.

3. **Spirilla** (*Sing.* **spirillum**). When the cells are elongated like filaments and have several spirals, the bacteria are known as **spirilla.** The typical example is *spirochaetes*, syphilis bacteria (*Treponema pallidum*).

STRUCTURE OF BACTERIA

Bacteria are unicellular, but multicellular in filamentous forms. The acerage diameter of a bacterial cell is 1.5 μm*. Each cell is composed of a mass of colourless, transparent colloidal substance known as Cytoplasm and a wall, the cell wall, surrounding it completely. The cell wall may be again surrounded by a layer of slimy or jelly-like substance. This layer is known as **capsule.** The cell wall is a non-living substance, while the cytoplasm is a living one. There is a nucleus inside the cytoplasm but it is not a true nucleus. Various ergastic substances are present in the cytoplasm. There may be one or more flagella at one or both ends of the body.

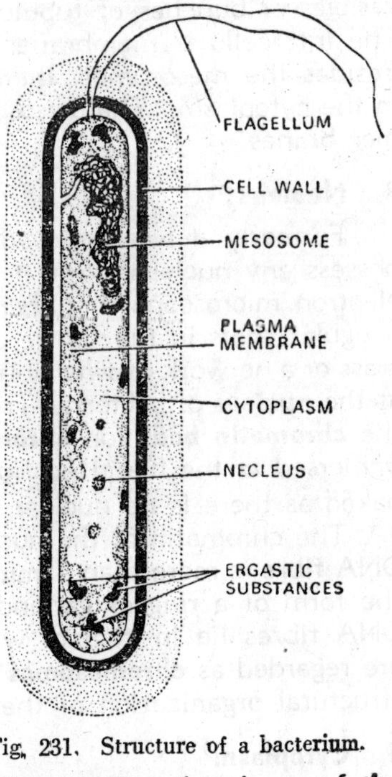

A detailed description of the different parts of the cell is given below :

Fig. 231. Structure of a bacterium.

1. **Cell wall**

The cell wall is comparatively hard and rigid. It protects the cytoplasm from external injuries and maintains the shape of the

*μm=a miclometep is used as a unit for measuring microscopic objects and is equivalent to 0.001 mm.

bacteria. The cell wall is usually composed of two layers : the inner flexible layer known as **cytoplasmic membrane** and the outer hard layer, the **cell wall proper.**

2. **Plasma membrane and Intracellular membranes**

(a) **Plasma membrane**—The plasma membrane lies just below the cell wall and surrounds the cytoplasm. It is made up of living substance and is selectively permeable. The plasma membrane is composed of three layers, **protein layers** present on the two sides and the **lipid layer** in between the two. The outer layer is rough as it bears numerous small particles and fibres and the inner layer, which lies in contact with the cytoplasm, is smooth. The intracellular membranes are connected with the plasma membrane at many points. Scientists are of the opinion that the intracellular membranes have been formed by invagination of the plasma membrane.

(b) **Intracellular membranes**—The intracellular membranes are spread to both nucleus and cytoplasm. These are like small vesicles or bunches of tubules or like wheels arranged in whorls. The intracellular membranes are usually denoted by **mesosomes.** Besides the mesosomes, there are other intracellular membranes in the cytoplasm. The mesosomes are denser than the cytoplasmic membranes.

3. **Nucleus**

Formerly it was believed that the bacterial cell does not possess any nucleus. But it is now known with the help of the electron microscope that there is one or more transparent and irregular spots in the centre of the cell in which there is a thick mass or a network of fine fibres. This transparent space is regarded as the **nucleus** of bacteria. The aforesaid mass or network is called the **chromatin body** or **chromatin reticulum.** The network lies immersed in the liquid portion of the nucleus. The nucleus is naked as there is no nuclear membrane.

The chromatin of the nucleus is composed of DNA fibres. A DNA fibre is more than 1 mm in length and it is usually coiled in the form of a ring or garland ; hence there is no free end. The DNA fibres lie in contact with the intracellular membrane and are regarded as **chromosomes** although they do not possess the structural organization of the chromosomes of eucaryotes.

4. **Cytoplasm**

Very little is known about the structure of the cytoplasm of bacteria. It is believed that there is a membrane system, which is spread over throughout the cell and is connected with the plasma membrane. Sometimes it becomes dense and forms the mesosomes.

5. **Ergastic substances**

The ergastic substances are formed as a result of metabolic activities of bacteria. These remain embedded in the cytoplasm. The common forms of ergastic substances are lipid granules, volutin granules, glycogen granules, bipyramidal protein crystalls, etc.

FLAGELLA

Bacterial movement is primarily due to **flagella** which are whip-like structures about 0.12 μm long and sometimes longer than a bacterial cell. Each flagellum is a protoplasmic structure with a basal granule. Depending upon the number and manner of attachment of flagella, the following 4 types of bacteria may be distinguished :

1. **Monotrichous**—Flagella attached singly at one end of the cell as in *Vilnis.*
2. **Lophotrichous**—Flagella many and attached at one end as in *Spirillum undula.*
3. **Amphitrichous**—Flagella many and attached at both ends as in **Spirilla.**
4. **Peritrichous**—Flagella many and attached all around the cell e.g. *Salmonella typhosa.*

Flagella occur in all forms of bacteria with the exception of **cocci.**

VIRUS

Viruses are smaller than bacteria and are sub-microscopic and can pass through very fine filters, which hold back bacteria.

FORMS OF VIRUS

The forms of virus are diverse. When observed under an electron microscope, they appear spherical or rod-like or cubical or filliform or polyhedral or coiled or twisted like a screw or bopyramidal or hexagonal or prism-like etc. On the basis of forms, the viruses may be grouped into three classes : (1) **Cubical** or box-like, e.g. **Vaccinia virus,** (2) **Helical,** when twisted like a screw or coiled e.g., *tobacco mosaic virus*, etc., (3) **Mixed symmetrics** or **Combined symmetrics,** e.g. bacterial virus, herpes simplex virus, etc.

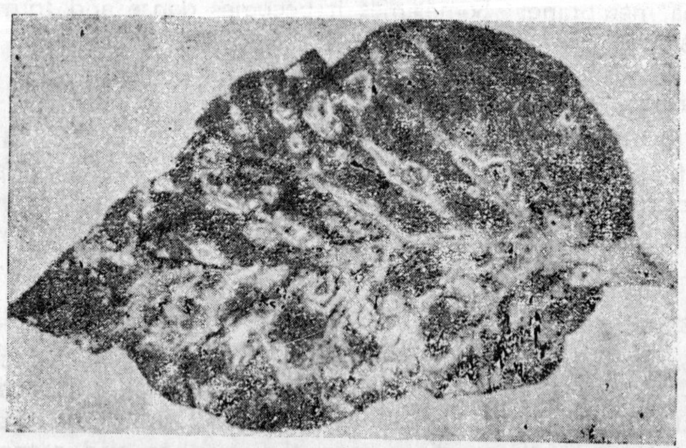

Fig. 232. Tobacco mosaic virus (×40,000)
(After J. Brandes, 1964)

STRUCTURE OF VIRUS

The virus is non-cellular and particulate. The present conception is that the body of virus is composed of a central core filled up with nucleic acid with a thick protein envelope. This protein envelope is called the **capsid.** There are numerous long protein particles, known as **capsomeres** inside it. Viruses either contain DNA or RNA but both do not occur in the same capsid. RNA of tobacco mosaic virus is embedded in the capsomeres. When the bacterial virus lives as a parasite inside the body of bacteria, it is known as **bacteriophage** or **phage.**

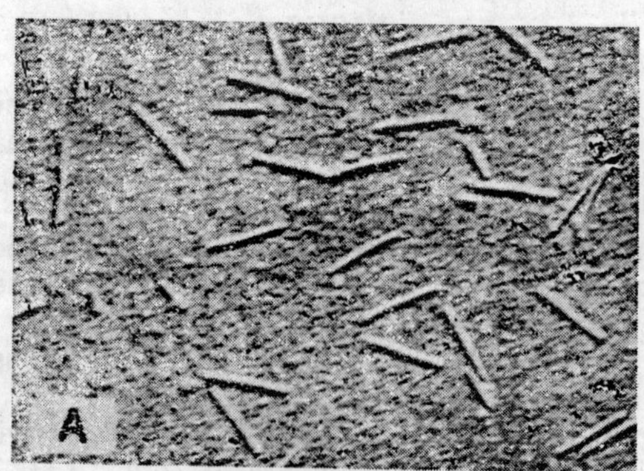

Fig. 233. Tobacco mosaic virtus on tobacco leaf.
(*After F. O. Holmes*)

REPRODUCTION

At the time of reproduction, a virus attaches itself to a bacterial cell or to the tissue of a host and an aperture appears on the host cell through which the nucleic acid only enters into the host and the protein coat is left on the outside as a "ghost". The nucleic acid then replicates inside the host cell and produces new viral protein and thus a new virus is formed. In this way numerous viruses are formed. Thus the viruses multiply to produce exact replicas of themselves in the tissue of hosts. The host cell ultimately dies and releases the numerous virus particles.

DNA viruses are bacterial virus, pox virus, herpes simplex virus, etc. and the RNA viruses are tobacco mosaic virus, spherical and rod-like plant virus, influenza virus, etc.

Symptoms of virus diseases

Viruses produce various symptoms or visible effects on their hosts. The symptoms may be primary or systemic.

(*a*) *Primary symptoms*. The primary is initial symptoms are local reactions at the actual spots of inoculation. They are usually of two kinds : *local lesions* and *clearing of veins*. The local lesions appear as dots or rings of various types. They are the result of death of cells in these areas. Clearing or chlorosis of the tissues and around the veins is known as vein clearing.

(*b*) *Systemic symptoms*. The prominent systemic symptoms are as follows :

1. *Mosaic*. In this case usually the leaves of host's show mosaic pattern or patches of yellow and green colours. These patches are due to chlorosis and may be circular or irregular.

2. *Chlorosis*. It is the uniform yellowing or formation of different shades of green without any pattern. This is due to disbalance of normal development of chlorophyll.

3. *Necrosis*. It implies the death or disintegration of the host cells. This is one of the symptoms of various virus diseases. Usually it appears as small spots on the leaves or streaks on the stems. Occasionally it extends over large areas causing the death of host plants.

4. *Rings*. These appear as light green or yellowish rings on the surface of leaves which are the results of chlorosis and necrosis. These rings are usually concentric to a central spot.

5. *Distortion*. It is common symptoms of virus diseases. In this case dwarfing and distortion of plant members or the entire plant takes place. Sometimes characteristic symptoms such as malformations and overgrowths are also found in some virus diseases.

Control measures

The following measures are adapted to check the spread of virus diseases :

1. Eradication of diseased plants.
2. Destruction of weeds which harbour viruses by burning.
3. Isolation of suspicious diseased plants.
4. Sanitation in case of highly infected plants is essential.
5. Removal of refuse of infected leaves of crop plants to a distant place far away from the healthy plants.
6. Heat treatment to kill or at least inactive viruses which cannot tolerate high temperature.
7. Inoculation of young plants with mild strains of virus for making them resistant to virulent strains.
8. Washing of hands with germicides before and after working in the field.
9. Sterilization of agricultural implements.
10. Preparation of virus-free seed beds.
11. Spraying of insecticides to kill insect vectors.
12. Growing resistant varieties of plants.

COMPARISON BETWEEN VIRUS AND BACTERIA

Virus	Bacteria
1. Parasite.	1. Saprophyte sometimes parasite.
2, Produces diseases like influenza, measles, chicken-pox, small-pox, polio, rabies, etc.	2. Produces diseases like cholera, typhoid, tuberculosis, etc.
3, Can be observed by an electron microscope	3. Can be observed by a compound microscope fitted with an oil-immersion lens.
4, Can be filtered by porcelain filters,	4. Cannot be filtered,
5, Forms are spherical, rod-like, filiforms, cubical, etc.	5, Forms are cocci bacilli and spirilla, etc.
6. Non-cellular	6 Unicellular, but multicellular in filamentous forms.
7. Body is composed of nucleic acid enveloped by protein,	7. Body is composed of cytoplasm with cell wall, surrounded by slime enclosing a primitive type of nucleus.
8, Non-flagellated,	8. Flagellated and sometimes non-flagellated,
9. Reproduction by repeated divisions of nucleic acid and enveloped by protein,	9. Reproduction vegetative, asexual and sexual.

The importance of study of Bacteria and Viruses

The study of Biology remains imcomplete without a comprehensive knowledge of bacteria and viruses. Microbes are miniature models for the study of various life processes that are going on in and around us. Thus, to understand life as a whole, the study of bacteria and viruses are imperative as they serve as simple platforms from which the other complex forms of life have emerged.

The bacteria, which are larger than the viruses, and altogether more organised, serve as unusual but useful models for understanding various biological phenomena. They have many characteristics in common with higher organisms—such as the mode of nutrition, respiration, growth and other metabolic processes. A knowledge of their life processes gives an insight into the processes being carried out in any living form. Even the mechanisms involving energy utilisation are common in the living world. Moreover, bacteria may be useful in studying space exploration, immunisation of populations and also genetic studies. The latter two issues have to be studied in lower life forms for the hazards and consequences of such experiments cannot be foreseen. In space travel, bacteria may be used as food, as a purifying agent and also as an energy source. However, a pre-requisite to all these major fields of study is a knowledge of the bacteria themselves, their physiology, structure and reproduction.

Viruses, on the other hand, show very few characteristics of living organisms. But they have a DNA or RNA thread surrounded by a protective protein covering. A well organised cell or nucleus is absent. So viruses serve as experimental tools for the study of DNA and RNA in their purest form. We know that it is the nucleic acid that carries the genetic information for all vital processes and to regulate any metabolic process, the nucleic acid has to be regulated. Such regulation studies can only be carried out with free nucleic acid, easy to handle, which is provided by a single virus. Thus, a study of viruses is important from the view-point of genetic regulation which remains the key to open all locks in any biological system.

SECTION V

LICHENS

General consideration

Lichens look like single plants, but they are associations of two different organisms, an alga and a fungus, living in close relationship. Formerly, they were placed under Thallophyta, but at present they have been removed from the group and constitute a distinct class. The word 'lichens' was first used by the Theophrastus, a disciple of Pluto and Aristotle, who lived during 371-284 B.C.

It has already been stated that an alga and a fungus live in close association forming lichens, which is usually a dorsiventral thallus. The alga due to presence of chlorophyll prepares carbohydrate food which is shared by the fungal partner, while latter fixes the thallus to the substratum, absorbs water and mineral salts in solution, supplies them to the algal partner for food manufacture, and carries on the process of reproduction. Thus, the two organisms derive mutual benefit and the mode of living is known as **symbiosis.** The alga may belong to Myxophyceae (e.g. *Nostoc, Stigonema*, *Rivularia*, *Gleocapsa*, etc.) or to Chlorophyceae (e.g. *Protococcus*, *Cladophora*, *Trentepohlia*, etc.) while the fungus is usually an ascomycete, but in some cases a basidiomycete. When the alga is uniformly distributed in the body of the thallus, it is said to be **Homoiomerous** (e.g. *Collema*, *Laptogium*, etc.) or it may be confined to localized areas below the upper cortex and is said to be **heteromerous** (e.g. *Parmelia*, *Usnea*, etc.).

Lichens may be of varied colours. They are usually grey or greyish green irregularly shaped structures, some lichens are yellow, orange, brown or red in colour.

Distribution and occurrence

There are about 16,000 species of lichens which are distributed throughout the world. Many of them grow profusely in humid tropical and subtropical regions. They are found growing on stones, bark of trees, leaves, walls and roofs, decaying lags, surface of soils, or remain hanging from rocks or branches of trees, some species are xerophytic and can withstand desiccation. Lichens which grow on stones are called **saxicoles** or stone lovers, whereas those which grow on barks are called **corticoles** or bark lovers. The former grow on firm substratum in cold regions, whereas the latter are mostly confined to tropical and subtropical regions where there is abundant moisture.

Classification

Lichens have been classified into two subclasses according to the nature of fungal partner.

Subclass I. Ascolichens, when the fungus is an ascomycete.

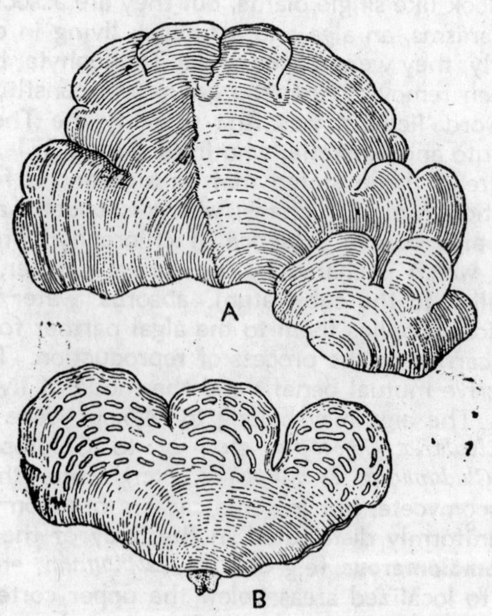

Fig, 234. *Basidiolichen.*
A, Dorsal view ; B, Ventral view.

This subclass has been further divided into two series on the basis of fruit body.

Series 1. Pyrenocorpeae, in which the fruit body is the perithecium.

Series 2. Gymmocarpeae, in which the fruit body is an apothecium.

Subclass II. Basidiolichens (Fig. 234) when the fungus is a basidiomycete, e.g. *Cora*, *Rhipidonema*, etc.

Types of Ascolichens (Fig. 235)

On the basis of the nature of thallus the Ascolichens are three types :

1. **Crustose** or crust-like type. The thallus is small, flat and thin incrustation on rocks and bark of trees. It is so very closely adpressed to the substratum that it is different to remove it without

any damage. The body is not differentiated into upper and lower surfaces. *Graphis*, *Leconora*, *Haematomma*, etc., are common examples.

2. **Foliose** or leaf-like type. The thallus is broad, much-branched and leaf-like structure with edges curled upwards. The body of the thallus is clearly differentiated into upper and lower surfaces. It is attached to rocks and twigs of branches by means of rhizoid-like outgrowths (rhizenes) developed from the lower surface, *Paramelia*, *Physcia*, *Pelligera*, *Gyrophora*, etc., are common examples.

3. **Fruticose** or shrub-like type. The thallus is slender and much-branched structure. The branches may be cylindrical to ribbon-like in form which may be erect or prostrate or hanging

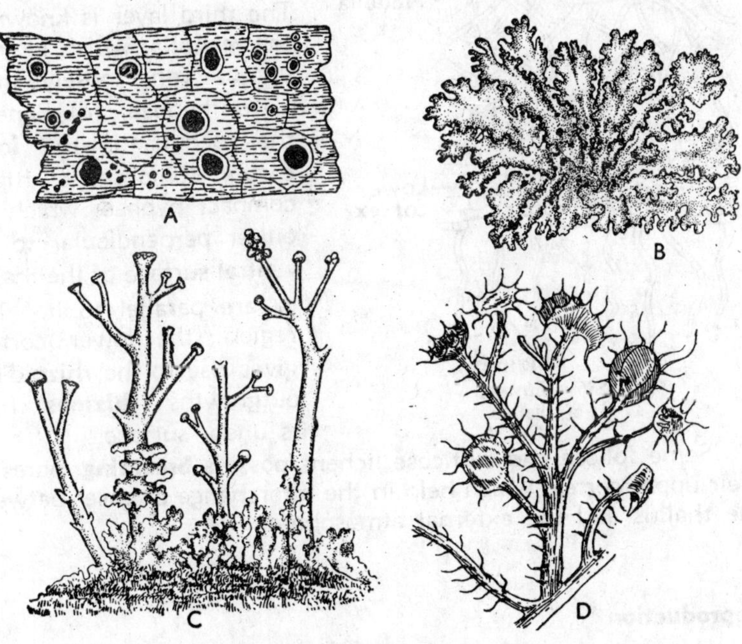

Fig. 235. Types of *Ascolichens*, A, Crustose ; B, Foliose ; C, Fruticose (e.g. *Cladonia*) ; D, Fruticose (e.g. *Usnea*).

from rocks and branches of trees. The thallus is attached to the substratum by a narrow basal point only. It is also differentiated into upper and lower surfaces, *Cladonia* (Fig. 235C), *Evernia*, *Usnea* (Fig. 235D), etc., are common examples.

Internal structure (Fig. 236)

In most foliose lichens the thalli are internally differentiated into four distinct regions : (*a*) The uppermost region is known as the **upper cortex,** which is usually composed of vertical hyphae and may be bounded externally by a single layer of hyphae representing an epidermis-like structure. (*b*) Below this region is the **algal layer** (also known as the **gonidial layer**) consisting of algae intermixed with loose hyphal elements. (*c*) The third layer is known as the **medulla,** which is made up of very loosely interwoven hyphae. (*d*) Beneath the medulla is the **lower cortex,** composed of highly compact hyphae, which are either perpendicular to the ventral surface of the thallus or are parallel to it. This region (the lower cortex) gives rise to the rhizoid-like outgrowths (**rhizines**) from its under surface.

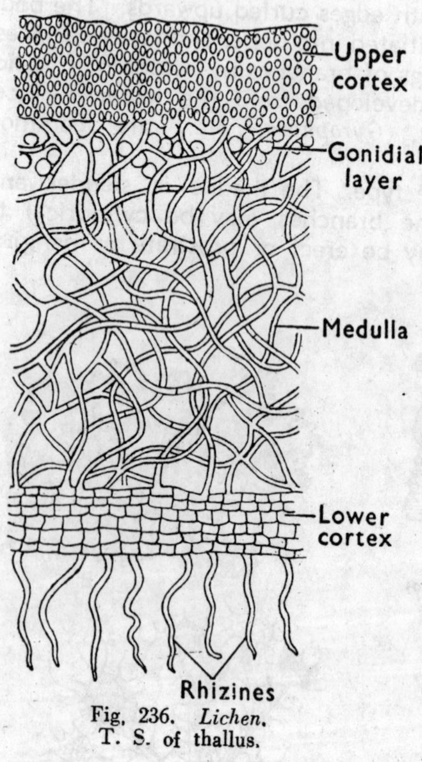

Fig. 236. *Lichen.* T. S. of thallus.

Some foliose and fruticose lichens possess **breathing pores** in their upper cortex, which help in the interchange of gases between the thallus and the external atmosphere.

Reproduction

Vegetative reproduction may take place in the following ways :

1. **Fragmentation.** In this process the thallus containing both the symbionts breaks up into many pieces, each of which produces a new lichen thallus.

2. **Soredia** (Fig. 237). These are greyish, minute, rounded bud-like outgrowths developed on the surface or margins of the thallus. They are composed of algal cells enclosed by a few hyphae. Soredia are usually dispersed by wind. Each soredium falling on

a suitable substratum germinates directly into a new lichen thallus or form new soredia.

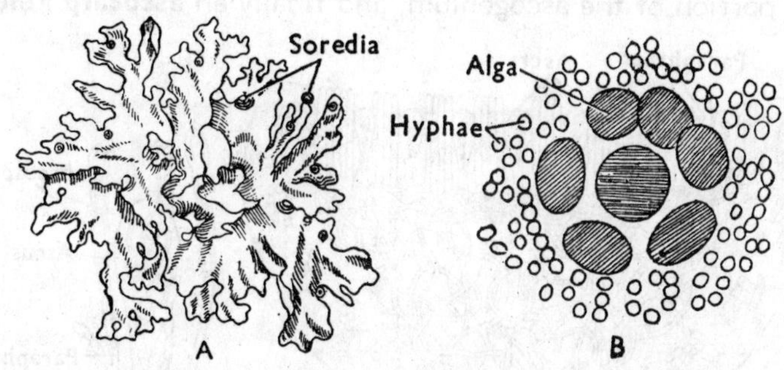

Fig. 237. *Lichen*.
A, Thallus with soredia ; B, A soredium (*magnified*).

3. **Isidia.** These are coral-like outgrowths developed from the surface of the thallus. They are composed of an external cortical layer of hyphae and an internal algal layer. Isidia help photosynthesis and also function as vegetative reproductive bodies. When detached isidium develops into a new lichen thallus.

4. **Cephalodia.** These are dark-coloured gall-like structures formed within or outside the body of the thallus. They are composed of one or more layer of algal cells. It is to be noted that the algal component is quite different from that of the thallus.

Asexual spores, like **oidia** or **pycnospores,** are regularly formed by the fungus of an ascolichen. These spores, falling on a suitable substratum, germinate very easily, and when the hyphae developed from them come in contact with the suitable alga, a lichen is produced. In some cases the alga of the lichen gives rise to typical zoospores.

The sexual reproduction takes place by fertilization organs, spermogonia and ascogonia are always produced by the fungal constituent. The male reproductive organs, called the **spermogonia,** are flask-shaped cavities developed on the body of the thallus, which contain inside them numerous small male cells, called **spermatia**. The female organ, the **ascogonium**, is a multicellular structure, the lower part of which is spirally coiled and is known as the **archicarp** ; the upper end is usually differentiated into a **trichogyne,** whose tip in most of the species projects slightly beyond the surface of the thallus. The spermatia become attached to the tips of the trichogyne and the contents of the spermatium pass into the trichogyne, but actual migration of the male nucleus has not yet been observed and practically nothing is known about nuclear fusion.

After fertilization, **ascogenous hyphae** are developed from the basal portion of the ascogonium, and finally an **ascocarp** (either an

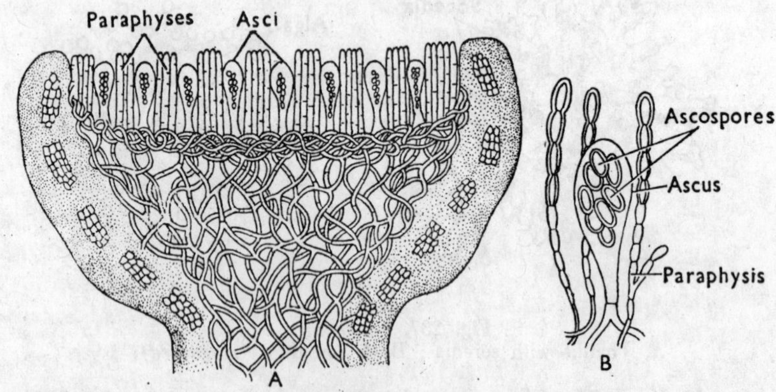

Fig. 238, *Lichen*.
A, V. S. of apothecium ; B, An ascus with ascospores and paraphysis.

apothecium (Fig. 238), when cup-shaped, or a **perithecium**, when (flask-shaped) is produced containing many **asci** and **paraphyses.** Each ascus usually contains eight **ascospores.** Ascospores are discharged in wet weather, and falling on suitable soil, germinate and give rise to hyphae. These hyphae coming in contact with suitable algae give rise to new lichens.

In some cases ascogenous hyphae are developed parthenogenetically without any formation of ascogonia.

Economic importance

Lichens are economically important, both for their harmful as well as beneficial effects. If we consider both the effects they will be found to be more helpful than harmful.

I. *Harmful lichens*

Many species of Lichens have harmful effects. Lichens growing on the window panes of old buildings corrode them by secreting organic acids and thus cause a great damage. Some lichens, such as *Letaria*, *Vulpina*, are poisonous.

II. *Beneficial Lichens*

The beneficial aspects of lichens are stated below :

1. **Soil formation and growth of new vegetation.** Lichens growing on rocks disintegrate them by secretion of organic acids and subsequently they are further broken down by the action of

snow and other physical causes forming crude soil. Lichens grow on such soil and after their death and decay enrich it by forming humus and thus paves the way for the growth of mosses and subsequently of ferns and higher plants. This is the reason why lichens are sometimes called 'soil builders' and 'farmers of nature'.

2. **Food.** Lichens contain *lichenin*, a carbohydrate substance, in their body, hence they are taken as food by man and animals. The people of Norway, Sweden and Ireland use Iceland moss (*Cetraria islandica*) as food. In China and Japan *Endocarpon miniatum*, popularly known as 'stone mushroom', is taken as a vegetable. In South India species of *Paramelia*, commonly known as 'rock flower', is used in preparing delicious curry. Besides these, *Umbellicaria*, *Lecanora*, etc., are used as food. In arctic region Reindeer moss (*Cladonia rangiferina*) is the only fodder for reindeer and cattle during winter. Lichens also afford food for the larvae of insects.

3. **Medicine.** A few species of Lichens are important from medicinal point of view. They are used for treatment of disease. Thus, *Pelligera caniana* is used for hydrophobia ; *Paramelia saxatilis* (the 'skull lichen') for epilepsy ; several species of *Cladonia*, *Pertusaria*, *Cetraria*, etc., for intermittent fever ; *Cladonia pyxidata* for whooping cough ; *Lobaria pulmonare* for lung disease. *Cetraria islandica* is used as a laxative.

4. **Dyes.** Some Lichens yield dyes. *Rocella tinctoria* yields litmus which is commonly used as an indicator in chemical laboratories. 'Orchil', a beautiful blue colour, is obtained from *Rocella*, is used for dyeing woollen and silken fabrics. 'Orcein', purified product of orchil is used for staining microscopic objects.

5. **Perfume.** Some species of Lichens contain cleoresinous substances, hence, they are used in perfumery. In France excellent perfumes are prepared from *Evernia prunastri* and *Lobaria pulmonaria*. Some lichens are used for preparation of cosmetics.

6. **Tanning.** In France and other European countries some species of lichens are used for tanning hides.

SECTION VI

BRYOPHYTA

INTRODUCTION

Bryophytes are autophytes which have migrated from water to terrestrial habit. They include groups of plants lying between Thallophytes and Pteridophytes in the plant kingdom. The favourable condition in which the plants thrive is a moist and shady place. There should be an ample supply of water for the existence of plant. They are more or less cosmopolitan in distribution and occur in all climates.

General characters

The plant body is a thallus and usually not differentiated into rest, stem and leaves, but in advanced forms it is differentiated into stem and leaves. The thallus or the leafy shoot is attached to the substratum by means of unicellular rhizoids developed from the ventral surface of the thallus or from the basal portion of the leafy shoot. These rhizoids perform the functions of fixation and absorption like the roots but they are not regarded as true roots. The Bryophytes reproduce sexually by fertilization. The sex organs, antheridia and archegonia, are *always multicellular structures* and *surrounded by a jacket layer of sterile cells* and contain the gametes, namely, antherozoids or spermatozoids and oosphere or ovum or egg respectively. They have a well-defined alternation of generations in their life cycles. The gametophyte is the conspicuous generation and it is an independent plant ; it is green in colour due to the presence of chlorophyll by which it can manufacture its own food. On the other hand, the sporophytic plant or the sporogonium is never totally independent. It always remains attached to the gametophyte and partially or wholly dependent on the gametophyte for nutrition.

In the absence of an up to date index of either mosses or liverworts it is impossible to state the number of described species except in the roundest of figures. Steere (1955) estimates 25,000 mosses, 350 sphagna, and 10,000 liverworts. To these figures new species are continually being added. Among the new taxa discovered in recent years are : *Cryptothallus mirabilis*, *Marchasta areolata*, *Takakia lepidozoides*, etc. *Cryptothallus*, a member of the Anacrogynae, is a colourless saprophyte often living in the surface little beneath *Molinia* or *Hylocomium*. *Marchasta* is a primitive member of the Marchantiales, in which the female receptacle is a twice bifurcated branch system. *Takakia* is a curious plant and appears to belong to an entirely new order of Hepaticae, the

Takakiales. It has peculiar and primitive features, the most remarkable being the cylinder **'phyllids'**, the leaf-like outgrowths on the stem.

The Bryophytes are ancient plants, and although they are not often preserved as fossils, we have a few records that are of exceptional interest. The oldest authentic liverwort is *Hapaticites kidstoni* from the upper carboniferous of England, described by Prof. Walton in 1925. Other important fossil genera are : *Marchantites*, *Metzgeriites*, *Muscites*, etc.

Origin of Bryophyta

The botanists are almost unanimous in believing that the bryophytes have taken their origin from some green algae. Confirmation to this idea has recently been obtained from the works of Stroin (1948), who has shown that the pigments, chlorophylls and xanthophylls of the Chlorophyceae only are identical with those found in the bryophytes. A few workers, like Haskall (1949), however, do not agree to this view and suggest that the bryophytes have been derived from the pteridophytes.

Previously, it was thought that an oogamous green alga, after its migration from water to land, gave rise to the sexual plant of a bryophyte, and simultaneously the phenomenon of alternation of generations also appeared. But, as it has been found out that an alternation of generations takes place independently in various diverse groups of green algae, like Ulotrichales, Chaetophorales and Cladophorales, there is the possibility that the ancestral form might be isogamous as well.

Whatever might be the ancestral algal type, there are two opposite schools of view as regards the structure of the primitive gametophyte in bryophytes. According to one school (Von Wettstein, 1908 ; Kashyap, 1919 ; Church, 1919 ; Harris, 1938 ; and Evans, 1939), the primitive gametophyte was an erect leafy shoot. The other school (Cavers, 1910 ; Campbell 1891, 1918, 1936) suggests that the gametophytic body was an undifferentiated thallus. The origin of the characteristic sex organs of bryophytes, however, presents some difficulty. The sex organs in the green algae are, as a rule, unicellular, and the majority of cells of a thallus can give rise to the gametes, while the sex organs of bryophytes are multicellular and the superficial cells constitute a sterile jacket of variable thickness. Davis (1903) put forward the hypothesis that both the sex organs, antheridia and archegonia, are fundamentally alike and evolved from a multicellular gametangium by gradual sterilization. According to this hypothesis, the hypothetical ancestral green alga bore superficially a number of multicellular gametangial outgrowths, more than one cell thick. At first, some of these outgrowths produced flagellate, motile male gametes, while the others produced similarly or dissimilarly sized, motile female gametes. Gradually, the cells in the surface layers began to fail to produce gametes and were converted into the sterile jacket. Those male outgrowths in which all the inner cells, excepting those of the jacket, retained their power of gamete-production, gave rise to the antheridia of the bryophytes. The bryophytic archegonium resulted by the complete sterilization of all the cells of the female outgrowths, excepting the lowermost as well as the innermost one, which lost its capacity to produce flagella and finally became an oosphere or egg.

As to the origin of the sporophyte in bryophytes, there are also two schools of view. According to the proponents of the **homologous (modification) theory** (Church, 1919 ; Zimmermann, 1932 ; and Fritsch, 1945), the sporophyte has evolved as a result of modification directly taking place in the gametophyte. According to these workers, both the gametophytic and sporophytic generations of the primitive bryophytes were externally complex, isomorphic, free-living plant bodies. In course of time the sporophyte got attached to the gametophyte and began to depend upon it for a partial food supply. Consequently, the sporophyte became less complex in structure. Advocates of the **antithetic (intercalation) theory** (Anderson, 1923), however, believe that the sporophyte became gradually more and more complex from a simple one by progressive sterilization of the spore-producing tissue. They believe that the sporophyte is a completely new structure placed in between two successive sexual or gametophytic generations. According to them, the first primitive sporophyte appeared from the zygote, enclosed within the venter of the archegonium. This zygote, instead of undergoing a meiotic division, divided equationally and gave rise to a number of diploid cells, each of which in its turn, divided mitotically and produced four haploid spores. Thus, in such a sporophyte all the cells were sporogenous. Gradual evolution resulted in the formation of a sporophyte, whose superficial cells were sterile and non-sporogenous. As a result of further sterilization, the sporophytes of the more advanced bryophytes have become differentiated into distinct foot, seta, and capsule.

Evolution among Bryophyta

Among Bryophytes evolution appears to have taken place along three different lines,—Hepaticae, Anthocerotae and Musci. If the view of Campbell and Cavers be accepted that the gametophyte of the most primitive bryophyte was a simple thallus body, then the simplest bryophytic gametophytes can be found among the family Sphaerocarpaceae of the liverworts (Hepaticae). The simplest sporophyte, on the other hand, will be found among the family Ricciaceae belonging to the same class. For this reason, Lotsy (1909) suggested an imaginary genus *Sphaero-riccia*, which was supposed to be the protobryophyte, the hypothetical ancestor of the present-day bryophytes.

Among the Hepaticae the Sphaerocarpales appear to be the most primitive, with which the Marchantiales are related to some extent. The Orders Jungermanniales and Calobryales, which are considered both as advanced as well as the most primitive by different workers, are rather remotely connected with the other groups of hepatics. Some workers believe that the leafy hepatics (Jungermanniales and Calobryales) have given rise to the true mosses. But taking the question of ontogeny of sex organs and the early developmental stage of the embryo into consideration, it seems more likely that the true mosses appeared quite independently of the hepatics. Both the classes Hepaticae and Musci, however, appear to be blind side lines from the evolutionary standpoint of view. On account of similarities existing in the structure of gametophytes as well as in the ontogeny of sex organs, it seems that the Anthocerotae might have originated and departed very early from some primitive Hepaticae. Further, due to the indeterminate growth of its sporophyte, the Anthocerotes are supposed by some workers to have given rise to the pteridophytes.

Classification of Bryophyta

The Bryophytes have been divided by many botanists into the following *three* Classes :

Class I. Hepaticae. The Hepaticae have dorsiventrally differentiated gametophytes, which are either externally simple (e.g. *Riccia* and *Marchantia*) or differentiated into stems and leaves (e.g. *Jungermannia*). Internally, they may be homogeneous or composed of different kinds of tissues. Sex organs are always formed on the dorsal surface of the thallus. The sporophytes may be extremely simple (e.g. *Riccia*) or differentiated into foot, seta and capsule (e.g. *Marchantia*) and these are always entirely parasitic upon the gametophytes for nourishment.

Class II. Anthocerotae. The gametophytes of the Anthocerotae have distinct dorsiventrality and are of simple external forms. The internal construction is homogeneous. The sex organs are developed on the dorsal surface and are embedded into the tissue of the thallus. The sporophytes are differentiated into capsule and foot. The lower part of the capsule, corresponding to the position of the seta, is highly meristematic. The sporogenous tissue is developed from the **amphithecium** instead of from the **endothecium**, which is transformed into **columella.**

Class III. Musci. The gametophytes of the Musci have a transitory prostrate stage bearing radially symmetrical, leafy, sexual branches (**gametophores**), which continue to grow as independent plants after the disappearance of the prostrate portion. Sex organs are developed near about the tips of the sexual branches and are produced either on the same plant (**monoecious**) or on different plants (**dioecious**). The sporophytes are differentiated into foot, seta and capsule and are semi-parasitic upon the gametophytes for nourishment.

CHAPTER I

CLASS HEPATICAE

Hepaticae has been divided into 4 Orders by Smith (1938, '55) incorporating the suggestions of Cavers (1910) and Campbell (1936): (1) **Sphaerocarpales**, e.g. *Sphaerocarpus*, (2) **Marchantiales,** e.g. *Riccia*, *Marchantia*, (3) **Jungermanniales**, e.g. *Lejeunea*, *Pellia*, *Porella*, etc., and (4) **Calobryales,** e.g. *Calobrya*.

ORDER 2. Marchantiales

The gametophyte is differentiated into a prostrate, ribbon-shaped, dorsiventral and dichotomously branched structure. Except in a very few genera, air chambers are present on the dorsal surface of the thallus. The ventral surface bears scales and two types of rhizoids: smooth-walled and pegged. Members of this Order have archegonia with six vertical tiers of neck cells.

The sporophyte may be very simple representing a spore-case (e.g. *Riccia*) or may be differentiated into foot, seta and capsule (e.g. *Marchantia*). The capsule never contains elaterophores although some short elater-like cells may remain attached at the basal region of the capsule in certain members like *Dumortiera hirsuta*, and there is no well-developed definite mechanism for the dehiscence of the capsule. The sterile jacket of the capsule is always one cell in thickness.

The Order Marchantiales has been divided into *five* families by Smith (1938, '55): (*a*) **Ricciaceae,** (*b*) **Corsiniaceae,** (*c*) **Targioniaceae,** (*d*) **Monocleaceae***, and (*e*) **Marchantiaceae.**

Evans (1939), on the other hand, grouped the Marchantiales into *six* families: (*a*) **Marchantiaceae,** (*b*) **Rebouliaceae,** (*c*) **Santeriaceae,** (*d*) **Targioniaceae,** (*e*) **Corsiniaceae,** and (*f*) **Ricciaceae.**

RICCIA

(Fam. RICCIACEAE)

Riccia, a common liverwort, grows usually during the rainy season on damp walls, moist places, etc., in dense patches, or rarely in pools of water as free-floating scum.

There are more than 130 species of *Riccia* distributed throughout the world, all are terrestrial, but only one species is aquatic,

---

* Verdoon (1932) and Evans (1939) do not include Monocleaceae in the Marchantiales.

viz., *R. fluitans*. The commonly occurring Indian species are *R. discolor* (=*R. himalayansis*), *R. gangetica*, *R. crystallina*, *R, pandei*, *R. sorocarpa*, etc.

The gametophyte

The vegetative body of each plant is a flat, dorsiventral thallus, wholly prostrate and typically rosette-like. It branches dichotomously. Each branch of the thallus is wedge-shaped and thickened on the middle line. On the ventral side of the thallus, there are numerous scale-like structures, one-cell in thickness, and many rhizoids which perform the function of the root. Rhizoids are of two kinds : smooth-walled and pegged, *i.e.*, with various types of ingrowths of the wall projecting into the lumen of the rhizoids.

Fig. 239. Gametophytic thallus of *Riccia*,

When a transverse section of the thallus of *Riccia* is examined under the microscope it is found that the upper or dorsal portion consists of vertical tiers of cells containing chloroplasts, while the

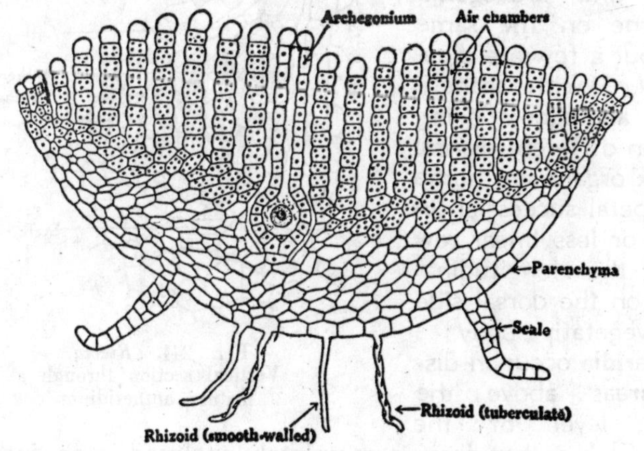

Fig. 240. *Riccia*,
Transverse section of the thallus.

lower or ventral part is a tissue of colourless parenchyma cells, which may contain starch. There is a single row of canals, extending throughout the entire length of the chlorophyll-bearing tissue ;

these canals are the air chambers. The air chambers are perfectly smooth and are without any ingrowths. At the top of the air chambers there is the so-called 'epidermis', which is only one cell in thickness. The air-pores are simple unicellular spaces bounded by several 'epidermal' cells. In older portions of the thallus and on the ventral surface are observed the unicellular rhizoids lying between the multicellular scales.

Reproduction

Riccia reproduces both by vegetative and sexual methods.

Vegetative reproduction takes place in five ways : (*a*) by the progressive growth of the apical region, followed by death and decay of the older portion ; as a result of decay, the two lobes of the dichotomy are ultimately separated and each of them develops into an independent plant, (*b*) by the formation of adventitious branches, developed from the ventral surface of the thallus, (*c*) by the growth of the surviving apical cell of the thallus of the previous season, (*d*) by the formation of tubers developed from the thallus, and (*e*) by the development of gemmae-like bodies from the rhizoid-tips ; these bodies detach themselves from the parent thallus and give rise to new individuals.

Most species of *Riccia* are monoecious, *i.e.*, antheridia and archegonia are borne on the same plant, but a few are dioecious, *i.e.*, with antheridia and archegonia being borne on different plants. The sex organs are borne in acropetal succession in a more or less linear row within the longitudinal furrow on the dorsal side of the vegetative body.

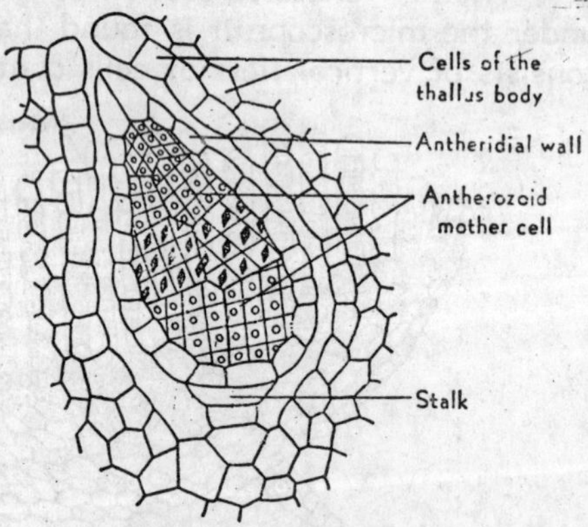

Fig. 241. *Riccia*. Vertical section through a mature antheridium.

Antheridia occur in discoid areas above the general level of the thallus. Each antheridium is completely enclosed in an antheridial chamber formed by the growth of the adjacent tissues and connected to the exterior by a narrow slit-like opening. Each antheridium is a pear-shaped body, stalked at the broader end. It is surrounded by a single layer of sterile cells at the exterior, forming the wall of the antheridium. Enclosed by this wall, there are numerous cells, each with a relatively large nucleus and dense cytoplasm. These are antherozoid mother cells or sperm mother cells. Each mother cell undergoes a single nuclear division and by an oblique partition forms two cells, each of which is metamorphosed into a single biflagellate **antherozoid** or **spermatozoid.** When the spermatozoids mature, there is a complete dissolution of the cell walls within the antheridium, so that the spermatozoids lie in a common cavity and are ultimately discharged.

Archegonia lie in the deep pits or furrows and are partially enclosed by the overgrowth of the surrounding tissues. Each archegonium is a flask-shaped body with a very short stalk and consists of two parts : an enlarged basal portion, called the **venter**, and an elongated, comparatively large, tubular portion known as the **neck.** The venter consists of **ventral canal cells** and a large **oosphere** or **ovum** or **egg,** and the neck consists of a number of **neck canal cells.**

When the archegonium matures, there is a complete dissolution of the canal cells, so that a passage is established. Biflagellate

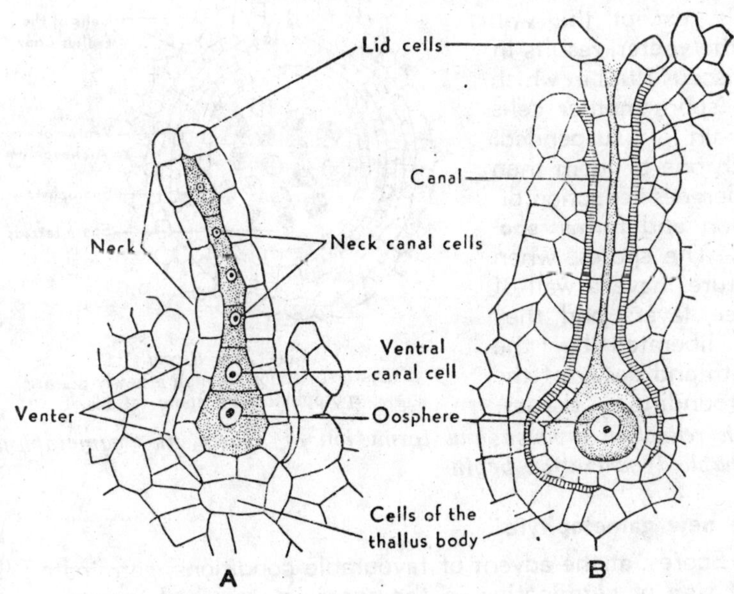

Fig. 242. *Riccia.*
A, A mature archegonium ; B, An archegonium ready for fertilization.

spermatozoids enter into the venter, one of which eventually fertilizes the egg. The fertilized ovum is then surrounded by a thin cellulose wall and becomes an **oospore.** *With fertilization and* *formation of the oospore, the sporophytic or diploid generation begins.*

The sporophyte

The oospore, as soon as formed, increases in size until the venter of the archegonium is almost completely filled up, and then undergoes a single division to form a two-celled **embryo.** This embryo by the process of repeated cell divisions grows into a multicellular structure, many times larger than the zygote in size. The sporophyte, when consists of 20-30 cells, becomes differentiated into an outer layer of sterile cells, called the **amphithecium**, and an inner mass of fertile sporogenous cells, known as the **endothecium.** Meanwhile, the venter also increases in size, and the entire sporophyte remains enclosed within the gametophytic tissue. Each cell of the endothecium, consisting of a relatively large nucleus and dense cytoplasm, is a **spore mother cell.** The spore mother cells undergo contraction of protoplast. The distintegration of the walls of the sterile cells, except the wall of the venter, results in a viscous fluid in which the spore mother cells remain suspended. Each one of them then undergoes reduction division and forms **spores.** The spores, when mature, have a wall of three layers and they are liberated by the death and decay of the surrounding tissues.

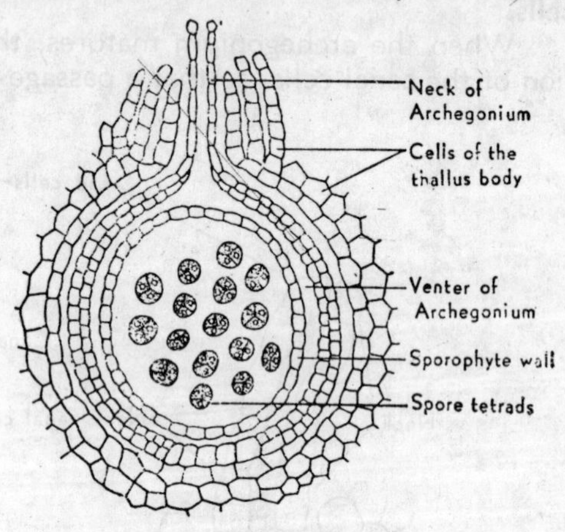

Fig. 243. *Riccia.* Transverse section through a newly mature sporophyte with spore tetrads.

With reduction division and formation of spores, the gametophytic or haploid generation begins.

The new gametophyte

Spores, at the advent of favourable conditions, germinate ; the first sign of germination in the spore is a marked increase in its size. Subsequently it becomes more or less transparent. This is followed by the appearance of a prominent pore opposite the **tri**radiate mark. The endospore comes out through this pore in the form of a colourless papilla. Later, a large number of chloroplasts make their appearance. The germ tube elongates, and by divisions forms an eight-celled germ plate. Subsequently a 2-sided apical cell is established, which cuts off segments adding to the tissues of the gametophyte. The first rhizoid develops when the germ plate is 2-celled.

MARCHANTIA

(Fam. MARCHANTIACEAE)

Marchantia, a common liverwort, is generally found on moist soils, rocks, etc. There are about 65 species of *Marchantia* distributed throughout the world. Of the 4 species, *M. palmata*, *M. nepalensis*, *M. simlana* and *M. polymorpha* growing in India, the last-named one is very common and, practically speaking, it is cosmopolitan in distribution.

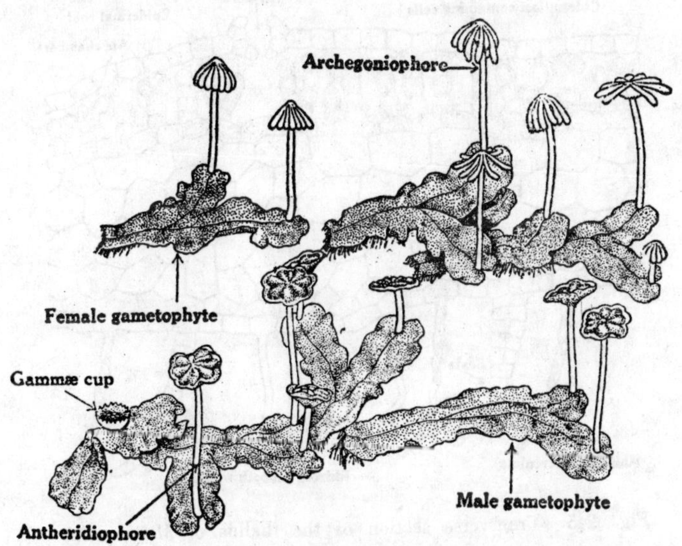

Fig. 244. *Marchantia*.
Thallus with antheridiophores and archegoniophores.

The gametophyte

The thallus is found creeping on the surface of the substratum in the form of a rosette and is closely attached to it by means of rhizoids and scales found on the under surface of the thallus. The branching of the thallus is dichotomous and there is a prominent midrib.

In transverse section of the thallus, it shows an upper epidermis containing many air-pores which open to the external surface. Beneath the upper epidermis lies the air chambers containing branched filaments of cells, which grow upwards from the layer of cells composing the floor of the chamber. The cells of these filaments contain chloroplasts and constitute the main photosynthetic tissue of the plant. Beneath the air chambers there are several layers of cells containing a few chloroplasts. From the lower surface of the thallus grow scales and rhizoids. The rhizoids are of two different kinds : some are smooth-walled, others are pegged, the inner surface of the walls of which are marked by localized thickenings.

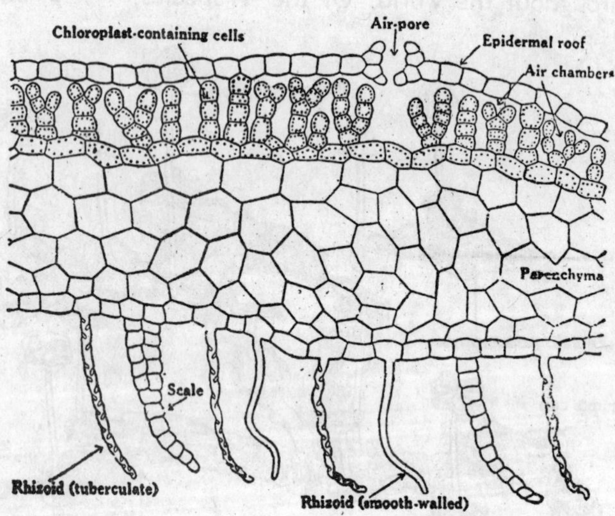

Fig. 245. Transverse section of the thallus of *Marchantia*.

Reproduction

Marchantia reproduces both by vegetative and sexual methods. The vegetative multiplication takes place by apical growth and branching, and by progressive death of the older parts of the thallus due to which the number of plants is increased. It also takes place by the formation of lens-shaped structures (**gemmae**) which are produced in a great number in goblet-shaped cups known as **gemmae cups.** Each gemma is attached to the thallus by means of a one-celled stalk, from which the gemma is easily detached. Each gemma is more or less round with two notches in the middle and when it falls on the substratum, cell divisions begin at the notches and two plants are consequently formed.

The sex organs of *Marchantia* are borne on special erect branches, each composed of a stalk and a terminal horizontal disc. The

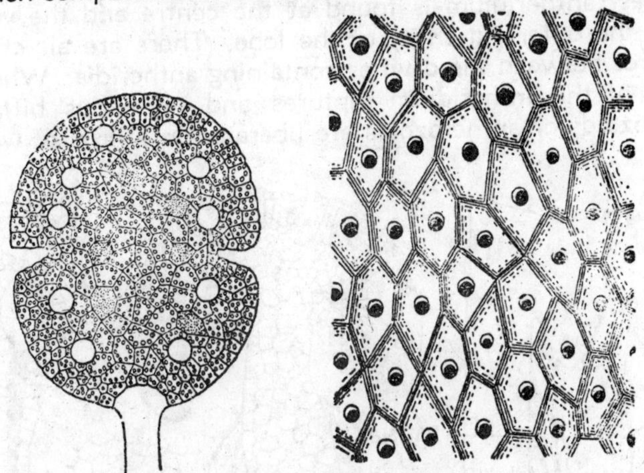

Fig. 246. *Marchantia.*
Thallus with gemmae cups containing gemmae ; an enlarged view of one of which is shown on the left-hand side.

male and female branches may be borne on the same plant (monoecious) or on different plants (dioecious).

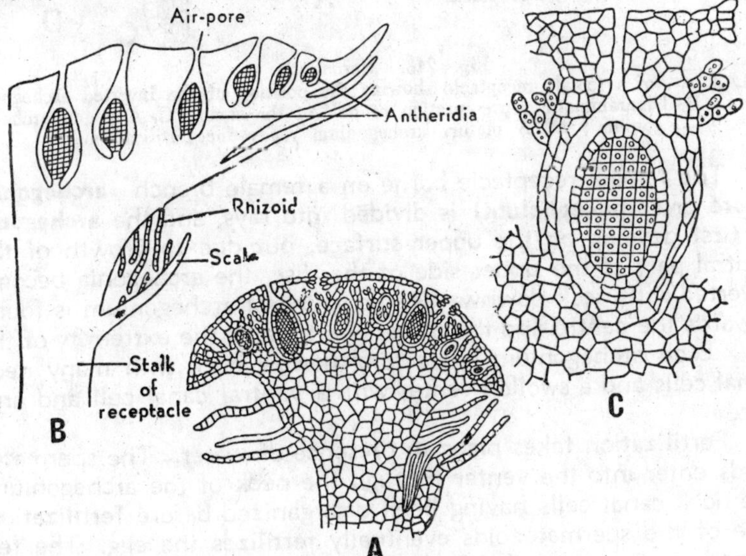

Fig. 247. *Marchantia.*
A, A v.s. of the disc of a male branch showing the position of the antheridia ; B, Diagrammatic representation of half of the same ; C, A v.s. through a mature antheridium.

The disc borne by a male branch (**antheridiophore**) is lobed and the **antheridia** are embedded on the upper surface of each lobe. The oldest antheridium is found at the centre and the youngest towards the outer extremity of the lobe. There are air chambers with pores between the cavities containing antheridia. When ripe, the wall of the antheridium ruptures and numerous biflagellate spermatozoids or antherozoids are liberated in a drop of water.

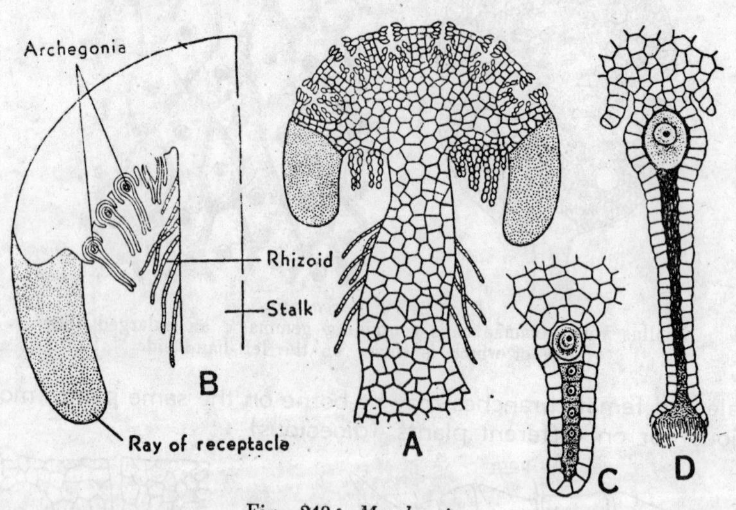

Fig. 248. *Marchantia.*
A, A v,s, of a female receptacle showing the position of the inverted archegonia ; B, Diagrammatic representation of half of the same ; C, A young archegonium ; D, A mature archegonium ready for fertilization.

The female receptacle borne on a female branch (**archegoniophore** or **carpocephalum**) is divided into rays, and the **archegonia** at first develop on the upper surface, but due to growth of the central part of the upper side of the disc, the archegonia become inverted with neck downwards, the youngest archegonium is found towards the centre and the oldest one towards the extremity of the ray. Each archegonium has a long narrow neck with many neck canal cells and a swollen venter with a ventral canal cell and an egg.

Fertilization takes place in presence of water. The spermatozoids enter into the venter through the neck of the archegonium, the neck canal cells having been disorganized before fertilization. One of the spermatozoids eventually fertilizes the egg. The fertilized egg is surrounded by a thin cellulose wall and becomes an **oospore.** *With fertilization and formation of oospore, the sporophytic or diploid generation begins.*

The sporophyte

The oospore develops immediately into a sporophyte within the venter of the archegonium. When fully developed, it is differentiated into (*i*) a broad basal **foot**, (*ii*) an elongated stalk or **seta,** and (*iii*) a terminal **capsule.**

As a result of fertilization, the ventral cells of the archegonium are stimulated to divide and re-divide forming a tissue, known as **calyptra**, which surrounds the developing sporophyte till the latter attains maturity. Some of the cells at the base of the archegonium also divide and form a cylindrical sheet-like outgrowth, known as **pseudoperianth,** surrounding the archegonial venter with its enclosed sporophyte. The oospore, first divides transversely into two cells—an upper and a lower. The second division is, however, at right angles to the first, so that a four-celled embryo is formed.

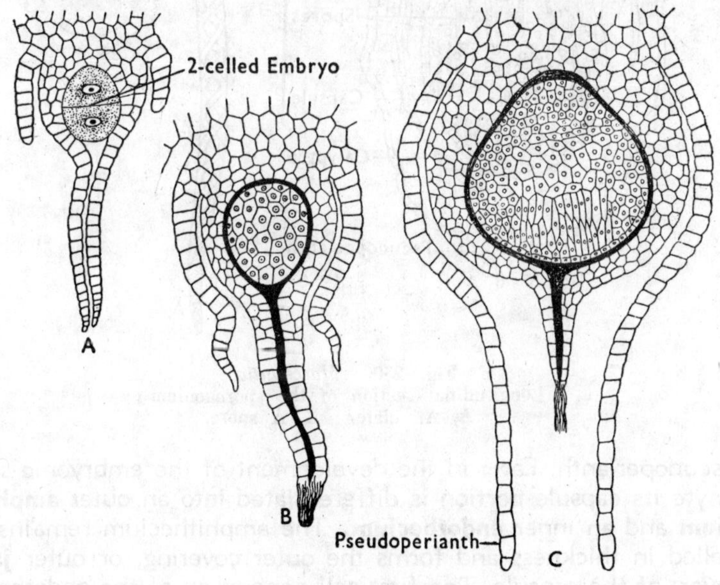

Fig. 249. *Marchantia,* A—C, Successive stages in the development of the sporophyte.

The two uppermost cells, the **epibasal cells,** by division and redivision give rise to the capsule and the upper part of the seta, and the two lowermost cells, the **hypobasal cells,** by subsequent divisions form the lower part of the seta and the foot. The foot is a broad, expanded tissue which fixes the sporophyte to the gametophyte and absorbs water and nutrient solutions from it. The seta consists of vertical rows of more or less isodiametric cells, which, during the later part of the development of the sporophyte, elongates considerably. Due to the elongation of the seta, the calyptra ruptures and the capsule is pushed outwards beyond the

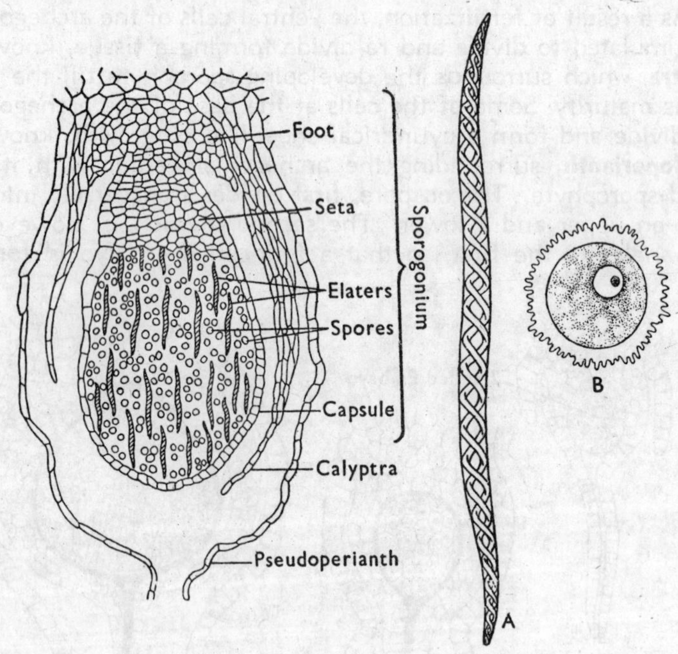

Fig. 250. *Marchantia.*
Longitudinal section of the sporogonium ;
A, An elater ; B, A spore.

pseudoperianth. Early in the development of the embryonic sporophyte its capsule portion is differentiated into an outer **amphithecium** and an inner **endothecium.** The amphithecium remains one-celled in thickness and forms the outer covering, or outer **jacket** layer, of the capsule. The first cell generation of the endothecium is the **archesporium,** which divides and re-divides to form a mass of **sporogenous tissue.** A few apical cells of this tissue remain sterile, while others elongate and divide obliquely. Finally, half of the sporogenous cells, by two or three successive divisions, gives rise to more or less isodiametric spore mother cells. The other half of the sporogenous cells becomes much elongated, each with two spiral thickenings on its wall, and forms the **elaters.** The spore mother cells and elaters are usually evenly distributed within the wall of the capsule. Each spore mother cell by reduction division forms four **spores.** *With reduction division and formation of spores, the gametophytic or haploid generation begins.*

At maturity, when the capsule is pushed outwards beyond the pseudoperianth, due to the sudden increase in length of seta, the jacket of the capsule splits up from the apex to about the middle into an indefinite number of segments and the spores are liberated. During the process the elaters coil and uncoil due to hygroscopic changes in their walls and assist in the liberation of spores.

The new gametophyte

The spores, after liberation, are dispersed and carried away by the wind. Each spore under suitable conditions germinates, increases considerably in size, divides to form a six- to eight-celled irregular filament (**protonema**), from which a typical gametophytic thallus is gradually differentiated.

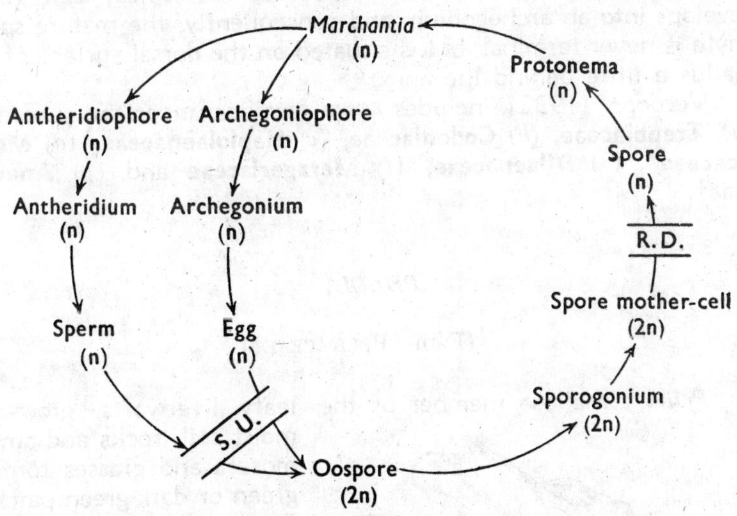

Fig. 251. Life cycle of *Marchantia*,

ORDER 3. **JUNGERMANNIALES**

The gametophyte may be thallose or foliose, or intermediate between the two. In no case, an air chamber is found in the gametophyte, and little internal differentiation is noticeable. The gametophyte bears smooth-walled rhizoids and mucilagenous hairs, but neither any scale nor any pegged rhizoid. The members of this Order have archegonia with five **vertical** rows of neck cells.

The sporophyte is always differentiated into foot, seta and capsule. The jacket of the capsule is usually more than one cell in thickness. The capsule always contains elaters and these may form a columnar structure, the **elaterophore**, which may be attached to the apex or to the base of the capsule. The capsule has a well-defined mechanism for dehiscence, and it splits up into four definite valves.

Smith (1938, '55) includes two suborders under the Order Jungermanniales : (*a*) **Metzgerineae (Anacrogynae)**, and (*b*) **Jungermannineae (Acrogynae)**.

SUBORDER METZGERINEAE (ANACROGYNAE)

The gametophyte is dorsiventral, and generally thallose, more rarely foliose in form. In this suborder the apical cell never develops into an archegonium and consequently, the mature sporophyte is never terminal, but is situated on the dorsal surface of the thallus a little behind the apex.

Verdoon (1932) includes *seven* families under the suborder : (*a*) **Treubiaceae**, (*b*) **Codoniaceae**, (*c*) **Haplolaenaceae**, (*d*) **Monocleaceae***, (*e*) **Dilaenaceae**, (*f*) **Metzgeriaceae** and (*g*) **Aneuraceae**†.

PELLIA

(Fam. PELLIACEAE‡)

Pellia, thallose member of the leafy liverworts, grows on moist soil, rocks and among mosses and grasses forming green or dark-green patches. It may also grow in running water.

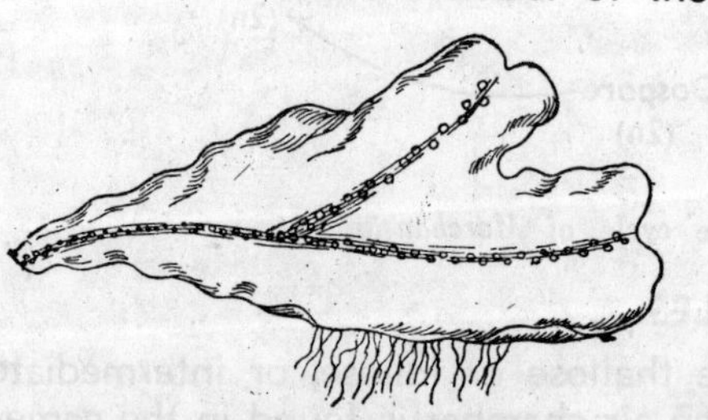

Fig. 252. *Pellia*. A gametophytic thallus.

There are 3 species of *Pellia* reported to be found in India — *P. epiphylla*, *P. fabbroniana* and *P. neesiana*.

* Smith includes the family Monocleaceae with the Order Marchantiales.
† Richardiaceae of Smith.
‡ Haplolaenaceae of Verdoon.

The gametophyte

The gametophyte is a simple, green, dorsiventral and dichotomously or pinnately branched structure. The thallus is externally differentiated into a **midrib** and **lateral wings,** the latter constituting the chief photosynthetic organs of the plant. The margins of the wings are undulated. On the ventral surface are present several smooth-walled rhizoids and a few mucilagenous hairs.

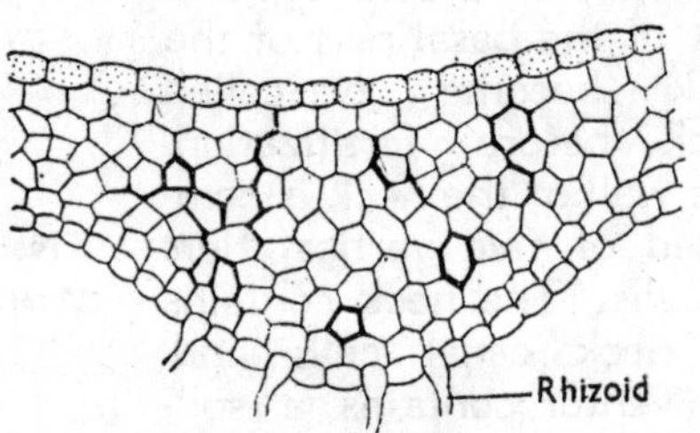

Fig. 253. *Pellia*, T.S. of thallus.

The internal structure of the gametophyte is very simple. It is mainly made up of parenchyma cells. The midrib portion is several cells in thickness, while the margins gradually become one cell in thickness. The cells of the wing and the superficial cells of the midrib contain chloroplasts, and practically all the cells contain starch grains.

Reproduction

Pellia reproduces both by vegetative and sexual methods.

Vegetative reproduction takes place by three different ways : (*a*) by the progressive growth of the thallus and subsequent death and decay of the older regions, (*b*) by multicellular **gemmae** formed from the superficial cells of the thallus, and (*c*) by the formation of underground **tubers.**

The plant is either monoecious or dioecious. The sex organs are borne dorsally on the midrib in two or more distinct rows. In homothallic species, antheridia are borne behind the archegonial clusters.

The **antheridia** develop from the superficial dorsal cells close to the apical cell. A mature antheridium is globose a subglobose with a short stalk and a jacket, one cell in thickness. The antheridia are slightly embedded in the tissue of the gametophytes. At maturity they burst suddenly, thereby liberating the relatively large biflagellate antherozoids.

The **archegonia** also develop from the superficial cells on the dorsal side. The archegonium initials, which give rise to the archegonia, lie very close to the apical cell, but unlike *Porella*, the apical cell itself never develops into an archegonium. The archegonia grow in clusters in pit-like depressions and are surrounded by an **involucre.** A mature archegonium has a venter and a neck. The neck is not very sharply delimited from the venter. The wall of the venter and that of the basal part of the neck become two-celled thick before fertilization. The wall of the neck is composed of five vertical tiers of cells. The neck contains 4-6 neck canal cells and the venter contains a solitary ventral canal cell and an egg.

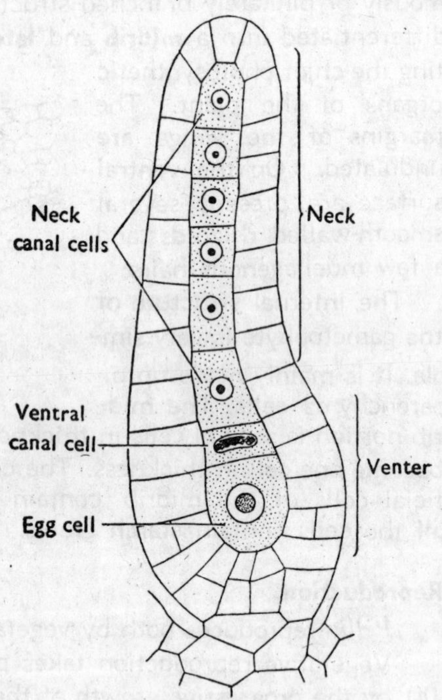

Fig. 254. *Pellia.* An archegonium,

Fertilization takes place in presence of water. The antherozoids swim into the venter through the passage formed by the disintegration of the neck canal and ventral canal cells. But, only one antherozoid enters into the archegonium and fertilizes the egg. The fertilized egg surrounds itself by a wall and forms the **oospore.** *With fertilization and formation of oospore, the sporophytic or diploid generation begins.*

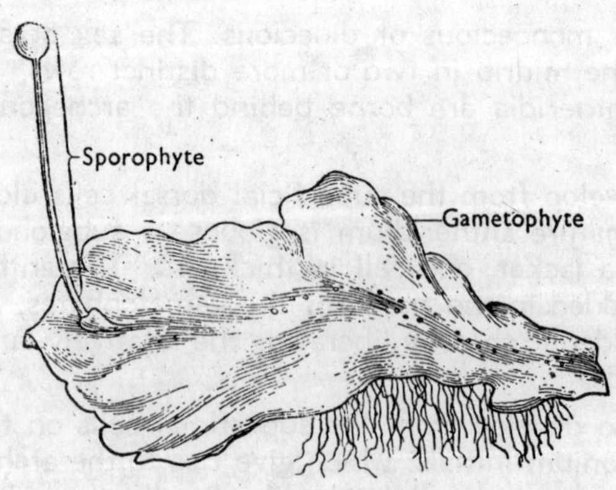

Fig. 255. *Pellia.* A gametophyte with attached sporophyte.

The sporophyte

The oospore enlarges filling the cavity of the venter. The venter by subsequent development forms the calyptra. Within each involucre, a single **sporogonium** (sporophyte) is developed and the remaining archegonia become abortive.

The oospore, by a transverse wall, forms a **hypobasal cell** and

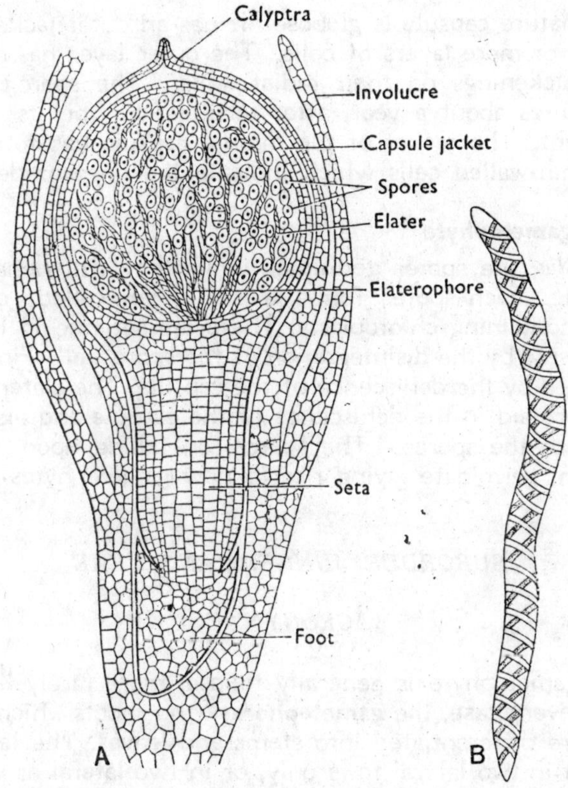

Fig. 256. *Pellia.*
A, v.s. through a mature sporogonium ; B, A single elater (magnified).

an **epibasal cell.** The hypobasal cell undergoes no further division but forms an **haustorium.** The sporogonium is wholly developed from the epibasal cell. The epibasal cell undergoes transverse divisions and from its four upper cells develop the **capsule,** while from the lower four develop the **seta** and the **foot.**

Within the capsule, by divisions, two regions are set apart, an outer wall of two layers of cells and an inner multi-layered mass. From the latter (endothecium) develops the sporogenous tissue and the sterile **elaters.** The elaters are long, slender with double spiral thickenings on their walls. Some of the sterile cells become compact at the base of the capsule and form the **elaterophore.** The spore mother cells, by meiotic division, from the **spore tetrads**. *With reduction division and formation of spores, the gametophytic or haploid generation begins.*

The mature capsule is globose. It has an outer jacket consisting of two or more layers of cells. The outer layer has cells with rod-like thickenings on their radial walls. The sporogonium of *Pellia* requires about a year, after fertilization, for its complete development. The jacket of the mature capsule has four vertical rows of thin-walled cells which indicate the lines of deniscence.

The new gametophyte

In *Pellia*, the spores germinate while they still remain inside the capsule. Each spore forms a small, few-celled, ellipsoidal structure containing chloroplasts. These are set free in the cavity of the capsule by the disintegration of the spore wall. Finally, they are liberated by the dehiscence of the capsule. The elaters and the elaterophore aid in the dehiscence of the capsule and also for the discharge of the spores. The spores, on falling upon a suitable substratum, germinate giving rise to new gametophytes.

SUBORDER JUNGERMANNINEAE

(*ACROGYNAE*)

The gametophyte is generally foliose, more rarely thallose in form. In every case, the **gametophores** (the shoots which bear sex organs) are differentiated into stems and leaves. The leaves may be present in two lateral rows only, or in two lateral as well as in one ventral rows. The leaves of the lateral sides are known as **lateral leaves** and those on the ventral side are known as **ventral leaves*** or **amphigastria.**

In this suborder the apical cell develops into an archegonium, and as such, the mature sporophyte is always terminal in position.

Verdoon (1932) includes 14 families under this suborder: (*a*) **Haplomitriaceae,** (*b*) **Macvicariaceae,** (*c*) **Epigonanthaceae,** (*d*) **Scapaniaceae,** (*e*) **Schistochilaceae,** (*f*) **Chephaloziellaceae,** (*g*) **Trigonanthaceae,** (*h*) **Ptilidiaceae,** (*i*) **Pleuroziaceae.** (*j*) **Goebeliellaceae,** (*k*) **Radulaceae,** (*l*) **Porellaceae (Madothecaceae),** (*m*) **Lejeuneaceae,** and (*n*) **Frullaniaceae.**

* These are also known as **under leaves.**

PORELLA (=*MADOTHECA*)

(Fam. PORELLACEAE=MADOTHECACEAE)

Porella, often termed as 'leafy liverwort', grows on rocks and barks of trees forming light-green or brownish green patches. The genus consists of about 180 species, found both in the tropical as well as in the temperate regions. In India there are about 34 species, mainly found in the Himalayas, of which the important ones are *P. decurrents*, *P. obtusifolia* and *P. platiphylla*.

The gametophyte

The gametophyte is a prostrate structure which is differentiated into the stem and leaves. The stem is pinnately branched with leaves arranged in three rows, two dorsal and one ventral. The dorsal rows form the lateral leaves, while the ventral row forms the **amphigastria** or under leaves. Each lateral leaf is unequally bilobed. In some epiphytic species, the under leaf is modified into a water sac. The arrangement of the lateral leaves is **incubous***, since they are obliquely inserted on the stem in such a way, so that the lower leaf overlaps the margin of the succeeding upper one on the dorsal surface. The lateral leaves are chlorophyllous and form the photosynthetic organs. Smooth-walled rhizoids are developed from the ventral surface of the stem and branches and fix the plant to

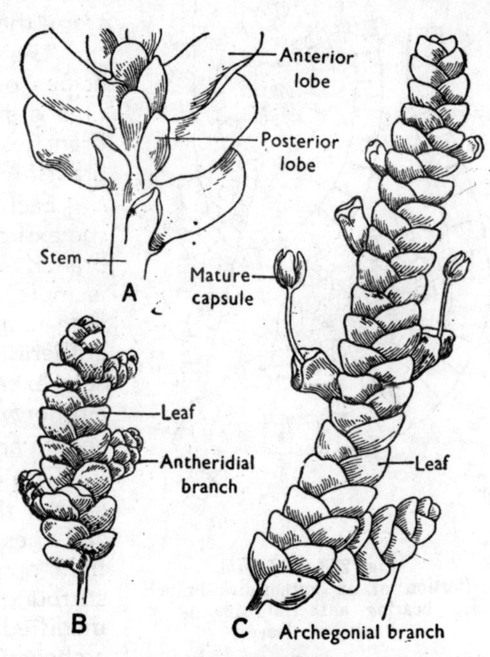

Fig. 257. *Porella*.
A, A portion of the vegetative body ; B, Same with antheridial branches ; C, Same bearing archegonial branches and mature capsules.

* In a **succubous** type of arrangement, the mode of overlapping is reversed

the substratum. It is to be noted that where branching takes place, the branches replace the lower lobes of the lateral leaves.

There is but little internal differentiation of the tissues of the thallus. All the cells of the gametophyte are parenchymatous. Air chambers and mucilagenous cavities are entirely absent.

Reproduction

Porella reproduces both by vegetative and sexual methods.

Vegetative reproduction takes place by three different ways : (*a*) by the progressive growth of the thallus and subsequent death and decay of the older parts, (*b*) by the formation of adventitious branches, and (*c*) by the production of one or two-celled **gemmae** from the leaf-margins.

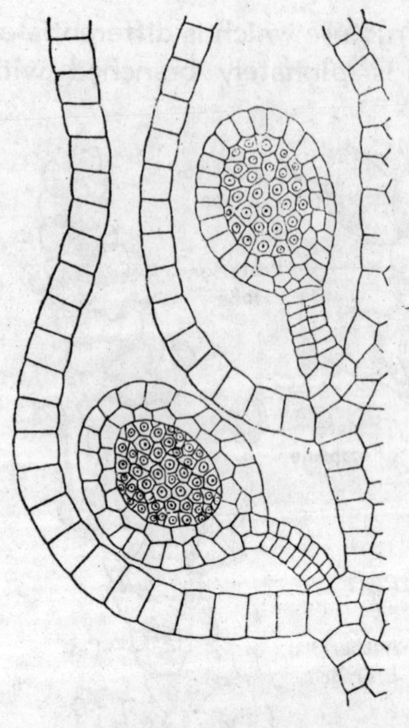

Fig. 258. *Porella*, Portion of an antheridial branch bearing antheridia in the axils of leaves.

The plants are either monoecious or dioecious, and the sex organs are borne on short lateral branches together with the bracts.

Each **antheridium** is borne in the axil of a leaf of an antheridial branch. A mature antheridium is more or less globose with a long stalk. The jacket of the antheridium is one cell in thickness except at the apical region. Antherozoids are typically biflagellate and crescent-shaped.

The archegonial branches are shorter than those of the antheridial ones and bear archegonia at their apices in groups. They are surrounded by a rosette of modified enlarged leaves. An archegonium develops from the apical cell, thereby checking further growth of the branch.

A mature **archegonium** has a broad venter containing a ventral canal cell and an egg. The wall of the venter is more than one cell in thickness. The neck is long and contains 6-8 neck canal cells. Each group of mature archegonia is surrounded by a thin sheath developed from the archegonial branch. This sheath is termed as **marsupium.**

The gametic union requires the presence of sufficient water. The antherozoids are carried by the current of water near the archegonium, one of which ultimately unites with the egg, thereby, effecting fertilization. *With fertilization and formation of oospore, sporophytic or diploid generation begins.*

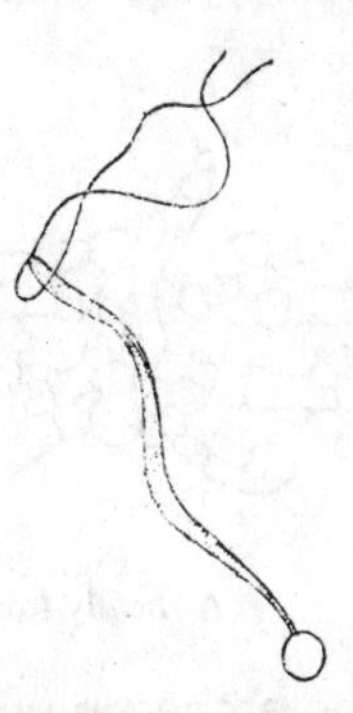

Fig. 259. *Porella.* A single antherozoid

The sporophyte

The oospore, produced as a result of fertilization, divides transversely into a **hypobasal cell** and an **epibasal cell.** The hypobasal cell produces an **haustorium** of two or more cells. The rest of the sporophyte develops entirely from the epibasal cell.

A mature sporophyte has a **foot,** a **seta** and a **capsule.** The foot is bulbous, the seta is short and the capsule is large and globose. The jacket of the capsule is more than one cell in thickness. The cells of the outermost layer are thick-walled, except along the four vertical lines which form the future lines of dehiscence of the capsule. The jacket develops from the amphithecium. The endothecium forms the sporogenous tissue. Certain portion of the sporogenous tissue is fertile and by reduction division forms the **spore tetrads,** while the

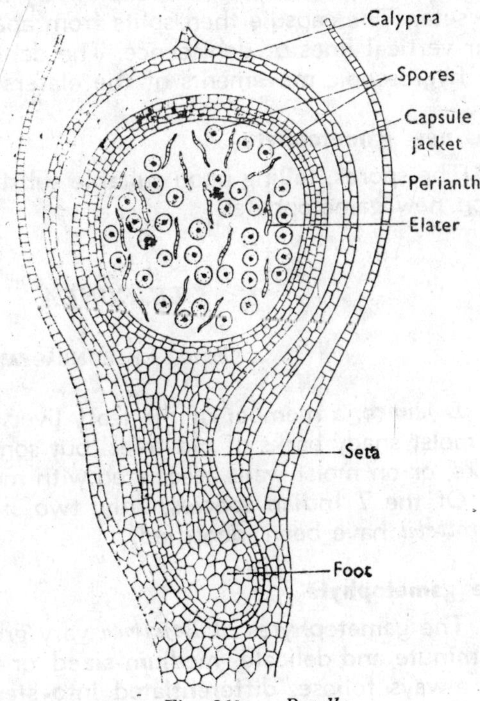

Fig. 260. *Porella.* v.s. through a mature sporogonium.

rest are sterile and develop into **elaters.** The spores may be brown or golden brown in colour and in many cases, they may be winged. *With reduction division and formation of spores, the gametophytic or haploid generation begins.* The elaters may be branched or unbranched.

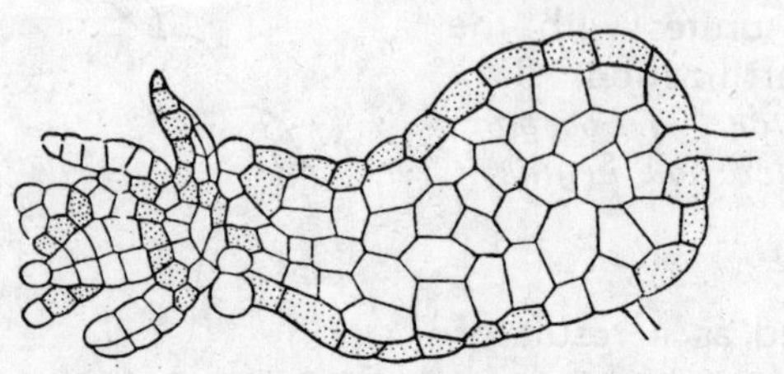

Fig. 261. *Porella.* A newly-formed gametophyte.

A mature sporophyte is protected by the **marsupium, perianth** (formed by the bracts of the archegonium) and the multi-layered **calyptra** (formed from the venter).

The mature capsule, prior to dehiscence, is carried up beyond the calyptra, perianth and marsupium by the sudden elongation of the seta. The capsule then splits from apex downwards along the four vertical lines of dehiscence. The dehiscence is mainly due to the hygroscopic movements of the elaters.

The new gametophyte

The spores, falling upon suitable substratum, germinate to produce new gametophytes.

LEJEUNEA

(Fam. LEJEUNEACEAE)

Lejeunea, a member of the leafy liverworts, is generally found on moist shady barks of old trees, but sometimes it also grows on rocks, or on moist walls associated with mosses.

Of the 7 Indian species, only two, viz., *L. chinensis* and *L. perrottetii* have been identified.

The gametophyte

The gametophytes of *Lejeunea* vary greatly in size. They may be minute and delicate, medium-sized, or large and robust. They are always foliose, differentiated into stem and leaves.

The branching of the stem is pinnate (alternate) and not dichotomous. When very young, the whorled leaves are in three vertical rows, but due to differential growth, leaves of the mature stem are alternately arranged and obliquely or almost longitudinally inserted. The bilobed leaves have their margins entire, or more or less toothed. The amphigastrias may be entire, or bifid, or rarely absent (e.g., *Lejeunea* sp. E).

The internal structure of the gametophyte is very simple and has but little differentiation of tissues. All the rhizoids are of the smooth-walled type.

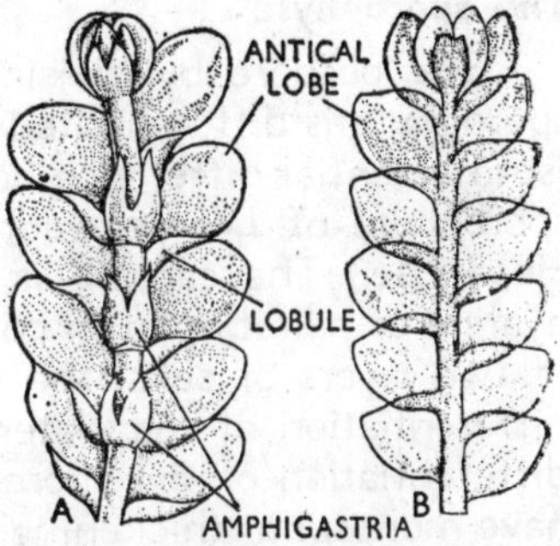

Fig. 262. *Lejeunea*, A, Dorsal view ; B, Ventral view.

Reproduction

Lejeunea reproduced both by vegetative and sexual methods.

Vegetative reproduction may take place by three different ways : (*a*) by the death and decay of the older parts, thus separating the branches, which by subsequent growth, become independent plants ; (*b*) by discoid **gemmae,** which are modified cells from the leaf margins ; and (*c*) by **tubers,** which are modified underground branches.

Lejeunea is either monoecious or dioecious. The sex organs may be borne on the main axis or on short lateral branches.

The **antheridia** are usually borne on short lateral branches, but occasionally they are also found on the main stem. They are protected by bracts, known as **antheridial bracts** or **perichaetial bracts,** which are sub-equal. An antheridium develops from any superficial cell close to the apex. The mature antheridium is globose and has a jacket enclosing a number of antherozoid mother cells, each of which gives rise to a biflagellate antherozoid. The cells of the jacket are strongly hygroscopic. The separation of jacket cells begin at the apex of an antheridium, due to an outward curvature immediately after they are wetted. The exposed mass of antherozoids begin to move freely in all directions.

A single **archegonium** develops from the apical cell of the female branch. The archegonia are protected by bracts (**perigonial bracts**) and bracteoles, which are different from the vegetative leaves. The archegonium consists of a **neck** and a **venter.** The neck consists of five vertical rows of neck cells and encloses 6-8 neck canal cells. The wall of the venter may be two-celled in thickness before fertilization.

At maturity, there is gelatinization of the neck canal as well as the ventral canal cells. Thus, the archegonium opens at the tip through which antherozoids enter. Only one of them fertilizes the egg and an oospore is formed. *With fertilization and formation of oospore, the sporophytic or diploid generation begins.*

The sporophyte

The oospore by divisions forms the sporophyte. The mature sporophyte is differentiated into a **foot,** a **seta** and a **capsule.** There is no essential difference between a foot and a seta of the mature sporophyte of *Lejeunea* and those of the sporophytes of other Hepaticae. The capsule is pedicellate and globose. It may be hyaline or pale brown in colour. The capsule has jacket consisting of two layers of cells, the inner wall being often spongy. The differentiation of the elaters usually takes place long before the differentiation of the spore mother cells. The elaters of *Lejeunea* have monospiral thickening, and each of them extends from top to bottom of the capsule with its upper end fixed to the capsule wall. The spore mother cells, by reduction division, give rise to the tetrads of **spores.** *With reduction division and formation of spores, the gametophytic or haploid generation begins.*

The mature capsule typically opens by four valves. The opening extends up to 2/3 of the length of the capsule from the apex. The lower 1/3 of the capsule is solid. The elaters assist in spore dispersal.

The new gametophyte

The spore, on liberation, germinates immediately to give rise to a protonema-like structure. Finally from the protonemal stage, the mature gametophore is developed.

CHAPTER II

CLASS ANTHOCEROTAE

Class Anthocerotae is a small but distinct group of Bryophytes which differs from the others in having a sporophyte which is of indefinite growth owing to the presence of a meristematic tissue at its base.

The Class Anthocerotae includes four genera : *Anthoceros*, *Megaceros*, *Dendroveros* and *Notothyllus*, of which the first-mentioned is the most common.

Salient features

1. Plants (gametophytes) are thallose with lobed margins and dichotomous branching. The thallus is dorsiventral and there is no internal differentiation of tissues. Rhizoids are present on its ventral surface but without scales or mucilagenous hairs.

2. Large intercellular spaces on the ventral surface of the thallus are filled up with mucilage which open to the external surface by means of narrow slit-like openings and these spaces often contain endophytic algae, like *Nostoc*.

3. Generally, a single large chloroplast is present in contact with or more or less inventing the nucleus in each cell of the thallus. Each chloroplast has a prominent pyrenoid.

4. All Anthocerotae are chiefly homothallic. Sex organs are deeply embedded in the dorsal surface of the thallus and are not borne on special branches as in many other bryophytes.

5. Antheridia arise in clusters from the hypodermal cells and these remain within a mucilage filled antheridial chamber. The sperms are biflagellate.

6. Archegonia arise singly and are embedded the thallus and are in direct contact with the vegetative cells, lateral to them, with neck projected upwards.

7. A meristematic tissue is present at the base of the capsule, by the activity of which the capsule has a continued apical growth. Ripe spores are towards the apex and young spore mature cells are below.

8. In the outer layers of the jacket of the capsule there are intercellular spaces and these are in communication with the exterior through stomata. Cells in the parenchymatous portion of the capsule contain chloroplasts.

9. Archesporial tissue is differentiated into alternate blocks of elaters and spore tetrads in the sporophyte.

10. A sterile central axis, known as columella, is present in the sporophyte.

Systematic position

Among the systematic hepatilogists, Endlicher was the first to recognise Anthoceratae as a distinct group within the Hepatics. Then Verdoon in his classification placed it at the end of the Hepatics, as the second subclass, co-ordinate in rank with the rest of the Hepatics included in the first subclass Hepaticales. This position was also maintained in the classifications of Buch. But, in the classification of Evans it was placed in the fourth Order under the Hepatics.

Anthoceros and its related genera have so many characteristic features, viz. indeterminately growing green sporophyte, with its broken up sporogenous tissue, photosynthetic equipment and central columella, which readily distinguish them from the rest of the bryophytes. Hence, Smith placed them under the class Anthocerotae, equal in rank with other Bryophytes (Hepaticae and Musci).

In the modern system of classification Anthocerotae has been placed between Hepaticae and Musci. Bold (1956), however does not believe that the liverworts and related to mosses, and as such he has put them its two divisions, Hepatophyta (containing liverworts and hornworts) and Bryophyta (containing only the mosses).

Affinity

(a) *Affinity with Hepaticae*

The gametophyte of Anthocerotae is very simple and similar to the Hepaticae, though in many respects it differs from the group. It also contains special characters of its own which are not found in any other group of Bryophyta. The dorsiventral thallose nature of the gametophyte, production of rhizoids on the ventral surfaces, the nature of the sex organs and gametes, etc., are characters allied to Hepatics. The characters by which it differs from Hepatics are embedded sex organs, internal homogeneous cell structure, antheridia developing from hypodermal cells on the dorsal surface of the thallus, etc.

The sporophyte of *Anthoceros*, on the other hand, is much more advanced than that of hepatics. The chief points of different between the two are as follows :

1. The base of the capsule is meristematic, which continually adds new cells giving rise to the respective tissues of the growing capsule.

2. The sporangium is differentiated into fact and capsule without seta.

3. Embryo, developed from the fertilized egg, is an octant.

4. The endothecium gives rise to the sterile columella, and the amphithecium gives rise to sporogenous tissue and sterile filamentous pseudoelaters.

(*b*) *Affinity with Musci*

The gametophyte of Musci is much advanced than that of Anthocerotae, where the mature of the plant is rather foliose than thallose, which is developed from filmentous protonema. The sex organs instead of being embedded are produced near about tips of the lateral leafy branches or on the main stems. The sporophyte of Musci is differentiated into capsule, seta and foot-like Anthocerotae, it contains chloroplasts and columella inside the capsule and stomata on its epidermis, and is partially dependent on the gametophyte for nutrition.

Evolutionary significance

Among this group there is a remarkable association of a primitive gametophyte with a highly developed sporophyte. It is evident that from *Riccia* to *Anthoceros* there is a progressive sterilization of sporogenous tissues, the sterilized tissue forming the vegetative structures. These noteworthy features found in the group are :

1. The beginning of independent sporophyte with the development of green tissue with stomata. In *A. fusiformis* (the Californian sp.) the capsule attains a length of 6 inches in exceptionally favourable conditions for growth and there was evidence that the surface of the foot, if exposed by the disorganization of the gametophyte, probably absorbed water from the soil.

2. Beginning of localised sporangia by breaking up of continuous sporogenous layer into smaller separate blocks, each separated from the other by sterile tissue.

3. Establishment of a sterile axis by transforming the sporogenous tissue from the central portion (endothecium) to the exterior region of the capsule (amphithecium). The chance suggests the beginning of a region for the development of the vascular tissue and superficial sporangia.

ANTHOCEROS

(Fam. ANTHOCEROTACEAE)

Most species of *Anthoceros*, commonly known as 'horned liverworts', occur frequently along hillside roads and on very moist clay banks. They differ so greatly from the Liverworts that the present-day workers separate them as a distinct Class co-ordinate with the Classes Hepaticae and Musci.

Anthoceros is a cosmopolitan genus with about 200 species and is found both in the hills as well as in the plains, in tropical and temperate regions. There are about 25 species occurring in India, of which the commonly growing ones are *A. himalayansis*, *A. erectus*, *A. crispulus*, etc.

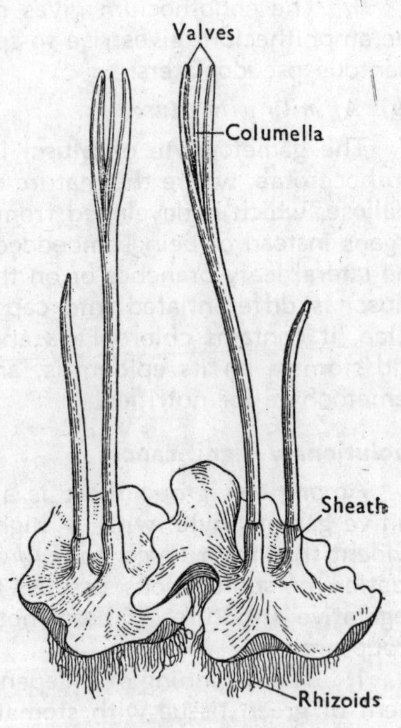

Fig. 263. *Anthoceros*. Thallus with sporophytes.

The gametophyte

The vegetative body of each plant is a small, dorsiventral and very simple, greasy dark-green gametophytic thallus, which is inconspicuously branched or somewhat lobed, and without any internal differentiation of tissues. There are numerous smooth-walled rhizoids on the under surface of the thallus, the scales being entirely absent. On the ventral side of the thallus there are numerous large intercellular spaces, each of which opens externally by a narrow slit. These cavities are usually filled up with mucilage and often contain colonies of an endophytic blue-green alga (e.g. *Nostoc*). Each cell of the thallus usually contains a single large chloroplast with a conspicuous pyrenoid, which is made up of numerous disc- or spindle-shaped bodies destined to be metamorphozed into small starch grains. Thus, it is evident that simplicity is the most prominent feature of the thallus in comparison with those of *Riccia* and *Marchantia*.

Reproduction

Anthoceros reproduces both by vegetative and sexual methods.

The vegetative reproduction is usually effected by progressive growth and death of the thallus. Under certain conditions of prolonged desiccation the gametophyte often produces **tubers,** formed due to marginal thickenings. Each tuber is externally protected by a cork layer and under favourable conditions gives rise to a new thallus.

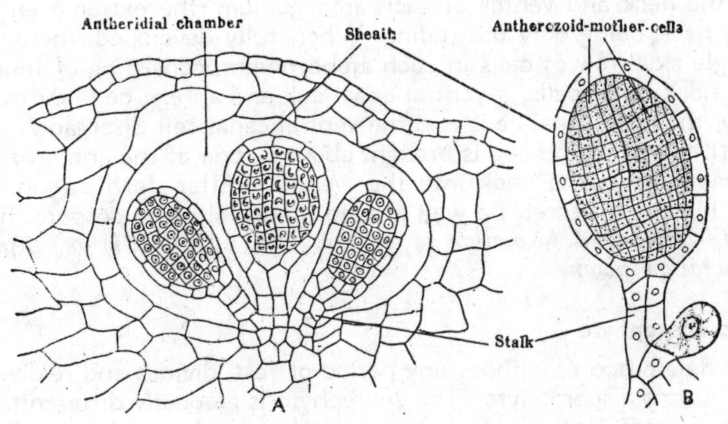

Fig. 264. *Anthoceros.*
A, Vertical section on a portion of thallus ;
B, An antheridium (enlarged).

Anthoceros is chiefly monoecious. though in some species the antheridia may attain maturity early (protandrous). It is a noteworthy feature that the sex organs are entirely embedded in the dorsal side of the thallus and not borne on special receptacles, as in *Marchantia*.

Antheridia develop in clusters within closed cavities (**antheridial chambers**) just beneath the upper surface of the thallus. From the floor of each antheridial chamber two to four antheridia develop. The sterile layer, over-roofing each antheridial chamber, may be one or more (usually two) cells in thickness. Each antheridium develops a stalk of several cells in height. Numerous biflagellate antherozoids are produced from each antheridium. When the antheridia attain maturity the sterile cell

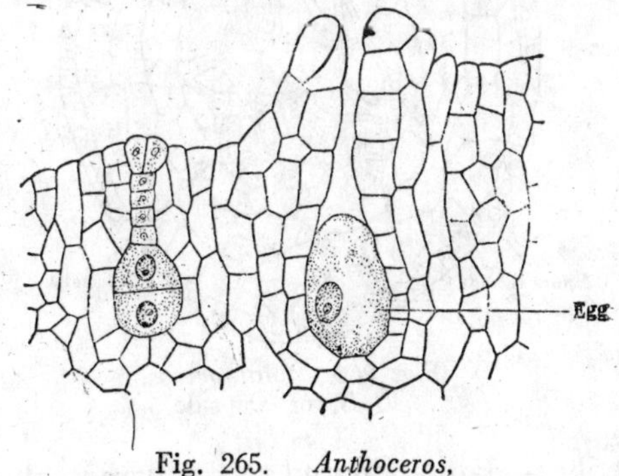

Fig. 265. *Anthoceros,*
Archegonia, young and mature.

layers, over-roofing each antheridial chamber, disintegrate and the antherozoids are liberated.

Archegonia develop singly and are closely embedded in the thallus. The vegetative cells of the thallus are confluent with a part of the neck and venter of each archegonium, the extreme end of the neck being only protruding. When fully developed, there is a single axial row of cells in each archegonium, consisting of four to six neck canal cells, a ventral canal cell and an egg cell. At maturity, the neck canal cells and the ventral canal cell disorganize and fertilization of the egg is brought about by one of the antherozoids passing down the neck into the venter. After fertilization the fertilized egg secretes a wall around it and forms an oospore. *With fertilization and formation of oospore, the sporophytic or diploid generation begins.*

The sporophyte

The oospore, without any period of rest, divides and re-divides and forms a sporophyte. The sporophyte is gradually differentiated into a basal **foot,** and an upper slender cylindrical structure of more or less uniform thickness, the **capsule.** The zygote usually first divides longitudinally and then transversely. This is followed by another longitudinal division of the four daughter cells forming an eight-celled embryo, made up of two tiers of four cells each. The foot develops by division and re-division of the cells of the lower tier. When fully formed, it becomes a massive inverted cap-like structure, by means of which the sporophyte does not only remain anchored to the gametophyte but also absorbs nourishment therefrom. The cells of the upper tier also by repeated divisions form the capsule, which when very young, becomes differentiated into **amphithecium** and **endothecium.** When fully developed, the capsule stands erect on the thallus and attains a height of 2.5 cm. or more in some cases.

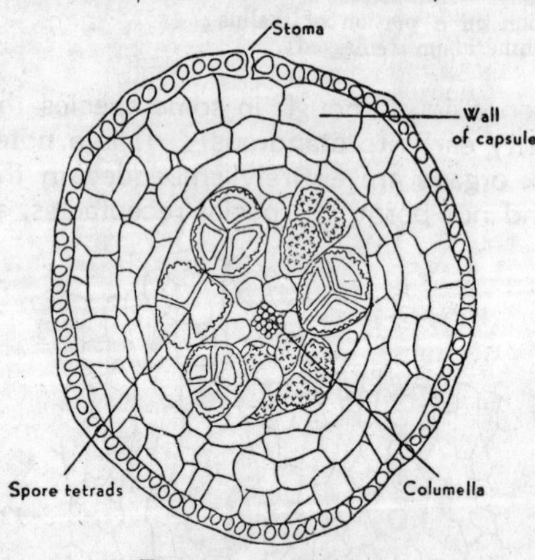

Fig. 266. *Anthoceros.* T. S, of Capsule,

The structure of a mature sporophyte is very complex. At the centre there are some elongated cells forming a sterile tissue called

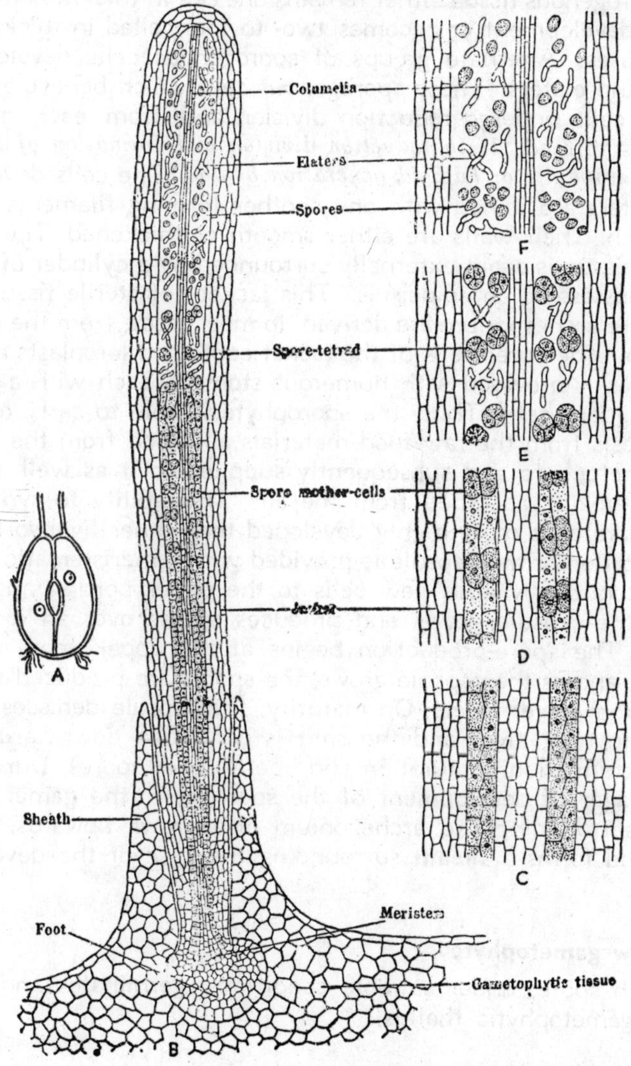

Fig. 267. *Anthoceros.*
A. A stoma ; B, Longitudinal section of the sporogonium *in situ* ;
C—F, Longitudinal views of the same at different levels.

columella. It appears 16-celled in rectangular arrangement in cross-section. The entire columella is derived from the endothecium. Surrounding and over-arching the top of the columella there is a cylindrical sheet of sporogenous tissue, the **archesporium.** The sporogenous tissue either remains one cell in thickness throughout its development or becomes two- to four-celled in thickness in some cases. Alternate groups of sporogenous cells develop into spores and elaters. Those sporogenous cells which behave as spore mother cells undergo reduction division and from each a **spore tetrad** is formed. *With reduction division and formation of spores, the gametophytic or haploid generation begins.* The cells developing into elaters are joined with one another forming filaments of 3-4 cells each. Their walls are either smooth or thickened. The sporogenous tissue is again externally surrounded by a cylinder of sterile tissue possessing an epidermis. This jacket (of sterile tissue) and the entire archesporium are derived, in most cases, from the amphithecium. The outer cells of the jacket contain chloroplasts and the epidermis is provided with numerous stomata, each with a typical pair of guard cells. Thus, the sporophyte is able to carry on photosynthesis from the raw food materials absorbed from the soil by the gametophyte and subsequently supplied to it as well as with carbon dioxide absorbed from the air. This ability to synthesize carbohydrates is more highly developed than other liverworts. The lower portion of the capsule is provided with a meristematic tissue, which continually adds new cells to the upper portion and, as a result, the capsule grows and produces spores over an extended period. The spore-production begins at the upper end of the capsule, and as the capsule grows, the spores are produced successively from lower layers. On maturity, the capsule dehisces at the apex into two valves and the split is continued downwards with gradual formation, maturation and liberation of spores. During the early stages of development of the sporophyte, the gametophytic tissue surrounding the archegonium also grows upwards, finally stops and forms a **sheath** surrounding the base of the developing capsule.

The new gametophyte

Each spore, under suitable conditions, germinates and forms a new gametophytic thallus.

Evolved characters

1. The sporophytes contain a few chloroplasts by which it can manufacture a portion of its food hence it is partially dependent on the gametophyte for nutrition. It depends on the gametophyte for supply of water only for manufacturing food.

2. In the Californian sp. of *Anthoceros* (*A. fusiformis*), the gametophyte sometimes disintegrates so the sporophyte becomes independent.

3. Like higher plants stomata are present in the epidermis of the capsule.

4. The columella acts as a conducting tissue and it seems that in higher plants the columella is replaced by conducting cylinders.

5. The amphithecium forms the sporogenous tissue and the jacket layer, while the endothecium forms only the columella—a higher character.

6. Presence of sterile filaments known as Pseudoelaters.

7. Owing to the presence of the meristematic tissue at the base of the capsule (sporophyte) is indeterminate in its growth.

8. Presence of single chloroplasts in the cell of the thallus suggests evolved characters, as in *Selaginella*, *Isoetses*, etc.

COMPARISON OF RICCIA, MARCHANTIA AND ANTHOCEROS

Riccia	*Marchantia*	*Anthoceros*
(*a*) *The gametophyte*		
1. Plant is rosette-like dorsiventral flat, green thallus with dichotomous branching and attached to the substratum by scales and rhizoids (both smooth and pegged).	1, Plant is dorsiventral, prostately, flat thallus with prominent midrib and dichotomous branching, and attached to the substratum, by scales and rhizoids (both smooth and pegged).	1. Plant is lobed, dorsiventral green thallus with irregular branching and attached to the substratum by rhizoids only.
2. Air-pores and air chambers present, the latter occur between vertical rows of cells containing chlorophyll.	2, Air-pores present on the dorsal surface, lead into large air chambers containing filamentous chloroplasts.	2. No air-pores or air chambers present, the cells on the dorsal surface contain large chloroplasts and prominent pyrenoids, on the ventral surface slits are present which has been *Nostoc*.
3. Sex organs usually homothallic.	3 Sex organs usually heterothallic.	3 Sex organs homothallic.

* In rare cases dehiscence by two sutures also has been recorded.

Riccia	*Marchantia*	*Anthoceros*
4. Antheridia develop singly within apex antheridial chambers embedded into the dorsal surface of the thallus.	4. Antheridium develops in groups on the upper surface of the lobes of antheridiophores and remains inside the antheridial chambers and arranged in centrifugal order.	4. Antheridia develop in clusters (4-6) within antheridial chambers deeply embedded into the dorsal surface of the thallus.
5. Each antheridium is shortly stalked, surrounded by a jacket of single layer of cells and contains sperm mother cells, each of which gives rise to a biflagellate sperm.	5. Same as in *Riccia.*	5. Same as in *Riccia,* but each antheridium is long-stalked.
6. Archegonia are deeply embedded into the thallus, when mature they are shortly stalked and flask-shaped ; the neck consists of row of neck canal cells, venter with a ventral canal cell and a large egg.	6. Archegonia develop on the upper surface of the lobes of archegoniophores and later on when inserted they are arranged in centripetal order ; the structure of archegonium is similar as in *Riccia.*	6. Archegonia develop singly on the dorsal surface of the thallus and almost embedded into it ; the neck consists of 4-6 neck canal cells, venter with a ventral canal cell and an egg.
(*b*) *The sporophyte*		
1. Zygote divides by a transverse wall forming a two-celled embryo.	1. Zygote divides by transverse and longitudinal wall forming a four-celled embryo.	1. Zygote divides by three successive walls for forming an eight-celled embryos.
2. Sporogonium is very simple erect and embedded into the thallus. It is not differentiated into foot, seta, stem and capsule, and is surrounded by a jacket of one layer of cells.	2. Sporogonium is a complex structure, invested and is surrounded by pseudo-perianth and calyptra. It is differentiated into foot, seta and capsule and has a jacket of one layer of cells.	2. Sporogonium is also complex structure, erect and arises from the upper surface of the thallus. It is differentiated into foot and capsule only and surrounded by a jacket of 4-6 layers of cells. The capsule is meristematic, green and possesses stomato on the epidermis, and enclosed by a sheath at the base.
3. Absence of columella.	3. Absence of columella.	3. Presence of columella in the capsule.
4. Sporogenous tissue is differentiated into spores only.	4. Sporogenous tissue is differentiated into spores and elaters.	4. Same as in *Marchantia.*
5. Sporophyte is completely dependent on the gametophyte for nutrition.	5. Same as in *Riccia,*	5. Sporophyte is partly dependent on the gametophyte for nutrition.

NOTOTHYLAS

(Fam. NOTOTHYLACEAE)

Notothylas is generally found in damp, shady places, either on moist soil or on rocks. Sometimes, it also grows on the walls and floors of old buildings.

The genus is with about 11 species distributed both in the tropical and the temperate regions. There are 3 Indian species so far recorded, viz., *N. indica*, *N. levieri* and *N. chaudhuri*.

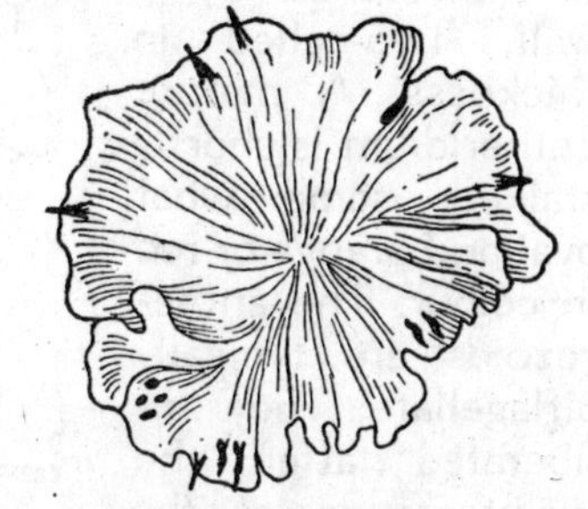

Fig. 268. *Notothyias*. Thallus with a few attached young sporophytes,

The gametophyte

The plant is thallose and prostrate with an orbicular or suborbicular form. It is thin and delicate, dichotomously branched, having a light green or yellowish colour. On the ventral surface it bears only smooth-walled rhizoids. The pegged rhizoids as well as the scales are entirely absent.

The thallus is marked for its external as well as internal simplicity. It has but little internal differentiation of tissues. The middle region of the thallus may be 6-8 cells in thickness, whereas the margin is 1-3-celled thrick. The epidermal cells are conspicuously smooth. Each epidermal cell contains a single large chloroplast with a pyrcnoid. Some of the internal cells may contain mucilage and harbour *Nostoc* colonies within them, but in some species, such as *N. javanicus*, the thallus is solid and there is no mucilage-containing cell.

Reproduction

Notothylas reproduces both by vegetative and sexual methods.

Vegetative reproduction takes place by the progressive growth of the apical portion followed by death and decay of the older one behind the dichotomy of the thallus. As a result of this, when the point of dichotomy is reached the two lobes separate out, and thus, from the older plant two new individuals are produced.

The plant body is either monoecious or dioecious*. Some of the former are protandrous.

The **antheridia** grow close to the growing point of the thallus and they develop endogenously in groups of 3 or 4

* It is interesting to note that the Indian species are monoecious.

(sometimes many) in chambers known as **antheridial chambers.** These chambers develop in the hypodermal region of the thallus. Each chamber is over-arched by a wall, two-celled in thickness. A mature antheridium is shortly stalked, some what oval and orange or red in colour. The antherozoids are typically biflagellate. They are liberated after the disintegration of the antheridial chambers.

Antheridial chamber

Fig. 269. *Notothylas.*
Transverse section of thallus showing antheridia.

The **archegonia** develop singly close to the apex of the thallus. They are usually embedded in tissues of the gametophyte. A mature archegonium has 3-5 neck canal cells. The canal of the neck is wide and may be as wide as the venter. Within the venter a ventral canal cell and an egg are found. There are 4 **cover cells** at the apex of the archegonial neck. At maturity, the neck canal cells and the ventral canal cell disintegrate, thereby forming a passage for the entrance of the antherozoids.

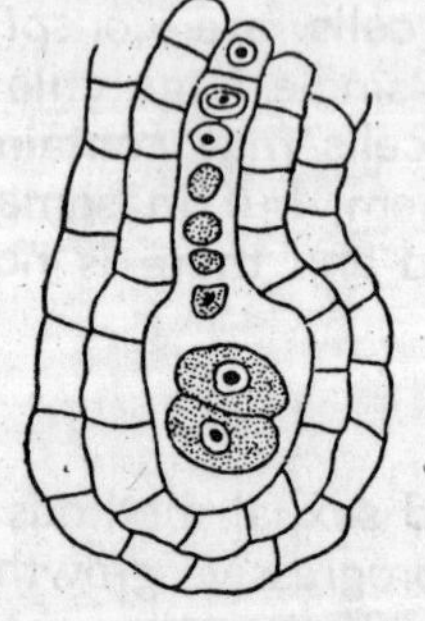

Fig. 270. *Notothylas.*
An archegonium.

Fertilization takes place by the union of an antherozoid with an egg. The entry of the former into the archegonium is facilitated by the presence of a thin film of water. The fertilized egg surrounds itself by a wall and forms the **oospore,** which almost completely fills the cavity of the venter. *With fertilization and formation of oospore, the sporophytic or diploid generation begins.*

The sporophyte

The oospore, by divisions and re-divisions, forms an *embryo* consisting of three tiers of cells. Of these three tiers, the uppermost one forms the **capsule** and the **seta,** while the two lower tiers produce the **foot.** From the very early stage the foot becomes bulbous. The seta remains rudimentary and remains ever meristematic.

The cells of the uppermost tier divide periclinally forming an outer amphithecium and an inner ndothecium. The behaviours of the amphithecium and the endothecium are variable, depending upon the species. In *N. levieri*, where the columella is absent, the sporogenous tissue develops from the endothecium, and the jacket from the amphithecium. In *N. indica*, the sporogenous tissue is developed from the amphithecium. Campbell has shown that in some species of *Notothylas*, the sporogenous tissue develops partly from the amphithecium and partly from the endothecium.

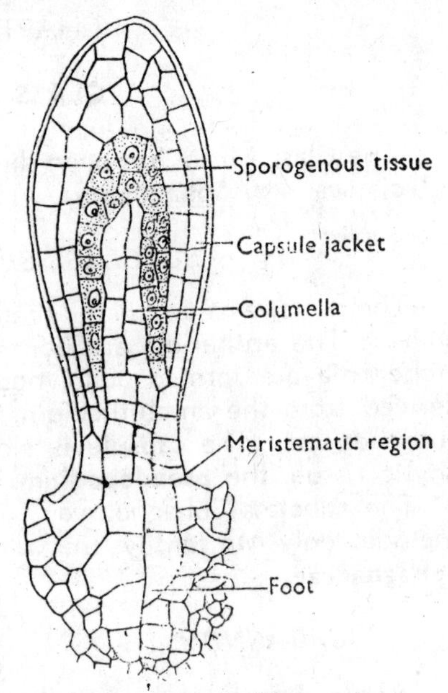

Fig. 271. *Notothylas*, V. S. of sporogonium.

The sporogonium, at maturity, becomes more or less cylindrical, sometimes tapering at both ends. They are borne horizontally along the margins of the thallus, either singly or in pairs. They are either partly or completely enshethed by an **involucre** (developed from the parent thallus). The jacket of the capsule is more than one cell in thickness, and its outermost layer is heavily cutinized forming the epidermis. The cells of the epidermal layer contain chloroplast, the stomata being absent entirely in this layer. The whole of the amphithecium or a part of it contributes to the formation of the jacket.

The sporogenous tissue differentiates into alternate transverse bands of sterile and fertile cells. The sterile cells ultimately form the **pseudoelaters,** while the fertile cells form **spore tetrads** by reduction divisions. *With reduction division and formation of spores, the gametophytic or haploid generation begins.*

Although the capsule is bi-valved with well-developed sutures for dehiscence, in most cases the spores are liberated by the decay of the capsule wall. However, in some cases, dehiscence has been observed only along one of the sutures*. It is probable that the sterile cells and the columella, when present, may help in spore dispersal. The spores are tetrahedral and dark-brown in colour.

The new gametophyte

A spore, on germination and subsequent development, gives rise to a new gametophyte.

CHAPTER III

CLASS MUSCI

The Class Musci has been divided by Smith (1955) into *three* sub-classes : (*a*) **Sphagnobrya***, (*b*) **Andreaeobrya,** and (*c*) **Eubrya†.**

SUBCLASS SPHAGNOBRYA

The protonema is broadly thallose and produces *only one gametophore.* The antheridia are borne in the axils of the leaves. The archegonia are formed acrogynously. The sporogenous tissue is derived from the amphithecium, whereas the columella from the endothecium. The capsule is elevated at maturity on a gametophytic tissue, the **pseudopodium.**

The subclass Sphagnobrya includes only *one* family, the **Sphagnaceae.**

SPHAGNUM

(Fam. SPHAGNACEAE)

Sphagnum, often known as 'bog- or peat-moss', is almost world-wide in distribution. It usually grows in swamps, ponds or other moist places on high altitudes, where the water is acidic and contains but little lime.

There are about 320 species of *Sphagnum*. The important Indian species are *S. ovatum*, *S. teres*, *S. robustum*, and *S. acutifolium*.

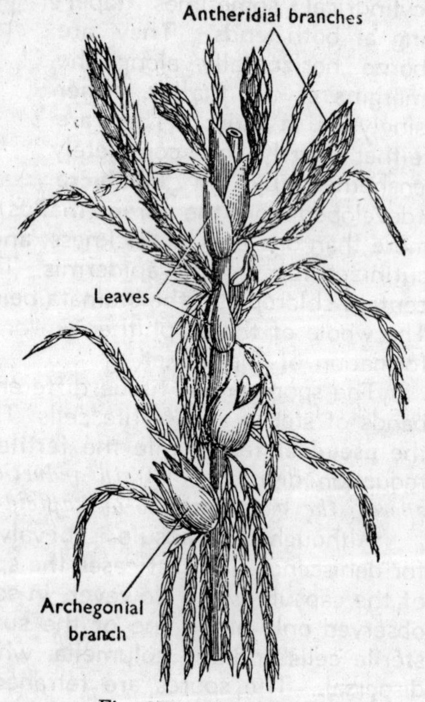

Fig. 272. *Sphagnum.*

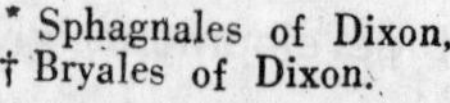

The gametophyte

The plant is an upright leafy shoot with radially arranged leaves, and is termed

* Sphagnales of Dixon.
† Bryales of Dixon.

as the **gametophore.** The gametophore consists of a central stem-like axis with many branches densely covered with leaves. The branches are usually of two kinds : (1) **short** and **erect** ones crowded at the apex forming the 'head' of the plant, and (2) **long** and **drooping** branches, which help in fixation of the plant and absorption of nutrient solution in a wick-like fashion.

The leaves are small, and while young, are arranged in three vertical rows on the stem, but later on due to torsion, the three-ranked arrangement is lost. They are one-celled in thickness and may be composed of cells which are all similar, or of two types of cells, living and dead. The dead cells are large and hyaline with thick walls and pores. The living cells are long, narrow and contain chloroplasts comprising the photosynthetic tissue. The hyaline cells are capable of absorbing and retaining water.

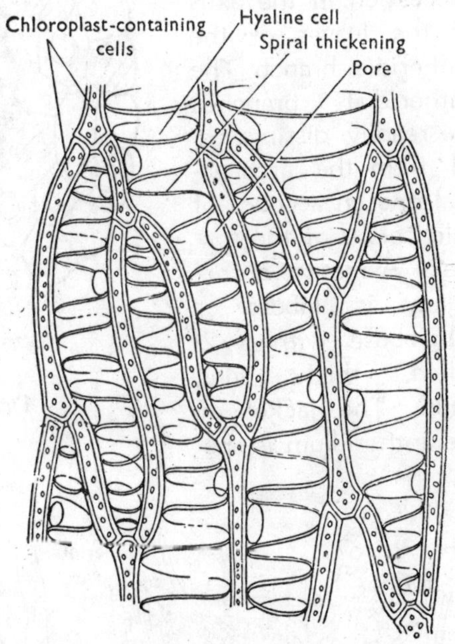

Fig. 273. *Sphagnum*, A portion of the leaf in surface view under microscope.

The stem is internally differentiated into a central cylinder and a cortex. The cortex is one-celled in thickness in the young stem and in lateral branches, but in mature main stem it is three or four cells in thickness. The cells of the central cylinder are elongated and may be homogeneous or heterogeneous. In the latter case, it contains dead and living cells, more or less similar to those of the leaves.

Reproduction

Sphagnum reproduces both by vegetative and sexual methods.

The only and efficient means of vegetative reproduction is by the lateral branches. The drooping lateral branches fix well within the substratum and after the death of the mother-plant become independent individuals.

The gametophyte may be monoecious or dioecious. The sex organs are borne on short, erect, lateral branches, and in the monoecious species the male and female sex organs are borne on separate branches.

The **antheridia** are developed in acropetal succession in the axils of the leaves of the antheridial branch. The antheridial branches are readily distinguished from the archegonial one on account of pale colour of the former. A mature antheridium is globose or subglobose with a 2-celled, thick, long stalk. The jacket of the antheridium is one-

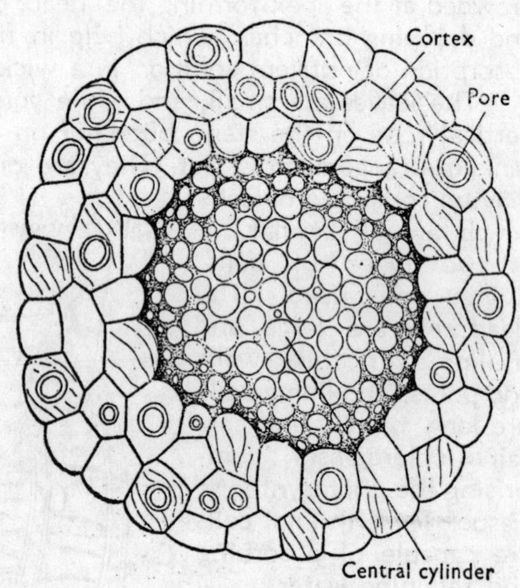

Fig. 274. *Sphagnum*. T. S, of stem,

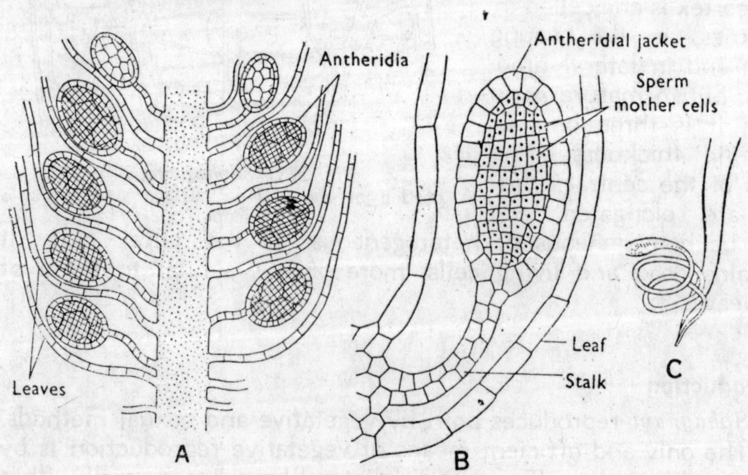

Fig. 275. *Sphagnum*. Portions of L,S. of antheridial branch showing the leaves and the antheridia ; B, An antheridium arising on a branch ; C, An antherozoid.

layered. The antherozoids are liberated by the rupture of the antheridial jacket. These are biflagellate, spirally coiled and elongated structures.

The **archegonia** are borne at the apices of the archegonial branches. Usually, there are three archegonia at the apex of each branch. A mature archegonium is relatively large with a stalk, a long neck and a massive venter. The neck contains several neck canal cells, whereas the venter contains one ventral canal cell and an egg.

The gametic union takes place during the spring. The liberated antherozoids swim towards the mature archegonium. Meanwhile, the neck canal and ventral canal cells disintegrate forming a continuous passage. Finally, only one antherozoid swims inside the archegonium and fertilizes the egg. The fertilization of an ovum by the ventral canal nucleus has also been reported in a number of cases. The fertilized egg surrounds itself by a wall forming the **oospore.** *With fertilization and formation of oospore, the sporophytic or diploid generation begins.*

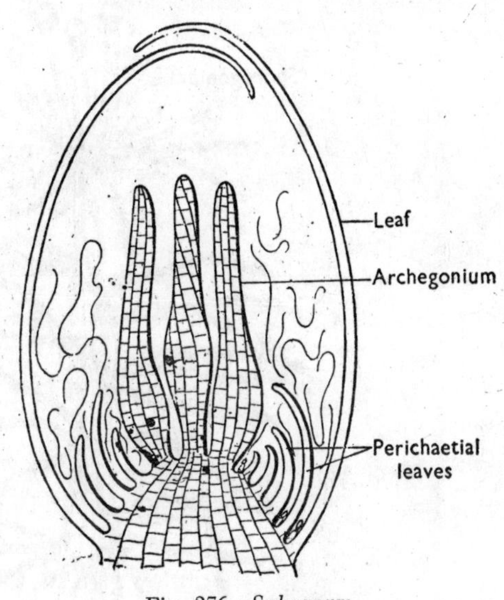

Fig. 276. *Sphagnum*. A cluster of archegonia,

The sporophyte

The oospore by repeated transverse divisions forms a filamentous embryo. The **capsule** develops from the upper portion of the filamentous embryo, the **seta** and **foot** from the submedian region, and the **haustorium** from the lowermost portion. The haustorium helps in the absorption of nutrients from the gametophyte and is obliterated when the sporophyte matures. The foot and the seta are rudimentary.

By successive cell divisions the capsular portion of the filamentous embryo forms a massive structure, within which periclinal divisions cut off an outer **amphithecium** and an inner **endothecium.** From the endothecium develops the **columella,** which occupies the central portion of mature capsule. The amphithecium, in its turn, by dividing periclinally gives rise to two regions, an outer and an inner. The sporogenous tissue, over-arching the columella, develops from the inner portion of the amphithecium, while the multi-layered jacket is developed from the outer region. The outermost layer of the jacket forms the epidermis bearing stomata. At the

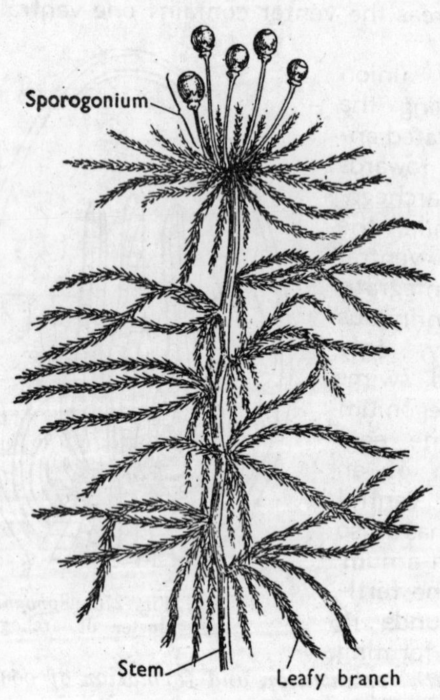

Fig. 277. *Sphagnum*,
Gametophyte with attached sporophyte.

apical region of the mature capsule, the outermost layer forms the thick-walled **lid** or **operculum.** The spore mother cells within the spore sac, by reduction divisions, forms the tetrads of **spores.** *With reduction division and formation of spores, the gametophytic or haploid generation begins.*

The mature capsule is dark-brown or black in colour. It is protected by the **calyptra**, the remnant of the archegonial venter. At the time of dehiscence, the mature capsule is elevated by a gametophytic tissue, known as **pseudopodium.** Due to the development of a differential air pressure inside the spore sac, the lid is explosively hurled off, thereby liberating the spores.

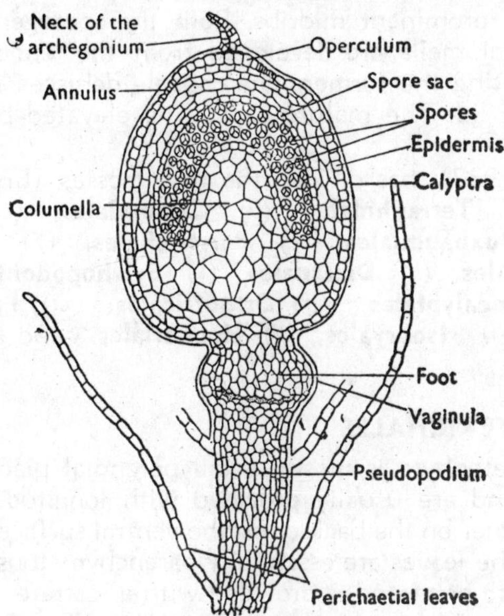

Fig. 278. *Sphagnum*, L.S, of capsule.

The new gametophyte

A spore, falling on a suitable substratum, germinates immediately into a few-celled, thalloid **protonema.** The protonema, by subsequent cell-divisions and growth, becomes a flat, green, prostrate and thalloid structure, which is irregularly lobed and is attached to the substratum by means of multicellular rhizoids. On this protonema, there develops a single lateral bud, which ultimately forms a new gametophore.

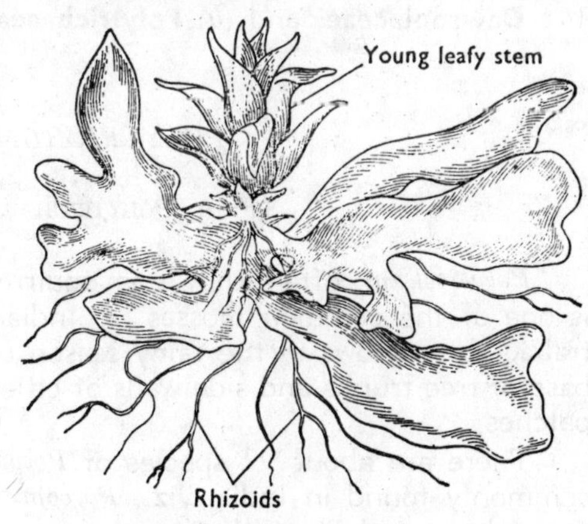

Fig. 279. *Sphagnum*, Development of a new gametophyte.

SUBCLASS EUBRYA

The protonema is filmentous and *develops more than one gametophores* with prominent midribs. Both the sporogenous tissue as well as the columella are developed from the endothecium, the latter penetrating the former. The capsule dehisces irregularly, or opening by a lid. The mature capsule is elevated by the seta at maturity.

Dixon (1932), has divided the true mosses (Bryales) into 17 Orders : (*a*) **Tetraphidales**, (*b*) **Calomniales**, (*c*) **Schistostegales**, (*d*) **Buxbaumiales**, (*e*) **Polytrichales**, (*f*) **Fissidentales**, (*g*) **Grimmiales**, (*h*) **Dicranales**, (*i*) **Syrrhopodontals**, (*j*) **Pottiales**, (*k*) **Encalyptales**, (*l*) **Orthotricaies**, (*m*) **Funariales**, (*n*) **Eubryales**, (*o*) **Isobryales**, (*p*) **Hookeriales**, and (*q*) **Hypnobryales.**

ORDER **POLYTRICHALES**

The gametophyte is mostly a tall perennial plant. The leaves are narrow and are usually provided with longitudinal lamellate structures, either on the back or on the ventral surface of the nerve. The cells of the leaves are essentially parenchymatous. The capsule is horizontal to erect and is provided with a rostrate lid. The calyptra is smooth, spinulose or hairy. There are 32 or 64 teeth in the peristome.

Two families are included by Dixon within the Order : (*a*) **Dawsoniaceae**, and (*b*) **Polytrichaceae.**

POLYTRICHUM

(Fam. POLYTRICHACEAE)

Polytrichum, often known as 'squirrel tail moss' or 'air moss', is one of the common mosses of Indian Archipelago and Australia, which grows in the rainy season on damp ground, near the base of tree trunks and side walls of cities forming dense tufts and patches.

There are about 92 species of *Polytrichum*, of which 4 are commonly found in India, viz., *P. commune*, *P. juniperinum*, *P. densifolium*, and *P. xanthopilum*.

The gametophyte

The gametophyte is differentiated into two portions : a prostrate and much-branched alga-like filamentous portion, the **protonema,** and an upright persistent leafy shoot, the **gametophore.** The filamentous protonema is transitory and shows two kinds of branches : the ordinary green ones with straight transverse septa, and the brown-walled ones with strongly oblique septa, the **rhizoids.** If abundant moisture is present, this protonema grows to a considerable extent and sooner or later there arise, from its distal end of the cells, lateral pear-shaped multicellular cell-masses (**buds**), from each of which a leafy gametophore is produced.

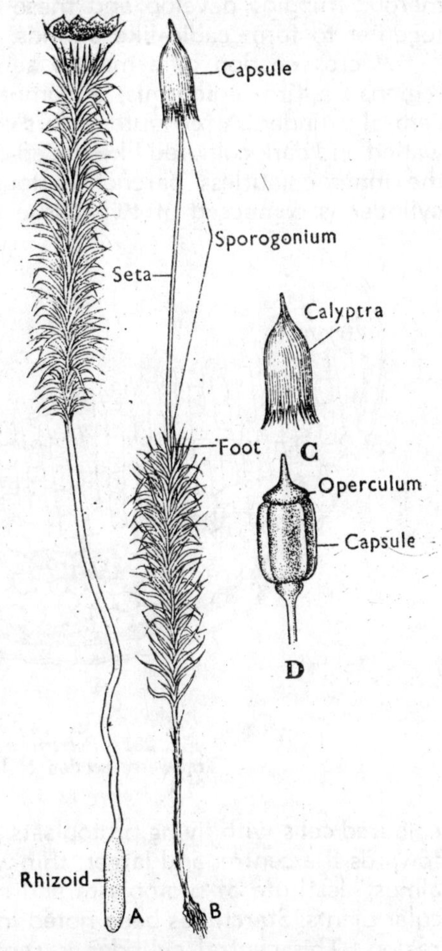

Fig. 280. *Polytrichum commune.* A, A male plant ; B, A female plant with sporogonium ; C. Calyptra ; D, Capsule with calyptra removed.

The gametophore, which is independent at maturity, often reaches a height of 20-40 cm. and is always differentiated into an angular stem and closely-set, thick, rigid, spirally arranged leaves (with angular divergence 5/13, 14/34, etc.). The leaves are small, very numerous, lanceolate to linear in outline, and with a very broad and strong midrib, projecting beyond the apex of the lamina. The lamina which develops only at the extreme margin of the midrib is usually more or less incurved. A leaf, when viewed with a pocket lens, shows that, as if, there are several narrow mid-ribs. But when sectioned and examined under microscope, these are found to be thin vertical plates of chloroplast-containing cells, the **lamella**, along the middle region of the leaf and are the incurved margins of the lamina.

which protect them in dry weather. At the base of the shoot numerous rhizoids develop and these often become closely twisted together to form cable-like strands.

A cross-section of a mature aerial stem shows three distinct regions : a firm epidermis, a comparatively thick cortex and a central cylinder. A few outer layers of cells of the cortex are thick-walled and dark-coloured like the epidermis, but more compact than the inner colourless parenchymatous ground tissue. The central cylinder is composed of two tissue elements ; thick-walled, dark-

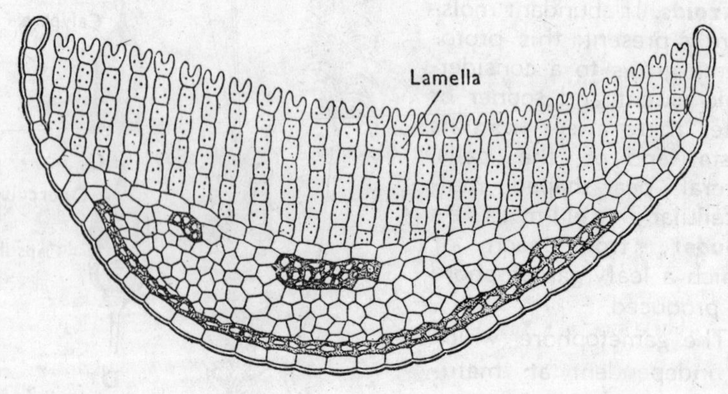

Fig. 281. *Polytrichum commune.*
Transverse section of leaf (in part).

coloured cells with living protoplasts (**stereids**) especially abundant towards the centre, and larger, thin-walled, empty cells (**hydroids**), almost destitute of protoplasm and resembling vessels of true vascular plants. Starch has been noted in the outer cells of the cortical region. This central cylinder is separated from the cortex by an incomplete pericycle-like sheath of thin-walled living cells. 'Leaf traces' are also present in the cortex and these are structurally similar to the central cylinder.

Reproduction

Polytrichum reproduces both by vegetative and sexual methods.

The protonema multiplies by the separation of its branches, which may grow into few protonemata. Often colourless **separation cells** appear and break the protonema into several filments. **Gemmae** are often developed from the terminal cells of the protonemal branches. These gemmae may directly give rise to new protonemata. Vegetative reproduction may also be carried on by the development of secondary protonemata, which are formed from any part of the plant, e.g. rhizoids, leaves or stem. Sometimes protonemata are produced from the sporogonium without the formation of spores. This is a case of **apospory.**

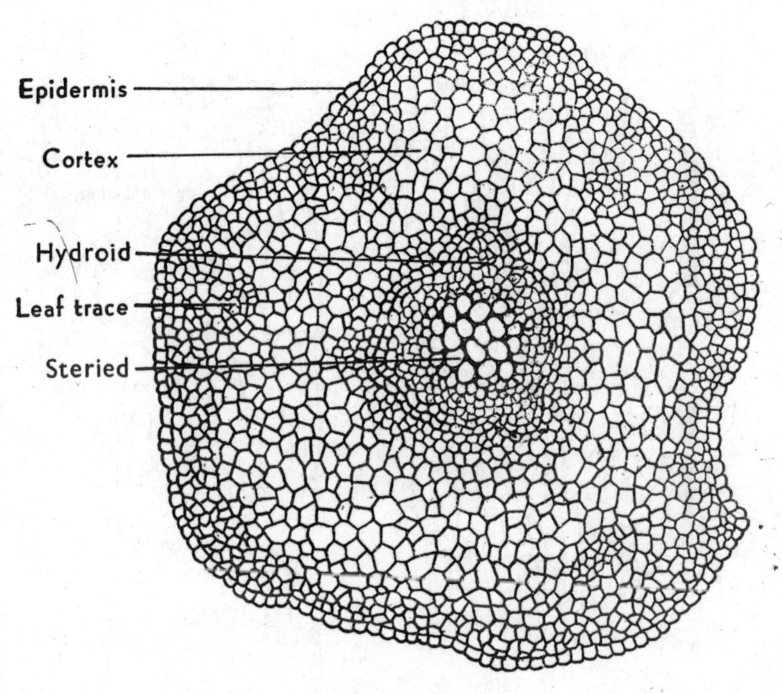

Fig. 282. *Polytrichum.*
Transverse section of the stem.

Polytrichum is usually dioecious and the sex organs, antheridia and archegonia, are borne separately at the apices of male and female gametophores respectively, forming the so-called 'inflorescences'. Each inflorescence consists of a group of sex organs which are surrounded by specialized leaves, **perichaetial leaves**, quite different in form and colour from those on the stem.

The conspicuous male inflorescence consists of a group of antheridia intermingled with peculiar sterile green hairs (**para-**

physes) and is surrounded by broad, reddish and membraneous perichaetial leaves The growth of the apical region of the stem is, however, not stopped by the formation of antheridia, and its further growth may be resumed when the formation of antheridia is totally stopped. This inflorescence is regarded as a compound structure, since groups of antheridia develop at the base of each

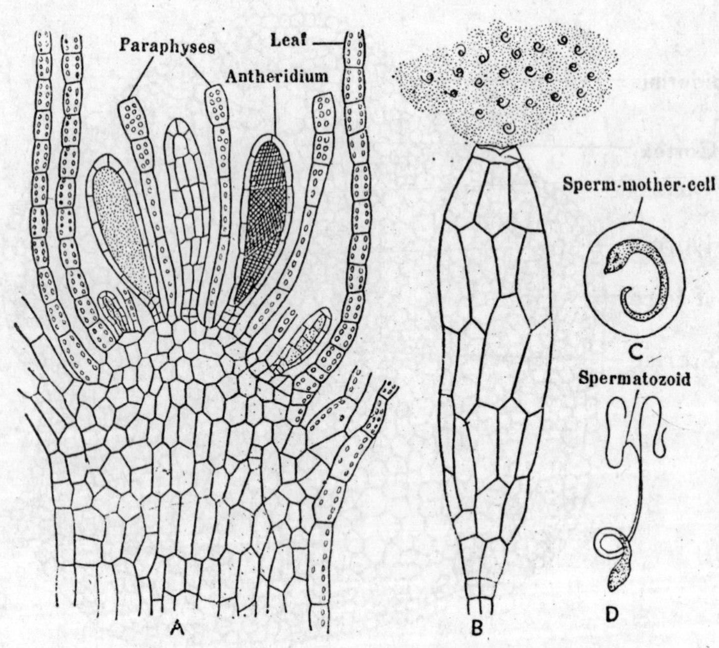

Fig. 283. *Polytrichum.*
A, Longitudinal section through the apex of a male plant showing antheridia and paraphyses ; B, A mature antheridium discharging spermatozoids ; C, Spermatozoid mother cell ; D, A spermatozoid.

leaf of the inflorescence and it is quite probable that each group represents a condensed branch.

Each **antheridium** is a shortly stalked, club-shaped body containing within it many mother cells of the spermatozoids (**androcyte cells**) and within each of which a biflagellate spermatozoid is developed. When ripe, the antheridium has a yellowish or orange colour and opens at the top (multicellular **opercular cap**), the whole mass of spermatozoids mother cells escape and finally from these mother cells the spermatozoids are discharged in the surrounding film of water, which wets the surface of the moss bed.

The **archegonia**, borne on a separate plant, are also in a cluster at the apex of the gametophore and the perichaetial leaves usually remain folded over them. Each archegonium is a flask-shaped body with a very short stalk and consists of two parts : a basal swollen portion, the **venter,** and a comparatively long upper portion, the **neck.** The venter contains a ventral canal cell and a female cell, the **oosphere,** or **ovum,** or **egg.** In this case there is a variable number of *neck cells*.

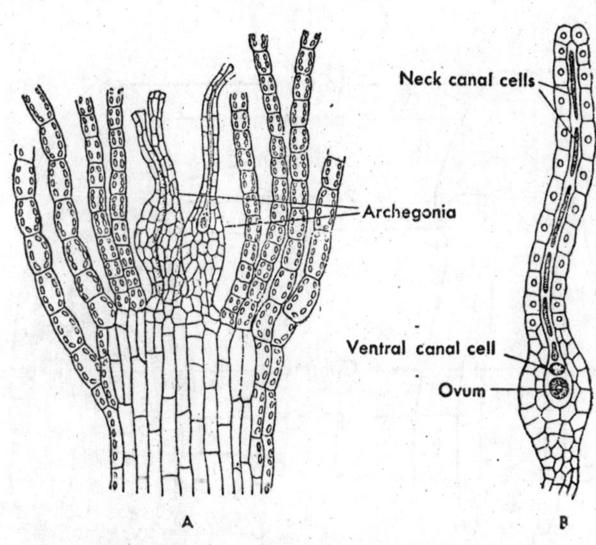

Fig. 284. *Polytrichum.*
A, Longitudinal section through the apex of a female plant showing archegonia ; B, A mature archegonium.

When an archegonium matures, a passage is established due to the disorganization of the canal cells. This passage becomes filled with a mucilagenous substance containing canesugar. Fertilization takes place in water. Biflagellate spermatozoids, swimming by means of flagella, come in the neighbourhood of archegonium ; these being attracted by the canesugar penetrate the neck, but only one of them fuses with the ovum. The fertilized ovum then surrounds itself with a cell wall and becomes an **oospore.** The ova of several archegonia may be fertilized forming oospores, but the one which is formed first begins to grow on getting food, while the rest dry up, so that only one sporophyte develops over a leafy gametophore. *With fertilization and formation of oospore, the sporophytic or diploid generation begins.*

The sporophyte

The oospore gradually passes into an embryo, which ultimately gives rise to the **sporogonium,** the sporophytic generation of the moss plant. Due to the rapid growth of the sporogonium, the upper portion of the archegonium-neck becomes torn off, so that it is carried off in the form of a cap, ultimately forming a very large hood-shaped **calyptra** covered with a dense growth of hairs.

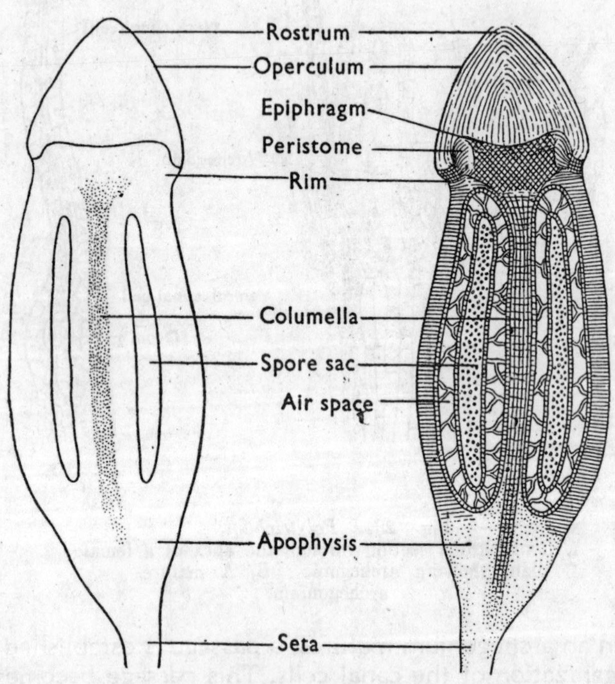

Fig. 285. *Polytrichum.* Median longitudinal section of a capsule (diagrammatic).

The sporogonium consists of three parts : (*a*) a sac-like upper part, the **capsule,** (*b*) a slender stalk called **seta**, and (*c*) a small **foot** by means of which it is attached to the gametophyte. The capsule is at first green in colour owing to the possession of chloroplasts and in its lower portion it bears a few stomata. Within the capsule the sporogenous tissue develops, from which ultimately **spores** are formed (four spores from each spore mother cell due to reduction division). A large part of the central tissue of the capsule remains sterile forming the so-called **columella** and the conical upper part, the **operculum**, which becomes detached from the lower part as lid in order to allow these spores to escape ; the operculum is prolonged into a beak-like **rostrum**. Just beneath the operculum there is a complicated structure known as **peristome** consisting of 32 or 64 'teeth' in a circle around the mouth of the

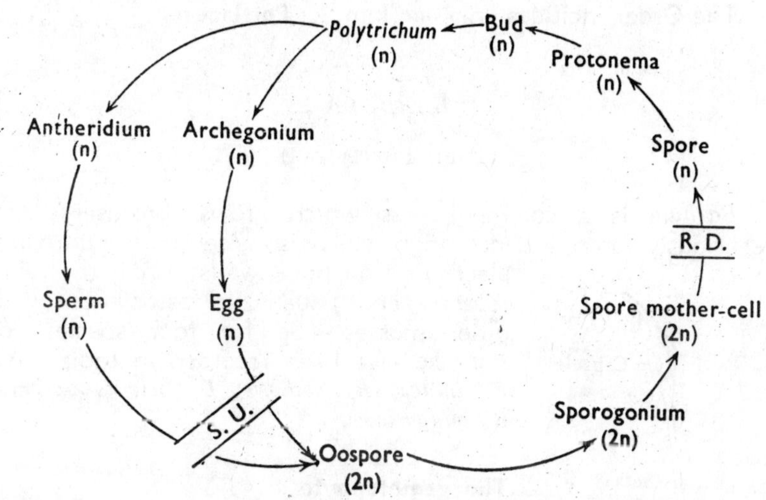

Fig. 286. Life cycle of *Polytrichum*.

spore-cavity of the capsule. These are nothing but bundles of thickened fibrous cells, regularly arranged in crescent form resembling the spokes in a wheel and have got a profound taxonomic importance. These teeth help to scatter the spores. The tip of the columella is expanded into the **epiphragm**, filling the space inside the peristome ring. There are two large intercellular spaces surrounding the sporogenous tissue, one on its outer side and the other between it and the columella, and are traversed by narrow filamentous strands of cells containing chloroplasts. At maturity the capsule finally becomes horizontal and dorsiventral. *With reduction division and formation of spores, the gametophytic or haploid generation begins.*

The new gametophyte

When the spores mature they are shed by means of peristome. These may rest for some time but when they germinate, under favourable conditions, they directly give rise to **protonemata.** Lateral buds arise from the protonema and each produces a new moss plant.

ORDER **POTTIALES**

The plants are mostly small and the leaves are variable. The mesophyll cells are isodiametric, usually opaque and small. The capsule is borne on a long and thin seta. It is cylindrical and erect. The calyptra is narrow. There are 16 teeth in the peristome.

The Order includes only *one* family : **Pottiaceae.**

BARBULA

(Fam. POTTIACEAE)

Barbula is a common moss which grows profusely and gregariously forming dense bright yellowish-green masses in damp places and on brick walls during the rainy season, and usually in association with other mosses. So far four species of *Barbula* have been recorded in India, viz., *B. indica*, *B. comosa*, *B. orientalis*, and *B. gangetica*.

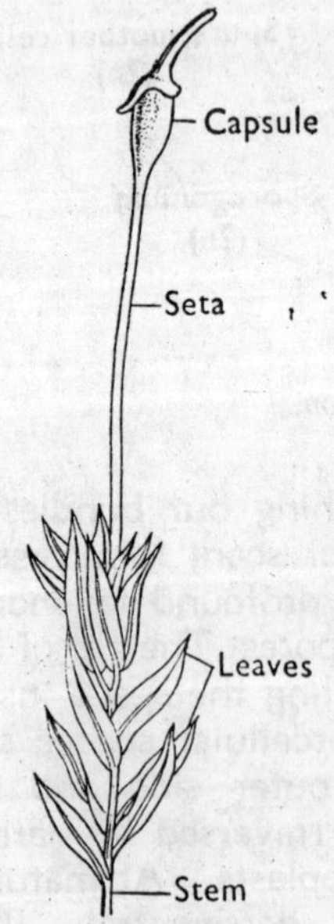

Fig. 287. *Barbula.* A gametophore with an attached sporophyte.

The gametophyte

The vegetative body of the gametophyte consists of two portions, viz., a prostrate, green, filmentous portion, called the **protonema** and a differentiated vegetative shoot, the **gametophore.**

The protonema is derived from a spore as a result of germination. When fully developed, it is a much-branched filamentous structure, which is differentiated into an extensive green portion, the **chloronema**, and a pale green slender branched portion that gives rise to rhizoids. Each portion consists of several cells, which are delimited from one another usually by walls. The chloronema is positively phototropic and remains on the surface of the substratum, while the rhizoidal system is negatively phototropic and grows vertically down into the substratum.

The gametophore takes its origin from the bud developed on the protonema. The bud is a two- or three-celled structure, which enlarges and becomes somewhat pear-shaped. By further divisions an apical cell is ultimately differentiated, and from this cell the gametophore develops. The gametophore, when fully developed, is erect and usually consists of a simple axis (stem) bearing numerous spirally-arranged minute leaves and with smooth-walled rhizoids at the base. The rhizoids have oblique walls and are brown in colour in older portion. The leaves are lanceolate with obtuse apex, margins recurved and minutely sinuate, and with a strong midrib projecting beyond the apex of the blade. In younger portion of the gametophores, the leaves show tristichous arrangement, but in the older portion this arrangement is lost.

A cross-section of the stem shows two distinct portions, namely, a central cylinder made up of thin-walled, narrow, polygonal cells (elongated in longitudinal section) and an outer cortical region with much larger cells with thicker and yellowish-brown cell walls at maturity. When young, the cortical cells contain chloroplasts. An epidermal layer is, however, not clearly differentiated.

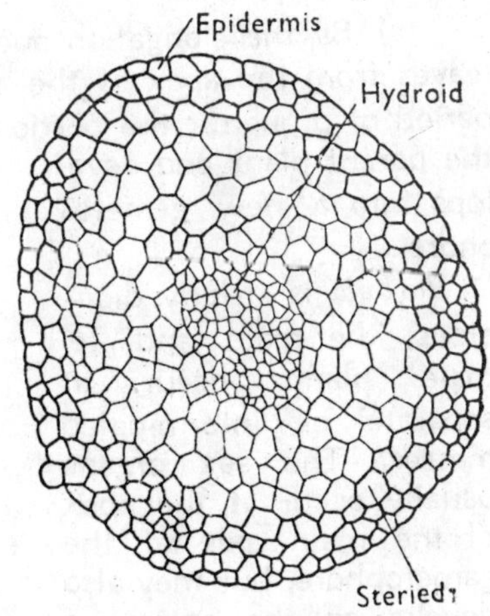

Fig. 288. *Barbula.* T.S. of stem.

Reproduction

Barbula reproduces both by vegetative and sexual methods.

Vegetative propagation takes place in three ways :

(*a*) By the formation of brute bodies, which arise as axillary multicellular, branched, filmentous bodies from a single or a group of superficial cells of the axis. The apical cells of these branches along with a few other cells, increase in volume, turn dark-green and become filled with dense cytoplasmic matter, and by a series of irregular division develop thick-walled, yellowish-brown multicellular bodies, known as **brute bodies (propagula)**. The brute bodies, on germination, produce protonema and rhizoids.

(*b*) By the production of protonema from any part of the mature gametophore.

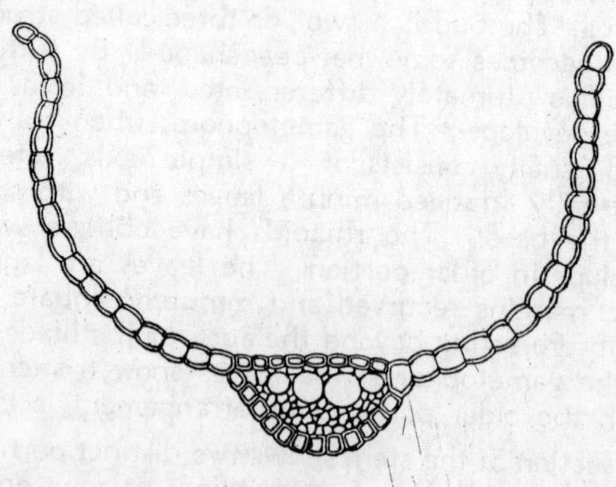

Fig. 289. *Barbula.* T,S. of leaf.

(*c*) By the elongation and subsequent development of a few leaves from the apex of the parent gametophore, after a long period of drought ; the portion finally gets itself detached from the parent plant and develops into a new gametophore.

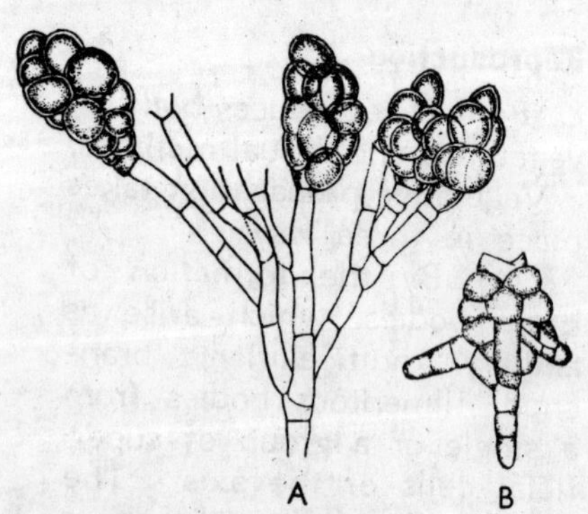

Fig. 290. *Barbula.* A, Brute bodies ; B, Germination of the same.

Barbula is strictly dioecious, the male and female plants occur in separate or intermingled masses. The sex organs usually occur at the apex of the main axis of the gametophore, but they also develop on the apices of the branches when the gametophore is branched. Both types of sex organs are associated with long, filmentous, multicellular **paraphyses** with pointed ends. They may remain intermingled with antheridia in male plants, but surround the central group of archegonia in female plants.

A mature **antheridium** is a club-shaped structure and shortly stalked, and contains within it numerous mother cells of the spermatozoids (**androcyte cells**), and each of which is metamorphosed into a long, slender, coiled spermatozoid with two flagella attached to one end. The spermatozoid mother cells lie entangled in a mucilagenous mass within the mature antheridium and are ultimately discharged through the apex by the rupture of its wall.

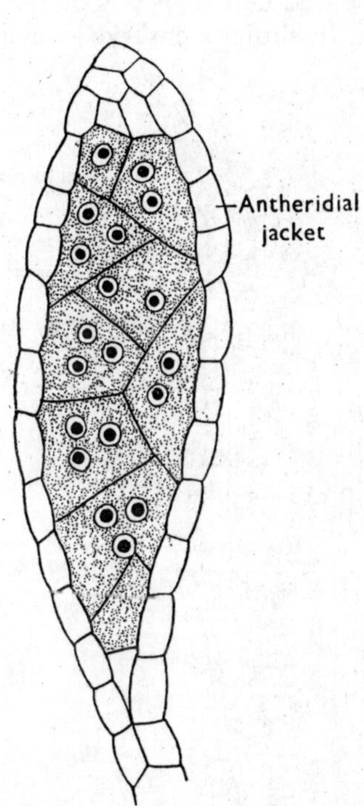

Fig. 291. *Barbula,* A developing antheridium.

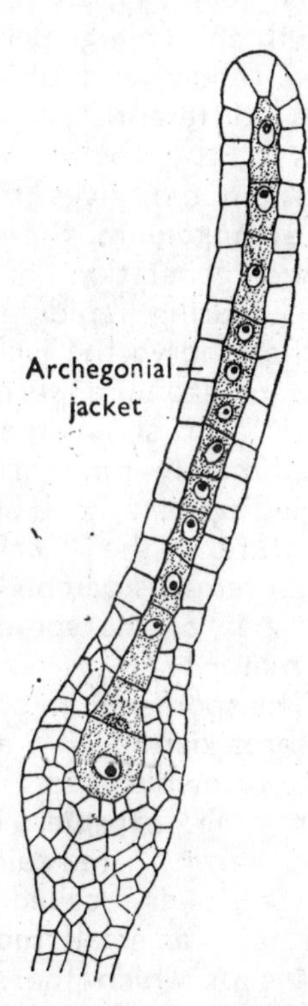

Fig. 292. *Barbula,* A mature archegonium.

An **archegonium** is a flask-shaped body with a very short stalk and consists of two portions : a basal portion called the **venter** and a comparatively long upper portion, the **neck.** The venter contains ventral canal cells and an egg or ovum. Within the neck there is a central row of 12 neck canal cells. At maturity, the apex of the neck splits open and all the neck canal cells and ventral canal cell disorganize to form a continuous passage.

In presence of water the spermatozoids swim out of an antheridium, enter the neck of the archegonium, reach the egg, but only one fuses with it. After fusion the egg secretes a wall around it and forms an **oospore.** *With fertilization and formation of oospore, the sporophytic or diploid generation begins.*

The sporophyte

At maturity, the oospore becomes yellowish-brown in colour. Growth and enlargement, due to repeated cell divisions of the oospore, follow and ultimately a multicellular **embryo** develops, with differentiated apical cells at both ends. This embryo gives rise to the **sporogonium,** the sporophytic generation of *Barbula.* During rapid growth of the embryo the jacket of the archegonium surrounding it at first enlarges and is ultimately torn off and carried up as a hood-shaped structure, the **calyptra,** which remains parched upon the apex of the sporophyte till maturity.

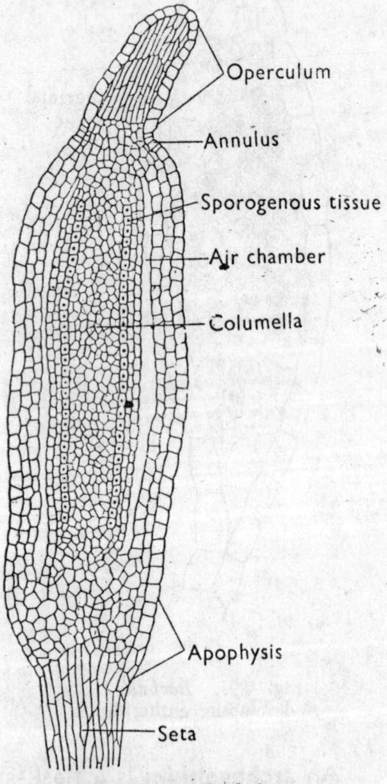

The sporogonium consists of three parts : (*a*) a sac-like brownish-red upper part, the **capsule,** (*b*) a long, thin, red-coloured, slender stalk, called **seta, and** (*c*) a small **foot,** by means of which the sporogonium is anchored to the gametophyte.

Fig. 293. *Barbula.* L.S. of a capsule.

A mature capsule is somewhat subcylindrical in shape and exerted on the seta. An upper lid-like structure, the **operculum,** is gradually differentiated from the body of the capsule. The operculum is conical and provided with a long beak. It is separated from the body of the capsule by a ring of very narrow, thin-walled cells forming the **annulus.** Internally, the capsule is differentiated into several regions. The basal portion, consisting of polygonal cells with chloroplasts and a few superficial stomata, is called the **apophysis.** At the centre, there is a cylindrical column of sterile tissue, called the **columella**, consisting of large cells and extending from the apophysis right up to the base of the operculum. Surrounding the columella a more or less barrel-shaped tissue develops, called the **sporogenous tissue**, consisting of 6-8 cell-layers in thickness. The cells of this tissue later on round up and form the spore mother cells. From each spore mother cell four **spores** are produced by reduction division. *With reduction division and formation of spores, the gametophytic or haploid generation begins.* Outside the sporogenous tissue there are other cellular layers and an air chamber extending up to the periphery. The outer cells of the body of the capsule also contain chloroplasts, when young. Finally, a cylindrical cavity develops around the sporogenous tissue due to the degeneration of some layers of cells.

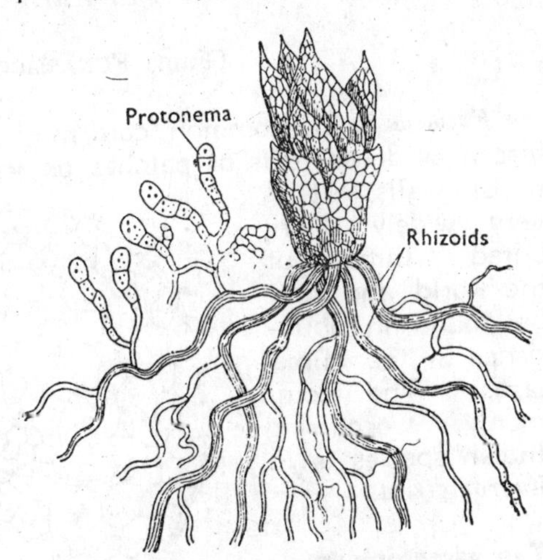

Fig. 294. *Barbula.* Development of the new gametophyte.

Just beneath the operculum there is a complicated structure, known as the **peristome,** consisting of 16 teeth, each of which divides to form 32 long, membraneous, reddish-brown, filiform branches with small, rod-like transverse thickenings. These remain in a circle and lie entangled with one another, covering the mouth of the body of the capsule. In presence of moisture, the peristome-teeth uncoil, become straight and help in the opening of the mouth of the capsule and scattering of spores.

The mature spores are somewhat spherical, variable in size and shape, brown in colour, unicellular and are provided with an outer smooth exospore and an inner, thin endospore.

The new gametophyte

The mature spores begin to germinate under favourable conditions. Each spore, on coming in contact with moisture, swells considerably, becomes turgid and green in colour. On germination, the endospore protrudes through the exospore as one or more papillate protrusions, which later on, by repeated divisions, give rise to the **protonema.**

ORDER **FUNARIALES**

These are annual or biennial mosses. The leaves form a terminal rosette. They are broad, ovate and thin-walled. The capsule is usually wide, and the lid is never prostrate. Peristome is normally double.

The Order contains 5 families : (*a*) **Gigiaspermaceae,** (*b*) **Funariaceae,** (*c*) **Disceliaceae,** (*d*) **Oedipodiaceae,** and (*e*) **Splachnaceae.**

FUNARIA

(Fam. FUNARIACEAE)

Funaria is the common 'cord moss', growing during the rainy season as dense tufts or patches on the surface of the soil and moist walls. It is very widely distributed throughout the world and may be found in abundance in the Himalayas. The commonly occurring Indian species is *F. hygrometrica*.

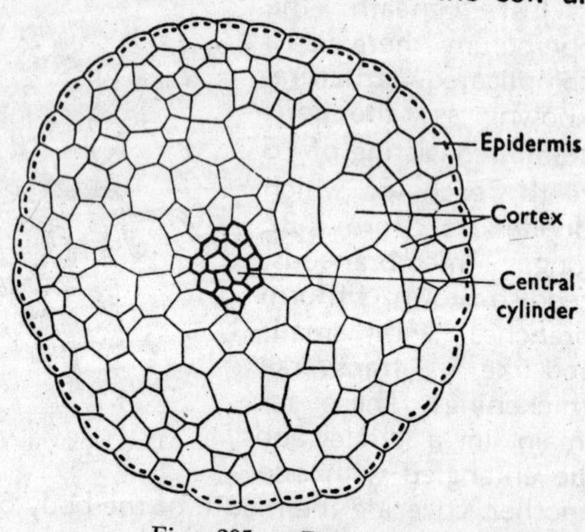

Fig. 295. *Funaria*. T.S. of stem.

The gametophyte

The gametophyte has two distinct phases : (*i*) a filamentous, prostrate, ephemeral structure, the **protonema**, and (*ii*) a leafy, erect persistent plant, the **gametophore,** developed from the protonema.

The gametophores are small, rarely exceeding an inch in height. They are differentiated into stem, leaves and rhizoids. The rhizoids are slender, dark-coloured, multicellular structures with oblique partition walls. They arise in clusters from the base of the stem penetrating the soil. There are also a few lateral extra-axillary branches. The leaves are simple, ovate and are arranged spirally in a 3/8th phyllotaxy. Each leaf has a well-defined midrib.

The stem is differentiated internally into epidermis, cortex and central cylinder. The epidermis is one-layered, being composed of thick-walled parenchymatous cells. The cortex is multi-layered, and the cells contain chloroplasts, and in the outer region their walls are thickened. The central strand is composed of thin-walled, elongated cells forming a conducting tissue.

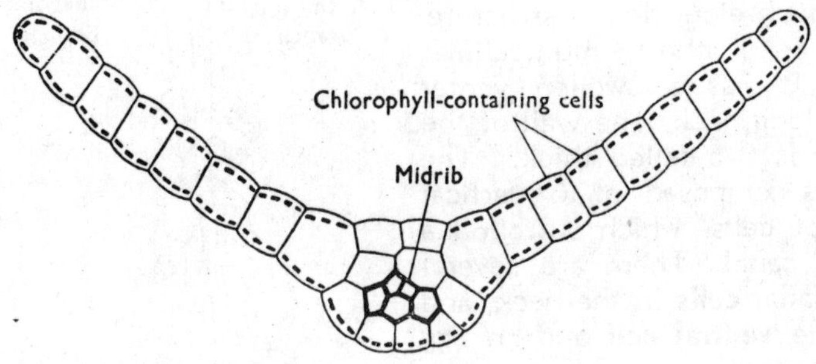

Fig. 296. *Funaria*.
T.S. of leaf.

The midrib of the leaf is multi-layered, thick and contains a stand of thin-walled conducting cells similar to those of the stem. The remaining portion of the leaves are one-celled in thickness, each of which contains chloroplasts. These cells constitute the photosynthetic tissue.

Reproduction

Funaria reproduces both by vegetative and sexual methods.

Vegetative reproduction takes place in the same way as in *Polytrichum*.

Funaria is monoecious, but the sex organs are borne on separate branches. The antheridia are borne at the apex of the main stem, while the archegonia at the apices of the lateral branches, which arise from the base of the main axis and soon overtop the latter.

The **antheridia** are produced in clusters in association with bract-like leaves, which form a rosette at the apex of the antheridial branch and form the **perichaetium.** A mature antheridium is an elongated, club-shaped structure borne on a short, stout, multicellular stalk. The antheridia are intermingled with a large number of multicellular hairs, known as **paraphyses.** The jacket of each antheridium is one-layered and encloses numerous biflagellate antherozoids. The mature antheridium, when comes in contact with water, bursts at the apical region, thereby liberating the antherozoids.

The **archegonia** are also produced in clusters, but here the leaves enclosing the archegonia are similar to ordinary foliage leaves. A mature archegonium is a much-elongated structure, borne on a short, multicellular stalk. It has a swollen venter and a long neck. The wall of the venter is two-celled thick. The neck is composed of 6 vertical rows of cells, which surround a central canal. There are several **neck canal cells** in the neck, and a single **ventral cell** and an **egg** in the venter.

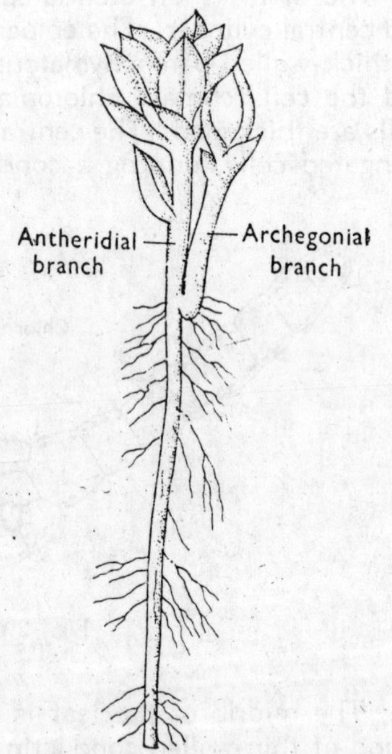

Fig. 297. *Funaria.* A portion of the gametophore bearing several branches.

Fertilization takes place in presence of water. The antherozoids reach the archegonium by swimming in water. Meanwhile, a continuous passage is formed within the archegonium by the dissolution of the neck canal cells and the ventral canal cell. The antherozoids are supposed to be attracted by a sugary fluid secreted from the archegonium. A single antherozoid enters the archegonium and ultimately fertilizes the egg. The fertilized egg soon surrounds itself by a wall forming the **oospore.** *With fertilization and formations of oospore, the sporophytic or diploid generation begins.*

The sporophyte

The oospore divides transversely into a lower **hypobasal cell** and an upper **epibasal cell.** The **capsule** develops from the epibasal cell, while the **foot** and **seta** from the hypobasal one. The cells of the epibasal region divide periclinally forming an outer **amphithecium** and an inner **endothecium.** From the inner region of the endothecium develops the **columella,** while from the outer region the **archesporium.** All the tissues external to the archesporium, including the outer wall of the spore sac, develop from the amphithecium. The amphithecium at the apex of the capsule forms the multi-layered **operculum**, while the innermost portion of the amphithecium in this region forms the **peristome.**

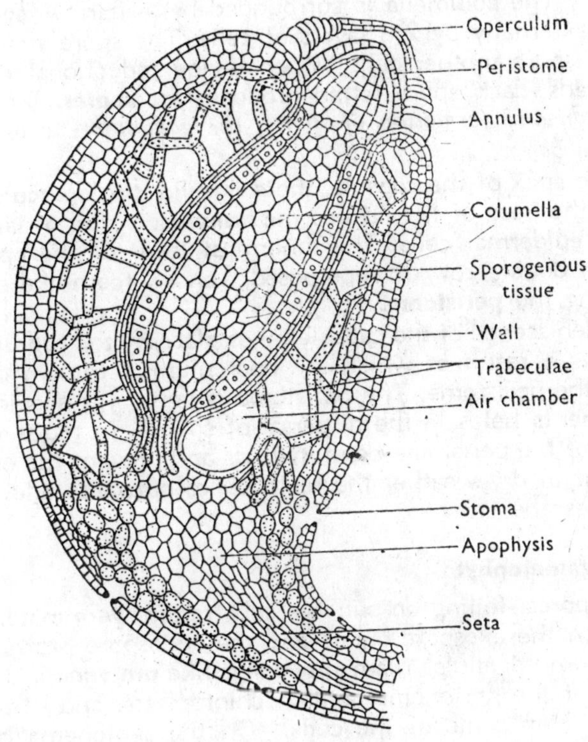

Fig. 298. *Funaria.* L.S. of capsule.

A mature sporogonium (sporophyte) has a foot, a seta and a capsule. The foot is small and conical embedding itself in the apex of the gametophyte. When young, the sporogonium is ensheathed by the base of the archegonium, but at maturity it ruptures and only the foot remains ensheathed. The seta is long, slender and reddish in colour.

The mature capsule is pear-shaped. Its basal part is solid and sterile and is known as **apophysis**, which bears a few stomata. This is chiefly concerned in supplying nutrition to the fertile part of the capsule. The outermost layer of the capsule is known as **epidermis.** Next to the epidermis, there is a mass of parenchyma tissue, the inner layers of which contain chloroplasts. These green cells constitute the photosynthetic tissue. Internal to the parenchyma layer, there is a large air space traversed by delicate strands of parenchyma cells, known as **trabeculae.** In the centre there is a mass of thin-walled, sterile, parenchyma cells constituting the **columella.** The columella is surrounded by a narrow **spore sac,** bounded externally by 2-3 layers of cells. The spore sac contains numerous spore mother cells, which divide reductionally to form spore tetrads. Each spore tetrad produces for **spores.** *With reduction division and formation of spores, the gametophytic or haploid generation begins.*

At the apex of the capsule, there is a lid, the **operculum.** Surrounding the base of the lid lies the **annulus**, a ring of large cuticularized epidermal cells. The innermost layer of the operculum contains a double row of superposed, yellow, teeth-like structure constituting the **peristome.**

The dehiscence of the capsule takes place by the rupture of the annulus, as a result of which the operculum is thrown off, thus exposing the peristome. The peristome is very hygroscopic and by its movements helps in the dispersal of spores. In moist weather, the teeth of the peristome bend inwards and prevent the escape of spores, but in dry weather the teeth curve outwards allowing the spores to escape.

The new gametophyte

The spores, falling on suitable substratum, germinate. During germination the exospore bursts and the endospore protrudes out. Later on, a multicellular filamentous alga-like **protonema** is formed. The cells of the protonema contain chloroplasts, and rhizoids are developed from some of the cells. On the protonema buds are developed, each of which subsequently gives rise to a gametophore.

EVOLUTION OF SPOROPHYTE AMONG BRYOPHYTA

It was first formulated by Bower (1890) that in the archegoniates, the spore-producing generation, the sporophyte, is an entirely new phase, derived from the progressive elaboration of zygote, and is intercalated within the gametophytic generation as a result of adaptation to land habit. This hypothesis was later supported by Chamberlain (1935), Smith (1938) and others. Further elaboration resulted in the sterilization of potentially sporogenous tissue. The most primitive sporophyte in the hepatics occurs in the genus *Riccia*. Such a sporophyte, according to some authors, is nearest to the hypothetical ancestors, represents the actual ancestors of the more highly evolved plants. Here, the entire structure is involved in the production of the spores with the exception of one layer of sporogenous wall. Frequent abortion of spore mother cells possibly represents the beginning of elaters. From this primitive type, complex sporophytes evolved in different directions, all having a foot, a seta and a capsule arising from the zygote. Each of these organs shows diversity in structure and form. In *Sphaerocarpus*, a step advanced more than *Riccia*, a sterile foot and a seta, each of a few cells are present ; the one-layered jacket of the capsule, apart from the spores, contains sterile cells homologous with elaters. These sterile cells, however, do not show the characteristic thickening. Another step in evolution is the sporophyte of *Targionia* with a broad foot and a narrow seta, and which contains spores intermingled with elaters. The jacket of the capsule consists of a layer of cells, except at the apex.

The highest evolved type among the Marchantiales, is found in *Marchantia*, where the upper half of the embryo gives rise to capsule and part of the seta, while the other half develops into the remaining part of the seta and the inverted hood-like foot. The jacket of the ovoid capsule is very similar to that of *Targionia*, in having a layer of cells except at the tip. It splits up, at maturity, into a number of segments. About half of the internal tissues develop into spirally thickened elaters, while the rest into spores.

A still more advanced type is to be seen in the leafy liverworts, where there is a well-developed foot, a long seta and a capsule with a jacket more than one-celled thick. The dependent sporophyte can partly manufacture its own food due to presence of chlorophyll, stomata and air spaces within the jacket layer. Dehiscence is regularly into 4 valves. Further sterilization is noted in the development of an elaterophore, arising from the base of the capsule in *Pellia* and from the apex in *Riccardia*.

The most complex sporophyte and culmination of this series is noted in the Anthocerotales. In *Anthoceros*, the foot is well developed, and the capsule is cylindrical in form. The latter has a jacket layer, 4-6 cells in thickness ; stomata and chlorophyllous tissue help in food manufacture. Under exceptional cases, the sporophyte of *Anthoceros fusiformis* can become an independent plant, characteristic of higher plants. The layer of sporogenous tissue within the capsule is very narrow and overarch the centrally situated columella, which is interpreted as the forerunner of vascular tissue. The jacket may split up into two valves. A nutritional independence and the provision for continued growth of the sporophyte due to the presence of meristematic tissue at the base of the capsule, have led many a pteridologists to believe the anthocerotean type of sporophyte as the ancestors of the Pteridophytes.

The often partially independent sporophytes of mosses though showing a greater amount of sterilization of potentially sporogenous tissue, and well-developed mechanism for spore dispersal, are considered due to their determinate growth, to represent a completely different, and blind evolutionary line. In *Sphagnum*, similar to that of *Anthoceros* the foot is bulbous and the seta is rudimentary. The Anthoceros-like feature is further emphasized by the production of columella from the endothecium, and the jacket layer as well as the sporogenous tissue from the amphithecium. The completely dependent sporophyte dehisces by an operculum and is elevated at maturity by pseudopodium, which is composed of the gametophytic tissue.

Of the Musci, *Sphagnum* is generally recognised as the most primitive, due to the significant points of structure between *Sphagnum* and *Anthoceros*, indicating a possible remote relationship. The sporophyte is the most characteristic and complicated structure in the true mosses, like *Funaria*, *Barbula*, etc., in having a foot, a long seta, the apophysis, the several-layered wall of the capsule, the columella, the wall of the spore sac, the peristome and the operculum. In these cases the columella and the sporogenous tissue are derived from the endothecium, while the amphithecium develops into jacket. Teeth of the peristome exhibit pronounced hygroscopic movements. In a moist weather the teeth bend down over the spore sac to stop spore liberation, while in a dry weather the peristome teeth bend outward to facilitate the shifting out of spores from the spore sac.

In about half a dozen genera of the mosses, the capsule does not open by a definite operculum and no peristome is present. The capsule opens irregularly ; and these genera were often grouped together as *Cleistocarpi*, contrasted with the remaining ones, known as *Stegocarpi*, which have a definite peristome and operculum. The ontogeny of cleistocarpous sporophytes is essentially the same as in stegocarpous mosses, and it is generally held that cleistocarpy has appeared in unrelated lines among the true mosses.

Chromosome number in Bryophytes

Until recently the range of chromosome numbers in the Hepaticae was thought to be $n=5$ in the Anthocerotales, $n=8$ or 9 in the Marchantiales, $n=9$ or 10 in the thalloid Jungermanniales, and $n=8$ or 9 in the leafy Jungermanniales, with occasional polyploid species in many genera. With the discovery of *Takakia* with a basic chromosome number of $n=4$, it has been suggested (Proskauer, 1962) that this is the basic number in the Hepaticae and that most of the genera are polyploids with $n=8$, or polyploids with an additional chromosome, $n=9$. It could be, as has been suggested by Fulford (1965) that possibly the number $n=4$ has been derived from a basic number of $n=8$ or 9.

In *Polytrichum* all species examined, with a few exceptions, have a chromosome number of 7. In *Sphagnum* most species have $n=19$ (with 2-6 '*m*' chromosomes in addition).

Economic importance of Bryophytes

The economic importance of the bryophytes is not obviously apparent, but they may be beneficial indirectly. The bryophytes are, practically speaking, the first colonizers on bare and exposed grounds. By their actions, which are partly mechanical and partly chemical, they can convert the top surface of rocks, lava or similar other substrata into soil. Then, when some of them die this soil becomes enriched with the organic matter. Subsequently, the pteridophytes and the seed-bearing plants appear in succession and finally a bare rocky surface is converted into a green forest. Further, on account of their extremely high capacity for absorbing and retaining water, they help in preventing soil erosion, and even may control flood to some extent.

The Bryophytes are very important economically as they form the peat, which can be used as a fuel in place of coal. The peat is produced as a result of accumulation of mosses, particularly *Sphagnum*, in huge numbers in swamps and bogs ; these mosses undergo slow decomposition and become compacted and carbonized. The 'peat moss' prepared from *Sphagnum* is used by the poultry people as bedding for the livestock as well as by the gardeners to increase the water-retaining capacity of the soil and for keeping it porous.

Sphagnum and other mosses, growing on the banks of ponds, jheels and lakes, form the quaking bogs, whose water appears to possess antiseptic and preserving properties. The larger mosses are sometimes used for packing delicate and fragile materials. Previously they were employed for stuffing cushions. The horticulturists and florists utilize *Sphagnum* for packing seedlings, cut flowers and other nursery stocks. It is also used as a substratum for germinating seeds. On account of the extermely efficient absorptive and antiseptic properties *Sphagnum* was used extensively for dressing wounds during the Russo-Japanese War as well as in World War I.

by Hufford (1958) that possibly the number n = 5 has been derived from a basic number of n = 4 and [illegible].

SECTION VII

PALAEOBOTANY

Introduction

Palaeobotany is the study of fossil plants. These plants had flourished in the early geological periods, but subsequently they gradually dwindled and ultimately became extinct. However, during the course of time the underground parts (i.e., the roots) and some sub-aerial parts of plants which laid buried inside the earth gradually petrified and finally transferred into rocks or fossils.

What is a fossil? Fossil is a relic of some former living thing (plant or animal) embedded in or dug out of the superficial deposits of past geological periods. Fossils usually occur as the hard parts of organisms such as woods, bones, shells, as moulds or casts and as impressions, e.g. leaves, flowers, fruits, seeds, etc., preserved in the rocks. The word fossil came from the Latin verb *federe* which means to dig.

Formation of fossils

Fossils are usually found in fine-grained sediments such as shales and sandstones. These consolidated sediments represent the muds and sands in which the plants were buried. Most plants, of course, decay completely and quickly, and it is only in exceptional cases that the delicate parts of organism are preserved. As a rule, a plant which falls into water becomes saturated and soon sinks to the botton where the progress of decay is retarded. If, instead of progressive but complete destruction, the tissues are incompletely decomposed, the accumulating sediment may enclose residual structures and arrest further decomposition.

Sometimes the plant besides or plant parts are buried under conditions in which not only decay is retarded, but in addition the water carries dissolved mineral substances. Such circumstances result in petrification or mineralisation. Silicified wood may reveal the minute detail of the ornamentation of cellwalls, or calcified nodules may preserve the nuclei in the cells of a developing megaspore.

Some kinds of plants are more liable to preservation than others, and some are of such delicate form and structure that they are seldom encountered as fossils. Calcareous or silicified parts of algae are frequently fossilised. The protoplasts are not preserved, but the calcified or solidified parts are diagnostic enough to permit accurate identification. On the other hand, fungi are infrequently observed as fossils, but their ravages can be detected in a great many petrifications.

KINDS OF FOSSIL PLANTS

According to the nature of fossilisation the fossils can be classified into the following types :

1. **Petrifications.** In this group are included those fossils preserving the external form, the internal structure, and sometimes substance of the original plant caused by cell to cell replacement of plant parts by mineral substances. Examples : Coalballs, silicified wood. Coalballs remain embedded in the coal and are of varying sizes. Silicified wood (thin sections) give microscopic structure.

2. **Incrustations** (cast). These are fossils with the external form as a cast. The internal structure is not preserved. Here the plant substances disappeared and a cavity is left. This cavity is filled up with mineral matter which forms a cast of original plant. The surrounding materials, the mould, form the incrustation, e.g. pith cast of calamites (trunk) or seeds.

3. **Compressions.** The external form of the plant is modified by vertical pressure of the sediments with which it is surrounded. When a plant is subjected to compression—leaves, seeds, fruits, trunks, etc., leave impressions on the rock surface. Coal is considered to be a complex kind of compression.

4. **Compactions** (mummified plant) are plants, or plant fragments, compressed by vertical pressure. Masses of plant fragments without intervening matrix, such as are found in peat and coal, are large-scale compactions.

Most of the deformations observed in this type of fossilisation are caused by the pressure of one fragment against another. Frequently remarkable conditions of preservations are found in compactions.

5. **Impressions.** The forms impressed by fossils of the incrustation or compression type as on coal and shale which hardens afterwards on the matrix are usually termed impressions. The external features of plant parts are thus preserved.

Plant bearing Strata in India

The Indian subcontinent can be divided into three distinct regions which differ from one another in geological as well as physical characteristics.

(1) The peninsula, consisting of Deccan and Ceylon is an extremely ancient and stable part of the earth's crust.

(2) The extra-peninsula comprising the Himalayan ranges has been a much disturbed area geologically. It lay for long periods

under the sea and now characterised by crumpling and folding due to mountain building movement.

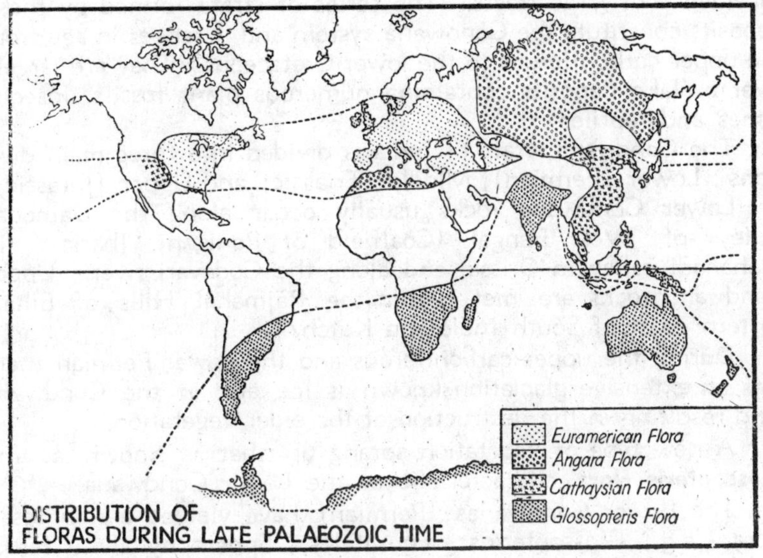

Fig. 299. Gondwana Land.

Distribution of floras during late Palaeozoic time after Wedey

Euamerican flora=Arcto-carboniferous provinces
Angara flora=Angaraland
Cathayria flora=China
Glossopteris flora=Gondwanaland

(3) The region lying between the two above is *Indo-gangetic* alluvium that has been filled up with the alluvial deposits brought down by the Himalayan rivers.

GONDWANA LAND (Fig. 299)

It is believed that peninsular India, Australia, South Africa, Antarctica, South America and Madagascar formed during Palaeozoic as a single large continent. This southern land mass was named **Gondwana land** after the Gond Kingdoms of Central India. It was separated from northern continents, including, Asia, Europe, North America by a sea, known as Tethys, a remnant of which is the Mediterranean sea. The present configuration of India was attained towards the end of the Tertiary era.

Gondwana System

Thick deposits of fresh water and subaerial sediments were laid as the peninsula in the basin-shaped depressions caused by subsidence of large tracts. The series of strata formed by these deposits constitute the Gondwana system and it ranges in age from the upper carboniferous to the lower Cretaceous. They are largely river or lake deposits containing numerous plant fossils, insects, fishes and reptiles.

The Gondwana strata of India is divided into three main divisions : Lower (Permian), Middle (Triassic) and Upper (Jurassic).

Lower Gondwana rocks usually occur along the Damodar valley of West Bengal (Coalfield of Raniganj, Jharia), in Mahanadi valley in Orissa, and along the Godavari river. Upper Gondwana rocks are met within the Rajmahal Hills of Bihar, eastern coast of South India and Kutch.

During the upper carboniferous and the Lower Permian there was an extensive glaciation known as Ice age in the Gondwana land resulting in the destruction of the elder vegetation.

A new type of vegetation sprang up that is known as the **Glossopteris flora**, characteristic of the Lower Gondwana.

The Lower Gondwanas (Permian) have yielded a rich fossil flora, e.g. Glossopterids, Equsetales, Spherophyllales, ferns, Cerdaitales and some conifers. The middle Gondwana (Triassic) was characterised by Dicroidium. The upper Gondwana (Jurassic) was predominated by Ptilophyllum flora and many other Cycadophytes, conifers, Gingakoales, ferns, and Equisetales.

Fossils of the main Gondwana Rocks of India

The earth's crust has experienced several revolutions involving change of topography, e.g. redistribution of land and water, elevation of submerged land, submergence of elevated levels, etc. The sediments transform into rocks, e.g. sedimentary rock with plant and animal remains preserved in it. These sedimentary rocks have been divided into geological periods on the basis of their fossil contents (see Table) Pteridophytes and gymnosperms consisting of hard parts are formed in large number as fossils while, bryophytes and algae mostly of soft parts are seldom encountered as fossils.

Palaeobotany has also its economic application, in the exploration of minerals, specially coal and oil (petroleum) and limestone formed by algal colonies. Ancient Carboniferous or Permian flora played an important role in the formation of coal.

Petroleum is possibly derived from marine planktonic flora and fauna of Eocene age.

Polynology dealing with fossil spores and pollen has proven to be a great value in the correlation of coal seams and in age determination of petroleum bearing rocks.

Upper Gondwana	Umia series	Lower Cretaceous
	Jabalpur Series Rajmahal Series Kota Series	Jurassic
Middle Gondwana	Mahadeva Series Panchet Series	Triassic
Lower Gondwana Damuda Series	Raniganj Iron stone shale Barakar	Permian
Talchir Series	Karharbari Talchir	Upper caboniferous

Table showing general sequence of the Gondwana group Fossils of the main Gondwana rocks of India

Lower Gondwana

1. Talchir series (Upper carboniferous)

Clossopteridales —*Glossopteris indica. G. communis G. angustifolia. Ganganiopteris, Cyclopteriods G. buriadica, Vertebraria indica Ottokaria katiwaiensis*

Cordaitales —*Naeggerathiopsis histopi Samaropsis mile cordaicarpus sahni*

Equisetales —*Schzoneura gondwanesis, Phyllothaca sahnie*

2. Damuda series (Permian)

Lycopodiales —*Nothrodendron*

Equisetales —*Schizoneura* (2 sp.) *Phyllotheca sp.*

Sphenophyllales —*Sphenophyllum speciosum*

Fillcales —*Alethopteris actinopteris*

Pteridospernale —*Glossopteris (General species) Sphenopteris, Vertebaria, Paleovittaria*

Cordaitales —*Naegerathiopsis, Dadoxylon* (wood)

Cycadales —*Taeniopteris danaeoides*

Coniferales —*Buriadia aewardiana*

Middle Gondwana Panchet and Mahadeva series Triassic

Filicales —*Danaeopsis hughesii*

Pteridospermales Thinnfeldia (several sp.)

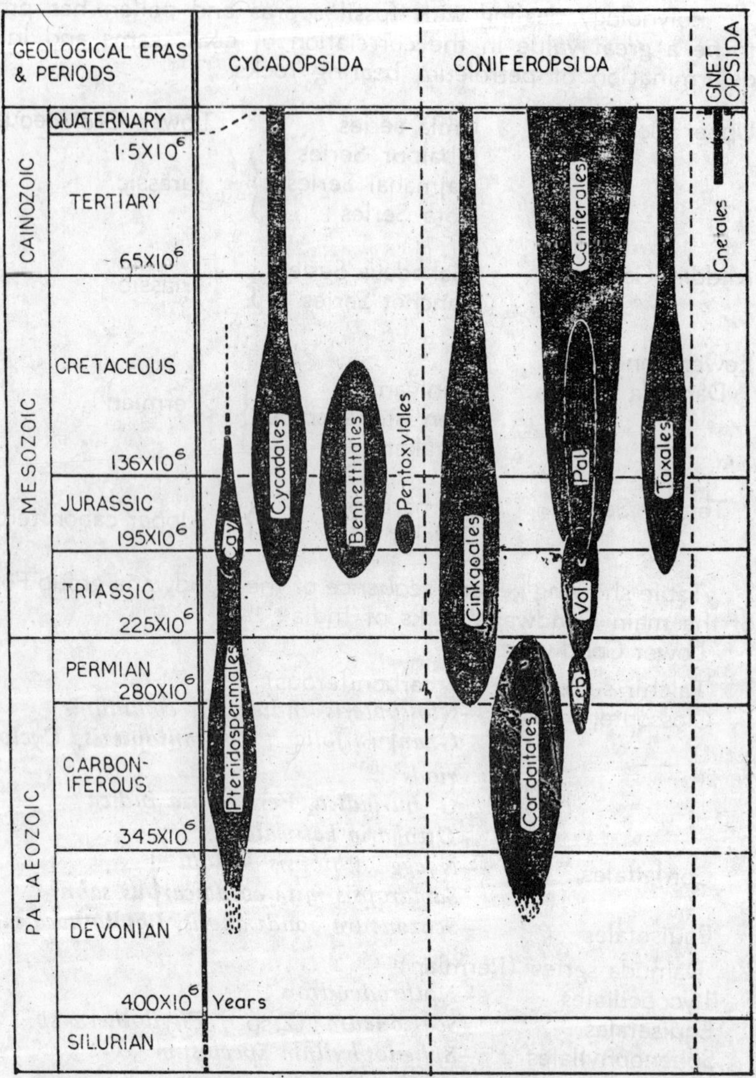

Geological history of gymnosperms

Cay-Caytoniaceae; Leb-Lebachiaceae; Pal-Palissyaceae; Vol-Voltziaceae.

Fig. 300.

Upper Gondwana

Era	Period/Epoch	Age	Events
Quanternary	Recent		Dominance of herbs
	Pleistocene		Increase of herbs
Cenozoic Tertiary	Pliocene	1,000,000 years ago	Decrease of trees Rise of herbs
	Miocene	13,000,000 years ago	Forests continuing
	Oligocene	25,000,000 years ago	
	Eocene	36,000,000 years ago	Worldwide tropical forests extension of angiosperms
	Palaeocene	58,000,000 years ago	Modernisation of angiosperms
Mesozoic	Cretaceous	63,000,000 years ago	Rise of flowering plants Decrease of Conifers
	Jurassic	136,000,000 years ago	Conifers and Cycad dominant
	Triassic	180,000,000 years ago	First known Cycads
Palaeozoic	Permian	230,000,000 years ago	Seed ferns extinct dwindling of ancient plants
	Carboniferous	310,000,000 years ago	Giant lyopods, horsetails and seed ferus appear
	Devonian	345,000,000 years ago	Early land plants Psilophytales
	Silurian	405,000,000 years ago	First known land plants Cooksonia
	Ordovocian	425,000,000 years ago	Marine algae dominant
	Cambrian	500,000,000 years ago	First plant spores Alga green and red
	Precambrian	600,000 000 years ago – 5,000,000,000 years ago	Bacteria, fungi, algae (blue green)

Table : A geological time scale with notes of events in the evolution of plants.

1. Kota and Rajmahal Series—Lower to middle Jurassic
   Lycopodiales —Lycopodites sp. Lycoxylon sp.
   Equisetales —Equisetites sp.
   Marattiales —*Marattiopsis* nacrolarpe
   Osmundaces Cladophetebis (several sp.)
   Gleicheniales —*Gleichenites gleichenoides*
   Benattiatales —*Ptillophyllum, Otozamites, Dictyozamites, Williamsonia Sewardiana*
   Nilssonia (Several sp.), *Taeniopteria* sp.
   Coniferales —*Elatocladus, Brachyphyllum,*
   Pentoxylales —*Pentaxylen, Carnoconites*
2. Jabalpur series (upper Jurassic to Lower Cretaceous)
   Osmundacede —*Chladophlebis*
   Gleicheniales —*Gleichonites*
   Cycadopsida —*Philophyllum, Otozamites, Williamsonias*
   Ginkgoales —*Ginkgoitas*
   Coniferales —*Elatocladus, Brachyphyllum*

Importance of the study of fossil plants

Palaeobotanical studies include two aspects, Botanical and Geological. The botanical aspects are concerned with morphology of fossil plants, their distribution, evidence of early plant life, past climate and environment and evolution. Paleobotany gives us indication to many extinct plants, Fossils of younger deposits help us in understanding modes of vegetation, the origin and development of agriculture and plant economy during courses of evolution.

Geological aspect help us in calculation of age of rocks and in stratigraphy, Microfossils, e.g. spores, pollen, algal remains, etc., have been recognised as a reliable tool in exploration of petroleum and coal.

Coal is proved as a mass of mummified plant and the value of various coals is based on original composition of its plant material.

SECTION VIII

PTERIDOPHYTA

INTRODUCTION

The Pteridophytes include plants like ferns, horse-tails, clubmosses and their allies, and are widely distributed in the temperate and tropical regions. They are frequently found in most terrestrial habitats but many grow as floating aquatics or may even be epiphytes on tree-trunks.

General characters

They have a well-defined alternation of generations in their life cycles and the *sporophyte is always an independent plant* and free from the gametophyte at maturity. The *gametophyte*, on the other hand, is either *wholly independent of the sporophyte or may be partially or wholly dependent on it* for nutrition and is always smaller than the sporophyte. The plant body is usually well differentiated into stem, root and leaves, and with an internal conducting system consisting of xylem and phloem. The asexual generation or the sporophyte may be **homosporous** (with spores of one kind) or **heterosporous** (with spores of two kinds, viz., small or **microspores** and large or **megaspores**). The Pteridophytes differ from the Bryophytes in having an independent sporophyte with well-differentiated vascular structures. They also differ from the seed-bearing plants (Spermatophytes) in the liberation of the female gametophyte from the sporangium. The method of sexual reproduction resembles that of the Bryophytes.

Similar to all vascular plants, the shoot of pteridophytes consists of the *cortex* and a central cylinder, which is known as the **stele.** The stele is mainly made up of xylem and phloem, and is delimited from the cortex by the endodermis. The histological structure of the protostele varies widely. A protostele with smooth core of xylem surrounded by phloem is termed a **haplostele** (e.g. *Rhynia*, *Horneophyton*, etc.). If the core of xylem of a protostele, in transectional view, is lobed or star-shaped, it is designated an **actinostele** (e.g. *Asteroxylon*, *Psilotum, Lycopodium selago*, etc.). The specialized type of protostele, in transection seems to consist of separate plates of xylem between and around which occurs the phloem—this form is designated a **plectostele** (e.g. *Lycopodium clavatum*, *Cladoxylon scoparium*, etc.). There are two principal types of steles : the **protostele** and the **siphonostele.** The protostele is characterized by the absence of a central column of pith, and from the phylogenetic as well as ontogenetic standpoint, it is the most primitive type of stelar construction.

A stele with a central column of pith is regarded phylogenetically as an advance in anatomical development and is known as a siphonostele. The pith in a siphonostele may have resulted either by the gradual inclusion of areas of cortical parenchyma or by the phylogenetic reduction of the original tracheids to parenchyma (Bower, 1911).

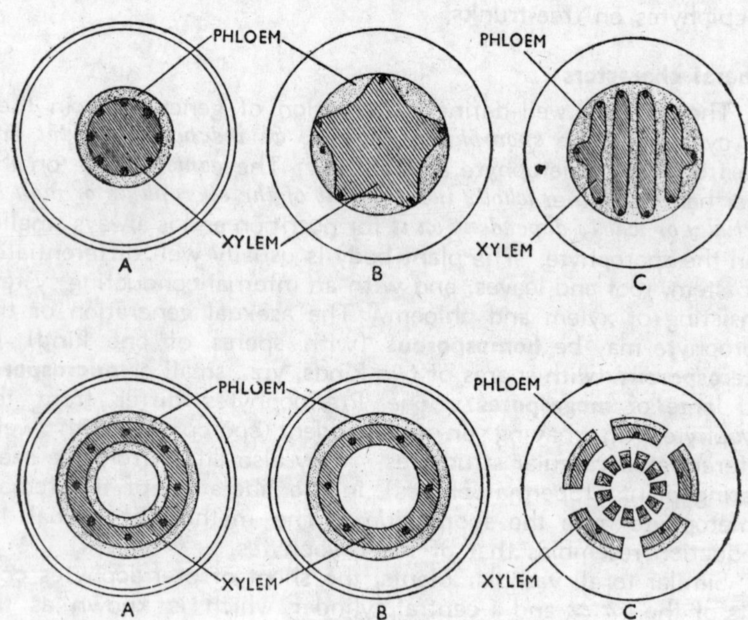

Fig. 301. *Stele.*
A, Protostele ; B, Actinostele ; C, Plectostele.
A, Ectophloic ; B, Siphonostele ; C, Dictyostele,

A siphonostele may be **amphiphloic** with phloem both external and internal to xylem (e.g. *Marsilea*, *Dicksonia*, etc.) or it may be **ectophloic** with pholem restricted to the external face of the xylem only (e.g. *Ophioglossum*, *Botrychium*, etc.

The evolution of siphonostele has been accompanied by the formation of parenchymatous gaps (leaf gaps and branch gaps) in the vascular cylinder. Siphonosteles without an overlapping of gaps are known as **solenosteles** (e.g. *Marsilea*, *Dennstaedtia*, etc.). and those with overlapping gaps are termed as **dictyosteles** (e.g. *Polypodium*, *Thelypteris*, etc.). The intervening vascular bundle to overlapping gaps is known as **meristele.** Dictyosteles with medullary bundles and often with cortical bundles are designated as **cyathean dictyosteles** (e.g. *Cyathea*, *Thyrsopteris*, etc.).

Origin of the Pteridophytes

The question of the origin of the present-day pteridophytes is a highly debated one, as a considerable gap exists in between the pteridophytes and other plants placed lower in the scale of evolution. There are two schools of view concerning the origin of pteridophytes, one proposing an origin from algae and the other from bryophytes.

According to the advocates of an algal origin, the similarities noted between the bryophytes and the pteridophytes are not due to any phylogenetic relationship existing in between the two groups, but these are the results of a parallel evolution. While Scott (1900), and Eames (1936) do not suggest any particular group of algae as the supposed ancestors, other workers like Church (1919), and Arnold (1947), are of opinion that the pteridophytes originated from some complex marine algae 'transmigrating' from the ocean to the land. Obviously, their idea implies that the pteridophytes evolved from the Phaeophyceae. On the other hand, Boblin (1901), Lotsy (1909), and Fritsch (1916) believe that this origin has taken place from some *Chaetophora*-like filamentous green algae. In a subsequent publication Fritsch (1945) expressed his idea that the hypothetical ancestor was a green alga with an erect parenchymatous body possessing an isomorphic type of alternation of generations in its life cycle.

Lignier (1903), Bower (1935), and Zimmermann (1930, 1938) believe that the bryophytes and the pteridophytes are phylogenetically connected but divergently developing evolutionary lines, which have separated early from very primitive archegonia-bearing hypothetical land plants. But Campbell (1895, 1899, 1924) is of opinion that the pteridophytes have originated from the true bryophytes of the anthocerotean type. This idea was opposed at first on the ground that wide differences exist between the sporophytes of the known pteridophytes and that of the anthocerotean type. But, when the rootless, non-leafy and dichotomously branched sporophytes of the psilophytes were discovered, this objection was rendered invalid. Further, though nothing is known about the embryology of the members of the Psilophytales, but a surprisingly superficial resemblance exists in between the embryos of the living Psilotales and the Anthocerotes.

Evolution among the Pteridophytes

Among the pteridophytes, the Psilophytales are very simple as well as very primitive, and they can be traced as far back as the Silurian. Their sporophytes were rootless and represented by either

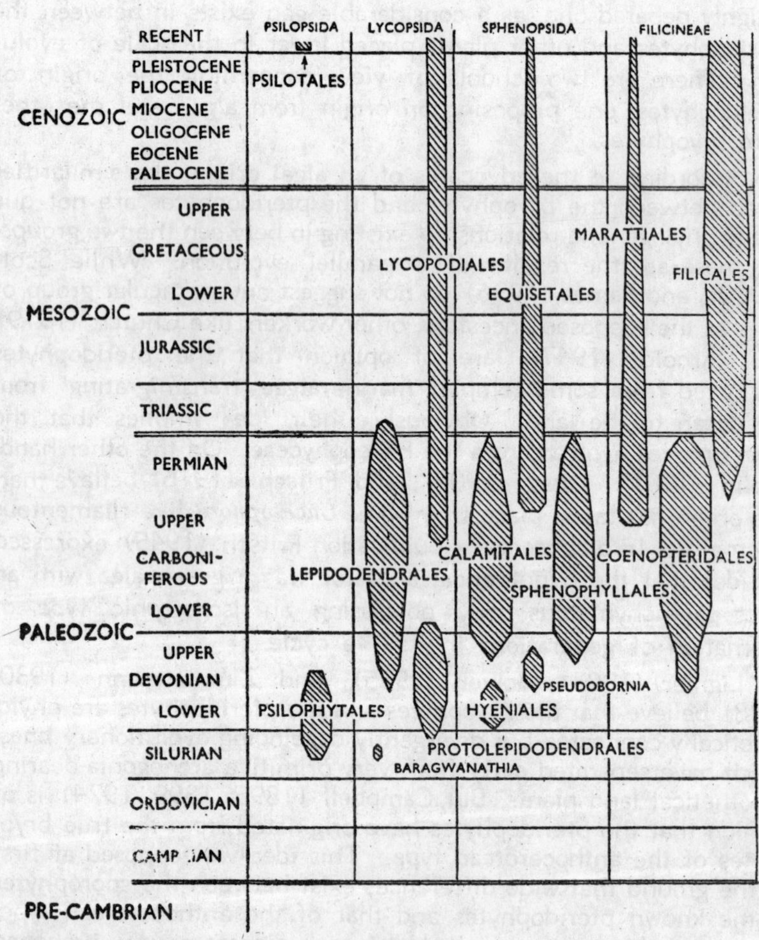

Fig. 302. Distribution of Pteridophytes in the geological periods.

completely leafless branches or by branches having minute veinless leaves. The sporangia were borne singly and terminally at the end of a branch. From this psilophytalean stock probably there appeared early in different divergent directions all the present-day pteridophytes.

It has, however, been suggested by many authors that the simplicity of the Psilophytales had resulted from reduction in response to some environmental stimulus, rather than being manifestation of genuine primitiveness. The much supporting evidence for such a hypothesis is that the Silurian *Baragwanathia*, a lycopod, was already well-defined and strongly established prior to the appearance of most of the psilophytaceous plants, which are conceived as ancestral to all other forms.

Classification of Pteridophytes

All the vascular cryptogams are generally put under the Division Pteridophyta, and are divided into *four* classes :

Class I. Psilophytineae. The sporophyte is leafless or provided with very minute leaf-like scales ; roots are also absent. The sporangia are terminal or lateral, and occur singly at the tips of the branches.

Class II. Lycopodineae. The sporophyte is differentiated into root, stem and leaf. The leaves are **microphyllous** and usually spirally arranged. The branching of the stem is typically dichotomous. Leaf-gaps are absent in the vascular cylinder. The sporangia are borne singly on the adaxial face of the sporophylls and contain either homospores (e.g. *Lycopodium*) or heterospores (e.g. *Isoetes* and *Selaginella*). The sporophylls may or may not form a *cone* or *strobilus*. Sperms are usually biflagellate excepting in *Isoetes* and *Stylites*.

Class III. Equisetineae. The sporophyte is differentiated into root, stem and leaf. The stem is provided with distinct nodes and internodes. The sterile leaves are usually arranged in whorls. Leaf-gaps are absent in the vascular cylinder. The sporangia are usually borne in groups on a special structure called the **sporangiophore** and form a distinct *cone*. Sperms are always multiflagellate.

Class IV. Filicineae. The sporophyte is differentiated into root, stem and leaf. In some exceptional cases roots are entirely lacking. The leaves are **macrophyllous** and are arranged spirally. Morphologically, the sporophylls and sterile leaves are alike and they never form any *cone* or *strobilus*. The sporangia are borne in groups forming *sori*, either on the margins or near about the centre on the under (abaxial) surface of the sporophylls. Leaf-gaps are present in the vascular cylinder. Sperms are always multiflagellate.

Bold (1957), however, does not accept the Division Pteridophyta, in its classical sense, and divides the vascular cryptogams into *four* Divisions : **Psilophyta**, **Microphyllophyta, Arthrophyta** and **Pterophyta.** Prof. Bold's system of classification is a negative and a retrogressive one, and it overlooks evidences of relationship and separates subdivisions of plants grouped together in other classifications.

Pichi-Sermolli (1958), although agrees that the Pteridophytes are not uniform as a taxon, still he considers that these plants should stand as a 'divisio' in its classical sense, because they share many fundamental characters. His Division Pteridophyta includes *six* classes : **Lycopsida, Sphenopsida, Noeggerathiopsida, Psilotopsida, Psilophytopsida,** and **Filicopsida.**

CHAPTER I

CLASS PSILOPHYTINEAE

The members of the Class Psilophytineae are the simplest as well as very primitive among the pteridophytes.

Plant rootless. Sporophyte differentiated into a rhizoid-bearing rhizomatous subterranean portion and an aerial erect shoot, which is sparingly or profusely branched. Protostelic, very rarely siphonostelic. Aerial shoot leafless, sometimes beset with small, simple, veinless leaf-like structures. Sporangia usually terminal, more rarely lateral, borne singly, less frequently in pairs or in groups. Gametophytes, in the living genera, are colourless and subterranean.

There is controversy of opinion as regards the origin of this Class, some suggesting that it has come from the algae, while others opine that the bryophyta has given rise to it. Whatever may be the origin, it may be considered that the remaining three Classes of the pteridophytes have come from this basic stock.

The Psilophytineae includes *two* Orders : (1) **Psilophytales,** an Order comprising fossil members only, and (2) **Psilotales,** an Order with the single family *Psilotaceae* having two living genera, *Psilotum* and *Tmesipteris*.

ORDER 1. PSILOPHYTALES

The Psilophytales are characterized in general in having a rootless, rhizomatous stem bearing rhizoids and a simple, sparsely-dichotomously branched subaerial shoot ; the subaerial branches are either leafless or provided with small, leaf-like outgrowths. The sporangia are terminal in a raceme-like fashion, or are lateral, and contain homospores ; in essence the sporangia represent the enlarged tips of the branches. The stele is a protostele, which may be either a haplostele or an actinostele.

Affinity

The habitat and the vegetative and reproductive structures of the group lead to the conclusion that the group is related algae and bryophytes on the one hand with other groups of pteridophytes (e.g., Lycopods, Equisetums and ferns) on the other.

(*a*) *Affinity with algae*

The swampy habit and dichotomous branching of the group, have got some affinities with some Phaeophyceae of ***Fucus*** type, which grow in the intertidal zones of the rock. Plants, like some higher algae, have rhizome-like basal portion, which supports cylindrical, dichotomously forked, upright stem.

(*b*) *Affinity with bryophytes*

Psilophytales and some bryophytes have simple leaf-like stems and terminal sporangia. The extremely simple structure of the sporangia of *Rhynia* is similar to the sporangial structure of many hepatics. The sporangium is borne singly at the end of a branch ; it has many-celled jacket layer ; the outermost wall is thick with a thick cuticle. In *Hornea*, columella is present in the central portion of the sporangium and it is like the columella in many bryophytes. The spores of *Asteroxylon*, like those of *Sphagnum*, are liberated through the apical region of the capsule.

Some morphologists have laid stress on the similarity between the telarous rhizome of *Hornea* and the fast of *Anthoceros*. They have tried to homologise the whole sporophyte of Rhyniaceae with *Anthoceros* by interpreting the naked subaerial stem portion between the rhyzome and the sporangium of the former as sterilized tissue, derived from the lower part of the capsule of Anthoceros type. The sporophyte of Rhyniaceae, like *Anthoceros*, bears chlorophyll and has stomato on the epidermis.

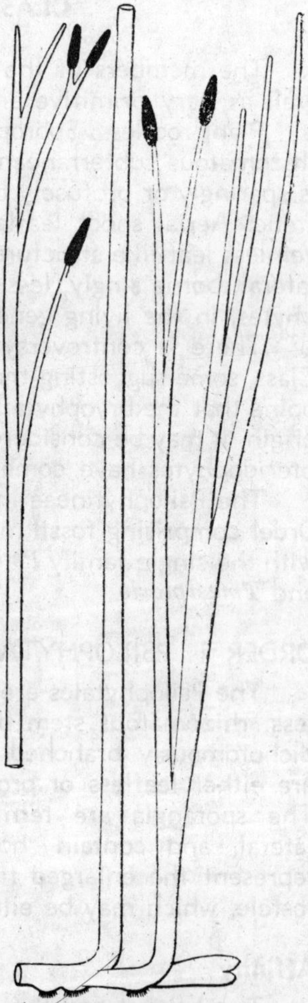

Fig. 303. *Rhynia*, The plant body.

(**c**) *Affinity with Lycopodium, Phylloglossum and higher plants*
Hynia is similar to *Psilophyton* in many respects.

(*d*) *Affinity with Primofilices*

The sterile leaf of *Cladoxylon* resembles *Rhynia*. The sporangia of *Etapteris* have similarity with the sporangia of Rhyniaceae.

(*e*) *Affinity with Psilotales*

Psilophytales and Psilotales are alike in many important characters : (*i*) Plant body is an axis without roots, (*ii*) with emergences rather than leaves, (*iii*) sporangia on axis-tips with massive differentiated wall with a central stelar columella, (*iv*) the emergences are flattened without vascular supply or with traces extending only to the cortex.

These characters are not found in any other group, and as such it may be said that Psilophytales and Psilotales belong to a major group (Psilophytineae).

The members of the Psilophytales, which are regarded as the oldest known vascular plants, appeared in the Silurian and existed up to the Upper Devonian, or probably early Carboniferous, but most of the records have been obtained from the Lower and Middle Devonian. The fossil remains are found in Scotland, Germany, Czekoslovakia, Norway, Australia, China and some parts of U.S.A.

Authorities differ in their opinions regarding the classification of the Order. Weitstein divides the Order into three families, Hirmer into five, and Kraussel into nine families. Arnold (1947) in his 'An Introduction to Palaeobotany' recognizes the following *five* families : **Rhyniaceae, Zosterophyllaceae, Psilophytaceae, Asteroxylaceae,** and **Pseudosporochraceae.**

Recent studies by Lyon (1964) show that *Asteroxylon* (Asteroxylaceae) is probably a lycopod, and as such should be included under the Lycopodineae. *Pseudosporochrus* 'Pseudosporochraceae) shows Cladoxylalean anatomy, and therefore is not a psilophyte (Leclarq and Banks, 1959).

RHYNIA

(Fam. RHYNIACEAE)

Uptil now the genus comprises of 2 species only : *R. major* and *R. gwynnevaughani* discovered from the Rhynie chert of Scotland in the Middle Devonian deposit.

The sporophyte

The plant body consists of a cylindrical, horizontally-growing subterranean rhizoid-bearing rhizome with dichotomously branched, leafless, aerial shoots, attaining a height of 20-50 cm.

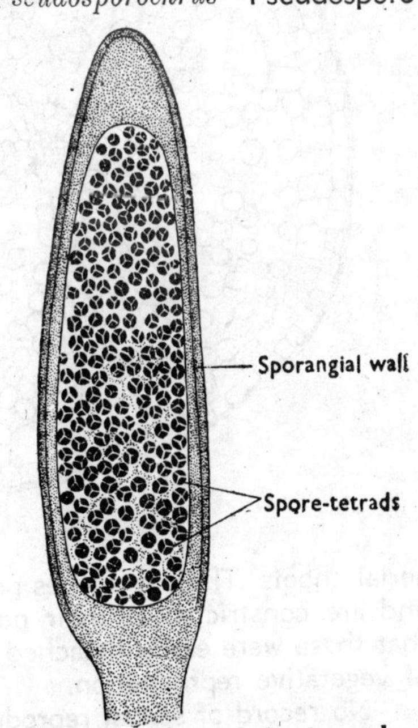

Fig. 304. *Rhynia.* L.S, of capsule,

and a diameter of 1.5-6 mm. The tips of the aerial branches are gradually tapering and in some cases end in oval sporangia. The heavily cutinized spores are borne in tetrads within large cavity of the sporangium and are homospores. The sporangial wall is differentiable into two layers, one outer and the other inner, the latter probably functioning as a tapetum.

Internally, the axis is differentiated into extrastelar and intrastelar regions. The former consists of an epidermis and a thick cortex with prominent intercellular spaces ; stomata occur on the epidermis. The stele is a protostele and the xylem is completely surrounded by the phloem ; the xylem is composed of annular tracheids only.

Reproduction

Rhynia reproduced by vegetative method only.

In some cases small outgrowths, occasionally developing into lateral branches, have been noted to appear on the body of the

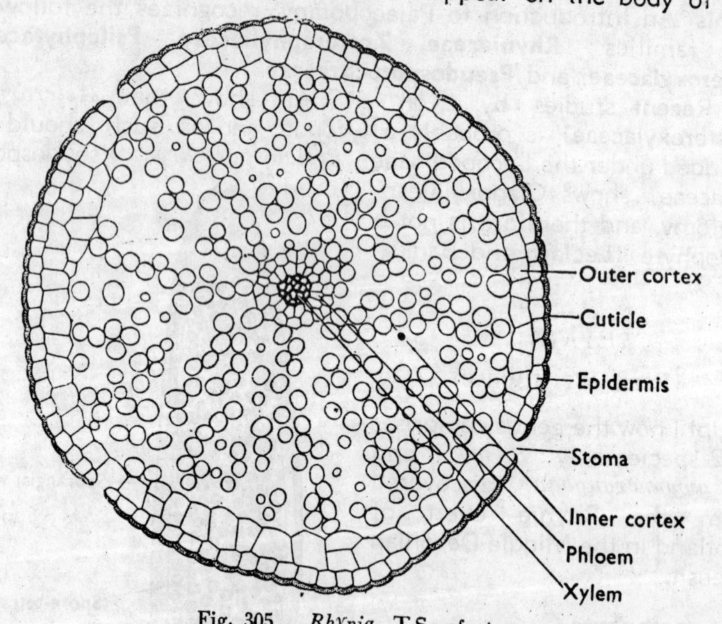

Fig. 305. *Rhynia.* T.S. of stem.

aerial shoots. These branches possess independent vascular strands and are constricted at their points of attachment, which suggest that these were easily detached and thus probably formed a means of vegetative reproduction.

No record of sexual reproduction has been found as yet.

It is interesting to note that Merker (1961) suggests that the creeping underground parts of *Rhynia* were not in actual fact the rhizomes of the sporophyte, but rather the gametophyte, and that the aerial part alone represents the sporophytic generation. This re-interpretation allows a closer comparison of the Psilophytales with the bryophytes, but it hardly adds support to the Homologous theory of the origin of sporophyte.

*HORNEOPHYTON**

(Fam. RHYNIACEAE)

This genus possesses only one species—*H. lignieri* and is found in the Rhynie chert, either independently or in association with *Rhynia*.

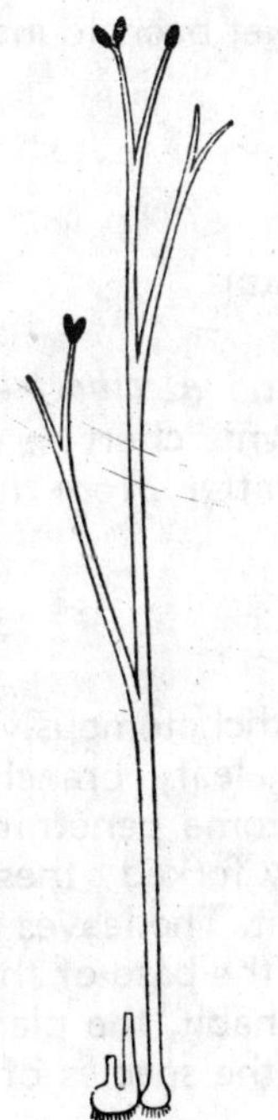

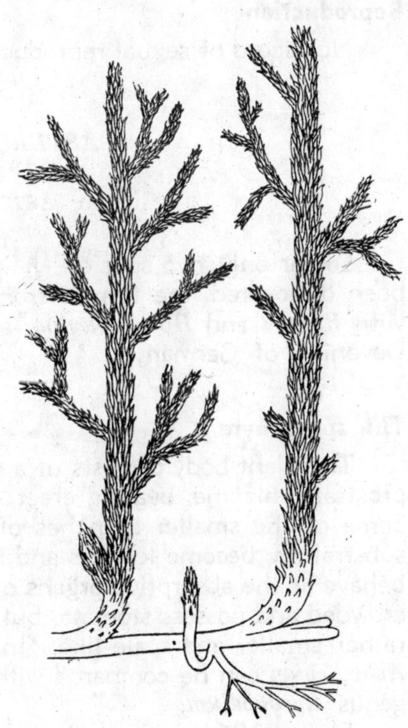

Fig. 306. *Horneophyton*, The plant body.

Fig. 307. *Asteroxylon*, The plant body.

* Originally named *Hornea* by Kidston and Lang (1917). But the same name was used in 1877 for a member of Sapindaceae.

The sporophyte

The plant is very similar to *Rhynia*, but is rather smaller and more delicate. The rhizome is a lobed, tuberous structure bearing rhizoids. The subaerial shoot is also dichotomously branched like *Rhynia* and is without any appendage. The sporangia are also borne at the tips of some of the branches as in *Rhynia*, but differ mainly in having a prominent sterile columella, which projects into the cavity of the sporangium from its base and extends very near to the apex. The tapetum is well defined and the spores occur in tetrads.

Internally, the rhizome is without a vascular system and consists of parenchymatous cells only, in the intercellular spaces of which some fungal hyphae are noted. The anatomy of the aerial shoot, however, represents that of *Rhynia*.

Reproduction

No record of sexual reproduction has yet been found.

ASTEROXYLON

(Fam. ASTEROXYLACEAE)

So far only two species—*A. mackiei* and *A. elberfeldenes* have been discovered, the former from the Rhynie chert in association with *Rhynia* and *Horneophyton*, and the latter from the Middle Devonian of Germany.

The sporophyte

The plant body consists of a rootless, dichotomously branched, prostrate rhizome, bearing erect, subaerial, leafy, branched shoots. Some of the smaller branches of the rhizome penetrate into the substratum, become leafless and repeatedly forked ; these probably behave as the absorptive organs of the plant. The leaves are closely crowded and possess stomata, but those at the base of the stem are rather smaller and scale-like. In general habit, the plant body of *Asteroxylon* can be compared with that of the species of the living genus *Lycopodium*.

Lyon (1964) reported the discovery of new, fertile axes associated with *Asteroxylon*. They bear vascularized sporangia laterally along the axis. Typical leaves of *Asteroxylon* are interspread among them. The stele of the axis resembles that of *Asteroxylon*. The tracheids of the stele are also similar to those of *Asteroxylon*. Lyon's material though unattached, still the similarity of the leaves, the stele, and the tracheids of the sterile and fertile stems provides a convincing case.

Internally, the rhizome as well as the leafy branches are differentiated into epidermis, cortex and stele. The cortical cells

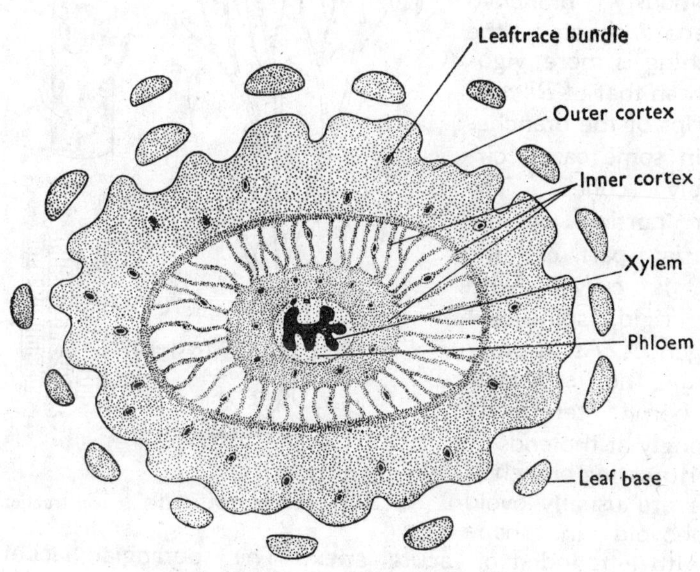

Fig. 308. *Asteroxylon*.
T.S. of stem.

contain fungal hyphae. The central cylinder is a mesarch actinostele with 4-10 rayed xylem. Practically speaking, the whole of the xylem mass is composed of spiral tracheids, though occasionally annular, scalariform and pitted tracheids are noted.

PSILOPHYTON

(Fam. PSILOPHYTACEAE)

This Devonian genus is widely distributed in several countries of Europe as well as in Canada and United States. The remains are generally fragmentary in nature.

The sporophyte

The plant body is small and possesses a prostrate, rootless but rhizoid-bearing rhizome, which gives rise to dichotomously branched subaerial shoots ; the branching is more vigorous than that of *Rhynia*. The tips of the branches are, in some cases, circinately coiled. The major portion of the subaerial part of the plant is curved with short, rigid, spinescent emergences. As in other genera, the sporangia are borne terminally and singly at the ends of the bifurcating branches. These are usually ovoid to obovoid in shape and with a rounded or acute apex. The sporangial jacket is several celled in thickness and the spores, though varying in size, are apparently homosporous.

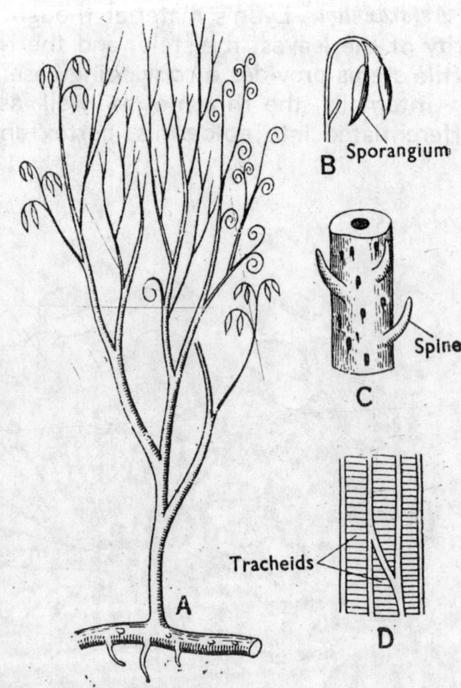

Fig. 309. *Psilophyton* (after reconstruction).

ORDER 2. PSILOTALES

The Order Psilotales is characterized by a rootless, dichotomously branched sporophyte, which is partly underground and partly subaerial. The latter part may be leafless or leafy. The sporangia are in diads (e.g. *Tmesipteris*) or triads (e.g. *Psilotum*). The gametophytes are entirely subterranean.

The Order includes two genera : *Psilotum* and *Tmesipteris*.

Affinity

Before the recognition of the group Psilophytineae, the Psilotales was included under Lycopodineae by Campbell, and under Equisetineae by Bower and as an independent series within the pteridophytes by Seward.

(*a*) *Affinity with Lycopodineae*

Campbell and his supporters mainly stressed on the resemblances between Psilotales and Lycopods in their gametophytic structure, *i.e.*, subterranean mycorhizal and radial form. The embedded nature of the antheridium resembles *Lycopodium* ; but unlike lycopods, there is a segregation of fertile and sterile regions. The sex organs and sperms differ in many important ways.

(*b*) *Affinity with Equisetineae*

Bower and his supporters claimed that Psilotales resembles Equisetineae in many important ways :

(*i*) Morphological and anatomical nature of the young shoot ; (*ii*) ribbed stem ; (*iii*) nature of the fructification which has been thought to be sporangiophoric in nature ; (*iv*) similarity in function of sporogenous cells during the development of the sporangium, all the cells do not develop into spores, some supplying nutrition to the developing spores.

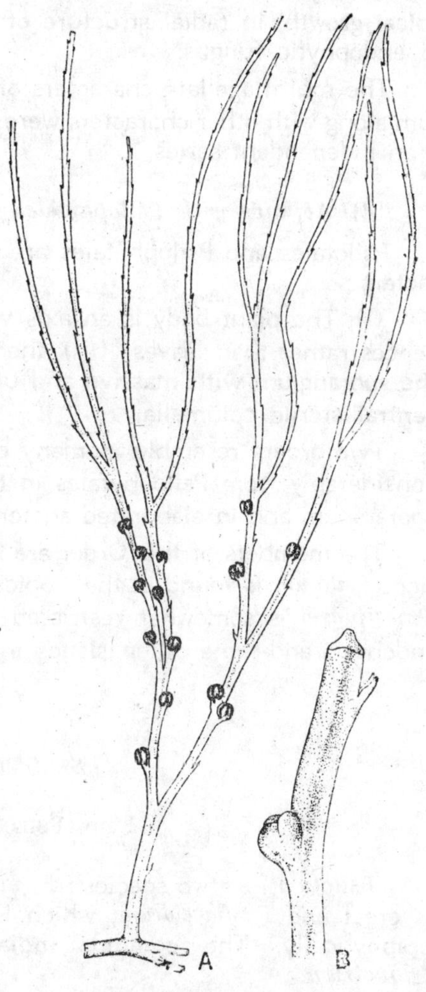

Fig. 310. *Psilotum.*
A, A portion of the plant ; B, Same showing sporangium (magnified).

But, in many other characters it differs from Equisetales.

(*c*) *Affinity with Ophioglossales*

The group resembles Ophioglossales in its gametophytic structures which are similar to that of the sporophyte. In both the groups the gametophytes are like the rhizomes in general appearance, in cylindrical form and dichotomous branching, in definite apical growth, in radial structure of rhizoids and in the presence of endophytic fungus.

The multiflagellate characters of sperms and absence of tapetum along with other characters were considered by Seward to make it an independent series.

(d) *Affinity with Psilophytales*

Psilotales and Psilophytales are alike in many important characters :

(*i*) The plant body is an axis without roots, (*ii*) with emergences rather than leaves, (*iii*) the sporangium on axis-tips, (*iv*) the sporangium with massive and undifferentiated wall, and with central sterile columella.

Two orders resemble in many characters but Psilotales differ considerably from Psilophytales in the position of the chambered sporangium and in elaborated anatomical structures.

The members of this Order are known only in the living condition. *Psilotum* is found in the tropical and subtropical regions, but *Tmesipteris* is somewhat restricted to Australia, New Zealand, Indonesia and some other islands in the Pacific ocean.

PSILOTUM

(Fam. PSILOTACEAE)

Psilotum has two species : *P. nudum* (=*P. triquetrum*), which is erect and *P. flaccidium*, which is lax and pending, and grows epiphytically. The common Indian species of *Psilotum* is *P. triquetrum*.

Psilotum is a rootless, slender plant, 20-100 cm. in length. The rhizome is covered with hair-like absorbing organs and frequently contains a mycorrhizal fungus. During the course of undergoing repeated dichotomous branching, the tip of any dichotomy comes out of the soil and develops into a subaerial shoot. These shoots are flattened or ridged, green in colour and are provided with minute, awl-shaped, scaly appendages in the upper portions only.

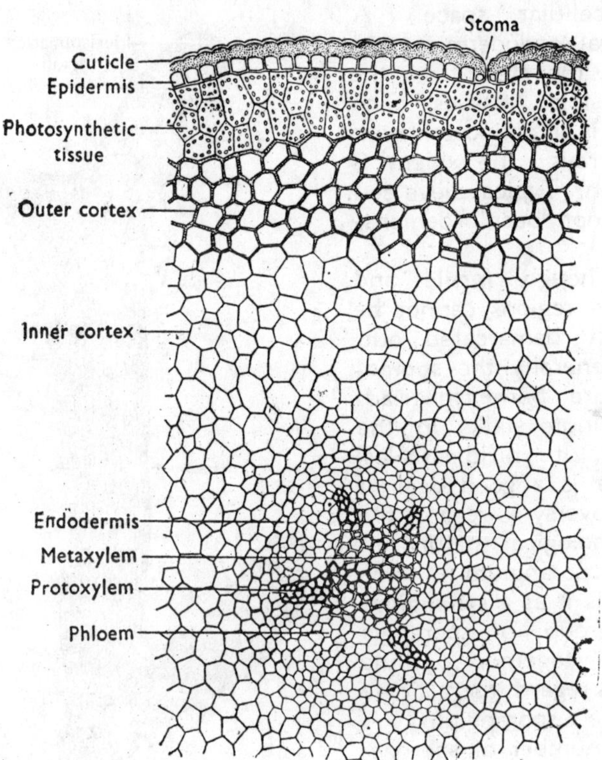

Fig. 311. *Psilotum*. T, S, of stem.

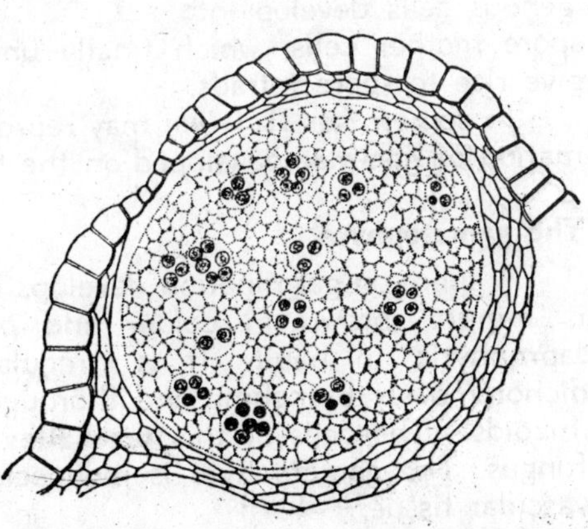

Fig. 312. *Psilotum*. T.S. of a sporangiophore (in part).

Internally, the subaerial shoot of *Psilotum* consists of an epidermis, interrupted frequently by stomata, below which there are a few layers of chlorenchyma cells. The cortex is differentiated into an outer sclerenchymatous and an inner parenchymatous zone ; the cells in the later region are without any intercellular space. A typical endodermis separates the stele from the extrastelar tissues. The stele is an actinostele with 5-6 rays ; the xylem is exarch. Typical sieve cell has not been demonstrated.

Though fertile and sterile regions cannot be strictly demarcated out, yet generally the **sporangia** are borne in triads on minute stalks in the axils of bifid scales. There is a good deal of controversy as regards the morphological nature of the sporangium ; some regards it as a **synangium** (a group of sporangia fused together), while others regard it as a single septate sporangium. A large number of sporogenous cells are produced from a single archesporial cell. Some of these sporogenous cells develop into spore mother cells, which finally undergoing reduction divisions give rise to spore tetrads.

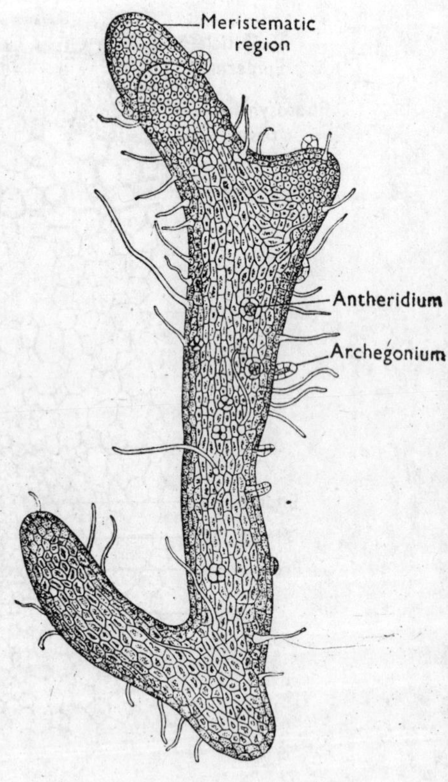

Fig. 313. *Psilotum*. The gametophyte.

In some cases *Psilotum* may reproduce vegetatively by the formation of **gemmae** developed on the rhizoids.

The gametophyte

A spore on germination develops into the gametophyte, which is minute, brown in colour and perfectly subterranean and saprophytic in habit. It is irregularly cylindrical, somewhat dichotomously branching and thoroughly covered with unicellular rhizoids. The cells of this **prothallus** are filled with a symbiotic fungus. The gametophyte is monoecious and often it develops vascular tissue.

The **antheridia** usually develop earlier than the archegonia.

These are spherical in outline with an antheridial jacket, which is single layer thick. Mature antheridia project above the gametophyte, and each one bears numerous spiral, multiflagellate sperms.

The **archegonia** are also projecting and formed from the superficial cells of the prothallus. The neck canal cells are probably two in number and within the venter there are ventral canal cell and egg cell.

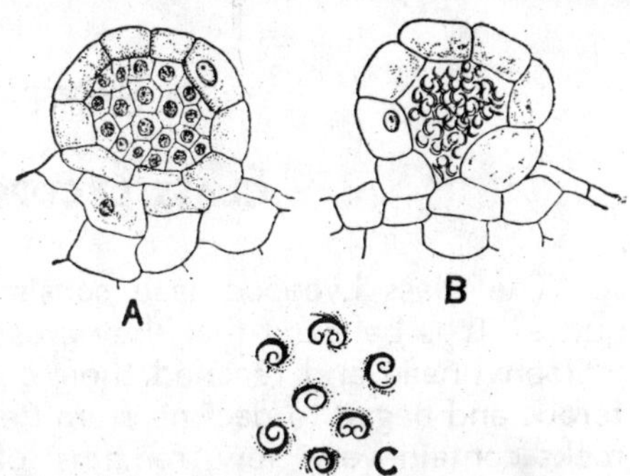

Fig. 314. *Psilotum*, A—B, Antheridium in different stages of development ; C, A few spermatozoids.

The new sporophyte

The development of the new sporophyte starts with the first division of the zygote, which is transverse, (*i.e.* a plane at right angles to the long axis of the archegonium) or very nearly so. From the outer part develops the axis, while the inner one gives rise to the *foot* of the embryo. This foot is very clearly distinguishable during the early stages of development. It enlarges downwards and sends out finger-like haustorial branches, which penetrate into the body of the adjoining gametophyte. Ultimately, when the young sporophyte becomes independent of the gametophyte for its food supply, the foot gets dissociated from the sporophyte and attaches itself to the gametophyte.

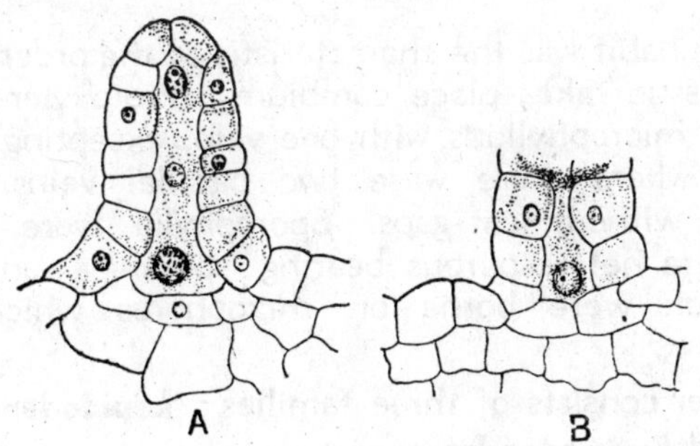

Fig. 315. *Psilotum*.
A—B, Archegonia in different stages of development.

CHAPTER II

CLASS LYCOPODINEAE

The Class Lycopodineae consists of an assemblage of antiquities. It is believed that they arose in the early Palaeozoic from Psilophytineae and reached their climax in the Middle Carboniferous and began to decline from Permian onwards ; the Mesozoic rocks contain very few remains of the ancient lycopods. The present-day flora is represented by only 5 genera : *Lycopodium*, *Phylloglossum**, *Selaginella*, *Stylites*. and *Isoetes*, all of which are insignificant herbs, while some of their ancestors were tall trees.

Sporophytes differentiated into stems, roots and leaves. Leaves microphyllous, arranged spirally in opposite pairs or in whorls (?) and without any leaf gaps. Protostelic, siphonostelic, or polystelic. Sporophylls with adaxial sporangia situated near the bases of the sterile regions, or they may occur in the strobili.

For the sake of convenience, the class Lycopodineae has been divided into 5 Orders : (1) **Lepidodendrales**, (2) **Lepidocarpales**†, (3) **Lycopodiales**, (4) **Selaginellales**, and (5) **Isoetales**, of which the first two Orders are found only in the fossil state.

ORDER 1. LEPIDODENDRALES

Tree-like habit was the characteristic of the order. Formation of secondary tissue takes place cambium. Protoxylem was exarch. Leaves were microphyllous with one vein, excepting some species of *Sigillaria* where there were two parallel veins, leaves were ligulate, but without leaf-gaps. Sporophylla were on strobilus. Members were heterosporous bearing sporangia on the adaxial surface. Roots were borne on rhizophores which secondarily thickened.

The order consists of three families : **Lepidodendraceae, Sigillariaceae** and **Bothrodendraceae.**

* Excepting *Phylloglossum* all other genera have been found in the fossil state.
† Prof. A.J. Eames includes *Lepidocorpales* along with *Lipidodendrales.*

Family 1. Lepidodendraceae

Plants were often tall trees. Trunk was a tall shaft that did not branch until some distance above the ground. Above the unbranched trunk there was a dichotomously branched crown, the smaller branches being clothed with simple linear leaves (up to 18 cm. in length). The trunk was attached to the soil by **stigmarian root system**. Most genera had secondary thickening of the stele, but certain species lacked a cambium. Stele was protostelic or siphonostelic. Protoxylem was exarch. The cortex consisted of different regions : (1) homogeneous inner cortex with leaf-traces, (*ii*) a secretory zone of large and small cells filled with dark substances, (*iii*) homogeneous middle cortex, (*iv*) the outermost cortex composed of alternate radial masses of thick- and thin-walled elements.

Fig. 316. *Stigmaria*.
tapering, dichotomously branched root.
Base of a lepidodendroid with a thick,

The family contains only 1 genus—*Lepidodendron*.

LEPIDODENDRON

(Fam. LEPIDODENDRACEAE)

Lepidodendron is the best known genus of the Palaeozoic and is with more than 100 species. It appeared in the Late Devonian, flourished most luxuriantly in the Carboniferous and probably declined during the Late Permian.

The sporophyte

The plant is a large tree with stigmarian root-system and a straight trunk, which remains unbranched for a considerable height and then gives rise to freely dichotomously dividing branches. The leaves are simple and deciduous, acicular to linear in shape, and ligulate. These are borne either spirally or in alternating whorls. The pyramidal leaf bases are persistent in nature and form the **leaf cushions,** which have got a great taxonomic importance. The leaf base possesses a single, small, median vascular strand, flanked on both

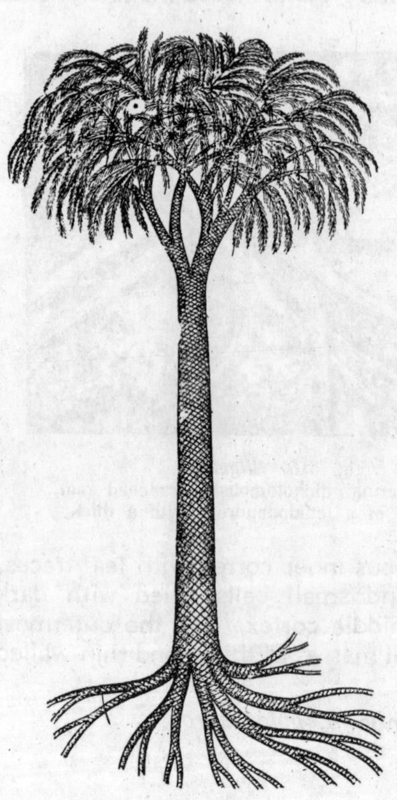

Fig. 317. *Lepidodendron* (after reconstruction), (*Redrawn after Hirmer*)

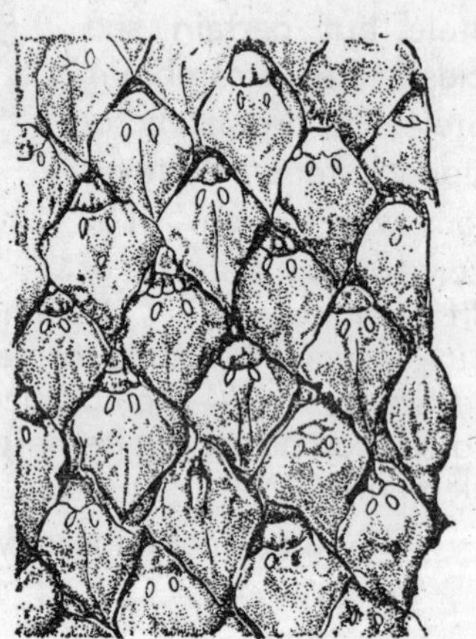

Fig. 318 *Lepidodendron*. A portion of the stem showing leaf cushions.

sides by a strand of parenchymatous cells forming the **perichnos.** The parichni run parallel to the vascular strands for some time but ultimately become lost in the mesophyll tissue ; these are supposed to be associated with the intake of air and its circulation through the body of the plant.

Internally, the stem can be differentiated into extrastelar and intrastelar regions. The cortex is very thick and is characteristically differentiated into : (1) a parenchymatous inner cortex, (2) a secreting zone, (3) a homogeneous middle cortex, similar to the inner one, and (4) an outer cortex composed of thin- and thick-walled cells. The stele is either a protostele or a siphonostele with exarch and polyarch xylem. In some cases, secondary growth has been recorded in the intrastelar region. The periderm is formed very early and may appear even before the intrastelar secondary thickening.

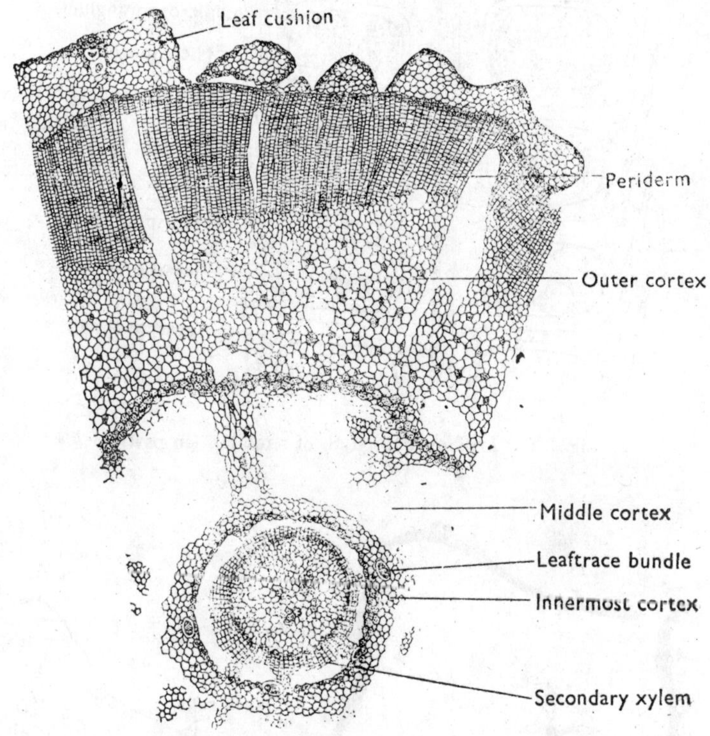

Fig. 319. *Lepidodendron*. T.S. of stem (in part).

Numerous fossil lepidodendroid cones have been discovered and these are usually referred to the form genus *Lepidostrobus*. The cones are cylindrical or elliptical in outline, about 3.30 cm. in length and 2.6 cm. in breadth ; these are usually slightly tapering both at the apex as well as at the base. The sporophylls are either spirally arranged or whorled, and standing out approximately at right angles from the central axis. Each sporophyll bears a ventral sporangium, whose wall is made up of a single layer of prism-shaped cells. The sporangia contain either microspores or megaspores.

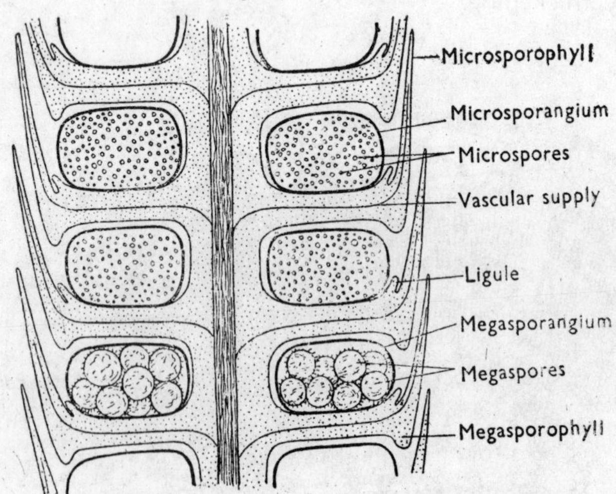

Fig. 320. *Lepidostrobus*, L.S. of strobilus (in part),

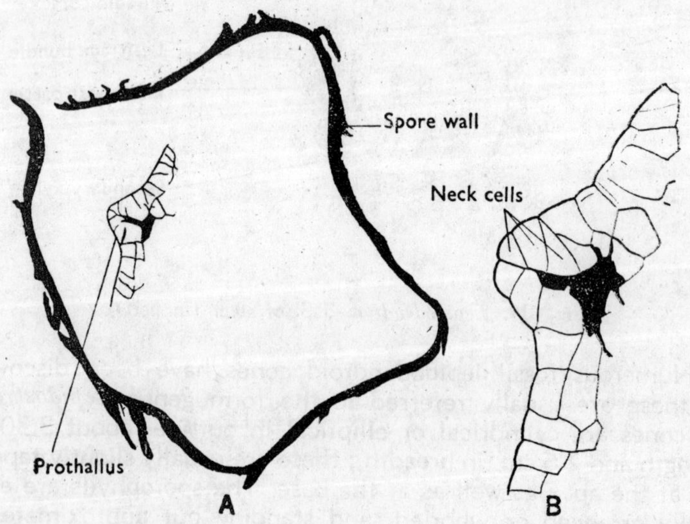

Fig. 321. *Lepidostrobus*. A, Female gametophyte ; B, An archigonium.

The gametophyte

No male gametophyte has yet been recorded, but Gordon (1910) discovered cellular female gametophytes bearing archegonia ; this suggests a possible relationship with the living *Selaginella.*

Family 2. Sigillariaceae

Trunk was sparingly branched and columnar. Leaves were ligulate with two-parallel veins and without leaf-gaps. Leaf-scars were in vertical sides and often lying between vertical ridges on the surface of the stem. Strobili were borne at the tips of short pendant fertile branches borne on transverse series below the vegetative branches. Micro- and megasporophylls were produced in a single strobilus.

The family contains only 1 genus—*Sigillaria.*

SIGILLARIA

(Fam. SIGILLARIACEAE)

Sigillaria. the 'seal tree', is another important Pálaeozoic lycopod found in Europe and America.

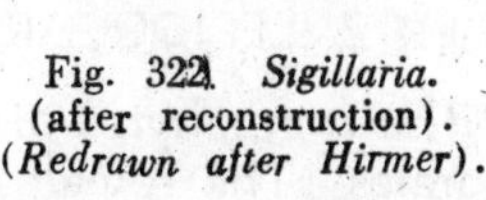

Fig. 322. *Sigillaria.* (after reconstruction). (*Redrawn after Hirmer*).

The sporophyte

The stem is arborescent like *Lepidodendron*, but branching is less profuse and the leaves are rather longer. In general appearance the plant looks somewhat like *Dracaena*, *Cordyline*, etc. The presence of the persistent leaf cushions in *Sigillaria*, as in *Lepidodendron*. is also a prominent feature ; the cushions of the former genus, however, are hexagonal or rounded and stand in more prominently raised vertical rows.

The species of *Sigillaria* are generally placed under two groups : (1) the **Eu-sigillariae** (plants possessing ribbed stems), and (2) the **Sub-Sigillariae** (plants without any ribs).

Anatomically, the general plan of construction of the stem of *Sigillaria* also resembles that of *Lepidodendron*. The primary xylem is either continuous or made up of strands and the protoxylem is exarch ; the tracheids are scalariform. A well-defined pith is always present. Secondary growth takes place both in the intrastelar as well as in the extrastelar regions. The tracheids of the secondary xylem are either scalariform or pitted.

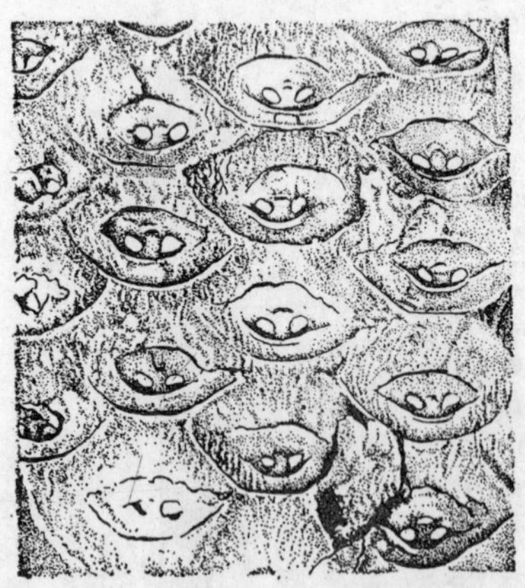

Fig. 323. *Sigillaria*, A portion of the stem showing leaf cushions.

Sigillariophylium, the leaf of *Sigillaria*, possesses double leaf traces (like the needles of some conifers) and stomata on the ventral surface.

There are two types of fructifications, the **Sigillariostrobus** and **Mazocarpon**, suggested to be the cones of *Sigillaria*. In Sigillariostrobus, as in *Lepidostrobus*, there is a central axis which bears a number of spirally-arranged or whorled sporophylls, each with a single adaxially borne sporangium. The cones are about 16-20 cm. long and all are heterosporus. The special feature of Mazocarpon is that there are 8 saucer-shaped megaspores, arranged in two rows within the megasporangium.

More than one spore, while still enclosed within the megasporangium, attain maturity and form prothallial tissue within, thus showing an advanced condition.

ORDER 2. LEPIDOCARPALES

The sporophytes of Lepidocarpales resembled those of Lepidodendrales. The remains were found in the Carboniferous.

The Order consists of 2 families : **Lepidocarpaceae** and **Miadesmiaceae.**

Family 1. Lepidocarpaceae

It is to be noted that in Lepidocarpaceae a seed-like structure was formed, but it is not regarded to be a true seed. The reasons are (*a*) no formation of pollen tube, (*b*) true integument absent, and (*c*) no resting period.

The family contains only 1 genus—*Lepidocarpon.*

LEPIDOCARPON

(Fam. LEPIDOCARPACEAE)

The genus with 3 species has been found only from the Carboniferous of Great Britain.

The sporophyte

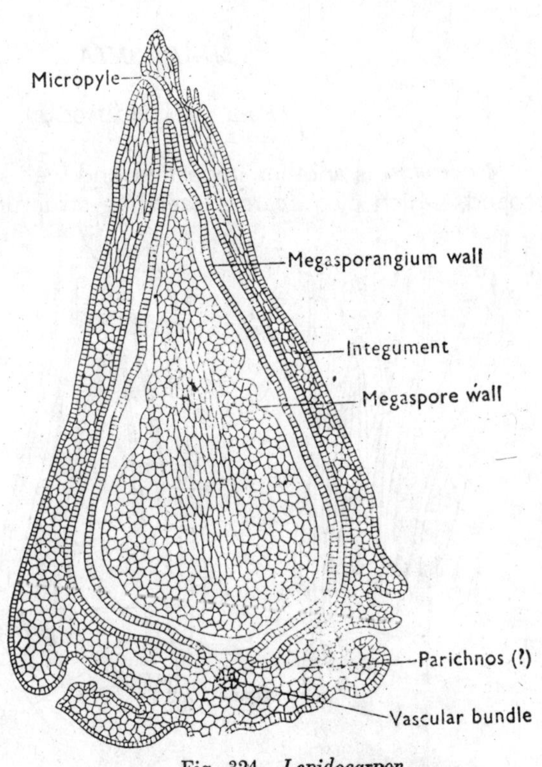

Fig. 324. *Lepidocarpon*. L.S. of a "seed".

The general appearance of the plant is similar to that of *Lepidodendron*. There are *Lepidostrobus*-like cones in which heterosporous sporangia are borne on the adaxial faces of the sporophylls. The tissue of the sporophyll lying beneath the mature megasporangium and flanking its two sides develops into an integument entirely surrounding the sporangium with a slit at its apex forming a micropyle - like structure. In a young megasporangium there are four megaspores, but in a mature one only of these develops and the other three degenerate.

The gametophyte

The solitary megaspore, while still enclosed within the megasporangium, develops the female gametophyte inside it. Nothing is known about fertilization. The whole structure, *i.e.*, the megasporangium, along with its permanently retained gametophyte and the integument, looks very much like a seed.

Family 2. Miadesmiaceae

This family occurred up the Carboniferous. It has many characters (both morphological and anatomical) similar to *Selaginella*. Like Lepidocarpaceae it has almost reached the seed-habit.

The family contains only 1 genus—*Miadesmia*.

MIADESMIA

(Fam. MIADESMIACEAE)

Miadesmia is another important and well-known Carboniferous lycopod, which also bears a seed-like structure.

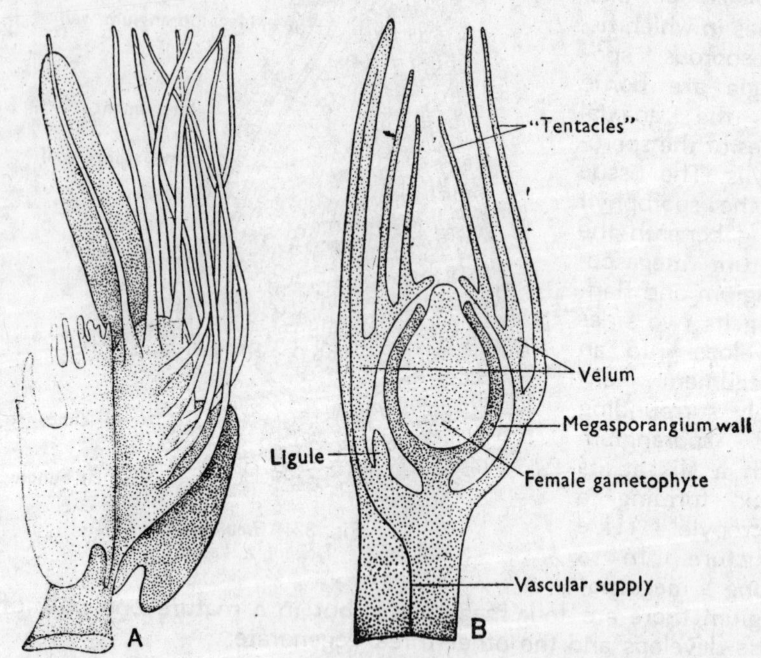

Fig. 325. *Miadesmia*, A, A megasporophyll : B, V.S. of the same.

The sporophyte

The plant is a *Selaginella*-like delicate herb, whose internal structure also resembles that of the living genus. The sporophylls are borne on lax strobili, but whether a strobilus bears both micro- and mega-sporophylls or one type of sporophyll only is not known. The megasporangium contains only one functional megaspore and no degenerating sister megaspores have yet been recorded. The sporophyll, as usual, by its upturning forms an elaborate, many-lobed, integument with a terminal micropyle, which is a rounded aperture in this case.

The gametophyte

The enclosed megaspore develops into a female gametophyte, which is never shed but remains permanently confined within the megasporangium, thus giving rise to an extremely seed-like structure.

ORDER 3. LYCOPODIALES

The members of the Order Lycopodiales are distinguished from other members of the Class Lycopodineae by being *homosporous* and having *eligulate* leaves. Sporophylls may or may not be aggregated into strobili. The sporangia are developed in the **eusporangiate** * fashion. Gametophytes are partly or entirely subterranean. Spermatozoids are typically *biflagellate*. Secondary thickening in stem or root is yet unknown.

The Order consists of *two* families : (1) **Protolepidodendraceae,** and (2) **Lycopodiaceae.**

Family Lycopodineae

Sporophyte herbaceous, eligulate bears microphyllous, foliage leaves and sporophylls similar or not, definite or no strobilus, homosporous, gametophyte partly or not subterranean, and nourished by phycomycetous fungi.

There are 3 genera (1) *Lycopodium.* (2) *Phylloglossum* and (3) *Lycopodites* (fossil)†

* Superficial group of 6-12 cells in the axil of a sporophyll may act as *sporangium initial,* which by repeated divisions ultimately forms the sporangium, Each of these cells divides by periclinal wall (*i.e.* parallel to the surface) forming rows of outer and inner cells. The inner cells, the *primary sporogenous cells,* by repeated divisions, give rise to the sporogenous tissue, while the outer cells ultimately form the wall of the sporangium consisting of a few layers of cell. This method of sporangium development is known as **eusporangiate** method and is characteristic of all vascular plants excepting the modern ferns. As opposed to this, the **leptosporangiate** method of development of sporangium is one in which a sporangium is developed from a solitary initial cell,

† It is to be noted that the Lycopodites is very similar to Lycopodium and only occurs in the upper Devonian.

LYCOPODIUM

(Fam. LYCOPODIACEAE)

Lycopodium, commonly known as 'club-moss' and 'ground pine', grows chiefly in tropical and subtropical forests but some species are also distributed in arctic and temperate regions.

The common Indian species are *L. hamiltonii*, *L. phlegmaria*, *L. cernuum*, *L. selago* and *L. clavatum*.

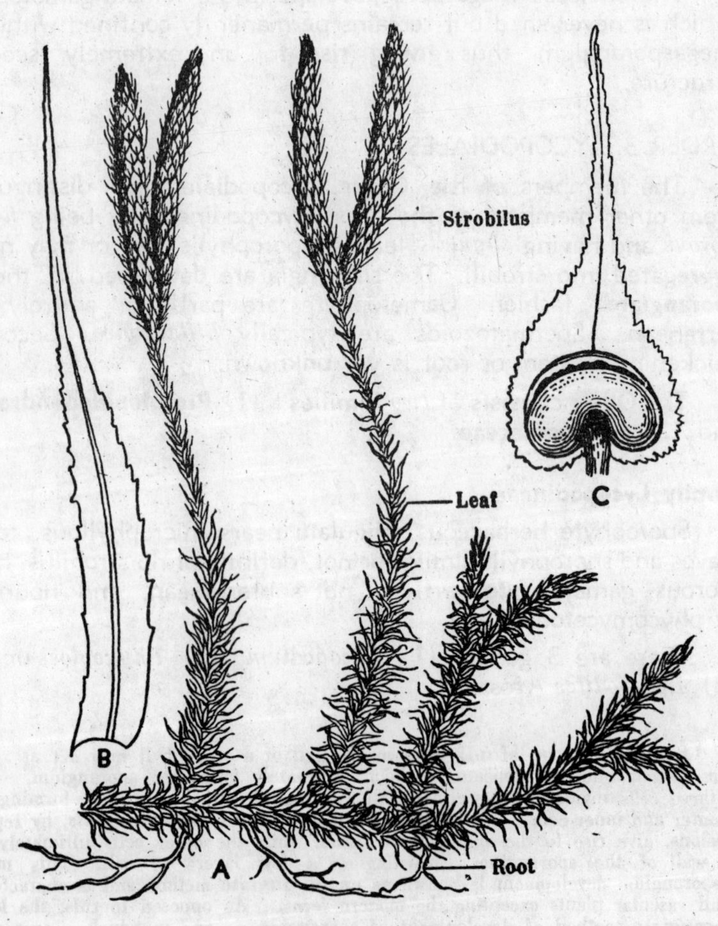

Fig. 326. ***Lycopodium.***
A, A portion of a plant ; B, A leaf ; C, A sporophyll with a sporangium.

The sporophyte

In habit, all species vary widely, but all have slender, weak-stemmed, comparatively small, herbaceous or shrubby sporophytes. Many species are somewhat prostrate with stems creeping above or below the surface of the soil. Other terrestrial species have upright or semi-erect stems, which later on become more or less horizontal. Some species may also be epiphytic with pendent bodies, while still others are twining to some extent.

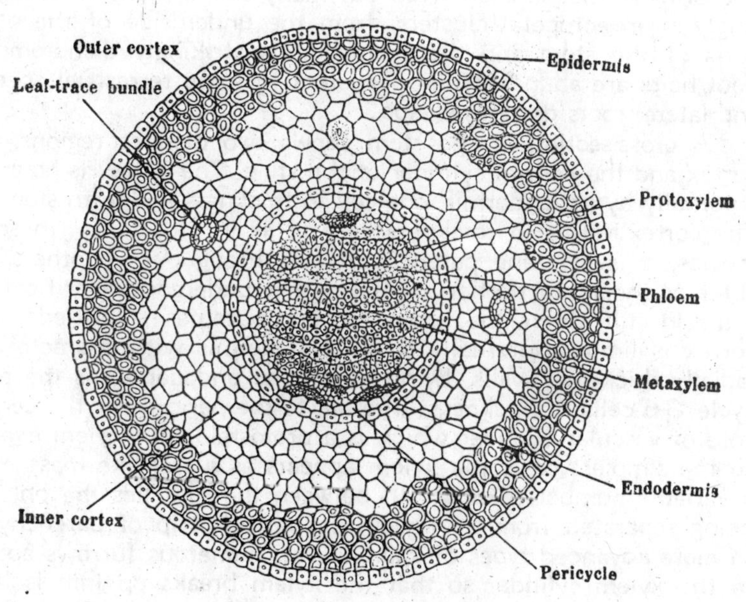

Fig. 327. *Lycopodium.*
Transverse section of the stem.

In the simplest case, the sporophyte has a simple stem covered with numerous, moss-like leaves, each bearing a single large sporangium on its upper side. In this sense *the whole sporophyte is a strobilus* (e.g. *L. selago. L. pitheyoides*, etc,), In more complex types, the sporophytes have much-branched stems whose lower leaves are sterile and act as foliage leaves, and this gradual sterilization process can be traced to more than one form, where the sporophyte is distinctly differentiated into a vegetative region bearing foliage leaves, and a reproductive region bearing the sporophylls. In such cases, the sporophylls are quite different in form from the foliage leaves and are localized and compacted to form a distinct strobilus (e.g. *L. clavatum*). These strobili are often separated from the vegetative body and are borne on slender stalks with rudimentary leaves.

Branching of the stem is characteristically dichotomous, the two branches of a forking may be equal or unequal. The leaves are very numerous, simple and small (usually 2-10 mm. long, sometimes up to 25-30 mm.), arranged in close spirals, whorls or opposite pairs, or the arrangement may be somewhat irregular. The primary root is short-lived but many adventitious roots arise, singly or in acropetal clusters, from the under side of the older parts of the stem and the branching is strikingly dichotomous. Root hairs are abundant and persistent in some terrestrial species and lateral roots do not develop.

A cross-section of the stem shows two distinct regions, the cortex and the central cylinder of the stele. The cortex is bounded externally by an epidermis, one cell in thickness and with stomata. The cortex varies in thickness as well as in structure. In some species, it is soft and parenchymatous throughout, in others the outer or the inner portion of the cortex undergoes sclerification, while in still others the entire cortex becomes sclerified. The cortex is limited internally by an endodermis with characteristic radially thickened walls. Lying within the endodermis is the pericycle, 3-6 cells in thickness. Internal to the pericycle is the central core of vascular cylinder which is a protostele with xylem exarch. In the simplest case, the xylem appears as a star-like mass, with a variable number of rays. In between the rays lies the phloem, being separated from the xylem by narrow strip of parenchyma. In more advanced types of sporophytes, numerous furrows appear in the xylem cylinder so that the xylem breaks up into isolated strands forming plate-like lobes or mesh-like mass, with included phloem bands.

Reproduction

Lycopodium reproduces both by vegetative and sexual methods

There are several means by which vegetative reproduction takes place : (1) Tips of lateral branches become flattened and with wing-like leaves, known as *bulbils* or *gemmae* annually fall to the ground, take roots and form new plants. (2) The rhizome progressively grows at the apex and its older part dies, the branches become separated and form new plants. (3) In some species during winter the entire plant dies, but the apical portion behaves as a resting bud. (4) In epiphytic species, portions of plant body may give rise to new plants. (5) Roots and detached leaves of bulbils can also give rise to new individuals.

Lycopodium is homosporous and the spores are produced within large-, short-stalked, reniform to somewhat subglobose sporangia, borne singly either in the axils or on the stem, a little above the sporophylls. The sporophylls are variable in form, size and colour in different species, sometimes resembling foliage leaves. These sporophylls usually become localized and aggregated to form *cones* or *strobili*, at the apex of the main stem or on lateral branches. The strobili are either stalked or sessile. The sporangium is eusporangiate in development. Within the jacket of the sporangium the *sporogenous tissue* is surrounded by a special nutritive layer known as **tapetum.** The cells of the sporogenous tissue ultimately cease to divide to form spore mother cells, each of which by reduction division gives rise to a **spore tetrad.** *With reduction division and formation of spores, the gametophytic or haploid generation begins.* Each spore shows a weak tri-radiate ridge and its wall is either smooth or shows honeycomb or net-like thickenings.

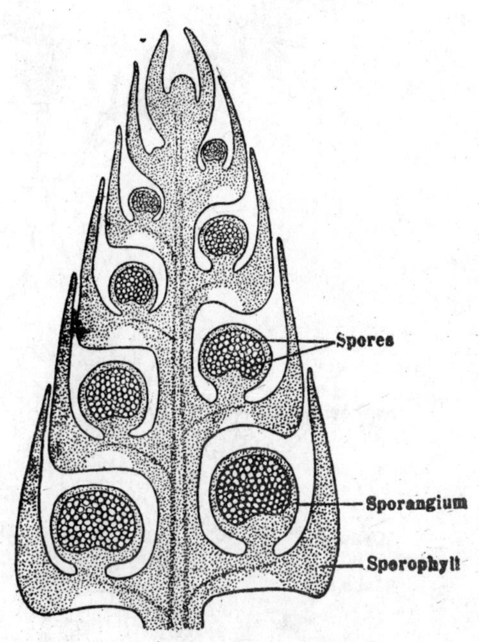

Fig, 328, *Lycopodium*. Longitudinal section of strobilus.

The gametophyte

When the spores are mature, a narrow transverse strip of cells (**stomium**) is gradually differentiated at the apex of the sporangium, which ruptures transversely and liberates the spores. Each spore, under favourable conditions, germinates and produces the gametophytic plant. There are two main types of gametophytes.

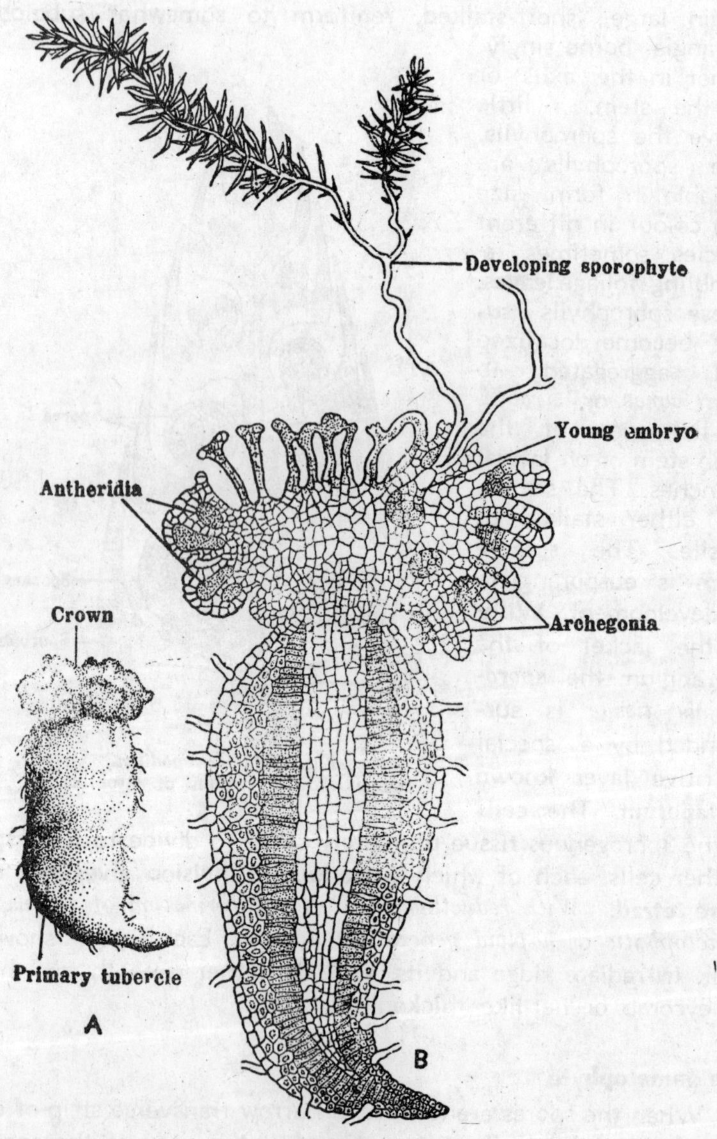

Fig. 329. *Lycopodium*.
A, A gametophyte ; B, Longitudinal section of the same showing a developing sporophyte.

In tropical species (*L. cernuum*) usually the spores after liberation germinate quickly and form short-lived gametophytes, on the surface of the ground, which are very small, green (excepting the basal portion), somewhat cylindrical to ovoid bodies with lobed apices. In other cases, especially in creeping and epiphytic species (*L. clavatum*), the spores after a shorter or longer period of rest (3-8 years) germinate and form non-green, subterranean, somewhat tuberous or carrot-shaped, much larger gametophytes, sometimes much convoluted, and these grow to maturity very slowly, taking several years (6-15 years) and nourishing the young sporophytes. In other species, transitional forms occur and these gametophytes are partly subterranean with a green, lobed, aerial portion (**crown**) bearing the sex organs. Usually, both types of gametophytes are associated with an endophytic fungus forming a **mycorrhiza**, which is a prominent feature of the gametophyte.

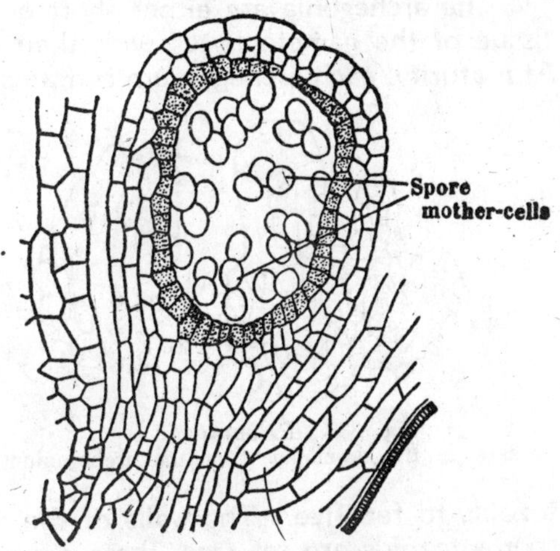

Fig. 330. *Lycopodium*. Longitudinal section of the sporangium containing spore mother cells.

The gametophyte of *Lycopodium* is monoecious (homothallic) and numerous sex organs, antheridia and archegonia, are borne either on the crown, or in between its lobes, or on the central cushion in flattened types of the gametophytes.

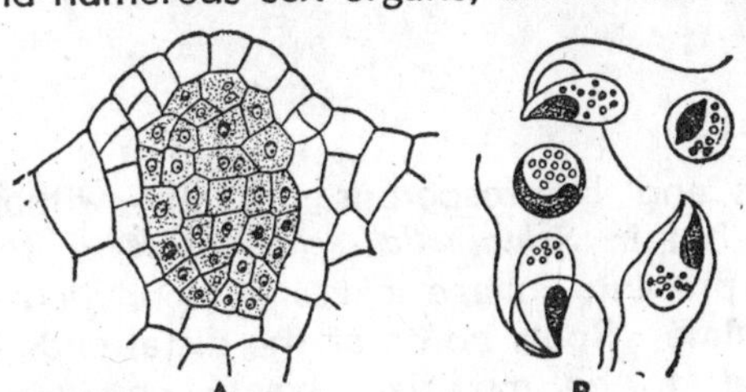

Fig. 331. *Lycopodium*. A, An antheridium ; B, Spermatozoids.

The antheridia vary in size, shape and number of spermatozoids and either project slightly or remain wholly embedded within the gametophytic tissue. There are many spermatozoid mother cells within the single-layered antheridial wall and each gives rise to a biflagellate (rarely three) spermatozoid resembling the spermatozoid of Bryophyta.

The archegonia are either short or long and embedded in the tissue of the gametophytes with their necks protruding upwards. At maturity, each archegonium contains an egg cell, a ventral canal cell and 6, sometimes 10-13, canal cells (but only one neck canal cell in shorter archegonium).

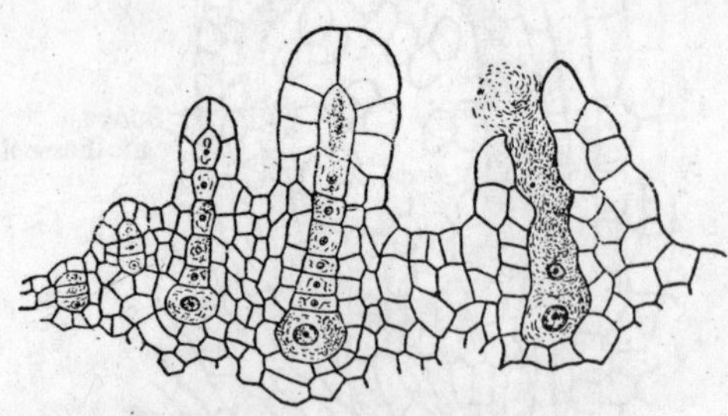

Fig. 332. *Lycopodium*. Stages in the development of the archegonium,

When the archegonium attains maturity its neck canal cells and ventral canal cell disintegrate forming a passage open to the ovum for the spermatozoids to fertilize. The walls of the antheridium breaks up, the spermatozoids are set free, these are washed to the archegonium and one of them, finding its way through the neck, ultimately fertilizes the ovum. The fertilized ovum soon covers itself with a wall and forms the **oospore.** *With fertilization and formation of oospore, the sporophytic or diploid generation begins.*

The new sporophyte

The oospore, by repeated divisions, gives rise to an embryo consisting of a *suspensor cell*, an absorbing organ called the *foot*, the stem, a leaf and a root belated in development. From this embryo the young sporophyte gradually develops and this may be supported and nourished by the gametophyte for several years. In some cases several young sporophytes may be borne simultaneously on the same gametophyte.

ORDER 4. SELAGINELLALES

Sporophyte herbaceous and heterosporous. Usually without any secondary thickening, but in *Selaginella selaginoides* a few secondary xylem elements present. Foliage leaves microphyllous—all alike, or dimorphic, ligulate. Roots borne at the distal ends of the branches (considered to be modified axes), known as *rhizophores*. Sporophylls always aggregated into well-organized strobili. Vegetative portions of micro-and mega-sporophylls alike, but micro-and mega-sporangia differing in size ; sporangia developing in eusporangiate fashion. Spermatozoids biflagellate,

There is only *one** family included under this Order : **Selaginellaceae.**

Family Selaginellaceae

The female gametophyte escapes partly from the megasporangium at some stage of the developments.

It contains 2 genera : (1) *Selaginella* (living) and (2) *Selaginellites* (extinct).

SELAGINELLA

(Fam. SELAGINELLACEAE)

Most species of *Selaginella* inhabit damp forests of tropical climates and are distributed all over the world ; some species also grow in the temperate regions. These are found in the hills and are abundantly cultivated in private gardens. Some are xerophytic and grow on rocky cliffs or dry sandy soil. They are mostly perennial, a few are small, delicate annuals.

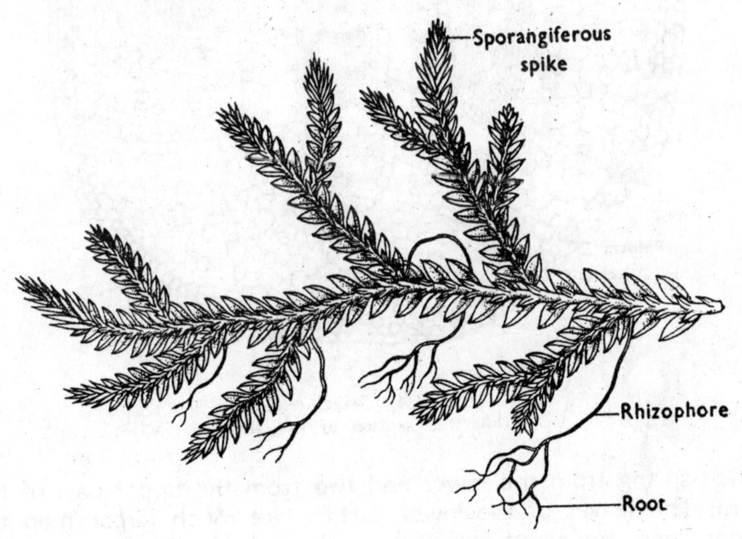

Fig. 333. A portion of plant body of *Selaginella*.

* According to some authorities the family Miadesmiaceae should belong to the Order Selaginellales instead of Lepidocarpales.

The common Indian species of *Selaginella* are *S. rupestris*, *S. pentagona*, *S. proniflora*, *S. semichordata* and *S. megaphylla*.

The sporophyte

In general appearance, they are usually long, slender, much-branched, dorsiventral, creeping stems. All forms branch freely, chiefly in one plane, and the branching is in most cases dichotomous or pseudo-monopodial.

The stems are thickly clothed with numerous small, more or less ovate leaves, usually of two distinct kinds : some large and some small, arranged usually in four longitudinal rows, two of

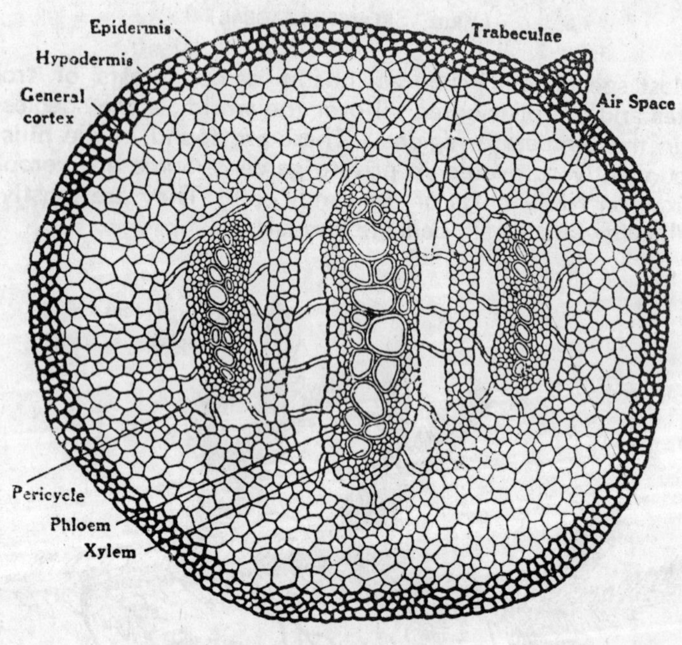

Fig. 334, *Selaginella.*
Transverse section of the stem.

which spring from the lower and two from the upper part of the stem. The leaves of the lower surface are much larger than the upper ones, one small leaf and one large leaf arise at each node. At the base of the ventral surface of the leaf, there is a membraneous **ligule** which is characteristic of the *Selaginella.*

The roots are mostly adventitious, because the first root dies early. The branching of the roots is dichotomous in alternate planes. At each ramification of the stem, a root-like organ, the **rhizophore,** is developed, which on reaching the soil produces the roots there.

Morphology of rhizophore

Three views have been put forward regarding the morphological nature of the rhizophore.

(*a*) *Root nature*

Rhizophores resemble the roots being positively geotropic and leafless, in having anatomical structure-like root and species with polystelic stem shows monostelic rhizophore, but they differ from the roots in having no root-caps and root-hairs and being exogenous in origin.

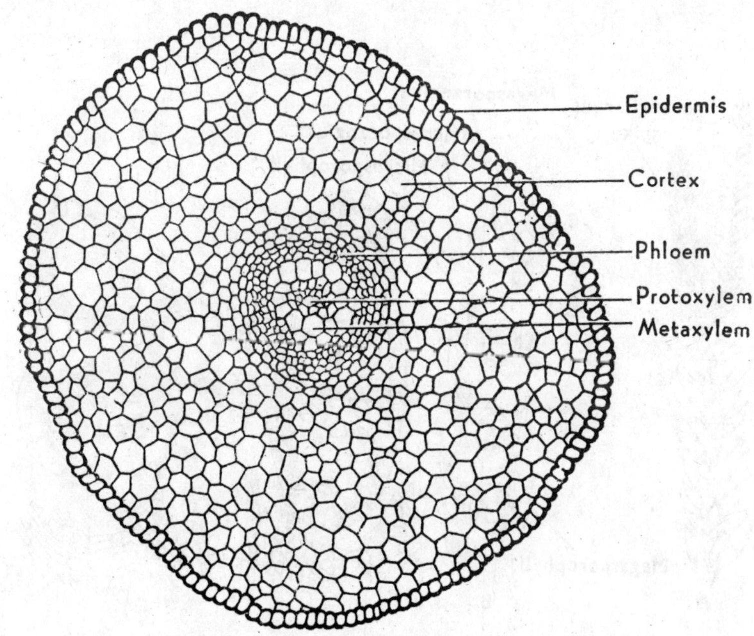

Fig. 335. *Selaginella.* T.S. of a rhizophore.

(*b*) *Stem nature* (Bruchmann, 1905)

Rhizophores resemble stems in being exogenous in origin, lack of root-caps and root-hairs, position definite in relation to stem, i.e., at basal dichotomy, and when decapitated develop sometimes leafy shoots.

(c) *Organs suigeneris* (Goebel 1905, Bower 1906, 1935)

Rhizophores are organs which are neither stems nor roots.

A cross-section of the stem shows two regions clearly differentiated into the cortex and the stele or steles. The cortex is many-layered consisting of either entirely thin-walled parenchyma or the outermost part of it being thick-walled and highly lignified (**sclerified parenchyma**), with or without intercellular spaces and is bounded on the outside by a single-layered epidermis, consisting of thick-walled cells and with a cuticle. The number of meristele ranges from one to three or more, each of which is surrounded by an air-space, which is bridged by radially elongated cells with prominent casparian strips, the **trabeculae,** which represent the endodermis. Surrounding each meristele there is a single layer of pericycle consisting of conspicuous parenchyma cells. The vascular bundles are hadrocentric ; the xylem is exarch and diarch.

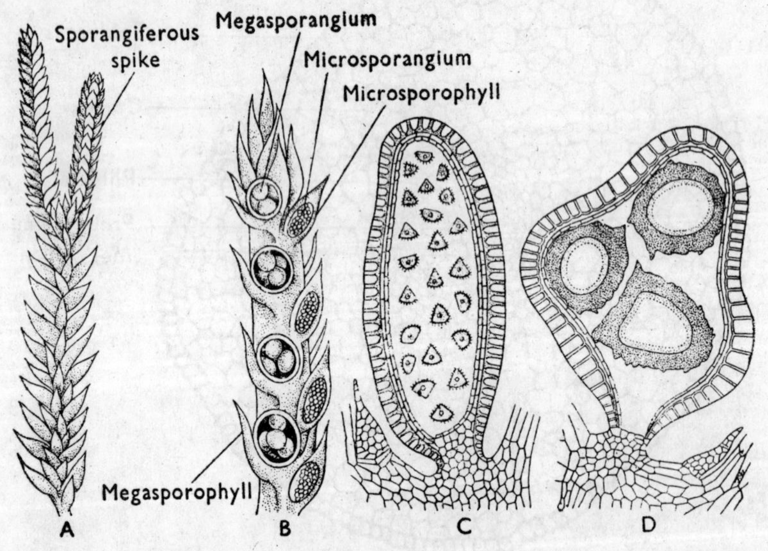

Fig. 336. *Selaginella.* A, Sporangiferous spike ; B, V. S. of the same ; C, Microsporangium ; D, Megasporangium.

A transverse section of the rhizophore shows an epidermis and a well-developed cortex enclosing the stele. The endodermis is not clearly marked out. There is a solitary protoxylem and the phloem entirely encircles the xylem.

Selaginella is heterosporous, because the asexual reproductive units, the spores, are of two kinds ; the smaller ones are **microspores** and the larger ones are **megaspores**, which are produced in different kinds of sporangia. The sporangia are mostly reniform or ovoid, sometimes flattened and shortly stalked. The two kinds of sporangia differ greatly in size, the **meagasporangia** being much larger than the **microsporangia.** The sporophylls bearing megasporangia are called **megasporophylls** and those bearing microsporangia are called **microsporophylls.** The sporophylls, which are nearly of equal size, are generally collected into more or less distinct, four-angled **cone** or **sporangiferous spike or strobilus.** These strobili are terminally situated at the apices of the branches. Each strobilus usually consists of both types of sporophylls, but in some species only one type of sporophylls may occur. The order of arrangement of the two types of sporophylls is variable in different species. Each megasporophyll bears in its axil a megasporangium within which occurs *only one functional megaspore mother cell* and it gives rise to four megaspores* due to reduction division. On the contrary, each microsporophyll bears in its axil a microsporangium containing *many microspore mother cells*, each of which produces four microspores due to reduction division, so that many microspores occur in each microsporangium. Both types of spores are tetrahedral and the wall shows a tri-radiate ridge and ornamentations. *With reduction division and formation of spores, the gametophytic or haploid generation begins.*

The gametophyte

Male gametophyte. The microspores, when still included within the microsporangium, begin to germinate but are ultimately set free by transverse rupture of the sporangium wall. The result of germination of each microspore is a **male prothallus (prothallial cell)** which is extremely reduced to a single cell.

It bears the so-called rudimentary *antheridium* (the *primary spermatogenous cells*—four in number) *being surrounded by a jacket of sterile cells* (*jacket cells*) and the whole remain included within the spore wall. From the primary spermatogenous cells about 128 to 256 *spermatozoid mother cells* are produced. Biflagellate spermatozoids are developed from the spermatozoid mother cells of the so-called antheridium and these ultimately float freely in the

---

* Occasionally 8 to 40 megaspores are found in a megasporangium.

cavity of the spore-wall. The spore wall bursts and liberates the spermatozoids in the surrounding film of water.

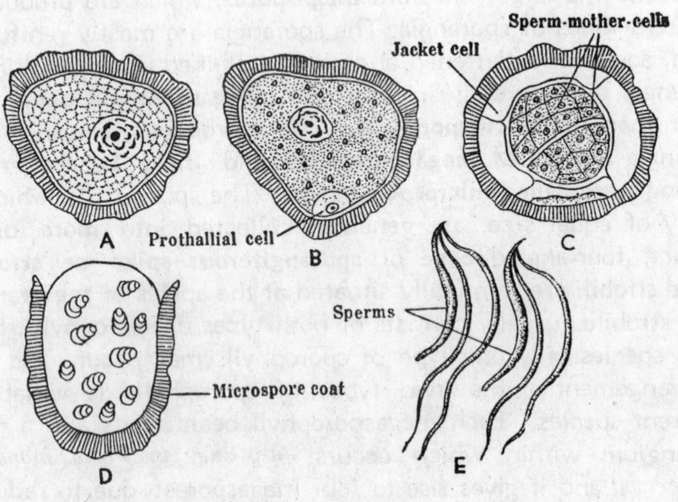

Fig. 337. *Selaginella.*
A—D, Successive stages in the development of male gametophyte and formation of spermatozoids ; E, Two spermatozoids.

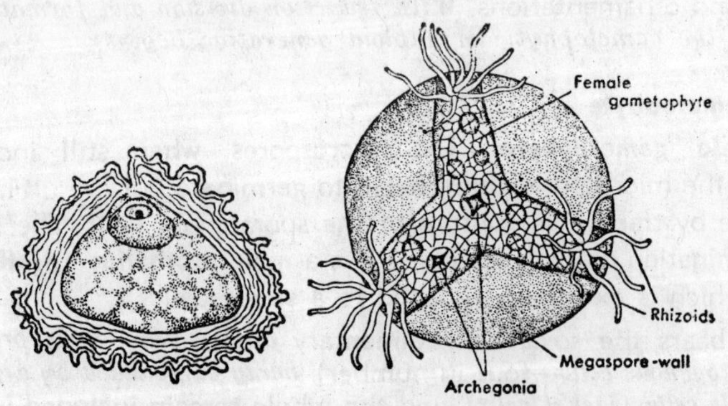

Fig. 338. A megaspore of *Selaginella* in section.

Fig. 339. Megaspore of *Selaginella* showing the female gametophyte exposed through the tri-radiate ridge.

Female gametophyte. Similarly megaspores germinate before they are set free from the megasporangium. On germination, the spore wall does not burst immediately and there follow within it free nuclear divisions forming a large number of nuclei, which are distributed in the general mass of cytoplasm surrounding a large

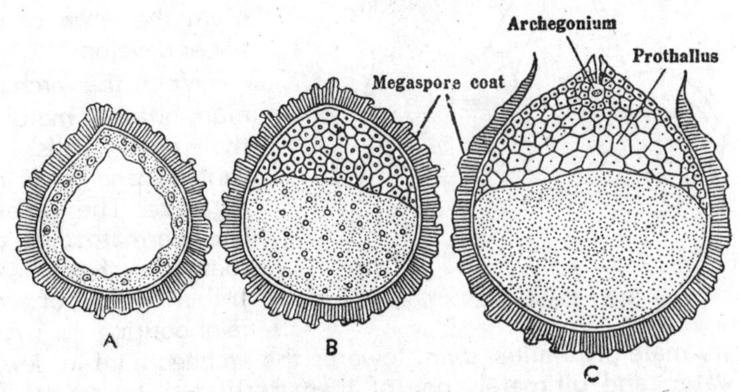

Fig. 340. *Selaginella.*
A—C, Stages in the development of female gametophyte and formation of archegonium.

central vacuole. As the nuclei increase in number, the cytoplasmic layer becomes thicker and the vacuole becomes smaller and smaller until it is completely filled up with cytoplasm. Wall formation about the nuclei follows from the periphery near the apical region (towards the tri-radiate ridge) forming a tissue which gradually extends inwards. In some cases, after forming a tissue consisting of 3-10 layers of cells from the periphery, the wall formation stops temporarily and the inner wall of the lowermost layer of cells becomes thickened to form so-called **diaphragm,** which separates the peripheral tissue from the non-cellular portion. The megaspores, at about this stage, are liberated from the megasporangium and the wall of each megaspore ultimately bursts along the tri-radiate ridge exposing the archegonia and part of the female gametophyte. The female gametophyte then becomes green and also develops rhizoids, which come out through the tri-radiate fissure. The female gameto-

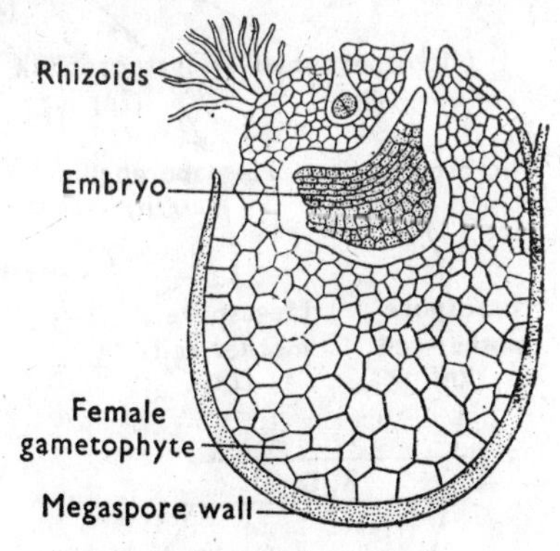

Fig. 341. *Selaginella.*
A longitudinal section through the female gametophyte showing the embryo sporophyte.

phyte, thus ultimately becomes independent of the sporophyte but not free from the megaspore, being still enclosed within spore wall.

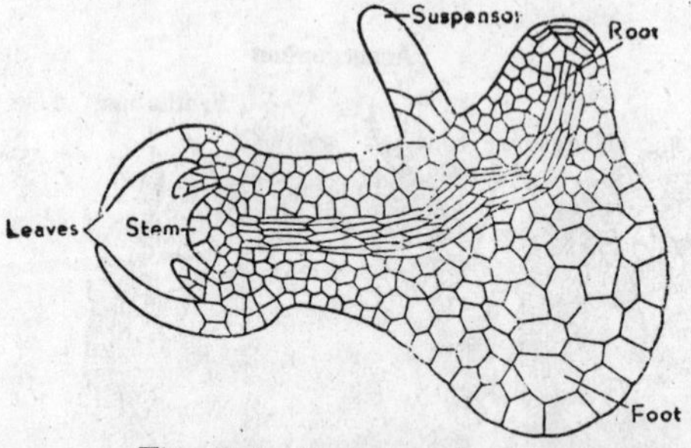

Fig. 342. Embryo of *Selaginella*.

Within each archegonium the *ovum* or *oosphere* develops.

When the archegonium attains maturity, the neck cells and ventral canal cells disorganize. The biflagellate spermatozoids, discharged from the antheridium of the neighbouring a rudimentary male prothallus, swim towards the archegonium in dew or rain water, and ultimately one of them fertilizes the ovum. The fertilized ovum, on secreting a wall around itself, becomes an **oospore.** *With fertilization and formation of oospore, the sporophytic or diploid generation begins.*

Life cycle

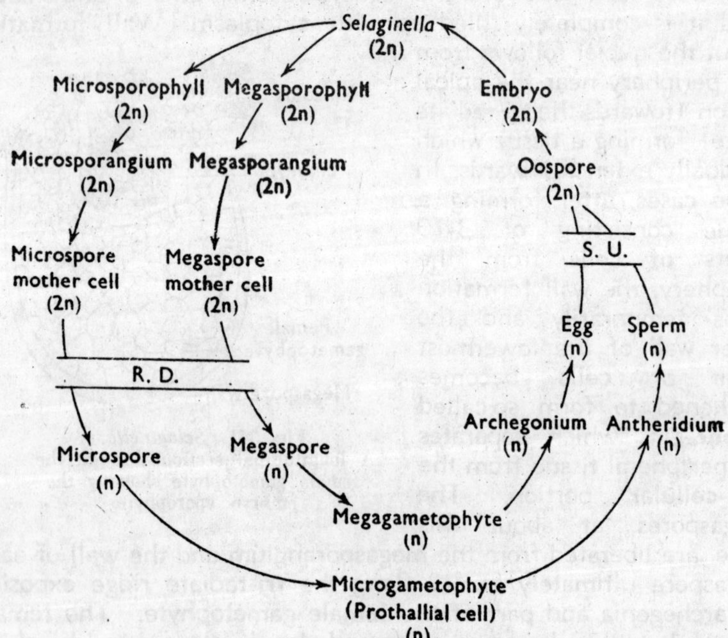

Fig. 343. Life cycle of *Seleginella.*

The new sporophyte

The oospore gradually gives rise to an embryo possessing a stem, two cotyledons, a foot, a root, and a suspensor, and from this embryo the *Selaginella* plant is derived.

ORDER 5. ISOETALES

Sporophyte herbaceous, rarely small trees, heterosporous. Massive rhizophore at the base of the stem. Leaves microphyllous and ligulate. Sporophylls aggregated into strobili, or lax. Sporangia incompletely trabeculated, and developed in eusporangiate fashion. Spermatozoids, in the living genera, multiflagellate. A special type of secondary growth noted in the axis of *Isoetes*.

There are *two* families belonging to this Order : (1) **Pleuromeiaceae**, and (2) **Isoetaceae.**

Family 1. Pleuromeiaceae

Sporophyte had an upright unbranched stem. Foliate leaves were restricted at the apex. Single strobilus was borne at the tip. The base of the stem was supported on a massive rhizophore which were provided with short arms.

It contains only 1 genus—*Pleuromeia*.

PLEUROMEIA

(Fam. PLEUROMEIACEAE)

Pleuromeia is a plant of the Middle Triassic and has been recorded from Europe and Eastern Asia.

The sporophyte

The stem is an unbranched erect trunk, about 2 metres high and with a girth of about 10 cm. The upper portion of the axis is thickly covered with long, linear-lanceolate, spirally arranged leaves, each having a prominent double mid vein and a broad base bearing ligule. On the other hand, the lower portion of the axis bears innumerable spirally arranged leaf scars. The base of the stem is divided dichotomously into four, six or eight short and thick lobes, covered with rootlets as in *Isoetes* and *Lepidodendron*.

In the subaerial portion of the axis the stele is an actinostele with exarch protoxylem. The secondary thickening is noted in the extra-stelar region only, where a thick periderm is produced.

Pleuromeia is heterosporous, two kinds of spores being borne by the plant : the reniform microspores and the tetrahedral megaspores. The spores are borne within the sporangia, which in their turn are borne apparently on the abaxial side of almost equal-sized

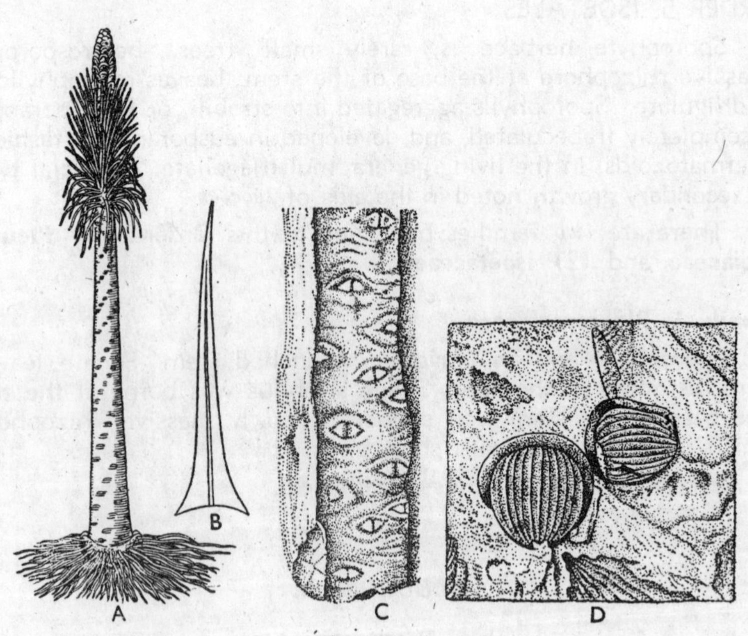

Fig. 344. *Pleuromeia.*
A, Plant (after reconstruction) ; B, Leaf ; C, A portion of stem showing leaf scars ; D, Sporophyll seen from above. (*Redrawn after Hirmer*),

sporophylls. The sporophylls, which are either oval and without any tip, or reniform or circular, are aggregated together on the axis giving rise to a solitary terminal cone.

Family 2. Isoetaceae

Sporophyta is corm-like, not externally differentiated into axis and rhizophore. Sporophylls are not borne in strobili. Leaves are ligulate. Members are heterosporous. Spermatozoids are multi-flagellate.

It contains 2 genera : (1) *Isoetes* (living) and (2) *Isotiles* (fossil, Lower Cretaceous).

ISOETES

(Fam. ISOETACEAE)

A great majority of the species of *Isoetes*, commonly known as 'quillworts' are hydrophytes which grow in water or on swampy lands.

A few species, however, grow in habitats that are completely dry for greater part of the year. The common Indian species of *Isoetes* are *I. coromandeliana*, *I. sampathkumaranii*, *I. indica*, etc.

The sporophyte

Isoetes suggests the appearance of a tufted grass, which consists of a very short, two- or three-lobed, tuberous corm densely covered by rosette of overlapping bases of stiff awl-shaped leaves. From the lower surface of the corm many dichotomously branched roots develop. The leaves are unique in structure, being arranged in a close spiral on the upper surface of the corm. *Each leaf is a sporophyll*, the outermost and lowermost leaves being sterile ; successively within these are sporophylls with mature and immature sporangia. In this sense *the entire plant body suggests the construction of a strobilus*. Each leaf consists of a basal sporangium-bearing region and a terminal foliage region. The awl-shaped foliage portion of the leaf contains within it four cylindrical air chambers, which may be transversely septate at intervals.

At the junction of the blade and basal portion of the leaf, there appears on the adaxial side a **ligule** being socketed in a small pit. Below

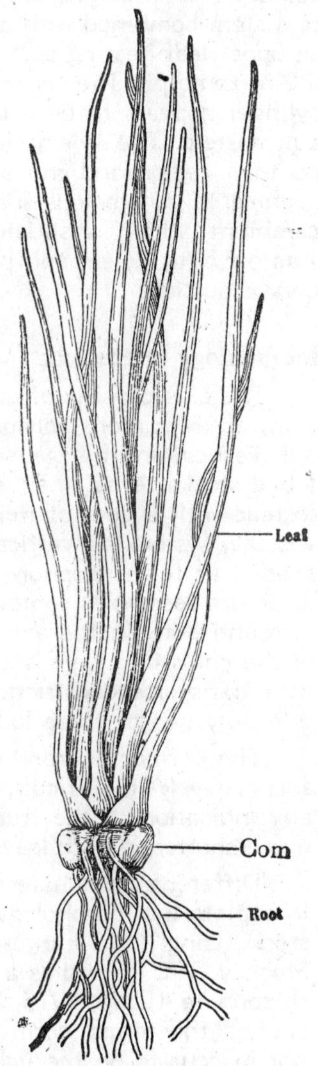

Fig. 345, *Isoetes*, An entire plant.

this ligule the broad sporangium-region occurs. There is a single flattened sporangium on the adaxial face of each leaf. This sporangium is situated within a depression in the leaf-base and is more or less completely or incompletely shut off from the outside by a curtain of tissue (**velum**) arising just below the ligule.

The morphology of the corm has been interpreted variously. It has been described as an erect rhizome ; as a stock ; as a stem ; as a stem combined with a stigmarian type of rhizophore ; and as an upper leaf bearing part, the stem, and a lower root-bearing part, the rhizomorph. The corm is so much compressed that the vascular cylinder appears to be a little more than a vascular plate and is a **protostele.** The xylem elements, however, do not completely fill up their region and the phloem elements are not completely recognizable. Anomalous secondary growth takes place by means of cambium, which is situated outside the phloem. The cambium cuts off both xylem and phloem elements inside, while secondary cortex outside.

Morphology of the axis

The axis consists of an upper leaf-bearing part—the stem, and a lower rhizophore portion from basal part of which roots come out, vertical and transverse sections of two-lobed as well as three-lobed stocks reveal their real nature. The central cylinder is protostelic with a core of mingled tracheids and parenchyma. The vascular system is a vertical cylinder at the stem portion and spade-shaped at the rhizophore portion of the corm. The entire axial structure resembles somewhat a chopper. Occasionally dichotomy is found both in the axis and rhizophore. Externally the division of the corm into stem and rhizophore can be seen in some cases, as a transverse constriction near the middle, sometimes the axis is deeply two or three lobed.

The correct interpretation of the morphological nature of the axis of *Isoetes* is difficult, because the external form does not give any indication of the true morphological nature. The axis being much shortened both leaves and roots are brought together.

Different views have been just forwarded by different workers to explain the morphology of the axis. The axis has been called a stock (Lang. 1915), interpreted as a stem (Scott & Hill, 1903 and Stockey, 1909), and as a stem, combined with stigmarian type of rhizophore (Lang, 1915, West and Takida, 1915). Many workers applied the terms 'corms' and 'rhizophore' which are considered not inaccurate on the light of recent anatomical researches. The exact interpretation rests upon the anatomy of the vascular system.

Isoetes is heterosporous. Both microspores and megaspores are produced in different types of sporangia, microsporangia and megasporangia, borne on microsporophylls and megasporophylls respectively. The method of development of both types of sporangia is somewhat alike in early stages. Within each sporangium a large mass of *sporogenous tissue* (up to 10,000—15,000 cells) is developed. At this stage the differences resulting in heterosporous conditions start. In those sporangia, which are destined to become microsporangia, differentiation of the sporogenous tissue begins. Some of the cells of the sporogenous tissue form alternating plates of sterile cells (**trabeculae**) across the sporangium with fertile

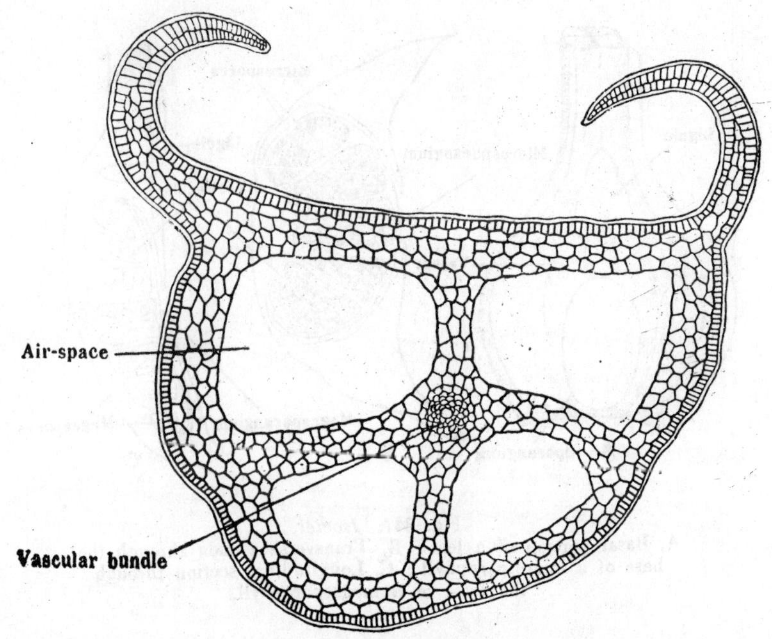

Fig. 346. *Isoetes,* Transverse section of leaf.

cells. which function as microspore mother cells. In those sporangia which are to become megasporangia, the trabeculae appear to be more massive and out of the thousands of sporogenous cells only 42-75 megaspore mother cells are fertile, others performing nutritive function. Reduction division of the spore mother cells follows and from each four spores are produced with the initiation of the gametophytic or haploid generation. The total output of microspores in a single microsporangium is 15,000-300,000 and that of megaspores in a single megasporangium is 150-300. At maturity, the sporangia are indehiscent in most cases and both types of spores are ultimately liberated by the death and decay of the sporophylls.

The gametophytes

Male gametophyte. The microspores, after liberation, germinate immediately and form male gametophytes within a few days. The nucleus of each microspore divides and the microspore is divided asymmetrically into a small **prothallial cell** and a large **antheridial initial cell.** The prothallial cell remains undivided, but

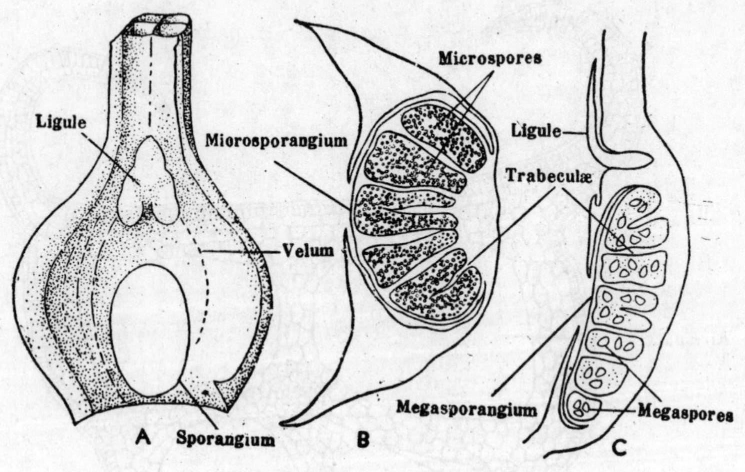

Fig. 347. *Isoetes.*
A, Basal portion of a leaf ; B, Transverse section through the base of a microsporophyll ; C, Longitudinal section through the base of a megasporophyll.

the antheridial initial divides repeatedly and ultimately forms a so-called rudimentary *antheridium*, consisting of an outer jacket layer of four cells and four inner spermatozoid mother cells. Each spermatozoid mother cell is ultimately metamorphozed into a large, spirally coiled, multiflagellate spermatozoid. The prothallial cell and the four jacket cells distintegrate and the spermatozoids are ultimately liberated by the decay of the spore wall.

Female gametophyte. Each megaspore germinates and forms a female gametophyte and its mode of development resembles that of *Selaginella* with the following differences :

The germination starts with a series of free nuclear divisions and a conspicuous central vacuole is never formed in the protoplast (as in *Selaginella*) in any stage of development. The nuclei gradually become more numerous in the apical portion of the multinucleate gametophyte and an apical tissue is formed at this

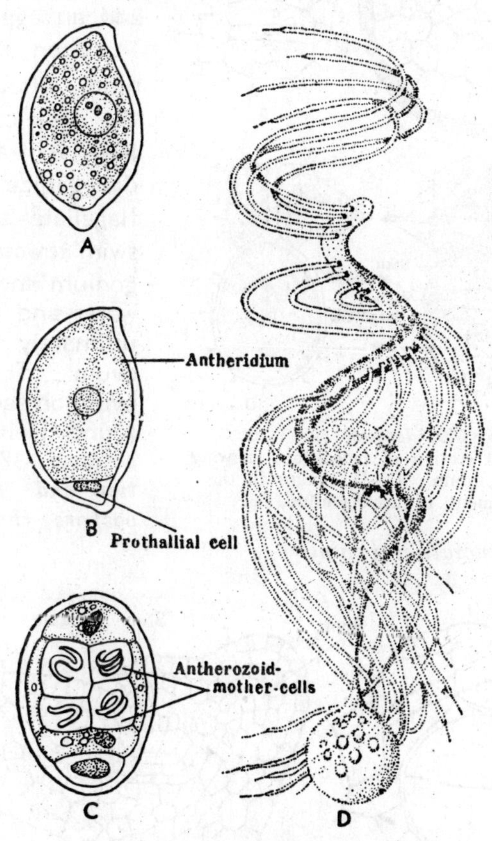

Fig. 348. *Isoetes*.
A—D, Stages in the development of antherozoid.

stage. The lower multinucleate portion of the gametophyte ultimately becomes cellular, but this process may be considerably delayed till the development of an adult embryo. The first-formed apical prothallial tissue is exposed by cracking of the spore wall along the tri-radiate ridge and is devoid of chlorophyll. The gametophyte does not protrude through the megaspore wall, but may

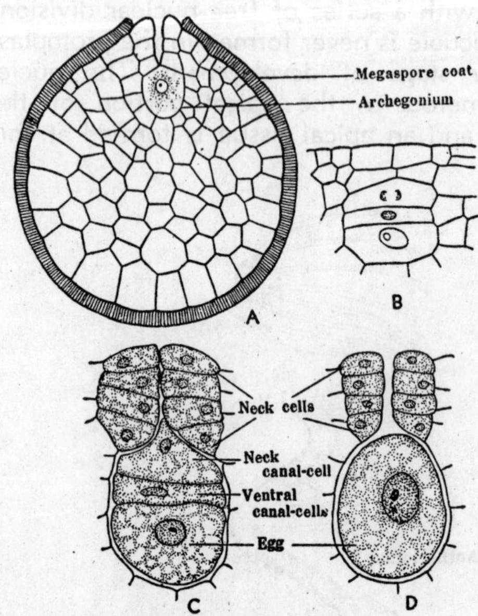

Fig. 349. *Isoetes*.
A. Longitudinal section of megaspore showing an archegonium ; B—D, Stages in the development of archegonium.

produce numerous rhizoids. The archegonium is broad and short, and consists of a single uninucleate neck canal cell, a ventral canal cell and an egg.

When the archegonium attains maturity the neck canal cell and the ventral canal cell disorganize. The multiflagellate spermatozoids swim towards the archegonium in dew or rain water and one of them ultimately fertilizes the ovum. The fertilized ovum on secreting a wall round itself becomes an *oospore*. *With fertilization and formation of oospore, the sporophytic or diploid generation begins.*

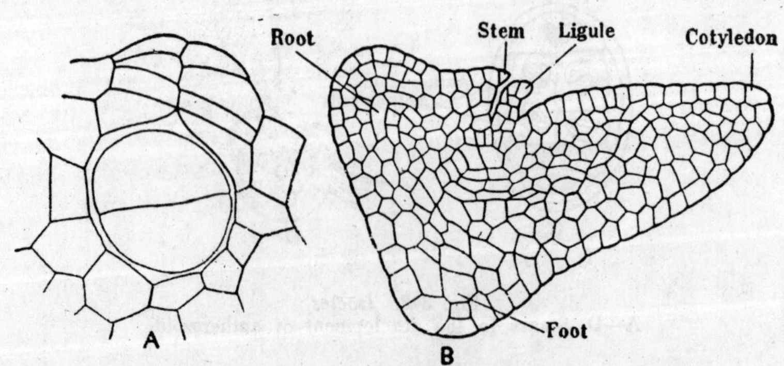

Fig. 350. *Isoetes*.
A, A developing embryo ; B, Developing sporophyte.

The new sporophyte

The oospore gradually gives rise to an embryo possessing a massive foot, a root, the stem and a leaf (cotyledon) with a ligule. It is a peculiar feature that the embryo of *Isoetes* has no suspensor.

Of the various parts of the embryo the stem appears to be a belated member. From this embryo the *Isoetes* plant is derived.

Systematic position

Isoetes differs so markedly from other pteridophytes that its systematic position has long been a matter of dispute. The genus shows a heterogeneous assemblage and characters common to several groups. Its multiflagellate sperm character led Campbell to suggest that it should be included in the Filicinean series. According to certain affinities with the spermatophytes in the character of the embryo, in the histology of the fully developed sporophyte, in the structure of the root as well as in the leaves with sheathing leaf bases surrounding the stout bulb-like stem.

Though the large multiflagellate sperm character, absence of the suspensor in the embryo, the general habit and the highly specialized leaves together find no parallel in any of the groups of pteridophytes, yet the presence of simple exarch vascular organization, the ligulate leaves and the solitary sporangium on the adaxial face of the sporophylls led majority of the pteridologists of recent years to include it in the Lycopodian series.

Moreover, the presence of stigmaria-like rhizophores, roots with the same distinctive structure as stigmarian rootlet, a vestigeal parichnos in the leaves, trabeculation of sporangia, the regular formation of 4 megaspores in the megasporangia are definitely Lepidodendroid characters. Though the heterosporous habit, ligulate character and the development of the female gametophyte are of much resemblance to *Selaginella*, yet it differs markedly from Selaginellales, Lycopodiales and Lepidodendrales in its sperm character, its root system and its large chambered sporangia. These characters themselves definitely justify its position in a separate order under the Lycopods.

In the modern system of classification Pleuromeiaceae has been placed together with Isoetaceae under the Order Isoetales. The genus *Pleuromeia* has so many characters in common with *Isoetes* that it definitely justifies its inclusion in the Order Isoetales. These are : (*a*) the leaves are of the same type and shape with broad bases and ring-like flange, (*b*) reniform microspores, and (*c*) large sporangia.

Moreover, the modern interpretation of the stock of *Isoetes*, i.e., it is a telescopic of the rhizophore, and stem of *Pleuromeia* also places it near Isoetales. The abaxial nature of the sporangia of *Pleuromeia* seems to be misinterpretation.

CHAPTER III

CLASS EQUISETINEAE

The members of the Class Equisetineae (also known as Articulatae) appeared in the Devonian, became very prominent in the Carboniferous and subsequently began to decline; at present the Class is represented by only one living genus *Equisetum*, the common 'horse-tail'.

Sporophyte differentiated into stem, root and leaves; homosporous. Protostelic or siphonostelic; protoxylem endarch, but exarch in Sphenophyllales. Internodes longitudinally ribbed throughout. Branches and leaves alternating with each other at the nodes. Leaves generally borne in transverse whorls, and of two types—microphyllous (in Equisetales) and macrophyllous (in Sphenophyllales). Spores with elaters. Prothallus dorsiventral. Antheridia in *Equisetum* many and sunken. Sperms multiflagellate. Archegonia many, sunken, with two neck canal cells.

The Class consists of 5 Orders: (1) **Hyeniales,** (2) **Pseudoborniales**, (3) **Sphenophyllales,** (4) **Calamitales,** and (5) **Equisetales.**

ORDER 1. HYENIALES

Sporophyte usually with jointed stem. Whorled arrangement of leaves but not conspicuous. Leaves elongate, narrow, once or twice dichotomously branched, each with a terminal sporangium. Sporangiophores in lax strobili, without sterile appendages.

There are two genera: (*a*) **Hyenia,** and (*b*) **Calamophyton.**

HYENIA

(Fam. HYENIACEAE)

The genus *Hyenia* is known only from the Middle Devonian and possesses some features which bring it nearer to the Psilophytineae than to the Equisetineae.

The plant is small and shrubby in nature, with short dichotomous appendages, a few of which are arranged in whorls. The aerial shoot is without any articulation and the internal structure is practically unknown. The appendages are of two types—sterile and fertile. The former are leafy and forked more than once. On the other hand, the latter ones have a single forking only with their tips either spreading or recurved. These fertile appendages

Fig. 351, *Hyenia* (after reconstruction) (*Redrawn after Krausel and Weyland*)

are also borne in whorls and are equivalent to the **sporangiophores,** because at the end of each of the bifurcations at the distal end of a fertile appendage there are more than one anatropous sporangia.

ORDER 3. SPHENOPHYLLALES

The Sphenophyllales first appeared in the Upper Devonian and persisted up to the Triassic. In all probability, the plants were herbaceous stem-climbers.

Sporophyte homosporous or incipiently heterosporous. Stem

longitudinally ribbed. Primary vascular cylinder actinostelic, tri- or hexa-arch ; secondary tissues formed. Leaves arranged in whorls at the nodes, sessile, wedge-shaped, entire or dichotomously divided, with dichotomously branched veins. Sporangiophores and bracts densely crowded in alternate whorls in the strobili.

SPHENOPHYLLUM

(Fam. SPHENOPHYLLACEAE)

Sphenophyllum, the best studied genus of the Order Sphenophyllales, forms a characteristic vegetation of the coal-swamp forests of Scotland, France, Germany and Bear island in the Arctic ocean.

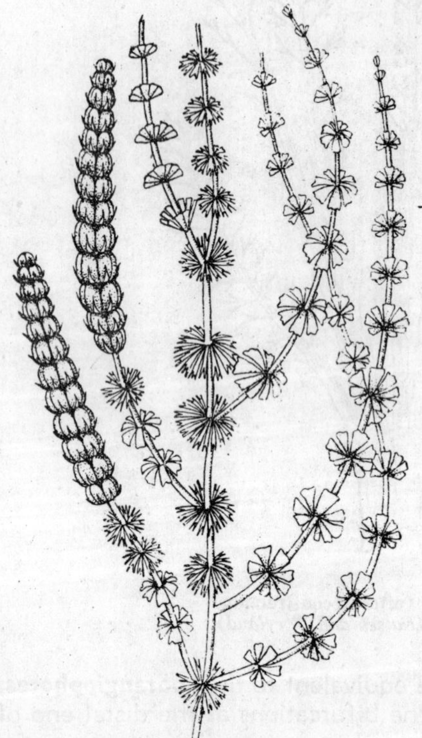

Fig. 352. *Sphenophyllum* Plant body.

The sporophyte

On the nature of the habitats of the plant, it can be supposed that probably though the trailing stem of *Sphenophyllum* was mainly aerial in habit, yet under certain circumstances it might have been partially submerged under the swamp. The stems are slender, about 5 mm. in diameter, and are provided with non-alternating ribs. The leaves are small, usually less than 2 cm. in length, and occur in some multiple of 3 at each node, usually 6 or 9, but sometimes becoming as many as 18. The apex of the leaf is variously toothed ; in some species (e.g. *S. myriophyllum*) the leaves are deeply notched. Each leaf possesses a number of diverging veins, produced from a single vein which undergoes several dichotomies.

Internally, the stem is rather confusing and appears to be like that of a root. The primary xylem occurs in the form of a triangle at the centre of the stem, thus making the stele an actinostele. The protoxylem is exarch. The primary phloem is not recognizable. The cortex is rather narrow and can be differentiated into an outer and an inner cortex. The whole of the cortex is used up in formation of a periderm. In the intrastelar region the secondary xylem, derived from the cambium ring, is made up of tracheids with multiseriate bordered pits and parenchymatous ray cells.

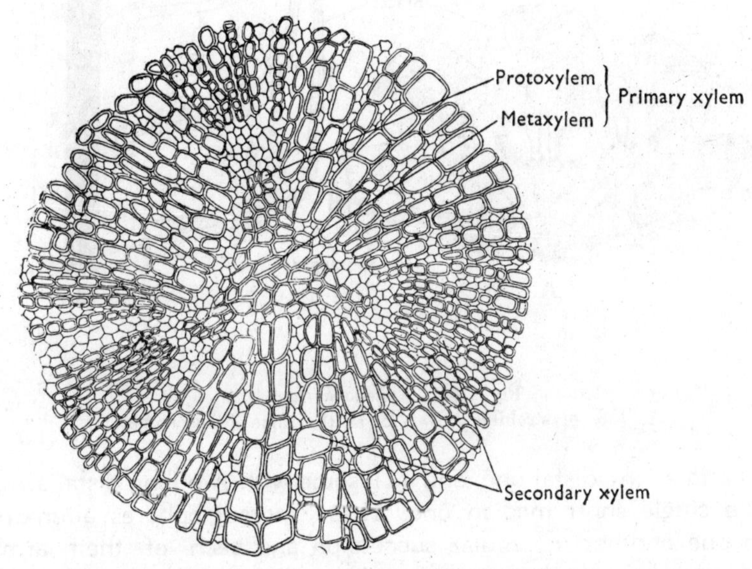

Fig. 353. *Sphenophyllum*.
T.S. of stem showing the xylem cylinder only.

Structurally, the internal organization of root is similar to that of the stem, excepting that the primary xylem is diarch instead of triarch.* The primary phloem is better preserved in the case of a root.

The strobili of *Sphenophyllum* are usually 1 cm. in diameter and with a variable length, and these are borne either terminally or laterally. The different types of sphenophyllean strobili are placed under the form genus *Bowmanites*, the best known species of which is *B. dawsoni*. In this case, there is a slender central axis

* In very few cases it may be triarch also.

bearing innumerable whorls of bracts at equal distances ; each whorl is composed of 14-20 bracts, which are free at their apices but laterally united at the bases. In the axil of each bract there is a solitary **sporangiophore** partially united with the bract. The sporangiophores are of two kinds : (1) some having two short median

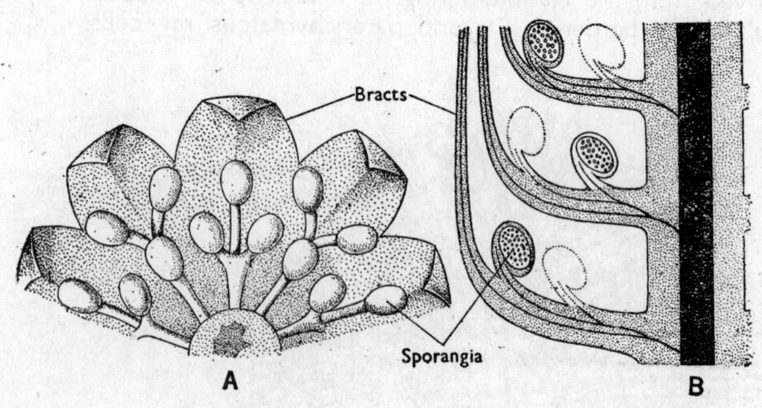

Fig. 354. *Sphenophyllum.*
A, T.S. of strobilus ; B. V.S. of the same (diagrammatic).

arms and a long distal one, and (2) some with two long distal arms and a single short median one. These sporangiophores alternate with one another in regular succession and each of their arms terminates in a single sporangium bearing mainly homospores.

ORDER 4. CALAMITALES

The members of the Calamitales constitute a diverse group of assemblage living in swampy habitats. The plants were both herbaceous and arborescent in habit representing the modern day equisetums. They appeared in the Upper Devonian, flourished luxuriantly forming one of the dominant elements of the Carboniferous flora, and finally declined in the Triassic.

Sporophytes mostly tall trees. Trunks usually unbranched, 20-30 metres high, and with a diameter of 1 meter ; siphonostelic. Secondary growth present. Leaves in one whorl at each node, and in most cases small and simple, free or more or less united at the base. Sporangiophores and leaf-like bracts alternately arranged in the strobili. Homosporous or heterosporous. Megaspores usually three times larger than the microspores.

CALAMITES

(Fam. CALAMITACEAE)

The genus *Calamites* is very widely spread and can be found wherever Carboniferous plant remains occur. The fossil remains, though quite common, are of a fragmentary nature and different parts of the plant are rarely found in an attached state. From the reconstructions, however, it appears that the main stems were large rhizomes bearing usually branched, ribbed, subaerial shoots, 20-30 metres high. The roots are adventitious. The leaves are simple, linear or linear-lanceolate and generally appear in whorls.

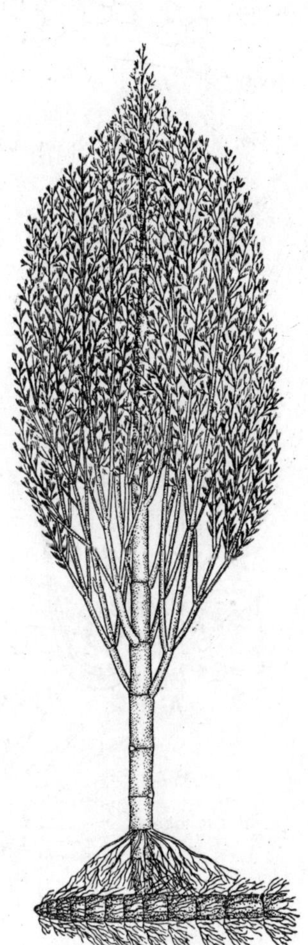

Fig. 355. *Calamites sp.* (after reconstruction). (*Redrawn after Hirmer*)

Internally, the stem of *Calamites* exactly represents that of *Equisetum*, excepting that in the former there is a clear secondary growth, both in the intrastelar as well as in the extrastelar regions. The secondary wood is very complex. The leaf-traces are also similar to those of *Equisetum*.

The strobili of *Calamites* consist of a number of sporangiophores bearing sporangia and resemble those of the present-day horse-tails. Up to the present, four types of fructifications have been described, viz., *Calamostachys*, *Palaeostachya*, *Macrostachya*, and *Cingularia*. In case of *Calamostachys* the leafy bracts and sporangiophores are borne in alternate whorls on the axis, while in *Palaeostachya* the sporangiophores appear in the axils of the bracts. In *Macrostachya* the

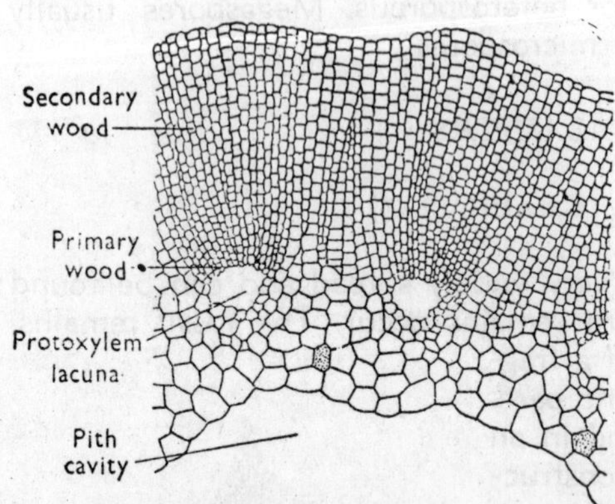

Fig. 356. *Calamites,* T. S. of stem (in part).

relation between the bracts and the sporangiophores is probably of the *Calamostachys* type, the difference in between the two being in size, as the former is much bigger than the latter. In *Cingularia* the sporangiophore, which is horizontally placed, is divided into two lobes, an upper and a lower, the former one

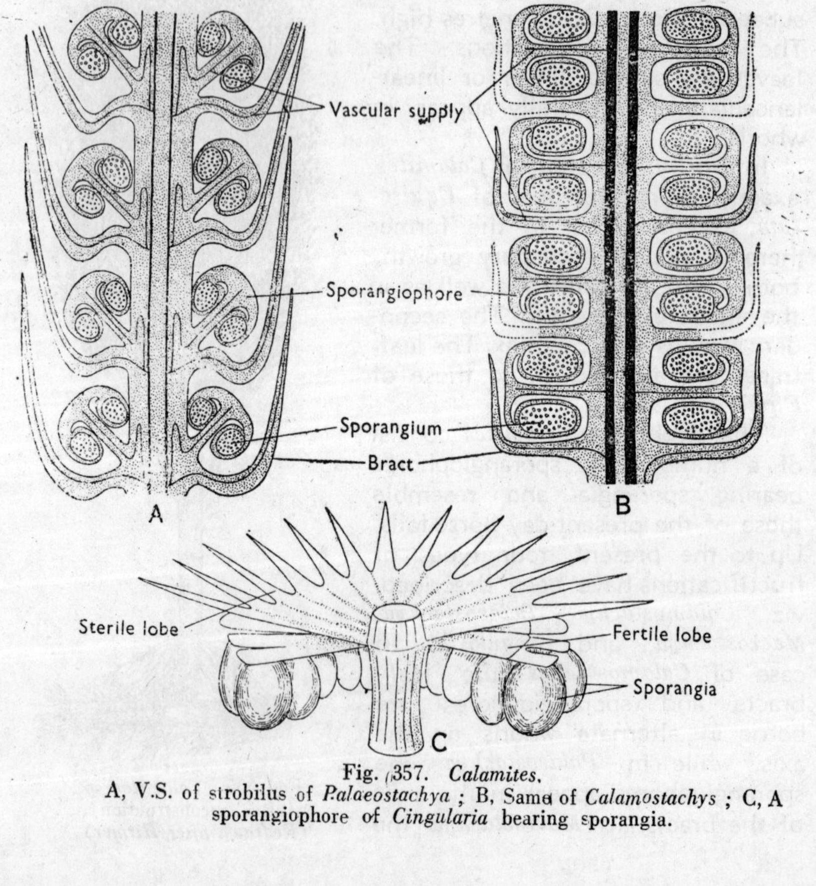

Fig. 357. *Calamites.*
A, V.S. of strobilus of *Palaeostachya* ; B, Same of *Calamostachys* ; C, A sporangiophore of *Cingularia* bearing sporangia.

being usually a sterile bract. The lower lobe, on the other hand, is notched at its apex and each division bears two hanging sporangia. The sporangia normally have homospores, excepting in *Calamostachys casheana*.

ORDER 5. EQUISETALES

The Equisetales are characterized by having two kinds of shoots, subterranean rhizomes and branched, green, phylloclade-like sub-aerial branches provided with ridges and furrows ; ribs of successive internodes usually alternating with one another. No secondary thickening ; vascular cylinder siphonostelic, endarch. The leaves are scaly and are produced in whorls at the nodes. The strobili consist of peltate sporangiophores bearing a number of sporangia, hanging from their under surfaces. The spores, though morphologically homospores, are physiologically different.

The Order appeared in the Upper Devonian and reached its zenith in the Carboniferous, and is represented at present by the only genus *Equisetum* belonging to the family Equisetaceae.

Family Equisetaceae

No distinct whorl of bracts is observed in the strobilus. Stem is without secondary thickening.

It contains 2 genera : (1) *Equisitiles* (extinct) and (2) *Equisetum* (living, world-wide in distribution).

Indian species of Equisetum are (a) *F. diffusum* (Kumayn, (2) *E. robustum* (Lahore and Pondicherry) and (3) *E. mobile* (Himalayas, Ceylon and also in plains).

Affinity

The Equisetineae are known mostly after the time when the Calamitaceae were becoming extinct. Possibly these are degenerating forms of Calamitaceae. Although there is no geological record it is equally possible that Equisetaceae diverged from the Calamitaceae very early in the evolution of the Order.

The Calamitaceae, instead of its tree-like habit had a horizontal underground rhizome with aerial branches, just as the present-day *Equisetum*, but the ribs of successive internodes were sometimes above, instead of alternating with one another. The cortex differs from that of *Equisetum* in having a cambium. The strobilus of *Equisetum* also lacks in distinct whorls of bracts.

The Equisetineae, as will be seen from the fossil forms, are a very ancient group and their relation to other pteridophytes or somewhat problematical. The modern forms being so much restricted in number and type offers but partial means of comparison, still a comparison of these with the simple Filicineae does indicate some affinity between the two groups, although as must be expected a very remote one. Van Tiegham has shown that the structure and arrangement of the vascular bundles in the stems of *Ophioglossum* and *Equisetum* have much in common. As we have seen the prothalium is not essentially different in *Equisetum* and eusporangiate ferns, and the sperms are almost similar to those of latter and quite dissimilar from Lycopodineae. The latter point is believed by Campbell to be one of great importance.

If the Equisetineae do come from common stock with the ferns, they must have branched off at a very early period, long before the latter had completely differentiated. The very different importance relatively of stems and leaves in the two groups point to this, as well as the extremely different character of the sporophylls.

The genus *Equisetum* is evidently a reduced remnant of a once predominant type of plants which has been crowded out by the more specialised ferns and spermatophytes. Their presence of heterospory in some fossil forms is interesting, but what are known at present it never developed to the same extinct as in the other groups of Pteridophytes.

The cosmopolitan genus *Equisetum* is the only genus of Equisetineae and the only living representative of Equisetales. Notwithstanding the difference of detail, the life cycle of a horse-tail is comparable to that of a fern.

The condition of syngamy and formation of embryo is essentially as ferns, but here the embryo has its apex directed towards the archegonial neck (exoscopic) and it grows out directly to the apex of the young plant.

A greatly added interest in *Equisetum* arises from the comparison with allied fossils which are grouped as Calamitaceae.

The Equisetales thus comprising Equisetaceae and Calamitaceae form a natural and closely related class, of which the present affinity was with Sphenophyllales, but with some degree of relationship also with Psilotales, all the three being sporangiophoric pteridophytes.

EQUISETUM

(Fam. EQUISETACEAE)

Equisetum, commonly known as 'horsetail' is found with about 25 species all over the world excepting Australia and New Zealand, and is mostly an inhabitant of the cool and temperate regions. It is

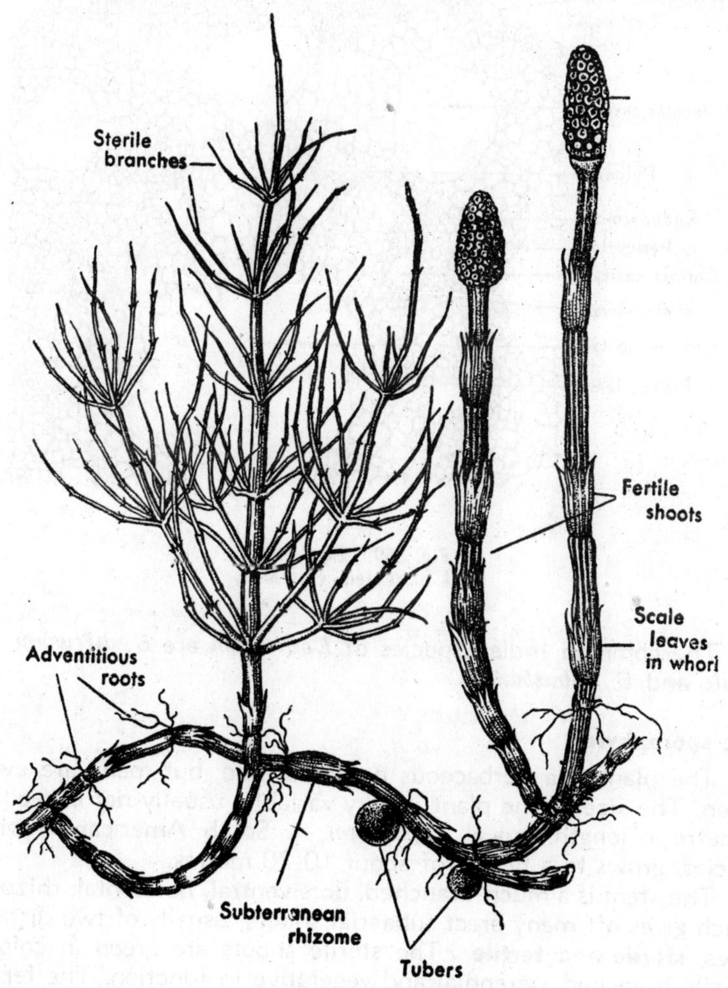

Fig. 358. *Equisetum.*
Sporophyte showing the horizontal rhizome with sterile and fertile shoots.

usually found in hills, especially in dark and marshy places, wet fields, gravelly or loamy soil.

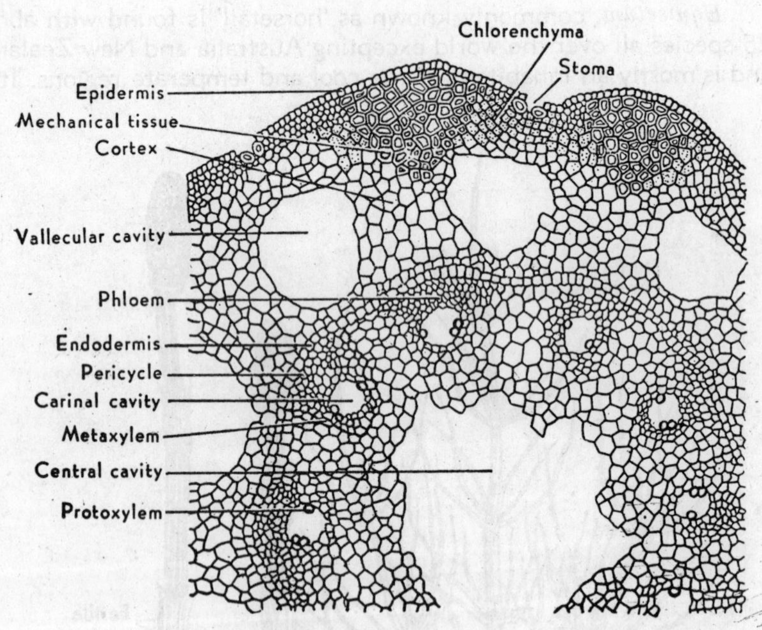

Fig. 359. *Equisetum*. T.S. of stem (in part),

The common Indian species of *Equisetum* are *E. diffusum*, *E. debile* and *E. robustum*.

The sporophyte

The plant is a herbaceous perennial one, but many are evergreen. The size of the plant is very variable, usually not exceeding a metre in length, but *E. giganteum*, a South American tropical species, grows to a height of about 10-20 metres.

The stem is a much-branched, dorsiventral, horizontal, rhizome which gives off many erect subaerial shoots, usually of two distinct types, **sterile** and **fertile**. The sterile shoots are green in colour, usually branched, perennial and vegetative in function. The fertile shoots are pale or brownish in colour, without chlorophyll, unbranched, short-lived and wither after discharging their function (the production of spores). Transitional forms between these two types are not uncommon. The stem is jointed with nodes and internodes, and each internode consists of distinct ridges and furrows, the number of ridges is equal to the number of leaves present at each node. At each node there is a whorl of minute scale leaves, which are mostly non-green and soon become dead. These are free at the tips but fused laterally with one another forming a sheath closely enveloping the base of each internode. The function of photosynthesis is, however, taken by the stem and branches. The branches are in whorls and usually equal in number to the leaves, a branch always developing between a pair of leaves. The whorls of leaves and branches of successive nodes alternate with one another.

Roots are slender, fibrous, adventitious in nature and arise endogenously from the bases of the lateral branches or dormant buds of the rhizome.

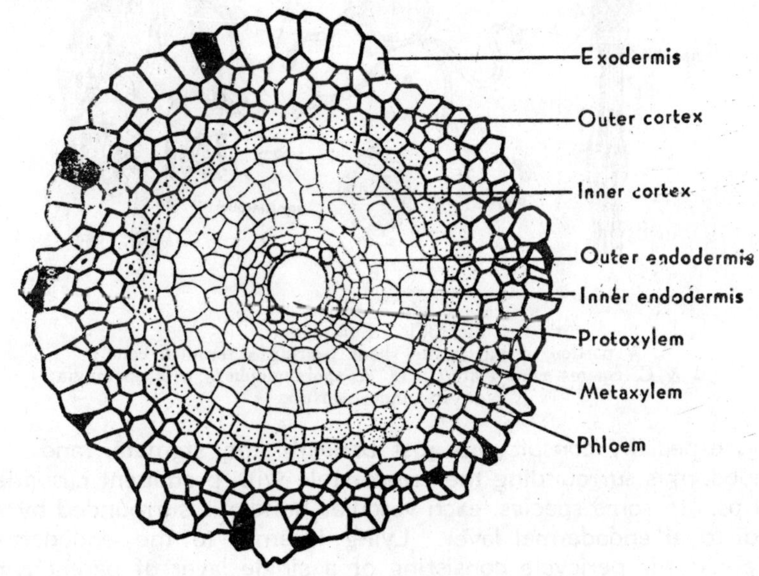

Fig. 36. *Equisetum*.
T.S. of root.

A cross-section of the stem shows two regions clearly differentiated, the cortex and the stele. The cortex is bounded on the outside by an epidermis which is single-layered and provided with a number of alternate ridges and furrows. The outer walls of the epidermal cells are highly silicified. Stomata are present in two vertical rows in each furrow. The cortex is highly differentiated into the following : (*a*) hypodermis consisting of sclerenchyma which may be restricted to the periphery of the cortex or may extend inwards to the stele ; below each ridge sclerenchyma is well-developed, (*b*) general cortex consisting of many-layered parenchyma with large air cavities (**vallecular cavities**), each corresponding to a furrow, and these alternate in position with usually water-filled cavities (**carinal cavities**) in the vascular bundles. The peripheral portion of the general cortex, lateral to the sclerenchyma, is chlorenchymatous with intercellular spaces

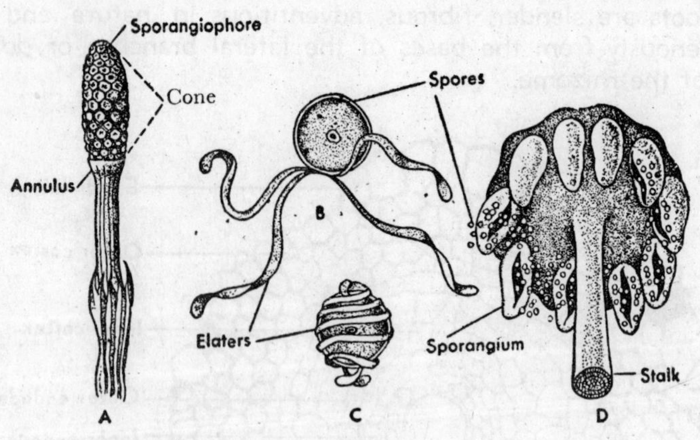

Fig. 361. *Equisetum*.
A, A portion of the fertile shoot bearing a terminal cone ;
B & C, Spores with elaters ; D, A sporangiophore with sporangia on its under surface.

and especially conspicuous just beneath the stomata, and (*c*) endodermis surrounding the entire stele with prominent casparian strips. In some species, each vascular bundle is surrounded by an individual endodermal layer. Lying internal to the endodermis there is the pericycle consisting of a single layer of parenchyma cells. The vascular bundles are closed, collateral, and conjoint being arranged in a ring and each containing a carinal cavity ; they are laterally separated from one another by a small mass of parenchyma cells. The protoxylem is endarch and in mature bundles these are found in a more or less disorganized condition within the carinal cavities. Outside the carinal cavity tsere is a mass of phloem consisting of phloem parenchyma and sieve tubes. On both sides of the phloem mass is a small metaxylem mass consisting of tracheids only. The pith lies at the centre. Occupying most of the pith there is a conspicuous space (the **central cavity**) in the internodes of the primary branches of the aerial shoots, and this central cavity may be entirely absent in the internodes of smaller branches and of the rhizome ; these cavities also are usually water-filled.

Internally, the root of *Equisetum* possesses an exodermis followed by a thick cortex. There are two endodermal layers.—the outer endodermis and the inner endodermis, which replaces the

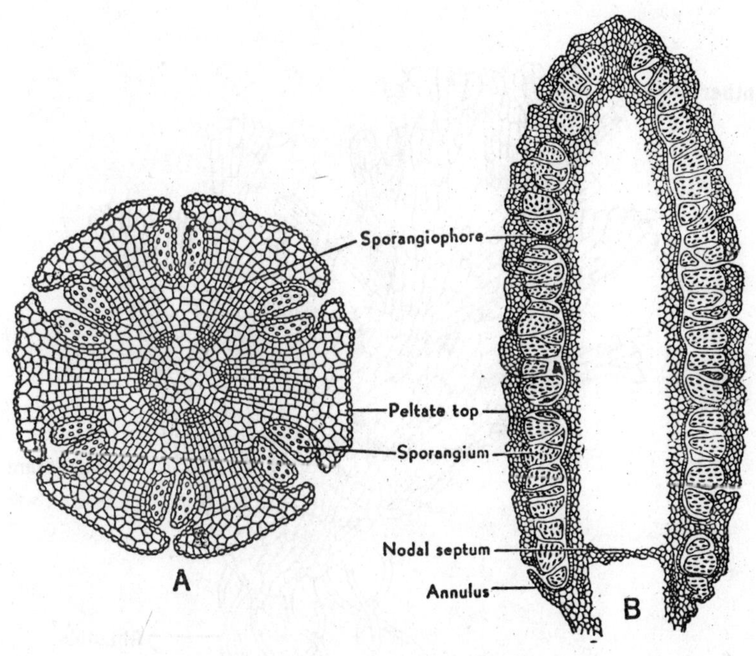

Fig. 362. *Equisetum*.
A, T.S, of a cone ; B, L,S, of the same.

pericycle. There are usually four protoxylem groups alternating with the phloem and a big central metaxylem.

At the apex of the fertile branch there is a cone-like structure, the **sporangiferous spike** or **cone** or **strobilus,** which consists of a central axis bearing a variable number of sporangium-bearing organs, the **sporangiophores**, in distinct but compact whorls. Each sporangiophore is a peltate structure with a somewhat flattened hexagonal disc and is attached to the main axis at right angles to each other. When young, these sporangiophores remain closely fitted together, but later on separate as distinct whorls. At the base of the strobilus, in some cases, a modified leaf-whorl is present forming the so-called **annulus.**

On the under surface of each sporangiophore, towards the circumference, sporangia, usually 5-10 in number, are borne on a ring and are projected horizontally towards the axis of the cone. Each sporangium is an elongated, sac-like body containing many spore mother cells, from each of which four spores are formed due

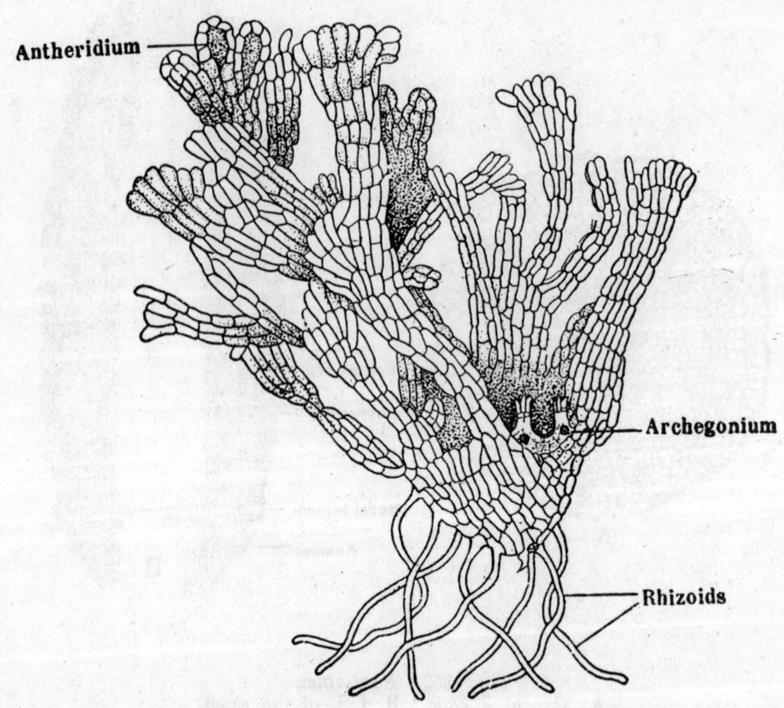

Fig. 363. Monoecious prothallus of *Equisetum.*

to reduction division, so that a mature sporangium contains many spores inside. *With reduction division and formation of spores, the gametophytic or haploid generation begins.*

The gametophytes

The sporangium, at maturity, bursts longitudinally and sets free a large number of green-coloured spores. Each spore, besides its usual two coats, has a delicate cuticular layer and a thick **perispore.** Later on, this last layer splits into four ribbon-like appendages, called **elaters,** with spoon-like tips and these remain attached to a common point. These elaters are hygroscopic in nature, which uncoil in dry air and recoil around the spore in moisture. The function of the elaters is uncertain. Possibly, their expansion may assist in the dehiscence of the sporangia, or possibly their expansion and contraction may assist in spore-dispersal. The spores are all of one kind. Hence, *Equisetum* is homosporous.

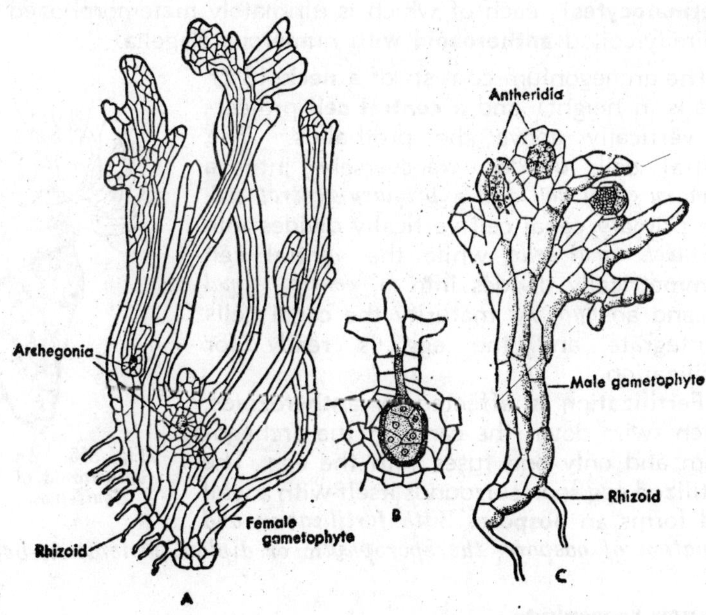

Fig. 364, *Equisetum arvense.*
A, A female prothallus ; B, An archegonium ;
C, A male prothallus.

On germination, each spore forms a small green prothallus which differs in form and in the position of sex organs (**antheridia** and **archegonia**) from that of a fern. At maturity, it looks like a disc-shaped thick cushion of tissue consisting of several layers of cells, from the upper surface of which there arise irregularly-lobed flattened branches, each one cell in thickness. It produces rhizoids from its lower surface. Antheridia usually develop at the upper ends of these flattened and vertical branches, while the archegonia are produced on the upper surface of cushion near the bases of these branches. Thus, the prothallus is monoecious. On the other hand, if the gametophytes remain small, each one-cell in thickness, probably due to nutritional deficiency, they bear antheridia only and it is for these reasons they were once thought to be dioecious. In some cases (*E. arvense*), half of the spores develop male gametophytes and the other half, female gametophytes under controlled conditions. In the latter case, if fertilization of the archegonia fails prothallia proceed to develop antheridia. The prothallia may be long-lived and may persist for more than two years.

Each antheridium consists of an outer jacket layer, one-cell in thickness, surrounding a number of spermatozoid mother cells (**spermatocytes**), each of which is ultimately metamorphozed into a spirally-coiled **antherozoid** with numerous flagella.

The archegonium consists of a **neck** (3 or 4 cells in height) and a **central cell** projecting vertically above the prothallus. The central cell divides transversely into a *primary canal cell* and a *primary ventral cell*. The primary canal cell vertically divides into two *neck canal cells*, while the ventral cell asymmetrically divides into a *ventral canal cell* and an *egg*. At maturity the canal cells disintegrate and the egg is ready for fertilization.

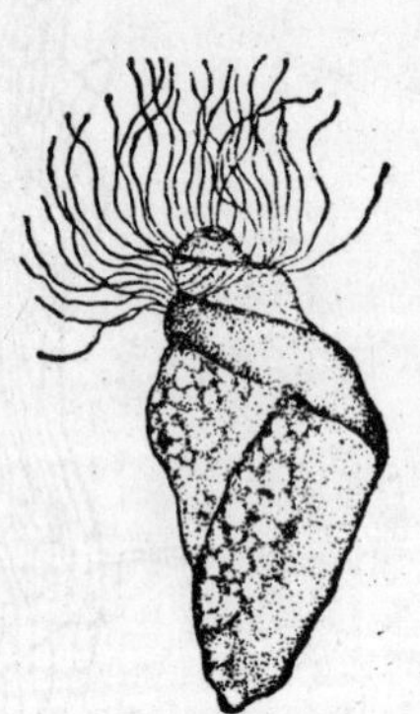

Fig. 365. An antherozoid of *Equisetum*.

Fertilization is effected by antherozoids, which swim down the canal of the archegonium and only one fuses with the egg. The fertilized egg soon surrounds itself with a wall and forms an **oospore.** *With fertilization and formation of oospore, the sporophytic or diploid generation begins.*

The new sporophyte

The oospore passes into an embryo (consisting of stem, root, cotyledon, and foot) which, without any period of rest, continues to grow until the *Equisetum* plant is established and thus completes the life cycle. It has been observed in the case of *E. debile* that a single gametophyte may bear eight to ten young sporophytes.

COMPARISON OF LYCOPODIUM, SELAGINELLA AND EQUISETUM

LYCOPODIUM	*SELAGINELLA*	*EQUISETUM*
(a) The Sporophyte		
1. Plants terrestrial herbs or epiphytes.	1. Plants-delicate herbs.	1. Plants-usually perennial herbs,
2. Stem is prosterate but the apex is upturned, densely covered with hairs, produces root branches.	2. Stem is creeping, apparently dichotomously branched, produces rhizophore at each bifurcation.	2. Stem is rhizome with nodes and internodes, produces two kinds of shoots : sterile and fertile, the sterile shoot is much branched and green while the fertile one is unbranched and non-green ; item ribbel
3. Roots adventitious, produced from the older parts of the stem.	3. Roots adventitious, produced from the ends of the rhizophores.	3. Roots adventitious, produced from the nodes of the rhizome,
4. Leaves small, narrow, arranged densely and spirally on the stem, eligulate.	4, Leaves are of two kinds in 4 vertical rows : dorsal 2 rows are small, venntral 2 rows large, ligulate.	4. Leaves small, scale like, fused to form a short sheath round the erect stems at the nodes.
5, Sporophylls are similar to foliage leaves and aggregated at the tips of the branches forming strobilus.	5. Sporophylls (both micro and mega) are spirally arranged at the tips of the lateral branches forming strobilus.	5, Sporophylls are not be of like but consld, of sporangiophores which are arranged in compact whorls at right angles to the fertile shoot forming the strobilus.
6, Sporongia arise on the abaxial surface of the sporophylls or in their axils.	6. Sporangia (both micro and mega) arise in the axils of sporophylls (mircro-and mega).	6, Sporangia hanging from the corners of the peltate disc of the sporangiophores,
7. Spores all alike, numerous and small.	7, Spores are of two kinds microspores and megaspores ; microspores are small, numerous and are contained in the microsporangia, while the megaspores are large, 4, in number and contained in the 4 angled sporangia. Both kinds of spores are provided with tri-radiate ridge.	7, Spores all alike, numerous, small green and provided with elaters.

(*b*) **The gametophyte**

LYCOPODIUM	*SELAGINELLA*	*EQUISETUM*
8. Spore is the first cell of the gametophyte it produces prothallus on germination.	8. Spores are the first cells of the gametophytes. These porduce two kinds of prothallimale. prothallus and female prothalles.	8. Spore is the first cell of the gametophyte. It produces one or two kinds of prothallus.
9. Gametophyte is of one kind and is represented by prothallus. it is small and round or tuberous, or carrot-like and infested by phycomycetous fungus.	9, Gametophytes are of two kinds Male gametophyte is represented by the prothallial cell, and the female gametophyte by the mass of exposed green cells of the megaspore.	9. Gametophyte is of one or two kinds. In the latter case the male gametophyte is smaller than that of female one,
10. Antheridium is embedded into the crown and surrounded by a jacket of sterile cells. It produces flagellate sperms.	10. Antheridium is rudimentary end surrounded by a jacket of sterile cells, It produces biflagellate sperms.	10. Antheridium is round and produces multi-flagellate sperms.
11. Archegonium is embedded into the crown and is flask-shaped. It consists of six neck canal cells, one ventral canal cell and an egg cell,	11, Archegonium is produced on the female prothallus. Its structure is the same as that of Lycopodium.	11. Archegonium is situated at the lips or margins of female prothallus. It is flask-shaped and consists of one or two neck canal cells, one ventral canal cell and one egg cell.
12. No suspensor.	12. Presence of suspensor.	12. No suspensor,

CHAPTER IV

CLASS FILICINEAE

The Class Filicineae is a comparatively larger group than other Classes of Pteridophytes and contains about 175 genera with 8,000 species. The members are very varied in their habit and habitat. Some of the genera are cosmopolitan in their distribution, while others are strictly endemic. The earliest members of Filicineae appeared in the Devonian but it is believed that the ancestors of the present-day ferns evolved during the Triassic and Jurassic.

Classification

Smith (1955) classified all the ferns in a single Class Filicineae which was divided into three Subclasses :

I. *Primofilices*. Sporangia are borne on pedicels with vascular bundles ; they are elongated and have a jacket more than one cell in thickness.

3 Orders : (*a*) *Protopteridales*, (*b*) *Coenopteridales* and (*c*) *Archaeopteridales*. (All fossil ferns are included in three Orders).

II. *Eusporangiatae*. Sporangia are borne on fertile spike or in sori on the upper surface of leaf blade. Each sporangium is developed from a group of initial cells. Sporangial jacket is more than one cell in thickness.

2 Orders : (*a*) *Ophioglossales* and (*b*) *Marattiales*.

III. *Leptosporangiatae*. Sporangium is developed from a single initial cell. Sporangial jacket is one cell in thickenings.

3 Orders : (*a*) *Filicales*, (*b*) *Marsilcales* and (*c*) *Salviniales*.

Pichi-Sermolli (1959) thinks that the Subdivisions of Filicineae into Eusporangiate and Leptosporangiate (a distinction established by Goebel) is rather artificial, since they include certain ferns for example, the Ophioglossales, and the Marattiales resembled in that the sporangia originated in the same way, but are not closely related. He has subdivided the Class Filicineae into seven Subclasses : Primofilicidae, Ophioglossidae, Marattiidae, Osmundidae, Filicidae, Marsileidiae and Salviniidae. Pichi-Sermolli, however, does not present any scheme of phylogenetic evolution of ferns.

Characters

(*i*) The plant body is an axis without roots, (*ii*) with emergences rather than leaves, (*iii*) the sporangium on axis-tips, (*iv*) the sporangium with massive and undifferentiated wall, and with central sterile columella.

These characters are not found in any other groups, Psilotaceae with their chambered sporangia and elaborated anatomical structure form on independent Order Psilotales under the Class Psilophytineae.

SUBCLASS I PRIMOFILICES

ARCHAEOPTERIS

(Fam. ARCHAEOPTERIDACEAE)

Archaeopteris is one of the most ancient plants, known only from the Devonian and that also from the Upper Devonian. The genus is based on leaf compressions. Recently, the leaves have been found attached to the *Callixylon* type of stem. The reconstruction by Beck (1962) shows that the plant was a tree of excurrent habit with an apical crown of branches much as living pines. The leaves are large and possess a rachis bearing almost opposite pairs of pinnae and a pair of stipules at the base of the rachis. A pinna, in its turn, bears a number of pinnules which are arranged in an alternate fashion. The pinnules on a pinna may be either all sterile or all fertile, or there may be an admixture of the two. The sterile pinnules are flat and oval or wedge-shaped with repeatedly dichotomous venation, which extend up to the entire or incised apices.

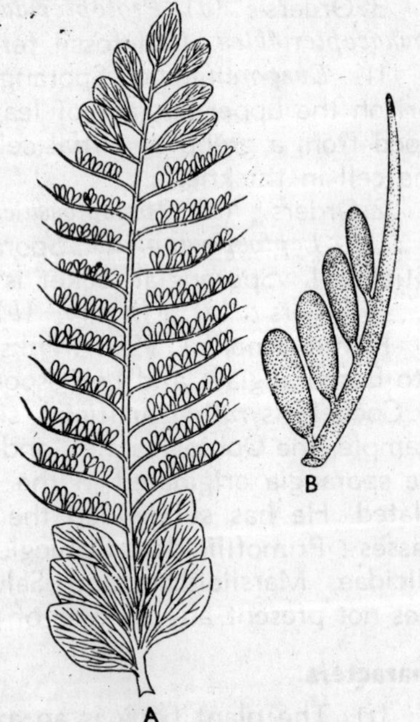

Fig. 366. *Archaeopteris.* A, Pinna with fertile and sterile pinnules ; B, Reconstruction of a portion of fertile pinnule with sporangia. (*Redrawn after Schimper and Arnold.*)

The sporangia are borne in a psilophyte-like fashion on the tips of branched or unbranched pedicels, which are borne adaxially on a fertile pinnule. The spores in one species can be differentiated into micro- or mega-spores and both kinds of sporangia are situated on the same pinnule. In size, the megaspores are about ten times in diameter than the microspores. It is interesting to note, however, that both the micro- and megasporangia are approximately of the same length, but the latter ar about double the former in breadth. A single microsporangium contains more than one hundred microspores, while a megasporangium contains only eight or sixteen megaspores.

Recent studies by Beck (1960, 62) show that *Archaeopteris* was neither a primitive fern nor a fern ancestor. The anatomy of the stem and the morphology of the leaf suggest that the plant was a 'progymnosperm'.

SUBCLASS II. EUSPORANGIATAE

The Order Ophioglossales includes a single family *Ophioglossaceae*, popularly known as 'Adder's tongue ferns'. It consists of three living genera only, of which *Ophioglossum* and *Botrychium* are cosmopolitan in their distribution, while the monotypic genus *Helminthostachys* is endemic to the Indo-Malayan region. This Order is regarded as a very primitive one.

OPHIOGLOSSUM

(Fam. OPHIOGLOSSACEAE)

The genus comprises of 28 species. The common Indian species are *O. gramineum*, *O. vulgatum*, *O. nudicaule*, *O. reticulatum*, etc.

The plant is characterized usually by the presence of a short, erect, rhizome, which rarely undergoes a dichotomous branching. Many adventitious roots are borne on the underground stem. In the majority of species there is only one leaf produced by the plant every year. Each leaf is clearly differentiable into a petiole and a lamina, the venation

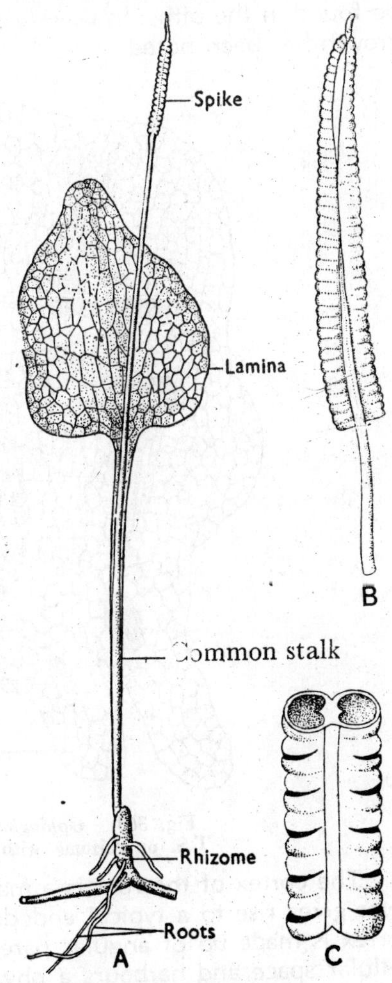

Fig. 367. *Ophioglossum*. **A,** An entire plant ; **B,** A mature spike ; **C,** T.S. through the apical portion of B.

being of the reticulate type. The leaves may be simple or lobed and sometimes forked in a dichotomous manner ; the phyllotaxy is spiral. The circinate type of ptyxis is unknown in this case.

Internally, the stem is siphonostelic as a rule, but occasionally the basal region of the stem may be protostelic with the upper part siphonostelic. The xylem is endarch with phloem lying external to xylem. The pith is generally homogenous and composed of comparatively large, thin-walled, parenchyma cells, but in some cases (e.g., *O. pendulum*) small scattered patches of xylem may be found in the pith. In *O. vulgatum* a small amount of secondary growth has been noted.

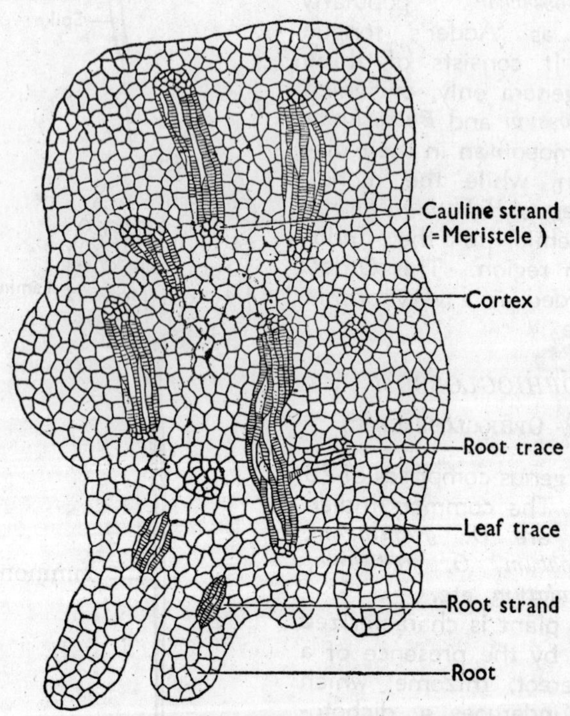

Fig. 368. *Ophioglossum reticulatum*, T.S. or rhizome with adventitious roots.

The cortex of the root is a massive structure whose innermost layer gives rise to a typical endodermis. The outer region of the cortex is made up of angular parenchyma cells without any intercellular space and harbours a phycomycetous mycorrhizal fungus. The inner region is composed of more or less rounded cells with prominent intercellular spaces. The stele may be monarch to tetrarch with radially arranged xylem and phloem ; xylem is exarch.

All the species of *Ophioglossum*, excepting *O. palmatum*, bear a single, linear, simple or slightly irregularly branched **fertile spike** at the junction of petiole and lamina. This spike resembles the tongue of an adder. There is a good deal of controversy regarding the morphological nature of the fertile spike in *Ophioglossum* (see below). The sporangia, however, are 0.5-3.0 mm. in diameter, subspherical and sunken within the leaf-tissue ; these are also regarded by some to be fused forming a **synangium** along the margin of the leaf. There are two marginal rows of sporangia which are eusporangiate in their mode of development. *With reduction division and formation of spores, the gametophytic or haploid generation begins*. At maturity, the sporangia turn yellowish or brownish in colour and dehisce by means of a 'lateral' slit, liberating the spores in multitude. The spores are originally tetrahedral but later on become subspherical ; the wall is thick and sculptured.

Morphology of the spike. Speculation on the morphological nature of the fertile spike of Ophioglossaceae dates at least from

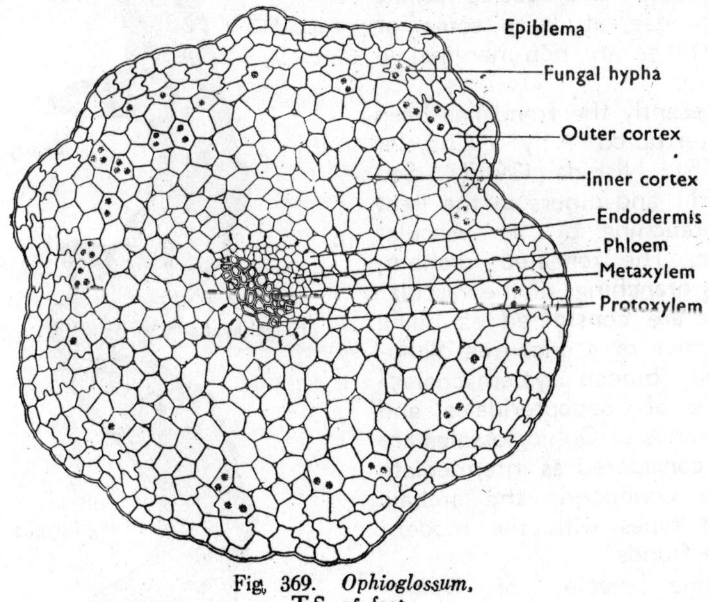

Fig. 369. *Ophioglossum*, T.S. of foot.

the time of Roeper (1826, 1859), who suggested that the spike in *Botrychium* has been derived from two basal pinnae of the sterile frond, and is secondarily erected upright, as in case of *Anemia*. It was later shown by Holle (1875) that Roeper's theory might be applied to *Ophioglossum*. Bower (1896), however, considered the spike of *Ophioglossum* as a septate sporangium, but this hypothesis was rejected by himself in 1911. Chrysler (1910) supported Roeper's view. He found that the fertile spike of *Botrychium* has the same number of vascular supply as would naturally go to a pair of pinnae. He further pointed out that in the abnormal specimens, where there is a pair of fertile spikes instead of one, each spike has the same number of vascular supply as would be present in a single pinna. The pinna-nature of the fertile spike is more evident in *Botrychium lanuginosum*, where the spike is situated in the middle of the lamina, and in the position of the third to the sixth leaflets from the base. However, the strongest evidence against the pinna-nature of the fertile spikes is found in *Ophioglossum palmatum* (Bower, 1911 ; Sen, 1961). In this species, unlike the pinnae, at least some of the spikes are non-marginal in position.

Recently the frond has been re-interrupted by Chrysler (1945), Nishida (1957), Sen (1961) and others in the light of branching of its vascular tissue. The repeated dichotomous branchings of the vascular tissue are considered as being indicative of a once-free dichotomous branch system characteristic of Coenopteridales, and the fronds of Ophioglossales are thus considered as intermediate forms, connecting the archaic radial types with the modern plane fronds.

Some species of *Ophioglossum* (*O. vulgatum*) can reproduce vegetatively by means of root buds.

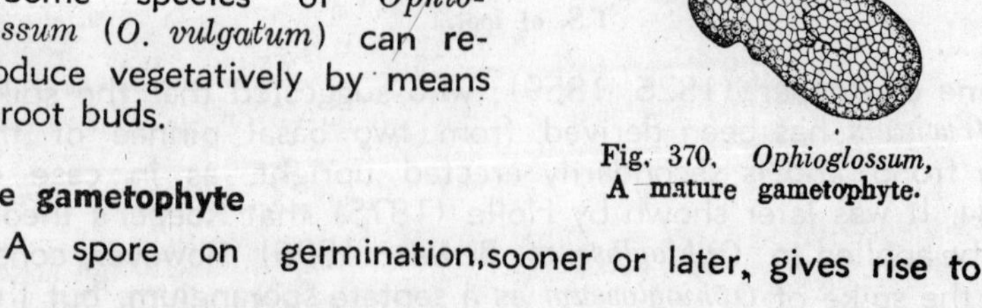

Fig. 370. *Ophioglossum*, A mature gametophyte.

The gametophyte

A spore on germination, sooner or later, gives rise to a

prothallus, which in its early stage of development becomes infected with an endophytic mycorrhizal fungus. In case of entirely subterranean prothalli, this fungus is responsible for the supply of food to the young gametophyte. In some cases, however, the prothalli possess small, subaerial green lobes. A mature prothallus of *Ophioglossum* is conical or irregularly cylindrical or stellate, a few mm. long, unbranched or copiously branched and perennial in habit. The sex organs are scattered generally near the growing tip of the prothallus and are formed in an irregular sequence, but in acropetal succession.

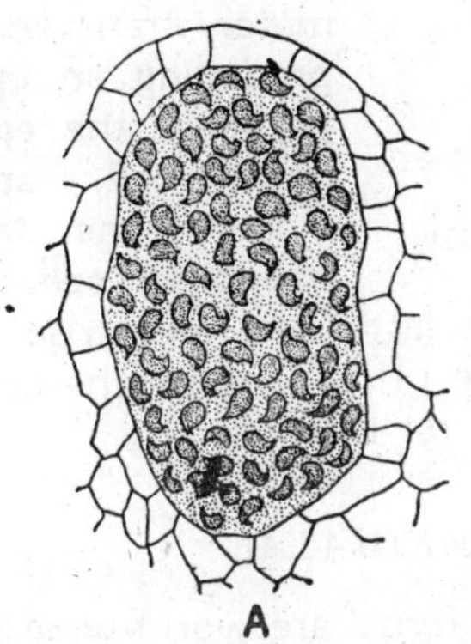

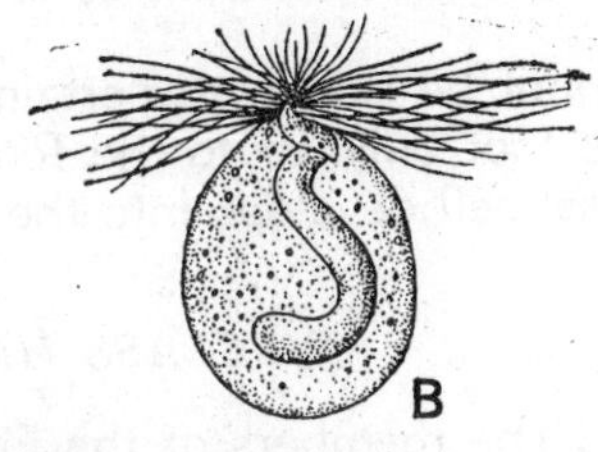

Fig. 371. *Ophioglossum*. A, A mature antheridium ; B. A single antherozoid.

An antheridium develops from a superficial cell (**antheridium initial cell**) of the prothallus, which divides periclinally into an outer and an inner cell. This inner cell gives rise to the antheridium proper. The antherozoids are coiled and multiflagellate.

An archegonium is also developed from a single superficial cell of the gametophyte. Here also, the first division of the **archegonial initial cell** is periclinal. The neck of the archegonium is slightly projecting beyond the surface of the prothallus. The ventral canal cell is extremely transitory in nature. By disintegration of the canal cell or canal cells an opening is formed in the neck of the archegonium, through which an antherozoid glides in and fuses with the egg cell, thereby causing fertilization. The fertilized egg soon covers itself by a wall and forms the **oospore.** *With ferti-*

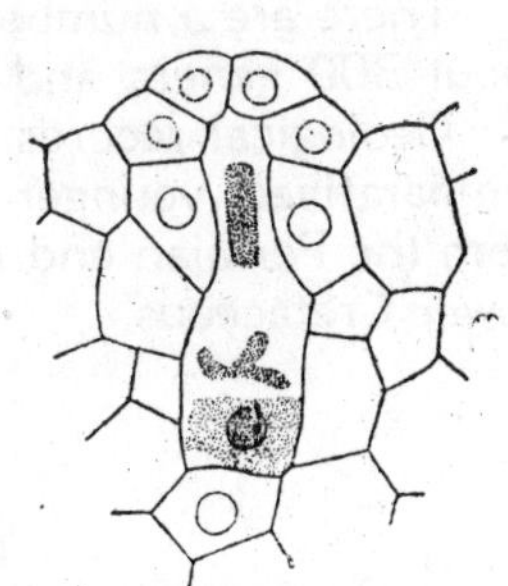

Fig. 372. *Ophioglossum*. A mature archegonium.

lization nnd formation of oospore, the sporophytic or diploid generation begins.

The new sporophyte

The new sporophyte develops from the oospore in course of a year, or the development may take place through a number of years. In all the species investigated so far, the first division of the oospore is approximately transverse, producing an upper cell, the **epibasal cell,** and a lower one, the **hypobasal cell.** It cannot be said with certainty whether the latter one gives rise to the foot only, or to the foot as well as the primary root. The epibasal cell develops into the stem and the first leaf.

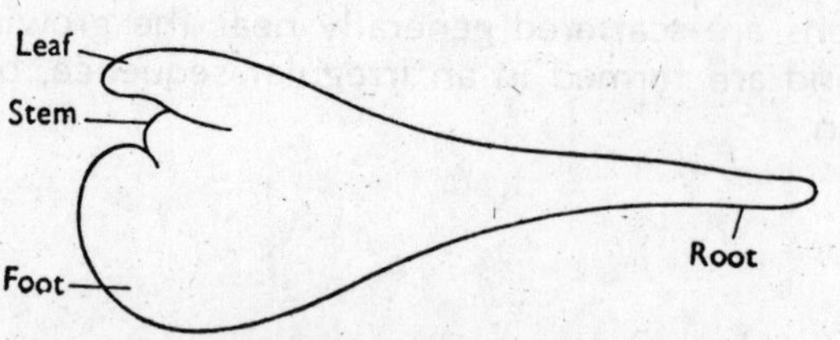

Fig. 373. *Ophioglossum.* Diagrammatic representation of a developing embryo.

SUBCLASS III. LEPTOSPORANGIATAE

The members of the Filicales or 'true ferns' are world-wide in their distribution. Like the eusporangiate ones, they also inhabit warm, moist and shady places, and the majority of them are mesophytes or hydrophytes, although xerophytic types are by no means uncommon. These are usually perennial plants. The Order is characterized by homospory. The sorus may be **simple** (all sporangia developing simultaneously), **gradate** (sporangia developing in a basepetal succession), or **mixed** (sporangia developing in an irregular sequence).

There are a number of Families included under the Order with about 300 genera and 9,J00 species (Copeland, 1947).

Geological records show that the members of this Order are comparatively younger than other groups of ferns and date back from the Permian and in all probability reached their climax in the Lower Cretaceous.

POLYPODIUM

(Fam. POLYPODIACEAE)

Polypodium is commonly found in tropical and temperate regions growing in the woods, hedge rows and near streams. Though it prefers shady places, it is sometimes found in more exposed situations, such as hill sides.

The genus comprises of 75 species. The common Indian species are *P. parasiticum*, *P. cucullatum*, *P. decorum* and *P. obliquatum*.

The sporophyte

The stem of *Polypodium* is a perennial, sparingly branched, erect or creeping rhizome, which when destitute of **fronds** (leaves) has the appearance of some kind of sea polypus. Usually, the greater part of the rhizome is subterranean, but it grows obliquely upwards and its apex rises a little above the surface of the ground and bears the leaves. This erect or ascending region is known as the **caudex,** often clothed with dense growth of scales, epidermal hairs or adventitious roots. The older portion of the stem shows the presence of persistent leaf-bases of the dead fronds, and when this portion dies the branches become disconnected and continue to develop as separate new plants.

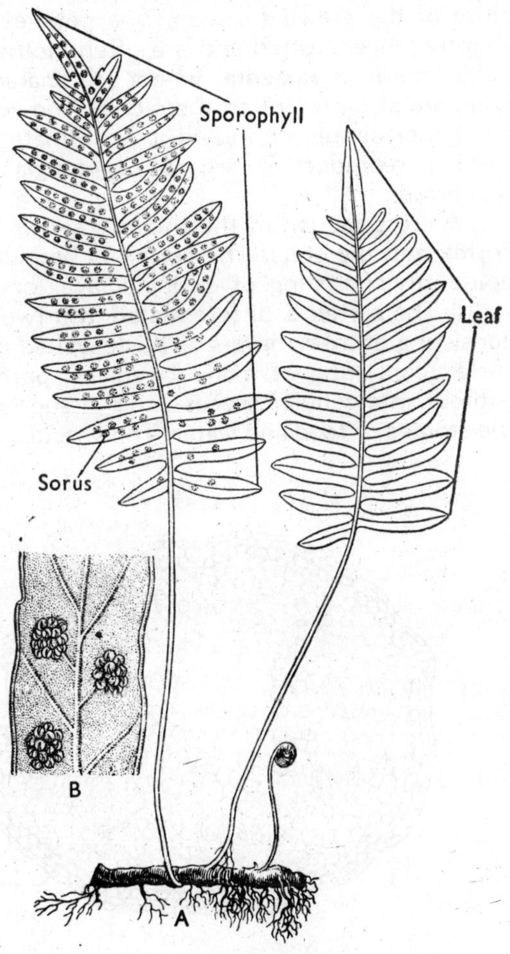

Fig. 374, *Polypodium.* A, An entire plant ; B, Portion of pinna with three sori.

The primary root dies early, all subsequent roots are adventitious and arise from lower side of the rhizome. Each root has a root cap and **root hairs.**

The leaves, often called **fronds,** are either simple, entire or pinnatifid or pinnately compound, and when young show characteristic **circinate ptyxis.** Annually, rosette of leaves unfold from the caudex portion of the rhizome and these ultimately die at the close of the growing season. The petioles (**stipes**) are short or slightly longer, tufted and are often clothed with numerous brown hairs known as **ramenta,** which are characteristic of ferns. These hairs are also present on the rachis. The veins of the leaf-segments are either simple or forked and ultimately bear groups (**sori**) of asexual reproductive organs (**sporangia**) and are, therefore, soriferous.

A cross-section of the rhizome shows two distinct regions, the cortex and the stele. The cortex is bounded on the outside by an epidermis consisting of a single layer of narrow cells with thick walls. The cortex is differentiated into two regions : (*a*) hypodermis consisting of a few layers of thick-walled parenchyma, (*b*) general cortex consisting of many layers of parenchyma cells with or without intercellular spaces ; this **tissue** is mainly concerned with the storage of food and water. The vascular bundles vary in number,

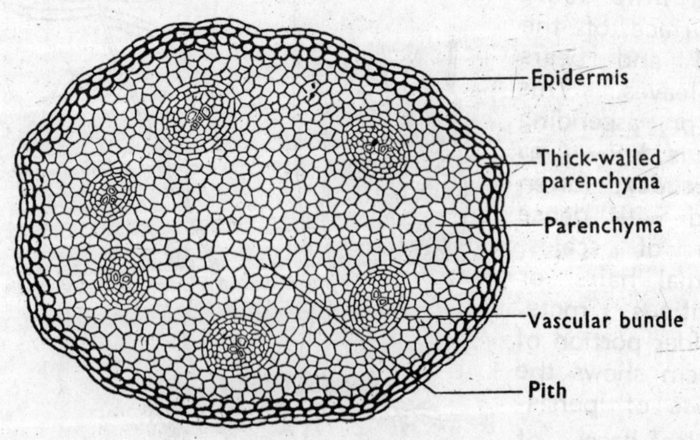

Fig. 375. *Polypodium.*
Transverse section of rhizome.

some of which are large and others are small and are generally found near about the centre of the stem. Each vascular bundle is discrete and hadrocentric and is surrounded by a typical endodermis, lying internal to which there is a single layer of pericycle ; the protoxylem is exarch. The phloem consists of **sieve** cells and 'conjunctive' parenchyma, and the xylem consists of tracheids varying in width with thick lignified walls and 'conjunctive' parenchyma like that of phloem. There is pith in the centre of the rhizome. Leaf-trace bundles are present in the cortex.

Early in summer, the foliage leaves bear on their under surface many greenish brown structures, called **sori,** which are developed directly over the veins so that the foliage leaves are now spoken of as **sporophylls.** Thus, in *Polypodium*, there is no differentiation into foliage leaves and sporophylls, both the functions of photosynthesis and spore-production are taken over by all the leaves. The sori are

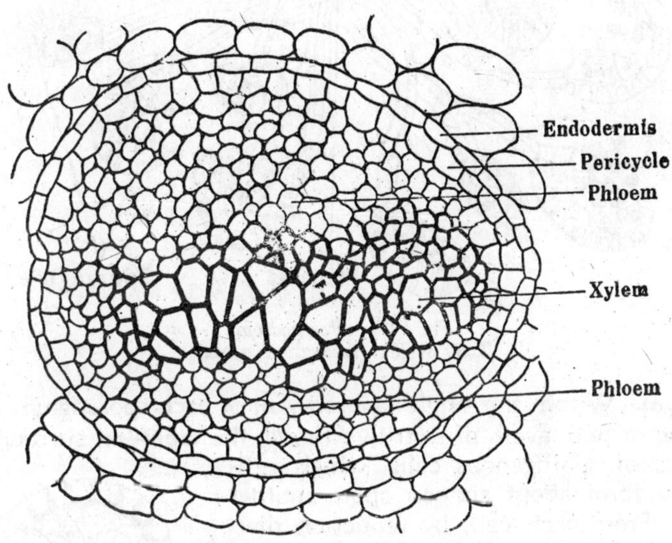

Fig. 376. *Polypodium*, A meristele (much enlarged).

generally round, large or small, and sometimes are mixed with hairs. They are generally terminal on the veinlets or at their bases forming a regular row on each side. Each sorus is naked and consists of a group of sporangia which arise from a tissue of the leaf, called **placenta** *. Each sporangium develops by the *leptosporangiate method.* ** The fully-formed sporangium is a lenticular **capsule** attached to the stalk. On the capsule there is a specialized,

* In some other genera of ferns it is protected by an **indusium,** outgrowth from the placenta.

** It means that the development of the sporogenous tissue takes place from the *outer* cell following the periclinal division of the superficial initial instead of from the *inner* cell, as in *Lycopodium*,

cutinized, incomplete cellular layer called **annulus.** Where the annulus stops short, the cells are thin and form what is called

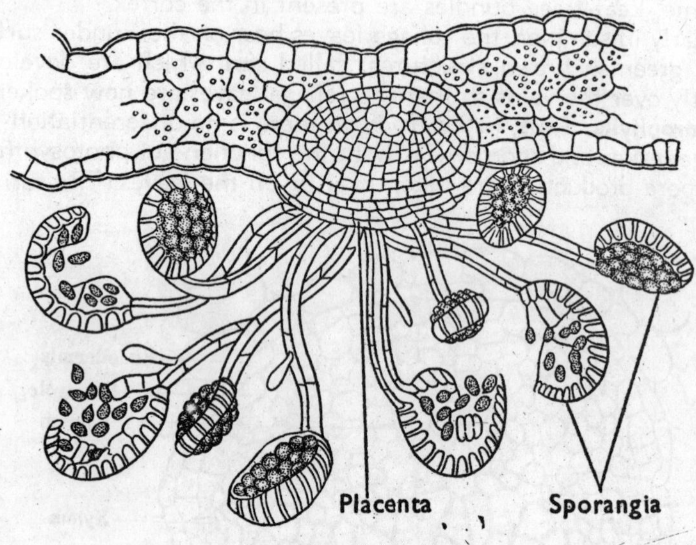

Fig. 377. *Polypodium.*
T.S. of leaf through a sorus.

stomium. Within the single-layered wall of each sporangium there are one or two layers of nutritive tissue, the **tapetum,** surrounding a mass of sporogenous cells, which ultimately form about sixteen spore mother cells. From each cell, by reduction division, a spore-tetrad is formed. When mature, the spores are dark-brown in colour and morphologically alike,—hence *Polypodium* is homosporous. *With reduction division and formation of spores, the gametophytic or haploid generation begins.*

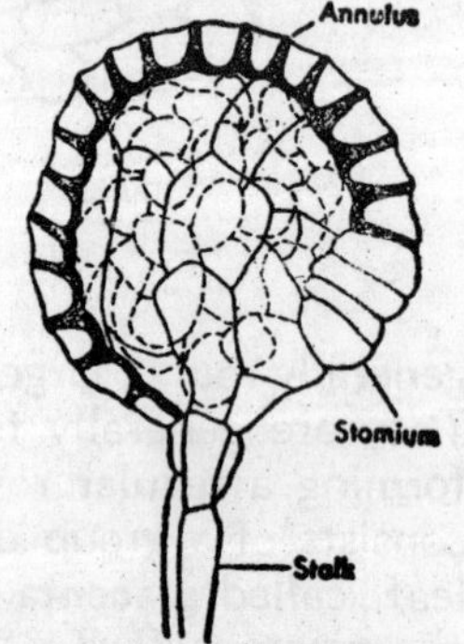

Fig. 378. *Polypodium.* A sporangium.

The gametophyte

When the sporangium ripens, it bursts at the stomium owing to the hygroscopic movement of the annulus and the spores escape. Each spore has two coats : the outer coat is called **exospore** and the inner coat, **endospore.** Under proper conditions of temperature and moisture each spore germinates. On germination, the outer coat bursts and the inner one elongates and protrudes into a multicellular filamentous structure, which when fully developed forms a flat, green, heart-shaped body called **prothallus.** The prothallus gives out from its under surface many delicate, unicellular, hair-like structures called **rhizoids,** by means of which the prothallus is not only attached to the substratum but it also draws nourishment therefrom. The prothallus is, therefore, an independent plant which can absorb raw food materials from the

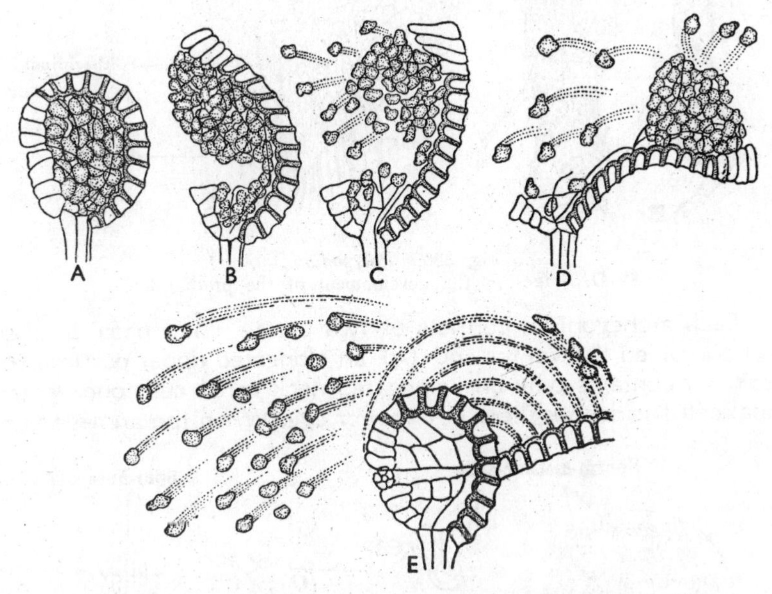

Fig. 379. *Polypodium.*
A—E, Successive stages in the dispersal of spores from sporangium (*after Atkinson*).

substratum and can carry on photosynthesis. The prothallus bears on its under surface, scattered among the rhizoids, especially on the thicker part of it, several multicellular bodies of two distinct kinds : (1) **antheridia** or the male sex organs, and (2) **archegonia** or the female sex organs.

Each antheridium is a spherical body and contains about thirty-two spermatozoid mother cells (**spermatocytes**), from each of which a spirally-twisted, multiflagellate **spermatozoid** or **antherozoid** is produced. When mature, the antheridium opens at the top and the mother cells are liberated; the spermatozoids set themselves free from the mother cells and begin to swim in the film of water already present on the surface of the prothallus.

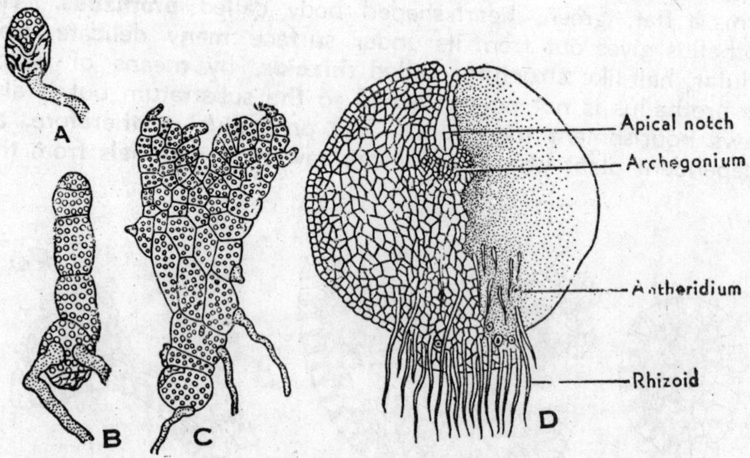

Fig. 380. *Polypodium.*
A—D, Stages in the development of the prothallus.

Each archegonium consists of two parts : (*i*) a basal swollen portion, called the **venter** and (*ii*) an elongated upper portion, the **neck.** It contains only one elongated neck canal cell, one ventral canal cell and an **oosphere** or **ovum** or **egg.** When the archegonium

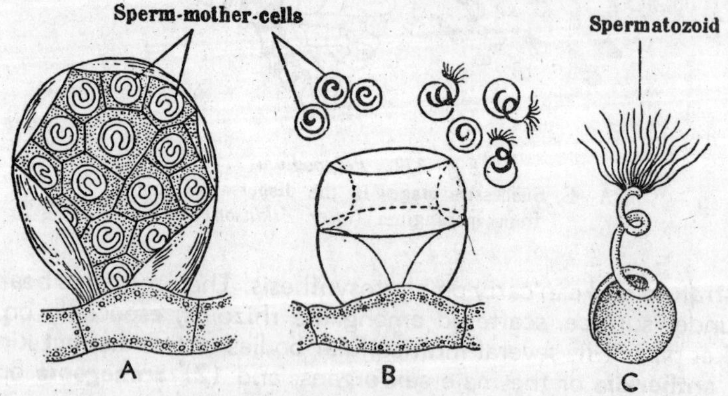

Fig. 381. *Polypodium.*
A, A mature antheridium ; B The same showing liberation of spermatozoids ;
C, A spermatozoid.

matures, its neck canal cell and ventral canal cell become disorganized so that a thorough passage is established between the exterior and interior of the archegonium. This passage becomes filled with a mucilagenous substance containing malic acid.

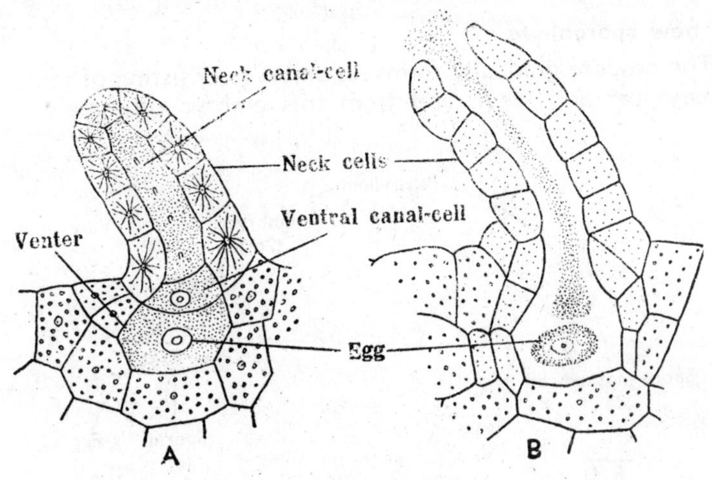

Fig. 382. *Polypodium.*
A, A young archegonium ; B, A mature archegonium discharging mucilage containing malic acid.

The spermatozoids, set free from the antheridium, move about by means of their flagella in the film of water already present on the surface of prothallus and are attracted towards the archegonium by the malic acid given out by it for the purpose. The spermatozoids enter the canal, pass down the venter but only one fertilizes the ovum. This fertilized ovum by secreting a wall round itself becomes an **oospore.** *With fertilization and formation of oospore, the sporophytic or diploid generation begins.*

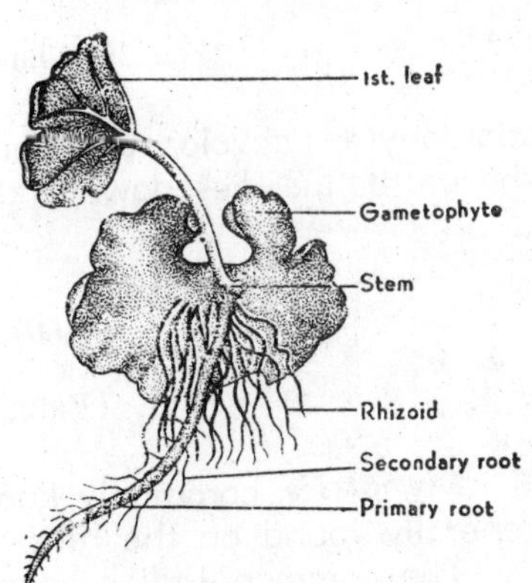

Fig. 383. *Polypodium.*
A young sporophyte still attached to the gametophyte.

It is to be noted that although the prothallus bears, as a rule, both kinds of sex organs, the antheridia and archegonia, cross-fertilization generally takes place, *i.e.*, spermatozoids developed on one prothallus pass into the archegonia of another. This is necessary because antheridium and archegonium are not developed on the same prothallus simultaneously.

The new sporophyte

The oospore gradually forms an **embryo** consisting of foot, root, primary leaf and stem, and from this embryo ultimately a new

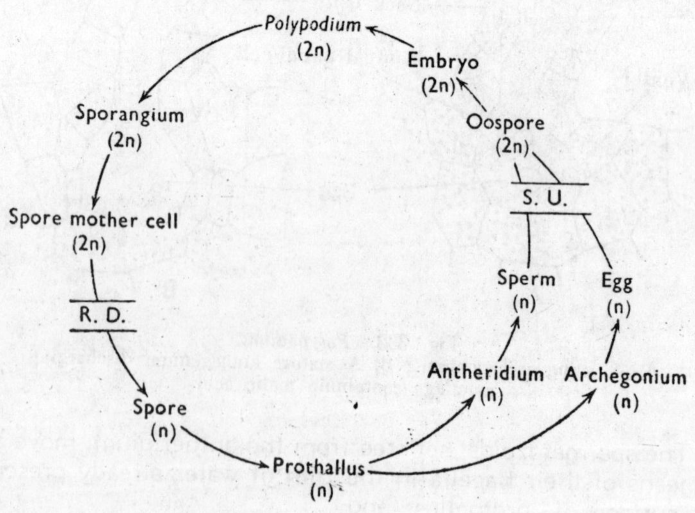

Fig. 384. Life cycle of *Polypodium*.

sporophyte is developed. After the establishment of new sporophyte the prothallus dies down and thus it becomes independent.

DRYOPTERIS

(Fam. ASPIDIACEAE)

Dryopteris, commonly known as 'male fern' or 'shield fern', is generally found on the hills.

The common Indian species of *Dryopteris* is *D. filix-mas*.

The sporophyte

Dryopteris presents a robust appearance and when fully developed, it consists of a short, unbranched, stout and massive rhizome, which grows obliquely upwards and its apex rises but little above the surface of the soil. The stem is entirely covered over by numerous persistent leaf bases. There is usually no lateral branching, but adventitious buds are developed at the bases of the leaves and these may separate to form new plants.

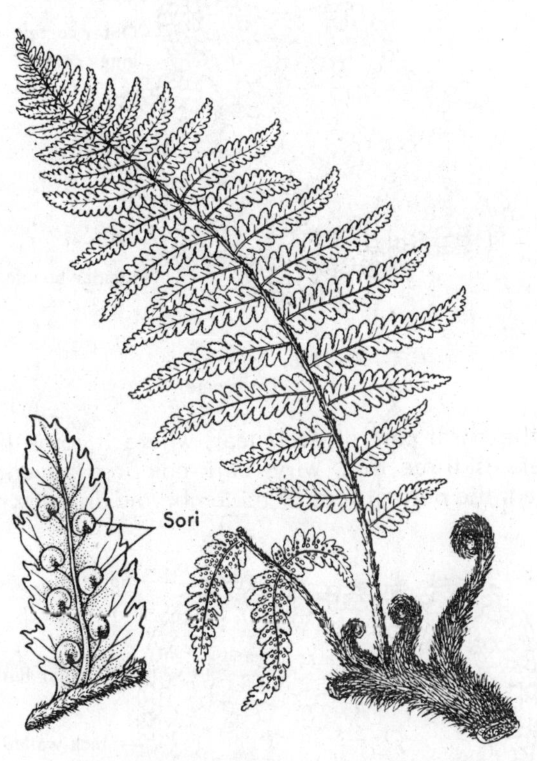

Fig. 385. *Dryopteris filix-mas.*
Portion of a plant on the right and portion of a pinna with sori on the left.

A transverse section of the rhizome shows two distinct regions : a large mass of ground tissue made up of parenchyma cells, and a vascular cylinder. The vascular cylinder is a typical dictyostele, with a number of meristeles embedded in the ground tissue forming an irregular ring. Each meristele is either round or elliptic in outline. The general mass of ground tissue lying internal to meristelar ring is the pith, while the tissue lying outside this ring constitutes the cortex. The cortex can be differentiated into two zones : an inner cortex made up of several layers of parenchyma cells with thin cellulose walls, and an outer cortex consisting of a few layers of cells with lignified thick walls. On the outermost surface there is the single-layered epidermis.

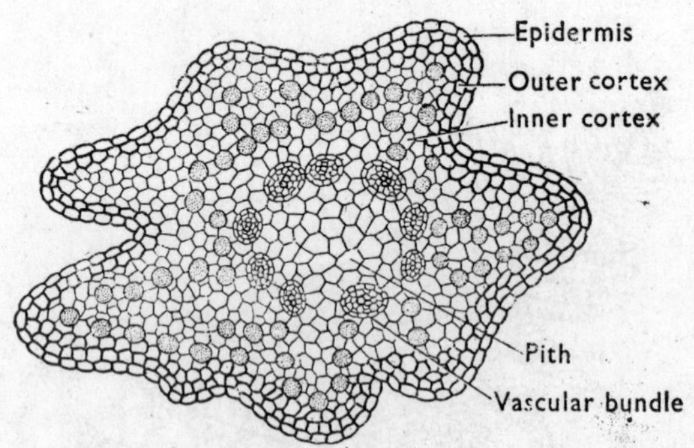

Fig. 386. *Dryopteris.*
T.S. of rhizome.

From the basal part of each leaf, where it joins the rhizome, usually there is three thin, wiry, dark-coloured adventitious roots are produced, the normal root of the embryo dying down very early.

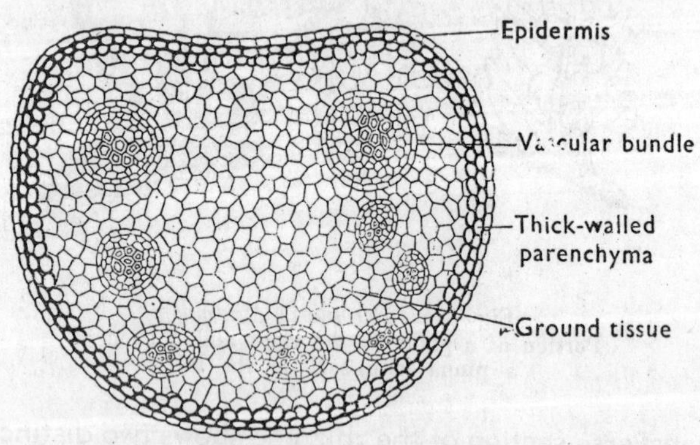

Fig. 387. *Dryopteris.*
T.S. of rachis.

These adventitious roots branch extensively and monopodially, the branches appearing in acropetal order of succession. As a result, the rhizome is clothed with a dense mass of adventitious roots.

Internally, the root represents that of *Polypodium* in essential characters.

The leaves, often called **fronds,** are large (may be up to 1 metre in length), pinnately compound and much subdivided and when young they show characteristic circinate ptyxis. Annually a rosette of leaves unfolds towards the growing region of the stem. The lower portion of the rachis and also the large veins of the leaflets are clothed with numerous brown scales, known as the **ramenta,** which are characteristics of ferns.

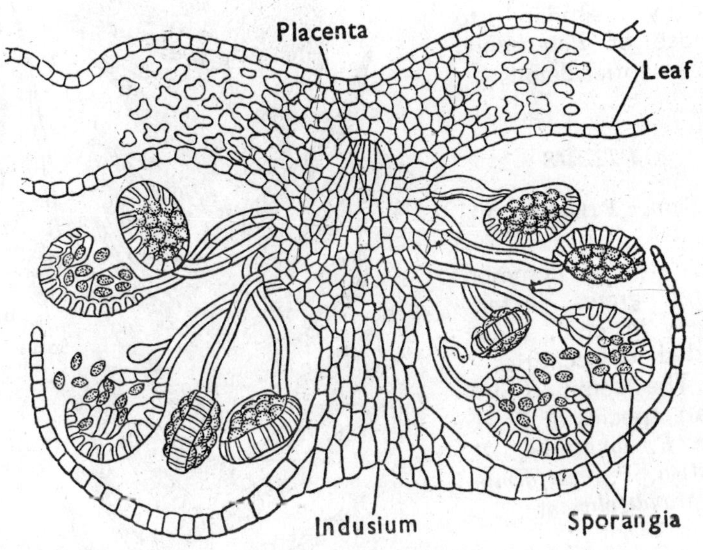

Fig. 388. *Dryopteris*, T.S, through a sorus.

A transverse section of the rachis reveals a number of isolated vascular strands embedded in a ground tissue giving rise to a somewhat horseshoe-shaped structure. The ground tissue is generally made up of several layers of parenchyma cells, of which a few outer layers are thick-walled. Each vascular bundle is hadrocentric.

During summer the sporangia are produced in groups forming small reniform **sori,** borne on the ventral surface of the pinnae of fertile leaves or **sporophylls.** The smaller pinnae usually bear only one or two sori each, while in the larger ones the sori are developed in two distinct rows, one on each side of the midrib. Each sorus is situated on a lateral vein and covered by a kidney-shaped **indusium.**

The structure of the sporangium as well as the process of fertilization are practically similar to those of *Polypodium* in essential details.

PTERIS

(Fam. PTERIDACEAE)

Pteris, a common fern, grows extensively in cool, moist and shady localities.

The common Indian species of *Pteris* are *P. longifolia*, *P. cretica*, *P. ensiformis*, *P. grandifolia*, etc.

The sporophyte

The rhizome may be either short and straight (as in *P. longifolia*, *P. cretica*, *P. ensiformis*, etc.), or long and creeping (as in *P. grandifolia*).

The internal anatomy of the rhizome is rather complicated and is very variable. Usually, in the cases of creeping rhizomes

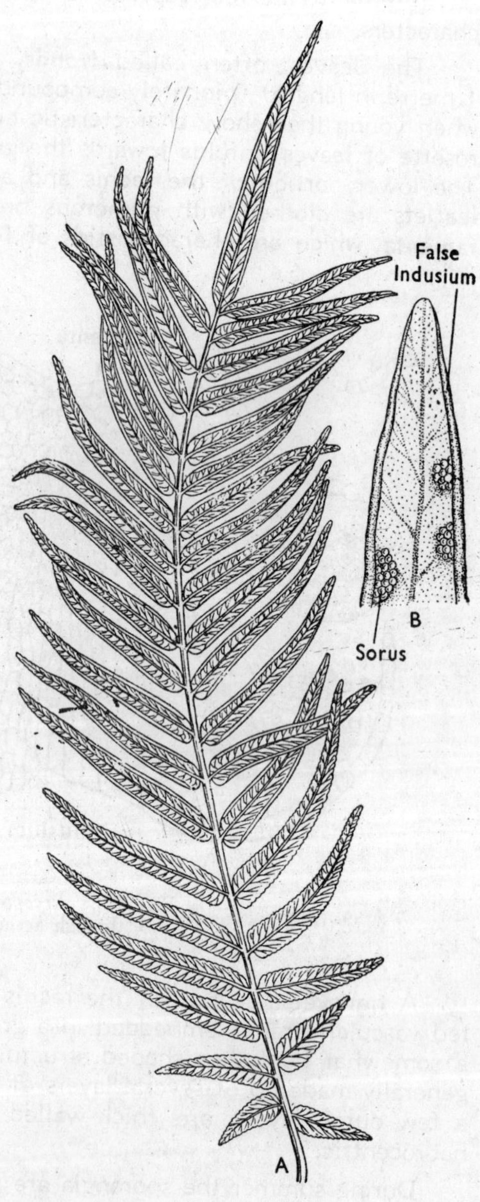

Fig. 389. *Pteris longifolia.* A, Portion of a shoot ; B, Portion of a pinna with coenosori.

the vascular cylinder is a solenostele, but in the species with upright rhizomes it is a polycyclic dictyostele with prominent overlapping leaf gaps.

The roots are adventitious in nature and develop from the rhizome. Internally, the root represents essentially the structure of that of *Polypodium*.

The leaves are variable and range from pinnate compound to decompound type. Scales and unbranched hairs are generally present at the leaf-bases as well as on the rhizomes forming **ramenta.** The leaves of the most commonly occurring species, *P. longifolia,* are imparipinnately compound and the pinnae are lanceolate in shape. The pinnae are sessile and situated laterally on both the sides of the rachis. Each pinna possesses a venation which is at first pinnate and then forked.

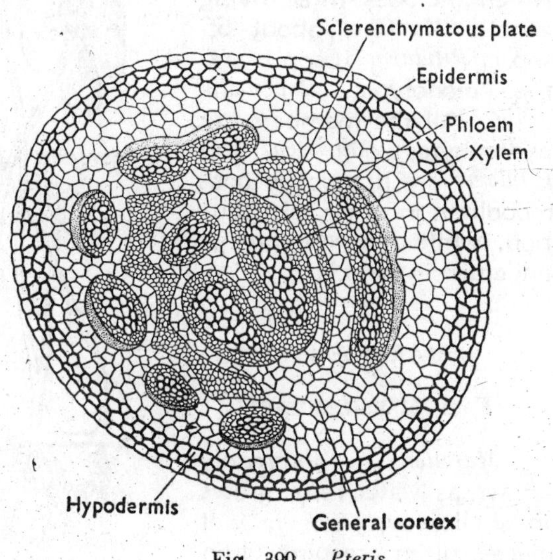

Fig. 390. *Pteris.* T.S. of rhizome.

A cross-section of the rachis reveals the presence of a single horseshoe-shaped hadrocentric bundle with exarch xylem embedded in the ground tissue, as in *Dryopteris*.

The sporangia are grouped together forming continuous linear sori, termed as **coenosori**, borne on the marginal connecting veins. As a rule, these coenosori are not produced near about the apices of the pinnae and their continuity may be interrupted at irregular intervals. Each sorus is protected by the reflexed margin of the pinna itself, which forms a **false indusium.**

The structure of the sporangium as well as the process of fertilization are practically similar to those of *Dryopteris* in essential details.

ORDER 4. MARSILEALES

The Order **Marsileales is characterized in having the sporangia** produced within a specialized structure, called the *sporocarp*. The sporocarp wall is produced by the modification of the leaf-blade. The sori borne within the sporocarp are of gradate type and the spores are heterospores.

The Order contains only one Family **Marsileaceae,** which includes three living genera : *Marsilea* (about 65 spp.), *Pilularia* (6spp.) and the monotypic *Regenellidium*. All the members are hydrophytes. *Marsilea* and *Pilularia* are practically cosmopolitan in their distribution, while *Regenellidium* is endemic in Brazil.

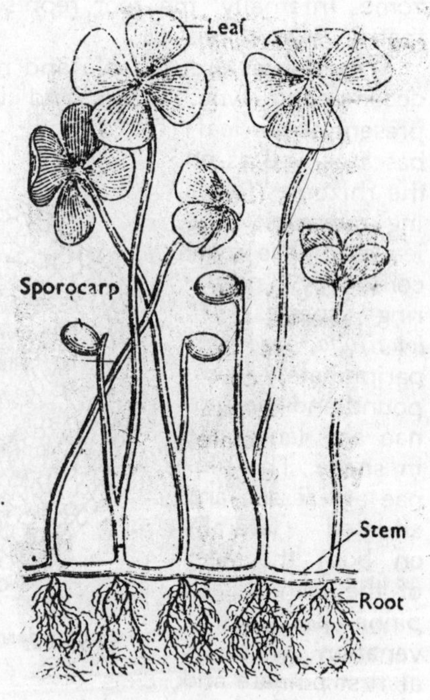

Fig. 391. *Marsilea*, An entire plant with sporocarps.

MARSILEA

(Fam. MARSILEACEAE)

Marsilea, commonly known as 'water fern', grows in shallow water or in wet places, often creeping upon the banks and growing in all directions. A few species, however, grow in dry situations throughout the year. The genus comprises of 70 species. The common Indian species are *M. minuta*, *M. quadrifolia*, *M. condensata*, and *M. poonensis*.

The sporophyte

The stem is rhizomatous, dichotomously branched and creeps on or just below the surface of the substratum. The internodes may be short or long. On the upper side of the rhizome there are two rows of alternating erect leaves. The branches are either axillary or arising below or lateral to each leaf. Adventitious roots develop on the outer side of each node of the rhizome. The leaves are typically peltate and quadrifoliate, each with a considerably long petiole. Young leaves, towards the growing apex of stem, show characteristic circinate ptyxis. The veins in the awl-shaped leaflets are dichotomously branched and are ultimately connected by short veinlets to form a reticulum.

Internally, the rhizomes of all species of *Marsilea* have an amphiphloic siphonostele, being limited internally and externally by endodermal layers, and with a central pith. The pith may be either parenchymatous or sclerotic, depending upon environmental conditions in which the plant grows, and is separated from the inner pericycle by a single layer of parenchymatous endodermis. In some species the protoxylem elements are not recognizable. Inside the outer endodermis there is a single layer of parenchymatous pericycle. External to the outer endodermis lies a comparatively thick

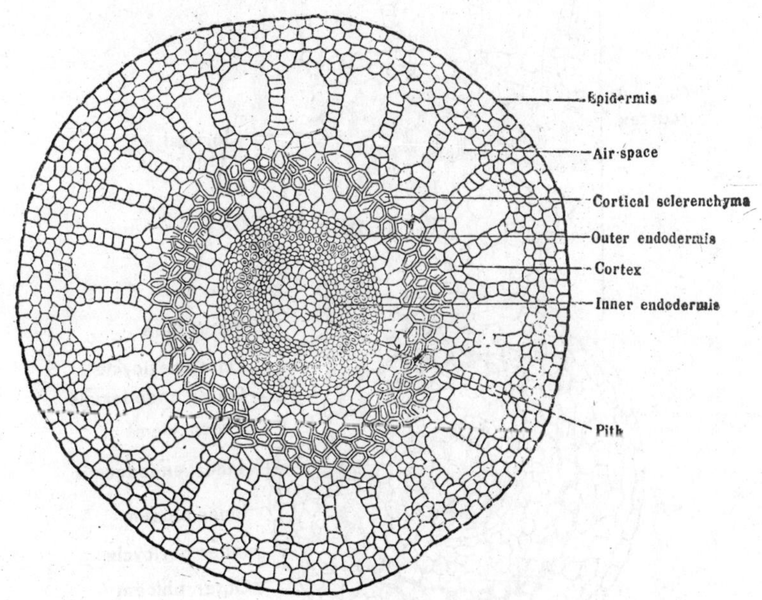

Fig. 392. *Marsilea.*
Transverse section of rhizome.

cortex extending up to the epidermis. This is differentiated into an inner solid thin-walled or sclerotic parenchyma and an outer parenchyma with a single ring of conspicuous air space, being limited externally by one to several layers of parenchymatous tissue.

At the time of reproduction prominent reproductive structures, known as **sporocarps,** which are usually borne laterally on short or long peduncles inserted a little above the base of the petioles (sometimes apparently adaxially or axillary). The sporocarps are stalked and somewhat bean-shaped to ovoid nut-like bodies. The wall is very hard and thick, strongly resistant to external influences and is capable of retaining its vitality for several years. The peduncle may be unbranched with a solitary terminal sporocarp, or in some species branches dichotomously and bears 2-20 or more

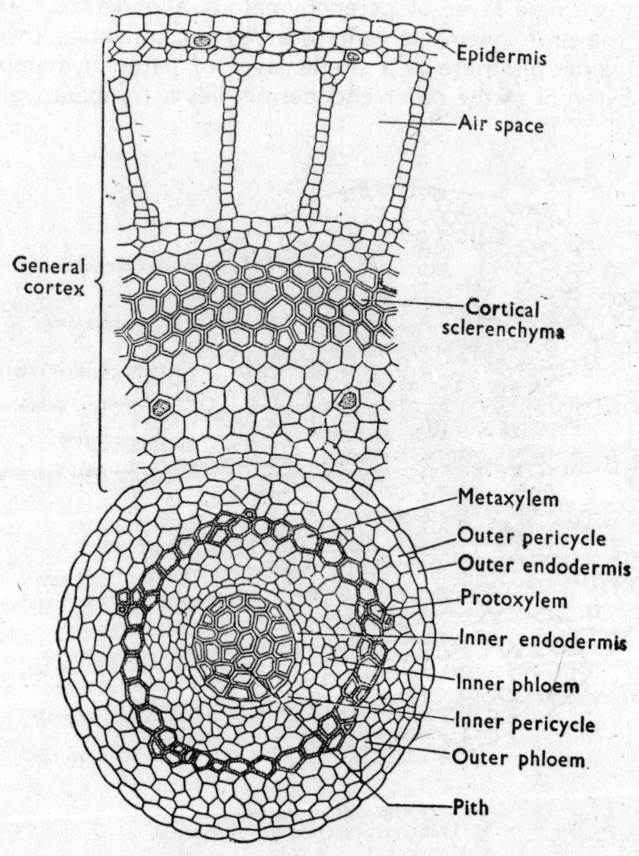

Fig. 393, *Marsilea*.
T.S. of rhizome (in part).

sporocarps. It has generally been interpreted that the sporocarp of *Marsilea* is 'a modified fertile segment from the lower part of a leaf, but it has also been considered to be homologous with the whole leaf'.

Morphology of sporocarp

The following views have been put forward to explain the morphology of the sporocarp of *Marsilea* :

1. The sporocarp has been interpreted as homologous with the whole leaf by Johnson (1933), because the apical growth of the sporocarp and an entire leaf is similar.

The argument against the view is that the vascular supply of the peduncle and a sporocarp is similar to that of a leaf segment.

2. According to Busgen (1890) the sporocarp is formed by two pinnae. But the single bundle in the peduncle and single main vein in the sporocarp show that it is not two pinnae but a single pinna.

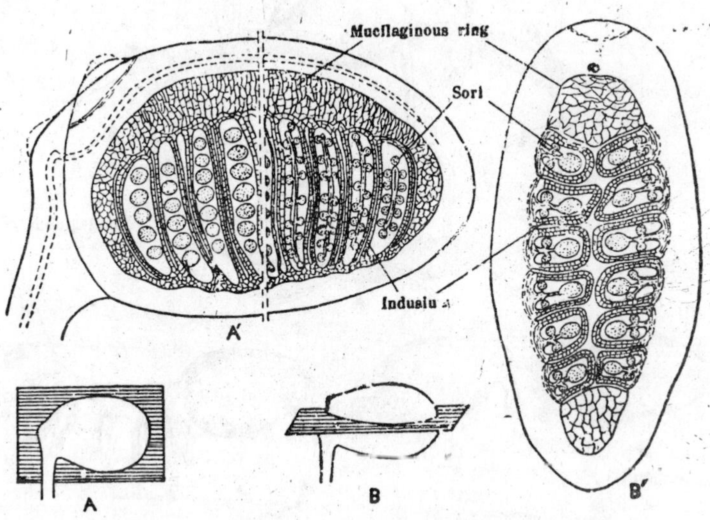

Fig. 394. *Marsilea*.
A—A′, Vertical section through the sporocarp ;
B—B′, Transverse section of the same.

Bower (1926) and Campbell (1903) believed that the sporocarp is formed by a pinnately divided pinna and the pinnules becoming fused.

4. Smith holds that in case of a single sporocarp at the base of a leaf (*M. vestita*) the infolding pinna is undivided. He suggested that the lateral margins of the abaxial side of the pinna is reflexed to oppose each other. Single pinna nature is evidenced by the presence of single main vein in the sporocarp and single bundle in the peduncle.

It is held that the sporocarp of *Marsilea* has been evolved due to an infolding of a fertile pinna of Cyathacious type of leaf. The Cyathacious nature is indicated by the presence of gradate sorus and enclosure of the receptacle by an indusium.

Within the inner wall of the sporocarp and attached to it, there are two rows of elongated, closely-packed **sori,** one on each side filling up the sporocarp cavity, and these extend transversely to the longitudinal axis of the sporocarp. Each sorus is enclosed by a delicate **indusium.** *Marsilea* is heterosporous and each sorus contains a row of megasporangia surrounded by many microsporangia.

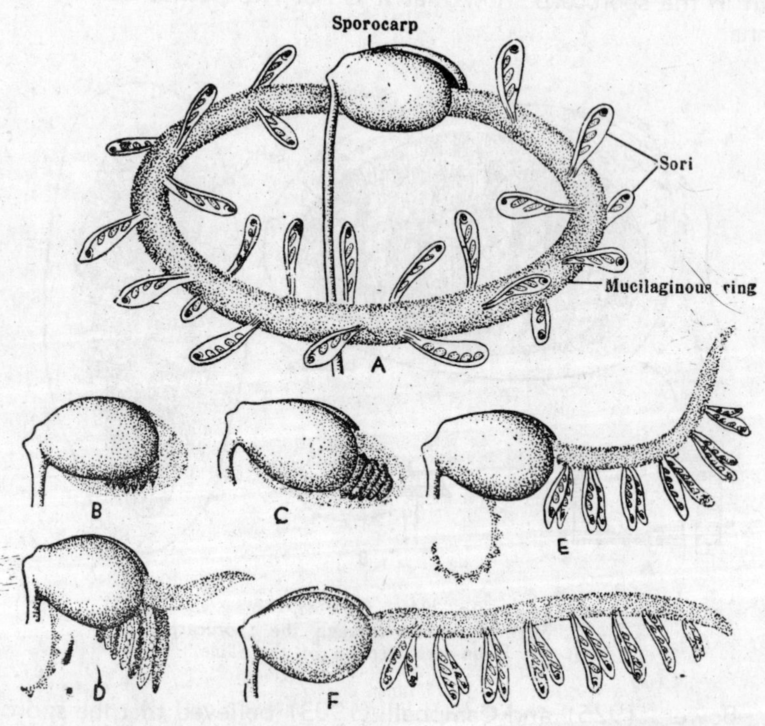

Fig. 395. *Marsitea,*
A—F, Successive stages in the germination of the sporocarp.

These sori are attached to a mucilagenous tissue, which swells remarkably on coming in contact with water at the time of germination. All the mother cells of the microsporangium undergo reduction division and form microspores. Within the megasporangium only one mother cell matures and by reduction division forms a sporetetrad, of which only one megaspore matures, while others degenerate. *With reduction division and formation of spores the gametophytic or haploid generation begins.*

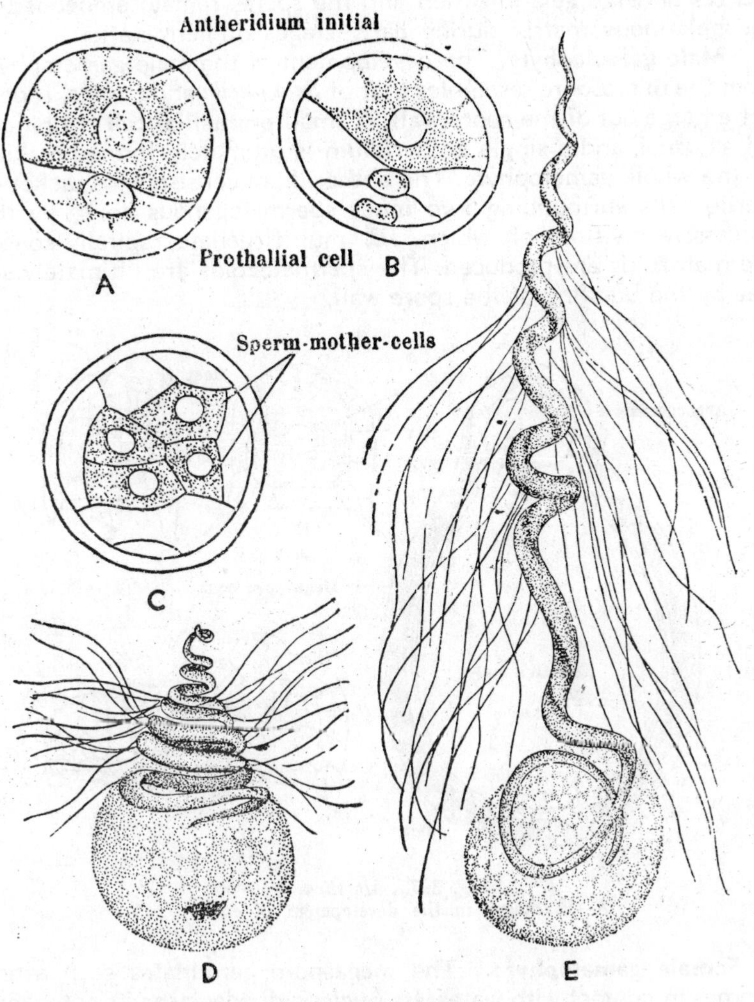

Fig. 396. *Marsilea.*
A—E, Stages in the Development of spermatozoids.

The gametophytes

When the spores attain maturity, the sporocarp germinates and opens in water along its ventral side and apex, splitting in a spreading bi-valved structure. The ring of internal mucilagenous tissue within the sori absorbs water, swells remarkably, comes out of the ruptured sporocarp and thus drags out the sori which are attached to the ring by their ends. Gradually the indusia and the sporangial jackets undergo gelatinization and the spores remain embedded in the gelatinous matrix during early stages of germination.

Male gametophyte. The development of the male gametophyte from the microspore resembles that of *Selaginella* and *Isoetes*. It does not emerge out of the spore wall. A small **prothallial cell** is first cut off as usual, and a single antheridium is ultimately formed making up the whole gametophyte. The antheridium consists of a jacket of sterile cells surrounding two inner spermatogenous cells, by the successive divisions of which 16, multiflagellate, spirally-coiled, spermatozoids are produced. The spermatozoids are ultimately set free by the bursting of the spore wall.

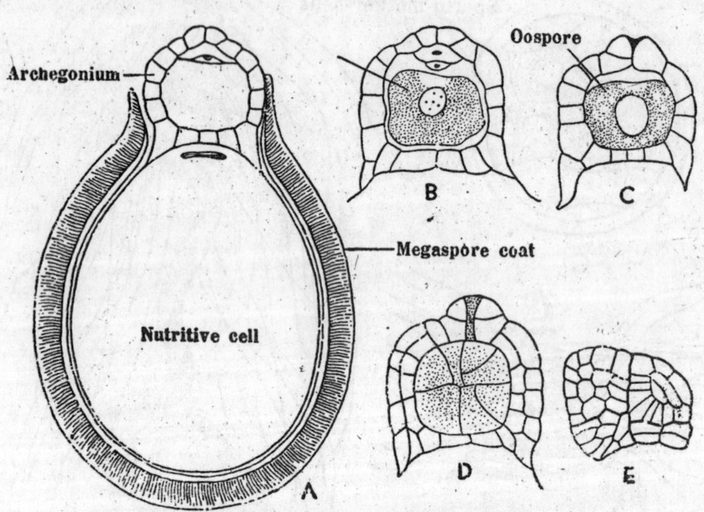

Fig. 397. *Marsilea*.
A—E, Stages in the development of embryo.

Female gametophyte. The megaspore germinates soon after it comes in contact with water. Its nucleus divides near its apex and a small apical cell is cut off by a wall. The large basal cell, with its undivided nucleus, contains abundant food materials, including starch grains, and is nutritive in function. The small apical cell protrudes through the megaspore wall and forms a small group of cells, the gametophyte proper, bearing a small and simple archegonium. The archegonium is broad but low and has only one neck canal cell.

The spermatozoids swim towards an archegonium and only one

finding its way down through the neck fertilizes the ovum and forms an **oospore.** *With fertilization and formation of oospore, the sporophytic or diploid generation begins.*

The new sporophyte

The oospore develops into an embryo consisting of a leaf, a root, a foot and the stem, and from this embryo the *Marsilea* plant is ultimately developed.

Comparison between Pteris and Marselia

Pteris	*Marselia*
(a) The Sporophyte	
1. Plants—terrestrial herbs growing in cool, moist and shady places.	1. Plants—delicate herbs growing in shallow water or wet places.
2. Stem—short and straight or long and creeping rhizome, bearing ramenta.	2. Stem—rhizomatous, dichotomously branched, creeping on just below the surface of the substratum.
3. Roots—adventitious growing from the rhizome.	3. Roots—adventitious growing from the nodes of the lower surface of the stem.
4. Leaves—usually imparipinnately compound ; pinnae lanceolate, sessile and situated laterally on both the sides of the reaches by veins at first pinnate and then forked ; circinate ptyxis.	4. Leaves—quadrifoliate with long petioles, growing from the nodes on the upper surface of stem veins dichotomously branched ; circinate ptyxis.
5, Sporangia of one kind, grouped in coenosori along the margins of pinnae and covered by false indusium. Each sporangium contains numerous small spores of one kind.	5. Sporangia of two kinds, micro- and mega- produced in sori in the sporocarp cavity and attached to its inner wall and covered by indusium. Each sorbs contains a row of megasporangia surrounded by microsporangia. Each microsporangium contains numerous small microspores and the megasporangium one functional megaspore.
(b) The gametophyte	
6. Spore is the first of all the gametophyte, It produces on germination, a flat, green, heart-shaped prothallus.	6. Spores are the first cells of the gametophytes, Microspore, on germination, produces prothallial cell and the megaspore, the female prothallus.
7. Gametophyte is of one kind and represented by prothallus which bears the sex organs (antheridium and archegonium) and rhizoids from its under surface,	7. Gametophytes are of two kinds : the male gametophyte is represented by the prothallial cell, and the female gametophyte by a group of cells formed near the apex of the megaspore.

Comparison between Pteris and Marselia

Pteris	*Marselia*
(b) The gametophyte	
8. Antheridium is a round body which is produced among the rhizoids of the prothallus. It gives rise to numerous multiflagellate sperms.	8. Antheridium consists of a jacket of cells enclosing two sperm atogenous cells which by successive divisions give rise to multi-flagellate sperms,
9. Archegonium is a flask-shaped body produced near the match of the prothallus and consists of only one, elongated neck canal cell, one ventral canal cell and an egg cell.	9. Archegonium is simple and broad, and consists of only one neck canal cell, one vertral canal cell and an egg cell,

ORDER 5. SALVINIALES

The Order Salviniales is also heterosporous and the sporangia are developed within *sporocarps*, each sporocarp containing either a number of microsporangia or a solitary megasporangium. The sporocarp wall is produced by the modification of the indusium.

The Order includes a single Family **Salviniaceae** with *two* living genera * : *Salvinia* (13 spp.) and *Azolla* (5 spp.). The plants are mainly inhabitants of tropical freshwaters.

SALVINIA

(Fam. SALVINIACEAE)

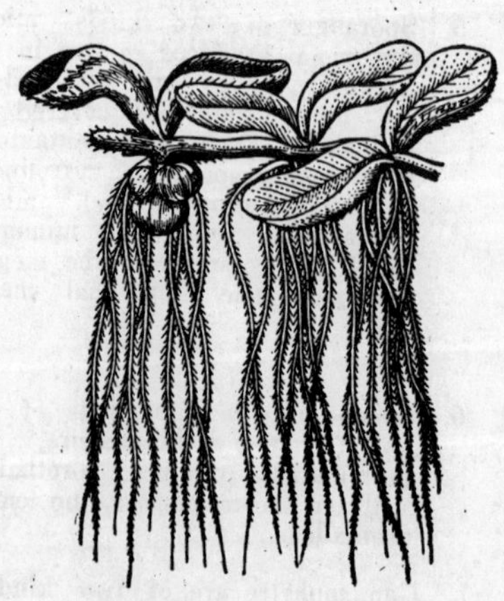

Fig. 398. *Salvinia natans.*

Salvinia is a free-floating hydrophyte and inhabits fresh-water pools, tanks and lakes gregariously. It is mainly an African genus, though a few species are very common in India.

The genus comprises of 10 species. The common Indian species are *S. natans* and *S. cucullata*.

The sporophyte

The stem is a branched rhizome attaining a length up to 10 cm. and the entire body is

* According to Christensen (1938) the two genera belong to two different Families.

densely clothed with short-stalked or sessile leaves, arranged in whorls of three * (two lateral and one submerged). The plant is rootless but the submerged leaf gets highly dissected and covered with multicellular hairs and thus resembles the root-system. The two lateral leaves are covered with stiff hairs and papilose projections and are highly modified as floating organs.

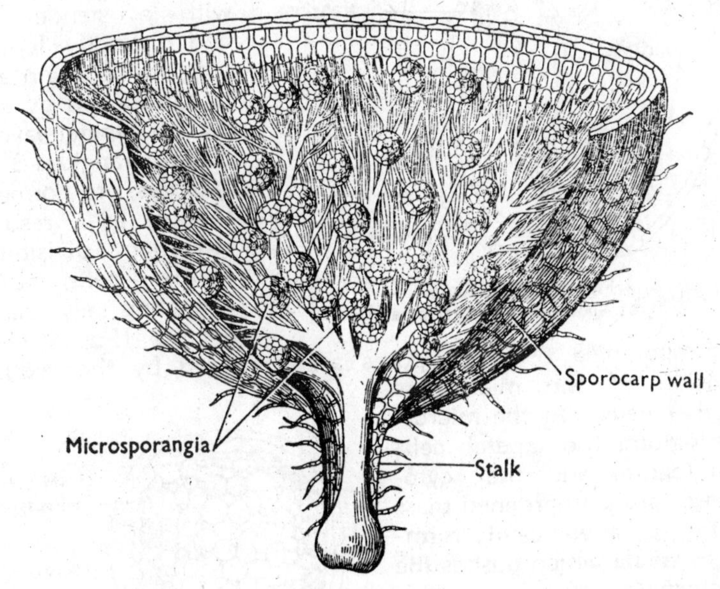

Fig. 399. *Salvinia.*
A sporocarp partially split open to show the microsporangia.

Internally, the rhizome has a siphonostele with greatly reduced vascular tissues and a broken cylinder of xylem.

The sporocarp

The sporocarps are oval, nut-like bodies which appear to arise in clusters near the base of the much dissected submerged leaf. Actually each segment of the leaf terminates into a sporocarp. The sporangia in each sporocarp arise on a raised Placenta, invested by

* The whorl of three leaves at a node regularly alternate with another whorl of three leaves, thus giving rise to six rows of leaves although due to the arrangement of leaves these appear to be present in three rows only.

an indusium. Thus each sporocarp is nothing but a sorus containing clustered sporangia. The sporocarps are differentiated into microsporocarps bearing microsporangia only and megasporocarps bearing megasporangia only (Fig. 400). Each sporangium is provided with a slender stalk and distinctly leptosporangiate in origin and it is surrounded by a wall with a tapetal layer. In megasporangium 32 megaspores are formed in tetrads, as a result of reduction division of mother cells but all excepting only one degenerate (Fig. 401). In microsporangia 64 microspores are produced by the reduction division of the microspore mother cells. In the microsporangium, the tapetal cells disintegrate and the cytoplasm forms a hardened mass in the sporangial cavity forming **massula** which pushes the microspores towards the periphery. In megasporangium, the hardened matrix formed from the tapetal cells and degenerated megaspores later become triangular, vacuolated and lobed at the tip forming **perespore** or **epispore**, with the formation of spores, gametophytic germination begins.

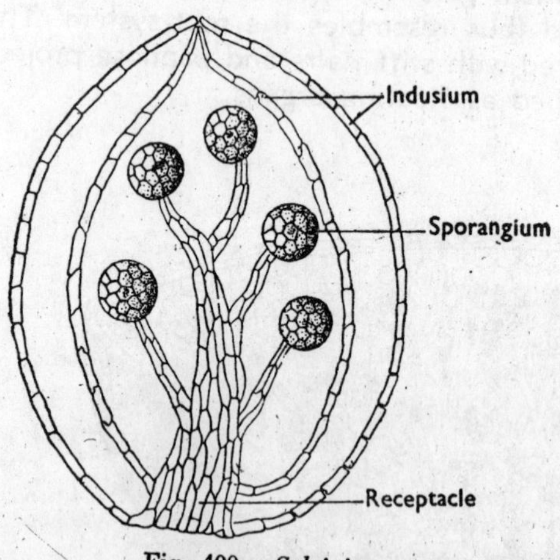

Fig. 400, *Salvinia*, L.S. of sporocarp (Diagrammatic).

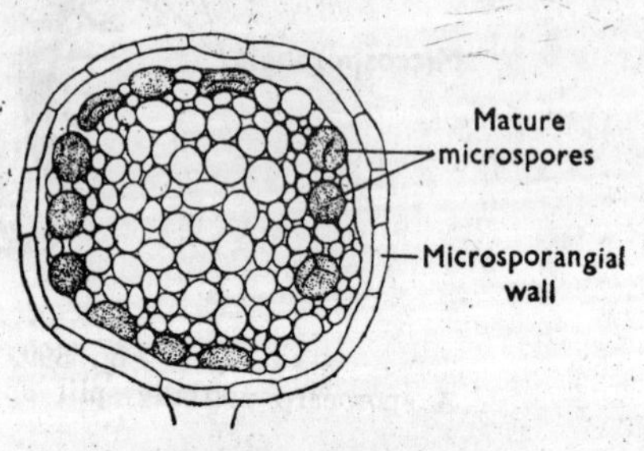

Fig. 401. *Salvinia*. A mature microsporangium in sectional view.

The gametophytes

Male gametophyte (Fig. 402). The **microspores germinate** within the massula of the microsporangium and develops into the male gametophyte. It cuts off a small prothalial cell and two antheridia. There is a large basal cell below the **antheridia** by which the antheridia are pushed out of the microsporangial wall. Each antheridium consists of four sperm mother cells within each of which a spirally coiled multiflagellate sperm is formed.

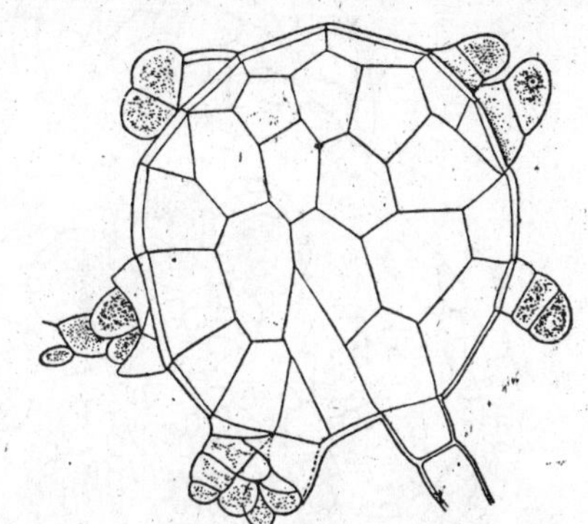

Fig, 402. *Salvinia,* Developing male gametophytes emerging out of the microsporangium,

Female gametophyte (Fig. 403). The single megaspore germinates within the perispore of the megasporangium and develops into the female gametophyte. A mature female gametophyte consists of a large basal, multinucleated nutritive cell and an archegonium which projects out of the triradiate ridge of the megaspore and gradually turns green. Each archegonium consist's of a neck made of binucleate neck canal and venter of a ventral canal cell and an egg.

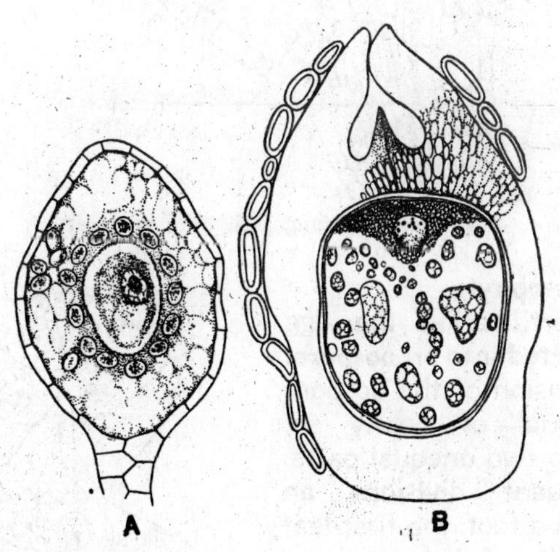

Fig. 403, *Salvinia,* A, The surviving megaspore in a megasporangium ; B, V,S, of a mature megaspore,

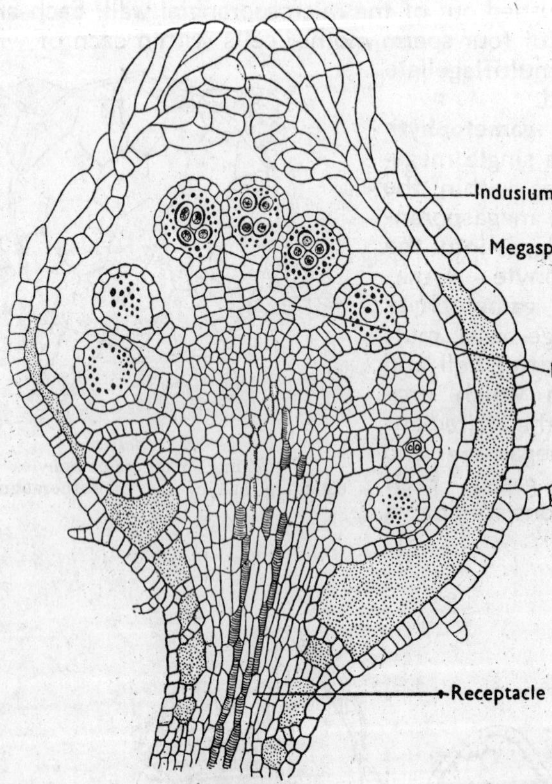

Fig. 404. *Salvinia,* L.S. of a sporocarp.

The new sporophyte

After fertilization the egg cell is converted into an **oospore.** The first division of the oospore is longitudinal or nearly so, giving rise to two unequal parts. By subsequent divisions an *embryo*, with a foot, the first leaf and a stem apex *, is formed and ultimately produces a new sporophyte.

* According to some workers the embryo possesses all the quadrants forming stem, leaf, foot and root, of which the last segment stops growing very early and cannot be distinguished from the foot.

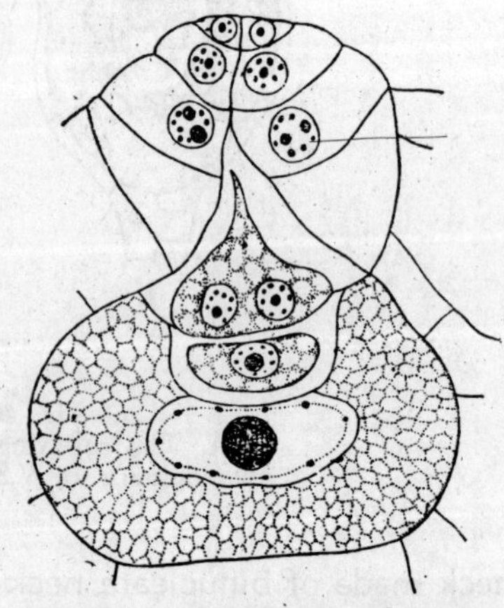

Fig. 405. *Salvinia,* An archegonium.

AZOLLA

(Fam. SALVINIACEAE)

Azolla is a free-floating plant occurring in fresh water pools, tanks and back waters. The genus comprises of 6 species, of which *A. filiculoides* may be regarded as a cosmopolitan one.

The common Indian species is *A. pinnata* (=*A. imbricata*).

No fossil representative is known from earlier than the Lower Caeneozoic bed.

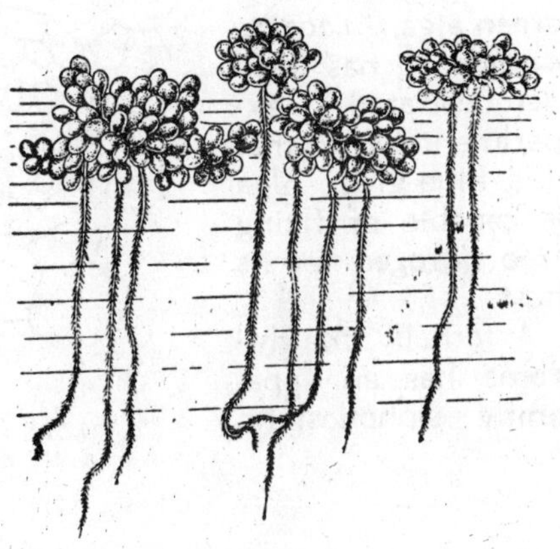

Fig. 406. *Azolla pinnata.* Plant body.

The sporophyte

The sporophyte of *Azolla* looks more or less like the gametophyte of a leafy Jungermannia. It has a freely branched, delicate rhizome, which is horizontally floating, bearing solitary or clustered adventitious roots on the underside, and alternately arranged two-ranked leaves on the dorsal side. Each leaf is dorsiventrally lobed,

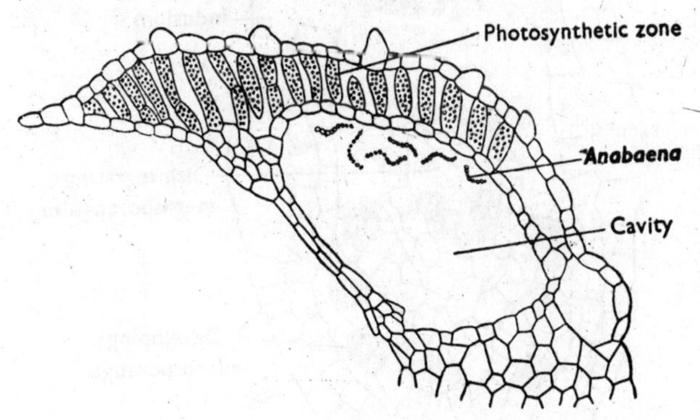

Fig. 407. *Azolla.*
L.S. through the dorsal lobe of a mature leaf.

the lobes being approximately of equal size ; the thick dorsal lobe is green and aerial, while the thin ventral one is almost hyaline and submerged. This ventral lobe is believed to be helpful in absorbing water. On the lower surface of the dorsal lobe there is a conspicuous cavity harbouring the blue-green alga, *Anabaena azollae*. It has been demonstrated experimentally that this blue-green alga is capable of fixing free nitrogen for its host.

Internally, the rhizome has an apparently siphonostelic

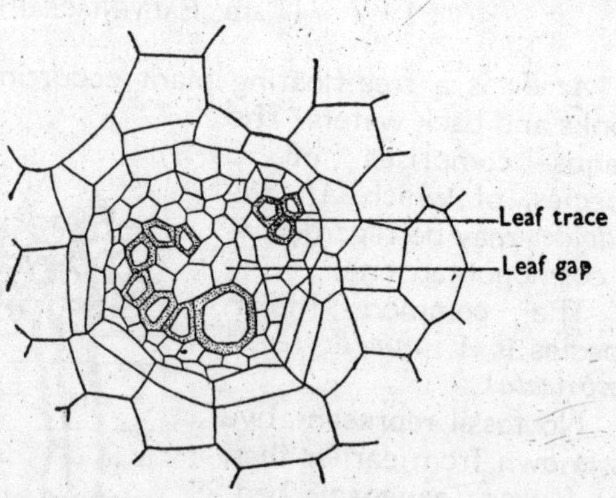

Fig. 408, *Azolla*, T.S. of stem (in part),

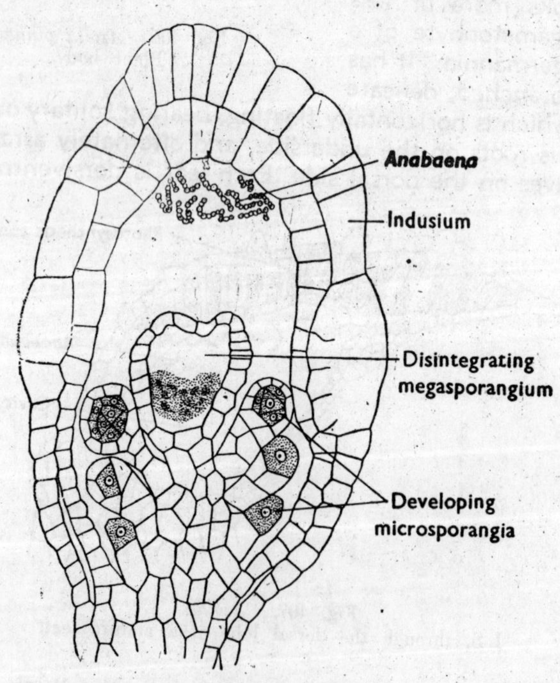

Fig. 409, *Azolla*, L.S. through a developing microsporocarp.

cylinder, but it is practically impossible to differentiate the central cylinder from the cortex. The vascular tissues are greatly reduced. The parenchyma cells in the cortical region are without intercellular spaces.

The sporocarp

The sporocarps are small globular nut-like bodies and formed on the submerged lobe of the lowermost leaf of a branch. Each submerged lobe gives rise to two sporocarps. The sporangia in each sporocarp arise on a raised placenta and incrusted by an indusium. Thus, each sporocarp is nothing but a sorus consisting of clustered sporangia. Early in the stage of development, a sporocarp contains both microsporangia and a single large terminal megasporangium. Later on the sporocarps are differentiated into microsporocarps and megasporocarps respectively. (Fig. 409). Thus, of the two sporocarps in a submerged lobe, the larger one is the microsporocarp bearing microsporangia only with abortive megasporangium and the smaller one is the megasporocarps bearing a megasporangium with abortive microsporangia. The sporangia are shortly stalked and the wall contains a layer of tapetium and these are distinctly leptosporangiate in origin. In the megasporangium, there is only one functioning megaspore matter cell which divides reductionally and form four megaspores of which three degenerate and only one persists. In the microsporangium 64 microspores are formed into tetrads as a result of reduction division of mother cells. The tapetal cells in the microsporangium as usual degenerate and cytoplasm organises into two to sight masses known as **massulae** embedding the microspores. The massulae are invested on the surface by hair-like appendages with sagittate tips known as **glochidia** (Fig. 410). In megasporangium four massulae are formed of which basal layer one contains

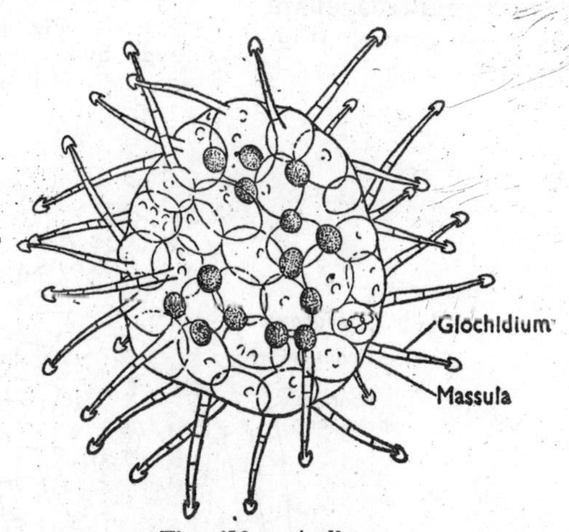

Fig. 410. *Azolla*. A microsporic massula with glochidia.

the functioning megaspore. With reduction division and formation of spores, the gametophytic generation begins.

The gametophytes

Male gametophyte (Fig. 411). The microspores germinate within the massulae and develop into male gametophytes. The microspore cuts off a small prothallial cell and a single antheridium. A large basal cell is also developed below the antheridium by which it is pushed out of the sporangial wall. The antheridium consists of eight sperm mother cells within each of which a spirally coiled multiflagellate sperm is formed (Fig. 412).

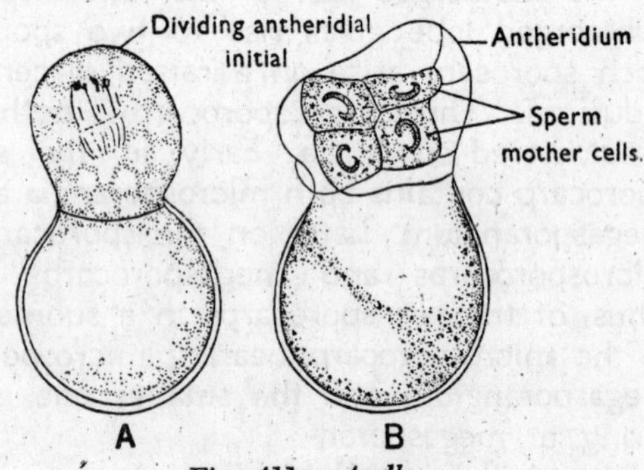

Fig. 411. *Azolla*, A—B, Stages in the development of the male gametophyte.

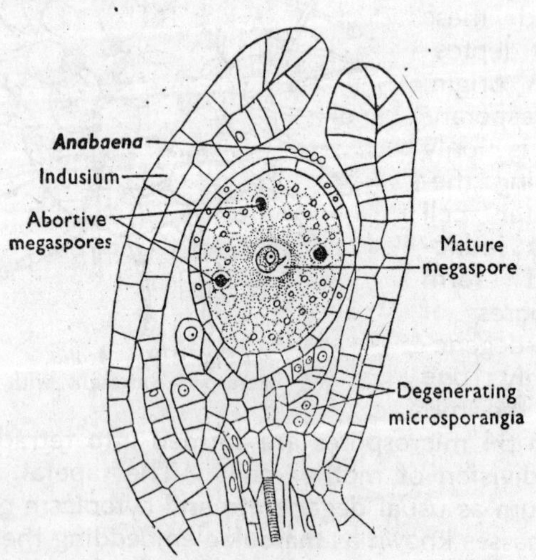

Fig, 412. *Azolla*. L. S. through a developing megasporocarp.

Female gametophyte (Fig. 413). The single megaspore germinates within the massula giving rise to the female gametophyte. A mature female gametophyte consists of a large basal multi-

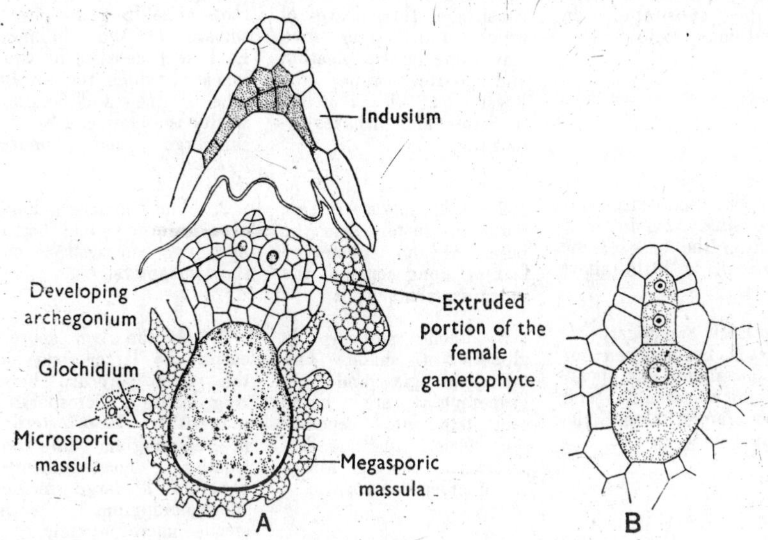

Fig. 413, *Azolla*.
A, A mature female gametophyte ; B, An archegonium.

nucleate nutritive cell and a number of archegonia which project out of the megaspore wall but never turn green. Each archegonium consists of neck of one neck canal cell and venter of a ventral canal cell and an egg.

The new sporophyte

As a result of fertilization the egg cell in the archegonium is converted into an **oospore.** This oospore becomes elongated vertically and undergoes a transverse division at first. By subsequent divisions the embryo forms a quadrant, from which develop the first leaf, the stem, the root and the foot. From this embryo ultimately a new adult sporophyte is established.

Comparison of Marsilea, Salvinia and Azolla

Marsilea	*Salvinia*	*Azolla*
(*a*) *The Sporophyte*		
1. The plant is an aquatic fern and consists of rhizomatous stem, adventitious roots and quadrifoliate leaves	1. The plant is a free floating aquatic fern with a delicate rhizomatous stem, The stem is densely covered with lea-	1. The plant is a minute free-floating fern and consists of a delicate rhizomatous stem on which extremely

Comparison of Marsilea, Salvinia and Azolla

Marsilea	*Salvinia*	*Azolla*
with long petioles. The plant remains attached to the substratum by adventitious roots.	ves which are arranged into whorls. Each whorl consists of three leaves of which the upper two leaves are green, floating and ovate while the lower leaf is root-like in habit and behaves as root,	minute leaves are densely arranged. Adventitious roots arise from the lower surface of the rhizome. Each leaf consists of two lobes of which the upper lobe is green and floating while the lower lobe is submerged and colourless.
2. The sporocarps are borne singly or in clusters from the base of the petiole or a little above it.	2. The sporocarps are borne in clusters near the base of the submerged leaf or along some of the inner segments of it	2, The submerged lobe of a lowermost leaf bears only two sporocarps on the two apices.
3, Each sporocarp is bivalved bean-shaped or oval in shape and bears both microsporangia and megasporangia along the margin.	3. Each sporocarp is globose in shape, The microsporangia and megasporangia are borne separately into separate sporocarps, the megasporocarps arising above the microsporocarps.	3. Of the two sporocarps, the larger one is the microsporocarp bearing fertile microsporangia with a large sterile megasporangium while the smaller megasporocarp contains a large fertile megasporangium with sterile microsporangia.
4, The sporangia are organised into sori, Each sorus is heterosporous and consists of a row of large megasporangia surrounded by smaller microsporangia below. Each sorus is covered by a layer of indusium,	4, Each sporocarp consists of a sorus of microsporangia or megasporangia and surrounded by a layer of indusium.	4. Each sporocarp is a sorus and surrounded by a layer of indusium,
5, Each sporangium is surrounded by a jacket-layer of cells without annulus,	5, Same as Marsilea and a layer of tapetum is formed inside the jacket-layer.	5 Same as Salvinia and the tapetum forms inside the sporangium into a many layered periplasmodium which gradually organises into four or more alveolar structures known as massulae within which the spores lie.
6. In the megasporangium, out of many megaspores formed as a result of reduction division of megaspore mother cells all but one degenerate but in the	6. Same as Marsilea.	6. Same as Marsilea.

Marsilea	*Salvinia*	*Azolla*
microsporangium a large number of small functioning microspores are formed by the reduction division of microspore mother cells.		

(*b*) *The gametophyte*

Marsilea	*Salvinia*	*Azolla*
1. The microspores and megaspores after liberation from the microsporangium germinate into male and female gametophytes respectively.	1. The microspores and megaspore are never set free from the micro- and megasporangia and germinate within them. Before germination of the microspores, the tapetal tissue forms a solid mass surrounding the spores known as massula and the spores gradually occupy the peripheral region of the microsporangium. In megasporangium, the tapetum and the degenerated megaspores forms a solid mass surrounding the megaspore which is lobed at the apex known as perispore.	1. The microspores and the megaspore germinate into male and female gametophyte while still within their massulae.
2. The male gametophyte consists of a small prothallial cells and two antheridia. Each antheridium consists of a jacket-layer of sterile cells of 16 sperm mother cells. Each mother cell forms a multiflagellate sperm.	2. The male gametophyte consists of a small prothallial cell and five antheridia with a large basal cell. Each antheridium consists of four sperm mother cells each of which forming a multiflagellate sperm.	2. The male gametophyte consists of a small prothallial cell and a single antheridium with 8 sperm mother cells. Each mother cell forms a multiflagellate sperm.
3. The mature female gametophyte consists of a layer basal multinucleate nutritive cell and an archegonium which is composed of a neck of only one neck canal cell and the venter of one ventral canal cell and an egg.	3. Same as Marsilea but the nutritive cell is multinucleated. The neck of the archegonium projects slightly along the triradiate ridge of the megaspore wall and turns green.	3. The female gametophyte consists of multinucleated nutritive cell and two archegonia. The structure of the archegonium is the same as that of Marsilea.

Marsilea	*Salvinia*	*Azolla*
4. When the antheridium matures, the prothallial cell disintegrates setting free the two antheridia in the cytoplasmic mass of the female gametophyte. The sperms are also liberated by decaying of the wall of the antheridium.	4. The male gametophytes peeping out of the microsporangium burst and remains embedded into the massula. The mode of liberation of sperms is the same as that of Marsilea.	4. Same as salvinia but the neck of the archegonium never turns green.
5. When the archegonium matures, the neck canal cell and ventral canal cell disintegrate forms a passage, through which sperms enter to fertilize the egg.	5. Same as Marsilea,	5. Same as Marsilea.

Origin of Seed Habit

The dominant plants of the present day are the Gymnosperms and the Angiosperms. It seems certain that the dominance of these groups of plants over the Vascular cryptogams, which reproduce by means of spores, is mainly due to their acquisition of the method of reproduction by seeds. In the cryptogamic type of reproduction, the spores, after liberation from the sporangium of the parent plants, produce very delicate sexual plants,—the gametophytes. The survival of these gametophytes, as well as their sexual reproduction, are mainly dependent on the presence of moisture, and as such is a matter of chance. In the seed plants, however, the spore, which produces the megagametophyte is retained within the sporangium, and once the male spore, which produce's the microgametophyte, comes in contact with the micropyle or the stigma. Further developments and fertilization are carried out within the integuments and are not at all dependent on environmental factors.

The process of the evolution of seed is thought to have commenced with an ancient homosporous form, which has given rise to the heterosporous condition. Most botanists regard the heterosporous condition as characteristic of all seed plants. The pollen is presumed to develop from a microspore, while the embryosac from the megaspore. The occurrence of many comparatively small spores within the megasporangia in *Selaginella* suggests a condition possibly not far advanced beyond the homosporous state. On the other hand, the sporangia with a fewer but comparatively larger spores, indicate an advance in the direction of seed habit. Further,

Selaginella rupestris and *S. apus* have progressed a long way in the direction of seed habit, as the megaspore in these cases is retained within the megasporangium, and the megaspore, while still within the sporangium, develops archegonia and forms embryo with roots and cotyledons. Thus, *Selaginella* is considered by many morphologists to illustrate the transformation from the strictly cryptogamic condition to the seed habit, that is, it shows the replica of stage through which the ancestor of the seed passed during its process of becoming a seed.

Thomson (1927, 1931, 1934) from his comparative studies of the sizes and other characteristics of pollen spores and seed spores concluded that seed plants are heterosporous and have evolved from homosporous ancestors, and *it is the heterothally and not heterospory that constitutes the important feature of the seed plants.*

Halle (1935) considered the terminal position of the primitive cupulate seed of the early lower carboniferous age, as significant and derived them from the terminal spore cases of the Psilophytales.

As long ago as 1904 Miss Bensen suggested that the cycado-filicinean seed may be interpreted as a synangium in which excepting a single sporangium, all are sterile. This means that the 'seed state' was preceded by one in which a sporangium was closely encircled by a ring of sporangia, and these sporangia became sterile and formed the integument by fusion. Walton has very recently simplified this concept and suggests that the encircling elements were not sterile sporangia, but sterile branch tips. There are many fossilized plant remains known to support Walton's hypothesis.

Economic Importance of Pteridophytes

In comparison with the seed-bearing plants, the pteridophytes are less important from the economic standpoint of view. *Lycopodium* and *Selaginella* are chiefly grown as ornamental plants and are utilized in the preparation of Christmas wreathes. Spores and stems of *Lycopodium* have got some medicinal importance, the former also being used in making fireworks. Species of *Selaginella*, e.g., *S. caesea*, and *S. wildenovii*, are used in decoration, because the leaves are remarkable for their metallic and many-hued tints, specially bronze and bluish colours, the latter being very uncommon among plants in general. *S. serpens* is well known for the periodic changes in the colour of its leaves. *S. lepidophyla* and

S. pilifera are sold as curios under the name 'Resurrection plants'. Ducks and other aquatic animals feed upon the corms of *Isoetes*. In early days people used *Equisetum* for polishing wood, floors and cooking utensils. The ferns are mostly ornamental plants of gardens and greenhouses. Some of them are used in the preparation of bouquets and are also placed in the buttonholes. Some species possess so dense and prominent epidermal hairs, that they are sometimes employed as stuffing material. In some tropical countries stems and leaves of tree ferns are used for building purposes. Some genera, like *Pteris*, *Ceratopteris* and *Marsilea*, are edible. The rhizomes and leaf bases of *Dryopteris filix-mas* are used in medicine as a taenifuge. Practically, all the members of the pteridophyta have contributed extensively to coal formation.

SECTION IX

GYMNOSPERMS

INTRODUCTION

General consideration

The idea of gymnospermy, as opposed to angiospermy, was first proposed by Robert Brown (1827). Since then, the question, which is not still clearly answered, is whether the group as a whole is monophyletic or polyphyletic in origin. The majority of workers, however, are of opinion that it is not monophyletic. Further, as the gymnosperms have been distinguished from the angiosperms mainly on the basis of the seed-character alone, they are to be considered as constituting an artificial group.

Whatever may be the validity or nature of the origin of the group, the gymnosperms or 'naked-seeded' plants are the most primitive of all seed-plants, as indisputable records of gymnosperms have been found in the Devonian (perhaps in the Silurian as well), whereas the angiospermous remains have been recorded only from the Jurassic onwards. They are of importance in the modern flora as they are well represented in the Himalayas and the coniferous vegetation is of importance as it produces timber and resin.

The gymnosperms are regarded as an intermediate group between the pteridophytes and angiosperms. The plant always represents the sporophyte, and is heterosporous. *The sporophylls are generally aggregated* ***into cone-like structures*** *or* ***strobili***, which are usually unisexual, and do not bear any accessory whorl. In the gymnosperms, *the carpels do not unite to form a closed chamber or ovary*, but *the magasporangium or the ovule is borne directly on the surface of the megasporophyll* as in the case of pteridophytes, and the *pollination is direct*, i.e., the pollen grains are transferred directly on the micropyle of the ovule. As in the heterosporous pteridophytes, *two kinds of gametophytes are produced, but they are highly reduced* as in angiosperms. Archegonia are still present. The fertilization is effected by means of motile spermatozoids in lower gymnosperms, but in higher ones by means of non-motile gametes. Unlike the angiosperms, the endosperm is normally formed directly from the megaspore before fertilization is effected ; as such, it is a haploid tissue, and is regarded as the female gametophyte in gymnosperms. As the carpel or carpels do not unite to form an ovary, the seeds are naked, and *there is no such organ as fruit* in the gymnosperms.

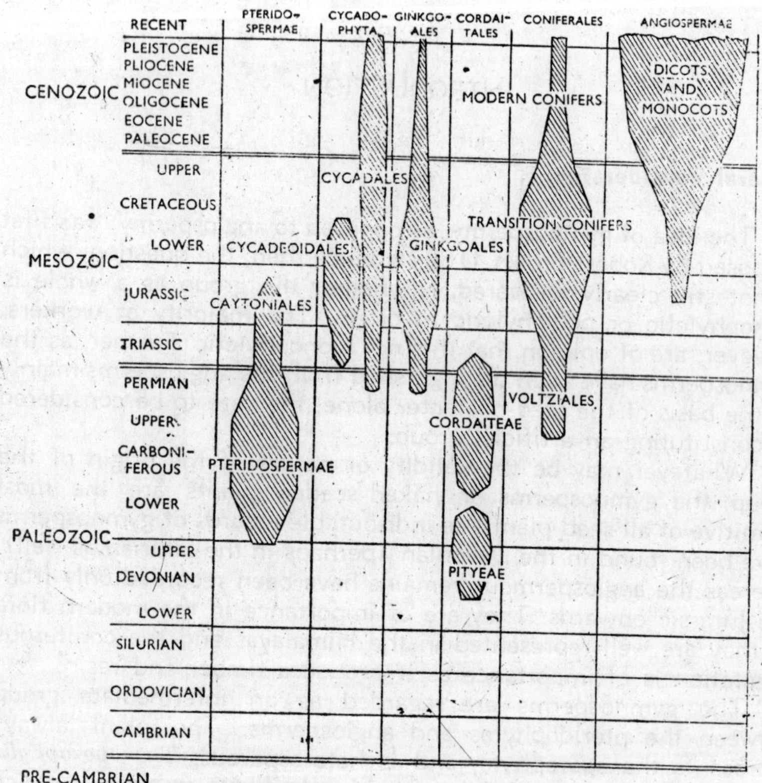

Fig. 414. Distribution of Gymnosperms in the geological periods.

Origin of Gymnosperms

When the anatomical and morphological features of the gymnosperms are taken into account, the division breaks itself into two separate groups, viz., cycadophytic and coniferophytic lines. The cycadophytic line contains the Pteridosperms, Cycads and Cycadeoids, and it shows evidences of derivation from the ferns. The coniferophytic one contains the Cordaites, Ginkgos and the Conifers. Its origin is unknown. The oldest known Coniferophyta belong to the Pityeae (upper Devonian). Pityeae were succeeded by the Cordaiteae (upper Carboniferous) from which the Ginkgoales and Coniferales were probably derived during the late Paleozoic (Permian). The Cycadophyta show evidence of fern ancestry. The oldest Pteridosperms appear in lower Carboniferous and oldest Cycads in late Paleozoic. Origin of Cycadeoideales, Ephedrales and Gnetales is not clear.

Classification of Gymnosperms

Of the different systems of classification, the one proposed by Prof. Chamberlain is adopted here. He divides the group into **Cycadophyta** and **Coniferophyta**, basing on the differences in the morphological and anatomical characters. The former section is characterized by plants of comparatively smaller size with unbranched stems, pinnately compound leaves, thicks cortex, scanty wood, large pith, and generally sporophylls are in simple cones. The Coniferophyta, on the other hand, are marked by having comparatively larger plants with extensively branched stems, simple leaves, scanty cortex, thick wood, small pith and usually the microsporophylls form simple cones and the megasporophylls form compound ones. Compound leaf is an outstanding character of Cycadophyta and the simple leaf of Coniferophyta.

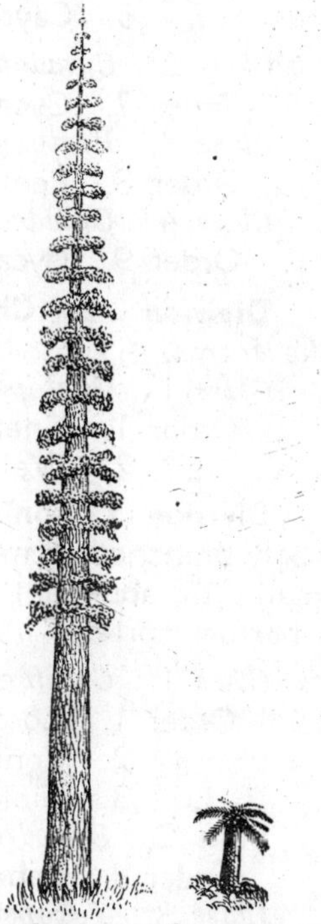

The Cycadophytes are divided into *three* orders—(1) **Cycadofilicales (Pteridospermae)** (Carboniferous, extinct), (2) **Bennettitales** (Mesozoic, extinct), and (3) **Cycadales** (Mesozoic to present day). On the other hand, the Coniferophytes include *four* orders—(4) **Cordaitales** (Paleozoic, extinct), (5) **Ginkgoales** (Mesozoic to present day), (6) **Coniferales** (Permian to present day), and (7) **Gnetales** (recent).

Coniferophyte Cycadophyte

Fig. 415 Showing relative sizes of a member of the Cycadophyte and another belonging to the Coniferophyte.

Prof. Sahni (1948) reported a unique group of Gymnosperms the **Pentoxyleae** from the Rajmahal Hills, Bihar. The group has a combination of characters suggestive of the affinities with the Cycadales, the Bennettitales and the Coniferales.

A new classification of Gymnosperms has been suggested by Pant (1957). A brief synopsis of Pant's scheme is given below:

Division 1. Cycadophyte.—Plants with relatively small, usually unbranched or poorly branched, aerial or subterranean trunk, their leaves are usually large and pinnate. The stems have a large pith, scanty wood, usually with wide medullary rays and a thick cortex.

Class 1. *Pteridospermopsida*

Order 1. Lyginopteridales

,, 2. Medullosales

,, 3. Glossopteridales

,, 4. Peltaspermales

,, 5. Corystospermales

,, 6. Caytoniales

Class 2. *Cycadopsida*

Order 7. Cycadales

Class 3. *Pentoxylopsida*

Order 8. Pentoxylales

Class 4. *Cycadeoideopsida* (Bennettitopsida)

Order 9. Cycadeoideales (Bennettiales)

Division 2. Chlamydospermaphyta.—Peculiar angiosperm-like forms.

Class 1. *Gnetopsida*

Order 1. Gnetales

,, 2. Welwitschiales

Division 3. Coniferophyta.—Usually large-sized trees with profusely branched stem and with simple leaves. Their stems have a small pith, abundant wood, usually with narrow medullary rays and a narrow cortex.

Class 1. *Coniferopsida*

Order 1. Cordaitales

,, 2. Coniferales

,, 3. Ginkgoales

Class 2. *Ephedropsida*

Order 4. Ephedrales

Class 3. *Taxopsida*

Order 5. Taxales

Characteristics of the principal Orders

1. **Pteridospermae (Cycadofilicales) :** Trees or smaller plants with fern-like foliage. Sporangia are borne on frond-like leaves more or less modified, but never grouped into a cone.

2. **Bennettitales :** Trees with stems covered with an armour of persistent leaf-bases. Microsporophylls frond-like forming a loose crown. Megasporophylls no longer leaf-like but found in a specialized cone-like structure.

3. **Cycadales :** Plants with palm-like habit. Micro- and megasporophylls grouped into cones, except in the genus *Cycas*, where the megasporophylls are collected into a loose crown as in the Bennettitales. Male cells motile.

4. **Pentoxylales :** Low shrubs. Female infructescence consisting of numerous cones specially attached on peduncles, each bearing numerous ovules on a central axis, with no megasporophylls, ovuliferous scales or interseminal scales. Male flowers terminally borne on dwarf shoots. Unilocular sporangia terminate short-branchlets of the appendages or microsporophylls.

5. **Cordaitales :** Large trees with flat strap-shaped leaves. Fructifications in cones.

6. **Coniferales :** Large trees or shrubs. Leaves needle or scale-like, sometimes flattened. The male flowers are arranged in more or less compact clusters or catkins and the female flowers are usually clustered to form a cone. Male cells never motile.

7. **Ginkgoales :** Medium-sized trees. Leaves flattened and lobed in various ways, with dichotomous venation. Male and female elements collected into strobili.

8. **Gnetales :** Small trees or shrubs or climbing shrubs. Opposite leaves, dicotyledonous embryos and compound cones in both male and female are the characteristics of the order.

Division I. Cycadophyta

Plants are relatively small, usually unbranched or poorly branched, aerial or subterranean trunk. Their leaves are usually large and pinnate. The stems have a large pith, scanty wood, usually with wide medullary rays and a thick cortex. There are three orders under the division, viz., Cycadofilicales, Bennettitales and Cycadales. The first two are extinct and the last one is still living.

CHAPTER I

CYCADOFILICALES (PTERIDOSPERMAE)

The Cycadofilicales or Pteridosperms are popularly known as 'seed ferns'. They were trees or small plants bearing fern-like foliage. They flourished greatly in the Carboniferous and the period was so very rich in fossil fern leaves that it was thought to be the 'Age of Ferns'. Owing to the presence of fern-like leaves they were formerly believed to be a kind of fern, but subsequently when fossil leaves with attached seeds were discovered (1903) the Cycadofilicales were designated as **Pteridosperms** by Oliver and Scott. They are regarded as the primitive group of seed-plants.

In the year 1877, Grand Eury first discovered a few species of fern leaves, which later on went by the name of the form genus *Myeloxylon*. In 1887 Williamson pointed out that *Heterangium* (stem) and *Kaloxylon* (root) combined characters of both ferns and cycads, which led potonie (1899) to create a new systematic group, the Cycadofilicales. With the discovery of the fact that *Lagenostoma lomaxi* belongs to the stem of *Lyginopteris oldhamia* by Oliver and Scott in 1903, the name **Pteridospermae** was proposed for the seed-bearing Cycadofilicales. The seed-bearing habit of the Pteridospermae was again verified next year by Kidston in *Neuropteris heterophylla*.

The Cycadofilicales or Pteridospermae are popularly known as 'seed ferns'. Though a few petrified stems have been discovered in the Devonian, yet no positive seed has been obtained before the Lower Carboniferous is reached. The plants first appeared in the Devonian, became very prominent in the Carboniferous, but remained wide-spread during the Permian, but a few survived even up to Mid-Jurassic. The best known Cycadofilicales are reported from Great Britain.

Characteristic features

(*a*) *Vegetative organs*

1. Plants were trees or small plants with monopodial branching and presence of ramentum.
2. Leaves were large and fern-like bearing micro- and megasporangia.
3. Leaf traces relatively large, single or double.
4. Leaves possessed resistant cuticle.
5. Primary xylem well-developed, usually mesarch or endarch.

6. Secondary xylem and phloem present, tracheids bearing numerous multiseriate bordered pits on the radial walls, and a large pith.

(*b*) *Spore-producing organs*

7. Pollen-producing microsporangia are of marattiaceous type. They are exannulate, sometimes grouped into synangia and difficult to distinguish from the fructifications of ferns, but never grouped into cone.

8. The ovule had an integument differentiated into three layers, the vascular supply was divided into two sets of branches, a well-developed nucellar beak and a pollen chamber.

9. Seeds were not in cones or inflorescences, but on slightly modified and undistinguished foliage and they resembled those of Cycads.

Classification of Cycadofilicales

The Cycadofilicales have been divided into *two* major groups : the *Paleozoic Cycadofilicales* and the *Mesozoic* ones. The former is further divided into *three* families, viz., **Lyginopteridaceae, Medullosaceae,** and **Calamopityaceae,** while the latter also consists of *three* families, viz., **Peltaspermaceae, Corystospermaceae,** and **Caytoniaceae.** Of the six families mentioned above, the most extensively studied one is Lyginopteridaceae.

A brief account of each of the families is given below :

1. **Lyginopteridaceae.** In the family the leaves are of the filicoid type, and the stem is of monostelic organization. The leaf traces and foliar bundles are single or double ; the xylem is mesarch. Seeds are of cycadean type, and the cupule is present. The best known lyginopterid is *Calymmatotheca hoeninghausi*. This is the plant to which both *Lyginopteris* and *Lagenostoma* belong.

2. **Medullosaceae.** In this family the stem is polystelic, and many bundles are scattered in the petiole. Seeds are large.

3. **Calamopityaceae.** This is the oldest and the largest of all the families of Pteridosperms. The stem is monostelic, and scattered bundles are present in the petiole.

4. **Peltaspermaceae.** The leaves in this family are small, bipinnate, and the rachis is characterized by swellings. The microsporophyll is branched, and microsporangia open longitudinally, and smooth pollens are discharged.

5. **Corystospermaceae.** The leaves in this family are linear-lanceolate and the seeds are characterized by ovoid, elliptic shape, and curved bifid micropyle.

6. **Caytoniaceae.** This family is characterized by leaves formed usually in two (occasionally three) pairs. Anatomically it has transfusion tissue and mesophyll with palisade layer. The pollen grains show a symmetrical bilobed structure, and these are winged. The ovules are orthotropous, and the nucellus is free from the integument except at the base. This is an advanced character. Formerly the Caytoniales were compared with the Angiosperms, but later on it was found out that members of this family are essentially gymnospermous.

CALYMMATOTHECA

(Fam. LYGINOPTERIDACEAE)

A chronological list of the names given to its various organs illustrating how this and many fossil plants are reconstructed by the gradual piecing together of detached organs is given below :

Stem : *Lyginopteris oldhamia* Binney (1866).
Leaf : *Sphenopteris hoeninghausi* Brongniart (1828).
Petiole : *Rachiopteris aspera* Williamson (1874).
Root : *Kaloxylon hookeri* Williamson (1876).
Seed : *Lagenostoma lomaxi* Oliver and Scott (1903).
Cupule : *Calymmatotheca stangeri* Stur (1877), Jongmans (1929).

Only pollen-bearing organs not yet determined with certainty are now needed to complete the list. It is possible these were of *Crossotheca* type or *Telangium*.

The sporophyte

The stem is long and slender with a presumed climbing habit, and bears spirally arranged fern-like leaves. The frond is compound with a gland, and the rachis divides equally. The pinnae are oppositely arranged.

The anatomy of the stem shows a large pith, which is parenchymatous, and stone cells in groups forming **sclerotic nests** are present. The mesarch primary wood surrounds the pith, and the protoxylem is surrounded by metaxylem.

The xylem of the root is mesarch, and undergoes secondary growth.

In the petiole the xylem is completely surrounded by the phloem. The anatomical structure of the leaf is not much different from that of the living ferns. The epidermis is cuticularized, and the palisade and spongy parenchymas are present. The stomata are situated on the lower surface.

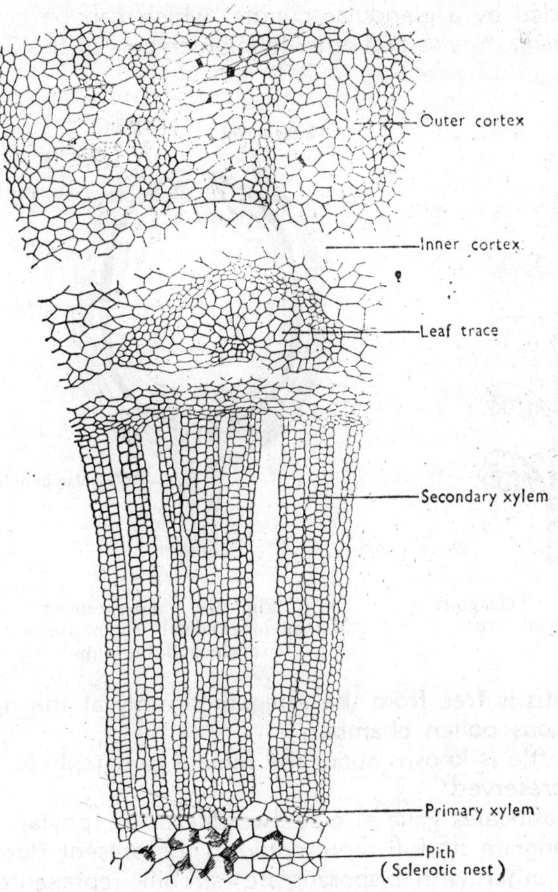

Fig. 416. *Calymmatotheca*.
T. S. of stem.

The stamen

The entire structure somewhat resembles the stamen of *Araucaria*. The fertile part is flattened into a paddle-shaped structure bearing a few pendant bilocular sporangia at its margin. In all probability the pollen grains did not give rise to pollen tubes, and the sperms would have been of the cycad type.

The seed

The seed is small, terminal and barrel-shaped. It is orthotropous and symmetrical in nature with a simple set of vascular supply. It is surrounded by a glandular cupule, which can be compared to that of *Juglans*, *Fagus*, and other living members of the Cupuliferae.

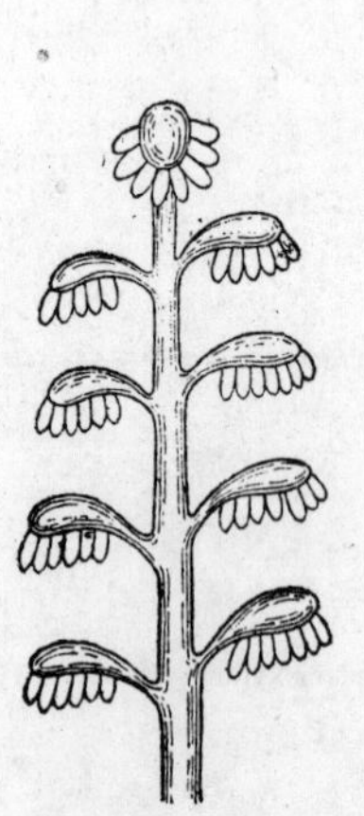

Fig 417. *Telangium* (=*Crossotheca*).

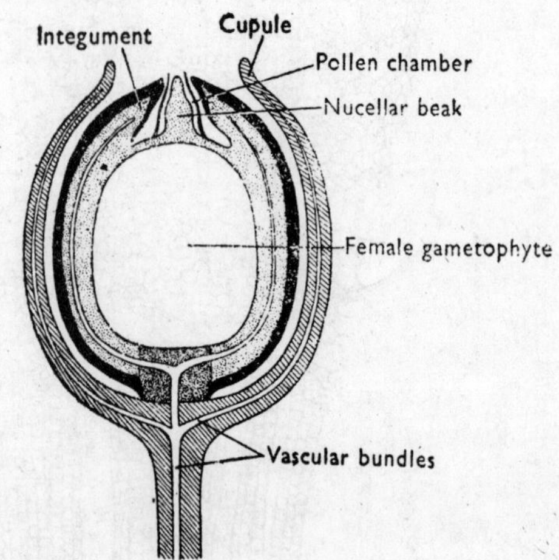

Fig. 418. *Lagenostoma*. Mec an longitudinal section through the ovule and the cupule.

The nucellus is free from the integument only at the tip, and has a conspicuous pollen chamber.

Very little is known about the female gametophyte, because it is hardly preserved.

Cycadofilicales gave rise to two Mesozoic phyla : one with monosporangiate strobili represented in the present flora by Cycadales, the other with bisporangiate strobili represented in the Bennettitales and not represented in the present flora.

GLOSSOPTERIDAE

Brongniart, in 1828, established the genus *Glossopteris* for leaves, believed to be ferns from the Paleozoic and early Triassic of the Southern Hemisphere. These were simple and entire and as the name suggest tongue-shaped or spathulate to ovate or linear-lanceolate in outline and either sessile or shortly and distinctly petiolate. They had a conspicuous midrib from which arise lateral and a network of small anastomosing veins. The leaves were often borne on characteristic rhizome-like stems, *Vertebraria*, bearing secondary wood with multiseriate pitted tracheids. Vascular skeleton appears to be constructed of several plates of vascular tissue radiating from a common centre. Cuticular studies have suggested that these represent seed plants. This is supported by the finding of unique types of reproductive organs, of varied morphological nature ; one of which (*Scutum leslium* Plumstead) has actually yielded seed-like structures.

Generally stalked reproductive structures of *Glossopteris* are either oval, round or lanceolate in shape and in most cases show a central seed-bearing portion surrounded by a marginal flap. Knowledge regarding the nature of the reproductive structures bearing pollen sacs is still lacking.

It has been suggested by some that the *Glossopteris* are to be included under Pteridospermae and a new class Glossopteridae should be created for them. They occur in various continents in the Southern Hemisphere previously connected together in the Gondwanaland. They are abundant in the Raniganj and Jharia coalfields.

Fig. 420. Reproductive organ attached to *Glossopteris* leaf.

Affinity

As the name indicates the order shows resemblance on the one hand with Filicales and on the other hand with Cycads.

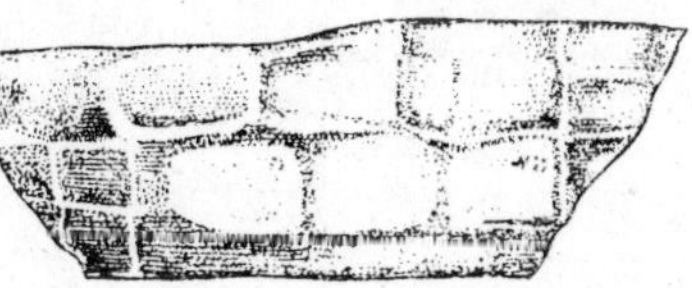

Fig. 419. Stem of *Glossopteris Vertebraria indica.*

(*a*) *Affinities with ferns*

1. They are ferns-bearing seeds.
2. In microsporangiate structure they can hardly be regarded above the level of ferns. These structures have resemblance with those of the marattiaceous ferns and some of the Botryopteridium.
3. Sporophylls are little modified from vegetative foliage.
4. The general form of the foliage is fern-like.
5. The vascular anatomy has got similarity except in the secondary growth in Cycadofilicales.

(*b*) *Affinities with Cycads*

1. They are Cycads without strobili. Though the primary stele of *Heterangium* or *Medullosa* resemble ferns yet when the stem structure is viewed, as a whole, it is decidedly Cycad-like.

2. Structure of petiole, stem and the seeds of the members of medullosae are closer to the Cycads.

3. The relationship with Bennettitales and Cycadales shows evidences that all the three have been grouped into one division Cycadophyta.

(*c*) *Affinities with higher Gymnosperms*

There is not much relationship with the Cordaitales, Coniferales and Gnetales. Although there is a suggestive connection between Calamopityaceae and Pityaceae particularly in the wood characters.

CHAPTER II

BENNETTITALES (=CYCADEOIDEALES)

Bennettitales resembled modern Cycads but had a more diversified habit with tuberous or columnar branched trunks with persistent leaf-bases. There was a crown of pinnate leaves. The reproductive organs were borne terminally on short axillary branches arising from the trunk. The strobili were typically bisporangiate unlike those of living Cycads.

The most common fossils among the Cycadophytes are leaves and it is difficult to distinguish the leaves of Mesozoic Cycadales and Bennettitales from their external features. Their stomatal characters are quite distinctive.

The Bennettitales, or the Cycadeoideales, appeared first in all probability in the Triassic*, flourished very luxuriantly in the Middle or Late Jurassic, and then went on declining in the Cretaceous. It is believed that this order arose side by side with the living Cycadales from a pteridospermous stock. The fossil remains are distributed extensively throughout the United States, Mexico, different parts of Europe, as well as India.

Classification

Bennettitales are divided into *three* families, viz., (1) Williamsoniaceae, (2) Wielandiellaceae and (3) Cycadeoideaceae.

Fam. 1. Williamsoniaceae. Plants are all older and primitive in age, mostly Triassic and Jurassic. Flowers were borne on relatively slender stems or pedicels and fully exposed. Materials are preserved as compressions.

Genera : *Williamsonia* (whole plants, male and female flowers), *Ptilophyllum* (fronds).

Fam. 2. Wielandiellaceae. These plants are also primitive and older like Williamsoniaceae. The chief difference is that their trunks are not covered by leaf armours as in Williamsoniaceae. Branches are slender and dichotomously branched.

Genus : *Wielandiella*, *Williamsoniella* (fronds).

Fam. 3. Cycadeoideaceae. Plants are younger and more advanced, mostly Cretaceous. The trunk is short, ovoid or columnar

* Chamberlain believes that they appeared first in the Upper Carboniferous.

with an armour of leaf-bases. Flowers are embedded within leaf-base layer.

Genus : *Cycadeoidea* (=*Bennettites*).

Comparison between Williamsoniaceae and Cycadeoideaceae

Williamsoniaceae	*Cycadeoideaceae*
1. Older and primitive, mostly Triassic and Jurassic.	1. Younger and more advanced, mostly Cretaceous.
2. Trunk elongated, slender and much-branched.	2. Trunk short, ovoid or columnar with armour of leaf-bases.
3. Flowers sessile or stalked but never embedded into leaf-base layer,	3. Flowers are embedded within the leaf-base layer.
4. Materials are preserved as compressions.	4. Materials are usually silicified and excellently preserved.

The valid name for Bennettitales is Cycadeoideales as explained by Arnold in 1947, but the former name is still frequently used by many workers. They were the characteristic flora of the Mesozoic era, and were distributed throughout both the hemispheres. They had many resemblances with Cycadofilicales and Cycads in their general habit.

Characteristic features

(*a*) *Vegetative organs*

1. Plants were unbranched trees, usually 1-2 metres in height, with compressed internodes and ramentum, bearing a crown of large pinnately compound leaves on the top.

2. The trunks were covered with an armour of persistent leaf-bases.

3. The outer walls of the epidermal cells are sinuous.

4. Guard cells and subsidiary cells are *syndetocheilic*, i.e., are produced by the division of the same initial.

5. The anatomical structure of the stem shows a thick cortex, a broad pith and narrow vascular cylinder composed of collateral bundles with exarch xylem.

(*b*) *Spore-producing organs*

6. Flowers unisexual or bisexual in strobili.
7. Microsporaphylls frond-like forming a loose cone.
8. Megasporophylls are not leaf-like, but found in specialised cone-like structure.

The following genera of Bennettitales are found in India :

1. **Williamsonia**

Several species of *Williamsonia* are represented in India. Of these *W. sewardiana* is the most completely worked out species, which is found in the Rajmahal Hills as reconstructed by Prof. Sahni.

Other Indian species of *Williamsonia* are *W. indica*, *W. microps*, *W. blanfordi*, etc. But, the vegetative parts of these species are not well preserved.

2. **Ptilophyllum**

It is a leaf genus belonging to *Williamsonia* and occurs in the Rajmahal and Jabalpur series of India. The two widely distributed species are : *P. acutifolium* and *P.* c.f. *cutchense*. The leaf is pinnate having the pinnae linear, straightly falcate with parallel or subparallel veins. The pinnae are characterised by their attachment to the upper surface of the rachis covering it almost completely. The base of the lamina is rounded.

3. **Bucklandia**

This is stem genus belonging to *Williamsonia*. It has only one species, viz., *B. indica*. It is regarded as the stem of *Williamsonia*.

4. **Otozamites**

It is also a leaf genus belonging to the Fam. Williamsoniaceae, and occurs in Upper Gondwana, Rajmahal and Jabalpur series. There are four species of the genus, viz., *O. bengalensis*, *O. parallelus*, *O. pecten* and *O. bunbaryanus*. The leaves resemble those of *Ptilophyllum* but differ in the points that the pinnae have acute base and also spreading venation.

5. **Dictyozamites**

It is also a leaf genus belonging to the Fam. Williamsoniaceae and occur in the Upper Gondwana of India. It has two Indian species *D. falcatus* and *D. indica*. The leaf resembles *Otozamites* but differs mainly in anastomosing veins.

Indian Bennettitales

The group is well represented in the Rajmahal Hills and other Upper Gondwana localities in India. No member of Cycadeoidaceae is known from India. Williamsoniaceae is represented in India by several species of *Williamsonia*. *W. sewardiana* found in Rajmahal Hill's is the most completely known species. This, as reported by Sahni (Fig. 421) is a small tree with a columnar trunk, covered with scars of foliage and scale leaves and a crown of slender pinnate leaves. Female flowers only are known and they are borne on short lateral branches, which are covered with leaf-bases and scales.

The flower consists of a conical fertile portion enclosed by linear heavy bracts and scales. The ovules are borne on long stalks and are surrounded by club-shaped interseminal scales (Fig. 424). The trunk of *W. sewardiana* is known as *Bucklandia indica* and its leaves *Ptilophyllum acutifolium*.

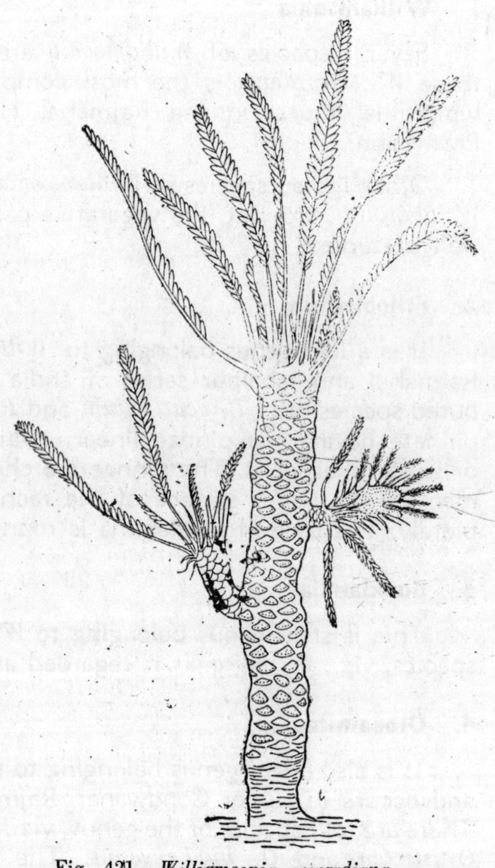

Fig. 421. *Williamsonia sewardiana*. (Redrawn after Sahni).

Other Indian Williamsonias are not well preserved and their vegetative parts are unknown, e.g., *W. indica*, *W. microps*, *W, blanfordi*. Microsporangiate Williamsonia's are *W. sahni*, *W. santalensis*, while *W. sewardiana* are unisexual. *W. santalensis* might be unisexual or bisexual.

Bucklandia has a compact secondary wood, uniseriate medullary rays and tracheids have multiseriate bordered pits.

Five genera based on foliage are known from India, viz., *Ptilophyllum*, *Pterophyllum*, *Zamites*, *Otozamites* and *Dictyozamites*. *Ptilophyllum* have linear leaves with pinnae attached to the upper face of the rachis, covering it almost completely. Base of pinna is rounded. Veins are parallel.

The sporophyte

The plant body of *W. sewardiana* is a small, stout tree resembling a miniature living *Cycas*. The trunk is columnar, bearing a cluster of pinnate compound leaves at its top. Intermingled with the leaves are scales, which leave small scars on the stem. There are lateral shoots, which are constricted at their bases. This suggests that they broke away, and served as propagative shoots. The leaf-bases formed an armour around the stem.

Internally, the pith of the stem is enclosed by a xylem ring. Tracheids of scalariform type are noted, and multiseriate bordered pits are present. The xylem rays are variable from uni- to multiseriate type. The protorylem is endarch, and secretory sacs are present in the cortex as well as in the pith.

The flower

Flowers are produced on short-branched lateral shoots, which project beyond the armour of leaf cushion. Each flower is unisexual and ovulate, having a receptacle bearing the stalked ovules intermingled with interseminal scales. The nucellus of the ovule is enclosed by an integument, which prolongs into a micropylar beak.

CYCADEOIDEA (=*BENNETTITES*)

(Fam. CYCADEOIDEACEAE)

The sporophyte

The main stem is ovoid or shortly columnar, stout, and covered by an armour of persistent leaf-bases and multicellular hairs. Mature leaves have not been observed in an attached condition with the trunk, but young fronds have been obtained in the form of terminal buds. The leaves are extremely cycad-like, but without any prominent midrib, and the venation is dichotomous.

Internally, the stem of *Cycadeoidea* shows endarch arrangement of the xylem. The pith is large, and is surrounded by a small layer of wood. Scalariform tracheids are present in the secondary xylem.

Anatomically, the leaf shows a xerophyllous structure. The epidermis is strongly cutinized, followed by one or two layers of thick-walled cells constituting the hypodermis. The mesophyll is differentiated into palisade and spongy parenchymas. Each of the mesarch bundles of the single median row is provided with a prominent bundle sheath, and connected with the dorsal face by

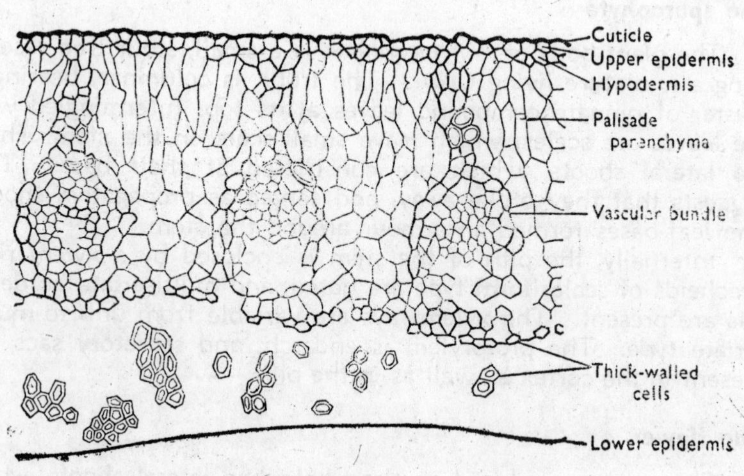

Fig. 422. *Cycadeoidea* (=*Bennettites*). T. S. of leaf.

sclerenchymatous cells. A wavy line of thick-walled cells occur below the bundles, and beneath this line is a thick zone of ill-defined sclerified cells extending up to the lower epidermis.

The flower

Flowers are sunken within the leaf-bases, and are, so far as known, bisexual. These are borne on axillary shoots. The axillary branch is expanded into a **receptacle,** which bears in the outermost region a dense cluster of bracts enclosing a number (about 10-20) of *microsporophylls* (*stamens*), and the innermost position is occupied by the *megasporophylls* (*carpels*), which are intermingled with interseminal scales. The whole structure resembles a flower of *Magnolia*.

Microsporophylls (or **stamens**). The microsporophylls or stamens bear two lateral rows of synangia of ordinary fern type. These are united at the base forming a sheath, and are not much advanced than the filicinean form.

Megasporophylls (or **carpels**). The megasporophylls or carpels are much more advanced than the microsporophylls or stamens. Each megasporophyll has a long, slender stalk bearing an ovule, and these lie intermingled with **interseminal scales**, which are probably nothing but sterile megasporophylls.

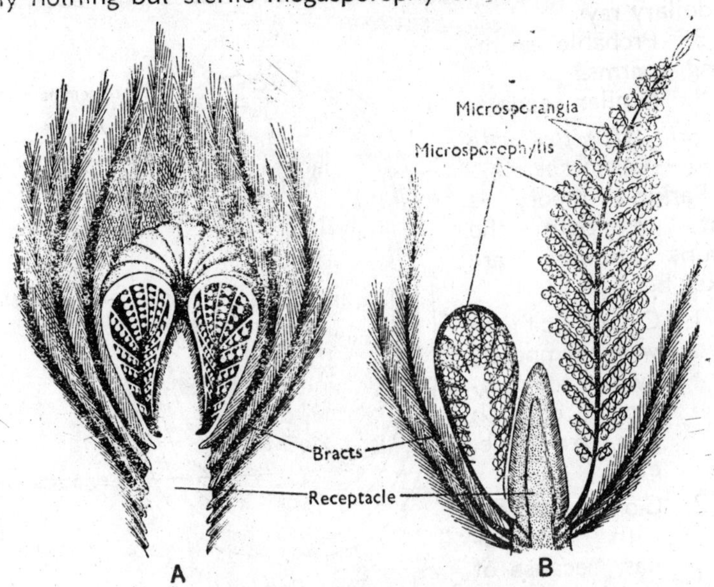

Fig. 423. *Cycadeoidea* (=*Bennettites*).
A-B, Male strobili with associated bracts. In B one of the sporophylls has been shown in an expanded condition.

The **ovule** is of the cycadean type with a three-layered integument, whose inner and outer layers are fleshy, and the middle one is stony. The nucellus is free from the integument. The embryo is large, dicotyledonous, and fills the seed completely, and during its development destroys the endosperm.

Affinity

Bennettitales have some resemblances with Ferns, Cycads and Angiosperms.

(*a*) *Affinities with Ferns*

1. Lateral branching.
2. Ramentum present.
3. Direct leaf trace.
4. Presence of synangia.
5. Scalariform thickening.

(*b*) *Affinities with Cycads*

1. Fronds of *Cycadeoidea ingens* similar to enfolding of *Encephalartos*, *Macrozamia* and *Bowenia*, otherwise frond character is different.

2. In general habit, to some extent, and anatomy Cycadeoids resemble Cycads, but no girdling of leaf traces and absence of medullary rays.

3. Probable swimming sperms.

4. Similar seeds.

(c) *Affinities with Angiosperms*

Parkin's theory is that, in both the groups flowers are alike, because :

1. Connection with sympetaly owing to common endarch siphonostele, etc.

2. Connection with Magnolias, because of floral analogies, but not true relations.

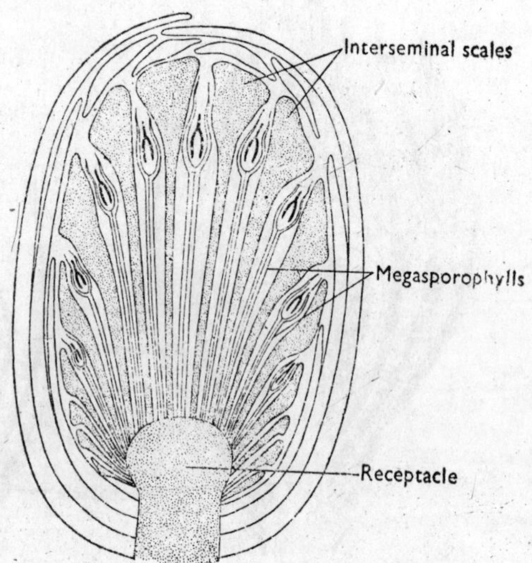

Fig. 424. *Cycadeoidea* (=*Bennettites*). L. S. of a female strobilus.

(i) Cycadeoidean bracts beneath stamen ring, homologous to the perianth.

(ii) Larger number of stamens on the staminate disc.

(iii) Cone-shaped ovuliferous receptacle bearing cluster of separate fruit-like structures.

(iv) Tracheids scalariform in all Cycadeoidaceae and most Williamsoniaceae, which is characteristic of *Magnolia*.

In certain respects the Cycadeoidales shows affinities with both the Pteridosperms and the Cycadales, particularly regarding the general habit, structure of wood, mesarch leaf trace, foliage and structure of the seed. Angiospermous affinities can also be considered by comparing their strobili with the flowers of *Magnolia*, but the similarity is only due to parallel evolution. The relationship is drawn with the ferns in having the ramentum, synangia, and direct leaf traces. Hence, this order represents a combination of characters of Cycadofilicales, Cycadales, and Filicales along with some characters of its own.

CHAPTER III

CYCADALES (CYCADOPHYTE)

The Cycadales were at their best during the Mesozoic and since then have been on the decline lingering on up to the present-day. They have many fern-like characters. Many of these characters were shared by Cycadofilicales and Bennettitales also. They resemble Cycadofilicales in the structure of their ovules, and Bennettitales in their general habit and in the internal structure of the stem.

During the Mesozoic, the Cycads were distributed all over the world, but at present they are restricted mainly to tropical and subtropical regions. Of a total number of 9 of the present-day living genera with about 90 species (65 spp. according to Schuster), 4 are Western and 5 are Oriental (2 African and 3 Eastern). Of the 4 Western Cycads, *Microcycas* is found only in Cuba, *Dioon* and *Ceratozamia* in Mexico alone, while *Zamia* occurs in both these places. The oriental genera, with the exception of only one are also strictly endemic. *Stangeria* and *Encephalartos* occur in South Africa. *Bowenia* and *Macrozamia* are restricted to Australia, while *Cycas*, which is abundant in Australia, is also found in India, China, Japan, and Polynesia. One species of Cycas (*Cycas madagascariensis*) is, however, reported from Madagascar.

In India, the genus grows in the plains of Orissa, Assam and the adjoining hills up to Nepal, Madras, Mysore, Malabar, Andaman and Nicobar Islands.

Plants woody, usually branched and dioecious; leaves bipinnate compound; sporophylls generally borne in cones (but not in the case of the megasporophylls of *Cycas*); microsporophylls bearing sporangia in groups of sori on the under-surface; spermatozoids multiflagellate, motile and 2 in number; megasporophylls usually bearing one to several erect, sessile, naked ovules; embryo in a ripe seed with generally two cotyledons, and attached to a long much-coiled suspensor; stems with large pith, little wood, and thick cortex; true vessels absent. It includes only one family, Cycadaceae.

This order includes only one family Cycadaceae consisting of 9 living genera, viz., *Cycas*, *Microcycas*, *Zamia*, *Microzamia*, *Ceratozamia*, *Stangeria*, *Dioon*, *Bowenia* and *Encephalartos*. Of those *Cycas* is the most primitive on account of its loose leaf-like megasporophylls.

Characteristic features

(*a*) *Vegetative organs*

1. Plants, palm-like, usually unbranched and dioecious. The trunk bears a crown of pinnate compound leaves on the top.

2. Stems with large pith, little wood and thick cortex but no true vessels are present.

3. Micro- and mega-sporophylls are grouped in cones, except in the genus *Cycas*, where the megasporophylls are collected into a loose crown as in the Bennettitales.

4. Microsporophylls bearing sporangia are in groups of sori on the under-surface.

5. Sperms multiflagellate, motile and 2 in number.

6. Megasporophylls usually bear one to several erect, sessile, naked ovules.

7. Embryo in a ripe seed contains generally two cotyledons and remains attached to a long, much-coiled suspensor.

CYCAS

(Fam. CYCADACEAE)

Cycas is the most prominent genus of the Eastern Hemisphere.

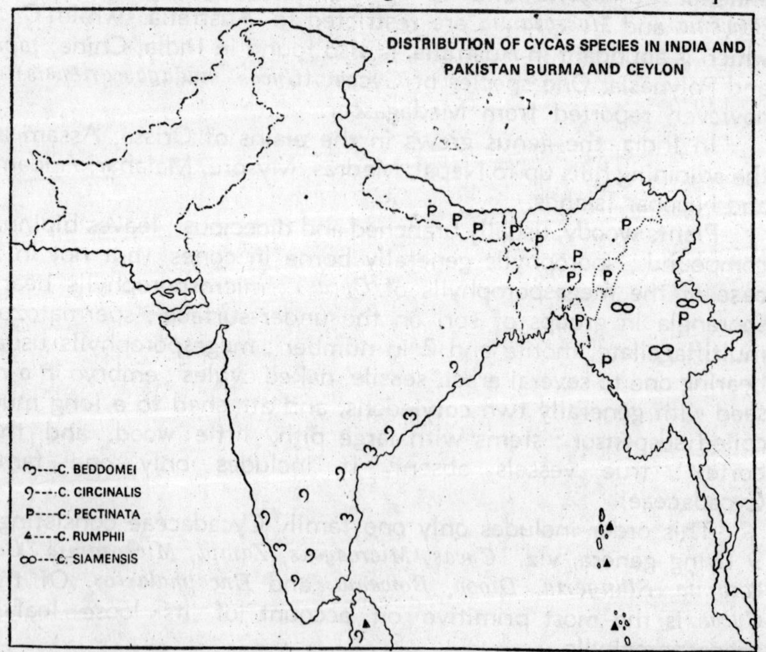

Fig. 425. Map of India showing the distribution of Cycas. (After *Pant*, 1962).

C. circinalis, *C. pectinata*, *C. rumphii*, and *C. beddomeii* are found wild in India. *C. revoluta* (native of Japan) is the most common cultivated species in Indian gardens. *C. siamensis* (found in Burma) is sometimes cultivated.

The sporophyte

The vegetative body of the sporophyte externally resembles a palm tree. The stem is typically unbranched, short, thick, cylindrical and more or less columnar, covered by an armour of persistent leaf-bases, and bearing a crown of leaves. Leaves are pinnate, tough, leathery, large (sometimes up to 3 metres in length), spirally arranged round the free-growing apex of the stem, and show circinate ptyxis characteristic of ferns. Each leaflet has only one midrib without branches. The primary root elongates as a strong tap root with scanty branches, but numerous secondary roots are present. These secondary roots, near the surface of the ground, branch profusely and dichotomously forming coralloid masses, known as **root tubercles***.

Fig. 426. A *Cycas*.

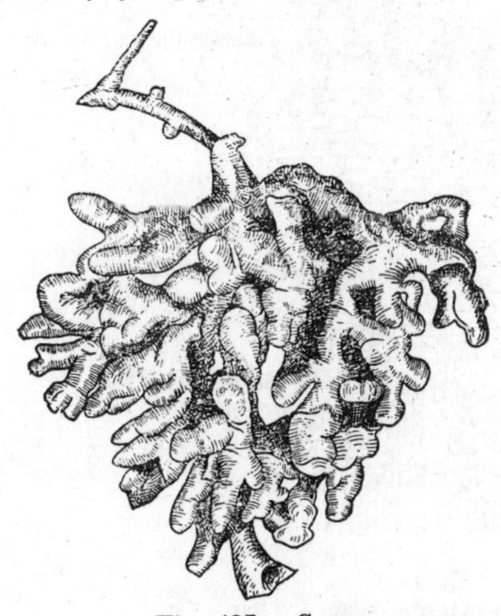

Fig. 427. *Cycas*. A group of root tubercles.

A cross-section of the stem shows a large pith, a comparatively thin vascular cylinder with conjoint, collateral, open and endarch bundles, and a

*Root tubercles are formed due to the entrance and subsequent multiplication of 'bacterioids' from the soil causing considerable enlargement of the intercellular spaces and disorganization of some of the cells. Algae (*Anabaena*, possibly *Nostoc* also) soon occupy these spaces and their multiplication still further enlarges the size of these cavities. These tubercles possibly serve both in aeration as well as in assimilation.

very thick cortex showing numerous leaf-traces (**girdles**), limited externally by an epidermis. Numerous canals filled with mucilage also occur in the cortex and in the pith, and these are connected with one another through leaf-gaps forming a network. The primary cambium is short-lived, and a succession of secondary cambiums is formed in the cortex producing concentric

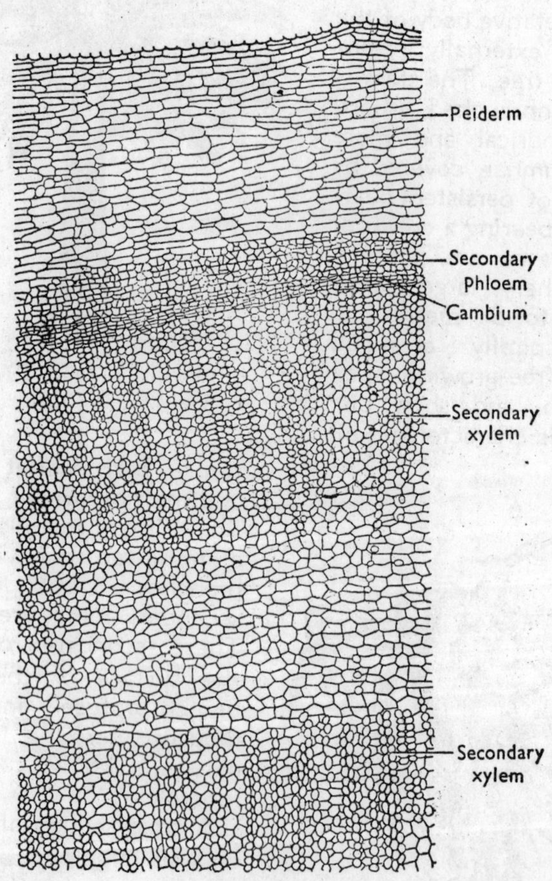

Fig. 428. *Cycas.*
T.S. of a two-year-old stem.

series of vascular cylinders. The first cortical cambium produces a prominent secondary vascular cylinder, the second cambium produces much narrower ones with widely separated vascular bundles, and as this process is continued the constructive power of the successive cambium layers is greatly reduced, which ultimately form isolated patches of smaller vascular bundles here and there at the periphery. These secondary cortical bundles are concentric.

The root is usually tetrach and the secondary growth begins early but in an irregular fashion.

In a cross-section of the petiole, numerous collateral and open vascular bundles are found to be present in a convoluted arc. The

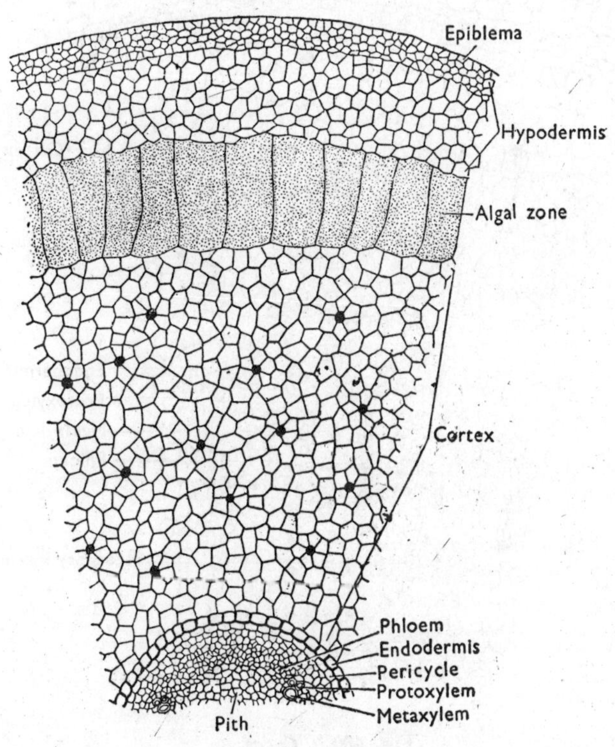

Fig. 429. *Cycas*.
T.S. of a root tubercle.

xylem of each bundle lies on the upper face with phloem below, and the former is composed of an endarch protoxylem with both centripetal and centrifugal masses of xylem, which are apparently secondary in origin (Legoc, 1914).

A cross-section of the leaf shows strongly cutinized epidermis on both sides of it and with deeply sunken stomata only on the under-surface. Below the upper epidermis there is a hypodermis, consisting of a few layers of thick-walled cells, and this tissue gives a tough and leathery texture to the leaf. The mesophyll tissue is differentiated into an upper palisade and a lower spongy paren-

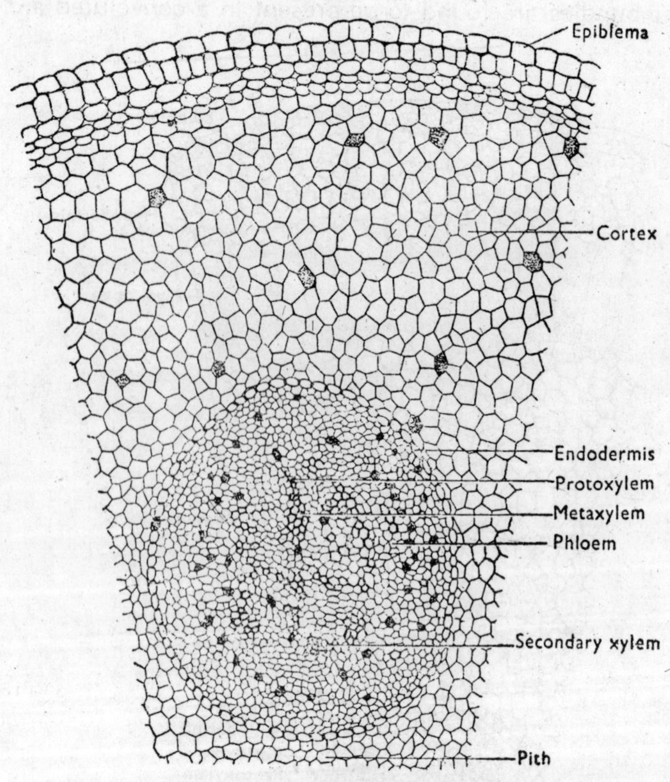

Fig. 430. *Cycas*.
T.S. of a root showing the beginning of the formation of secondary xylem.

chyma, full of chloroplasts, and these two tissues are separated by colourless, elongated cells forming the **transfusion tissue**, which runs parallel to the leaf-surface. The vascular bundle is usually mesarch.

Cycas is strictly dioecious and heterosporous, the micro- and mega-sporophylls being borne on different plants. In this case, the microsporophylls only are in compact *strobili*, while the megasporophylls are arranged spirally like the ordinary crown of foliage leaves around the terminal vegetative bud of the shoot-axis. The staminate

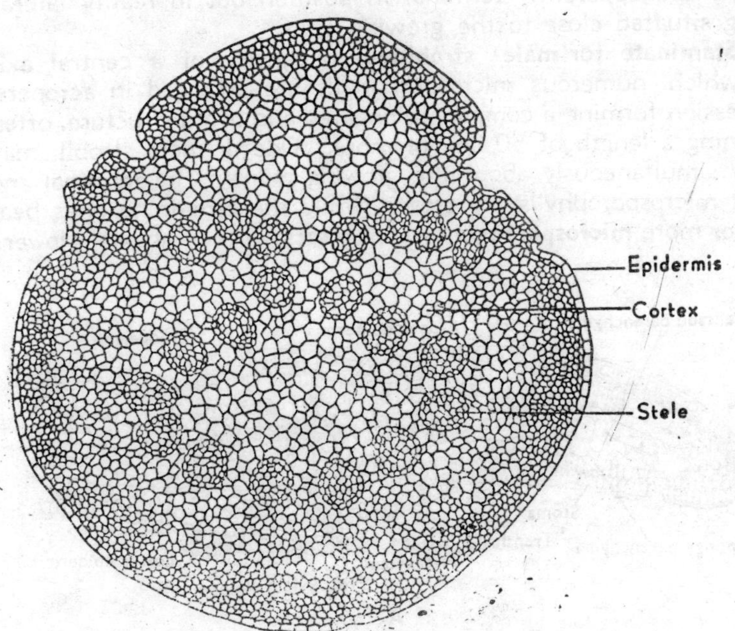

Fig. 431. *Cycas.* T.S. of the petiole.

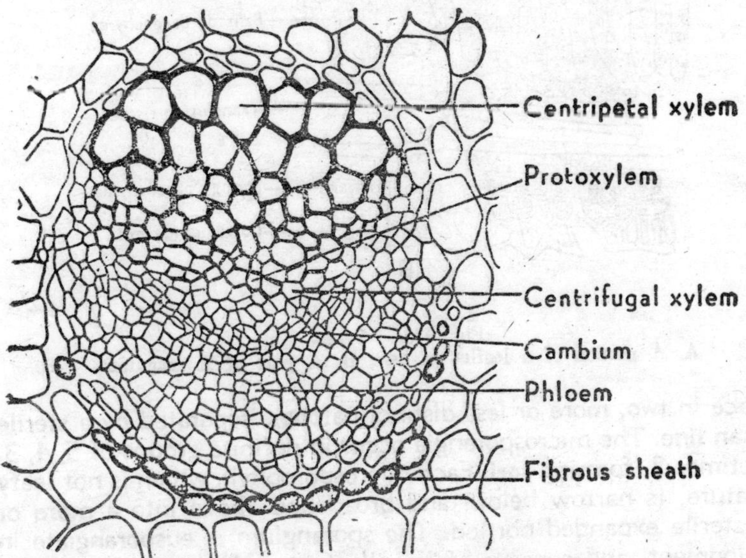

Fig. 432. *Cycas.* A single vascular bundle from Fig. 431, magnified.

strobili are apparently terminal in position but in reality lateral, being situated close to the growing apex.

Staminate (or **male**) **strobillus**. It consists of a central axis on which numerous microsporophylls are arranged in acropetal succession forming a compact, elongated and ovoid structure, often attaining a length of 50 cm. or more. One or more strobili may grow simultaneously about the growing point. The terminal and basal microsporophylls are sterile, while the remaining ones bear 700 or more **microsporangia** or **pollen sacs** on their abaxial (lower)

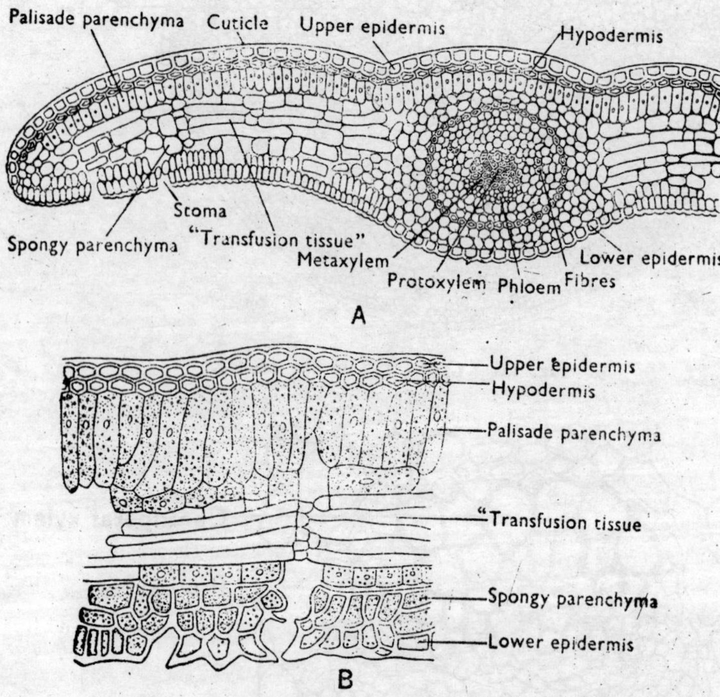

Fig. 433. *Cycas*.
A, A portion of a leaflet in t.s.; B, A part of A magnified.

surface in two, more or less distinct patches, separated by a sterile median line. The microsporangia occur in definite groups of 5, 4, 3, sometimes 2, forming **sori.** Each microsporophyll, which is not leafy in nature, is narrow below, and broadened above into a more or less sterile expanded portion. The sporangium is eusporangiate in development, and consists of a wall of several layers of cells surrounding an inner large mass of **sporogenous tissue,** from the surface of which a comparatively scanty tapetum is developed. From each spore mother cell, by reduction division, four **microspores** or **pollen grains** are produced.

Ovulate or female strobilus.

The megasporophylls do not form compact strobili, as in the case of microsporophylls, but are spirally and loosely arranged like ordinary crown of

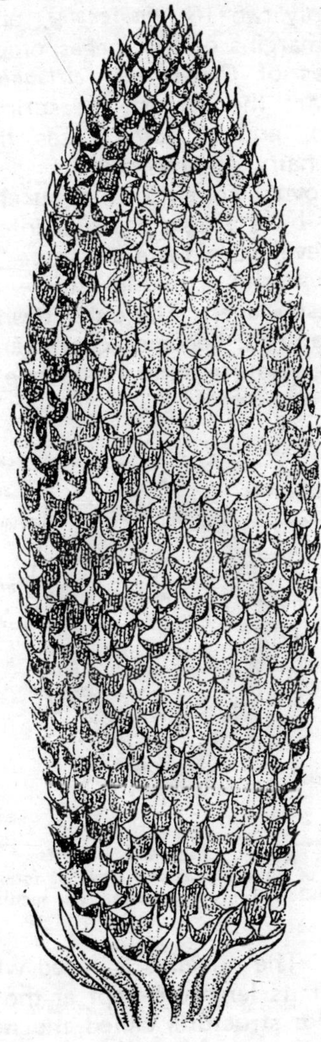

Fig. 434. *Cycas.* A male strobilus.

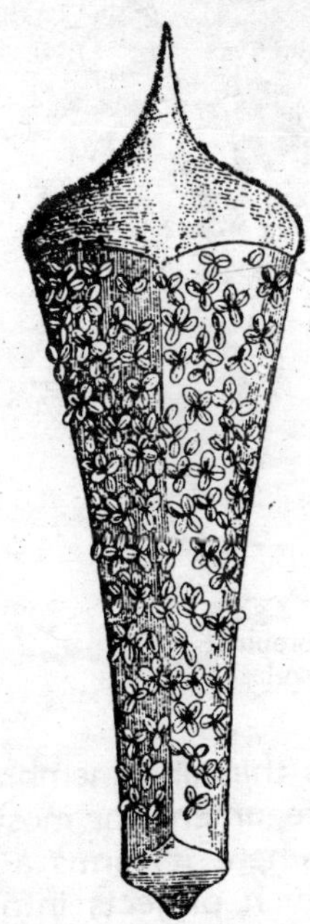

Fig. 435. *Cycas.* A microsporophyll in ventral view showing a few sori.

foliage leaves around the terminal vegetative bud of the shoot-axis. The megasporophylls, in some cases bear considerable resemblance to foliage leaves (*e.g., C. revoluta, C. circinalis,* etc.), are devoid of chlorophyll, and covered with short brownish hairs. Several **ovules** or **megasporangia**, sometimes only two (*C. siamensis*), are borne on the margins of the megasporophyll. In a species of *Cycas* (*C. circinalis*) the ovules are the largest, measuring about 6×4 cm., and in some cases they are densely hairy (*C. revoluta*).

The ovule consists of a **nucellus** surrounded by a single massive integument which develops a testa of three layers: an outer fleshy, a middle stony, and an inner fleshy layer. The outer fleshy layer, in a ripe seed, becomes characteristically coloured, and the inner fleshy one usually

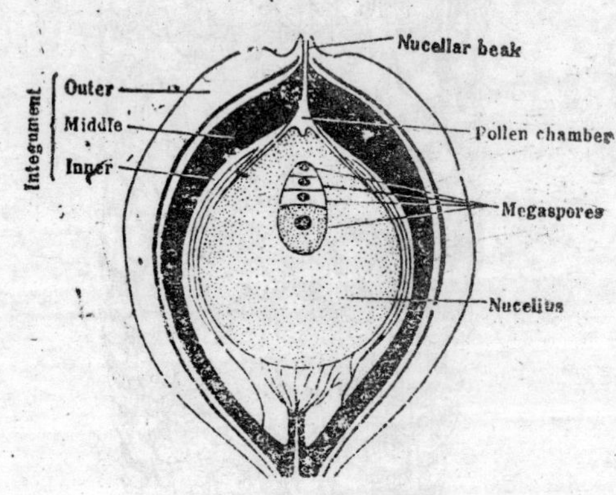

Fig. 436. *Cycas*. A megasporophyll with ovules.

Fig. 437. *Cycas*. Structure of an ovule at the stage of formation of linear tetrad of megaspores (in median l.s.).

becomes thin and membraneous. The nucellus is fused with the thick integument for most part of its length, except at the apical region, where it forms a beak-like structure, called the **nucellar beak**, which projects into the micropyle. Within the nucellar beak develops a conspicuous chamber, called the **pollen chamber**, in which the pollen grains are collected. The vascular supply of the ovule is divided into two sets, the outer set enters the outer fleshy layer, and the inner set traverses the inner fleshy layer just within the stony coat, and continues beyond the free portion of the nucellus. Deep within the tissue of the nucellus a **spore mother cell** soon becomes differentiated, which by reduction division, forms a linear tetrad of four **megaspores** or **embryosacs**, of which the innermost one is functional, while the others disorganize.

The gametophytes

Male gametophyte. The microspore, the first cell of the male gametophyte, has two coats : the *exine* and the *intine*. It germinates while still within the microsporangium ; its nucleus divides and two unequal cells are formed, a small persistent **prothallial cell** or **vegetative cell**, and a large cell, the **antheridial initial.** The

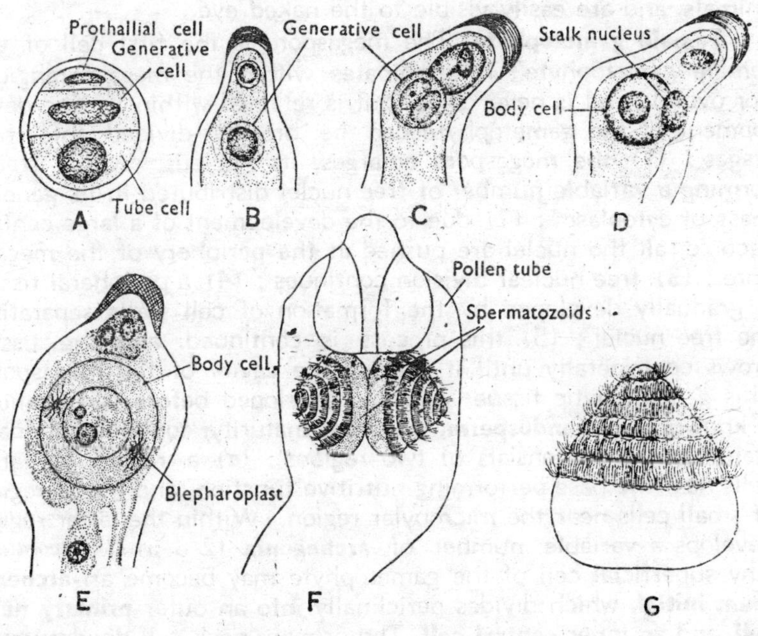

Fig. 438. *Cycas.*
A—F, Successive stages in the development of the male gametophyte ; G, A mature spermatozoid.

larger cell in its turn, divides again into two unequal cells, one, a small cell closely in contact with the prothallial cell, is the **generative cell**, and the other larger cell is the **tube cell.** It is at this three-celled condition the microspores or pollen grains are discharged from the microsporangium, and are disseminated by wind. It has been accepted that *Cycas* is wind-pollinated. The three-celled microspores are carried by the wind to the ovules of the neighbouring female plants. They are caught by a mucilagenous secretion from the micropyle. and as the fluid dries up, they are sucked into the pollen chamber. The tube cell elongates and penetrates the tissue of the nucellus forming the **pollen tube**, and the tube nucleus passes into it. The pollen tube often branches, and always functions as an absorptive organ. The generative cell then divides into a **stalk cell** and a **body cell.** The former is functionless, but the latter again undergoes division producing two **spermatozoid mother cells,** in each of which a large spirally coiled, multiflagellate **spermatozoid** is produced. These spermatozoids are remarkably large, larger than any known in other plants and animals, and are easily visible to the naked eye.

Female gametophyte. The megaspore is the first cell of the female gametophyte. It germinates within the megasporangium (or ovule), and is never shed, but is retained within it. The development of the gametophyte can be broadly divided into five stages : (1) the megaspore enlarges, its nucleus divides freely forming a variable number of free nuclei distributed in its general mass of cytoplasm ; (2) due to the development of a large central vacuole, all the nuclei are pushed at the periphery of the megaspore ; (3) free nuclear division continues ; (4) a peripheral tissue is gradually developed by the formation of cell walls separating the free nuclei ; (5) this process is continued, and the tissue grows centripetally until it fills up the cavity of the megaspore. This gametophytic tissue, which is developed before fertilization, is known as the **endosperm,** which, at maturity, contains abundant starch grains. It consists of two regions : (*a*) a region of large cells near the base performing nutritive function, and (*b*) a region of small cells near the micropylar region. Within the latter region develops a variable number of **archegonia** (2-8 in *C. revoluta*). Any superficial cell of the gametophyte may become an **archegonium initial,** which divides periclinally into an outer **primary neck cell**, and an inner **central cell.** The primary neck cell divides vertically to form two *neck cells*, while the central cell enlarges remarkably and gradually becomes surrounded by a special jacket of nutritive cells, known as the **archegonial jacket.** The nucleus of the central cell finally divides to form a *ventral nucleus*, and an *egg nucleus*, and there is no wall in between the two. The absence of such a wall is regarded as an advanced character. Around the latter an *oosphere* is gradually differentiated. The ventral nucleus soon disorganizes. The oosphere and its nucleus have been described as the largest among plants, and can be detected by the unaided eye. During the development of the archegonia at the micropylar surface of the gametophyte, its neighbouring cells continue to grow upwards, so that the archegonia are left in a shallow depression, known as the **archegonial chamber.**

After penetrating the nucellus the pollen tube bursts, when

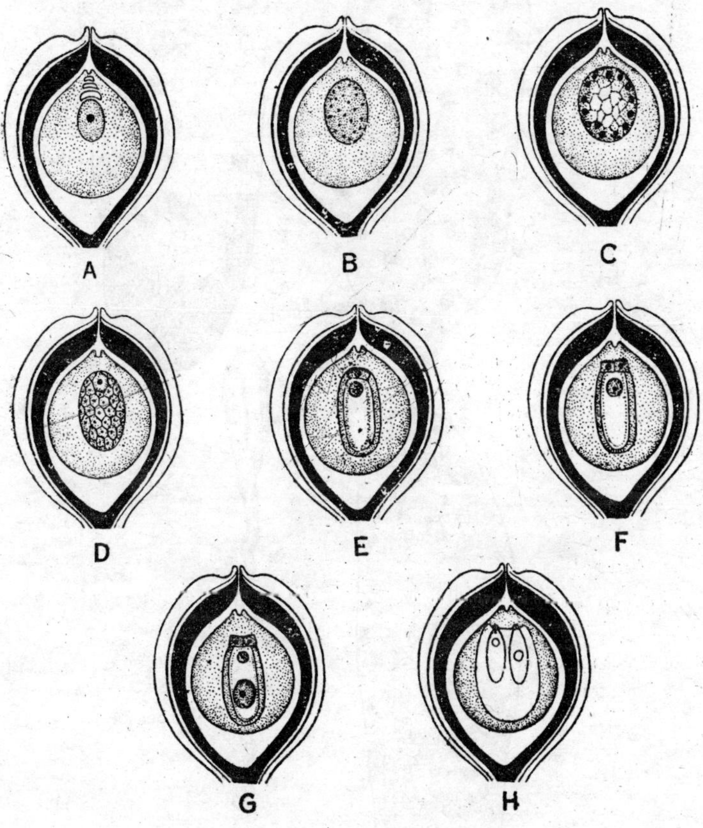

Fig. 439. *Cycas.*
A—H, Successive stages in the development of the female gametophyte.

the spermatozoids are set free in the archegonial chamber. The spermatozoids then make their way into the archegonium, anr one of them fertilizes the oosphere. The fertilized oosphere surrounds itself by a wall, and forms an **oospore.**

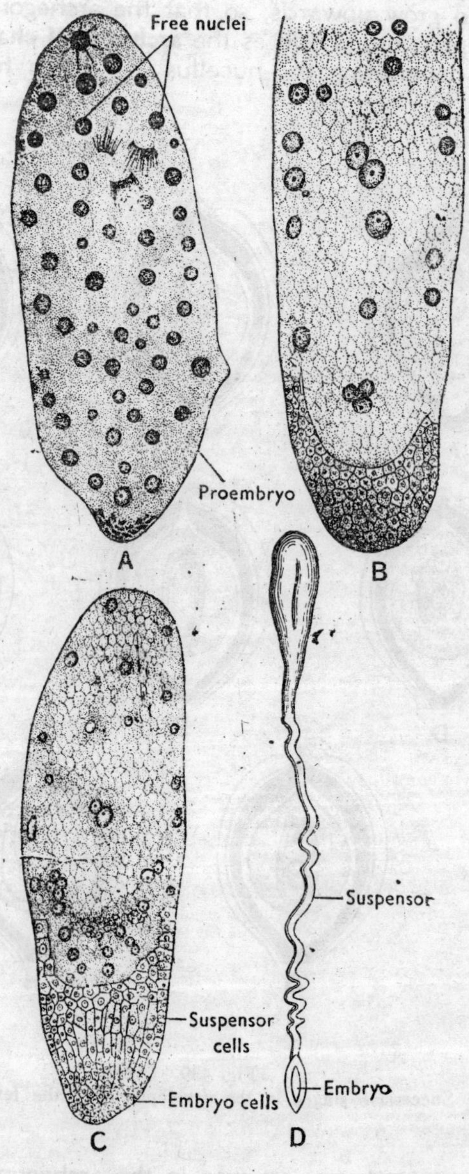

Fig. 440. *Cycas*.
A—C, Successive stages in the development of the embryo of a Cycad (*Zamia*) ; D, A mature embryo.

The new sporophyte

After fertilization the oospore enlarges, its nucleus by free cell-formation produces as many as 256 or probably more (*C. revoluta*) nuclei, distributed through the cytoplasm of the oospore. A large central vacuole soon appears (*C. circinalis*), followed by the formation of a peripheral tissue. This tissue is the **proembryo**. Further details are not known in *Cycas*. But in another genus, *Zamia*, the development has been fairly worked out. In *Zamia* the proembryo is formed only at the lower end of the developing oospore. The cells below the tip-cells of this proembryo elongate remarkably, and ultimately form a long, coiled, flexuous and massive filamentous structure, called the **suspensor**, which forces the tip-cells out of the archegonium into the nutritive gametophytic tissue (endosperm). From the tip-cells a dicotyledonous embryo is produced. The embryo and the endosperm remain within the three-layered testa, and the ovule is gradually transformed into a seed. The seed, on germination, gives rise to a new seedling sporophyte, and the mode of germination is hypogeal.

Fossil Cycads

The Cycadales first appeared in Upper Triassic and are the only group out of all the Cycadopsida that has survived until the present-day. Among the living plant they are extremely ancient and retained primitive features both in their morphology and life cycle.

The fossil cycads are mostly included in the order Nilssoniales by the following Cycas :

Leaves : *Nilssonia*.

Seed-bearing organs : *Beania*.

Pollen-bearing organs : *Androstrobus*.

Nilssonia is a common form that have large frond, and the lamina is often cut into segments of various sizes and shapes. The common Indian species are *N. princeps*, *N. morrisiana*, *N. medlicottiana*, etc.

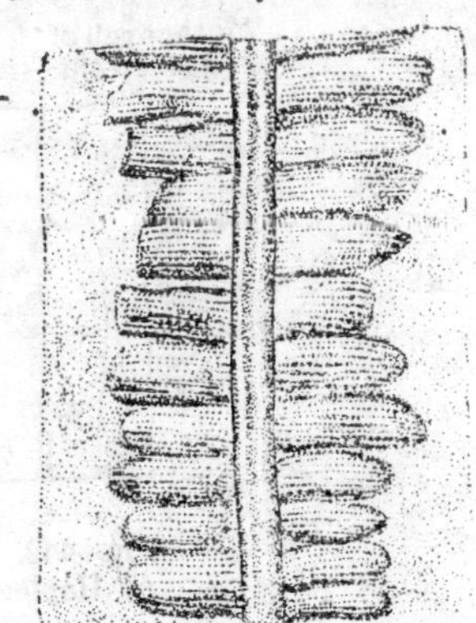

Fig. 441. Leaf of Cycadales. *Nilssonia*.

The leaves are with strong midribs, undivided lamina forked or simple veins pass to the margins at right angles to the midrib or slightly upwardly bent.

Haplocheilic type of stoma typical of the fossil Nilssoniales shows its resemblances with Cycadales. Hence the leaves of Nilssoniales represent the foliage of fossil member of Cycadales.

The pistillate fructification of fossil Cycads is *Beania* from the Jurassic of Yorkshire. Each of the peltate sporophylls bears two ovules, sporophylls are arranged spirally in a loose cone, and the structure of the ovule shows close resemblance with that of Cycas.

The male cone referred to *Androstrobus*, belonged to the same plant as *Beania*, because they are associated together in the rocks, and the pollen grains inside the micropyle of *Beania* are same as obtained from the male cones of *Androstrobus*.

Phylogeny of Cycadales

It is generally agreed that the Cycadales are evolved from some of the Paleozoic Pteridosperms, because both these groups possess typical cycadophytic characters. Centripetal xylem of the vascular

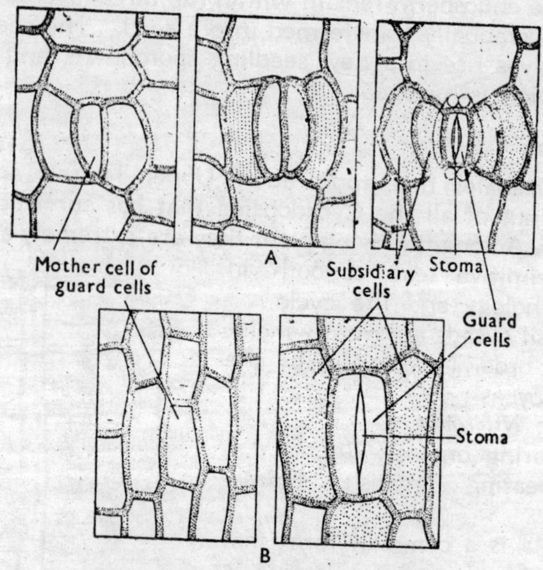

Fig. 442. Development of stomata. A, Haplocheilic ; B, Syndetocheilic.

bundles in the leaves and cone peduncles, seed structure, and megasporophyll of Cycas have pteridospermic (Paleozoic) resemblances. Anatomical studies of Cycads suggest they have descended either from the Medullosaceae, which possess a hollow stelar cylinder, or Lyginopteridaceae, which have monostelic stem as in the *Cycas*. Bennettitales resemble the Cycadales in their vegetative characters, but differ in their stomatal structure and their very different fructification is indicative of a common ancestry or parallel evolution. *Cycas* has been considered to be the most primitive because of the lack of ovulate strobili. Fossil foliage of Cycadales and Bennettitales can be distinguished by the arrangement of the cells surrounding the guard cell-pair and other stomatal characters. In Cycadales the arrangement of the cell is **haplocheilic** in which two guard cells originate from a common mother cell and the neighbouring cells become modified as subsidiary cells. This character is shared by Pteridosperms, Conifers, Cordaitales, Ginkgoales and Ephedrales. In Bennettitales a common mother cell gives rise by two divisions to three cells, the median one dividing to form two guard cells, the latter cells becoming specialized as subsidiary cells. **Syndetocheilic** character is shared by *Gnetum*, *Welwitschia* and some angiosperms. These differences raise doubts if Cycads and Cycadeoids are closely related, regardless of the resemblances in general habit and internal structure.

The Cycadales are remarkable in the retention of more primitive characters than are possessed by any living group of Gymnosperms. The swimming sperms are shared by the Ginkgoales along with the structure of the ovule. But the vegetative structures are more fernlike.

Because of their adaptation to the arid environment the Cycads survived the adverse conditions of the Permian much better than did the Pteridosperms.

Affinity

Cycadales have some relationship with Cycadofilicales, Bennettitales and Cordaitales.

(*a*) *Affinity with Cycadofilicales*

1. Frond-like leaves.
2. Large leaf stalks with copious supply of supporting tissue.
3. Thick persistent cortex.
4. The pronounced tendency to undergo anomalous development.
5. Loosely constructed secondary wool with numerous large rays.
6. A large pith, which sometimes contains mucilage ducts.
7. Presence of centripetal xylem in the cone-stalk.
8. Highly specialised staminal strobili.
9. Structure of the ovules.

(*b*) *Affinity with Bennettitales*

1. External appearance similar.
2. Megasporophylls are collected into loose crown.

3. Anatomical structures of stem and leaves similar.

(*c*) *Affinity with Cordaitales*

1. Large pith.
2. Abundant sclerenchyma in leaf.
3. Relative simple structure of wood.
4. Simple and fairly large seed.

Fern-characters in Cycas

1. The sporophyte of *Cycas* has a columnar and an unbranched stem covered over with persistent leaf-bases and bearing a crown of large pinnate compound leaves towards the apex, as in tree ferns.

2. Rachis and leaflets enrolled from the apex in a circinnate manner.

3. Megasporophylls are leaf-like as is indicated by their arrangement on the stem, where they take the place of foliage leaves ; by their approach to pinnate character, especially in *Cycas revoluta*, and by their developing chlorophyll, as in *C. circinalis*. In ferns also the sporophylls are either leaves or resemble them very much.

4. In the arrangement of microsporangia in sori on the undersurface of the microsporophylls, presence of indusial hairs beneath the sori, structure and eusporangiate development of the microsporangia and their dehiscence and their large output of microspores, *Cycas* resembles Marattiaceae.

5. Motile and flagellate sperms.

6. Xylem has no vessels and phloem is without companion cells. Sieve plates are present on the longitudinal walls of the sieve tubes and sometimes even concentric bundles are found in the leaf, cone-axis and stalks of sporophylls. The entire cortical bundles of the stem are concentric. All these are fern characters. Further, like them in ferns, pith and cortex are large.

7. Presence of leaf gaps in the cortex.

All these characters lead one to believe that *Cycas* might have evolved from the ferns.

CHAPTER IV

CORDAITALES

The Cordaitales appeared in the Devonian period or perhaps in Silurian, reached their climax in the Carboniferous, and finally disappeared in the Permian, although some believe that they continued up to the Triassic. Fossil remains are distributed over North America, some parts of South America, Great Britain, France, Russia, India, China, Australia and Africa.

Prof. Sahni has placed this order in **Stachyospermae,** because the ovules are stem-borne. The stele is cylindrical, and leaf traces are conspicuous.

Classification of Cordaitales

The order is usually divided into *three* families : **Pityeae, Cordaiteae.** and **Poroxyleae.** Of the three families, the best known as well as most extensively studied one is the Cordaiteae.

A brief account of each of the families is given below :

1. Pityeae. The important genera belonging to this family are *Pitys*, *Archaeopitys* and *Callixylon.* The foliage structure is only known in case of *Pitys dayi*, which is fleshy and about 4-6 mm. in diameter. There is no definite leaf gap present. The structure of the stem is known. A cross-section of the stem of *Callixylon* shows a parenchymatous pith, mesarch primary wood, compact secondary wood with characteristically alternately pitted tracheids, feeble growth rings and uni- to multi-seriate rays. A group of pits (occurring on the radial walls) alternating with an unpitted area in a regular pattern is a unique feature of this wood only. No fructification is known as yet.

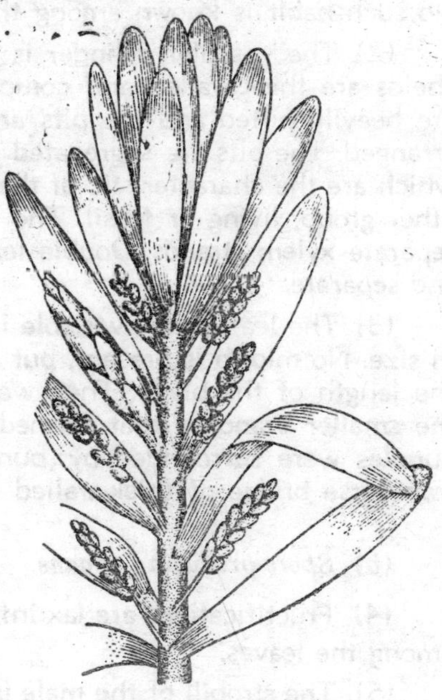

Fig. 443. *Cordaites.*

2. Cordaiteae. The important genus is *Cordaites,* which is an assemblage of different form genera. For details—see below.

3. Poroxpleate. This family is very restricted in its distribution and consists of only one genus, *Poroxylon*, with two species. The structure of the stem comprises of a large pith, surrounded by a primary exarch wood. The secondary wood is loose, and the leaves are strap-shaped. The seed is known as *Rhabdocarpus.*

The Cordaitales constitute a group of Paleozoic arborescent gymnosperms which together with the Cycadofilicales contributed the bulk of the seed plants of the Permo-carboniferous coal forests.

Characteristic features

(*a*) *Vegetative organs*

(1) The members of Cordaitales were tall and slender trees, the trunks often reaching a height of 10-30 metres before branching. The long slender shaft bore a dense crown of branches, on which were produced an abundance of large and simple leaves. No such habit is known among the existing gymnosperms.

(2) The vascular cylinder is collateral and endarch. The tracheids are thick-walled and compactly arranged. The radial walls are heavily pitted and the pits are alternately and multiserially arranged. The pits are segregated into groups with unpitted spaces which are the characteristic of the group. This is not found in any other group, living or fossil. The innermost wood forms a ring of separate xylem strands. Double leaf trace is present. Pith is large and separate.

(3) The leaf is very variable in shape, rounded to very slender in size. No midrib is present, but a series of parallel lines traverse the length of the blade. They were borne on spiral sequence on the smaller branches that formed the crown of the tree. The bundles were surrounded by bundle sheath and connected by transverse bridge of thick-walled cells.

(*b*) *Spore-producing organs*

(4) Fructifications are lax inflorescences on the slender stems among the leaves.

(5) The strobili of the male inflorescence contain 1-6 or more fertile bracts (microsporophylls), each of which supports as many as 6 terminal elongated pollen sacs.

(6) Each female strobilus usually contains 1-4 ovuliferous appendages (megasporophylls). In some cases, megasporophylls are forked and bear two terminal flattened ovules.

(7) Air sacs rendered the pollen bouyant and facilitated easy dispersal by wind.

(8) The winged seeds are flattened and heart-shaped, the nucellus is free from the integument except at the base and the vascular supply is double. The nucellar beak of the pollen chamber projects into the micropyle. Fertilization probably took place by swimming sperms. If a pollen tube was present, it probably functioned as an absorptive organ as in recent Cycads and Ginkgos.

Fossil Cordaitales

The Cordaitales, with the Pteridosperms, formed the vegetation of the late Palaeozoic era. The Lower Gondwana rocks of India have yielded potrified wood which are presumably cordaitean.

The fossil Cordaitales which are found in India are as follows :

1. *Neoggerathiopsis.* It is a leaf genus which occurs in the Lower Gondwana in India. It has two most common species *N. hislopi* and *N. stoliczkanus* ; leaves are elongate to spathulate in shape with broadly rounded apex. They vary in size, larger ones reaching more than 20 cm. in length.

2. *Samaropsis.* It is the seed genus with few species and occurs in the Karbarbari and Raniganj series of Lower Gondwana in India. The seeds are winged, ovate or flat with emarginate apex and found in close association with *Neoggerathiopsis hislopi.*

3. *Cordaicarpus.* It is also a seed genus with more than one species, and occurs in the Talchir of Lower Gondwana of India. The base is slightly cordate and the apex pointed. They are small, oval or pear shaped and vary in size.

b. *Dadoxylon.* It is the stem genus with more than one species.

The important Indian species are *D. indicum*, *D. bengalense* and *D. zalesskyi.* These occur in the Barakar series of Lower Gondwana. The species are silicified stems with a large pith containing sclerotic cells. The secondary wood has sharply marked growth rings.

CORDAITES

(Fam. CORDAITEAE)

Cordaites is the most important genus in the family Cordaiteae. The genus is an assemblage of different form genera. The stem genera are termed as *Mesoxylon*, *Dadoxylon*, etc., the root as *Amyelon*, the inflorescence as *Cordaianthus*, the seed as *Samaropsis*, *Cordaicarpus*, etc.

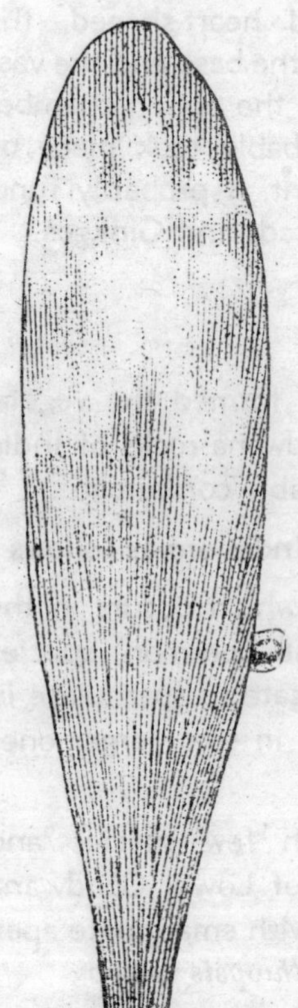

Fig. 444.
Leaf of Cordaitales
Neoggerathiopsis.

The sporophyte

Tree-like in habit, tall and slender trunks, branching only at the top, and bearing long, slender, spirally arranged leaves. The leaves are tough, leathery, linear, lanceolate to spathulate in shape, and there is no midrib. The veins are arranged in a parallel fashion.

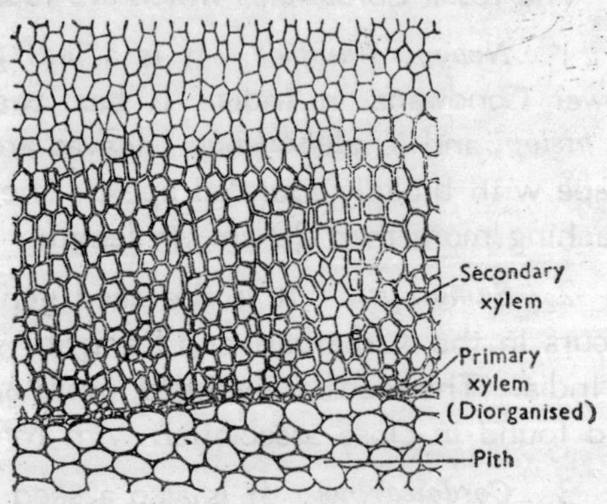

Fig. 445. *Cordaites.*
T.S. of the stem (in part).

The structure of the stem shows a large parenchymatous pith, which is partly septate due to the formation of diaphragms, as is found in the modern *Fuglans*. The primary wood is small and endarch. The secondary wood forms a thick layer ; tracheids are pitted. Pits are uni-, di-, or tri-seriate ; the rays are simple. Growth rings are rare.

The central cylinder of the root is a di-, tri-, or tetrach

protostele, and is surrounded by secondary wood. The periderm is much well-developed.

Internally, the leaf shows xerophytic characters, and possesses a thick cuticle. The upper epidermis is highly cuticularized, below which there is a thin hypodermis, composed of one or two layers of thick-walled cells. The mesophyll is mainly composed of palisade parenchyma cells ; the cells towards the lower epidermis are angular, closely set, and without any intercellular

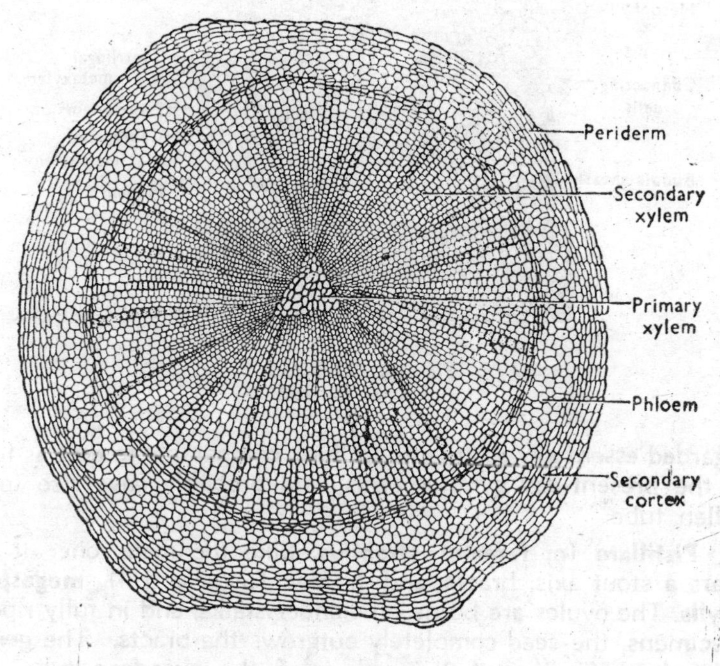

Fig. 446. *Cordaites*.
T.S. of the root.

spaces. The vascular bundles are arranged in a parallel series ; each bundle is surrounded by a sheath, and is connected with the hypodermis by means of a band of thick-walled cells. Though the lower epidermis is not found in a very well-state of preservation, the guard cells are noted to be provided with 4-6 subsidiary cells.

Cordaites may be either monoecious or dioecious, and bear small monosporangiate strobili on stalks, the male one's being more numerous than the female ones.

Staminate (or **male**) **strobilus**. It consists of a short axis bearing spirally arranged, sterile bracts, and fertile **microsporophylls,** each of the latter supporting a number of **microsporangia** or **pollen sacs.** The microspores or pollen grains are globose, and the exine is inflated forming a big air-containing sac, which, with the exception of a small area at one corner of the pollen grain, can be

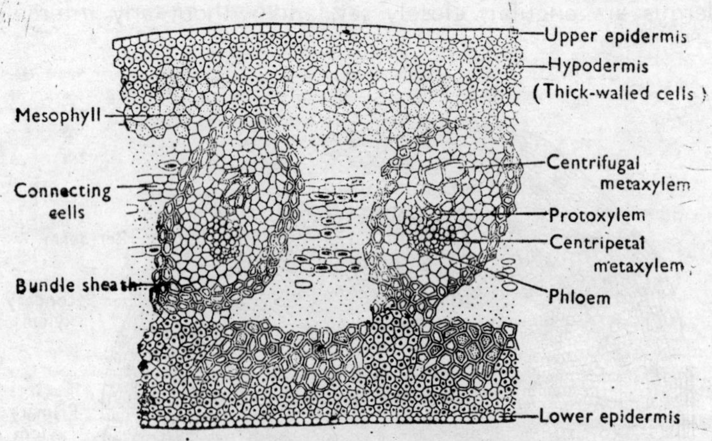

Fig. 447. *Cordaites*. T.S. of the leaf.

regarded essentially as an antheridium, comparable to that as found in the present-day gymnosperms, and probably gave rise to the pollen tube.

Pistillate (or **female**) **strobilus**. Like the male one, it also bears a stout axis, bracts and a few (usually 1-4) **megasporophylls.** The ovules are borne on slender stalks, and in fully ripened specimens, the seed completely outgrows the bracts. The general plan of construction of the ovule is of the cycadean type. The nucellus is practically free from the three-layered, solitary integument, excepting at the base ; the nucellar beak projects into the micropyle. The pollen chamber is conspicuous.

The gametophytes

Male gametophyte. Soon after the shedding of the winged pollen grain, a large number of cells develop within its body. The nature of the cells is not properly known.

Female gametophyte. There are two archegonia present and the structure is an elongated one.

In all probability the fertilization was effected with the help of motile sperms.

Seed. The seed is flattened and winged.

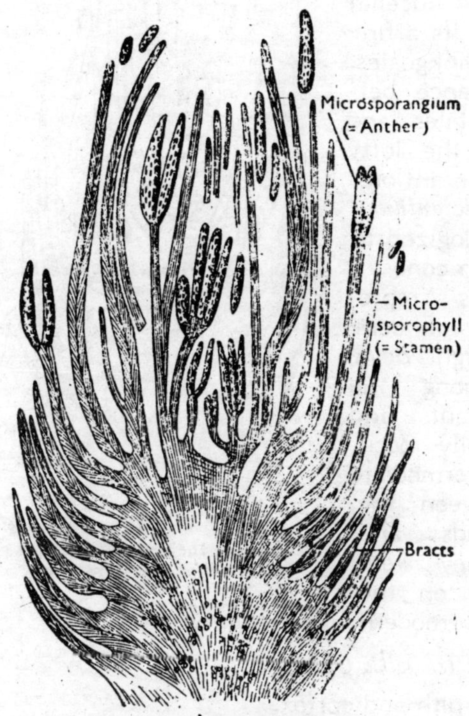

Fig. 448. *Cordaites*.
L.S. of the male strobilus.

Embryo. Regarding the embryo nothing is practically known, excepting the recent findings of Darrah from the coal balls of Iowa.

Affinity

This order exhibits a combination of characters of the Pteridosperms, Cycadeoideales, Cycadales, Ginkgoales, and Coniferales, together with peculiarities of its own. As to the structure of the seed, large pollen chamber and two sets of vascular strands, it resembles the Pteridosperms. It shows an affinity with the Cycadeoidales in the general organization of strobili and reduction of bracts, but it differs from the latter in its monosporangiate nature.

Its resemblances with the Cycadales are also very prominent, because of the large pith, the abundance of sclerenchyma in the leaf, the general structure of seed, and the probable presence of swimming sperms. The anatomical evidence, general habit, leaf structure, and nucellar beak suggest its affinity with the Ginkgoales. The resemblance between Cordaitales and Conifers in the lofty habit, and the inflorescence (*Cordaianthus*) can be homologized to the abietinean cone.

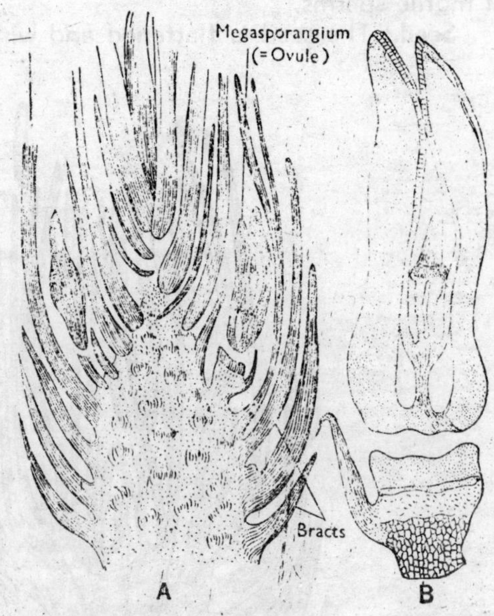

Fig. 449. *Cordaites*. A, L.S. of the female strobilus ; B, L.S. of a mature ovule.

Cordaitales represent a state of comparatively high development among the Paleozoic plants and phylogenetically occupy an intermediate position between the recent Cycads and Conifers. They were more or less on the same level of modern Gymnosperms.

(*a*) *Affinities with Cycads*

1. Large pith and cortex.
2. Abundant sclerenchyma in the leaf.
3. Relatively simple and fairly large seeds.
4. Probability of motile sperms.
5. Relatively simple structure of the wood.

(*b*) *Affinities with Ginkgoales*

1. Lofty and branching habit as in Pityeae and Poroxylaceae.
2. Fan-shaped leaves were probably borne by some cordaitalean trunk.
3. Probable motility of sperms.
4. General anatomical plan and the occurrence of double leaf trace—indicate the similarity of both the groups.

(*c*) *Affinities with Pteridosperms*

1. Structure of the seed—from nucellus and integument in certain seeds of both the groups ; large pollen chamber, two sets of vascular strands and the absence of embryo in both the groups.

2. Anatomy—large pith, primary wood mesarch in ***Mesoxylon***, lyginopterid-like secondary wood in *Poroxylon*, double leaf trace, etc.

(*d*) *Affinities with Coniferales*

1. Lofty and arborescent habit—a feature shared by Pityeae and possibly by Poroxylaceae.
2. Leaves of Pityeae have been compared to those of *Araucaria* by Prof. Gardon.
3. Similarities in general plan of anatomy (*a*) the presence of multiseriate bordered pits and (*b*) absence of resin canal in the wood of Cordaitae suggest they are more related to the Araucariaceae than the Pinaceae.
4. Cordaitean inflorescence (*Cordaianthus*) and abietinean cone are probably homologous with intermediate graduations noticed in some Paleozoic Conifers, e.g., ***Ernestiodendron, Lebachia***, *Pseudovoltzia* and *Ullmannia*.

CHAPTER V

GINKGOALES

The Ginkgoales were widely distributed during the Mesozoic. They reached their climax in the Jurassic and then began to decline. At present the order is represented by a single family, *Ginkgoaceae*, with only one genus, *Ginkgo*. The name of common plant is *Ginkgo biloba* (maiden-hair tree), which is generally referred to as the 'living fossil'. It is found in an apparently wild condition in some mountainous regions of Eastern China and is cultivated as a temple tree in China and Japan. The Order has been probably derived from the Cordaitales.

Characteristic features

(*a*) *Vegetative organs*

1. Medium-sized trees with spreading branches, dioecious.
2. Leaves long-stalked, flattened and lobed in various ways with dichotomous venation.
3. A thick cortex, a comparatively thin vascular cylinder and a large pith with mucilage canals or reservoirs.
4. Vascular cylinder is made up of collateral and endarch bundles.
5. No direct leaf trace.

(*b*) *Spore-producing organs*

6. Flowers unisexual.
7. Microsporophylls in loose catkin-like structure; each microsporophyll bears 2 pendant microsporangia.
8. Megasporophylls collected in strobili.
9. Ovules generally in pairs, one ovule on each side of the apex of a long stalk, which arises in the leaf-axis at the end of a short shoot.
10. Fertilization by flagellated sperms.
11. No formation of proembryo or suspensor.
12. Seed drupe-like containing a dicotyledonous embryo embedded in the copious endosperm.

The Ginkgoales appeared in the Permian or probably in the Carboniferous, reached their climax in the Jurassic, and began to decline before the Jurassic came to an end. At present they are found growing in an apparently wild condition in some mountainous places of Western China. The majority of the plants are cultivated as temple trees in China and Japan. There is only one living genus *Ginkgo** under the order with one **species** ***biloba***, and the plant is included under the single family **Ginkgoaceae.**

GINKGO

(Fam. GINKGOACEAE)

The sporophyte

The plant, popularly known as 'maiden-hair tree', is a beautiful tree of pyramidal habit, reaching a height of about 30 metres, and with a girth of more than 1 metre. In case of an old tree, the outline may be rounded at the top. There are two kinds of branches : **long shoot** and **dwarf shoot** or **spur**. The branches, in addition to bearing normal long-pointed leaves, possess scale leaves. On the long shoot, the leaves are spirally-arranged, whereas on the spur, due to the suppression of the internodes, the leaves appear to be whorled. Furthermore, the scattered leaves are broadly fan-shaped with a repand margin, and are provided with a deep apical notch, giving the blade its characteristic bilobed appearance. On the other hand, the leaves on the spur shoot are, as a rule, undivided. The venation is rather characteristic. The two main strands from the petiole enter into the lamina, and by forking repeatedly give rise to a symmetrical dichotomous venation. The leaves are deciduous, and fall off in winter. It is interesting to note, however, that in fact, no rigid line of demarcation can be drawn in between the two kinds of lateral shoots, as, in some cases, spurs may grow out into long shoots.

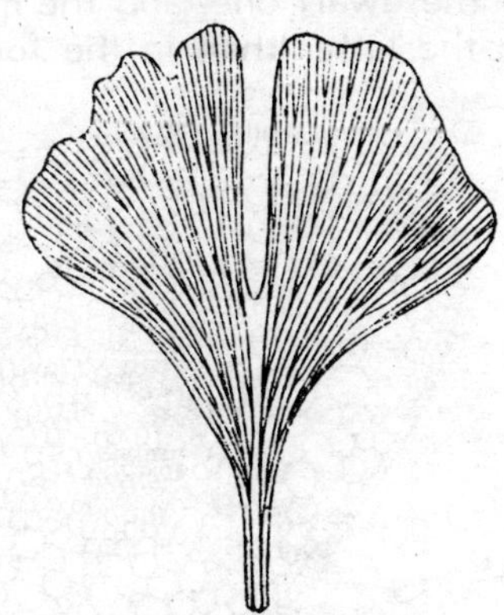

Fig. 450. *Ginkgo*. A single leaf.

Internally, the stem resembles the structure of that of the *Pinus*. Particularly, the wood structure can be regarded as strictly abietinean. The protoxylem is composed of spiral elements, and the metaxylem of bordered pitted ones, the pits occurring irregularly either in a single row or in two rows. Bars of Sanio between the pits, as well as trabeculae crossing the interior of the tracheids, are noted in the

* The proper spelling should be *Ginkyo*.

secondary wood. The wood of the long shoot is harder than that

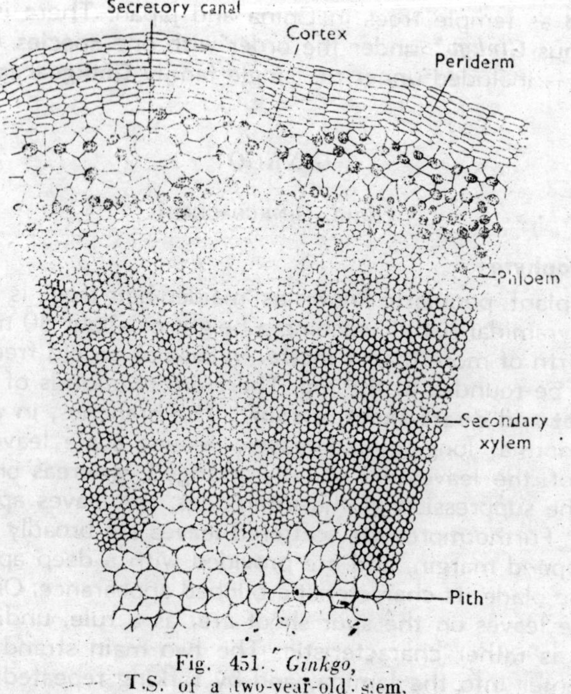

Fig. 451. *Ginkgo*, T.S. of a two-year-old stem.

of the dwarf one, and the mucilage canals are far more numerous in the latter than in the former. The annual rings, though not so

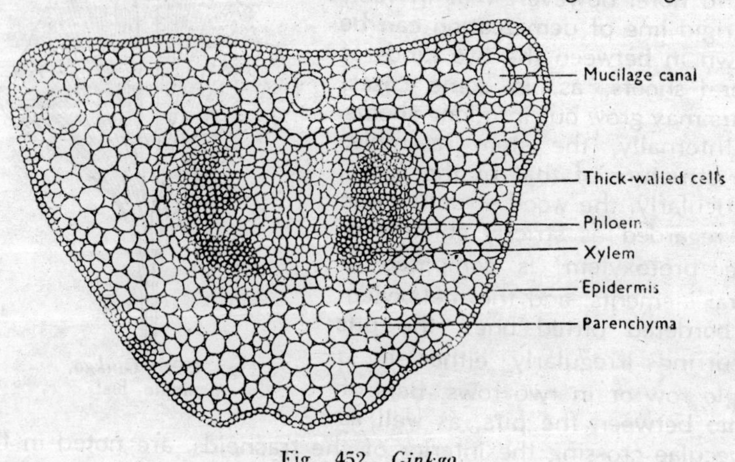

Fig. 452. *Ginkgo*, T.S. of the petiole,

prominent as in the *Pinus*, can be clearly marked out. In both the shoots the periderm develops to a considerable extent.

Normally, the root possesses a diarch cylinder, but the same

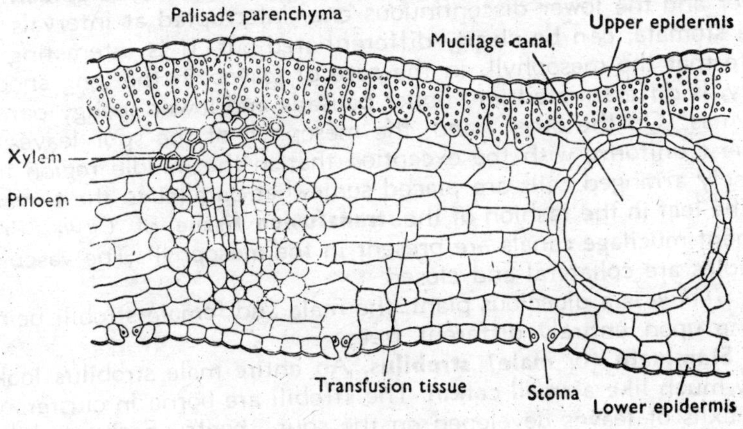

Fig. 453. *Ginkgo*, T.S. of the leaf.

becomes triarch, when the embryo contains three cotyledons. The mature root possesses annual rings like a mature stem.

In the petiole there is a double leaf trace, each one being

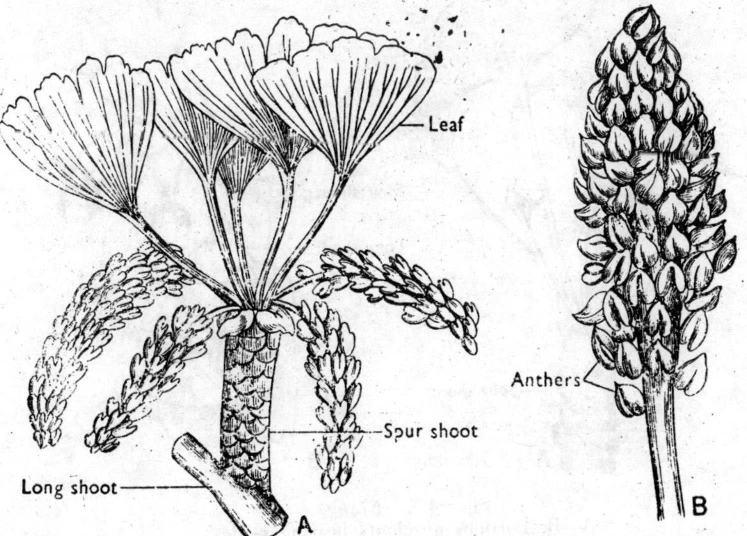

Fig. 454. *Ginkgo*.
A, A portion of the shoot bearing a number of male strobili ; B, A single male strobilus (magnified).

composed of a collateral bundle, and surrounded by a sheath made up of thick-walled cells. The bundles exhibit secondary growth.

In a cross-section of the leaf, the upper continuous epidermal layer and the lower discontinuous one, interrupted at intervals by the stomata, can be clearly differentiated out. It is interesting to note that the mesophyll, in the case of leaves on the long shoots only, is differentiated into upper palisade and lower spongy parenchymas. On the other hand, the mesophyll of the spur leaves is almost uniform, with the exception that in the middle region the loosely arranged cells are placed somewhat parallel to the surface of the leaf in the fashion of the **transfusion tissue** of *Cycas*. Prominent mucilage canals are present in the mesophyll. The vascular bundles are collateral and closed.

Ginkgo is a dioecious plant, the male and female strobili being borne upon entirely different trees.

Staminate (or **male**) **strobilus.** An entire male strobilus looks very much like a small catkin. The strobili are borne in clusters in the axils of leaves developed on the spur shoots. Each strobilus consists of a slender axis, which bears a number of spirally arranged, ebracteate *sporophylls*. A sporophyll bears normally two, hanging *microsporangia* at its tip, surmounted by a sterile **hump**, but occasionally 3-4 sporangia may be found. According to some,

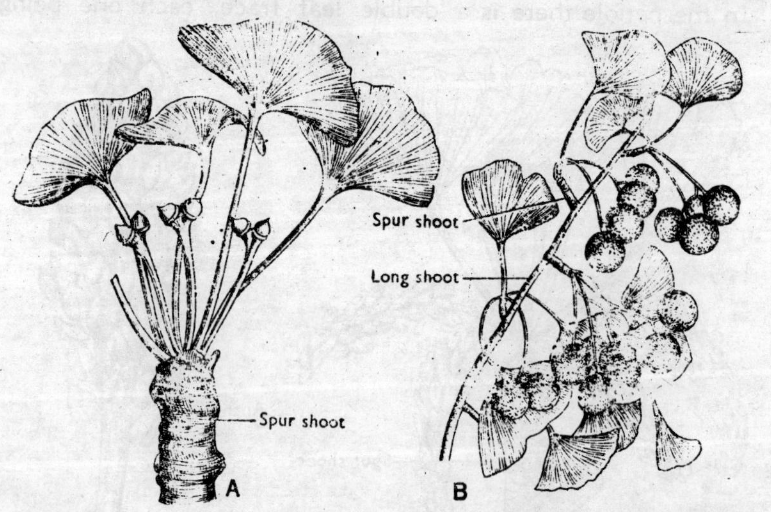

Fig. 455. *Ginkgo*.
A—B, Portions of plants bearing ovules.

the hump may be regarded as a sterile microsporangium. The *microspores* or *pollen grains* are produced by reduction division of spore mother cells. Each pollen grain is provided with two coats : the *exine* and the *intine*. The former does not cover the whole of the pollen grain, and thus, there are two little lateral **ears** resembling the wings of the pollen of *Pinus* in a miniature scale.

Pistillate (or **female**) **strobilus**. Like the male strobili. the female ones also are borne in the axils of leaves or scales, developed on the spur shoots of the female trees. Each female strobilus consists of a simple stalk, which bifurcates at its tip, and each branch bears a solitary, terminal, sessile *ovule*, the lower part of which remains encircled by a fleshy, cup-like structure, known as the **collar** or **ring**. The morphological nature of this collar is a much-debated point, but the majority of workers like to interpret it as a modified megasporophyll. Usually, only one of the pair of ovules attains maturity.

The structure of the ovule is very much similar to that of *Cycas* with a striking point of difference, in the fact, that there is no

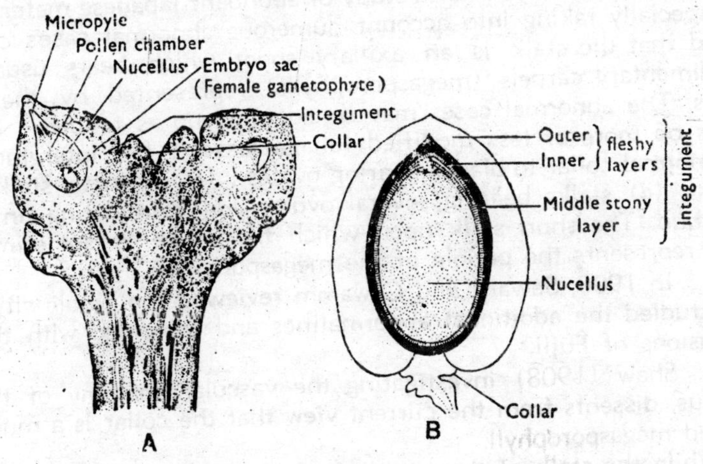

Fig. 456. *Ginkgo*.
A, Median longitudinal section through the apex of an ovuliferous axis ; B, L.S. of an ovule.

vascular supply to the integument. By the breaking down of the free apex of the nucellus, a conspicuous **pollen chamber** is produced.

Morphology of the collar of Ginkgo

There has been a considerable difference of opinion as to the morphology of the structures associated with the ovule.

1. In 1869, Van Tieghem interpreted the stalk as a petiole, the 2 ovules as determined by the characteristic lobes of the leaf-blade ; the collar as a reduced aril, and hence, the whole structure as a single megasporophyll (carpel).

2. In 1872, 1879, Strasburger suggested that the stalk as a shoot bearing a pair of flowers, each reduced to an ovule surrounded by an aril (collar) the whole structure is thus an inflorescence of 2 flowers in which the carpels are suppressed.

3. In 1873, Eichler interpreted tht collar as the outer integument of the ovule, which view is not necessarily inconsistent with the preceding views that, it stands for an aril ; later (1889) he called the collar 'a rudimentary carpel'.

4. Celakovsky (1890, 1900) stated that the stalk is an axillary shoot bearing 2 or more carpels, and that each carpel is represented only by an ovule, which means that the existence of the carpel is only theoretical.

5. In 1896, Fujii after a study of abundant Japanese materials and specially taking into account numerous abnormal cases concluded that the stalk is an axillary shoot which bears usually 2 rudimentary carpels (megasporophylls) represented by the 2 collars. The abnormal cases may be summed up as follows : (*a*) ovules on more or less modified foliage leaves ; (*b*) intergrades from normal collar to blades bearing ovules ; (*c*) distinctly stalked ovules ; (*d*) stalks bearing several ovules and terminating in a scaly bud. The short stalk upon which the ovule is sometimes borne represents the petiole of the megasporophyll.

6. In 1900, Seward and Gowamm reviewed the whole situation, studied the additional abnormalities and coincided with the conclusions of Fujii.

7. Shaw (1908) investigating the vascular anatomy of the strobilus, dissents from the current view that the collar is a much reduced megasporophyll.

While the stalk of the strobilus resembles the petiole of the leaf, it is quite different in structure. A T. S. of petiole shows only 2 bundles representing the double leaf trace, while a T. S. of the stalk of the strobilus shows the 4 bundles which would be expected in a stem bearing 2 leaves (collars) at its apex. When more than 2 ovules are borne on one stalk there are twice as many bundles as there are ovules at the apex, so that in a T. S. it has zone of wood-like that in a stem.

The evidences from the abnormalities which may be interpreted as reverse ones, together with the testimony of the vascular anatomy, strongly support the view that the stalk is a stem bearing 2 megasporophylls (collars), each of which bears a single ovule.

The whole structure is then a strobilus with 2 or more megasporophylls which are reduced to the so-called carpels.

The gametophytes

Male gametophyte. The microspore is the first cell of the male gametophyte. It germinates while still enclosed within the microsporangium. The microspore-nucleus divides mitotically, and two highly unequal cells are produced, the lower one being known as the **first prothallial** (or **vegetative**) **cell.** The larger cell undergoes a second mitotic division giving rise to a smaller cell, the **second prothallial cell**, and a larger **antheridial initial cell.** The first prothallial cell degenerates very quickly, while the second one is persistent. The antheridial initial cell then divides in its turn, and produces a **generative cell,** lying in contact with the second prothallial cell, and a **tube cell.** As in *Pinus*, the microsporangium

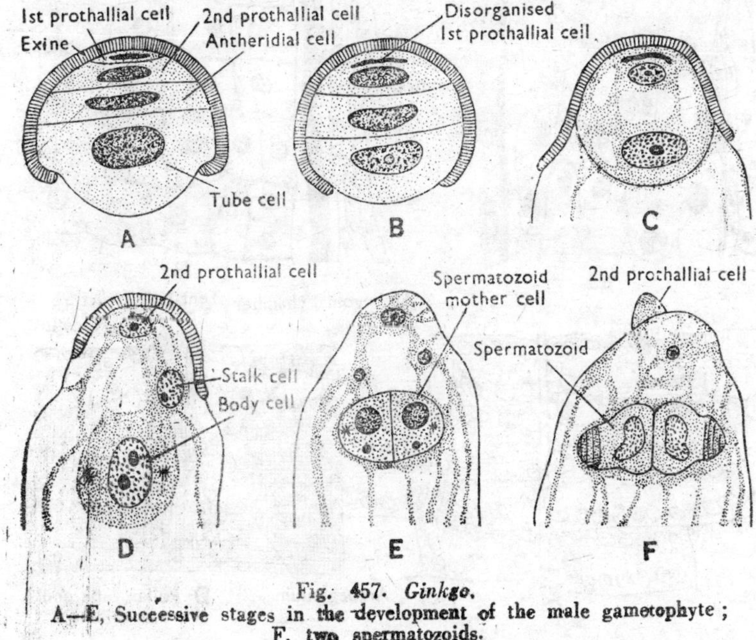

Fig. 457. *Ginkgo.*
A—E, Successive stages in the development of the male gametophyte ; F, two spermatozoids.

opens by a longitudinal slit, and the pollens are liberated at this four-celled stage. The pollen grains are dispersed by the wind, and get deposited on the open micropylar end of the ovule, where they are stuck up in the pollination drop, and subsequently brought within the pollen chamber. This constitutes the pollination in *Ginkgo*, which occurs in the beginning of May. The generative cell divides within the pollen chamber, and produces a non-functional **stalk cell**, and a **body cell.** As in *Cycas*, by the division of the body cell, two multiflagellate, swimming *sperms* are produced. Meanwhile, the tube cell has protruded out, and formed a *pollen tube*, which is more or less haustorial in nature, and it makes its way through the nucellus towards the female gametophyte.

Female gametophyte. The megaspore is the first cell of the female gametophyte. The development of the female gametophyte and that of the pollen tube start almost simultaneously. During its early stage of development, the female gametophyte is surrounded by a zone of spongy tissue which absorbs the tissue lying outside it ; but, later on, it is itself used up by the developing gametophyte. The mode of development of the female gametophyte of *Ginkgo* is

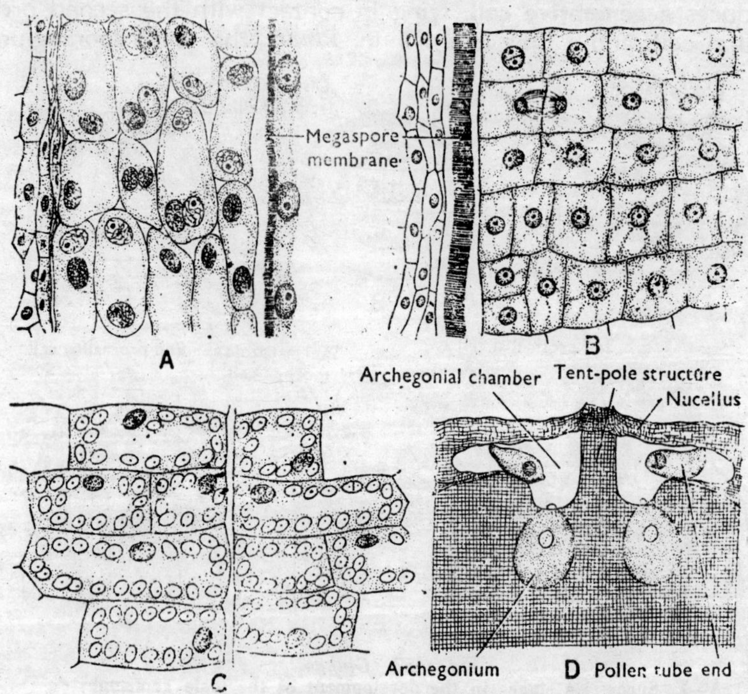

Fig. 458. *Ginkgo,*
A—C, Stages in the development of endosperm ; D, Formation of the tent-pole structure.

also like that of *Cycas* with a few interesting deviations. For instance, when the free nuclear period is coming to a close, a delicate membrane, very much distinct from the megaspore-membrane, is laid down on the outer surface of the protoplasmic layer. At the time of cell-formation cellwalls begin to be laid at right angles to this membrane. Primarily, the inner side of the innermost cell remains naked, but when the wall-formation stops, a wall is deposited on the naked face of the cell. Consequently, the innermost cells, coming from opposite directions within the developing megaspore, do not have a common wall, but each one is provided with a wall of its own, so that the female gametophyte has a plane of cleavage along the middle region. It is to be noted that chloroplasts are present in the cells of the female gametophyte (**endosperm**).

Archegonia, as usual, are developed towards the micropylar end of the endosperm. There are usually two, occasionally three, archegonia formed. Each archegonium has a two-celled *neck*, a distinct *ventral canal cell*, and an *egg cell*. But, here, instead of a cup-shaped archegonial chamber, as is found in *Cycas*, a circular trough is developed, surrounding a central mass of beak-like tissue supporting the remnant of the nucellus ; this is known as the **tent-pole structure.**

Fertilization takes place in late September, *i.e.*, four months after pollination has been effected. The tip of the pollen tube, carrying the two sperms, bursts open, and the contents are discharged within the archegonial chamber. The sperm-nucleus unites with the egg-nucleus near about the centre of the egg, and brings about fertilization. The fertilized egg cell develops into an **oospore**.

The new sporophyte

The oospore enlarges, and a period of free nuclear division commences. The nuclei (usually 256 in number) are evenly distributed throughout the cytoplasm of the oospore. Subsequently, simultaneous wall-formation takes place, and the whole interior of the archegonium becomes filled up with cells of approximately the same size. Later on, the cells near the base become numerous and small, from which the *embryo* is developed. On the other hand, the cells of the developing sporophyte in the neck region of the archegonium enlarge, but there is no organized suspensor formed. The embryo is typically dicotyledonous. The mode of germination of the seed is hypogeal, and a seed, on germination, gives rise to a seedling sporophyte.

Living Fossil

The Cycads and the *Ginkgo biloba* or maiden-hair tree exist on the earth today as surviving types of ancient primitive seed plants. Hence they are often referred to as living fossils. They represent the last remnants of diversified and widely distributed lines of fossil gymnosperm plants since the Palaeozoic and Mesozoic times.

Living Cycads are the remnant of Cycadophytes and *Ginkgo* represent the remnant of Coniferophyte stock.

Cycads and *Ginkgo* resemble in their methods of pollination and pollen tube development, the morphology of male gametophytes, the possession of motile multiflagellated sperms, and the general structure of the ovule and seed.

Such similarity do prove a phylogenetic relationship between these two groups but indicate retention of very ancient patterns of reproduction by both Cycads and *Ginkgo*.

Cycads and *Ginkgo* have persisted in little change until the present through a long succession of ages. They illustrate continuity and exceptional power of endurance in a changing world.

Fossil Ginkgoales

There are about 7 closely related fossil genera of Ginkgoales. They are distinguished on the basis of leaf structure.

1. *Baiera*. It is abundant in the Lower Permian of Europe and North America. The genus became extinct in the Cretaceous. Usually leaves are found, very rarely in an attached condition. They differ from the living *Ginkgo* in being more deeply incised and in having narrow lobes and sessile petioles. The venation is distinctly dichotomous as in ferns. Several seeds were borne on the branched axis of the female shoot. The sporangia were in strobili on the male shoot consisting of sporophylls, each with several microsporangia.

2. *Ginkgoites* (Fossil *Ginkgo*). It is a leaf genus. The leaves are more or less lobed and petiolate. *G. crassipes* occurs in Rajmahal series of Upper Gondwana, and *Ginkgoites lobata* in Jabalpur stage.

Ginkgoites are identical with *Ginkgo*, while *Baiera* differs from *Ginkgoites* in its deeply cut leaves and the absence of a distinct petiole. *Baiera* is also recorded from India.

Affinity

The Ginkgoales have some resemblances with Pteridosperms, Cycadales and Coniferales.

(*a*) *Affinity with Pteridosperms*

1. Fern-like leaves.
2. Motile sperms.
3. Erect ovule.
4. Double leaf trace.
5. Structure of seed.

(*b*) *Affinities with Cycadales*

1. Presence of thick cortex, a comparatively thin vascular cylinder and a large pith with muncilage canals—these are all striking characters of Cycadean stems.

2. Motile sperms.

(*c*) *Affinities with Coniferales*

1. The coniferous habit of trees.
2. Character of wood.
3. Similar gametophyte structure.
4. Sporophylls collected into strobili.

CHAPTER VI

CONIFERALES

Fossil remains of the Coniferales in very large quantity supply undoubted evidence of the great antiquity of the order, which are known to have existed from later Paleozoic period. It reached its climax in Jurassic and then began to decline. Coniferales is still a dominant vegetation of the temperate regions of the world. In India, they are mostly confined in the Himalayas and the adjoining areas, except *Podocarpus*, which is found to occur in South India.

Coniferales can be distinguished in the structure of the reproductive organs and the manner in which the seeds are borne. The female flowers forming cones is characteristic of the order. Taxaceae and Podocarpaceae are exceptions. They are Conifers without cones.

Classification of Coniferales

Chamberlain (1935) divided the order into the following *six* families, *viz.*, (1) **Abietaceae**, (2) **Taxodiaceae**, (3) **Cupressaceae**, (4) **Araucariaceae**, (5) **Podocarpaceae** and (6) **Taxaceae** *

The principal characters of the families and their distribution are as follows :

1. **Abietaceae**. Leaves and sporophylls are developed spirally in definite cones ; the bract and ovuliferous scale are distinct, ovules two on the surface of the scale. Pollen sacs two ; pollen grains winged. Leaves are of needle type.

There are 9 genera and about 130 species. Indian genera are *Abies, Cedrus, Larix, Picea, Pinus* and *Tsuga*. *Pinus, Larix, Abies, Picea* have also the widest distribution in the Northern Hemisphere.

2. **Taxodiaceae**. Leaves are also spiral but the bract and ovuliferous scale are almost completely united ; pollen grains wingless. Ovules two to eight.

There are 8 genera and 15 species, mostly distributed in China, Japan, Formosa and the U.S.A. ***Taxodium*** and ***Cryptomeria*** are

* On account of some peculiar features of *Taxus*, Prof. Sahni suggests that the genus, along with *Cephalotaxus* and *Torreya*, should form a new order Taxales, which should be equal in rank with the Coniferales.

exotic in India. *Sequoia*, occurring in Pacific coast of the U.S.A. (California), reaches a height of 300 feet and a diameter of 40 feet.

3. **Cupressaceae**. The arrangement of leaves and sporophylls is cyclic and strobili ripen fleshy. Ovules erect.

There are 12 genera and about 120 species. Indian genera are *Cupressus, Juniperus, Libocedrus. Callitris* and *Thujá* are exotic genera. *Cupressus* and *Juniperus* have also the widest distribution in the Northern Hemisphere.

4. **Araucariaceae**. Sporophylls are spirally arranged in perfect cones ; the bract and ovuliferous scale are united. The ovules are solitary and the microsporangia hang from a peltate sporophyll. Stamens with 4-19 pollen sacs. Ovules solitary on the cone scale. Trees with broad leathery spiral leaves.

There are 2 genera and 30 species. *Araucaria* is exotic in India.

5. **Podocarpaceae**. Stamens with two pollen sacs and winged pollen. Ovules solitary. Shrubs or trees with scale-like, needle-like, linear or lanceolate leaves.

There are 7 genera and 100 species. These belong mostly to the Southern Hemisphere. Indian genus *Podocarpus*, which is found in a wild state in South India, is *P. wallichianus* Presl (=*P. latifolia* Wall).

6. **Taxaceae**. Stamens with 3-8 pollen sacs. Pollen wingless. Ovules erect, terminal seeds with a fleshy aril or drupe-like. Leaves linear.

There are 4 genera and 18 species. Indian genera are *Taxus* and *Cephalotaxus* *. *Taxus baccata*, the Yew, is found in the Himalayas. Flowers are dioecious. A scarlet fleshy aril renders the seeds attractive to birds and thus favours distribution.

Prof. Sahni proposed grouping the Cordaitales, Ginkgoales, Taxales and the Coniferales into a major division of the Gymnospermae. He designated this division **Stachyospermae** as the seeds are borne upon an axis. As a contrast the Cycadofilicales, Bennettitales and Cycadales are **Phyllosperms** as the seeds are borne on leaves.

Taxads stand clearly apart from the true Conifers. Of these, the position of the ovule is the most important. In Taxads it is always a direct continuation of the flower-axis, while in Conifers it is essentially terminal on more or less stalk-like lateral appendage of the flower-axis. Unlike the Conifers, the Taxads always bear erect ovules, each of which is enclosed by an aril arising as an outgrowth

* *Cephalotaxus* are now separated from *Taxus* and raised to a separate family Cephalotaxaceae.

from the flower-axis. All Taxads are distinguished from the majority of the Conifers by the absence of bladders (wings) on their pollen grains. On these grounds, Taxads are excluded from the Coniferales and is raised to the rank of a separate order Taxales.

The Coniferales probably first appeared in the later Palaeozoic, reached their climax in the Mesozoic and then began to decline. But still it is the largest order of the gymnosperms. They are the inhabitants of the temperate regions of the world.

Distribution of wild Conifers in India (including Pakistan, Ceylon and Burma)

The wild Conifers of India are chiefly distributed in the Himalayas and connecting ranges of Himachal Pradesh, Kashmir, Assam and Burma. In the Himalayas, particularly the Conifers are the flourishing group, covering extensive areas in a more or less pure forest formation. In contrast to this, peninsular India has only a single species (*Podocarpus latifolia*) to offer, while in Ceylon there is no Conifer.

Hooker enumerates 13 genera and 26 species, of which 23 are wild. The following account gives a brief survey of the various members of the Conifers.

1. *Cupressus torulosus*. It is the only Cupress in India and is confined to outer ranges of North-Western Himalayas and extending up to Central Nepal. Its occurrence is distinctly noticed between 6,000 to 13,000 ft. It also occurs in the Western Himalayas and ascends from 5,000 to 15,000 ft. being abundant between 10,000 to 15,000 ft.

2. *Juniperus* (4 species)

   (*a*) *J. communis*—spreads mostly over to the North-Western Himalayan ranges from Afganistan to Kumaon, between 5,000-14,000 ft.

   (*b*) *J. pseudosabina*, *J. reccuva* and *J. macropoda*—purely natives of the Western Himalayas, occurring in higher altitudes, 7,500-15,000 ft.

3. *Cephalotaxus* (2 species)

   (*a*) *C. griffithi* predominates over the Mishmi Hills and Upper Assam between Burma, etc. It ascends from 3,000-8,000 ft.

   (*b*) *C. manii* is only confined to Khasia Hills and Assam between 3,000-6,000 ft.

4. *Taxus baccata.* It occurs in Bhutan, Assam and Upper Burma. In Himalayas it extends both over the Eastern and Western from 5,000 to 12,000 ft.

5. *Podocarpus* (4 species)

(*a*) *P. latifolia* may be considered to be originally growing in lower hill forests of South India, Assam and Burma.

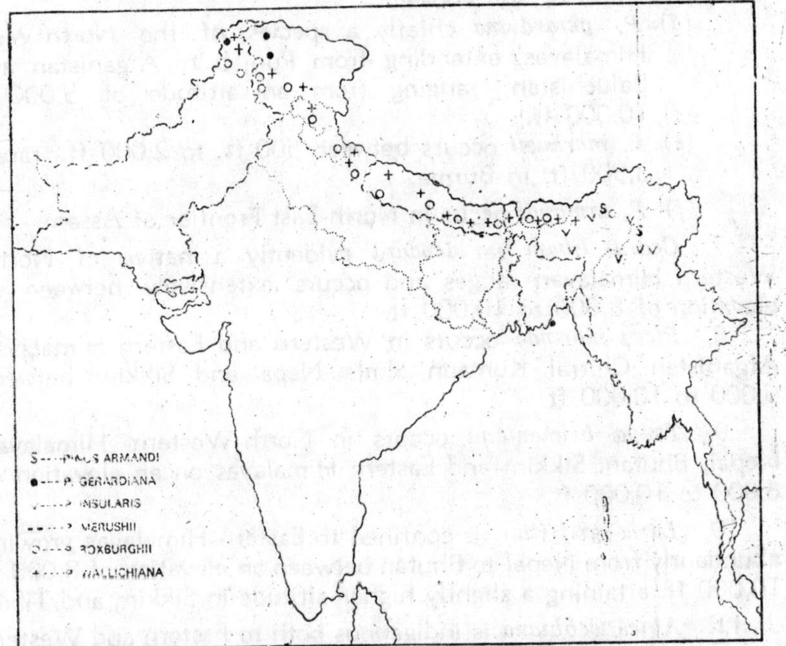

Fig. 459. Map of India showing the distribution of *PINUS* (after Raizada and Sahni 1960).

(*b*) *P. nerifolia* grows in Annamalies, has a wide range of distribution ascending up to 5,000 ft. It also grows abundantly in the lower hill forests of Central Himalayas, Eastern Himalayas, Bangla Desh, Assam, Andaman Islands, South Burma, etc.

(*c*) *P. Cupressina* spreads over the hills of Burma.

6. *Pinus* (6 species)

(*a*) *P. wallichiana*—evidently a North-West Himalayan species, ranging from an elevation of 5,000 to 10,000 ft.

(*b*) *P. roxburghii* is mainly confined to the lower hill ranges, descending to the valleys of Western and Eastern Himalayas, where it extends up to Bhutan. It is abundant in the wild state of growth between 1,000 to 3,000 ft. and ascends up to 6,000 ft. It has adapted itself to grow in the plains.

(*c*) *P. insularis*—native of Eastern Himalayas, spreading over Khasia, Jaintia and Naga Hills. It ascends from an elevation of 2,000 to 5,000 ft. It is also found in 7,000 ft. and above.

(*d*) *P. gerardiana* chiefly a species of the North-West Himalayas, extending from Punjab to Afganistan and Baluchistan, ranging from an altitude of 5,000 to 10,000 ft.

(*e*) *P. merkusii* occurs between 500 ft. to 2,000 ft., rarely 3,500 ft. in Burma.

(*f*) *P. armandi* occur in North-East Frontier of Assam.

7. *Cedrus libani* var *deodara* evidently a native of North-Western Himalayan ranges and occurs extensively between an elevation of 8,000 to 10,000 ft.

8. *Picea morinda* occurs in Western and Eastern Himalayas, Afganistan, Chitral, Kumaun, Simla, Nepal and Sikkim between 6,000 to 10,000 ft.

9. *Tsuga brunoniana* occurs in North-Western Himalayas, Nepal, Bhutan, Sikkim and Eastern Himalayas on an elevation of 6,000 to 10,000 ft.

10. *Larix griffithii* is confined to Eastern Himalayas growing abundantly from Nepal to Bhutan between an elevation of 8,000 to 10,000 ft. attaining a slightly higher altitude in Sikkim and Tibet.

11. *Abies webbiana* is indigenous both to Eastern and Western Himalayas, ranging from 7,000 to 12,000 ft. and sometimes up to 14,000 ft. altitude.

Characteristic features

(*a*) *Vegetative organs*

1. Large trees or shrubs.
2. Leaves needle or scale-like, sometimes flattened.
3. Epidermis is irregular in outline.
4. Large number of resin ducts.
5. Xylem is made of tracheids with bordered pits on their radial walls.
6. Phloem consists of sieve-tubes and phloem parenchyma.

(*b*) *Spore-producing organs*

7. Flowers are unisexual.

8. Male flowers are arranged in more or less in compact clusters or catkins.

9. Female flowers are usually clustered to form a strobilus or cone.

10. Winged pollens.

11. Male cells never motile.

PINUS

(Fam. ABIETACEAE)

Pinus, the familiar pine tree, is represented by nearly 90 species, which are widely distributed throughout the Northern Hemisphere, specially in extra-tropical regions (Fig. 454). In India, the different species of *Pinus* are mainly restricted to the Western Himalayas, while only *P. insularis* is found to be growing in the Khasia and Jaintia Hills of Assam. On the basis of the number and forms of leaves, *Pinus* is divisible into the following species : *P. wallichii* (=*P. excelsa* Wall), *P. roxburghii* Saig (=*P. longifolia* Roxb), *P. insularis* Endl (=*P. khasya* Royle) and *P. gerardiana* Wall (=*P. merkusi* Jungh).

The sporophyte

The plants are tall trees, which are characterized by the excurrent type of branching, and fascicles of slender, needle-like, evergreen foliage leaves. The main stem is stout, cylindrical, bearing a series of wide-spreading branches, and covered by a scaly bark. At its apex there is a relatively large terminal bud. It bears two kinds of shoots : (*a*) one of unlimited growth or **long shoot,** and (*b*) the other of limited growth or **dwarf shoot**. The long shoots usually bear scale leaves, in the axils of

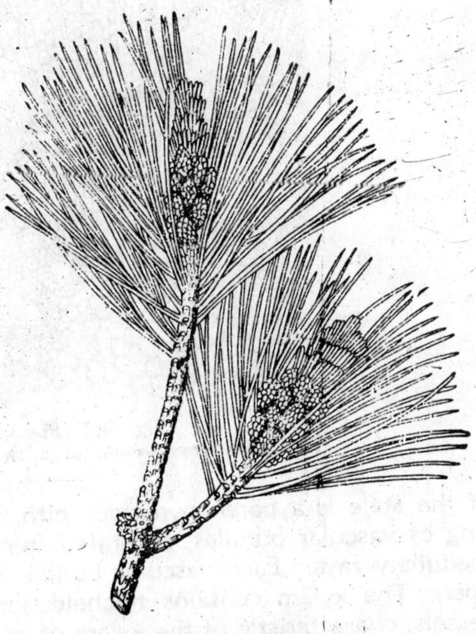

Fig. 460. *Pinus*. Branches bearing staminate strobili.

which numerous dwarf shoots appear. There is a fascicle of two or more needle-like leaves, closely held together at the base by a circle of scales, at the apex of each dwarf shoot. The primary root-system is persistent and perennial, and consists of a large and deeply penetrating tap root, which branches extensively. In some species the tap root may die early.

The primary structure of a young stem in a cross-section shows three distinct regions : epidermis, cortex and stele. At the centre

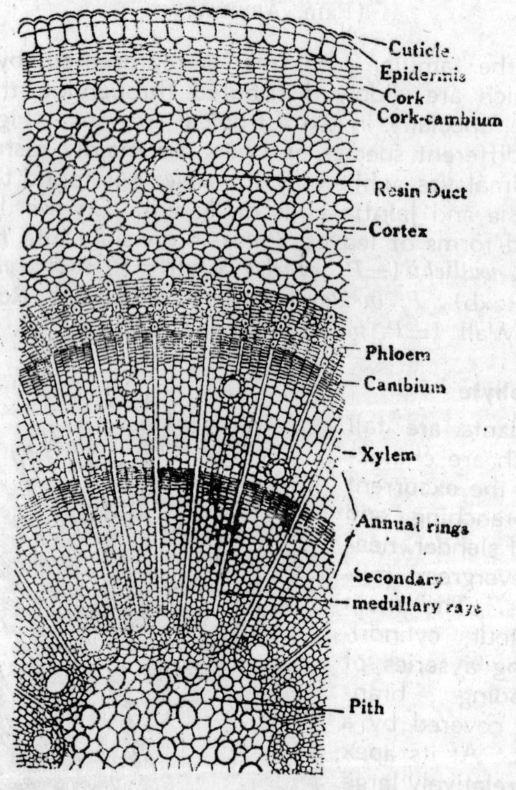

Fig. 461. *Pinus*.
Part of a cross-section of a two-year-old stem.

of the stele is a parenchymatous pith, which is surrounded by a ring of vascular bundles, separated from one another by primary medullary rays. Each vascular bundle is conjoint, collateral, and open. The xylem contains tracheids, and not tracheae or true vessels, characteristic of the xylem of an angiosperm. The phloem consists of sieve-tubes, and phloem parenchyma. In between xylem and phloem there is a strip of cambium. The cortex is made up of parenchyma, frequently with chloroplasts, and is traversed by longitudinal resin canals (ducts). On the outside there is an epidermis with heavily cutinized outer wall. During secondary growth, secondary xylem and phloem are produced by the cambial activity, as in the dicotyledons, and conspicuous annual rings are gradually developed. Secondary medullary rays are formed in the usual way. Resin canals also appear in the secon-

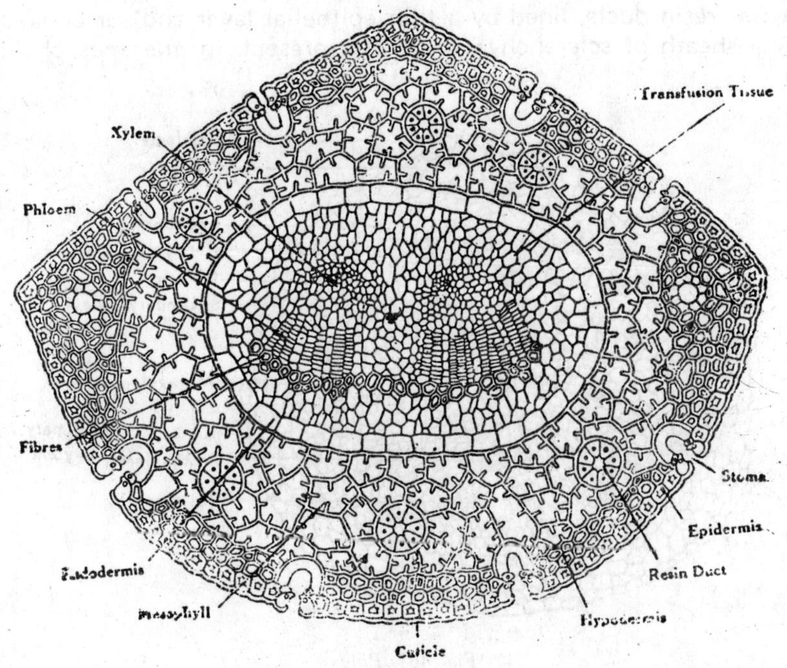

Fig. 462. *Pinus*.
Cross-section of a needle.

dary xylem. At the time of cambial activity within the stele, a complete ring of cork cambium appears in the hypodermal region of the cortex, which eventually gives rise to the periderm. Later on, successive layers of cork cambium appear deeper and deeper in the cortex, and finally in the outer part of the phloem. In this way a thick protective bark develops on the outside of the stem of *Pinus*.

A cross-section from the middle of a leaf of the current year shows from outside inwards a single-layered epidermis composed of thick-walled cells with a heavy cuticle, the lumen of each cell being often nearly obliterated. The hypodermis is sclerenchymatous, with fine pits on the lignified walls ; it is several cells deep, specially at the ridges. A few stomata are noted ; each stoma interrupting the epidermis and the hypodermis, and opening into a respiratory cavity in the mesophyll, which consists of several layers of large, polygonal, thin-walled, parenchyma cells containing cytoplasm, nucleus and abundant chloroplasts ; their cellulose walls are infolded to form peculiar projections into the cell cavities. A few resin ducts, lined by a thin epithelial layer and surrounded by a sheath of sclerenchyma, are also present in the mesophyll.

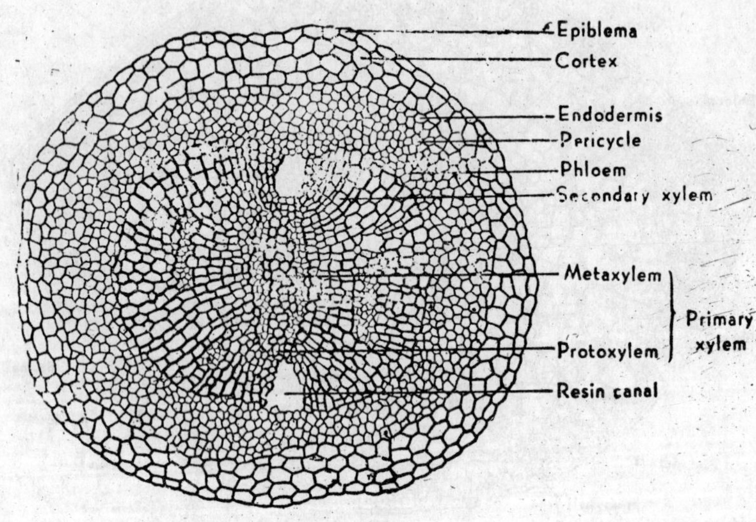

Fig. 463. *Pinus*. T.S. of a root.

There are two vascular bundles, each one having its xylem towards the upper side of the leaf, and its phloem facing the lower side, which is usually more or less convex ; the bundles are embedded in a many-layered ground tissue, the pericycle, which is surrounded by an endodermis, consisting of a single layer of parenchyma clearly separating the central region from the mesophyll. The pericycle consists of two kinds of parenchyma cells, termed collectively the **transfusion tissue,** and an irregular band of sclerenchyma lying across and below the phloem of each bundle, and connecting them. The transfusion tissue consists of (*a*) **albuminous cells,** that is, cells with cellulose walls, containing protein and starch, and serving for the translocation of prepared foods from the mesophyll to the phloem, and (*b*) **tracheidal cells,** which are empty dead cells with lignified walls possessing bordered pits, functioning as channels for water and dissolved salts from xylem to mesophyll.

The primary structure of a root in a cross-section shows, as usual, three distinct regions, *viz.*, epidermis, cortex and stele. There are two, three or four groups of primary xylem, alternating with the corresponding number of phloem groups. A small parenchymatous pith may or may not be present. The outer region of the stele constitutes the pericycle composed of several layers of cells. A resin canal is usually formed just within the forking of each protoxylem. Outside the stele is the parenchymatous cortex, limited internally by the endodermis with characteristically thickened walls. Next comes the epiblema as that in a dicotyledonous root. The secondary growth in thickness takes place in the same manner, as in a dicotyledonous root, by the activity of a layer of secondary cambium, which first appears as strips of cambium from the thin-walled cells between primary xylem and primary phloem. The cork cambium also originates from the outermost cells of the pericycle, and gives rise to cork outside, so that the cortex and the epiblema die to form a bark.

Pinus is monoecious, and bears both microsporophylls in *staminate strobili*, and megasporophylls in *carpellate strobili*. But bisporangiate strobili may occur in exceptional cases, as in *P. maritima* and *P. laricio*.

Morphology of the ovuliferous scale of Conifers

Different views have been put forward, from time to time, to explain the morphology of the ovuliferous scale of Conifers, a brief account of which is stated below :

1. In 1827, Robert Brown interpreted ovules as pistils and *ovuliferous scale* as *open cerpel.* But his statement that a carpel (leaf) produced at the axil of a bract (leaf) met strong opposition.

2. In 1839, Schleiden stated that *ovuliferous scale is a placenta,* which is a flattened axis. This branch nature was later on supported by Baillon, Dickson, Strasburger and others, but without regarding as placenta.

3. In 1842, Braun from the study of the cone of *Larix* represents *ovuliferous scale as the first two leaves* of the axillary shoot, which were fused by their adaxial margins. This view was accepted by Oersted, Von Mohl and others.

4. In 1860, Dickson observed in some cones of *Picea excelsa* that lower bracts and the *ovuliferous scales are the axes of the next higher order*. Similar cones have been reported by Shaw from *Sequoia*, and by Goebel from *Pinus*. These illustrations support the sporophyll character of a bract, which is a carpel.

5. In 1864, Parlatore recorded in a cone of *Pinus pinaster* that at the axil of every alternate bract, dwarf shoot bearing two needle leaves sprang and, therefore, *he supports Braun's view*.

6. In 1864, Oersted in some cones that lower bracts were foliar in nature bearing a number of scales as on a suppressed axis, the two outermost being the largest and opposite ; higher up, the bracts becoming smaller and smaller and the axillary scales becoming less numerous, but the two outermost scales gradually increased in size and became connate by their adaxial margins bearing rudimentary ovules at the base and in the uppermost part, the bracts were reduced to its normal forms, the scales enlarged and fused into a single structure. He, therefore, *supports the axis nature of the ovuliferous scales* by Braun.

7. In 1868, Sachs and Eichler supported that the *ovuliferous scale is a ligular outgrowth of the bract*, which is a carpel as in the leaves of *Selaginella*, *Isoetes*, etc.

8. In 1869, Van Tieghem from his study of vascular anatomy of the bract and ovuliferous scale stated that the vascular supply of these organs start separately from the axes and are, therefore, independent in origin. The bundles from the base of the scale undergoes inversion and then divides into an arc of bundles. *This supports the axis nature of the scale* and the inverse circulation shows that a leaf belongs upon the suppressed branch opposite the branch.

9. In 1876, Braun's view was further supported by Stenzel from his study of abnormalities in cones of *Picea excelsa*.

10. In 1879, Celakovsky *confirmed the axis nature of the scale* which contains the blended characters of the integuments of the ovule. There is, therefore, no carpel present.

11. Kaubart suggested that the *ovuliferous scale is an arch* from his study of Junipers.

12. In 1892, Bessey suggested that the *ovuliferous scale is a continuation of the chalaza* and that the staminate and ovulate strobili are homologous.

Of all the views, Braun's view regarding the axis nature of the ovuliferous scale appears to be correct as it reasonably relates megasporangia to the abaxial surface of the sporophylls, the relation held by the microsporangia.

Staminate (or **male**) **strobilus**. The staminate strobilus is found in clusters towards the apex of some branches. It is simple in nature, and consists of a short axis, on which there are *microsporophylls* (or *stamens*), arranged spirally. Each microsporophyll consists of a *stalk* subtending an expanded *scale-like portion*. On the under side of this scale, and to the side of the stalk, there are two *microsporangia* (or *pollen sacs*). The wall of the microsporangium consists of several layers of cells, whose inner layer, at least, forms the *tapetum*, surrounding the spore mother cells as in the pteridophytes. As a result of reduction division, four *microspores* (or *pollen grains*) are produced from each microspore mother cell. Usually, the microspores are shed within a few weeks after the appearance of the strobili, which, having performed their function, ultimately wither, and fall off from the tree.

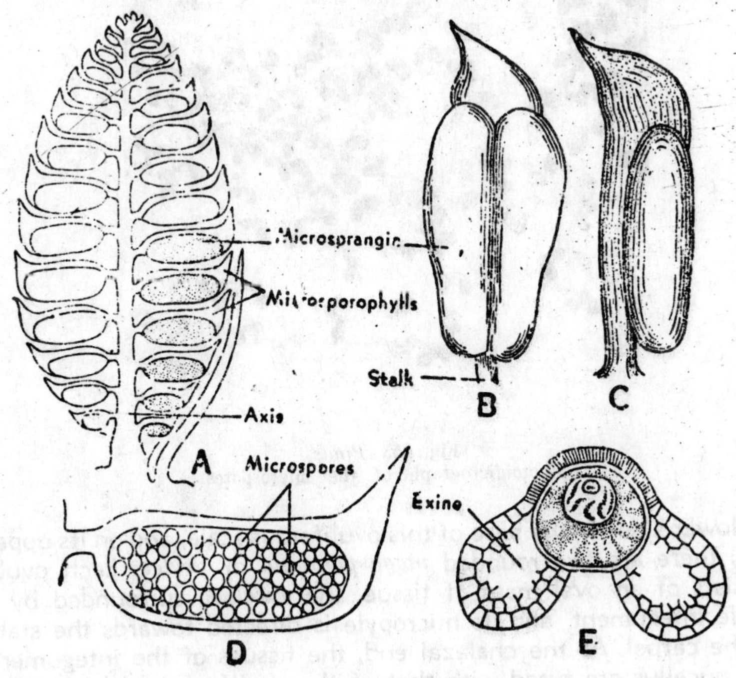

Fig. 464. *Pinus*.
A, A staminate strobilus in l.s. ; B—C, Microsporophyll with microsporangia in front and side views respectively ; D, A single microsporophyll with microsporangium and microspores in l.s. ; E, mature microspore.

Each microspore consists of an oval cell with a conspicuously large nucleus, and has two balloon-like, air-filled **wings,** formed by the separation of the exine layer from the intine at two places, and subsequent inflation of the spaces, thus formed, between the two layers.

Carpellate (or **female**) **strobilus.** The carpellate strobili remain on the tree for a much longer period than do the staminate ones. When first formed near the tips of certain branches, they are deep red in colour, and about 1 cm. in length. Each strobilus is compound and consists of a central axis, on which *megasporophylls* (or *carpels*) are spirally arranged. A megasporophyll, when removed and viewed with a pocket lens, is found to consist of a very short *stalk* and a *scale* (**ovuliferous scale**) to which a *bract* is attached on

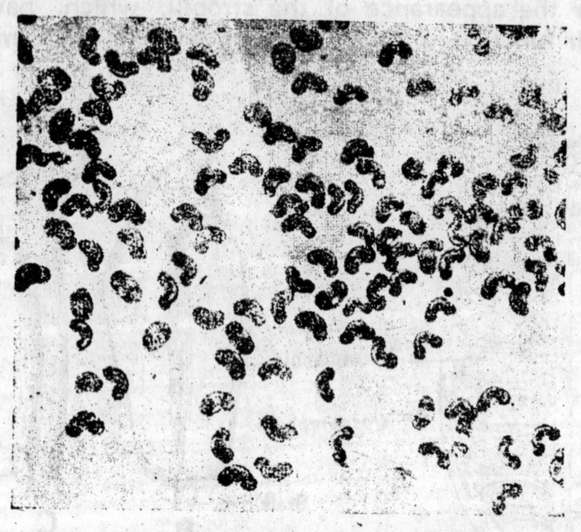

Fig. 465. *Pinus.*
Photomicrograph of the micro-pores.

the lower side. At the base of this ovuliferous scale, and on its upper side, there are two rounded *megasporangia* or *ovules.* Each ovule consists of an oval mass of tissue, the *nucellus*, surrounded by a single integument, and its micropyle is directed towards the stalk of the carpel. At the chalazal end, the tissues of the integument and nucellus are fused with that of the ovuliferous scale. Within this nucellar tissue there is a single central *megaspore mother cell,* whose nucleus, by two successive divisions (reduction division), forms a linear **tetrad of** *megaspores* (or **embryosacs**), of which, the one, furthest away from the micropyle functions, and enlarges considerably at the expense of the three others, which are finally absorbed.

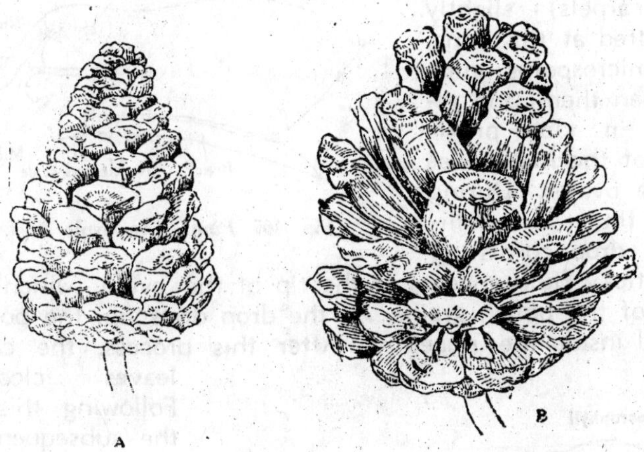

Fig. 466. *Pinus*.
A, A carpellate strobilus at the time of fertilization ; B, The same several months later with scales spread apart and seeds shed.

The gametophytes

Micro (or **male**) **gametophyte**. The microspores (pollen grains) begin to germinate, about a month before they are set free from the microsporangium. The nucleus first divides to form two daughter nuclei, one of which flattens out against the spore-wall, and is cut off from the other daughter nucleus, and most of the cytoplasm by the formation of a thick wall. The cell, thus cut off, is the **first vegetative cell** (**first prothallial cell**), whose nucleus rapidly degenerates. The nucleus of the larger sister cell divides again, and forms a **second vegetative cell** (**second prothallial cell**), whose nucleus also behaves in the same manner, while the large persistent cell, with its prominent nucleus and cytoplasm, is called the **antheridial cell**. A little before the microspores are liberated, the antheridial cell divides to form a smaller cell, the **generative cell**, cut off against the second vegetative cell, and a larger cell, the **tube cell**. It is at this stage the microsporangia burst longitudinally, and the microspores (pollen grains) are liberated. The amount of pollen grains liberated by the micro-sporangia is astonishingly large ; **these fill the surrounding atmosphere**, and are commonly known as **flowers of sulphur** which are disseminated by wind. During transport most of the pollen grains are wasted, but some of them reach the mature carpellate cones with their megasporophylls (or carpels) slightly separated at this time. The microspores glide between them, and remain in close proximity of the micropyles of the ovules. During this time a pollination drop consisting of a sticky fluid appears at the tip of the ovule, which catches some of the pollen grains. As the drop dries up, the pollens are sucked inside the nucellus. After this process, the carpellary leaves close up. Following this, during the subsequent eleven months, male gametophytes do not develop further considerably, but a short **pollen tube** may be formed from each pollen grain. The tube may branch somewhat, penetrates the nucellus, and grows very slowly, till winter sets in.

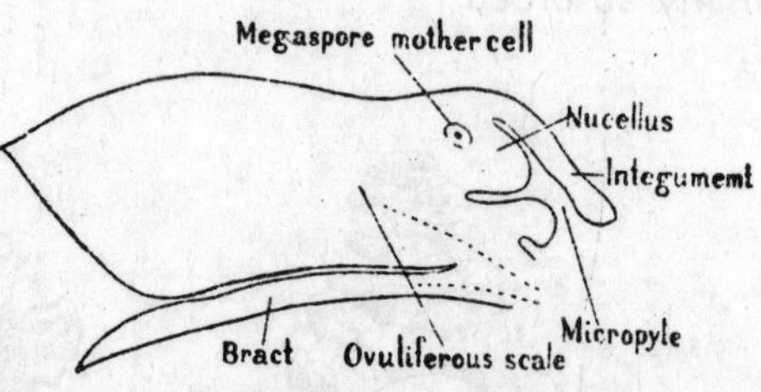

Fig. 467. *Pinus*. An ovule in l.s.

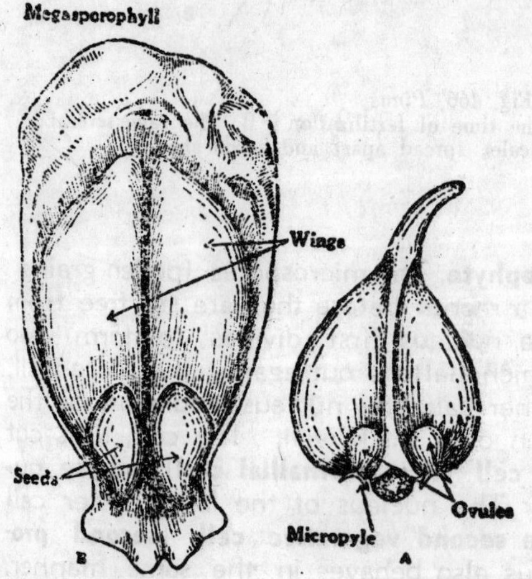

Fig. 468. *Pinus*.
A, A megasporophyll at the time of pollination ;
B, The same with mature seeds.

During the second spring, the pollen tube grows slowly downwards, penetrates the nucellus, and finally its tip reaches the surface of the female gametophyte. During the development, the tube nucleus first enters the pollen tube. The generative cell also divides into a **stalk nucleus** and a **body nucleus**, which also enter into the tube, where the body nucleus again divides to form two **male** or **sperm nuclei**. About the stalk nucleus cytoplasm is organized to form a definite *stalk cell*, around which there is a definite membrane. The male gametes have clearly differentiated cytoplasm, and a large nucleus.

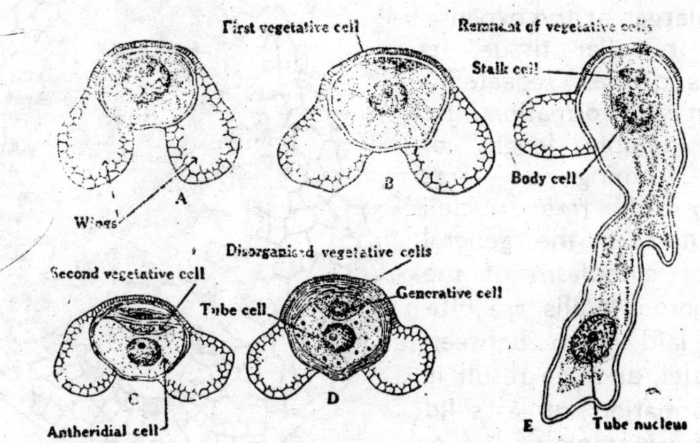

Fig. 469. *Pinus.*
A—E, Successive stages in the development of the male gametophyte.

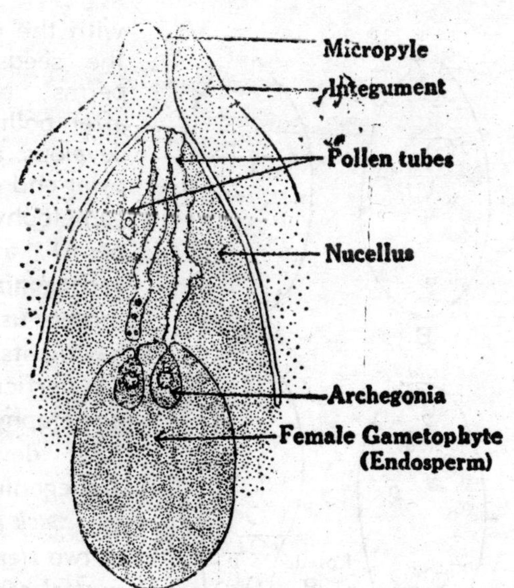

Fig. 470. *Pinus.*
Part of a longitudinal section through a megasporangium (ovule) ; three pollen tubes growing down into the nucellus and effecting fertilization.

Mega (or **female**) **gametophyte.** During the year, following pollination, development of the female gametophyte takes place.

The megaspore germinates within the megasporangium, and it is never set free. It first enlarges at the expense of the nucellar tissue, its nucleus divides repeatedly, without wall-formation, for a considerable length of time, forming a large number of free nuclei, **distributed in the general** mass of cytoplasm of the megaspore. Walls are ultimately laid down between the nuclei, and the result is the formation of a solid mass of gametophytic tissue, **known as the endosperm,** which is not homologous

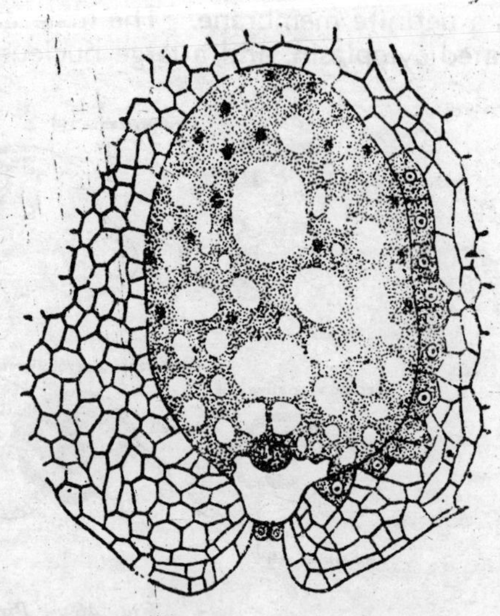

Fig. 471. *Pinus*.
Longitudinal section of an archegonium.

with the endosperm in the seeds of angiosperms. Nearly a year after pollination, there develops, at the micropylar end of the female gametophyte (endosperm), a number of **archegonia** (two or three usually), each having its origin from a superficial cell of the gametophyte. When fully developed, each archegonium consists of a *neck* of eight cells, in two tiers of four, the *ventral canal cell*, and a very big cavity containing an *egg*. Before fertilization the ventral canal cell disorganizes.

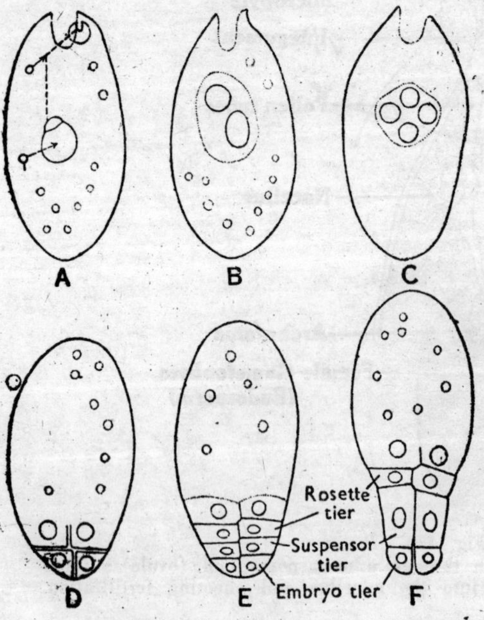

Fig. 472. *Pinus*.
A—F, Stages in the development of the **embryo.**

The neck canal cells are entirely wanting, and the large cavity, containing the egg, is surrounded by a jacket layer of cells, which supplies food to the egg cell, and ultimately to the developing embryo. The archegonia mature and are ready for fertilization about a year after pollination.

The tip of the pollen tube, on reaching an archegonium at the surface of the female gametophyte, destroys the neck cells and discharges its contents into the cytoplasm of the egg. The nucleus of one male cell moves towards the egg nucleus, and fertilizes it. The other male nucleus, the tube nucleus as well as the stalk nucleus soon disintegrate. The fertilized egg surrounds itself with a wall, and forms an **oospore.**

The new sporophyte

The fusion nucleus then passes to the base of the oospore, and, by repeated divisions, forms four nuclei, which become

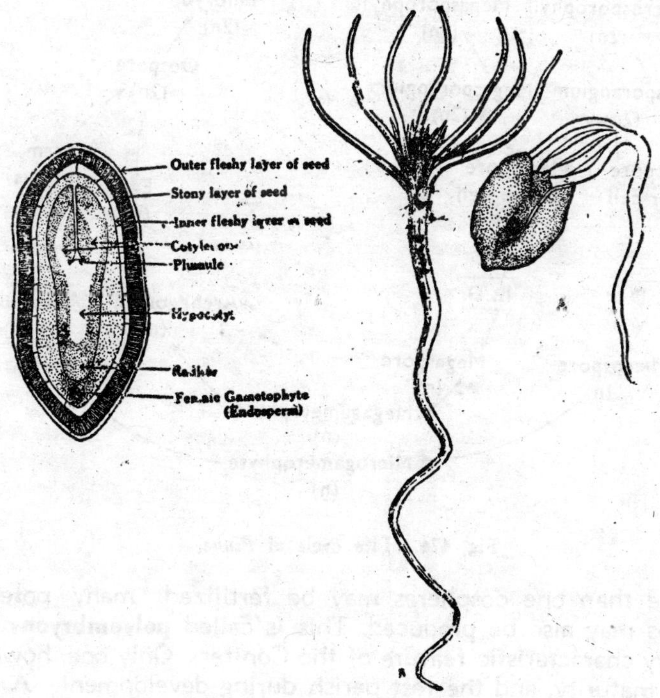

Fig, 473. *Pinus.*
A—B, Stages in the development of a seedling ; C, Longitudinal section of a mature seed.

arranged at right angles to the long axis of the oospore. Two further divisions occur, resulting in the production of *four tiers*, each tier containing four nuclei. Partition walls develop separating all the nuclei, excepting those of the uppermost tier. The three lower tiers are known respectively, from below upwards, as the **embryo tier**, **suspensor tier** and **rosette tier**, and the whole structure is termed as the **proembryo**. The embryos develop from the lowermost or embryo tier, the other tiers being only nutritive in function. The suspensors rapidly elongate and diverge, so that the embryos are pushed deep within the tissue of the female gametophyte, which now becomes laden with food matters diffusing into it from the placenta. Each suspensor bears at its apex one of the four *embryo cells*. Four potential embryos are produced by rapid division of each of the embryo cells. It is to be noted that,

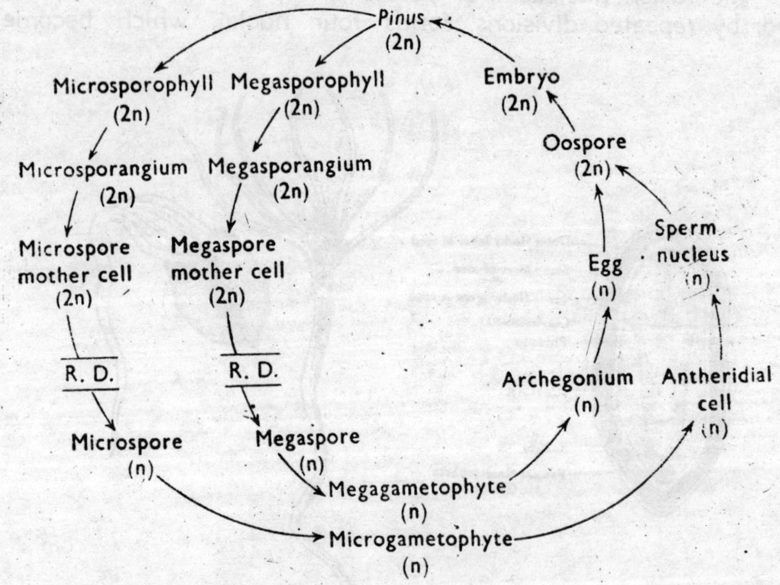

Fig. 474. Life cycle of *Pinus*.

as more than one oospheres may be fertilized, many potential embryos may also be produced. This is called **polyembryony**, and is a very characteristic feature of the Conifers. Only one, however, attains maturity, and the rest perish during development. A fully developed embryo consists of a radicle, the hypocotyl, three to many cotyledons, and a small plumule. As the endosperm expands, the nucellus is generally crushed out, but sometimes it persists as a thin layer forming the so-called **perisperm**. The integument is gradually converted into the seed coat, and the ovule develops into a seed.

Fossil Conifers

Several fossil Conifers have been recorded from India ; of these mention may be made of :

1. *Walkomiella indica*, a Palaeozoic Conifer, from the Lower Gondwana beds, has recently been described by Dr. Surange.

2. *Mesembrioxylon schmidianum* has been recorded from Miocene of South India.

TAXUS

(Fam. TAXACEAE)

There is only one species *Taxus baccata* (common Yew) under the genus, though, occasionally, some authors have recognized a number of species. The plant is extensively distributed over Great Britain, Germany, America, Mexico, Iran, Japan, Philippines, and India (in the Western Himalayas).

The sporophyte

The plant is a slow-growing tree with an usual height of 30-40 feet, and bearing horizontally growing branches of unlimited growth forming a thick canopy. Dwarf shoots are absent. The leaves are simple, dorsiventral, slightly stalked, and are twisted at their bases, giving rise to a two-ranked arrangement. They contain silica particles, particularly so at the sharp-pointed tips. Scale leaves are absent.

Internally, the stem shows a general arrangement of the *Pinus* type, with the exception that the resin canals are entirely absent, and the tracheids of the secondary wood possess spiral thickenings in addition to the usual uniseriate bordered pits. The medullary rays are also uniseriate, and wood parenchymas are absent.

The root is diarch, and is also devoid of resin canals, and possesses spiral thickenings in the tracheids.

The internal structure of leaf resembles that of a leaflet of *Cycas* in some respects. There are two cuticularized epidermal layers, the upper one being continuous, while the lower one is interrupted at intervals by sunken stomata. The mesophyll is differentiated into upper palisade and lower spongy parenchymas ; sometimes the latter may contain some resinaceous, yellow-coloured matter within some cells. There is a solitary vascular bundle in the centre surrounded by an endodermal layer, with xylem towards the upper surface and phloem towards the lower one. The pericycle is modified into **transfusion tissue**.

Taxus is dioecious, and the male flowers are borne in strobili, while the female ones do not form any cone.

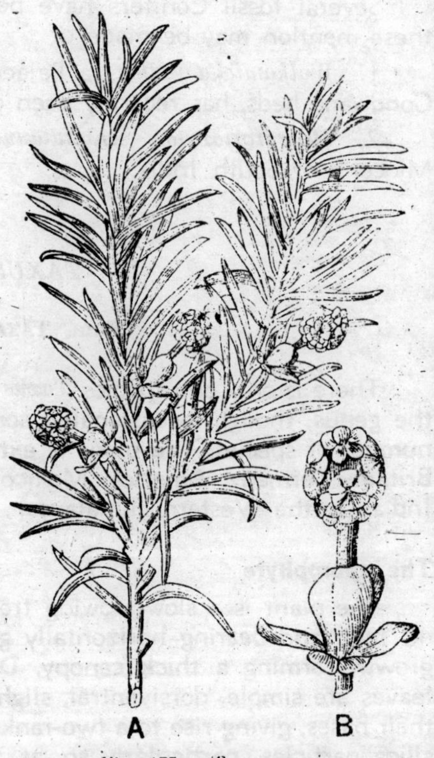

Fig. 475. *Taxus*.
A, A portion of the plant bearing male strobili ; B, A male strobilus.

Staminate (or **male**) **strobilus**. The staminate strobili are borne in the axils of leaves, produced on branches of the previous year. Each strobilus consists of a short central axis, bearing about a dozen of spirally arranged scales, in basipetal order of development, at their bases and a cluster of closely inserted, umbellate *microsporophylls* at the top. It is to be noted that the vegetative apex is also utilized in the production of sporophyll. Each microsporophyll is a peltate, shield-like body with 6-8 pendant *microsporangia*, hanging from the under-surface of the shield. These sporangia are united with one another, as well as with the sporophyll-stalk. The microsporangia contain numerous microspore mother cells, each of which on undergoing reduction division, gives rise to a tetrad of *microspores* or *pollen grains*. The pollen grains are liberated by the dehiscence of the sporangium, and are dispersed by the wind. They come in the neighbourhood of the ovule, and are caught by the pollination drop, exuded from the micropylar end of the ovule.

Megasporangium (or **Ovule**). The ovules occupy the same axillary position on the female plants, just as the male cones do in the male ones. There is also a short central axis, which is known as the **primary axis**, bearing a number of closely imbricated, overlapping, sterile scale leaves on its basal region. In the axil of the uppermost scale there arises the fertile shoot, the **secondary axis**, which bears three pairs of decussately arranged minute scale leaves, the lowermost pair of which stands at right angles to the subtend-

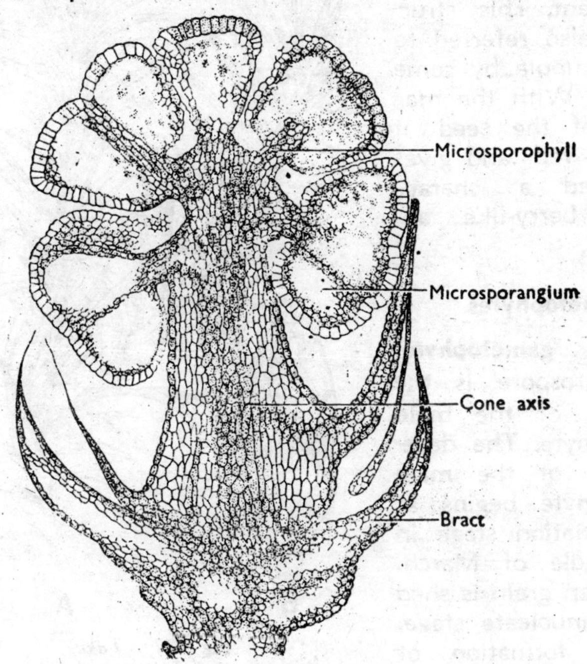

Fig. 476. *Taxus.*
L. S. of a male cone.

ing bracts. This secondary axis apparently terminates in a solitary ovule. The vegetative apex of the primary shoot may occasionally proliferate, producing another secondary axis, bearing an ovule in the next year.

The ovule is orthotropous. The nucellus is free from the integument. The latter is three-layered as usual and forms a prominent micropylar canal above the nucellus. In some cases, in the adult stage the nucellus and the integument may be fused. Just below the integument, there appears a slowly growing ring-like structure, which later on surrounds the entire ovule. This is usually known as **the aril**, but it cannot be compared to the structure bearing the same designation as is found in the angiosperms. On the contrary, it can be compared with the epimatium of the *Podocarpus*, while others consider it to be an outer integument. This structure is also referred to as the cupule by some authors. With the maturity of the seed it becomes red, and gives the seed a characteristic berry-like appearance.

Fig. 477. *Taxus*.
A, A portion of the plant showing female flowers ; B, A female inflorescence.

The gametophytes

Male gametophyte. The microspore is the first cell of the male gametophyte. The development of the male gametophyte begins at the pollination stage in the middle of March. The pollen grain is shed in a uninucleate stage, and the formation of any prothallial cell is completely eliminated. Pollination takes place by the agency of wind. The division of the pollen-nucleus results into an **antheridial cell**, and a **tube cell**. The former divides later on into a **stalk cell** and a **body cell**. The body cell, by undergoing another division, gives rise to two unequal cells, which finally develop into two dissimilar non-flagellate *male gametes*.

Female gametophyte. The megaspore is the first cell of the female gametophyte. The megaspore nucleus divides freely, and gives rise to 256 nuclei. The cell, in the meanwhile, enlarges rapidly, and these nuclei are placed peripherally around a central vacuole. Subsequent to this, wall-formation begins. The walls are laid down at right angles to the megaspore membrane, and they extend to the middle of the megaspore cavity, giving rise to long tube-like cells known as the **alveoli**. In almost all cases, the centripetal ends of the alveoli are provided with walls only at a later

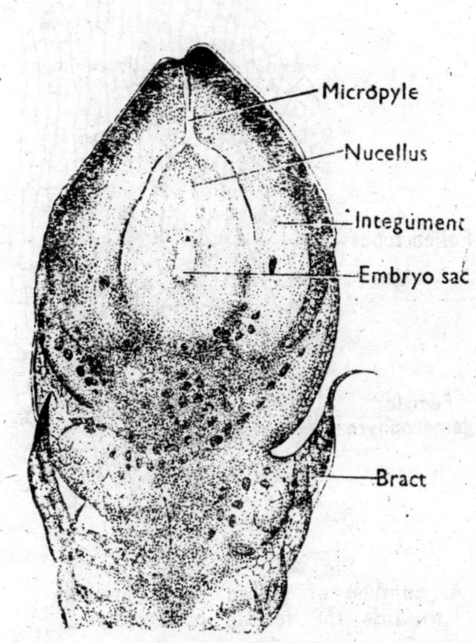

Fig. 478. *Taxus*.
L.S. through an ovule and an ovuliferous branch.

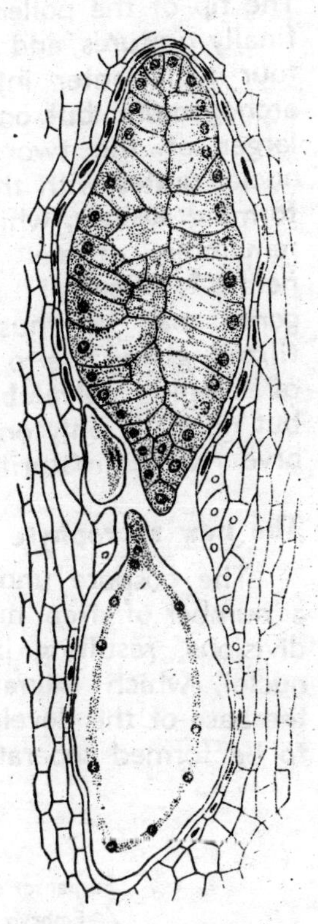

Fig. 479. *Taxus*.
Development of endosperm.

stage. Subsequently, further divisions of the alveoli take place, resulting in a large number of cells forming the **endosperm** (the female gametophyte). The cells of the endosperm are uninucleate at first, but later on the number of nuclei in each may multiply during the month of July. Ultimately, the nuclei in each cell degenerate, and undergo fusion forming a single, large, irregular body. The *archegonia*, 5-8 in number, develop from the superficial cells at the top of the endosperm. The structure of the archegonium is rather simple. There are four *neck cells*, and only one *egg cell* in the venter ; no ventral canal cell has yet been recorded.

The interval between pollination and fertilization is a short period of one month only. The pollen tube, developed from the tube cell, reaches the female gametophyte at a period, when the latter may be in a comparatively early stage of development, or in other words, the archegonium-initial may not have yet been recognized. The tip of the pollen tube finally ruptures, and all the four nuclei enter into the archegonium, but only the larger of the two male nuclei unites with the egg forming *oospore*, while the remaining three degenerate'*. Several archegonia may be thus fertilized, giving rise to a case of simple **polyembryony**, but normally only one embryo reaches maturity.

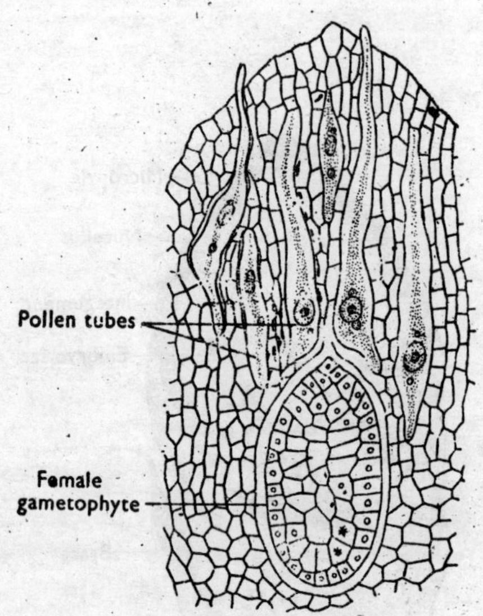

Fig. 480. *Taxus*.
A number of pollen tubes growing towards the female gametophyte.

The new sporophyte

The oospore undergoes a number of free nuclear divisions, resulting in 32 nuclei, which migrate to the base of the developing sporophyte. At this stage walls begin to be formed separating the nuclei into cells, constituting the

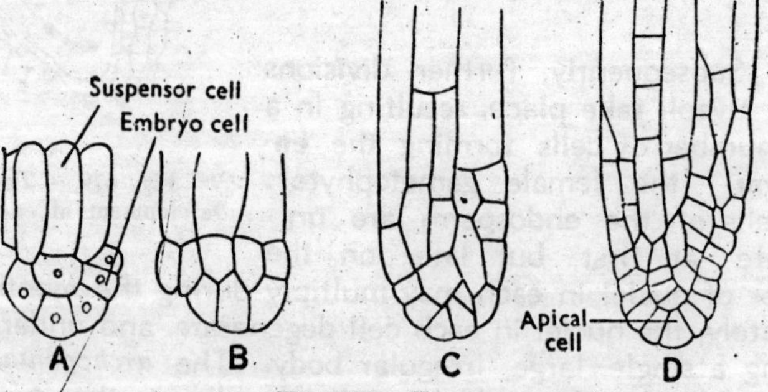

Fig. 481. *Taxus*.
A—D, Successive stages in the development of the embryo.

proembryo. The cells of the proembryo are arranged in three tiers. From the lowermost tier (which as a rule is composed of one cell

* According to Chamberlain. "In *T. baccata* only the larger sperm enters the egg, the smaller sperm, and both the stalk and tube nuclei remaining in the pollen tube."

only) the *embryo* is developed. The other tiers of cells give rise to the *suspensor*. The mature embryo is dicotyledonous, and in course of its attaining maturity, consumes the endosperm wholly. The aril of the mature seed, on account of its red colour, attracts the birds, and thus the seed is dispersed through their agency. The germination of the seed is hypogeal, and on germination, it gives rise to a seedling sporophyte.

Systematic position of Taxads

Taxads include recent *Taxus* (5-spp.), *Nototaxus*, *Amantotaxus* and *Torreya*.

In many respects Taxads are clearly apart from the true Conifers.

1. The most important is the position of ovules. In the Taxads it is always a direct continuation of the floral axis, while in the Conifers and Cordaites the ovule is borne on more or less a stalk-like sterile appendage (megasporophyll) of the floral axis.

2. In Conifers the female flower is biaxial, in nature, while in the Taxads it is strictly uniaxial (even in the fossil members).

3. Unlike the Conifers, the Taxad ovule is enclosed by an aril, which arises as an outgrowth from the floral axis.

4. The male flowers of Taxads are remarkable for the characteristic sporophylls which are perisporangiate in some, changing to dorsiventral, in others, by the presence of sterile scales in some (e.g., *Nototaxus*) in between the sporophylls.

5. Finally, Taxads are distinguished from the majority of the Conifers by the wingless pollen.

These unique characters of Taxads have made their systematic position a controversial one. The modern trend in Conifer taxonomy is to find whether Taxads should be included in the Conifers or excluded from them.

(*a*) Pilger (1926) called Taxaceae as Conifers without cones. He liked to keep them with Conifers but later doubted their inclusion.

(*b*) Sinnot (1913) grouped Taxaceae and Podocarpaceae together.

(*c*) Later authors increased this scope of grouping and put Cephalotaxaceae and Ginkgoaceae in the same group. Later on Ginkgos were removed from the Taxads basing on (*i*) nature of leaf, (*ii*) long stalk of flower and (*iii*) motile sperms.

(*d*) Wilde (1944) constituted a separate family Podocarpaceae which has been subsequently universally accepted. So, the relation of Cephalotaxaceae with Taxaceae remains to be judged.

(e) Pulle (1936) partially following Niger and Pilger puts both Taxaceae and Cephalotaxaceae together under Conifers in the order Taxales.

(f) Prof. Sahni (1920) considered *Taxus*, *Torreya* and *Cephalotaxus* as distinct from Podocarps and the Conifers. Under the circumstances they should constitute a separate phylum Taxales equivalent in rank with Coniferales, contrary to Pilger but in conformity with Pulle he considers Taxaceae and Cephalotaxaceae as closely related groups.

(g) Florin (1948) also has shown inclination to consider a separate phylum Taxales from Coniferales. He was supported by Arnold (1948) and others.

So, the modern trend is to exclude the Taxales from the Conifers and to include them in a separate Class (or order as the case may be) of the Gymnospermae, provisionally the Class might be called Taxales.

Affinity

The Coniferales have some relationship with Cordaitales, Ginkgoales and Gnetales.

(a) *Affinities with Cordaitales*

1. Reduction of foliage leaves.
2. Similarity of female strobili.
3. Structure of secondary wood.

(b) *Affinities with Ginkgoales*

1. Male flowers arranged in catkin-like structure.
2. Female flowers are collected into strobilus or cone.

CHAPTER VII

GNETALES

The 'Gnetales' comprise a small group of gymnosperms which have recently appeared on the surface of hte globe. This is the reason why no fossil of any member of order has been obtained below the Tertiary*. The Gnetales seem to form a connecting link between gymnosperms and angiosperms.

Characteristic features

(*a*) *Vegetative organs*

1. Small trees or shrubs or climbing shrubs, sparsely branched and usually dioecious.
2. Leaves simple, opposite and net-veined, or scale-like, or long strap-shaped.
3. Presence of true vessels in the secondary wood.

(*b*) *Spore-producing organs*

4. 'Flowers' with a distinct perianth.
5. Micro- and mega-sporangiate strobili compound.
6. Single integument of the ovule becomes elongated as a tube.
7. Embryo with two cotyledons.
8. Copious endosperm.

The 'Gnetales' comprise a small group of plants—*Gnetum*, *Welwitschia* and *Ephedra* and they seem to form a connecting link between gymnosperms and angiosperms. They are characterized by their extraordinary morphology and diverse habit.

Morphological evidence strongly supports a break-up of the old Order with the setting up of three families (Ephedraceae, Welwitschiaceae, Gnetaceae) and the establishment of three Orders Ephedrales, Welwitschiales and Gnetales. Ephedrales have phylogenetic relationships to the Welwitschiales and the Gnetales. Stomatal apparatus of *Ephedra* belongs to a primitive basic type different from that of *Welwitschia* and *Gnetum*. In the structure of the cone, in nodal anatomy, in primary stem structure and in wood structure *Ephedra* differs from the other two genera. Ovule position and morphology of the fertile shoot of the *Ephedra* suggest relationship of Ephedrales to Cordaites stock or to an ancestral stock common to Cordaites and Conifers.

* Pollen of *Ephedra* and *Welwitschia* have recently been obtained from the Permian of Lower Gondwana in India.

Among the angiospermic features are : (1) The compound nature of both the microsporangiate and megasporangiate strobili, which are similar to the inflorescences of angiosperms. (2) The presence of vessels in the xylem.

The relation of the three genera to any known angiosperm is highly improbable and their affinities with modern gymnosperms seem equally obscure. The leaves of the three genera differ widely in size, form and venation. In *Ephedra* the leaves are scale-like, basically fused to form a sheath. The leaves of *Welwitschia* are long and strap-shaped. *Gnetum* is particularly unusual among gymnosperms, because of pinnate reticulate venation (angiosperm-like). Regarding stomata *Ephedra* are haplocheilic as in most gymnosperms, whereas syndetocheilic stomata occur in both *Gnetum* and *Welwitschia*.

Evolution of vessels in angiosperms and the Gnetales illustrates parallel evolution and there is no evidence of phyletic relationship between the two groups of plants.

In all members of the Gnetales, the micro- and mega-sporangiate strobili are compound. In all gnetalean plants the single true integument of the ovule becomes elongated as a tube.

While *Ephedra* has an archegonium, the complex female gametophytes of both *Gnetum* and *Welwitschia* are devoid of archegonia.

The members of *Gnetales* are specialized endpoints in evolution which are not closely related to any present-day gymnosperms or angiosperms.

No fossil record the Gnetales have been obtained below the Tertiary, and consequently, the order may be regarded as a comparatively younger one. The members of this order occur both in the Eastern as well as in the Western Hemispheres, excepting *Welwitschia mirabilis*, which is practically endemic to the Namib desert area of South-West Africa.

Plants woody, sparsely branched and usually dioecious ; leaves simple, opposite and net-veined like those of the dicotyledons ; 'flowers' with a distinct perianth and generally forming cones ; embryo with two cotyledons ; endosperm copious ; true vessels present in the secondary wood ; resin canals absent.

The order includes only *one* family **Gnetaceae**. Person records about 66 species under Gnetales—35 species for *Ephedra*, 30 for *Gnetum*, and only 1 for *Welwitschia*.

Classification

The Gnetales have been divided into *three* families :

(1) ***Ephedraceae*** (with one genus ***Ephedra***). (2) ***Wel-***

witschiaceae (with one genus *Welwitschia*), and (3) *Gnetaceae* (with one genus *Gnetum*). But according to modern classification the Gnetales have been split up into three orders : *Ephedrales*, *Welwitschiales* and *Gnetales*.

In this book the three genera are included in the single order Gnetales purely for convenience in discussion.

Distribution

The two genera, *Ephedra* and *Gnetum*, occur both in the Eastern as well as in the Western Himalayas, but *Welwitschia* (*W. mirabilis*) is confined only to the Namib desert area of South-West Africa.

Relation of the three genera

The relation of the three genera to any known angiosperm is highly improbable and their affinities with modern gymnosperms seem equally obscure. The leaves of the three genera differ widely in size, form and venation. In *Ephedra* the leaves are scale-like, basically fused to form a sheath. The leaves of *Welwitschia* are long and strap-shaped. *Gnetum* is particularly unusual among gymnosperms because of the pinnate reticulate venation (angiosperm-like). Regarding stomata *Ephedra* are haplocheilic whereas, syndetocheilic stomata occur in both *Gnetum* and *Welwitschia*. *Ephedra* differs from the other two genera while *Ephedra* has got an archegonium, the complex female gametophyte of both *Gnetum* and *Welwitschia* are devoid of archegonia. Ephedraceae has phylogenic relationship with Welwitschiaceae and Gnetaceae, in the structure of the cone, nodal anatomy, in primary stem structure and in wood structure.

Relationship of Gnetales with other Gymnosperms

1. The relationship of Gnetales with other gymnosperms and angiosperms are not clear. Of the origin of the group also nothing is known particularly.

2. There are good reasons to believe that the three existing genera are the remnants of an ancient race.

3. The somewhat diverse views as to the natural position of the Gnetales, most of the authors agree in placing the group at the top of the gymnosperms and at the bottom of the angiosperms. Some of the recent investigators point out the angiospermic characters of *Gnetum* and have gone so far as to include the whole group among the angiosperms ; but it is difficult to accept this view as the endosperm of Gnetales is somewhat different from any other living angiosperms.

4. Thompson points out the arrangement of the parts of so-

called flower in *Gnetum*, presence of an ovary with a style, and the germination of a microspore at some distance from the nucellus, and concludes that the ancestors of the angiosperms are not far remote from the genus.

5. As regards to the affinities of Gnetales with other gymnosperm groups the anatomy is, on the whole, in favour of some connection with the Conifers, the gametophytes of *Ephedra* also in general show various points of resemblance to the more primitive Conifers. Of course, a few small anatomical features are Cycadean.

6. There are some resemblances in between the flowers of *Ephedra* and *Taxus*. Thompson emphasises that *Ephedra* and *Welwitschia* have most probably been derived from primitive hermaphrodite flowers. In this connection Bennettitalean derivation is of great importance.

7. The dichasial cyme, which is the characteristic of Gnetalean inflorescence, although it has no parallel among the recent gymnosperms, yet dichasially branched inflorescence is found in *Wielandiella*.

8. The resemblances between the ovules and the seeds of Gnetales and Bennettitales, especially in the long micropylar tube and the configuration of the integuments, have been given much stress by Thoddy and Birrage.

9. There are not much resemblances by which it can safely be said that Gnetales arose from angiosperms ; a more congenial and logical conclusion can be drawn that the plants like *Gnetum* originated from a stock of ancestral plants related to gymnosperms and from which angiosperms arose. *Ephedra* is more closer to the gymnosperms, whereas *Gnetum* represent another arm of evolution, which shows more angiospermic in character. It may be concluded that the angiospermic characters particularly in *Gnetum*, are due to parallel evolution and not direct relation.

EPHEDRA

(Fam. GNETACEAE)

The species of *Ephedra* are found distributed in North as well as in South America, Spain, France, the Mediterranean regions, and India. It is interesting to note that, not a single species has yet been recorded, which is common to both the Hemispheres. According to Hooker, there are three species of *Ephedra* growing in India : *E. vulgaris*, *E. pachyclada*, and *E. peduncularis*. From *Ephedra* a valuable alkaloid '*ephedrine*' is extracted, which is extensively used in bronchial troubles.

The sporophyte

Plants are low-growing shrubs, while a few are woody climbers, or prostrate. In some places they serve as sand-binders. The plant is highly xeromorphic, and grows on rocks or in sandy places. The leaves are rudimentary, and practically of no importance to the plant, as the stem itself is ribbed phylloclade. They are usually decussately arranged, but may occur in whorls of three, very rarely of four. They are connate at their bases forming a small sheath. The branches appear in two's or three's from the axillary buds, and may fall off in some species at the end of the growing season, and are replaced by new ones in the next season ; such species may be regarded as **deciduous** ones, by analogizing them with trees shedding off their leaves in winter.

Internally, the stem has got a conspicuously thick epidermis, and groups of sclerenchyma cells occur below each rib. Sunken

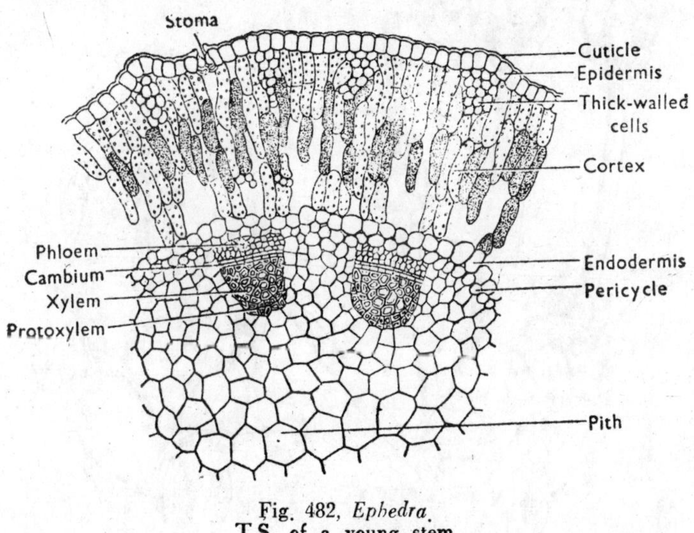

Fig. 482, *Ephedra*. T.S. of a young stem.

stomata occur in the furrows. The cortex is loose in texture, and differentiated into an outer palisade and inner spongy tissues, the cells of both of which contain abundant chloroplasts. Below the cortex there is an endodermal layer, encircling an endarch, siphonostelic vascular cylinder, the bundles of which are conjoint, collateral, and open. The tracheids are provided either with single or alternating double rows of bordered pits, with Bars of Sanio and trabeculae. In young stems, the medullary rays are uniseriate. At or near about the nodes, the cells of the pith get highly lignified, and form transverse plates. Resin canals are entirely absent, but cells containing large, stellate, calcium oxalate crystals are frequently met with. A group of thick-walled cells with dense cell-contents (most probably tannin) occur in the centre of the pith. The stem grows in girth due to secondary growth, and prominent annual rings are formed. The secondary wood possesses vessels in addition to tracheids.

Ephedra is dioecious. It is interesting to note, however, that though normally male and female strobili are borne on different individuals, yet monoecious plants are not rare in nature, e.g., *E. foliata.* Furthermore, bisporangiate flowers may be found in species like *E. camphylopoda*, *E. trifurca,* etc.

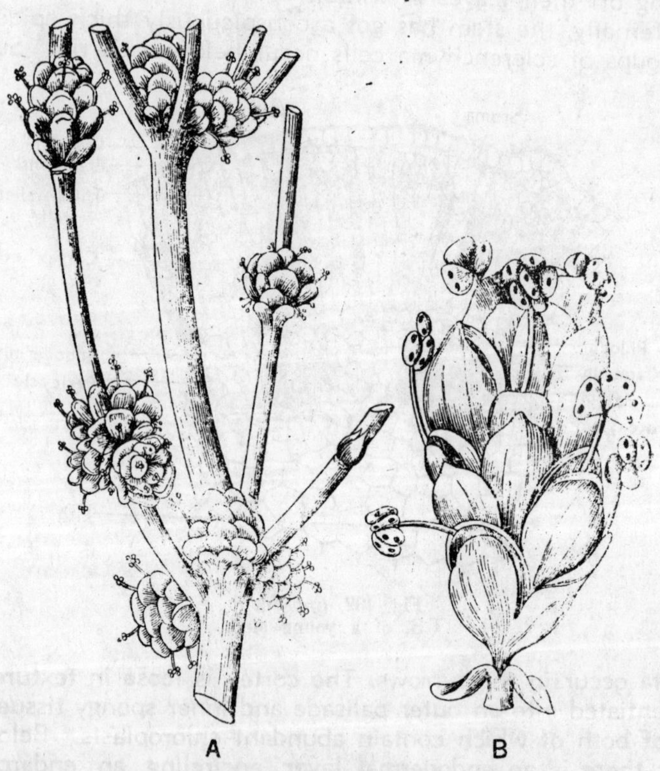

Fig. 483, *Ephedra*
A, A portion of the plant bearing male strobili ; B, A single male strobilus.

Staminate (or **male**) **strobilus**. Staminate strobili occur in groups of two, three or four, from the nodes of the branches. Each strobilus is a compound one, appears in the axil of a leaf, and consists of a short axis, bearing 2-8 decussately arranged bracts ; the lower 1-2 pairs of bracts are usually sterile, while each of the rest bears a single male flower. Each male flower is represented by a single stamen, having a stalk bearing a variable number of *microsporangia* (or *anthers*) at its tip, subtended at the base by a pair of delicate, oppositely placed **scales**, which coalesce together forming a structure that has been doubtfully interpreted as a **perianth**. The stalk bearing the microsporangia has been referred to by some as **sporangiophore** or **antherophore**. Each microsporangium is 2-3 lobed, and the lobes open by apical slit. The microspore mother cells (or pollen mother cells) inside the microsporangium, on undergoing reduction division, give rise to *microspores* or *pollen grains*.

Pistillate (or **female**) **strobilus**. The mode of distribution of

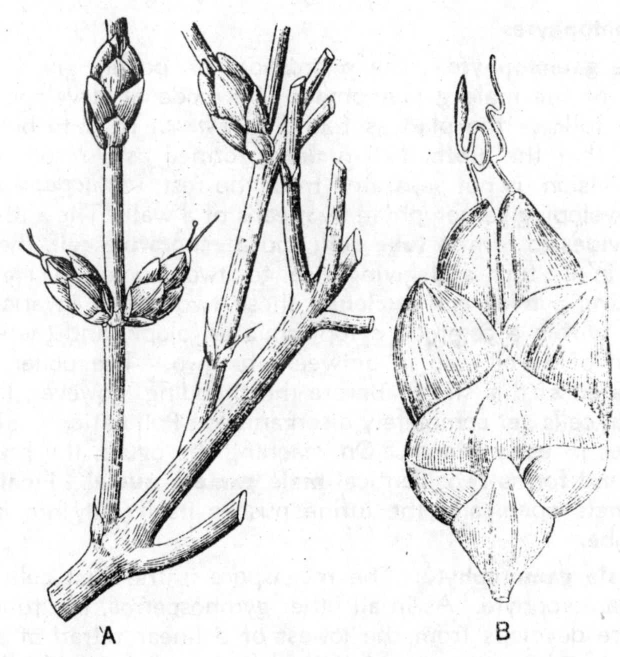

Fig. 484, *Ephedra*.
A, A portion of the plant bearing female strobili ;
B, A female strobilus.

the female strobili is practically the same as that of the male ones, and their structures are also very similar. The former ones are, however, rather shorter and more pointed, than the latter. Each strobilus consists of a few pairs (usually 4) of sterile bracts, and either a solitary *ovule* or 2-3 of them. The bracts may be fleshy or dry, and winged, and sometimes highly coloured for the purpose of effective dispersal by animals or wind, as the case may be.

The structure of the ovule is fundamentally the same as in other gymnosperms. There is the **nucellus** surrounded by two integuments, the outer one being formed by four segments (**bracts**), coalescent at the base, and the inner integument is formed of two such coalescent bracts. The upper portion of the nucellus is separate from the inner integument, which, at the time of pollination, prolongs out considerably, giving rise to a smooth or spirally coiled **micropylar tube**. The pollination drop is exuded at the tip of this micropylar tube. At the tip of the nucellus there is a conspicuously deep **pollen chamber**, whose bottom actually touches the apex of the female gametophyte (endosperm).

The gametophytes

Male gametophyte. The microspore or pollen grain is the first cell of the male gametophyte. The mode of development in this case follows the plan as found in *Pinus*. It is to be noted, however, that the **prothallial nucleus,** formed as a result of the second division, is not separated from the rest (*antheridial initial*) of the developing gametophyte by means of a wall. The antheridial initial divides to form a **tube cell**, and a **generative cell**, the latter dividing in its turn and giving rise to two nuclei, a **stalk cell nucleus** and a **body cell nucleus** ; these two nuclei invariably lie enclosed within a common cytoplasmic envelope, and there is no formation of a cell wall in between the two. The pollen grains are liberated at this stage. Before the shedding, however, the two prothallial cells get completely disorganized. Pollination is effected sometimes in early March. On reaching the ovule, the body cell divides, and forms two identical **male gamete nuclei**. Finally, the exine bursts open, and the intine pushes itself out into a short pollen tube.

Female gametophyte. The megaspore is the first cell of the female gametophyte. As in all other gymnosperms, the functional megaspore develops from the lowest of a linear tetrad of megaspores, and undergoes a period of free nuclear division. At the 256 nuclear stage, cell walls begin to be laid down rapidly in a centripetal fashion, and finally the female gametophyte (endosperm) becomes entirely cellular. Even before the female gametophyte is cellular throughout, a differentiation takes place inside it forming two regions, an *upper reproductive* one composed of large elongated cells, and a *lower nutritive* one made up of comparatively much smaller cells. Finally, the lower nutritive region gets further differentiation into an upper tissue performing the function of reservoir of food, and a lower mass of cells constituting a **haustorium**, which absorbs nutrients from the nucellus.

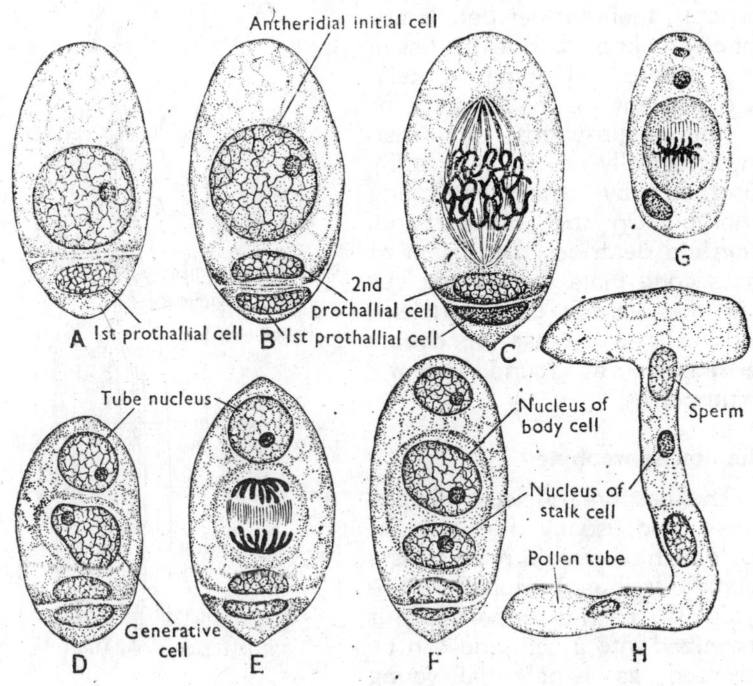

Fig. 485, *Ephedra*.
A—H. Successive stages in the development of the male gametophyte.

At the micropylar end of the endosperm, **archegonia** develop, usually two in number ; occasionally, there is only one archegonium, and rarely there are three. The number of neck cells are rather heavy in *Ephedra,* and stands at 32 or more. There is no wall formed in between the ventral canal nucleus and the egg nucleus.

The time interval in between pollination and fertilization is exceptionally short for a gymnosperm, and is less than a period of 12 hours. The short pollen tube pierces through the neck of the archegonium, and by the bursting of its tip, the contents are discharged in the egg. The first male gamete nucleus actually unites with the egg nucleus forming **oospore**, while the second male gamete nucleus and the ventral canal nucleus undergo divisions producing the nuclei for a few, minute, very short-lived cells at the top of the oospore ; their further details are not clearly known. But this tissue is considered, by some workers, as equivalent to the endosperm of the angiosperms, at least physiologically, as it is readily absorbed by the developing embryo. On the other hand, Herzfeld describes the fusion of the second male gamete nucleus with the ventral canal nucleus, and calls it a case of **double fertilization** as found in the angiosperms.

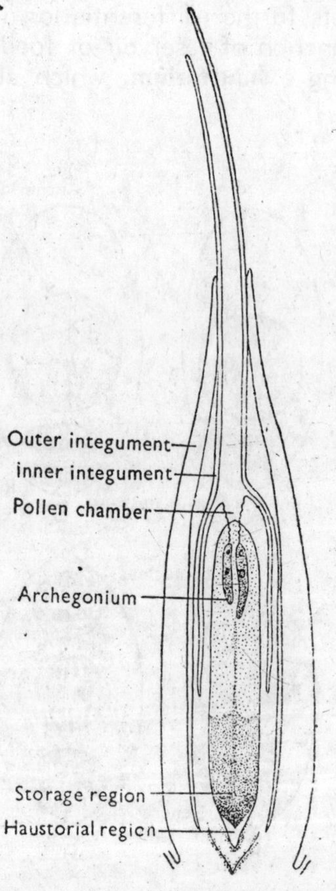

Fig. 486. *Ephedra*. L.S. of a mature ovule.

The new sporophyte

The oospore nucleus divides freely, and usually forms eight nuclei, which remain more or less evenly distributed throughout the cytoplasm. Each of these nuclei is organized into a cell, and can be regarded as a potential young embryo ; this is an instance of **polyembryony,** where no cleavage takes place. Normally, 3-5 of these embryos begin further development. At first, the embryo cell nucleus divides into two unequal parts without any corresponding cellwall formation. A small tubular outgrowth is developed, and the larger nucleus passes into it moving towards the tip, behind this, a transverse wall is formed. The terminal cell, thus cut off, divides and forms the **proembryo,** from the tip of which the *embryo* is developed. The remaining portion of the tube with its nucleus forms the **suspensor**, which elongates subsequently and helps in pushing the developing sporophyte (embryo) down within the nutritive tissue. The cells of the proembryo lying behind the tip also elongate to some extent, and form the **secondary suspensor**. Only one embryo, however, usually reaches maturity. The seed is dicotyledonous with

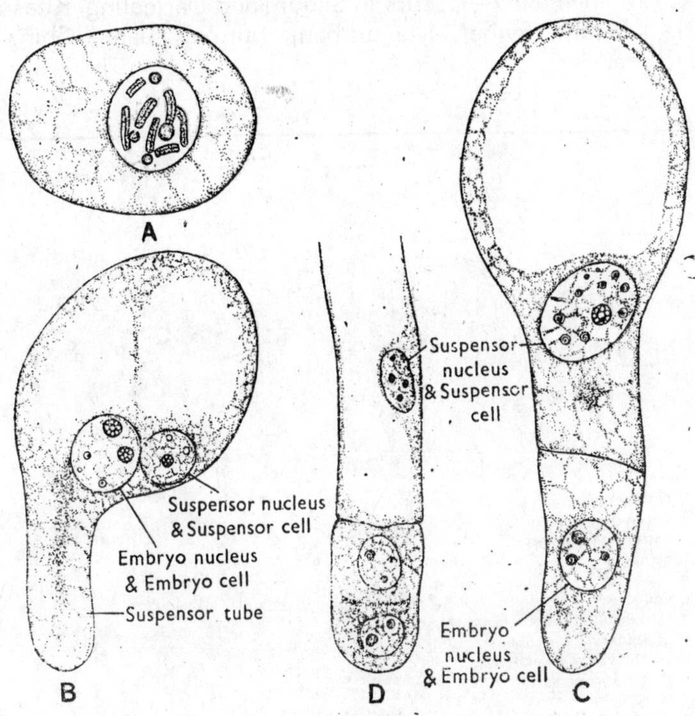

Fig. 487, *Ephedra*.
A—D, Successive stages in the development of the embryo.

two linear cotyledons, and the mode of germination is hypogeal. On germination the seed gives rise to a seedling sporophyte.

GNETUM

(Fam. GNETACEAE)

Distribution of Gnetum

1. *Gnetum gnemon*—Occurring in Nefa, Assam, Manipur, Burma, Malay, Moluccas, Sunda Islands, Celebes, Borneo, Phillippines, New Guinea.

var. *brunonianum* and var. *griffithii* occurs in Nefa and Assam.

2. *G. ula.*—Found in Tropical forests of South India occurring as far north as Orissa. Also found in Andaman Islands.

3. *G. montanum*—Occurs in Sikkim and Darjeeling, Khasia and Jaintia, Assam, Sylhet, Mayurbhanj, Burma, Siam, China and Indo-China.

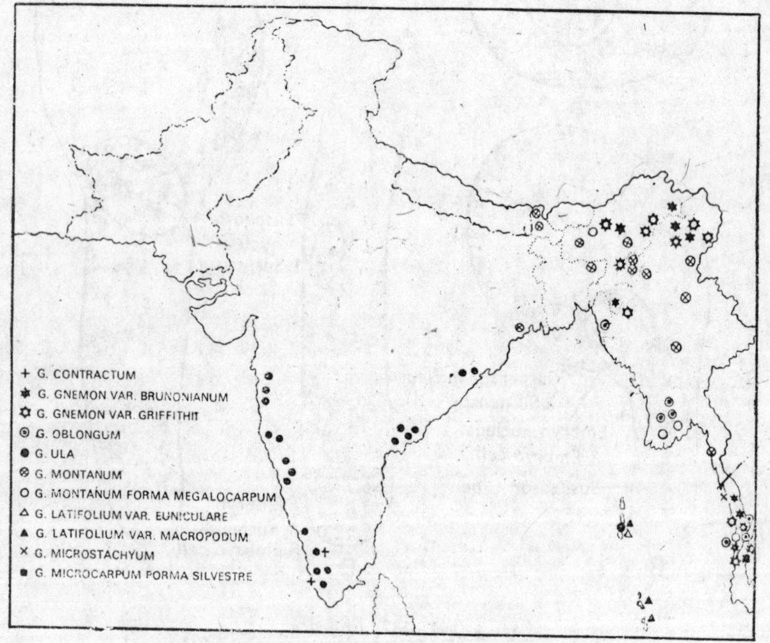

Fig. 488. Map of India including Pakistan showing the distribution of *GNETUM* (after Bharadavaja 1957).

4. *G. contractum*—Occur in Keralla and Nilgiri hills.

5. *G. latifolium*—Occur in Andaman and Nicobar Islands, Malay, Siam, Sumatra and Java.

var. *macropodum*—known in Andaman and Nicobar Islands.

var. *funiculare*—known from South Andaman.

Gnetum grows luxuriantly in the tropical and humid firests of South America (2 sp.), West Africa (2 sp.) being mostly distributed in tropical Asia, and in the lands between Asia and Australia, in Andaman and Nicobar Islands, Phillippines, New Guinea, Siam, Indo-China, China, Burma, Pakistan, India, etc. According to Hooker, there are 6 species of *G: etum* in India, viz., *G. gnemon*,

G. macrostachyum, *G. scandens* (?), *G. funiculare*, *G. neglectum*, and *G. macropodum*. Maheshwari and Vasil (1961) record 5 species of *Gnetum* from India. These are *G. ula*, *G. gnemon*, *G. latifolium*, *G. contractum*, and *G. montanum*. Of these the first-named species is the most common. *G. gnemon* and *G. latifolium* possess two varieties each, namely, *G. gnemon* var. *brunonianum*, *G. gnemon* var. *griffithii*, *G. latifolium* var. *macropodum* and *G. latifolium* var. *funiculare*.

The sporophyte

The plants are mostly lianes (*G. ula*), which climb or trail over other vegetation, often reaching the tops of the tallest trees. A few species are, however, small trees (*G. gnemon*, *G. costatum*) and shrubs. The leaves are simple, large, oval, entire, exstipulate, leathery, and with short petioles. They show pinnately reticulate venation resembling the foliage leaves of dicotyledons, and are arranged on the stem in opposite-decussate pairs. The branches are of two kinds : one of limited growth or **dwarf shoot**, and the other of unlimited growth or **long shoot**. In climbing species the foliage leaves are borne on dwarf shoots only, while those on long shoots are usually reduced to scales. In case of a tree (*G. gnemon*), the differences between these shoots are very much reduced.

In transverse section of a young stem of *Gnetum*, whether belonging to the arborescent types (*G. gnemon*) or to the climbing ones (*G. ula*), shows a somewhat circular outline. The epidermis in single-layered and made up of rectangular cells, whose outer walls are thick and heavily cuticularized ; sunken stomata are present. The cortex is many-layered and consists of polygonal or rounded parenchyma cells with chloroplasts. Lying within the cortical tissue a number of scattered sclerotic cells or sclereids are found, which in little older stems form a conspicuous irregular ring. This is commonly known as the ring or zone of **spicular cells**. The endodermis as well as the pericycle, however, cannot be clearly differentiated. The vascular bundles, varying in number, are arranged in a circle, and are collateral and open in nature. The phloem consists of sieve-tubes, phloem parenchyma and well-developed phloem fibres. The xylem is endarch and made up mainly of tracheids and a few vessels or trachea. *The presence of true vessels is an angiospermic character found in Gnetum.* Broad and long, conspicuous medullary rays separate the vascular bundles from one another. The pith is more or less circular and consists of thinwalled parenchyma cells. In somewhat older stems, however, the cells of the pith lying towards the vascular bundles become lignified.

Secondary growth in the stems of *Gnetum* takes place in the

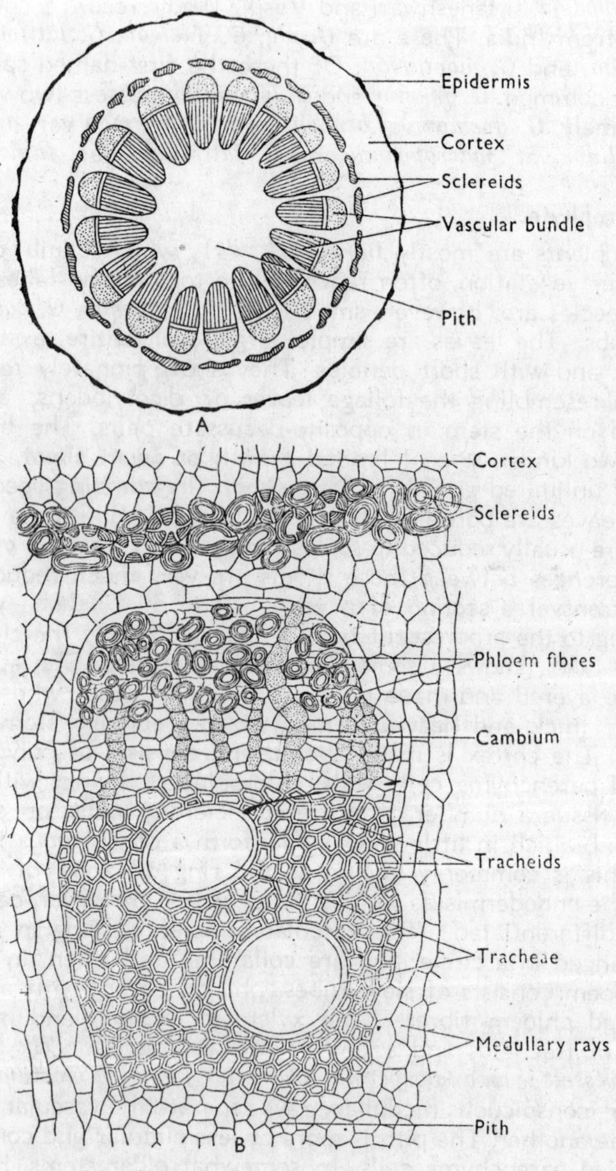

Fig. 489. *Gnetum.*
A, A transverse section of a young stem ; B, A portion of the same (magnified) to show the different tissues.

normal fashion. In the case of lianes, however, though secondary growth commences normally, during later stages, secondary cambium arises at different regions within the deeper layers of the cortex. As a result, anomalous rings of secondary vascular bundles (either complete or incomplete) are produced successively.

A transverse section of a young root of *Gnetum* exhibits the following structure : The epiblema is single-layered. The cortex is composed of a large number of layers made up of conspicuous starch grain-containing polygonal cells ; within these cortical cells numerous fibres can be observed. Below the cortex there is an endodermis, which encloses within it a few-layered pericycle. The

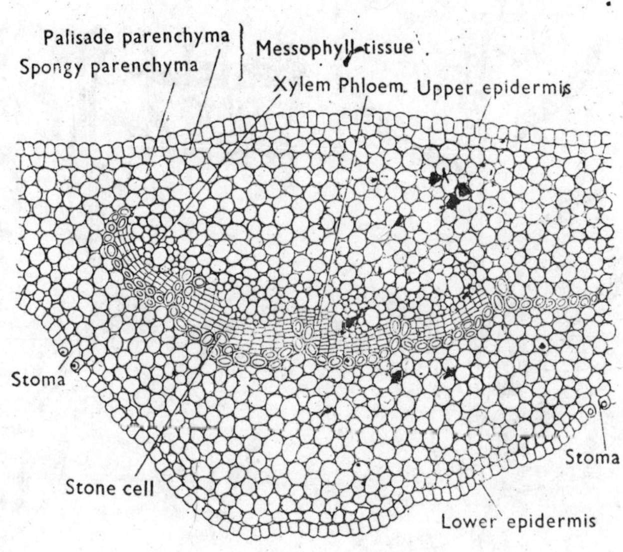

Fig. 490. *Gnetum*.
A transverse section of a leaf (in part).

vascular bundles are diarch with a rather poor amount of primary xylem. The pith is also inconspicuous. Secondary growth is of the normal type, some of the xylem elements in a mature root contains starch grains.

A cross-section of the leaf of *Gnetum* seems to differ in no essential feature from that of a dicotyledon. The epidermal layers are provided with a thick cuticle. Numerous stomata occur entirely on the lower epidermis. The mesophyll consists of a single layer of upper palisade cells, and a well-developed lower spongy tissue.

Within the latter stellately branched sclereids occur, particularly near the lower epidermis. A large number of latex tubes and fibres are present within the mesophyll tissue, more conspicuously in the midrib region of the leaf. In the midrib the vascular bundles are arranged forming a distinct curve. In some species a curved ring of sclereids is formed outside the phloem zone, whose cells are arranged in regular rows. Above the phloem there lies the xylem consisting of tracheids, vessels and xylem parenchyma.

In *Gnetum* the microsporophylls and megasporophylls form different strobili and the plants are mostly dioecious.

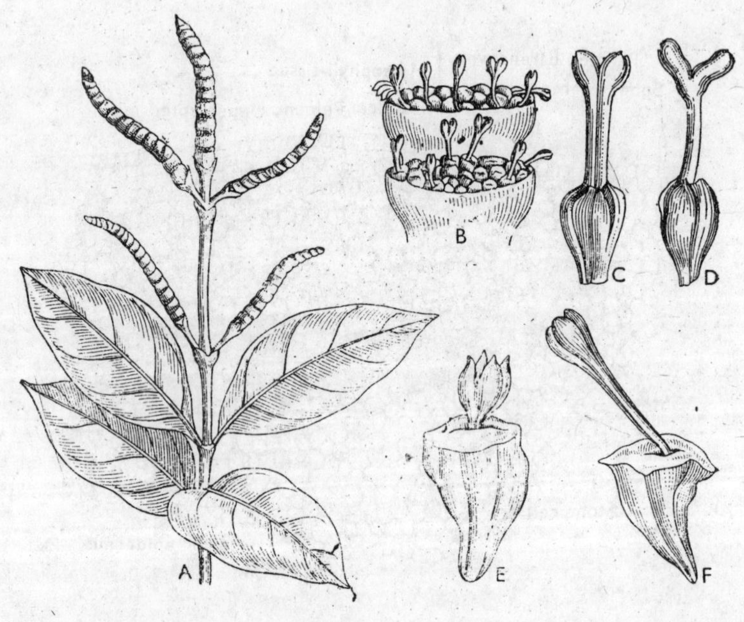

Fig. 491. *Gnetum*.
A. A branch bearing a cluster of staminate strobili ; B, A portion of the same (enlarged) ; C—F, Male flowers in different stages of development.

Staminate (or male) strobilus is a cone-like structure formed by the aggregation of several pairs of decussate bracts on a slender axis. It is axillary or terminal, solitary or catkin-like cluster. The bracts are connate throughout and look like small cups. In the axils of these bracts end surrounding the axes, numerous microsporophylls forming **staminate flowers** develop. Each staminate flower consists of a stalik, bearing at its tip, two anthers, each with a single microsporangium, and invested at the base by two connate bracts (the **perianth**). *The presence of the perianth is a striking angiospermic character.* The flowers mature in an acropetal order. Our knowledge about the development of microsporangium and *microspores* (*pollen grains*) is still very incomplete. Within the microsporangium gradually sporogenous cells become differentiated, and from these ultimately, by reduction division, spore tetrads are formed. The outer wall of the anther consists of a single layer of cells, and the tapetum is formed from the outer sporogenous tissue, and not from the wall. As the microsporangia mature, all the cells between the microspores and the epidermis break, and the microspores are liberated.

Ovulate strobilus. The structure of the ovulate strobili resembles, in general, that of the staminate strobili, but are compound, since the megasporangia or ovules are borne on the

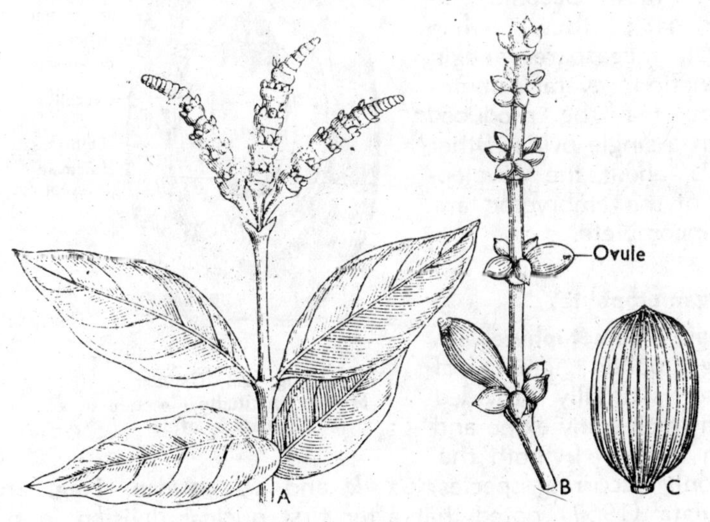

Fig. 492. *Gnetum*.
A, A branch bearing a cluster of ovulate strobili ; B. An older ovulate strobilus bearing a few mature ovules ; C, A ripe seed.

secondary axis. The *ovules* or *megasporangia* arising in the axils of connate bracts. These are five or six whorls of ovules surrounding the axis, and with five to seven ovules in each whorl. Sometimes the axis is terminated by a single ovule. Though there are numerous ovules, only a few attain maturity. Each ovule is invested with two integuments ; the inner one becomes prolonged into a **micropylar tube**, which is a characteristic feature of the genus. The nucellus has all the characteristic features of the gymnosperms, consisting of a heavy mass of sterile tissue overlying the megaspore mother cell. It is quite probable that in some cases more than one megaspore mother cells may be organized within a single ovule. The tip of the nucellus becomes more or less disorganized and shallow (*G. gnemon*), and this is the only trace of the pollen chamber found in other gymnosperms. A deeper and narrower pollen chamber may be formed in some cases (*G. africanum*). The megaspore mother cell, as usual by reduction division, forms four cells, each of which may become an **embryosac** ; thus, when several megaspores begin to function, several gametophytes may be produced within a single ovule. Other details about the development of the embryosac are still incomplete.

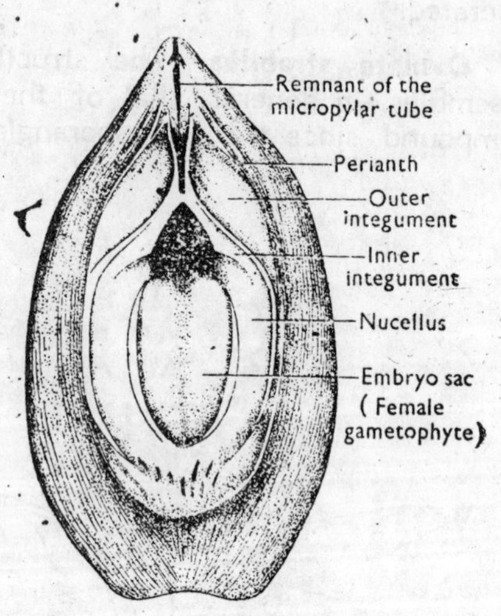

Fig. 493. *Gnetum*. Median longitudinal section of a mature ovule.

The gametophytes

Male gametophyte. A young pollen grain of *Gnetum* is usually provided with a thick spiny exine and a thin intine. In both the commonly occurring species, *G. ula* and *G. gnemon*, Negi and Madhulata (1957) noted that after first nuclear division in the microspore or pollen grain, a small lens-shaped cell is cut off at one end. This subsequently becomes rounded but neither divides any further nor it does take part in the development of the pollen tube. On the other hand, it degenerates *in situ*, and is, therefore, regarded as a **prothallial cell**. The sister nucleus, however, divides again giving rise to two nuclei, the **tube nucleus** and the **generative nucleus**. This generative nucleus soon develops a cytoplasmic sheath around itself to form a **generative cell**. Thus, a mature pollen grain contains a prothallial cell, a generative cell and a tube nucleus, lying in close proximity.

At the time of germination of the pollen grain, which takes place inside the pollen chamber, the exine is cast off and the intine is pushed out in the form of **pollen tube**. The tube nucleus is the first to enter the pollen tube and is followed later on by the generative cell. The generative cell finally divides to form two **male cells**.

Female gametophyte. The development of female gametophyte in *G. gnemon* and *G. ula* is distinctly tetrasporic. So far as known *Gnetum* is the only gymnosperm showing this type of development of the female gametophyte, though such a condition can be frequently met with in a number of angiospermic plants.

At the end of meiosis in the megaspore mother cell, a four nucleate **coenomegaspore** is formed. Further development takes

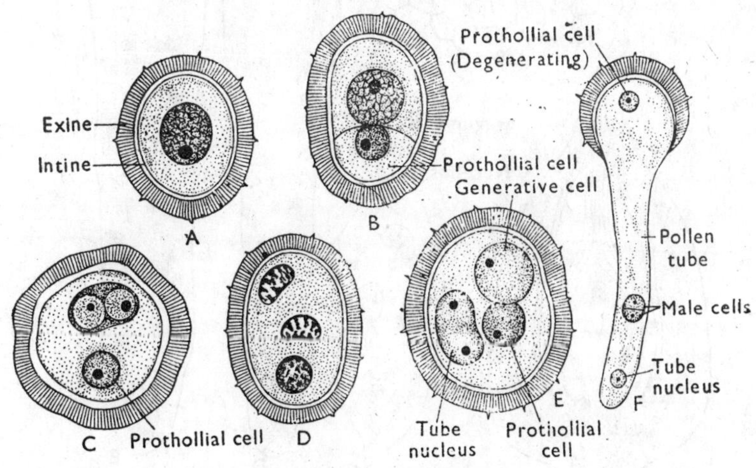

Fig. 494. *Gnetum*.
A, A mature pollen grain ; B—F, Stages in the development of male gametophyte.

place with free nuclear divisions within the megaspore. A conspicuous vacuole appears in the central portion of the developing gametophyte and the nuclei lying in the peripheral layer of cytoplasm undergo further divisions ; these number of divisions vary in different species. In addition to a normally developing main gametophyte, there may be 2-4 accessory gametophytes (which are smaller in size and contain a few nuclei only). These accessory gametophytes are usually placed above the main gametophyte and ultimately undergo degeneration. *No archegonium is present within the gametophyte which is an angiospermic character.*

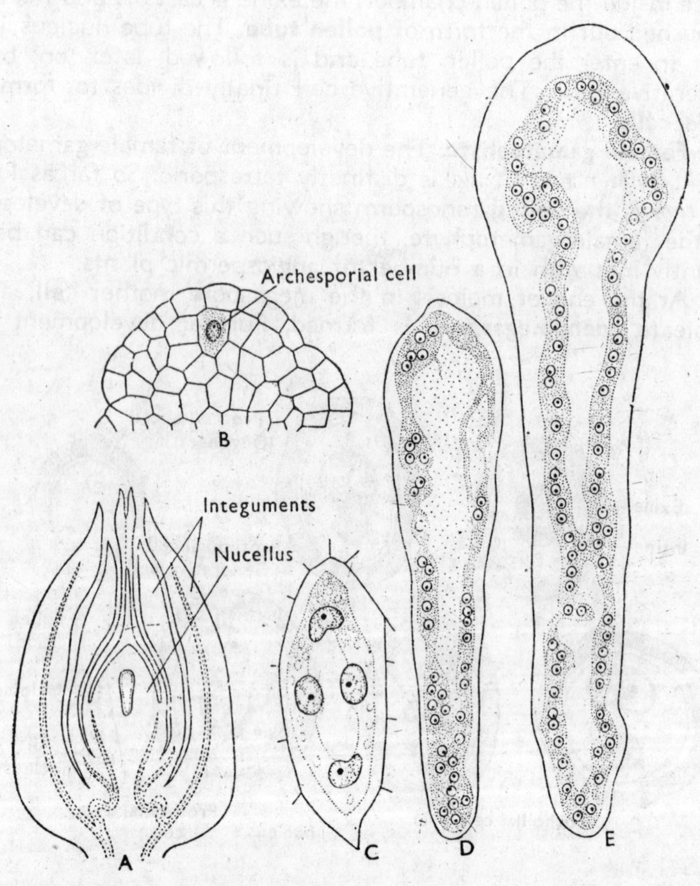

Fig. 495. *Gnetum*.
A, L.S. of an ovule (diagrammatic) ; B—E, Stages in the development of female gametophyte.

Fertilization

After the entry of pollen tube into the female gametophyte, whose lower end has become partly cellular, one or more nuclei (3-8) at its upper end also become delimited by cellwalls. These groups of cells are usually present in the neighbourhood of the pollen tube. Out of each such group, one or rarely two cells behave as egg cells, which often become surrounded by one or two layers of minute and degenerated cells. In all probability these inconspicuous cells provide nourishment to the egg and become used up at the time of fertilization. Only a male nucleus enters the egg, while its sheath is left outside. In cases where two eggs are present in the vicinity of the pollen tube, double fertilization may result.

Gnetum is remarkable among gymnosperms in the fact that a typical gymnospermic endosperm, which is formed prior to fertilization, is lacking here. Madhulata (1960) reports in *G. gnemon* that while eggs are being differentiated, the female gametophyte remains in a free nuclear condition, and only when zygotes are produced in the micropylar region of the ovule, the first walls are laid down in the chalazal region producing in an upward direction. Very rarely the cellwall formation may take place simultaneously throughout the gametophyte. Sometimes walls may be laid down even when eggs are not differentiated within the gametophyte.

The new sporophyte

After fertilization, the zygote develops into the embryo. The details of the embryo development, however, are not clear and much confusion exists, which may be attributed to variations existing among the different species of the genus.

In *G. gnemon*, Madhulata (1960) has shown that a small tuber-like projection may be developed directly from one side of the zygote, or in some ovules the zygote divides forming a two-celled structure, each of which on germination gives rise to a short tube ; frequently, only one of these two cells germinates. In rare cases, instead of a single tube, two or three tubes are developed from a zygote. The particular tube which receives the zygote nucleus remains functional while the others become abortive. The tube containing the nucleus grows in a downward direction, pushes inside the endosperm, grows through intercellular spaces and finally gives rise to a number of elongated uninucleate cells by the formation of septa. This is the **primary suspensor tube** or **suspensor tube** or **proembryo tube**. Usually, a small protuberance appears either above or below a septum. This, later on, becomes elongated forming a more or less tube-like structure, into which passes a nucleus. Thus, the primary suspensor tube usually becomes much branched. After the formation of the primary suspensor tube is completed, a small cell is cut off at its tip which first divides transversely and then longitudinally to give rise to a tetrad of cells. From these apical cells by further divisions there appears a more or less globose mass of cells which constitute the **embryonal cells.**

Sometimes the primary suspensor itself undergoes divisions. Of the group of embryonal cells, those which are terminal in position develop into an **embryo**, while those which are situated behind the embryo become considerably elongated and divide further to give rise to a long **secondary suspensor**. This secondary suspensor helps in pushing the embryo deeper within the endosperm for obtaining better nutrition.

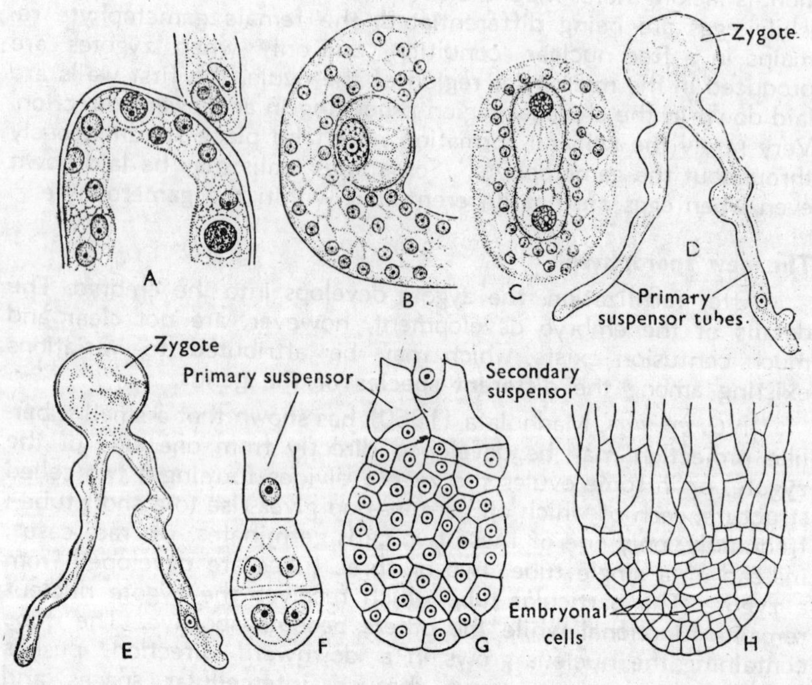

Fig. 496, *Gnetum*.
A—H, Stages in fertilization and development of new sporophyte.

In some species, *like G. ula, G. gnemon* and others, polyembryony is frequently met with, which may originate in several ways.

A mature seed is usually elongated but may be slightly oval also. Its colour varies from green to red. The endosperm is very conspicuous and remains enveloped by three envelopes. The cotyledons are two in number.

Economic Importance of Gymnosperms

The members of the gymnosperms are utilized for various purposes. The chief uses of them are, however, as fuel, timber, lumber and materials for making building and furniture. Some of them are used for ceremonial decorations as well as ornamental garden plants. The tubers of the cycads yield the arrowroot starch. Some of the pines are sources of the pulp for the paper industry. Previously, the pine wood was employed in the preparation of match sticks. Some of the valuable pine products, which are obtained by distillation and other processes, are methyl alcohol, charcoal, resin, wood gas, turpentine, various kinds of oil and others. The bark of hemlock (*Tsuga canadensis*) gives tannins, which are extensively used for the purpose of tanning animal skins into leather, for making ink, as well as for manufacturing drugs. *Pinus gerardiana* and several others supply edible seeds. Amber, which is utilized for making ornaments and art curios, is nothing but the resin of a fossil pine. An important medicinal plant is *Ephedra*, from which is obtained the alkaloid 'ephedrine'. The inflorescence and young leaves of *G. gnemon* are taken as vegetables in some parts of South-East Asia. The seeds also are edible after cooking or roasting. From the bark is obtained a kind of fibre, which is used for making ropes, fishing nets, etc. In South India the seeds of *G. ula* are taken as food. The plant also possesses some properties detrimental to the fishes. The kernel of the seed of *G. latifolia* is also taken as a food after boiling or roasting. Its bark is also utilized for preparation of nets and ropes. The fossil gymnosperms, particularly the Pteridosperms, have contributed to a large extent to the formation of coal.

COMPARISON OF CYCAS, PINUS AND GNETUM

CYCAS	PINUS	GNETUM
A. The Sporophyte		
1, *Plants* : Resemble dwarf date palms, unbranched or branched, dioecious.	1. *Plants* : Tall tree characterisel by excurrent branching and evergreen leaves, monoecious.	1. *Plants* : Mostly woody climbers, sometimes small trees or shrubs, mostly dioecious.
2. *Stem* : Shoot, thick, cylindrical, covered by leaf-bases, and bearing a crown of leaves.	2. *Stem* : Robust cylindrical by scaly bark, bears two kinds of shoots, dwarf and long.	2. *Stem* : Stout, usually bears two kinds of shoots, dwarf and long.
3. *Roots* : Primary ones are long, very large, but some species have nodules.	3. *Roots* : Long tap root.	3. *Roots* : Tap root.
4. *Leaves* : Large, Pinnate, spirally arranged and with circinate-ptyxis.	4. *Leaves* : Of two kinds : (a) Scale like 2 or more in a bunches, on dwarf shoots in their axils and (b) needle-like one or more in a bunches, on dwarf shoots.	4. *Leaves* : Usually of two kinds (a) scale leaves on long shoots and (b) ordinary green leaves on dwarf shoots. These leaves are simple, large, oval, leathery, exstipulate, pinnately reticulate and are arranged in opposite decussate manner.
5. *Strobili* : Of two kinds, male and female.	5. Strobili : Of two kinds, male and female,	5. *Strobili* : Of two kinds, staminate or male and ovulate.

CYCAS	PINUS	GNETUM
(a) **Male Strobilus**—Is small, compact and consists of a central axis on which the microsporophylls are spirally arranged. Each sporophyll is narrow below and broadened above, bearing numerous microsporangia in which a large number of microspores are produced, on lower side. 2-6 sporangia are grouped in *sori*.	(a) **Male Strobilus**—Is found in clusters near the apex of a branch and consists of a short axis on which the microsporophylls are spirally arranged. Each sporophyll bears on its underside two sporangia containing numerous microspores or pollen grains. Each microspore is provided with two coats, *exine* and *intine*, the former bears two wings.	(a) **Male Strobilus**—Is a cone like structure formed by the aggregation of numerous pairs of opposite decussate bracts on a slender axis. It is axillary or terminal, solitary or catkin-like cluster. The bracts are united forming small cups. In the axils of these cups and surrounding axis numerous microsporophylls forming *staminate flowers* develop. Each staminate flower consists of a stalk, bearing at its tip two *anthers*, each with a microsporangium containing numerous microspores and subtended at the base by two united *perianth*. Each microspore is provided with two coats, *exine* and *intine*, the former is thick and spiny and the latter thin.
(b) **Female Strobilus**—Consists of loosely arranged non-green leaf megasporophylls arising spirally at the apex of the stem and alternating with foliage. The megasporangia or *ovules* arise in place of pinnae. Ovule consists of nucellus surrounded by *an integument* which develops a testa of three layers, *a nucellar beak* and a *pollen chamber*. Within the nucellus there is a megaspore mother cell which by reduction	(b) **Female Strobilus**—Is compound and consists of an elognated axis which the megasporophylls are spirally arranged. On the upper surface of each scale there is another stouter scale, *ovuliferous scale*, which bears two megasporangia or *ovules* on the upper surface. Ovule consists of nucellus surrounded by *an integument* and a *pollen chamber*. The micropyle is	(b) **Ovulate Strobilus**—Resembles that of male strobilus but is compound, since the megasporangia are borne on the secondary axil. *Ovules* or megasporangia arise in the axils of united bracts. There are 5 or 6 whorls of ovules surrounding the axis and with 5 or 7 ovules in each whorl. Sometimes the axis is terminated by an ovule. Ovule consists of *nucellus* sur-

CYCAS	PINUS	GNETUM
division forms a linear tetrad of 4 *megaspores*, of which the innermost one is functional.	directed towards the stalk of carpers. Within the nucellus there is a megaspore mother cell which produces one functional *megaspore*, as in *Cycas*.	rounded by *two integuments*, a *micropylar tube* and a shallow *pollen chamber*. Within the nucellus there is one or more megaspore mother cell, which by reduction division forms 4 cells, each of which may become a *megaspore*. In most cases the megaspore mother cell at the end of reduction division forms a four nuclears *cenomegaspore*.
B. The Gametophytes		
(a) Male gametophyte	**(a) Male gametophyte**	**(a) Male gametophyte**
1. **Microspore is the first cell of the male gametophyte and begins to germinate inside the microsporangium before it is shed.**	1. Same as in CYCAS.	1. Same as in CYCAS
2. Microspore cuts off a small *prothallial cell*, the male gametophyte, and the rest of the spore divides into a *generative cell* and a *tube cell*.	2. Microspore cuts off a small cell, the *first prothallial cell* which soon degenerates, then it produces another small cell, the *second prothallial cell* and an *antheridial cell*. This entheridial cell gives rise to a *generative cell* and a *tube cell*.	2. Microspore germinates to produce a *generative nucleus* and a *tube nucleus*. The generative nucleus is provided with a wall forming a *generative cell*.
3. Generative cell produces a *stalk-cell* and a *body-cell*.	3. Generative cell produces a *stalk nucleus* and a *body nucleus*.	3. No formation of stalk nucleus or body nucleus.

CYCAS	PINUS	GNETUM
4. Tube cell prolongs into *pollen tube* carrying the stalk-cell, body-cell and tube nucleus inside it.	4. Tube cell prolongs into a *pollen tube* carrying the stalk nucleus, body nucleus and tube nucleus.	4. Exine of the microspore *prolongs into pollen tube* carrying the generative cell and the tube nucleus.
5. The stalk-cell is functionless but the body-cell produces two *spermatocytes*, each of which contains a *spermatozoid*.	5. Body nucleus divides into two *male nucleus*.	5. Generative cell divides into two *male cells*.
(b) **Female gametophyte**	(b) **Female gametophyte**	(b) **Female gametophyte**
1. Megaspore is the first cell of the female gametophyte and germinates inside the megasporangium, which is never shed.	1. Same as in CYCAS.	1. Megaspore or cenomegaspore is the first cell of the female gametophyte and germinates inside the megasporangium.
2. Megaspore becomes larger and by free nuclear division produces numerous nuclei, round each of which cytoplasm collects and cell-wall is formed and thus a tissue, known as *endosperm*, is formed. The endosperm represents the female gametophyte and is formed before fertilization.	2. Same as in CYCAS	2. Cenomegaspore produces numerous nucleus by free nuclear division which lie in the cytoplasm. Surrounding a large vacuole. Wall formation begins around the free nuclei, from base upwards but it is not complete. This tissue represents the female gametophyte. Sometimes 2-4 accessory female gametophytes are formed above the main gametophyte but these undergo degeneration.

CYCAS	PINUS	GNETUM
3. Endosperm is vacuolated and consists of two regions : (a) a region of large cells near the base and (b) a region of small cells near the micropyle.	3. Endosperm is solid and consists of two regions (a) a region of small cells towards the top and (b) a region of large cells towards the base.	3. Endosperm is formed after fertilization.
4. In the latter region *archegonia* develop in *archegonial chamber* and these are surrounded by a jacket of sterile cells.	4. In the former region 2 or 3 *archegonia* develop and these are separated from one another.	4. No forma ion of archegonia.
5. Archegonium consists of two *neck cells*, a *venter* and a large *ovum* or *egg*.	5. Archegonium consists of a *neck* composed of 8 cells in two tiers of 4, a *ventral canal cell* and a very large cavity surrounded by a layer of jacket cells and containing or *ovum* or *egg*.	5. One or two free nuclei situated towards the microstyle are covered by cytoplasm and form one or two *ova* or *eggs*.

Section X

ANGIOSPERMS

Origin of Angiosperms

The origin of the present-day angiosperms is a very knotty problem, and is not yet properly understood. The phylogenists have put forward some theories from time to time, a brief resume of some of which is presented below.

Though there is a lack of adequate palaeobotanical records, a large number of workers try to establish the origin or angiosperms from some gymnospermous stock or from some of their ancestral forms, and as such, angiosperms may be monophyletic or polyphyletic in origin. Arber and Parkin (1907) suggested a hypothetical connecting link in between the Cycadeoidaceae and the Angiospermae. They gave the name **Hemiangiospermae** to this link, whose imaginary reproductive organs were constructed as in the cycadeoid flower in having an elongated axis bearing spirally arranged perianth leaves, the androecial branch of numerous stamens, and a large number of open carpels with marginal megasporangia. From such a type the magnoliaceous flower is supposed to have originated. According to this view, therefore, the angiosperms are monophyletic in origin, as all of them have come from the same ranalian stock; the dicotyledons have come first, and the monocotyledons constitute an offshoot of them. But there is no fossil record to prove that such a structure was ever present. It is interesting to note, however, that this theory was nevertheless accepted by workers like Bessey, Hutchinson and others. Wettstein (1910-11) postulates that the ancient angiosperms were monosporangiate, and were derived from a gnetalian inflorescence. He regards *Casuarina* as the most primitive of the existing angiosperms. According to him, the bisexual flower came into existence by the appearance of a terminal pistillate flower on a staminate inflorescence. Wettstein does not support the view that the origin of the dicots is from the monocots. Markgraf (1930) also lays emphasis on the Gnetales for providing a solution to this problem of angiosperm origin, Fagerlind (1947) considers that there was a common ancestral stock, which had given rise to a line, from which have originated the present-day *Gnetum*, *Ephedra*, and *Welwitschia* among the gymnosperms on one hand, and another in the other direction, from which have evolved the modern angiosperms polyphyletically; he terms the latter as the **Proangiosperms**. Andrews (1947) and Arnold (1947) are both of opinion that the angiosperms have come from the pteridosperms, but Darrah (1939) considers it to be an entirely debatable point. A few workers suggested that the angiosperms might have been evolved from the Caytoniales, a Jurassic group of angiosperm-like plants, recorded by Thomas (1925). But Arnold has shown that they are simply some Mesozoic remnants of the pteridosperms. Campbell (1925) rejects the idea of the derivation of angiosperms from the cycadeoidean stock, and suggests their origin from some pteridophytic ancestor. According to him, the monocotyledons are more primitive than the dicotyledons. Engler (1936) however, discredits both the cycadeoidean as well as the gnetalian theories of origin, and suggests that the monocotyledons and dicotyledons have arisen independently from a hypothetical group, called the **Protangiosperms,** existing in the Mesozoic. The Protangiosperms themselves might have come from some *Ophioglossum*-like eusporangiate pteridophytic stock, and bore flowers, which were bisporangiate and were either completely achlamydeous or were provided with a very rudimentary perianth. Rendle (1904) supports this idea of Engler.

A view quite different from the previous ones was expressed by Sahni (1920), and later on elaborated by Lam (1948). According to this theory, which is being known as the *Stachyosporous theory* of the origin of the angiosperms, the seed plants belong to two *taxa* : **Phyllospermae** and **Stachyosporae**. In the former, the megasporangia lie enclosed within leafy carpels and contain the majority of the apocarpous dicotyledonous plants and their derivatives. In the Stachyosporae, on the other hand, the megasporangia remain covered by some sterile organ ; this latter taxon comprises of the Monochlamydeae of Bentham and Hooker and 'perhaps some monocotyledons and sympetalae'.

Anderson (1934) suggests that the angiosperms might have been evolved as a result of hybridization between very widely different gymnosperms. Goldschimdt (1940) is also of opinion that the evolution of the major angiospermic taxa might have taken place as a result of direct mutations.

General consideration

The Angiosperms or 'closed-seeded' plants are very complex seed-bearing plants (Spermatophytes).. They include the great majority of seed plants. The most distinguishing feature of this group is that the *carpels unite by their margins to form an ovary in which the ovules are enclosed,* and the *pollen grains fall upon a receptive surface known as the stigma.* The plant is the sporophyte which is more highly differentiated than those of the gymnosperms. As in gymnosperms, *the sporophylls are aggregated to form 'flowers' but they are provided with one or two accessory whorls.* The sporophyte is *always heterosporous* producing two kinds of spores. The micro- and mega-sporophylls are usually found in the same flower. As in gymnosperms, two kinds of gametophytes, micro- and mega-gametophytes, are produced but they are extremely reduced. *No organ corresponding to archegonium is found.* The reproduction is effected by motionless gametes. *The endosperm is produced after fertilization.* Seeds are enclosed within fruit.

Alternation of Generations

In the angiosperms there is an 'alternation of generations' but it is very much less distinct. The plant itself is the sporophyte because it bears spores (e.g., microspores or pollen grains and megaspores) and it is more conspicuous of the two generations. The microgametophyte is represented by the pollen tube and the megagametophyte by the embryosac. The female organs or archegonia themselves have perished though their essential cells, the oospheres or eggs, have still persisted. It is to be noted that the gametophyte is completely dependent upon the sporophyte.

It is seen that the sporophyte is followed by the gametophyte and the gametophyte by the sporophyte, and so on. Thus, one stage is alternated by the other. This phenomenon of alternation of two stages or phases is spoken of as 'alteration of generations'.

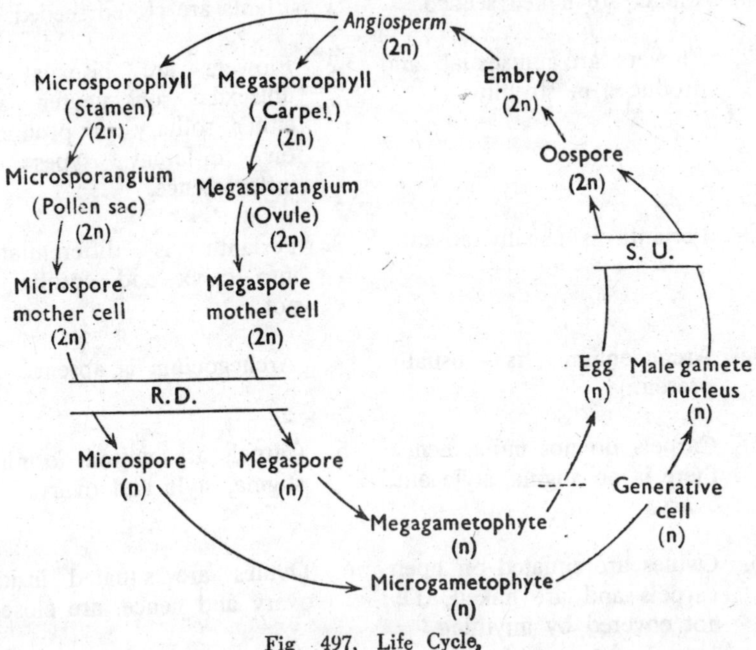

Fig. 497, Life Cycle,

Homology of Vascular Cryptogams and Angiosperms

We are now in a position to correlate the main facts in the life history of the angiosperms with those of the Vascular Cryptogams.

Reproductive structures of Vascular Cryptogams		*Corresponding structures in Angiosperm*
Microsporophylly	..	Stamens
Microsporangium	..	Pollen sac
Microspore	..	Pollen grain
Megasporophyll	..	Carpel
Megasporangium	..	Ovule
Megaspore	..	Ovum

Comparison between Gymnosperms and Angiosperms

Gymnosperms	Angiosperms
1. Plants are naked seeded.	1. Plants are closed seeded.
2. Flowers are unisexual and produced in strobitus.	2. Flowers are bisexual or unisexual or neuter and either solitary or produced on different types of inflorescence.
3. Perianth is usually absent.	3. Perianth is differentiated into calyx and corolla or not.
4. Archegonium is usually present.	4. Archegonium is absent.
5. Carpels do not unite, hence there is no stigma, style and ovary.	5. Carpels are united forming stigma, style and ovary.
6. Ovules are situated on open carpels and are naked, i.e. not covered by anything.	6. Ovules are situated inside ovary and hence, are closed.

7. Pollen grains tall directly on the micropyle of the ovule.	7. Pollen grains tall on the stigma.
8. Endosperm is formed before fertilization.	8. Endosperm is formed after fertilization.
9. Xylem is usually composed of tracheids.	9. Xylem is composed of true vessels.

Difference between Gymnospermous and Angiospermous ovules

(a) The ovules of Gymnosperms usually have one integument, but these of Angiosperms have two integuments. (b) The ovule of Gymnosperms has a cavity, known as *pollen chamber* but there is no such chamber in Angiosperms. (c) In Gymnosperms the endosperm is developed before fertilization, but in Angiosperms it is developed after fertilization.

Classification of Angiosperms

Angiosperms have been divided into two classes : **Monocotyledons** and **Dicotyledons.**

Section XI

TAXONOMY

INTRODUCTION

There are thousands of plants in the universe, and it is not possible to obtain a satisfactory knowledge of such a diverse multitude of plants without arranging them systematically according to some definite rules or plans.

Taxonomy is that branch of Botany which deals with nomenclature, identification and classification of plants. In its extended sense, the object of Systematic Botany is the naming, describing and arrangement of plants in such a way as to indicate as far as possible their probable line of descent, so that one can at once ascertain their names and at the same time get an insight into their affinities and general properties.

The study of Taxonomy involves (1) **nomenclature**, *i.e.*, the naming of plants which may or may not indicate any relationship, (2) **identification**, *i.e.*, whether the taxon is identical with or similar to another already described element, or it is determined to be an unidentified and completely a new one, and (3) **classification**, *i.e.*, the arrangement of such units according to some definite plans.

According to H. L. Manson, 1950 'Taxonomy' includes four different but related branches and they are :—

(i) **Systematics**—it covers the informative branch of taxonomy and it is mainly based on exomorphological characters.

(ii) **Taxonomic systems**—by this system, on the basis of systematic informations, an idea of species and genus may develop, line of evolution can be traced, and a classification can be suggested.

(iii) **Nomenclature**—according to international code a name should be given, and

(iv) **Documentation**—maintenance of herbarium specimens as evidence.

Principles of classification

1. **Species**. Botanists are almost unanimous in looking upon the species as the unit adopted in formulating the principles of classification, and then building the higher units upon this concept. By the term **species** is understood a collection of individuals, which resemble one another closely in all important characters of vegetative and reproductive organs and are, therefore, supposed to have descended from a common ancestor. If we walk in a rice field we observe thousands of individuals, which, though differing

in some respects from one another, are commonly associated under a common name. Such a collection of individuals resembling one another in all important characters constitute what is known as a **species**, and this can at once be verified if they breed true from generation to generation, *i.e.*, produce offspring exactly resembling their parents. It should, however, be remembered that such a thing is only possible if the individuals in question are exposed to the influence of the same environmental factors, such as soil, heat, light, moisture, etc., as the parents.

Under certain conditions, however, particularly under changed external conditions, a species may exhibit certain variations in form, size, colour, taste, etc., in the young plants. In this way are produced what are known as **varieties** or **subspecies**. In some cases the variations are only temporary, the individuals reverting to the parent type or perishing altogether. In other cases, however, they are permanent, persisting throughout the life of the individual. But even then, the successive generations of these new individuals will have a tendency to revert to the original specific type from which they have been derived, so that the nature of the plants will depend entirely upon soil characters and other external conditions to which they are exposed. Hence, a variety differs essentially from a species in that it cannot be propagated without tending to revert to the parent type.

Besides the transient varieties referred to above, there are others, which are called **permanent varieties** or **races**, because their characters can be transmitted by seed. The cereal grains, such as wheat, barley, etc., and the vegetables, such as radishes, cabbages and cauliflowers afford good examples. It is impossible to say with certainty how they arose in nature. They, however, present definite or well-marked characters by which they are readily distinguished from the true species.

Another cause which leads to constant variation from the specific type is **hybridization**, a method widely practised by gardeners in raising new forms, which are commonly known as **hybrids** or **cross-breeds**. The hybrid roses and the hybrid mangoes are good examples. But these again are rarely constant and always tend to revert to the original specific type.

Thus, a species must be regarded as a permanent production of nature, which, though varying within certain limits, can never be capable of being modified or altered to such an extent as to resemble a different species. Nothing should be regarded as a new species unless it exhibits some important and distinctive characters in the wild condition.

2. **Genera**. As some individuals resemble one another more closely than others, so there are some species which resemble one another more closely than other species. Such allied species are placed under a higher group, called the **genus**. A genus, therefore, is an assemblage of species, which resemble one another in general structure and appearance more than they resemble any other species. Thus, the fig, the banyan, and the India-rubber plant, although constituting different species, present well-marked resemblances to one another in certain characters, and are, therefore, placed under one common genus, viz. *Ficus*. The characters of a genus are derived exclusively from the reproductive organs, while those of the species are generally taken from all parts of the plant body. A genus, therefore, may be strictly defined as a collection of species, which bear similarity to one another in the general characters of their organs of reproduction. A genus does not necessarily contain a number of species. A single species on account of its presenting certain well-marked peculiarities may itself constitute a genus. Such genera are known as **monotypic** ones.

3. **Families.** If we follow this principle of classification, we find that some genera are more allied to one another than to other genera. Such allied genera are grouped together into a still higher grade, called the **family**. Thus, the thorn apples, potatoes and chillies, although belonging to different genera, present certain well-defined resemblances to one another, and are, therefore, included in the family Solanaceae. Again, the roses, apples and plums all belong to different genera but to one family, viz. Rosaceae.

It is, however, often found that there are certain genera, which more closely resemble one another than they do other genera of the same family. Thus, the pulses, indigo, tamarind, *Acacia*, and the sensitive plants all belong to the same family, but the *Acacia* and the sensitive plant show more resemblances to each other than do the tamarind and the indigo. Hence, while all of them belong to the same family Leguminosae, they are at the same time placed under three different **subfamilies**. Thus, the indigo and pulses belong to the subfamily Papilionaceae, the tamarind to the subfamily Caesalpinieae, and the *Acacia* as well as the sensitive plant to the subfamily Mimosae.

Following the same principle of resemblances and differences, the families are grouped into **Orders**, orders into **Subclasses**,

subclasses into **Classes,** classes into **Divisions** till we arrive at the whole collection of plants known as the **Vegetable Kingdom**.

Nomenclature

The art of naming and describing a plant accurately is one of the main objects of Taxonomy. This involves the use of certain technical terms, so that it may be readily recognized by one, who has a knowledge of these terms but to whom the plant was previously unknown. Every species of a plant has a name by which it is distinguished from any other species. Thus, the thorn apple is named *Datura fastuosa*, the custard apple as *Anona squamosa*, and the apple as *Pyrus malus*. The name of each plant thus consists of two parts; the first part indicates the genus to which the plant belongs and is always placed before the second part, which indicates its species. It is thus seen that the three plants mentioned above not only belong to different species but also to different genera. The first part of each name is called the **generic** name and the second, the **specific** one. Two or more species belonging to the same genus have, of course, the same generic name. Thus, the custard apple and the bullock's heart both belong to the same genus *Anona*, but to two different species, viz. *squamosa* and *reticulata* respectively.

This system of naming plants is called the **binomial nomenclature.** It is customary to put the name of the author in an abbreviated form after the specific name of the plant* in order to denote the name of the person, who described the plant for the first time, or to avoid confusion which may arise from the description of the same plant published by a different author from a different part of the globe. For example, the common mango is termed *Mangifera indica* Linn. after the well-known botanist **Linnaeus**.

Specific names are derived from various sources. Sometimes they are derived from the name of the country to which a plant originally belonged, for example, *Argemone mexicana* means that the native home of the plant is Mexico, *Ficus indica* means that the plant is indigeneous to India, etc. Sometimes they refer to the habit of a plant, such as *Mentha arvensis*, which is found in fields; or they may express some obvious morphological character of the species, such as *Butomopsis lanceolata*, with lanceolate

* Both the generic and specifiic names are, as a rule, indicated in italics, while the author's name is printed in Roman script, e.g., *Polyalthia longifolia* Benth, & Hook. (the common devdaru),

leaves, *Ruellia tuberosa*, with tuberous roots. *Viola tricolor* with tricoloured flowers, and so on.

The generic names may also be variously derived. They may refer to the names of some eminent botanists, such as *Jussiaea* after Jussiaeu, *Caesalpinia* after Caesalpinus, or to some peculiarity of structure, or habit, or to various other sources. Thus, *Sagittaria* is derived from its arrow-shaped leaves, *Campanula* from its bell-shaped corolla, *Lactuca* from its milky juice, etc.

On similar principles the names of families are also derived in various ways. They are usually taken from some well-known genus. Thus, the genus *Malva* gives the name Malvaceae to the family to which it belongs. Likewise, the genera *Lilium, Orchis, Cyperus, Asclepias, Convolvulus, Amarantus*, etc., give name respectively to the families Liliaceae, Orchidaceae, Cyperaceae, Asclepiadaceae, Convolvulaceae, Amaranthaceae, and so on. At other times, however, they are derived from some characteristic feature of the plants included in them. Thus, the name Cruciferae is derived from flowers having cruciform corolla, Umbelliferae, from the umbel inflorescence, Leguminosae, from the fruit which is a legume, etc.

The names of the Classes, Divisions, etc., are derived from some permanent characters of the plants placed in them and refer either to the structure or mode of development. Familiar examples are the Dicotyledons and the Monocotyledons meaning that the former have two cotyledons and the latter only one.

History of Taxonomy

Taxonomy, in its wide sense, includes the study of the various types of plants, their identification, their characteristics, habitats and distribution as well as their affinities. Thus, it helps in a scientific reconstruction of the entire plant kingdom. With this end in view, various attempts have been made from the times of the earliest Indian and Greek savants like **Charak**, **Sushrut**, **Plato**, **Aristotle**, **Pliny**, and **Dioscorides**. These sages were, however, concerned more with philosophy than with nature. **Theophrastus** (370-285 B.C.), a disciple of Aristotle, is regarded as the father of Botany. Though he made an attempt to a more intelligent approach to the groupings of plants, yet he could not tide over the influence of philosophy of his teacher.

The aim and object of Taxonomy, as already stated, is, apart from naming and describing the plants, to arrange them in such a way as to indicate as far as possible their probable line of descent. The numerous **systems** that have been devised for this purpose do not, however, conform to this view. For, while some systems readily enable us to ascertain their names, others not only fulfil it, but at the same time give us an idea as to their relationships. Based on this, the different systems have been broadly divided under two heads, namely, **artificial** and **natural**, the former enabling us to ascertain the names only, while the latter fulfil all the conditions, which come within the scope of Systematic Botany. The artificial system places together in a group those plants that resemble one another mainly in *one* prominent character (*i.e.*, sex character), while the natural system places together in a group those plants that *resemble one another in a number of prominent characters indicating a close relationship amongst them.* Furthermore, in the artificial systems closely allied plants are widely separated and placed in different groups, because of the absence of one particular character, while plants, which have no relation to one another, are brought together under the same group, because of the presence of that character alone.

The ultimate object of Systematic Botany should be the development of a natural system, which would aim to arrange plants in such a way as to give us an idea of the sequence of evolution in the Plant kingdom. It should naturally start with forms which are simple and are, therefore, regarded as primitive, and gradually advance to higher and more complex forms till the highest group of plants is attained. Such a system is called **phylogenetic**. The systematist tries to make his system phylogenetically true as far as possible. A perfectly phylogenetic system is, therefore, an ideal system, but so far it is far from being achieved. The reason of this lies in the fact that the assumptions on which such a system is to be based are theoretical, and the data that have so far been available are very imperfect. But this can only be remedied as our knowledge of plants inhabiting the different parts of the globe becomes more and more extended.

The credit of the present-day form of Systematic Botany must go to the herbalists of the sixteenth and seventeenth centuries, like **Otto Brunfels** (1464—1534), **Jerome Bock** (1498—1554), **Leonhard Fuchs** (1501—1566), **Mattias de L'Obel** (1538—1616), **John Gerard** (1545—1612), and **Charles L'Ecluse** (1526—1609).

Andrea Cesalpino (1519—1603) is usually regarded as the first plant taxonomist. He classified plants first on the basis of habit, and secondarily on the characters of fruits and seeds. In this connection of the systems of classification based on the habits

Fig. 498. Andrea Cesalpino.

Fig. 499. Gaspard Bauhin.

of plants, mentions must be made of the names of **Jean (Johna) Bauhin** (1541—1631), **Joseph Pitton de Tournefort** (1656—1708), the father of the modern concept of genera, and **Gaspard (Casper** or **Kaspar) Bauhin** (1560—1624), brother of Jean Bauhin. It is of interest to note that in the works of Gaspard Bauhin the plants were frequently referred to with a binary nomenclature, thus distinguishing between genera and species.

John Ray (1628—1705), an English philosopher and naturalist, propounded a system of plant classification. In this

Fig. 500. John Ray.

system he gave much importance to the habits of plants no doubt, yet laid the first foundation of the natural system. In his *Historia plantarum* (1686—1704), Ray classified about 18,000 species of plants under two major divisions, namely, **Herbae**, (herbs) and **Arbores** (trees). He subdivided the Herbae into **Imperfectae** and **Perfectae**. The Perfectae and the Arbores were further divided into **Dicotyledons** and **Monocotyledons**. Ray was the first to recognize positively the two taxa of monocotyledonous and dicotyledonous plants, basing on the presence of either one or two cotyledons in the embryo.

About thirty years later **Carolus Linnaeus** or **Carl Linne** (1707—1778), a Swedish naturalist, regarded as the father of taxonomy, brought out his system known as the **Sexual system** in his *Systema Naturae* (1735).

Fig. 501. Carolus Linnaeus.

The Classes and Orders in this system are based exclusively upon the sporophylls (stamens and carpels of higher plants), which were considered to be the sexual organs of the plant. Hence, the Linnaean system is also known as the **Sexual system**. Linnaeus divided plants primarily into 24 **Classes**, (one of which is *Cryptogamia*), according to the number, nature and distribution of their stamens. Thus, plants with one stamen are placed in the Class *Monandria*, those with two stamens in the Class *Diandria*, those with three in the Class *Triandria*, and so on. The Classes were again subdivided into smaller groups or **Orders**, according to the number and condition of their carpels, styles or stigmas, or according to the number and condition of stamens which have not been used as the basis of classes, or according to the nature of flowers or fruits. Thus, plants with one carpel were placed in the Order *Monogynia*, those with two carpels in the Order *Digynia*, those with three in the Order *Trigynia*, and so on.

A detailed scheme of the Linnaean system of classification is given below :

Classes		Orders
I. **Monandria** (stamen one)	..	Monogynia
II. **Diandria** (stamens two)	..	Monogynia Trigynia
III. **Triandria** (stamens three)	..	Monogynia Digynia Trigynia
IV. **Tetrandria** (stamens four)	..	Monogynia Digynia Tetragynia
V. **Pentandria** (stamens five)	..	Monogynia Digynia Trigynia Pentagynia
VI. **Hexandria** (stamens six)	..	Monogynia Digynia Trigynia Hexagynia
VII. **Heptandria** (stamens seven)	..	Monogynia
VIII. **Octandria** (stamens eight)	..	Monogynia Trigynia Tetragynia
IX. **Enneandria** (stamens nine)	..	Monogynia Hexagynia
X. **Decandria** (stamens ten)	..	Monogynia Digynia Trigynia Pentagynia Polygynia
XI. **Dodecandria** (stamens twelve)	..	Monogynia Trigynia
XII. **Icosandria** (stamens more than twelve, attached to the calyx)	..	Monogynia Digynia Pentagynia Polygynia
XIII. **Polyandria** (stamens more than twelve, attached to the receptacle)		Monogynia Tetragynia Pentagynia Polygynia

Classes	*Orders*
XIV. **Didynamia** (stamens didynamous) ..	Gymnospermia Angiospermia
XV. **Tetradynamia** (stamens tetradynamous)	Siliculosa Siliquosa
XVI. **Monadelphia** (stamens in one bundle)	Pentandria Hexandria Decandria Dodecandria Polyandria
XVII. **Diadelphia** (stamens in two bundles)	Triandria Hexandria Octandria Decandria
XVIII. **Polyadelphia** (stamens in several bundles)	Icosandria Polyandria
XIX. **Syngenesia** (stamens with united anthers)	Aequalis Superflua Frustranea Segregata
XX. **Gynandria** (stamens adnate to the pistils)	Monandria Hexandria
XXI. **Monoecia** (plants monoecious)	Monandria Diandria Triandria Tetrandria Pentandria Hexandria Polyandria Monadelphia Syngenesia Gynandria
XXII. **Dioecia** (plants dioecious) ..	Monandria Diandria Triandria Tetrandria Pentandria Hexandria Enneandria Decandria Icosandria Polyandria Monadelphia

	Classes		*Orders*
XXIII.	**Polygamia** (plants polygamous)	..	Monoecia Dioecia Trioecia
XXIV.	**Cryptogamia** (flowers concealed)	..	Miscellanea Filices

The special merit of the Linnaean system lies in the fact that it is an excellent example of the limitation of the artificial system. Here we depend for the groupings on characters derived from one set of organs instead of considering the aggregate of characters as we should do in a natural system. It is just like a dictionary where the words arranged alphabetically have no relationship to one another, or like a library where the books are placed side by side purely depending upon the subject matter, so that any word in the dictionary or any book in the library can be readily referred to. It is to Linnaeus that we owe the foundation of a true binomial system of nomenclature, though many plants had been known by a binomial title long before Linnaeus' time. Linnaeus made binomial nomenclature a fixed rule, and his careful study of the whole plant world and the indication and definition of genera and species were perhaps the most important contributions ever made to Systematic Botany.

The system of Linnaeus gained a wider circulation due to the efforts of some of his students like **Pehr (Peter) Kalm** (1716—1779), **Frederick Hosselquist** (1722—1752), and **Carl Peter Thunberg** (1743—1828).

It was actually in France that the first seed for a natural system of classification was sown. **Bernard de Jussieu** (1699—1776), Professor and Demonstrator of Botany at the Royal Garden of La Trianon, Versailles, modified the system of Linnaeus to a great extent, but never published his work. Later on, his nephew **Antoine Laurent de Jussieu** (1748—1836) made some improvement over his uncle's system and published the same in his *Genera Plantarum secundum Ordines naturales disposita.* The Orders or Families (which he termed as 'Ordines naturales') in his system numbered one hundred, all of which are practically still recognized. They were arranged in fifteen Classes, of which Class I was termed the **Acotyledons**, which contained algae, fungi, hepaticae, musci, filices and an Order Naiades including large number of aquatic flowering plants having no affinities. Classes II, III and IV belonged to the **Monocotyledons,** while the rest were all included under the **Dicotyledons**. In his system Jussieu adopted the distinction between Monocotyledons and Dicotyledons, as suggested by Ray, but at the same time regarded the Acotyledons (equivalent to the present-day Cryptogams) as a Class of the same status or rank with either of the Classes of seed plants.

Fig. 502. Antoine de Jussieu.

Another great pioneer in the field of the system of plant classification was **Augustus Pyrame de Candolle** (1778—1841). While working as the Professor of Botany at Montpellier, he published his epoch-making book *Theorie elementaire de la botanique* in 1813, in which he suggested that morphology of plants and not their physiology must be considered as the primary basis of classification. It is, however, a very interesting as well as strange fact that in presenting his system he selected an anatomical character, namely, the presence or absence of vessels which were, according to him, organs of prime importance in nutrition). On the basis of this, he classified plants broadly into two main groups, **Vascular plants** or plants with cotyledons and **Cellular plants** or plants without cotyledons. The former group was again divided into **Exogens** or Dicotyledons and **Endogens** or Monocotyledons, which differed not only in the number of cotyledon or cotyledons in the embryo, but also were supposed to differ in the mode of growth in thickness.

Fig. 503. A. P. de Candolle.

Robert Brown (1773—1858), an English botanist, published his work entitled *Botanicorum facile princeps*, wherein he did not suggest any new system of classification but classified some intricate and difficult points of floral morphology as well as problems on the unknown or doubtful affinities of some families.

Fig. 504. Robert Brown.

During the period of twenty years extending from 1825—1845 about two dozens of different systems of plant classification were proposed by various workers like **Brongniart** (1770—1847), **John Lindley** (1799—1865) and **Endlicher** (1805—1849).

Almost all the systems of classification up to 1850 were mainly concerned with the asexual plants (Cryptogams). This was rather an unsatisfactory state of affairs. It was **Hofmeister,** who in 1851 explained clearly the phenomenon of alternation of generations, and thus the relationships of the flowerless plants amongst themselves as well as to the flowering plants were brought into light. Hofmeister's theory, in fact, suggested the key to the establishment of a natural system.

Fig. 505. Sir Joseph Dalton Hooker.

Of all the natural systems announced so far, Bentham and Hooker's system had gained the maximum popularity. **George Bentham** (1800—1884) and **Joseph Dalton Hooker** (1817—1911), two Englishmen, jointly produced the monumentous work *Genera plantarum* (1862—1883) in which all the genera of seed plants, known up to that time, were described and classified according to a definite system. It is of interest to note that the pattern of the system of Bentham and Hooker is based mainly on that of de Candolle.

Bentham and Hooker divided plants into two great **Subkingdoms**—*Cryptogamia* and *Phanerogamia*. The latter subkingdom was divided into two **Divisions**—*Gymnospermia* and *Angiospermia*. The Angiospermia were divided into two **Classes**—*Dicotyledons* and *Monocotyledons*. The Dicotyledons were divided into three **Subclasses**—*Polypetalae*, *Gamopetalae* and *Monochlamydeae*. Polypetalae were divided into three **Series**—*Thalamiflorae*, *Disciflorae* and *Calyciflorae*, and the Gamopetalae into three Series—*Inferae*, *Heteromerae* and *Bicarpellatae*. The Monochlamydeae were divided into eight Series, and the Monocotyledons into seven Series. The Series were next divided into **Cohorts**, Cohorts into **Orders**, Orders into **Genera**, and finally each Genus into **Species**. The *Gymnospermia* were placed in between Dicotyledons and Monocotyledons. There are altogether 202 Orders, the Dicotyledons beginning with *Ranunculaceae* and ending in *Labiatae*. while the Monocotyledons beginning with *Hydrocharideae* and ending in *Gramineae*.

Subkingdom I. Cryptogamia (*kryptos*=hidden ; *gamos*=marriage) or "flowerless plants", are those plants which have no evident flowers with stamens or pistils, and reproduce by spores or spore-like bodies which are usually unicellular and never contain anything like an embryo. The Cryptogamia have been divided into Thallophyta, Bryophyta and Pteridophyta.

Subkingdom II. Phanerogamia (*phaneros*=evident ; *gamos*=marriage) or "flowering plants", are those plants which produce evident flowers with stamens or pistils or both, and usually with a perianth. They usually reproduce by seeds which are complex multicellular bodies and usually contain an embryo. Hence, they are also known as "seed-plants" or **Spermatophytes**.

Division 1. Gymnospermia (*gymnos*=naked ; *sperma*=a seed) or "naked-seeded" plants, are those plants in which the carpellary leaves do not unite to form an ovary and the seeds are, therefore, exposed. The pollen grains fall directly upon the micropyle of the ovule. True vessels and perianth are absent (except in Gnetales).

Division 2. Angiospermia (*angeion*=a vessel ; *sperma*=a seed) or "closed-seeded" plants, are those in which the carpellary leaves unite by their margins to form an ovary with styles and stigmas, so that the seeds lie within a chamber. Pollen grains fall directly on the stigma. True vessels are present. They include the largest majority of existing flowering plants.

Class I. Dicotyledons—These plants bear two cotyledons in their embryo ; the radicle on germination produces a tap-root ; leaves with reticulate venation ; flowers usually pentamerous. Vascular bundles of the stem open and arranged in a ring, and those of the root di-, tri- or tetra-arch.

Class II. Monocotyledons—These plants bear only one cotyledon in their embryo ; the radicle on germination produces a number of adventitious roots ; leaves with parallel venation and sheathing bases ; flowers usually trimerous. Vascular bundles of the stem closed and scattered irregularly, and those of root polyarch.

A tubular classification of the Dicotyledons and the Monocotyledons is given below :

Dicotyledons

SUBCLASS. 1. POLYEPETALAE

Series i. THALAMIFLORAE. Petals and stamens hypogynous.

Cohort 1. *Ranales.* Natural Orders : *1, Ranunculaceae ; 2, Dilleniaceae ; 3, Calycanthaceae ; *4, Magnoliaceae ; *5, Anonaceae ; 6, Menispermaceae ; 7, Berberideae ; *8, Nymphaeaceae.

" 2. *Parietales.* Natural Orders : 1, Sarraceniaceae ; *2, Papaveraceae ; *3, Cruciferae ; *4, Capparideae ; *5, Resedaceae ; 6. Cistineae ; 7, Violarieae ; 8, Canellaceae ; 9, Bixineae.

" 3. *Polygalineae.* Natural Orders : 1, Pittosporeae ; 2, Tremandreae ; 3, Polygaleae ; 4, Vochysiaceae.

" 4. *Caryophyllinae,* Natural Orders : 1, Frankeniaceae ; *2, Caryophylleae ; *3, Portulacaceae ; 4, Tamariscineae.

" 5. *Guttiferales.* Natural Orders : 1, Elatineae ; 2, Hypericineae ; *3, Guttiferae ; 4, Ternstroemiaceae ; *5. Dipterocarpeae ; 6, Chlaenaceae.

" 6. *Malvales.* Natural Orders : *1, Malvaceae ; *2. Sterculiaceae ; *3, Tiliaceae.

Series ii, DISCIFLORAE, Stamens usually definite, inserted upon or inside or outside of a development of the floral axis which forms a ring or cushion at the base of the ovary, or is broken up into glands. Ovary superior.

Cohort 7. *Geraniales.* Natural Orders : 1, Lineae ; 2, Humiriaceae ; 3, Malpighiaceae ; 4, Zygophylleae ; *5, Geraniaceae ; *6, Rutaceae ;

*Natural Orders or Families marked with an asterisk are treated in this book.

7, Simarubeae ; 8, Ochnaceae ; 9, Burseraceae ; *10, Meliaceae ; 11, Chailletiaceae.

Cohort 8. *Olacales,* Natural Orders : 1, Olacineae ; 2, Ilicineae ; 3, Cyrilleae.

„ 9. *Celastrales,* Natural Orders : 1, Celastrineae ; 2, Stackhousieae ; *3, Rhamneae ; *4, Ampelideae.

„ 10. *Sapindales,* Natural Orders : *1, Sapindaceae ; 2, Sabiaceae ; 3, Anacardiaceae.

Ordines anomali : 1, Coriarieae ; 2, Moringeae.

Series iii. CALYCIFLORAE, Petals and stamens perigynous. Ovary often more or less enclosed by the development of the floral axis, sometimes inferior.

Cohort 11. *Rosales,* Natural Orders : 1, Connaraceae ; *2, Leguminosae ; *3, Rosaceae ; 4, Saxifrageae ; *5, Crassulaceae ; 6, Droseraceae ; 7, Hamamelideae ; 8, Bruniaceae ; 9, Halorageae.

„ 12. *Myrtales,* Natural Orders : *1, Rhizophoreae ; *2, Combretaceae ; *3, Myrtaceae ; *4, Melastomaceae ; *5, Lythraceae ; *6, Onagraceae.

„ 13. *Passiflorales.* Natural Orders : 1, Samydaceae ; 2, Loaseae ; 3, Turneraceae ; *4, Passifloreae ; *5, Cucurbitaceae ; 6, Begoniaceae ; 7, Datisceae.

„ 14. *Ficoidales,* Natural Orders : *1, Cacteae ; 2, Ficoideae.

„ 15. *Umbellales.* Orders : *1, Umbelliferae ; 2, Araliaceae ; 3, Cornaceae.

SUBCLASS 2. GAMOPETALAE

Series i. INFERAE. Ovary inferior. Stamens as many as the corolla-lobes, rarely fewer.

Cohort 1. *Rubiales.* Natural Orders : 1, Caprifoliaceae ; *2, Rubiaceae.

„ 2. *Asterales.* Natural Orders : 1, Valerianeae ; 2, Dipsaceae ; 3, Calycereae ; *4, Compositae.

„ 3. *Campanales.* Natural Orders : 1, Stylideae ; 2, Goodenoviae ; 3, Campanulaceae.

Series ii. HETEROMERAE. Ovary generally superior. Stamens as many as the corolla-lobes, or more ; epipetalous or free from the corolla. Carpels more than two.

Cohort 4. *Ericales.* Natural Orders ; 1, Ericaceae ; 2, Vaccinieae ; 3, Monotropeae ; 4, Epacrideae ; 5, Diapensiaceae ; 6, Lennoaceae.

„ 5. *Primulates.* Natural Orders : 1, Plumbagineae ; 2, Primulaceae ; 3, Myrsineae.

„ 6. *Ebenales.* Natural Orders : *1, Sapotaceae ; 2, Ebenaceae ; 3, Styraceae.

Series iii. BICARPELLATAE. Ovary generally superior, Stamens alternate with the corolla-lobes and equal in number or fewer. Carpels usually two.

Cohort 7. *Gentianales.* Natural Orders : *1, Oleaceae ; 2, Salvadoraceae ; *3, Apocynaceae ; *4, Asclepiadaceae ; 5, Loganiaceae ; 6, Gentianaceae.

Cohort 8. *Polemoniales.* Natural Orders : 1, Polemoniaceae ; 2, Hydrophyllaceae ; *3, Boragineae ; *4, Convolvulaceae ; *5, Solanaceae.

„ 9. *Personales.* Natural Orders : *1, Scrophularineae ; 2, Orobanchaceae ; *3, Lentibulariaceae ; 4, Columelliaceae ; *5, Gesneraceae ; *6, Bignoniaceae ; *7, Pedalineae ; *8, Acanthaceae.

„ 10. *Lamiales.* Natural Orders : 1, Myoporineae ; 2, Selagineae ; *3, Verbenaceae ; *4, Labiatae.

Ordo amomalus : Plantagineae.

SUBCLASS 3. MONOCHLAMYDEAE

Series i. CURVEMBRYEAE. Embryo curved round the generally mealy albumen. Ovules generally solitary, Flowers usually hermaphrodite. Stamens equal in number to or fewer than the perianth segments.

Natural Orders : *1, Nyctagineae ; 2, Illecebraceae ; *3, Amarantaceae ; *4, Chenopodiaceae ; 5, Phytolacaceae ; 6, Batideae ; *7, Polygonaceae.

Series ii. MULTIOVULATAE AQUATICAE, Submerged herbs. Ovary syncarpous. Ovules numerous.

Natural Order : 8, Podostemaceae,

Series iii. MULTIOVULATAE TERRESTRES. Terrestrial herbs or shrubs, Ovary syncarpous. Ovules numerous,

Natural Orders : 9, Nepenthaceae ; 10, Cytinaceae ; 11, Aristolochiaceae.

Series iv. MICREMBRYEAE. Embryo very small in a copious albumen, Ovary syncarpous or apocarpous. Ovules usually solitary.

Natural Orders : *12, Piperaceae ; 13, Chloranthaceae ; 14, Myristicaceae ; 15, Monimiaceae.

Series v. DAPHNALES, Ovary usually monocarpellary, Ovules solitary or in pairs. Generally trees or shrubs with hermaphrodite flowers. Perianth sepaloid in one or two series.

Natural Orders : *16, Laurineae ; 17, Proteaceae ; 18, Thymeleaceae ; 19, Penaceae ; 20, Elaeagnaceae.

Series vi. ACHLAMYDOSPOREAE. Ovary unilocular ; 1-3- ovuled, Seeds devoid of testa. Albumen naked. Perianth sepaloid or petaloid.

Natural Orders : *21, Loranthaceae ; *22, Santalaceae ; 23, Balanophoreae.

Series vii. UNISEXUALES. Flowers unisexual, Ovary syncarpous or monocarpellary. Ovules solitary or in pairs. Seeds albuminous or exalbuminous. Perianth sometimes absent.

Natural Orders : *24, Euphorbiaceae ; 25, Balanopseae ; *26, Urticaceae ; 27, Platanaceae ; 28, Leitneriaceae ; 29. Juglandeae ; 30, Myricaceae ; *31, Casuarineae ; 32, Cupuliferae.

Series viii. ORDINES ANOMALI. Near the last Series but not closely allied to any other Order. Flowers often unisexual.

Natural Orders : *33, Salicineae ; 34, Lacistemaceae ; 35, Empetraceae ; 36, Ceratophylleae.

Gymnospermae

Natural Orders : *1, Gnetaceae ; *2, Coniferae ; *3, Cycadaceae.

Monocotyledons

Series i. MICROSPERMAE, At least the inner perianth petaloid, Ovary inferior, generally unilocular with three parietal placentae. Seeds very small, numerous and exalbuminous.

Natural Orders : *1, Hydrocharideae ; 2, Burmanniaceae ; *3, Orchidaceae.

Series ii. EPIGYNAE. At least the inner perianth petaloid, Ovary with a few exceptions inferior. Albumen copious,

Natural Orders : *4, Scitamineae ; 5, Bromeliaceae ; 6, Haemodraceae ; 7, Irideae ; *8, Amaryllideae ; 9, Taccaceae ; 10, Dioscoreaceae.

Series iii, CORONARIEAE. At least the inner perianth petaloid, Ovary free, Albumen copious.

Natural Orders : 11, Roxburghiaceae ; *12, Liliaceae ; *13, Pontederiaceae ; 14, Philydraceae ; 15, Xyrideae ; 16, Mayaceae ; *17, Commelinaceae ; 18, Rapataceae.

Series iv. CALYCINAE. Perianth small, sepaloid, somewhat stiff or herbaceous. Ovary free. Albumen copious,

Natural Orders : 19, Flagellarieae ; 20, Juncaceae ; *21, Palmae.

Series v. NUDIFLORAE, Perianth 0 or reduced to scales or setae. Ovary superior, carpels solitary or, if many, syncarpous, 1—many-ovuled. Seeds usually albuminous.

Natural Orders : *22, Pandaneae ; 23, Cyclanthaceae ; *24, Typhaceae ; *25, Aroideae ; *26, Lemnaceae.

Series vi. APOCARPEAE, Perianth in 1 or 2 series or 0, Ovary superior, Carpels solitary or free. Seeds exalbuminous.

Natural Orders : 27, Triurideae ; *28, Alismaceae ; 29, Naiadaceae.

Series vii. GLUMACEAE. Flowers in heads or spikelets, subtended by generally imbricated bracts. Perianth small, scale-like, or glumaceous, or 0. Ovary 1-ovuled or divided into 1-ovuled loculi, Seeds albuminous.

Natural Orders : 30, Friocauleae ; 31, Centrolepideae ; 32, Restiaceae ; *33, Cyperaceae ; *34, Gramineae.

Merits and Demerits

Merits :

1. It is a great natural system, perhaps the first of its kind.
2. It is very suitable for all practical purposes.
3. Beginning of Polypetalae with Ranales, composed of the well-known Ranunculaceae and its allies,
4. Monocotyledons are derived from Dicotyledons.

Demerits :

1. The classification is based mainly on single and mostly artificial characters. Hence, closely related orders are often widely separated,

2. It is not phylogenetic.

3. Monochlamydeae are grouped apart from Polypetalae.

4. Some orders with simple flowers have close relationship with some orders with well-developed floral configuration, hence, they should be placed nearer in a natural system of classification. For example, Chenopodiaceae should be brought nearer to Caryophyllaceae.

5. In the classification of Monocotyledons, Sci'amineae and Orchideceae are placed at the very beginning, but these cannot be regarded as primitive with so many advanced charac ers.

6. In the subdivision of Monocotyledons, stress has been laid on the relative position of ovary and the character of the perianth. Thus, Irideae and Amaryllideae are more nearly related to Liliaceae than to Scitamineae or Bromeliaceae with which they are associated on account of the epigynous character. Juncaceae, which is associated with Palmae, should be placed close to Liliaceae. Hydrocharideae, though wi h an inferior ovary, should be placed close to aquatic orders with non-endospermic seed.

7. The authors are silent about the phylogeny of Dicotyledons and Monocotyledons and the anomalous position of Gymnosperms.

The publication of the theories of Organic evolution by **Darwin** and by **Wallace** brought an end to the period of classification of plants based on their forms and relationships, and new systems based on the phylogenetic relationships of plants began to see the light of the day. **Julius von Sachs** (1832—1897), Professor of Botany at Wurzburg, was one of the pioneers to give up de Candollean idea of classification and substituted it by a new system in 1868. But his theory was never widely accepted.

By accepting the concept of evolution, **August Wilhelm Eichler** (1839—1887), another renowned German botanist, proposed a system of classification in 1875, and later on elaborated his own work in 1883. In the light of present-day idea of phylogeny, Eichler's system was not a truly phylogenetic one, but still it gained a wide-spread acceptance.

The best-known development of a phylogenetic system is that by **Adolf Engler** (1844—1930), Professor of Botany in the University of Berlin. He published a system of classification in 1892, mainly based on that of Eichler, in *Syllabus der Vorlesungen*, meant to be used as a guide to the plants growing in the Breslau Botanic Garden. During the years 1887—1899 Engler and his associate **Prantl** brought out a monographic work, entitled *Die naturlichen Pflanzenfamilien*, in which all the known genera of plants from the algae to the seed plants were recorded, and keys to their identification were given. Later on in 1924, Engler in collaboration with **Gilg** (**and** afterwards with **Diels**) published the single-volume work *Syllabus der Pflanzenfamilien*. This work has been published in several editions, the latest or the eleventh one, of which came out in 1936.

Fig. 506. Adolf Engler.

Engler's system has been very widely used, especially on the continents of Europe and America. He divided the Plant Kingdom into 13 **Divisions**. In this system the seed-bearing plants (Spermatophyta) are designated as *Embryophyta siphonogama* and are divided into two **Subdivisions**—*Gymnospermae* and *Angiospermae* and the Angiospermae into two **Classes**—*Monocotyledonae* and *Dicotyledonae*. The former is divided into 11 **Orders,** while the latter into two **Subclasses**—*Archichlamydeae* (or lower Dicotyledons) and *Metachlamydeae* or *Sympetalae* (or higher Dicotyledons) and *Metachlamydeae* or *Sympetalae* (or higher Dicotyledons). The former contains 33 Orders and the latter 11 Orders. The Orders are further divided into **Suborders, Families**, and **Genera**. This system is based on the assumption that in flowering plants the absence of a perianth is a primitive character. Thus, the woody plants with unisexual apetalous flowers borne in aments (willows birches, oaks, etc., often called Amentiferae) are treated as among the most primitive Dicotyledons. Monocotyledons begin with *Typhaceae* and end in *Orchidaceae*, while the Dicotyledons begin with *Casuarinaceae* and end in *Compositae*.

The chief differences between this system and that of Bentham and Hooker are the amalgamation of Polypetalae and Monochlamydeae under one single group Archichalmydeae, and the Monocotyledons taking precedence over the Dicotyledons. The groups of the Families of Angiosperms have been arranged in ascending series according to the increasing complexity of the flower, as indicated specially by the character of floral envelope.

The term 'Natural Order' has been replaced by the term 'Family' and the 'Class or Series' by the term 'Order'.

A tabular view of Engler's system of classification is given below :

Divisions

I. **Schizophyta—**
   1. Class Schizomycetes
   2. „ Schizophyceae.

II. **Myxothallophyta, Myxomycetes,** etc.

III. **Flagellatae**

IV. **Dinoflagellatae**
   ? **Silicoflagellatae**

V. **Bacillariophyta**

VI. **Conjugatae**

VII. **Chlorophyceae**
   1. Class Protococcales
   2. „ Ulotrichales
   3. „ Siphonocladales
   4. „ Siphonales

VIII. **Charophyta**

IX. **Phaeophyceae**

X. **Rhodophyceae**
   1. Class Bangiales
   2. „ Florideae

XI. **Eumycetes**
   1. Class Phycomycetes
   2. „ Ascomycetes
   3. „ Protomycetes
   4. „ Basidiomycetes

Divisions

XII. **Embryophyta asiphonogama** (Archegoniatae)

A. Subdivision Bryophyta
   1. Class Hepaticae
   2. „ Musci

B. Subdivision Pteridophyta
   1. Class Filicales
   2. „ Sphenophyllales
   3. „ Equisetales
   4. „ Lycopodiales
   5. „ Psilotales
   6. „ Isoetales

XIII. **Embryophyta Siphonogama**

A. Subdivision Gymnospermae
   1. Class Cycadofilicales
   2. „ Cycadales
   3. „ Bennetti'ales
   4. „ Ginkgoales
   5. „ Coniferae
   6. „ Cordaitales
   7. „ Gnetales

B. Subdivision Angiospermae
   1. Class Monocotyledoneae
   2. „ Dicotyledoneae
   1. Subclass Archichlamydeae
   2. „ Metachlamydeae (Sympetalae)

The classes Monocotyledoneae and Dicotyledoneae are described in detail below :

Monocotyledoneae

Order 1. PANDANALES

Fam : *Typhaceae, *Pandanaceae, Sparganiaceae.

„ 2. HELOBIAE

Potamogetonineae

Fam : Potamogetonaceae, Najadaceae, Aponogetonaceae, Scheuchzeriaceae.

Alismatineae

Fam : *Alismataceae.

Butomineae

Fam : Butomaceae, *Hydrocharitaceae.

Order 3. TRIURIDALES

Fam : Triuridaceae.

„ 4. GLUMIFLORAE

Fam : *Gramineae, *Cyperaceae.

„ 5. PRINCIPES

Fam : *Palmae.

„ 6. SYNANTHAE

Fam : Cyclanthaceae.

„ 7. SPATHIFLORAE

Fam : *Araceae, *Lemnaceae

„ 8. FARINOSAE

Flagellariineae

Fam : Flagellariaceae.

Enantoblastae

Fam : Restionaceae, Centrolepidaceae, Mayacaceae, Xyridaceae, Eriocaulaceae.

Bromelineae

Fam : Thurniaceae, Rapatiaceae, Bromeliaceae.

Commelinineae

Fam : *Commelinaceae.

Pontederineae

Fam : *Pontederiaceae, Cyanastraceae.

Philydrineae

Fam : Philydraceae.

„ 9. LILIIFLORAE

Juncineae

Fam : Juncaceae.

Lilineae

Fam : Stemonaceae, *Liliaceae, Haemodoraceae, Amaryllidaceae, Velloziaceae, Taccaceae, Dioscoreaceae.

Iridineae

Fam : Iridaceae.

„ *10. SCITAMINEAE

Fam : Musaceae, Zingiberaceae, Cannaceae, Marantaceae.

„ 11. MICROSPERMAE

Burmanniineae

Fam : Burmanniaceae.

Gynandrae

Fam : *Orchidaceae.

Dicotyledoneae

SUBCLASS ARCHICHLAMYDEAE (**Choripetalae** and **Apetalae**)

Order 1. VERTICILATAE
Fam : *Casuarinaceae.

„ 2. PIPERALES
Fam : Saururaceae, *Piperaceae, Chloranthaceae.

„ 3. HYDROSTACHYALES
Fam : Hydrostachyaceae.

„ 4. SALICALES
Fam : *Salicaceae.

„ 5. GARRYALES
Fam : Garryaceae.

„ 6. MYRICALES
Fam : Myricaceae.

„ 7. BALANOPSIDALES
Fam : Balanopsidaceae.

„ 8. LEITNERIALES
Fam : Leitneriaceae.

„ 9. JUGLANDALES
Fam : Juglandaceae.

„ 10. JULIANIALES
Fam : Julianiaceae.

„ 11. BATIDALES
Fam : Batidaceae.

„ 12. FAGALES
Fam : Betulaceae, Fagaceae.

„ 13. URTICALES
Fam : Ulmaceae, *Moraceae, *Urticaceae.

„ 14. PODOSTEMONALES
Fam : Podostemonaceae.

„ 15. PROTEALES
Fam : Proteaceae.

„ 16. SANTALALES
Santalineae
Fam : Olacaceae, Opiliaceae, Octoknemataceae, Grubbiaceae, *Santalaceae, Mezodendraceae.
Laranthineae
Fam : *Loranthaceae.

„ 17. ARISTOLOCHIALES
Fam : Aristolochiaceae, Rafflesiaceae, Hydnoraceae.

„ 18. BALANOPHORALES
Fam : Balanophoraceae.

„ 19. POLYGONALES
Fam : *Polygonaceae.

„ 20. CENTROSPERMAE
Chenopodiineae
Fam : *Chenopodiaceae, *Amaranthaceae.
Phytolaccineae
Fam : *Nyctaginaceae, Phytolaccaceae, Gyrostemonaceae, Achatocarpaceae, Aizoaceae.

Portulacineae

Fam : *Portulacaceae, *Basellaceae.

Caryophyllineae

Fam : *Caryophyllaceae.

Order 21. RANALES

Nymphaeineae

Fam : *Nymphaeaceae, Ceratophyllaceae.

Trochodendrineae

Fam : Trochodendraceae, Cercidiphyllaceae.

Ranunculineae

Fam : *Ranunculaceae, Lardizabalaceae, Berberidaceae, Menispermaceae.

Magnoliineae

Fam : *Magnoliaceae, Himantandraceae, Calycanthaceae, Lactoridaceae, *Anonaceae, Eupomatiaceae, Myristicaceae, Gomortegaceae, Monimiaceae, *Lauraceae, Hernandiaceae.

22. RHOEADALES

Rhoeadineae

Fam : *Papaveraceae.

Capparidineae

Fam : *Capparidaceae, *Cruciferae, Tovariaceae.

Resedineae

Fam : Resedaceae.

Moringineae

Fam : Moringaceae.

Bretschneiderineae

Fam : Bretsohneideraceae.

23. SARRACENIALES

Fam : Sarraceniaceae, Nepenthaceae, Droseraceae.

" 24. ROSALES

Podostemonineae

Fam : Podostemonaceae, Hydrostachyaceae.

Saxifragineae

Fam : *Crassulaceae, Cephalotaceae, Saxifragaceae, Pittosporaceae, Byblidaceae, Brunelliaceae, Cunoniaceae, Myrothamnaceae, Bruniaceae, Hamamelidaceae, Roridulaceae, Eucommiaceae.

Rosineae

Fam : Platanaceae, Crossosomataceae, *Rosaceae, Connaraceae ; *Leguminosae.

" 25. PANDALES

Fam : Pandaceae.

" 26. GERANIALES

Geraniineae

Fam : Oxalidaceae, *Geraniaceae, Tropaeolaceae ; *Linaceae, Humiriaceae, Erythroxylaceae, Zygophyllaceae, Cneoraceae, *Rutaceae, Simarubaceae, Burseraceae, *Meliaceae, Akariaceae.

Malpighineae

Fam : Malpighiaceae, Trigoniaceae, Vochysiaceae.

Polygalineae

Fam : Tremandraceae, Polygalaceae.

Dichapetalineae

Fam : Dichapetalaceae.

Tricoccae

Fam : *Euphorbiaceae Daphniphyllaceae.

Callitrichaneae

Fam : Callitrichaceae.

Order 27, SAPINDALES

Buxineae

Fam : Buxaceae.

Empetrineae

Fam : Empetraceae

Coriarineae

Fam : Coriariaceae.

Limnanthineae

Fam : Limnanthaceae.

Anacardineae

Fam : *Anacardiaceae

Celasarineae

Fam : Cyrillaceae, Pentaphylacaceae, Corynocarpaceae, Aquifoliaceae, Celastraceae, Hippocrateaceae, Salvadoraceae, Stackhousiaceae, Staphyleaceae.

Icacinineae

Fam : Icacinaceae.

Sapindineae

Fam : Aextoxicaceae, Aceraceae, Hippocastanaceae, *Sapindaceae.

Sabineae

Fam : Sabiaceae.

Melianthineae

Fam : Melianthaceae.

Didiereineae

Fam : Didiereaceae.

Balsamininineae

Fam : Balsaminaceae.

,, 28. RHAMNALES

Fam : *Rhamnaceae, *Vitaceae.

,, 29. MALVALES

Elaeocarpineae

Fam : Elaeocarpaceae.

Chlaenineae

Fam : Chlaenaceae.

Malvineae

Fam : Gonystilaceae, *Tiliaceae, *Malvaceae, *Bombacaceae, *Sterculiaceae.

Scytopetalineae

Fam : Scytopetalaceae.

Order 30. PARIETALES

Theineae

Fam : Dilleniaceae, Actinidiaceae, Eucryphiaceae, **Medusagynaceae**, Ochnaceae, Strasburgeriaceae, Caryocaraceae, Maregraviaceae, Quiinaceae, Theaceae, ***Guttiferae**, ***Dipterocarpaceae.**

Tamaricineae

Fam : Elatinaceae, **Frankeniaceae, Tamaricaceae.**

Foquierineae

Fam : Foquieraceae.

Cistineae

Fam : Cistaceae, **Bixaceae.**

Cochlospermineae

Fam : Cochlospermaceae.

Flacourtineae

Fam : Winternaceae, Canellaceae, *Violaceae, **Flacourtiaceae**, Stachyuraceae, Turneraceae, Maleshorbiaceae, ***Passifloraceae**, Achariaceae.

Papayineae

Fam : Caricaceae.

Loasineae

Fam : Loasaceae,

Datiscineae

Fam : Datiscaceae.

Begoniineae

Fam : Begoniaceae.

Ancistrocladineae

Fam : Ancistrocladaceae.

„ 31. OPUNTIALES

Fam : *Cactaceae.

„ 32. MYRTIFLORAE

Thymelaeineae

Fam : Geissolomataceae, Penaceaceae, Oliniaceae, **Thymelaeaceae, Elaeagnaceae.**

Myreineae

Fam : *Lythraceae, Heteropyxidaceae, Sonneratiaceae, **Crypteroniaceae.** Punicaceae, Lecythidaceae, ***Rhizophoraceae, Nyssaceae, Alangiaceae, *Combretaceae, *Myrtaceae, *Melastomaceae, Hydrocaryaceae, Oenotheraceae, Haloragidaceae.**

Hippuridineae

Fam : Hippuridaceae, **Thelygonaceae.**

Cynomorineae

Fam : Cynomoriaceae.

Order 33. UMBELLIFLORAE
Fam : Araliaceae, *Umbelliferae, Cornaceae.

SUBCLASS METACHLAMYDEAE (**Sympetalae**)

Order 1. DIAPENSIALES
Fam : Diapensiaceae.

„ 2, ERICALES

Ericineae
Fam : Clethraceae, Pirolaceae, Lennoaceae, Ericaceae.

Epacridineae
Fam : Epacridaceae.

„ 3. PRIMULALES
Fam : Theophrastaceae, Myrsinaceae, Primulaceae.

„ 4. PLUMBAGINALES
Fam : Plumbaginaceae.

„ 5. EBENALES

Sapotineae
Fam : *Sapotaceae, Hoplestigmataceae.

Diospyrineae
Fam : Ebenaceae, Diclidantheraceae, Symplocaceae, Sytracaceae, Lissocarpaceae.

„ 6, CONTORTAE

Oleineae
Fam : *Oleaceae.

Gentianineae
Fam : Desfontaineacaceae, Loganiaceae, *Gentianaceae, *Apocynaceae, *Asclepiadaceae.

„ 7. TUBIFLORAE

Convolvulineae
Fam : *Convolvulaceae, Polemoniaceae, Fouquieraceae.

Lennoineae
Fam : Linnoaceae.

Boraginineae
Fam : Hydrophyllaceae, *Boraginaceae.

Verbenineae
Fam : *Verbenaceae, *Labiatae.

Solanineae
Fam : Nolanaceae, *Solanaceae, *Scrophulariaceae, *Bignoniaceae, *Pedaliaceae, Martyniaceae, Orobanchaceae, Gesneriaceae, Columelliaceae, *Lentibulariaceae, Globulariaceae.

Acanthineae
Fam : *Acanthaceae.

Myoporineae
Fam : Myoporaceae.

Phrymineae
Fam : Phrymaceae.

„ 8. PLANTAGINALES
Fam : Plantaginaceae.

Order 9. RUBIALES

Fam : *Rubiaceae, Caprifoliaceae, Adoxaceae, Valerianaceae, Dipsacaceae.

„ 10. CUCURBITALES

Fam : *Cucurbitaceae.

„ 11. CAMPANULATAE

Fam : Campanulaceae, Goodeniaceae, Brumoniaceae, Stylidiaceae, Calyceraceae, *Compositae,

Merits and Demerits

Merits :

1. The chief merit lies in the broad treatment of the entire Plant Kingdom, its excellent illustrations and its phylogenetic arrangement of many groups.
2. Amalgamation of Polypetalae and Monochlamydeae into Archichlamydeae.
3. Orchidaceae is placed at the end of the Monocotyledons and Compositae at the end of the Dicotyledons, since they are most highly evolved.
4. Juncaceae, Iridaceae and Amaryllidaceae are placed closer to Liliaceae.

Demerits :

1. The union of Choripetalae and Apetalae is an improvement over that of Bentham and Hooker's system, but in other respects not so—it is a far cry from a salix to a buttercup.
2. Amentiferae and Centrospermae are placed at the beginning of the Dicotyledons even before Ranales. The foliar nature of carpels is fatal to the primitiveness of Amentiferae. Centrospermae are highly specialized. Caryophyllaceae with two whorls of perianth, central placentation and syncarpous ovary can never precede Ranales.
3. Grouping of all sympetalous forms under one assemblage (Metachlamydeae) has led to Orders being distantly removed.
4. Monocotyledons are placed before the Dicotyledons. It is generally agreed that Monocotyledons have arisen from Dicotyledons by reduction.
5. Placing of Helobiae between two more advancd Orders, Pandanales and Glumiflorae.
6. Araceae is inserted a long way before the Liliaceae, from which it has been derived (*not vice versa*).
7. Recent works on the fossil records give little support to this system.

Richard von Wettstein (1862—1931), a German botanist, published his *Handbuch der systematischen Botanik* in 1901, in which he presented his ideas on the phylogenetic classification of plants. Though the basic structure of his system is somewhat like that of Engler's, yet in general his was a better phylogenetic classification than that suggested by Engler. But the system was never widely accepted.

Charles E. Bessey (1845—1915) of the University of Nebraska was the first American who made a significant contribution to a really phylogenetic classification of plants. He thoroughly rejected the ideas of Eichler and Engler, and based his system mainly on that of Bentham and Hooker, re-arranged and re-named in the majority of cases, basing on evolutionary principles. Bessey regarded the seed plants as polyphyletic in origin, which had developed along three independent lines. Of these, in his system of classification, he dealt with the *Anthophyta* (Angiosperms) only. He classified the Angiosperms into two main **Classes** — *Alternifoliae* (Monocotyledoneae) and *Oppositifoliae* (Dicotyledoneae). Each of these classes was subdivided into two **Subclasses**—*Strobiloideae* and *Cotyloideae*. These Subclasses under the Class Alternifoliae were again divided into several **Orders**, each consisting of a few to one **Family.** The Subclass under the Class Oppositifoliae, on the other hand, were first divided into some **Super Orders**, which, in their turn, were further subdivided into **Orders** and **Families**.

Fig. 507. Charles Edwin Bessey.

The system of **Alfred Baston Rendle** (1865—1938), late Keeper of the Department of Botany, British Museum of Natural History, London, was published in his book *Classification of Flowering plants*, Vols. I (1904) and II (1925).

This system follows in the main that of Engler with some deviations. The Archichlamydeae has been broken up into **Grades**, *Monochlamydeae* and *Dialypetalae*, but Sympetalae has been arranged under several **Orders**, and these have been distributed under the three grades mentioned above corresponding to the grades of differentiation of the floral structure.

The first Grade. Monochlamydeae, includes on the whole comparatively simple types of flowers which are either naked or have a monochlamydeous bract-like perianth. It includes 13 Orders and 31 Families.

In the second Grade, Dialypetalae, the Orders are arranged as far as possible in the ascending sequence. It is characterized by "a diminution in the number of members of each whorl, and in the higher groups, a tendency to their union, a whorled instead of a spiral arrangement of parts, a passage from hypogyny through perigyny to epigyny and a development of zygomorphic form from a regular flower". It includes 17 Orders and 95 Families.

The last Grade, Sympetalae, includes 11 Orders and 51 Families. It represents still higher grade of floral development and comprises, first, a pentacyclic group with typically two whorls of stamens ; secondly, a higher group with tetracyclic hypogynous flowers, and thirdly, a group with tetracyclic epigynous flowers in which the highest form of floral complexity is attained.

In the classification of Monocotyledons slight deviations from Engler are also noticeable. The arrangement, however, follows closely with that of Engler.

John Hutchinson (1884—) of the Royal Botanic Gardens, Kew, England, has proposed a new system of classification on strictly phylogenetic lines in his *The Families of Flowering Plants*. The first volume on Dicotyledons was published in 1926, and the second on Monocotyledons in 1934*. Its chief feature is the renewal of the ancient emphasis on the distinction between arborescent and herbaceous habits, in conjunction with other floral characters. Hutchinson opines that Ranales and Magnoliales form the starting point of the phylogenetic system, the former giving rise to other Orders that are mostly herbaceous, and the latter to those ones that are mostly woody, and from these branches each of the existing

Fig. 508. John Hutchinson.

* Recently a revised second edition of the book has been published in 1960.

families has been derived by specialization. In this system Hutchinson established that plants with sepals and petals are more phylogenetically ancient than those without them. His system is woven round the following criteria : (1) of the free and connate or adnate parts, the latter are the more recent ; (2) the spiral arrangement of parts is more primitive than the cyclic one ; (3) numerous, free stamens have evolved before the few and united ones, and (4) hermaphrodite flowers have come earlier than the unisexual ones. In this system resemblances are emphasized rather than differences. Hutchinson has distributed Monochlamydeae of Bentham and Hooker among Polypetalae, and at the same time has deemed them as more recent. The Monocotyledons have come later than Dicotyledons and they have a polyphyletic origin from Ranunculaceae and it's allies. He opines that Amentiferae are more evolved due to their united carpels, and the anemophilous pollination found therein cannot be regarded as a primitive one. On the whole, this re-arrangement of the Orders of Bentham and Hooker's system has been made on a phylogenetic basis. Hutchinson has classified the flowering plants into two **Phyla**—*Gymnospermae* and *Angiospermae*. Angiospermae have been divided into two **Subphyla**—*Dicotyledons* and *Monocotyledons*. The former have been divided into two **Divisions**—*Archichlamydeae* and *Metachlamydeae* ; and the latter into three **Divisions**—*Calyciferae* (calyx-bearers), *Corolliferae* (corolla-bearers) and *Glumiflorae*. The Divisions are further subdivided into **Orders**, **Families**, and **Genera**. The Dicotyledons begin with Magnoliaceae and end in Labiatae, while the Monocotyledons begin with Butomaceae and end in Gramineae. The Orders here recognized are much smaller concepts than those of Bentham and Hooker or of Engler, and correspond more with the Suborders of the latter.

The Subphyla Dicotyledons and Monocotyledons are described in detail below :

DICOTYLEDONS

DIVISION I. ARCHICHLAMYDEAE

Order 1. MAGNOLIALES

Fam : *Magnoliaceae, Winteraceae, Schizandraceae, Himatandraceae, Lactoridaceae, Trochodendraceae, Cercidiphyllaceae.

Order 2. ANONAIES

Fam : *Anonaceae, Eupomatiaceae.

" 3. LAURALES

Fam : Monimiaceae, *Lauraceae, Gomortegaceae, Hernandiaceae, Myristicaceae.

" 4. RANALES

Fam : *Ranunculaceae, Cabombaceae, Ceratophyllaceae, *Nymphaeaceae.

" 5. BERBERIDALES

Fam : Berberidaceae, Circaeasteraceae, Lardizabalaceae, Sargentadoxaceae, Menispermaceae.

" 6. ARISTOLOCHIALES

Fam : Aristolochiaceae, Cytinaceae, Hydnoraceae, Nepenthaceae.

" 7. PIPERALES

Fam : *Piperaceae, Saururaceae, Chloranthaceae, Lacistemaceae.

" 8. RHOEADALES

Fam : *Papaveraceae, Fumariaceae.

" 9. LOASALES

Fam : Turneraceae, Loasaceae,

" 10. CAPPARIDALES

Fam : *Capparidaceae, Moringaceae, Tovariaceae.

" 11. CRUCIALES

Fam : *Cruciferae.

" 12. VIOLALES

Fam : *Violaceae, Resedaceae,

" 13. POLYGALALES

Fam : Polygalaceae, Trigoniaceae, Vochysiaceae.

" 14. SAXIFRAGALES

Fam : *Crassulaceae, Cephalotaceae, Saxifragaceae.

" 15. SARRACENIALES

Fam : Droseraceae, Sarraceniaceae,

" 16. PODOSTEMONALES

Fam : Podostermonaceae, Hydrostachyaceae.

" 17. CARYOPHYLLALES

Fam : Elatinanceae, *Caryophyllaceae, Molluginaceae, Ficoidaceae (Aizoaceae), *Portulacaceae.

" 18. POLYGONALES

Fam : *Polygonaceae, Illecebraceae.

" 19. CHENOPODIALES

Fam : Phytolaccaceae, Cynocrambaceae, *Chenopodiaceae, Batidaceae, *Amarantaceae, Basellaceae.

" 20. GERANIALES

Fam : *Linaceae, Zygophyllaceae, *Geraniaceae, Limnanthaceae, Oxalidaceae, Tropaeolaceae, Balsaminaceae.

Order 21. LYTHRALES
Fam : *Lythraceae, Crypteroniaceae, Sonneratiaceae, Punicaceae, Oliniaceae, *Onagraceae, Holorrhagaceae, Callitrichiaceae.

" 22. THYMELAEALES
Fam : Geissolomataceae, Thymeleaceae, Penaeaceae, *Nyctaginaceae.

" 23. PROTEALES
Fam : Proteaceae.

" 24. DILLENIALES
Fam : Dilleniaceae, Crossosomateceae.

" 25. CORIARIALES
Fam : Coriariaceae.

" 26. PITTOSPORALES
Fam : Pittosporaceae, Byblidaceae, Tremandaceae.

" 27. BIXALES
Fam : Bixaceae, Cochlospermaceae, Flacourtiaceae, Samydaceae, Canellaceae, Cistaceae.

" 28. TAMARICALES
Fam : Frankeniaceae, Tamaricaceae, Fouquieraceae.

" 29. PASSAFLORALES
Fam : Malesherbiaceae, *Passifloraceae, Achariaceae.

" 30. CUCURBITALES
Fam : *Cucurbitaceae, Begoniaceae, Datiscaceae, Caricaceae.

" 31. CACTALES
Fam : *Cactaceae.

" 32. THEALES
Fam : Theaceae (Ternstroemiaceae), Medusagynaceae, Marcgraviaceae, Caryocaraceae, Actinidiaceae, Saurauiaceae, Ochnaceae, Ancistrocladaceae, *Dipterocarpaceae, Chlaenaceae.

" 33. MYRTALES
Fam : *Myrtaceae, Lecythidaceae, *Melastomaceae, *Combretaceae, *Rhizophoraceae.

" 34. GUTTIFERALES
Fam : Hypericaceae, Eucryphiaceae, Quinaceae, *Guttiferae.

" 35. TILIALES
Fam : Scytopetalaceae, *Tiliaceae, Gonystylaceae, *Sterculiaceae ; * Bombacaceae.

" 36. MALVALES
Fam : *Malvaceae.

" 37. MALPIGHIALES
Fam : Malpighiaceae, Humiriaceae, Erythroxylaceae.

Order 38. EUPHORBIALES
Fam : *Euphorbiaceae.

„ 39. CUNONIALES
Fam : Cunoniaceae, Brunellaceae, Escalloniaceae, Greylaceae ; Grosasulariaceae, Hydrangeaceae.

„ 40. ROSALES
Fam : *Rosaceae, Chailletiaceae, Calycanthaceae.

„ 41. *LEGUMINOSAE
Fam : Caesalpiniaceae, Mimosaceae, Papilionaceae.

„ 42. HAMAMELIDALES
Fam : Bruniaceae, Stachyuraceae, Hamamelidaceae, Eucommiaceae, Myrothamnaceae, Buxaceae, Plantanaceae.

„ 43. SALICALES
Fam : *Salicaceae.

„ 44. GARRYALES
Fam : Garryaceae.

„ 45. LEITNERIALES
Fam : Leitnerlaceae.

„ 46. MYRICALES
Fam : Myricaceae.

„ 47. BALANOPSIDALES
Fam : Balanopsidaceae.

„ 48. FAGALES
Fam : Betulaceae, Corylaceae, Fagaceae.

„ 49. CASUARINALES
Fam : *Casuarinaceae.

„ 50. URTICALES
Fam : Ulmaceae, Barbeyaceae, *Moraceae, Scyphostegiaceae, *Urticaceae, Cannabinaceae.

„ 51. CELASTRALES
Fam : Aquifoliaceae, Empetraceae, Celastraceae, Corynocarpaceae, Cyrillaceae, Cneoraceae, Pandaceae, Hippocrateaceae, Icacinaceae, Salvadoraceae, Stackhousiaceae.

„ 52. OLACALES
Fam : Olacaceae, Opiliaceae.

„ 53. SANTALALES
Fam : Octoknemataceae, *Loranthaceae, *Santalaceae, Grubbiaceae, Myzodendraceae, Balanophoraceae.

„ 54. RHAMNALES
Fam : *Rhamnaceae, Elaeaginaceae, Hetropyxidaceae, *Ampelidaceae (Vitaceae).

„ 55. RUTALES
Fam : *Rutaceae, Simarubaceae, Burseraceae.

„ 56. MELIALES
Fam : *Meliaceae.

Order 57. SAPINDALES

Fam : * Sapindaceae, Akaniaceae, Aceraceae, Sabiaceae, Melianthaceae, Didieraceae, Staphyleaceae, *Anacardiaceae, Connaraceae.

„ 58. JUGLANDALES

Fam : Juglandaceae, Julianiaceae.

„ 59. UMBELLIFLORAE

Fam : Cornaceae, Alangiaceae, Nyssaceae, Araliaceae, *Umbelliferae.

DIVISION II. METACHLAMYDEAE

Order 60. ERICALES

Fam : Clethraceae, Ericaceae, Vacciniaceae, Epacridaceae, Monotropaceae, Diapensiaceae, Lennoaceae.

„ 61. EBENALES

Fam : Ebenaceae, *Sapotaceae.

„ 62. MYRSINALES

Fam : Myrsinaceae.

„ 63. STYRACALES

Fam : Styracaceae, Symplocaceae, Diclidantheraceae, Lissocarpaceae.

„ 64. LOGANIALES

Fam : Loganiaceae, *Oleaceae.

„ 65. APOCYNALES

Fam : *Apocynaceae, *Asclepiadaceae.

„ 66. RUBIALES

Fam : * Rubiaceae, Caprifoliaceae.

„ 67. ASTERALES

Fam : Adoxaceae, Valerianaceae, Dipsacaceae, Calyceraceae, *Compositae.

„ 68. GENTIANALES

Fam : *Gentianaceae,

„ 69. PRIMULALES

Fam : Primulaceae, Plumbaginaceae.

„ 70. PLANTAGINALES

Fam : Plantaginaceae.

„ 71. CAMPANALES

Fam : Campanulaceae, Lobeliaceae, Goodeniaceae, Stylidiaceae.

„ 72. POLEMONIALES

Fam : Polemoniaceae, Hydrophyllaceae.

„ 73. BORAGINALES

Fam : *Boraginaceae.

„ 74. SOLANALES

Fam : *Solanaceae, *Convolvulaceae.

Order 75. PERSONALES

Fam : *Scrophulariaceae, Orobanchaceae, *Lentibulariaceae, Columelliaceae, Gesneriaceae, *Bignoniaceae, *Pedaliaceae, *Acanthaceae.

„ 76. LAMIALES

Fam : Globulariaceae, Myoporaceae, Selaginaceae, *Verbenaceae, *Labiatae.

MONOCOTYLEDONS

vision I. Calyciferae

Order 77. BUTOMALES

Fam : Butomaceae, * Hydrocharitaceae.

„ 78. ALISMATALES

Fam : * Alismataceae, Scheuchzeriaceae, Petrosaviaceae.

„ 79. TRIURIDALES

Fam : Triuridaceae,

„ 80. JUNCAGINALES

Fam : Juncaginaceae, * Liliaceae (Heterostylaceae), Posidoniaceae.

„ 81. APONOGETONALES

Fam : Aponogetonaceae, Zosteraceae.

„ 82. POTAMOGETONALES

Fam : Potamogetonaceae, Ruppiaceae.

„ 83. NAJADALES

Fam : Zannichelliaceae, Najadaceae.

„ 84. COMMELINALES

Fam : * Commelinaceae, Flagellariaceae, Mayaceae.

„ 85. XYRIDALES

Fam : Zyridaceae, Rapateaceae.

„ 86. ERIOCAULALES

Fam : Eriocaulaceae.

„ 87. BROMELIALES

Fam : Bromeliaceae.

„ 88. ZINGIBERALES

Fam : *Musaceae, *Strelitziaceae, Lowiaceae, *Zingiberaceae, * Cannaceae, * Marantaceae.

ivision II. Corolliferae

Order 89. LILIALES

Fam : * Liliaceae, Tecophilacaceae, Trilliaceae, * Pontederiaceae, Smilaceae, Ruscaceae.

„ 90. ALSTROEMERIALES

Fam : Alstroemeriaceae, Petermanniaceae, Philesiaceae.

Order 91. ARALES
Fam : * Araceae, * Lemnaceae.

" 92. TYPHALES
Fam : Sparganiaceae, * Typhaceae.

" 93. AMARYLLIDALES
Fam : * Amaryllidaceae.

" 94. IRIDALES
Fam : Iridaceae.

" 95. DIOSCORELAES
Fam : Stenomeridaceae, Trichapodaceae, Roxburghiaceae, Dioscoreaceae.

" 96. AGAVALES
Fam : Xanthorrhoeaceae, Agavaceae.

" 97. PALMALES
Fam : * Palmae.

" 98. PANDANALES
Fam : *Pandanaceae.

" 99. CYCLANTHALES
Fam : Cyclanthaceae.

" 100. HEAMODORALES
Fam : Haemodoraceae, Hypoxidaceae, Velloziaceae, Apostasiaceae, Taccaceae, Philydraceae.

" 101. BURMANNIALES
Fam : Burmanniaceae, Thismiaceae, Corsiaceae.

" 102. ORCHIDALES
Ram : *Orchidaceae,

Division III. Glumiflorae

" 103. JUNCALES
Fam : Juncaceae, Thurniaceae, Centrolepidaceae, Restienaceae.

" 104. CYPERALES
Fam : * Cyperaceae.

" 105. GRAMINALES
Fam : * Gramineae.

Merits and Demerits

Merits : 1. The placing of Ranunculaceae and its allies at the beginning of the Dicotyledons.

2. Amentiferae is deemed as a reduced form and is placed later in the Dicotyledons.

3. In Dicotyledons the woody forms are derived from the Magnolian stock and herbaceous ones from the Ranunculian one.

4. Dicotyledons at first started as bisexual flowers while unisexual ones are derived from them by reduction.

5. Monocotyledons are derived from Dicotyledons, and the origin is polyphylectic from Ranunculaceae and its allies.

6. Helobiae is placed at the beginning of Monocotyledons.

7. Re-shuffling of Liliaceae and Amaryllidaceae solely on inflorescence characters, irrespective of epigyny or hypogyny.

8. The foliar origin of carpels has become the basis of this system of classification. Recent cytogenetical and anatomical studies support this contension.

Demerits : 1. Delimitation of small groups based on resemblances. Relative groups as a result have been shown to be distantly related.

2. Polyphylectic origin of Amentiferae from herbaceous and woody forms.

3. Polyphylectic origin of such natural groups as Asterales, Umbelliferales, Urticales, etc.

4. Sometimes too much stress is laid on habit and habitat.

5. In Monocotyledons related Orders like Scitamineae and Microspermae are placed apart.

6. So far Zingiberaceae is concerned, it is separated from Liliales because the former is rhizomatic while the latter is bulbous.

7. The origin of Monocotyledons from a single source Ranales is unlikely (as postulated in his Monocotyledons).

8. The phylogenetic line demarcating Sympetalae from Dialypetalae should be removed.

9. Proteales of Apetalae though characterized by woody habit have been derived from herbaceous Ranales.

Oswald Tippo* (1911—) of Illinois University, U. S. A., published an outline of suggested system of classification in 1942. In this system the entire Plant Kingdom has been divided into two **Subkingdoms**, each one of which consists of several **Phyla** and **Subphyla**. All the vascular plants (Pteridophytes, Gymnosperms and Angiosperms) have been placed under one Phylum, the *Tracheophyta*. An outline of Tippo's classification is given below :

Plant Kingdom

I. SUBKINGDOM : **Thallophyta**

Phylum Cyanophyta (blue-green algae)	.. ..	"Algae" of older system
„ Euglenophyta (euglenoids)	.. ..	
„ Chlorophyta (green algae)	.. ..	
„ Chrysophyta (yellow green algae, golden-brown algae, and diatoms)	..	
„ Pyrrophyta (cryptomonads and dinoflagellate)		
„ Phaeophyta (brown algae)	.. ..	
„ Rhodophyta (red algae)	.. ..	

* Chronica Botanica. 7 : 5 : 203-206; 1942.

Phylum Schizomycophyta (bacteria) .. .. } "Fungi" of older system
" Myxomycophyta (slime moulds) .. ..
" Eumycophyta (true fungi) .. ..

II. SUBKINGDOM :

Phylum Bryophyta (or Atracheata) .. .. } "Bryophytes" of older system
Class Musci (mosses) .. ..
" Hepaticae (liverworts) .. ..
" Anthocerotae (hornworts) .. ..

Phylum Tracheophyta (or Tracheata)—vascular plants } "Pteridophytes" of older system

Subphylum Psilopsida
Class Psilophytineae
Order *Psilophytales* .. .. ..
" *Psilotales*

Subphylum Lycopsida (club-mosses)
Class Lycopodineae
Order *Lycopodiales* (club-mosses)
" *Selaginellales* (small club-mosses) ..
" *Lepidodendrales* (giant club-mosses) ..
" *Pleuromeiales* .. ..
" *Isoetales* (quillworts) .. ..

Subphylum Sphenopsida (horsetails)
Class Equisetineae
Order *Hyeniales*
" *Sphenophyllales*
" *Equisetales* (horsetails) .. ..

Subphylum Pteropsida
Class Filicineae (ferns)
" *Ophioglossales* .. .. ..
Order *Coenopteridales* .. .. ..
" *Marattiales* .. ..
" *Filicales* .. .. ..

Class Gymnospermae (Conifers and their allies) } "Spermatophytes" of older system

Subclass Cycadophytae
Order *Cycadofilicales* (or Pteridospermae)—seed ferns ..
" *Bennettitales* .. .. ..
" *Cycadales*—cycads .. .. ..

Subclass Coniferophytae	"Spermatophytes" of older system
Order *Cordaitales*	
,, *Ginkgoales*—maiden-hair tree	
,, *Coniferales*—conifers	
,, *Gnetales*	
Class Angiospermae—flowering plants	
Subclass Dicotyledoneae	
Subclass Monocotyledoneae	

Recently, **R. C. Maclean** and **W. R. Ivimey-Cook**, two British authors, in their *Textbook of Theoretical Botany, Vol. II* (1956), have suggested an outline classification of the Angiosperms, in which they have made a departure from the existing systems. These authors have rejected Bentham and Hooker's Apetalae, and have accepted Engler's Archichlamydeae and Metachlamydeae. They have retained the Ranales, however, in their age-old traditional position as the most primitive Order in the Plant Kingdom, and have placed the Dicotyledons before the Monocotyledons in opposition to Engler's idea. Moreover, they do not follow Hutchinson even in not accepting the separation of the Orders into two distinct lines—one predominantly herbaceous, and the other predominantly woody.

Characters used in a phylogenetic system

In a phylogenetic system the following salient characters are usually taken into consideration for differentiating a "primitive plant" from an "advanced one".

Primitive characters	*Advanced characters*
(*a*) *Morphological* :	
1, Plants, woody and erect, monoecious.	1. Plants herbaceous and weak, dioecious.
2. Leaves simple, net-veined, spirally arranged.	2. Leaves parallel-veined, compound with opposite or whorled phyllotaxy.
3. Flowers regular, solitary, bisexual, hypogynous, acyclic, radially symmetrical.	3. Flowers irregular, aggregated, unisexual or neuter, perigynous or epigynous, cyclic, bilaterally symmetrical.
4. Perianth consists of like segments.	4. Perianth absent or consists of dissimilar segments.
5. Petals free.	5. Petals united or absent.
6. Stamens numerous and free.	6. Stamens a few and united.

7. Carpels numerous and free.	7. Carpels solitary, or a few and united.
8. Placentation axile.	8. Placentation parietal.
9. Ovules numerous.	9. Ovules solitary or central.
10. Fruit simple or aggregate,	10. Fruit multiple.
11. Seed endospermic with a small, straight embryo.	11. Seed endospermic with a large, curved embryo.

(b) *Anatomical* :

12. Cortical cells contain chloroplasts.	12. Cortical cells are without chloroplasts.
13. Bundles of the stem are collateral, open and arranged in a ring,	13. Bundles of the stem are collateral, closed and scattered.
14. Tracheids present and vessels less prominent,	14. Tracheids usually absent and vessels predominant.
15. Vessels with scalariform thickenings and scalariform perforations.	15. Vessels with pitted thickenings and simple perforations.

FIELD AND HERBARIUM TECHNIQUES AND MAINTENANCE

A herbarium is a collection of plants that usually have been pressed, dried, mounted on sheets and arranged in accordance with any accepted system of classification for future reference and study.

There are three different means of handling fresh material for processing into herbarium specimens. The most easy and satisfactory method is to press each plant as it is collected, in between the folded blotting papers or sheets of newsprint. The second method is to accumulate the material in a **Vasculum** (a metal collecting can). But plants should be pressed as soon as opportunity permits. The third method is to carry collected specimens in a rucksack. They are then pressed as soon as possible after return to headquarters.

At the time of collection care should be taken to have the specimens in flowering stages. Vegetative parts without flowers are absolutely useless for herbarium as their identification becomes almost impossible. Certain items of equipments are indispensable while attending an excursion for collection of materials (i) a strong knife, (ii) a pair of pruning shears, (iii) a collecting pick, (iv) a plant press containing blotting papers, (v) a field record book with voucher numbers, and (vi) a small note book.

Drying technique : The collected specimens are placed in between the blotting papers which are then placed one above the other and then tied tightly in a field press, which is efficient in holding the specimen under a constant and firm pressure. The press is locked up for twenty-four hours—the **'sweating period'**. After the sweating period the press is opened, the pressing papers are changed and the specimens are rearranged. The rearrangement of specimens is very important as during this process the plant parts can be put in a desired position. The press is locked up again and allowed to remain as such for forty-eight to seventy-two hours. This process is repeated for several time until the specimens become completely dried.

Mounting and levelling of the specimen : After drying the specimens should be mounted on mounting papers or herbarium sheets. These sheets must be of good quality and heavy to support the specimens as a permanent record. The standard size of a herbarium sheet is 29×42 cm. The specimens are fixed to the sheets with the help of quick drying adhesives. Each herbarium sheet should be provided with a level (6×10 cm.), either pressed or printed on the lower right-hand corner. The label should give the following information :

FLORA OF ....

Voucher No......... Date of collection........
Name................
Family................
Habit..................
Locality............... Attitude..............
Collection................
Remarks................

Preservation of herbarium sheets : If not properly preserved, the insects and fungi do irreparable damage to the herbarium sheets. The most common pests are the **silver fish**, herbarium bettle, etc. and the fungus is **Eurotium herbariorum**. Different chemicals, such as **cyanide gas, paradichlorobenzene**, DDT, naphthaflaker are generally used as preservatives.

Alternation of generations

Every plant possesses what is termed a **life history**, *i.e.* every plant has got a beginning, passes through certain stages, attains maturity, reproduces, becomes old and ultimately dies. All these changes from the beginning to the end collectively constitute its life history. In all groups of plants, beginning from the thallophytes right up to the spermatophytes, there is very frequently found an alternation of two stages, or phases, or generations in the life history of the individual. The two alternating generations may be morphologically distinct and independent individuals, or they may not be so. That stage, which bears the sex organs, is called the **gametophyte** or **sexual generation**, and that which bears the assexual bodies called **spores**, is known as the **sporophyte** or **asexual generation**. The spore produced by the sporophyte always develops into a gametophyte, while the zygote produced by the gametophyte develops into a sporophyte. This phenomenon of alternation between the gametophyte and the sporophyte is spoken of as the '*alternation of generations*'.

Generally, the alternation of the nuclear phases is closely associated with the alternation of generations. Thus, the sporophyte nucleus is **diploid** (with $2n$ number of chromosomes), while the gametophyte nucleus is **haploid** (with n number of chromosomes). The gametophyte or the haploid generation begins with meiotic division, while the sporophyte or diploid generation starts with sexual fusion (conjugation or fertilization) and with the formation of the zygote (zygospore or oospore).

This alternation of generations is not always obligatory, for, in certain cases, the vegetative propagation of a gametophyte, for example, may result in a life cycle in which there is a succession of gametophytic individuals before the formation of a sporophyte takes place. Moreover, in some remarkable cases, the alternation of generations is not connected with the alternation of the phases of the nucleus. Thus, in the phenomenon of **apogamy**, the vegetative budding of a gametophytic tissue may give rise to a sporophyte, while in the case of **apospory**, a gametophyte is produced from the sporophyte without the formation of any spore.

The chief advantage in the 'alternation of generations' is supposed to be that the sporophyte by producing abundant spores helps in multiplication and dispersal, while the gametophyte by the production of gametes facilitates the merging of characters of different individuals. There are some disadvantages also ; for example, in some mosses, the conditions for the fusion of gametes are often lacking, hence development of the sporophyte is practically impossible.

Alternation of generations

Every plant possesses what is termed a **life history**. Every plant has got a beginning, passes through certain stage, attains maturity, reproduces, becomes old and ultimately dies. All these changes from the beginning to the end collectively constitute its life history. In all groups of plants beginning from the thallophytes right up to the spermatophytes, there is very frequently found an alternation of two stages, or phases, or generations in the life history of the individual. The two alternating generations may be morphologically distinct and independent individuals, or they may not be so. That stage, which bears the sex organs, is called the **gametophyte** or **sexual generation** and that which bears the asexual bodies called **spores**, is known as the **sporophyte** or **asexual generation**. The spore produced by the sporophyte always develops into a gametophyte, while the zygote produced by the gametophyte develops into a sporophyte. This phenomenon of alternation between the gametophyte and the sporophyte is spoken of as the '*alternation of generations*'.

Generally, the alternation of the nuclear phases is closely associated with the alternation of generations. Thus, the sporophyte nucleus is **diploid** (with 2*n* number of chromosomes), while the gametophyte nucleus is **haploid** (with *n* number of chromosomes). The gametophyte or the haploid generation begins with meiotic division, while the sporophyte or diploid generation starts with sexual fusion (conjugation or fertilization), and with the formation of the zygote (zygospore or oospore).

This alternation of generations is not always obligatory, for in certain cases, the vegetative propagation of a gametophyte, for example, may result in a life cycle in which there is a succession of gametophytic individuals before the formation of a sporophyte takes place. Moreover, in some remarkable cases, the alternation of generations is not connected with the alternation of the phases of the nucleus. Thus in the phenomenon of **apogamy**, the vegetative budding of a gametophytic tissue may give rise to a sporophyte, while in the case of **apospory**, a gametophyte is produced from the sporophyte without the formation of any spore.

The chief advantage in the 'alternation of generations' is supposed to be that the sporophyte by producing abundant spores helps in multiplication and dispersal, while the gametophyte by the production of gametes facilitates the merging of characters of different individuals. There are some disadvantages also. For example, in some mosses, the conditions for the fusion of gametes are often lacking, hence development of the sporophyte is practically impossible.

FAMILIES OF ANGIOSPERMS

CHAPTER I

MONOCOTYLEDONS

The plants under the category of Monocotyledons bear only one cotyledon in their embryo. The radicle on germination produces a number of adventitious roots. Leaves have parallel venation and sheathing leaf-bases. Flowers are usually trimerous. Vascular bundles of the stem are closed and scattered in the ground tissue, and those of root polyarch.

ORDER 1. PANDANALES

Marsh-herbs, shrubs or trees, monoecious or dioecious; leaves linear; flowers unisexual, naked; or with a simple inconspicuous perianth; stamens 1-many; carpels 1-many; fruit more or less nut-like; seeds rich in endosperm.

According to Engler's system of classification this order has been placed at the beginning of the monocotyledons and comprises three families, viz., Typhaceae*, Pandanaceae* and Sparganiaceae. Bentham and Hooker have put the first two families under the series Nudiflorae. Hutchinson, however, has separated Pandanaceae from Typhaceae and Sparganiaceae, and has put it under the order Pandanales. The aforesaid three families are now regarded to be simple by a reduction of reproductive organs and believed to have been derived from liliaceous stocks.

TYPHACEAE

General characters

Plants—perennial herbs of marshy places, monoecious; stem rhizomatous and creeping. Leaves—alternate, 2-ranked, *erect*, *very long* and *linear*, sessile with sheathing leaf-base, mostly radical. Inflorescence—dense cylindric spike (*spadix*). Flowers—minute, unisexual, hypogynous, naked; the male flowers are situated on the upper portion of the spadix and the female ones on the lower portion; both kinds of flowers are subtended by one caducous bract-like spathe. Perianth—represented by bristles. Stamens—in male flowers usually

3, rarely 1–7, monadelphous. Carpel—in the female flowers one; ovary superior, situated on a gynophore, 1-celled with 1 pendulous ovule; style 1, persistent; many silky hairs present at the base of the gynophore. Fruit—a minute nutlet. Seed—albuminous with a straight embryo.

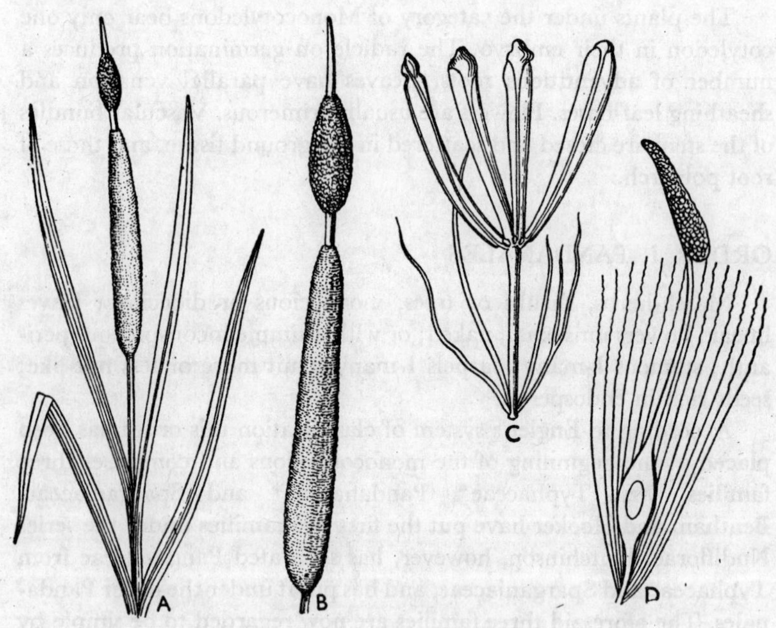

Fig. 509. Typhaceae (*Typha angustata*).
A, Portion of a flowering shoot; B, Inflorescence; C, Staminate flower; D, Pistillate flower.

Floral formula

♂ flowers—P_0 $A_{(1-7)}$ G_0

♀ flowers—P_0 A_0 $\underline{G_1}$

Number and distribution

This family contains a single genus *Typha* with about 15 species. The genus is of cosmopolitan distribution throughout the marshes of temperate and tropical countries of both the hemispheres.

Common plants

(1) Bulrush (*Typha elephantina* Roxb. and *T. angustata* Chaub.), (2) *T. latifolia* L., (3) *T. angustata* Chaub.

Affinity

Typhaceae is the most primitive family of the monocotyledons. It has close affinity with Pandanaceae and Araceae but is readily distinguished by its very long erect linear leaves, and dense spicate inflorescence (spadix), which is fuzzy brown at maturity.

Economic importance

This family is of little economic importance. The leaves of *T. elephantina* are often woven in making mats and screens, and for thatching temporary sheds. The pollens of *T. angustata* are often made into cakes which are taken by the poor people.

PANDANACEAE

General characters

Plants—often branched ***palm-like trees*** or shrubs, sometimes root-climbers, dioecious; usually with stout, stilt roots. Leaves—spirally arranged in crowns, simple, long and narrow having spines along the

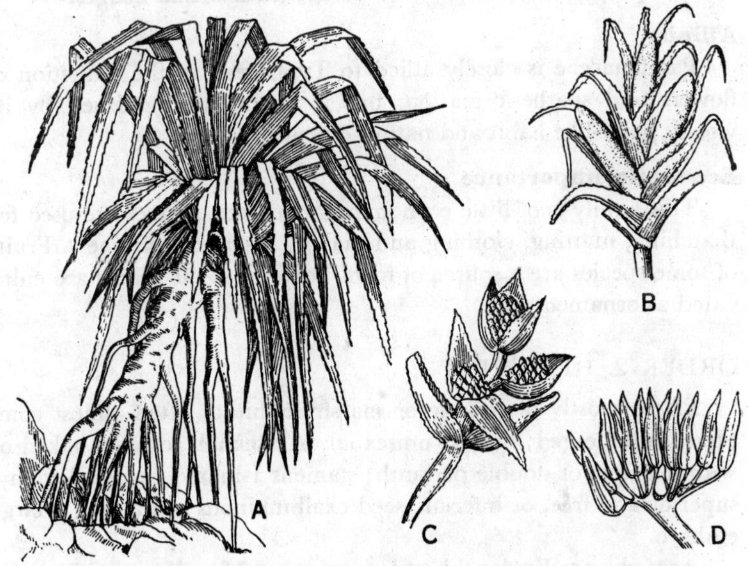

Fig. 510. Pandanaceae (*Pandanus fascicularis*). A, Plant; B, An inflorescence; C, Staminate flowers; D, A single staminate flower cut open.

margins and the midrib, sessile with sheathing leaf-base. Inflorescence—spadix, enclosed in a spathe-like bract. Flowers—small, unisexual, mostly achlamydeous. Perianth—rudimentary or absent. Stamens—in male flowers numerous; filaments distinct or united; anthers basifixed, dehiscing longitudinally. Carpels—in female flowers, numerous; ovary superior, 1-celled with 1-infinite anatropous ovules; stigma as many as the carpels, sessile. Fruit—*drupaceous* or woody. Seed—albuminous (oil present) with basal small embryo.

Floral formula

♂ flowers—P_0 A_∞ G_0

♀ flowers—P_0 A_0 $\underline{G_\infty}$

Number and distribution

This family consists of 3 genera with about 300 species and occurs in the tropics, a few are temperate.

Common plants

(1) The Screw-pine (*Pandanus fascicularis* L.), a small tree 10–12 ft. high, very common in Sundribans. (2) *P. foetida* Roxb., a bush with no proper stem, common in village thickets and hedges.

Affinity

Pandanaceae is closely allied to Typhaceae in the reduction of flowers and spathe-formation, but is readily distinguished by its woody palm-like habit and nature of fruit.

Economic importance

This family is of little economic importance. Leaves are used for thatching, matting, clothing and making assorted containers. Fruits of some species are a source of food. Sometimes the plants are cultivated as ornamentals.

ORDER 2. HELOBIEAE

Plants mostly of aquatic or marshy habitats, often almost completely submerged; flowers unisexual or bisexual, regular, naked or with a simple or double perianth; stamens 1-many; carpels 1-many, superior and free, or inferior; seed exalbuminous containing a large embryo.

According to Engler this order comprises 7 families, viz., Potamogetonaceae, Najadaceae, Aponogetonaceae, Scheuchzariaceae, Alismataceae*, Butomaceae and Hydrocharitaceae*. There is no mention of this order in the Bentham and Hooker system. Alismataceae is, however, has been put under the series Apocarpeae.

ALISMATACEAE

General characters

Plants—perennial or annual *aquatic* or *marshy herbs*, with generally a stout rhizome, monoecious or polygamous. Leaves—radical or clustered at the nodes, entire with long petioles, sagittate or hastate. Inflorescence—*panicle* or *raceme* or *cymose umbel on scape*. Flowers—regular, bisexual (but unisexual in *Sagittaria*), bracteate, hypogynous. Perianth —3+3, free, *outer* 3 *sepaloid* and inner 3 petaloid, free, imbricate. Stamens—6-many. Carpels—3–6 or more, *apocarpous;* ovary superior, 1-celled with 1 or *more basal* anatropous ovules; placentation marginal or superficial. Fruit—*etaerio of achenes*, rarely of follicles. Seeds—minute, *exalbuminous*. Embryo—large, straight or curved.

Floral formula

$\oplus$ ⚥ P_{3+3} $A_{6-\infty}$ $\underline{G_{3-\infty}}$

Number and distribution

This family consists of 17 genera and about 82 species which are

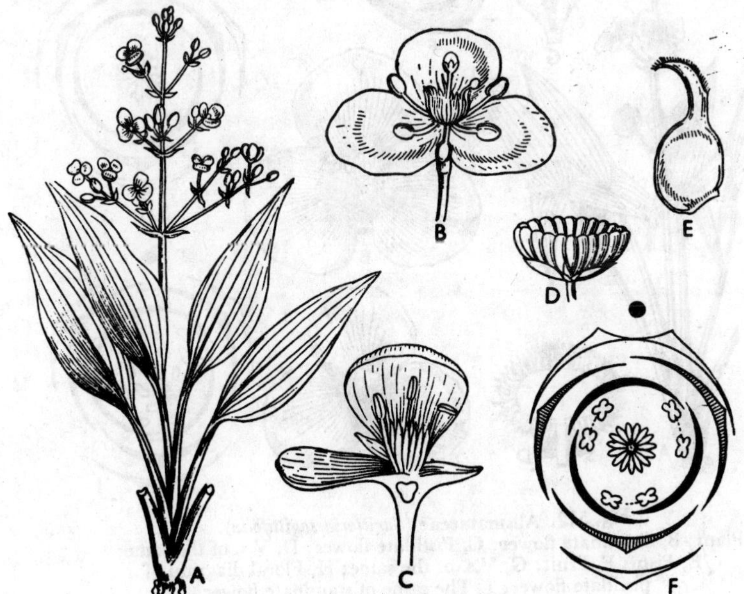

Fig. 511. Alismataceae (*Alisma plantago*). A, Plant; B, Flower; C, The same with a perianth lobe removed; D, Fruit; E, Pistil; F. Floral diagram.

hydrophilous in habit and are confined to the temperate and warmer regions.

Key to Genera

A. Fls. hermaphrodite

(*a*) Fruit dehiscent of 6–7 follicles; stamens 8–12; ovules many .. .. *Butomopsis.*

(*b*) Fruit indehiscent of 3 or more achenes; stamens 6–9; receptacle flat; ovule solitary .. .. *Alisma.*

B. Fls. polygamous; fruit indehiscent

(*a*) Unisexual fls.; receptacle globose; stamens 6-many .. *Sagittaria.*

(*b*) Bisexual fls.; receptacle flat; stamens 6, 2-seriate .. *Limnophyton.*

Common plants

(1) Water plantain (*Alisma plantago* L.), a common aquatic plant. (2) Arrow-head (*Sagittaria sagittifolia* L.), commonly found in tanks

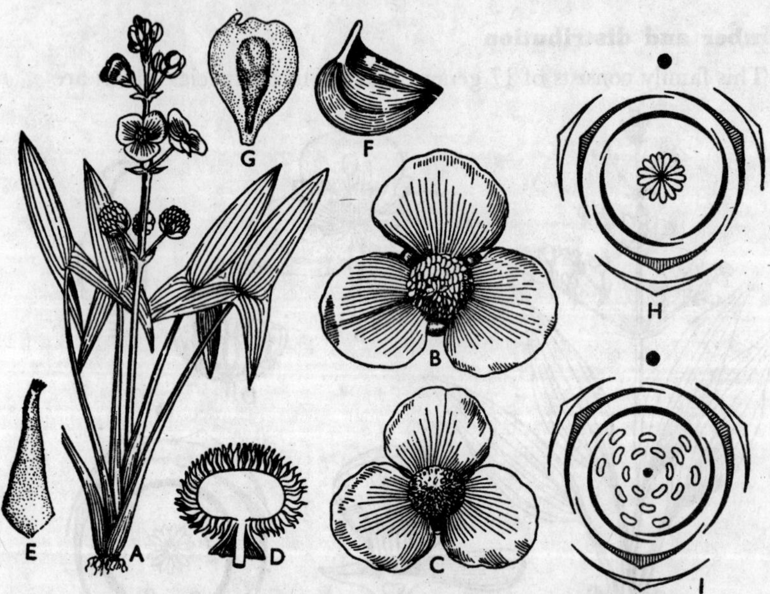

Fig. 512. Alismataceae (*Sagittaria sagittifolia*). A, Plant; B, Staminate flower; C, Pistillate flower; D, V.s. of the same; E, Pistil; F, Fruit; G, V.s. of the same; H, Floral diagram of pistillate flower; I, The same of staminate flower.

with sagittate leaves. (3) *Butomopsis lanceolata* Kunth. = *Tenagocharis lanceolata* Kunth., a common herb of marshes and rice-fields with lanceolate leaves, milky juice and bisexual flowers. (4) *Limnophyton obtusifolium* Miq., another common aquatic plant.

Affinity

Alismataceae closely resembles Ranunculaceae in having hypogynous flowers with free sepals, petals and numerous stamens and carpels, and also in etaerio of achenes or follicles) and Commelinaceae, but readily distinguished by the aquatic habit, form of inflorescence, two whorls of perianth and exalbuminous seeds. This does not necessarily indicate an affinity. It has been compared to Nymphaeaceae on account of superficial placentation but there is hardly any relationship between them. It differs from Hydrocharitaceae in the ovary having 1 or more basal ovules and the flowers usually arranged in whorls.

Economic importance

This family is of little economic importance. Rhizomes of *Sagittaria* are often eaten as an article of food by the Red Indians. The cultivation of Asiatic species is adopted by the Chinese people for their greater food value. Some plants are used as ornamentals, such as *Alisma* and *Sagittaria*.

HYDROCHARITACEAE

General characters

Plants—floating or submerged aquatic herbs, dioecious, sometimes monoecious. Leaves—radical or cauline (alternate, opposite or whorled), sessile. Inflorescence—umbel. Flowers—enclosed in an entire or 2-leaved spathe, regular, unisexual (sometimes bisexual, e.g., *Ottelia*), epigynous. Perianth—3+3, generally distinguished into calyx and corolla, or 3 (e.g., *Vallisneria*), valvate. Stamens—in male flowers 3–12, but 9 in *Elodea* and 3 in *Hydrilla*. Carpel—in female flowers usually one; style bipartite; ovary inferior, 1-celled with numerous ovules on parietal placenta. Fruit—berry-like. Seed—exalbuminous containing a large embryo.

Floral formula

♂ flowers—$\oplus P_{3+3}\ A_{3-12}\ G_0$

♀ flowers—$\oplus P_{3+3}\ A_0\ \overline{G_1}$

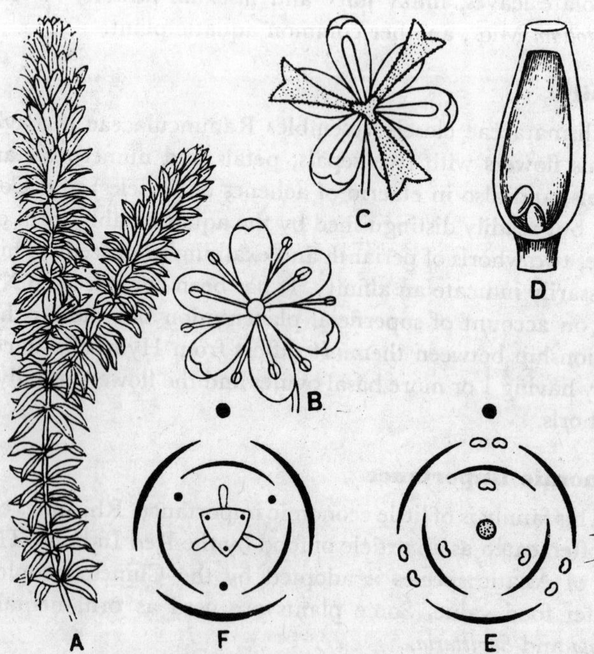

Fig. 513. Hydrocharitaceae (*Elodea canadensis*).
A, Portion of a plant; B, Staminate flower; C, Pistillate flower; D, L.s. of ovary; E, Floral diagram of staminate flower; F, Same of pistillate flower.

Number and distribution

This family consists of 16 genera with 80–90 species; 13 species occur in fresh-water and 3 are marine.

KEY TO GENERA

A. Stems branching, leafy; leaves small: spathes small, sessile:

(*a*) Leaves whorled; styles undivided; ovules anatropous .. *Hydrilla.*

(*b*) Leaves scattered; styles cleft; ovules orthotropous .. *Lagerosiphon.*

B. Stems none, or with stolons only, or a creeping rootstock

(*a*) Leaves all long or narrow, sessile; male scapes several flowered—

(*i*) Perianth single .. .. .. *Vallisneria.*

(*ii*) Perianth double .. .. .. *Blyxa.*

(*b*) Leaves mostly or all petioled—

(*i*) Ovary not beaked; fruit not winged; leaves all petioled; male scapes several flowered .. *Hydrocharis*.

(*ii*) Ovary beaked; fruit winged; submerged leaves narrow, others long-petioled; fls. solitary .. *Ottelia*.

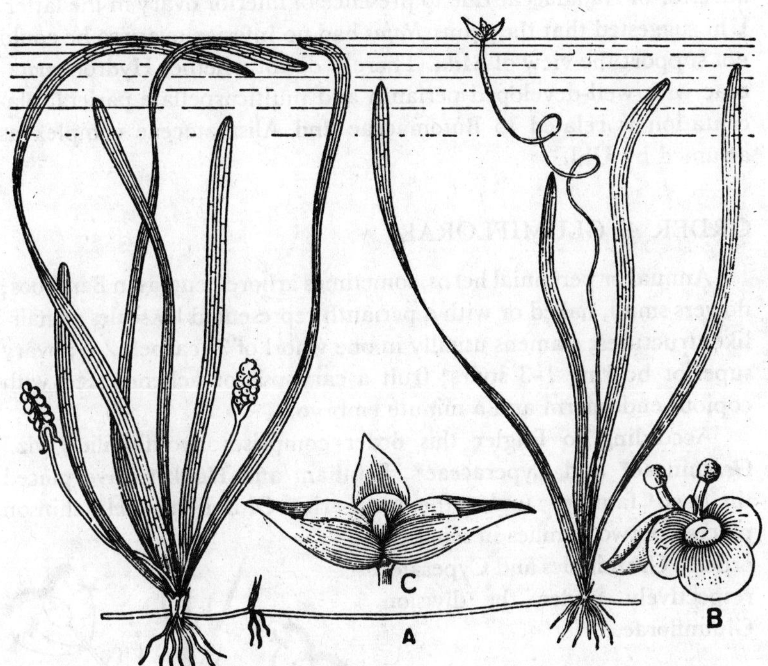

Fig. 514. Hydrocharitaceae (*Vallisneria spiralis*). A, Portion of a plant; B, Staminate flower; C, Pistillate flower.

Common plants

(1) *Hydrilla verticillata* Casp., a submerged, leafy dioecious herb. (2) *Lagerosiphon roxburghii* L., a filiform tank herb. (3) *Vallisneria spiralis* L., a submerged, stoloniferous, dioecious herb with long ribbon-shaped leaves. (4) *Blyxa roxburghii* Rich., a submerged, tufted, aquatic annual. (5) *Hydrocharis cellulosa* Buch.-Ham., a floating monoecious herb. (6) *Ottelia alismoides* Pers., a marsh herb with long-stalked leaves, white flowers and ovoid fruits enclosed in a 6-winged spathe. (7) *Elodea canadensis* Michx., very common in ponds.

Affinity

Hydrocharitaceae are considered to be closely related to Butomaceae and differ from the latter by the presence of inferior ovary, the spathe or paired floral bracts and the monocarpellary pistil. Miki (1937) has opined that Hydrocharitaceae may be regarded as the ancestor of Najadaceae due to presence of inferior ovary in the latter. Uhl suggested that the genus *Najas* had no inferior ovary so he could not support the view of Miki. There is doubt whether Hydrocharitaceae with well-developed perianth and multicarpellate parietal placentation is related to Butomaceae and Alismataceae complex as assumed by Uhl.

ORDER 4. GLUMIFLORAE

Annual or perennial herbs, sometimes arborescent, as in Bamboos; flowers small, naked or with a perianth represented by scales or hair-like structures; stamens usually in one whorl of 3; carpels 2–3; ovary superior bearing 1–3 styles; fruit a caryopsis or achene; seed with copious endosperm and a minute embryo.

According to Engler this order comprises two families, viz., Gramineae* and Cyperaceae*. Bentham and Hooker have placed the two families under the last series Glumiferae. Hutchinson places the two families in separate orders, Graminales and Cyperales respectively under the division Glumiflorae.

GRAMINEAE (*POACEAE*)

General characters

Plants—mostly perennial, sometimes annual or biennial herbs, rarely arborescent (e.g., *Bambusa*). Stem—*cylindrical*, generally *fistular*, i.e., solid at the nodes and hollow in the internodes, rarely solid throughout (e.g., *Zea, Saccharum*, etc.). Leaves—alternate, 2-ranked, linear to lanceolate, with leaf-sheath which

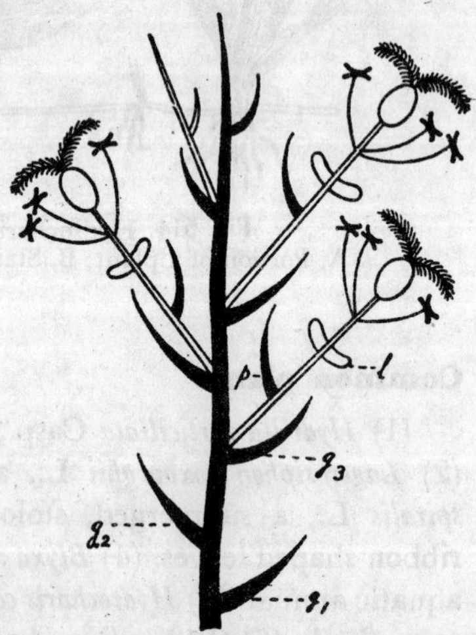

Fig. 515. Grass spikelet (*Diagrammatic*). g_1, g_2, Empty glumes; g_3, Flowering glume; *p*, Palea; *l*, Lodicule.

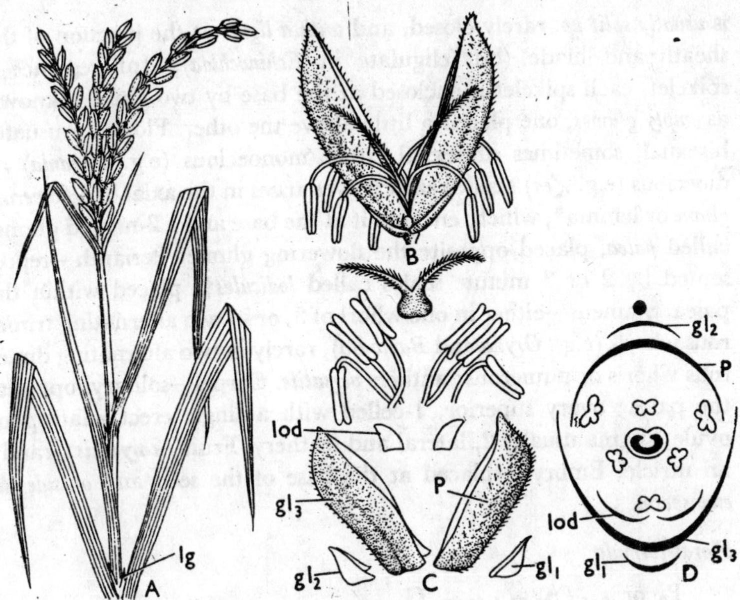

Fig. 516. Gramineae (*Oryza sativa*).
A, Portion of a flowering shoot; B, Flower; C, The same dissected out; D, Floral diagram. gl_1, Glume one; gl_2, Glume two; gl_3, Glume three; *lod*, Lodicules; *lg*, Ligule; P, palea.

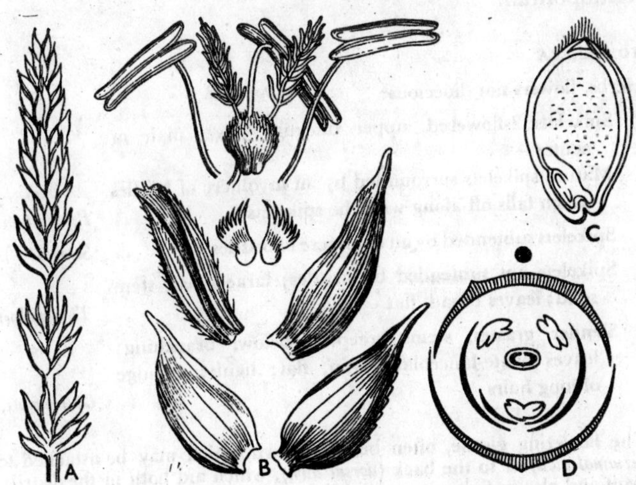

Fig. 517. Gramineae (*Triticum sativum*).
A, Portion of the inflorescence; B, Flower dissected out; C, L.s. of grain; D, Floral diagram.

is *usually split up*, rarely closed, and *with a ligule* at the junction of the sheath and blade (but eligulate in *Echinochloa*). Inflorescence spikelet, each spikelet is enclosed at the base by two glumes, known as *empty glumes*, one placed a little above the other. Flowers—usually bisexual, sometimes unisexual either monoecious (e.g. *Zizania*) or dioecious (e.g. *Zea*) sessile; each flower arises in the axial of a *flowering glume* or lemma*, which, encloses it at the base and a 2-nerved glume, called *palea*, placed opposite the flowering glume. Perianth—represented by 2 or 3 minute scales called *lodicules*†, placed within the palea. Stamens—either in one whorl of 3, or in two alternating trimerous whorls (e.g., *Oryza* and *Bambusa*), rarely in two alternating dimerous whorls or numerous; anthers *versatile*. Carpel—solitary, opposite the palea; ovary superior, 1-celled with a single erect anatropous ovule; stigma usually 2, lateral and feathery. Fruit—*caryopsis*, rarely an utricle. Embryo—placed at the base of the seed and *outside the endosperm*.

Floral formula

$$P_0 \text{ or } _{2-2} \quad A_{3 \text{ or } 6\ (3+3)},\ \underline{G_1}$$

Number and distribution

This family consists of about 500 genera and 4,000 species which are cosmopolitan.

KEY TO GENERA

A. Herbs, flowers not dioecious:

(*a*) Spikelets 2-flowered, upper bisexual, lower male or neuter—

Mature spikelets surrounded by an involucre of bristles which falls off along with the spikelets .. *Pennisetum*.

Spikelets subtended by an involucre of bristles .. *Setaria*.

Spikelets not subtended by bristles; large grass; stem solid; leaves broad, flat .. *Thysanolaena*.

Slender grasses, stems creeping below, branching; leaves ovate-lanceolate, thin, flat; ligules a ridge of long hairs .. *Oplismenus*.

* The flowering glume, often bears an awn which may be attached to the apex (*terminal awn*) or to the back (*dorsal awn*), which aid both in the distribution of the fruit and also in fixing it to the soil.

† The lodicules separate the palea and the glume to allow the stamens and stigmas to protrude out of flower by virtue of the swelling and consequent pressure upon the bracts.

Annual or perennial grasses; leaves broad or narrow, flat, or rarely plicate; ligules O or hairy; glume II not fimbriate, glume III with a palea or quite empty .. .. *Panicum.*

Annual or perennial grasses; flowers (spikelets) in digitate spikes; lowest glume minute but usually present; glume III with a minute palea .. .. *Digitaria.*

(*b*) Spikelets 1-flowered

(*i*) Spikelets articulated on their pedicels and deciduous from them—

Glumes I, II minute .. .. .. *Oryza.*

Floating grass, diffusely branched, rooting in dense masses at the nodes; glumes I and II absent .. .. *Hygroryza.*

(*ii*) Spikelets usually in pairs—

Spikelets all similar—

Racemes of spikelets in compound panicles—

Panicle spiciform, silky, rachis tough; erect perennial grasses, stem leafy, internode solid, leaves narrow .. .. .. *Imperata.*

Panicle much-branched, silky, rachis fragile, spikelets awnless; tall perennial grasses .. .. *Saccharum.*

Spikelets dissimilar—

Spikelets in alternating pairs or the lower solitary—

Sessile spikelet usually many, inflorescence long .. *Andropogon.*

(*iii*) Male and female spikelets in different spikes—

Fruiting spikelets crowded on a spongy rachis, the grain exposed; a tall annual cultivated grass .. *Zea.*

Fruiting spikelet enclosed in the stony polished nut-like bract .. .. .. *Coix.*

(*c*) Spikelets 2- or more-flowered; annual or perennial cultivated grasses; leaves flat; spikelet with twisted awns .. .. *Avena.*

(*d*) Spikelets 3- . -flowered, in decompound panicles; tall perennial grasses with long leaves .. .. *Phragmites.*

(*e*) Spikelets many-flowered, not pedicellate, with long silky hairs; outer glumes shorter than the lowest flowering glume; grain very minute; annual or perennial glabrous grasses, stems erect, leaves narrow .. *Eragrostis.*

(*f*) Spikelets 2-seriate and secund—

Spikelets not clustered, 1-flowered, awnless, spikes digitate; perennial creeping grasses, leaves narrow, flat .. .. *Cynodon.*

(*g*) Spikelets 3–12-flowered in numerous digitate or whorled spikes .. .. *Eleusine.*

(*h*) Spikelets inserted in notches or pits of a simple rachis—

Spikelets solitary at the nodes of the spikes; plane of spikelets tangential to the rachis; annual or biennial cultivated grass .. .. .. *Triticum.*

Spikelets 2 or more, collected in fascicles at the nodes of the spikes; an annual cultivated grass .. *Hordeum.*

B. Shrubs or trees, rarely climbing; stem-sheaths broad, blade often triangular; leaves short-petioled .. .. *Bambusa.*

Range of floral structures

There may be one flower in a spikelet, as in *Agrostis*, 2 to many, as in *Arrhenatherum*, *Bambusa*, *Festuca*. The rachilla may or may not be continued beyond the flower. Thus, in many 1-flowered spikelets the flower is terminal, i.e., barren glumes, fertile glumes and palea are on the same axis (e.g., *Anthoxanthum*, *Agrostis*, *Oryza* and Andropogoneae). On the other hand, in *Gastridium* the solitary flower is lateral—the rachilla being produced beyond it. The lower barren glumes are rarely absent, as in *Coleanthus*. *Luveria* is distinguished from *Oryza* by their almost complete abortion. In *Brachiaria* (American genus), there is but one barren glume, generally there are two, sometimes more than 2, as in *Anthoxanthum*.

The empty glumes may closely resemble flowering ones, as in *Poa*, *Festuca*, etc., or be different in form, as in *Avena*, where they are much larger and envelope the rest of the several-flowered spikelets. In *Oryza*, they are less than half the length of the single-flowered spikelets. *Stipa* and some *Bambusa* have a third posterior lodicule, the perianth accordingly form a trimerous whorl. In *Melica*, there is only one lodicule.

In the great majority of cases there are 3 stamens. Only one stamen is present in *Uniola;* this is generally the anterior one, which on the contrary is suppressed in *Coleanthus* and the androecium becomes diandrous with 2 lateral stamens; in *Anthoxanthum*, the 2 stamens are antero-posterior. Most of the Bambusae and some *Oryza* have two alternate trimerous whorls (i.e., 6 stamens). In *Microlaena*, there are two alternating dimerous whorls (i.e., 4 stamens). There are rarely more than 6 stamens. *Pariana*, a tropical South American genus, with unisexual flowers has 10–40 stamens in the male flower and *Ochlandra* has large 1-flowered spikelet with 3–7 empty glumes, numerous lodicules and 6–30 polyadelphous or monadelphous stamens. (In *Neohouzeaua* the stamens are strictly monadephous.)

The ovary bears 1–3 styles, each terminating in a long densely papillate stigma, which is rarely simple but generally plumosely branched. *Nardus* has a single simple style and stigma. *Zea mays* has a single stigma formed by the union of 2. In the great majority of cases there are 2 styles. Many Bamboos have a third style. The solitary ovule is sessile on the ventral surface.

Common plants

(1) Paddy (*Oryza sativa* L.). (2) Wheat—*Triticum aestivum* L. (*Syn. T. sativum* Lam.). (3) Barley (*Hordeum vulgare* L.). (4) Oat (*Avena sativa* L.). (5) Maize or Indian corn (*Zea mays* L.).

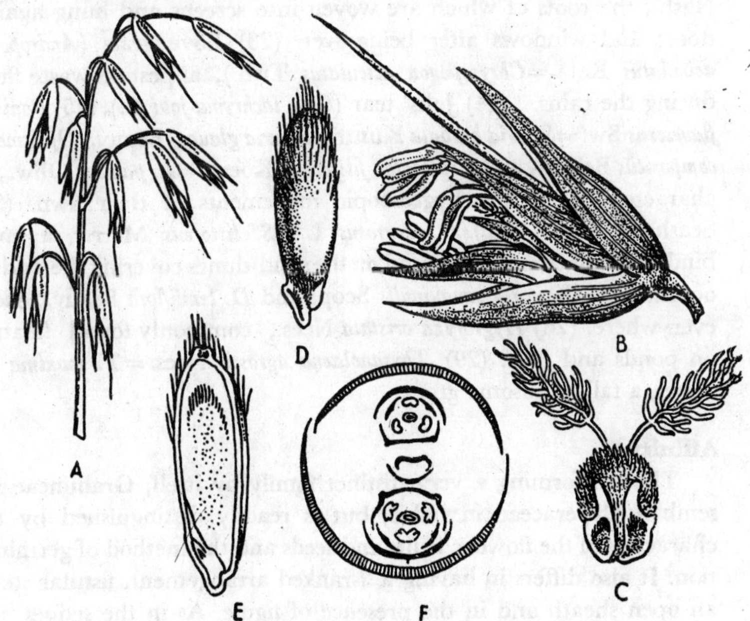

Fig. 518. Gramineae (*Avena sativa*).
A, Portion of a branch with spikelets; B, A spikelet; C, Pistil with lodicules; D, Grain; E, L.s. of the same; F, Floral diagram of a spikelet.

(6) *Pennisetum typhoideum* Rich., *P. typhoides* Staff & C. E. Hubb. (7) *Panicum frumentaceum* Roxb. (8) *P. miliaceum* L., *P. miliare* Lamk., Ragi (*Eleusine coracana* Gaertn.), are small-grained cereals commonly known as 'millets'. (9) *Andropogon sorghum* Brot. =*Sorghum vulgare* Pers. (10) Rye (*Secale cereale* L.) from which rye-bread is produced. (11) Bamboo (*Bambusa arundinacea* Willd.). (12) Sugarcane (*Saccharum officinarum* L.). (13) *Saccharum munja* Roxb., used in making crude writing pens for village school children. (14) *Saccharum spontaneum* L., used in inferior thatching and sand binding. (15) *Imperata arundinacea* Cyrill., used in superior thatching. (16) *Phragmites karka* Trin., the split stems of which are woven into mats. (17) *Cynodon dactylon* Pers., a favourite pasture grass. (18) *Eleusine aegyptiaca* Desf. =*Dactyloctenium aegypticum* Beauv., a common grass used as fodder. (19) *Eleusine indica* Gaertn., a common weed. (20) *Eragrostis cynosuroides* Beauv. =*Desmostachya bipinnata* Stapf., used in religious ceremonies. (21) *Ischaemum angustifolium* Hack. =*Eulaliopsis binata* C. E. Hubb used in manufacturing paper. (22) *Andropogon squarrosus* Hack. =*Vetiveria zizanoides* Nash., the roots of which are woven into screens and hung against doors and windows after being wet. (23) Love grass (*Andropogon aciculatus* Retz. =*Chrysopogon aciculatus* Trin.), a pest of waste fields during the rains. (24) Jobs' tear (*Coix lachryma-jobi* L.). (25) *Panicum flavescens* Sw. =*Setaria barbata* Kunth., *Setaria glauca* Beauv., *Oplismenus compositus* Beauv., and *Leptochloa filiformis* Koem. =*L. panicea* Ohw. are characterized by the hygroscopic movements of their awn. (26) Seashore grass (*Spinifex squarrosus* L. =*S. littoreus* Merr.), a sand-binding plant commonly found on the sand-dunes covering the Indian ocean. (27) *Digitaria sanguinalis* Scop. and *D. tenuiflora* Beauv., occur everywhere. (28) *Hygroryza aristata* Nees., commonly found floating on ponds and jhils. (29) *Thysanolaena agrostis* Nees. =*T. maxima* O. Ktze., a tall handsome grass.

Affinity

Though forming a very distinct family by itself, Gramineae resembles Cyperaceae in habit, but is readily distinguished by the characters of the flowers, fruits and seeds and the method of germination. It also differs in having a 2-ranked arrangement, fistular stem, an open sheath and in the presence of ligule. As in the sedges, the flowers are associated with scale-like glumes, but the arrangement of the floral members conforms to the typical trimerous type. The florets of gramineae borne terminally, while those of cyperaceae are axillary in position. A definite perianth cannot be recognized while the fruit with its one or two carpels is less specialized than those of sedges. The form and position of the embryo are also different. Moreover, the process of germination agrees to some extent with those of Palmae and Liliaceae.

Economic importance

This family stands first among angiosperms in economic importance. *Oryza sativa* and *Triticum sativum* supply the staple foodgrains the people of the whole world and are being cultivated from very ancient time. Millet is obtained from *Pennisetum typhoideum*, *Panicum miliaceum*, *P. miliare*, *Eleusine coracana*, etc. Barley is obtained from *Hordeum vulgare*. *Eleusine aegyptica* and *Panicum sativum* are used as fodder grass. *Secale cereale* is a medicinal plant. Several cultivated species are used for making fermented liquors. Sugar is obtained from the stem of Sugarcane. Bamboo is used all over India for erecting huts. Few grasses yield essential oils, e.g., Ginger grass (*Andropogon odoratus* Dna.), Citronella grass (*Cymbopogon nardus* L.), Lemon grass (*C. citratus* Stapf.) and Geranium oil grass (*C. schoenonthus* Spreng.). Some are used for thatching and paper-manufacturing.

CYPERACEAE

General characters

Plants—annual or more often perennial grass-like herbs, persisting in damp situations with a sympodial rhizome. Stem—*triangular* and *solid throughout*. Leaves—3-*ranked* with a narrow blade, *leaf-sheath closed* eligulate. Inflorescence—spikelets, arranged in spike, receme, panicle or umbel and frequently subtended by foliaceous bracts, spikelets may be one flowered (e.g. *Diplacrum*) or may be many flowered (e.g. *Schoenus*). Flowers—*very minute*, usually bisexual (but unisexual in *Carex*), subtended by chaffy bracts. Perianth—represented by bristles or scales or absent. Stamens—usually in one whorl of 3, rarely only 1, with *basifixed* anthers. Carpels—(3) or (2), ovary 1-celled with a solitary basal, erect, anatropous ovule; style 1, with tripartite stigma. Fruit—*achene*, *utricle* or *nut*. Embryo—smaller than those of Gramineae and lies at the base of the seed in the central line surrounded by endosperm; the cotyledon comes out of the sheath at the time of germination.

Floral formula

$P_0, A_3, \underline{G}_{(2)\text{ or }(3)}$

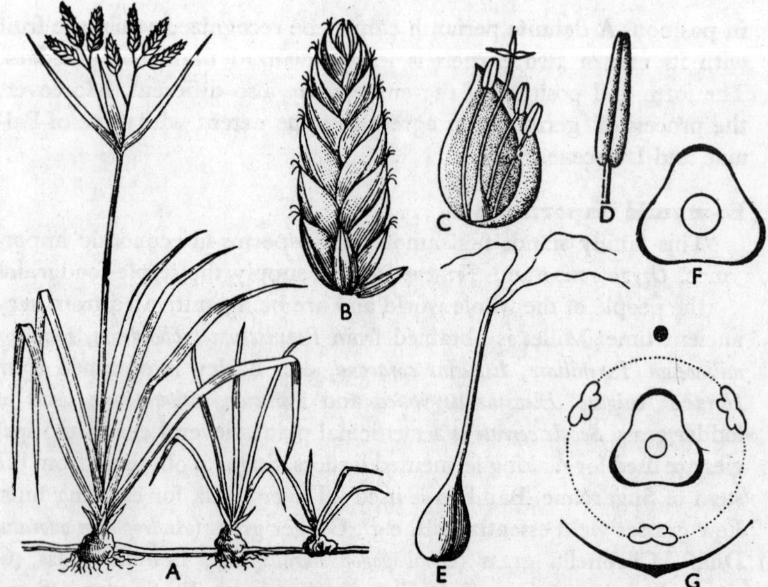

Fig. 519. Cyperaceae (*Cyperus rotundus*).
A, An entire plant; B, An inflorescence; C, Flower; D, Stamen; E, Pistil; F, T.s. of ovary; G, Floral diagram.

Number and distribution

This family consists of about 72 genera and 3,200 species distributed everywhere as marsh plants.

KEY TO GENERA

A. Ovary and fruit enclosed in a utricle .. .. *Carex.*

B. Ovary and fruit not enclosed in a utricle—

(*a*) Flowering glumes distichous, scales or bristles *O*

(*i*) Style 2-fid; rachilla of spikelets deciduous; perennial herbs; stem trigonous; leaves narrow, radical .. *Kyllinga.*

(*ii*) Style 3-fid; rachilla of spikelets persistent; fruit trigonous; perennial or annual herbs; leaves all towards the base of stem or sometimes a few cauline, occasionally reduced to sheaths .. .. *Cyperus.*

(*b*) Flowering glumes spirally arranged; base of style passing gradually into the fruit, and constricted or articulated; glabrous herbs, often tall, leafless or leafy at the base only; stem terete, trigonous or triquetrous .. *Scirpus.*

Range of floral structures

The flowers are usually bisexual, but naked unisexual flowers occur in *Carex*. In this genus the male flowers form a simple spike, each of which being subtended by a bract, whereas the female flowers form a compound spike. The bract subtending the flower is represented by utricle. In *Uncinia*, the secondary axis becomes elongated and forms a bristle-like projection. The secondary axis in *Elyna* bears a male flower above the female one.

The perianth is represented by hairs (e.g., *Eriophorum*), or bristles (e.g., *Scirpus*), or scales. In *Oreobolus*, the perianth is glumaceous which consists of 6 members arranged in two whorls of 3 each. The members of the perianth may be reduced by abortion of one member or they may become numerous, as in *Rhynochospora* and *Eriophorum*.

Androecium consists of 6 stamens, usually arranged in two whorls of 3 each or only 3 stamens sometimes occur, the inner whorl being entirely absent. In *Hemicarpha* and *Bisboeckelera*, the number of stamen is only one.

Gynoecium consists of either 3 or 2 carpels, which are united. Both forms of carpel occur in the species of *Carex*. The number of stigma corresponds to the number of carpels. The style often becomes thickened at its base and forms a beak-like structure which crowns the fruit. The ovary is superior, 1-celled with a single basal ovule.

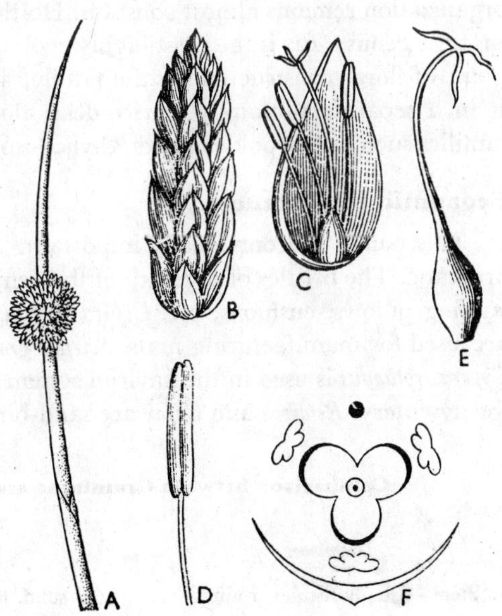

Fig. 520. Cyperaceae (*Scirpus articulatus*). A, Portion of a flowering shoot; B, Inflorescence; C, Flower; D, Stamen; E, Pistil; F, Floral diagram.

Common plants

(1) Common Sedge (*Cyperus rotundus* L.), a weed of cultivated lands. (2) Mat-grass (*Cyperus tegetum* Roxb.), the split stems of which are woven into ordinary mats. (3) *Scirpus grossus* L.f., the black tubers of which are edible.

(4) Club-rush (*Scirpus littoralis* Schrad.), commonly found in the Sundribans. (5) *Fimbristylis junciformis* Kunth., commonly found on wet lands. (6) *Fimbristylis complanata* Link., a common weed with glabrous stem flattened under the umbel. (7) *Juncellus inundatus* Clarke, the split stems of which are also woven into mats. (8) *Kyllinga brevifolia* Rottb., a common weed with white globose heads. (9) Slough grass (*Carex indica* L.), also commonly found on sandy places and very efficient in binding sand.

Affinity

Cyperaceae has been found to be basically similar to Gramineae, particularly from the standpoint of origin. Hutchinson has regarded Gramineae (Graminales) to be the more highly advanced than Cyperaceae and opined that both the families have been derived from spikaceous ancestors through Juncaceae complex. Snell and Blaser were of opinion that Gramineae could not be taken as close allies to Cyperaceae. Blaser (1940) indicated that the spikelets of Cyperaceae could not be homologous with those of the grasses, as the former family varies widely regarding organization, but in the latter the organization remains almost constant. Holthem (1948) has indicated that the genus *Carex* is the most highly evolved when treated from the point of floral construction in the family, and hence he has placed it in a separate subfamily Caricoideae along with other two subfamilies such as Scirpoideae and Rhynchosperaceae.

Economic importance

This family is economically important. The roots of *Kyllinga* are aromatic. The bristles of perianth of the genus *Eriophorum* are used in stuffing pillows, cushions, etc. *Cyperus tegetum* and *Juncellus inundatus* are used for manufacturing mats. *Scirpus grossus* yields edible tubers. *Cyperus rotundus* is used in the kaviraji system of medicine as a specific for dysentery. *Remirea* and *Carex* are sand-binding plants.

Comparison between Gramineae and Cyperaceae

Gramineae	*Cyperaceae*
1. Stem—usually fistular, round.	1. solid, triangular, sympodial rhizomes.
2. Leaves—2-ranked, sheath split up, with ligule.	2. 3-ranked, sheath closed, without ligule.

Comparison between Gramineae and Cyperaceae—(*Contd.*)

Gramineae	*Cyperaceae*
3. Perianth—represented by 2 or 3 lodicules.	3. represented by bristles or scales or absent.
4. Stamens—usually 3, sometimes 6, with versatile anthers.	4. usually 3, rarely 1, with basi-fixed anthers.
5. Carpel—1.	5. (3) or (2).
6. Style—usually 2 with feathery stigmas.	6. always one, with 3-partite stigma.
7. Fruit—caryopsis.	7. achene, utricle or nut.

ORDER 5. PRINCIPES

Generally woody plants with a stout unbranched stem ending in a crown of leaves; flowers small trimerous, usually on compound spadices which are enclosed by one or more large spathaceous bracts in bud; carpels 3, free or variously united; fruit a fibrous drupe or berry; seed with copious endosperm and a minute embryo.

According to Engler and Prantl, this order constitutes the 5th order of monocotyledons which includes a single family Palmae. Bentham and Hooker have placed this family under the series Calycinae. Hutchinson has designated this family as Palmaceae and as well as McLean and Cook have followed the same designation. Lawrence has placed the family in the order Principes after Glumi-floreae and before Synanthae.

PALMAE (*ARECACEAE*)

General characters

Plants—predominantly trees with a stout, erect, unbranched cylindrical stem, having short internodes covered with leaf-scars (or the bases of leaf-stalks), and ending at the top in crown of a few large foliage leaves closely packed together (excepting *Calamus*), sometimes scrambling, occasionally acaulescent; the erect types may be sometimes branched, as in Doum palm (*Hyphaene theboica*) and several others. Leaves—simple, pinnate or palmate, often very large, with well-developed petiole and a broad persistent sheathing base, *plicate*. Inflorescence—usually lateral, *simple* or *compound spadix* or a richly branched panicle, often very large, bearing numerous small flowers enclosed either in one woody, boat-shaped spathe or several spathes, in the latter case, one for each branch, infra-, intra- or supra-foliar. Flower—sessile, *generally unisexual* (bisexual in *Licuala* and *Livistona*), monoecious or dioecious, regular, arranged in a close spiral upon the axis of the inflorescence. Perianth—3+3, green, yellow or white, *persistent* and more or less leathery or fleshy. Stamens

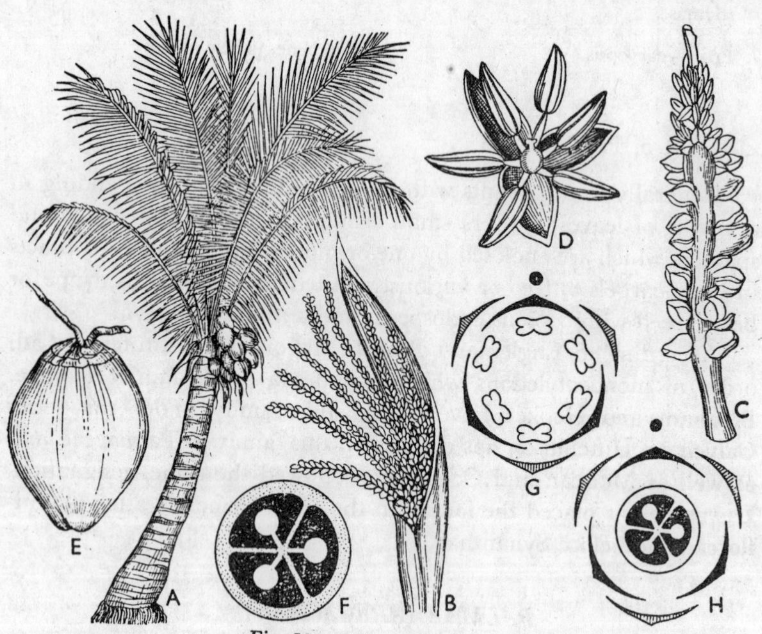

Fig. 521. Palmae (*Cocos mucifera*).
A, Plant; B, Inflorescence enclosed in a spathe; C, A rachilla with the spathe removed; D. Staminate flower; E, Fruit; F. T.s. of ovary; G, Floral diagram of staminate flower; H, The same of pistillate flower.

usually 6, in 2 whorls, rarely 3 (e.g., *Nipa*). Carpels—3, either free or united; *ovary superior, 3-celled* with 1 anatropous or orthotropous ovule in each cell, but often during ripening 2 carpels with their ovules become abortive (e.g., Coconut); style short. Fruit—berry or fibrous drupe. Seeds—albuminous. Embryo—minute, embedded in a copious endosperm.

Floral formula

♂ flowers—$P_{6(3+3)}$, $A_{6(3+3)}$ G_0

♀ flowers—$P_{6(3+3)}$, A_0 $\underline{G_{(3)}}$

Number and distribution

This family consists of 210 genera and about 4,000 species which are chiefly confined to the tropical regions.

KEY TO GENERA

A. Leaves flabelliform, fan-shaped or orbicular:

(a) Monocarpic palms, flowering once and then dying; flowers bisexual .. .. *Corypha.*

(b) Polycarpic palms, flowering year after year—

(i) Flowers bisexual—

Ovary of 3 triangular carpels .. .. *Licuala.*

Ovary of 3 globose carpels .. .. *Livistona.*

(ii) Flowers unisexual; male flowers small, female flowers very large .. .. .. *Borassus.*

B. Leaves pinnate:

(a) Fruit not covered with scales—

(i) Leaves twice pinnatisect .. .. .. *Caryota.*

(ii) Leaves completely or partially once pinnatisect—

Dwarf palms of tidal swamps, branching (buried) .. *Nipa.*

Tall palms with erect unbranched stems; fruit large ovoid nut with a fibrous husk .. .. *Cocos.*

Tall or short palms with pinnatisect leaves, segments lanceolate or ensiform with margins induplicate; flowers dioecious, small, yellowish; fruit yellow or bright-red to blue-black .. .. *Phoenix.*

Slender palms with erect annulate stems; leaves pinnatisect, distal segments confluent; flowers monoecious on branched intrafoliar spadices, male flowers minute, female much larger; perianth accrescent .. .. .. *Areca.*

(b) Fruits covered with imbricating scales; stems climbing, rarely erect, armed .. .. .. *Calamus.*

Range of floral structures

The flowers are generally unisexual, but bisexual flowers also occur sometimes, as in *Livistona*, *Licuala*, *Trachycarpus*, etc. The male and female flowers occur either on the same plant (e.g., *Cocos*) or on different plants (e.g., *Phoenix*). The arrangement and the position of the male and female flowers vary in different genera. In *Raphia ruffia*, the female and the male flowers are arranged in the lower and the upper halves respectively. In *Geonoma*, the male and female flowers become intermingled. In such case, a central female flower with one male on both sides is enclosed by a bract of the so-called fleshy spike. There occurs considerable variation in the size of the flowers, as in *Borassus*, where the female ones are larger than the minute male ones.

The number of the perianth is 6, arranged in two whorls of 3 each. They are generally polyphyllous, but sometimes united. In *Areca catechu*, the inner whorl of perianth leaves becomes very much larger than the outer whorl.

Variation in the number of stamens takes place. Usually there are 6 stamens arranged in 2 whorls of 3 each. But 3 stamens are found in *Nipa*, which is due to the suppression of the stamens of the inner whorl. The stamens sometimes are of indefinite number, as in *Pinanga*, *Caryota*, etc. 'Horn'-like stominodes are found in *Borassus*.

Variation in the number of carpels and position of the ovules are noted occasionally. Usually the pistil is tricarpellary but monocarpellary one occurs in *Cocos nucifera*, where out of 3 carpels two abort during the process of ripening of the fruit. In *Corypha* it is monoearpic from the very beginning, it has no abortive carpels.

The ovary is generally 3-celled, but it is 1-celled in *Areca catechu*. The form of ovules varies from anatropous (e.g., *Geonoma*, *Areca*) to orthotropous which is very rarely found.

Common plants

(1) Palmyra palm (*Borassus flabellifer* L.). (2) Coconut palm (*Cocos nucifera* L.). (3) Date palm (*Phoenix sylvestris* Roxb. and *P. dactylifera* L.). (4) Betelnut palm (*Areca catechu* L.). (5) Cane palm (*Calamus tenuis* Roxb.); Rattan cane (*C. rotang* L.). (6) Water coconut (*Nipa fructicans* Wurmb.), chiefly found in the Sundribans. (7) *Phoenix paludosa* Roxb., also found in the Sundribans. (8) Sago palm (*Metroxylon rumphii* Mart.=*M. sagus* Roltb.). (9) Fish-tail palm (*Caryota urens* L.), commonly planted in gardens. (10) Royal palm (*Oreodoxa regia*=*Roystonia regia* O. F. Cook) is one of the finest specimens of the family and can be seen planted on both sides of the Oreodoxa Avenue in the Indian Botanic Garden. (11) Talipot palms (*Corypha elata* Roxb. and *C. umbracaulifera* L.), are very common in gardens. (12) *Licuala peltata* Roxb., a gregarious shrub. (13) *Livistona chinensis* R. Br., a tree, 20–30 ft. high, frequently cultivated.

Affinity

Bentham and Hooker placed this family under the series Calycinae for its sepaloid calycine perianth. On the basis of homochlamydeous, trimerous, unisexual flowers the family has been placed under Principes by Engler. The presence of universal spadix and unisexual flowers led Rendle to put Palmae with Araceae under Spadiciflorae. Hutchinson is of opinion that the palms have been derived from liliflorean stock and he placed the group under separate order Palmales. According to Wettstein, Palmae seem to be closely related to Pandanaceae and Cyclanthaceae. This family is also allied to Araceae but readily distinguished by the habit, character of ovary, fruit and seeds. The two-whorled trimerous perianth, 6 stamens and tricarpellary superior ovary bring it in close relation to Liliaceae. Hutchinson traces the origin from Liliaceae through *Dracaena-Cordyline*. Erdtnan shows a resemblance between *Palm* and *Dracaena* in the nature of their pollen grains.

Economic importance

This family is of great economic importance as it includes a large number of economic plants. *Cocos nucifera* is one of the most important economic plants, which yields coconut oil of commerce. In addition to this product, it also produces various other substances which are utilized for different purposes. The fibrous mesocarp is utilized in the production of ropes, mats, brushes, etc. The sugary sap derived by tapping the young inflorescence is used for alcoholic drink and toddy yields vinegar. *Phoenix dactylifera* produces common edible dates; the wood of this plant is used in making water-pipes; the leaves are used for thatching purposes mats, baskets, fans, etc. *P. sylvestris* is a common sugar-yielding plant. The common fan-palm (*Borassus flabellifer*), produces molasses and sugar from its juice secreted by tapping the inflorescence; it also yields strongest timber in making the posts, pillars, etc. *Elaeis guineensis* Jacq., yields a valuable oil. *Copernicia*, the common Cannuba palm, is a wax-yielding plant and it is used for making gramophone records, candles, etc. *Corypha umbracaulifera* (Talipot palm) produces umbrella from the leaves; the split leaves are utilized in making mats, baskets, fans, etc. *Calamus rotang* yields valuable canes. *Areca catechu* is the common betel-nut palm, the seeds of which are cut into slices and taken with the leaves of betel; a sort of powder is derived from the roasted seeds; the leaves are used for thatching purpose. *Phytelephas*, the common vegetable ivory, is largely used by American people; the hard endosperm of the seed is generally edible. *Metroxylon rumphii* produces common sago which is derived from the pith by crushing and washing. *Caryota urens* produces a sort of

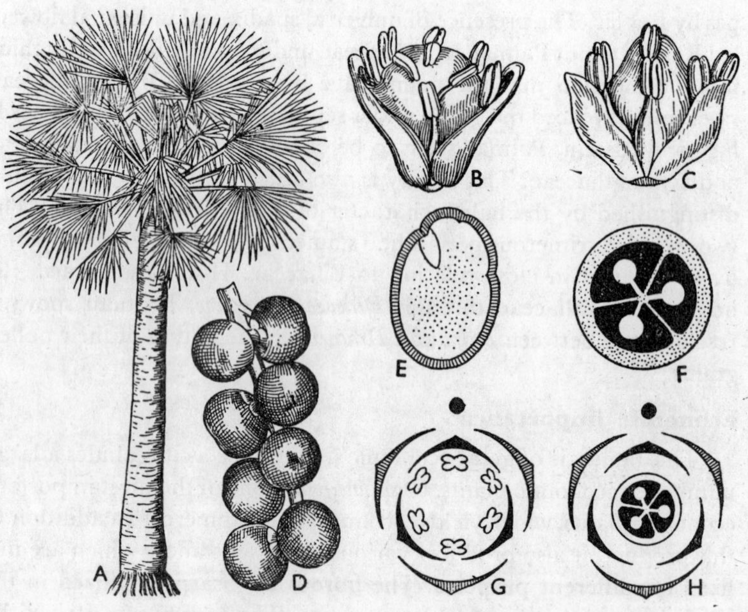

Fig. 522. Palmae (*Borassus flabellifer*).
A, The plant; R, Staminate flower; C, Pistillate flower; D, Fruits; E, L.s. of seed; F, T.s. of ovary; G, Floral diagram of staminate flower; H, The same of pistillate flower.

toddy rich in vitamins, which is used in tuberculosis. Many species are cultivated in gardens as ornamentals.

ORDER 7. SPATHIFLORAE

Generally herbs or climbers; leaves large; flowers small, unisexual or bisexual, crowded on a fleshy spadix which is subtended by a single large bract or spathe; perianth absent or much reduced but never petaloid; ovary superior; fruit berry; seed with copious endosperm and a minute embryo.

According to Engler, this order comprises of two families, viz., Araceae* and Lemnaceae*. Bentham and Hooker have placed these families under the series Nudiflorae. Hutchinson, however, places these families under the order Arales.

ARACEAE

General characters

Plants—usually terrestrial herbs (but aquatic in *Pistia*), often large or even tree-like, rarely shrubs, sometimes climbing, generally with acrid watery latex. Stem—rhizomatous, tuberous or corm-like, resin passages and mucilage sacs sometimes occur. Leaves—radical or alternate (in climbing species), generally net-veined, sometimes long and

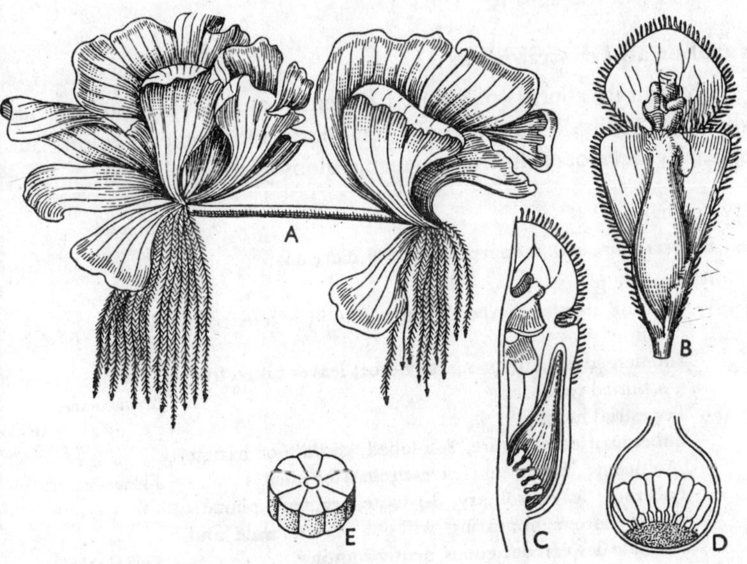

Fig. 523. Araceae (*Pistia stratiotes*).
A, Plant; B, Inflorescence enclosed in the spathe; C, V.s. of the same; D, L.s. of ovary; E, Fruit.

narrow with parallel veins (e.g., *Acorus calamus*). Inflorescence—*spadix with a spathe* which may be green (e.g., *Colocasia*), petaloid (e.g., *Richardia*), or brilliant scarlet (e.g., *Anthurium*). Flowers—small, inconspicuous with dimerous or trimerous whorls, bisexual or unisexual, closely crowded on the spadix without bracteoles, mostly zoophilous. Perianth—absent (in unisexual flowers) but present in bisexual flowers, of 4–6 scales which may be free or united. Stamens—

2, 4 or 8, with the filaments more or less united at the base (e.g., *Arisaema*), or throughout their length (e.g., *Colocasia, Alocasia*), or to a single stamen (e.g., *Arisarum*); in *Pistia* the male flower is reduced to two anthers which are united; staminodes sometimes present in the female flowers. Carpels—(3), usually reduced to one (e.g., *Colocasia, Pistia*); ovary superior, sometimes inferior, 1-many-celled, ovules few to numerous in each cell on basal, parietal or axile placentae; stigma 1 or more. Fruit—berry. Seed—albuminous, embedded in a mucilaginous pulp, or exalbuminous. Embryo—*minute* and *straight*.

Floral formula

$$P_{(4-6)\text{ or }0}\ A_{(2-8)\text{ or }1}\ \underline{G_{(1-3)}}$$

Number and distribution

This family consists of about 105 genera and about 1,500 species which are generally found in the temperate and tropical regions but especially developed in the warmer regions of the globe.

Key to Genera

A. Flowers unisexual, monoecious, rarely dioecious:

(*a*) Aquatic plants—

Floating stemless herbs; leaves sessile in a rosette-like tuft .. .. *Pistia*.

Submerged aquatic or marsh herbs; leaves tufted from a buried rootstock .. .. .. *Cryptocoryne*.

(*b*) Terrestrial herbs—

Tuberous; leaves entire, 3–5-lobed, cordate or hastate or pedate; flowers and leaves present together .. *Typhonium*.

Tuberous; leaves solitary, 3-partite, segments pinnatisect; flowers appearing without leaves, male and female flowers contiguous, neuter wanting .. *Amorphophallus*.

Herbs, usually tall, coarse; leaves and scapes arising from the rhizome; leaves may be peltate; spadix with a barren appendage, not adnate to the spathe—

Ovules few, basal .. .. .. *Alocasia*.

Ovules many, parietal .. .. .. *Colocasia*.

B. Flowers bisexual:

(*a*) Epiphytic climbing herbs—

Perianth absent, berries free, ovule solitary .. *Scindapsus*.

Perianth of 4–6 segments, ovule solitary, plant unarmed .. .. .. *Pothos*.

(*b*) Stout spinous aquatic or marsh herbs .. .. *Lasia*.

Range of floral structures

This family shows great variations in floral structures. The flowers are bisexual with typical trimerous arrangement $P_{3+3}A_{3+3}G_{(3)}$ (e.g., *Acorus*), or with dimerous whorls (e.g., *Anthurium*), or dimerous arrangement with reduction to one in gynoecium (e.g., *Gymnostachys*). The flowers are bisexual and naked, as in *Calla*, or unisexual and naked with male flowers on the upper and female on the lower portions of the spadix, as in *Colocasia*, *Alocasia* and others.

The spathe is green, as in *Colocasia*, or petaloid, as in *Richardia*, or it assumes brilliant scarlet colour, as in *Anthurium*.

Perianth is either present or absent. The perianth leaves are united (e.g., *Spathiphyllum*), or free (e.g., *Acorus*). They are generally absent in unisexual flowers but are present in bisexual flowers.

Androecium forms two whorls or a single whorl and in the latter case, the filaments are connate to some extent at the base (e.g., *Dracunculus*, *Arisaema*), or filaments are united throughout their length and form a synandrium, as in *Colocasia*, *Alocasia*. The male flowers are found to be reduced to form synandrium by two anthers, (e.g., *Pistia*). In *Arisarum* and *Biarum*, there is a single stamen.

Carpels are generally three, but one carpel is present in *Colocasia* and *Pistia*. Ovary is superior or sessile. The ovary becomes 1-many chambered with few to indefinite ovules. The placentation may be of various types, such as, parietal, axile or marginal.

Common plants

(1) Common Arum or Taro (*Colocasia antiquorum* Schott. =*C. esculenta* Schott.), a herb chiefly cultivated for its edible rhizome. (2) *Alocasia indica* Schott., also cultivated for its rootstock. (3) *Scindapsus officinalis* Schott., a root-climber of gardens. (4) *Typhonium trilobatum* Schott., commonly found in waste places. (5) Teliga potato (*Amorphophallus campanulatus* Bl.), commonly cultivated for the edible corm, also found wild. (6) Water lettuce (*Pistia stratiotes* L.), a common floating herb with rosettes of radical leaves. (7) *Cryptocoryne ciliata* Fisch., an aquatic herb on the muddy banks of the Ganges, characterized by the viviparous mode of germination of the seeds. (8) *Pothos scandens* L., a gigantic root-climber, common in gardens. (9) Arum lily (*Richardia ethiopica* Kunth.), a herb with thick rootstock and large white trumpet-like spathe; very common in Darjeeling. (10) *Arisaema speciosum* Mart., grows in Darjeeling and has a long tail and a spotted hood-like spathe which looks like a fearful snake from a

distance, an instance of mimicry. (11) *Lasia heterophylla* Schott., occurs in swampy places.

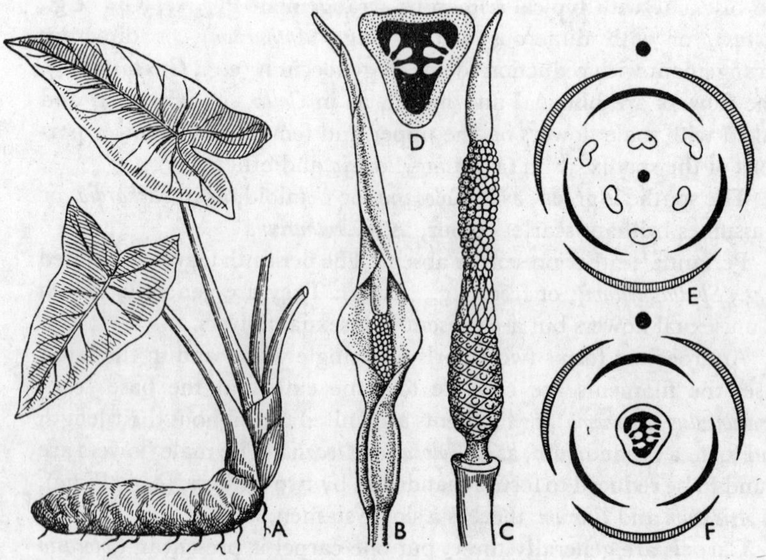

Fig. 524. Araceae (*Colocasia antiquorum*).
A, The plant; B, Inflorescence enclosed in a spathe; C, The same with the spathe removed; D, T.s. of ovary; D, Floral diagram of staminate flower; E, The same of pistillate flower.

Affinity

Hutchinson is of opinion that Araceae has been developed as a separate phylum from Liliflorae. Lotsy assumes that Palms, Aroids and Pandanales have been derived from the Piperales. Such contrast with Piperaceae is mainly based on the floral structure and inflorescence of the latter which simulate with such trend of Araceae. The plants of this family, though strikingly different in general habit, are closely allied to Palmae in such important characters, as the relative size of the embryo and endosperm, while in both we notice the large development of the spathe and the association of a large number of small, inconspicuous flowers in often huge, indefinite inflorescences. Araceae, on the other hand, is closely allied to Lemnaceae which is evidently a much reduced member of Aroid type, the reduction proceeding so far as to affect the vegetative and reproductive organs.

Economic importance

This family consists of several economic plants. An aromatic essential oil is obtained from Sweet flag (*Acorus calamus*). The underground stems of *Colocasia*, *Alocasia* and *Amorphophallus* are eaten as vegetables. A kind of fibre is derived from the stem of *Scindapsus*. The fruits of *Monstera* are often taken for delicate flavour. Some plants are cultivated as ornamentals, such as *Philodendron*, *Anthurium*, *Caladium*, *Pothos*, *Scindapsus*, etc.

LEMNACEAE

General characters

Plants—small, floating, perennial herbs with a *thalloid leaf-like shoot*, monoecious. Flowers—unisexual, naked or enclosed by a membraneous sheathing spathe. Stamens—in male flower *one;* anther 1–2-celled; filament absent or if present filiform or fusiform. Carpel—in

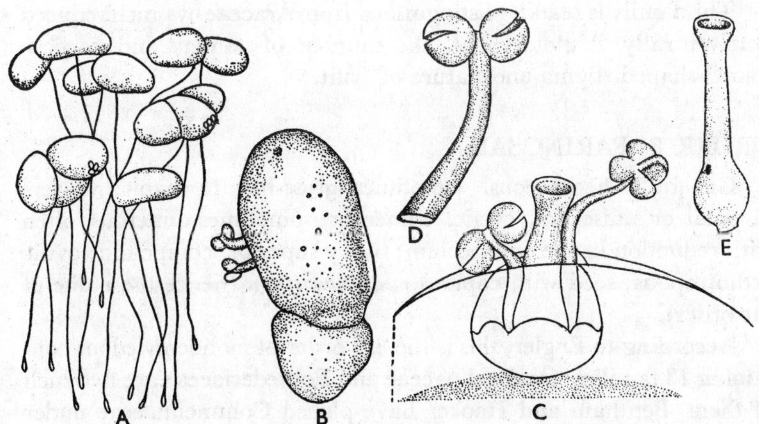

Fig. 525. Lemnaceae (*Lemna minor*).
A, A group of plants; B, Portion of a flowering shoot; C, A three-flowered inflorescence enclosed in a sheath; D., Staminate flower; E. Pistillate flower.

female flower *one;* ovary superior, flask-shaped, 1-celled with 1–7, basal, erect ovules; stigma short, *funnel-shaped*. Fruit—*utricle*. Seed—with or without endosperm.

Number and distribution

This family consists of 3 genera with 25 species, which are distributed throughout the world except the Arctic region.

Common plants

(1) Duck weeds (*Lemna trisulca* and *L. minor*) are common floating herbs, measuring about 1/8th to 3/4ths of an inch, covering the surface of tanks and pools as a compact green mass. (2) *Wolffia arrhiza* L., smallest flowering plant measuring about 1/20th of an inch. (3) *Spirodela polyrrhiza* L., another common floating herb.

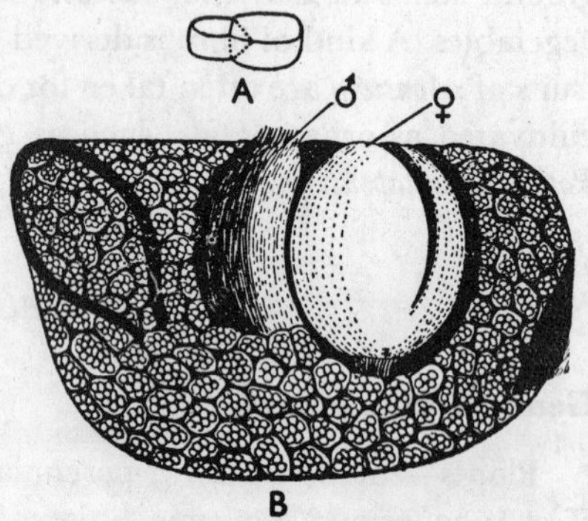

Fig. 526. Lemnaceae (*Wolffia arrhiza*). A, Plant; B, V.s. of the same (highly magnified).

Affinity

This family is readily distinguished from Araceae by much reduced dorsiventrally thalloid shoot, the number of stamens and carpels, funnel-shaped stigma and nature of fruit.

ORDER 8. FARINOSAE

Generally herbaceous, sometimes grass-like in habit; flowers bisexual or unisexual, cyclic, trimerous, sometimes dimerous, often with reduction in the androecium; ovary superior, compound; ovule orthotropous; seed with copious *mealy endosperm* (hence the name of the order).

According to Engler, this is the 8th order of monocotyledons containing 13 families. Commelinaceae and Pontederiaceae are two such of them. Bentham and Hooker have placed Commelinaceae under the series Coronarie. Rendle following Engler has put the family in Farinosae. Hutchinson has made a separate rank of the order Commelinales.

COMMELINACEAE

General characters

Plants—annual or perennial herbs with swollen nodes. Leaves—alternate, simple, with prominent sheath. Inflorescence—monochasial (helicoid) cymes arising from the axil of a foliage leaf or of a spathe-like bract; bracteoles sometimes present. Flowers—*irregular*, sometimes zygomorphic, bisexual, hypogynous. Perianth—3+3, distinguished into calyx and corolla; sepals generally free, petals commonly *blue*, generally free. Stamens—6, all perfect or only 3, outer being staminodes (but staminodes absent in *Collisea*); filaments often hairy. Carpels—(3); ovary superior, 3-celled, rarely 2-celled by suppression, with solitary or few orthotropous ovules in each cell; style terminal; stigma generally capitate. Fruit—*capsule*. Seed—*angled*, albuminous (mealy endosperm). Embryo—at the apex of the opposite end of the hilum.

Floral formula

$P_{6(3+3)}, A_{6(3+3) \text{ or } 6}, \underline{G_{(3)}}$

Number and distribution

This family consists of 37 genera and about 600 species distributed throughout the tropics but absent from Europe and temperate Asia.

KEY TO GENERA

A. Stamens 3 perfect, and 1–3 staminodes:

(*a*) Cymes solitary, enclosed in spathaceous bract; one petal larger than others and often clawed .. .. *Commelina*.

(*b*) Cymes paniculate, not enclosed in spathes; petals all equal .. .. *Aneilema*.

B. Stamens 6 perfect:

Petals united below in a tube .. .. .. *Cyanotis*.

Common plants

(1) *Commelina benghalensis* L., a very common weed of ditches and other moist places with ordinary subaerial flowers and cleistogamous flowers buried under the ground. (2) *Commelina appendiculata* Clarke and *C. obliqua* Ham., are common weeds of ditches. (3) Spiderwort (*Tradescantia virginiana* L.), and *T. bicolor*=*Rheo discolor* Hance, common garden herbs, the staminal hairs of which exhibit circulatory motion of the protoplasm. (4) *Cyanotis axillaris* Roem. & Schult., a common weed found in cultivated lands. (5) *Aneilema spiratum* R. Br. =*Murdania spirata* Bruckner, *A. vaginatum* R. Br.=*Murdania vaginatum* Bruckner and *A. nudiflorum* R. Br. are common weeds of fields and in wet places.

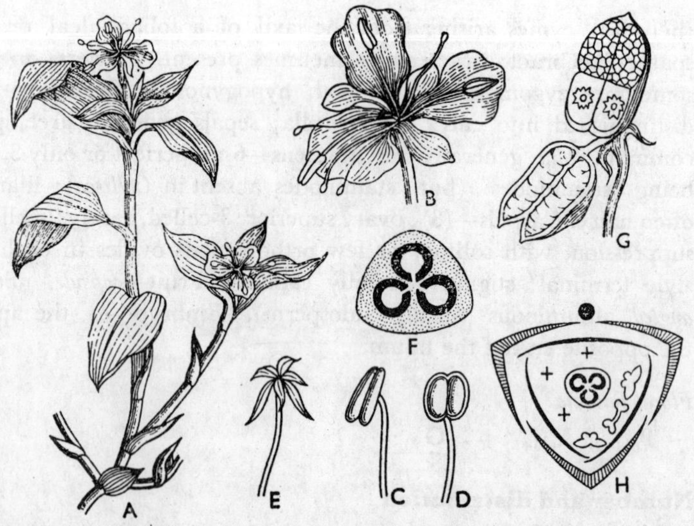

Fig. 527. Commelinaceae (*Commelina benghalensis*).
A, Portion of a flowering shoot; B, Flower; C–D, Fertile stamens; E, Sterile stamen; F, T.s. of ovary; G, Dehiscence of fruit; H, Floral diagram.

Affinity

The affinity of Commelinaceae is still problematic. According to Hutchinson Commelinaceae establishes a close link between Helobiae and Liliflorae. He has also asserted that Commelinaceae is phylogenetically related to different taxa of the families of the order Farinosae, regarding the characters of mealy endosperm and the perianth differentiation into calyx and corolla. The Commelinaceae may be closely related to Pontederiaceae on the basis of mealy endosperm, ligular ochrea-like sheath and in the resemblance of floral structure of *Pontederia* (Pontederiaceae) and *Spironema* (Commelinaceae).

Economic importance

This family is of little economic importance. The leaves of *Commelina benghalensis* are edible. *Rheo discolor* is a favourite garden plant. Other ornamental plants are *Cyanotis*, *Aneilema*, *Floscopa*, etc.

PONTEDERIACEAE

General characters

Plants—*aquatic perennial herbs*, erect or floating or rooting in the substratum. Stem—main stem slender or stout, buried or unraised rootstock with fibrous roots. Leaves—arising singly on the stem, mostly enveloped with sheathing leaf-base, *fleshy, with long swollen petiole.* Inflorescence—terminal raceme or spike, rarely panicle, with spathaceous bracts. Flowers—slightly irregular, *medianly zygomorphic*, bisexual, hypogynous, with minute or obsolete bracts and bracteoles. Perianth—(3+3), petaloid, usually tubular below, persistent, imbricate. Stamens—usually 3+3, rarely uniseriate with outer row of 3 stamens absent, adnate to the perianth lobes; anthers elongated, basifixed or dorsifixed, with longitudinal or porous dehiscence; filaments filiform. Carpels—(3); ovary superior, 3-*celled* with axile placentation or 1-*celled* with parietal placentation with many ovules, arranged in two series. Fruit—a loculicidal 3-valved capsule or 1-seeded achene. Seeds—with cylindrical embryo and *mealy endosperm.*

Floral formula

$\uparrow$ ⚥ $\overline{P_{(3+3)}\ A_{(3+3)}}$ $\underline{G_{(3)}}$

Number and distribution

This family consists of 7 genera and about 28 species. All are aquatic or marsh plants distributed in the warm parts of the globe.

KEY TO GENERA

A. Ovary trilocular:
Stamens 6 in two series .. .. .. *Eichhornia.*

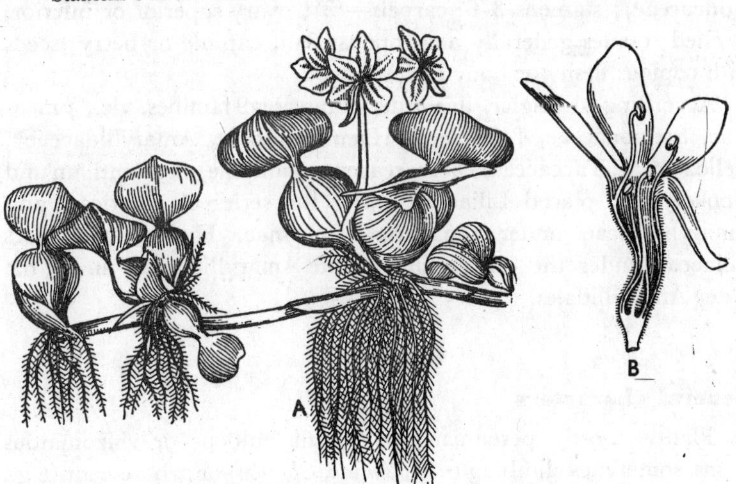

Fig. 528. Pontederiaceae (*Eichhornia crassipes*). A, An entire plant; B, L.s. of a flower.

Stamens 3 in one series .. .. .. *Heteranthera.*

B. Ovary unilocular .. .. *Pontederia.*

Common plants

(1) *Eichhornia crassipes* Solms. (Water hyacinth), widely distributed in stagnant or slow moving fresh-water, (2) *Pontederia sagittata* L., *P. vaginalis* L. and *P. plantaginea* L. are aquatic herbs, distributed in all provinces.

Affinity

According to Hutchinson and Schwartez presence of six petaloid perianth lobes suggests an affinity with Liliaceae but is separated from the latter family by the presence of zygomorphic flowers and seeds with mealy endosperm.

Economic importance

Eichhornia and *Pontederia* are usually cultivated in pools and lakes as aquatic ornamentals.

ORDER 9. LILIFLORAE

Generally perennial herbs; flowers bisexual, regular or sometimes irregular, typically 3-merous; perianth petaloid but glumaceous (Juncaceae); stamens 3–6; carpels—(3); ovary superior or inferior, 3-celled; ovules generally anatropous; fruit capsule or berry; seeds with copious fleshy or bony endosperm.

According to Engler, this order comprises 9 families, viz., Juncaceae, Stemonaceae, Liliaceae*, Haemodoraceae, Amaryllidaceae*, Velloziaceae, Taccaceae, Dioscoreaceae, Iridaceae, etc. Bentham and Hooker have placed Liliaceae under the series Coronarieae, and Amaryllidaceae under the series Epigynae. Hutchinson places Liliaceae under the order Liliales and Amaryllidaceae under the order Amaryllidales.

LILIACEAE

General characters

Plants—mostly perennial herbs with bulbous or rhizomatous stems, sometimes climbing (e.g., *Smilax*, *Gloriosa*) or arborescent (e.g., *Dracaena*, *Yucca*, *Aloe*). Leaves—simple, radical or cauline (alternate or whorled, but opposite in *Scolyopus*), rarely compound (e.g., *Paris polyphylla*). Inflorescence—generally racemose, sometimes cymose. Flowers—regular, bisexual, rarely unisexual (e.g., *Smilax*), hypogynous. Perianth—3+3, free or united, petaloid, sometimes sepaloid. Stamens—3+3; anthers introrse or extrorse. Carpels—(3); *ovary superior*, 3-celled with many or few anatropous ovules in each cell; styles separate or united. Fruit—a septicidal or loculicidal capsule, sometimes berry. Seed—with a small embryo and copious fleshy or bony endosperm.

Floral formula

$\oplus$ ⚥ $P_{6(3+3)}, A_{6(3+3)}, \underline{G_{(3)}}$

Number and distribution

This family consists of about 240 genera and 4,000 species of world-wide distribution.

KEY TO GENERA

A. Shrubs with perennial stems above ground; fruit berry-like:

(*a*) Stems without green leaves, usually straggling, leaves replaced by linear or acicular cladodes with minute scales .. .. *Asparagus*.

(*b*) Stems leafy—

(*i*) Leaves 3–5-nerved, reticulately veined; leaf-base with 2 tendrils .. .. .. *Smilax*.

(*ii*) Leaves parallel veined, numerous, usually clustered at the apex of an erect caudex; each cell of ovary 1-ovuled .. .. *Dracaena*.

B. Climbing herbs with leafy stems; leaves with a long, tendril-like apex; flowers large, showy .. .. *Gloriosa*.

C. Herbs with tunicated bulbs and characteristic odour. strong or pungent; leaves radical, fistular or flat, enveloping the scape below; flowers umbellate or capitate at the top of the scape, at first enclosed in an involucre of bracts .. .. *Allium*.

Common plants

(1) Onion (*Allium cepa* L.), and (2) Garlic (*Allium sativum* L.) are chiefly cultivated for their edible bulbs. (3) *Asparagus racemosus* Willd., a common prickly climber with fasciculated roots and cladodes. (4) Glory lily (*Gloriosa superba* L.), a climber commonly found in dry places with apices of leaves converted into tendrils. (5) Sarsaparilla ((*Smilax macrophylla* Roxb. =*S. zeylanica* L.). a prickly climber

with reticulate venation and stipular tendrils. (6) *Aloe perfoliata* Willd. and *A. vera* L., common herbs with dentate fleshy leaves. (7) *Drácaena terniflora* Jack. and *Yucca gloriosa* L. are common tree-like shrubs, often

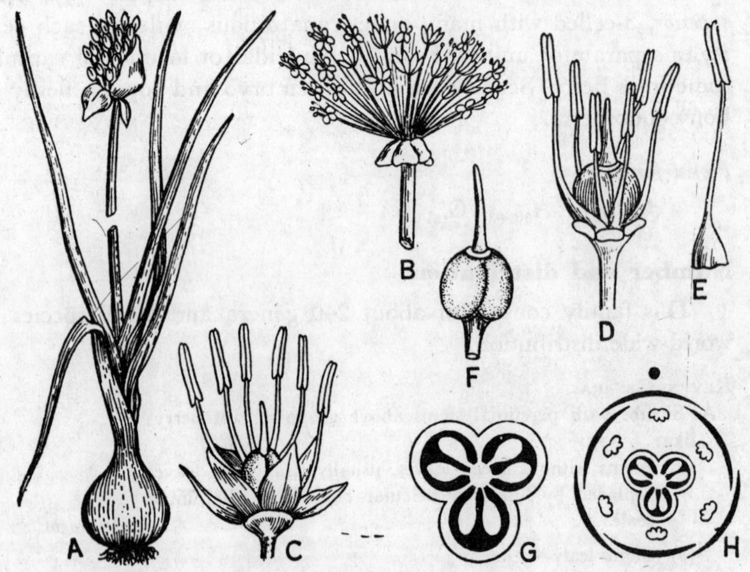

Fig. 529. Liliaceae (*Allium cepa*).
A, Plant; B, Inflorescence; C, Flower; D, The same after removal of perianth; E, Stamen; F, Pistil; G, T.s. of ovary; H, Floral diagram.

cultivated in gardens. (8) *Hemerocallis fulva* L., and *Asphodelus tenuifolius* Cav., are common garden plants. (9) *Colchicum luteum* Baker., a medicinal plant chiefly found in the hills.

Affinity

Liliaceae resembles very much Amaryllidaceae except in the character of superior ovary. Juncaceae also bears a close affinity to Liliaceae. It is considered to be polyphyletic in origin from the standpoint of cytological variabilities, embryological and anatomical structures. Liliaceae is also supposed to have been derived from Helobieae or its ancestor based on the floral structures of a few genera belonging to Liliaceae, such as, *Petrosavia*, *Protolirion*, etc., which possess semi-free carpels.

Economic importance

This family is of some economic importance. Tulips, Lilies, Hyacinths, Scillas, autumn Crocuses and others constitute the bulk of the Dutch bulb trade. The day lilies (*Hemerocallis*) merit special attention. *Asparagus* is an important vegetable crop. The onion and garlic are of great commercial value. The red squill, used in rodent control, is obtained from the bulbs of *Urginea*. *Aloin*, important in drug trade, is obtained from large acerage of the genus *Aloe*. *Colchicum* is an important medicinal plant. Many plants are used as ornamentals, such as, *Gloriosa*, *Hemerocallis*, *Asphodelus*, *Dracaena*, *Yucca*, etc.

AMARYLLIDACEAE

General characters

Plants—mostly perennial herbs with bulbous, sometimes rhizomatous stems, rarely shrubby or arborescent. Leaves—radical, distichous. Inflorescence—monochasial cymes, subtended by 2-many

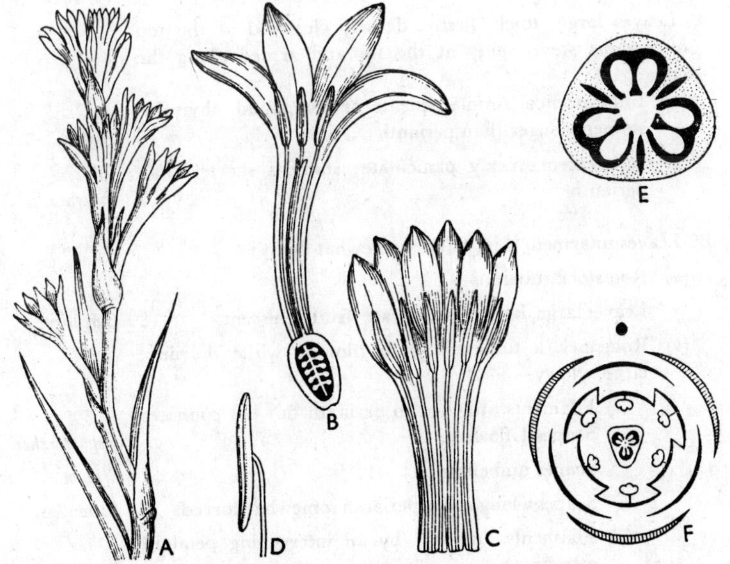

Fig. 530. Amaryllidaceae (*Polianthes tuberosa*).
A. Portion of a flowering shoot; B, V.s. of a flower; C, Perianth-tube split open showing epiphyllous stamens; D, Stamen; E, T.s. of ovary; F, Floral diagram.

spathe-like bracts and borne on a leafless scape. Flowers—regular or zygomorphic, bisexual, epigynous. Perianth—3+3, petaloid, sometimes gamophyllous with a corona (e.g., *Narcissus*, *Pancratium*, some species of *Crinum*), united below into a shorter or longer tube, imbricate or valvate. Stamens—6, with introrse anthers, epiphyllous. Carpels—(3); *ovary inferior*, usually 3-celled with numerous anatropous ovules arranged in two series on axile placenta. Fruit—usually a 3-celled capsule, sometimes berry. Seeds—few to many. Embryo—small, embedded in a copious fleshy endosperm; radicle turned towards the hilum.

Floral formula

$$\uparrow \text{ or } \oplus ⚥ \overline{P_{6(3+3)}, A_{6(3+3)}}, \overline{G_{(3)}}$$

Number and distribution

This family consists of 86 genera and about 1,310 species confined to the warmer regions of both hemispheres. Chiefly xerophytic.

KEY TO GENERA

A. Leaves large, thick, fleshy, densely clustered at the top of a short stem, spiny at the tip and armed along the edge:
- (*a*) Inflorescence, simple, spicate or compound, thyrsoid; stamens longer than perianth .. .. .. *Agave.*
- (*b*) Inflorescence laxly paniculate; stamens shorter than perianth .. .. *Furcraea.*

B. Leaves unarmed, thin, flat or somewhat fleshy:
- (*a*) Rootstock tuberous—
  Leaves large, lanceolate, plicate; fruit dehiscent .. *Curculigo.*
- (*b*) Rootstock a tunicated bulb; flowers white or pink, large, showy—
  - (*i*) Filaments attached to perianth but not connate:
    Scapes 1-flowered .. .. .. *Zephyranthes.*
    Scapes umbellate .. .. .. *Crinum.*
    Scapes a long spike, perianth somewhat curved .. *Polianthes.*
  - (*ii*) Filaments united by an intervening petaloid membrane .. .. *Pancratium.*

Range of floral structures

The plan of the flower in Amaryllidaceae resembles Liliaceae excepting the character of an inferior zygomorphic flower is often noted, as in *Alstroemeria*, by reduction of perianth, stamens and style. Perianth members are generally connate but free perianths are also found in *Galanthus*, *Leucojum*, etc. In *Galanthus*, the outer three perianth-segments become larger and spreading, whereas the inner ones are smaller and straight. The members of the perianth are 6, which generally form a longer or shorter tube.

The corona or paracorolla met with in many genera of this family exhibits the most exquisite and curious morphological structure. The so-called corona or paracorolla is supposed to be the basal outgrowth of the filaments which are united together to form funnel-shaped structure, or inner outgrowth of perianth constituting the infundibular structure. The corona is either staminal or perigonal from the view-point of origin. In *Narcissus* and *Cryptostephanus*, the nature of corona is perigonal but it becomes staminal in *Pancratium*. Considerable debate has been made about the nature of paracorolla and it has been interpreted by many authors, and according to others it has been considered as nectar-secreting disc.

Variation in the number of stamens is also noted. In the genus, *Gethyllis*, 12–18 stamens are found to be united in many bundles. In *Vellozia*, the number of stamens is some multiple of 6.

The ovary is usually 3-celled, but 1-celled ovary with parietal placentation is found in *Leontochir*.

Common plants

(1) Tuberose (*Polianthes tuberosa* L.), commonly cultivated in gardens for the sweet-scented white flowers. (2) *Crinum asiaticum* L. and *C. latifolium* L., common garden plants with flowers in cymose umbels. (3) *Pancratium verecundum* Ait., another common garden plant with staminal coronas which are united forming a cup-like structure. (4) *Curculigo orchioides* Gaertn., a garden plant very common in dry situations with yellow flowers. (5) *Curculigo recurvata* Dryand., a native of the tropical Himalayas is found in Darjeeling; it is a highly interesting plant likely to be mistaken for a dwarf palm on account of its corrugated palm-like leaves. (6) *Agave americana* L. and *A. cantula* Roxb., commonly planted in gardens and along the railway lines for hedging purpose. (7) Star-grass (*Hypoxis aurea* Lour.), a small weed with tubercled seeds. (8) Daffodil (*Narcissus pseudo-narcissus*), a common garden plant with prominent corona. (9) *Furcraea gigantea*

Vent., a short-stemmed large shrub. (10) *Zephyranthes tubispatha* Herb., a bulbous herb of the gardens.

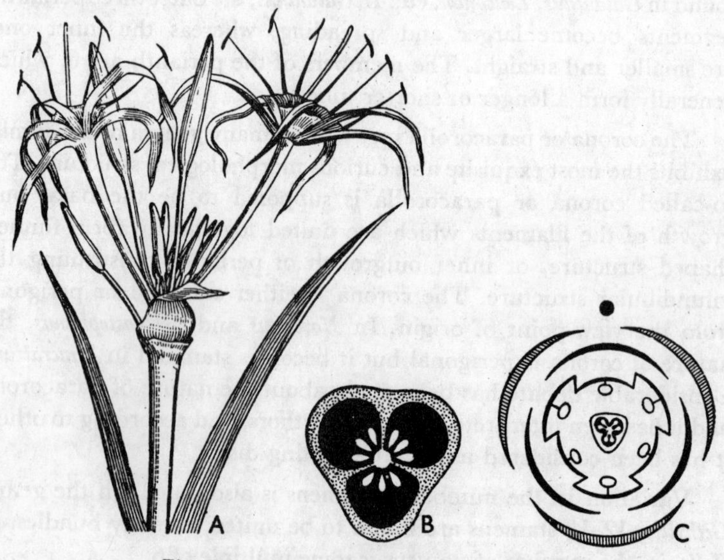

Fig. 531. Amaryllidaceae (*Crinum asiaticum*).
A, Portion of a flowering shoot; B, T.s. of ovary; C, Floral diagram.

Affinity

Amaryllidaceae is closely allied to Liliaceae but readily distinguished by the inferior ovary. It is also allied to Dioscoreaceae but the latter is distinguished by its habits: climbing plants with net-veined leaves and small, often unisexual flowers. Iridaceae, while resembling Amaryllidaceae in the inferior ovary, is distinguished from the latter as well as other epigynous petaloid families in having only three stamens.

Economic importance

This family is of some economic importance. *Agave americana* is one of the most important economic plants of Mexico and is widely cultivated in the tropics for the tough bast fibres of the leaf which yield the 'false manila hemp' of commerce; the sap which exudes from the terminal bud on removal yields, when fermented, a drink known as '*pulque*'. Other species are also useful fibre-plants, e.g., Sisal hemp (*A. rigida* var *sisalana*). *Furcraea* is another fibre-yielding plant. The South American genus *Alstroemeria* yields a kind of flour from its root. Many plants are used as ornamentals, such as *Crinum*, *Polianthes*, *Curculigo*, *Amaryllis*, *Narcissus*, *Pancratium*, *Zephyranthes*, etc.

Comparison between Liliaceae and Amaryllidaceae

Liliaceae	*Amaryllidaceae*
1. Modified stems are either rhizomes, bulbs or tubers.	1. Modified stems are usually bulbs, rarely rhizomes.
2. Leaves are either radical or cauline or both.	2. Mostly radical leaves.
3. Flowers hypogynous.	3. Flowers epigynous.
4. Inflorescence—either simple or compound racemes or spikes or umbellate cymes.	4. Usually umbellate cymes.
5. Absence of corona in staminal filaments.	5. Presence of corona.
6. Anthers versatile, introrse and extrorse.	6. Anthers versatile, introrse.
7. Superior ovary.	7. Inferior ovary.

ORDER 10. SCITAMINEAE (ZINGIBERALES)

Generally large perennial herbs with rhizomatous stems; leaves distichous or in spirals, but the leaf-sheath is not entire; flowers bisexual, usually irregular; perianth in two trimerous whorls, petaloid or differentiated into calyx and corolla; functional stamens 1 or 5 (but 6 in *Ravenala*); carpels—(3); ovary inferior, usually 3-celled, with 1-many ovules in each cell; fruit capsule or berry; seed with small endosperm and copious perisperm, embryo straight or curved.

According to Engler this order comprises 4 families, viz., Musaceae, Zingiberaceae, Cannaceae, and Marantaceae. In Bentham and Hooker's system this order is designated as family Scitamineae consisting of 3 subfamilies Zingiberaceae, Cannaceae or Marantaceae and Musaceae and they have placed it under the series Epigynae. Hutchinson places the aforesaid families under the order Zingiberales.

MUSACEAE

General characters

Plants—perennial large herbs with rhizomatous stems or rarely with woody stems (e.g., *Ravenala* and some species of *Strelitzia*).

Leaves—large, glabrous, simple, lanceolate or oblong, entire, with prominent midrib and sheathing leaf-base. Inflorescence—spadix enclosed by fleshy spathaceous bracts. Flowers—zygomorphic, usually bisexual, epigynous, often large and showy. Perianth—3+3, petaloid or distinguished into calyx and corolla, free or united. Stamens—5, only the posterior is rudimentary (staminode) or wanting, sometimes

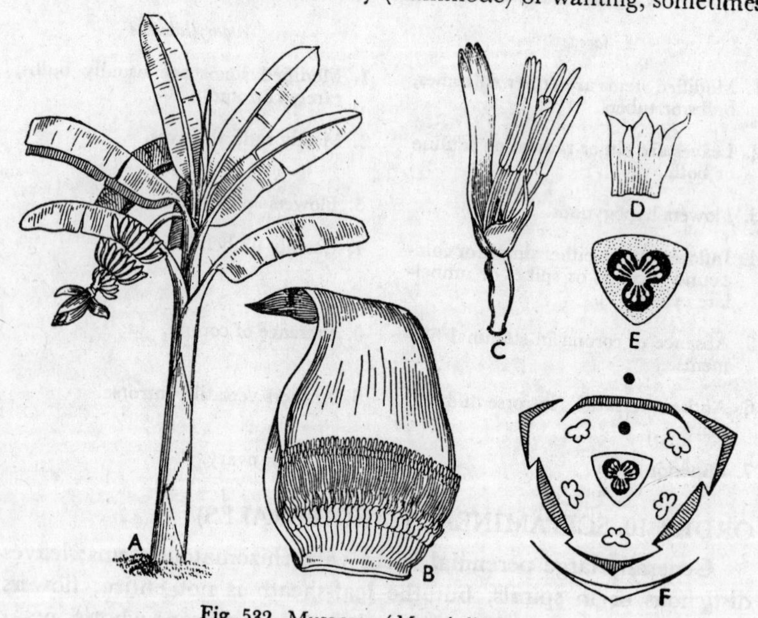

Fig. 532. Musaceae (*Musa balbisiana*).
A, The plant; B, A spathe enclosing two rows of flowers; C, Flower; D, Calyx split open; E, T.s. of ovary; F, Floral diagram.

6 perfect (e.g., *Ravenala*). Carpels—(3); ovary inferior, 3-celled, with numerous ovules on the inner angle of each cell, but often they are suppressed by cultivation. Fruit—berry or capsule (e.g., *Ravenala*). Seeds—often arillate with mealy endosperm and with straight embryo.

Floral formula

$\uparrow$ ⚥ $P_{6(3+3)}, A_{6 \text{ or } 5}, \overline{G_{(3)}}$

Number and distribution

This family consists of 5 genera and about 150 species which are commonly distributed in the tropics of both the old and new worlds.

KEY TO GENERA

(*a*) Sepals free; petals long and narrow; stamens 6 perfect; stem tree-like, marked with annular leaf-scars; leaves distichous, very large; fruit capsule .. .. *Ravenala.*

(*b*) Sepals united into a split spathaceous tube; leaves spiral, oblong; stamens 5 perfect; fruit a berry .. .. *Musa.*

Common plants

(1) Plantain (*Musa paradisiaca* L.), commonly cultivated for unripe fruits, which are taken as vegetables and for disorder of the stomach. (2) Banana (*Musa balbisiana* Colla.), commonly cultivated for delicious fruits. (3) *Musa textilis* Nees., fibres of which yield the 'manila hemp' of commerce. (4) Traveller's tree (*Ravenala madagascariensis* Sonn.), native of Madagascar often planted in gardens and is well-known for the exudation of watery sap from the petiole, when incised.

Economic importance

The family is of some economic importance. *Musa balbisiana* Colla. (banana) and *M. paradiasiaca* (plantain) are extensively cultivated for ripe and unripe fruits respectively. *M. textilis* yields a kind of fibre known as 'manila hemp' of commerce. Some plants are ornamentals, such as, *Ravenala madagascariensis* (traveller's tree), *Strelitzia reginae* Ait. (bird-of-paradise) and species of *Heliconia.*

ZINGIBERACEAE

General characters

Plants—perennial herbs usually with horizontal rhizomatous stems. Leaves—simple, with petiole, lamina and sheath; sheath bears a ligular outgrowth. Inflorescence—spike or raceme, subtended by a bract. Flowers—medianly zygomorphic, bisexual, epigynous. Perianth—3+3, usually distinguished into calyx and corolla. Stamens—*only 1 fertile* (the median posterior one belonging to the inner whorl), 1 suppressed (the anterior one belonging to the outer whorl) and remaining 4 are converted into petaloid staminodes, of which 2 of the inner whorl are united forming the *labellum*, the landing stage of the insect. Carpels—(3); ovary inferior, 3-celled, rarely 1-celled (e.g., *Globba*), with many ovules in each cell. Fruit—capsule or berry. Seeds—generally arillate with straight embryo.

Floral formula

$\uparrow \; ⚥ \; P_{6(3+3)}, A_5, \overline{G}_{(3)}$

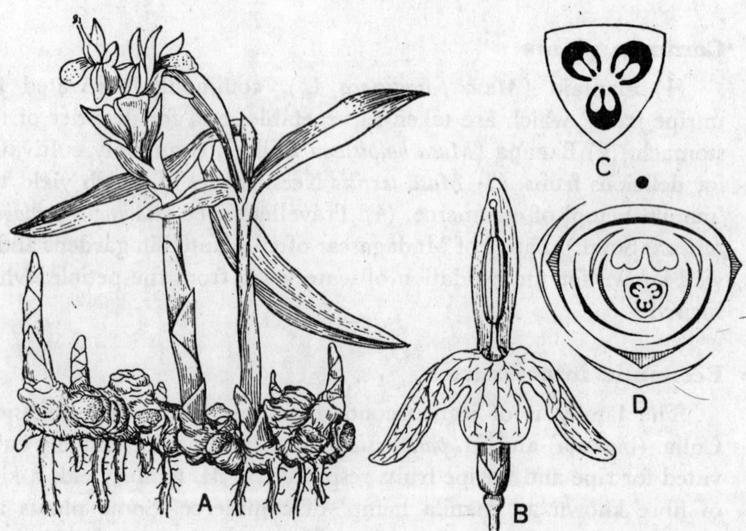

Fig. 533. Zingiberaceae (*Zingiber officinale*).
A, Portion of a plant; B, Flower; C, T.s. of ovary; D, Floral diagram.

Number and distribution

This family consists of about 47 genera and 1,400 species which are distributed in the tropics and subtropics.

KEY TO GENERA

A. Ovary 1-celled; stem leafy; flowers yellow; herbs with creeping rhizomes and erect stems; buds often replaced by bulbils .. .. *Globba.*

B. Ovary 3-celled with axile placentation:

(*a*) Lateral staminodes broad—

(*i*) Connective not spurred at the base; corolla tube long and slender

(1) Filaments short; connectives broad, crested; stem short with a few leaves, or no aerial stem *Kaempferia.*

(2) Filaments long; connectives not crested; stem elongated, leafy .. .. *Hedychium.*

(*ii*) Connective spurred at the base; stemless herbs; leaves often very large; flowering spike surmounted by a coma of coloured bracts .. .. *Curcuma.*

(*b*) Lateral staminodes small or 0 or adnate to the lip—

(*iii*) Flowering spikes dense cone-like, but not surmounted by a coma of bracts—

(3) Filaments short, not petaloid .. .. *Zingiber*

(4) Filaments petaloid bearing the anther on its middle .. .. *Costus.*

(5) Filaments short, with or without petaloid crest .. .. *Amomum.*

(*c*) Flowers in racemes or panicles at the top of tall leafy stems .. .. *Alpinia.*

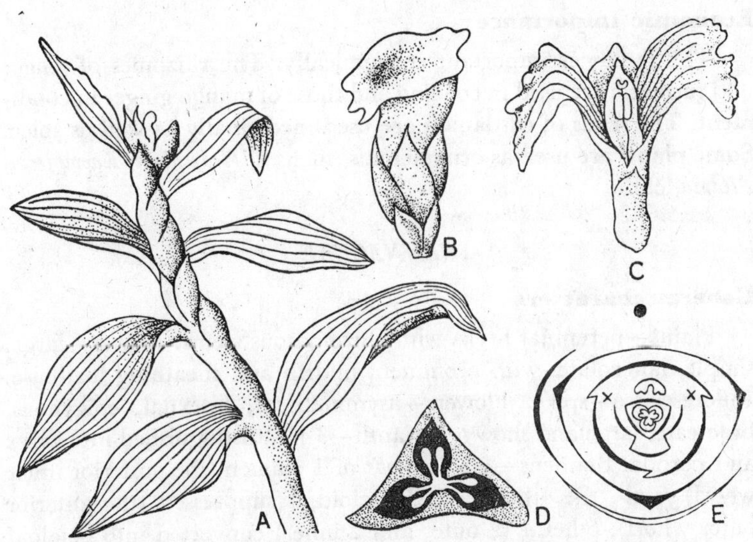

Fig. 534. Zingiberaceae (*Costus speciosus*).
A, Portion of a flowering shoot; B, Flower; C, Corolla split open; D, T.s. of ovary; E, Floral diagram.

Common plants

(1) Ginger (*Zingiber officinale* Roxb.), the dried rhizome of which yields the 'ginger' of commerce. (2) Mango ginger (*Curcuma amada*

Roxb.), the rhizome of which has the smell of mango and hence used as a condiment. (3) Turmeric (*Curcuma longa* L.=*C. domestica* L.), the rhizome of which is used in cooking. (4) Indian arrowroot (*Curcuma zedoaria* Roscoe), the rhizome of which yields an inferior quality of arrowroot. (5) Ginger-lily (*Hedychium coronarium* Koen.), commonly planted in gardens for its sweet-scented flowers. (6) *Kaempferia rotunda* L., another common garden plant with scented flowers. (7) Cardamon (*Amomum subulatum* Roxb. and *Elettaria cardamomum* Maton.), commonly cultivated in the hills for the sake of its seeds. (8) *Globba bulbifera* Roxb., common in marshy places and banks of rivers with terminal panicles, the lower flower buds of which are converted into bulbils which get easily detached and reproduce the plant. (9) Shell ginger (*Alpinia galanga* Sw.), a common garden plant with scented flowers. (10) *Costus speciosus* Smith, common in shady waste places.

Economic importance

This family is important economically. The rhizomes of ginger and turmeric are used in cooking and those of mango ginger in condiment. The seeds of cardamon are used medicinally as well as spice. Some plants are used as ornamentals, such as, *Hedychium*, *Kaempferia*, *Alpinia*, etc.

CANNACEAE

General characters

Plants—perennial herbs with rhizomatous stems. Leaves—large, simple, lanceolate, with prominent midrib and sheathing leaf-base. Inflorescence—spike. Flowers—asymmetrical, bisexual, epigynous, bracteate, large and showy. Perianth—3+3, distinguished into calyx and corolla. Stamens—$\frac{1}{2}$ *anther-lobe* of 1 stamen (the posterior inner whorl) *fertile*, the other half is petaloid, 1 suppressed (the anterior outer whorl), other 4 (2 outer and 2 inner) converted into petaloid staminodes, of which one of the inner whorl is the largest and forms the labellum. Carpels—(3); ovary inferior, 3-celled with numerous ovules in each cell; style petaloid; stigma terminal, oblique. Fruit—a capsule with warty or spinous projections. Seed—small, subglobose with very hard endosperm. Embryo—straight.

Floral formula

Asym. ⚥ $P_{6\,(3+3)}, A_5, \overline{G_{(3)}}$

Number and distribution

This family consists of 1 genus and 60 species which are distributed in the tropics.

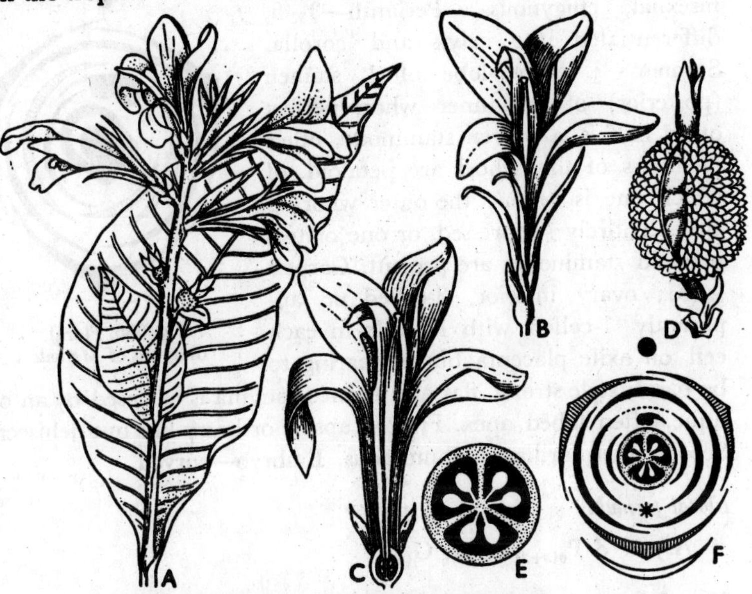

Fig. 535. Cannaceae (*Canna indica*).
A, Portion of a flowering shoot; B, Flower; C, V.s. of the same; D, Fruit; E, T.s. of ovary; F, Floral diagram.

Common plant

Indian shot (*Canna indica* L.), commonly cultivated in the garden for its showy flowers.

Economic importance

This family is of little economic importance. Different species of *Canna* are planted as ornamentals.

MARANTACEAE

General characters

Plants—perennial herbs with rhizomatous stems. Leaves—distichous, simple, with distinct petiole, lamina and sheath; a pulvinus-like swelling is present below the lamina. Inflorescence—spicate cyme (monochasium) or panicle, usually subtended by spathe-like bracts. Flowers—irregular, bisexual, epigynous. Perianth—3+3, differentiated into calyx and corolla. Stamens—½ anther-lobe of 1 stamen (posterior) of the inner whorl perfect other half is a barren staminode, other members of this whorl are petaloid, of which one is *hooded;* the outer whorl is either entirely suppressed, or one or two petaloid staminodes are present. Carpels —(3); ovary inferior, 3-celled or apparently 1-celled with 1 ovule in each cell on axile placenta but appearing to be basal; style strong, flat and twisted; stigma is enclosed by an oblique, often lobed apex. Fruit—capsule or berry-like but dehiscent Seeds—often arillate, albuminous. Embryo—curved.

Fig. 536. Floral. diagram of *Maranta*.

Floral formula

Asym. ⚥ $P_{6(3+3)}$ $A_{4 \text{ or } 5}$ $\overline{G_{(3)}}$

Number and distribution

This family consists of 26 genera and about 350 species which are chiefly distributed in the tropics.

Key to Genera

(*a*) Ovary apparently 1-celled; 1 ovule with 2 empty cells; stem with a terminal few-flowered inflorescence .. *Maranta*.

(*b*) Ovary 3-celled, 3-ovuled; leafy stem with terminal panicled, scattered flowers; bracts and bracteoles deciduous .. .. *Clinogyne*.

Common plants

(1) Arrowroot (*Maranta arundinacea* L.), the rhizomes of which yield the 'arrowroot' of commerce. (2) Mat-grass (*Clinogyne dichotoma* Salisb.), a cane-like plant, the split stems of which are woven into mats.

Economic importance

This family is economically important. *Maranta* yields the arrowroot of commerce. The split stems of *Clinogyne* are woven into mats.

Some plants are ornamentals, such as, *Maranta*, *Calathea* and *Thalia dealbata* (an aquatic plant).

Range of floral structures

The Musaceae approaches most nearly the common monocotyledonous arrangement. *Ravenala* has 6 fertile and equal stamens, and the zygomorphy of the flower is due merely to a small median petal. Generally, however, only 5 stamens are fertile, the sixth being absent or represented by a small petaloid structure. The flowers are rendered attractive by the large, often brilliantly coloured spathe-like bracts and also by the perianth. In *Strelitzia*, the united anterior petals form a landing stage for the honey-bird which visits the flower. The small tribe *Lowioideae* is of special interest from the orchid-like development of petals.

In the other families, the androecium plays the most important part in attracting the visitors and facilitating their entrance to the nectar-passage.

In Zingiberaceae, one stamen is fertile, but in Cannaceae and Marantaceae only half anther is functional, the rest of the stamens being more or less petaloid.

Marantaceae differs from other families in the reduction of the number of ovules, there being only one in each ovary-chamber, while frequently 2 of the 3 ovary-chambers become abortive, so that only one-seeded fruit results.

ORDER 11. MICROSPERMAE

Flowers cyclic, usually irregular, bisexual; stamens adherent or adnate in whole or in part to the style; carpels 3; ovary inferior, 1-celled or 3-celled with numerous small ovules; fruit capsule; seeds very numerous, minute with an undifferentiated embryo and with or without endosperm.

According to Engler this order comprises two families, viz., Burmanniaceae and Orchidaceae* and it has been placed at the end of the monocotyledons, since it is regarded as the most highly evolved. Bentham and Hooker have designated this order as a series and have placed it at the beginning of the monocotyledons. Hutchinson has separated the families of this order into two orders, Burmaniales and Orchidales, containing the families Burmanniaceae and Orchidaceae respectively.

Comparison of Musaceae, Zingiberaceae, Cannaceae and Marantaceae

	Musaceae	*Zingiberaceae*	*Cannaceae*	*Marantaceae*
(1) Leaves—	(1) Leaf base sheathing.	(1) Sheath ligulate.	(1) Leaf base sheathing.	(1) Pulvinus present at the leaf base.
(2) Flowers—	(2) Zygomorphic, bi- or unisexual.	(2) Medianly zygomorphic, bisexual.	(2) Asymmetrical, bisexual.	(2) Asymmetrical, bisexual.
(3) Perianth—	(3) 6, petaloid, similar or distinguished into K and C.	(3) 3+3, generally the outer sepaline and the inner petaline.	(3) 3+3, the outer sepaline and the inner petaline.	(3) 6, generally distinguished into K and C.
(4) Stamens—	(4) 5 (rarely 6), perfect, no petaloid staminode.	(4) Stamen (posterior one of the inner whorl) perfect; 1 stamen (posterior one of the outer whorl) suppressed, others are modified into petaloid staminodes, two such of the inner whorl are united forming the labellum.	(4) $\frac{1}{2}$ stamen of the posterior whorl perfect, one of the anterior whorl suppressed; other 4 are converted into petaloid staminodes; one staminode of the inner whorl forms the labellum.	(4) $\frac{1}{2}$ anther-lobe of the posterior stamen of the inner whorl perfect other members are petaloid, one is hooded.
(5) Ovary—	(5) Usually 3-celled with many ovules on axile placentae.	(5) 3-celled with axile placentation.	(5) 3-celled with 2 series of anatropous ovules on axile placentae.	(5) 3-celled or 1-celled; ovules on axile placentae, but appears to be basal.
(6) Style—	(6) Simple.	(6) Slender, lies in a channel of the fertile stamen.	(6) Petaloid.	(6) Stout, flat and twisted.
(7) Stigma—	(7) More or less lobed or capitate.	(7) Variously developed.	(7) Terminal, oblique.	(7) Terminal and sometimes truncate.

ORCHIDACEAE

General characters

Plants—perennial herbs, terrestrial or epiphytic, a few saprophytic (e.g. *Didymoplexis*) deriving their nourishment from humus since their roots or rhizomes are associated with endotropic mycorrhiza rarely climbers (e.g. *Bulbophyllum*). Roots—the main root is always absent, its place being taken by adventitious roots which arise especially from the nodes; they are generally of three kinds: (1) normal cylindrical earth-roots, (2) tuberous roots which serve for storage

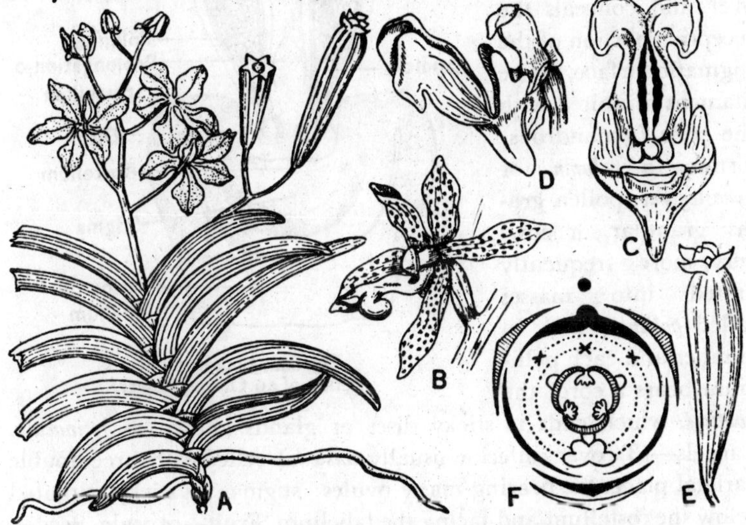

Fig. 537. Orchidaceae (*Vanda roxburghii*).
A, Portion of a shoot with flowers and fruits; B, Flower; C, Column; D, Back view of the same; F, Fruit; F, Floral diagram.

of reserve food materials and (3) aerial roots in which the epidermis is specially developed to form the *velamen*, special water-absorbing tissue, rarely absent. Leaves—thick, usually alternate with closed sheaths. Inflorescence—raceme or spike. Flowers—bisexual, epigynous, medianly zygomorphic, usually very showy. Perianth—free, 3+3; the outer consisting of 3 sepals, more or less similar, and the inner of 3 petals, more or less dissimilar; the two lateral petals are alike and resemble the sepals but the median petal is usually much larger and known as the *labellum* or lip; the labellum is provided with a spur, variously shaped and normally posterior in position but becomes anterior by the twisting of the ovary. Stamen—1 (in *Monandrae*) or 2 (in *Diandrae*) in *Monandrae* the column bears an anther at the top and just under it there is a more or less projecting beak, the *rostellum* and under this there lies two fertile stigmas which are more or less united into one; but in *Diandrae* the three stigmas are united into one, on which the two anthers are placed and there is no rostellum. (The rostellum is only the projecting portion of the stigma; it is itself functionless but bends over and conceals the receptive portion of the stigmatic surface.) The filament is united with the style (gynandrous) forming a *column* or *gynostegium*; pollen grains granular, or powdery, more frequently united into masses called *pollinia*, 2–8 in number and each pollinium bears a cord, the *caudicle*, which ends in sticky discs or glands known as *retinacula*. Carpels—(3); ovary inferior, usually *twisted*, 1-celled with three double parietal placentae bearing many ovules; stigmas 3, sticky, situated below the rostellum and facing the labellum. Fruit—capsule. Seed—very numerous, minute, exalbuminous. Embryo—undifferentiated.

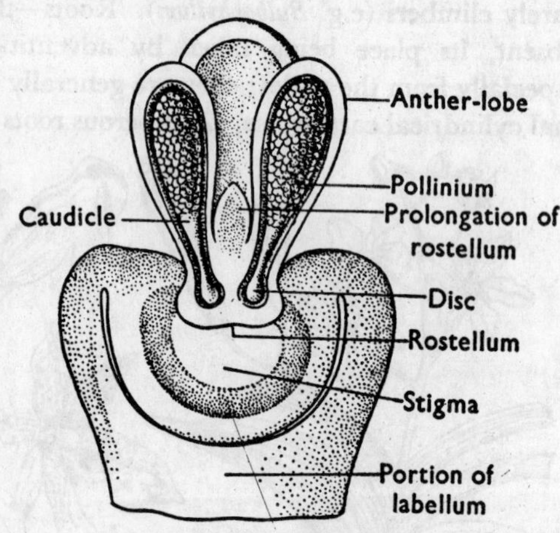

Fig. 538. Longitudinal section of an Orchid flower.

Floral formula

$$\uparrow \ ⚥ \ P_{6(3+3)}, A_{1 \text{ or } 2}, \overline{G_{(3)}}$$

Number and distribution

This family consists of about 450 genera and 10,000–15,000 species widely distributed in the tropical and temperate regions of the world. This is the largest family of flowering plants in India. It is only in the Eastern Himalayas, Burma and Malaya Peninsula that the family predominates.

KEY TO GENERA

(*a*) Terrestrial herbs with underground rhizomes; leaves elliptical, plicate, sheaths forming a pseudo-stem; lip white with pink lines or streaked with purple or red .. *Geodorum*.

(*b*) Terrestrial herbs, leafless, saprophytic, with tuberous roots; inflorescence a scanty raceme of white flowers .. *Didymoplexis*.

(*c*) Terrestrial 1-leaved tuberous herbs; leaf broadly cordate or orbicular, strongly plicate, lying on the surface of the ground; flowers on scapes arising from the tuber .. *Pogonia*.

(*d*) Terrestrial herbs with succulent glabrous stem; leaves membraneous, often withering at flowering times; flowers small, in racemes or spikes .. .. .. *Zeuxine*.

(*e*) Epiphytic herbs with leafy stems; leaves thickly coriaceous or fleshy, flat, keeled or terete; flowers large often showy in dense racemes or sometimes solitary; petals like sepals; lip large, base saccate or spurred; caudicle very broad .. *Vanda*.

(*f*) Epiphytic herbs; leaves coriaceous, flat, often keeled; flowers small in racemes, corymbs, umbels or panicles; petals like sepals; lip small, sessile, forms a cylindric or saccate spur; caudicle very narrow .. .. *Saccolabium*.

(*g*) Epiphytic herbs with pseudo-bulbs; leaves sessile, bases sheathing; flowers large and showy, solitary or in racemes; petals like sepals; lip sessile or clawed at the base; anther 2-celled; pollinia 4, usually slightly coherent .. *Dendrobium*.

(*h*) Epiphytic shrub; stem terete or angled; leaves coriaceous or fleshy or *0*; pollinia granular .. .. *Vanilla*.

Range of floral structures

A wide variation occurs in the floral structures of this family.

The sepals and petals may be quite different in form or they seem to be almost alike. The sepals are generally minute and indistinct but sometimes become somewhat conspicuous and larger, as in *Masdevallia*. The sepals may be free or more or less united. The odd sepal becomes spurred in *Disa*, but in *Haemaria*, it joins with the lateral petals forming hood-like structure.

Variation in the form of petals is also noticeable. The lateral petal is obliterated in *Coryanthes*, but in *Epicranthes* the petals are usually filiform. The petals become usually smaller than the lip, but sometimes become larger, as in *Oncidium*. In *Cypripedium*, the petals look like narrow ribbon and occasionally they are one yard long. In *Disa*, the labellum becomes sometimes minute and narrow or becomes large with spreading limbs, as in *Odontoglossum*, or they are curved, as in *Cattleya*. The labellum becomes slipper-like in *Cypripedium*, but in *Coryanthes* it assumes a bucket-like structure. The spurred petals may or may not be present. The origin of the spur is supposed to have been derived from the lip (labellum) or partly from the floral axis. The incision of the lip may be various; it becomes either trifid or tripartite or the middle segment of the lip becomes 4-partite when re-divide or it may often represent the simplest type of lip which conform to the structure of the lateral petals, such as, in *Thelymitra*.

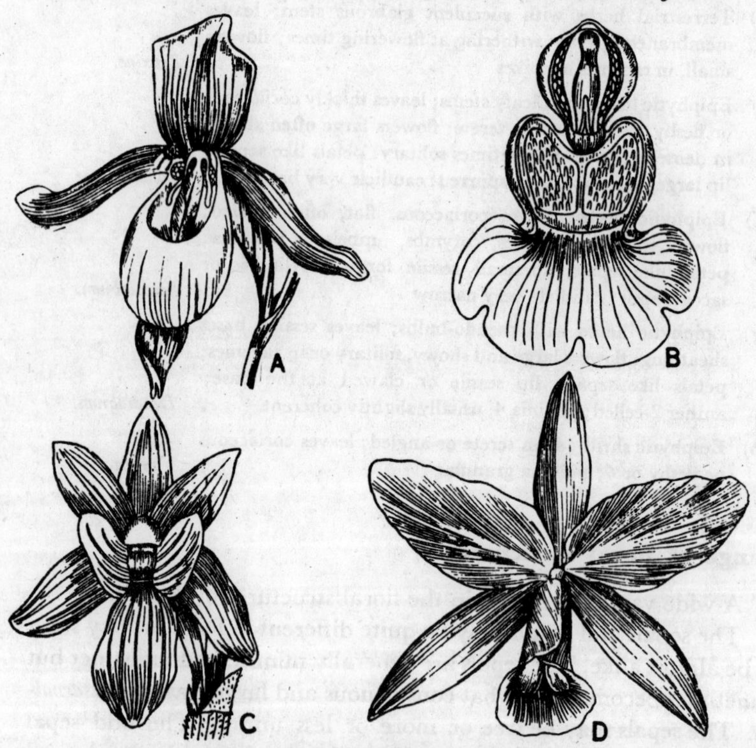

Fig. 539. Orchidaceae.
A, *Dendrobium*; B, *Orchis*; C, *Cypripedium*; D, *Cattleya*.

The odd member of the outer whorl of stamens, which is situated opposite the sepal, becomes generally fertile but a fleshy staminode is formed by that very stamen, as in *Cypripedium* and allied genera. In *Arundina pentandra*, they are found to be present and fertile, but in *Diuris*, they assume the form of leaf-like staminodes. In *Orchis*, they are represented by small auricles.

The lateral pair of the inner whorl of stamens becomes fertile, as in *Cypripedium*, but in others they form staminodes of different shapes, such as *Epipactis*, or are foliaceous, as in *Thelymitra*.

The anther may become erect and free on the top of the column, as in *Ophrys*, *Orchis* and others, but generally it becomes bent over the inner face of the latter. In *Coelogyne*, the anther seems to be hanged downwards vertically from the apex.

The union of column with anther may also vary. In the tribe Ophrydeae, it is provided with a broad, short filament from which it is quite unseparable. The anther remains strongly coherent with the column and it is not pulled off with the removal of pollen.

The anthers are either 2-, 4- or 6-chambered which correspond to the number of pollen masses. Pollen masses become either granular or powdery, as in *Cephalanthera*, or they are found to be united in packets by some sort of elastic net, as in *Orchis*, or waxy pollinia being united in a chamber are formed in *Cattleya*. A slender process is often formed by the drawing out of the lower part of the anther on each side and ultimately this process covers the lower sterile portion (caudicle) of the pollinium.

All three stigmas become functional in Cypripedeae and Apostasieae, but in some cases the lateral pair, the third being sterile and finally forms the rostellum. The stigmas originate as smooth, viscous, flat or cushion-like spots on the inner side, or sometimes on the end of the column, or often forms special processes that are carried up on the style-like projection, as in *Habenaria*.

The ovary manifests wide variations, but it is usually cylindrical or spindle-shaped. The ovary is often provided with longitudinal lines, ridges or wings which later on become more prominent with the ripening of the fruits.

The Orchids represent inferior and 1-locular ovary which bears numerous small ovules borne on three double parietal placentae.

Common plants

(1) *Vanda roxburghii* R. Br., an epiphytic herb commonly found on mango trees. (2) *Zeuxine sulcata* Lindl., a common terrestrial grass-like herb. (3) *Dendrobium* is found on the hills as well as in the Sundribans; *D. nobile* Lindl. is one of the noblest and finest specimens of the genus. (4) *Vanilla planifolia* L., cultivated for the fruits. (5) *Saccolabium papillosum* Lindl., epiphytic on trees. (6) *Pogonia plicata* Lindl. and *P. carinata* Lindl., common in shady thickets. (7) *Geodorum dilatum* R. Br., a terrestrial herb on grassy lawns. (8) *Didymoplexus pallens* Griff., commonly found in shady thickets.

Affinity

Orchidaceae established a link with that of epigynous members of Liliflorae. Hutchinson considers the family to be derived from Haemodoraceae or Amaryllidaceae for higher and complex development of floral parts and the reduction of stamens during evolution. Moreover, the families Burmaniaceae and Apostasiaceae of the order Orchidales resemble closely with those of epigynous Liliflorae. Orchidaceae is also supposed to have been derived from Musaceae based on the similar structure and construction of flowers of *Orchidantha* (a member of Musaceae) and a few genera of Orchids. On the whole, Orchidaceae represents the highest evolved family among the monocotyledons in the presence of floral complexity and general plant of construction.

There are certain reasons for considering Orchidaceae as one of the highest evolved family of monocotyledons. These are as follows—

(1) Zygomorphy of flowers accompanied with different types of labellum-formations along with spur containing nectar.

(2) Epigynous flowers.

(3) Constant reduction and suppression of the members of androecium.

(4) Reduction in the stigmatic lobes which often develop into rostellum.

(5) Diversity in shape and size of the flowers which may be of various types.

Economic importance

This family is less important economically. The roots of *Vanda* are used as curative for rheumatism and as an antidote for scorpion-stings. The dried pulpy fruit of *Vanilla planifolia* furnishes the 'vanilla' of commerce, used for flavouring chocolate and confectionary. Many species are cultivated as ornamentals, such as, *Cypripedium*, *Cattleya*, *Cymbidium*, *Dendrobium*, etc.

Comparison between Scitaminae and Orchidaceae

Scitaminae	*Orchidaceae*
(1) Plants—perennial herbs with rhizomatous stems.	(1) perennial herbs, terrestrial or epiphytic, a few saprophytic.

	Scitaminae		*Orchidaceae*
(2)	Roots—adventitious, one kind (earth-root).	(2)	adventitious, 3 kinds—earth-roots, fleshy tuberous roots and aerial roots with velamen.
(3)	Leaves—large with prominent midrib and sheathing leaf-bases.	(3)	thick and coriaceous.
(4)	Inflorescence—spike or raceme with spathe-like bracts.	(4)	raceme or spike.
(5)	Flowers—usually bisexual, zygomorphic or asymmetrical, epigynous.	(5)	bisexual, medianly zygomorphic, epigynous, gynandrous.
(6)	Perianth—3+3, petaloid or distinguished into sepals and petals.	(6)	3+3, distinguished into sepals and petals; sepals similar, petals dissimilar, the median petal is the largest and forms the labellum.
(7)	Stamens—½ or 1 or 5 (rarely 6) perfect, others converted into petaloid staminodes; one or two staminodes may form the labellum; pollen grains powdery.	(7)	1 or 2; pollen grains frequently united forming pollinia; filament united with the style forming a column.
(8)	Carpels—(3); ovary inferior, 3-celled, with 1-many ovules in each.	(8)	(3); ovary inferior, twisted, 1-celled with many ovules on double parietal placentae.
(9)	Stigma—variously developed.	(9)	situated below the rostellum.
(10)	Fruit—capsule or berry.	(10)	capsule.

CHAPTER II

DICOTYLEDONS

The plants under the category of Dicotyledons bear two cotyledons in their embryo. The radicle on germination produces a taproot. Leaves have reticulate venation. Flowers are usually pentamerous. Vascular bundles of the stem are open and arranged in a ring and those of the root di-, tri-, or tetrarch.

SUBCLASS 1. ARCHICHLAMYDEAE

Flowers with or without perianth, mono- or dichlamydeous, in the latter case petals free. Carpels free or united.

ORDER 1. VERTICILLATAE

Flowers monoecious. Male flowers verticillate. Stem anomalous anatomically. Fruit winged nut.

According to Engler Verticillatae is the 1st order of Archichlamydeae as he regards it the most primitive one. Bentham and Hooker have placed Casuarinaceae in the series Unisexuales under subclass Monochlamydeae. Hutchinson has put the family under the order Casuarinales.

CASUARINACEAE

General characters

Plants—evergreen much-branched drooping trees or shrubs with *jointed whorled branches*, monoecious or dioecious; internodes with striate grooves like that of *Equisetum*. Leaves—*minute, scale-like in whorl* of 4–16, usually linear to lanceolate, basaly united forming a sheath round the twig, exstipulate. Flowers—unisexual, naked; male flowers verticillate in terminal spikes (catkin-like) and female flowers in ovoid or globose heads, subtended by bracts. Perianth—1 or 2, concave in male flowers but absent in female flowers. Stamens—in male flowers 1, subtended by 4 scale-like bracteoles. Carpels—in female flowers 2, subtended by 1 bract and a pair of bracteoles; ovary superior, 2-celled but afterwards 1-celled bearing 2 ascending orthotropous ovules on a single *parietal placenta;* style 1, very short; stigma 2, long. Fruit—1-seeded winged nut, enclosed by 2 bracteoles and a bract; *many such fruits are aggregated into a dry, woody, cone-like, multiple fruit.*

Floral formula

Br. ♂ flowers—P_{1-2} A_1 G_0

Br. ♀ flowers—P_0 A_0 $\underline{G_{(2)}}$

Number and distribution

This family contains a single genus *Casuarina* with about 40 species. It is a native of Australia.

Common plant

Beef-wood tree (*Casuarina equisetifolia* Forst.), a tall tree planted usually in avenues.

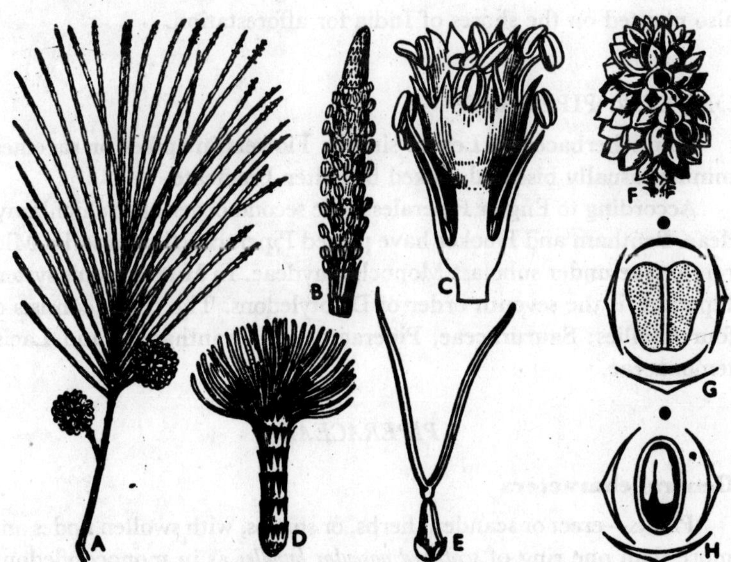

Fig. 540. Casuarinaceae (*Casuarina equisetifolia*).
A, Portion of a flowering shoot; B, Staminate inflorescence; C, V.s. of a staminate flower; D, Pistillate inflorescence; E, Pistillate flower; F, Fruit; G, Floral diagram of staminate flower; H, The same of pistillate flower.

Affinity

Casuarinaceae resembles strikingly to the Betulaceae in the structure and development of the pistil and ovary. The characteristic stem and leaf of the genus *Casuarina* are highly adaptive but it is very difficult to ascertain any trace of affinity with the Fagales. The habit of *Casuarina* recalls the habit of *Ephedra*, a gymnosperm, thereby suggesting the derivation of gymnosperms from Casuarina-like primitive plant. This view has been propounded by Wettstein.

This family is readily distinguished from others by its equisetum-like jointed branches, whorled, minute leaves, and its woody cone-like fruit. Engler considers that the apparently simple anemophilous flowers, the approach to a catkin-like staminate inflorescence and the large rays in the wood of the family as a most primitive of dicotyledons.

Economic importance

Economically the family is important as a timber tree. Several species are cultivated extensively in our garden as ornamentals and also planted on the shores of India for afforestation.

ORDER 2. PIPERALES

Plants herbaceous. Leaves simple. Flowers in spikes or racemes, minute, usually bisexual, naked but often bracteate.

According to Engler Piperales is the second order of Archichlamydeae. Bentham and Hooker have placed Piperaceae in the series Micrembryeae under subclass Monochlamydeae. In Hutchinson's system Piperales is the seventh order of Dicotyledons. The order consists of four families: Saururaceae, Piperaceae, Chloranthaceae and Lacistemonaceae.

PIPERACEAE

General characters

Plants—erect or scandent herbs, or shrubs, with swollen nodes and more than one ring of *scattered vascular bundles* as in monocotyledons. Leaves—usually alternate, simple, often oblique, *fleshy*, exstipulate or with two adnate stipules. Inflorescence—*spike* (catkin). Flowers—*minute*, bisexual, sometimes unisexual (e.g., *piper*), nakel, hypogynous, bracteate. Perianth–*absent*. Stamens–10-10; filaments usually distinct.

Carpels—(2–5); ovary superior, *1-celled, with 1 basal orthotropous ovule;* style 0–1; stigmas 1–5 (often brush-like as in *Peperomia*). Fruit—small drupe. Seed—*with endosperm and perisperm* and minute embryo.

Floral formula

$⚥$ Br. $P_0\ A_{1-10}\ \underline{G}_{(2-5)}$

Number and distribution

This family consists of about 10–12 genera and about 1,300 species, which are widely distributed in the tropics of both hemispheres.

KEY TO GENERA

Fruit conspicuous, anther cells distinct, stigmas 3–5 confluent .. .. .. *Piper.*

Fruit minute, anther cells confluent, stigma penicellate .. *Peperomia.*

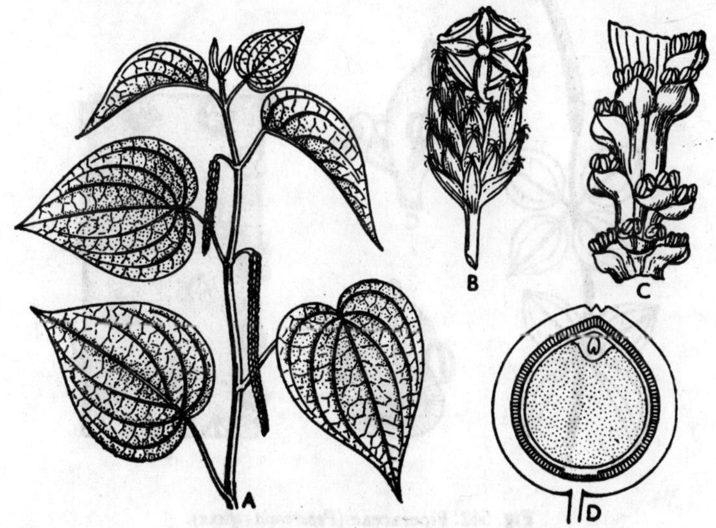

Fig. 541. Piperaceae (*Piper betle*).
A, Portion of a plant; B, Female inflorescence; C, Male inflorescence; D, L.s. of a seed.

Common plants

(1) Betle leaf plant (*Piper betle* L.), a stout climber, cultivated largely for its leaves, which are used as a masticatory. (2) *P. chaba* Hunter, another stout climber, the wood of which is used as a pungent

condiment. (3) Long pepper (*P. longum* L.), a slender creeper. (4) Black pepper (*P. nigrum* L.), another slender climber. (5) White pepper (*P. caninum* L.). (6) *Peperomia reflexa* Dietr., a common herbaceous tufted weed of waste places.

Affinity

Engler and Rendle believed that the family belonged to the most primitive dicotyledons. But it is now generally held that the family has an indeterminate origin which may be an offshoot from ranalian ancestry. This family is readily distinguished by the presence of succulent habit, very minute naked flowers in spike inflorescence, and 1-celled ovary with solitary basal orthotropous ovule.

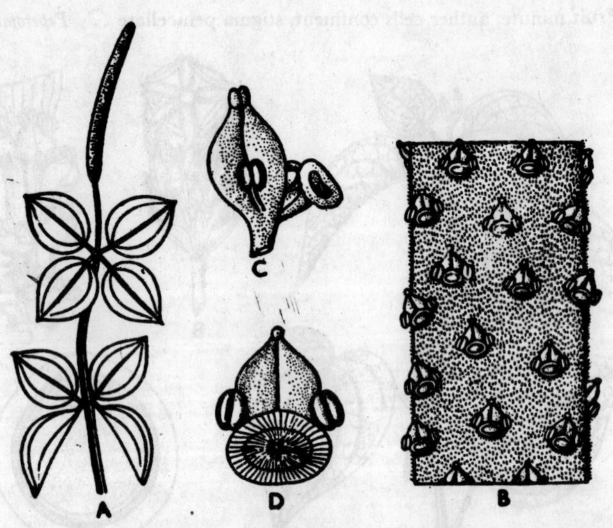

Fig. 542. Piperaceae (*Peperomia reflexa*).
A, Portion of a plant; B, A portion of a spike (enlarged);
C, V.s. of a flower; D, Flower.

Economic importance

This family is of some economic importance. Fruit of *Piper nigrum* and *P. caninum* are used as spice. *P. longum* is used in medicine. Some species are ornamental, such as *Macropiper*, *Piper*, *Peperomia*, etc.

ORDER 3. SALICALES

Flowers dioecious. Perianth absent. Bracteoles absent. Fruit capsule.

According to Engler this order is also regarded as a primitive one and has been placed at the beginning. Bentham and Hooker have placed the family Salicaceae in the series Ordines anomali under the subclass Monochlamydeae. In Hutchinson's system Salicales comprises only 1 family, Salicaceae.

SALICACEAE

General characters

Plants—trees or shrubs, dioecious. Leaves—alternate, simple, vary from linear to cordate, stipulate. Inflorescence—*catkin*, erect or pendulous. Flowers—*unisexual*, sessile or shortly pedicellate, subtended by a hairy bract and a *cup-like disc* (an expanded floral axis), hypogynous.

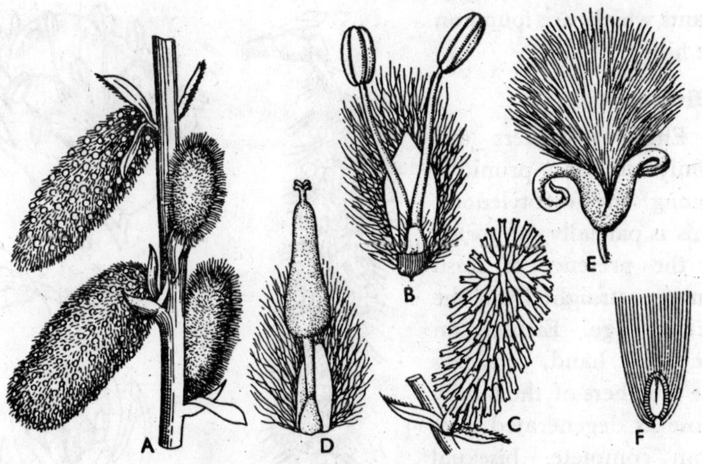

Fig. 543. Salicaceae (*Salix tetrasperma*).
A, Staminate catkins; B, Staminate flower; C, Pistillate catkin; D, Pistillate flower; E, Fruit; F, Seed.

Perianth—*0*. Stamens—in male flowers 2 or more; filaments slender, free, or more or less united at the base, transversely placed. Carpels—in female flowers (2–4); ovary sessile superior, 1-celled with numerous anatropous ovules arranged on 2–4 *parietal placentae;* style short or long, lateral or antero-posterior to the carpel; stigma 2–4-fid. Fruit —a small *capsule* dehiscing by two valves. Seed—very small with a thin testa, exalbuminous, comose; embryo straight.

Floral formula

♂ flowers Br.—$P_0\ A_{2-\infty}\ G_0$

♀ flowers Br.—$P_0\ A_0\ \underline{G_{(\dot{2-4})}}$

Number and distribution

This family consists of 2 genera and 300 species mostly confined to the temperate, alpine or artic zones.

KEY TO GENERA

Catkin pendulous, disc cupular or annular cut-bract .. *Populus.*
Catkin erect, disc of 1 or 2 separate glands, entire bract .. .. *Salix.*

Common plants

(1) Willow (*Salix tetrasperma* Roxb.) and (2) Poplar (*Populus alba* L.) are the common plants which are found on the hills.

Affinity

Engler considers this family to be primitive among the dicotyledons. This is partially supported by the presence of fossil remains straight from the tertiary age. Eichler, on the other hand, considers the members of the family arose as degenerated ones from complete, bisexual flowers. This family can be readily distinguished from the allied catkin-bearing families by dioecious plants, flowers subtended by hairy bracts and cup-like discs, and comose seeds.

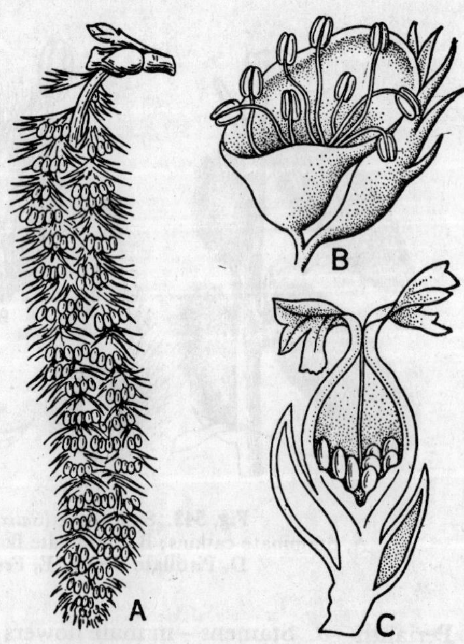

Fig. 544. Salicaceae (*Populus alba*). A, An inflorescence; B, Staminate flower; C, Pistillate flower.

Economic importance

This family is of little economic importance. Many species are ornamentals. The wood of *Salix* is used as a fuel and the twigs of Willows for basketry.

ORDER 12. URTICALES

Flowers generally unisexual. Stamens few to many. Ovary 2-carpellate, superior, unilocular with a single ovule. Fruit a nut or drupe. Seed with fleshy or oily endosperm.

According to Engler this order has been divided into 3 families: (*a*) Ulmaceae, (*b*) Moraceae and (*c*) Urticaceae. Bentham and Hooker have designated this order as family Urticaceae under the series Unisexuales of Monochlamydeae and have divided it into 4 tribes: Urticeae, Cannabinae, Artocarpae and Moreae. Hutchinson, however, has divided this order into 6 families: Ulmaceae, Urticaceae, Cannabinaceae, etc.

MORACEAE

General characters

Plants—trees or shrubs, rarely herbs (e.g., *Dorstenia*), monoecious

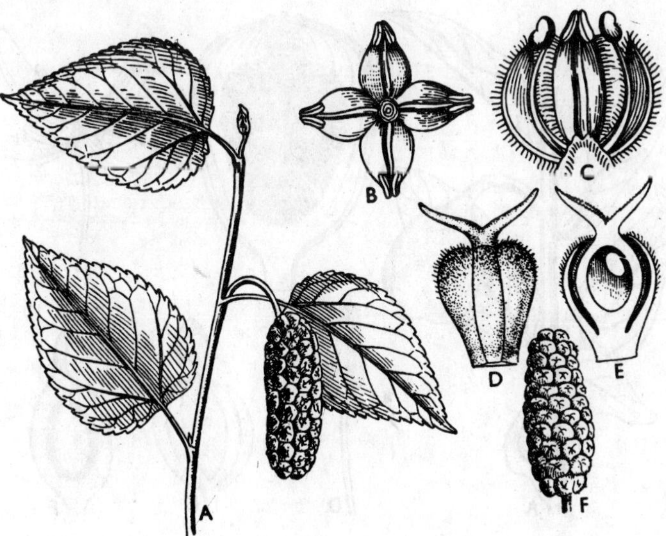

Fig. 545. Moraceae (*Morus indica*).
A, Portion of a flowering shoot; B, Staminate flower; C, V.s. of the same; D, Pistillate flower; E, V.s. of the same; F, Fruit.

or dioecious, evergreen or deciduous, usually with *milky latex* (absent in *Cannabis* and *Humulus*). Leaves—alternate, simple, entire, serrate or lobed, stipulate. Inflorescence—condensed spike or cymose, sometimes hypanthodium (e.g., *Ficus*). Flowers—small, regular, *unisexual*, hypogynous. Perianth—usually 4 in two whorls, sometimes 2 or 6, free or more or less united, valvate or imbricate. Stamens—in male flowers generally equal in number and opposite the perianth-lobes, sometimes 2 or 1 (e.g., *Ficus*, *Morus*, *Artocarpus*, *Dorstenia*); filaments bent inwards in bud (e.g., *Morus*), but straight in *Ficus*; anthers mostly versatile. Carpels—in female flowers (2); ovary superior, usually 1-*celled with* 1 *pendulous ovule in each; stigma usually* 2-*fid*. Fruit—drupe, syconus (e.g., *Ficus*) or sorosis (e.g., *Artocarpus* and *Morus*). Seeds—with fleshy endosperm or without curved.

Floral formula

$$\oplus \ \text{⚥} \ P_{2-6} \ A_{2-6} \ \underline{G_{(2)}}$$

Number and distribution

This family consists of nearly 73 genera and over 1,000 species, which are widely distributed in the tropics.

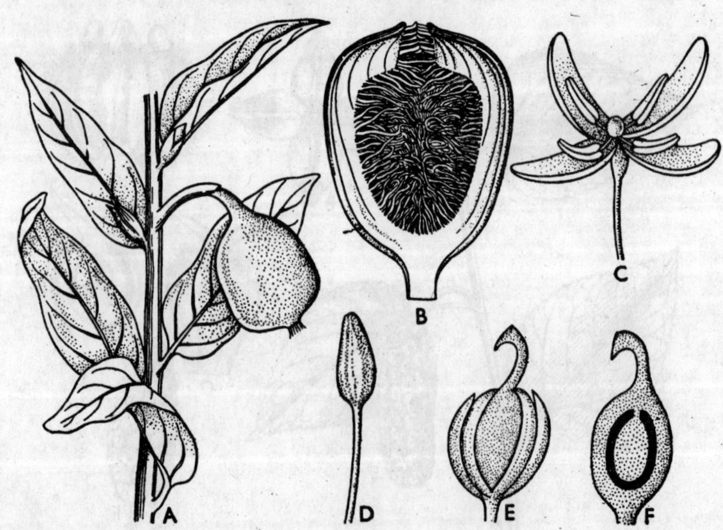

Fig. 546. Moraceae (*Ficus pumila*).
A, Portion of a flowering shoot; B, L s. of an inflorescence; C, Staminate flower, D, Staminode; E, Pistillate flower; F, L.s. of ovary.

KEY TO GENERA

A. Trees or shrubs:

(*a*) Male flowers spicate, female ones in globose head; style undivided; achenes stipitate; dioecious trees *Broussonetia*.

(*b*) Male flowers in minute heads, female flowers solitary axillary; small trees with rigid and scabrid (both sides) leaves .. .. .. *Streblus*.

Flowers concealed inside fleshy receptacles .. *Ficus*.

Flowers covering the outside of fleshy receptacles .. *Artocarpus*.

(*c*) Leaves alternate, entire, toothed or 3-lobed; flowers monoecious, male spikes elongated, female spikes long cylindric, or short oblong, or nearly globose; style divided .. .. .. *Morus*.

B. Tall erect herb:

Leaves opposite below, alternate above, lanceolate, serrate; stipules 2, lateral; flowers dioecious .. *Cannabis*.

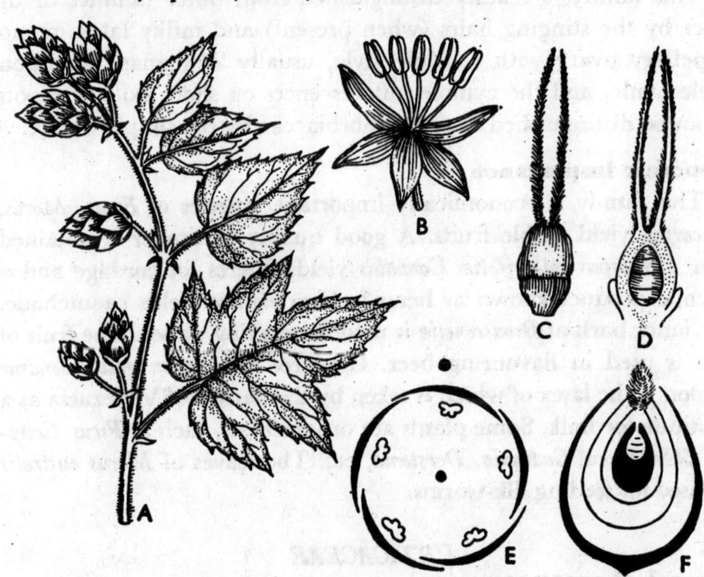

Fig. 547. Moraceae (*Humulus lupulus*).
A, Portion of a flowering shoot; B, Staminate flower; C, Pistillate flower; D, V.s. of the same; E, Floral diagram of staminate flower; F, Same of pistillate flower.

Common plants

(1) Banyan tree (*Ficus benghalensis* L.). (2) Peepul tree (*Ficus religiosa* L.). (3) Fig tree (*Ficus cunia* Ham., *Ficus hispida* L. f.). (4) *F.*

infectoria Roxb. =*F. lacor* Buch-Ham. (5) Ivy fig (*Ficus stipulata* Wall)., a common herb found climbing on walls. (6) India Rubber tree (*F. elastica* Roxb.). (7) Jackfruit tree (*Artocarpus integrifolia* L. =*A. heterophyllus* Lamk.). (8) Breadfruit tree (*A. incisa* L. f.), a native of Sunda islands, occasionally planted in gardens. (9) Monkey jack (*A. lakoocha* Roxb.), another fruit-tree. (10) Mulberry—*Morus australis* Poir (Syn. *Morus indica* L.), chiefly cultivated for rearing silk-worms. (11) Paper Mulberry (*Broussonetia papyrifera* Vent.), occasionally cultivated, the bark of which is chiefly used for manufacturing paper. (12) *Streblus asper* Lour., a rigid shrub found on roadsides. (13) Hemp. (*Cannabis sativa* L.), a tall erect annual herb. (14) Hop (*Humulus lupulus* L.), a shrub cultivated in gardens.

Affinity

This family is readily distinguished from other families of the order by the stinging hairs (when present) and milky latex, monocarpellary ovary with a single style, usually 2 stigmas, pendulous single ovule, and the cymose inflorescences on short axillary shoots. It can be distinguished from Euphorbiaceae by the simple ovary.

Economic importance

This family is economically important. Species of *Ficus*, *Morus*, *Artocarpus* yield edible fruits. A good quality of timber is obtained from *Atrocarpus integrifolia*. *Cannabis* yields fiberes for cordage and a narcotic product known as hemp*. *Ficus elastica* yields caoutchouc. The inner bark of *Broussonetia* is used for making paper. The fruit of Hop is used in flavouring beer. Cow-tree (*Brosimum galactodendron* D. Don.), the latex of which is taken by the natives of Venezuela as a substitute for milk. Some plants are ornamentals, such as *Ficus*, *Cecropia*, *Chlorophora*, *Cudrania*, *Dorstenia*, etc. The leaves of *Morus australis* are used for feeding silk-worms.

URTICACEAE

General characters

Plants—usually herbs, rarely small trees (e.g., *Holoptelea*) or climbers, with *watery latex*, and sometimes with *stinging hairs* (e.g., *Urtica*, *Fleurya*); monoecious or dioecious. Leaves—alternate or opposite, simple, usually stipulate (exstipulate in *Parietaria*). Inflorescence

* The leaves of this plant are used in preparing an intoxicating beverage known as 'bhang'; the young inflorescences are smoked as 'ganja', and the resinous exudation is also smoked as 'charas'

—cymose, sometimes catkin-like (e.g., *Boehmaria*), on short axillary shoots. Flowers—small, green, regular, *unisexual* (bisexual in *Parietaria*), hypogynous. Perianth—4 in two whorls, sometimes 5, free in male flowers but more or less united in female flowers, persistent. Stamens—in male flowers usually 4, sometimes 5, opposite the perianth-leaves; filaments *bent inwards in bud*, but when mature spring elastically backwards and outwards discharging cloud of pollen. Carpel—in female flowers 1; ovary superior, sometimes inferior, *1-celled with 1 basal orthotropous ovule; style 1*, ends in brush-like stigma. Fruit—an *achene* or drupe. Seeds—with oily endosperm and a straight embryo.

Floral formula

$\oplus$ ⚥ $P_{4-5}\ A_{4-5}\ \underline{G_1}$

Number and distribution

This family consists of about 42 genera and nearly 600 species which are chiefly tropical.

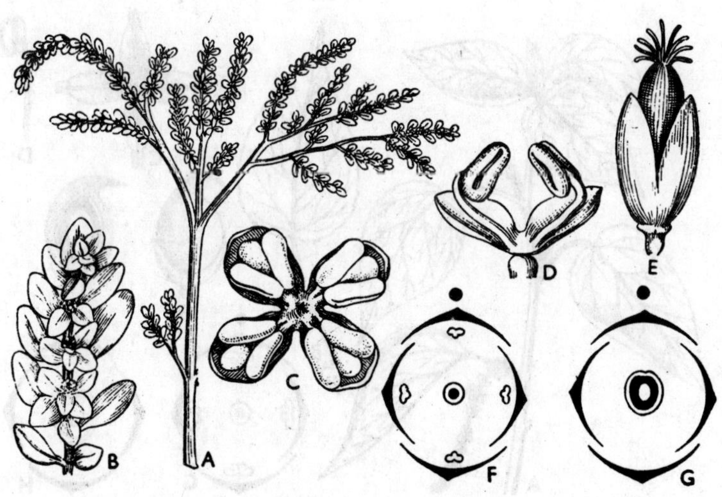

Fig. 548. Urticaceae (*Pilea microphylla*).
A, Portion of a flowering shoot; B, Magnified view of the same; C, Staminate flower; D, V.s. of the same; E, Pistillate flower; F, Floral diagram of staminate flower; G, Same of pistillate flower.

Key to Genera

(*a*) Trees or shrubs

(*i*) Flowering before the leaves; leaves entire, fruit samaroid; tree .. .. .. *Holoptelea.*

(*ii*) Flowering with the leaves; fruit small, drupaceous; leaves serrate .. *Trema.*

(*iii*) Flowers axillary spikes or racemes, monoecious or dioecious; stipules free; stigma persistent; leaves alternate or opposite, toothed .. *Boehmeria.*

(*b*) Herbs

(*i*) Leaves and stems beset with stinging hairs; leaves alternate, stipulate; fls. in axillary clusters, 1-sexual, monoecious or dioecious; ovary oblique .. .. *Fleurya.*

(*ii*) Common on damp walls and less-used paths; leaves opposite; infl. cymose .. .. *Pilea.*

(*iii*) Leaves usually alternate, entire; flowers in axillary clusters, minute, usually monoecious; stipules free; stigma jointed, dioecious .. *Pouzolzia.*

Common plants

(1) Nettle (*Fleurya interrupta* Gaud. and *Urtica urens* L., *U. dioica*

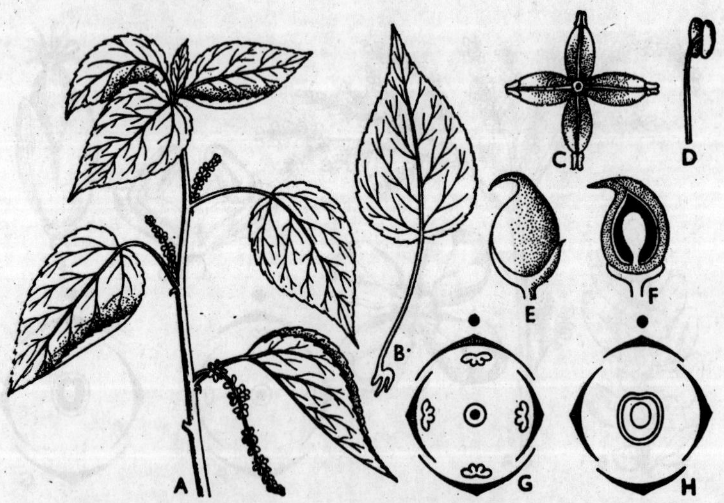

Fig. 549. Urticaceae (*Fleurya interrupta*).
A, Portion of a flowering shoot; B, A leaf with stipules; C. **Staminate flower;** D, Stamen; E, Pistillate flower; F, L.s. of ovary; G of staminate flower; H, Same of pistillate

L.), a common weed with stinging hairs. (2) Rami grass (*Boehmeria nivea* Hook. & Arn.), commonly cultivated for its silky fibre. (3) Gunpowder plant (*Pilea microphylla* Liebm.), so-called from the cloud of pollen discharged from the anthers when the plant is shaken; commonly found on damp walls. (4) *Pouzolzia indica* Gaud., a common weed of waste places. (5) *Trema orientalis* Bl., a very common shrub. (5) *Holoptelea integrifolia* Planch, a large spreading tree.

Affinity

This family is regarded to be most highly advanced in the order Urticales as evidenced by the abortion of the second carpel, basal

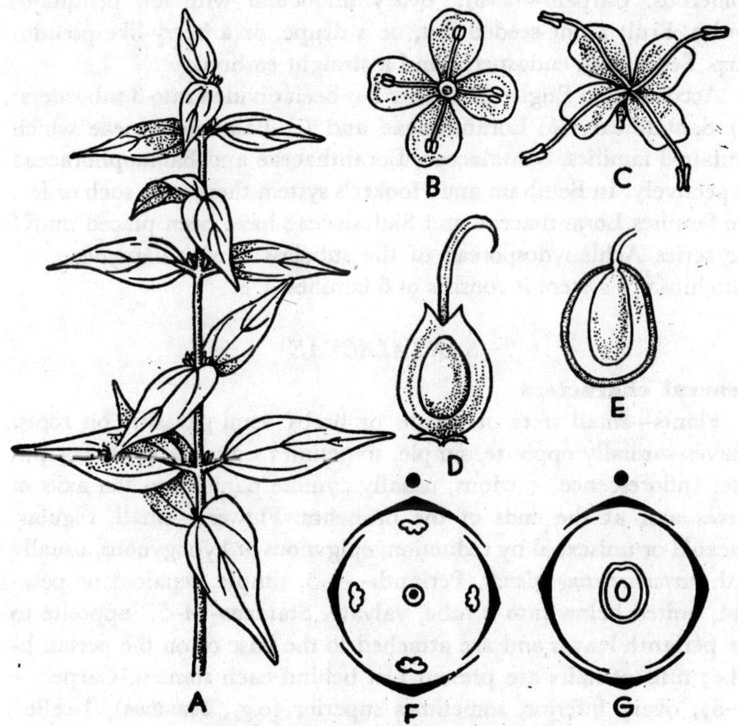

Fig. 550. Urticaceae (*Pouzolzia indica*).
A, Portion of a flowering shoot; B, A young staminate flower; C, An old staminate flower; D, Pistillate flower; E, L.s. of ovary; F, Floral diagram of staminate flower; G, Same of pistillate flower.

position of the ovule and herbaceous habit. It is distinguished from other families of the order by the stinging hairs (when present), monocarpellary ovary with single basal orthotropous ovule, single style and cymose inflorescences on short axillary shoots.

Economic importance

This family is of little economic importance. *Boehmeria* furnishes fibre for Chinese 'grass cloth' known as Ramia. Species of *Pilea, Pillionia,* etc., are ornamentals.

ORDER 14. SANTANALES

Flowers usually unisexual, cyclic, regular, sometimes irregular. Perianth leaves small and opposite to the adnate stamens. Stamens isomerous. Carpels—(2–3), ovary unilocular with few pendulous ovules. Fruit a one-seeded nut, or a drupe, or a berry-like pseudocarp. Seeds with endosperm and a straight embryo.

According to Engler this order has been divided into 3 suborders: (*a*) Santalineae, (*b*) Loranthineae and (*c*) Balanophorineae which contain 3 families, Santalaceae, Loranthaceae and Balanophoraceae respectively. In Bentham and Hooker's system there is no such order, the families Loranthaceae and Santalaceae have been placed under the series Achlanydosporeae of the subclass Monochlamydeae. Hutchinson's system it consists of 6 families.

SANTALACEAE

General characters

Plants—small trees or shrubs or herbs, semi-parasitic on roots. Leaves—usually opposite, simple, sometimes scale-like or 0, exstipulate. Inflorescence—various, usually cymose panicles in the axils of leaves and at the ends of the branches. Flowers—small, regular, bisexual or unisexual by reduction, epigynous or hypogynous, usually with *nectar-secreting glands*. Perianth—4–5, simple, sepaloid or petaloid, united below into a tube, valvate. Stamens—4–5, opposite to the perianth leaves and are attached to the base or on the perianth-tube; tufts of hairs are present just behind each stamen. Carpels—(3–5); ovary inferior, sometimes superior (e.g., *Santalum*), 1-celled with *central placenta* bearing usually *3 ovules, each with 1 integument.* Fruit—a drupe or an achene. Seed—*without testa,* albuminous; embryo straight.

Floral formula

$\oplus$ ⚥ $\overline{P_{(4-5)}\ A_{4-5}}\ \overline{G}_{(3-5)}$

Number and distribution

The family consists of about 26 genera with 250 species widely distributed in the tropics.

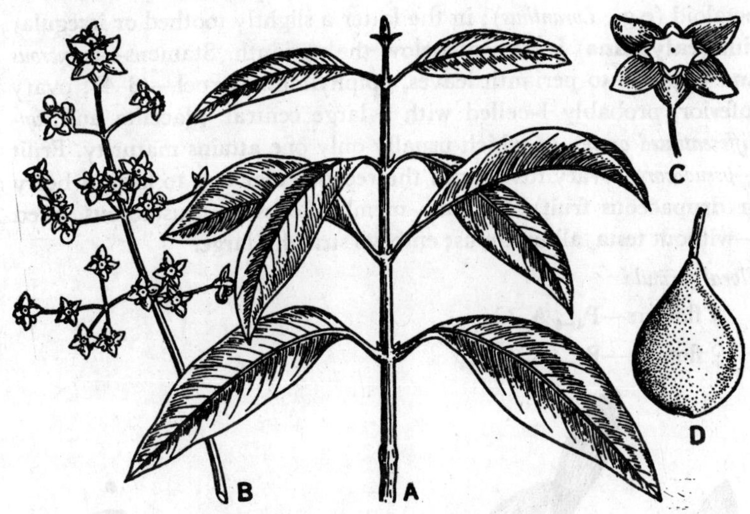

Fig. 551. Santalaceae (*Santalum album*).
A, A vegetative shoot; B, An inflorescence; C, Flower; D, Fruit.

Common plant

The Sandal wood tree (*Santalum album* L.), common in South India and often planted in gardens.

Affinity

This family is closely allied to Loranthaceae but readily distinguished by the presence of central placenta, 3–5 carpellate ovary with 3 ovules, ovule with one or no integument, and the seed without testa.

Economic importance

This family is less important economically. *Santalum* yields the 'sandal wood'. Only *Buckleya* and *Pyrularia* are ornamentals.

LORANTHACEAE

General characters

Plants—*hemi-parasitic herbs* with sympodial (but dichasial in *Viscum*) stems attached to the hosts by haustoria. Leaves—usually *opposite*, simple, entire, leathery, persistent, exstipulate. Inflorescence —solitary or dichasia in the axils of leaves. Flowers—almost regular, bisexual or unisexual and dioecious (e.g., *Viscum*), epigynous. Perianth—generally of two similar 2–3-merous whorls, free or united into a tube which is *often split down one side*, sepaloid (e.g., *Viscum*) or petaloid (e.g., *Loranthus*); in the latter a slightly toothed or irregular rim (**calyculus**) is present below the perianth. Stamens—*isomerous* and opposite to perianth leaves, epiphyllous. Carpel—(3–4); ovary inferior, probably 1-celled with a large central placenta and *undifferentiated ovules*, of which usually only one attains maturity. Fruit —*pseudocarp* (ovary fused with the receptacular cup to form a berry or drupaceous fruit), pericarp membraneous or crustaceous. Seed —without testa, albuminous; embryo straight, large.

Floral formula

♂ flowers—$P_{4-6}\ A_6\ G_0$

♀ flowers—$P_{4-6}\ A_0\ \overline{G_{(3-4)}}$

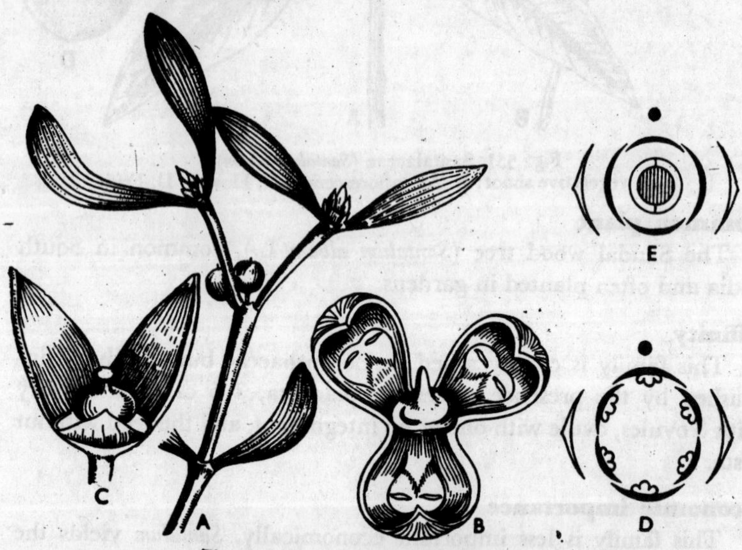

Fig. 552. Loranthaceae (*Viscum album*).
A, Portion of a flowering shoot; B, Staminate flower; C, Pistillate flower; D, Floral diagram of a staminate flower of the terminal dichasium; E, Same of pistillate flower.

Number and distribution

This family consists of 21 genera and over 500 species, mostly distributed in tropical and subtropical regions.

GENERA

Fls. bisexual, calyculus present .. .. *Loranthus*.

Fls. unisexual, calyculus absent .. .. *Viscum*.

Common plants

(1) Mistletoe (*Viscum album* L.) and (2) *Loranthus longiflorus* Deser. =*Dendrophthoe falcata* E. Hing. and *L. globossus* Roxb. are commonly found on mango trees.

Affinity

This family is related to Santalaceae in their habit, undifferentiated ovules and anomalous development of embryosac, but readily distinguished from it by the aerial parasitic habit, nature of the perianth, number of carpels, cup-shaped receptacle, absence of distinct ovules, and character of fruit.

Economic importance

Economically this family is not important.

ORDER 16. POLYGONALES

Plants herbs, shrubs or rarely trees. Leaves usually with ochreate stipules. Flowers bisexual consisting of similar members of perianth. Ovary 2–4-carpellate, superior, 1-celled with solitary orthotropous ovule. Fruit a nutlet or achene.

According to Engler this order contains a single family Polygonaceae. Bentham and Hooker have put this family along with Nyctaginaceae, Amaranthaceae and Chenopodiaceae in the series Curvembryeae under the subclass Monochlamydeae. In Hutchinson's system it consists of 2 families.

POLYGONACEAE

General characters

Plants—usually herbs *with swollen nodes*, sometimes climbing (e.g., *Antigonon*), seldom trees (e.g., *Coccoloba uvifera*). Leaves—alternate, simple, entire, usually with *ochreate stipules* (absent in *Antigonon*). Inflorescence—mixed in most cases, commonly a raceme or panicle of cymes. Flowers—small, regular, usually bisexual (unisexual in *Rumex*), trimerous, cyclic or acyclic. Perianth—3–6, free, green, sometimes 5, petaloid, persistent. Stamens—6–9. Carpels—(3), rarely (2), united; ovary *triangular*, *1-celled with 1 basal orthotropous ovule*;

style 1; stigma, 2–4. Fruit—triangular or biconvex nut. Seed—with mealy endosperm. Embryo—curved.

Floral formula

$\oplus$ ⚥ $P_{6(3+3)\text{ or }5}$, A_{6-9}, $\underline{G}_{(2)\text{ or }(3)}$

Number and distribution

This family consists of about 32 genera and about 800 species which are chiefly found in the north temperate zone.

KEY TO GENERA

A. Inflorescence ending in a tendril, stipule 0
Perianth 5-cleft; climbing plant .. .. *Antigonon.*

B. Inflorescence not ending in a tendril, stipulate
(*i*) Perianth 4–5; capitate stigmas .. .. *Polygonum.*
(*ii*) Perianth 6-fid, inner 3 usually enlarged in fruit; stigmas horseshoe-shaped or peltate, fimbriated .. .. *Rumex.*

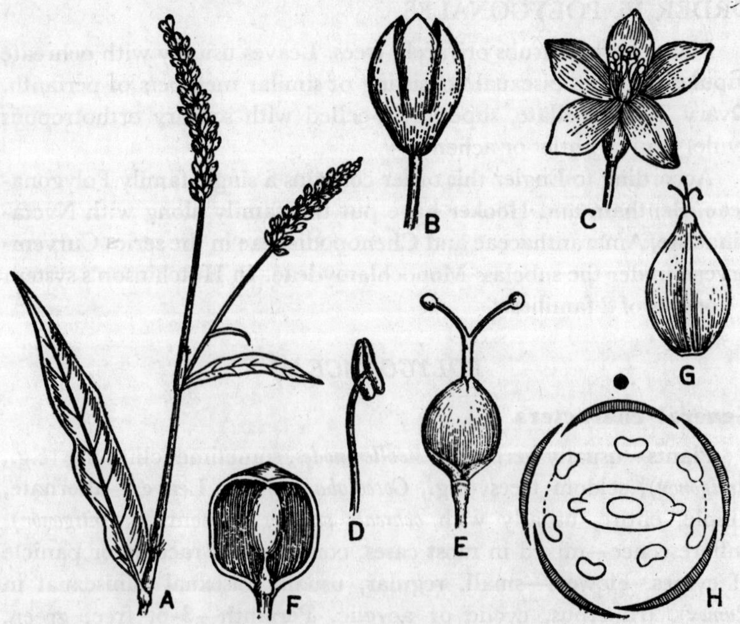

Fig. 553. Polygonaceae (*Polygonum orientale*).
A, Portion of a flowering shoot; B, Flower bud; C, Flower; D, Stamen; E, Pistil; F, L.s. of ovary; G, Fruit; H, Floral diagram.

Common plants

(1) Knot-weed (*Polygonum hydro-piper* L.), a common weed of damp places. (2) *Polygonum orientale* L. and *P. barbatum* L. are common weeds of ditches. (3) *Polygonum plebejum* R. Br., a diffusely branched prostrate herb. (4) *Rumex maritimus* L., a marshy weed. (5) Dock (*Rumex vesicarius* L.) commonly cultivated for its acid leaves. (6) Railway creeper (*Antigonon leptopus* Hook. & Arn.=*Corculum leptopus* Stuntz.), a common garden climber with small pink or white flowers. (7) *Muehlenbeckia platyclada* Meisn.—*Homalocladium*, *Platycladium* (Muell.), Baily, are often planted in gardens for flattened leaf-like stems (phylloclades). (8) Sea-grape (*Coccoloba uvifera* L.), a tree found in the Indian Botanic Garden, the leaves of which resemble *Ficus benghalensis* and likely to be mistaken for it. (9) Rhubarb (*Rheum emodi* Wall.), a medicinal plant commonly found in the hills.

Affinity

This family is closely allied to Chenopodiaceae, Amaranthaceae and Nyctaginaceae but readily distinguished by the ochreate stipules, triangular 1-celled ovary, with solitary basal ovule, 1-seeded fruit and curved embryo. It bears some affinity with Urticaceae in the orthotropous ovule and stipule.

Economic importance

This family is not much important economically. *Fagopyrum* (buck-wheat) and *Rheum* (rhubarb) are useful as food in the western countries. *Rumex vesicarius* is used as a vegetable. *Rheum emodi* is used in medicine. Some plants are also recognized as ornamentals, such as, *Antigonon*, *Coccoloba uvifera*, *Polygonum aubertii*, etc.

ORDER 17. CENTROSPERMAE

Plants annual and perennial herbs with alternate or opposite exstipulate leaves. Flowers bisexual or unisexual by reduction, usually pentamerous. Perianth typically biseriate. Stamens in 1 or 2 series, hypogynous, or sometimes perigynous. Carpels with monocarpellary to pentacarpellary pistil; ovary superior, unilocular with 1-many campylotropous ovules. Fruit a capsule or nut, rarely baccate. Embryo large and curved or coiled.

According to Engler this order consists of 4 suborders containing families Chenopodiaceae, Amaranthaceae, Nyctaginaceae,

Portulacaceae, Caryophyllaceae, etc. Bentham and Hooker have put the families Nyctaginaceae, Amaranthaceae and Chenopodiaceae under the series Curvembryeae of subclass Monochlamydeae, and Caryophyllaceae and Portulacaceae under the series Thalamiflorae of subclass Polypetalae. Hutchinson, however, has discarded the name of this order and has placed Caryophyllaceae and Portulacaceae under the order Caryophyllales and the rest under the order Chenopodiales.

CHENOPODIACEAE

General characters

Plants—usually annual or perennial succulent herbs, sometimes shrubs, very rarely trees (e.g., *Haloxylon*), monoecious or dioecious

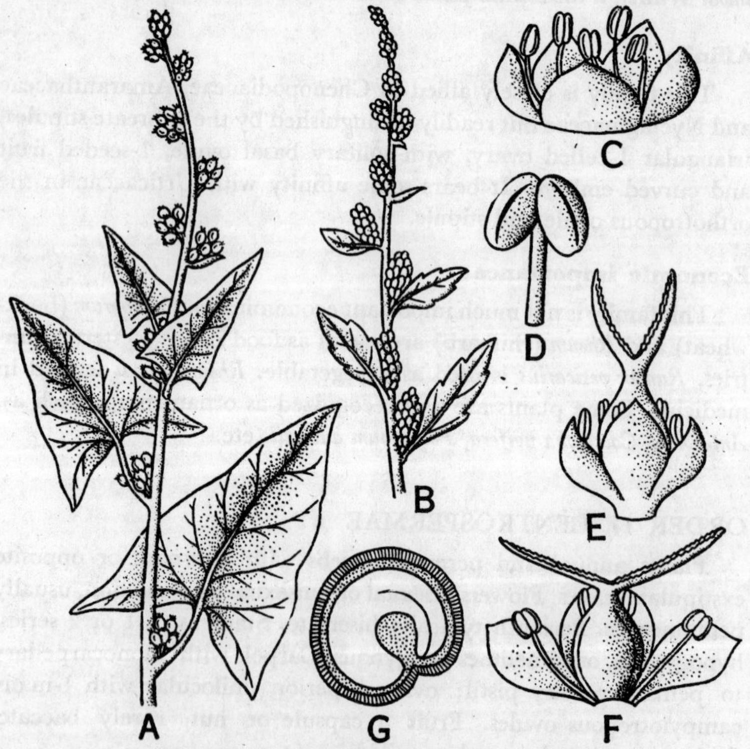

Fig. 554. Chenopodiaceae (*Chenopodium album*).
A, Portion of a flowering shoot bearing staminate flowers; B, The same with pistillate flowers; C, Staminate flower; D, Stamen; E, Pistillate flower; F, Hermaphrodite flower; G, T.s. of seed.

with swollen nodes. Leaves—usually alternate, rarely opposite (e.g., *Salicornia*), simple, fleshy, entire or variously lobed (but in halophytic species, such as *Suaeda*, *Salsola*, *Salicornia*, etc., are much reduced in size, linear or even scale-like), glabrous (but covered with mealy hairs in *Chenopodium*, *Artiplex*, *Salsola*), *exstipulate*. Inflorescence—dense spike or panicle or cymose (at first dichasia but soon change into monochasia). Flowers—regular, bisexual (but unisexual in *Spinacia* and *Artiplex*), hypogynous (but epigynous in *Beta*), often with scarious bracts and bracteoles. Perianth—5, usually more or less dry and membraneous, free or more or less united, persistent. Stamens—5 (but 2 in *Salicornia*), *opposite the perianth leaves*; filaments united at the base into a short tube. Carpels—(2–3); ovary superior, sometimes inferior (e.g., *Beta*), *1-celled with a campylotropous erect or pendulous ovule*; style short or long; stigma usually 2–3-fid. Fruit—lens- or kidney-shaped nutlet. Seeds—albuminous or exalbuminous with horny testa; *embryo curved* (e.g., *Chenopodium*, *Artiplex*, *Salicornia*, *Beta*, etc.) or *coiled* (e.g., *Suaeda*, *Salsola*, etc.).

Floral formula

$\oplus$ ⚥ $P_{5 \text{ or } (5)}\ A_{(5)}\ \underline{G_{(2-3)}}$

Number and distribution

This family consists of about 102 genera and 1,400 species which are cosmopolitan.

KEY TO GENERA

A. Stem not jointed:

(*a*) Leaves fleshy; fls. minute, axillary, 2-sexual; stamens almost hypogynous .. .. .. *Suaeda.*

(*b*) Leaves membraneous; fls. clustered; stamens perigynous—

(*i*) Fls. all similar, 2-sexual

Perianth 5-partite, hardly altered in fruit; fls. without bracts and bracteoles .. .. *Chenopodium.*

Perianth 5-lobed, base thickened in fruit; fls. bracteate .. .. *Beta.*

(*ii*) Fls. dissimilar, 1-sexual

Male fls. in terminal spike; stamens 4–5; female fls. in axillary clusters, with 2–4 toothed perianth but without bracteole .. .. .. *Spinacia.*

Male fls. with 3–5 sepals; female fls. without perianth .. .. *Artiplex.*

B. Stem jointed; leaves 0; fls. bisexual:

Fls. 2–6 in spike; perianth-mouth narrow, 3–4-fid .. *Arthrocnemum.*

Fls. in 3, sunk in cavities near joints; perianth-mouth wide, truncate or with 3–4 minute teeth .. .. *Salicornia.*

Common plants

(1) Spinach (*Spinacia oleracea* L.) commonly cultivated. (2) Lamb's quarters (*Chenopodium album* L.) and *C. ambrosoides* L., tall herbs which are also cultivated. (3) *Suaeda maritima* Dumort, commonly found in saline regions. (4) Salt-bush (*Atriplex hortensis* L.).

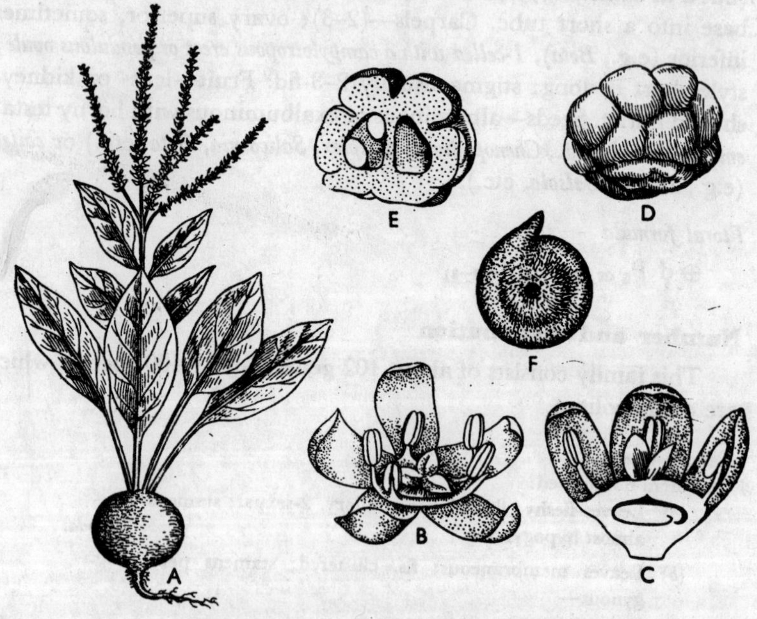

Fig. 555. Chenopodiaceae (*Beta vulgaris*).
A, An entire plant with foliage and inflorescence; B, Flower; C, V.s. of the same; D, Fruit; E, V.s. of the same; F, Seed.

(5) *Salicornia brachiata* Roxb. and (6) *Arthrocnemum indicum* Moq., prostrate woody shrubs commonly found in the Sundribans. (7) Sugar-beet (*Beta vulgaris* L.), commonly cultivated for obtaining sugar.

Affinity

This family is allied to Amaranthaceae in the presence of monochlamydeous flowers, uniseriate stamens and a single basal ovule in 1-celled ovary. It is also allied to Phytolaccaceae in the plan of floral structure, and is supposed that the family has been derived from Phytolaccaceae. Chenopodiaceae is readily distinguished from allied families by the fleshy habit, absence of scarious bracts, 2–3-carpellate ovary which is 1-celled and 1-ovuled, and the nature of the embryo.

Economic importance

This family is not of much economic importance. *Spinacia oleracea*, the common spinach, is used as a vegetable. Some plants are considered to be fodder plants, such as, species of *Artiplex*, *Kochia*, etc. *C. quinoa* yields a sort of grain with mealy perisperm. The seeds of *C. anthelminticum* yield a kind of oil which is used as a vermifuge. *Chenopodium bonus* and *Hemichroa* are cultivated as pot-herbs.

AMARANTHACEAE

General characters

Plants—mostly annual or perennial herbs, sometimes shrubs (e.g., *Deeringia*). Leaves—alternate or opposite, simple, generally entire,

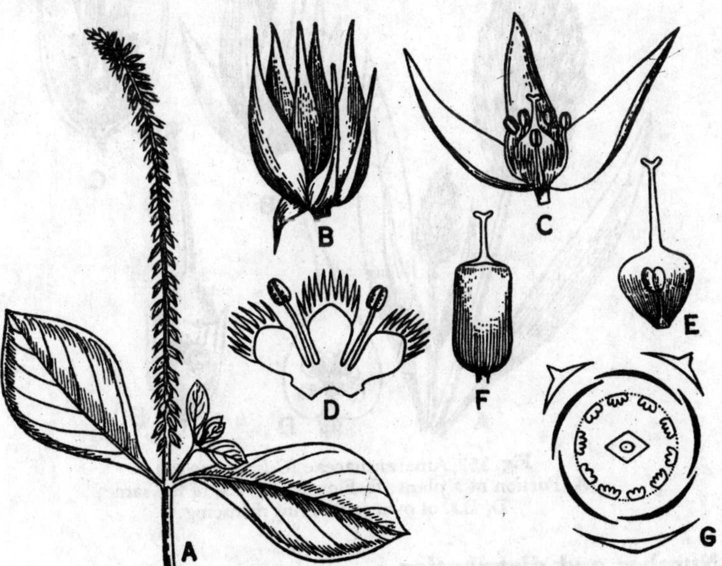

Fig. 356. Amaranthaceae (*Achyranthes aspera*).
A, Portion of a flowering shoot; B, Flower; C, The same cut lengthwise; D, Androecium; E, Pistil; F, Fruit; G, Floral diagram.

often more or less hairy, exstipulate. Inflorescence—simple or compound *spike*, or raceme, or dichasia. Flowers—small, regular, bisexual, sometimes unisexual (e.g., *Amaranthus*), hypogynous, with a *pair of membraneous, persistent, bracteoles*. Perianth—5, dry and *membraneous*, often *white* and *shining* or coloured, free or more or less united, persistent, imbricate. Stamens—5, opposite the perianth segments; filaments *often united* into a membraneous tube which may bear simple, lobed or fringed, petaloid outgrowths between two stamens. Carpels—(2–3); ovary superior, 1-celled, frequently with solitary basal or campylotropous ovule; style 1–3. Fruit—a *nutlet* or *utricle* (e.g., *Achyranthes*) or pyxis (e.g., *Celosia*). Seed—black with bony *shining testa*, and mealy endosperm. Embryo—horseshoe-shaped or annular.

Floral formula

$\oplus$ ⚥ $P_5\ A_5\ \underline{G_{(2\ \text{to}\ 3)}}$

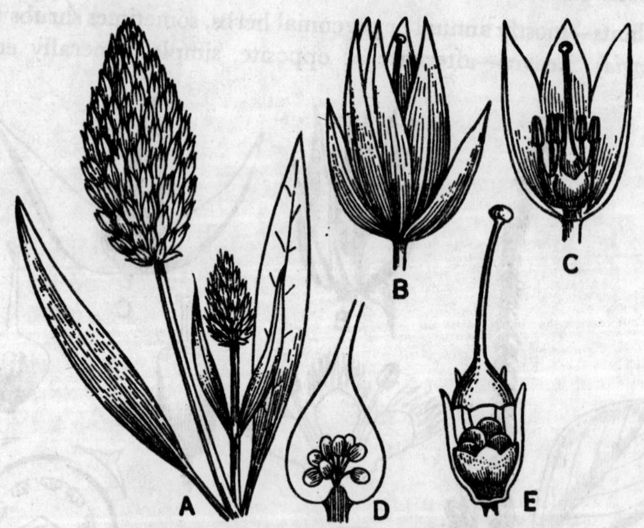

Fig. 557. Amaranthaceae (*Celosia argentea*). A, Portion of a plant; B, Flower; C, V.s. of the same; D, L.s. of ovary; E, Fruit dehiscing.

Number and distribution

This family consists of 64 genera and about 800 species which are chiefly found in the tropical or subtropical regions.

Key to Genera

A. Leaves usually alternate:
- (*a*) Ovary 2-many-ovuled—
  - Plant climbing, undershrub; fruit a berry .. *Deeringia.*
  - Annual herb, flowers white or pink, fruit a circumsessile capsule .. .. *Celosia.*
- (*b*) Ovary 1-ovuled—
  - (*i*) Ovules erect
    - Flowers 1-sexual .. .. .. *Amaranthus.*
    - Flowers bisexual:
      - Fls. spicate in threes, the outer two reduced to crested scales; fruit a nut .. .. *Digera.*
      - Fls. capitate, fruit a circumsessile capsule .. *Allmania.*
  - (*ii*) Ovules suspended; fls. perfect; stamens with interposed staminodes .. .. .. *Aerva.*

B. Leaves opposite, ovary 1-celled:
- (*a*) Anthers 2-celled—
  - Flowers all perfect—
    - Stamens with interposed staminodes, bracts spinous *Achyranthes.*
    - Staminodes absent .. .. .. *Psilotrichum.*
  - Flowers perfect and deformed, clustered together—
    - Stamens with interposed staminodes .. .. *Cyathula.*
    - Staminodes none .. .. .. *Pupalia*
- (*b*) Anthers 1-celled—
  - Flowers small, white, in heads; staminal tube short; stigma capitate, subsessile .. .. *Alternanthera.*
  - Flowers short, white or coloured, usually capitate; staminal tube long; stigma 2-fid; style long .. *Gomphrena.*

Common plants

(1) *Amaranthus spinosa* L., a common spinous weed. (2) *Amaranthus viridis* L. and *A. gangeticus* L. are cultivated as vegetables. (3) Cocks' comb (*Celosia cristata* L.), commonly planted in gardens. (4) *Celosia argentea* L., a weed found in waste places. (5) *Achyranthes aspera* L.=*Aerva aspera* Spreng., a common weed. (6) *Alternanthera sessilis* R. Br., a very common weed found in moist places. (7) *A. paronychioides* St. Hil., common in the vicinity of Railway lines near Calcutta. (8) *Aerua scandens* Wall.=*Aerva sanguinolenta* Bl. and *A. lanata* Juss., common weeds. (9) Globe Amaranth (*Gomphrena globosa* L.), commonly cultivated in gardens. (10) *Deeringia celosioides* Br.=

D. amaranthoides Merr., a climbing shrub with purple berries. (11) *Pupalia atropurpurea* Moq., a common weed with hooked fruits. (12) *Digera arvensis* Forsk.=*D. muricata* Mart., a weed. (13) *Psilotrichum ferrugineum* Moq., a weed of fields and waste places. (14) *Allmania nodiflora* R. Br., a dichotomously branched annual. (15) *Cyathula prostrata* Bl., a slender erect weed.

Affinity

This family is closely allied to Chenopodiaceae but readily distinguished by the dense spicate inflorescence, scarious bracts and bracteoles, membraneous and shining perianth, and usually connate filaments.

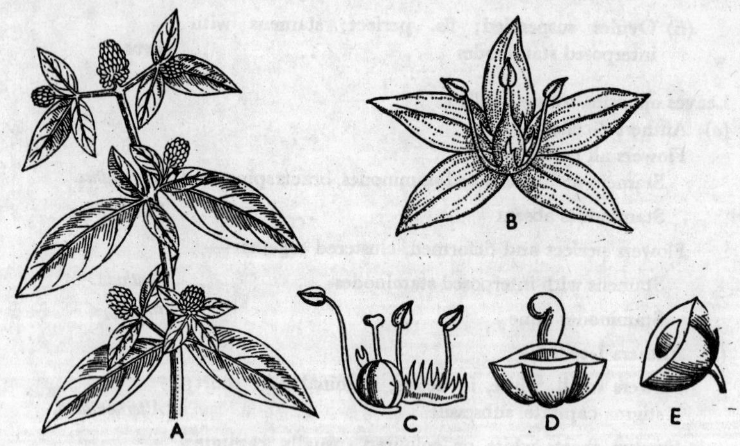

Fig. 558. Amaranthaceae (*Alternanthera sessilis*).
A, Portion of a flowering shoot; B, Flower; C, Stamen; D–E, Dehiscing fruit.

Economic importance

This family is of little economic importance. Some plants are used in medicine, such as, *Achyranthes*, *Aerua*, *Amaranthus*, etc., and as pot-herbs. A few are ornamentals, such as, *Celosia*, *Gomphrena*, etc.

NYCTAGINACEAE

General characters

Plants—usually herbs or shrubs (e.g., *Mirabilis*), sometimes climbers (e.g., *Bougainvillaea*, *Pisonia*). Leaves—usually opposite, simple, entire, more or less unequal, exstipulate. Inflorescence—cymose. Flowers—regular, usually bisexual (unisexual in *Pisonia*), hypogynous with involucre. Perianth—5, usually petaloid, *united* (tubular or funnel-shaped), the *lower part inflated* and *persistent* in fruit forming anthocarp. Stamens—usually 5–8, unequal. Carpel—one; ovary superior, 1-celled with *basal*, *anatropous* or *campylotropous ovule.* Fruit—achene, enclosed in the perianth base. Seed—albuminous, with mealy perisperm. Embryo—curved or folded, with broad leaf-like cotyledons and an *inferior radicle.*

Floral formula

$\oplus$ ⚥ $P_{(5)}\ A_{5-8},\ \underline{G_1}$

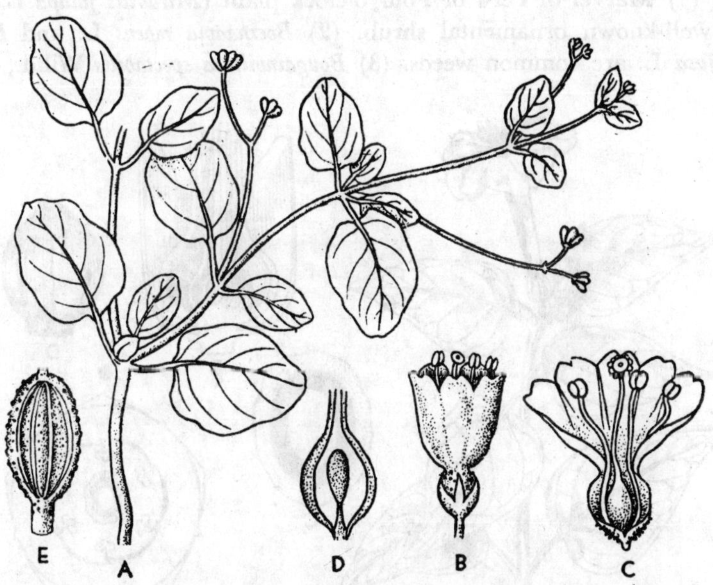

Fig. 559. Nyctaginaceae (*Boerhaavia repens*).
A, Portion of a flowering shoot; B, Flower; C, Perianth split open; D, L.s. of ovary; E, Fruit.

Number and distribution

This family consists of 28 genera and about 250 species which are found both in tropical and subtropical regions.

KEY TO GENERA

A. Embryo hooked; radicle long; limb of perianth plicate:

(*a*) Leaves opposite, herbs—

(*i*) Flowers very small; leaves often in unequal pairs .. .. *Boerhaavia.*

(*ii*) Flowers large, showy; lower leaves petioled, upper ones sessile .. .. .. *Mirabilis.*

(*b*) Leaves alternate; climbing shrubs; flowers in threes, attached to midribs of large coloured bracts .. *Bougainvillaea.*

B. Embryo straight; radicle short; limb of perianth induplicate-valvate; fls. small in panicled cymes .. .. *Pisonia.*

Common plants

(1) Marvel of Peru or Four o'clock plant (*Mirabilis jalapa* L.), a well-known ornamental shrub. (2) *Boerhaavia repens* L. and *B. diffusa* L. are common weeds. (3) *Bougainvillaea spectabilis* Willd., a

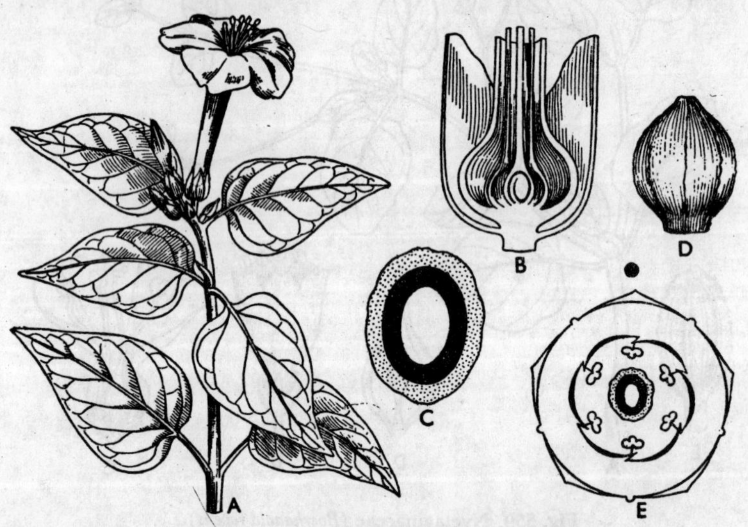

Fig. 560. Nyctaginaceae (*Mirabilis jalapa*).
A, Portion of a flowering shoot; B, V.s. of the lower portion of a flower; C, T.s. of ovary; D, Fruit; E, Floral diagram.

handsome climber with 3 brightly coloured bracts, often planted in gardens. (4) *Pisonia aculeata* L., a large spinous straggling shrub.

Affinity

This family is closely allied to Polygonaceae but readily distinguished by the sepaloid bracts, unicarpellate ovary, and the peculiar fruit enclosed in the persistent base of the perianth (anthocarp).

Economic importance

This family is of little importance economically. *Boerhaavia* is used in medicine. Some plants are used as ornamentals, such as, *Mirabilis*, *Bougainvillaea*, *Abronia*, etc.

Comparison of Chenopodiaceae, Amaranthaceae and Nyctaginaceae

Chenopodiaceae	*Amaranthaceae*	*Nyctaginaceae*
1. Plants—succulent herbs or shrubs with swollen nodes.	1. Herbs or shrubs.	1. Herbs or shrubs, sometimes climbers.
2. Leaves—alternate, sometimes opposite, simple, fleshy, entire or variously lobed, sometimes scale-like, exstipulate.	2. Alternate or opposite, simple, exstipulate.	2. Opposite, simple, more or less unequal, exstipulate.
3. Inflorescence—dense spike or panicle or cymose.	3. Simple or compound spike or raceme, or dichasia.	3. Cymose.
4. Flowers—regular, bisexual sometimes unisexual, hypogynous, rarely epigynous, with scarious bracts and bracteoles.	4. Regular, bisexual sometimes unisexual, hypogynous, with scarious bracts and bracteoles.	4. Regular, bisexual rarely unisexual, hypogynous with involucre.

Comparison of Chenopodiaceae, Amaranthaceae and Nyctaginaceae—(*Contd.*)

Chenopodiaceae	*Amaranthaceae*	*Nyctaginaceae*
5. Perianth — usually 5, free or united, dry and membraneous.	5. 5, membraneous, dry and shining, persistent.	5. (5), usually petaloid, tubular or funnel-shaped, the lower part inflated and persistent.
6. Stamens—5, rarely 2, opposite the perianth leaves; filaments free or united at the base forming a short tube.	6. 5, opposite the perianth lobes; filaments often united at the base forming a membraneous tube.	6. 5–8, unequal, epiphyllous.
7. Carpels—(2–3)	7. (2–3).	7. One.
8. Ovary—superior, rarely inferior, 1-celled with a campylotropous erect or pendulous ovule.	8. Superior, 1-celled with a campylotropous ovule.	8. Superior, 1-celled with a basal anatropous or campylotropous ovule.
9. Fruit—nutlet.	9. Nut or utricle or pyxis.	9. Achene.

PORTULACACEAE

General characters

Plants—usually annual or perennial herbs. Leaves—opposite or alternate, entire, *succulent*, usually stipulate (scarious stipules). Inflorescence—cymose or racemose. Flowers—regular, bisexual, hypogynous without disc. Sepals—*usually* 2, placed antero-posteriorly, imbricate. Petals—usually 4–6, free. Stamens—4–6 or more, antipetalous and united with the petals at the base. Carpels—(2–3), ovary superior (half-inferior in *Portulaca*), sunk in torus, 1-celled with 2 to many campylotropous ovules on a central basal placenta; styles and stigmas 2–5. Fruit—capsule, dehiscing circumscissilely. Seed—albuminous. Embryo—curved.

Floral formula

$$\oplus ⚥\ K_2\ \overline{C_{4-8}\ A_{4-6\text{ or }\infty}}\ \underline{G_{(2-3)}}$$

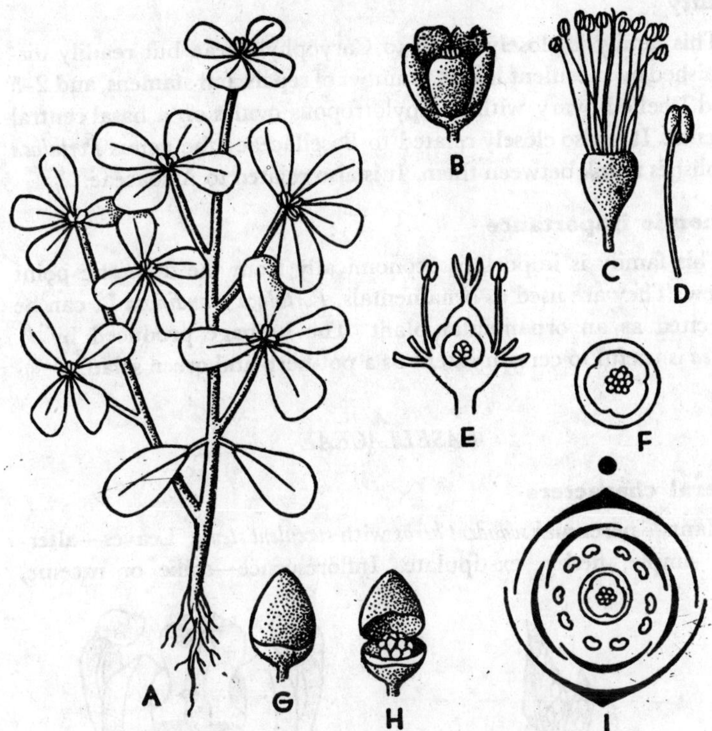

Fig. 561. Portulacaceae (*Portulaca quadrifida*).
A, An entire plant; B, Flower; C, The same with sepals and petals removed; D, Stamen; E, L.s. of ovary; F, T.s. of ovary; G, Fruit; H, Same splitting open; I, Floral diagram.

Number and distribution

This family consists of 16 genera and 500 species which are generally distributed in tropical and temperate regions.

KEY TO GENUS

Ovary half-adnate; styles 3–5-fid; fruit capsule; seeds many, reniform; fls. terminal surrounded by whorls of leaves or clustered .. .. *Portulaca*.

Common plants

(1) Purslane (*Portulaca oleracea* L.), (2) *P. quadrifida* L. and (3) *P. tuberosa* Roxb. are very common weeds growing in nooks and corners.

Affinity

This family is closely allied to Caryophyllaceae but readily distinguished by succulent leaves, number of sepals and stamens, and 2–5 styled 1-celled ovary with campylotropous ovules on a basal central placenta. It is also closely related to Basellaceae; the genus *Portulaca* establishes a link between them. It is also related to Aizoaceae.

Economic importance

This family is important economically from the domestic point of view. They are used as ornamentals. *Portulaca grandiflora* L. can be best cited as an ornamental plant. The herbage produced by *P oleracea* is useful to certain extent as a pot-herb and green salad.

BASELLACEAE

General characters

Plants—perennial *scandent herbs* with *succulent stems.* Leaves—alternate, simple, fleshy, exstipulate. Inflorescence—spike or raceme.

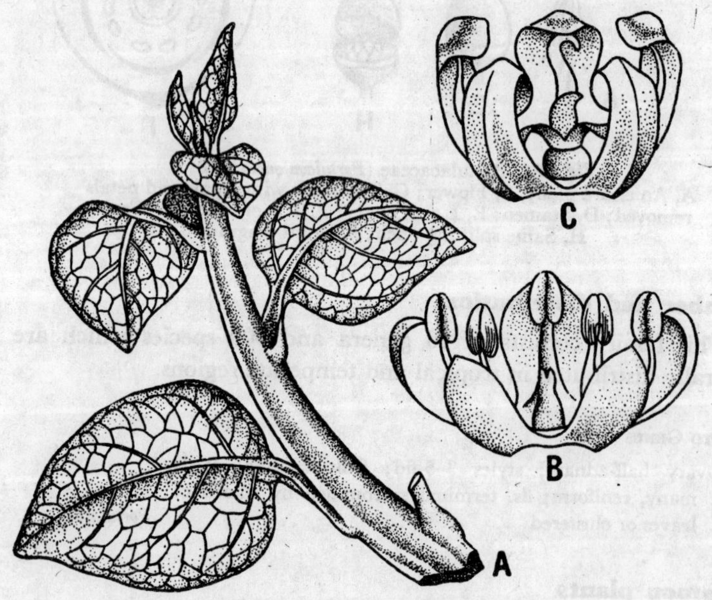

Fig. 562. Basellaceae (*Basella rubra*).
A, Portion of a shoot; B, Staminate flower; C, Pistillate flower.

Flowers—small, regular, incomplete, bisexual, hypogynous. Perianth—represented by 5 sepals, white or reddish, more or less united at the base, subtended by a pair of bracts forming an involucre, imbricate, *persistent*. Stamens—5, antisepalous, united with the bases of the sepals. Carpels—(3); ovary superior, 1-celled with solitary, campylotropous ovule or basal placenta; style 1; stigma usually 3-fid. Fruit—drupe, invested by the persistent perianth. Seeds—with scanty endosperm and a *rolled embryo*.

Floral formula

$\oplus$ ⚥ $\overline{P_{(5)}}\ A_5\ \underline{G_{(3)}}$

Number and distribution

This family consists of 5 genera and about 22 species which are commonly found in the tropics.

Common plant

Basella rubra L., shoots of which are taken as spinach.

Affinity

This family is readily distinguished from other members of Centrospermae by the scandent succulent character, bisexual apetalous flowers, fleshy persistent perianth leaves enveloping the fruit, and spirally twisted embryo. Bentham and Hooker included this family under Chenopodiaceae, but it differs from the latter by the biseriate perianth. It is related very closely to Portulacaceae and it is believed it arose as an offshoot of the latter.

Economic importance

This family is of little economic importance. The shoots of *Basella* are taken as spinach. The tuberous roots of *Ullucus tuberosus* are eaten in America as a substitute for potato. The Madeira vine (*Boussingaultia*) is an ornamental garden plant.

CARYOPHYLLACEAE

General characters

Plants—annual or perennial herbs with swollen nodes. Leaves—usually *opposite*, simple, linear to lanceolate, slightly amplexicaul, usually exstipulate (excepting *Spergula*). Inflorescence—cymose (*dichasium* or *dichotomous cyme*). Flowers—regular, usually bisexual, hypogynous or perigynous. Sepals—4–5, free or united, imbricate, persistent. Petals—4–5, often clawed, free. Stamens—8 or 10, *in two whorls*, or fewer, *apparently obdiplostemonous*. Carpels—(5), often fewer with 2–5 *styles* free or united below; ovary superior, usually 1-celled with numerous ovules on the *free central placentae*. Fruit—usually a capsule, breaking into valves equal to or double the number of styles. Seeds—more or less flattened, albuminous, usually with a curved embryo (but straight in *Dianthus*).

Floral formula

$$\oplus ⚥ \; K_{4-5 \text{ or } (4-5)} \; C_{4-5} \; A_{8-10} \; G_{(5)}$$

Number and distribution

This family consists of about 80 genera and 2,100 species which are mostly found in the temperate regions of the Northern Hemisphere and in the mountains of the tropics.

Key to Genera

A. Calyx gamosepalous; stipules 0:

(*a*) Petals clawed; disc small or elongated into a gynophore; styles free—

(*i*) Sepals veined; 4-valved capsule; embryo ring-like; styles 2 .. .. .. *Saponaria*.

(*ii*) Sepals bracteate, striated; embryo straight .. *Dianthus*.

(*iii*) Sepals 5-nerved; capsule 1-celled, 4-valved; embryo annular; styles 2–3 .. .. *Gypsophila*.

B. Calyx polysepalous:

(*b*) Petals subsessile; stamens originating from annular disc; styles free—

(*iv*) Stipule 0; petals bifid or 0; styles 3–5; capsule globose .. .. *Stellaria*.

(*v*) Stipule dry and membraneous; petals entire; capsule valved .. .. .. *Spergula*.

(*c*) Petals subsessile; stamens on annular disc; stipule scarious; style connate—

(*vi*) Petals 2–6-fid; sepals herbaceous .. .. *Drymaria*.

(*vii*) Petals entire; sepals keeled; style 3-fid .. *Polycarpon*.

(*viii*) Petals entire; sepals scarious; style connate; stigma 3-toothed .. .. .. *Polycarpaea*.

Range of floral structures

The flowers are typically pentamerous with formula $K_5 C_5 A_{5+5} \underline{G_{(5)}}$. But deviation from the normal plant of flowers occurs either by elaboration or reduction. This family has been divided into 2 subfamilies: (a) *Alsinoideae*, where the flower is simpler or reduced type, and (b) *Silenoideae*, where the flower is highly elaborated, characterized by the tubular development of the members of the calyx.

Subfamily 1. Alsinoideae—Sepals and petals are simple in form or absent, styles free or connate. In *Spergula arvensis*, the flower is simple with white petals, 2 whorls of stamens, and 5 carpels. *Sagina* also resembles *Spergula* in floral structure but the parts are found often in 4. In *Sagina apetala* L. the petals are very much reduced or totally absent. The petals are notched in *Cerastium* and *Stellaria*. In *Stellaria* the flower is usually pentamerous, rarely tetramerous. In *Polycarpon*, the flower is reduced, the petals are sometimes absent and the stamens also are reduced in number; the styles are connate below it. In *Lyallia*, the flower is apetalous and the number of stamens is 3.

Subfamily 2. Silenoideae—The sepals are connate into a tube. The petals are found often coloured and distinguished into a claw and a limb. An outgrowth or *ligule* is found sometimes on the throat of the corolla-tube or at the junction of the claw and limb. This sort of structure (ligule) is also present in *Dianthus*, *Silene* and *Lychnis*, but it is obliterated in the genera, like *Githago* and *Gypsophila*. The flower has pentamerous arrangement with 2 whorls of stamens. The styles are free. The number of carpels is 5 in *Lychnis*, 3 in *Silene*, and 2 in *Dianthus* and *Saponaria*.

Common plants

(1) Pink (*Dianthus chinensis* L.), Carnation (*D. caryophyllus* L.) and Sweet-William (*D. barbatus* L.) are common season flowers. (2) Cow cockle (*Saponaria vaccaria* L.), a commonh erb. (3) Chickweed (*Stellaria media* L.), a common weed of gardens in cold weather. (4) *Polycarpon loefliangiae* Benth. & Hk. f., used as a vegetable. (5) *Gypsophila elegans* L. and Baby's breath (*G. paniculata* L.) are common season flowers. (6) *Lychnis* (maltese cross) and *Silene* (catchfly) are handsome garden plants. (7) *Spergula arvensis* L. and *Drymaria cordata* Willd. are common weeds found in Darjeeling, Shillong and other hilly places. (8) *Polycarpaea corymbosa* Lamk. is a decumbent herb found on the river banks.

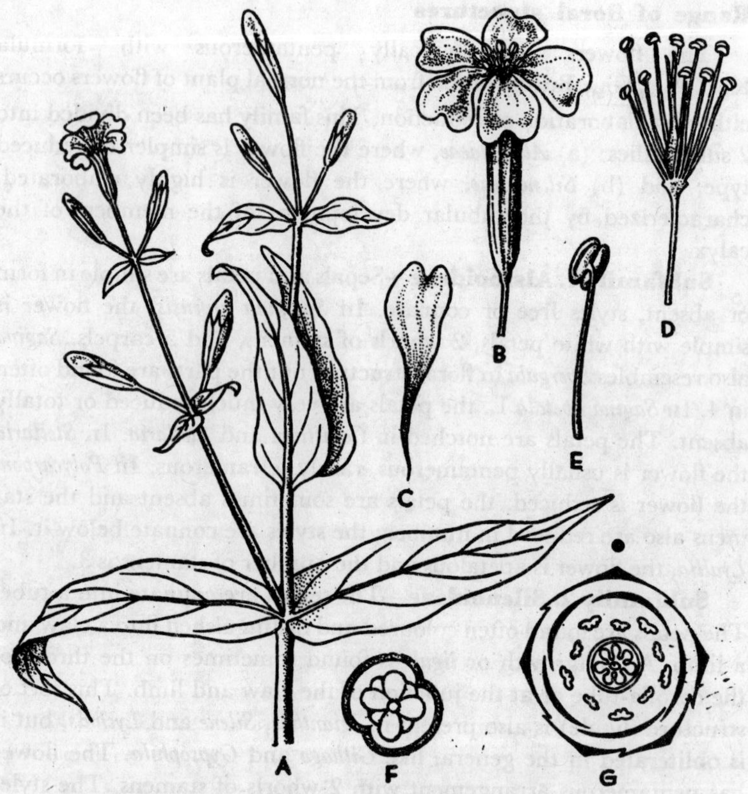

Fig. 563. Caryophyllaceae (*Gypsophila elegans*).
A, Portion of a flowering shoot; B, Flower; C, Petal; D, Flower with sepals and petals removed; E, Stamen; F, T.s. of ovary; G, Floral diagram.

Affinity

This family is allied to Phytolaccaceae from which it has originated by conversion of the outer stamen-whorl to petals and of the outer carpel-whorl to stamens. This view was expressed by Eichler and accepted by Pax, Wettstein and Rendle. Wernham is of opinion that this family was evolved from Ranalian ancestors and Primulaceae might have arisen from Caryophyllaceae. This family is also allied to reduced families, such as Chenopodiaceae and Amaranthaceae, a view has been accepted by Bessey, Hutchinson and others. It is also related to Geraniaceae according to Dickson. This family is related to Portulacaceae but distinguished by the

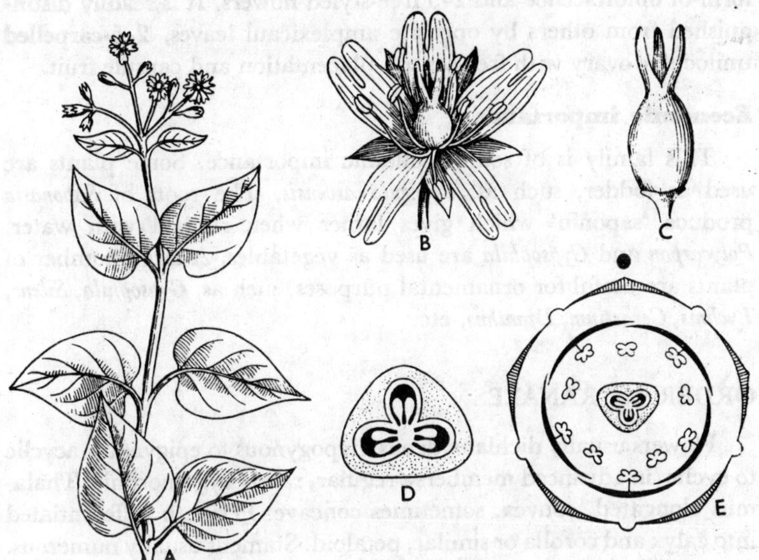

Fig. 564. Caryophyllaceae (*Stellaria media*).
A, Portion of a flowering shoot; B, Flower; C, Pistil; D, T.s. of ovary; E, Floral diagram.

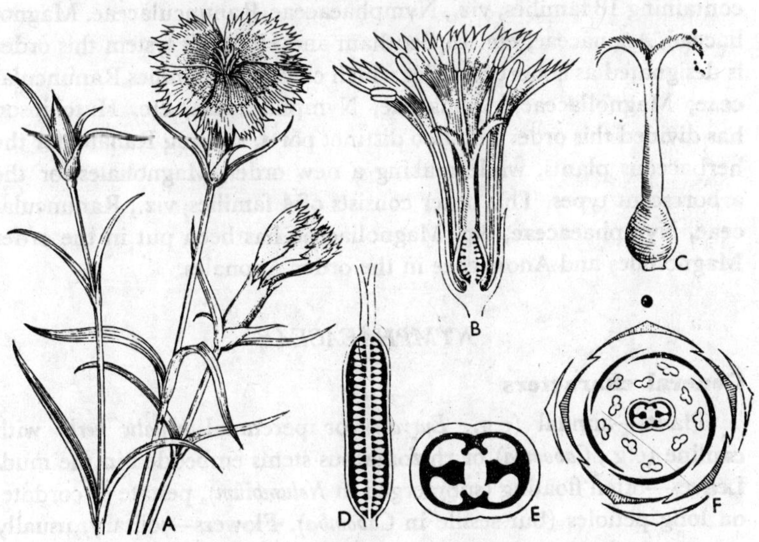

Fig. 565. Caryophyllaceae (*Dianthus chinensis*).
A, Portion of a flowering shoot; B, V.s. of a flower; C, Pistil; D, V.s. of ovary; E, T.s. of the same; F, Floral diagram.

form of inflorescence and 2–5 free-styled flowers. It is readily distinguished from others by opposite amplexicaul leaves, 2–5-carpelled unilocular ovary with free central placentation and capsule fruit.

Economic importance

This family is of some economic importance. Some plants are used as fodder, such as, *Spergula arvensis*. The roots of *Saponaria* produce 'saponin' which gives lather when rubbed with water. *Polycarpon* and *Gypsophila* are used as vegetables. A large number of plants are useful for ornamental purposes, such as, *Gypsophila*, *Silene*, *Lychnis*, *Cerastium*, *Dianthus*, etc.

ORDER 18. RANALES

Flowers usually dichlamydeous, hypogynous to epigynous, acyclic to cyclic (in advanced members), regular, rarely zygomorphic. Thalamus elongated, convex, sometimes concave. Perianth differentiated into calyx and corolla or similar, petaloid. Stamens usually numerous. Carpels many to one, often free. Seeds with copious endosperm, sometimes with perisperm.

Engler has placed this order under subclass Archichlamydeae containing 18 families, viz., Nymphaeaceae, Ranunculaceae, Magnoliaceae, Anonaceae, etc. In Bentham and Hooker's system this order is designated as cohort Ranales which consists of families Ranunculaceae, Magnoliaceae, Anonaceae, Nymphaeaceae, etc. Hutchinson has divided this order into two distinct parts, keeping Ranales for the herbaceous plants, while making a new order Magnoliales for the arborescent types. This order consists of 4 families, viz., Ranunculaceae, Nymphaeaceae, etc. Magnoliaceae has been put in the order Magnoliales and Anonaceae in the order Anonales.

NYMPHAEACEAE

General characters

Plants—annual (e.g., *Euryale*) or perennial *aquatic herbs* with cauline (e.g., *Cabomba*) or rhizomatous stems embedded in the mud. Leaves—often floating (submerged in *Nelumbium*), peltate or cordate, on long petioles (but sessile in *Cabomba*). Flowers—solitary, usually on a scape, large and showy, regular, **bisexual**, hypogynous to epigynous (e.g., *Euryale*), **acyclic**, hemicyclic, or cyclic. Sepals—3–6, or adnate to the torus. Petals—3 (e.g., *Cabomba*) to numerous, *often gradually passing into stamens*, imbricate. Stamens—3–6 (e.g., *Cabomba*) or numerous; filaments foliaceous. Carpels—3-many, united into a many-celled ovary (e.g., *Nymphaea* and *Nuphar*) or free and sunk in spongy thalamus (e.g., *Nelumbium*); ovary superior or inferior (e.g., *Victoria* and *Euryale*); ovules 1 to many on the inner walls or from the apex of the carpels. Fruit—a follicle (e.g., *Cabomba*), or aggregate of achenes (e.g., *Nelumbium*) or spongy berry (e.g., *Euryale*). Seeds—often arillate, generally with both perisperm and endosperm, and a straight embryo.

Floral formula

$\oplus$ ⚥ K_{3-6} $C_{3-\infty}$ $A_{6-\infty}$ $\underline{G_{3-\infty}}$ or $\overline{G_{3-\infty}}$

Number and distribution

This family consists of 8 genera and about 90 species which are cosmopolitan.

Key to Genera

A. Carpels embedded irregularly in the pits of obscure thalamus:

 (*a*) Sepals 4–5; petals and stamens numerous; seeds exalbuminous .. .. *Nelumbium.*

B. Carpels confluent with one another or with the ovary:

 (*b*) Sepals, petals and stamens half-inferior, inserted on a disc, confluent with the carpels .. .. *Nymphaea.*

 (*c*) Sepals, petals and stamens inferior; ft. a prickly berry .. .. *Euryale.*

Range of floral structures

The chief constant floral characters of the family are spirocyclic, regular, bisexual flowers or rarely cyclic with gradual change from sepals to petals and to stamens.

This family has got wide variation in the construction of floral parts. The variation occurs mainly due to number of sepals and petals, nature of thalamus, apocarpy or syncarpy.

This family has been subdivided into 3 subfamilies based on the floral range and construction of floral parts.

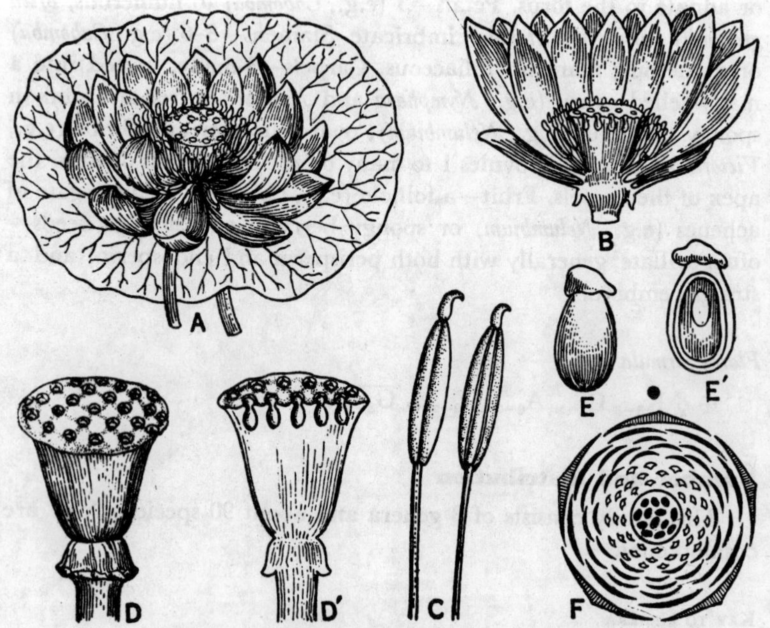

Fig. 566. Nymphaeaceae (*Nelumbium speciosum*).
A, A flower with a leaf on the background; B, L.s. of a flower; C, Stamens; D, Thalamus; D′, L.s. of the same; E, Seed; E′, L.s. of the same; F, Floral diagram.

Subfamily 1. Cabomboideae

The subfamily is represented by the genus *Cabomba*, which consists of 6 perianth-leaves in two whorls 3+3, the outer one forms the calyx and the inner one corolla. Stamens 6. Carpels 3, free. Flowers are cyclic, trimerous and hypogynous.

Floral formula

$\oplus$ ⚥ $P_{3+3}\ A_6\ \underline{G_3}$

Subfamily 2. Nelumboideae

The subfamily is represented by the only genus, *Nelumbo*, which consists of indefinite perianth leaves, the outer whorl of 5 sepals. Stamens indefinite. Carpels free, numerous, spirally arranged. Flowers are spirocyclic and hypogynous.

Floral formula

$\oplus$ ⚥ $P_\infty\ A_\infty\ \underline{G_\infty}$

Subfamily 3. Nymphaeoideae

This subfamily is represented by the most prominent genus *Nymphaea*. It consists of 4–5 sepals in whorls and indefinite petals; stamens indefinite; carpels numerous, fused. Flowers are spirocyclic, hypo-, peri-, or epigynous (e.g., *Euryale*).

Floral formula

$\oplus$ ⚥ K_{4-5} C_{∞} A_{∞} $\underline{G}_{(\infty)}$ or $\overline{G}_{(\infty)}$

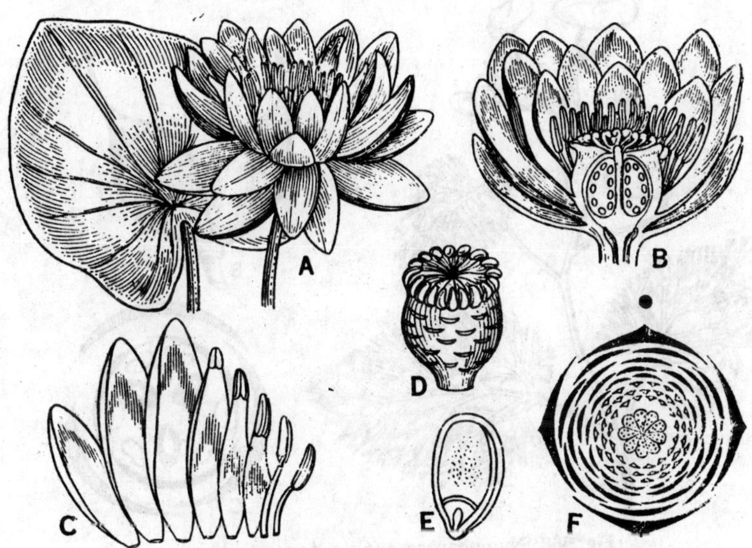

Fig. 567. Nymphaeaceae (*Nymphaea lotus*).
A, A flower with a leaf on the background; B, L.s. of a flower; C, Transition of petals into stamens; D, Pistil; E, L.s. of a seed; F, Floral diagram.

Common plants

(1) Water-lily or Pond-lily (*Nymphaea lotus* L.), *Nymphaea pubescens* Willd.). (2) Red water-lily (*Nymphaea rubra* Roxb.). (3) Blue water-lily (*Nymphaea stellata* Willd.). (4) Lotus (*Nelumbium speciosum* Willd. =*Nelumbo nucifera* Gaertn.). (5) *Euryale ferox* Salisb., commonly found in the tanks of Bangla Desh, all parts of which are beset with prickles. (6) Yellow water-lily (*Nuphar luteum* L.). (7) *Cabomba aquatica*, commonly cultivated in the aquarium.

Affinity

This family bears relationship with Papaveraceae in the character of superficial placentation of the ovary and large peltate-rayed stigmas. It is allied to Magnoliaceae in the character of accessory whorls and stamens. It also established a close link with Alismataceae in the structure of the ovary. Nymphaeaceae is readily distinguished by the aquatic habit, usually long-petioled peltate leaves and long-peduncled flowers, and parietal or superficial placentation.

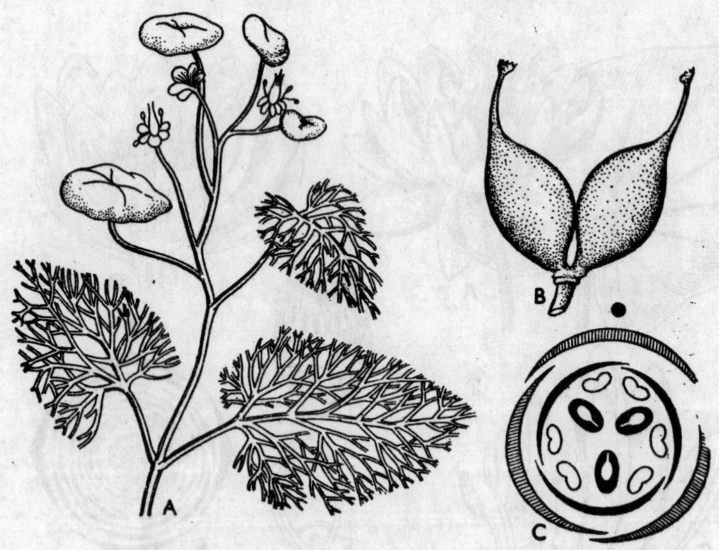

Fig. 568. Nymphaeaceae (*Cabomba aquatica*).
A, Portion of a flowering shoot; B, Fruit; C, Floral diagram.

Economic importance

This family has very little economic importance. Many plants have medicinal value. Fruits and rhizomes of many species are edible. Most plants are cultivated as ornamentals.

RANUNCULACEAE

General characters

Plants—generally annual or perennial herbs, sometimes woody (e.g., *Paeonia*) and climbing (e.g., *Clematis* and *Naravelia*). Leaves—radical or cauline, alternate, rarely opposite (e.g., *Clematis* and

Naravelia), simple (sometimes compound, e.g., *Caltha*), shape varies from entire to decompound (e.g., *Thalictrum*), *with sheathing leaf-bases*, exstipulate. Inflorescence—cymose, sometimes racemose (e.g., *Delphinium*, *Aconitum*, etc.). Flowers—generally bisexual (unisexual in *Thalictrum*), acyclic or hemicyclic, mostly regular (irregular in *Delphinium* and *Aconitum*), hypogynous. Perianth—simple and petaloid, generally succeeded by various forms of nectaries (*honey leaves*), or differentiated into distinct calyx and corolla, imbricate; sepals 5 or more, deciduous, often petaloid; petals 5 or more. Stamens—*numerous*, *spirally arranged* on the thalamus, free with extrorse anthers. Carpels—usually *numerous*, rarely reduced to one; free, rarely partly united (e.g., *Nigella*); ovary superior, 1-celled with numerous to few ovules on the ventral suture. Fruit—usually an etaerio of many-seeded follicles or 1-seeded achenes with long persistent styles (e.g., *Clematis*, *Naravelia*), or rarely berry (e.g., *Actaea*). Seeds—with copious oily endosperm and a small embryo.

Floral formula

$⚥\ K_5\ C_5\ A_{5 \text{ or } \infty}\ \underline{G_{1-5 \text{ or } \infty}}$

Number and distribution

This family contains about 35 genera and 1,500 species which are usually found in the temperate and colder parts of the globe.

Key to Genera

A. Carpels 1 ovuled; fruit achenes:

(*a*) Leaves opposite, compound; plants usually climbing

(*i*) Sepals 4, petaloid; petals 0; no tendril .. *Clematis*.

(*ii*) Sepals as many as petals, 4 or 5; third or terminal leaflet modified into tendril .. .. *Naravelia*.

(*b*) Leaves alternate or radical; plants usually herbs—

(*iii*) Sepals petaloid; petals 0; fls. involucrate .. *Anemone*.

(*iv*) Sepals petaloid; petals 0; fls. non-involucrate .. *Thalictrum*.

(*v*) Sepals 3–5, deciduous; petals 5 .. .. *Ranunculus*.

B. Carpels many-ovuled; fruit follicles:

(*c*) Leaves alternate or radical; plants usually herbs—

(1) Carpels united at the base; fls. regular—

(*vi*) Sepals petaloid and as many as petals; 5 petals long, clawed and bifid; leaves bi-pinnate .. .. .. *Nigella*.

(2) Carpels free; fls. irregular—

(vii) Sepals 5, yellow or white, posterior one helmet-shaped; leaves palmatipartite or seldom entire; plants usually twining .. *Aconitum.*

(viii) Sepals 5, pale blue or purplish, dorsal members spurred like those of petals; leaves palmately lobed; plants erect .. .. *Delphinium.*

Range of floral structures

The family Ranunculaceae has wide range of variation in the floral construction. The members of the family generally consist of regular flowers but zygomorphic flowers are often noted, as in

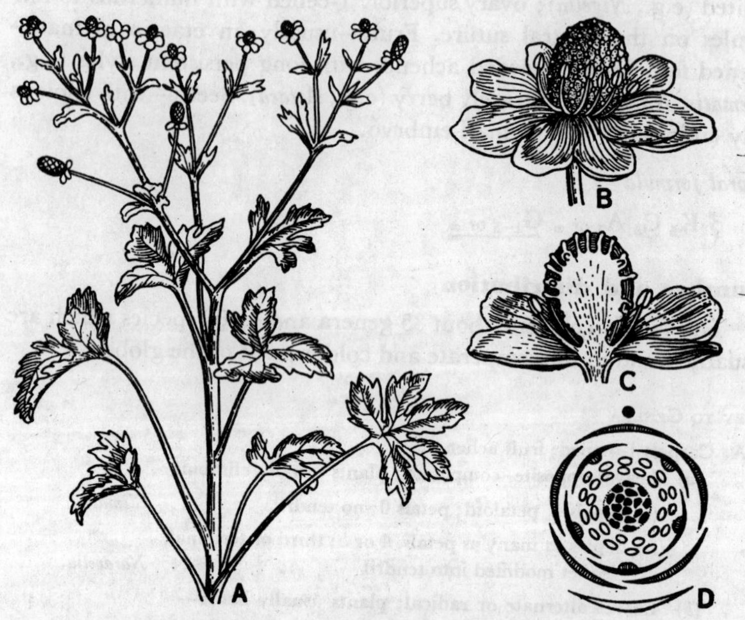

Fig. 569. Ranunculaceae (*Ranunculus sceleratus*). A, Portion of a flowering shoot; B, Flower; C, Vertical section of the same; D, Floral diagram.

Aconitum and *Delphinium*. In *Caltha* and *Paeonia*, the flowers are acyclic or hemicyclic. There is also found a gradual transition from sepals to petals as in *Nymphaea* of Nymphaeaceae. In *Caltha*, number of perianth leaves being 5–15, deciduous; stamens are very numerous in many rows; carpels 5–10.

Typical pentamerous flowers are very rare and it is only seen in specimens *Xanthorrhiza* and *Aquilegia*. In *Nigella* the perianth-leaves are generally five which are petaloid—true petals absent, honey leaves present and they are 8 in number. Stamens numerous, arranged in 8 rows; carpels 5, connate in a 5-celled syncarpous pistil.

Prantl classified the family into *three* tribes according to the construction of flowers:

Tribe I. Paeonieae: Flowers usually solitary, acyclic or hemicyclic. Perianth double, the outer perianth calyx-like but sometimes petaloid to some extent. Honey leaves are absent. Stamens numerous. Ovules in two rows, longitudinally disposed on the ventral suture of the carpel. Examples: *Paeonia* and *Caltha*.

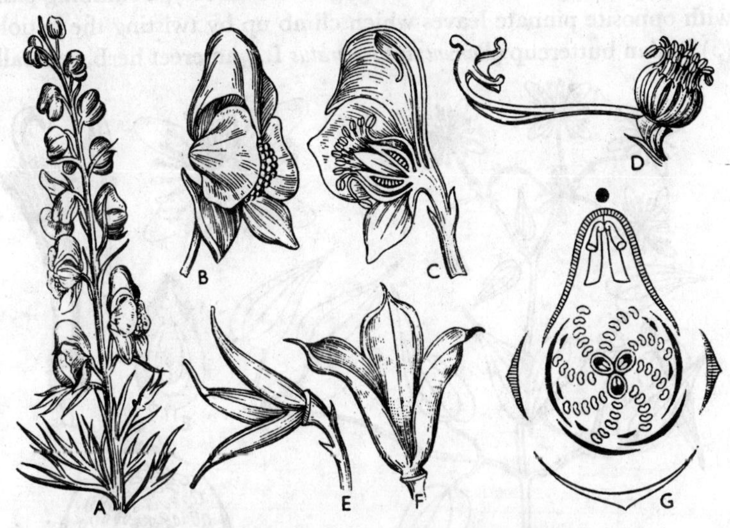

Fig. 570. Ranunculaceae (*Aconitum napellus*).
A, Portion of a flowering shoot; B, Flower; C, V.s. of the same; D, The same after removal of calyx and corolla; E, Pistil; F, Fruit; G, Floral diagram.

Tribe II. Helleboreae: Flowers in raceme or cyme or solitary, cyclic or acyclic. Honey leaves present. Perianth double due to formation of honey leaves, inner half of the perianth petaloid, rarely sepaloid, honey leaves small generally. Ovules in two rows, rarely 1 or 2, longitudinally disposed on ventral suture.

(a) Perianth petaloid and the honey leaves are tongue-shaped, as found in *Helleborus*.

(b) Perianth sepaloid and honey leaves are petaloid, as found in *Aquilegia*.

Tribe III. Anemoneae: Flowers regular, acyclic or hemicyclic. Perianth is double or single or it consists of 2 or more whorls, petaloid or sepaloid. Honey leaves absent or rarely present. Carpels numerous. Ovules solitary, mostly basal. Examples: *Anemone*, *Naravelia*, *Clematis* etc.

Common plants

(1) *Naravelia zeylanica* DC., a common wild climbing plant with ternate leaves, the terminal leaflet of which is converted into a tendril. (2) Virgin's bower (*Clematis gouriana* Roxb.), a climbing plant with opposite pinnate leaves which climb up by twisting the petiole. (3) Indian buttercup (*Ranunculus sceleratus* L.), an erect herb, generally

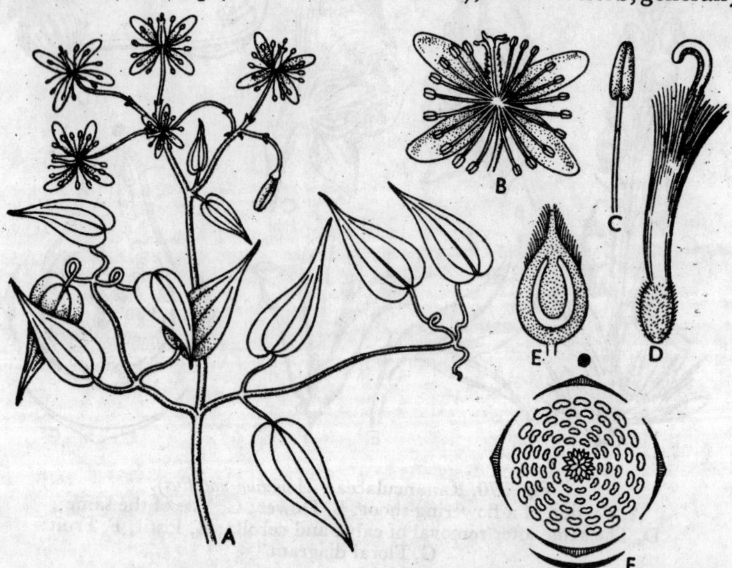

Fig. 571. Ranunculaceae (*Clematis gouriana*).
A, Portion of a flowering shoot; B, Flower; C, Stamen; D, Carpel; E, L.s. of ovary; F, Floral diagram.

found on the banks of rivers and marshes. (4) Larkspur (*Delphinium ajacis* L.), a commonly cultivated garden annual. (5) Fennel flower or Black cumin (*Nigella sativa* L.), cultivated for its seeds which are largely used as a condiment and also as a preservative of clothes against the attacks of vermins. (6) Monkshood (*Aconitum napellus* L.), a commonly cultivated garden annual. (7) *Anemone pulsatilla* and (8) *Delphinium staphysagria* are medicinal plants. (9) Meadow rue (*Thalictrum javanicum* Bl.), a slender herb with decompound leaves, chiefly found on the hills.

Affinity

The structure of the essential organs relates the family closely to Magnoliaceae, which is readily distinguished by having distinct stipules and different habit. The dimorphic leaves, small flowers with free, hypogynous parts and fruit of *Cabomba* establish a close link with that of the genus *Ranunculus*. It resembles the family Papaveraceae but

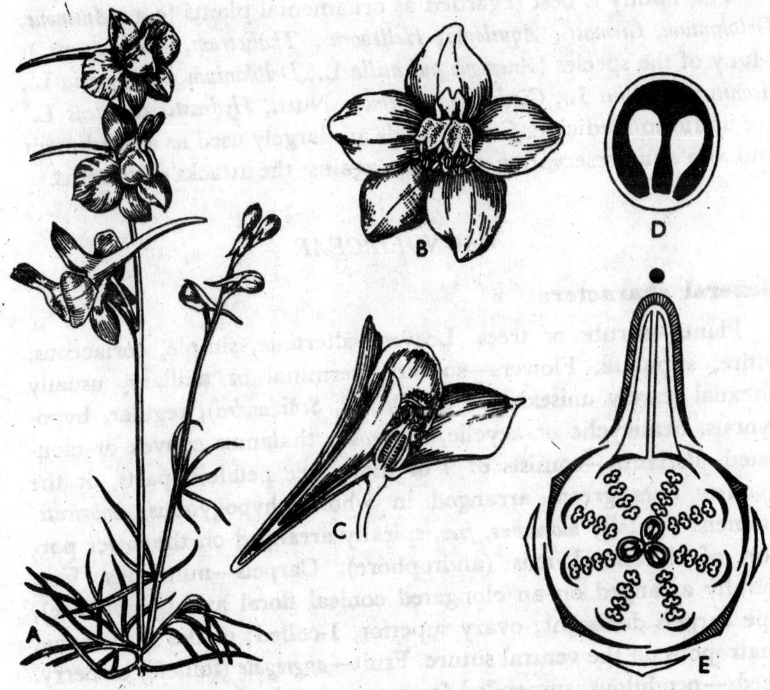

Fig. 572. Ranunculaceae (*Delphinium ajacis*).
A, Portion of a flowering shoot; B, Flower; C, V.s. of the same; D, T.s. of ovary; E, Floral diagram.

it is distinguished by having distinct carpels. It is also readily distinguished from Rosaceae by its hypogynous stamens, abundant perisperm and general properties. The most remarkable feature in the family lies in its close link with the monocotyledons. The presence of tubular cotylar sheath and union of two cotyledons in *Ranunculus ficaria*, indicate a probable affinity with the monocotyledons. The presence of free carpels and general habit of Alismataceae with Ranunculaceae, have established a close relationship. Ranunculaceae is distinguished from allied families by the usually herbaceous habit, the leaves often divided or compound, the flowers mostly bisexual with reduced or modified petals, the stamens usually numerous and spirally arranged, the gynoecium of generally several to many carpels, and the ovary unicarpellate. The genus *Actea* with its solitary carpel forms a link with Berberidaceae.

Economic importance

This family is best regarded as ornamental plants (e.g., *Anemone, Delphinium, Clematis, Aquilegia, Helleborus, Thalictrum, Paeonia*, etc.). Many of the species (*Anemone pulsatilla* L., *Delphinium staphysagria* L., *Aconitum napellus* L., *Cimicifuga racemosa* Nutt., *Hydrastis canadens* L.) are useful in medicine. Cumin seeds are largely used as a condiment and also as a preservative of clothes against the attacks of vermins.

MAGNOLIACEAE

General characters

Plants—shrubs or trees. Leaves—alternate, simple, coriaceous, entire, stipulate. Flowers—solitary, terminal or axillary, usually bisexual (rarely unisexual, e.g., *Drimys, Schizandra*), regular, hypogynous, hemicyclic or acyclic, *trimerous;* thalamus convex or elongated. Perianth—consists of 9 or more free petaloid parts, or the 3 outer ones green, arranged in whorls, hypogynous, *imbricate*. Stamens—usually *numerous, free*, spirally arranged on the lower portion of the floral axis (androphore). Carpels—numerous, free, spirally arranged on an elongated conical floral axis (gynophore), ripe carpels dehiscent; ovary superior, 1-celled; ovules 2 to many, anatropous on the ventral suture. Fruit—*aggregate* (follicle) or berry. Seeds—pendulous, suspended for a time by slender threads, one or few, with a copious endosperm and a small embryo.

Floral formula

$\oplus$ ⚥ $P_{9-\infty}\ A_{\infty}\ \underline{G_{\infty}}$ (or $K_3\ C_{\infty}\ A_{\infty}\ \underline{G_{\infty}}$)

Number and distribution

This family consists of 10 genera and over 100 species, which are found mostly in the tropics but a few may be found in the temperate zone.

KEY TO GENERA

Erect trees or shrubs; conspicuous:

(*a*) Gynophore absent—

Carpels closely aggregated; ft. dehiscing dorsally; ovules 2 or few; fls. terminal .. .. *Magnolia*.

(*b*) Gynophore present—

Carpels in loose spike; gynophore stalked, persistent; fls. axillary, solitary .. .. *Michelia*.

(terminal in *M. cathcartii* Hk. f. & T.=*Alcimandra cathcartii* Dandy, reported from the temperate forest of Sikkim Himalayas)

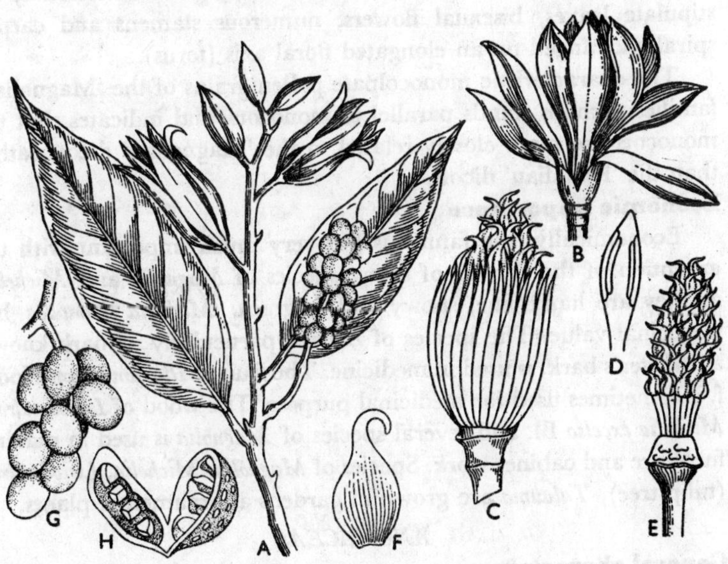

Fig. 573. Magnoliaceae (*Michelia champaca*).
A, Portion of a flowering shoot; B, Flower; C, The same after removal of petals; D, Stamen; E, Pistil; F, Carpel; G, Aggregate fruit; H, Fruit split open.

Common plants

(1) The Champak (*Michelia champaca* L.), (2) *Magnolia pterocarpa* Roxb., (3) *Magnolia grandiflora* L., all of which produce fragrant

flowers and for this reason are cultivated in the gardens. (4) *Magnolia campaellii*, a shrub producing beautiful flowers can be found in Darjeeling.

Affinity

This family is considered to be as most primitive among the dicotyledons. The primitive character is exemplified by spiral arrangement of stamens and carpels, and apocarpous pistil. It also establishes a close link with gymnosperms. The gymnospermous character of wood, i.e., tracheids with bordered pits, has been revealed in the genus *Drimys*. It has been presumed by some authors that the elongated floral axis of a *Magnolia*, which bears numerous spirally arranged free sporophylls indicate a probable relationship with *Bennettites*, a genus of Bennettitales, particularly in the presence of sporophyll-bearing axis of the same. Magnoliaceae is also allied to Anonaceae from which it is readily distinguished by having imbricate corolla and uniform albumen. The family is characterized by the stipulate leaves, bisexual flowers, numerous stamens and carpels spirally arranged on an elongated floral axis (torus).

The characteristic monocolpate pollen grains of the 'Magnolian' families perhaps stands parallel to monocots, and indicates that the monocots are more closely related to the 'Magnolian' dicots rather than the 'Ranalian' dicots.

Economic importance

Economically, the family is not very much important with the exception of the flowers of many species of *Magnolia* and *Michelia*, as they are handsome, showy and fragrant. *Michelia champaca* has medicinal value. The species of *Drimys*, particularly its bark known as Winter's bark, is used in medicine. The fruit of *Illicium verum* Hook. f. is sometimes used for medicinal purpose. The wood of *Liriodendron*, *Michelia excelsa* Bl. and several species of *Magnolia* is used in making furniture and cabinet work. Species of *Magnolia*, *Michelia*, *Liriodendron* (tulip tree), *Talauma* are grown in gardens as ornamental plants.

ANONACEAE

General characters

Plants—trees or shrubs, sometimes woody climbers (e.g., *Artabotrys*). Leaves—alternate, simple, entire, *gland-dotted*, exstipulate. Flowers—solitary, regular, usually bisexual, hypogynous, spirocyclic, *trimerous*. Sepals—3, small, usually free or united below, *valvate*. Petals—6 (in two series) or 3 (e.g., *Anona*), *valvate* or imbricate (e.g., *Uvaria*). Stamens—numerous, spirally set on a slightly elongated convex thalamus; filaments short and thick; anthers linear with *prolonged truncate connective*, extrorse. Carpels—usually numerous, free and spirally set on the thalamus, ripe carpels indehiscent; ovary superior, 1-celled; ovules usually numerous in a double row on the ventral suture of the carpel; style short or absent. Fruit—an *etaerio of drupes*, but in *Anona* the ripe carpels are fused together forming a large fleshy fruit (*composite berry*). Seed—often arillate with *ruminated albumen* and a minute embryo.

Floral formula

$\oplus$ ⚥ K_3 or $_{(3)}$ C_{3-6} A_{∞} $\underline{G_{\infty}}$

Number and distribution

This family consists of about 80 genera and 850 species which are widely spread in the tropics.

Key to Genera

A. Carpels numerous, distinct, indehiscent:

- (*a*) Petals imbricate in bud—
  - (*i*) Corolla-members biseriate; sepals valvate; connective truncate; torus flat .. .. *Uvaria*.
- (*b*) Petals valvate in bud—
  - (*ii*) Corolla-members conniving at the concave base covering the stamens with truncated or produced anther cells; peduncles hooked .. .. *Artabotrys*.
  - (*iii*) Corolla-members spreading from the base, flat, lanceolate; anther cells lanceolate—
    - (1) Ovules numerous in 2 series on the ventral suture .. .. *Cananga*.
    - (2) Ovules 2–6, uniseriate on the ventral suture *Unona*.
    - (3) Ovules 1–2, basal or subbasal; stamens cuneate; ft. 1-seeded .. .. *Polyalthia*.

B. Carpels numerous, united into a fleshy fruit:

- (*c*) Petals 3–6 in 2 series, valvate in bud; stamens numerous; ovaries numerous, partially united: ovule 1, erect .. .. *Anona*.

Common plants

(1) Custard apple (*Anona squamosa* L.). (2) Bullock's heart (*Anona reticulata* L.). (3) *Polyalthia longifolia* Benth. & Hook. f., an ornamental tree whose foliage is largely used for decorative purpose on festive

occasions. (4) *Polyalthia cerasoides* Benth. & Hook., a tree commonly found in the thickets. (5) *Artabotrys odoratissimus* R. Br. =*A. uncinatus* Merr., a hook climber which is usually cultivated in gardens for its fragrant flowers. (6) *Uvaria macrophylla* Roxb. =*Fissitigma macrophylla* Merr., a woody climber found in Bangladesh. (7) *Cananga odorata* Hook. & Thoms. =*Desmos chinensis* Lour., a small tree often planted in gardens.

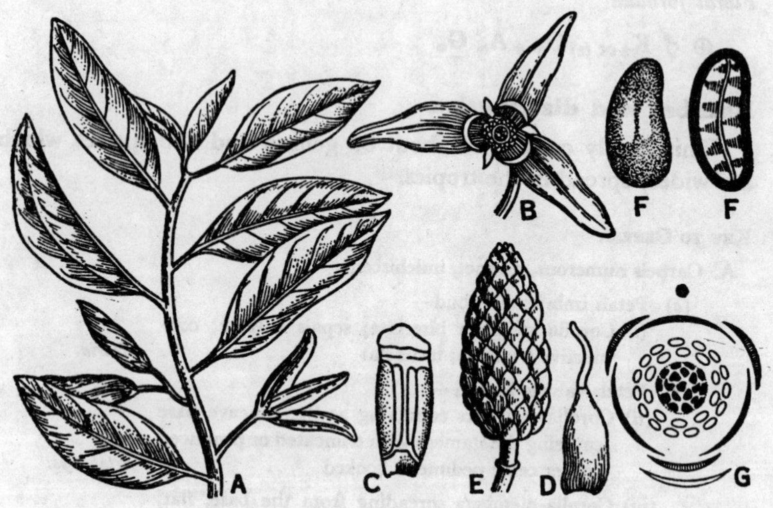

Fig. 574. Anonaceae (*Anona squamosa*).
A, Portion of a flowering shoot; B, Flower; C, Stamen; D, Pistil; E, Fruit; F, Seed and L.s. of the same; G, Floral diagram.

Affinity

This family shows an affinity with Magnoliaceae but ruminate endosperm, valvate corolla, prolonged connective, and exstipulate leaves separate it from the latter. The trimerous flower and small embryo establish a close relationship with monocotyledons.

Economic importance

This family is of some economic importance. *Anona squamosa* and *A. reticulata* yield sweet and fleshy edible fruits. Species of *Polyalthia* are grown as ornamental trees; its wood is used for making masts.

Comparison between Magnoliaceae and Anonaceae

Magnoliaceae	*Anonaceae*
1. Leaves—coriaceous, stipulate.	1. gland-dotted, exstipulate.
2. Flowers—large, showy.	2. small.
3. Sepals petaloid.	3. petals sepaloid.
4. Petals—6-many, imbricate.	4. never more than 6, valvate.
5. Anthers—generally introrse.	5. extrorse, linear with prolonged connective.
6. Fruit—etaerio of follicles or drupes.	6. etaerio of drupes or a composite berry.
7. Albumen—uniform.	7. ruminated.

LAURACEAE

General characters

Plants—trees or shrubs (excepting *Cassytha*, a twining parasitic perennial herb), *with aromatic bark and foliage.* Leaves—usually alternate, simple, entire, coriaceous, gland dotted, mostly curviveined (but

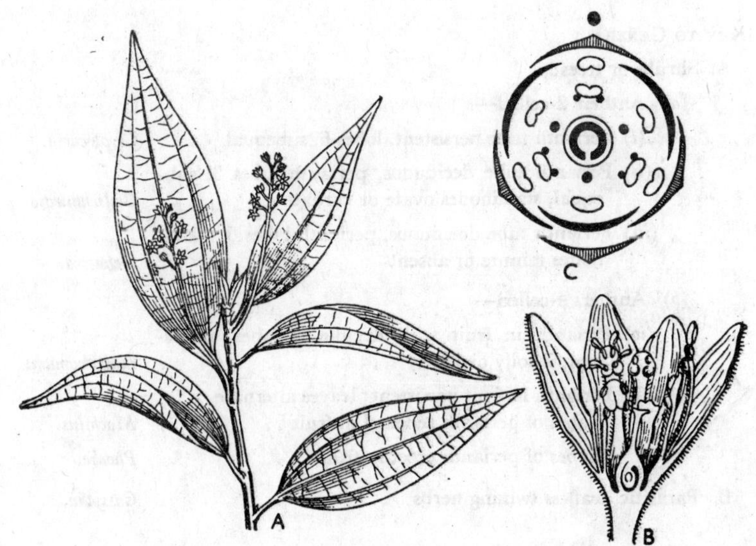

Fig. 575. Lauraceae (*Cinnamomum zeylanicum*).
A, Portion of a flowering shoot; B, V.s. of a flower; C, Floral diagram.

in *Cassytha* reduced to scales or absent), exstipulate. Inflorescence—raceme, spike, umbel or panicle. Flowers—small, greenish or yellowish, regular, bisexual (sometimes unisexual), hypogynous, trimerous. Perianth—3+3, more or less united at the base, *sepaloid, persistent,* imbricate. Stamens—12, *usually in 4 whorls of 3 stamens* each, generally the innermost is reduced to a whorl of staminodes (e.g., *Cinnamomum*), the third whorl usually bears a pair of glandular protuberances, inserted to the perianth tube; anthers 2–4-celled, *usually with valvular dehiscence.* Carpel—1; ovary superior, 1-celled with 1 anatropous pendulous ovule, placentation marginal. Fruit—*drupe,* sometimes berry and more or less enveloped by the cup-shaped receptacle, and sometimes also by the persistent base of the perianth (e.g., *Cassytha*). Seed—*exalbuminous with large straight embryo.*

Floral formula

$$\oplus ⚥ P_{(3+3)} A_{3+3+3+3s} \underline{G_1}$$

Number and distribution

This family contains about 45 genera with 1,100 species, distributed in the tropical and subtropical regions.

KEY TO GENERA

A. Shrubs or trees:

(*a*) Anthers 2-celled—

(*i*) Perianth tube persistent, lobes 6, subequal .. *Cryptocaria.*

(*ii*) Perianth tube deciduous, perianth lobes 5, subequal, staminodes ovate or cordate .. *Beilschmiedia.*

(*iii*) Perianth tube deciduous, perianth lobes 6, staminodes minute or absent .. .. *Dehassia.*

(*b*) Anthers 4-celled—

(*iv*) Perianth in fruit with deciduous lobes, persistent, wholly or partly .. .. .. *Cinnamomum.*

(*v*) Perianth in fruit persistent; leaves alternate

Lobes of perianth reflexed in fruit .. .. *Machilus.*

Lobes of perianth erect in fruit .. .. *Phoebe.*

B. Parasitic, leafless twining herbs .. .. .. *Cassytha.*

Common plants

(1) *Cryptocaria floribunda* Nees., a tree. (2) *Beilschmiedia roxburghiana* Nees., a deciduous tree. (3) Camphor tree (*Cinnamomum camphora* Nees.), yields camphor. (4) *C. tamala* Nees., a medium tree, the leaves

of which are used as a spice in cooking. (5) Cinnamon (*C. zeylanicum* Breyn.), a small tree, the bark of which is used as a spice. (6) *Cassytha filiformis*, a common leafless thread-like greenish parasite. (7) *Dehassia kurzi* King, an evergreen tree, commonly found in Bangladesh. (8) *Machilus vilosa* Hook. f., a large tree. (9) *Phoebe lanceolata* Nees., an evergreen tree grows at the foot of East Himalayas.

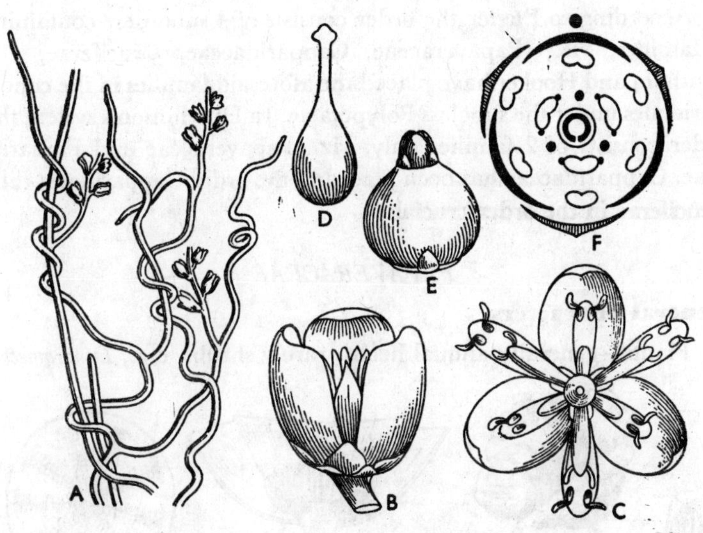

Fig. 576. Lauraceae (*Cassytha filiformis*).
A, Portion of a plant; B, A flower bud; C, A flower; D, Pistil; E, Fruit; F, Floral diagram.

Affinity

This family is readily distinguished from allied families by the presence of small undifferentiated perianth, trimerous stamens in several whorls, valvular dehiscence of anthers, drupe-like fruit and single exalbuminous seed with large straight embryo.

Economic importance

The family is economically important. Many plants yield aromatic oils. Camphor is obtained from *Cinnamomum camphora*; *C. tamala* and *C. zeylanica* yield spices. Some plants of this family, viz., *Persea*, *Sassafras*, etc., yield fragrant wood for cabinet work. *Persea americana* yields a kind of edible fruit (Avocado pear). A few species are ornamentals.

ORDER 19. RHOEDALES

Plants usually herbs. Flowers hypogynous, regular, cyclic with perianth members usually 4 in number, rarely 3. Carpels two or more, united. Placentation parietal. Seeds usually small with curved embryo.

According to Engler the order consists of 4 suborders containing 6 families, viz., Papaveraceae, Capparidaceae, Cruciferae, etc. Bentham and Hooker have placed the aforesaid families in the cohort Parietales under the subclass Polypetalae. In Hutchinson's system this order consists of 2 families only, viz., Papaveraceae and Fumariaceae. Capparidaceae has been placed in the order Capparidales and **Cruciferae in the order cruciales.**

PAPAVERACEAE

General characters

Plants—generally annual herbs (rarely shrubs, e.g., *Dendromecon*)

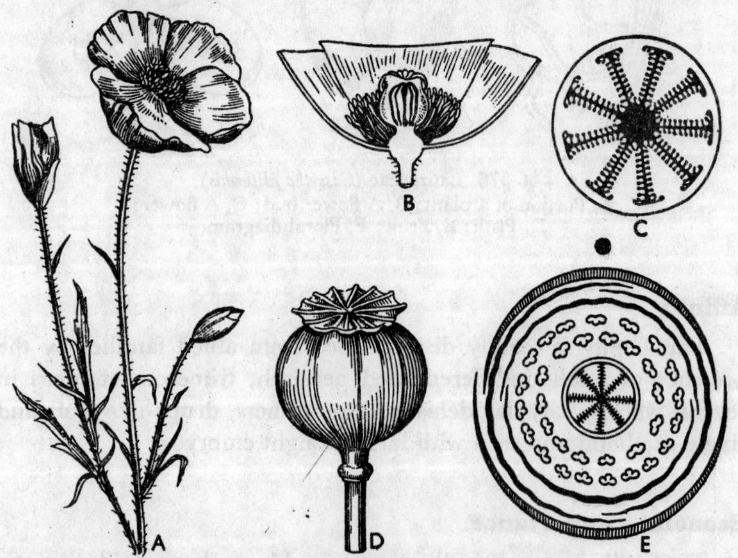

Fig. 577. Papaveraceae (*Papaver orientale*).
A, Portion of a flowering shoot; B, V.s. of a flower; C, T.s. of ovary; D, Fruit; E, Floral diagram.

with milky or coloured *latex*. Leaves—alternate, simple, entire or more often lobed or much divided, exstipulate. Inflorescence—racemose or cymose. Flowers—bisexual, regular, hypogynous. Sepals—2 (sometimes 3), free, caducous, imbricate. Petals—usually 2+2 (sometimes 3+3), absent in *Macleaya*, *crumpled*, deciduous. Stamens—numerous, in *several alternating whorls* (generally multiple of 2 or 3); anther bilocular. Carpels—2-many, syncarpous; ovary superior 1-celled, with numerous anatropous or campylotropous ovules on *parietal placentae*, (but basal placentation in *Bocconia*) or many-celled; stigma radiating from the centre, either sessile or supported on a distinct style. Fruit—capsule, opening by apical pores or valves. Seeds—with oily endosperm and a minute embryo.

Floral formula

$\oplus$ ⚥ $K_{2-3}\ C_{2+2 \text{ or } 3+3}\ A_{\infty}\ \underline{G_{(2-\infty)}}$

Number and distribution

This family consists of 28 genera and about 250 species which are usually found in the North temperate zones.

KEY TO GENERA

Capsule opening by apical pore or valve:

(*a*) Stigmas sessile, radiating from disc; capsule globose; floral symmetry 2 or its multiple; latex white .. .. *Papaver*.

(*b*) Stigmas arising from the depressed style; capsule oblong; floral symmetry 3 or its multiple; latex yellow .. .. *Argemone*.

(*c*) Stigmas decurrent with the style; capsule elongated; floral symmetry 2 or 3; latex yellow .. *Meconopsis*.

Common plants

(1) Opium poppy (*Papaver somniferum* L.), only white-flowered forms are commonly cultivated for obtaining opium. (2) Mexican poppy or Prickly poppy (*Argemone mexicana* L.), a prickly erect herb with yellow flowers which grows wild on roadsides and rice-fields. (3) Oriental poppy (*Papaver orientale* L.) and (4) *P. argemone* L. are common garden annuals. (5) *Meconopsis nepalensis* DC. and *M. wallichii*

Hook., are the commonly occurring plants in Darjeeling at a varying altitude of 8,000–11,000 ft.

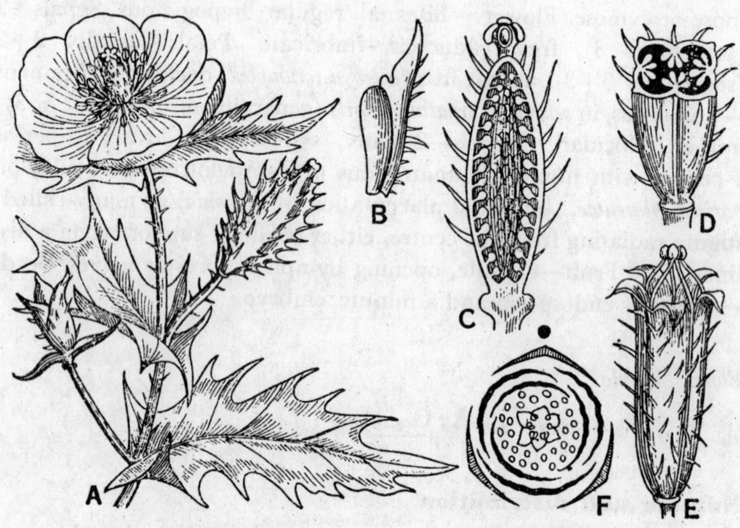

Fig. 578. Papaveraceae (*Argemone mexicana*).
A, Portion of a branch with flower and fruit; B, Sepal; C, L.s. of ovary; D, T.s. of the same; E, Fruit, F, Floral diagram.

Affinity

This family differs from Ranunculaceae by dimerous calyx, syncarpous ovary and milky or coloured latex. It forms a link with Cruciferae and Capparidaceae in the character of dimerous arrangement of the accessory sets and pod-shaped ovary, but differs from them in the character of the seed, and narcotic milky latex. It is also allied to Nymphaeaceae in the general structure of the flower. Papaveraceae is characterized by caducous calyx, usually crumpled corolla, numerous stamens in several whorls, unilocular ovary with parietal placentation and capsule fruit.

Economic importance

Papaveraceae is economically important. The opium of commerce is obtained from the dried latex of unripe capsules of *Papaver somniferum*; an alkaloid known as '*morphine*' is obtained from it. *Chelidonium majus* L. and *Sanguinaria canadensis* L. are medicinal plants. Some ornamental plants belong to the family. About 20 genera especially the oriental poppy (*Papaver orientale*), californian poppy (*Eschscholtzia* sp.), blue poppy (*Meconopsis* sp.), prickly poppy (*Argemone mexicana*), etc., are useful for decorative purposes.

CAPPARIDACEAE

General characters

Plants—chiefly herbs or shrubs, sometimes small trees (e.g., *Crataeva*) or climbing (e.g., *Capparis*), without latex. Leaves—usually alternate, simple or digitately 3–7 foliate, with or without stipules. Inflorescence—cymose, axillary or terminal, or racemose. Flowers—slightly irregular, rarely irregular (e.g., *Capparis*), bisexual (but unisexual in *Podandrogyne*), hypogynous, tetramerous, bracteate, *often with gynophore*, sometimes with androphore. Sepals—generally 4, free (sometimes more or less united), valvate or imbricate. Petals—usually 4, free, imbricate. Stamens—usually numerous, sometimes 8 or 6 (but *not tetradynamous*, e.g., *Gynandropsis*), rarely 4, free, with long filaments, sometimes supported on a stalk (androphore, e.g., *Gynandropsis*). Carpels—usually 2, sometimes 4; ovary superior, 1-celled with parietal placenta, but sometimes 2-chambered by replum (e.g., *Capparis*), usually supported on a long or short gynophore (excepting *Cleome*); ovules numerous and campylotropous. Fruit—siliquose (e.g., *Cleome*), capsule or berry (e.g., *Capparis*), rarely nut. Seeds—reniform, albuminous with curved embryo.

Floral formula

$$⚥\ K_{4\ (2+2)}\ C_4\ A_{4-\infty}\ \underline{G_{(2)}}$$

Number and distribution

This family consists of 46 genera and about 700 species which are abundantly found in the tropics and subtropics.

KEY TO GENERA

A. Fruit capsular; plants usually herbs:

(*a*) Stamens 12–20, sessile; corolla imbricated in bud; leaves digitately compound .. .. *Cleome*.

(*b*) Stamens 6 on androphore; corolla open in bud; leaves compound 5–7-foliate .. .. *Gynandropsis*.

B. Fruit berry or capsule:

(*c*) Disc present below sepaline tube; sepals 4, open in bud; plants usually small trees .. .. *Crataeva.*

(*d*) Disc hemispheric; sepals 4, 2-seriate; stamens 8-numerous, long, purple, inserted at the base of the gynophore; plants climbing with spinous stipule .. *Capparis.*

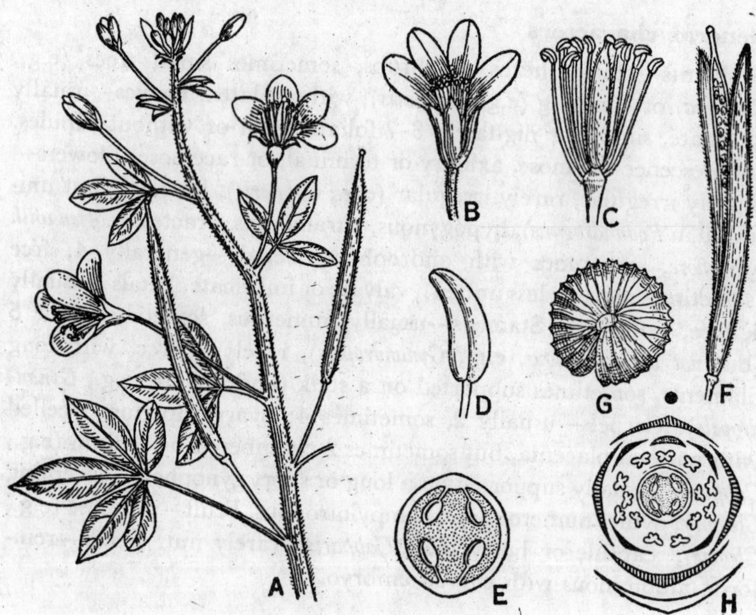

Fig. 579. Capparidaceae (*Cleome viscosa*).
A, Portion of a branch with flower and fruit; B, Flower; C, The same after removal of calyx and corolla; D, Stamen; E, T.s. of ovary; F, Fruit; G, Seed; H, Floral diagram.

Range of floral structures

This family also shows variations in their floral structure. *Cleome tetrandra* represents the most reduced type of flower, where two sepals are outer, and two inner are transverse. The four petals are found to be diagonally placed. Ovary consists of 2 carpels. Variations may occur from this plan by the multiplication of the median stamens alone, or both median and lateral, or by conversion of one or more stamens into petaloid staminodes. Suppression of floral parts may sometimes occur. The flower of *Cleome spinosa* resembles that of a cruciferous one in its horizontal plan but the tetradynamous stamens never occur in the family Capparidaceae. The multiple stamens sometimes develop in certain genera by the serial and lateral splitting of the 4 stamens, e.g., *Capparis*.

Zygomorphy of flower is attained due to unequal development of members. In *Pteropetalum*, the posterior petals are larger than the

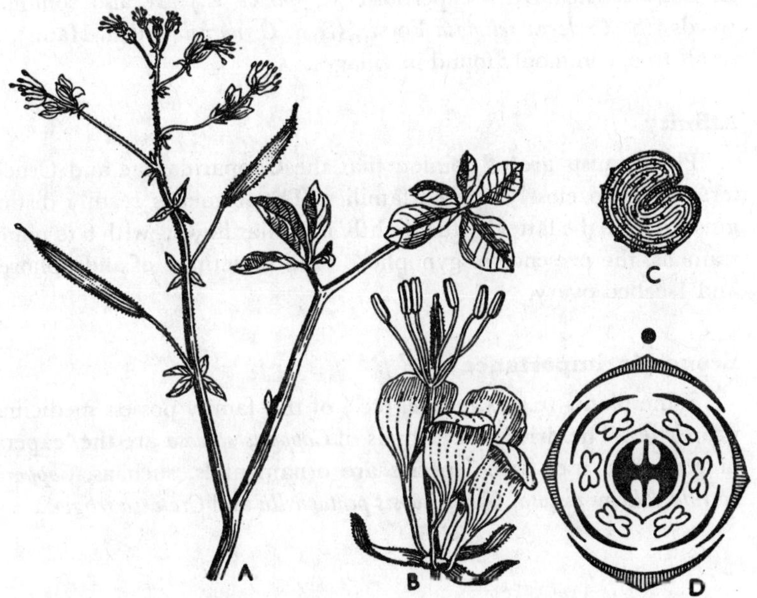

Fig. 580. Capparidaceae (*Gynandropsis pentaphylla*).
A, Portion of a flowering shoot; B, Flower; C, Seed; D, Floral diagram.

anterior ones. In many species of *Capparis* the posterior sepal develops a hood-like structure; in *Emblingia* the formation of a 4-lobed calyx takes place by the union of sepals below. The sepals are generally found to be free, but occasionally they are united below.

The members of corolla are generally free. But in the anomalous genus *Emblingia*, the petals are united. In many a genera the petals are lacking.

The pistil is carried upon the long gynophore. It consists of two, rarely several carpels; forming a 1-celled ovary. This 1-chambered ovary may sometimes become multilocular by the growth of parietal placentae inwards.

Common plants

(1) *Cleome viscosa* L. = *Polanisia viscosa* DC., a common glandular weed, with yellow flowers, found everywhere. (2) *Gynandropsis pentaphylla* DC. = *G. gynandra* Briq., a common weed of waste and cultivated places with white flowers. (3) *Capparis sepiaria* L., a climbing plant chiefly found in scrubby jungles. (4) *Capparis horrida* L. f., *C. zeylanica* L. = *C. brevispina* DC., caperbush (*C. spinosa* L.) are also common weeds. (5) *Crataeva religiosa* Forst., (Syn. *C. nurvala* Buch.-Ham.), a small tree, commonly found in villages.

Affinity

Phylogenists are of opinion that the Capparidaceae and Cruciferae are two closely related families. The former is readily distinguished from the latter by the slightly irregular flower, with 6 to many stamens, the presence of gynophore (and sometimes of androphore) and 1-celled ovary.

Economic importance

Some plants (e.g., *Crataeva*, etc.) of this family possess medicinal properties. The dried flower-buds of *Capparis spinosa* are the 'capers' of economic use. Some species are ornamentals, such as, *Capparis horrida, Cleome viscosa, Gynandropsis pentaphylla* and *Crataeva religiosa*.

CRUCIFERAE (*BRASSICACEAE*)

General characters

Plants—annual or biennial herbs, often with *pungent watery* latex. Leaves—*radical* or *cauline* (usually *alternate*), simple, more or less lobed, sometimes compound (e.g., *Cardamine*), exstipulate with 1-celled simple or branched hairs. Inflorescence—usually a *raceme*, sometimes corymb (e.g., *Iberis*), ebracteate. Flowers—bisexual, regular (irregular in *Iberis*), actinomorphic, hypogynous. Sepals—2+2, free, imbricate. Petals—4, free, *cruciform*, clawed, imbricate or twisted. Stamens—2+4, *tetradynamous*, with nectaries present at the base of long stamens. Carpels—(2); ovary superior, 1-celled with parietal placentation, but afterwards 2-celled by a false septum (*replum*) connecting the two parietal placentae; ovules many, ylotropous. Fruit—usually a *siliqua*, sometimes a silicula. Seeds—numerous, round, exalbuminous, oily with curved embryo.

Floral formula

⚥ $K_{4\ (2+2)}\ C_4\ A_{6\ (2+4)}\ \underline{G}_{(2)}$

Number and distribution

This family consists of 350 genera and about 2,500 species which are chiefly found in the North temperate regions and in the plains during winter.

KEY TO GENERA

A. Fruit indehiscent:

(*a*) Pod long, hollow or septate, breaking into 1-seeded fragments; seeds globose; sepals pouched at the base *Raphanus*.

(*b*) Pod short, globose; sepals spreading, not pouched at the base .. .. *Senebiera*.

B. Fruit dehiscent:

(*c*) Pod short, cylindric; seeds minute, biseriate; sepals spreading; stigma shortly divided; fls. yellow .. *Nasturtium*.

(*d*) Pod short, flattened, acute, unnerved; seeds uniseriate; sepals erect; fls. white .. .. .. *Cardamine*.

(*e*) Pod with indehiscent beak; cotyledons incumbent or folded—

(*i*) Beak cylindric or conical; seeds uniseriate; sepals yellow, pouched at the base and marked with green veins .. .. .. *Brassica*.

(*ii*) Beak flattened; seeds biseriate; sepals lilac, pouched at the base .. .. .. *Eruca*.

Range of floral structures

The regular flowers (e.g., *Brassica*, *Raphanus*) are *bisexual* and *hypogynous*, with *four free sepals* in two whorls, median and transverse, and *four free diagonally placed petals*. The androecium is typically of 6 stamens in 2 whorls, usually tetradynamous. The pistil consists of 2 transversely placed carpels bearing a double row of pendulous, campylotropous ovules on the parietal placentae formed at two sutures.

Departures from the normal type of flower occur. In *Iberis* and

Teesdalia the flower becomes zygomorphic by the enlargement of the two outer petals. The petals are infrequently small or absent totally, as in species of *Lepidium*, *Coronopus*, *Nasturtium* and others; in *Capsella bursa pastoris*, the petals are occasionally replaced by 4 stamens.

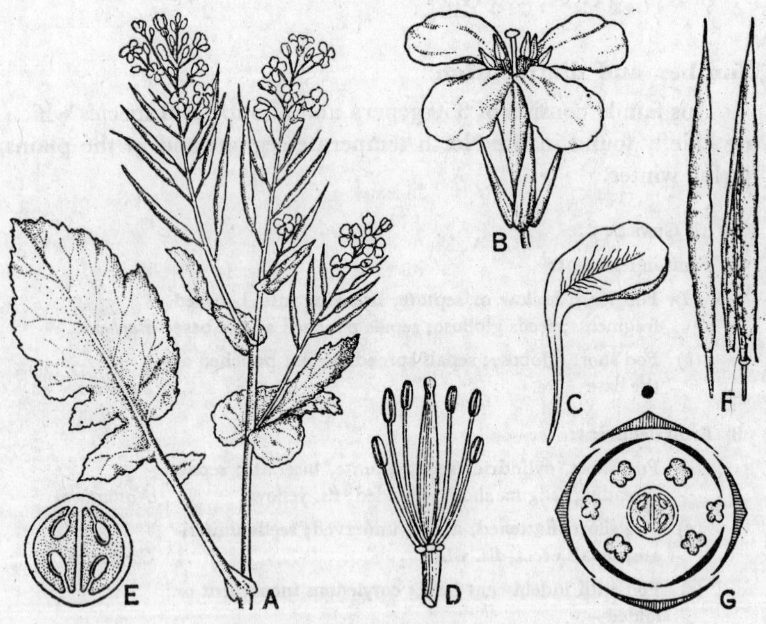

Fig. 581. Brassicaceae (*Brassica nigra*). A, Portion of a flowering shoot; B, Flower; C, Petal; D, Tetradynamous stamens; E, T.s. of ovary; F, Fruit; G, Floral diagram.

Reduction in the number of stamens is also found to occur. In *Cardamine hirsuta*, the lateral stamens are generally absent; in species of *Lepidium* and *Coronopus* doubling of the median stamens may also fail to take place and the flower ultimately becomes diandrous. In the Asiatic genus *Megacarpaea*, the number of stamens reaches up to 16.

Three or four carpels occur abnormally in many genera of Cruciferae. The genera *Tetrapoma* and *Holargidium* have four- (or more) carpelled ovary. *Lepidium sativum* represents the tricarpellary pistil. Multicarpellary pistils have also been recorded in abnormal flowers in a considerable number of genera.

The pistil sometimes presents difficulties in the almost universal position of the stigmas above the commissure, or the vertical line of tissue at the junction of the two carpels, and in the presence of false septum. In *Matthiola incana* and *Moricandia* the stigmas occupy the usual position above the midrib of the carpel.

Common plants

(1) *Mustard plants*, e.g., Mustard or Indian rape (*Brassica napus* L.), White mustard (*B. alba* Hook. & Thom.), Black mustard (*B. nigra* Koch. =*B. juncea* Hook. & Thom.), are all cultivated for oil. (2) Radish (*Raphanus sativus* L.), is cultivated for the swollen fleshy root. (3) *Turnip* (*Brassica campestris* L.), *is taken as a vegetable.* (4) *Nasturtium indicum* DC. =*Rorippa indica* Hochr, a weed. (5) Candytuft (*Iberis amara* L.), a common garden plant. (6) Cauliflower, cabbage, knol-kohl and broccoli are the different varieties of *Brassica oleracea* L., which are cultivated as vegetables. (7) *Cardamine debilis* Don., a garden weed of the cold weather. (8) *Eruca sativa* Lamk., a cold weather crop is occasionally cultivated. (9) Shepherd's purse (*Capsella bursa pastoris* Moench.), a common weed. (10) *Senebiera pinnatifida* DC. =*Coronopus didymus* Sm., a common weed in garden and roadside.

Affinity

Phyletically, the position of Brassicaceae is in the Rhoedales. But there are discrepancies of opinion between Bentham & Hooker and Hutchinson, as to whether it has been derived from papavarous ancestors or from capparidaceous ancestors. Capparidean alliance is more tenable being based on the morphology of androecium and gynoecium and anatomy therein. However, this family can be readily distinguished from Capparidaceae by having cruciform corolla, tetradynamous stamens, the absence of a gynophore, and the nature of the fruit. It is also related to Papaveraceae.

Economic importance

There is considerable importance of the family for the production of fodder crops, weeds and ornamentals. The most important and edible food crops are cabbage, cauliflower, broccoli, brussel's sprouts, knol-kohl, turnip and radish. Economic weeds include mustards (*Brassica*), shepherd's purse (*Capsella*) and pepper grass (*Lepidium*). Oil is extracted from the mustard seeds and the oil-cake is used as manure and fodder. The table mustard is obtained from the seeds of black and white mustards. The ornamental plants are stocks (*Matthiola*), candytuft (*Iberis*), wallflower (*Cheiranthus*), etc.

Comparison between Brassicaceae and Capparidaceae

Brassicaceae	*Capparidaceae*
1. Leaves—radical or cauline, simple. lobed or pinnatifid, exstipulate.	1. simple or palmately compound, with or without stipules.
2. Flowers—regular, ebracteate.	2. slightly irregular, bracteate, usually with gynophore and sometimes with androgynophore.
3. Petals—4, cruciform.	3. 4, but never cruciform.
4. Stamens—6, tetradynamous.	4. numerous, sometimes 8 or 6 (but never tetradynamous), rarely 4.
5. Ovary—1-celled, but afterwards 2-celled by replum.	5. 1-celled but sometimes chambered by replum.
6. Fruit—siliqua or silicula.	6. siliquose or berry.

ORDER 21. ROSALES

Flowers bisexual (unisexual by abortion), cyclic, regular (sometimes zygomorphic), typically pentamerous, hypogynous to epigynous (usually perigynous). Stamens numerous in many whorls, usually free. Carpels numerous, free or united, but the styles generally distinct.

According to Engler this order consists of 3 suborders containing 17 families, viz., Crassulaceae, Rosaceae, Leguminosae, etc. Bentham and Hooker have placed the aforesaid families in the cohort Rosales under the subclass Polypetalae. In Hutchinson's system Crassulaceae has been put under the order Saxifragales. The order Rosales contains 3 families only in his system. Leguminosae is designated as an order consisting of 3 families, viz.; Caesalpinieae, Mimosae and Papilionaceae. Later, in the year 1959, Hutchinson renamed the family Papilionaceae as Fabaceae, and Lawrence described it as subfamily Lotoideae.

CRASSULACEAE

General characters

Plants—annual or perennial herbs or undershrubs with *succulent stems*. Leaves—alternate, sometimes opposite or whorled, simple, entire but sometimes lobed, *succulent*, usually persistent, exstipulate.

Inflorescence—usually cymose, sometimes spike or panicle. Flowers—regular, bisexual (sometimes unisexual), hypogynous. Sepals—4, sometimes 5, free (but united in *Kalanchoe*), valvate or imbricate. Petals—4, sometimes 5, free, valvate or imbricate. Stamens—*as many as or twice as many as the petals in two whorls*, situated on a swollen or

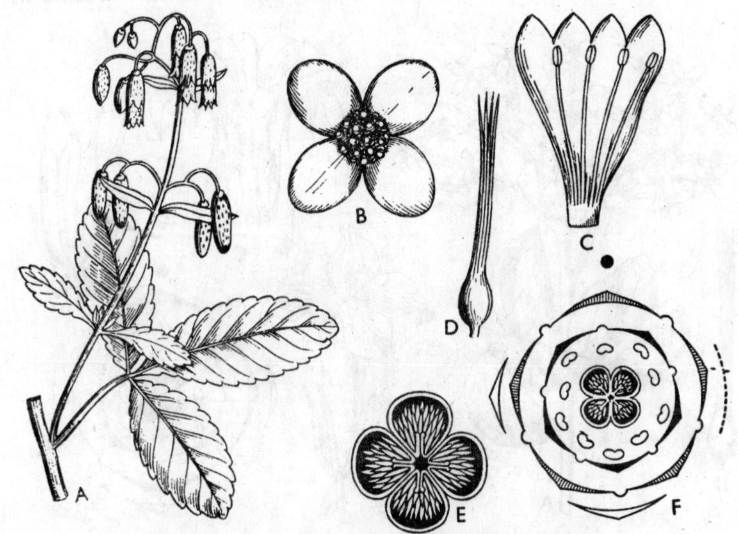

Fig. 582. Crassulaceae (*Bryophyllum calycinum*).
A, Portion of a flowering shoot; B, Flower; C, Corolla split open; D, Pistil; E, T.s. of ovary; F, Floral diagram.

cup-like disc, free. Carpels—*usually equal to the number of petals*, free or united below, *each usually subtended by a scale-like nectar gland at the base;* ovary superior, 1-celled with parietal placentation. Fruit—*follicle.* Seeds—with fleshy endosperm and straight embryo.

Floral formula

$\oplus$ ⚥ K_{4-5} C_{4-5} A_{4-10} $\underline{G_{(4-5)}}$

Number and distribution

This family consists of 30 genera with about 1,300 species, which are widely distributed in the world excepting Australia and Oceania.

Key to Genera

Calyx with a long inflated tube and a shortly 4-fid limb; corolla tube campanulate with a shortly 4-fid limb .. *Bryophyllum.*

Calyx with a short tube and deeply 4-partite limb; corolla tube flask-like with a spreading, 4-fid limb .. .. *Kalanchoe.*

Common plants

(1) *Bryophyllum calycinum* Salisb., a stout fleshy herb. (2) *Kalanchoe heterophylla* Prain, a stout fleshy herb, chiefly found in Pareshnath

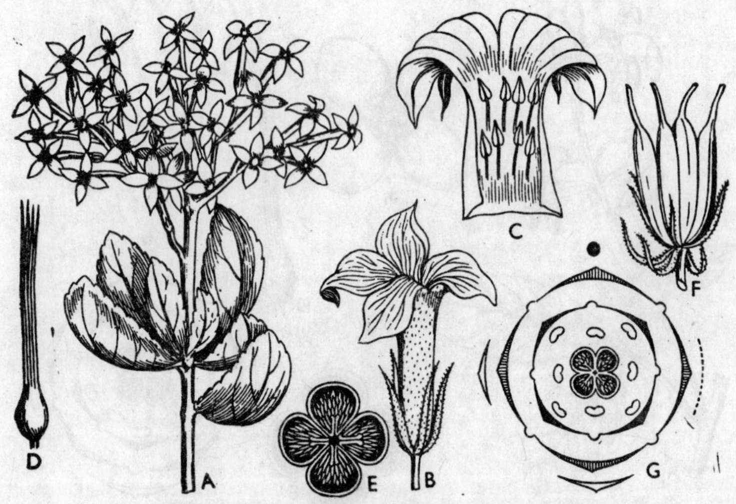

Fig. 583. Crassulaceae (*Kalanchoe spathulata*).
A, Portion of a flowering shoot; B, Flower; C, Corolla split open; D, Pistil; E, T.s. of ovary; F, Fruit; G, Floral diagram.

Hill. (3) *K. laciniata* Adams., found in Bangla Desh, Behar and other places. (4) *K. spathulata* Adams., a common weed.

Affinity

This family is readily distinguished from others by the succulent character of stems and leaves, the gynoecium composed of usually as many carpels as there are petals, a like number of stamens in each whorl and by the presence of scale-like gland at the base of each carpel.

Economic importance

This family is of little economic importance. *Bryophyllum* is used in medicine. Some are planted in our gardens as ornamentals.

ROSACEAE

General characters

Plants—herbs, shrubs or trees (e.g., Apple, Pear, Cherry, Plum,

Loquat, etc.), sometimes climbing, often prickly. Leaves—alternate, usually pinnately compound, stipulate (*adnate stipules*). Inflorescence —cymose. Flowers—regular (but sometimes zygomorphic, as in *Chrysobalanus*), usually bisexual (unisexual in *Aruncus*), *perigynous*, sometimes epigynous, with *odd sepal posterior*. Sepals—usually 5, connate to receptacle imbricate. Petals—5 to ∞, free, imbricate. Stamens—free (but monadelphous in *Chrysobalanus*), usually numerous, in 1-many whorls of 5 stamens, sometimes 5 or 10; bent inwards in bud, perigynous (but epigynous in *Pyrus*, *Eriobotrya*). Carpels—1 (e.g., *Prunus*) to numerous, free or united; ovary superior or inferior (e.g., *Pyrus*), 1-celled or 2–5 celled, usually with 2 pendulous or ascending, anatropous ovules. Fruit—drupe, pome or aggregate of follicles or achenes or berries. Seed—generally without endosperm. Embryo—plano-convex, often with fleshy cotyledons.

Floral formula

$⚥\ K_{(5)}\ C_{5\ \text{or}\ \infty}\ A_{\infty}\ \underline{G_{1-\infty\ \text{or}\ (\infty)}}$

Number and distribution

This family consists of about 115 genera and 3,200 species which

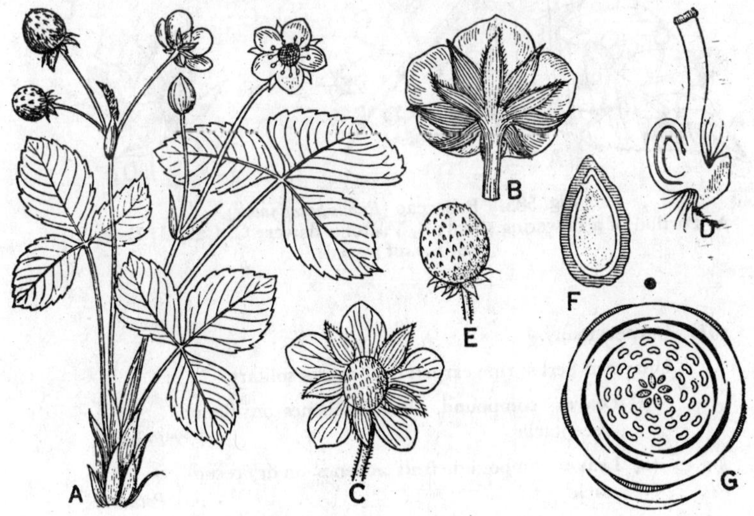

Fig. 584. Rosaceae (*Fragaria vesca*).
A, Portion of a flowering shoot; B, Flower as seen from the underside; C, Flower; D, L.s. of a carpel; E, Fruit; F, Seed; G, Floral diagram.

are chiefly found in the temperate regions (in India in the Northern Himalayas).

Key to Genera

A. Ovary superior; ripe carpels not enclosed within the calyx-tube:

(*a*) Carpel solitary—

(*i*) Leaves simple, quite entire, fruit 2-seeded .. *Pygeum*.

(*ii*) Leaves simple, serrate, fruit 1-seeded .. *Prunus*.

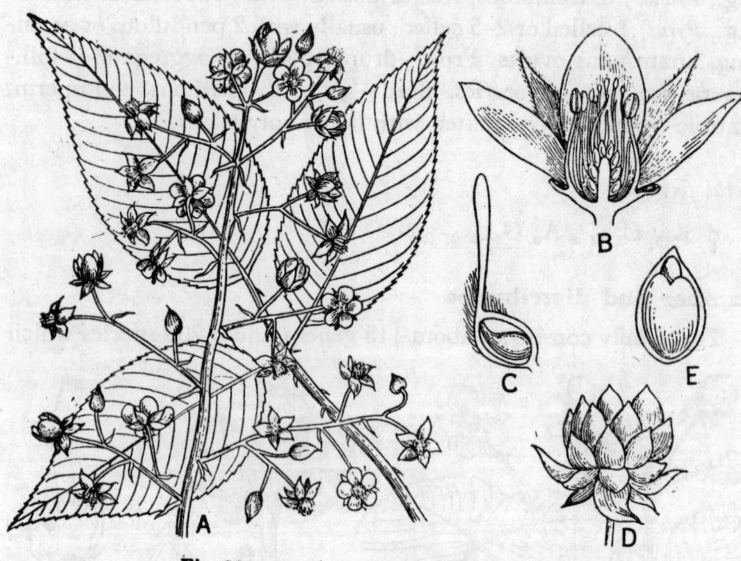

Fig. 585. Rosaceae (*Rubus hexagynous*).
A, Portion of a flowering shoot; B, V.s. of a flower; C, Carpel; D, Fruit; E, L.s. of a seed.

(*b*) Carpels many—

Unarmed herbs; ripe carpels dry; ovules solitary

(*i*) Leaves compound, fruit achenes on fleshy receptacle .. .. .. *Fragaria*.

(*ii*) Leaves compound, fruit achenes on dry receptacle .. .. *Potentilla*.

Armed shrubs; leaves simple or compound, with stipules adnate or free; carpels many or few on a convex receptacle; fruit drupe .. .. *Rubus*.

B. Ovary inferior; ripe carpels enclosed within the calyx-tube:

(*c*) Carpels many, not confluent when ripe—

Armed shrubs; leaves compound with adnate stipules; fruit a fleshy calyx-tube enclosing bony achenes .. *Rosa*

Shrubs or trees; leaves simple, coriaceous, usually serrate; flowers white, panicled; fruit 1-seeded dry or succulent berry, endocarp membraneous .. *Eriobotrya.*

Shrubs or trees; leaves simple or compound; flowers white, red or pink, in terminal corymbs .. *Pyrus.*

Range of floral structures

This family has wide range of variation in the construction of flowers regarding the structure of receptacle, union of carpels and the nature of fruit. It has been divided into *six* subfamilies according to the floral construction by Focke.

Subfamily I. Spiraeoideae

The receptacle is somewhat flat but never forms a deep cup or convex structure. Stamens—10-many. Carpels—5, free, situated in the centre of the receptacle. Fruit—a follicle or capsule. Example —*Spiraea*, found in the Eastern Himalayas.

Floral formula

$⚥\ K_{(5)}\ C_{5-\infty}\ A_{10-\infty}\ \underline{G_5}$

Subfamily II. Pomoideae

The flowers are usually epigynous. The receptacle is deeply concave. Stamens—many. Carpels—2–5, more or less united and adnate to the cap of the receptacle (inferior ovary); each carpel contains two ovules. Fruit—a pome. Examples—*Pyrus malus* L. (Apple), *Cotoneaster*, etc.

Floral formula

$⚥\ K_{(5)}\ C_{5-\infty}\ A_{\infty}\ \overline{G}_{(2-5)}$

Subfamily III. Rosoideae

The receptacle is deeply concave in nature. Stamens—many. Carpels—many and free, situated in the cup-shaped receptacle, as in *Rosa*, or the receptacle is swollen nd convex, or slightly elongated, as in *Rubus*, on which many free carpels are seated. Each carpel contains 1 or 2 ovules. Examples—*Rosa alba* L., a common garden rose, *Potentilla fulgens* L. found in the Eastern Himalayas, *Fragaria vesca* L. (Strawberry), *Rubus hexagynous* Roxb. (Bramble), etc.

Floral formula

$⚥\ K_{(5)}\ C_{5-\infty}\ A_{\infty}\ \underline{G_{\infty}}$

Subfamily IV. Neuradoideae

The receptacle is cup-shaped, enlarging in fruit. Carpels—5–10, united at the base of the receptacle. Example—*Neurada procumbens* L. found in the desert of India.

Floral formula

$⚥\ K_{(5)}\ C_{5-\infty}\ A_{\infty}\ \underline{G_{(5-10)}}$

Subfamily V. Prunoideae

Flowers regular. The receptacle is somewhat cup-shaped. Stamens —10–20 or more. Carpel—1, contains two pendulous ovules. Style—terminal. Fruit—drupe. Examples—*Prunus*, etc.

Floral formula

$\oplus\ ⚥\ K_{(5)}\ C_{5-\infty}\ A_{10-\infty}\ \underline{G_1}$

Subfamily VI. Chrysobalanoideae

Flowers irregular. The receptacle is deeply cup-shaped. Stamens —10–15 or more; filaments are united (monadelphous). Carpel—one; ovules erect; style basal. Fruit—berry. Examples—*Chrysobalanus*, etc.

Floral formula

$\uparrow\ ⚥\ K_{(5)}\ C_{5-\infty}\ A_{(10-\infty)}\ \underline{G_1}$

Common plants

(1) Cabbage-rose (*Rosa centifolia* L.), Wild rose of Bengal (*R. involucrata* Roxb.), *R. damascena* Mill., commonly cultivated for attar, *R. indica* L., (Syn. *Rosa chinensis* Jacq.), a small spreading shrub frequent in gardens, White rose (*R. alba* L.). (2) Cherry (*Prunus cerasus* L.). (3) Plum (*P. domestica* L.). (4) Apricot (*P. armeniaca* L.).

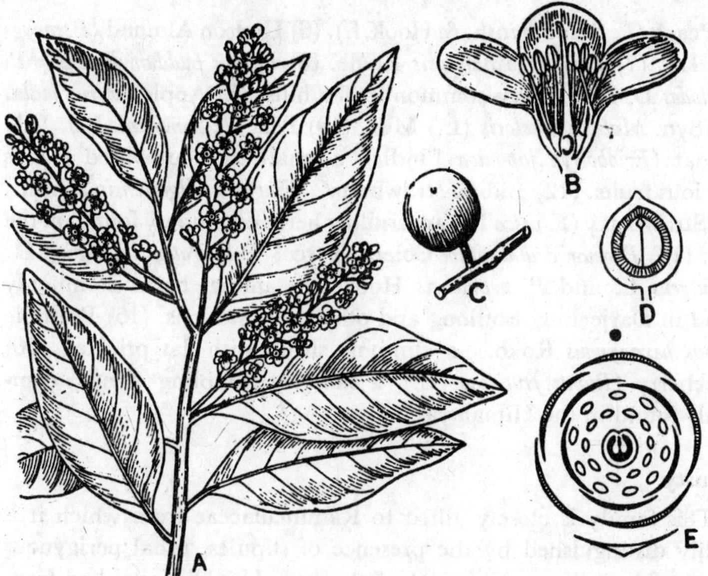

Fig. 586. Rosaceae (*Prunus persica*).
A, Portion of a flowering shoot; B, V.s. of a flower; C, Fruit; D, L.s. of the same; E, Floral diagram.

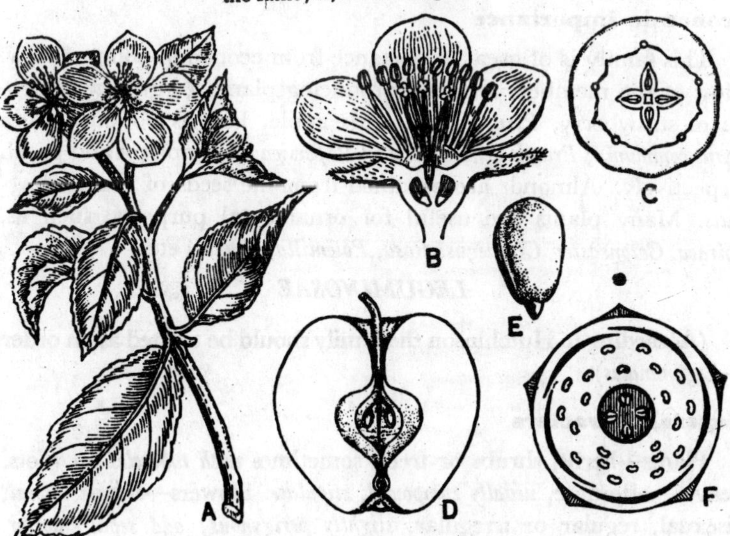

Fig. 587. Rosaceae (*Pyrus malus*).
A. Portion of a flowering shoot; B, V.s. of a flower; C, T.s. of fruit; D. L.s. of fruit; E, Seed; F, Floral diagram.

(5) Peach (*P. persica* Benth. & Hook. f.). (6) Hudson Almond (*P. amygdalis* L.). (7) *Prunus bokhariensis* Royle. (8) *Prunus puddum* Roxb. = *P. ceraslodes* D. Don., very common in the hills. (9) Apple (*Pyrus malus* L.) (Syn. *Malus sylvestoris* (L.) Mill. (10) Pear (*P. communis* L.). (11) Loquat (*Eriobotrya japonica* Lindl.), a small tree cultivated for its delicious fruits. (12) Indian strawberry (*Fragaria nilgerrensis* Schldl.) and Strawberry (*F. vesca* L.) are trailing herbs commonly found on the hills. (13) *Pygeum acuminatum* Coleb., a tree. (14) *Potentilla supina* L., *P. fulgens* L. and *P. nepalensis* Hook. are annual herbs commonly found in Darjeeling, Shillong and other hilly stations. (15) Bramble (*Rubus hexagynous* Roxb.), a climbing shrub with flat prickles. (16) Blackberry (*Rubus fruticosus* L.), a suberect rambling shrub, commonly found in the Himalayas.

Affinity

This family is closely allied to Ranunculaceae from which it is readily distinguished by the presence of stipules, usual perigynous flower and cyclic arrangement of stamens. It is distinguished from Leguninosae by the position of odd sepal.

Economic importance

This family is of great importance from economic point of view. Most of the members are fruit-producing plants. *Frageria vesca* produces strawberry, *Pyrus malus* yields apple. Pear is obtained from *Pyrus communis*; *Prunus armeniaca* and *P. persica* yield apricot and peach respectively. Almonds are obtained from the seeds of *Prunus amygdalis*. Many plants are useful for ornamental purposes, such as, *Spiraea*, *Cotoneaster*, *Crataegus*, *Rosa*, *Potentilla*, *Prunus*, etc.

LEGUMINOSAE

(According to Hutchinson the family should be treated as an order —*Leguminales*).

General characters

Plants—herbs, shrubs or trees, sometimes *with tubercles* on roots. Leaves—alternate, *usually compound*, *stipulate*. Flowers—*always lateral*, bisexual, regular or irregular, *slightly perigynous; odd sepal anterior*. Carpel—1; ovary superior, 1-*celled* with *marginal placentae*, bearing ovules in two alternating rows along the ventral suture. Fruit—usually a *legume*, sometimes lomentum. Seed—exalbuminous. Embryo—consists of two large flat [illegible]dons.

Number and distribution

This family consists of about 550 genera and more than 13,000 species which are widely distributed all over the globe, particularly in the tropics. Along with Orchidaceae, Leguminosae compete for the second place, largest being the family Compositae.

Subdivisions of the Family

Leguminosae is the second largest family of flowering plants. Hence, it has been divided into three subfamilies—(*a*) **Papilionaceae,** (*b*) **Caesalpinieae** and (*c*) **Mimosae,** the differences being based upon the characters of the corolla and the androecium.

Range of floral structures

This family exhibits a good deal of variation in the arrangement and form of the segments of perianth, particularly of corolla. There has been observed much wide variations in the number and cohesion of the androecium.

The *subfamily Papilionaceae* is characterized by the presence of the prominent zygomorphic and papilionaceous flowers. The sepals are generally connate and their aestivation is imbricate. The number of petals is 5 and they are unequal with vexillary aestivation. The outermost (posterior) petal becomes the biggest, forming the standard (*vexillum*), the lateral pair forms the wings (*alae*) and the anterior pair forms the keel (*carina*). In the genus *Amorpha*, the wings and keel are not found.

The number of stamens is 10; they are usually diadelphous, sometimes monadelphous, as in *Crotalaria, Arachis;* they are in two bundles of 5 each, as in *Aeschynome*. Sometimes the posterior stamen is obliterated, as in *Chorizema*.

The *subfamily Caesalpinieae* contains 133 genera. Flowers are usually medianly zygomorphic and they are either penta- or tetramerous. In *Tamarindus*, two upper sepals are connate, but in other genera the sepals are free and with imbricate aestivation. But *Cercis* represents the valvate type of aestivation. There also occurs variation in the pentamerous corolla. In *Cassia*, the 5 petals are subequal. The anterior pair of petals becomes small or suppressed, as in *Amherstia nobiles*. In *Krameria*, the glandular scales represent the anterior pair of petals. They are obliterated in *Tamarindus*. Species of *Ceratonia* and *Copaifera* are without petals.

The last *subfamily Mimosae* contains 40 genera. Flowers are usually regular. Valvate type of aestivation is manifested by both calyx and corolla, but imbricate type of aestivation is found in *Parkia*. The number of perianth is 5, but tri-, tetra- or hexamerous flowers do occur. In *Mimosa pudica*, the flower is tetramerous but in *Acacia* the flower may be tri- or tetramerous. The stamens also show a great variation in their number. The stamens are numerous and free as in *Acacia;* they are numerous and more or less forming a single bundle (monadelphous) as in *Inga*.

A marked variation in the number of carpels is found to occur here and there in some genera. The carpel is usually single and median. Two carpels are found in the genus *Tounatea* (Caesalpinieae). Some under the tribe Ingeae (Mimoseae), *Medicago* (Papilionaceae) have only single carpel.

The styles are terminal and bending in two subfamilies Caesalpinieae and Papilionaceae, but the straight or rolled styles occur in *Phaseolus*.

The ovules are either amphitropous or anatropous, occasionally Campylotropous. They are either ascending or pendulous having one or two integuments.

SUBFAMILY 1. PAPILIONACEAE (Family FABACEAE—Hutchinson)

Characters

Leaves—usually imparipinnate. Flowers—solitary or in racemes very irregular (*papilionaeous*), posterior petal biggest and outermost Petals—5, *vexillary* in aestivation. Stamens—10, *usually diadelphous* (9)+1, sometimes monadelphous (e.g., *Arachis*, *Crotalaria*, etc.) rarely 9 (e.g., *Abrus*). Embryo—curved.

Floral formula

$$⚥\ K_{(5)}\ C_5\ A_{(9)+1 \text{ or } (10)}\ \underline{G_1}$$

Key to Genera

A. Stamens free:

(*a*) Straggling or scandent shrubs; leaves 1-foliate; bracteoles large, hiding flowers .. .. *Dalhausiea*.

(*b*) Shrubs; leaves imparipinnate; bracteoles 0 *Sophora*.

(*c*) Erect trees; leaves imparipinnate; bracteoles minute *Ormosia*.

B. Stamens monadelphous:

(a) Prostrate herbs (cultivated); leaves pinnately compound with 2 pairs of leaflets; fruit hypogeal burying itself to ripen underground .. .. *Arachis*.

(b) Annual herbs; leaves digitately 3- or 4-foliate, gland-dotted .. .. *Zornia*.

(c) Herbs or shrubs; leaves simple, sessile, or digitately 3–7-foliate; fruit turgid, non-septate, dehiscent .. *Crotalaria*.

(d) Stem woody and twining; leaves paripinnate; stamens (9), vexillary filament absent .. .. *Abrus*.

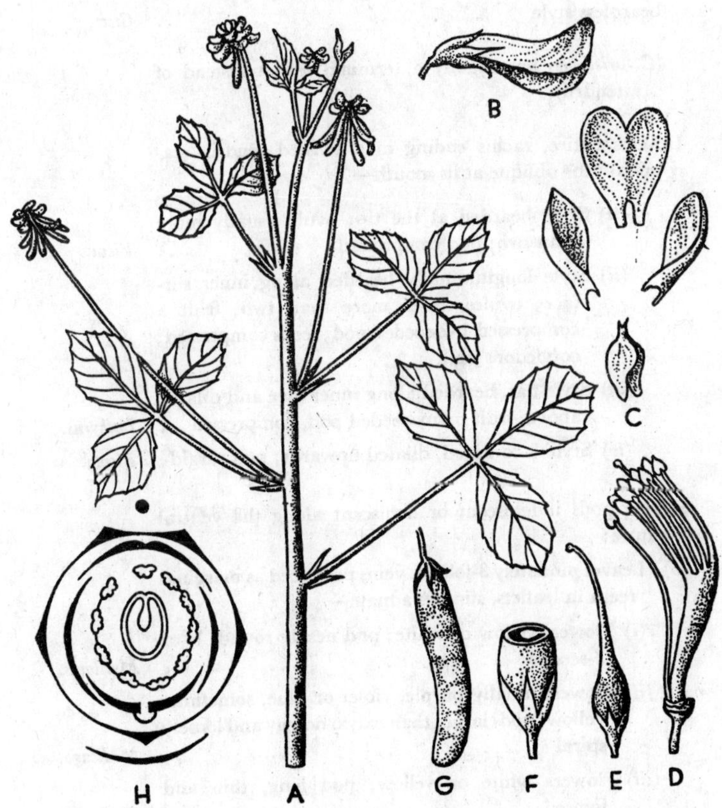

Fig. 588. Papilionaceae (*Trigonella corniculata*).
A, Portion of a flowering shoot; B, Flower; C, Petals; D, Flower with sepals and petals removed; E, Pistil; F, T.s. of ovary: G, Fruit: H, Floral diagram.

(*e*) Large twining or prostrate herbs—

(*i*) Leaves pinnately 3-foliate .. .. *Canavalia.*

(*ii*) Leaves pinnately 3-foliate, leaflets lobed .. *Pueraria.*

(*iii*) Leaves pinnately 3-foliate, 5 alternate stamens sterile .. .. *Teramnus.*

C. Stamens diadelphous:

Herbs; pods dehiscent by both sutures—

(*a*) Leaves paripinnate, rachis ending in a bristle or tendril—

Leaflets deeply toothed; pod turgid, sessile, tipped with beardless style .. .. *Cicer.*

(*C. arietinum* has usually a terminal leaflet instead of a tendril).

Leaflets entire, rachis ending in a twisted tendril, staminal tube oblique at its mouth—

(*i*) Style bearded at the tip; ovule usually more than two; pod compressed .. .. *Vicia.*

(*ii*) Style longitudinally bearded along inner surface; ovules never more than two; fruit a compressed 1–2-seeded pod; seeds compressed; cotyledons pink .. .. .. *Lens.*

(*iii*) Style flat, bearded along inner face and dilated above; fruit many-seeded pod, compressed .. *Lathyrus.*

(*iv*) Style 3-cornered, dilated upwards; pod turgid *Pisum.*

Herbs; pods indehiscent or dehiscent along the ventral suture:

(*b*) Leaves pinnately 3-foliate, veins produced as marginal teeth in leaflets, stipules adnate—

(*i*) Flowers yellow or white; pod nearly round, 1- or 3-seeded .. .. *Melilotus.*

(*ii*) Flowers usually purple, violet or blue, sometimes yellow; pods larger than calyx, downy and loosely spiral .. .. *Medicago.*

(*iii*) Flowers white or yellow; pod long, thin and jointed .. .. *Trigonella.*

(*iv*) Flowers usually reddish or purple; pod slender, 1- or more seeded .. .. .. *Indigofera.*

(*v*) Flowers blue; pod 1-seeded, indehiscent .. *Psoralea.*

Herbs or undershrubs; leaves pinnate, sensitive, 3–5 pairs, exstipulate, the rachis ending in a bristle or leaflet; flowers bright yellow; stamens in 2-bundles of 5 each; fruit a lomentum, folded inside the calyx .. .. *Smithia.*

Undershrubs growing in jheels and ditches, soft-wooded; leaves imparipinnate, numerous, sensitive; flowers bright yellow or orange-yellow; stamens in 2 bundles of 5 each; fruit a long lomentum, exserted .. *Aeschynomene.*

Herbs or undershrubs; leaves stipulate, leaflets 1–9; stamens (9)+1; fruit lomentum, coiled and more or less folded within the calyx .. .. .. *Uraria.*

Herbs or undershrubs; leaves 3–1-foliate; pod flat not coiled; stamens (10) or (9)+1 .. .. *Desmodium.*

Herbs or undershrubs; leaves pinnately 3-foliate, not glandular beneath

Twining, style bearded below stigma—

Keel spirally twisted; stigma oblique .. .. *Phaseolus.*

Keel not spiral; stigma oblique .. .. *Vigna.*

Leaflets lobed, stigma oblique, tuberous rootstocks .. *Pachyrrhizus.*

Stigma terminal; pod flattish, winged .. .. *Dolichos.*

Pod square, winged .. .. *Psophocarpus.*

Standard shorter than keel and wings; pods usually beset with stinging hairs .. .. .. *Mucuna.*

Trees with prickly branches; keel and wings shorter than standard; leaflets more or less cordate .. .. *Erythrina.*

Trees or woody climbers; flowers large showy, orange-red; calyx silky, wings free from keel .. .. *Butea.*

Woody twiners; flowers small; corolla not much larger than calyx; wings adnate to the keel .. .. *Spatholobus.*

(*c*) Leaves pinnately 5 or more foliate with terminal leaflet—

(*i*) Pod flat, indehiscent

Woody climbers or trees—

Leaflets alternate; stamens (9)+1 or (10) or (5)+(5) .. .. .. *Dalbergia.*

Timber trees; flowers yellow—

Leaflets alternate; stamens as above; pod thin, orbicular .. .. .. *Pterocarpus.*

Trees; leaflets opposite; flowers pink or white; ovary 2-ovuled; pod almost woody, wingless .. *Pongamia.*

(*ii*) **Pod dehiscent**

Herbs or shrubs, usually climbing

Flowers blue, white or purple; standard spoon-shaped; stamens (9)+1 or (10); anthers uniform .. .. .. *Clitoria*.

Erect herbs or undershrubs, more or less hairy with an offensive smell; leaflets imparipinnate, with 6–10 pairs; flowers red or purple .. *Tephrosia*.

Herbs, shrubs or soft-wooded trees, sometimes prickly; leaves paripinnate; leaflets may be 40 pairs; flowers large, yellow, dotted with purple or white or red; roots with copious tubercles .. .. *Sesbania*.

Common plants

(1) Pulses: Pea (*Pisum sativum* L.), Gram (*Cicer arietinum* L.), Lentil (*Lens esculentus* Moench. = *L. culinaris* Medic.), Pigeon pea

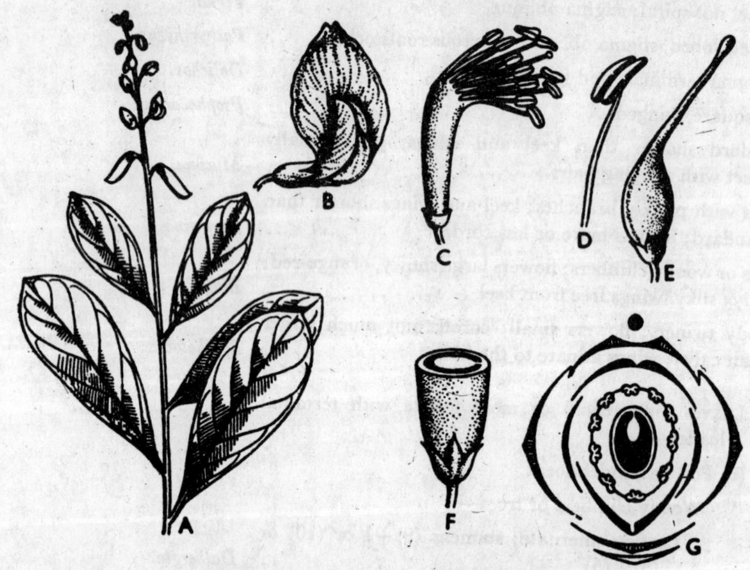

Fig. 589. Papilionaceae (*Crotalaria juncea*).
A, Portion of a flowering shoot; B, Flower; C, Monadelphous stamen; D, Stamen; E, Pistil; F, T.s. of ovary; G, Floral diagram.

(*Cajanus indicus* Spreng. = *C. cajan* Mill.), Chick pea (*Lathyrus sativus* L.), Green gram (*Phaseolus aurieus* L.), Black gram (*Phaseolus mungo*

L.). (2) Vegetables: Windsor bean or Broad bean (*Vicia faba* L.), Lablab or Black bean (*Dolichos lablab* L.), Cow-pea (*Vigna catjang* Endl.). (3) Butterfly pea (*Clitoria ternatea* L.), a common perennial twiner of gardens. (4) Coral tree (*Erythrina indica* Lamk. =*E. variegata* L.), a common tree planted along hedges. (5) *Sesbania grandiflora* Pers. (6) The flame of the forest (*Butea frondosa* Roxb. =*B. monosperma* Taub.), commonly planted for its beautiful flowers. (7) Groundnut or Pea-nut (*Arachis hypogaea* L.), commonly cultivated for its

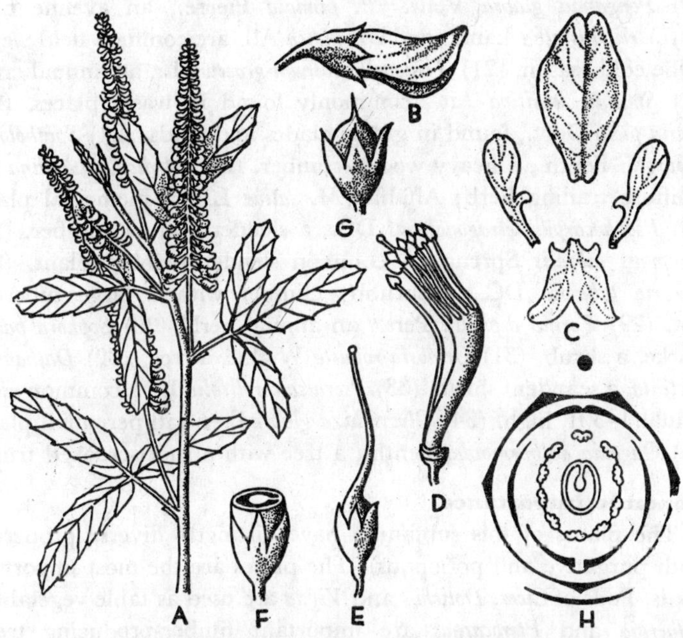

Fig. 590. Papilionaceae (*Melilotus alba*).
A, Portion of a flowering shoot; B, Flower; C, Petals; D, Flower with sepals and petals removed; E, T.s. of ovary; G, Fruit; H, Floral diagram.

edible seeds. (8) *Dalbergia sisso* Roxb., a timber tree. (9) Indian cork plant (*Aeschynomene aspera* L.), yields the 'shola' of commerce. (10) Indigo (*Indigofera tinctoria* L.), a dye-yielding plant. (11) Crab's eye or Indian liquorice (*Abrus precatorius* L.), a perennial twiner, the red and black seeds of which are used as small weights by the jewellers. (12) Red sandal wood (*Pterocarpus santalinus* L.), and Gum kino tree (*P. marsupium* Roxb.), are timber trees. (13) *Mucuna prurita* Hook., a semiwoody climber whose pods are provided with stinging hairs. (14) Telegraph plant (*Desmodium gyrans* DC.=*D. motorium* Merr.), a common weed of waste places, well-known for its variation movements. (15) Sunn-hemp (*Crotalaria juncea* L.), a fibre-yielding plant; *C. retusa* L., a common garden plant. (16) Yam bean (*Pachyrhizus angulatus* Rich.), a climber with woody stems and large tuberous roots. (17) Sword bean (*Canavalia ensiformis* DC.=*C. gladiata* DC.), a large climber. (18) Hoary pea or Wild indigo (*Tephrosia purpurea* Pers.), commonly found in waste places and roadsides. (19) *Pongamia glabra* Vent.=*P. pinnata* Pierre., an avenue tree. (20) *Melilotus alba* Lamk. and *M. indica* All. are common field weeds in the cold season. (21) *Trigonella foenum-graecum* L., an annual crop. (22) *Smithia sensitiva* Ait., commonly found in waste places. (23) *Uraria picta* Desv., found in grassy glades and fields. (24) *Spatholobus roxburghii* Benth., a heavy woody climber. (25) *Medicago lupulina* L., a diffuse trailing herb; Alfalfa (*M. sativa* L.), a medicinal plant. (26) *Psophocarpus tetragonolobus* DC., a slender annual climber. (27) *Teramnus labialis* Spreng., a common slender twining plant. (28) *Pueraria tuberosa* DC., a shrubby climber with a large tuberous root. (29) *Zornia diphylla* Pers., an annual herb. (30) *Sophora bakeri* Clarke, a shrub. (31) *Ormosia robusta* Wight., a tree. (32) *Dalhausiea bracteata*, a scandent shrub. (33) *Psoralea corylifolia* L., a common erect annual, 1–3 ft. high. (34) *Glycyrrhiza glabra* L., a tall perennial plant. (35) *Ougenia dalbargioides* Benth., a tree with a short-crooked trunk.

Economic importance

The plants of this subfamily have distinctly diverse properties (both purgative and poisonous). The pulses are the most important plants. Pods of *Cicer*, *Dolichos* and *Vigna* are used as table vegetables. *Dalbergia* and *Pterocarpus* are important timber-producing trees. *Crotalaria* yields hemp-like strong fibres. *Indigofera* was formerly extensively cultivated for producing dye. *Butea* is chiefly used as a lac-rearing tree. Seeds of *Trigonella*, *Melilotus*, *Medicago* and *Psoralea* and root of *Glycyrrhiza* have medicinal importance. *Aeschynomene aspera* yields 'shola' of commerce which is extensively used for making hats. The seeds of *Abrus* are used as jewellers' weights.

SUBFAMILY 2. CAESALPINIEAE
(Family CAESALPINIACEAE—Hutchinson)

Characters

Leaves—usually paripinnate or bipinnate. Flowers—in panicles, *slightly irregular* (but not papilionaceous), posterior petal smallest

and innermost. Petals—5, *imbricate* in aestivation. Stamens—5+5, or *less* (due to abortion), *free*. Embryo—straight.

Floral formula

⚥ $K_{(5)}$ or $_5$ C_5 A_{10} $\underline{G_1}$

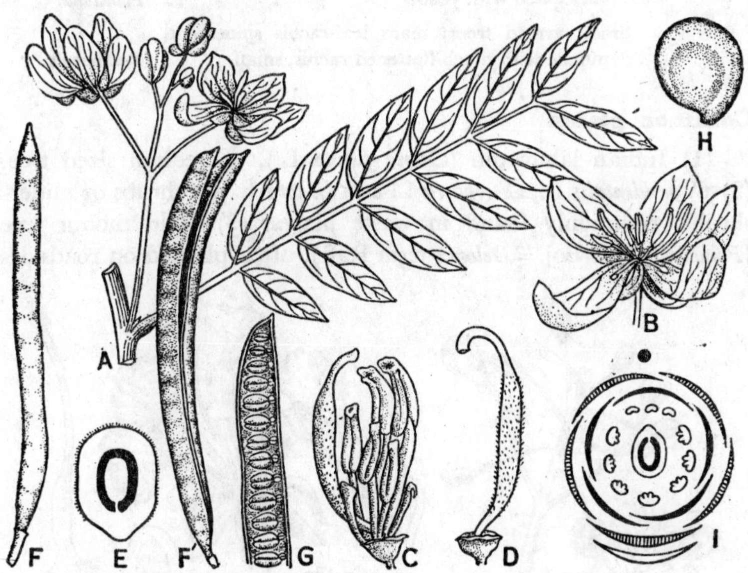

Fig. 591. Caesalpinieae (*Cassia fistula*).
A, Portion of a flowering shoot; B, Flower; C, The same after removal of calyx and corolla; D, Pistil; E, T.s. of ovary; F, Fruit; G, Magnified view of a portion of the same; H, Seed; I, Floral diagram.

Key to Genera

(*a*) Leaves simple, 2-lobed .. .. .. *Bauhinia.*

(*b*) Leaflets paripinnate—

Petals 5, anthers basifixed .. .. .. *Cassia.*

Calyx petaloid, scarlet, 4-lobed; corolla 0; sts. 8 .. *Saraca.*

Petals 0; calyx 5-lobed, green; stamens 10; leaflets 1–3, jugate .. .. *Hardwickia.*

Petals 3; stamens 3, monadelphous .. .. *Tamarindus.*

(*c*) Leaflets bipinnate—

Trees, rusty tomentose shoots and rusty panicles of showy yellow flowers .. .. .. *Peltophorum.*

Trees, shrubs or prickly climbers

Calyx deeply cleft, the lowest lobe largest; petals orbicular, usually clawed .. .. *Caesalpinia.*

Calyx-lobes valvate and almost equal

Unarmed trees; flowers large, bright scarlet and variegated with yellow .. .. *Poinciana.*

Small armed trees; main leaf-rachis spinescent, pinnae with much-flattened rachis, small .. *Parkinsonia.*

Common plants

(1) Indian laburnum (*Cassia fistula* L.), a medium sized tree. (2) *C. occidentalis* L., *C. sophera* L. and *C. tora* L. are shrubs or under-shrubs, commonly found in waste places. (3) Gold mohur tree (*Poinciana regia* Boj.=*Delonix regia* Raf.), often planted on roadsides

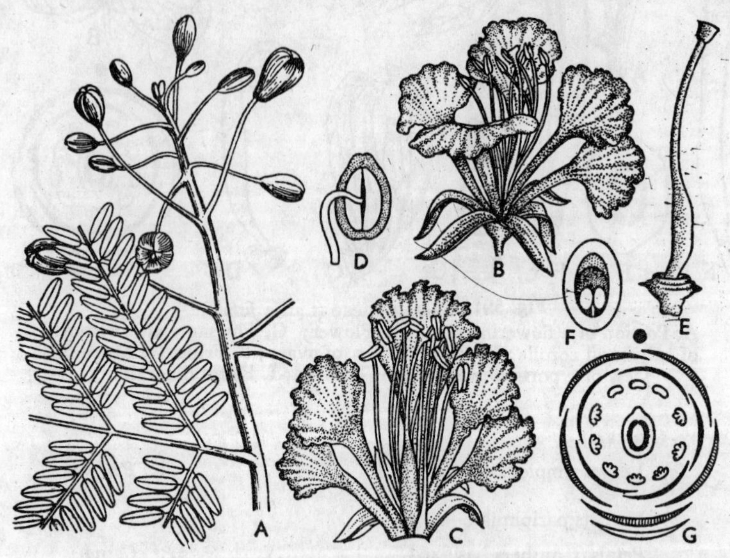

Fig. 592. Caesalpinieae (*Caesalpinia pulcherrima*).
A, Portion of a flowering shoot; B, Flower; C, Vertical section of the same; D, Stamen; E, Pistil; F, T.s. of ovary; G, Floral diagram.

and produces cream-yellow flowers just before the rainy season. (4) Peacock flower (*Caesalpinia pulcherrima* Swartz.), also planted on roadsides and produces crimson flowers. (5) Tamarind (*Tamarindus indica* L.), a tall tree often planted for fruit. (6) Fever nut

(*Caesalpinia bonducella* Fleming=*C. crista* L.), a hook climber. (7) The Ashoka tree (*Saraca indica* L.), often planted on roadsides and in gardens and has medicinal importance. (8) Camel's foot plants (*Bauhinia acuminata* L., *B. variegata* L., *B. purpurea* L.), small trees or woody climbers with emarginate leaves. (9) *Peltophorum ferrugineum* Benth.=*P. pterocarpum* Backer and *P. inerme* are trees with beautiful yellow flowers blossoming on the advent of summer, planted commonly in parks and along roadsides. (10) *Parkinsonia aculeata* L., a large shrub. (11) *Hardwickia pinnata* Roxb.=*Kingiodendron pinnata* Harms., a small tree.

Affinity

This subfamily is allied to Anacardiaceae but readily distinguished by having single carpel.

Economic importance

The plants of this subfamily usually have purgative but non-poisonous properties. The tamarind is the most important plant. *Saraca* is of medicinal importance. *Bauhinia* yields good fibres. *Haematoxylon* yields haemotoxylin, a kind of stain for microscopical work.

SUBFAMILY 3. MIMOSAE
(Family MIMOSACEAE—Hutchinson)

Characters

Leaves—usually bipinnate. Flowers—in spikes, regular, usually 4-merous, less frequently 5- or 3-merous. Petals—4, united or free, *valvate* in aestivation. Stamens—numerous, sometimes definite, exerted. Embryo—straight.

Floral formula

$\oplus$ ⚥ $K_{(4) \text{ or } (5)}$ C_{4-5} $A_{\infty \text{ or } 10 \text{ or } 4}$ $\underline{G_1}$

Key to Genera

A. Stamens definite, 4, 5, 8 or generally 10:

Marsh plants with flattened or angular stems; heads of flowers on long stalks; flowers hermaphrodite, male or neuter .. .. .. *Neptunia*.

Flowers in round heads, all flowers similar—

(*a*) Leaf with one pair of pinnae .. .. *Xylia.*

(*b*) Woody climber with tendrils .. .. *Entada.*

(*c*) Erect unarmed tree with bipinnate leaves, fruit linear, falcate, seeds scarlet .. .. *Adenanthera.*

(*d*) Prickly trees or shrubs, pod turgid and spongy inside .. .. *Prosopis.*

(*e*) Herbs or shrubs with sensitive leaflets, pod flat and jointed .. .. *Mimosa.*

B. Stamens indefinite, much exerted:

(*a*) Erect or climbing shrubs or trees armed with spiny stipules or recurved prickles; flowers white, yellow or purple in round heads or cylindrical spikes .. *Acacia.*

(*b*) Large unarmed trees, rarely climbing; leaves bipinnate, pinnae and leaflets several; flowers in round heads; stamens monadelphous; pods thin, strap-shaped, continuous within .. .. *Albizzia.*

(*c*) Tall trees; leaves bipinnate with pinnae one pair and leaflet one pair only, sometimes spinescent; stamens monadelphous; pod twisted .. .. *Pithecolobium.*

(*d*) Big trees; leaves bipinnate, leaflets many; stamens monadelphous; pod septate between seeds, valves spongy or fleshy .. .. .. *Enterolobium*

Common plants

(1) Sensitive plant (*Mimosa pudica* L.), a common straggling herb. (2) The Babul or Gum tree (*Acacia arabica* Willd.), a small tree which yields gum. (3) Cutch tree (*Acacia catechu* Willd.), the wood of which on distillation produces 'cutch' of commerce. (4) *Acacia moniliformis* Griseb., commonly planted on roadsides and parks and bears phyllodes. (5) *Acacia recurva* also bears phyllodes, common in Darjeeling. (6) Silk flower (*Albizzia lebbek* Benth.), commonly planted on roadsides. (7) *Entada scandens* Benth.=*E. phaseoloides* Merr., a woody climber with snake-like branches, the seeds of which are used for curling garments. (8) *Neptunia oleracea* Lour, and *N. plena* Benth., common water-weeds with sensitive leaves. (9) *Prosopis spicigera* L. (10) *Xylia dolabriformis* Benth., Iron wood tree of Burma. (11) Manila tamarind (*Pithecolobium dulce* Benth.=*Inga dulcis* Willd., a medium tree, common. (12) Rain tree (*Enterolobium saman* Prain=*Samanea saman* Merr.), an avenue tree. (13) Red wood (*Adenanthera pavonina* L.), a tree.

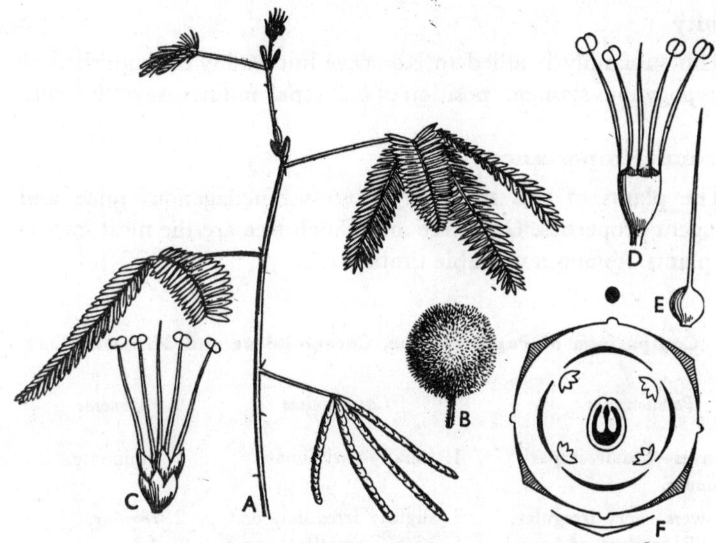

Fig. 593. Mimosae (*Mimosa pudica*).
A, Portion of a flowering shoot; B, Inflorescence; C, Flower; D, The same after removal of calyx and corolla; E, Pistil; F, Floral diagram.

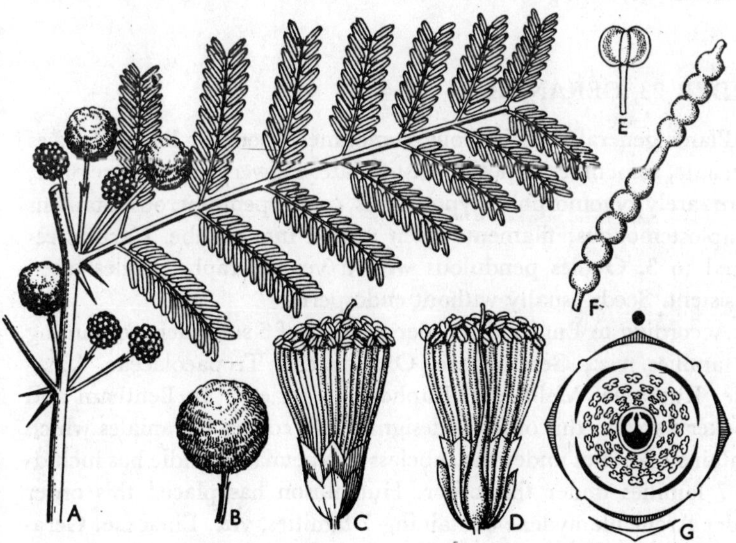

Fig. 594. Mimosae (*Acacia arabica*).
A, Portion of a flowering shoot; B, Inflorescence; C, Flower; D, V.s. of the same; E, Stamen; F, Fruit; G, Floral diagram.

Affinity

This subfamily is allied to Rosaceae but readily distinguished by the hypogynous stamens, position of odd sepal and nature of the fruit.

Economic importance

The plants of this subfamily possess mucilagenous juice and astringent properties. Gum tree and Cutch tree are the most important plants. *Xylia* is a valuable timber tree.

Comparison of Papilionaceae, Caesalpinieae and Mimosae

Papilionaceae	*Caesalpinieae*	*Mimosae*
1. Leaves—usually imparipinnate.	1. usually paripinnate.	1. bipinnate.
2. Flowers—very irregular, papilionaceous, odd petal biggest and outermost.	2. slightly irregular, odd petal smallest and innermost.	2. regular, 4-merous.
3. Aestivation—vexillary.	3. imbricate.	3. valvate.
4. Stamens—(9)+1 or (10).	4. 5+5 or less, free.	4. ∞ or definite.

ORDER 23. GERANIALES

Plants generally herbaceous, sometimes woody or lianes. Leaves alternate, sometimes opposite, exstipulate. Flowers bisexual, regular, more rarely zygomorphic, hypogynous, cyclic, pentamerous. Stamens obdiplostemonous; filaments often united into a tube. Carpels reduced to 3. Ovules pendulous with a ventral raphe. Styles often persistent. Seeds usually without endosperm.

According to Engler this order consists of 6 suborders containing 20 families, viz., Geraniaceae, Oxalidaceae, Tropaeolaceae, Linaceae, Rutaceae, Meliaceae, Euphorbiaceae, etc. In Bentham and Hooker's system this order is designated as cohort Geraniales which contains 7 families under the subclass Polypetalae. Rendle has included 7 families under this order. Hutchinson has placed this order under Archichlamydeae containing 7 families, viz., Linaceae, Geraniaceae, Oxalidaceae, Tropaeolaceae, Balsaminaceae, etc. Rutaceae has been put under the order Rutales, Meliaceae under the order Meliales and Euphorbiaceae under the order Euphorbiales.

GERANIACEAE

General characters

Plants—annual herbs, often with fleshy stems. Leaves—alternate rarely opposite, compound but sometimes simple, usually palmiveined, stipulate. Inflorescence—cymose. Flowers—regular, sometimes

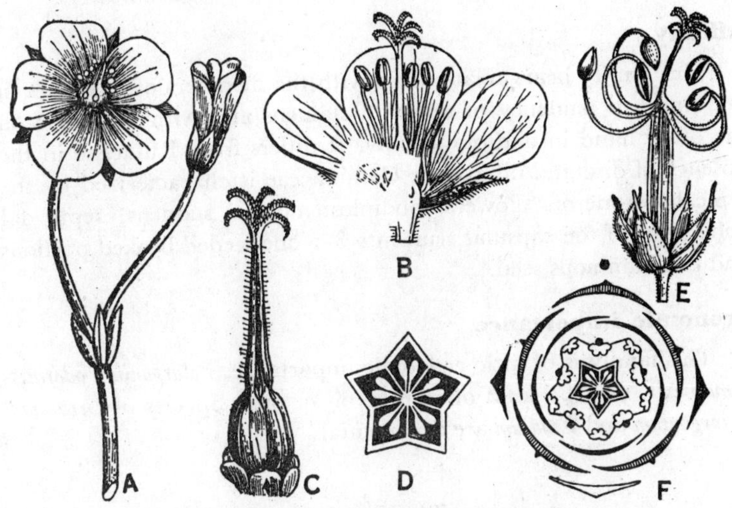

Fig. 595. Geraniaceae (*Geranium ocellacum*).
A, Portion of a flowering shoot; B, V.s. of a flower; C, Pistil; D, T.s. of ovary; E, Dehiscence of fruit; F, Floral diagram.

slightly irregular (e.g., *Pelargonium*), bisexual, hypogynous. Sepals—usually 5, (4 in *Vivania*) imbricate. Petals—usually 5, with nectar glands alternating with them, imbricate. Stamens—*usually 10 in 2 series, obdiplostemonous*, rarely 15; filaments united at the base. Carpels—(3–5); ovary superior, beaked, 3–5-celled with 1 or 2 ovules in each; style 3–5, slender. Fruit—capsule, *dehiscing septicidally into 3–5 one-seeded beaked portions* (loculicidal in *Vivania*). Seeds—exalbuminous with a straight or curved embryo.

Floral formula

⚥ K_{4-5} C_5 $A_{5+5 \text{ or } 15}$ $\underline{G_{(3-5)}}$

Number and distribution

This family consists of 11 genera and about 850 species which are widely distributed in the temperate zone and in the hills and in subtropical regions.

Common plants

(1) *Geranium ocellatum* Camb., a small straggling herb producing rose-coloured flowers with a purple 'eye', commonly found on the hills. (2) *G. nepalense* Sw., a common herb found in Darjeeling. (3) *Pelargonium* sp., a garden plant, producing beautiful flowers.

Affinity

This family bears relationship with the members of Malvales in one hand in tendency of union of stamens and with Rutaceae on the other hand in obdiplostemony. It differs from Rutaceae in the absence of disc and oil-glands. Geraniaceae is characterized by the typically 5-merous flowers, obdiplostemonous stamens, septicidal dehiscence of the capsular fruit into 3–5 one-seeded beaked portions and exalbuminous seed.

Economic importance

This family is of little economic importance. *Pelargonium odoratissimum* Ait. yields a kind of scented oil or otto. Species of *Geranium*, *Pelargonium* and *Erodium* are ornamentals.

OXALIDACEAE

General characters

Plants—perennial herbs, sometimes trees (e.g., *Averrhoa*). Leaves—alternate, usually pinnately or palmately compound, exstipulate. Inflorescence—cymose. Flowers—regular, bisexual, hypogynous. Sepals—5, imbricate. Petals—5, twisted. Stamens—10 in 2 series, obdiplostemonous, *united at the base* (*shortly monadelphous*). Carpels—(5); ovary superior, 5-celled with 1-many anatropous ovules in each; *style 5, free*. Fruit—capsule, *dehiscing along the dorsal suture*, or berry (e.g., *Averrhoa*). Seeds—sometimes *arillate*, albuminous with a straight embryo.

Floral formula

$\oplus$ ⚥ $K_5\ C_5\ A_{(5+5)}\ \underline{G_{(5)}}$

Number and distribution

This family consists of 7 genera and about 1,000 species which are chiefly distributed in the tropics.

KEY TO GENERA

(*a*) Fruits of loculicidally dehiscent capsules; stamens all perfect; herbs—
- (*i*) Valves cohering with axis; leaves trifoliate .. *Oxalis.*
- (*ii*) Valves dehiscing from axis; leaves pinnately compound .. .. *Biophytum.*

(*b*) Fruits of indehiscent berries; often the stamens reduced to staminodes; leaves pinnate; trees .. .. *Averrhoa.*

Common plants

(1) Wood-sorrel (*Oxalis corniculata* L.), a weed very common on roadsides and especially on cultivated lands. (2) *Biophytum sensitivum* DC., another common weed with sensitive leaves, chiefly found on

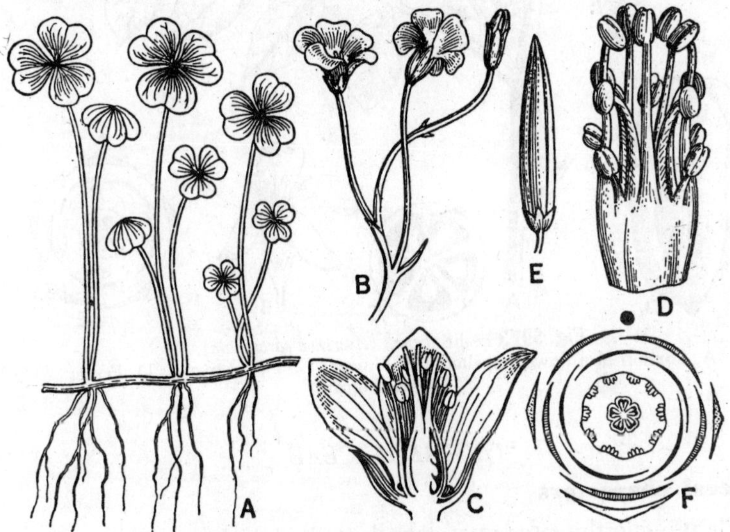

Fig. 596. Oxalidaceae (*Oxalis corniculata*).
A, Portion of a plant; B, Inflorescence; C, V.s. of a flower; D, Androecium; E, Fruit; F, Floral diagram.

cultivated lands. (3) Carambola (*Averrhoa carambula* L.), a tree commonly planted for its fruits. (4) The Bilimbi (*A. bilimbi* L.), a small cultivated tree.

Affinity

This family is allied to Geraniaceae but readily distinguished by the palmately compound leaves, shortly monadelphous stamens, 5 free styles, 5-celled ovary, mode of dehiscence of fruit and arillate seeds.

Economic importance

This family is of little economic importance. The gooseberry-like fruits of Carambola (*Averrhoa*) are edible. Many species of *Oxalis* have medicinal value. A few species are ornamental.

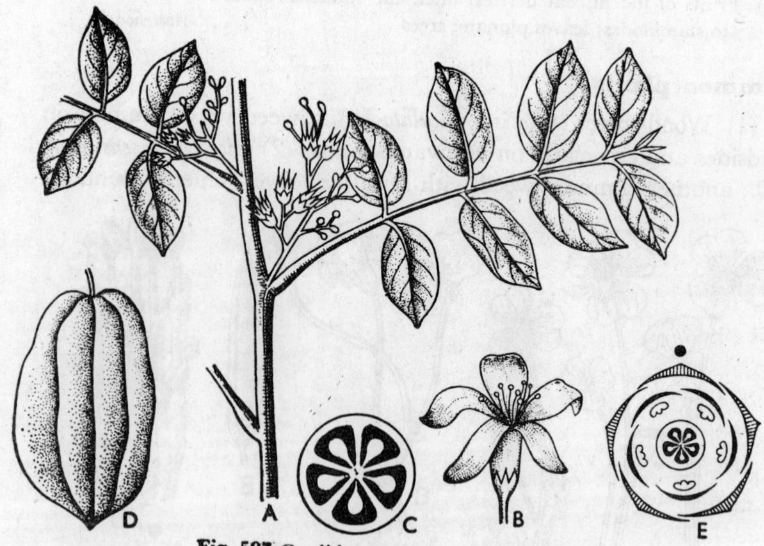

Fig. 597. Oxalidaceae (*Averrhoa carambula*).
A, Portion of a flowering shoot; B, Flower; C, T.s. of ovary; D, Fruit; F, Floral diagram.

TROPAEOLACEAE

General characters

Plants—mostly prostrate succulent herbs. Leaves—alternate, simple, *peltate*, sometimes lobed, exstipulate. Flowers—irregular, bisexual, hypogynous. Sepals—5, petaloid, *the dorsal one prolonged into a spur*. Petals—5, clawed, the upper 2 petals differ in shape from the lower 3 (usually smaller and situated in the opening of the spur), imbricate. Stamens—*8 in 2 whorls*, unequal. Carpels—(3); ovary superior, *3-celled* with 1 pendulous anatropous ovule in each; *style 1*; *stigma 3-fid*, linear. Fruit—a *3-seeded schizocarp*. Seeds—exalbuminous with a straight embryo.

Floral formula

$\uparrow$ ⚥ $K_5\ C_5\ A_{4+4}\ \underline{G_{(3)}}$

Number and distribution

This family consists of 1 genus, *Tropaeolum* with about 60 species which are chiefly found on the hills.

Common plants

Garden Nasturtium (*Tropaeolum majus* L.), a common garden plant.

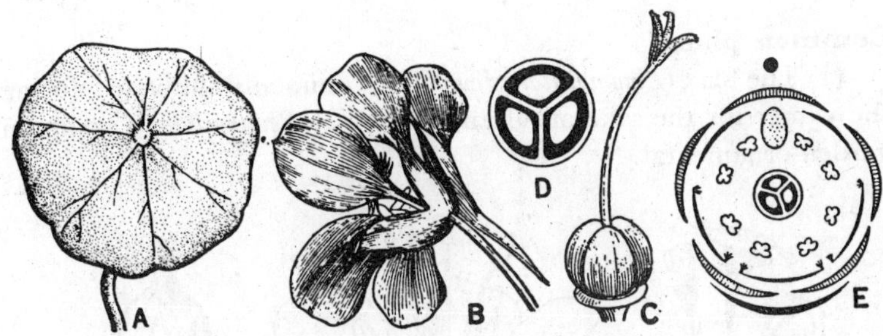

Fig. 598. Tropaeolaceae (*Tropaeolum majus*).
A, A single leaf; B, Flower; C, Pistil; D, T.s. of ovary; E, Floral diagram.

Affinity

This family is characterized by the peltate leaves, petaloid spurred sepal, 8 stamens in 2 whorls, 3 carpels, and the nature of the fruit.

Economic importance

This family is of very little economic importance. *Tropaeolum* is an ornamental plant.

LINACEAE

General characters

Plants—usually annual herbs, sometimes shrubs. Leaves—alternate rarely opposite, simple, entire, stipulate or exstipulate. Infloresence—usually cymose (a dichasial cyme). Flowers—pentamerous, regular, bisexual, hypogynous. Sepals—5, free or slightly united at the base, imbricate. Petals—5, often *clawed, twisted*. Stamens—5 or 10, the fertile stamens equal to the number of petals and antisepalous; *filaments united at the base* forming a ring, outside which nectar glands are present. Carpels—usually (5), antipetalous; ovary superior, usually 5-celled with 2 pendulous and anatropous ovules in the inner angle of each cell; styles free. Fruit—capsule. Seed—with fleshy endosperm and a straight embryo.

Floral formula

$\oplus$ ⚥ $K_{5 \text{ or } (5)}$ C_5 $A_{(5 \text{ or } 10)}$ $\underline{G_{(5)}}$

Number and distribution

This family consists of 9 genera and about 200 species which are chiefly distributed in the temperate zone.

Common plants

(1) The Flax (*Linum usitatissimum* L.), commonly cultivated during the winter for the sake of oil and fibre. (2) *Reinwardita*, a common garden ornamental.

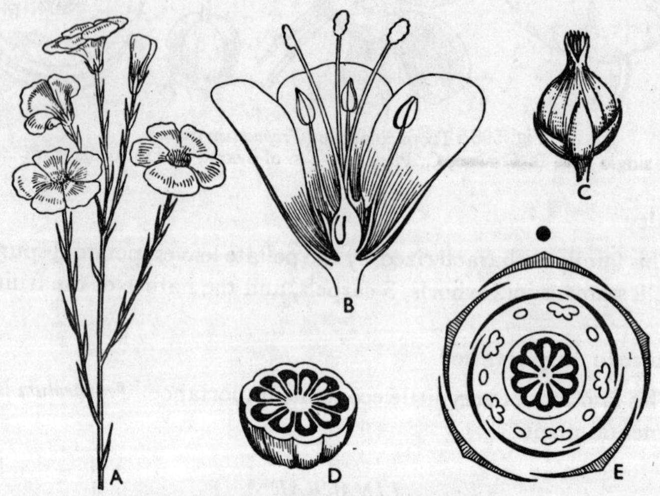

Fig. 599. Linaceae (*Linum usitatissimum*). A, Portion of a flowering shoot; B, V.s. of a flower; C, Pistil; D, T.s. of ovary; E, Floral diagram.

Affinity

This family is closely related to Geraniaceae and Malvaceae but readily distinguished from them by the pentamerous flowers, clawed petals with twisted aestivation, short connate filaments and septicidally dehiscent capsule.

Economic importance

This family is economically important. *Linum usitatissimum* yields a kind of fibre which is used for preparing linen cloth, and also a kind of oil (linseed oil). A few species of *Linum* and *Reinwardtia* are ornamentals.

RUTACEAE

General characters

Plants—usually shrubs or trees, sometimes climbing, often provided with spines. Leaves—alternate or opposite, simple or compound, smooth, mostly *gland-dotted*, exstipulate. Inflorescence—usually cymose. Flowers—regular (sometimes slightly irregular), usually bisexual (unisexual in *Zanthoxylum*), with an annular or cushion-like disc generally between or above the stamens. Sepals—4–5, free or united, *glandular*, imbricate. Petals—4–5 (but united in *Correa*), *glandular*, imbricate. Stamens—generally 8 or 10, *obdiplostemonous*, sometimes equal in number to the petals, or numerous (e.g., *Citrus* and *Aegle*), free or polyadelphous. Carpels—usually (4–5), sometimes free below and united above; ovary superior, often 4–5-celled, usually deeply *lobed, situated on a disc;* ovules 1–2 or more in each cell; style short; stigma capitate; placentation axile (but parietal in *Feronia*). Fruit—a *hesperidium* or *amphisarca*, sometimes a capsule. Seeds—with or without endosperm, and with a large straight or curved embryo.

Floral formula

$⚥\ K_{4-5}\ C_{4-5}\ A_{8-10}\ \underline{G_{(4-5)}}$

Number and distribution

This family consists of about 140 genera and 1,300 species which are found in tropical and temperate climates.

KEY TO GENERA

A. Fruit syncarpous; ovary entire; fls. polygamous;
 (*a*) Stem unarmed
  (*i*) Fls. usually 5-merous, leaves simple .. *Skimmia.*
  (*ii*) Fls. 4-merous, leaves 1–3-foliate .. .. *Acronychia.*
 (*b*) Stem armed
  Fls. 2–5-merous, 1–3-foliate .. .. *Toddalia.*

B. Fruit capsular; ovary deeply 2–5-lobed; fls. polygamous; leaves 3-foliate or imparipinnate .. .. *Zanthoxylum.*

C. Fruit berry; ovary entire; fls. bisexual; leaves compound:
 (*a*) Ovules solitary or 2 in a loculus—
  (*i*) Petals 4–5, imbricate; ovary 2–5-celled; style very short; persistent .. .. .. *Glycosmis.*

(*ii*) Petals 4–5, imbricate or valvate; stamens 8 or 10, inserted on a columnar disc, filaments free; anther linear-oblong; fls. large, axillary, solitary or fascicled .. .. .. *Paramignya.*

(*iii*) Petals 5; stamens 8 or 10; filaments dilated below; style deciduous .. .. .. *Clausena.*

(*iv*) Petals 5, imbricate; stamens 10, short and long filaments alternating; style deciduous, flattened below .. .. *Murraya.*

(*b*) Ovules many in each loculus—

(*v*) 20–60; leaves unifoliate .. .. .. *Citrus.*

(*vi*) Stamens 10–12; fruit large, many-seeded, woody rind .. .. *Feronia.*

(*vii*) Stamens 30–60; leaves 3-foliate; fruit large, globose; testa mucilagenous .. .. *Aegle.*

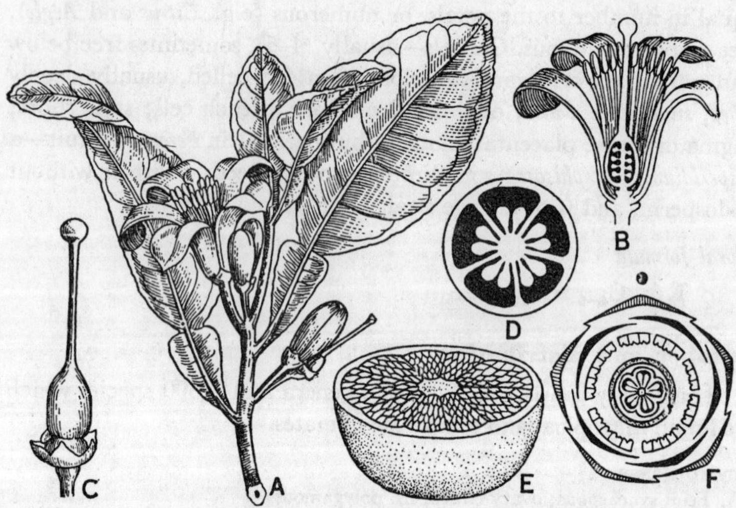

Fig. 600. Rutaceae (*Citrus aurantium*).
A, Portion of a flowering shoot; B, L.s. of a flower; C, Pistil; D, T.s. of ovary; E, T.s. of fruit; F, Floral diagram.

Common plants

(1) Orange (*Citrus aurantium* L.=*C. reticulatus* Blanco.). (2) Lemon (*Citrus medica* L.). (3) Shaddock or Pumelo (*Citrus decumana* L.= *C. maxima* Merr.). (4) Wood apple (*Aegle marmelos* Correa), a tree cultivated throughout India for its fruits, which are of great medicinal value. (5) Elephant apple (*Feronia elephantum* Correa=*F. limonia*

Swingle), a fruit tree. (6) Tooth-brush plant (*Glycosmis pentaphylla* Correa), a common shrub the twigs of which are used as tooth-brushes. (7) Orange jessamine (*Murraya exotica* L.=*M. paniculata* Jack.), a garden plant. (8) Curry-leaf plant (*Murraya koeningii* Spreng.), the leaves of which are extensively used as a condiment in South India. (9) Common rue (*Ruta graveolens* L.), a medicinal plant. (10) *Atalantia monophylla* DC., a shrub often planted in gardens. (11) *Acronychia laurifolia* Bl.=*A. pedunculata* Miq., found in

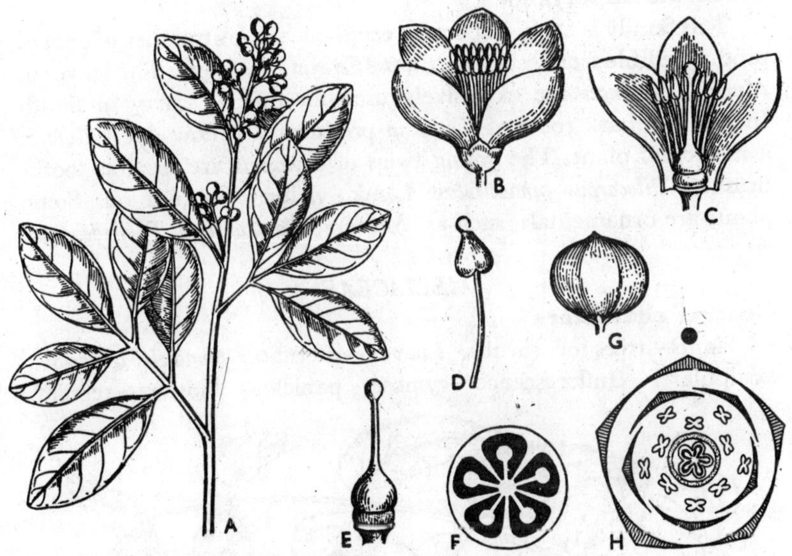

Fig. 601. Rutaceae (*Glycosmis pentaphylla*).
A, Portion of a flowering shoot; B, Flower; C, Corolla cut open showing androecium and gynoecium; D, Stamen; E, Pistil; F, T.s. of ovary; G, Fruit; H, Floral diagram.

scrub jungles near Canning. (12) *Clausena heptaphylla* W. & A., generally found in village-shrubberies. (13) Prickly ash (*Zanthoxylum trifoliatum* L.=*Acanthopanax trifoliatum* Merr.), a small tree armed with prickles. (14) *Paramignya citrifolia* Hook. f. and *P. angulata* Kurz.=*Merope angulata* Swingle, are thorny undershrubs common in Sundribans. (15) *Skimmia laureola* Hook. f., a glabrous shrub 3–5 ft. high, chiefly found in the hills. (16) *Toddalia aculeata* Pers.=*T. asiatica* Lamk., a rambling prickly shrub. (17) *Zanthoxylum budranga* L., a common prickly shrub.

Affinity

Engler placed Rutaceae under Geraniales, whereas Hutchinson places it under separate order Rutales. This family resembles Meliaceae, Anacardiaceae and Sapindaceae in obdiplostemonous stamens, structure of leaf, heath-like habit, but readily distinguished from them by the presence of gland-dotted leaves, lobed ovary situated on a disc and the character of fruit. The family is also closely related to Euphorbiaceae in the presence of ventral raphe of the ovule in some genera.

Economic importance

This family is fairly important economically. A number of genera produce edible fruits, such as, *Citrus*, *Feronia*, *Aegle*, etc. The leaves of *Murraya koeningii* are extensively used for making curry in South India. The bark roots of *Toddalia* produces a yellow dye. *Ruta* is a medicinal plant. The young twigs of *Glycosmis* are used as tooth-brushes. *Pilocarpus pinnatifolius* Lamk. yields jaborandi oil. Some plants are ornamentals, such as, *Murraya*, *Zanthoxylum*, *Phellodendron*, etc.

MELIACEAE

General characters

Plants—trees or shrubs. Leaves—alternate, *pinnately compound*, exstipulate. Inflorescence—cymose panicle. Flowers—regular

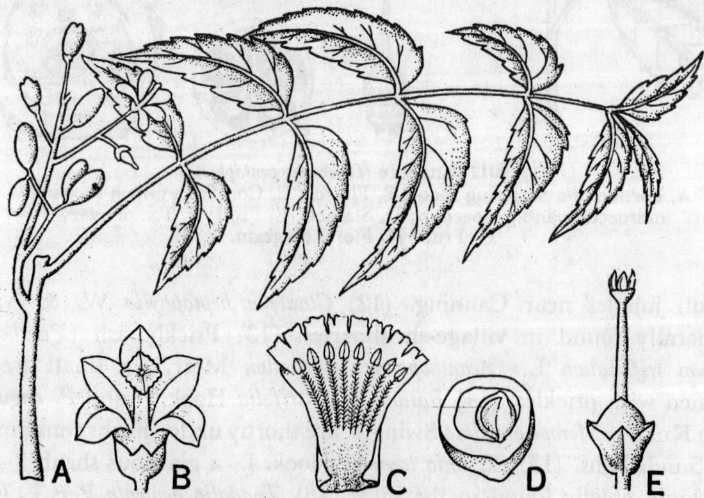

Fig. 602. Meliaceae (*Melia azadirachta*).
A, Portion of a flowering shoot; B, Flower; C, Staminal tube split open; D, T.s. of ovary; E., Pistil.

bi-sexual, hypogynous, usually with an annular disc between stamens and petals. Sepals—(4–5), small, imbricate. Petals—4–5, twisted or imbricate, distinct or adnate to the staminal tube and then valvate. Stamens—8–10 in 2 whorls, mostly monadelphous (but free in *Cedrela*, and *Chloroxylon*), sometimes are converted into staminodes; filaments *usually united*, rarely free; *anthers often sessile, inserted in the tube*. Carpels—(2–5); ovary superior, often 2–5-celled with mostly 2,

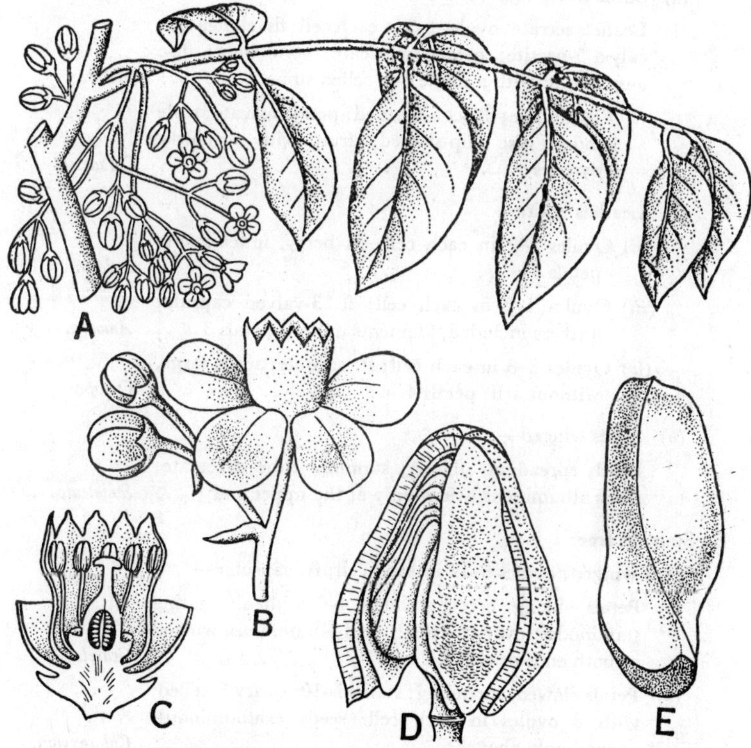

Fig. 603. Meliaceae (*Swietenia mahogoni*).
A, Portion of a flowering shoot; B, Inflorescence;
C. V.s. of a flower; D, Fruit; E, Seed.

rarely more (12 in *Swietenia*), ovules in each cell; stigma often *disciform* or *capitate*. Fruit—capsule or berry, rarely drupe. Seeds—with or without endosperm, *often winged*.

Floral formula

$\oplus$ ⚥ $K_{(4-5)}\ \overline{C_{4-5}A_{(8-10)\ \text{or}\ 8-10}}\ G_{\underline{(2-5)}}$

Number and distribution

This family consists of 50 genera and about 800 species, widely distributed in the tropics.

KEY TO GENERA

A. Stamens connate in a tube:

(*a*) Seeds not winged—

(1) Leaflets serrate; ovules 1–2 in each cell; fls. elongated; calyx 5-partite; petals imbricate; style long; disc annular; ft. with a single 1–5-celled stone .. *Melia.*

(*i*) Fls. globose; calyx 5-toothed; petals valvate; style short; disc cup-shaped; fruit with 5 horny pyrenes .. .. *Cipadessa.*

(2) Leaflets entire—

(*ii*) Ovules 1–2 in each cell; ft. berry, indehiscent; petals 5 .. .. *Aglaia.*

(*iii*) Ovules 1–2 in each cell; ft. 3-valved capsule; anthers included, filaments united; petals 3 .. *Amoora.*

(*iv*) Ovules 3–8 in each cell; ft. capsule; seeds large, without aril; petals 4 .. .. .. *Carapa.*

(*b*) Seeds winged—

Petals spreading, oblong; staminal tube urceolate; seeds albuminous, wings only at the upper end .. *Swietenia.*

B. Stamens free:

Seeds winged; ovules 8–12 in each cell; ft. capsular—

(*a*) Petals oblong, erect; stamens 4–6 with alternating staminodes; ovary 5-celled; seed albuminous, winged at both ends or only below .. .. .. *Cedrela.*

(*b*) Petals clawed, spreading; stamens 10; ovary 3-celled, with 8 ovules in each cell; seeds exalbuminous, winged only above .. .. .. *Chloroxylon.*

Common plants

(1) Neem or Margosa tree (*Melia azadirachta* L.=*Azadirachta indica* A. Juss.), commonly found throughout India, possesses bitter taste in leaves and bark. (2) Persian lilac or Chinaberry tree (*Melia azedarach* L.), larger than the former one, cultivated. (3) Mahogany tree (*Swietenia mahogoni* L.), a valuable timber tree; *S. microphylla* and *S. macrophylla* are commonly planted on roadsides. (4) Satin-wood (*Chloroxylon swietenia* DC.), another valuable timber tree.

(5) Moulmein cedar on Toon wood (*Cedrela toona* Roxb.), a tall timber tree. (6) *Amoora cucullata* Roxb. and *A. rohituka* W. & A. = *Aphanamixis polystachya* Parker, commonly planted on roadsides. (7) *Aglaia roxburghiana* Miq. (8) *Carapa obovata* Bl., a small tree with large round fruit, chiefly found in the Sundribans. (9) *Cipadessa fruticosa* Bl., a much-branched shrub.

Affinity

This family is allied to Rutaceae and Sapindaceae but readily distinguished from them by the monadelphous stamen, deciform or capitate stigma, and winged seeds. It is distinguished from Burseraceae by the absence of resin ducts.

Economic importance

This family is of some economic importance. *Melia* is a medicinal plant. Many are valuable timber trees, e.g., *Swietenia*, *Chloroxylon* and *Cedrela*.

EUPHORBIACEAE

General characters

Plants—minute herbs to huge trees, monoecious or dioecious, often with milky latex. Leaves—usually alternate, may be opposite or whorled (in many cases the upper ones are opposite while lower ones alternate), simple, entire or palmately lobed, very rarely compound (e.g., species of *Bischofia*), while in others reduced to spines usually stipulate. Inflorescence—various, raceme, sometimes cyathium or spike, or mixed, or a dichotomous cyme, subtended by involucral or brightly coloured bracts. Flowers—usually small, incomplete, *unisexual*, regular or slightly irregular. Perianth—usually varies from 3–5, when present, often small, green, sometimes absent; rarely differentiated into calyx and corolla (e.g., *Jatropha*), valvate or imbricate. Stamens—in male flowers as many as the perianth leaves or double as many, or very numerous or few or one (e.g., *Euphorbia*); filaments free or united, rarely branched (e.g., *Ricinus*); anthers 2-celled; rudiments of ovary present or absent. Carpels—in female flowers (3); ovary superior, *generally 3-celled* with axile placentation, each cell containing *1* or *2 pendulous* anatropous ovules with ventral raphe; micropyle carunculate, staminodes present or absent; styles 3, free or united at the base, each often 2-lobed; stigmas 3 or 6. Fruit—

schizocarp-capsule (*regma*), sometimes drupe-like. Seeds—albuminous, *carunculate*. Embryo—straight or bent.

Floral formula

♂ flowers—P_{3-5} $A_{1-\infty}$ G_0

♀ flowers—P_{3-5} A_0 $G_{(3)}$ or more

Number and distribution

This family consisting of 283 genera and about 7,300 species which are chiefly found in the tropics, shows a considerable variety of habit from mesophytic to xerophytic tendencies, the latter being much more common to dry rocky soils of India.

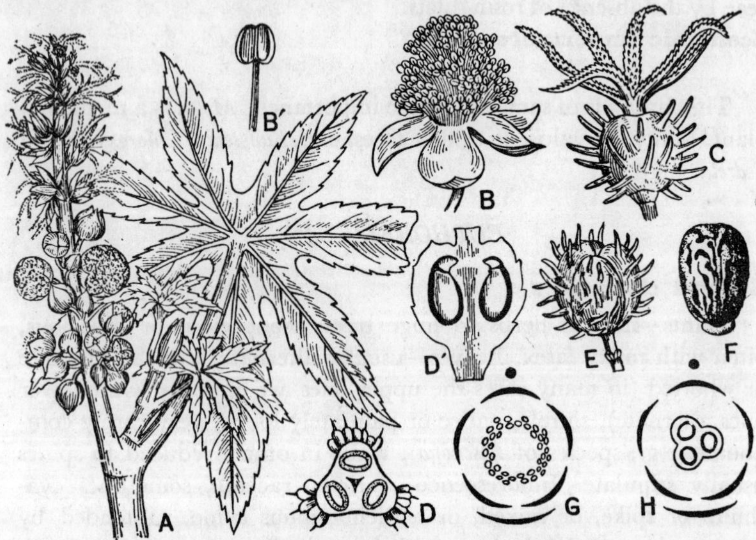

Fig. 604. Euphorbiaceae (*Ricinus communis*).
A, Portion of a flowering shoot; B, Staminate flower; B′, Stamen; C, Pistillate flower; D′, T.s. of ovary; D, L.s. of the same; E, Fruit; F, Seed; G, Floral diagram of a staminate flower; H, The same of a pistillate flower.

KEY TO GENERA

A. Flowers aggregate, monoecious (in cyathium):

Involucre regular, each segment alternates with free gland; ovary 3-locular with 8 ovules in each .. .. *Euphorbia*.

Involucre slipper-shaped, drawn into a spur, glandular within .. .. *Pedilanthus*.

Involucre urn-shaped, single stamen .. .. *Poinsettia*.

B. Flowers separate, monoecious, not reduced to single stamens and pistils:

(*a*) Cells of ovary 2-ovuled—

Herbs, shrubs or trees; leaves distichous, alternate; branchlets often resembling pinnate leaves; petals 0; disc of distinct scales .. .. .. *Phyllanthus.*

(*b*) Cells of ovary 1-ovuled; flowers in spikes or racemes; sepals imbricate; petals present in male fls.—

Petals present or obsolete in female flowers; disc of 4–6 glands opposite the sepals .. .. *Croton.*

Petals absent in female flowers; disc of 5–6 glands alternate with petals; garden shrubs with ornamental leaves .. .. *Codiaeum.*

(*c*) Cells of ovary 1-ovuled; flowers in spikes or racemes; calyx segments 5, valvate; petals 5 in male flowers, disc of 5 glands alternate with petals; herbs or undershrubs; leaves sinuate, toothed; wavy or plicate, 2-glandular at the base .. .. *Chrozophora.*

(*i*) Herbs or shrubs; leaves toothed or crenate, rarely entire; flowers in racemes or spikes, male flowers without bracts, female flowers with accrescent leafy bracts; sepals 4; petals 0 .. .. *Acalypha.*

(*ii*) Tall annuals, sometimes shrubs; leaves large, broad, palmately lobed, lobes 7 or more, serrate; calyx of 3–5 valvate segments; petals of male and female flowers 0; stamens numerous, filaments united, branched; flowers in terminal panicles .. *Ricinus.*

(*iii*) A climbing herb with hispid stinging hairs; male sepals valvate and female sepals imbricate .. *Tragia.*

(*iv*) Trees and shrubs; leaves serrate or toothed; flowers in terminal spikes or racemes; calyx of 2–3 valvate segments; stamens 2 or 3; petals 0 in male and female flowers .. .. *Sapium.*

(*v*) Herbs, shrubs or trees, often glandular or prickly; leaves often lobed; sepals and petals 5; stamens many, filaments of inner series united; central flowers in the cyme or in forks usually female, flowers scarlet, purple or yellow .. .. *Jatropha.*

C. Fls. dioecious:

Trees with compound leaves .. .. .. *Bischofia.*

Plants with simple leaves—

(*i*) Large shrubs or trees; fls. axillary or leaf-opposed clusters; petals 0; stamens 10–60; pistillode absent; disc obsolete; fruit 3–4-gonous or 2–4-lobed fleshy capsule; leaves alternate .. *Gelonium.*

(*ii*) Trees; male flowers clustered, female subsolitary; calyx 3–6-lobed; stamens 2–4; style short, dilated into broad fleshy arms; fruit a one-celled drupe .. *Putranjiva.*

(*iii*) Shrubs or trees flowers in spikes or racemes; calyx 3–8-toothed; stamens 2–5; fruit a small drupe crowned with terminal stigmas .. .. *Antidesma.*

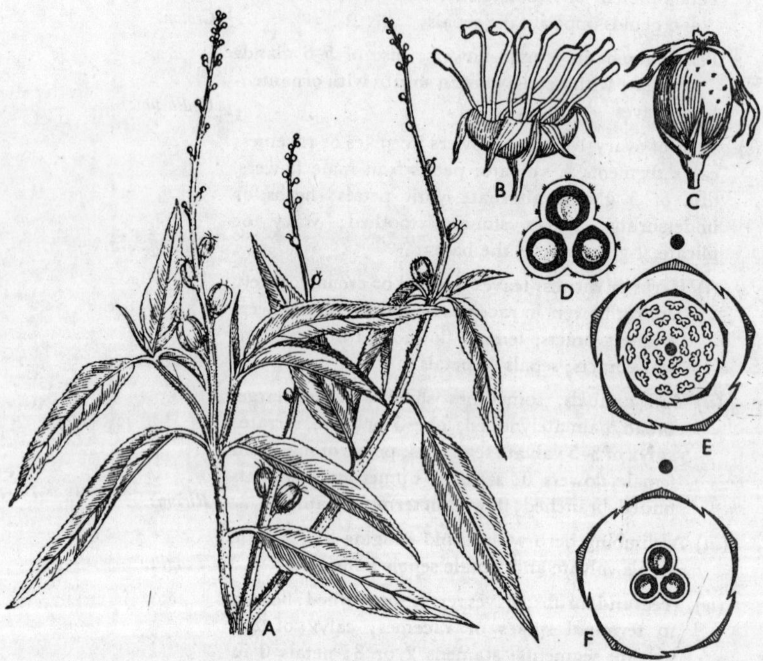

Fig. 605. Euphorbiaceae (*Croton bonplandianum*). A, Portion of a flowering shoot; B, Staminate flower; C, Pistillate flower; D. T.s. of ovary; E, Floral diagram of a staminate flower; F, The same of a pistillate flower.

(*iv*) Trees; fls. in racemes; stamens 4–8, filaments short; ovary 2–3-celled; fruit fleshy capsule; testa with a thick fleshy covering .. .. *Baccaurea.*

(*v*) Trees or shrubs; leaves opposite or alternate; fls. minute, apetalous in spike or panicle; stamens numerous, anther cells 2, globose, adnate to the broad connective; fruit capsule; female fls. often with disc .. .. *Mallotus.*

(*vi*) Trees, with opposite leaves; male flowers in raceme, female flowers few, disc never present; fruit drupe; gall structures commonly occur in leaves .. .. *Trewia*.

(*vii*) Shrubs or small trees; leaves alternate or opposite; flowers rarely monoecious; petals in male and female flowers 0, disc 0; fruit a capsule of 3 cocci separating from the columella with twisted valves; common in salt areas of Sundribans .. *Excoecaria*.

Range of floral structures

This family has a wide range in floral structures and organization.

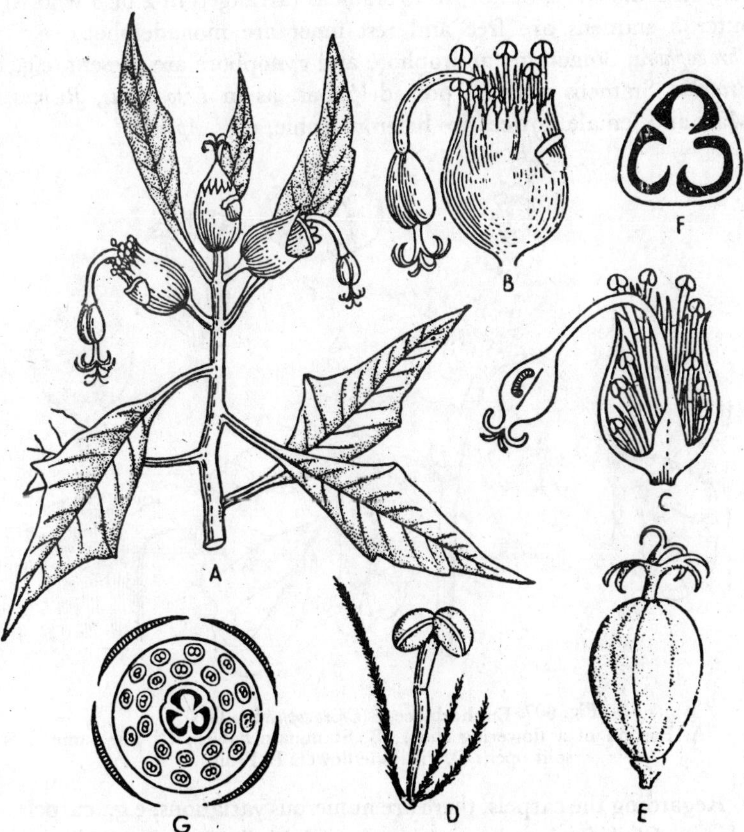

Fig. 606. Euphorbiaceae (*Poinsettia pulcherrima*).
A, Portion of a flowering shoot; B, Inflorescence; C, T.s. of the same; D, Staminate flower; E, Pistillate flower; F, T.s. of ovary; G, Floral diagram of cyathium.

The flowers may be diplochlamydeous, bisexual and pentamerous. The perianth leaves are free or connate. Number of sepals and petals varies in different cases which may be more or less than 5, as in *Phyllanthus* sp. Sepals and petals range from 4–6. Regarding the number of stamens and their disposition there are extraordinary variations. The stamens may be single, as in all members of the genus *Euphorbia*, or may be 3, 10 to several hundred, as in *Trewia*, *Ricinus*, etc. According to Eames, the stamens of *Ricinus* is the inflorescence. In many cases, about 20-25 per cent. of the total genera, the stamens are monadelphous, e.g., *Wielandia*, *Phyllanthus*, *Jatropha*, etc. In some cases, out of 10–15 stamens (arranged in 2 or 3 whorls) outer 5 stamens are free and rest inner are monadelphous, e.g., *Chrozophora*. Sometimes androphore and gynophore are present, e.g., *Bridelia*. Stamens may be polyadelphous, as in *Lesoecoccus*, *Ricinus*. Male and female flowers are heteromorphic, e.g., *Aposora*.

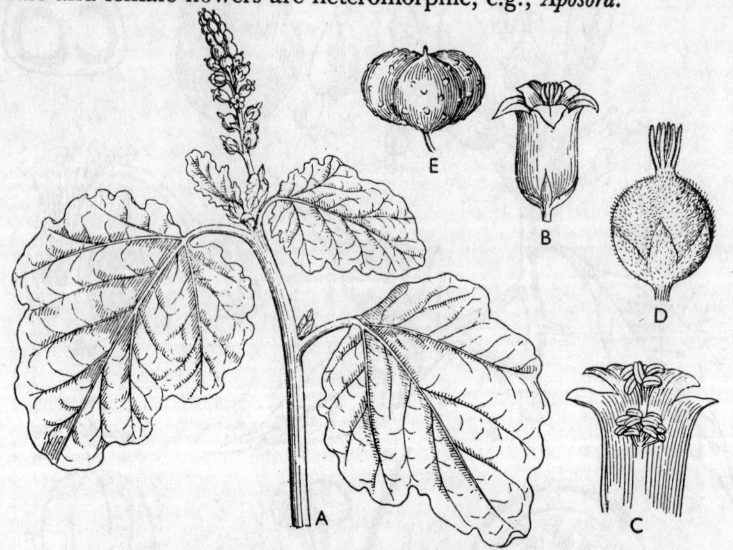

Fig. 607. Euphorbiaceae (*Chorozophora rottleri*).
A, Portion of a flowering shoot; B, Staminate flower; C, The same split open; D, Pistillate flower; E, Fruit.

Regarding the carpels, there are numerous variations, e.g., carpels 2–15 in *Glochidion*, and some species of *Phyllanthus*. In *Artilesma*, *Cometia*, etc. owing to the abortion of other carpels the ovary is 1-celled. In *Baccaurea* the ovary is 2–5-celled. In many genera, e.g., *Pridetia*, either pistillode or staminode is present.

Common plants

(1) Castor-oil plant or Castor bean (*Ricinus communis* L.), a shrub commonly cultivated for the seeds from which castor-oil is extracted. (2) Physic-nut (*Jatropha curcas* L.), and *J. gossypifolia* L. and *J. glandulifera* Roxb., are common shrubs on roadsides or hedges. (3) *Jatropha multifida* L., a common garden plant with red flowers. (4) *Jatropha thomsoni*, a favourite garden plant. (5) *Euphorbia pulcherrima* Willd. =*Poinsettia pulcherrima* R. Garh., a common garden plant with vermilion-coloured leafy bracts. (6) *E. antiquorum* L., another common hedge plant with fleshy three-angled stem. (7) *Pedilanthus tithymaloides* Poit., a common hedge plant. (8) *Croton sperciflorum* Morr. =*C. bonplandianum* Baill, a common weed of waste places. (9) *Euphorbia neriifolia* L., a shrub with obovate

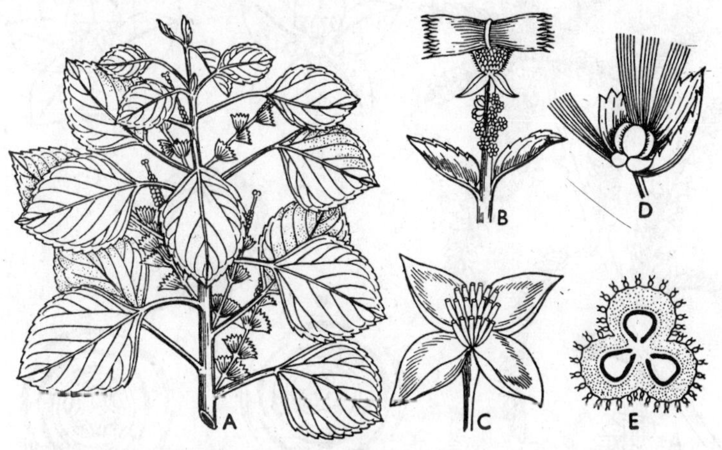

Fig. 608. Euphorbiaceae (*Acalypha indica*).
A, Portion of a flowering shoot; B, Inflorescence; C, Staminate flower; D, Pistillate flower; E, T.s. of ovary.

leaves; Milk hedge (*E. tirucauli* L.) is cultivated as a hedge plant. (10) *Euphorbia thymifolia* Burm. =*E. nivulla* L., *E. pilulifera* L. =*E. hirta* L. and *E. macrophylla* Heyne, are very small prostrate weeds of pathways. (11) *Phyllanthus emblica* L. =*Emblica officinalis* Gaertn. and *P. distichus* Muell. =*Cicca acida* Merr. are common fruit trees. (12) *Phyllanthus-raternus* L., and *P. simplex* Retz., common weeds. (13) *Trewia nudiflora* L., a common, deciduous tree. (14) Indian stinging nettle (*Tragia involucrata* L.) a comon weed with stinging hairs. (15) *Acalypha indica* L. and *A. fallax* Muell.-Arg., are common weeds of waste places with a green bract enclosing the female flowers. (16) *Acalypha hispida*, a favourite garden plant with long pendulous catkins. (17) Croton-oil plant (*Croton tiglium* L.). (18) Chrozophora rattleri Klotz. f. (Syn. *C. Plicata Jook.*) a common weed. (19) *Baccaurea sapida* Muell., commonly found in Bangla Desh which produces delicious edible fruits like mangosteen. (20) *Excoecaria agallocha* L., commonly found in Sundribans whose latex produces blisters on skin. (21) Monkey-face tree (*Mallotus philippinensis* Muell.-Arg.), a tree known for its anthelmentic, vermifugal and purgative properties. (22) Manihot (*Manihot utilissima* Pohl. = *M. esculenta* Crantz.), produces the cassava starch. (23) Para-rubber (*Hevea brasiliensis*), a

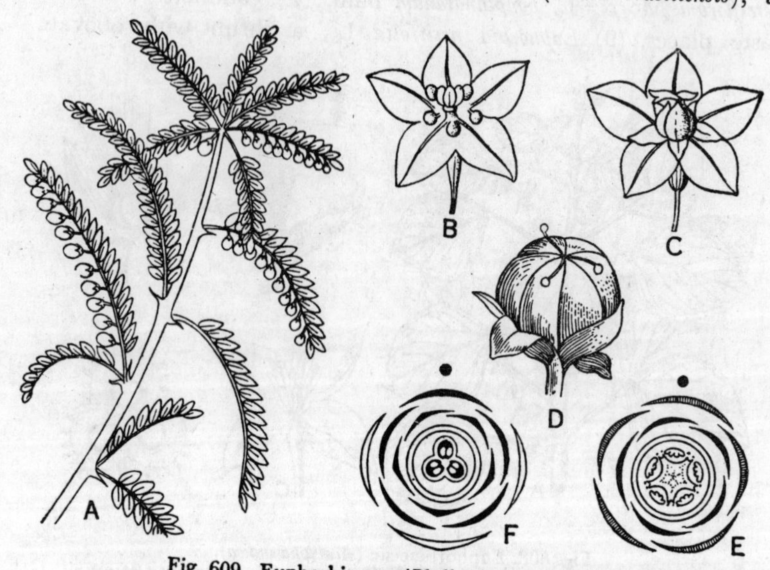

Fig. 609. Euphorbiaceae (*Phyllanthus-raternus*).
A. Portion of a flowering shoot; B, Staminate flower; C, Pistillate flower; D, Fruit; E, Floral diagram of staminate flower; F, The same of pistillate flower.

rubber-producing plant. (24) *Bischofia javanica* Bl. and *Putranjiva roxburghii* Wall., are common avenue trees. (25) *Antidesma ghesembilla* Gaertn., a common shrub of villages. (26) Garden croton (*Codiaeum variegatum* Bl.), (27) *Sapium indicum* Willd. found in the Sundribans. (28) *Sapium sebiferum* Roxb., very common. (29) *Gelonium multiflorum* A. Juss., very common.

Affinity

This family is closely allied to Malvales, particularly Sterucliaceae, owing to the presence of monadelphous stamens in about 25 per cent. of the total genera, the presence of pistillode and staminode and occasionally androphore and gynophore and in nature of embryo. The family might have been evolved from the ancester of Malvales by suppression of inner whorl of perianth and abortion of one of the stamens or carpels. Bentham and Hooker placed the

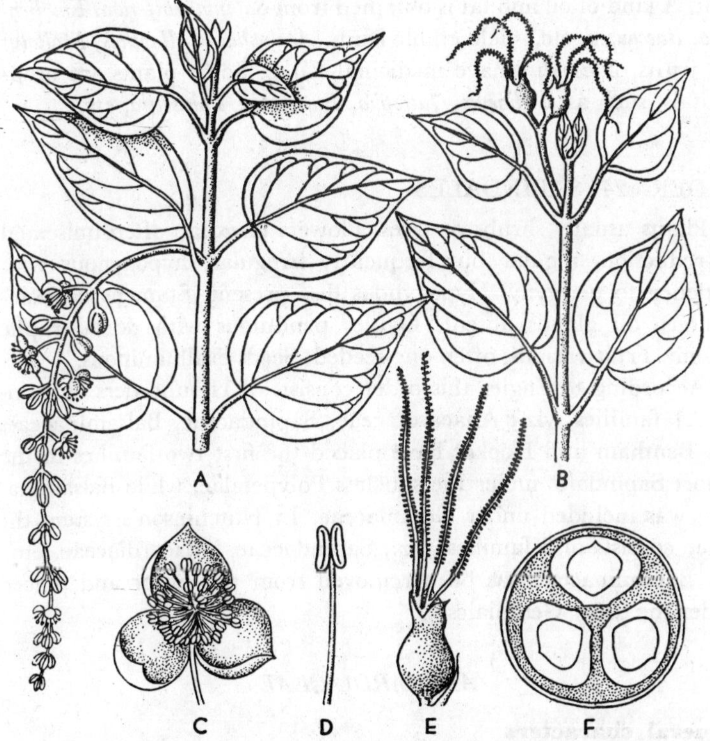

Fig. 610. Euphorbiaceae (*Trewia nudiflora*).
A, Portion of a staminate shoot; B, Portion of a pistillate shoot; C, Staminate flower; D, Stamen; E, Pistillate flower; F, T.s. of ovary.

family in series Unisexuales under the subclass Monochlamydeae. Wettstein is of opinion that it is primitive due to unisexual monochlamydeous flower. Euphorbiaceae is readily distinguished by the milky latex, unisexual flowers, 3-carpellate and 3-celled ovary with

1 or 2 pendulous ovules having ventral raphe in each cell, and carunculate seed.

Economic importance

This family is of great economic importance. Rubber is obtained from *Hevea brasiliensis* and *Manihot glaziovii*. A kind of starch and Brazilian arrowroot are obtained from *Manihot utilissima*. Castor-oil is obtained from *Ricinus communis* and tung oil from *Aleurites fordii*. A kind of oil and fat is obtained from *Sapium sebiferum*. *Emblica*, *Cicca*, *Baccaurea*, etc., yield edible fruits. *Acalypha*, *Phyllanthus*, *Mallotus* and fruits of *Emblica* have medicinal value. Some plants are ornamentals, such as, *Codiaeum*, *Jatropha*, *Euphorbia*, *Poinsettia*, etc.

ORDER 24. SAPINDALES

Plants usually shrubs or trees. Flowers bisexual, often unisexual by reduction, regular but frequently irregular, hypogynous with tendency to perigyny. Hypogynous disc present. Stamens diplostemonous, oil glands absent. Ovules pendulous with dorsal raphe present. Fruit various, often one-seeded. Seeds exalbuminous.

According to Engler this order consists of 11 suborders containing 21 families, viz., Anacardiaceae, Sapindaceae, Balsaminaceae, etc. Bentham and Hooker have placed the first two families in the cohort Sapindales under the subclass Polypetalae, while Balsaminaceae was included under Geraniaceae. In Hutchinson's system the order consists of 9 families, viz., Sapindaceae, Anacardiaceae, etc., but Balsaminaceae has been removed from this order and placed under the order Geraniales.

ANACARDIACEAE

General characters

Plants—trees or shrubs, *often with resinous juice*. Leaves—alternate (but opposite in *Dobinea*), usually *simple* (but compound in *Spondias*, *Odina* and *Rhus*), exstipulate. Inflorescence—cymose panicle, terminal or axillary. Flowers—small, regular, bisexual but often unisexual by reduction, with more or less *cup-shaped glandular disc between the stamens*. Sepals—usually 5, connate, united at the base. Petals usually 5, free. Stamens—10 in 2 whorls, free, usually fewer (1 in *Anacardium*, 5 in *Rhus*) arising from the rim of an intrastaminal disc. Carpels—usually 3–5, united, but functionally 1; ovary 1-celled (rarely 5-celled, e.g., *Spondias* and *Buchanania*), *ovule solitary, anatropous with a dorsal raphe;* style usually 1, eccentric. Fruit—usually a *drupe*, sometimes nut. Seed—exalbuminous. Embryo—curved, with fleshy cotyledons.

Floral formula

$\oplus$ ⚥ $K_5\ C_5\ A_{10}\ \underline{G}_{(1-5)}$

Number and distribution

This family consists of 73 genera and about 600 species which are chiefly found in the tropics.

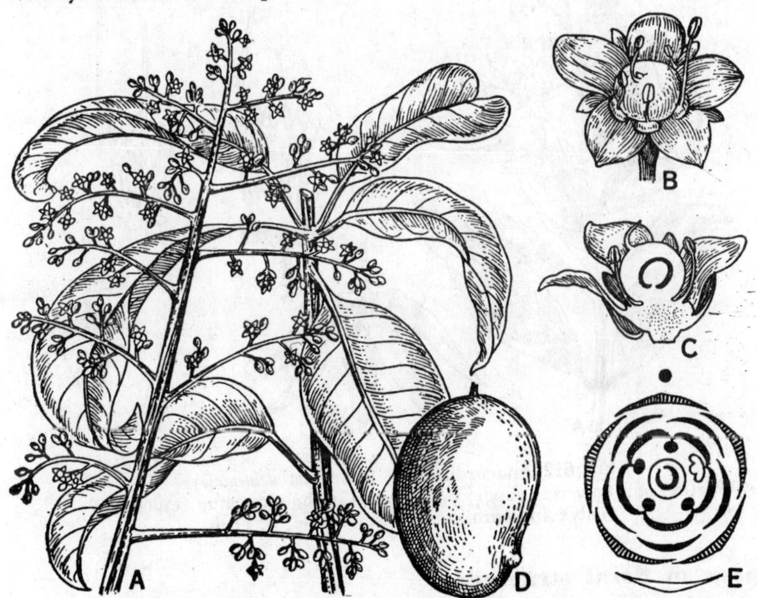

Fig. 611. Anacardiaceae (*Mangifera indica*).
A, Portion of a flowering shoot; B, Flower; C, V.s. of the same; D, Fruit; E, Floral diagram.

KEY TO GENERA

A. Ovary 1- or 2-celled:

(*a*) Leaves alternate; perianth not fleshy—

(*i*) Calyx 4–5; corolla 4–6; leaf pinnate .. *Rhus.*

(*ii*) Calyx 4–5; stamens 5 (usually 1 fertile); style 1, filiform; leaf simple .. .. .. *Mangifera.*

(*iii*) Calyx 5; stamens 8–10 (usually with staminodes); style 1, filiform; torus striated; leaf simple .. *Anacardium*.

(*iv*) Calyx 3–5; stamens 10; carpels 5 or 6 (all but one sterile), leaf simple .. .. *Buchanania*.

(*b*) Leaves 3-foliate or pinnate; petals imbricate; stamens 8–10; styles 3–4; fls. polygamous .. .. *Odina*.

(*c*) Leaves simple
Petals imbricate; stamens 5; styles 3; ft. drupe on an enlarged peduncle .. .. .. *Semecarpus*.

B. Ovary 2–5-celled; ovules pendulous from the top; leaves compound; fls. polygamous; stamens 8–10; styles 4–5, free above .. .. *Spondias*.

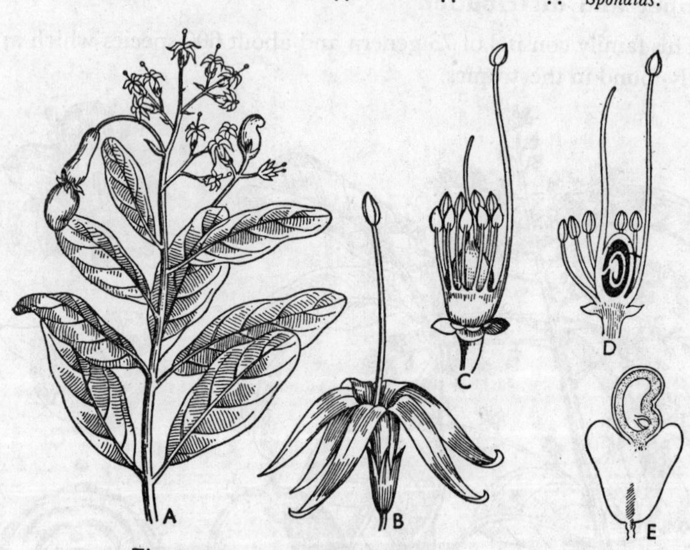

Fig. 612. Anacardiaceae (*Anacardium occidentale*).
A, Portion of a flowering shoot; B, Flower; C, The same after removal of calyx and corolla; D, V.s. of same; E, Fruit.

Range of floral structures

This family also exhibits a little variation in the floral parts.

The flowers are generally bisexual but sometimes unisexual by the obliteration of stamens or pistils.

The members of this family show wide variation in the form of floral axis. The floral disc is generally convex in form. In some cases a cup-like floral disc (receptacle) is found between stamens and pistil, e.g., *Rhus*, or the floral axis becomes occasionally lengthened or thickened, as in *Mangifera indica*.

The variation in the number of stamens is also noticeable. In the genus *Buchanania*, all the 10 stamens are fertile; *Rhus* has only 5 stamens; 10–7 stamens occur in *Anacardium* but 1 stamen is found to be fertile; there are 5 antisepalous stamens in *Mangifera* but ultimately 1 stamen becomes fertile.

The variation in the number of carpels and chambers of ovary is also manifested in many genera of this family. The number of carpels is 5 in *Buchanania*, where only one ovule develops into seed on maturation. In the genera, such as, *Mangifera* and *Anacardium* there occur 1 carpel in each. Ovary is usually 1-celled, rarely 5-celled, as in *Buchanania*.

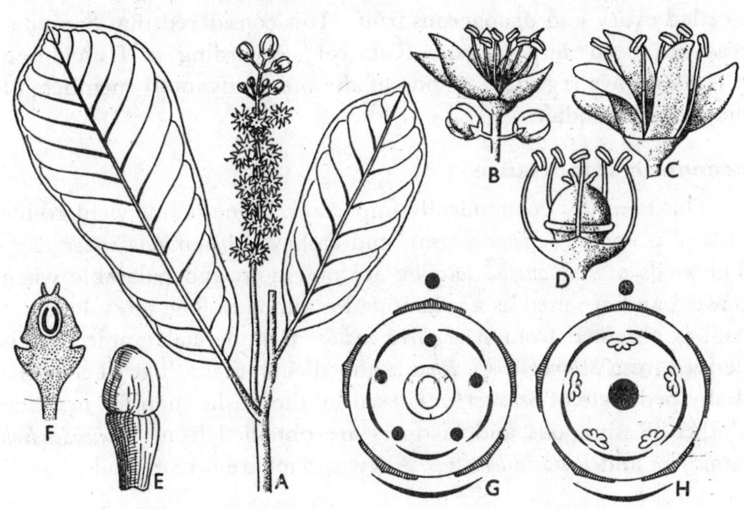

Fig. 613. Anacardiaceae (*Semecarpus anacardium*). A, Portion of a flowering shoot; B, A part of an inflorescence; C, A bisexual flower; D, The same after removal of sepals and petals; E, Fruit; F, L.s. of ovary; G–H, Floral diagrams of pistillate and staminate flowers respectively.

Common plants

(1) Mango (*Mangifera indica* L.), a common fruit tree found throughout India. (2) Cashew-nut (*Anacardium occidentale* L.), abundantly found along the coast of Bay of Bengal and remarkable for the fleshy enlargement of the peduncle supporting the kidney-shaped nut. (3) Marking-nut (*Semecarpus anacardium* L.), found in

villages with a fleshy enlargement of the peduncle bearing a roundish nut, the juice of which is chiefly used by the washerman for marking clothes. (4) Hogplum (*Spondias dulce* Willd.). (5) Indian hogplum (*Spondias mangifera* Willd.=*S. pinnata* Kurz.). (6) Indian ash tree (*Odina woodier* Roxb.=*Lannea coromandelina* Merr.) yields copious gummy substance. (7) Sumac (*Rhus succedanea* L.), commonly found in Assam. (8) *Buchanania latifolia* Roxb.=*B. lanzan* Spreng., a medium-sized tree. (9) Green almond (*Pistacia vera* L.) yields pistacia nuts.

Affinity

This family is allied to Sapindaceae but readily distinguished by the presence of resinous juice and intrastaminal disc, the usually 1-celled ovary and drupaceous fruit. It is considered that Sapindaceae has been derived from Rutaceae. According to Hutchinson it is nowadays regarded as one of the more advanced members of the order Sapindales.

Economic importance

This family is economically important. Some plants yield edible nuts of pistachio (*Pistacia vera*), and cashew (*Anacardium occidentale*). The seeds of *Buchanania latifolia* are nutritious and palatable when roasted and are used as a substitute for almonds. The most delicious fruit is obtained from *Mangifera indica*. Commercial tannic acid is derived from *Schinopsis* sp. *Rhus* is a medicinal plant. The juice of the fleshy peduncle of *Semecarpus* is used by the washerman for marking clothes. Resins, oils and lacquers are obtained from *Toxicodendron vernicifera* and *Pistacia lentiscus*. A few species are ornamentals.

SAPINDACEAE

General characters

Plants—trees or shrubs, sometimes tendril-climbers (e.g., *Cardiospermum*). Leaves—alternate, usually pinnately *compound*, exstipulate (but stipulate in climbing species). Inflorescence—*cymose panicle* (excepting *Cardiospermum*, which has a dichotomous cyme). Flowers—small, regular or irregular, bi- or unisexual, apparently polygamous, with an annular or oblique *disc between the petals and stamens*, pentamerous. Sepals—5, generally free, but in regular flowers frequently 4 by the union of the third and the fifth, imbricate. Petals—5, but become 4 by suppression of a petal, rarely 0, free, *often provided with scales,* imbricate. Stamens—usually 8 or 10 in two whorls, free, inserted inside the disc or outside it or on it. Carpels—(3); ovary 3-celled, lobed or entire, with one *ascending ovule with a ventral raphe* in each cell; style terminal. Fruit—dry (a nut or capsule), or fleshy (berry or drupe). Seed—exalbuminous, *often with an aril.* Embryo—curved or convoluted.

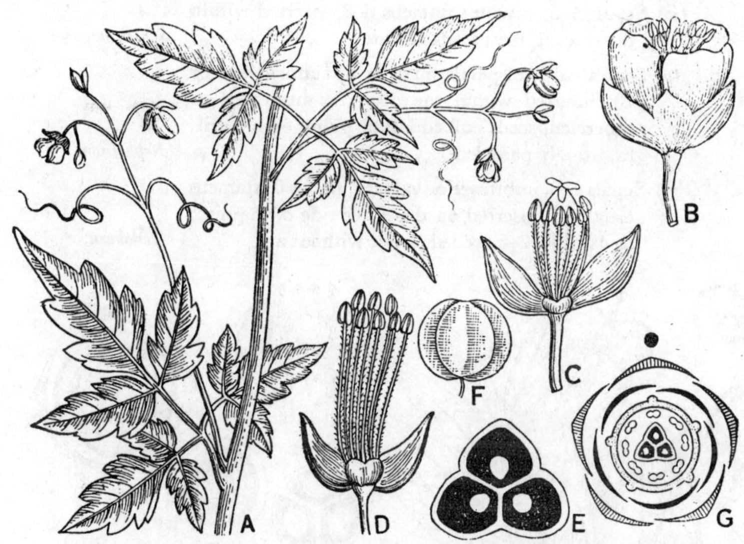

Fig. 614. Sapindaceae (*Cardiospermum halicacabum*). A, Portion of a flowering shoot; B, Flower; C, The same after removal of corolla; D, Stamens; E, T.s. of ovary; F, Fruit; G, Floral diagram.

Floral formula

⊕ or ↑ ⚥ K_5 $C_{5 \text{ or } 0}$ A_{8-10} $\underline{G_{(3)}}$

Number and distribution

This family consists of 130 genera and about 1,100 species which are chiefly found in the tropics.

Key to Genera

A. Irregular flowers; disc one-sided:

(*a*) Fruit capsule, inflated; ovule solitary; inflorescence axis turns into tendril .. .. .. *Cardiospermum.*

(*b*) Fruit divides into 1 or 3 indehiscent oblong lobes; leaves pinnate .. .. *Erioglossum.*

(*c*) Fruit indehiscent—

(*i*) Leaves digitately 3- or 1-foliate .. .. *Allophylus*.

(*ii*) Leaves paripinnate; stamens outside the disc .. *Aphania*.

B. Regular flowers; disc central:

(*d*) Fruit deeply divided into 1–3 lobes—

(*iii*) Sepals 4–5, imbricate; ft. smooth; seed without aril; stamens usually 8 .. .. *Sapindus*.

(*iv*) Sepals 4–5, valvate; stamens 6–8, inserted within the disc; ft. dry; seeds arillate .. .. *Schleichera*.

(*v*) Sepals valvate; petals small or 0; stamens 6–8 or 10, inserted within the disc; ft. muricated or tubercled, seeds embedded in pulpy edible aril; fls. usually panicled .. .. .. *Nephelium*.

(*vi*) Sepals 2–5, imbricate or valvate; petals 0; stamens usually 8, inserted on the outer side of the disc; ft. capsule, 2–6-seeded; seeds without aril .. *Dodonaea*.

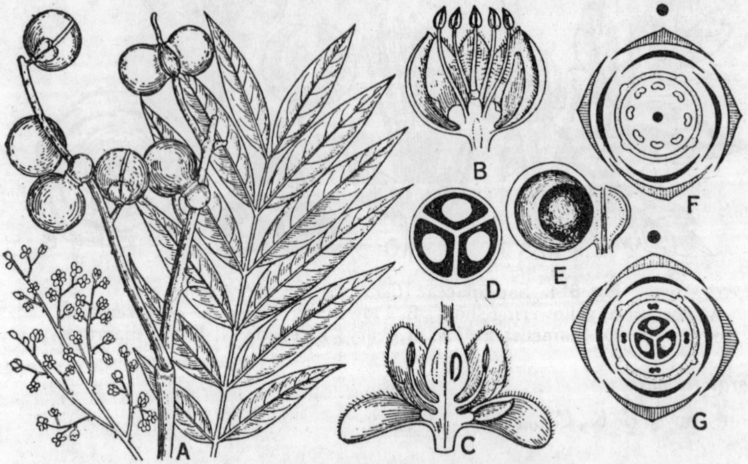

Fig. 615. Sapindaceae (*Sapindus trifoliatus*).
A, Portions of twigs with flowers and fruits; B, V.s. of a staminate flower; C, L.s. of a pistillate flower; D, T.s. of ovary; E, T.s. of a fruit; F, Floral diagram of staminate flower; G, The same of pistillate flower.

Range of floral structures

Variation in floral structures is also noted in this family. Both regular and zygomorphic flowers occur. *Sapindus*, *Nephelium* and *Litchi* have regular flowers; irregular flowers occur in *Cardiospermum*, *Erioglossum*, *Allophylus* and *Aphania*.

Flowers may be unisexual or bisexual. Bisexual and staminate flowers are found in some species, while bisexual and pistillate flowers occur in others.

Variation in the number of petals also occurs. Petals are found to be absent in some genera, such as, *Dodonaea*, *Schleichera*, etc.

The number of stamens also differs in different genera. Stamens are usually 8. The typical pentamerous genus *Turpinia* possesses 5 stamens. Multiple stamens are noted in the African genus *Deinbollia*.

The number of style in most cases is one, but it varies from 2–4; ovary 3-locular, but rarely number of the loculi is reduced to 1, 2 or 4.

Common plants

(1) Litchi (*Nephelium litchi* Camb. = *Litchi chinensis* Sonner), a common fruit tree. (2) Longan (*Nephelium longana* Camb. = *Euphoria longana* Lamk.), often cultivated for its edible fruits. (3) Soapberry trees (*Sapindus trifoliatus* L. = *S. emarginatus* Vahl. and *S. mukorossi* Gaertn.), yield fruits which make lather with water. (4) Balloon-vine (*Cardiospermum halicacabum* L.), a common weed with wiry stem found in waste places. (5) *Allophylus cobbe* Blume = *A. serratus* Radlk., a small tree or shrub sometimes met with in hedges. (6) *Aphania danura* Radlk., chiefly found in the Sundribans. (7) *Erioglossum edule* Blume, usually found in village-shrubberies. (8) Ceylon oak (*Schleichera trijuga* Willd. = *S. olesa* Oken.), a large tree. (9) *Dodonaea viscosa* Jacq., a twining undershrub.

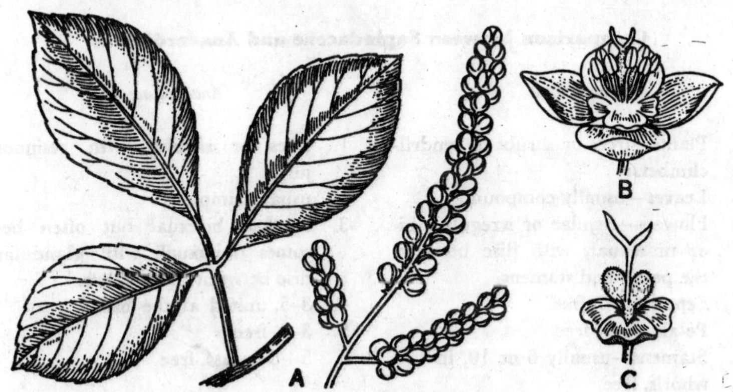

Fig. 616. Sapindaceae (*Allophylus cobbe*).
A, A compound leaf and inflorescence; B, Staminate flower; C, Pistillate flower.

Affinity

This family is allied to Anacardiaceae from which it is distinguished by the pinnately compound leaves, mostly irregular polygamous flowers, scaly outgrowths on petals, usually eight stamens, tricarpellate ovary and arillate seeds. Warburg is of opinion that Sabiaceae and Sapindaceae are two closely related families. The arillate seed establishes a link with Euphorbiaceae.

Economic importance

Economically, this family is not of much importance. *Nephelium litchi* yields a fleshy edible aril. Longan (*Nephelium longana*) also yields an inferior quality of edible aril. The pericarp of the fruits of soapberry trees (*Sapindus trifoliatus* and *S. mukorossi*) produces lather with water, which is used for cleansing woollen garments. *Cardiospermum*, *Allophylus*, *Dodonaea* are medicinal plants. The varnish tree (*Koelreuteria paniculata*), *Xanthoceras sorbifolia*, *Melicocca*, *Ungnadia* are ornamental plants.

Comparison between Sapindaceae and Anacardiaceae

Sapindaceae	*Anacardiaceae*
1. Plants—trees or shrubs or tendril-climbers.	1. trees or shrubs, with resinous juice.
2. Leaves—usually compound.	2. usually simple.
3. Flowers—regular or irregular, bi- or unisexual, with disc between the petals and stamens.	3. regular, bisexual but often becomes unisexual, with glandular disc between the stamens.
4. Sepals—4–5, free.	4. 3–5, united at the base.
5. Petals—4–5, free.	5. 3–5, free.
6. Stamens—usually 8 or 10, in two whorls, free.	6. 5+5 or less, free.
7. Carpels—(3); ovary 3-celled, each cell containing one ascending ovule with a ventral raphe.	7. 1; ovary usually 1-celled, containing one anatropous ovule with a dorsal raphe.
8. Fruit—usually a nut or capsule.	8. usually a drupe, sometimes nut.

BALSAMINACEAE

General characters

Plants—annual terrestrial herbs, sometimes aquatic (e.g., *Hydrocera*), with succulent stems. Leaves—alternate, opposite or whorled, simple, serrate, exstipulate. Flowers—irregular, bisexual, hypogynous. Sepals—5, *petaloid, the posterior one is very large and spurred*, imbricate. Petals—5, the anterior one is the largest. Stamens—5; filaments short and broad; *anthers united covering the pistil like a hood.* Carpels—(5); ovary superior, oblong, 5-celled with a row of pendulous anatropous ovules in each cell, *stigma sessile*, often *5-toothed*. Fruit—capsule, *dehisces elastically into 5 valves.* Seeds—exalbuminous with a straight embryo.

Floral formula

↑ ☿ $K_5\ C_5\ A_5\ \underline{G_{(5)}}$

Number and distribution

This family consists of 2 genera, *Impatiens* and *Hydrocera*, and about 450 species which are commonly distributed on the hills.

Common plants

(1) Balsam (*Impatiens balsamina* L.), a herb commonly planted in gardens. (2) *I. roylei* is very common in the Himalayas. (3) *Hydrocera triflora* W. & A., an annual aquatic weed rooting at the nodes.

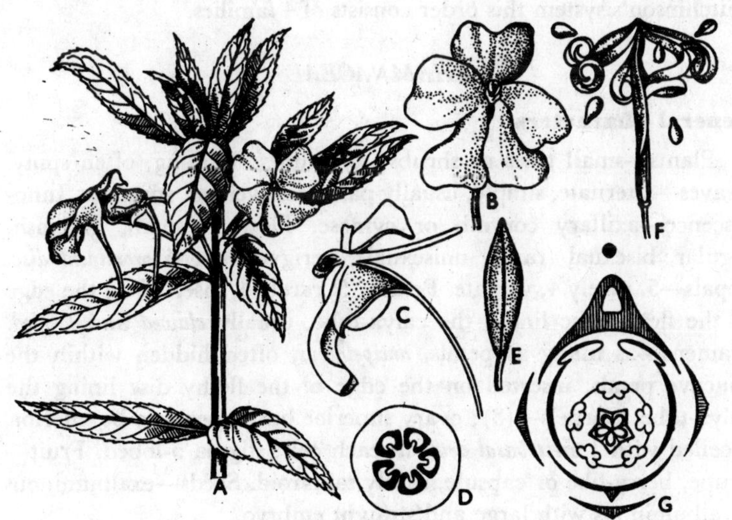

Fig. 617. Balsaminaceae (*Impatiens balsamina*).
A, Portion of a flowering shoot; B, Flower; C, V.s. of the same; D, T.s. of ovary; E, Young fruit; F, Dehiscing mature fruit; G, Floral diagram.

Affinity

Balsaminaceae is distinguished from its allied families by the presence of a spurred sepal, union of anthers round the pistil, and elastic dehiscence of capsular fruit.

Economic importance

This family is of very little economic importance. Different species of *Impatiens* are planted in gardens as ornamentals.

ORDER 25. RHAMNALES

Usually woody plants, mostly climbing. Flowers bisexual, often with a tendency of unisexuality. Calyx-lobes very small or calyx entire. Intrastaminal disc well-developed. Stamens in one whorl, as many as the sepals, antipetalous. Ovary usually with 1 or 2 ascending ovules.

According to Engler this order consists of 2 families, viz., Rhamnaceae and Vitaceae. Bentham and Hooker have placed the aforesaid families in the cohort Celastrales under the subclass Polypetalae. In Hutchinson's system this order consists of 4 families.

RHAMNACEAE

General characters

Plants—small trees or shrubs, sometimes climbing, often spiny. Leaves—alternate, simple, usually palmately veined, stipulate. Inflorescence—axillary corymb or cymose. Flowers—small, greenish, regular, bisexual (rarely unisexual), perigynous *with prominent disc.* Sepals—5, rarely 4, valvate. Petals—5, rarely 4, inserted on the edge of the fleshy disc lining the calyx-tube, usually *clawed* and *hooded.* Stamens—as many as petals, *antipetalous*, often hidden within the concave petals, inserted on the edge of the fleshy disc lining the calyx-tube. Carpels—(3); ovary superior but appears to be inferior, 3-celled with 1 *erect basal ovule* in each cell; stigma 5-lobed. Fruit—drupe, berry-like or capsule, rarely samaroid. Seeds—exalbuminous or albuminous with large and straight embryo.

Floral formula

$\oplus$ ⚥ $K_{5 \text{ or } 4} C_{5 \text{ or } 4} A_{5 \text{ or } 4} \underline{G_{(3)}}$

Number and distribution

This family consists of 45 genera with 550 species, which are found in the tropical and subtropical regions.

KEY TO GENERA

A. Armed shrubs and trees with prominent 3-nerved leaves; ovary sunken in disc; fruit fleshy with hard 1–3-celled, 1–3-celled core; seed albuminous .. .. *Zizyphus*.

B. Unarmed climbers:

(*a*) Fruit samaroid, 1-celled, 1-seeded; seed exalbuminous *Ventilago*.

(*b*) Fruit 3-winged; fls. in panicled fascicles .. *Gouania*.

(*c*) Fruit terete; fls. subumbellate .. .. *Helinus*.

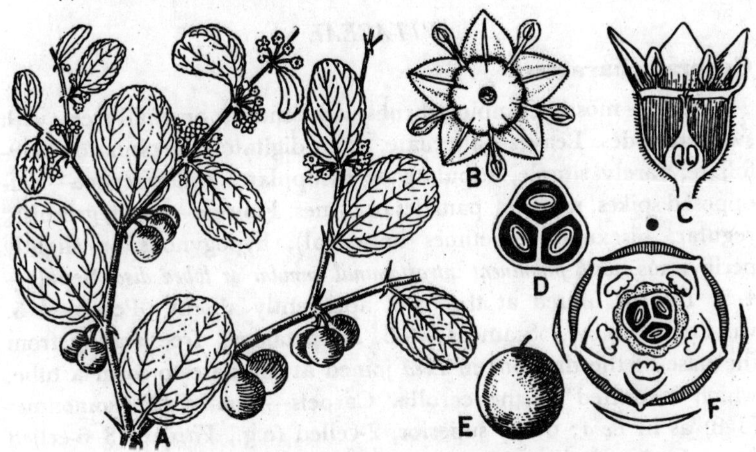

Fig. 618. Rhamnaceae (*Zizyphus jujuba*). A, Portion of a flowering shoot; B, Flower; C, V.s. of the same; D, T.s. of ovary; E, Fruit; F, Floral diagram.

Common plants

(1) The Jujube tree (*Zizyphus jujuba* Lamk. = *Z. mauratiana* Lamk.), a small tree generally cultivated for its edible fruits. (2) *Z. oenoplia* Mill., a straggling shrub, commonly found in hedges. (3) *Ventilago maderaspatana* Gaertn., a strong climber. (4) *Gouania leptostachya* DC., another strong climber. (5) *Helinus lanceolatus* Brand., a scandent cirrhose shrub.

Affinity

This family is closely related to Vitaceae, as it is evident from almost similar floral structures. It also bears affinity with Celastraceae, the main distinction is the antipetalous stamens. It differs from

Vitaceae in having simple leaves and in the structure of the receptacle. Rhamnaceae is readily distinguished by the simple unlobed leaves, perigynous flowers, antipetalous stamens and basal ovules.

Economic importance

This family contains some ornamental plants, such as, *Rhamnus*, *Ceanothus*, *Zizyphus*, *Hovenia spyridum*, etc. *Zizyphus jujuba* yields edible and tasty fruits. A pugative, *cascara sagrada*, is obtained from the Californian species, known as *Rhamnus purshiana* DC. *Rhamnus infectoria* L. and *R. chlorophora* Decene are dye-yielding plants. The wood of *R. frangula* yields a kind of fine charcoal for making cheap gunpowder.

VITACEAE

General characters

Plants—mostly climbing shrubs with tendrils, or small trees, with swollen nodes. Leaves—alternate, often digitately or pinnately 3–9-foliate, rarely simple, stipulate or exstipulate. Inflorescence—leaf-opposed spikes, racemes, panicles or cymes. Flowers—small, greenish, regular, bisexual (sometimes unisexual), hypogynous or slightly perigynous, *with prominent intrastaminal annular or lobed disc.* Sepals—4–5, free or united at the base, apparently absent. Petals—4–5, valvate, *caducous.* Stamens—4–5, antipetalous, free arising from the base of the disc but in *Leea* joined at the base to form a tube, which is united to the corolla. Carpels—usually (2), sometimes (3–8) as in *Leea;* ovary superior, 2-celled (e.g., *Vitis*) or 3–6-celled (e.g., *Leea*), usually with 1–2 ovules in each cell; stigma *capitate* or *discoid.* Fruit—*berry.* Seeds—with a strong or bony coating, and with *copious oily endosperm and a small straight embryo.*

Floral formula

$$\oplus \ ⚥ \ K_{4-5} \ \overline{C_{4-5} A_{4-5}} \ \underline{G_{(2) \text{ or } (3-8)}}$$

Number and distribution

This family consists of 11 genera and about 600 species which are chiefly found in the tropical and subtropical regions.

Key to Genera

A. Tendril-climbers; fls. in raceme or cyme clusters; stamens free; ovary 2-celled, ovules 2 in each cell .. .. *Vitis.*

B. Erect shrubs; large leaves with sheathing petioles; stamens connate; ovary 3–6-celled, 1 ovule in each cell .. *Leea.*

Common plants

(1) *Vitis quadrangularis* Wall. =*Cissus quadrangularis* L., a common climber with square stems. (2) *Vitis pedata* Vahl. =*Cayratia pedata* Gagnep., and *Vitis setosa* Wall. =*Cissus setosa* Roxb., commonly found in villages and have medicinal value. (3) *Vitis trifolia* L. =*Cayratia carnosa* Gagnep., very common. (4) Grape-vine (*Vitis vinifera* L.). (5) *Leea macrophylla* Roxb., an erect herb without tendrils, chiefly found along Siliguri Road to Sukna. (6) *Leea aequata* L., a shrub 4–10 ft. high. (7) *L. herbacea* Ham., another shrub 12–16 ft. high.

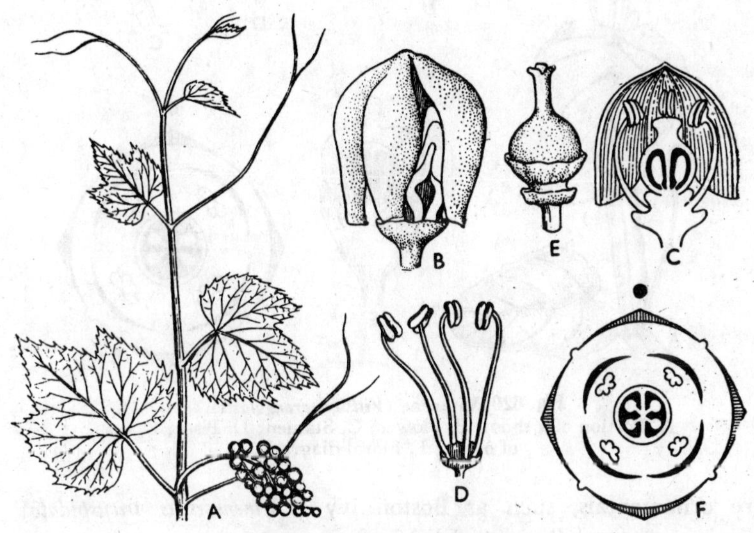

Fig. 619. Vitaceae (*Vitis vinifera*).
A, Portion of a plant; B, Flower; C, V.s. of the same; D, Stamens; E, Pistil; F, Floral diagram.

Affinity

This family bears an affinity with Rhamnaceae and members of Celastrales in the plan of floral structures, but is readily distinguished by the climbing habit, berried fruit, leaf-opposed inflorescence, antipetalous stamens, capitate or discoid stigma, and seeds with copious endosperm and small embryo. This family is considered to have been derived from Rutaceae by the suppression of antisepalous whorl of stamens.

Economic importance

This family is economically important. *Vitis vinifera* yields edible fruits from which raisins and a sort of wine are obtained. *Vitis quadrangularis*, *V. pedata* and *V. setosa* are medicinal plants. Some plants

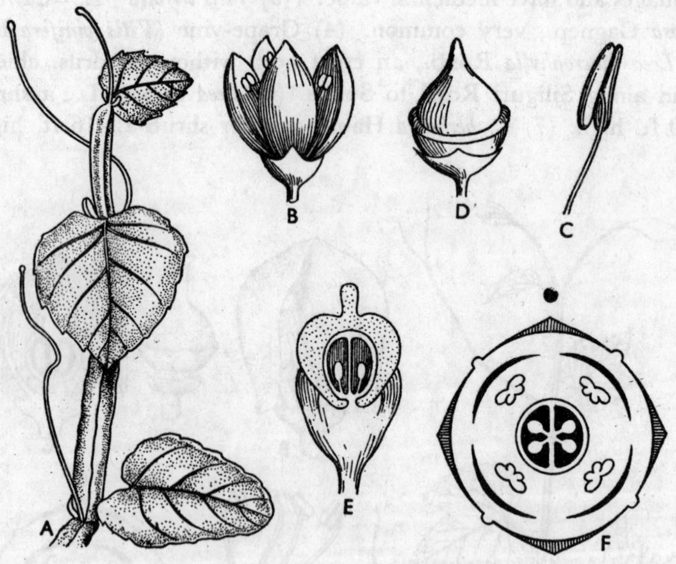

Fig. 620. Vitaceae (*Vitis quadrangularis*). A, Portion of a shoot; B, Flower; C, Stamen; D, Pistil; E, L.s. of ovary; F, Floral diagram.

are ornamentals, such as Boston ivy (*Parthenocissus tricuspidata*), Virginia creeper (*P. quinquefolia*), etc.

ORDER 26. MALVALES

Plants herbs, shrubs or trees, often with mucilage and stipulate leaves. Flowers usually bisexual, actinomorphic, cyclic, hypogynous. Perianth mostly pentamerous. Calyx valvate. Stamens usually numerous, monadelphous, polyadelphous or free with tendency of union at the base. Ovary multicarpellary. Placentation axile. Ovules anatropous.

According to Engler this order consists of 4 suborders containing 8 families, viz., Tiliaceae, Malvaceae, Bombacaceae, Sterculiaceae, etc. Bentham and Hooker designated this order as cohort Malvales consisting of 3 families, viz., Malvaceae, Sterculiaceae and Tiliaceae; Bombacaceae had no separate existence and was included in Malvaceae. In Hutchinson's system this order consists of 1 family Malvaceae only, while the other families have been put under the order Tiliales which contains 5 families.

TILIACEAE

General characters

Plants—generally trees or shrubs, sometimes herbs (e.g., *Corchorus*) with mucilage. Leaves—alternate, simple, entire or toothed, often oblique, stipulate. Inflorescence—typically *cymose*. Flowers—regular, bisexual (rarely unisexual), hypogynous. Sepals—5, free or

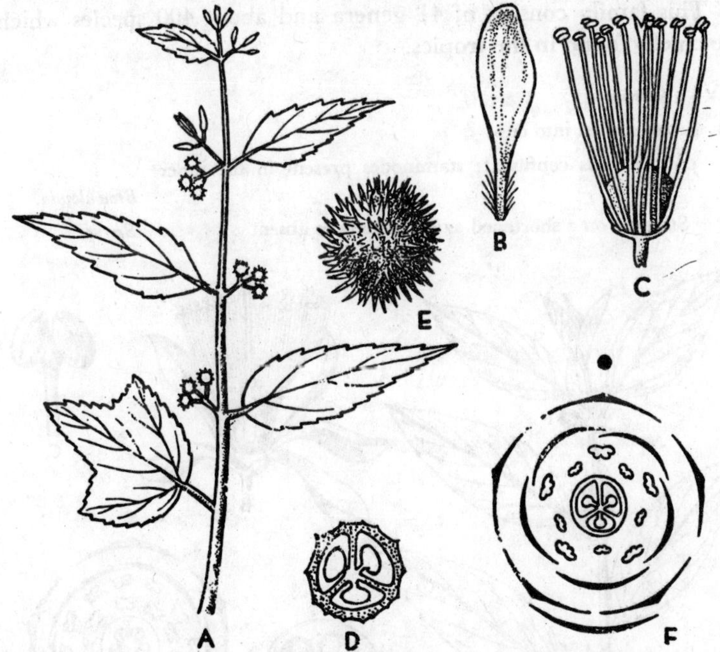

Fig. 621. Tiliaceae (*Triumfetta rhomboidea*).
A, Portion of a flowering shoot; B, Petal; C, Flower with sepals and petals removed; D, T.s. of ovary; E, Fruit; F. Floral diagram.

united at the base, caducous, valvate. Petals—5, or fewer or 0, free, imbricate or valvate. Stamens—10-numerous, free or slightly united at the base or in 5–10 bundles (*polyadelphous*), *usually inserted at the base of the petals*, but sometimes raised above the corolla by the development of an internode (*androgynophore*), as in *Grewia*, intrastaminal disc present; anthers 2-celled. Carpels—(2–5); ovary superior, 2–10-celled with 1-many ascending or pendulous ovules; style 1; stigmas as many as the locules. Fruit—fleshy (drupaceous) or dry (capsule), indehiscent or dehiscent. Seed—albuminous with a curved embryo and leafy cotyledons.

Floral formula

$\oplus$ ⚥ $K_5\ C_5\ A_{\infty \text{ or } 10}\ \underline{G_{(2-5)}}$

Number and distribution

This family consists of 41 genera and about 400 species which are chiefly found in the tropics.

KEY TO GENERA

A. Sepals united into cup:

Anther-cells confluent; staminodes present in the inner whorl .. .. *Brownlowia*.

Stamens on a shortened axis, staminodes absent .. *Berrya*.

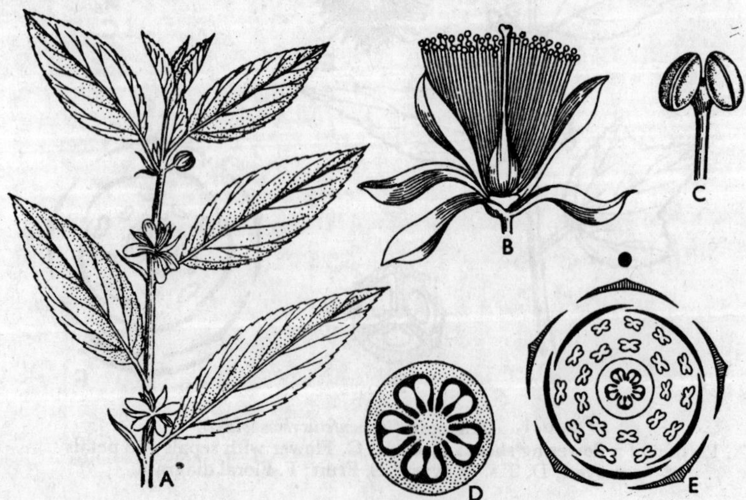

Fig. 622. Tiliaceae (*Corchorus capsularis*).
A, Portion of a flowering shoot; B, Flower; C, Stamen; D, T.s. of ovary; E, Floral diagram.

B. Sepals free:

(a) Petals not clawed or glandular—

(i) Fruit a many-seeded capsule; plant usually herb .. .. *Corchorus.*

(ii) Fruit a fleshy drupe; plant tree or shrub .. *Elaeocarpus.*

(b) Petals with a thickened or glandular claw—

(iii) Fruit smooth, drupaceous; leaves 3–9-nerved .. *Grewia.*

(iv) Fruit prickly, globose, indehiscent or separating into 3–5 cocci .. .. .. *Triumfetta.*

Common plants

(1) Jute (*Corchorus capsularis* L. and *C. olitorius* L.). (2) *Corchorus acutangulus* Lamk. =*C. aestuans* L., a common weed of waste places,

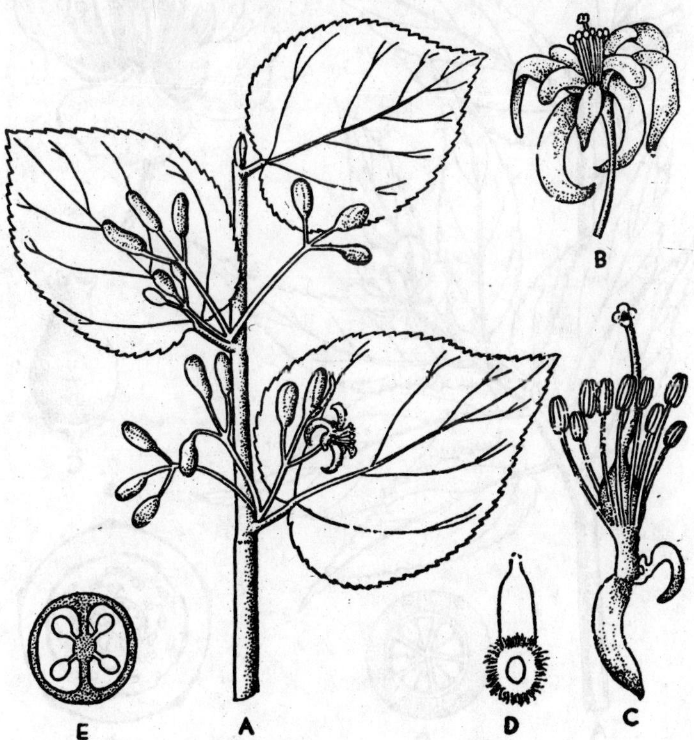

Fig. 623. Tiliaceae (*Grewia asiatica*).
A, Portion of a flowering shoot; B, Flower; C, The same after removal of all but one sepal and one petal; D, Gland at the base of the petal; E, T.s. of ovary.

the leaves of which have medicinal value. (3) *Grewia asiatica* L.= *G. subinaequalis* DC., a commonly planted fruit tree. (4) Spiny cocklebur (*Triumfetta rhomboidea* Jacq.=*T. bartramia* L.), a common weed with hooked spines on fruit. (5) Bead-tree (*Elaeocarpus ganitrus* Roxb. =*E. sphaericus* K. Schum.), the seeds of which are ornamented and strung together into beads. (6) *E. floribundus* Bl., commonly found in North Bengal. (7) *Brownlowia lanceolata* Benth., commonly found in Sundribans. (8) *Muntingia callabura* L., a common garden plant. (9) *Berrya ammonilla* Roxb., a timber tree.

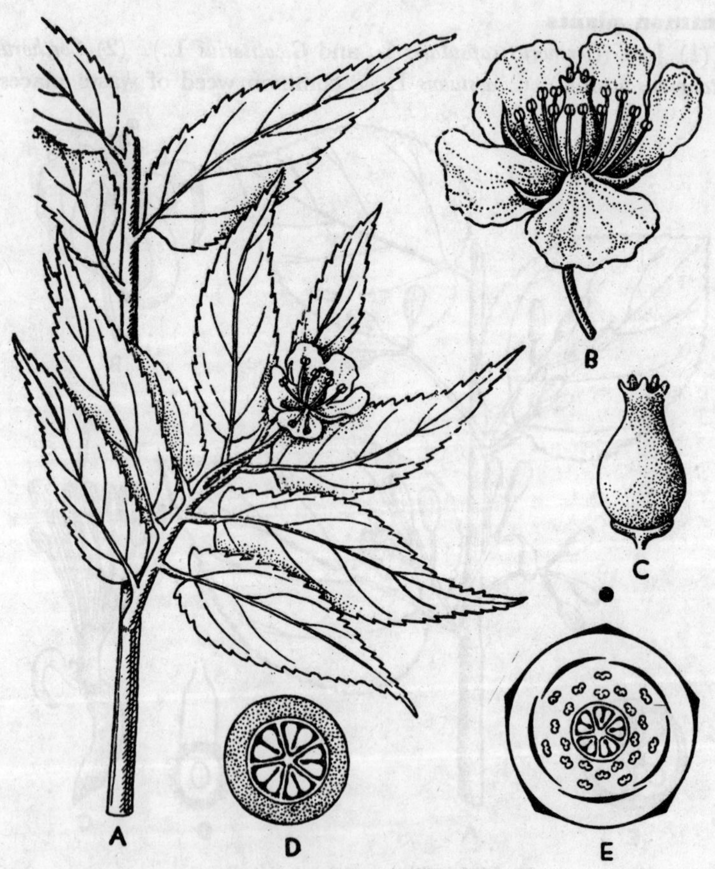

Fig. 624. Tiliaceae (*Muntingia callabura*).
A, Portion of a flowering shoot; B, Flower; C, Pistil; D, T.s. of ovary; E, Floral diagram.

Affinity

This family is allied to Malvaceae and Steruliaceae but readily distinguished by the free or polyadelphous stamens, 2-celled anthers, presence of a disc, and typically cymose inflorescence.

Economic importance

Tiliaceae is economically important. The plants of this family generally possess mucilagenous juice and fibrous bark. The most important plants are *Corchorus capsularis* and *C. olitorius* which yield fibres. *Grewia* yields edible fruits. The seeds of *Elaeocarpus* are strung into beads. *Berrya ammonila* and *Tilia cordata* are timber-yielding plants. The leaves of *Corchorus acutangulus* have medicinal property. Species of *Grewia, Corchoropsis, Entelea, Muntingia*, etc., are ornamentals.

MALVACEAE

General characters

Plants—usually herbs or shrubs, *often mucilagenous* and with stellate hairs on young parts. Leaves—alternate, simple, entire or variously

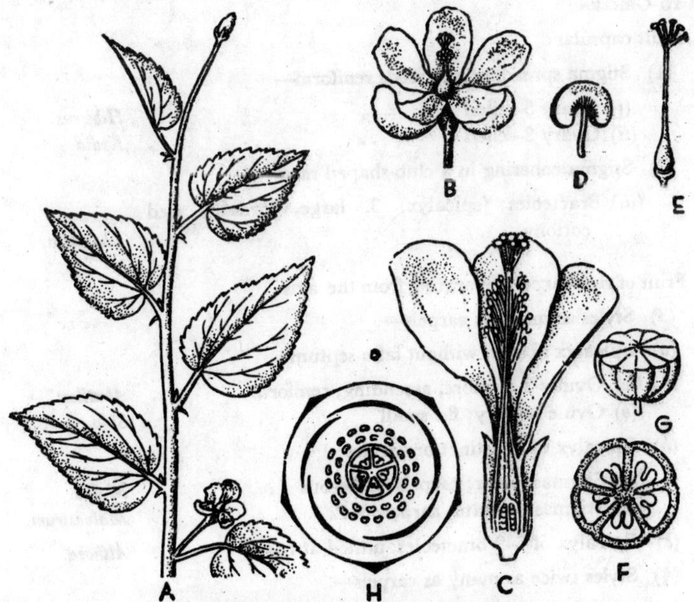

Fig. 625. Malvaceae (*Sida cordifolia*).
A, Portion of a flowering shoot; B, Flower; C, V.s. of the same; D, Stamen; E, T.s. of ovary; G, Fruit; H, Floral diagram.

lobed, mostly palmately veined, stipulate (*free-lateral stipules*). Inflorescence—cymose. Flowers—regular, bisexual (unisexual in *Napaca*), hypogynous, often showy, cyclic. Sepals—5, more or less united, *often subtended by an epicalyx* (excepting *Sida*, *Abutilon*, etc.), valvate. Petals—5, free from one another but adnate at the base to the staminal tube, *twisted*. Stamens—numerous, usually *monadelphous*, with *reniform*, 1-*celled anthers; pollen grains large* and *spiny*. Carpels—(1 to numerous); ovary—1-many-celled, but often 5-celled, with 1-*many anatropous ovules in each cell* and placed at the bottom of the staminal tube; style 1; stigmas as many or twice as many as carpels. Fruit—capsule or schizocarp, sometimes berry (e.g., *Malvaviscus*). Seeds—reniform, naked or comose with *curved embryo* and folded *cotyledons*.

Floral formula

$$⚥\ K_{(5)}\ C_5\ A_{(\infty)}\ \underline{G_{(5)\ \text{or}\ (10)}}$$

Number and distribution

This family consists of about 82 genera and 1,500 species which are cosmopolitan excepting in very cold regions.

KEY TO GENERA

A. Fruit capsular:

(1) Stigma spreading and seeds reniform—

(*i*) Ovary 5-celled .. .. .. *Hibiscus*.
(*ii*) Ovary 3-celled .. .. .. *Kydia*

(2) Stigma cohering in a club-shaped mass

(*iii*) Bracteoles (epicalyx) 3, large, cordate; seed cottony .. .. *Thespesia*.

B. Fruit of ripe carpels separating from the axis:

(3) Styles as many as carpels—

(*a*) Epicalyx absent, without false septum:

(*iv*) Ovules 2 or more, ascending, reniform .. *Abutilon*.
(*v*) Ovule solitary; fls. small .. .. *Sida*.

(*b*) Epicalyx of 3 distinct bracteoles:

(*vi*) Stigmas linear; carpels numerous .. .. *Malva*.
(*vii*) Stigmas capitate; carpels 8–12 .. .. *Malvastrum*.

(*c*) Epicalyx of 6–9 bracteoles, united at base .. *Althaea*.

(4) Styles twice as many as carpels—

(*viii*) Bracteoles 10; carpels opposite to sepals .. *Pavonia*.

(*ix*) Bracteoles 5; carpels opposite to petals .. *Urena.*

(*x*) Bracteoles 0 or mixed with fls. in dense heads; carpels unarmed .. .. .. *Malachra.*

(*xi*) Epicalyx present; carpels 10 .. .. *Malvaviscus.*

Range of floral structures

This family does not show wide variation in floral structure. Epicalyx is present in *Malva*, *Hibiscus*, *Althaea* and *Lavetere*, but absent in *Sida* and *Abutilon*. There are 3 epicalyces in *Gossypium.*

Variation in the number of carpels also occurs. Its number ranges from one to many. The number of carpels in *Abutilon* is 15–20; in *Malva* numerous; in *Malvastrum* 8–10 carpels; in *Plagianthus* 2 or 1; in *Malope trifida* numerous carpels are vertically arranged.

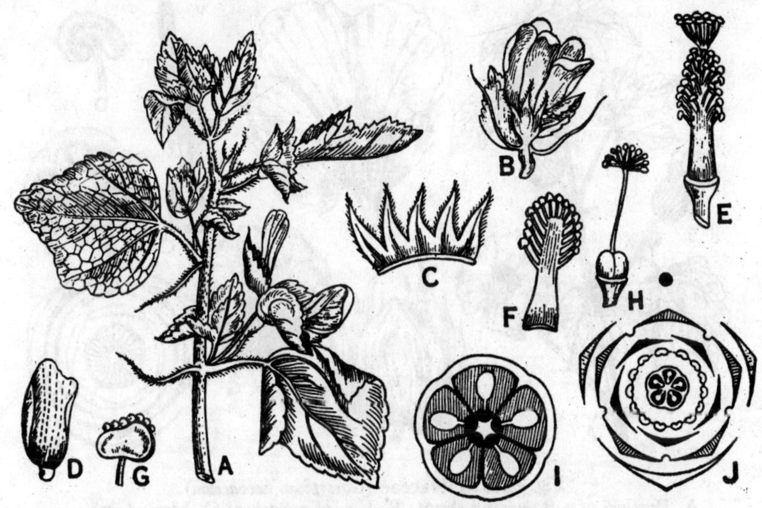

Fig. 626. Malvaceae (*Malachra capitata*).
A, Portion of a flowering shoot; B, Flower; C, Calyx; D, Petal; E, The same after removal of calyx and corolla; F, Stamens; G, Anther; H, Pistil; I, T.s. of ovary; J, Floral diagram.

Styles as many as carpels, e.g., *Abutilon*, *Sida*, *Malva*, and *Althaea;* but twice as many as carpels in *Pavonia*, *Kydia*, *Urena*, and *Malachra.*

Stigma is spreading in *Hibiscus* and *Kydia*, but connate into a club-shaped mass in *Thespesia;* ovary 3-celled in *Kydia*, but 5-celled in *Hibiscus.*

The position and number of ovules in the ovarian chamber also varies. Generally, the ovules are ascending but may be pendulous or horizontal; 2-ovuled ovary-chamber is found in *Abutilon*, but 1-ovuled ovary-chamber occurs in *Sida* and *Malachra*.

Common plants

(1) Cotton-plant (*Gossypium herbaceum* L.), a shrub commonly cultivated for cotton. (2) China-rose (*Hibiscus rosa-sinensis* L.), a common ornamental shrub. (3) Lady's-finger (*Hibiscus esculentus* L. =*Abelmoschus esculentus* Moench.), cultivated throughout India for its fruit which is a vegetable; Roselle (*H. sabdariffa* L.), commonly cultivated for its fleshy calyx which is used in making pickles and jelly. (4) Changeable rose (*Hibiscus mutabilis* L.), often planted in gardens for the sake of flower, the petals of which change from white

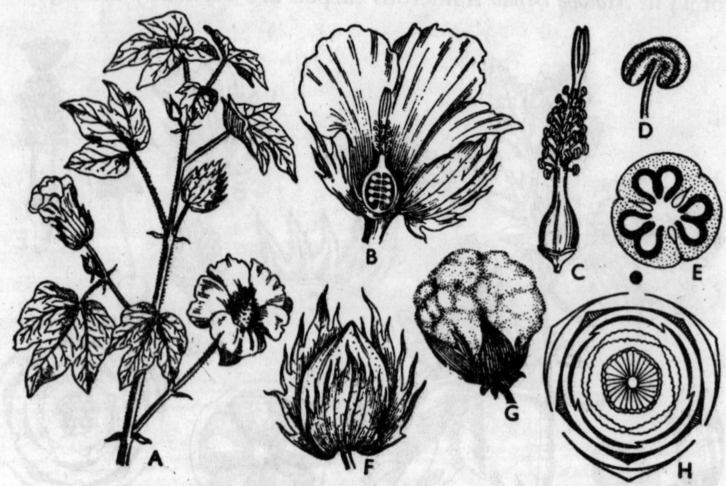

Fig. 627. Malvaceae (*Gossypium herbaceum*).
A, Portion of a flowering shoot; B, V.s. of a flower; C, Monadelphous stamen; D, Stamen; E, T.s. of ovary; F, Young fruit; G, Ripe dehiscent fruit; H, Floral diagram.

to red in the course of a day. (5) Deccan hemp (*Hibiscus cannabinus* L.), commonly cultivated for fibres. (6) *Urena lobata* L. and *U. sinuata* L. are common weeds found everywhere. (7) Indian mallow (*Abutilon indicum* Don.), commonly found in bushes; *A. hirtum* G. Don., an erect woody herb. (8) Different species of *Sida*, e.g., *S. cordifolia* L., *S. acuta* Burm., *S. rhombifolia* L., *S. rhomboidea* Roxb., and *S. humilis* Willd. =*S. veronicaefolia* L. are common weeds on waste places and roadsides. (9) Portia tree or Tulip tree (*Thespesia populnea* Corr. =*Hibiscus populneus* L.), often planted as an avenue tree. (10) *Malachra capitata* L., a common weed of waste places. (11) Tree mallow (*Hibiscus tiliaceous* L.), a small tree found in Sundribans and also along river banks as far north as Calcutta. (12) *Malvastrum tricuspidatum* Gray =*M. coromandelianum* Garcke, found in hedges and waste places. (13) *Pavonia odorata* Willd., a weed of fields and waste places. (14) *Kydia calycina* Roxb., a tree. (15) *Malva verticillata* L., a very common plant. (16) Hollyhock (*Althaea rosea* L.), a common garden plant.

Affinity

This family is closely allied to Tiliaceae, Bombacaceae and Sterculiaceae in its general characters and aestivation of calyx but readily distinguished by monadelphous stamens, 1-celled anthers, large, spiny pollen grains, twisted corolla and presence of epicalyx.

Economic importance

Malvaceae is of great economic importance. *Gossypium* is the most important plant which produces cotton of commerce; oil is extracted from the seeds for burning lamps and the oil-cake may be used as a fodder. *Hibiscus cannabinus* yields good fibres. Fruits of lady's-finger (*Abelmoschus esculentus*) are used as vegetable. *Hibiscus*, *Althaea*, *Malva*, *Malvaviscus*, *Thespesia*, *Callirhoe*, etc., are ornamentals.

BOMBACACEAE

General characters

Plants—tall trees, often with very thick base and spreading branches. Leaves—alternate, usually palmately compound (digitate), stipulate. Flowers—large and showy, regular, bisexual, hypogynous, bracteate, sometimes subtended by an epicalyx (e.g., *Adansonia*). Sepals—5, free or slightly united at the base, valvate. Petals—5, sometimes 0, twisted. Stamens—5-numerous, free or *polyadelphous* (e.g., *Bombax*); *staminodes often present; anthers* 1-*celled; pollen grains smooth*. Carpels—(2–5); ovary superior, 2–5-celled with 2 or more erect anatropous ovules in each cell; style 1, capitate or lobed; stigmas 1–5. Fruit—capsule or berry-like. Seeds—smooth, occasionally arillate, with or without endosperm, *often embedded in the pith-like tissue or in a woolly outgrowth of the pericarp*.

Floral formula

$\oplus$ ⚥ $K_{5 \text{ or } (5)}\ C_{5 \text{ or } 0}\ A_{5-\infty}\ \underline{G_{(2-5)}}$

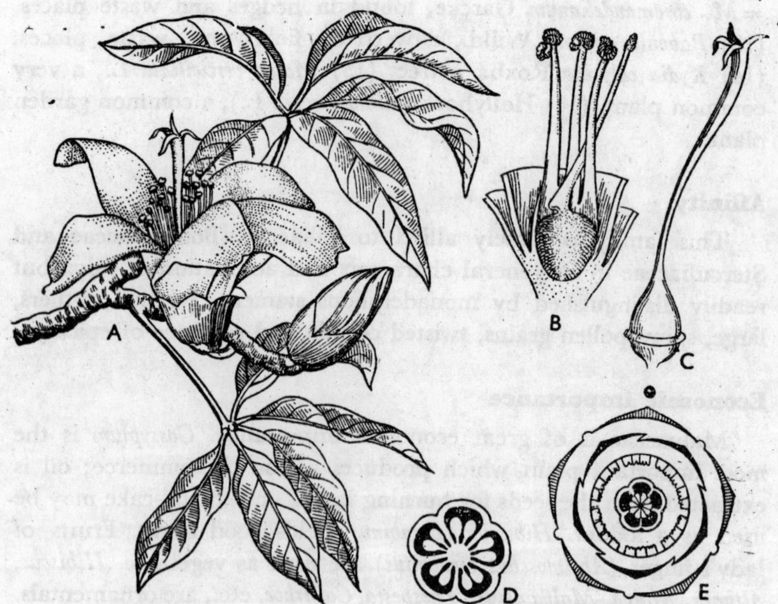

Fig. 628. Bombacaceae (*Bombax malabaricum*).
A, Portion of a flowering shoot; B, V.s. of a flower after removal of calyx and corolla; C, Pistil; D, T.s. of ovary; E, Floral diagram.

Number and distribution

This family consists of 22 genera and 140 species which are exclusively distributed in the tropics.

Key to Genera

(*a*) Fruit dehiscent; seeds packed; calyx truncate or toothed—

(*i*) Fls. red, stamens many .. .. .. *Bombax*.

(*ii*) Fls. white, stamens few .. .. *Eriodendron*.

(*b*) Fruit indehiscent; seeds embedded in a mealy pulp; epicalyx present .. .. .. *Adansonia*.

Common plants

(1) Red silk-cotton tree (*Bombax malabaricum* DC. =*Salmalia malabarica* Schott.), a huge tree with buttressed trunk which yields stuffing-cotton. (2) White silk-cotton tree (*Eriodendron anfractuosum* DC. =*Ceiba pentandra* Kurz.), a tall tree which yields 'kapok' of commerce. (3) The Baobab tree (*Adansonia digitata* L.), a thick-based spreading tree.

Affinity

This family is allied to other families under the order Malvales but is readily distinguished by the smooth pollen grains, presence of many staminodes and the pericarp of the fruit (pithy to woolly).

Economic importance

This family is economically important. Red silk-cotton tree (*Bombax*) yields cotton for stuffing pillows. White silk-cotton tree (*Eriodendron*) yields the 'kapok' of commerce. *Durio zebethinus* Murr. yields edible fruits. *Ochroma lagopus* Sw. yields very light and soft wood. The Baobab tree (*Adansonia*), Bombax, the Brazillian floss-silk tree (*Chorisia*), the guinea chestnut (*Pachira*), etc., are ornamentals.

STERCULIACEAE

General characters

Plants—generally trees or shrubs, sometimes herbs, with stellate hairs and mucilage. Leaves—alternate, simple, entire or palmately lobed, or compound, stipulate. Inflorescence—usually cymose, axillary or terminal. Flowers—regular or less often zygomorphic, bisexual (sometimes unisexual, e.g., *Heritiera*, *Sterculia*), hypogynous. Sepals—3–5, more or less slightly united at the base, valvate Petals—5, often reduced in size (sometimes absent, e.g., *Heritiera*, *Sterculia*), free, sometimes adnate to the base of the staminal column, twisted. Stamens—numerous in two whorls (those of outer whorl staminodial or 0, and those of inner whorl usually fertile) or monadelphous; *anthers. 2-celled*. Carpels—usually 5, syncarpous, sometimes almost free excepting the styles and stigmas (e.g., *Sterculia*); ovary superior, *often stalked*, 4–5-celled with two to numerous anatropous ovules in each cell; styles as many as carpels, free or united. Fruit—capsule or follicle, dehiscing along the ventral suture. Seeds—with fleshy endosperm and an embryo with *flat, folded* or *rolled, leafy cotyledons*.

Floral formula

$\text{⚥}\ K_{(3-5)}\ C_5\ A_{(\infty)}$ or $\infty\ \underline{G_{(5)}}$

Number and distribution

This family consists of 50 genera and about 750 species which are found in tropical and subtropical regions.

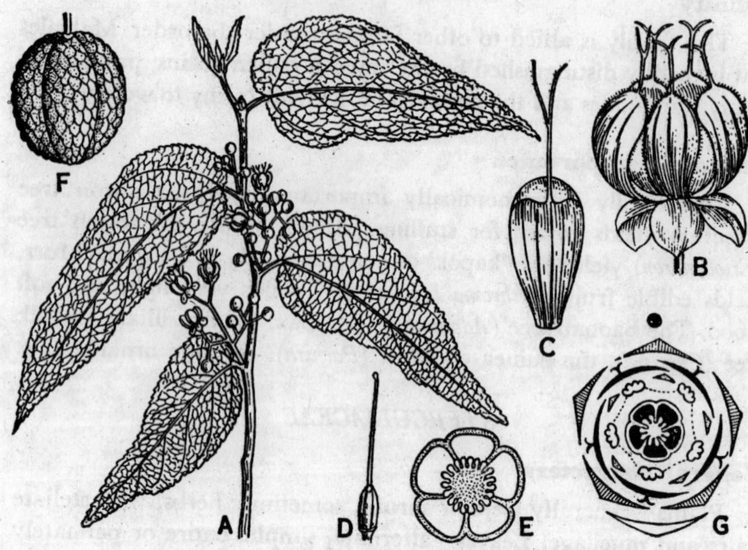

Fig. 629. Sterculiaceae (*Guazuma tomentosa*).
A, Portion of a flowering shoot; B, Flower; C, Petal; D, Pistil; E, T.s. of ovary; F, Fruit; G, Floral diagram.

Key to Genera

A. Flowers unisexual or polygamous; petals 0:

(*a*) Staminal column with ring of sessile anthers—

(*i*) Anthers 5–25; ripe carpels dehiscent .. *Sterculia*.

(*ii*) Anthers 5; ripe carpels indehiscent .. .. *Heritiera*.

B. Flowers bisexual:

(*b*) Petals flat, deciduous; anthers alternating with staminodes—

(*iii*) Leaves oblique below; ovary at the base of the staminal column; anther-cells parallel; seeds winged *Pterospermum*.

(*iv*) Leaves simple; ovary at the top of the staminal column; anther-cells divaricate; capsule woody with wingless seed .. .. .. *Helicteres*.

(*c*) Petals flat, persistent; anthers alternating with staminodes—

(*v*) 15 anthers in 5 groups of 3, alternating with staminodes .. .. .. *Pentapetes*.

(*vi*) Ovary 5-celled; styles 5 .. .. .. *Melochia*.

(*vii*) Ovary 1-celled, monocarpellary .. . *Waltheria*.

(*d*) Petals deciduous, unequal; capsule, inflated pyriform *Kleinhovia*.

(*e*) Petals concave; anthers in groups between each pair of staminodes—

(*viii*) Petals clawed; fruit membraneous; 5-angled 5-winged capsule, truncated above; ovules many in each loculus .. .. .. *Abroma*.

(*ix*) Fruit woody, tubercled capsule, globose; ovules many in each loculus .. .. .. *Guazuma*.

(*x*) Petals ligulate; fruit armed, prickly or bristly capsule; ovules 2 in each loculus .. .. *Buettneria*.

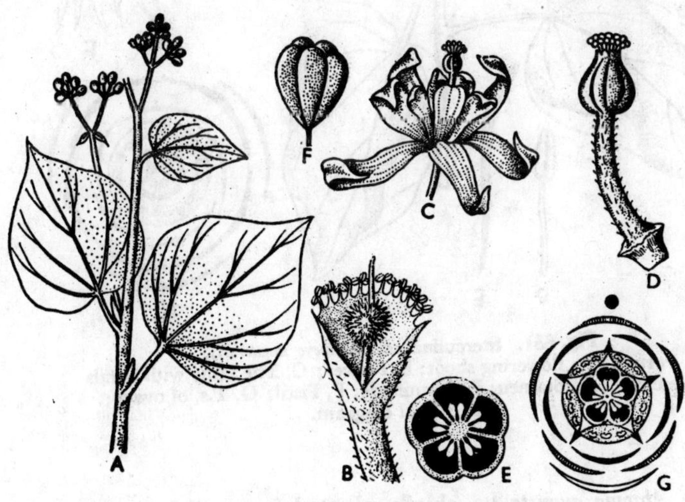

Fig. 630. Sterculiaceae (*Kleinhovia hospita*).
A, Portion of a flowering shoot; B, Flower bud; C, Flower; D. Staminal column; E, T.s. of ovary; F, Fruit; G, Floral diagram.

Common plants

(1) *Sterculia foetida* L. and *S. colorota*=*Firmiana colorata* R. Br. are large trees planted on roadsides. (2) *S. alata* Roxb., an avenue

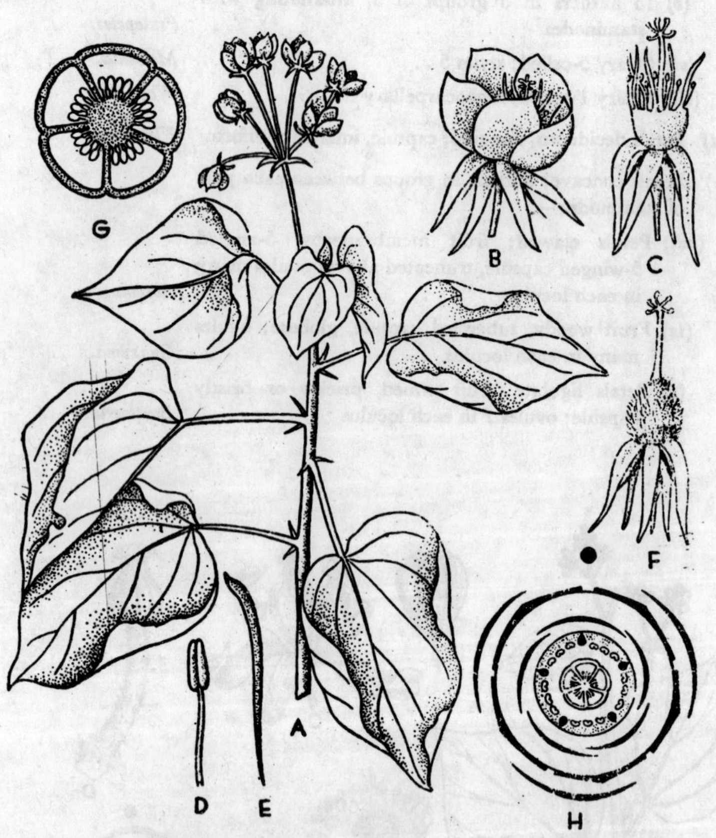

Fig. 631. Sterculiaceae (*Dombeya mastersii*). A, Portion of a flowering shoot; B, Flower; C, The same with petals removed; D, Stamen; E, Staminode; F, Pistil; G, T.s. of ovary; H, Floral diagram.

tree. (3) *Abroma augusta* L., chiefly planted for medicinal purposes. (4) *Pterospermum acerifolium* Willd., an avenue tree which produces fragrant flowers with fleshy sepals; *P. semisagittatum* Ham., another common tree. (5) *Heritiera minor* Roxb., abundantly found in the Sundribans which yields the best fire-wood. (6) *Helicteres isora* L., a shrub with spirally twisted follicles. (7) *Kleinhovia hospita* L., commonly planted on roadsides. (8) *Melochia corchorifolia* L., a common weed of waste places, dry-fields and grassy glades. (9) Bastard cedar (*Guazuma tomentosa* Kunth.). (10) Noon-flower (*Pentapetes phoenicea* L.), a common garden herb with pink-red flowers.

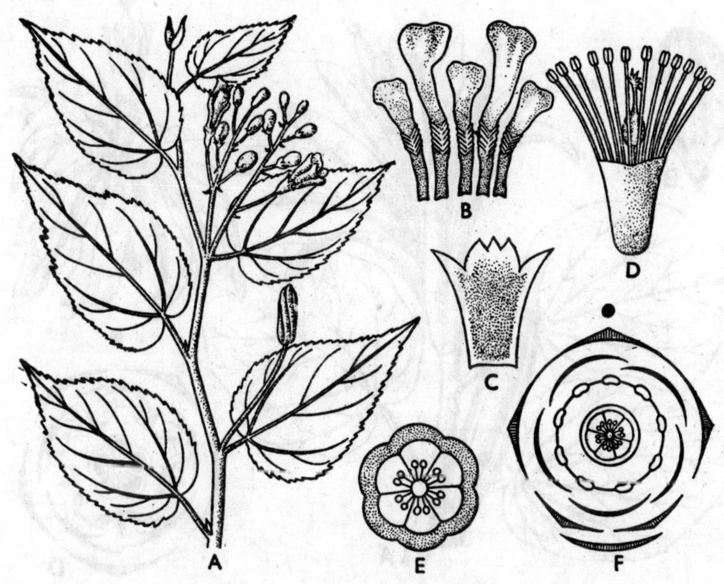

Fig. 632. Sterculiaceae (*Helicteres isora*).
A, Portion of a flowering shoot; B, Petals; C, Calyx split open; D, Flower with sepals and petals removed; E, T.s. of ovary; F, Floral diagram.

(11) Cocoa-tree (*Theobroma cacao* L.), chiefly cultivated in Southern India and Ceylon for preparing cocoa and chocolate from the roasted seeds. (12) *Waltheria indica* L., a common weed of waste places. (13) *Buettneria herbacea* Roxb., a herb. (14) *Dombeya mastersii*, a common garden plant.

Affinity

This family is allied to Tiliaceae, Malvaceae and Bombacaceae, but readily distinguished by the absence of epicalyx, definite number of stamens and stalked ovary. It differs from Malvaceae in having 2-celled anthers, and from Bombacaceae in presence of copious endosperm, androecium of typically 5 fertile stamens alternated with equal number of staminodes, and absence of a pithy or woolly pericarp.

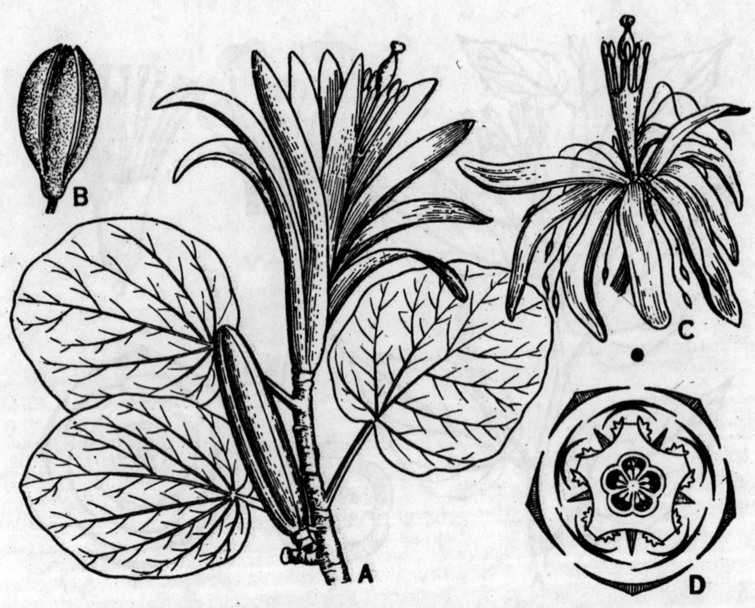

Fig. 633. Sterculiaceae (*Pterospermum acerifolium*).
A, Portion of a flowering shoot; B, Fruit; C, Flower; D, Floral diagram.

Economic importance

This family is economically important. The most important plant is *Theobroma cacao* from the seeds of which cocoa and chocolate are prepared. The root of *Abroma* is used in medicine. *Heritiera* supplies fire-wood. *Cola vera* Schum. yields a kind of nut. Some plants are ornamentals, such as, *Sterculia*, *Dombeya*, *Cola*, *Pterospermum*, *Kleinhovia*, *Guazuma*, etc.

Comparison of Tiliaceae, Malvaceae, Bombacaceae and Sterculiaceae

Tiliaceae	*Malvaceae*	*Bombacaceae*	*Sterculiaceae*
1. Plants—usually trees or shrubs, sometimes herbs.	1. Usually herbs or shrubs, often with mucilage.	1. Tall trees often with thick base.	1. Usually trees or shrubs, sometimes herbs.
2. Leaves—alternate, simple, often oblique, stipulate.	2. Alternate, simple, stipulate.	2. Alternate, usually digitate.	2. Alternate, simple, stipulate.
3. Flowers—regular, bi- or unisexual, hypogynous.	3. Regular, bisexual, hypogynous.	3. Regular, bisexual, hypogynous.	3. Regular or irregular, bi- or unisexual.
4. Sepals—5, free or united.	4. 5, usually surrounded by epicalyx.	4. 5, free or slightly united at the base, sometimes surrounded by an epicalyx.	4. 3–5, free or slightly united at the base.
5. Petals—5 or less or 0, free, imbricate.	5. 5, almost free, twisted.	5. 5, sometimes 0, twisted.	5. 5, often reduced in size or 0, twisted.
6. Stamens—10-numerous, free or slightly united, or polyadelphous, usually inserted at the base of the petals, rarely situated on an androgynophore.	6. Numerous, usually monadelphous.	6. 5-numerous, free or polyadelphous, staminodes often present.	6. Numerous in two whorls, those of the outer whorl staminodial or 0 but of the inner whorl fertile, or monadelphous.
7. Anthers—2-celled.	7. Reniform, 1-celled; pollen grains spiny.	7. 1-celled; pollen grains smooth.	7. 2-celled.
8. Carpels—(2–5).	8. (2-many).	8. (2–5).	8. Usually 5, syncarpous.
9. Ovary—2–10-celled with 1-many ascending or pendulous ovules in each cell.	9. 1-many-celled with 1 or more ovules in each cell.	9. 2–5-celled with 2 or more erect anatropous ovules in each cell.	9. Often stalked, 4–5-celled with 2-numerous anatropous ovules in each cell.
10. Fruit—fleshy or dry (capsule), dehiscent or indehiscent.	10. Capsule or schizocarp.	10. Capsule or berry-like.	10. Capsule or follicle.

ORDER 27. PARIETALES

Flowers regular or zygomorphic, usually bisexual. Perianth pentamerous or tetramerous, differentiated into calyx and corolla. Calyx imbricate. Stamens isomerous with the perianth members or more. Carpels (3); ovary unilocular with parietal placentation; ovules many. Disc is often present. Seeds albuminous.

According to Engler, this order consists of 11 suborders containing 29 families, viz., Guttiferae, Dipterocarpaceae, Violaceae, Passifloraceae, etc. Rendle has divided this order into 10 families. Bentham and Hooker have put Guttiferae and Dipterocarpaceae in the cohort Guttiferales, Passifloraceae in the cohort Passiflorales and Violaceae in the cohort Parietales under the subclass Polypetalae. In Hutchinson's sytsem the name of the order has been discarded. Guttiferae has been put under the order Guttiferales, Dipterocarpaceae under the order Theales, Violaceae under the order Violales and Passifloraceae under the order Passiflorales.

GUTTIFERAE (CLUSIACEAE)

General characters

Plants—trees or shrubs with yellowish or greenish resin. Leaves—usually opposite or whorled, simple, entire, coriaceous, exstipulate. Inflorescence—cymose. Flowers—regular, usually bisexual (rarely unisexual), hypogynous. Sepals—2–6, or more, imbricate. Petals—4–12, imbricate. Stamens—few or numerous, free or more or less united into several bundles (*polyadelphous*). Carpels—usually (3 or 5), sometimes more or fewer (2–1); ovary superior, generally 1-many-celled, with 1 to numerous anatropous ovules in each cell; styles equal to the number of carpels or chambers, and united. Fruit—drupe or capsule. Seed—exalbuminous with large straight embryo.

Floral formula

$$\oplus \; ⚥ \; K_{2-6}\, C_{4-12}\, A_{\infty}\, \underline{G_{(3-5)\ \text{or}\ (2-1)}}$$

Number and distribution

This family consists of about 35 genera and 400 species which are chiefly tropical

KEY TO GENERA

A. Ovary with 2 erect ovules in each cell:
Ovary 2-celled; style long; embryo with a small radicle and 2 large cotyledons; petals 4 .. .. *Mesua.*

B. Ovary with ovules solitary in each cell:
(*a*) Ovary 1-celled with solitary erect ovule; style long; embryo with a small radicle and 2 large cotyledons; petals 4 or 0 .. .. *Calophyllum.*
(*b*) Ovary 2–12 celled with a solitary ovule attached to the inner angle of each cell; embryo with a large radicle and 2 small cotyledons; petals 4–5 .. *Garcinia.*

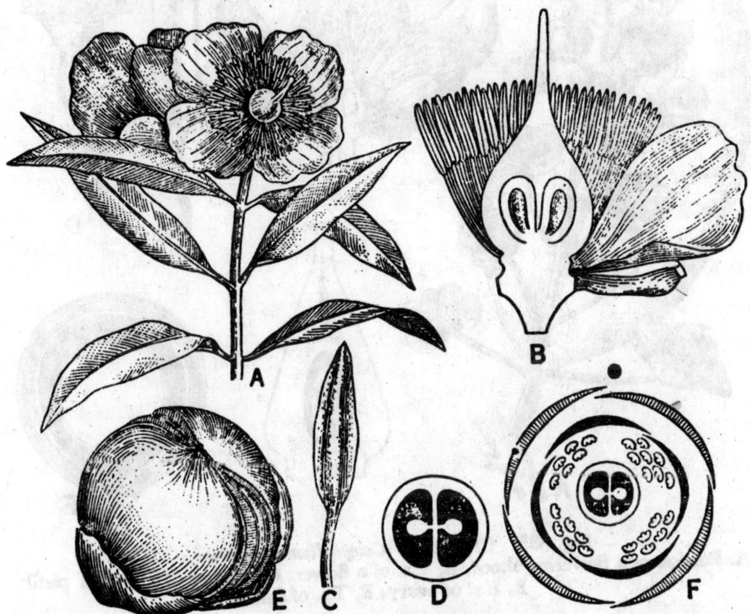

Fig. 634. Clusiaceae (*Mesua ferrea*).
A, Portion of a flowering shoot; B, V.s. of the flower; C, Stamen; D, T.s. of ovary; E, Fruit: F, Floral diagram.

Common plants

(1) Cowa tree (*Garcinia cowa* Roxb.). (2) *G. xanthochymus* Hook. f. (3) Mangostene (*G. mangostena* L.), often planted in gardens for its delicious aril. (4) Alexandrian laurel (*Calophyllum inophyllum* L.), often grown in gardens as an avenue tree. (5) *Mesua ferrea* L., often planted in gardens for its fragrant flowers.

Affinity

This family bears close affinity with Theaceae and Dipterocarpaceae. It is distinguished from the former by the absence of oil glands and from the latter by the absence of alternate stipulate leaves. From the study of floral morphology of various genera with special reference to 4-merous arrangement of the perianth members, its relationship may be suggested with the members of the Parietales.

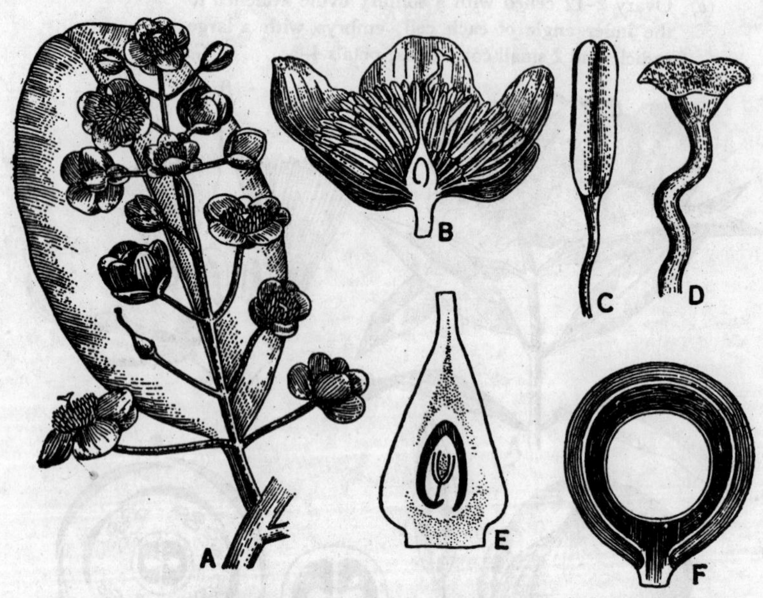

Fig. 635. Clusiaceae (*Calophyllum inophyllum*).
A, Portion of a flowering shoot; B, V.s. of a flower; C, Stamen; D, Part of pistil; E, L.s. of ovary; F, T.s. of fruit.

Economic importance

This family is of little economic importance. The sweet-scented flowers of *Mesua ferrea* are used in perfumery and in medicine. The wood of *Garcinia* and *Calophyllum brasiliense* Camb. are timber-yielding plants. The seeds of *Allanbackia stahlmanni* yield oil. Gamboge, the yellow pigment of commerce, is obtained from *Garcinia morella* Desr. *Garcinia mangostena* yields highly delicious fruits. Some plants are also cultivated as ornamentals, such as, *Garcinia*, *Mesua*, *Calophyllum*, etc.

DIPTEROCARPACEAE

General characters

Plants—usually huge trees with copious *resinous juice*. Leaves—alternate, simple, entire, coriaceous, stellately pubescent, stipulate (convolute stipules). Inflorescence—raceme or panicle. Flowers—regular, bisexual, hypogynous pentamerous. Sepals—5, united at the base forming 5 lobes, imbricate, *persistent* (in *Dipterocarpus* only two calyx-lobes grow out into wings, but in *Shorea* all five develop into wings). Petals—5, free, twisted. Stamens—numerous or less, free or slightly polyadelphous; connective often prolonged. Carpels—(3); ovary superior, *3-celled with 2 pendulous ovules in each.* Fruit—*samara*, enclosed in the persistent sepals. Seed—exalbuminous, with straight or curved embryo.

Floral formula

$\oplus$ ⚥ $K_{(5)}\ C_5\ A_\infty\ \underline{G_{(3)}}$

Number and distribution

This family consists of 16 genera and 300 species which are commonly found in the tropics.

KEY TO GENERA

A. Calyx forming a distinct tube, 2 lobes accrescent and erect; fruit tree .. .. *Dipterocarpus.*

B. Calyx-tube short or rudimentary, segments subvalvate:

(*i*) 2 calyx-lobes winged; stamens 15; fruit a 3-valved coriaceous capsule or indehiscent; fls. in axillary panicles .. .. .. *Vatica.*

(*ii*) calyx-lobes equal; stamens 16; anthers apiculate; fruit a capsule; fls. in axillary panicles .. *Isauxis.*

C. Calyx-lobes imbricate:

(*iii*) 3 or all segments enlarged in fruit, indehiscent; stamens 15-numerous, subulate or cuspidate .. *Shorea.*

(*iv*) 2 calyx-segments enlarged; stamens 10–15, subulate or cuspidate .. .. .. *Hopea.*

Common plants

(1) Sal tree (*Shorea robusta* Gaertn.), a huge timber tree, (2) Garjan balsam (*Dipterocarpus turbinatus* Gaertn.), a gigantic tree

commonly found in Bangladesh (Chittagong and Tipperah). (3) *Isauxis lancaefolia* King, found in Chittagong. (4) *Vatica scaphula* Dyer., commonly occurring in Chittagong, can also be found in the Indian Botanic Garden. (5) *Hopea odorata* Roxb., a tall tree.

Affinity

This family resembles Guttiferae in possessing resin. It is also allied to Magnoliaceae by the presence of large convolute stipules but readily distinguished by the enlarged persistent calyx.

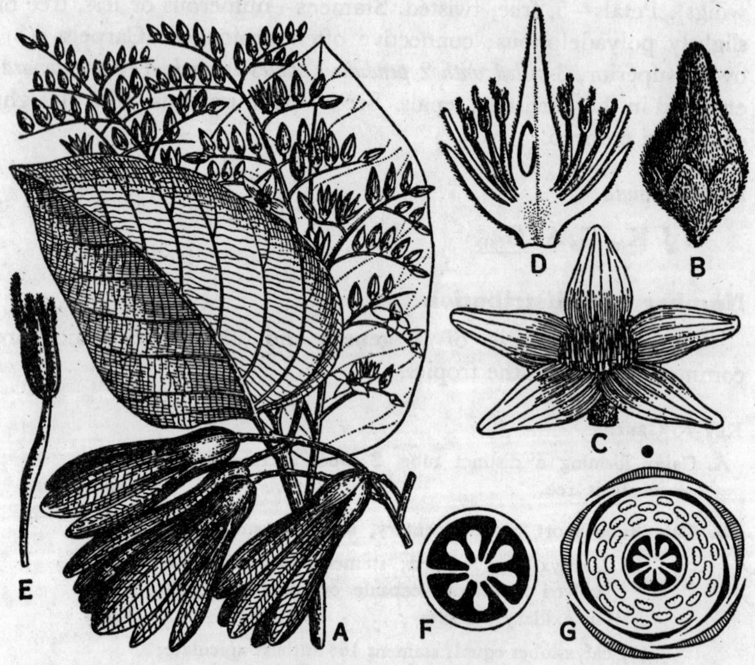

Fig. 636. Dipterocarpaceae (*Shorea robusta*).
A, Portion of a flowering shoot; B, Flower bud; C, Flower; D, V.s. of the same; E, Stamen; F, T.s. of ovary; G, Floral diagram.

Economic importance

This family is somewhat economically important. *Shorea* yields timber of great value and a resin, known as dumar resin, much used as an incense. *Dipterocarpus* yields a liquid balsam or resin known as Garjan-oil. *Dryobalanops aromatica* Gaertn. yields yellow camphor. The seeds of *Vatica*, *Vateria* and *Doona* are edible. *Isauxis* produces a kind of scented oil. *Vateria indica* yields a gum-resin used for making varnish.

VIOLACEAE

General characters

Plants—annual or perennial herbs. Leaves—usually alternate, simple, sometimes lobed, *stipulate*. Inflorescence—solitary (e.g.

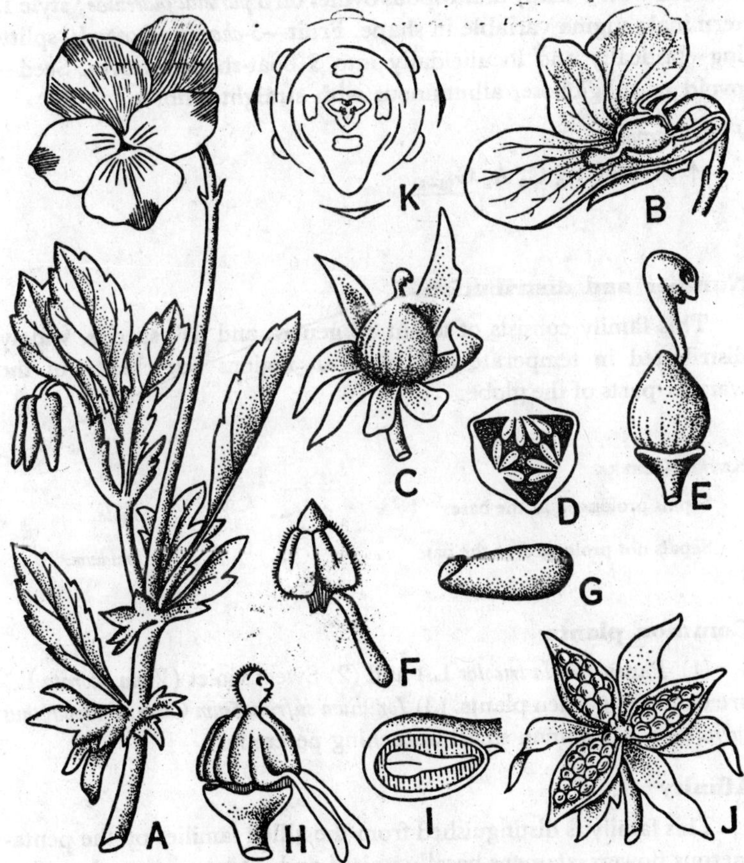

Fig. 637. Violaceae (*Viola tricolor*).
A, Portion of a flowering shoot; B, Flower cut lengthwise; C, Pistil; D, T.s. of ovary; E, Young pistil; F, Stamen; G, Seed; G, Fruit; I, L.s. of a seed; J, Dehiscence of fruit; K, Floral diagram.

Viola) or terminal spike with bracts and bracteoles. Flowers—*irregular* or regular, bisexual, hypogynous, sometimes cleistogamous.

Sepals—5, uniform in size or prolonged at the base (e.g., *Viola*), persistent, imbricate. Petals—5, of which the *lowermost one largest* and *spurred* or saccate, imbricate or twisted. Stamens—5, with short filaments, *introrse; the connective of anterior pair of anthers often spurred at the base* in irregular flowers or otherwise appendaged in regular flowers, *forming a cone round the ovary*. Carpels—(3–5); ovary superior, 1-celled with 1-many anatropous ovules on 3 *parietal placentae;* style 1, terminal; stigma variable in shape. Fruit—3-*chambered capsule*, splitting elastically and loculicidally into 3 boat-shaped valves. Seed—ovoid or subglobose, albuminous with straight embryo.

Floral formula

$\uparrow$ or $\oplus$ ⚥ $K_5\ C_5\ A_5\ \underline{G_{(3-5)}}$

Number and distribution

This family consists of about 16 genera and 850 species, widely distributed in temperate and tropical regions but chiefly in the warmer parts of the globe.

Key to Genera

Sepals prolonged at the base	*Viola.*
Sepals not prolonged at the base	*Ionidium.*

Common plants

(1) Pansy (*Viola tricolor* L.) and (2) Sweet violet (*Viola odorata* L.) are common garden plants. (3) *Ionidium sufruticosum* Cing. =*Hybanthus sufruticosa*, a common small branching perennial.

Affinity

This family is distinguished from the allied families by the pentamerous flowers, stamens basally united and introrse, spurred corolla, and 3-chambered capsule fruit.

Economic importance

This family is of very little economic importance. The leaves of *Rinorea* sp. are used as vegetables. *Leonia glycecarpa* yields edible fruits. Different species of *Viola* (*V. odorata, V. tricolor*, etc.) are ornamentals.

PASSIFLORACEAE

General characters

Plants—mostly climbing herbs, sometimes shrubs. Leaves—alternate, simple or compound, generally lobed, *stipulate.* Inflorescence solitary or cymose. Flowers—regular, bisexual (unisexual in *Modecca*), bracteate with prominent receptacle. Sepals—usually 5, free or united at the base, persistent, imbricate. Petals—usually 5, often smaller than sepals, free, imbricate, with *corona*. Stamens—5, originally free but become *uplifted by androphore;* anthers 1-celled. Carpels —(3–5); ovary superior, often raised on a gynophore, 1-celled with many anatropous ovules on parietal placentae; styles 3–5, free or united at the base, each bears a capitate stigma. Fruit—*berry* or *capsule*. Seeds—*arillate with perisperm*. Embryo—straight.

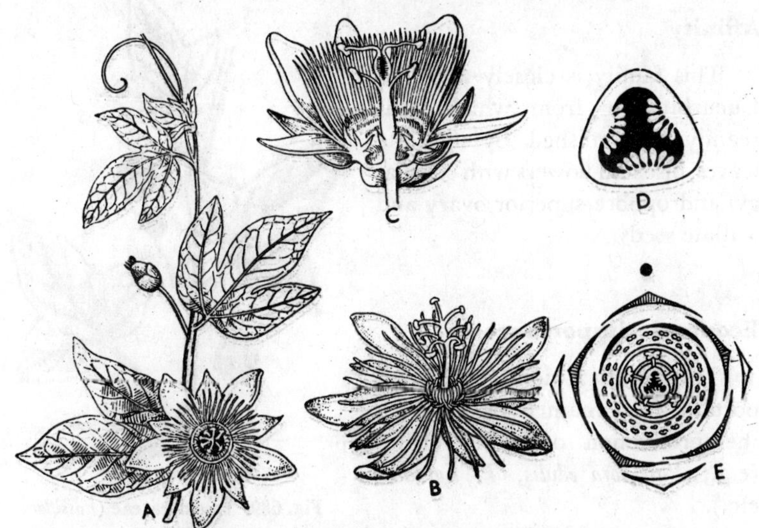

Fig. 638. Passifloraceae (*Passiflora suberosa*).
A, Portion of a flowering shoot; B, Flower; C, V.s. of the same; D, T.s. of ovary; E, Floral diagram.

Floral formula

$\oplus$ ⚥ $K_{5 \text{ or } (5)}$ C_5 A_5 $G_{(3-5)}$

Number and distribution

This family consists of 12 genera and about 600 species which are chiefly found in the tropics.

KEY TO GENERA

A. Fls. bisexual, stamens hypogynous, plants usually twining herbs .. .. *Passiflora.*

B. Fls. unisexual:

Corollas of male and female fls. similar; stamens perigynous; plants twining herbs or undershrubs .. *Modecca.*

Common plants

(1) Passion-flower (*Passiflora foetida* L., *P. suberosa* L., *P. lunata* L.). (2) *Modecca cordifolia* Bl. and *M. palmata* Lam., very common.

Affinity

This family is closely allied to Cucurbitaceae from which it is readily distinguished by stipulate leaves, bisexual flowers with corona, gynandrophore, superior ovary and arillate seeds.

Economic importance

This family is domestically important for ornamentals, and for the production of edible fruits (e.g., *Passiflora edulis*, *P. ligularis*, etc.).

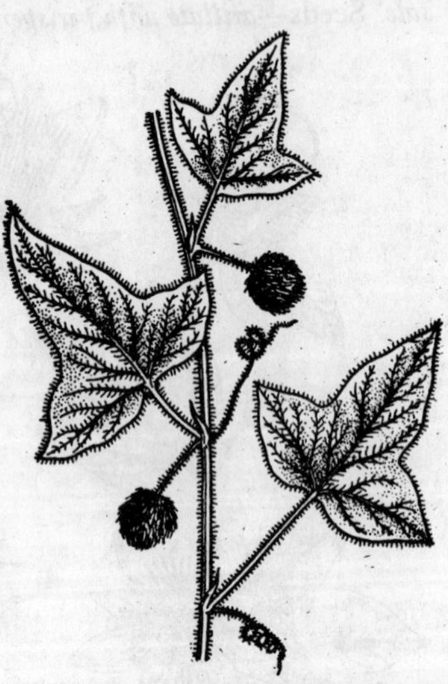

Fig. 639. Passifloraceae (*Passiflora foetida*).

ORDER 28. OPUNTIALES

Plants generally succulent with reduced leaves. Flowers bisexual, regular or irregular, epigynous. Stamens numerous. Ovary inferior. Fruit berry.

According to Engler this order contains only one family Cactaceae. Bentham and Hooker have placed Cactaceae in the cohort Ficoidales under the subclass Polypetalae. Hutchinson designated this order as Cactales which contains a single family Cactaceae.

CACTACEAE

General characters

Plants—succulent herbs and shrubs, usually with thick angular or flattened or cylindrical stems (phylloclades), which are simple or branched, and most of them have prominent vertical ridges and

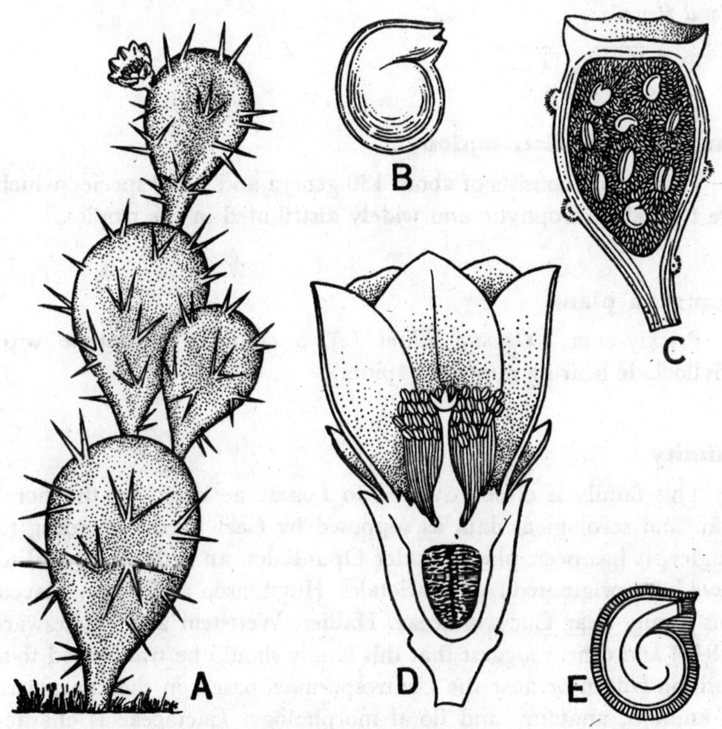

Fig. 640. Cactaceae (*Opuntia dilleni*).
A, A phylloclade bearing a flower; B, Seed; C, L.s. of a fruit; D, V.s. of a flower; E, L.s. of a seed.

spines. Leaves—usually modified into spines*, or sometimes developed which are flat or cylindrical in shape but soon fall off. Flowers—regular or nearly so, bisexual (sometimes unisexual), epigynous. Perianth—numerous in *several series*, generally more or less united

* Spines grow from rounded cushions or *tubercles* composed of a combination of leaf-base and rudimentary branch.

to form a tube, sometimes free. Stamens—numerous, epiphyllous, rarely arise from the thalamus. Carpels—(3-many); ovary *inferior*, 1-celled with 3 or more *parietal placentae* bearing numerous anatropous ovules; style simple; stigma equal to the number of carpels. Fruit—berry, often glochidiate, spiny or bristly, many-seeded. Seed—usually exalbuminous, often with black testa. Embryo—straight or curved.

Floral formula

$\oplus$ ⚥ $\overline{P_{\infty}}\ A_{\infty}\ \overline{G_{(3-\infty)}}$

Number and distribution

This family consists of about 130 genera and 1,200 species which are typically xerophytic and widely distributed in the tropics.

Common plant

Prickly-pear (*Opuntia dilleni L.*), a common xerophyte with phylloclade bearing numerous spines.

Affinity

This family is closely related to Loasaceae based on the floral plan and serological data as supposed by Carl Mez. According to Engler, it has been placed under Opuntiales, an order supposed to have been originated from Parietales. Hutchinson and Bessey placed this family near Cucurbitaceae. Hallier, Wettstein and Maheswari (1945) and others suggest that this family should be transferred to a position within or near the Centrospermae, based on the characters of embryo, anatomy and floral morphology. Cactaceae is characterized by the fleshy habit with spines, solitary flowers with an undifferentiated perianth, numerous spirally arranged stamens and glochidiate berry.

Economic importance

This family is of domestic importance as it contains ornamentals, and they are extensively cultivated in Europe. The fruit of the Prickly-pear (*Opuntia* sp.) is edible.

ORDER 29. MYRTIFLORAE

Plants herbs, shrubs or trees. Leaves opposite, simple, exstipulate. Flowers regular, bisexual, cyclic, perigynous to epigynous, generally tetra- or pentamerous. Stamens diplostemonous or obdiplostemonous. Pistil frequently oligomerous. Ovary multilocular to unilocular with numerous ovules on axile placentae. Seeds exalbuminous.

According to Engler this order consists of 4 suborders containing 20 families, viz., Lythraceae, Rhizophoraceae, Combretaceae, Myrtaceae, Melastomaceae, Onagraceae, etc. Benthem and Hooker have placed the aforesaid families in the cohort Myrtales under subclass Polypetalae. In Hutchinson's system, Lythraceae and Onagraceae have been put under the order Lythrales while Myrtaceae, Melastomaceae, Combretaceae and Rhizophoraceae under the order Myrtales.

LYTHRACEAE

General characters

Plants—trees, shrubs or herbs, often with square stems. Leaves —opposite or whorled, simple, entire, with or without minute

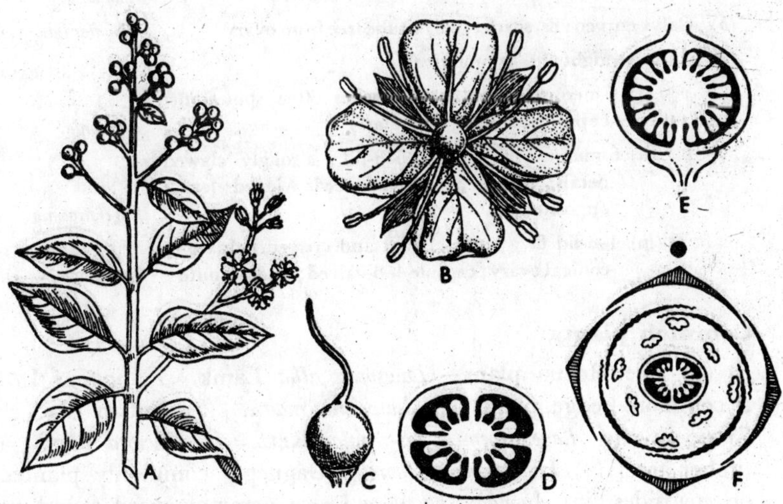

Fig. 641. Lythraceae (*Lawsonia alba*).
A, Portion of a flowering shoot; B, Flower; C, Pistil; D, T.s. of ovary; E, L.s. of the same; F, Floral diagram.

stipules. Inflorescence—raceme or cymose. Flowers—medium (e.g., *Lagerstroemia*) or minute (e.g., *Ammania*), regular (sometimes irregular e.g., *Cuphea*), bisexual, perigynous. Sepals—4–8, united into a tube, *valvate*. Petals—4–8, (sometimes absent, e.g., *Peplis*), free, inserted at the mouth of the corolla, crumpled, usually with *crisped margins*. Stamens—usually twice as many as petals in 2 whorls, inserted on the calyx-tube, generally bent in bud. Carpels—(2–6); ovary superior, usually 2–6-celled with many anatropous ascending ovules in each on axile placentae. Fruit—*capsule*. Seed—exalbuminous. Embryo—large, usually straight with flat cotyledons.

Floral formula

$\oplus . ⚥\ K_{4-8}\ C_{4-8}\ A_{8-16}\ \underline{G_{(2-6)}}$

Number and distribution

This family consists of about 23 genera and 475 species which are chiefly distributed in the tropics.

KEY TO GENERA

(*a*) Calyx membraneous; fls. minute; stem quadrangular, reddish; herbaceous .. .. *Ammania*.

(*b*) Calyx curved; fls. scarlet; calyx-tube free from ovary .. *Woodfordia*.

(*c*) Calyx straight; fls. symmetrical—

(*i*) 4-merous white fls.; branches often spinescent; capsule dehiscing irregularly .. .. *Lawsonia*.

(*ii*) 6-merous fls., rarely 5–8-fid.; strongly clawed petals; capsule 3–6-valved; seeds winged; leaves opposite .. .. *Lagerstroemia*.

(*iii*) 4–8-fid fls.; petals clawed and crisped, adnate to conical ovary; capsule 4–8-valved; seeds minute *Duabanga*.

Common plants

(1) The Henna plant (*Lawsonia alba* Lamk. = *L. inermis* L.), a common hedge plant. (2) *Lawsonia indica*. (3) Indian lilac or Crepe myrtle (*Lagerstroemia flos-reginae* Retz. = *L. speciosa* Pers.), a timber tree. (4) *Lagerstroemia thorellii* Gagnep., commonly planted on roadsides. (5) *Ammania baccifera* L., a common weed found on roadsides and wet places. (6) *Woodfordia floribunda* Salisb. = *W. fruticosa* Kurz., a common shrub with di- and trimorphic flowers.

(7) *Duabanga sonneratioides* Ham., occurs in North Bengal, also can be seen in the Indian Botanic Garden.

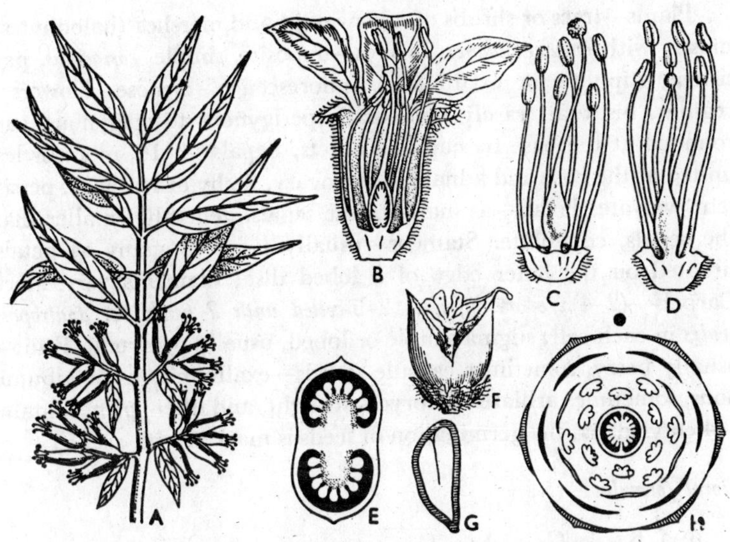

Fig. 642. Lythraceae (*Woodfordia floribunda*).
A, Portion of a flowering shoot; B, V.s. of a flower; C, Medium and short stamens with long stigma; D, Long and medium stamens with short stigma; E, T.s. of ovary; F, Fruit; G, L.s. of seed; H, Floral diagram.

N. B. The genus *Punica* (*P. granatum* L., the pomegranate plant) has now-a-days been placed in the Family Punicaceae.

Affinity

This family is closely allied to Melastomaceae, Onagraceae, Saxifragaceae, and Myrtaceae but readily distinguished by the crumpled corolla, stamens twice the number of petals, superior ovary and exalbuminous seeds.

Economic importance

This family is economically important from the standpoint of ornamental value. Among the ornamental plants are *Lagerstroemia indica* and *Lawsonia inermis*, abundantly cultivated in the warmer countries of the world. Some species of *Cuphea* are also useful for decorative purposes. *Lagerstroemia speciosa* Pers. yields good quality of timber. The leaves of *Lawsonia alba* produce hair dye.

RHIZOPHORACEAE

General characters

Plants—trees or shrubs of salt swamps and marshes (halophytes), mostly with *pneumatophores*. Leaves—opposite, simple, *coriaceous*, persistent, stipulate or exstipulate. Inflorescence—cymose. Flowers—regular, bisexual (rarely unisexual), perigynous to epigynous, surrounded at the base by cup-like bracts. Sepals—3–16, more or less united at the base and adnate to the ovary, fleshy or leathery, persistent, valvate. Petals—as many as the sepals, generally smaller than the sepals, convolute. Stamens—usually twice as many as petals, situated on the outer edge of a lobed disc; filaments very short. Carpels—(2–4); *ovary inferior*, 2–5-*celled with 2 pendulous anatropous ovules* in each cell; stigma simple or lobed, usually persistent. Fruit—usually berry, sometimes capsule. Seeds—exalbuminous or albuminous, sometimes arillate. Embryo—straight, and often *green*, contains 3–4 cotyledons; the germination of seeds is marked with *vivipary*.

Floral formula

$$\oplus ⚥ K_{(3-16)} C_{3-16} A_{6-\infty} \overline{G_{(2-4)}}$$

Number and distribution

This family consists of about 17 genera with 70 species. Many plants form characteristic components of the mangrove vegetation of muddy coasts and estuaries.

Key to Genera

A. Sea-shore trees (mangrove); seeds exalbuminous; embryo with a large hypocotyl germinating while the fruit is still on the tree:

(*a*) Calyx-segments and petals each 4; petals entire; stamens 8; ovary 2-celled .. .. .. *Rhizophora.*

(*b*) Calyx-segments and petals each 5–6; petals not entire, emarginate; stamens 10–12; ovary 3-celled .. *Ceriops.*

Petals lacerate; stamens infinite; ovary 1-celled .. *Kandelia.*

(*c*) Calyx-segments and petals 8–14; calyx without bracteoles; petals 2-fid.; stamens 16–28; ovary 2–4-celled .. .. *Bruguiera.*

B. Inland trees; seeds albuminous; embryo not germinating till fruit falls; calyx-tube minutely bracteolate *Carallia*.

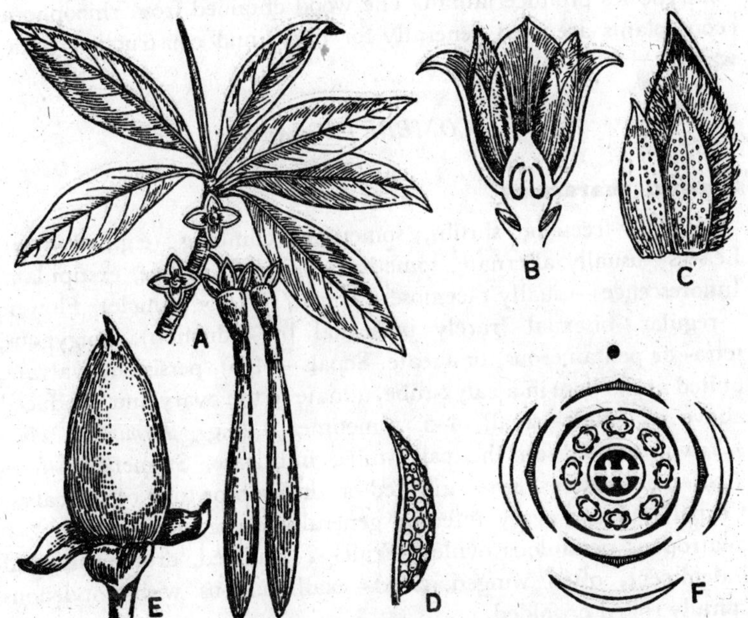

Fig. 643. Rhizophoraceae (*Rhizophora mucronata*).
A, Portion of a shoot with flowers and germinating seeds; B, V.s. of a flower; C, A petal with two opposite stamens; D, Stamen; E, Fruit: F, Floral diagram.

Common plants

(1) *Rhizophora mucronata* Lamk., a small evergreen tree found in the Sundribans. (2) *R. conjugata* L.=*R. candelaria* DC., a small tree. (3) *Ceriops roxburghiana* Arn., a large shrub of the Sundribans. (4) *Kandelia rheedi* W. & A.=*K. candel* Druce, a small tree. (5) *Bruguiera gymnorhiza* Lamk.=*B. conjugata* Merr., a large tree. (6) *Carallia lucida* Roxb., an evergreen tree with shining leaves.

Affinity

This family closely resembles Combretaceae and Myrtaceae, but is readily distinguished by the presence of pneumatophores, coriaceous leaves, numerous stamens, 2–5-celled ovary with 2 ovules in each cell, green cotyledons and viviparous germination of seeds.

Economic importance

This family is less important economically. Bark and foliage of some species produce tannin. The wood obtained from rhizophoraceous plants are used generally for piling and construction under water.

COMBRETACEAE

General characters

Plants—trees or shrubs, sometimes climbing (e.g., *Poivera*). Leaves—usually alternate, sometimes opposite, simple, exstipulate. Inflorescence—usually racemose (raceme, spike or panicle). Flowers—regular, bisexual (rarely unisexual by reduction), epigynous, tetra- or pentamerous, bracteate. Sepals—(4–5), persistent, valvate, united at the base in a calyx-tube, adnate to the ovary and produced above it. Petals—small, 4–5, sometimes 0 (e.g., *Terminalia*, *Anogeissus*), inserted on the calyx-tube, imbricate. Stamens—4–5 *in 1 series*, or 8–10 *in 2 series*, inserted on the limb or tube of the calyx. Carpels—(4–5); ovary inferior, generally *angled*, *1-celled* with 2–6 anatropous pendulous ovules. Fruit—2–5-angled, drupaceous and indehiscent, often winged. Seed—exalbuminous with cotyledons spirally rolled or folded.

Floral formula

$$\oplus ⚥ K_{(4-5)}\ C_{4-5}\ A_{4-5 \text{ or } 8-10}\ \overline{G}_{(4-5)}$$

Number and distribution

This family consists of 18 genera with 500 species occurring in the tropical region.

KEY TO GENERA

A. Inflorescence racemose (raceme, spike or head); calyx-lobes valvate; stamens without glands or staminodes; ovules 2–4:

(*a*) Petals 0—

Calyx-limb deciduous; erect trees or shrubs:

Flowers in heads .. .. *Anogeissus*.

Flowers in spikes or racemes .. .. *Terminalia*.

(*b*) Petals 5 or 4—

(*i*) Calyx-limb deciduous; climbers with opposite leaves:

Calyx-tube not or shortly produced beyond ovary .. .. *Combretum.*

Calyx-tube much produced beyond ovary .. *Quisqualis.*

(*ii*) Calyx-limb persistent; shrubs or trees with alternate leaves .. .. .. *Lumnitzera.*

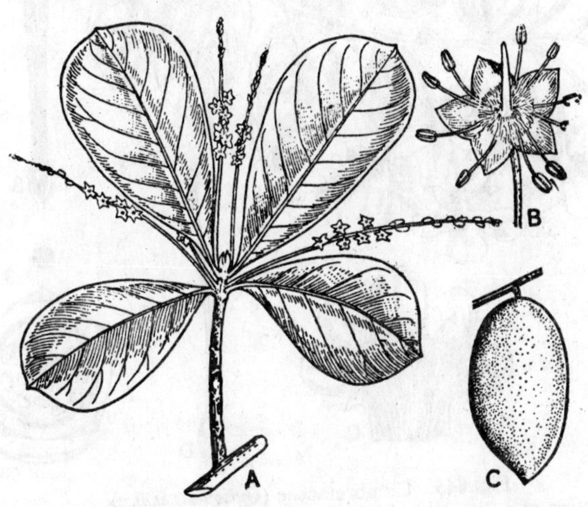

Fig. 644. Combretaceae (*Terminalia catappa*).
A, Portion of a flowering shoot; B, Flower; C, Fruit.

B. Inflorescence cymose; calyx-lobes imbricate; stamens with glands or staminodes; ovule solitary .. .. *Gyrocarpus.*

Common plants

(1) *Anogeissus latifolia* Wall., a tree. (2) The Indian almond (*Terminalia catappa* L.), frequently cultivated. (3) Myrobolan (*T. chebula* Roxb.). (4) The Beleric myrobolan (*T. belerica* Roxb.). (5) *T. arjuna* W. & A., a common avenue tree, occasionally planted in gardens. (6) *T. tomentosa* W. & A., a large tree with villous twigs. (7) Rangoon creeper (*Quisqualis indica* L.), a common climbing garden plant. (8) *Lumnitzera littoria* Voigt., a small tree found in the Sundribans. (9) *Gyrocarpus americana* Jacq., a large tree. (10) *Combretum*

decandrum Roxb., a large shrub. (11) *Combretum ovalifolium* Roxb., a large climbing shrub.

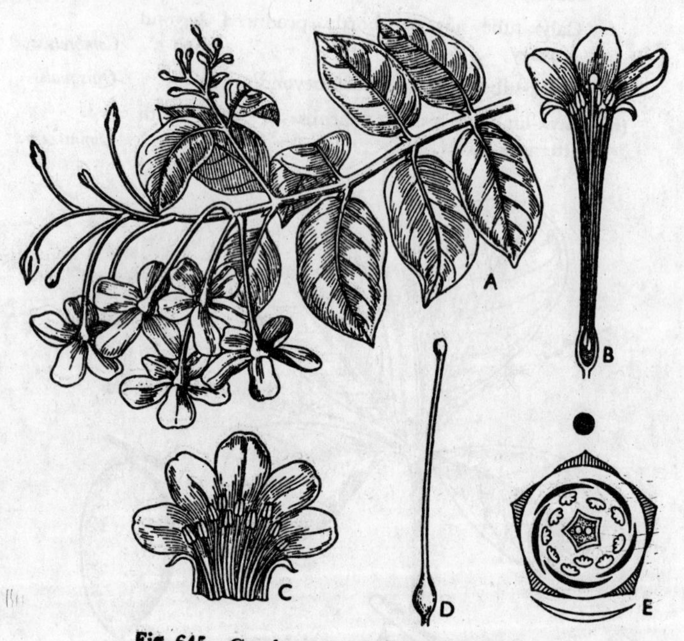

Fig. 645. Combretaceae (*Quisqualis indica*).
A, Portion of a flowering shoot; B, V.s. of a flower; C, Upper portion of the corolla tube split open; D, Pistil; E, Floral diagram.

Affinity

This family is closely related to Myrtaceae in the inferior ovary and number of perianth leaves, but readily distinguished by the number of stamens, 1-celled ovary with 4–6 pendulous ovules and drupaceous indehiscent fruit.

Economic importance

This family has some economic importance. The Indian almond (*Terminalia catappa*) yields edible nuts. *Terminalia chebula*, the common myrobolan, is one of the important commercial products of India. Many plants of this family are medicinal. The bark of *Terminalia arjuna* is used in cardiac trouble. Myrobolans are used in medicine and in tanning. Some plants are useful for timbers. Species of *Combretum* and *Quisqualis* are ornamentals.

MYRTACEAE

General characters

Plants—trees or shrubs. Leaves—usually opposite, simple, entire, coriaceous, *gland-dotted,* exstipulate, usually with *submarginal veins.*

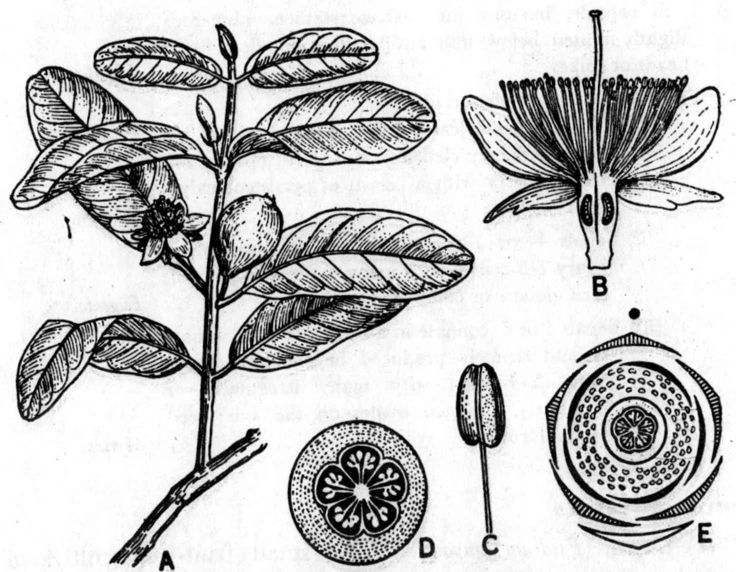

Fig. 646. Myrtaceae (*Psidium guyava*).
A, Portion of a flowering shoot; B, V.s. of a flower; C, Stamen; D, T.s. of ovary; E, Floral diagram.

Inflorescence—cymose (solitary in *Psidium*). Flowers—regular, bisexual, epigynous. Sepals—4–5 (but absent in *Eucalyptus*), usually free, sometimes more or less persistent or thrown up as a cup, quincuncial. Petals—4–5, free, inserted on a disc forming a lining to the calyx-tube, imbricate. Stamens—*numerous, free* or polyadelphous (e.g., *Melaleuca*), *bent inwards in bud*, inserted on the disc, with 2-celled anthers; connective often prominent and gland-tipped. Carpels—(2–5) or numerous; ovary *inferior*, 1-many-celled with 2-many ovules situated on axile placenta; style long. Fruit—berry or capsule, tipped by calyx-limbs. Seeds—exalbuminous. Embryo—thick, often curved.

Floral formula

$\oplus$ ⚥ $K_{4-5}\ C_{4-5}\ A_{\infty}\ \overline{G}_{(2-5)}$

Number and distribution

This family consists of about 80 genera and 3,000 species which are chiefly distributed in tropical regions.

KEY TO GENERA

A. Fruit capsule, bursting into valves; stamens numerous, slightly united below into antipetalous bundles; fls. in heads or spikes .. .. *Melaleuca*.

B. Fruit fleshy berry (indehiscent):

(*i*) Sepals subimbricate and closed in bud but become deeply cleft and valvate in opened fls.; fruit a berry with a crown of persistent calyx; seed reniform .. .. .. *Psidium*.

(*ii*) Sepals 4- or 5-lobed both in bud and flower; ovary 2–3-celled, with many ovules in each cell; seed globose or compressed .. .. *Eugenia*.

(*iii*) Sepals 4 or 5, connate in a turbinate tube, adnate to and scarcely produced beyond the ovary; ovary 2–4-celled with many irregularly or biseriately arranged ovules on the axis; seed subreniform .. .. .. *Myrtus*.

Common plants

(1) *Guava* (*Psidium guyava* L.), a small fruit-tree cultivated throughout India. (2) Black plum or Jambu (*Eugenia jambolana* Lamk. =*Syzygium cuminii* Skeels), a large fruit-tree. (3) Rose-apple (*Eugenia jambos* L.=*Syzygium jambos* Alston), a small fruit-tree. (4) Malay apple (*Eugenia malaccensis* L.=*Syzygium malaccense* Merr. & Perry), another small fruit-tree. (5) Clove (*Eugenia caryophyllaea* Wight= *Syzygium aromaticum* Merr. & Perry), cultivated in South India and Ceylon, yields cloves which are dried unopened flower buds. (6) *Melaleuca leucadendron* L., a native of Malacca Islands, yields the 'cajeput oil' of commerce. (7) *Eucalyptus globosus* Labille, cultivated throughout India which produces timber and an oil. (8) Myrtle (*Myrtus communis* L.=*Acmena communis* Merr. & Perry), a shrub of hedges. (9) Bottle brush tree (*Callistemon linearis* L.), commonly planted in gardens.

Affinity

This family is closely allied to Rosaceae on the one hand and to Melastomaceae, Lythraceae and Onagraceae on the other, but

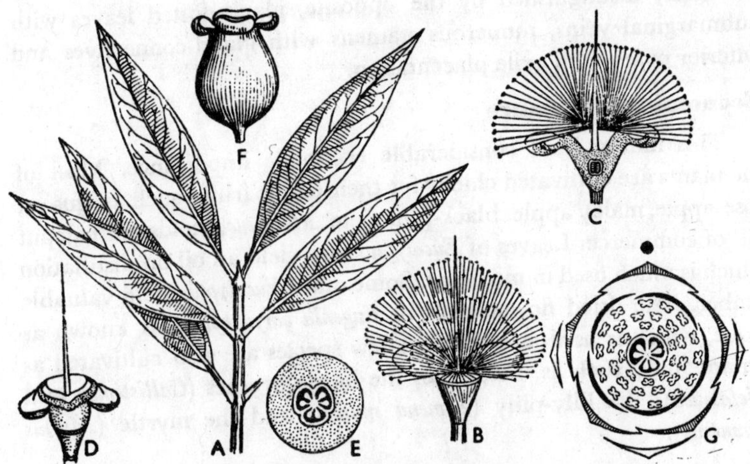

Fig. 647. Myrtaceae (*Eugenia jambos*).
A, Portion of a shoot; B, Flower; C, V.s. of the same; D, Pistil; E, T.s. of ovary; F, Fruit; G, Floral diagram.

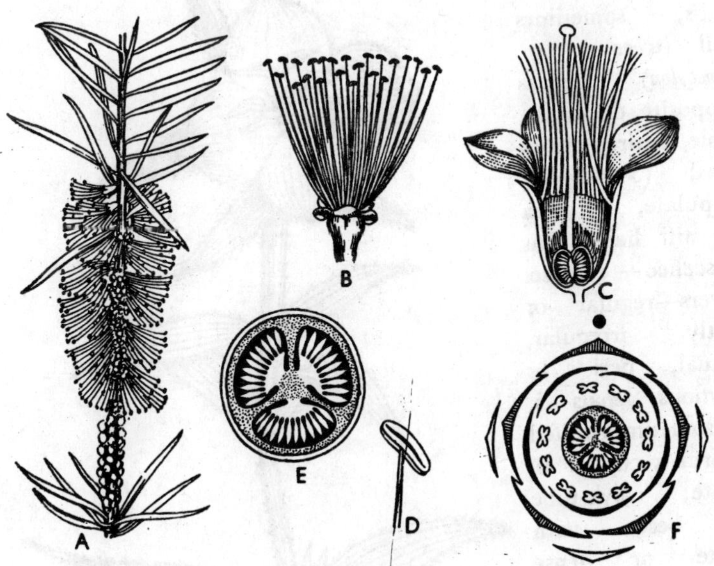

Fig. 648. Myrtaceae (*Callistemon linearis*).
A, Portion of a flowering shoot; B, Flower after removal of calyx and corolla; C, V.s. of a flower; D, Stamen; E, T.s. of ovary; F, Floral diagram.

is readily distinguished by the opposite, gland-dotted leaves with submarginal veins, numerous stamens with gland-connectives and inferior ovary with axile placentation.

Economic importance

This family is of considerable economic importance. Most of the plants are cultivated chiefly for their edible fruits, such as, guava, rose-apple, malay apple, black-plum, etc. *Melaleuca* yields the 'cajeput oil' of commerce. Leaves of *Eucalyptus* also yield an oil on distillation which is much used in medicine. Some other *Eucalyptus* yield valuable timber. The dried flower buds of *Eugenia caryophylloea* is known as clove, which is used as a spice. A few species are also cultivated as ornamentals, such as, *Eucalyptus*, the bottle brushes (*Callistemon* and *Melaleuca*), the lilly-pilly (*Acmena smithii*) and the myrtle (*Myrtus communis*).

MELASTOMACEAE

General characters

Plant—herbs or shrubs, sometimes small trees (e.g., *Memecylon*). Leaves—opposite, decussate, simple, entire, curvi-veined (*3–9-nerved*), exstipulate, often with stiff hairs. Inflorescence — cymose. Flowers—regular or slightly irregular, bisexual, peri- or epigynous. Sepals—5, free, sometimes united to form a cup or 0, valvate; calyx-tube often beset with stellate or dense tomentum. Petals—usually 5, free, *twisted*. Stamens—usually

Fig. 649. Melastomaceae (*Osbeckia chinensis*).

double the number of petals, and in two whorls, either all alike (e.g., *Osbeckia*), or alternately different in length and form (e.g., *Melastoma*); anthers long and linear, *beaked*, opening by apical pores and variously curved; filaments bent inwards. Carpels—(4–5); ovary usually inferior, sometimes superior, usually 4–5 celled with numerous

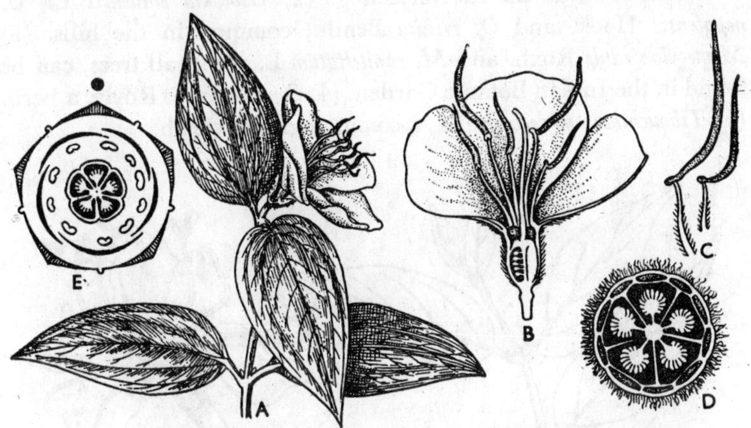

Fig. 650. Melastomaceae (*Tibouchina semidecandra*). A, Portion of a flowering shoot; B, V.s. of a flower; C, Stamens (dimorphic); D, T.s. of ovary; E, Floral diagram.

anatropous ovules in each cell, style and stigma 1 and simple. Fruit—usually capsule or berry. Seed—exalbuminous, with minute embryo.

Floral formula

$\oplus$ ⚥ $K_{5 \text{ or } 0}\ C_5\ A_{5+5}\ \overline{G}_{(4-5)}$

Number and distribution

This family consists of about 150 genera and 4,000 species which are chiefly found in the hills.

Key to Genera

A. Fruit capsule; seeds many; ovary 4–5-celled; placentation axile; leaves 3- or more-nerved from base:

(*a*) Petals 4–5; seeds curved—

(*i*) Stamens all alike .. .. .. *Osbeckia.*

(*ii*) Stamens unequal .. .. .. *Melastoma.*

(*b*) Petals 3: seeds straight .. .. .. *Sonerila.*

B. Fruit berry; seeds solitary; ovary 1-celled; placentation free central; leaves pinnately nerved .. .. *Memecylon.*

Common plants

(1) *Melastoma malabathricum* L., commonly found from the foot of the Himalayas up to Darjeeling. (2) *Osbeckia chinensis* L., *O. nepalensis* Hook. and *O. crinita* Benth., common in the hills. (3) *Memecylon edule* Roxb. and *M. capitellatum* L. are small trees, can be found in the Indian Botanic Garden. (4) *Sonerila tenera* Royle, a herb. (5) *Tibouchina semidecandra* L., a common garden shrub.

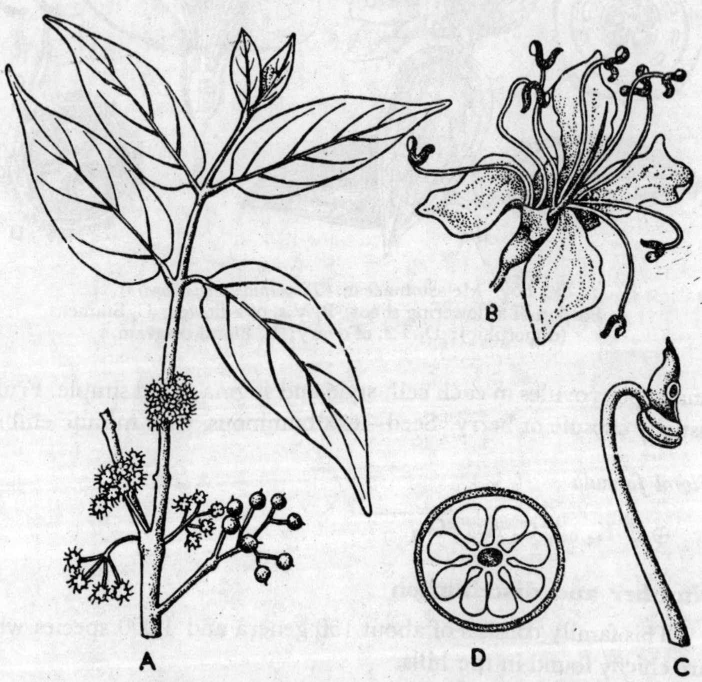

Fig. 651. Melastomaceae (*Memecylon edule*).
A, Portion of a flowering shoot; B, Flower; C, Stamen; D, T.s. of ovary.

Affinity

This family is allied to Myrtaceae and Lythraceae but readily distinguished by 3–9-nerved leaves, valvate calyx, twisted corolla and beaked anthers.

Economic importance

This family is of little economic importance. Certain genera are important for ornamentals, such as, *Memecylon*, *Tibouchina*, *Medinella*, *Melastoma*, etc.

ONAGRACEAE

General characters

Plants—mostly annual or perennial herbs (occasionally aquatic e.g., *Jussiaea*), sometimes shrubs (e.g., *Fuchsia*). Leaves—opposite or alternate, always simple, entire, exstipulate or stipulate (e.g., *Fuchsia*). Inflorescence—racemose (raceme or spike). Flowers—usually regular, bisexual, epigynous, *tetramerous*, sometimes pentamerous (e.g.,

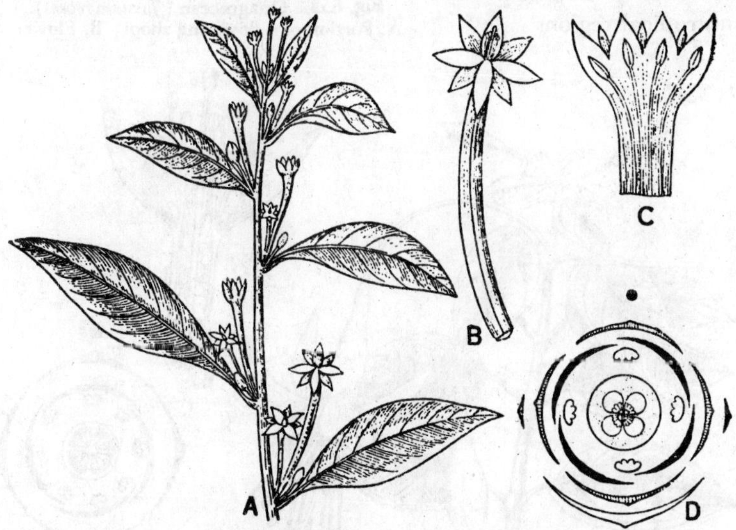

Fig. 652. Onagraceae (*Ludwigia parviflora*).
A, Portion of a flowering shoot; B, Flower; C, L.s. of the same; D, Floral diagram.

Fuchsia). Sepals—usually (4), but 6 in *Jussiaea*, tubular, adnate to the ovary and often extended far above it, valvate, persistent (e.g., *Ludwigia* and *Jussiaea*). Petals—usually 4 imbricate. Stamens—4 or 4+4, obdiplostemonous, rarely 6 (e.g., *Jussiaea*). Carpels—usually (4); ovary *inferior*, *usually 4-celled* with 1 to numerous anatropous ovules in each cell; style 1, slender. Fruit—a capsule or nut-like, sometimes berry (e.g., *Fuchsia*). **Seed**—exalbuminous. **Embryo**—straight.

Floral formula

$$\oplus ⚥ K_{(4)}\ C_4\ A_4 \text{ or } {}_{4+4} \text{ or } {}_6\ \overline{G}_{(4)}$$

Number and distribution

This family consists of 20 genera with about 650 species widely distributed but mostly abundant in subtropical regions.

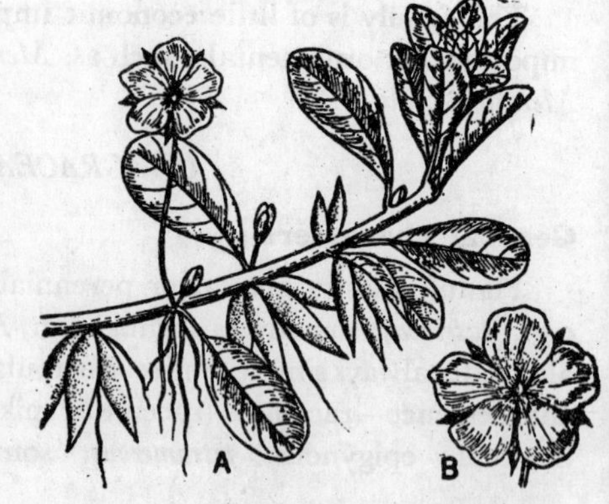

Fig. 653. Onagraceae (*Jussiaea repens*). A, Portion of a flowering shoot; B, Flower.

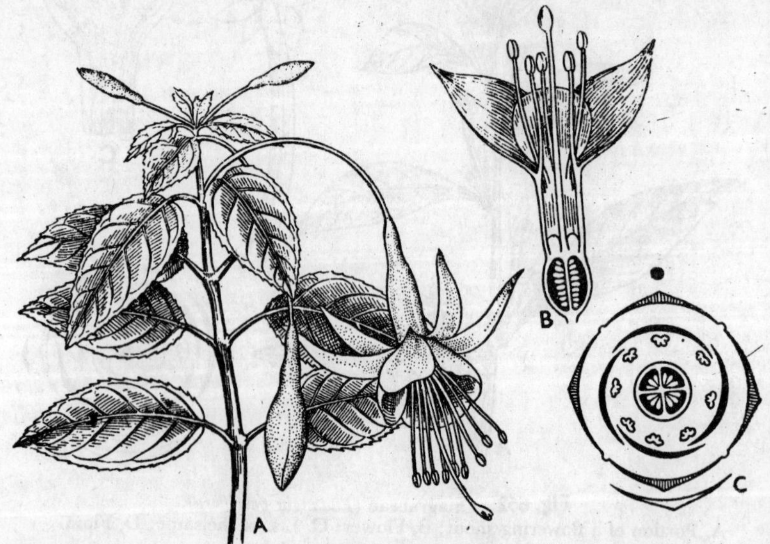

Fig. 654. Onagraceae (*Fuchsia hybrida*). A, Portion of a flowering shoot; B, V.s. of a flower; C, Floral diagram.

Key to Genera

Seeds numerous; plants growing in swamps—

(*i*) Stamens twice as many as the calyx-lobes .. .. *Jussiaea*.

(*ii*) Stamens equal in number to the calyx-lobes .. *Ludwigia*.

Common plants

(1) *Jussiaea repens* L., a herb commonly found creeping on the margins of tanks and floating on the surface of water. (2) *J. suffruticosa* L., a semishrubby erect perennial. (3) *Ludwigia parviflora* Roxb., an erect herb commonly found in rice-fields. (4) *L. prostrata* Roxb., a prostrate herb found in rice-fields. (5) *Fuchsia hybrida* L., a garden plant with handsome flowers, commonly found in the hills.

N.B. The genus *Trapa* (*Trapa bispinosa* L., the water chestnut) has now-a-days been placed in the Family Trapacae.

Affinity

This family is closely allied to Lythraceae but readily distinguished in having 4-merous flowers, inferior many-ovuled ovary, and exalbuminous seeds.

Economic importance

This family is of little economic importance. Some plants, such as, *Fuchsia* and others are ornamentals.

ORDER 30. UMBELLIFLORAE

Plants woody or herbaceous. Leaves alternate, often large with a sheathing base, exstipulate. Inflorescence, generally umbellate, (simple or compound). Flowers regular, bisexual, epigynous. Stamens episepalous. Carpels often reduced to two. Ovule solitary in each chamber, pendulous, anatropous with one integument. Seeds with copious endosperm. Oil or resin-passages often present.

According to Engler this order consists of 3 families, viz., Araliaceae, Umbelliferae and Cornaceae. Bentham and Hooker have placed the family Umbelliferae in the cohort Umbellales under the subclass Polypetalae. This order of Hutchinson contains 5 families.

UMBELLIFERAE (*APIACEAE*)

General characters

Plants—biennial or perennial herbs with furrowed stems, usually with hollow internodes; schizogenous oil ducts present in the stems, roots and mostly also among the mericarps; these are known as '*vittae*'. Leaves—alternate (but opposite in *Apiastrum*), often decompound, sometimes simple (e.g., *Hydrocotyle* and *Bupleurum*), with *sheathing leaf-bases*, exstipulate. Inflorescence—usually compound umbel, sometimes simple umbel (e.g., *Hydrocotyle*), subtended by involucel. Flowers—small, bisexual (sometimes unisexual), regular, epigynous. Sepals—5, free, often scarcely indicated. Petals—5, free, often unequal, with short claws, imbricate. Stamens—5, free, alternating with petals and arising from an epigynous disc. Carpels—(2), median, mostly prominently ribbed and often with parallel resinous canal; style 2, free but swollen at the base to form a *stylopodium;* ovary inserted on a disc, *inferior*, 2-celled with one pendulous ovule in each cell; stigma bifid. Fruit—*cremocarp* or *nut-like*. Seed—albuminous with minute embryo.

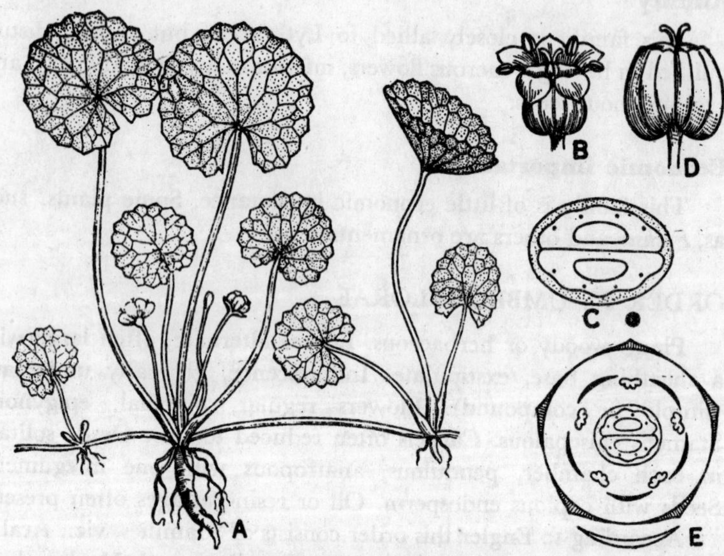

Fig. 655. Apiaceae (*Centella asiatica*). A, Portion of a plant with flowers; B, Flower; C, T.s. of ovary; D, Fruit; E, Floral diagram.

Floral formula

$\oplus$ ⚥ $K_5\ C_5\ A_5\ \overline{G}_{(2)}$

Number and distribution

This family consists of about 270 genera and 2,900 species which are cosmopolitan but chiefly temperate, specially in the Northern Hemisphere.

KEY TO GENERA

A. Leaves simple:

Umbels simple .. .. *Hydrocotyle.*

Umbels compound .. .. *Bupleurum.*

B. Leaves compound:

(*a*) Secondary ridges of the fruit not prominent—

(*i*) Primary ridges not winged:

Flowers yellow, furrows of the fruit vittate .. *Foeniculum.*

Flowers white—

Furrows of the fruit 1-vittate:

Lobes of leaves linear, fruit ovoid, laterally compressed .. .. .. *Carum.*

Each leaflet pinnate or partite, fruit not laterally compressed .. .. *Seseli.*

Marshy herbs, leaves 1–3-pinnate, fruit longer than broad, carpophore 0 .. .. *Oenanthe.*

(*ii*) Primary lateral ridges of the fruit excurrent, winged .. .. .. *Peucedanum.*

(*b*) Secondary ridges of the fruit prominent

Involucre of bracts none, fruits glabrous .. *Coriandrum.*

Bracts of involucre numerous, pinnate, cultivated for its edible root, fruit hirsute .. .. *Daucus.*

Range of floral structures

The constant feature of this family is the presence of umbellate inflorescence. The most commonest form of inflorescence is compound umbel, but simple umbels do also occur, e.g., *Hydrocotyle* and *Astrantia.* Occasionally, the umbel is reduced to a single flower, as in species of *Hydrocotyle* and *Azorella*. In *Eryngium*, the flowers are aggregated into dense heads being enclosed by a whorl of bracts; each flower is again surrounded by a bract. The terminal flower is represented by the genus *Daucus*.

As a matter of fact, the floral development is very much astounding, because the stamens grow out first followed usually by petals and then by sepals. The presence of calyx is less perceptible. The two rudimentary carpels develop later on. Firstly they separate and become joined at their margins, whereas the stylopodium is formed by the roof.

Calyx is usually much smaller than the corolla, and they are represented by inconspicuous teeth being present on the upper edge of the ovary. In *Eryngium*, *Astrantia*, *Sanicula* these structures are best developed; the sepals are with slight imbricate aestivation. The corolla is either with open, valvate or imbricate aestivation. The apex of corolla becomes sometimes pointed and the length of the point and the extent of inflexion in the bud give characters for recognition of different genera.

The aggregation of flowers into more or less dense inflorescences tenders them conspicuous. The flowers in the circumference are often sterile (male) and become zygomorphic. The outer petals become much larger than the inner ones of the same flower and of the other flowers of the head. The flowers are usually white and sometimes become pink or yellow in colour, and very rarely they appear as blue.

The fruit is crowned by the ring of calyx and the remains of the styles, and finally divides into two carpels. Before falling, two mericarps often hang for a short period on a thin simple or bifurcated stalk, the *carpophore*. There are found great variations in the nature and structure of the mericarps and these variations ultimately provide characters for the identification of genera and larger groups.

This family has been divided into 3 subfamilies based on the characters of fruits:

(a) **Hydrocotyloideae:** The fruit is with a woody endocarp but with no free carpophore. Vittae (oil-glands) absent or sunk in the main ribs only.

(b) **Apioideae:** The endocarp is soft and parenchymatous but sometimes with subepidermal layers of wood fibres. Vittae are of various types; style on the apex of stylopodium.

(c) **Saniculoideae:** The endocarp is soft and parenchymatous, exocarp rarely smooth; style is surrounded by a ring-like disc (stylopodium).

Common plants

(1) Coriander (*Coriandrum sativum* L.). (2) Anise or Fennel (*Foeniculum vulgare* Gaertn.). (3) Ajowan (*Carum copticum* Benth. = *Trachyspermum amni* Sprague). (4) *Carum roxburghianum* Benth. = *Trachyspermum burghianum* Craib. (5) Caraway (*Carum carui* L.). (6) Point caraway (*Cuminum cyminum* L.). (7) Carrot (*Daucus carota* L.). (8) *Peucedanum sowa* Kurz. = *Anethum graveolens* L. (9) *Ferula asafoetida* Boiss. (10) Pennywort (*Hydrocotyle asiatica* L. = *Centella asiatica* Urban), occurs as weed. (11) Celery (*Apium graveolens* L.), used as a vegetable. (12) Parsnip (*Pastinaca sativa*), also used

as a vegetable. (13) *Bupleurum mucronatum* W. & A., occurs as a weed in the hills. (14) *Seseli indicum* W. & A., an annual much branched herb, common. (15) *Oenanthe benghalensis* Benth. and *O. stolonifera* Wall. = *O. javanica* DC., commonly found in moist shady places near ponds and ditches.

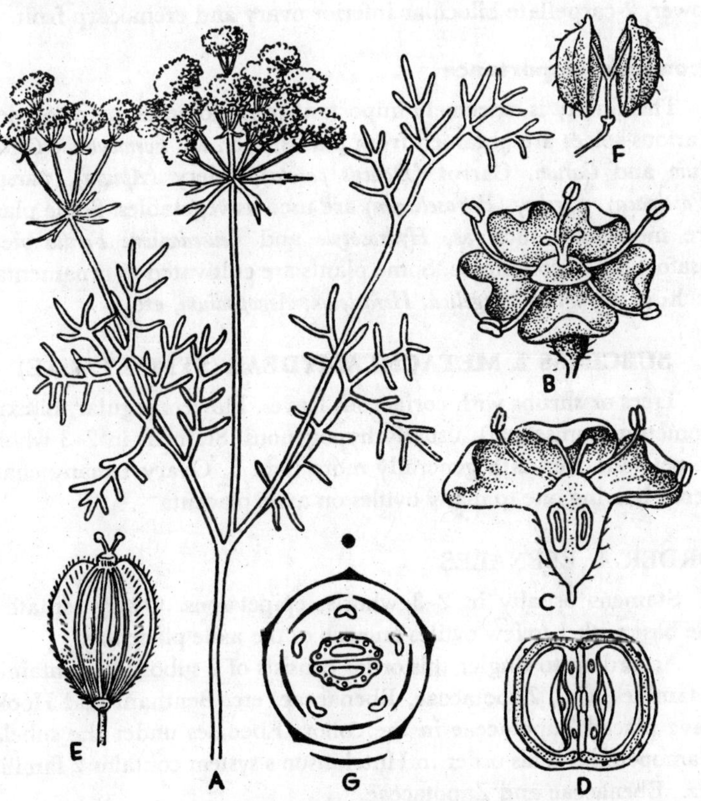

Fig. 656. Apiaceae (*Coriandrum sativum*).
A, Portion of a flowering shoot; B, Flower; C, L.s. of the same; D, T.s. of ovary; E, Fruit; F, The same split open showing the carpophore; G, Floral diagram.

Affinity

This family recalls that of Compositae in the reduction of calyx, bicarpellate pistil, and two distinct styles, but readily distinguished by the character of the fruit. It is also related to Rhamnales in the reduction of calyx, single staminal whorl, the prominent disc, and solitary ovule. Hutchinson has not kept Umbelliferae apart from Rhamnales. So according to him, a phylogenetic relationship can be drawn as such, Rhamnales→Umbelliferae→Compositae. Umbelliferae is readily distinguished from the allied families by the aromatic odour, sheathing leaf-base, umbellate inflorescence, pentamerous flower, 2-carpellate bilocular inferior ovary and cremocarp fruit.

Economic importance

This family is extremely important from domestic point of view. Various spices are obtained from plants, such as, *Foeniculum*, *Coriandrum* and *Carum*. Carrot (*Daucus carota*), celery (*Apium*), parsnip (*Pastinaca*), parsley (*Petroselinum*) are used as vegetables. Some plants are medicinal, such as, *Hydrocotyle* and *Peucedanum*. *Ferula* yields 'asafoetida' of commerce. Some plants are cultivated as ornamentals, such as, *Eryngium*, *Angelica*, *Heracleum*, *Aegopodium*, etc.

SUBCLASS 2. METACHLAMYDEAE (SYMPETALAE)

Trees or shrubs with coriaceous leaves. Flowers regular, bisexual (sometimes unisexual), usually hypogynous. Stamens in 2–3 whorls, epipetalous. Perianth generally more than 5. Ovary 1-many chambered bearing one to many ovules on axile placenta.

ORDER 4. EBENALES

Stamens usually in 2–3 whorls, epipetalous. Ovary septate at the base with 1 to few ovules on each of the axile placentae.

According to Engler this order consists of 2 suborders containing 5 families, viz., Zapotaceae, Ebenaceae, etc. Bentham and Hooker have placed Zapotaceae in the cohort Ebenales under the subclass Gamopetalae. This order in Hutchinson's system contains 2 families, viz., Ebenaceae and Zapotaceae.

ZAPOTACEAE

General characters

Plants—trees or shrubs with milky latex, the young twigs have woolly coverings. Leaves—alternate, simple, entire, coriaceous, exstipulate or stipulate. Inflorescence—cymose in the axils of leaves or an old stem. Flowers—regular, bisexual, hypogynous. Sepals—(4–12), the lobes subequal or the inner larger, imbricate. Petals—as many as or 2–4 times as many as the calyx-lobes, united into a tube shorter than the calyx. Stamens—usually in 2 or 3 whorls of 4–5 each, but usually only the inner whorl fertile, others reduced to staminodes, epipetalous. Carpels—(4–5); ovary superior, 4–5-celled with 1 anatropous ascending ovule in each cell, integument one; style simple; stigma not prominent. Fruit—berry or rarely 1-seeded drupe-like. Seeds—with hard shining testa; endosperm oily.

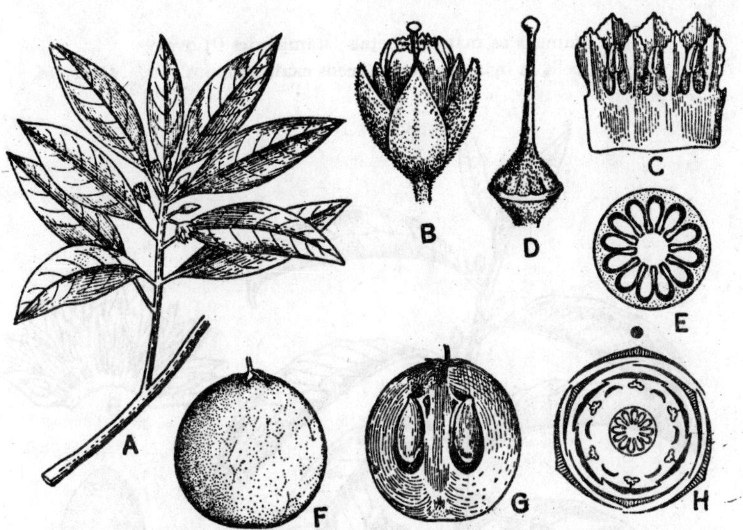

Fig. 657. Zapotaceae (*Achras zapota*).
A, Portion of a flowering shoot; B, Flower, C, Corolla-tube split open; D, Pistil; E, T.s. of ovary; F, Fruit; G, L.s. of the same; H, Floral diagram.

Floral formula

$$\oplus ⚥ K_{(4-12)} \overline{C_{(4-\infty)} A_{4-\infty}} \underline{G}_{(4-5)}$$

Number and distribution

This family consists of about 40 genera and 600 species. They are widely distributed in the tropics.

Key to Genera

A. Corolla-lobes and calyx-lobes equal in number:

(*a*) Calyx-segments in 1 series only; parts of fls. in whorl of 5; stamens as many as petals; staminodes as many as stamens and alternating with them; seeds exalbuminous—

(*i*) Fls. sessile in branched panicles; ovary glabrous, cells 1–2 .. .. *Sarcosperma.*

(*ii*) **Fls. pedicellate in axillary fascicles; ovary villous; cells 4–5 .. ..** ***Sideroxylon.***

(*b*) Calyx-segments in 2 distinct series; parts of flowers in whorls of 6—

(*i*) Stamens as many as petals; staminodes as many as stamens and alternating with them; ovary cells as many as petals; seeds albuminous .. .. *Achras.*

(*ii*) Stamens as many as petals; staminodes 0; ovary-cells as many as petals; seeds exalbuminous .. *Dichopsia.*

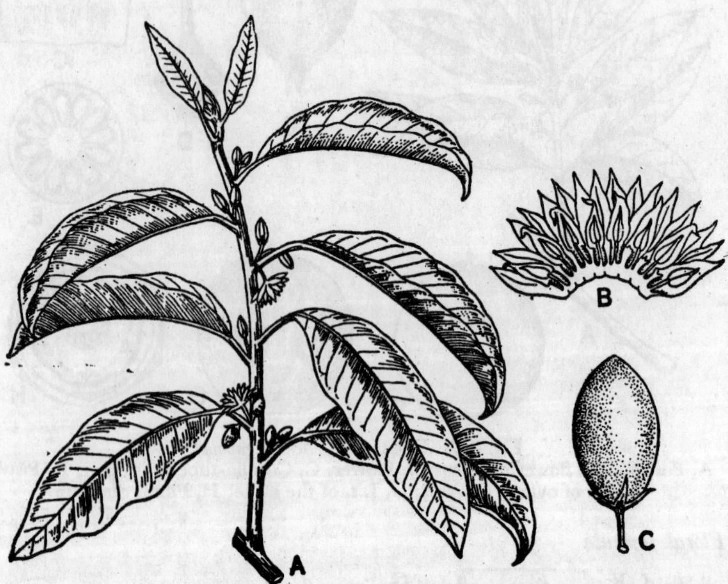

Fig. 658. Zapotaceae (*Mimusops elengi*).
A, Portion of a flowering shoot; B, Corolla-tube split open; C, Fruit.

B. Corolla-lobes more numerous than calyx-lobes; ovary-cells as many as calyx-lobes:

(*a*) Staminodes 0; stamens about 2–3 times as many as corolla-lobes, in 1–3 series; corolla 8–14; calyx-lobes and ovary-cells 4 or 6; seeds exalbuminous .. *Bassia.*

(*b*) Staminodes 6 or 8; stamens also 6–8, fewer than the corolla-lobes; corolla-lobes 18–24 in 2–3 series; calyx-lobes and ovary-cells 6 or 8; seeds albuminous .. *Mimusops.*

Common plants

(1) *Sarcospermum arboreum* Hook. f., a large tree with spreading branches. (2) *Sideroxylon tomentosum* Roxb., a large tree. (3) The Sapota or Sapodilla plum (*Achras zapota* L.), a medium tree cultivated for edible fruits. (4) The Mahua (*Bassia latifolia* Roxb. =*Madhuca indica* Gemel.), a common tree. (5) *Mimusops elengi* L. and *M. hexandra* Roxb. =*Manilkara hexandra* Dub., are trees often planted in gardens for fragrant flowers. (6) *Dichopsia pentaphylla* Hook. f., a tree.

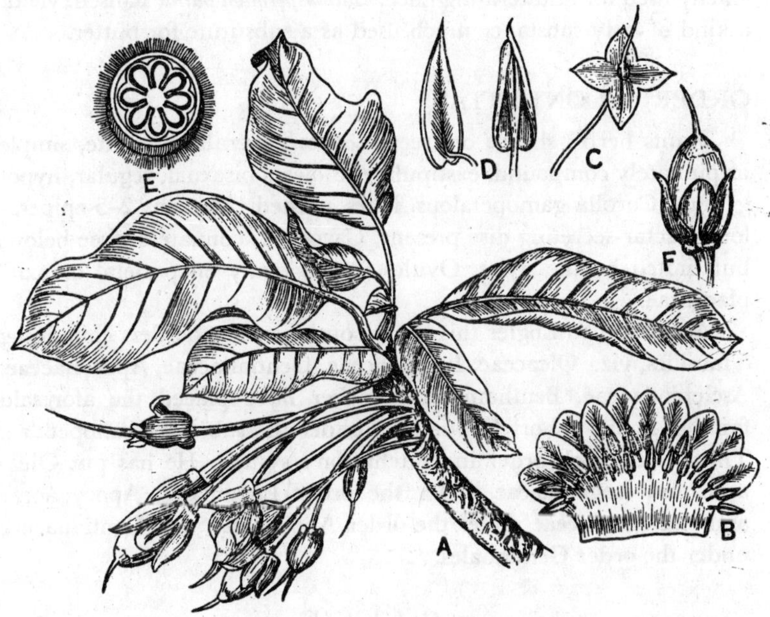

Fig. 659. Zapotaceae (*Bassia latifolia*).
A, Portion of a flowering shoot; B, Corolla-tube split open; C, Calyx; D, Stamen (front and back view); E, T.s. of ovary; F, Fruit.

Affinity

This family is related to Ebenaceae in the habit and structure of fruit but differs from it in having the completely septate superior ovary, each loculus containing a single ascending ovule having a single integument, and presence of milky latex.

Economic importance

This family is economically useful. The fruits of some species are edible, such as, *Achras zapota* (the sapodilla plum), *Chrysophyllum cainoto* L. (star-apple), *Vitellaria mammosa* Rdklf. (marmalade plum), *Mimusops elengi*, etc. The wood of *Sideroxylon* is very stiff and yields valuable timber, often known as Iron wood. The bark of some species is frequently used in medicine. *Mimusops*, *Payena* and *Palaquium gutta* Bureck. yield latex, which is a source of guttaparcha of commerce. The waxy flowers of *Bassia latifolia* produce a kind of country liquor, while the seeds yield a kind of oil, known as 'vegetable butter', chiefly used for adulterating ghee. *Butryospermum parkii* Kotsch. yields a kind of fatty substance much used as a substitute for butter.

ORDER 5. CONTORTAE

Plants herbs, shrubs or trees. Leaves generally opposite, simple or pinnately compound, exstipulate. Flowers bisexual, regular, hypogynous. Corolla gamopetalous, lobes twisted. Stamens 2–5-epipetalous, nectar-secreting disc present. Carpels 2, connate or free below, but united by the styles. Ovules few to many on parietal or axile placentae.

According to Engler this order consists of 2 suborders containing 5 families, viz., Oleaceae, Loganiaceae, Gentianaceae, Apocynaceae, Asclepiadaceae. Bentham and Hooker have placed the aforesaid families in the cohort Gentianales under the subclass Gamopetalae. There is no such order in Hutchinson's system. He has put Oleaceae and Loganiaceae under the order Loganiales, Apocynaceae and Asclepiadaceae under the order Apocynales, and Gentianaceae under the order Gentianales.

OLEACEAE

General characters

Plants—shrubs, sometimes climbing (e.g., *Jasminum*) or trees (e.g., *Olea*, *Linociera*, etc.). Leaves—usually opposite, simple, or pinnately compound, entire or toothed, exstipulate. Inflorescence—cymose, usually 3-chotomous cyme. Flowers—regular, usually bisexual (unisexual in *Fraxinus* and *Olea*), hypogynous. Sepals—(4–5), small, valvate. Petals—(4–5), sometimes free or 0, *mostly imbricate*. Stamens—*usually* 2, inserted on corolla-tube. Carpels—(2); ovary superior, 2-celled, usually with 2 *pendulous* or *ascending anatropous ovules* in each cell; style simple; stigma 1–2. Fruit—capsule (e.g., *Syringa*), berry (e.g., *Ligustrum*) or drupe (e.g., *Olea*,

Linociera, etc.), sometimes samara (e.g., *Fraxinus*). Seed—with abundant *fleshy endosperm*. Embryo—straight.

Floral formula

$\oplus$ ⚥ $K_{(4-5)}\ C_{(4-5)\ or\ 0}\ A_2\ \underline{G_{(2)}}$

Number and distribution

This family consists of 22 genera and about 500 species which are distributed from the temperate to the warmer regions.

Key to Genera

(*a*) Corolla-lobes imbricate, more than 4 in number—

(*i*) Fruit a didymous berry, 2- or 1-lobed; seeds single, erect, rarely 2 in each cell; fls. in 2- or 3-chotomous or simple cymes; plants usually erect or suberect shrubs with simple or compound leaves .. *Jasminum*.

(*ii*) Fruit a compound capsule; fls. in bracteate heads of 3-chotomous cymes; seeds orbicular, erect, stigma shortly 2-fid .. .. *Nyctanthes*.

(*b*) Corolla-lobes valvate never exceeding 4 in number; fruit a drupe; shrubs or trees—

(*iii*) Petals shortly united or sometimes absent; leaves with feathered leaf-veins; fls. in axillary panicles; seeds pendulous with fleshy albumen .. .. *Olea*.

(*iv*) Petals showy, free or united, induplicate; seeds solitary, pendulous, exalbuminous .. .. *Linociera*.

Range of floral structures

The flowers are usually small and they form compound raceme, as in *Ligustrum* and *Fraxinus*, while the flowers in *Jasminum nudiflorum*, remain united together in threes at the end of a shoot bearing scale. The flowers are generally axillary to bracts and a pair of bracteoles are found to be present.

The flowers are usually bisexual but unisexual flowers occur in *Fraxinus* and in some species of *Olea*.

The calyx is obliterated in *Fraxinus excelsior* and others. If calyx is found, it is tetramerous, sometimes the 5th sepal occurs in the species of *Jasminum*.

The number of petals is equal to the number of sepals and alternate with the latter. The aestivation is valvate in *Syringa* or imbricate in *Jasminum*. The petals become free or united in the genus *Fraxinus*. *Jasminum nudiflorum* has 6 petals. The corolla is generally tubular or rotate with its flattened limbs, as in ***Olea***, ***Ligustrum***, and ***Jasminum***.

The stamens are generally 2 and transverse but occasionally they are median. Sometimes 4 stamens occur in the monotypic genera *Hesperella* and *Tessarandra*, and these alternate with petals.

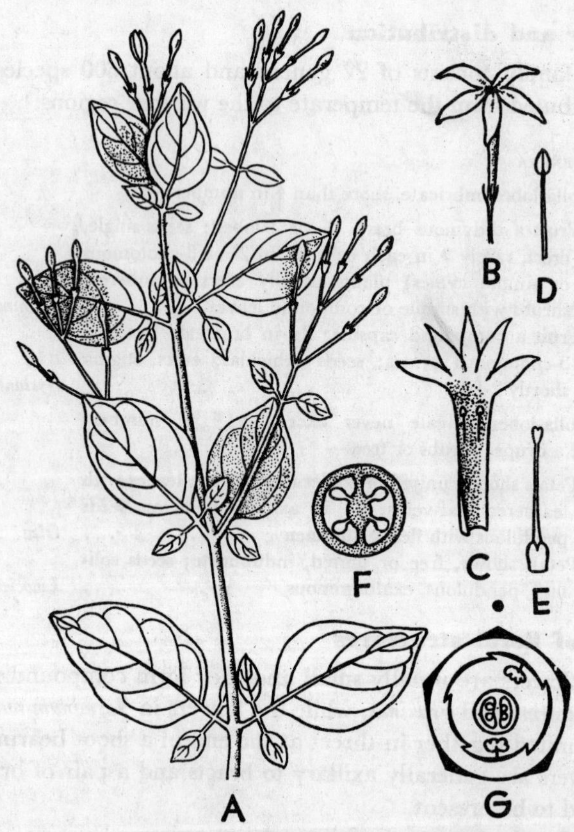

Fig. 660. Oleaceae (*Jasminum auriculatum*).
A, Portion of a flowering shoot; B, Flower; C, Corolla split open; D, Stamen; E, Pistil; F, T.s. of ovary; G, Floral diagram.

Two carpels are found to alternate with the stamens and they are generally median. The chamber of ovary becomes sometimes three to four. The ovules are generally 2 in each chamber, pendulous or ascending on axile placenta. One ovule is also sometimes found to occur.

Common plants

(1) Arabian Jasmine (*Jasminum sambuc* Ait.). (2) *Jasminum auriculatum* Vahl. and *J. grandiflorum* are commonly cultivated in gardens. (3) *Jasminum pubescens* Willd. (4) Night flowering jasmine (*Nyctanthes arbor tristis* L.=*J. multiflorum* Andr.), often planted in gardens. (5) Privet (*Ligustrum robustum* Bl.), a tree found in Bangla Desh and Assam. (6) *Olea dioica* Roxb., a tree 30–60 ft. high, chiefly found in North Bengal. (7) *Linociera ternifolia* Wall., a tree.

Affinity

According to Hutchinson this family is also allied to Melastomaceae. Some phylogenists consider this family to be related to Loganiaceae. It is allied to Rubiaceae and Apocynaceae but distinguished by the typically 2-merous flowers, aestivation of corolla, number of stamens, and 2-celled superior ovary with 2 ovules in each cell.

Economic importance

This family is of great economic importance. *Olea europaea* yields edible fruits and is the source of olive-oil of commerce. *Fraxinus excelsior* L. produces a valuable timber known as 'ash wood' for cabinet work. The corolla of *Nyctanthes* yields an orange dye. Some plants are ornamentals, such as, Privet (*Ligustrum*), Jasmine (*Jasminum*), fragrant olive (*Osmanthus*), Lilac (*Syringa*), etc.

GENTIANACEAE

General characters

Plants—generally annual or perennial herbs, often with dichotomous branching. Leaves—usually opposite and decussate (alternate in *Menyanthes*), sessile, simple, entire, 3–5-nerved, exstipulate. Inflorescence—cymose, often dichasial. Flowers—regular, bisexual, hypogynous, bracteate. Sepals—(4–5), tubular, persistent, imbricate. Petals—(4–5), tubular, rotate or salver- or funnel-shaped, twisted. Stamens—4–5, epipetalous, alternating with corolla-lobes. Carpels—(2); ovary superior, generally 1-celled (rarely 2-celled owing to the projection of two *parietal placentae* towards the centre) with numerous anatropous ovules; style simple; stigma simple or bilobed. Fruit—capsule. Seed—small with fleshy perisperm. Embryo—minute.

Floral formula

$\oplus$ ⚥ $K_{(4-5)}\ C_{(4-5)}\ A_{4-5}\ \underline{G_{(2)}}$

Number and distribution

This family consists of 70 genera and about 800 species which are chiefly found in the hills in temperate and tropical regions.

KEY TO GENERA

Style short, leaves opposite or rarely alternate:

(*i*) Corolla tubular-campanulate, without pits or depression; twiners .. .. .. *Crawfurdia.*

(*ii*) Corolla-lobes twisted, with pits at the base .. *Swertia.*

(*iii*) Corolla-lobes twisted clockwise; stigma divided; fls. irregular; minute herbs .. .. *Hoppea.*

(*iv*) Stigmas 2 .. .. *Canscora.*

(*v*) Corolla-lobes induplicate-valvate in bud; aquatic floating herbs with opposite leaves .. *Limnanthemum.*

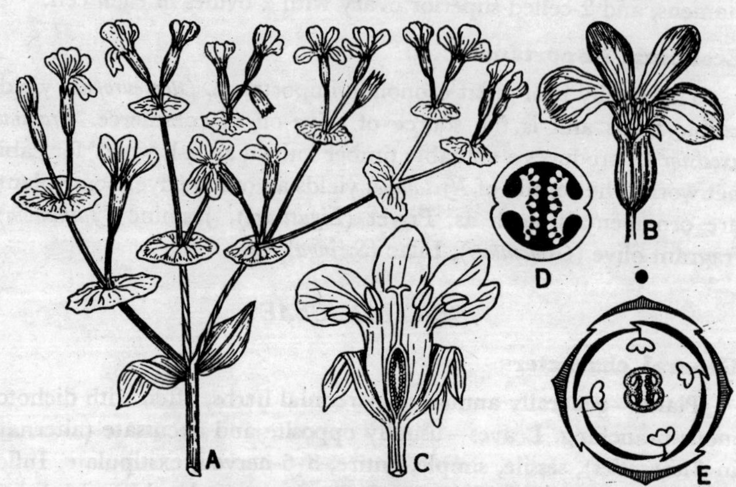

Fig. 661. Gentianaceae (*Canscora diffusa*).
A, Portion of a flowering shoot; B, Flower; C, V.s. of the same; D, T.s. of ovary; E, Floral diagram.

Common plants

(1) *Swertia chirata* Ham. grows in Darjeeling and other hilly places and is of great medicinal importance. *S. bicalyculata* L., a very common weed on the hills. (2) *Canscora decussata* R. & S. has amplexicaul leaves. (3) *Canscora grandiflora* Weight, has perfoliate bracts. (4) *Canscora diffusa* R. Br., a dichotomously branched herb with

connate leaves. (5) Snowflake (*Limnanthemum cristatum* Griseb.), a floating herb with white flowers, very common in tanks. (6) Gentian (*Gentiana lutea* L.), a medicinal plant. (7) *Hoppea dichotoma* Willd., a small much-branched, glabrous herb.

Affinity

This family is allied to Apocynaceae and Loganiaceae but readily distinguished from them by the nature of placentation, completely coherent carpels and absence of milky latex. Hutchinson has removed it from Loganiales and placed under the order Gentianales near the Primulales. This family also bears a close link with Caryophyllaceae basing on the nature of inflorescence and mode of branching.

Economic importance

This family is of little economic importance. *Gentiana*, *Swertia* and *Canscora* are used in medicine. Some plants are ornamentals, such as, *Gentiana*, *Exacum*, *Menyanthes*, *Nymphoides*, etc.

APOCYNACEAE

General characters

Plants—trees, shrubs, herbs or woody climbers (e.g., *Beaumontia*, *Ichnocarpus*, *Aganosma*, etc.) with *milky latex*. Leaves—usually opposite or whorled, simple, entire, *exstipulate*. Inflorescence—cymose or racemes passing into cymes. Flowers—regular, bisexual, hypogynous, bracteate. Sepals—(5), often glandular, imbricate. Petals—(5), usually salver- or funnel-shaped (but bell-shaped in *Allamanda*), the *throat* or *interior of the tube often with hairs*, *scales* or *other outgrowths* (corona), *twisted*, rarely valvate. Stamens—5, epipetalous, almost sessile in the corolla-tube or throat of corolla; anther often *sagittate;* filaments very short. Carpels—2, completely united or *united by their styles* and *free below;* ovary superior, 1- or 2-celled with few to many anatropous, generally pendulous, ovules on the partition walls; stigma often thickened and *dumbel-shaped*. Fruit—usually a *pair of follicles*, sometimes drupe or berry or capsule. Seeds—often flat, *winged* or *comose*, with cartilagenous or fleshy endosperm. Embryo—straight, nearly as long as the seed with flat, seldom folded, cotyledons.

Floral formula

$\oplus$ ⚥ $K_{(5)}\ \overline{C_{(5)}\ A_5}\ \underline{G}_{(2)}$

Number and distribution

This family consists of about 300 genera and 1,300 species which are chiefly found in the tropical and subtropical regions.

KEY TO GENERA

I. Corolla-lobes overlapping to the left; anthers included, free from the stigma; anther-cells round at the base.

A. Calyx glandular:

(*i*) Carpels-2, syncarpous; ovary 2-celled with axile ovules; fruit large, fleshy or pulpy within; seeds wingless or with pencil of hairs; spiny shrubs .. .. *Carissa.*

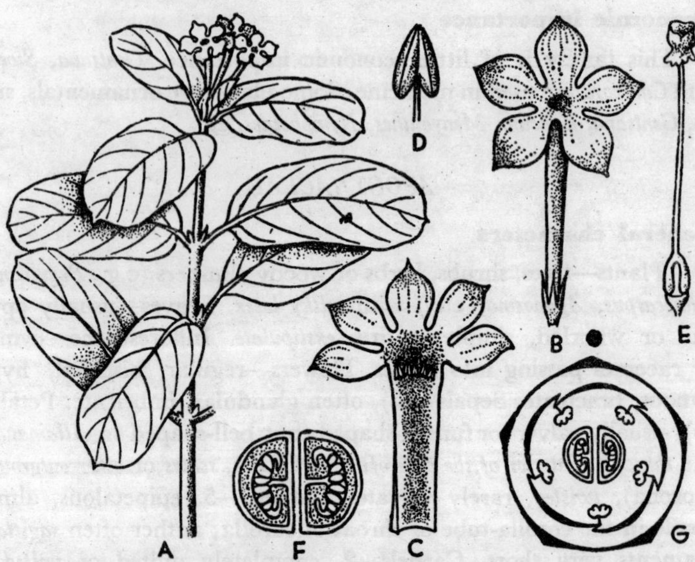

Fig. 662. Apocynaceae (*Vinca rosea*).
A, Portion of a flowering shoot; B, Flower; C, Corolla split open; D, Stamen; E, Pistil; F, T.s. of ovary; G, Floral diagram.

(*ii*) Carpels- 2, wholly united; corolla salver-shaped; ovary 1-celled with parietal ovules; indehiscent ft.; seeds without albumen; climbing .. .. *Willughbeia.*

(*iii*) Carpels-2, united by the style; fruit various, rarely a pair of follicles; seeds peltate, winged; trees with alternate leaves .. .. .. *Plumeria.*

(*iv*) Carpels-2, thoroughly distinct or united, style ealyptriform at the base, bifid at the top; fruit usually a double berry; disc present; undershrubs .. *Rauwolfia.*

(*v*) Corolla-lobes long, yellow or white; fruit a drupe; leaves whorled .. .. .. *Thevetia.*

B. Calyx glandular, carpels—2, distinct:

(*a*) Disc present—

(*i*) Fruit a product of 2 ripe carpels, usually 1 abortive; leaves opposite; corolla salver-shaped; shrubs .. .. *Kopsia.*

(*ii*) Stigma annulate, viscid, sometimes with reflected membrane; ovules 6-many; follicular fruit with truncated seeds, subcylindric; herbs .. *Vinca.*

(*iii*) Fruit 2 slender follicles; style filiform; seeds comose; disc various or absent; leaves whorled; trees .. .. *Alstonia*

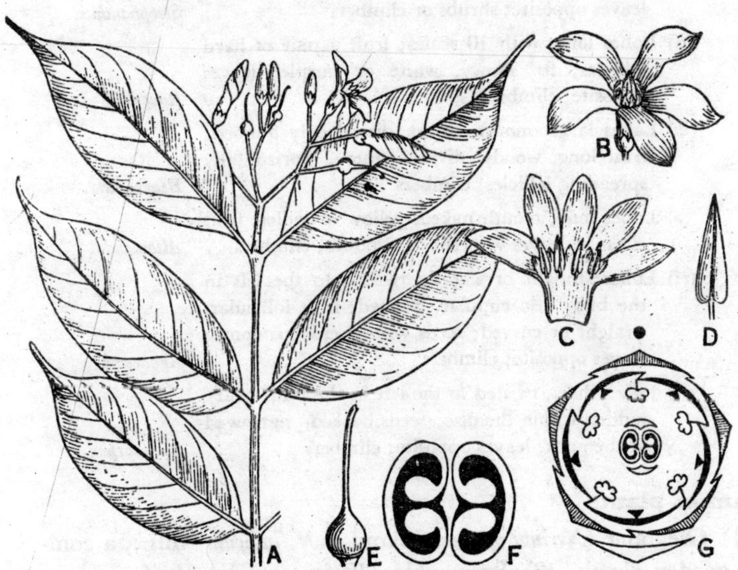

Fig. 663. Apocynaceae (*Wrightia tomentosa*).
A, Portion of a flowering shoot; B, Flower; C, Corolla split open; E, Pistil; F, T.s. of ovary; G, Floral diagram.

(*b*) Disc absent—

(*iv*) Corolla tubular; style short; fruit 2 elongated follicles; seeds comose; leaves membraneous; trees .. .. .. *Holarrhena.*

(*v*) Corolla salver-shaped with cylindric slender tube; fruit of 2 reniform or oblong-ovoid ribbed seeds, buried in scarlet pulpy aril, compressed; stamens sagittate; leaves opposite; shrubs .. .. *Tabernaemontana.*

(*vi*) Corolla rotate or salver-shaped; mouth of corolla with a ring of scales; anthers conniving in a cone around the top of the style and attached to it by a point on the connective; carpels free except at the styles; erect shrubs or small trees .. *Wrightia*.

II. Corolla-lobes overlapping to the right; anthers included or exserted; anther-cells conniving in a cone around the top of the style:

Corolla-throat broad with 5–10 scales, fruit 2 follicles—

(*i*) Lobes short with 5 broad scales; fruit elongate, erect follicles; seed villous, oblong; leaves whorled; shrubs .. .. .. *Nerium*.

(*ii*) Lobes long or tailed, with 10 scales; fruit elongate, hard, spreading; seeds compressed, fusiform; leaves opposite; shrubs or climbers .. *Strophanthus*.

(*iii*) Lobes long, with 10 scales; fruit a pair of hard follicles; fls. showy, white or purple; leaves opposite; climbers .. .. .. *Roupellia*.

(*iv*) Lobes large, mouth naked, disc deeply 5-lobed; fruit long, woody, dividing into 2 horizontally spreading follicles; climbers .. .. *Beaumontia*.

(*v*) Lobes long, mouth naked, yellow or violet; fruit capsule; leaves whorled or opposite; climbers .. *Allamanda*.

(*vi*) Lobes straight or slightly twisted to the left in the bud; disc cupular, 5-lobed; fruit follicular, straight or curved; seeds with deciduous coma; leaves opposite; climbers .. .. *Aganosma*.

(*vii*) Lobes short, twisted to the left in the bud; ovary hidden within the disc; seeds beaked, narrowed at the apex; leaves opposite; climbers .. *Ichnocarpus*.

Common plants

(1) Oleander (*Nerium odorum* Soland. = *N. indicum* Mill.), a common garden shrub. (2) Periwinkle (*Vinca rosea* L. = *Lochnera rosea* Reichb.), a common garden herb and also garden escape. (3) *Thevetia neriifolia* Juss. = *T. peruviana* Merr., common in gardens and also garden escape. (4) *Tabernaemontana coronaria* L. = *Ervatamia divaricata* Burhill, a cultivated garden shrub. (5) Natal plum (*Carissa carandas* L.), a spinous shrub cultivated for its acid berries. (6) Devil tree (*Alstonia scholaris* R. Br.), a tall tree with whorled leaves. (7) The Pagoda or Temple tree (*Plumeria acutifolia* Poir. = *P. rubra* L.), a small-sized tree found everywhere and very seldom fruits in our country. (8) *Ichnocarpus frutescens* R. Br., a much branched large

twining shrub. (9) *Aganosma caryophyllata* G. Don. = *A. dichotoma* K. Schum., very common in Bengal. (10) *Willughbeia edulis* Roxb., a climbing shrub with peduncles modified into tendrils. (11) *Holarrhena antidysenterica* Wall., a wild tree, the bark of which is used in dysentery.

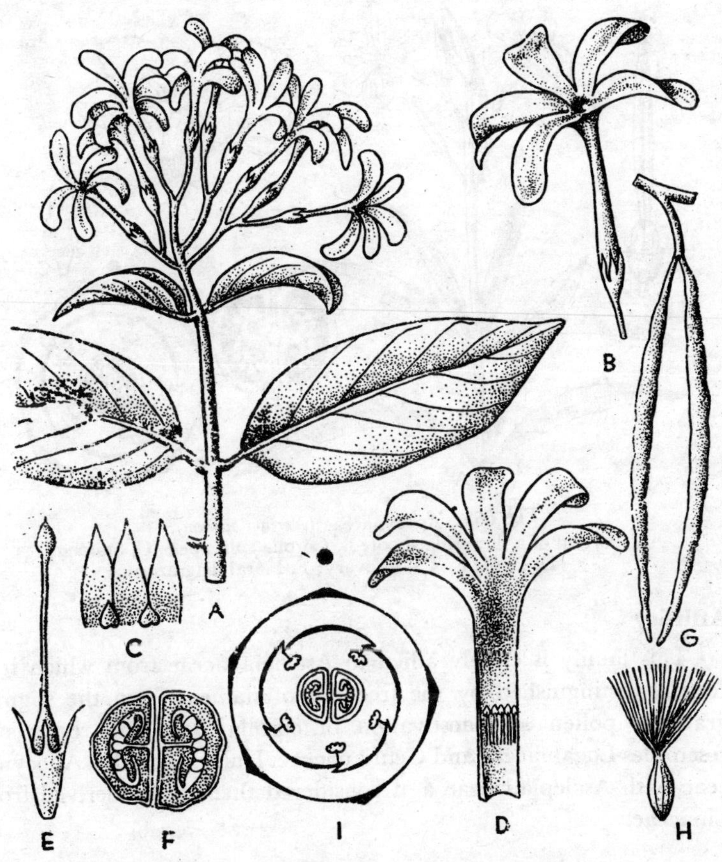

Fig. 664. Apocynaceae (*Holarrhena antidysenterica*). A, Portion of a flowering shoot; B, Flower; C, Calyx split open showing glands at the bases of sepals; D, Corolla split open; E, Pistil; F, T.s. of ovary; G, Fruit; H, Seed; I, Floral diagram.

(12) *Kopsia fruticosa* DC., a large evergreen shrub frequent in gardens. (13) *Allamanda cathartica* L., a climbing shrub in gardens. (14) *Rauwolfia serpentina* Benth. and *R. canescens* L. are medicinal plants found in shady waste places. (15) *Roupellia grata* Wall., a climber in gardens.

(16) *Beaumontia grandiflora* Wall., a lofty climber, often planted in gardens. (17) *Wrightia coccinea* Sims. and *W. tomentosa* Roem. & Schult., small trees commonly planted in gardens. (18) *Strophanthus combe* DC., yields the 'strophanthus' of allopathic medicine.

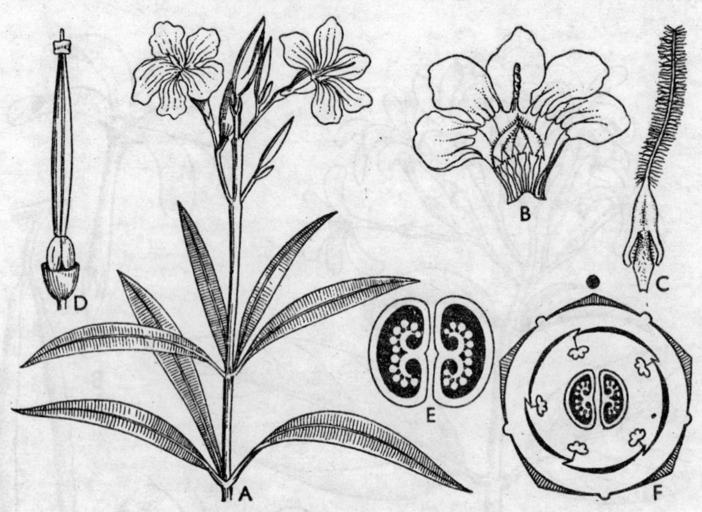

Fig. 665. Apocynaceae (*Nerium odorum*).
A, Portion of a flowering shoot; B, Corolla split open; C, Stamen; D, Pistil; E, T.s. of ovary; F, Floral diagram.

Affinity

This family is closely allied to Asclepiadaceae from which it is readily distinguished by the freedom of stamens from the stigma, granular pollen and aestivation of corolla. In some respects it resembles Loganiaceae and Gentianaceae. Hallier included Apocynaceae with Asclepiadaceae and considered them to be derived from Linaceae.

Economic importance

This family is domestically important. Some plants, such as, *Nerium*, *Alstonia*, *Holarrhena*, *Rauwolfia* and *Strophanthus* are most important from medicinal standpoint of view. *Carissa* yields edible fruits. The economic plants are *Dyera latifolia* Hook. f., *Urceola elastica* Roxb., *Ecetinos achinthes mucronata*, *Landolphia kirki* Dyer and *Carpodinus lanceolatus* Schum., which yield rubber. *Apocynum cannabinum* yields fibre which is used in making rope and cord. Some plants are ornamentals, such as, *Nerium*, *Vinca*, *Carissa*, *Allamanda*, *Plumeria*, *Thevetia*, *Ervatamia*, etc.

ASCLEPIADACEAE

General characters

Plants—perennial herbs or shrubs, or woody climbers (e.g., *Dregea*, *Finlaysonia*, etc.), with milky latex. Leaves—usually opposite and decussate, simple, entire, usually exstipulate. Inflorescence—usually cymose. Flowers—regular, bisexual, hypogynous, *gynandrous*, either petals or stamens or both may bear appendages of various forms forming a single or double corona. Sepals—(5), very deeply partite, quincuncial. Petals—(5), generally rotate, sometimes campanulate or salver-shaped or funnel-shaped, imbricate, rarely valvate (e.g., *Dregea*). Stamens—5, usually *adnate to the pistil forming a gynostegium; filaments united into a hollow column enclosing the style;* pollen grains united into 1 or 2 *pollinia* in each antherlobe (in subfamily Cynanchoideae) or remain in tetrads (in subfamily Periplocoideae); the pollinia usually being united in pairs to a gland (*retinaculum*) on the 5-angular stigma and covered by a membrane (cf. Orchidaceae). Carpels—2, *united only by their styles and free below;* ovary superior with numerous, anatropous and pendulous ovules situated on the ventral suture; styles 2, cohering above and dilating to form a flat, 5-angular or lobed stigmatic head. Fruit—of 2 *follicles*. Seed—comose, with bony endosperm and large embryo.

Floral formula

$\oplus$ ⚥ $K_{(5)}\ C_{(5)}\ \overline{A_5\ \underline{G_{(2)}}}$

Number and distribution

This family consists of 280 genera and about 1,800 species which are chiefly tropical.

KEY TO GENERA

A. Filaments free; anthers acute or appendicular; pollinia granular, in pairs in each cell:

(*a*) Coronal scales corolline, free, short, thick; seeds with coma—

(*i*) Corolla small, rotate, lobes valvate .. .. *Hemidesmus*.

(*ii*) Corolla small, rotate, lobes overlapping .. *Cryptolepis*.

(*iii*) Corolla large, funnel-shaped, lobes overlapping .. *Cryptostegia*.

(*b*) Coronal scales filiform, 5, free, close to or adnate to the filaments—

Corolla-lobes short and broad; filaments without intervening glands; seeds without coma; fls. in pubescent stout cyme .. .. .. *Finlaysonia.*

B. Filaments connate; anthers with membraneous tips inflexed; pollinia waxy, single in each cell, sessile or pedicelled in pairs, usually pendulous:

(*c*) Coronal appendages double, outer corolline and inner staminal, with ligulate scales—

Corolla wide rotate-campanulate, angularly 5-lobed; plant usually a twiner .. .. .. *Oxystelma.*

Corolla campanulate; processes of inner corona free from smooth staminal tube .. .. *Cynanchum.*

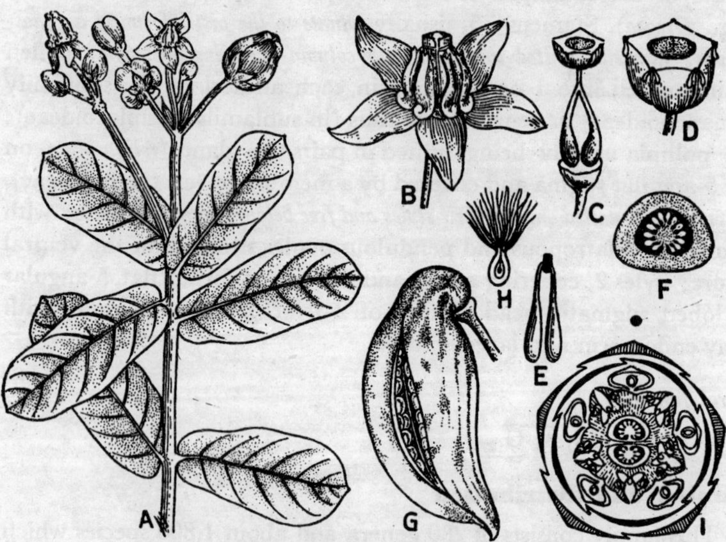

Fig. 666. Asclepiadaceae (*Calotropis procera*).
A, Portion of a flowering shoot; B, Flower; C, Pistil; D, Stigmatic head; E, Pollinia; F, T.s. of ovary; G, Fruit; H, Floral diagram.

(*d*) Coronal appendages single (or while double both are staminal)—

(*i*) Corolla wide campanulate; staminal corona-radiating and laterally compressed, spurred on the back; plant erect .. .. .. *Calotropis.*

(*ii*) Corolla rotate; coronal processes staminal, spoon-shaped; ligulate at the face .. .. *Asclepias.*

(*iii*) Corolla twisted, rotate; outer coronary scales cupular, membraneous and the inner ones erect with a dorsal ligulary processes connecting the anthers .. .. *Sarcostemma.*

(*e*) Coronal appendages or only corona suppressed—

(*i*) Corolla rotate, outer corona absent or rudimentary with larger or only lobes opposite the anthers .. .. *Pentatropis.*

(*ii*) Corolla funnel-shaped; outer corona conspicuous, 5–10-lobed, laterally compressed; stem twining *Daemia.*

(*iii*) Corolla campanulate, twisted, lobes short; corona 0; stem twining.. .. .. *Sarcolobus.*

(*iv*) Corolla funnel- or salver-shaped; coronary scales erect or rarely absent; climbing shrub .. *Stephanotis.*

(*v*) Corolla campanulate or salver-shaped; coronal scales on the back of the anthers, simple .. *Marsdenia.*

(*vi*) Corolla rotate or salver-shaped; coronal scales on the back of the anthers, notched; fls. yellow or orange .. .. *Pergularia.*

(*vii*) Corolla rotate; coronal processes fleshy; stamens originating from the throat of the corolla-tube *Tylophora.*

(*viii*) Corolla rotate, green; coronal scales spreading in stellate processes, fleshy and thick; fls. in pendulous umbel .. .. .. *Dregea.*

(*ix*) Corolla rotate; coronal processes large; stellate anthers occasionally without membraneous tip *Hoya.*

(*x*) Corolla urceolate; scales of corona erect, mem braneous .. .. *Dischidia.*

Range of floral structures

The plan of the flower is remarkably uniform with three regularly alternating pentamerous whorls of sepals, petals and stamens respectively and a bicarpellary pistil crowning the axis. The corolla is usually divided forming a rotate structure but the tube sometimes becomes longer, forming a salver-shaped corolla, as in *Stephanotis*, or pitcher-form corolla, as found in *Ceropegia.* Flowers are generally regular, but zygomorphic flower is found in *Ceropegia.* There are often found great variations in the form of corona-like petaloid appendages which arise just from the back of the stamens or sometimes from the corolla.

The shapes of the flowers are generally small; but relatively large flowers are found in *Ceropegia*, *Stapelia* and *Stephanotis.*

The five stamens and two carpels have separate origin on the floral axis. The ovaries are generally apocarpous, but the styles uniting to form a swollen stigma-head. It may become flattened, or more or less conical, or beaked.

The anthers are united laterally to form a 5-sided blunt cone which remains attached to the stigma-head. This sort of union of anthers and pistil forms a structure, known as *gynostegium.*

This family has been divided into 2 subfamilies based on the pollen structure. The first subfamily is **Periplocoideae,** characterized by the presence of granular pollen tetrads and translators spoon-shaped provided with an adhesive disc. Examples—*Hemidesmus, Cryptolepis,* etc. The second subfamily is **Cynanchoideae,** characterized by the pollens aggregated in 2–4 wax-like bodies known as pollinia. It contains the following genera, each has different pollinia construction. In genera *Asclepias* and *Calotropis,* pollinia are two in each anther, i.e., 10 in all; in *Secamone* and *Genianthus,* the pollinia are four in each anther, i.e., 20 in all; in genera, such as, *Tylophora* and *Dregea,* pollinia two in each anther but erect. In genus *Gonolobus,* the pollinia are in pairs in each anther but transverse.

Common plants

(1) *Calotropis procera* R. Br., a shrub with purplish flower growing throughout the plains of India. (2) *Calotropis gigantea* R. Br. (3) Indian sarsaparilla (*Hemidesmus indicus* R. Br.), a twining shrub. (4) Milk weed or Silk weed (*Asclepias acida* Roxb. =*Sarcostema acidum* Voigt.). (5) *Asclepias curassavica* L., an erect perennial herb found in gardens and waste places near villages. (6) *Finlaysonia obovata* Wall. =*F. maritima* Backer, a large climbing plant found in Sundribans. (7) *Sarcolobus globosus* Wall., another climbing plant found in Sundribans. (8) *Cynanchum callialata* Ham., a twining shrub. (9) Wax-plant (*Hoya parasitica* Wall.), a twining epiphyte bearing wax-like leaves and flowers. (10) *Daemia extensa* Br. =*Pergularia daemia* Chois., a common climbing plant with spinous follicles. (11) *Dischidia rafflesiana* Wall., a stout twiner with pitchers 2–5 inches long, commonly found in Assam. (12) Rubber vine (*Cryptostegia grandiflora* R. Br.), a large stout climber in gardens. (13) *Pentatropis microphylla* W. & A., a slender twining herb, can be found from the salt lakes southwards to Sundribans. (14) *Dregea volubilis* Benth. =*Marsdenia volubilis* T. Cooke, a stout tall climber. (15) *Sarcostemma brevistigma* Wight, grows wild. (16) *Tylophora*

asthmatica W. & A. = *T. indica* Merr., a slender twining herb, very common. (17) *Oxystelma esculentum* R. Br., a climbing perennial herb. (18) *Cryptolepis buchanani* R. & S., common in hedges and village-shrubberies. (19) *Pergularia minor* Andr. = *Telosnia minor* Craib., a glabrous twining undershrub of gardens. (20) *Marsdenia tenacissima* W. & A., very common.

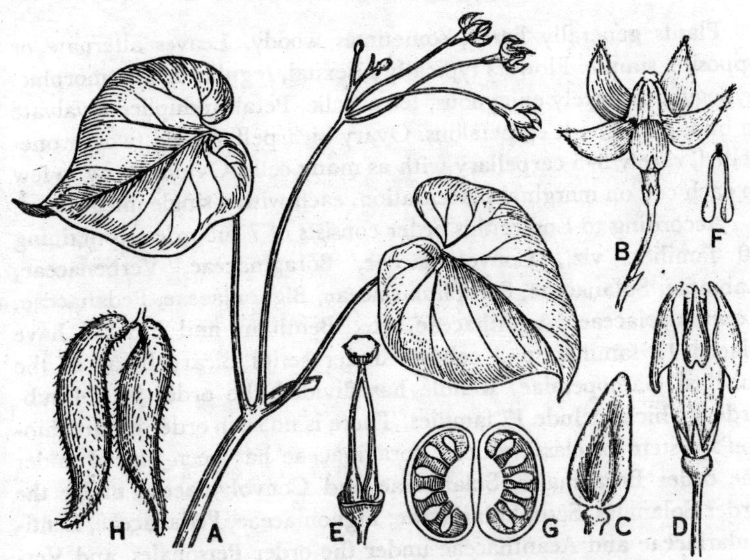

Fig. 667. Asclepiadaceae (*Daemia extensa*). A, Portion of a flowering shoot; B, Flower; C, Petal; D, Flower with sepals and petals removed; E, Pistil; F, Pollinia; G, T.s. of ovary; H, Fruit.

Affinity

This family bears an affinity with families, such as, Oleaceae, Loganiaceae, Gentianaceae and Apocynaceae in the characters of aestivation, in the form and shape of calyx and the number of carpels, but readily distinguished from them by gynandrous flowers, valvate corolla, presence of pollinia and gynostegium.

Economic importance

This family is of economic importance. Some plants, such as, *Hemidesmus*, *Calotropis*, *Tylophora*, etc., have medicinal properties. Some species of *Asclepias* are deadly poisonous. The Ceylon milk plant (*Gymnema lactiferum*) is used as an article of food. An inferior quality of rubber is obtained from *Cryptostegia grandiflora.* A few plants are ornamentals, such as, *Asclepias*, *Hoya*, *Stapelia*, *Periploca*, *Ceropegia*, *Cryptostegia*, etc.

ORDER 6. TUBIFLORAE

Plants generally herbs, sometimes woody. Leaves alternate or opposite, simple. Flowers typically bisexual, regular or zygomorphic, hypogynous, rarely epigynous, tetracyclic. Petals induplicate-valvate in bud. Stamens 4, epipetalous. Ovary bicarpellary and two- or one-celled, rarely 3–5 carpellary with as many cells. Ovules many to few in each cell on marginal placentation, each with a single integument.

According to Engler this order consists of 7 suborders containing 20 families, viz., Convolvulaceae, Boraginaceae, Verbenaceae, Labiatae, Solanaceae, Scrophulariaceae, Bignoniaceae, Pedaliaceae, Lentibulariaceae, Acanthaceae, etc. Bentham and Hooker have placed 17 families in 3 cohorts under series Bicarpellatae of the subclass Gamopetalae. Rendle has divided the order into 4 suborders which include 17 families. There is no such order in Hutchinson's system of classification. Boraginaceae has been placed under the order Boraginales, Solanaceae and Convolvulaceae under the order Solanales, Scrophulariaceae, Bignoniaceae, Pedaliaceae, Lentibulariaceae and Acanthaceae under the order Personales, and Verbenaceae and Labiatae under the order Lamiales.

CONVOLVULACEAE

General characters

Plants—usually annual or perennial twining herbs (twining to the left), sometimes erect (e.g., *Cressa cretica*) or leafless parasites (e.g., *Cuscuta*), with watery latex. Leaves—alternate, simple, entire, or pinnately or palmately lobed, exstipulate. Inflorescence —dichasium or racemose (e.g., *Porana*). Flowers—regular, bisexual, hypogynous, bracteate. Sepals—5, usually free, quincuncial, often persistent. Petals—(5), usually *funnel-* or *salver-shaped*, *twisted*. Stamens —5, *unequal*, epipetalous, inserted at the base of the corolla tube and alternating with petals; pollen ellipsoid or round. Carpels—(2); ovary superior, often surrounded by a disc, usually 2-celled with 2 *erect anatropous ovules*, or sometimes 4-celled with one anatropous ovule in each cell; style 1 (but 2 in *Cressa* and *Cuscuta*); stigma terminal and most frequently bilobed. Fruit—usually *capsule*, sometimes berry (e.g., *Argyreia*, *Cuscuta*). Seed—smooth or hairy, exalbuminous. Embryo—curved with *folded green cotyledons* (e.g., *Ipomoea*), or without cotyledons, or very rudimentary ones (e.g., *Cuscuta*), radicle directed towards the hilum.

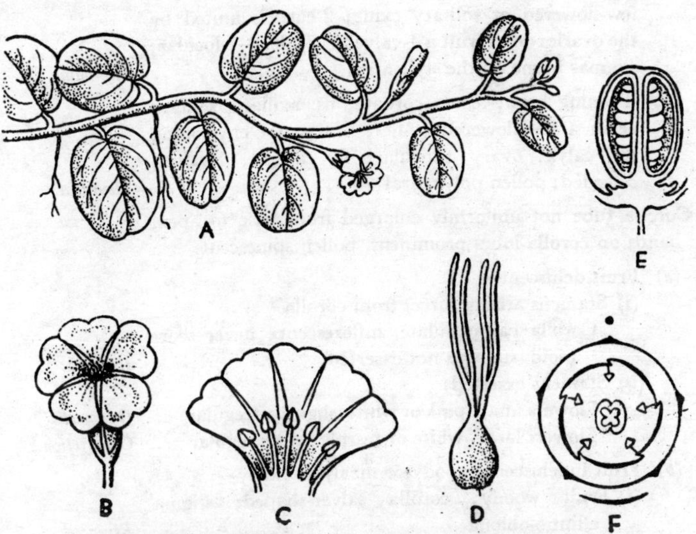

Fig. 668. Convolvulaceae (*Evolvulus nummularius*).
A, Por ion of a flowering shoot; B, Flower; C. Corolla split open; D, Pistil; F, Floral diagram.

Floral formula

$\oplus$ ⚥ $K_5\ \overline{C_{(5)}\ A_5}\ \underline{G_{(2)}}$

Number and distribution

This family consists of about 50 genera and 1,200 species, which are chiefly found in tropical and subtropical regions.

KEY TO GENERA

A. Corolla tube usually enlarged uniformly from base to apex. the 5 bands on the lobes not well-marked, pollen not spinescent:

(*a*) Yellow parasites without leaves .. .. *Cuscuta.*

(*b*) Large climbers; flowers white, blue or purple; handsome garden plants .. .. .. *Porana.*

(*c*) Flowers in cymes or solitary; plants small, erect or diffuse annual, grey, pubescent .. .. *Cressa.*

(*d*) Climbing herbs; leaves cordate or elliptical; flowers blue, pink or white in umbellate or capitate cymes; ovary 2-locular; fruit capsule, hairs 3-many branched; garden plants .. .. *Jacquimontana.*

(*e*) Prostrate herbs or undershrubs; inflorescence is a few-flowered or solitary cyme; 2-carpels united by the ovaries only; fruit a 4-valved capsule, 2–1-locular; stigmas borne on the style arms .. .. *Evolvulus.*

(*f*) Twining herb; leaves cordate; fls. axillary, solitary or in a few-flowered cymes; bracts not enveloping the calyx; ovary 1-locular; ft. capsule, 4-valved 3-seeded; pollen polyhedral .. .. *Hewittia.*

B. Corolla tube not uniformly enlarged from base to apex, bands on corolla-lobes prominent, pollen spinescent:

(*a*) Fruit dehiscent—

(*i*) Stamens arising direct from corolla

Corolla campanulate, inflorescence never scorpioid, stamens not exserted .. .. *Ipomoea.*

(*ii*) Stamens exserted:

Flowers small, pink or white, slightly irregular .. *Quamoclit.*

Flowers large, white or purple, quite regular .. *Calonyction.*

(*b*) Fruit indehiscent, woody or mealy or fleshy—

(*i*) Fruit woody; corolla salver-shaped; stigma elliptic-oblong .. .. .. *Rivea.*

Fruit mealy or fleshy, corolla rarely or not salver-shaped—

(1) Sepals large, orbicular, accrescent, ultimately completely enveloping the fruit .. *Sticlocardia.*

(2) Sepals small, ovate, not enlarging to envelop the fruit:

Ovary 2-celled .. .. .. *Lettsomia.*

Ovary 4-celled .. .. .. *Argyreia.*

(3) Sepals unequal, outer 3 not larger than the inner 2; carpels—2; style entire; stigma globose; ovary 2-celled; bands of corolla demarcated by purple lines .. .. *Merremia.*

Common plants

(1) *Ipomoea reptans* Poir. =*I. aquatica* Forsk., an aquatic herb with very long-jointed, hollow stem. (2) Moon-flower (*Ipomoea bona-nox* L. =*Calonyction bona-nox* Boj.), a large climber with white flowers, opening at sunset. (3) Sweet potato (*Ipomoea batatas* Lamk.

=*Batatas edulis*), a creeping herb with edible tuberous root. (4) *Ipomoea paniculata* R. Br.=*Jacquimontea paniculata* Hall. f., a medicinal plant with palmatisect leaves. (5) *Ipomoea pes-tigridis* L., a twining hairy plant with white or pale-pink flowers, very common on waste places. (6) *I. hederacea* Jacq., a slender climber with pink or blue flowers, very common in waste places near villages during the rainy season. (7) Morning-glory (*Ipomoea purpurea* Lamk.), a very common twiner found in gardens. (8) Cypress vine or Needle creeper (*Quamoclit pinnata* Boj.=*I. quamoclit* L.), a small annual garden

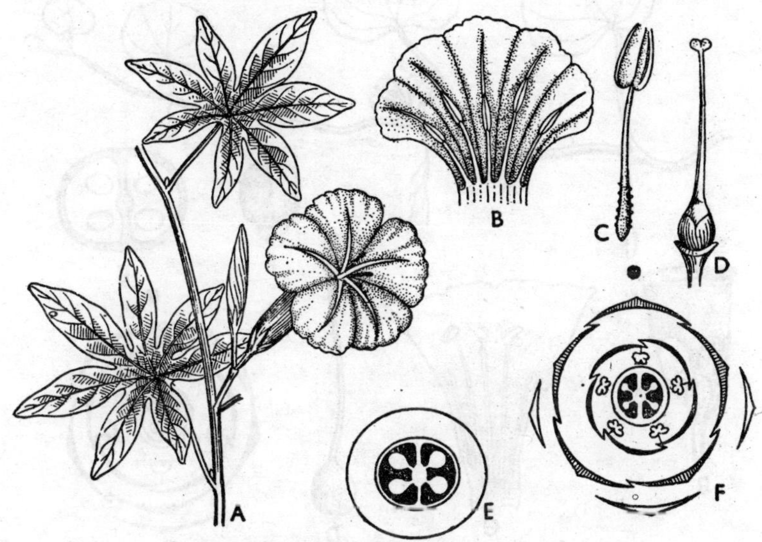

Fig. 669. Convolvulaceae (*Ipomoea purpurea*).
A, Portion of a flowering shoot; B, Corolla split open; C, Stamen; D, Pistil; E, T.s. of fruit; F, Floral diagram.

twiner with pinnatisect leaves and crimson flowers. (9) Christmas vine (*Porana paniculata* Roxb.), a common garden climber. (10) *Argyreia speciosa* Sw.=*A. nervosa* Boj., a garden climber with cordate leaves. (11) *Evolvulus nummularius* L., a common weed which is found on pathways; *E. alsinoides* Wall., also a common weed of grassy places. (12) *Merremia emarginata* Hallier f., a prostrate creeping herb rooting at the nodes. (13) Bindweed (*Convolvulus arvensis* L.), a common weed found on sands. (14) Goat's foot (*Ipomoea biloba* Forsk.), the leaves of which resemble the hoofs of a goat, is a sand-binder found on sea-shores; *I. pes-caprae* Sweet, another sand-binding herb. (15) Dodder (*Cuscuta reflexa* Roxb.), a common twining golden-yellow leafless thread-like parasite. (16) *Rivea hypocrateriformis* Choisy, a large climber. (17) *Stictocardia tilaefolia* Hallier, f., a large climber found in salt-lakes and Sundribans. (18) *Cressa cretica* L., found in dried-up muddy places near salt-lakes. (19) *Jacquimontana cerulea* Choisy, a garden plant. (20) *Lettsomia strigosa* Roxb. = *Argyreia capitata* Choisy, a strong climber commonly found in hedges

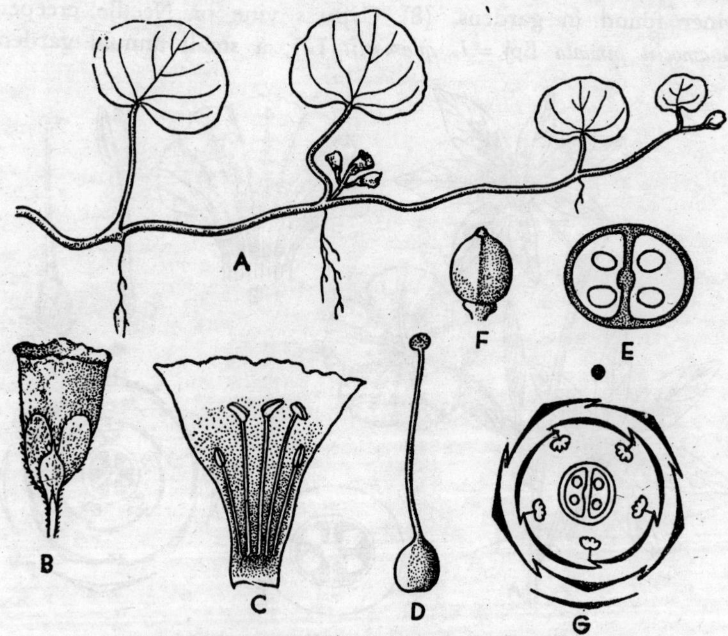

Fig. 670. Convolvulaceae (*Merremia emarginata*).
A, Portion of a flowering shoot; B, Flower; C, Corolla split open; D, Pistil; E, T.s. of ovary; F, Fruit; G, Floral diagram.

and village shrubberies. (21) *Hewittia bicolor* Wight, a perennial twining herb, bearing pale-yellow flower with dark purple eye, very common.

Affinity

Convolvulaceae establishes a close relationship with Solanaceae in the presence of false septum, persistent calyx, structure of corolla and intraxylary phloem, hence, the families Convolvulaceae, Solanaceae, Nolanaceae and Scrophulariaceae have been grouped into a single order Solanales, next to Loganiales. The family is also allied to Polemoniaceae and Boraginaceae, but readily distinguished by the watery latex, twisted corolla, terminal style, structure of ovary and nature of the embryo.

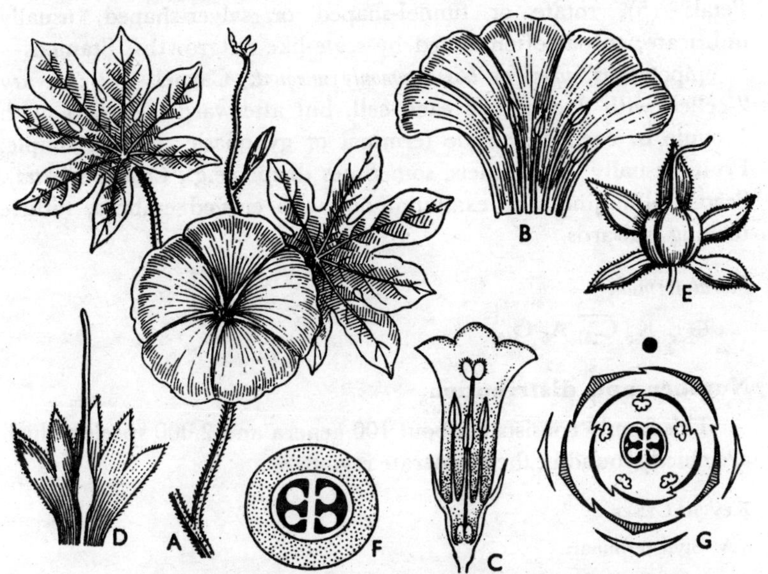

Fig. 671. Convolvulaceae (*Ipomoea pes-tigridis*).
A, Portion of a flowering shoot; B, Corolla tube split open; C, V.s. of flower; D, Calyx split open showing pistil; E, Fruit; F, T.s. of ovary; G, Floral diagram.

Economic importance

Economically this family is less important. *Ipomoea paniculata* is used medicinally. The tuberous root of *I. batatas* is edible. The latex of *Exogynum purga* is used as a purgative. Some plants are cultivated as ornamentals, such as, cypress vine (*Quamoclit pinnata*), moon-flower (*Calonyction bona-nox*), morning-glory (*Ipomoea purpurea*), christmas vine (*Porana paniculata*), etc.

BORAGINACEAE

General characters

Plants—pubescent annual or perennial herbs, sometimes shrubs or trees (e.g., *Cordia*, *Ehretia*). Leaves—usually alternate, simple, entire, often hispid, exstipulate. Inflorescence—simple or double *scorpioid cymes* which are spirally coiled in the young condition.

Flowers—*regular* (but slightly zygomorphic in *Lycopsis*), bisexual, hypogynous, with a disc beneath the ovary. Sepals—5, free or united below into a longer or shorter tube, generally bell-shaped, imbricate. Petals—(5), rotate or funnel-shaped or salver-shaped, usually imbricate; throat often closed by scale-like outgrowths. Stamens—5, epipetalous, *equal* or *less commonly unequal*. Carpels—(2); ovary 2-celled with 2 ovules in each cell, but afterwards 4-celled with 1 ovule in each cell; style terminal or gynobasic; stigma simple. Fruit—usually of 4 nutlets, sometimes drupe (e.g., *Cordia*, *Ehretia*). Seeds—albuminous or exalbuminous with curved embryo, radicle turning upwards.

Floral formula

$\oplus$ ⚥ $K_5\ \overline{C_{(5)}\ A_5}\ G_{(2)}$

Number and distribution

This family consists of about 100 genera and 2,000 species which are chiefly found in the temperate regions.

KEY TO GENERA

A. Style terminal:

(*a*) Style 2-partite on ovary; fruit a drupe with four 1-seeded stone; calyx enlarging in fruit; usually trees or shrubs .. .. .. *Cordia*.

(*b*) Style 2-fid at the apex; pyrenes 2 or 4 or rarely 1-seeded; trees or shrubs .. .. .. *Ehretia*.

(*c*) Style more or less separate; pyrenes 4, 1-seeded; prostrate herbs .. .. *Coldenia*.

(*d*) Style filiform; stamens 5, anthers lanceolate conniving in a cone; calyx enlarged in fruit; ovary deeply 4-lobed and 4-celled; fruit pyramidal; erect herbs .. *Trichodesma*.

(*e*) Style on entire ovary, dilated at the apex or above the base; plants herbaceous .. .. *Heliotropium*.

B. Style gynobasic:

Fls. all sessile or only the lower ones pedicelled; stamens included; nutlets obovoid, glochidiate, depressed .. *Cynoglossum*.

Range of floral structures

The flowers are radially symmetrical but a deviation from the normal symmetry takes place also, as in *Echium* and some other genera. In *Lycopsis*, the corolla tube becomes bent, as a result of which it assumes zygomorphy.

The aestivation of the sepals is usually imbricate but sometimes valvate type of aestivation also occurs. The sepals may be free at the base, as in *Lythospermum*, or connate in *Myosotis*.

Corolla shows also variation in their form. Rotate corolla is seen in the genus *Symphytum*, salver-shaped corolla occurs in *Anehusa*, but funnel-shaped in *Cynoglossum*. The throat of the corolla tube is either naked or closed, as in *Lythospermum*, and there are five pencils of hairs found in the funnel-shaped corolla, as in *Pulmonaria*.

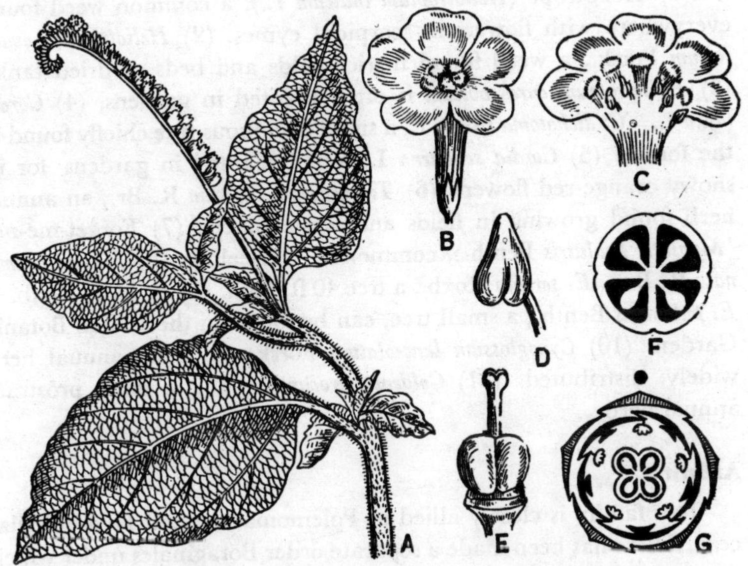

Fig. 672. Boraginaceae (*Heliotropium indicum*).
A, Portion of a flowering shoot; B, Flower; C, The same split open; D, Stamen; E, Pistil; F, Fruit; G, Floral diagram.

The ovary is situated on a nectar-secreting disc which looks like a ring. The two carpels are median. They become divided by a sort of medium constriction or divided into four prominent one-ovuled portions, the style springing from the central portion rather the focus of the group. In the subfamilies **Cordioideae** and **Ehretioideae,** the ovary is seen to maintain its original structure and bears the style on its apex. One ovule is found to be attached at the inner angle of each ovary-chamber; it is usually anatropous with an up-wardly directed micropyle. In the subfamily **Heliotropioideae,** the ovule becomes descending with a downwardly projected micropyle.

The style usually becomes ended in a simple stigma, such as, *Symphytum, Myosotis;* the stigma becomes bilobed, as in *Anchusa, Pulmonaria,* whereas the style becomes bipartite in *Echium.*

The styles are generally terminal in the genera, such as, *Cordia, Ehretia, Heliotropium;* but gynobasic styles are found in *Borago, Cynoglossum* and others.

Common plants

(1) Heliotrope (*Heliotropium indicum* L.), a common weed found everywhere with flowers in scorpioid cymes. (2) *Heliotropium ovalifolium* Forsk., a weed found in rice-fields and beds of dried tanks. (3) *Heliotropium curassavicum* is often planted in gardens. (4) *Cordia myxa* L. = *C. dichotoma* Forst. f., a small deciduous tree chiefly found in the forests. (5) *Cordia sebestena* L., often planted in gardens for its showy orange-red flowers. (6) *Trichodesma indicum* R. Br., an annual herb found growing in fields and waste places. (7) Forget-me-not (*Myosotis paulutris* Benth.), common in Darjeeling. (8) *Ehretia acuminata* R. Br. = *E. serrata* Roxb., a tree 40 ft. high. (9) *E. laevis* Roxb. = *E. pubescens* Benth., a small tree, can be found in the Indian Botanic Garden. (10) *Cynoglossum lanceolatum* Forsk., an erect annual herb widely distributed. (11) *Coldenia procumbens* L., a flatly prostrate annual herb.

Affinity

This family is closely allied to Polemoniaceae and Hydrophyllaceae. There has been made a separate order Boraginales under which the above three families have been placed. The Boraginales establish a link between Solanales and Verbenales. Boraginaceae also bears a close relationship with Solanaceae. It has resemblance with that of Labiatae in the structure of fruits and in the presence of nectar-secreting disc which is hypogynous, but it is readily distinguished by alternate leaves, scorpioid inflorescence, regular corolla with scales at the throat and character of fruit. It also bears affinity with Verbenaceae in the general organization of flowers.

Economic importance

This family is of little economic importance. The roots of *Alkanna tinctoria* yield a dye which is used in colouring oil, wine, etc. Some plants are ornamentals, such as, *Cordia, Ehretia, Myosotis,* etc.

VERBENACEAE

General characters

Plants—herbs, shrubs or trees, often with square stems. Leaves—usually opposite or whorled, simple, sometimes pinnately or palmately compound (e.g., *Vitex*), exstipulate. Inflorescence—racemose or cymose, often with well-developed bracts. Flowers—usually zygomorphic, bisexual, hypogynous. Sepals—(5), tubular or bell-shaped,

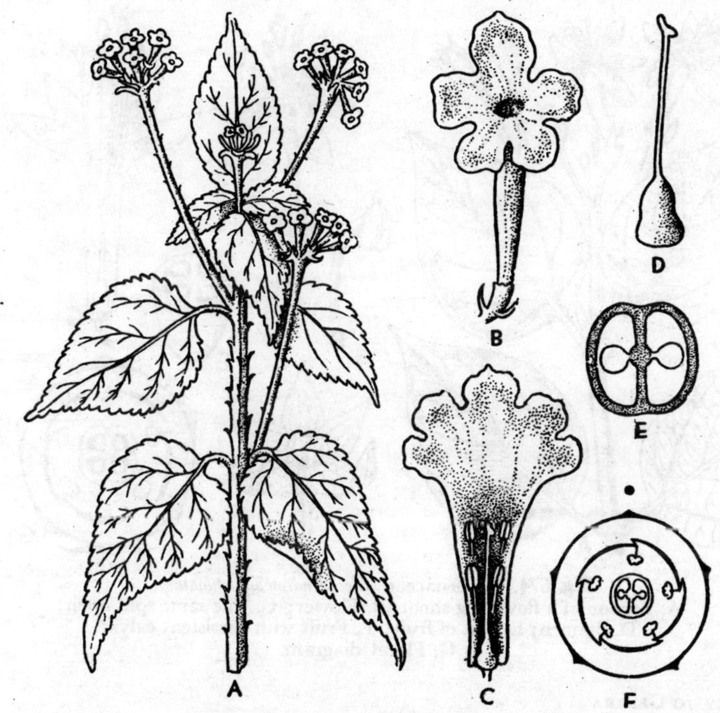

Fig. 673. Verbenaceae (*Lantana camara*).
A, Portion of a flowering shoot; B, Flower; C, Corolla tube split open; D, Pistil; E, T.s. of ovary; F, Floral diagram.

persistent. Petals—(5), *tubular*, *often oblique* with a spreading limb, imbricate. Stamens—4, didynamous or 2, rarely 5 (e.g., *Tectona*), epipetalous. Carpels—(2), (but (4) in *Duranta*); ovary superior, more or less lobed, often 2–4-*celled* with 2 or 1 *ovule in each cell;* style terminal. Fruit—usually *drupaceous* or of 4 nutlets (e.g., *Verbena*), rarely capsule (e.g., *Avicennia*). Seed—exalbuminous. Embryo—straight, with radicle turned downwards.

Floral formula

$\uparrow$ ⚥ $K_{(5)}$ $\overline{C_{(5)} A_4}$ $\underline{G_{(2)}}$

Number and distribution

This family consists of 80 genera and about 800 species belonging to the southern tropical and temperate regions.

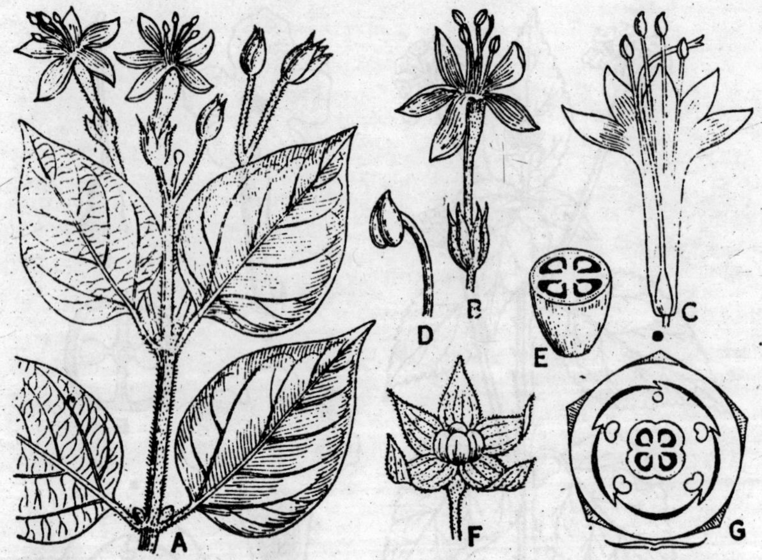

Fig. 674. Verbenaceae (*Clerodendron infortunatum*).
A, Portion of a flowering shoot; B, Flower; C. The same split open: D, Stamen; E, T.s. of fruit; F, Fruit with persistent calyx: G, Floral diagram.

KEY TO GENERA

A. Inflorescence racemose centripetal spicate:

Small flowers, sessile, clustered in heads, corolla 4 or 5 (2-lobed)—

(*i*) Fruit drupe; 2 pyrenes; small calyx; shrubs .. *Lantana*.

(*ii*) Fruit capsule, 2 pyrenes; small calyx .. *Lippia*.

(*iii*) Fruit separating into two 1-seeded pyrenes .. *Stachytarpheta*.

(*iv*) Fruit pyrenes 4 or 1; calyx tubular, non-accrescent: herb .. .. .. *Verbena*.

(*v*) Fruit fleshy. 2-seeded pyrenes .. .. *Duranta*.

B. **Inflorescence cymose, centrifugal or panicled;**

Small flowers; corolla regular; stamens isomerous; leaves entire—

(*vi*) **Fls. 4–6-merous; anthers exserted; fruit a drupe with 1, 4-celled pyrenes, enclosed in fleshy calyx** .. .. *Tectona.*

(*vii*) **Fls. 4-merous; anthers exserted; fruit a round drupe with 4 pyrenes** .. .. *Callicarpa.*

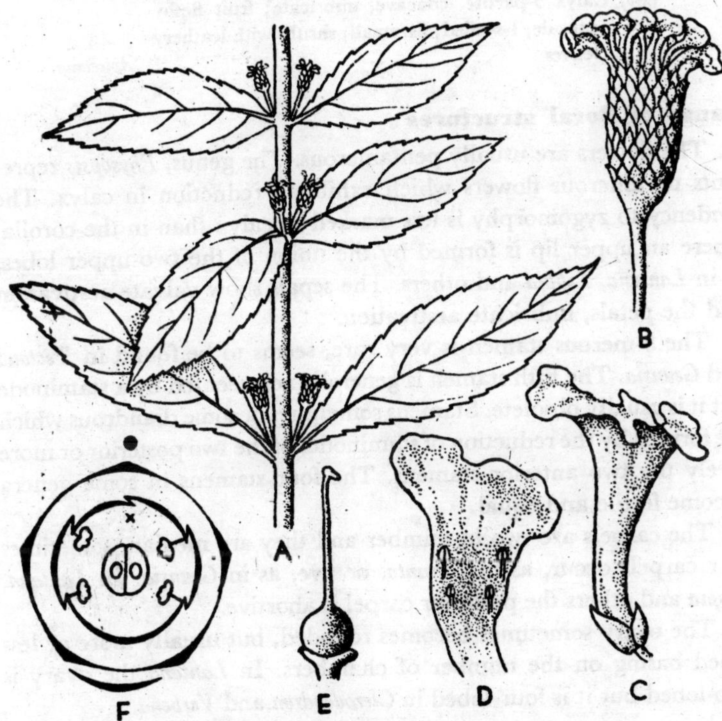

Fig. 675. Verbenaceae (*Lippia geminata*).
A, Portion of a flowering shoot; B, Inflorescence; C, Flower; D, Corolla tube split open; E, Pistil; F, Floral diagram.

Small flowers; corolla 2-lipped; stamens didynamous:

(*a*) **Succulent drupe with ingle pyrene—**

(*viii*) **Leaves entire or toothed** .. .. *Premna.*

(*ix*) **Leaves entire; fls. large 1 inch long** .. *Gmelina.*

(*x*) **Leaves digitate, 3–5-foliate** .. *Vitex.*

(*b*) Fruit drupe with 4 pyrenes; leaves simple—

(*xi*) Calyx bell-shaped; corolla tube long slender; stamens equal or didynamous; drupe round .. *Clerodendron.*

(*xii*) Calyx large, petaloid (red), rotate; usually a climbing or straggling shrub .. .. *Holmskioldia.*

C. Inflorescence capitate cyme:

(*xiii*) Bracts (involucral) 6 or 3–4; large; fruit usually dry; corolla 2-lipped; large climber .. *Congea.*

(*xiv*) Calyx 5-partite, concave, imbricate; fruit fleshy capsule, 1-seeded; fls. small; shrubs with leathery leaves .. .. *Avicennia.*

Range of floral structures

The flowers are usually pentamerous. The genus, *Physopsis* represents tetramerous flowers which exhibit a reduction in calyx. The tendency to zygomorphy is less marked in calyx than in the corolla, where an upper lip is formed by the union of the two upper lobes, as in *Lantana*, *Lippia* and others. The sepals show valvate aestivation and the petals, imbricate aestivation.

The 5-merous stamen is very rare, seems to be found in *Tectona* and *Geunsia*. The fifth stamen is generally represented by a staminode but it is usually obsolete. Stamens sometimes become diandrous which are formed by the reduction of staminodes of the two posterior or more rarely the two anterior stamens. The four stamens in some genera become fertile and equal.

The carpels are two in number and they are median, sometimes four carpels occur, as in *Duranta*, or five, as in *Geunsia*. In *Lantana*, *Lippia* and others the posterior carpel is abortive.

The ovary sometimes becomes rounded, but usually more or less lobed basing on the number of chambers. In *Lantana* the ovary is two-lobed but it is four-lobed in *Clerodendron* and *Verbena*.

Common plants

(1) Teak (*Tectona grandis* L. f.), an useful timber tree. (2) Chaste-tree (*Vitex negundo* L.), a common shrub with trifoliate or quadrifoliate leaves. (3) *Clerodendron infortunatum* Gaertn. =*C. viscosum* Vent. and *C. inerme* Gaertn., common herbs chiefly found on waste lands; *C. siphonanthus* R. Br. =*C. indicum* Ktze., a tall shrub about 6 ft. high with hollow stems. (4) *Petrea volubilis* Jacq., a climber, very common in gardens. (5) *Duranta plumieri* Jacq., a common hedge-plant with blue flowers and succulent yellow berries. (6) *Lantana*

indica Roxb. and *L. camara* L.=*L. aculeata* L. weeds chiefly found along roadsides. (7) *Lippia nodiflora* Rich.=*Phyla nodiflora* Green, a herb commonly found in moist places, and *L. geminata* H. B. & Kunth., a shrub 3–8 ft. high. (8) Verbain (*Verbena officinalis* L.), a small weed of waste places. (9) *Holmskioldia sanguinea* Retz., a shrub commonly planted in gardens for the sake of its flowers. (10) The white Mangrove (*Avicennia officinalis* L.), a common tree with long pneumatophores found in the salt-lakes near Calcutta and Sundribans, the seeds of which are viviparous.

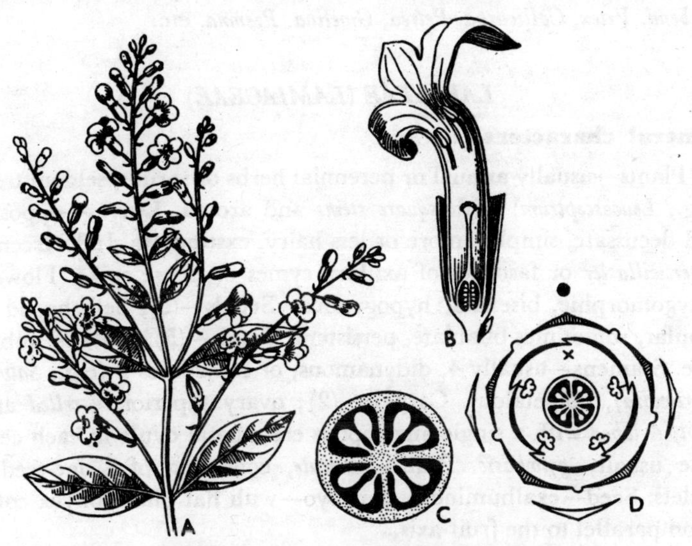

Fig. 676. Verbenaceae (*Duranta plumieri*).
A, Portion of a flowering shoot; B, Flower cut lengthwise;
C, T.s. of ovary; D, Floral diagram.

(11) *Gmelina arborea* Roxb., a tree 60 ft. high. (12) *Gmelina hystrix* Schult.=*G. philippensis* Cham., a garden plant. (13) *Premna integrifolia* L., a shrub or small tree, chiefly found in the Sundribans. (14) *Callicarpa macrophylla* Vahl., common on roadsides and village shrubberies. (15) *Callicarpa arborea* Roxb., a tree about 40 ft. high. (16) *Congea tomentosa* Roxb., a large climber. (17) Aron's rod (*Stachytarpheta indica* Vahl.), a herb 1–2 feet high.

Affinity

This family is closely allied to Acanthaceae and Labiatae but readily distinguished from the former by 2–4-celled ovary with 2 or 1 ovule in each cell and character of fruit, and from the latter by the form of the inflorescence and terminal style. It also establishes a link with Boraginaceae, but distinguished by the ascending ovule.

Economic importance

This family is perhaps most important economically. The leaves of *Vitex* are reputed as febrifuge. *Clerodendron siphonanthus* is a medicinal plant. *Tectona grandis* produces a useful timber. Some plants are ornamentals, such as, *Clerodendron*, *Duranta*, *Holmskioldia*, *Lantana*, *Verbena*, *Vitex*, *Callicarpa*, *Petrea*, *Gmelina*, *Premna*, etc.

LABIATAE (*LAMIACEAE*)

General characters

Plants—usually annual or perennial herbs or shrubs, seldom trees (e.g., *Leucosceptrum*) with *square stems* and aroma. Leaves—opposite and decussate, simple, more or less hairy, exstipulate. Inflorescence —*verticillaster* or fascicles of axillary cymes or dense spike. Flowers —zygomorphic, bisexual, hypogynous. Sepals—(5), bell-shaped or tubular, sometimes bilabiate, persistent. Petals—(5), *bilabiate*, imbricate. Stamens—usually 4, didynamous, or sometimes 2 (e.g., *Salvia*, *Meriandra*), epipetalous. Carpels—(2); ovary superior, 4-*celled* and *deeply* 4-*lobed* with a single anatropous erect basal ovule in each cell; style usually *gynobasic*. Fruit—*carcerule*, consisting of 4 one-seeded nutlets. Seed—exalbuminous. Embryo—with flat planoconvex cotyledon parallel to the fruit-axis.

Floral formula

$\uparrow$ ⚥ $K_{(5)}\ \overline{C_{(5)}\ A_4}\ \underline{G_{(2)}}$

Number and distribution

This family consists of about 200 genera and 3,200 species which are chiefly found in the warmer and temperate regions.

KEY TO GENERA

A. Stamens 4 perfect, rarely 2; anther-cells 2, confluent; ovary 4-partite; dry nutlets with basal scars:

(*a*) Lower corolla-lip flat—

(*i*) Calyx segments deflexed in fruit; upper lip large, decurrent; stigma bifid; racemes bearing whorls of 6–10 fls.; herbs or shrubs .. .. *Ocimum*.

(*b*) Lower corolla-lip concave, boat-shaped—

(*ii*) Calyx-segments 5, equal or rarely toothed; filaments free .. .. .. *Plectranthus.*

(*iii*) Calyx 5, always 2-lipped; stamens 4; filaments connate below; herbs or shrubs with fleshy stem and leaves .. .. .. *Coleus.*

(*c*) Corolla obscurely 2-lipped with 2 upper lobes flat, similar and subequal to two laterals, all about as long as the abruptly deflexed, saccate lower lip; calyx teeth subequal .. .. *Hyptis.*

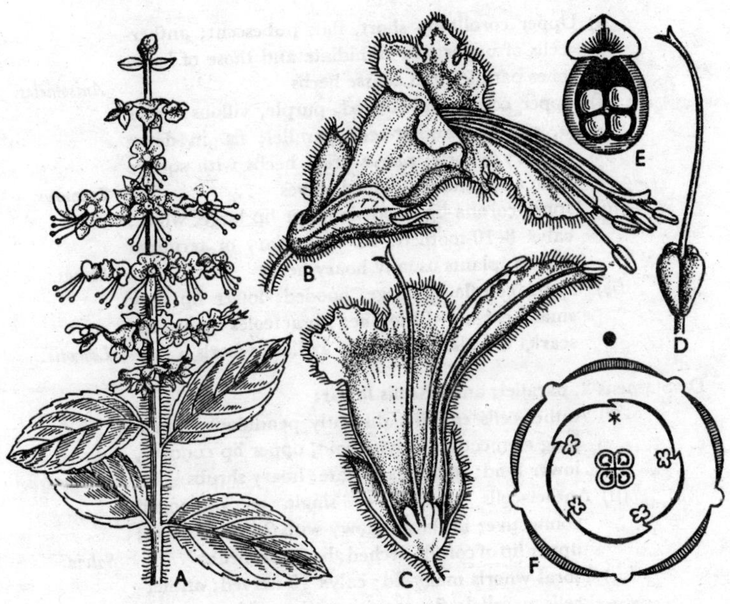

Fig. 677. Lamiaceae (*Ocimum sanctum*). A, Portion of a flowering shoot; B, Flower; C, V.s. of the same; D, Gynobasic style; E, Fruit; F, Floral diagram.

B. Stamens 4, upper pair long; anthers 1- or 2-celled; corolla flat:

(*i*) Calyx 5-toothed, ovoid; core subequally 4-lobed; stamens exserted; filaments bearded; small plants with whorled leaves and densely spicate fls. .. *Dysophylla.*

(*ii*) Calyx 5-toothed; lower corolla-lobe subpatent; stamens exserted; whorls in glomerate or panicular spike; filaments bearded or naked .. *Pogostemon.*

(*iii*) Calyx 5-partite, plumose segments; stamens included; fruit-nutlets ovoid; hairy plants, usually hoary shrubs, with opposite crenulate leaves .. *Colebrookia.*

(*iv*) Calyx 5-toothed, often enlarged and inflated in fruits; corolla tubular, incurved or straight; stamens diverging with divaricate anther-cells; plants herbs or undershrubs with opposite leaves .. .. *Elsholtzia.*

C. Stamens 4, perfect, lower pair longest; calyx 5–10-nerved; upper lip of corolla hooded, villous; anther-cells 2, diverging:

(*i*) Upper corolla-lip short, flat, pubescent; anther-cells of upper pair dimidiate and those of lower ones parallel; tall coarse herbs .. .. *Anisomeles.*

(*ii*) Upper corolla-lip hooded, purple, villous; calyx 5, spinous; anther-cells parallel; fls. in dense axillary whorls; plants erect herbs with square stem and pinnately lobed leaves .. .. *Leonurus.*

(*iii*) Upper corolla-lip hooded; lower lip large, white; calyx 8–10-toothed; fls. in axillary or terminal whorls; plants usually hoary herbs .. *Leucas.*

(*iv*) Upper corolla-lip large, hooded; lower lip very small; calyx 8–10-toothed; bracteoles many; fls. scarlet or yellow, borne in axillary whorls .. *Leonotis.*

D. Stamens 2, parallel; anther-cells linear:

(*i*) Anther-cells equally, distantly pendulous from a long connective; calyx ovoid, upper lip concave, lower 2-fid; style bilamellate; hoary shrubs .. *Meriandra.*

(*ii*) Anther-cells unequal or single on prolonged connective; fls. large showy with 2-lipped calyx; upper lip of corolla arched; herbs or shrubs .. *Salvia.*

(*iii*) Floral whorls many-fid; calyx 10-nerved; anther-cells parallel; fls. sometimes borne in terminal spike; corolla 4-lobed, subequal; a strongly scented perennial herb with creeping root-stock *Mentha.*

Range of floral structures

Labiatae includes a group of plants which are found to possess variable characters in their floral parts.

The calyx may be tubular, bell-shaped or spherical, straight or bent. The variation in the form of teeth or lobes is noticeable. Calyx is regularly 5-toothed; it may be 2-lipped, as in *Plectranthus*, *Thymus* and *Salvia*, or a fleshy calyx, as found to occur in *Hoslundia*.

The corolla also shows a great variation in their structure. It can be differentiated into two portions—the tube and limb. The tube is generally found to be straight or variously bent. The limb is equally 5-toothed. The general arrangement of corolla is bilabiate, as in *Thymus;* in *Mentha,* the corolla is tetra- or pentamerous. 4/1 arrangement (4 petals forming the upper lip and a single petal, the lower lip) is found to occur in *Ocimum*, *Hyptis*. 0/5 arrangement exists in the genus *Teucrium.*

The development of 5th posterior stamen is very rare. It is sometimes found as a staminode, but usually it is totally suppressed. The

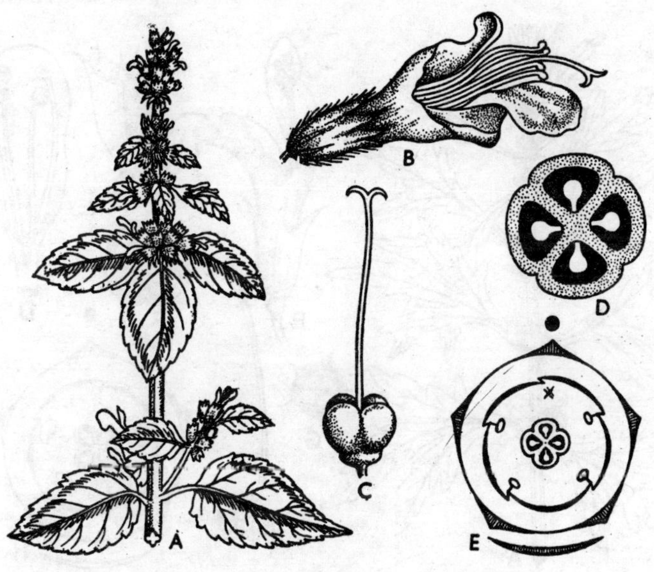

Fig. 678. **Lamiaceae (*Anisomeles ovata*).**
A, Portion of a flowering shoot; B, Flower; C, Pistil; D, T.s. of ovary; E, Floral diagram.

two upper stamens are reduced to staminodes or they are found to be completely suppressed, as in *Lycopus*, *Salvia*. In *Coleus* the stamens are found to unite into a bundle; in *Nepeta,* the anterior pair is longer. A variation is also noticeable in the connectives of anthers. The presence of number of connectives is not broad and generally with two parallel theca, occurs in Ocimoideae; the wide transverse connective with two fertile anther-lobes is found in the genus *Meriandra.* The long connectives with one sterile anther-lobe are found in the species of *Salvia*, *Hemigenia*.

The style is generally gynobasic, except in *Teucrium* and *Ajuga*.

Common plants

(1) Basil (*Ocimum sanctum* L.). (2) *Ocimum basilicum* L., commonly found on roadsides; *O. canum* Sims., a herb 1–2 ft. high. (3) *Ocimum gratissimum* L., a shrub. (4) Sage (*Salvia plebeja* R. Br.), an annual weed and *S. coccinea* L., a commonly cultivated garden plant with brightly coloured sepals and petals. (5) Motherwort (*Leonurus sibiricus* L.), a common weed on roadsides, with pink flowers and

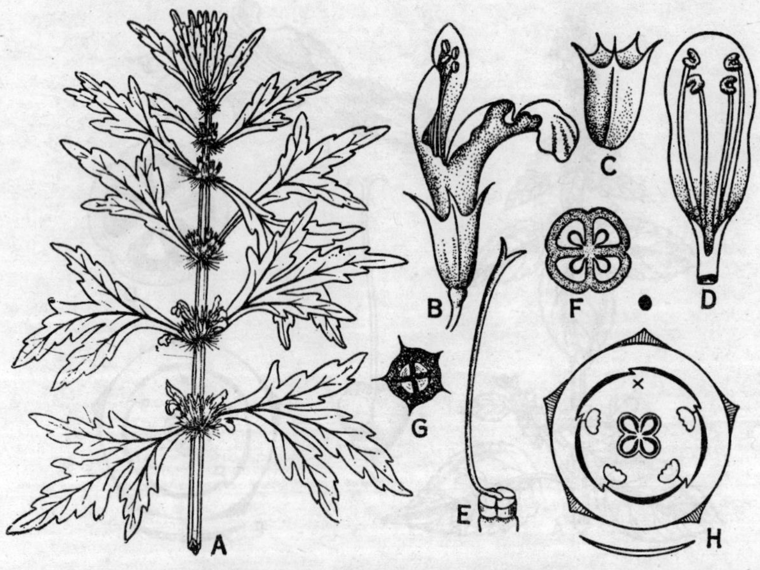

Fig. 679. Laminaceae (*Leonurus sibiricus*).
A, Portion of a flowering shoot; B, Flower; C, Calyx; D, V.s. of corolla; E, Pistil; F, T.s. of ovary; G, Fruit; H, Floral diagram.

heteromorphic foliage. (6) *Leucas aspera* Spreng. = *L. mollisima* Wall. and *L. linifolia* Spreng. = *L. lavendulaefolia* Nees., common annual herbs with white flowers; *L. procumbens* Desf., a slender procumbent herb. (7) Mint (*Mentha viridis* L.), cultivated in gardens for leaves which are used as condiment. (8) Peppermint (*Mentha piperita* L.), the leaves of which on distillation yield menthol. (9) *Lavandula vera* DC., produces oil of lavender. (10) *Anisomeles ovata* Br. = *L. indica*. Ktze., a weed of waste places. (11) Thyme (*Thymus vulgaris* L.).

thymol-producing plant. (12) *Pogostemon heyneanus* Benth. (*Patchouli*), used in perfumery. (13) Rosemary (*Rosmarinus officinalis* L.), a medicinal plant. (14) Several species of *Coleus* (e.g., *C. aromaticus* Benth.) are ornamental garden plants. (15) *Leucosceptrum canum* Sm., a

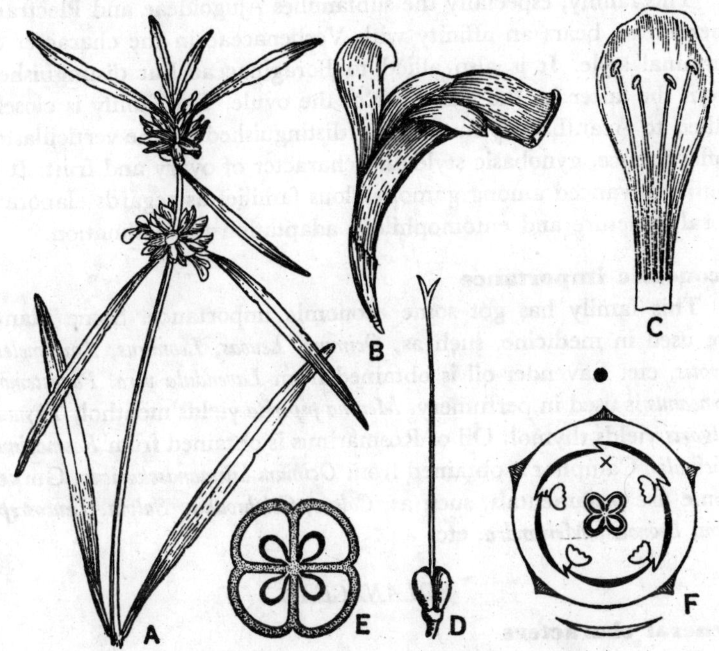

Fig. 680. Labiatae (*Leucus linifolia*).
A, Portion of a flowering shoot; B, Flower; C, V.s. of the same; D, Pistil; E, T.s. of ovary; F, Floral diagram.

native of the Himalayas, is a tall tree, very common in Darjeeling; it has long upright spikes of yellow-white flowers resembling a bottle-brush when old; a quantity of sweet juice exudes from the flowers and this is sucked up by the herdsmen. (16) *Dysophylla verticillata* Benth., a variable weed of rice-fields and swamps, much-branched or simple. (17) Lion's ear (*Leonotis nepetifolia* R. Br.), an annual herb, 4–6 ft. high. (18) *Meriandra benghalensis* Benth., a large straggling shrub found in the gardens. (19) *Plectranthus ternifolius* Don., a bushy herb 3–5 ft. high commonly found in North Bengal. (20) *Colebrookia oppositifolia* Sm., a shrub 5–10 ft. high, can be found in the Indian Botanic Garden. (21) *Elsholtzia polystachya* Benth., occasionally found. (22) *Hyptis suaveolens* Poit., a very common rigid annual, 2–4 feet high. (23) *Pogostemon plectranthoides* Desf., a large bush, can be found in all the provinces.

Affinity

This family, especially the subfamilies Ajugoideae and Plectrantheroideae, bears an affinity with Verbenaceae in the character of terminal style. It is also allied to Boraginaceae but distinguished from the latter by the character of the ovule. The family is closely allied to Acanthaceae but readily distinguished by the verticillaster inflorescence, gynobasic style and character of ovary and fruit. It is highly advanced among gamopetalous families as regards elaborate floral structure and entomophilous adaptation for pollination.

Economic importance

This family has got some economic importance. Some plants are used in medicine, such as, *Ocimum*, *Leucas*, *Leonurus*, *Anisomeles*, *Hyptis*, etc. Lavender-oil is obtained from *Lavendula vera*. *Pogostemon heyneanus* is used in perfumery. *Mentha piperita* yields menthol, *Thymus vulgaris* yields thymol. Oil of Rosmarinus is obtained from *Rosmarinus officinalis*. Camphor is obtained from *Ocimum kilimandscharicum* Gurke. Some are ornamentals, such as, *Coleus*, *Colebrookia*, *Salvia*, *Leucosceptrum*, *Leonotis*, *Meriandra*, etc.

SOLANACEAE

General characters

Plants—herbs or shrubs, rarely small trees, sometimes climbing. Leaves—alternate, simple, often lobed, exstipulate. Inflorescence—often cymose. Flowers—regular, sometimes zygomorphic, bisexual, hypogynous. Sepals—(5), persistent, often enlarging in the fruit, imbricate. Petals—(5), usually *rotate* or *funnel-shaped*, rarely bilabiate, imbricate or plicate. Stamens—usually 5, alternating with the corolla-lobes, rarely 4, didynamous (e.g., *Brunfelsia*, *Browallia*, *Salpiglossis* and *Schizanthus*), epipetalous; anthers bilocular, dehiscing by apical pores or longitudinally. Carpels—(2), *obliquely placed;* ovary superior, generally 2-celled or falsely 3–5-celled with numerous anatropous ovules on axile placenta; stigma bilobed. Fruit—usually many-seeded *berry*, sometimes capsule (e.g., *Datura*). Seeds—more or less uniform, albuminous. Embryo—usually *curved*, sometimes straight.

Floral formula

$\oplus$ or $\uparrow$ ⚥ $K_{(5)}\ \overline{C_{(5)}\ A_5}\ \underline{G_{(2)}}$

Number and distribution

This family consists of about 85 genera and over 2,200 species which are widely distributed throughout tropical and temperate regions.

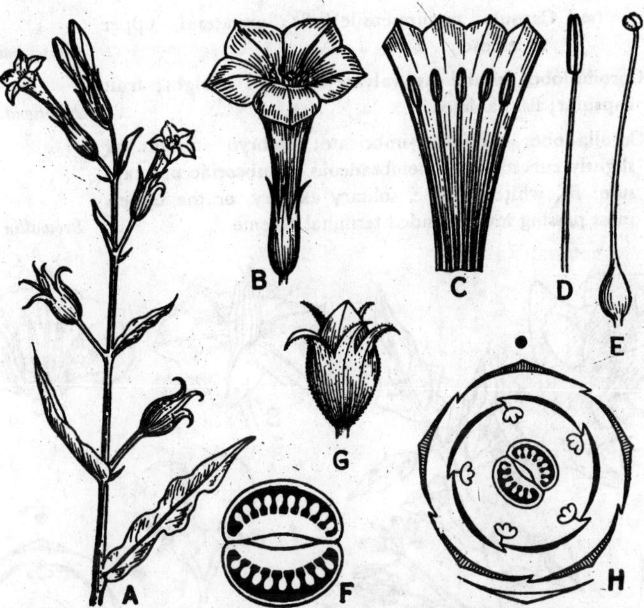

Fig. 681. Solanaceae (*Nicotiana plumbaginifolia*). A, Portion of a flowering shoot; B, Flower; C, The same cut open; D, Stamen; E, Pistil; F, T.s. of ovary; G, Fruit; H, Floral diagram.

Key to Genera

A. Corolla-limb valvate; fruit usually a berry; seeds more or less discoid, compressed; embryo peripheric:

(*a*) Anthers opening through 2 apical pores, connivent in a cone—

(*i*) Leaves simple, lobed or pinnatifid .. .. *Solanum.*

(*b*) Anthers dehiscing by longitudinal slit—

(*ii*) Dehiscence introrse, leaves pinnate .. .. *Lycopersicum.*

(*iii*) Calyx small in fruit; anthers equal or shorter than the filament; fls. small, in paired pedicels or simple .. .. .. *Capsicum.*

(*iv*) Calyx enlarging in fruit, covering the berry, shortly lobed; pedicels solitary .. .. *Physalis.*

(*v*) Calyx enlarging in fruit, overtopping the berry; pedicels clustered .. .. .. *Withania*.

B. Corolla-lobes imbricate; embryo curved:

(*vi*) Capsule 4-valved, semi-indehiscent; fls. solitary, axillary; stamens all perfect .. .. *Datura*.

(*vii*) Capsule circumscissile; fls. unilateral, upper racemose .. .. *Hyoscyamus*.

C. Corolla-lobes induplicate-valvate; embryo straight; fruit capsular; fls. panicled .. .. .. *Nicotiana*.

D. Corolla-lobes subplicate-imbricate; embryo straight or slightly curved; fruit membraneous or subcoriaceous capsule; fls. white or blue, solitary axillary, or the uppermost passing into a 1-sided terminal raceme .. *Browallia*.

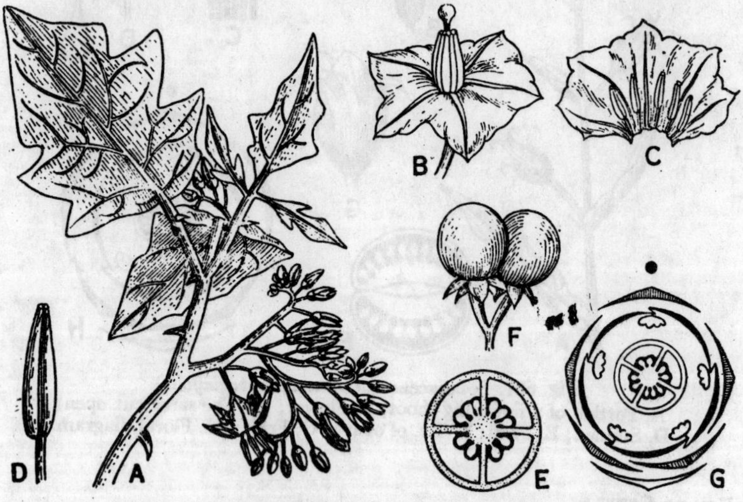

Fig. 682. Solanaceae (*Solanum torvum*).
A, Portion of a flowering shoot; B, Flower; C, Corolla split open; D, Stamen; E, T.s. of ovary; F, Fruit; G, Floral diagram.

Range of floral structures

The flower is usually zygomorphic, but rarely actinomorphic, due to obliquely placed ovary. The corolla is found to be regular as in *Solanum*, which consists of rotate corolla, or the bell-shaped corolla of *Atropa*, or irregular to some extent, as in *Hyoscyamus*.

Zygomorphy is very prominent in *Salpiglossis*. In this genus there are two or four fertile stamens. The corolla may be two-lipped, as in *Schizanthus*. The stamens are usually unequal in their length.

The ovary becomes 1-celled in *Henoonia*, but in *Capsicum* the ovary is also 1-celled in the upper portion. In many genera false partitions are laid down as a result of which 3–5-celled chambers are formed. In *Datura*, 4-celled chamber is seen, but in *Nicandra*, the ovary becomes 3–5-celled.

The number of ovules is generally numerous but occasionally few ovules are found, as in *Cestrum*.

Common plants

(1) Brinjal or Egg plant (*Solanum melongena* L.), a common herb cultivated throughout India. (2) Potato (*Solanum tuberosum* L.). (3) *Solanum xanthocarpum* Schrad. & Wendle, a prickly weed found on roadsides, much used by Indian Kabirajes. (4) *Solanum torvum* Swartz., a common shrub. (5) *Solanum ferox* L. (6) *Solanum*

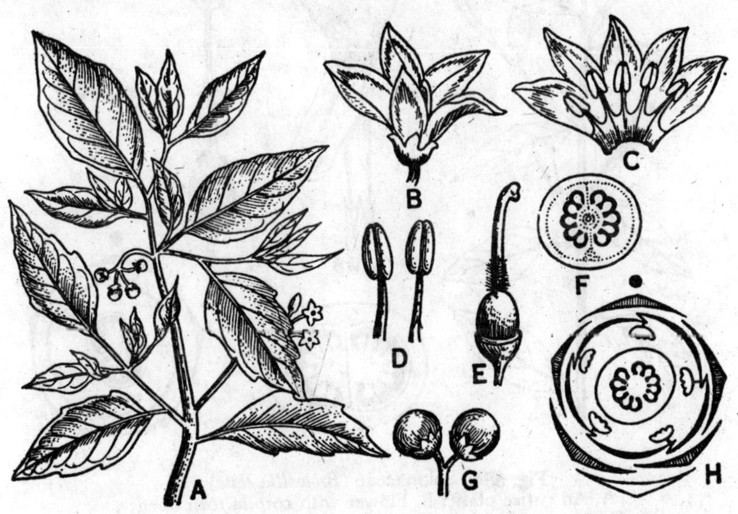

Fig. 683. Solanaceae (*Solanum nigrum*).
A, Portion of a flowering shoot; B, Flower; C, Corolla split open; D, Stamens; E, Pistil; F, T.s. of ovary; G, Fruit; H, Floral diagram.

verbascifolium L., a large shrub or small tree about 12 ft. in height. (7) Nightshade (*Solanum nigrum* L.), a common weed found everywhere. (8) *Solanum indicum* L., a prickly herb commonly found on roadsides and rubbish heaps. (9) *Solanum trilobatum* L., a prickly climbing plant found in salt-lakes near Calcutta. (10) Tomato

(*Lycopersicum esculentum* Mill. = *S. lycopersicum* Mill.), a tall herb, commonly cultivated for globose pulpy fruits. (11) Chilli or red pepper (*Capsicum frutescens* L. = *C. annum* L.), cultivated for the scarlet or orange-yellow fruits which are used as condiment. (12) Thorn-apple (*Datura fastuosa* L. = *D. metel* L.), a common herb whose seeds are highly poisonous; Jimson weed (*D. stramonium* L.), another highly poisonous plant from which alkaloid 'daturin' is extracted. (13) Tobacco (*Nicotiana tabacum* L.), a small shrub with sticky glandular hairs. (14) *Nicotiana plumbaginifolia* Viv., a common weed. (15) *Withania somnifera* Dun., a medicinal plant cultivated in gardens.

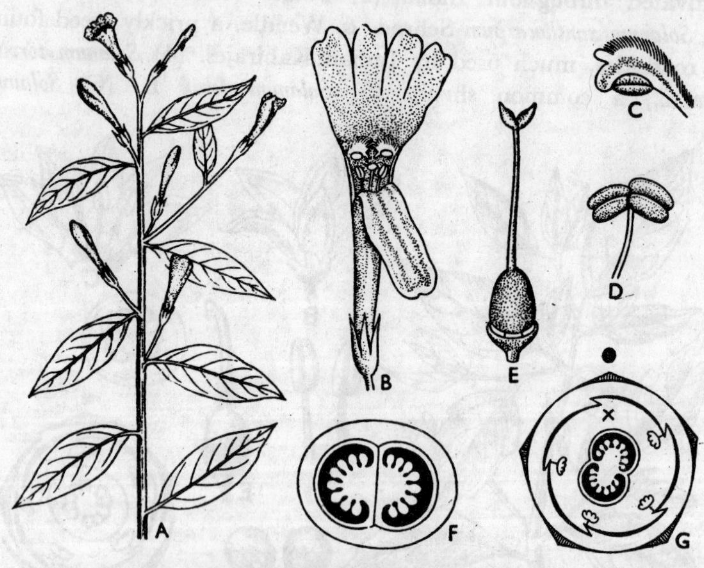

Fig. 684. Solanaceae (*Browallia elata*).
A, An entire plant; B, Flower with corolla torn open; C, A stamen with hood; D, A shorter stamen; E, Pistil; F, T.s. of ovary; G, Floral diagram.

(16) Cape gooseberry or Ground cherry (*Physalis peruviana* L.), commonly cultivated for the edible fruits which lie concealed within accrescent calyx; *P. minima* L., a common weed in waste places and on the borders of cultivated land. (17) *Cestrum nocturnum* Murray, a common garden plant, the flowers of which emit a sweet odour at night. (18) *Solanum macranthum*, a tree-like plant with pale-blue flowers, often cultivated in gardens. (19) *Solanum seaforthianum*, a

climber, very commonly found in Darjeeling with small white flowers. (20) *Brunfelsia, Salpiglossis, Schizanthus* and *Petunia* are garden plants. (21) Deadly nightshade (*Atropa belladonna* L.), (22) Woody nightshade or Bitter-sweet (*Solanum dulcamara* L.)., and (23) Henbane (*Hyoscyamus niger* L.), are medicinal plants. (24) *Browallia elata* L., an annual garden herb. (25) *Solanum glaucum*, very common at Diamond Harbour. (26) *Cestrum diurnum*, very common on roadsides.

Affinity

This family is allied to Scrophulariaceae but distinguished by the form of the corolla, number of stamens and oblique position of carpels. It differs from Convolvulaceae in having numerous seeds.

According to Engler, this family occupies a position under order Tubiflorae in the subseries Solanineae. Hutchinson considers this family is related to Convolvulaceae and Boraginaceae. Wettstein accepts the view that Solanaceae is closely associated with Convolvulaceae, that is why he has put the family under Tubiflorae. Rendle is of opinion that the family Solanaceae be placed under Tubiflorae. Hallier considers it as a primitive member of the Tubiflorae and has derived from Linaceae.

Economic importance

This family is of considerable economic importance. Some plants are used as vegetables, such as, *Solanum tuberosum* (potato), *S. melongena* (brinjal), *S. lycopersicum* (tomato), *Capsicum* and others. Some genera are important from medicinal standpoint of view, such as, *Atropa, Datura, Solanum, Withania, Hyoscyamus*, etc. Tobacco (*Nicotiana tabacum*) is an important economic plant. Alkaloids, such as, *nicotin* and *daturin* are obtained from *Nicotiana tabacum* and *Datura stramonium* respectively. Some plants are ornamentals such as, *Petunia, Cestrum, Datura, Browallia, Brunfelsia, Schizanthus*, etc.

SCROPHULARIACEAE

General characters

Plants—usually herbs or undershrubs, rarely parasitic on roots (e.g., *Lathrea, Striga*). Leaves—alternate throughout, or the lower opposite and the upper alternate, or all opposite or whorled, exstipulate. Inflorescence—racemose (raceme or spike) or cymose (dichasia). Flowers—zygomorphic (sometimes almost regular in

Scoparia), bisexual, hypogynous, generally *with bracts.* Sepals—(5), more or less deeply 4–5-partite, imbricate or valvate. Petals—usually (5), *personate,* sometimes spurred or saccate, rarely rotate (e.g., *Scoparia*), imbricate. Stamens—usually 4, didynamous, sometimes 5 (e.g., *Verbascum*) or 2 (e.g., *Veronica*), epipetalous. Carpels—(2), medianly placed; ovary superior, *usually 2-celled,* rarely 4-celled

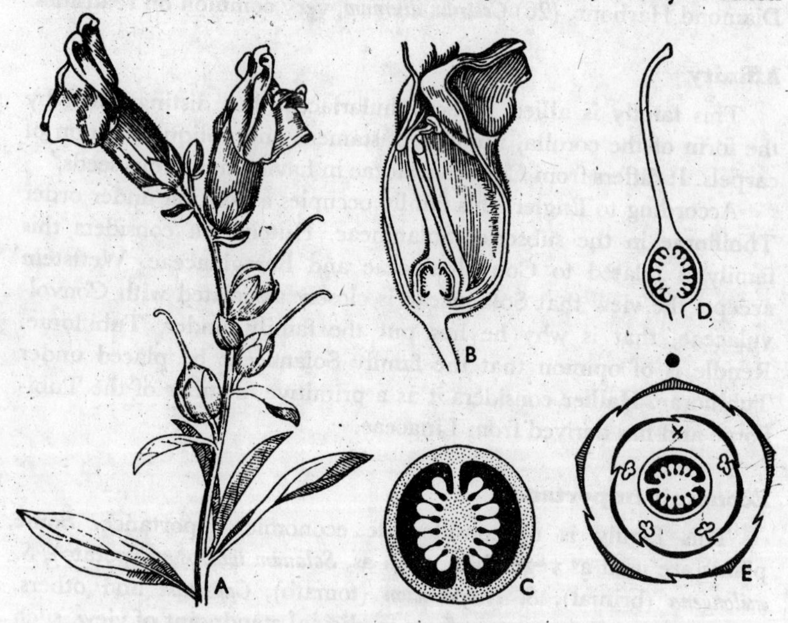

Fig. 685. Scrophulariaceae (*Antirrhinum majus*).
A, Portion of a flowering shoot; B, V.s. of a flower; C, T.s. of ovary; D, V.s. of ovary; E, Floral diagram.

with *numerous anatropous ovules* on *axile placenta* (but free-central in *Scoparia*); stigma simple or bilobed; style terminal. Fruit—usually a *capsule,* sometimes berry. Seed—albuminous. Embryo—*straight* or *slightly curved.*

Floral formula

$\uparrow$ ⚥ $K_{(5)}\ \overline{C_{(5)}\ A_{4 \text{ or } 5}}\ \underline{G_{(2)}}$

Number and distribution

This family consists of about 210 genera and nearly 3,000 species which are cosmopolitan but chiefly confined to temperate regions.

Key to Genera

A. Corolla tubular, tube saccate to spurred; capsule opening by pores; inflorescence uniform:

(*i*) Corolla spurred; anther-cells distinct .. *Linaria*.

(*ii*) Corolla large, saccate below .. .. *Antirrhinum*.

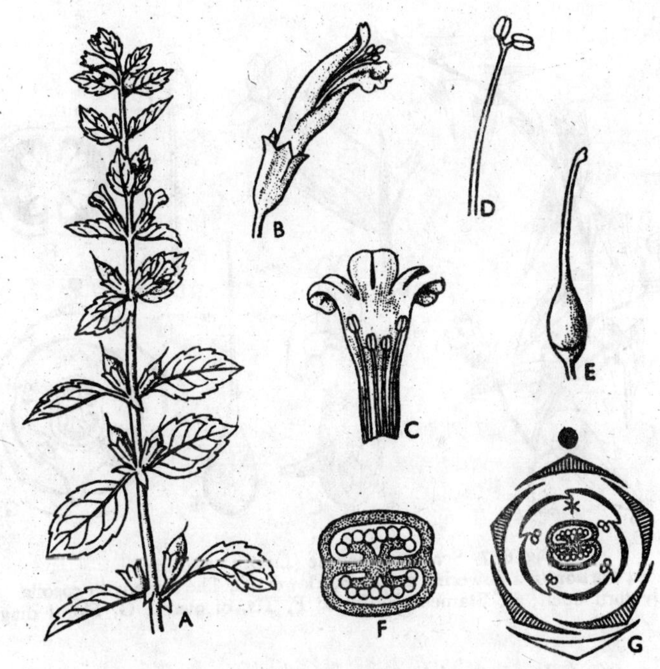

Fig. 686. Scrophulariaceae (*Lindenbergia urticaefolia*). A, Portion of a flowering shoot; B, Flower; C, Corolla split open; D, Stamen; E, Pistil; F, T.s. of ovary; G, Floral diagram.

B. Corolla personate, with 2 parallel ridges:

(*iii*) Calyx campanulate, 5-partite, equal; stamens all perfect; seeds angular; plants usually aquatic with submerged leaves multifid .. *Limnophila*.

(*iv*) Calyx campanulate, 5-fid; anther-cells disjoined; capsule loculicidal .. .. .. *Lindenbergia*.

C. Corolla distinctly bilabiate; the anther-cells contiguous but distinct; calyx wide campanulate, 2-fid .. .. *Mazus*.

D. **Corolla** 5-lobed, without parallel ridges:

(*v*) Calyx 5-partite, imbricate; stamens inserted; anther-cells contiguous; corolla white, tinged with purple and yellow; creeping or erect .. *Herpestis.*

(*vi*) Calyx deeply 5-fid; corolla-throat much widened; stamens 2 perfect, 2 staminodes; fls. violet; annual marshy herbs .. .. .. *Dopatrium.*

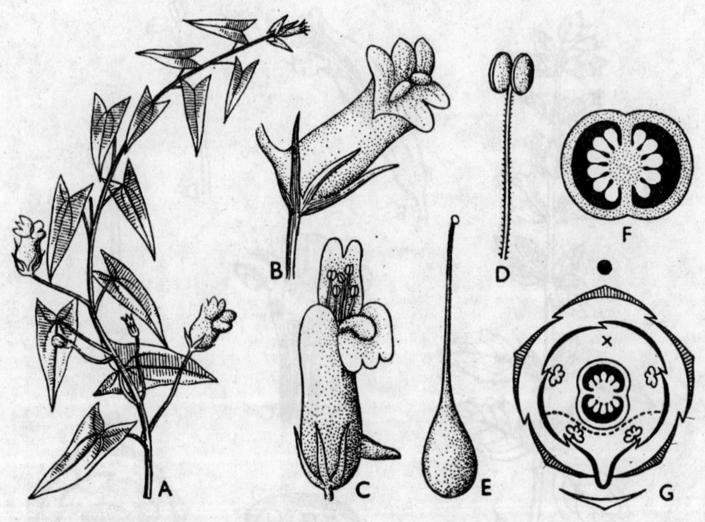

Fig. 687. Scrophulariaceae (*Linaria ramosissima*).
A, Portion of a flowering shoot; B, Flower; C, The same with corolla slightly torn open; D, Stamen; E, Pistil; F, T.s. of ovary; G, Floral diagram

(*vii*) Calyx 5-toothed; 2 stamens attached to upper lobes, the other 2 stamens to lower lobes, all anthers conniving or cohering in pair .. *Vandellia.*

(*viii*) Calyx tubular, sometimes winged or obliquely 2-lipped; stamens 4, didynamous; fls. showy; fruit a linear capsule .. .. *Torenia.*

(*ix*) Calyx segments 5; stamens 2, both perfect; capsule long .. .. .. *Bonnaya.*

E. Corolla-lobes 4, rotate, white, almost regular; stamens 4, perfect with staminal hairs; fruit a small globular capsule with free central placenta .. .. .. *Scoparia.*

F. Corolla-lobes 5, rotate; calyx partite; stamens equal; anthers sagittate or horseshoe-shaped .. .. *Hemiphragma.*

G. Corolla-lobes 5, subovate, with two upper lobes exterior in bud; stamens 4; leaves all alternate .. .. *Celsia*.

H. Corolla tubular, with spreading limbs, abruptly incurved; calyx subcampanulate, 5-toothed; ovary 1-celled, tip mucronate .. .. .. *Striga*.

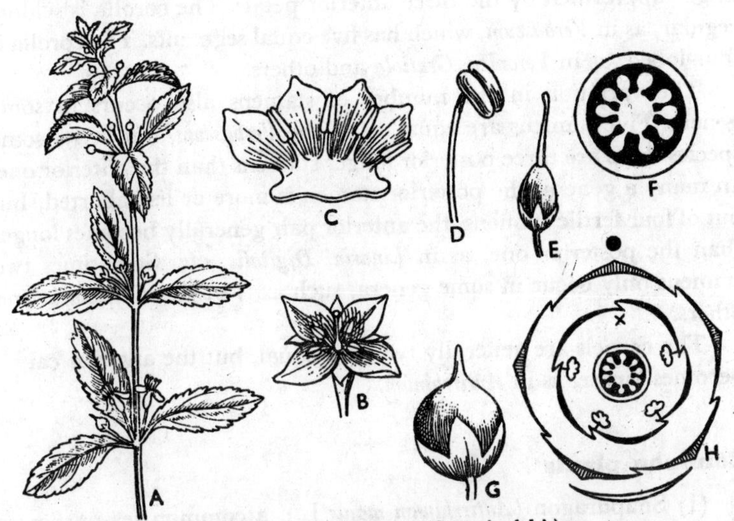

Fig. 688. Scrophulariaceae (*Scoparia dulcis*).
A, Portion of a flowering shoot; B, Flower; C, Corolla tube split open; D, Stamen; E, Pistil; F, T.s. of ovary; G, Fruit; H, Floral diagram.

Range of floral structures

This family shows a considerable variation in their floral structures.

Flowers are usually bracteate and there are also bracteoles. Calyx is generally pentamerous, but reduction in the number of calyx is also manifested in *Euphrasia* and many *Veronicas*, where the general suppression of the posterior sepal occurs. In *Pedicularis*, there are 2–5-toothed calyx and in *Calceolaria*, the two anterior sepals are found to be entirely connate.

The usual zygomorphic corolla shows wide variation in its form based on the length and breadth of the tube. The corolla may be absent in *Veronica* or the corolla may be large and bell-shaped, as in *Digitalis purpurea*. In *Veronica*, the corolla is provided with spreading limbs. It is small and suberect, as in *Scrophularia*, or the corolla forms a pair of closed lips, as in *Linaria* and *Antirrhinum*. The genus *Linaria* shows a petal which is spurred at the anterior region. In *Diascia*, the lateral anterior petals are spurred. The corolla tube is very short in *Calceolaria*. In this case two lips are found, an upper smaller lip formed by the union of the posterior petals, and a lower larger lip, formed by the three anterior petals. The corolla is seldom regular, as in *Verbascum*, which has five equal segments. The corolla is four-lobed, as in *Veronica*, *Gratiola* and others.

The variation in the number of stamens also occurs in some genera. Five stamens are equal, as in the *Verbascum*, but in its some species there are three posterior longer stamens than the anterior one. In many a genera, the posterior stamen is more or less aborted, but out of four fertile stamens, the anterior pair generally becomes longer than the posterior one, as in *Linaria*, *Digitalis*, etc. Sometimes two stamens only occur in some genera, such as, *Veronica*, *Calceolaria* and others.

The carpels are generally two and equal, but the anterior car becomes larger, as in *Antirrhinum*.

Common plants

(1) Snapdragon (*Antirrhinum majus* L.), a common season flower of gardens. (2) *Lindenbergia urticaefolia* Link & Otto.=*L. indica* O. Ktze. and *L. polyantha* Royle, very common on old walls and edges of roofs bearing small yellow flowers. (3) *Scoparia dulcis* L., a rigid perennial herb, common in waste places with almost regular flowers and corolla-throat densely bearded. (4) Toad-flax (*Linaria ramosissima* Wall.), a prostrate herb with sagittate leaves, commonly found in waste places, (5) *Herpestis monnieria* H. B. & K.=*Bacopa monnieri* Pennel, a small weed reputed for nervine properties. (6) *Mecardonia diathera* L., common on pathways. (7) *Celsia coromandeliana* Vahl.=*Verbascum coromandelianus* O. Ktze., a weed. (8) *Bonnaya brachiata* Link & Otto.=*Linderia brachiata* Link & Otto., a weed. (9) *Vandellia crustacea* Benth.=*Linderia crustacea* F. Muell., a common weed. (10) *Limnophila gratioloides* R. Br., a weed of rice-fields and damp places; *Limnophila heterophylla* Benth., an aquatic plant with highly dissected submerged leaves, is a typical example of heterophylly. (11) Coral plant (*Russelia juncea* Jacq.=*R. equisetiformis* Schlecht & Cham.), a closely tufted perennial herb with numerous slender green

branches; leaves opposite or whorled, those on the stem often reduced to scales; very common in garden with crimson-red flowers. (13) Purple foxglove (*Digitalis purpurea* L.), a medicinal plant, abundant in Darjeeling. (14) *Torenia cordata* (Griff.) Dutta, a medicinal plant

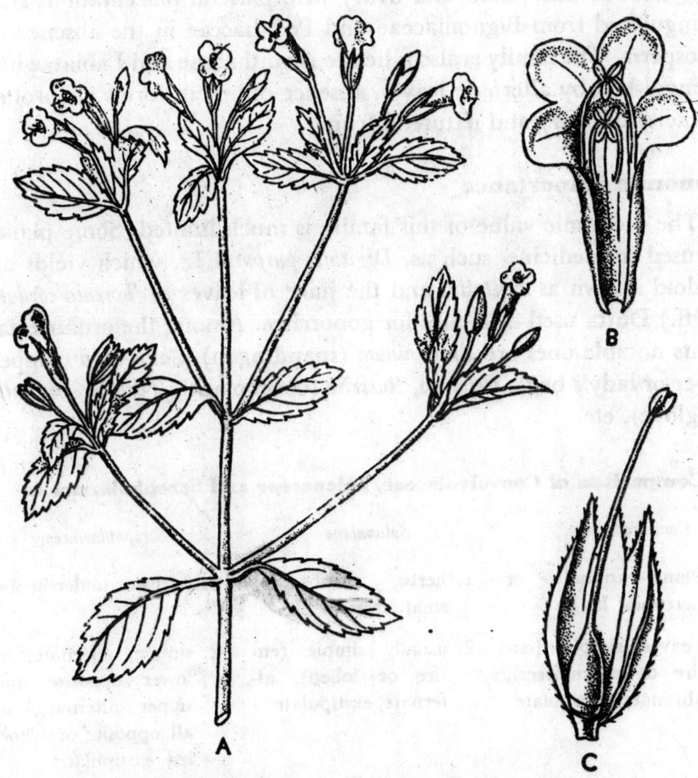

Fig. 689. Scrophulariaceae (*Torenia calcarata*).
A, Portion of a flowering shoot; B, Corolla tube split open; C, Pistil with calyx split open and corolla removed.

common in the hills of West Bengal and Assam. (15) *T. calcarata* Griff. and *Verbascum celosiodes* Benth. are season flowers. (16) *Dopatrium junceum* Ham., a weed of rice-fields and swamps. (17) *Striga densiflora* Benth., a herb 6–8 in. high. (18) *Mazus rugosus* Lour.=*M. japonicas* O. Kunth., a small annual with tufted radical leaves. (19) *Hemiphragma heterophyllum*, commonly found in the hills.

Affinity

This family is much allied to Solanaceae, especially with the tribe Salpiglossideae in the floral structure but distinguished by medianly placed ovary, the aestivation of corolla and zygomorphic corolla. Scrophulariaceae also bears an affinity with other allied families, such as, Orobanchaceae and Gesneraceae, but distinguished from them in their unilocular ovary with parietal placentation. It is distinguished from Bignoniaceae and Pedaliaceae in the absence of endosperm. The family is also allied to Acanthaceae and Labiatae but distinguished by alternate leaves, absence of bracts, forms of corolla, character of ovary and nature of fruit.

Economic importance

The economic value of this family is much limited. Some plants are used in medicine, such as, *Digitalis purpurea* L., which yields an alkaloid known as *digitalin*, and the juice of leaves of *Torenia cordata* (Griff.) Dutta used as a cure for gonorrhea. Among the ornamental plants notable ones are *Antirrhinum* (snapdragon), *Calceolaria* (slipper flower or lady's bag), *Veronica*, *Russelia* (coral plant), *Torenia*, *Digitalis* (foxglove), etc.

Comparison of Convolvulaceae, Solanaceae and Scrophulariaceae

Convolvulaceae	*Solanaceae*	*Scrophulariaceae*
1. Plants—annual or perennial herbs.	1. herbs, shrubs or small trees.	1. herbs or undershrubs.
2. Leaves—simple (entire or palmatisect), alternate, exstipulate.	2. usually simple (entire or lobed), alternate, exstipulate.	2. simple, alternate, or lower opposite and upper alternate, or all opposite or whorled, exstipulate.
3. Inflorescence–racemose or dichasium.	3. cymose.	3. racemose (raceme or spike) or cymose.
4. Flowers—regular, bisexual, hypogynous.	4. apparently regular, sometimes zygomorphic, bisexual, hypogynous.	4. zygomorphic, bisexual, hypogynous.
5. Sepals—5, free or united, often persistent.	5. (5), persistent, often enlarging in fruit.	5. (5), more or less deeply 4–5 partite.

Convolvulaceae	*Solanaceae*	*Scrophulariaceae*
6. Petals—(5), funnel- or salver-shaped, twisted.	6. (5), rotate or funnel-shaped, plicate.	6. usually (5), personate, imbricate.
7. Stamens—5, unequal.	7. 5, but 2+2 in zygomorphic flowers.	7. usually 2+2, rarely 5 or 2.
8. Carpels—(2), medianly placed.	8. (2), obliquely placed.	8. (2), medianly placed.
9. Ovary—2-celled with 2 erect anatropous ovules in each or 4-celled with 1 ovule in each.	9. 2-celled or falsely 3–5-celled with many anatropous ovules in each.	9. 2-celled with many anatropous ovules in each.
10. Fruit—capsule, sometimes berry.	10. berry, sometimes capsule.	10. capsule, sometimes berry.

BIGNONIACEAE

General characters

Plants—trees or shrubs, often climbers. Leaves—usually opposite, simple or pinnately compound, often glandular, exstipulate. Inflorescence—usually cymose (dichasial cyme). Flowers—zygomorphic

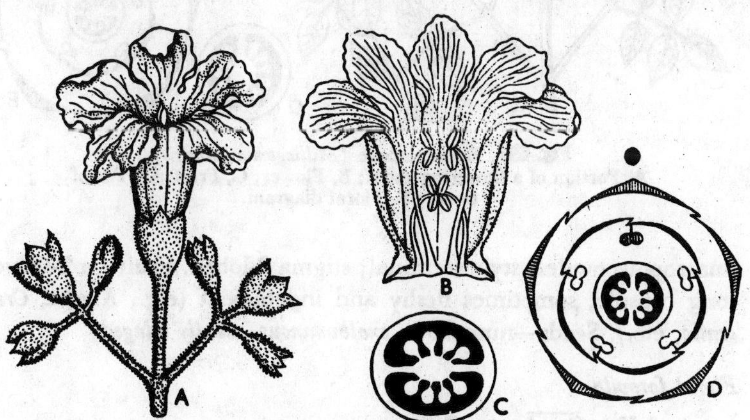

Fig. 690. Bignoniaceae (*Stereospermum suaveolens*). A, Portion of an inflorescence; B, Corolla tube split open; C, T.s. of ovary; D, Floral diagram.

bisexual, hypogynous, bracteate. Sepals—(5), with 5 teeth or lobes, sometimes bilabiate (e.g., *Spathodea*) or truncate imbricate. Petals—

(5), bell- or funnel-shaped, rarely bilabiate, imbricate. Stamens—4, didynamous, with a posterior staminode or rarely perfect (e.g., *Oroxylon*), sometimes 2, inserted on the lower part of the corolla-tube, epipetalous; anther cells parallel or divaricate. Carpels—(2); ovary superior, usually 2-celled with axile placentation, sometimes 1-celled with parietal placentation (e.g., *Kigelia*) having numerous

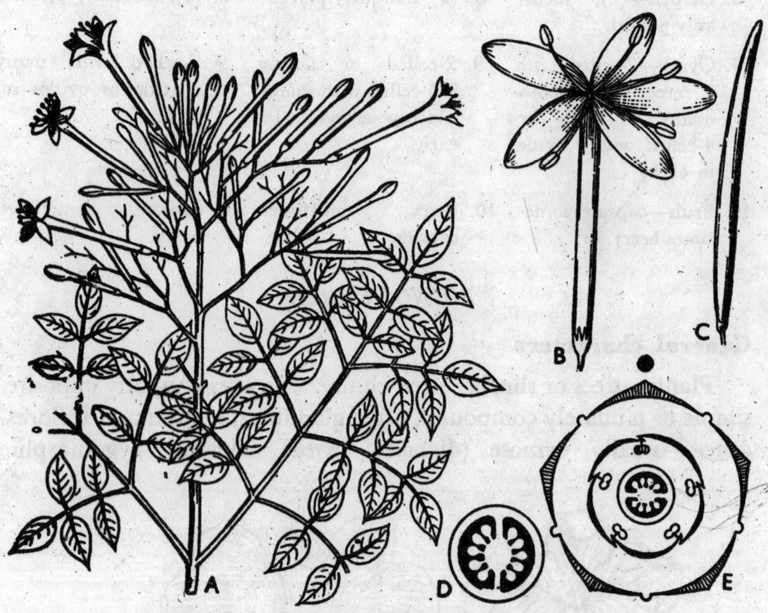

Fig. 691. Bignoniaceae (*Millingtonia hortensis*).
A, Portion of a flowering shoot; B, Flower; C, Fruit; D, T.s. of ovary; E, Floral diagram.

anatropous ovules; style terminal; stigma 2-lobed. Fruit—a 2-valved long capsule, sometimes fleshy and indehiscent (e.g., *Kigelia*, *Crescentia*, etc.). Seeds—numerous, *exalbuminous*, *usually winged*.

Floral formula

↑ ⚥ $K_{(5)}$ $\overline{C_{(5)} A_{4 \text{ or } 2}}$ $\underline{G_{(2)}}$

Number and distribution

This family consists of about 110 genera and 750 species which are chiefly distributed in the tropics.

Key to Genera

A. Stamens 5 perfect, leaves 2–3 pinnate; capsule septifragal, calyx large coriaceous; corolla tube wide campanulate .. *Oroxylon.*

B. Stamens 4, perfect:

(*a*) Capsule septifragal; leaves 2–3 pinnate; calyx small cup-shaped; corolla long, slender .. .. *Millingtonia.*

(*b*) Capsule loculicidal; leaves 1–2 pinnate or rarely simple; calyx large; corolla tube short or long and much reduced at the mouth—

(*i*) capsule with double wings at the margins; calyx large, swollen, campanulate .. .. *Pajanelia.*

(*ii*) capsule not winged:

(1) calyx tubular, campanulate, equally 5-toothed .. .. .. *Tecoma.*

(2) calyx ovoid and oblong, never equally 5-toothed; corolla tube long or short cylindric below and campanulate above .. *Dolichandrone.*

(3) calyx spathaceous; corolla tube ventricular; corolla irregular; deeply 3–5-lobed; capsule falcate or twisted .. .. .. *Heterophragma.*

(4) calyx truncate or shortly unequally lobed; capsule with thick spongy septum .. *Stereospermum.*

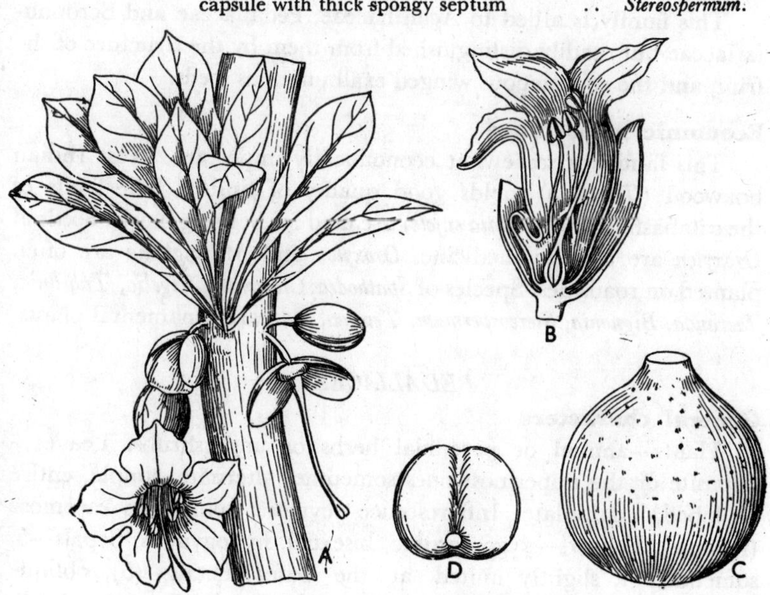

Fig. 692. Bignoniaceae (*Crescentia cujete*).
A, Portion of the trunk with foliage leaves and flowers; B, V.s. of a flower; C, Fruit; D, Seed.

Common plants

(1) *Oroxylon indicum* Vent., a small tree often planted on roadsides. (2) Indian cork tree (*Millingtonia hortensis* L.), a tall tree often planted on roadsides and gardens. (3) *Pajanelia rheedei* DC. (4) Yellow elder (*Tecoma stans* L.), a garden shrub. (5) *Dolichandrone spathaceae* K. Schum., a fairly tall tree. (6) *Heterophragma adenophyllum* Seems., a large tree. (7) *Bignonia venusta* Ker. =*Pyrostegia venusa* Miers., a common garden climber with orange-coloured flowers. (8) African tulip tree. (*Spathodea campanulata*, Beauv.). (9) The Sausage tree (*Kigelia pinnata* DC.). (10) Calabash (*Crescentia cujete* L.) and (11) Jacranda (*Jacranda mimosifolia* D. Don) are beautiful flowering trees. (12) Cat's claw (*Bignonia unguis-cati*), a slender climber, the terminal leaflets of which are modified into hook-like structures. (13) *Tabebuia rosea* DC., another tall tree with rosy-pink flowers. (14) *Stereospermum suaveolens* DC., *S. chelonoides*, very common tall trees. (15) Candle tree (*Parmentiuros cerifera* Seems.) can be found in the Indian Botanic Garden.

Affinity

This family is allied to Acanthaceae, Pedaliaceae and Scrophulariaceae but readily distinguished from them by the structure of the fruit, and the conspicuous winged exalbuminous seeds.

Economic importance

This family is somewhat economically important. West Indian boxwood (*Tabebuia*) yields good quality of timber. The fruits of the calabash tree (*Crescentia cujete*) are used for begging bowls. Seeds of *Oroxylon* are used in medicine. *Oroxylon* and *Millingtonia* are often planted on roadsides. Species of *Spathodea*, *Crescentia*, *Kigelia*, *Tabebuia*, *Jacranda*, *Bignonia*, *Stereospermum*, *Tecoma*, etc., are ornamental plants.

PEDALIACEAE

General characters

Plants—annual or perennial herbs or undershrubs. Leaves—opposite or the uppermost ones sometimes alternate, simple, entire or lobed, exstipulate. Inflorescence—cymose, sometimes racemose (raceme). Flowers—zygomorphic, bisexual, hypogynous. Sepals—5, sometimes 4, slightly united at the base. Petals—(5), oblique or slightly bilabiate, tubular below, imbricate. Stamens—2+2, didynamous or 2 (e.g., *Martynia*), epipetalous. Carpels—(2); ovary superior, seated on a large fleshy or glandular disc, usually *4-celled* sometimes 1- or 2-celled, with many or few anatropous ovules; stigma slightly 2-lobed; style slender. Fruit—capsule, or nut, often *beaked*, or *barbed*, or with wings. Seeds—albuminous.

Floral formula

$\uparrow$ ⚥ $K_{(5 \text{ or } 4)}$ $\overline{C_{(5)} A}_{4 \text{ or } 2}$ $G_{\underline{(2)}}$

Number and distribution

This family consists of 16 genera and about 50 species, mostly tropical.

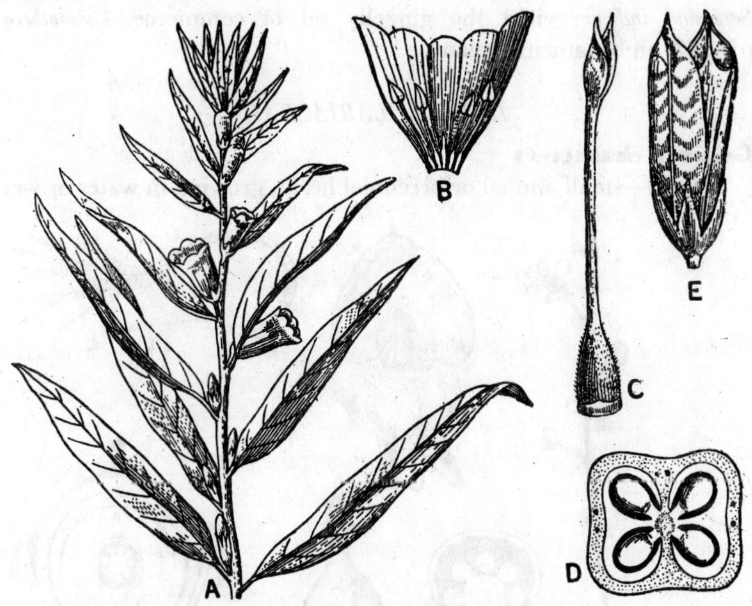

Fig. 693. Pedaliaceae (*Sesamum indicum*).
A, Portion of a flowering shoot; B, Corolla tube split open; C, Pistil; D, T.s. of ovary; E, Fruit.

Key to Genera

Anther-cells divariacate; ovary 1-celled; placenta parietal; capsule beaked; racemes terminal .. .. *Martynia*.

Anther-cells subparallel; ovary 2-celled and spuriously 4-celled; placenta axile; capsule not beaked; fls. axillary .. *Sesamum*.

Common plants

(1) The Tiger's claw plant (*Martynia diandra* Glox. =*Martynia annua* L.), a tall coarse herb, very common on roadsides and near

villages. (2) The Gingelly or Sesame (*Sesamum indicum* DC.), a herb commonly cultivated for the sake of oil.

Affinity

This family is related to Acanthaceae in the zygomorphy of flowers and nature of fruits. It resembles Solanaceae in the presence of false septa. Pedaliaceae is readily distinguished by the 4-celled ovary, and usually beaked or barbed fruits.

Economic importance

This family has got some economic importance. The seeds of *Sesamum indicum* yield the gingelly oil of commerce. *Ceratotheca triloba* is an ornamental plant.

LENTIBULARIACEAE

General characters

Plants—small annual or perennial herbs, growing in water or wet

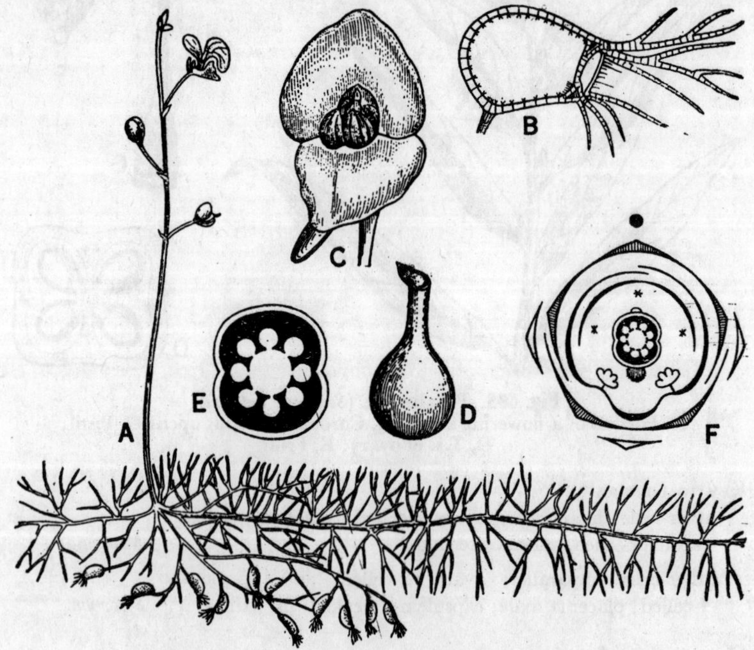

Fig. 664. Lentibulariaceae (*Utricularia stellaris*).
A, Portion of a flowering shoot; B, Bladder in section; C, Flower; D, Pistil; E, T.s. of ovary; F, Floral diagram.

places. Leaves—alternate or in basal rosette, often dimorphic, the submerged ones are much dissected bearing small bladder-like appendages, while the subaerial ones composing floating rosette. Inflorescence—raceme produced on a scape. Flowers—zygomorphic, bisexual, hypogynous, bracteate. Sepals—(2–5), bilabiate, usually persistent, valvate. Petals—(5), ***bilabiate***, sometimes personate, the lower lip much the larger and 3-lobed, spurred or saccate at the base. Stamens—2, epipetalous, adnate to the base of the corolla tube and alternating with the lower 3-lobed lip. Carpels—(2); ovary superior, 1-celled with many anatropous ovules on *free central placenta;* stigma bifid, unequal. Fruit—capsule. Seed—minute, exalbuminous, with a poorly differentiated embryo.

Floral formula

$$\uparrow ⚥\ K_{(2-5)}\ \overline{C_{(5)}\ A_2}\ \underline{G_{(2)}}$$

Number and distribution

This family contains about 5 genera and 260 species which are mainly tropical and temperate.

Common plants

(1) *Utricularia stellaris* L., a common floating herb. (2) *U. flexuosa* Vahl., another common floating herb. (3) *U. Seanders* Benj., a terrestrial plant of marshy places.

Affinity

This family is related to Scrophulariaceae in having zygomorphic flowers but readily distinguished by stamens 2, free central placentation and presence of tiny bladders.

Economic importance

This family is less important economically. Some species of butterwort (*Pinguicula*) are used as ornamentals and a few species of bladderwort (*Utricularia*) are grown in aquaria.

ACANTHACEAE

General characters

Plants—perennial herbs or shrubs, sometimes climbing, (e.g., *Thunbergia*), rarely trees (e.g., *Strobilanthus*), with *branches swollen at the nodes.* Leaves—opposite and decussate, simple, entire, often with *cystoliths,* exstipulate. Inflorescence—racemose (dense spike) or cymose, often with *copious bracts* and *bracteoles.* Flowers—zygomorphic, bisexual, hypogynous, bracteate. Sepals—(5), often unequal, much reduced (e.g., *Thunbergia*), usually imbricate. Petals—(5), often *bilabiate*, sometimes *oblique*, imbricate or twisted. Stamens—4, didynamous, sometimes 2 (e.g., *Justicia*, *Adhatoda*, etc.), epipetalous, sometimes 1–3 staminodes present; anthers sometimes spurred and hairy. Carpels—(2), medianly placed; ovary superior, *beaked* (prolonged but does not bear any ovule), 2-celled, with 2 or more anatropous ovules in each cell on the axile placenta; style simple, *terminal;* stigma often unequal, sometimes spoon-shaped. Fruit—usually a loculicidal capsule. Seeds—generally supported on a development (often hook-like) of the funicle (*jaculator*), exalbuminous. Embryo—*curved*, radicle pointed downwards.

Floral formula

$\uparrow \text{⚥}\ K_{(5)}\ \overline{C_{(5)}\ A_{4 \text{ or } 2}}\ \underline{G_{(2)}}$

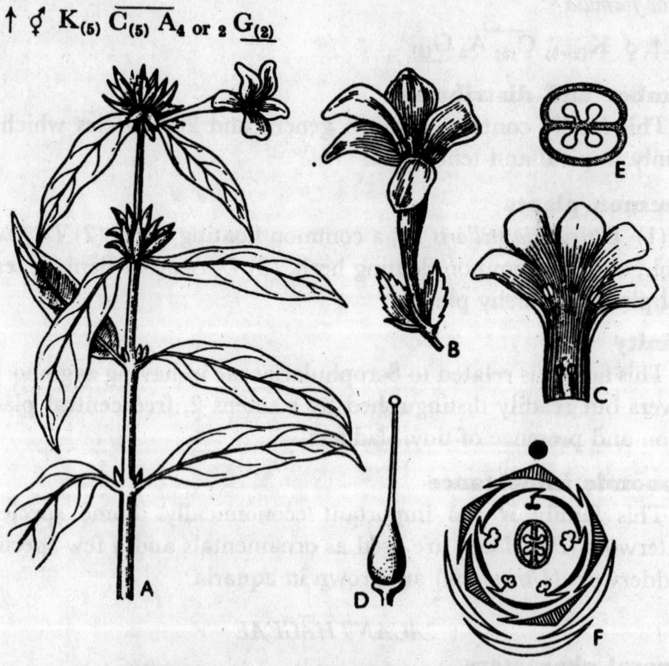

Fig. 695. Acanthaceae (*Barleria cristata*).
A, Portion of a flowering shoot; B, Flower; C, Corolla-tube split open; D, Pistil; E, T.s. of ovary; F, Floral diagram.

Number and distribution

This family consists of about 240 genera and over 2,200 species which are commonly found in the tropical regions.

KEY TO GENERA

A. Corolla-lobes imbricate in bud; ovules numerous in two long rows; seeds mounted in papilla:

(a) Stamens 2; calyx 4-sect; herbaceous bracts .. *Nelsonia.*

(b) Stamens 4; calyx 5-partite .. .. *Ebermaiera.*

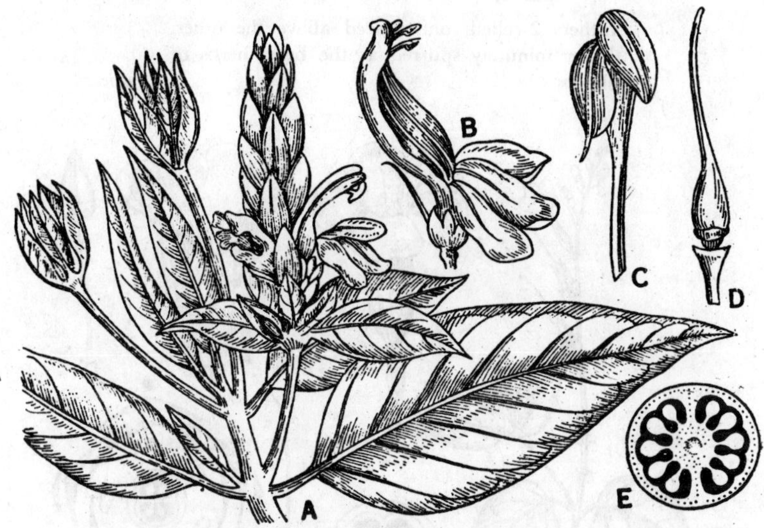

Fig. 696. Acanthaceae (*Adhatoda vasica*). A, Portion of a flowering shoot; B, Flower; C, Stamen; D, Pistil; E, T.s. of ovary.

B. Corolla-lobes imbricate; jaculators curved; anthers 2–1-celled, often spurred at the base:

(a) Ovules 3–10 in each cell; capsule more or less few-seeded, compressed at right angles to septum; fls. panicled .. .. .. *Andrographis.*

(b) Ovules 2–1 in each cell; corolla-lobes subequal; stamens 4, of which 2 are small or obsolete

(i) Anthers 2-celled .. .. .. *Barleria.*

(ii) Anthers 1-celled .. .. .. *Crossandra.*

(iii) Anthers 2-celled, all equal, calyx deeply 5- or 4-lobed .. .. *Lepidagathis.*

(iv) Anthers 2-celled; stamens 4; corolla tube long; limb enlarged .. .. .. *Asystasia.*

(v) Anthers 2-celled; stamens 2; placenta originating from the base—

(1) Single-sided bracts, spicate; short-stalked capsule .. .. .. *Rungia.*

(2) Clustered bracts, 2 unequal; fls. shortly pedicellate; club-shaped capsule; calyx 5-partite .. .. .. *Dicliptera.*

(vi) Anthers 2-celled, one placed above the other, lower minutely spurred at the base; herbs or shrubs .. .. *Justicia.*

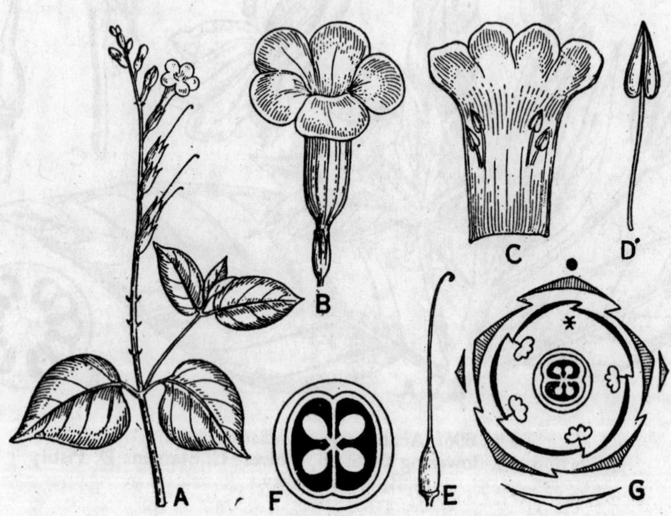

Fig. 697. Acanthaceae (*Asystasia gangetica*).
A, Portion of a flowering shoot; B, Flower; C, The same split open; D, Stamen, E, Pistil; F, T.s. of ovary; G, Floral diagram.

(vii) Anthers 2-celled, apiculate, scarcely spurred; corolla 2-lipped, short-tubed; bracts leafy; placentae not originating from the base of the capsule .. .. *Adhatoda.*

(1) Fls. long, narrow, clustered; bracts narrow, small; plants usually shrubs .. .. *Rhinacanthus.*

(2) Fls. in axillary or terminal clusters; bracts larger than the bracteoles in opposite valvate pairs; corolla rose or purple; plants spreading herbs .. .. .. *Peristrophe.*

(*c*) Ovules 2 in each cell; stamens 2—

(*i*) Corolla cylindric, widened at the base; anther-cells parallel, equal with widened connective .. *Eranthemum.*

(*ii*) Corolla tube long, filiform; anther-cells parallel, subequal; large bracts imbricated .. .. *Ecbolium.*

C. Corolla-lobes twisted in bud:

(*a*) Stamens 4, didynamous; bracts large, foliaceous; ovules in collateral pairs in each cell; fruit beaked capsule; jaculator absent; plant usually a climber with yellow or blue fls. .. .. .. *Thunbergia.*

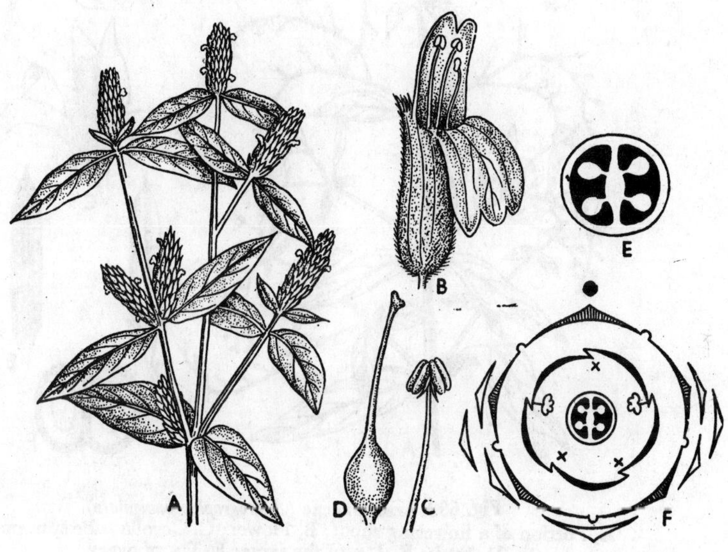

Fig. 698. Acanthaceae (*Justicia simplex*).
A, Portion of a flowering shoot; B, Flower; C, Stamen with appendage; D, Pistil; E, T.s. of ovary; F, Floral diagram.

(*b*) Stamens 4, didynamous; seeds mounted on jaculator; style 2-fid, one lobe often suppressed—

(1) Ovules 3–12 in each cell:

(*i*) Corolla 2-lipped; fls. sessile, axillary, lower leaves often toothed; jaculator not hooked .. .. .. *Cardenthera.*

(*ii*) Corolla 2-lipped; fls. subsessile, axillary; leaves entire; jaculator hooked; capsule narrow; spinescent herb .. .. *Hygrophila.*

(*iii*) Corolla regular, 5-lobed; large bracteole; stamens muticous; clavate capsule with solid base .. .. *Ruellia*.

(*vi*) Corolla 5-lobed; bracteole small or absent; fls. capitate; capsule with seeds from the base .. .. *Hemigraphis*.

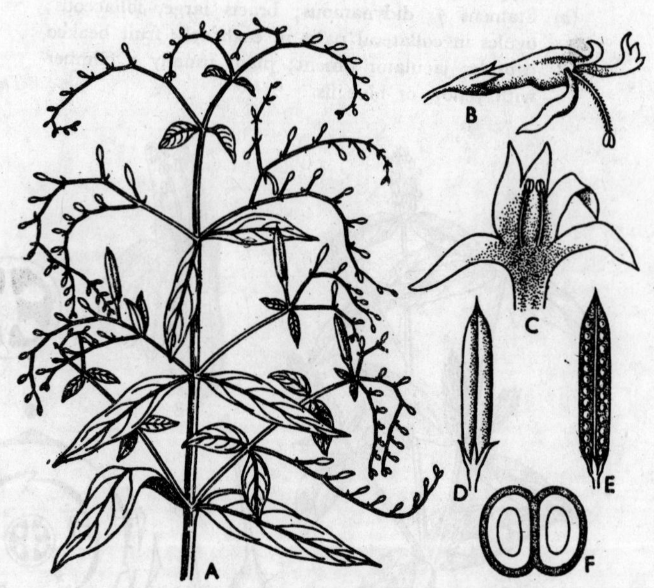

Fig. 699. Acanthaceae (*Andrographis paniculata*).
A, Portion of a flowering shoot; B, Flower; C, Corolla tube split open; D, Fruit; E, L.s. of the same; F, T.s. of ovary.

(2) Ovules 2 in each cell:

(*i*) Corolla 5-lobed; stamens 4 or 2; anthers muticous; placenta from the base of the capsule .. .. .. *Strobilanthes*.

(*ii*) Corolla 5-lobed, slightly unequal; stamens 4, didynamous; anthers 2-celled, parallel, base mucronate; placenta from the base of the capsule .. .. .. *Phaylopsis*.

D. Corolla-lobes short, upper lip reduced, lower one 3-lobed; ovules 2 in each cell; jaculator curved and hardened; anterior filaments with process .. .. .. *Acanthus*.

Common plants

(1) *Adhatoda vasica* Nees., a common densely growing erect shrub. (2) *Barleria prionitis* L., a shrub, commonly found in bushes with two prolonged thorns at each node. (3) *Barleria cristata* L., an erect undershrub. (4) *Hygrophila spinosa* T. And. =*Asteracantha longifolia* Nees., an erect highly spinous marshy herb extensively used as a remedy for diarrhoea; *H. phlomoides* Nees., an erect herb without any spine, commonly found in wet places. (5) *Andrographis paniculata* Nees., a common herb with square stems used as a febrifuge and liver tonic; *A. echioides* Nees., common in waste places and on old

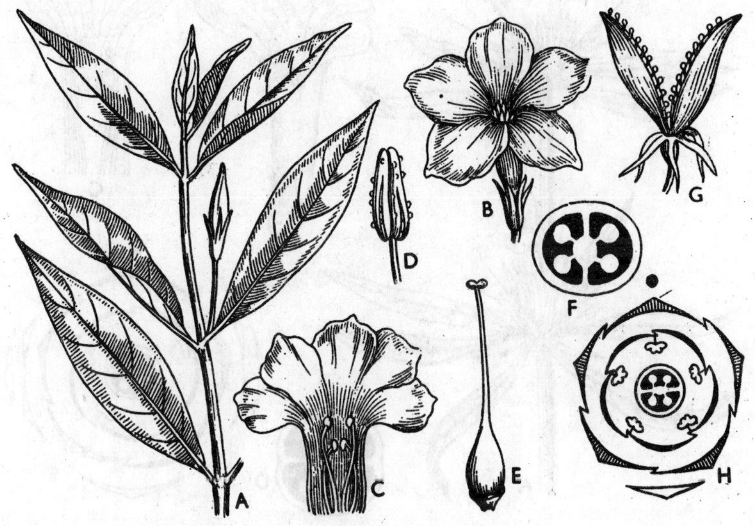

Fig. 700. Acanthaceae (*Ruellia tuberosa*).
A, Portion of a plant; B, Flower; C, Corolla split open; D, Stamen; E, Pistil; F, T.s. of ovary; G, Fruit dehiscing; H, Floral diagram.

brick walls. (6) *Justicia gendarussa* L., often planted in gardens. (7) *J. simplex* Don., *J. diffusa* Willd. and *J. procumbens*=*Rostellularia procumbens* Nees., are common weeds; *J. betonica* L., an erect shrub with pale-violet flowers, often planted in gardens. (8) *Ruellia prostrata* Lamk. =*Dipteracanthus prostratus* Nees., and *R. tuberosa* L. =*Dipteracanthus tuberosus* Nees., very common in and about gardens. (9) *Cardenthera triflora* Ham., a weed of marshy places. (10) *Ecbolium linneanum* Kurz., a small shrub commonly found in bushes and roadsides. (11) *Nelsonia campestris* R. Br., a diffuse herb found on grassy lands. (12) *Thunbergia grandiflora* Roxb., a big twining plant planted in gardens. (13) *Acanthus ilicifolius* L., a very prickly mangrove plant. (14) *Rungia parviflora* Nees., a common procumbent weed bearing one-sided spike. (15) *Rhinacanthus communis* Nees., a garden plant. (16) *Dicliptera roxburghiana* Nees., a common weed. (17) *Hemigraphis hirta* T. And., *H. latebrosa* Nees., and *Phaylopsis parviflora* Willd. =*Micranthus oppositifolius* Wendl., are common weeds of grassy lands. (18) *Crossandra undulifolia* Salisb., a small shrub.

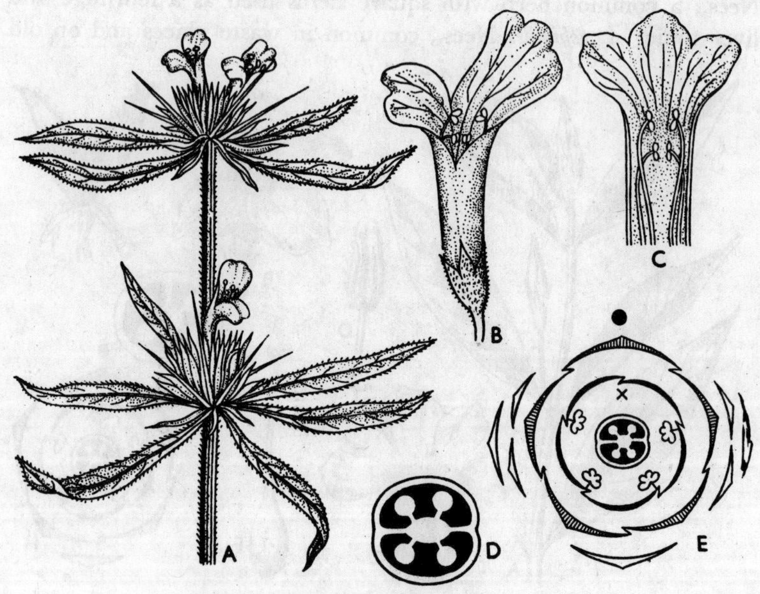

Fig. 701. Acanthaceae (*Hygrophila spinosa*).
A, Portion of a flowering shoot; B, Flower; C, V.s. of the same; D, T.s. of ovary; E, Floral diagram.

(19) *Eranthemum platiferum* Nees. =*Daedalacanthus platiferus* Gamble, a perennial undershrub. (20) *Lepidagathis hyalina* Nees. = *L. incurva* D. Don., a suberect perennial herb, occasionally found. (21) *Peristrophe bicalyculata* Nees., a paniculately branched herb with 6-angled stems. (22) *Ebermaiera glutinosa* Wall., a trailing herb found in rice-fields. (23) *Strobilanthes auriculatus* Nees. =*Pteracanthus auricularis* Bran., a shrub; *S. scaber* Nees. =*Sericocalyx scaber* Nees., a herb. (24) *Asystasia gangetica* T. And., a procumbent perennial weed found near the banks of the Ganges.

Affinity

This family is closely allied to Scrophulariaceae and Bignoniaceae but readily distinguished by the presence of cystoliths in leaves, copious bracts and bracteoles, imbricated calyx of unequal sepals, 2-celled beaked ovary and exalbuminous seeds with jaculator and curved embryo. It differs from Labiatae by its 2-celled unlobed ovary, terminal style, many-seeded capsule and bracteated inflorescence.

Economic importance

This family is of little economic importance. *Adhatoda vasica* and *Hygrophila spinosa* are used in Kabiraji medicine. *Andrographis paniculata* is used as a liver tonic for children. Some plants are ornamentals, such as, *Acanthus, Barleria, Ruellia, Thunbergia, Justica, Jacobinia*, etc.

Comparison of Verbenaceae, Labiatae and Acanthaceae

Verbenaceae	*Labiatae*	*Acanthaceae*
1. Plants—herbs, shrubs or trees, often with square stems.	1. usually herbs or shrubs with square stems.	1. usually herbs or shrubs rarely with square stems; branches swollen at the nodes.
2. Leaves — simple, sometimes compound, opposite or whorled.	2. simple, usually opposite, decussate.	2. simple, opposite, sometimes decussate.
3. Inflorescence — racemose or cymose, often with well-developed bracts.	3. usually cymose, sometimes verticillaster.	3. condensed spike, sometimes cymose, usually with copious bracts and bracteoles.
4. Flowers — zygomorphic, bisexual, hypogynous.	4. zygomorphic, bisexual, hypogynous.	4. zygomorphic, bisexual, hypogynous.
5. Sepals—(5), tubular or bell-shaped, often persistent.	5. (5), tubular or bilabiate, persistent.	5. (5), often unequal.
6. Petals—(5), oblique or tubular.	6. (5), bilabiate.	6. (5), oblique or bilabiate.

Verbenaceae	*Labiatae*	*Acanthaceae*
7. Stamens—2+2, or 2, rarely 5.	7. 2+2, or 2.	7. 2+2, or 2; anthers often spurred or hairy.
8. Carpels—(2).	8. (2).	8. (2).
9. Ovary — 2-4-celled with 1 or 2 ovules in each cell.	9. deeply 4-lobed and 4-celled, with 1 ovule in each cell.	9. beaked, 2-celled, with 2-many ovules in each cell.
10. Style—terminal.	10. gynobasic.	10. terminal.
11. Fruit—usually drupe or berry.	11. carcerule.	11. capsule; seeds usually with jaculator.

ORDER 8. RUBIALES

Plants herbs, shrubs or trees. Leaves opposite. Inflorescence cymose. Flowers tetracyclic, actinomorphic or zygomorphic. Petals 4–5. Stamens as many as petals, distinct anthers. Ovary inferior, 1–5-celled, usually 2–3-celled.

According to Engler this order consists of 5 families, viz., Rubiaceae, Caprifoliaceae, etc. Bentham and Hooker have placed Rubiaceae in the beginning of Gamopetalae under the cohort Rubiales. This order under Hutchinson's system consists of 2 families only, viz., Rubiaceae and Caprifoliaceae.

RUBIACEAE

General characters

Plants—minute herbs (e.g., *Galium*) to huge trees (e.g., *Anthocephalus*). Leaves—*opposite* or *whorled*, simple, entire, usually with *interpetiolar* or less often with intrapetiolar stipules. Inflorescence —dichasial cymes, sometimes aggregated into heads (e.g., *Anthocephalus*, *Morinda*). Flowers—usually regular, bisexual, epigynous. Sepals—(4–5), rarely unequal, valvate. Petals—(4–5), funnel- or salver-shaped or rotate, imbricate, valvate or twisted. Stamens—4–5, alternating with petals, epipetalous, inserted on the corolla tube or at its mouth; anthers introrse, 2-celled. Carpels—usually (2); ovary *inferior*, usually 2-celled, with numerous anatropous ovules in each cell on axile placenta (but 1-celled with parietal placenta, as in *Gardenia*). Fruit—capsule or berry (e.g., *Coffea*), sometimes aggregate (e.g., *Morinda*). Seed—with bony or horny endosperm. Embryo —straight or curved.

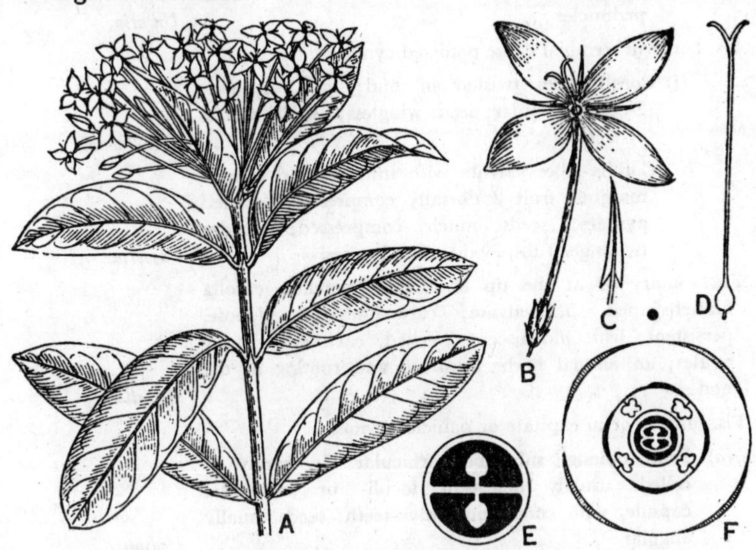

Fig. 702. Rubiaceae (*Ixora coccinea*).
A, Portion of a flowering shoot; B, Flower; C, Stamen; D, Pistil; E, T.s. of ovary; F, Floral diagram.

Floral formula

$\oplus$ ⚥ $K_{(4-5)}$ $C_{(4-5)}$ A_{4-5} $\overline{G}_{(2)}$

Number and distribution

This family consists of about 400 genera and 4,800 species extending from the tropical to the frigid regions.

KEY TO GENERA

A. Fls. borne in globose head and with funnel-shaped corolla:

(*a*) Ovaries confluent; fruit a globose fleshy mass; ovary 4-celled above but 2-celled below; ovules many; heads not bracteated; usually trees .. .. *Anthocephalus.*

(*b*) Ovaries free, 2-celled; fruit capsular, free—

(*i*) Ovules many, imbricated on pendulous placenta in each cell; heads bracteated; calyx 5-lobed; corolla valvate .. .. .. *Adina.*

(*ii*) Ovules many, imbricated upwards on pendulous placenta in each cell; bracteated heads united by their confluent calyx-tube, entire; corolla valvate .. .. *Stephegyne.*

(*iii*) Ovules many, ascending on projecting placentae; heads ebracteated; climbers with hooked peduncles .. .. *Uncaria.*

B. Fls. borne in terminal dense panicled cyme:

(*i*) Corolla-lobes twisted in bud; fruit capsular, 2-celled, angular; seeds wingless; usually shrubs or trees .. .. *Wendlandia.*

(*ii*) Corolla-lobes valvate with inflexed and crisped margins; fruit 2 dorsally compressed 1-seeded pyrenes; seeds much compressed; slender twining shrubs, foetid when bruised .. *Paederia.*

C. Fls. solitary or at the tip of forked branches; corolla funnel-shaped, 5, valvate; calyx-limb 5, globose, persistent; fruit indehiscent 2-celled, each with many ovules; an annual herb, prostrate and rooting at the nodes .. .. *Dentella.*

D. Fls. solitary or in capitate or panicled cyme:

(*a*) Fruit oblong, subglobose-orbicular, 2-, rarely 4-celled, usually dehiscent loculi- or septi-cidal capsule, with contiguous calyx-teeth; seeds usually angular .. .. *Hedyotis.*

(*b*) Fruit oblong 2-celled capsule; corolla-lobes 4; stipules bristly non-entire, fls. in cyme; calyx-teeth remote—

(*i*) Seeds minute and angular; fls. in paniculate cyme .. .. *Oldenlandia.*

(*ii*) Seeds globose or planoconvex with a cavity on the ventral surface .. .. .. *Anotis.*

(*c*) Fruit a fleshy berry; seeds many, small—

(*i*) Corolla valvate; terminal inflorescence; calyx with one limb forming coloured flag (flag apparatus) .. .. *Mussaenda.*

(*ii*) Corolla imbricate, rarely twisted; stamens inserted at the base of the corolla tube; inflorescence terminal .. .. .. *Hamelia.*

(*iii*) Corolla imbricate; stamens inserted at the mouth of the corolla tube; inflorescence axillary:

(1) Ovary 1-celled, many-ovuled; stigma fusiform .. .. .. *Gardenia.*

(2) Ovary 2-celled, many-ovuled; stigma fusiform .. .. .. *Randia.*

(3) Ovary 2-celled; few-ovuled; style arm bifid; fls. in axillary spikes .. .. *Petunga.*

(*iv*) Corolla-lobes twisted; stipules interpetiolar:

(1) Fls. in long corymb—
Petals 5; bracts thin, membraneous .. *Pavetta*.
Petals 4; bracts coriaceous .. .. *Ixora*.

(2) Fls. axillary, solitary or fascicled; style arms 2, linear; petals 4–5 .. .. *Coffea*.

(*v*) Corolla-lobes valvate; stipules interpetiolar:

(1) Fls. in dense heads; fruit a globose or oblong solid mass; erect shrubs or small trees .. .. *Morinda*.

(2) Fls. free, densely panicled; fruit capsular, 5-valved at the apex; stigma papillate, 5-fid .. .. *Hamiltonia*.

(3) Fls. free; setaceous stipule, connate with the petiole into toothed cup; fruit of 2 separable cocci; leaves opposite—
Ovules pendulous; dorsally compressed seeds; fruit small .. .. *Knoxia*.
Ovules attached to ovarian septum; seeds oblong; fruit small, crustaceous, one or both dehiscent into separate cocci *Spermacoce*.

(4) Leaves whorled; stipules foliar; fruit of 2 leathery or fleshy lobes .. .. *Rubia*.

E. Fls. in axillary fascicle; corolla-lobes valvate with a ring of deflexed hairs inside and a smooth or villous throat; disc swollen; ovule solitary, pendulous; fruit drupaceous:

(*a*) Ovary 2-celled; fls. very small, 4-merous; plants usually erect, sometimes climbing .. .. *Canthium*.

(*b*) Ovary 3–5-celled; fls. 5-merous; plants always erect .. *Vangueria*.

(*c*) Ovary 2-celled; fls. 5-merous, plants shrub .. *Psychotria*.

Range of floral structures

Flowers are generally bisexual, regular, tetra- or pentamerous; calyx with valvate aestivation; corolla usually funnel-shaped, salver-shaped or rotate with valvate, imbricate or contorted aestivation. Stamens inserted on the corolla-tube, 2-celled. Carpels (2), sometimes provided with a fleshy disc; ovary inferior, 1-many-celled, usually 2-chambered, with numerous to 1 anatropous ovules in each; style filiform, bifid or multifid.

Variation in the floral structure is also remarkable in the different genera. Regular flowers occur in *Oldenlandia*, *Rondeletia*, *Cinchona*, *Ixora*, *Hamelia*, but zygomorphy of flower is found in *Posoqueria*, *Henriquezia*.

Unisexuality is often noted in some genera. The dioecious flowers are found in *Anthospermum*, *Coprosma*.

Calyx becomes enlarged and leaf-like, as in *Mussaenda*, *Warscewiczia* and also in *Nematostylis*.

Ovary is generally inferior, but semi-inferior ovary is also found to occur in *Synaptantha;* the superior ovary is sometimes found in the genus *Gaertnera* (Tropical Africa and India) and *Pagamea* (Brazil, Guiana).

Variations in the number of chambers of ovary, number of ovules in each chamber, and attachment of ovules also occur in many genera. Exceptions to the two-chambered ovary with parietal placentation occur in the genera *Gardenia*, *Oldenlandia*, *Rondeletia*, *Cinchona; Pavetta* is uniovulate with the ovule sunken in the fleshy funiculus. The genera *Vangueria*, *Knoxia*, *Ixora*, *Hamelia*, etc., represent the uniovulate one-chambered ovary.

The attachment of the ovules either at the base of the ovary or to the septum is variable in different genera. Basal attachment of ovules is found in the genera *Psychotria* (*Uragoga*), *Hydnophytum*, *Myrmecodia*, *Paederia* and others. Septal attachment of ovules is noted in some genera, such as, *Galium*, *Asperula*, *Rubia*, *Crucianella* and others.

Common plants

(1) *Ixora coccinea* L. and *I. parviflora* Vahl. =*I. arborea* Roxb., are common garden shrubs. (2) *Oldenlandia corymbosa* L., *O. umbellata* L. and *O. paniculata* L., are common weeds in rice-fields. (3) *Anthocephalus cadamba* Miq. =*A. indicus* Rich., a common large tree. (4) *Adina cordifolia* Hook. f. (5) Cape jasemine (*Gardenia florida* Willd.= *G. jasminoides* Ellis.), a much-branched shrub grown in gardens. (6) *Vangueria spinosa* Roxb. =*Meyna laxiflora* Robins, a spinous tree. (7) *Paederia foetida* L., a foetid slender twining shrub, the leaves of which are reputed as a good stomachic. (8) Indian madder (*Rubia tinctoria* L.), a climbing herb with big stipules. (9) *Mussaenda frondosa* Hook., a small shrubby plant, one of the calyx-lobes of which grows out into a large white leaf-like expansion, common in nurseries. (10) *Catesbaea spinosa*, a highly spinous herb with showy white

tubular flowers which hang vertically downwards; very common in the Indian Botanic Garden. (11) Coffee plant (*Coffea arabica* L.), usually cultivated in Southern India for coffee. (12) Cinchona plant (*Cinchona succirubra* Pavon ex Klotzsch, *C. officinalis* L., *C. ledgeriana* Moens, *C. calisaya* Wedd.), cultivated on the hills for its bark which

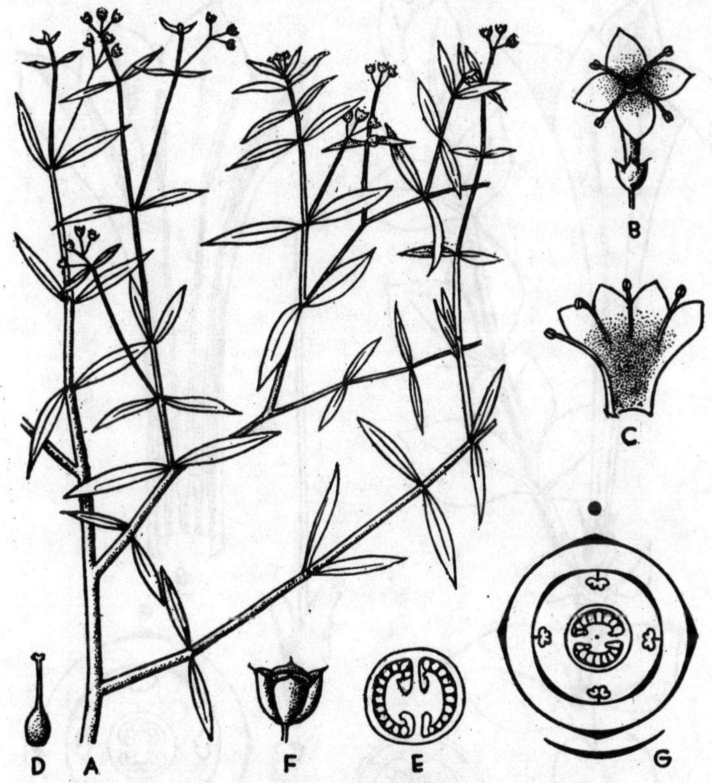

Fig. 703. Rubiaceae (*Oldenlandia corymbosa*).
A, Portion of a flowering shoot; B, Flower; C, Corolla split open; D, Pistil; E, T.s. of ovary; F, Fruit; G, Floral diagram.

yields quinine. (13) Ipecac (*Psychotria ipecacuanha* Stocks = *Uragoga ipecacuanha* Bail.), a medicinal plant with moniliform roots. (14) *Dentella repens* Forst., a common weed. (15) *Morinda citrifolia* L., a garden plant which produces multiple fruit. (16) *Randia dumetorum* Lamk., a large shrub with spines; *R. uliginosa* DC., a small tree that can be found in Indian Botanic Garden.

(17) *Hamelia patens* Jacq., a common garden plant. (18) *Stephegyne parvifolia* Korth. =*Mytragyna parvifolia* Korth., often mistaken for *Anthocephalus*. (19) *Canthium angustifolium* Roxb., a spreading shrub of the Sundribans. (20) *Hedyotis auricularia* L., a herb.

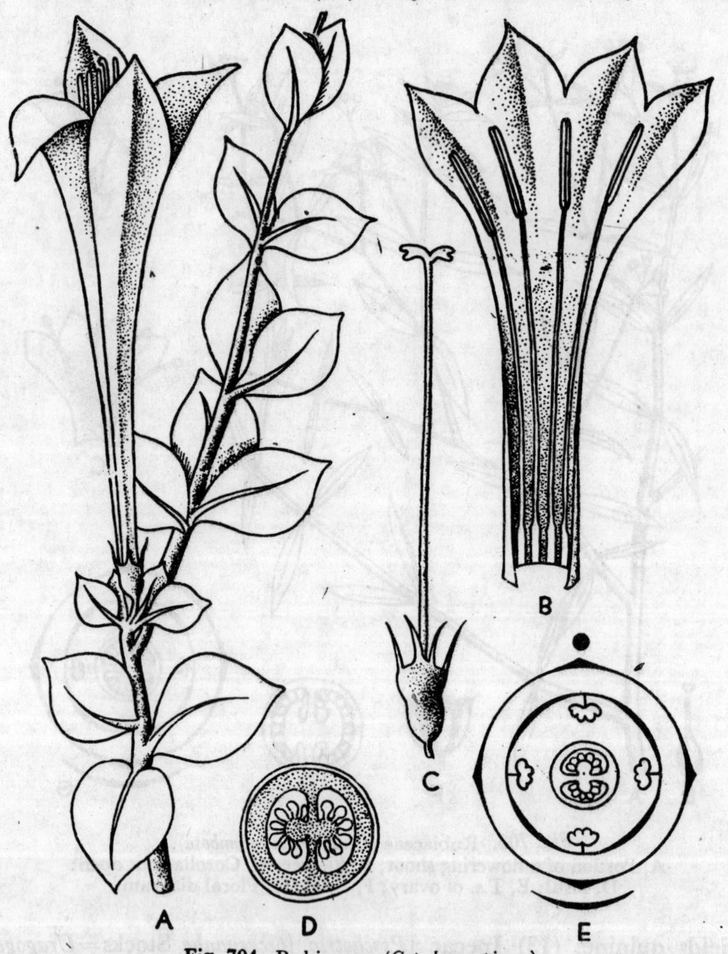

Fig. 704. Rubiaceae (*Catesbaea spinosa*).
A, Portion of a flowering shoot; B, Corolla split open; C, Pistil; D, T.s. of ovary; E, Floral diagram.

(21) *Uncaria macrophylla* Wall., a strong climber. (22) *Wendlandia exserta* DC., a small crooked tree. (23) *Anotis calycina* Hook. f., a slender annual herb. (24) *Petunga roxburghii* DC., an evergreen

shrub of the Sundribans. (25) *Pavetta indica* L., a small tree. (26) *Knoxia corymbosa* Willd., a common erect annual. (27) *Spermacoce hispida* L.=*Borreria hispida* K. Schum., a common perennial herb. (28) *Hamiltonia suaveolens* Roxb., a small shrub.

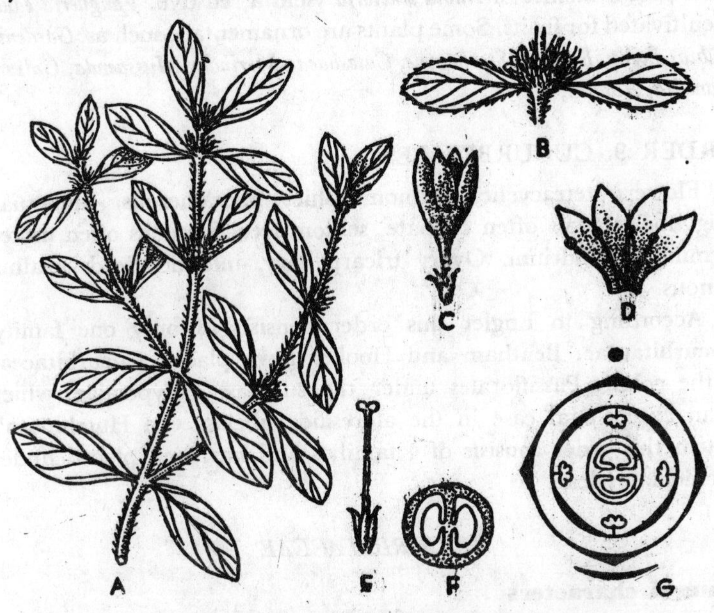

Fig. 705. Rubiaceae (*Spermacoce hispida*).
A, Portion of a flowering shoot; B, Inflorescences in the axils of opposite leaves; C, Flower; D, Corolla split open; E, Pistil; F, T.s. of ovary; G, Floral diagram.

Affinity

This family can be traced phylogenetically from Umbelliferae, particularly allied to Cornaceae, in the morphological aspects, such as, presence of interpetiolar stipules, cymose umbel-like inflorescence, suppression of calyx, epigyny, etc. The family is also allied to Adoxaceae, Caprifoliaceae under the order Rubiales. Rubiaceae is apparently related to Compositae. The derivation of head can be traced from the head-like inflorescence of some members of Rubiaceae and Dipsaceae.

Economic importance

This family is of economic importance. Coffee is obtained from

Coffea arabica. Quinine is obtained from the bark of *Cinchona*. *Paederia*, *Oldenlandia* and *Anthocephalus* are of medicinal importance. *Psychotria ipecacuanha*, which is the source of 'vinum ipecac', is also a valuable medicinal plant; the alkaloid '*emetine*' is extracted from the plant. The roots and branches of *Rubia tinctoria* yield a red dye. *Vangueria edulis* is cultivated for fruits. Some plants are ornamentals, such as, *Gardenia*, *Rubia*, *Ixora*, *Knoxia*, *Stephegyne*, *Catesbaea*, *Morinda*, *Mussaenda*, *Galium*, *Hamelia*, *Randia*, etc.

ORDER 9. CUCURBITALES

Flowers tetracyclic, actinomorphic, pentamerous, unisexual, epigynous. Petals often connate, seldom free. Stamens often united forming synandrium. Ovary tricarpellary, inferior. Seeds exalbuminous.

According to Engler this order consists of only one family, Cucurbitaceae. Bentham and Hooker have placed Cucurbitaceae in the cohort Passiflorales under the subclass Polypetalae, which is an exceptional case in the aforesaid subclass. In Hutchinson's system this order consists of 4 families and has been placed under Archichlamydeae.

CUCURBITACEAE

General characters

Plants—climbing or procumbent herbs with *extra-axillary*, simple or branched tendrils, monoecious or dioecious (e.g., *Trichosanthes dioica*, *Bryonia dioica*), often with 5-angled stems. Leaves—alternate, simple, often lobed, palmi-veined, exstipulate. Inflorescence—cymose. Flowers—*unisexual*, regular, epigynous, usually yellow or white. Sepals—(5), tubular, imbricate. Petals—(5), inserted on the calyx-tube, bell-shaped or rotate, imbricate. Stamens—5 in the male flowers, usually all united into a column (*syngenesious*), or appear to be 3 owing to 4 of them uniting in two pairs; anthers extrorse, straight or sinuous; one anther always 1-celled, the other 2-celled. Carpels—in the female flowers, (3); ovary *inferior*, 1-celled, but sometimes becomes spuriously 3-celled owing to the projection of the *parietal placentae* towards the centre; style one, short and thick, generally divided into 3 branches with a horseshoe-shaped stigma on each branch. Fruit—usually a *pepo*, sometimes berry. Seed—exalbuminous. Embryo—straight with large oily cotyledons.

Floral formula

♂ flower—$K_{(5)}\ C_{(5)}\ A_{(5)}\ G_0$

♀ flower—$K_{(5)}\ C_{(5)}\ A_0\ \overline{G}_{(3)}$

Number and distribution

This family consists of about 100 genera and 850 species which are commonly found in the tropics.

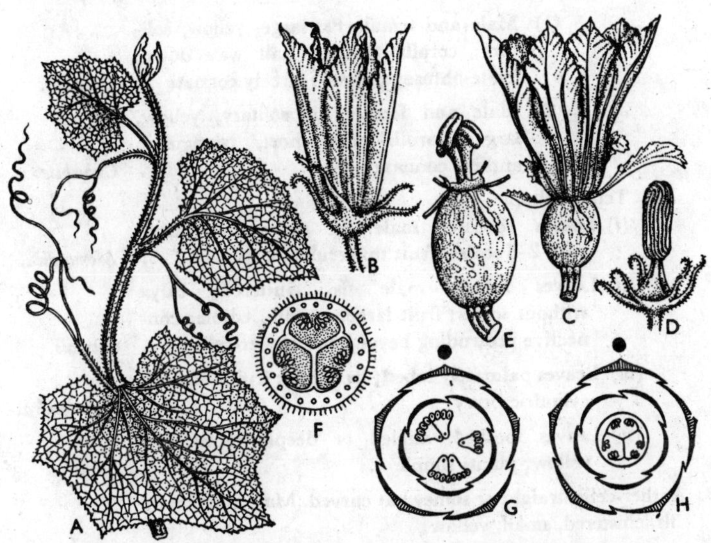

Fig. 706. Cucurbitaceae (*Cucurbita maxima*).
A, Portion of a shoot; B, Staminate flower; C, Pistillate flower; D, Androecium; E, Pistil; F, T.s. of ovary; G, Floral diagram of staminate flower; H, The same of pistillate flower.

KEY TO GENERA

Female fls. usually single; ovules pendulous or horizontal—

A. Anther-cells 'S'-shaped or folded. Corolla rotate or campanulate, divided or nearly so into 5 petals above:

(*a*) Tendril divided—

(*i*) Fls. white; petals fimbriated at the margin; seeds many .. .. .. *Trichosanthes*.

(*ii*) Fls. large, white; petals entire; anthers included; petiole with 2 glands .. .. .. *Lagenaria*.

(*iii*) Fls. pale yellowish-white; petals fimbriated; seeds many .. .. *Hodgsonia*.

Stamens inserted at the mouth of the calyx-tube; anthers free; fls. yellow:

(1) Fruit dry, angled or ribbed, rarely smooth; endocarp fibrous, opening by special lid; male fls. borne in raceme .. .. *Luffa.*

(2) Fruit fleshy, soft, indehiscent; male and female fls. both solitary .. .. *Benincasa.*

Stamens inserted below the mouth of the calyx-tube:

(1) Male and female fls. large, yellow, solitary; corolla divided half way down, ovate-obtuse; anthers scarcely connate .. *Citrullus.*

(2) Male and female fls. solitary, yellow, large; corolla-lobes short, triangular; anthers connate .. .. *Cucurbita.*

(*b*) Tendril simple—

(*i*) Leaves cordate; male fls. subracemic; calyx with 2–3 scales; fruit tuberculated, spinous .. *Momordica.*

(*ii*) Leaves lobed; male fls. clustered; calyx without scales; fruit large, smooth, edible; connective protruding beyond the anther-cells .. *Cucumis.*

(*iii*) Leaves palmately lobed; fls. white; fruit a smooth cylindric berry .. .. .. *Cephalandra.*

(*iv*) Leaves toothed, angled or deeply lobed; fls. yellow; plants simple .. .. .. *Zehneria.*

B. Anther-cells straight or somewhat curved. Male and female fls. clustered, small, yellow:

(*a*) Tendril simple .. .. *Mukia*
(*b*) Tendril divided .. .. .. *Bryonia.*

Common plants

(1) Gourd (*Cucurbita maxima* Duchesne = *Cucurbita moschata*). (2) Pumpkin or white gourd (*Benincasa cerifera* Savi. = *B. hispida* Cogn.). (3) Bottle gourd (*Lagenaria vulgaris* Ser. = *Lagenaria sicerara*). (4) Cucumber (*Cucumis sativus* L.). (5) Melon (*Cucumis melo* L.). (6) Water melon (*Citrullus vulgaris* Schrad.). (7) *Trichosanthes dioica* Roxb. (8) Snakegourd (*Trichosanthes anguina*). (9) *Trichosanthes palmata* Roxb. = *T. bracteata* Voigt. (10) Bath-sponge (*Luffa aegyptiaca* Mill. = *Luffa cylindrica* M. V. Roem.). (11) *Luffa acutangula* Roxb. (12) Bitter gourd (*Momordica charantia* L.). (13) *Momordica cochinchinensis* Spreng. (14) Scarlet gourd (*Cephalandra indica* Naud. = *Coccinia cordifolia* Cogn., very common in hedges and thickets. (15)

Colocynth (*Citrullus colocynthis* Schrad.), and (16) Bryony (*Bryonia dioica* Jacq.) are medicinal plants. (17) *Mukia scabrella* Arn. = *Melothria maderaspatana* Cogn., very common in hedges, thickets and waste places. (18) *Zehneria umbellata* Thw. = *Melothria heterophylla* Cogn., generally found in hedges and thickets. (19) *Hodgsonia heteroclita* Hook. f. & Thoms., a gigantic climber, stem sometimes 100 ft. long.

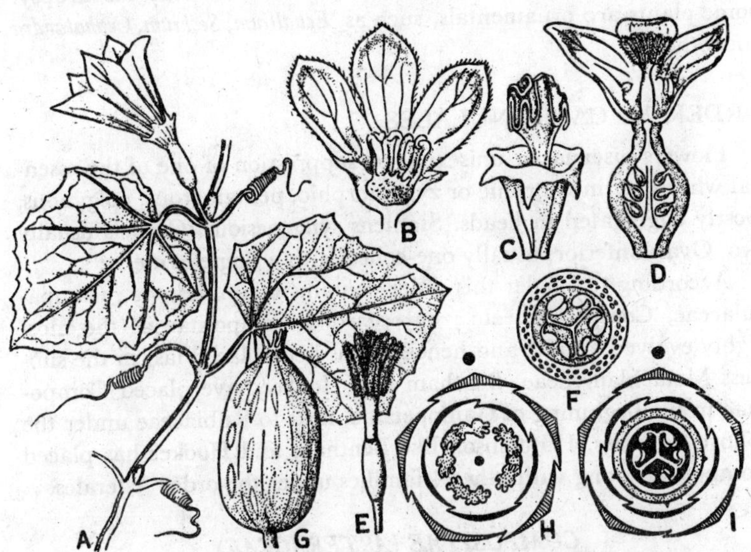

Fig. 707. Cucurbitaceae (*Cephalandra indica*).
A, Portion of a branch with female flower; B, Staminate flower cut lengthwise; C, Stamens after removal of calyx and corolla; D, Pistillate flower cut lengthwise; E, Pistil; F, L.s. of ovary; G, Fruit; H, Floral diagram of staminate flower; I, The same of pistillate flower.

Affinity

This family is allied to Campanulaceae based on the characters of corolla, androecium and ovary. It also bears an affinity with Passifloraceae in the presence of parietal placentation and the presence of tendril, but readily distinguished by the palmi-veined and exstipulate leaves, unisexual flowers, gamopetalous corolla and inferior ovary. It has been considered, by some taxonomists, to be related to Begoniaceae and Datiscaceae, and therefore it should form a distinct taxon Cucurbitales. The recent interpretation is that Cucurbitaceae should be removed from the Campanulales and be treated as an advanced form of Archichlamydeae.

Economic importance

This family is of considerable economic importance. A large number of plants produce edible fruits. Among them are *Trichosanthes*, *Cucumis*, *Benincasa*, *Cucurbita*, *Citrullus*, etc. Some plants are of medicinal importance, e.g., Colocynth and Bryony. *Luffa echinata* produces a bitter alkaloid which is used as a remedy for dropsy. Some plants are ornamentals, such as, *Ecballium*, *Sechium*, *Cephalandra* and others.

ORDER 10. CAMPANULALES

Flowers bisexual or unisexual by suppression of one of the essential whorls, actinomorphic or zygomorphic, pentamerous, epigynous, mostly aggregated in heads. Stamens syngenesious. Carpels usually two. Ovary inferior, usually one-celled with a single ovule.

According to Engler this order contains 6 families, viz., Campanulaceae, Compositae, etc.; he regarded Compositae as the most highly evolved family, and hence, it has been placed last in the subclass Metachlamydeae. Bentham and Hooker have placed Compositae in the beginning of Gamopetalae, next to Rubiaceae under the cohort Asterales. Hutchinson like Bentham and Hooker has placed Compositae along with other 4 families under the order Asterales.

COMPOSITAE (ASTERACEAE)

General characters

Plants—usually herbs, sometimes shrubs (e.g., *Eupatorium*). Leaves—alternate (sometimes opposite), simple or variously lobed, exstipulate. Inflorescence—*capitulum* (excepting *Caesulia*, *Layascea* and *Echinops*), homogamous (e.g., *Launaea*, *Emilia*, *Vernonia*, etc.) or heterogamous, surrounded by an *involucre* of bracts. Florets of the capitulum—sessile, bisexual or unisexual, or the outer (ray-florets) female or neuter, palacated or non-palaeated. Sepals—absent or *modified into pappus*. Petals—(5), tubular, ligulate or bilabiate, valvate. Stamens—5, *syngenesious*, epipetalous. Carpels—(2); ovary *inferior*, 1-celled with one ascending, anatropous ovule borne on basal placenta; stigma bifid. Fruit—*cypsella*, often crowned by persistent pappus. Seed—exalbuminous. Embryo—straight.

Floral formula

$⚥\ K_{P \text{ or } 0}\ C_{(5)}\ A_{(5)}\ \overline{G}_{(2)}$

Number and distribution

This family consists of about 950 genera and probably 20,000 species which are cosmopolitan.

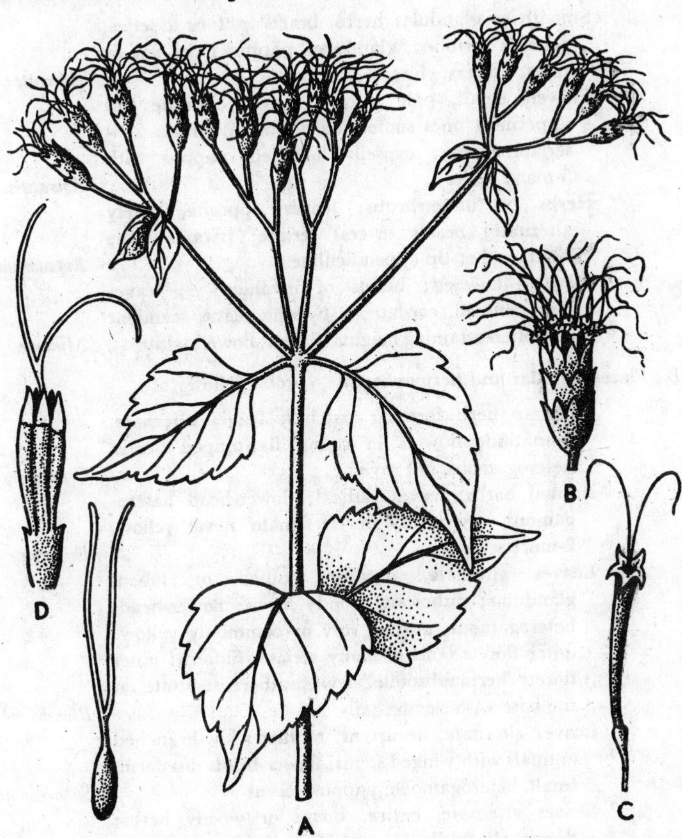

Fig. 708. Asteraceae (*Eupatorium odoratum*).
A, Portion of a flowering shoot; B, Inflorescence; C, Flower; D, The same with petals removed; E, Pistil.

KEY TO GENERA

A. Florets all tubular and hermaphrodite, corolla never yellow, no rays, bracts in many series:

(*a*) Leaves alternate, heads many-flowered—

Pappus absent, achenes 4–5-angled .. .. *Ethulia*.

Pappus short, falling off early, achenes 10-ribbed .. *Centrotherum*.

Pappus of many long hairs and bristles, achenes angled or ribbed or not so, but rounded .. *Vernonia*.

Rigid herbs, heads of 2–5 florets, clustered in dense masses, corolla 4-lobed, pappus of shining bristles, cypsella 10-ribbed .. .. .. *Elephantopus.*

(*b*) Leaves opposite—

Smooth or glandular herbs, bracts in 1 or 2 series, achenes 5-ribbed, glandular, pappus hairs few or short, flowers white .. .. .. *Adenostemma.*

Flowers small, pale purple; leaves opposite but uppermost ones sometimes alternate; bracts 2–3-seriate, linear; cypsella 5-angled, pappus with 5-many scales .. .. .. *Ageratum.*

Herbs or undershrubs; leaves opposite, rarely alternate; bracts several seriate; pappus hairs rigid, anther-tip appendiculate .. .. *Eupatorium.*

Head 4-flowered; bracts of involucre 4; leaves long-petioled, cordate; a twining plant, scandent and often attaining heights of trees; flowers white .. *Mikania.*

B. Florets tubular and hermaphrodite, corolla yellow:

Prostrate herb forming patches; leaves alternate, pinnatifid; flowers in round flat-topped heads, heterogamous, not rayed .. .. .. *Grangea.*

Annual herbs; leaves radical; flower-head heterogamous, rayed; ray florets female, never yellow, 2-more seriate .. .. .. *Erigeron.*

Leaves alternate, usually toothed or lobed, glandular; pubescent woody herbs; flower-heads heterogamous, purple, rosy or commonly yellow; outer florets female, many seriate, filiform; inner florets hermaphrodite, few; anthers sagittate at the base with slender tails .. .. *Blumea.*

Leaves alternate, decurrent, toothed; low-branched annuals with winged stems; flower-heads disciform, small, heterogamous; pappus absent .. .. *Sphaeranthus.*

Leaves alternate, entire; hoary or woody herbs; florets all fertile in corymbose leafless heads or leafy spikes or clusters .. .. .. *Gnaphalium.*

Glabrous marsh herbs; leaves alternate, serrulate, dilated into a broad stem-clasping base; stem purple; flower-heads each 1-flowered; pappus absent .. .. *Caesulia.*

Annual coarse herbs; leaves alternate, toothed, heart-shaped or 3-lobed; heads 1-sexual:

Female florets apetalous, 2-together, united with the involucre to form a 2-beaked utricle covered with hooked spines; male florets many in upper globular heads .. .. .. *Xanthium.*

C. Flower-heads rayed, leaves opposite:

Leaves pinnatisect; pappus present; heads large showy, involucre of bracts fused, cylindrical and green .. .. *Tagetes*.

Leaves quite entire; heads large, rayed; involucre of bracts 3- or more-seriate, imbricate, gradually shorter from within outwards; capitulum large, showy .. .. *Zinnia*.

Marsh herb used in kitchen; leaves sessile; ray florets many-seriate, involucre of bracts in four pairs *Enhydra*.

Small herbs; capitulum small, peduncled, white, bracts in one or two series, outer large; disc florets 4-toothed .. .. *Eclipta*.

A procumbent herb growing in wet places near ponds or shrub, sometimes climbing; ray florets large, yellow, female, fertile; outer bracts of involucre 3–5, herbaceous, inner dry; pappus united at the base .. .. *Wedelia*.

Pappus scales free from the base, ray florets large, yellow, sterile—

Leaves always alternate, entire or toothed; capitulum large; bracts 2-many-seriate; corolla of tubular florets elongated, enlarged and 5-fid .. .. *Helianthus*.

Leaves opposite, ovate-lanceolate; capitula small, ovoid and yellow; cypsella of ray florets usually ciliate .. .. *Spilanthes*.

Leaves opposite or upper alternate; achene without pappus but crowned with base of corolla and almost 4-cornered .. .. *Guizotia*.

Annual branched herb; leaves opposite, petioled, toothed; flower-heads very small, yellow, axillary terminal, heterogamous and rayed; calyx and corolla of ray florets 2–3-toothed, tubular; corolla 4-toothed; cypsella of ray florets with 2-lacerated wings; pappus represented by spines .. .. *Synedrella*.

Tall annual herbs; leaves opposite, 2–3-pinnatisect or lobed or entire; capitulum white, pink or yellow, long-stalked, rayed, heterogamous; ray florets 1-seriate, neuter; bracts of involucre 2-seriate, united below; petals of ray florets united, ligulate; pappus 2 or 4, persistent .. .. .. *Cosmos*.

A weak, straggling perennial herb; leaves opposite, pinnatisect, segments few and narrow; capitulum long-stalked, rayed, heterogamous, bracts few-seriate; ray florets yellow, corolla bilabiate or ligulate with a large 3-fid or 3-partite outer and a small 2-fid or obsolete inner lip; pappus of short feathery bristle .. .. *Tridax*.

Strong smelling herbs or shrubs; leaves alternate, 1–3-pinnatisect or entire or serrate; flower-heads small, greenish white or greenish yellow .. *Artemisia.*

Annual or perennial herb; leaves alternate, pinnately lobed or entire; capitulum large, showy on long peduncles, rayed, or sometimes homogâmous due to abortion of rays; ray florets female, 1-seriate; disc florets hermaphrodite; bracts of involucre many-seriate; pappus of short scales may be present .. .. *Chrysanthemum.*

Thistle-like herbs; leaves and involucre of bracts spinescent—

Flower-heads 1-flowered, crowded into spherical masses, greenish-white .. .. .. *Echinops.*

Flower-heads many-flowered, separate; flower hermaphrodite or by abortion 1-sexual; cypsella 1-angled, ribbed; pappus-hairs feathery .. *Cnicus.*

Herbs with milky juice, leaves radical or alternate, branches divaricate, sometimes spinescent—

Flowers blue .. .. *Cichorium.*

Flowers yellow—

Cauline leaves stem-clasping and auricled, flower-heads terminal:

Achenes not beaked, compressed, many-ribbed *Sonchus.*

Achenes beaked .. .. .. *Lactuca.*

Annual weeds with long leaves, radical leaves crowded, petioled, entire or lyrate; cauline leaves often auricled and stem clasping—

Heads homogamous, florets purple .. *Emilia.*

Heads heterogamous, florets all yellow .. *Senecio.*

Thistle-like herbs; leaves alternate, white-veined above, sinuately lobed; lobes and teeth spinescent—

Flower-heads homogamous, terminal, large, nodding: bracts spinescent, fimbriate .. *Silybum.*

Annual milky herbs; leaves radical or cauline, often stem-clasping, spinose, toothed; flower-heads yellow, homogamous, ligulate, bell-shaped—

Perennial glabrous herbs with yellow juice .. *Launaea.*

Common plants

(1) Sunflower (*Helianthus annuus* L.). (2) Marigold (*Tagetes patula* L.). (3) Chrysanthemum (*Chrysanthemum coronarium* L.). (4) Garden zinnia (*Zinnia elegans*, *Z. pauciflora* L.). (5) Lettuce (*Lactuca sativa* L.), used as a salad. (6) *Enhydra fluctuans* Lour., commonly

found in marshes, used as a vegetable and reputed to induce sleep. (7) Jerusalem artichoke (*Helianthus tuberosus* L.), cultivated for its tubers. (8) Niger seed (*Guizotia abyssinica* Cass.) yields an oil much used for adulterating purpose. (9) Safflower (*Carthamus tinctorius* L.), cultivated in cold weather for the orange dye from the petals and for oil from the seeds. (10) Climbing hemp weed (*Mikania scandens* Willd.), a climber. (11) *Tridax procumbens* L., very common in grassy waste lands and old walls, bearing cream-coloured flower-heads on long stalks during the dry season. (12) *Blumea lacera* DC., a very

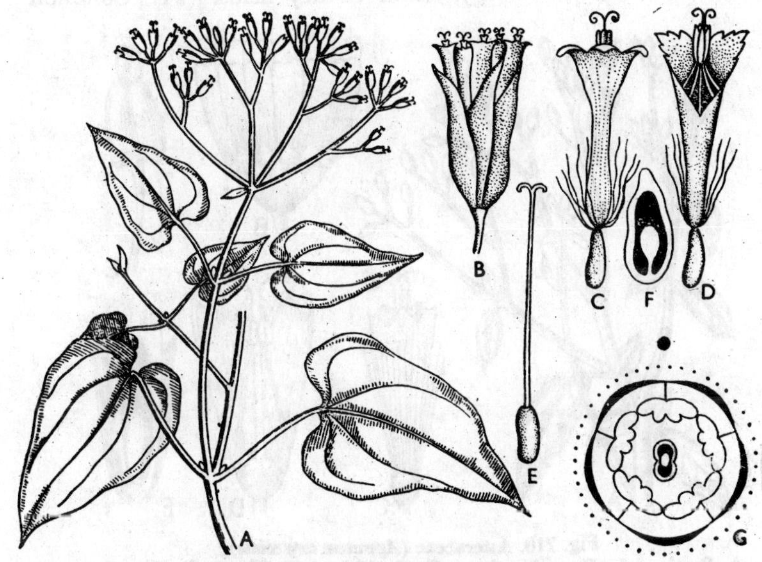

Fig. 709. Asteraceae (*Mikania scandens*).
A, Portion of a flowering shoot; B, Inflorescence; C, Floret; D, The same split open showing syngenesious stamens; E, Pistil; F, L.s. of ovary; G, Floral diagram.

common annual weed with yellow flowers. (13) Iron weed (*Vernonia cineria* Less.), another common weed with purplish flowers. (14) *Vernonia anthelmentica* Willd., a medicinal plant. (15) *Eclipta alba* Hassk. =*E. prostrata* L., also a common weed, the juice of the leaves of which is used in tattooing. (16) *Eupatorium ayapana* Vent., a medicinal plant, the leaves of which are reputed as a specific for stopping internal haemorrhage; *E. odoratum* L., a common weed. (17) *Wedelia calendulacea* Less., a medicinal plant, the leaves of which are used for promoting the growth of hair. (18) *Adenostemma viscosum* DC., a common weed. (19) *Ageratum conyzoides* L., Elephant's foot (*Elephantopus scaber* L.), *E. spicatus* L., Milk-thistle (*Sonchus oleraceus* L.), *S. asper* Vill., *Sphaeranthus indicus* L., *Cnicus arvensis* Hoffm. and *Emilia sonchifolia* DC. are common weeds. (20) *Senecio nudicaulis* Ham., *Caesulia axillaris* Roxb. and *Crepis japonica* Benth., are common in the rice-fields. (21) *Dahlia*, *Cosmos*, Daisy, *Aster*, *Calendula*, *Gallardia* are common garden plants. (22) *Grangea maderaspatana* Poir., generally found on roadsides, dry fields and waste places. (23) *Gnaphalium indicum* L. and *G. luteoalbum* L., commonly found in dry fields. (24) Common

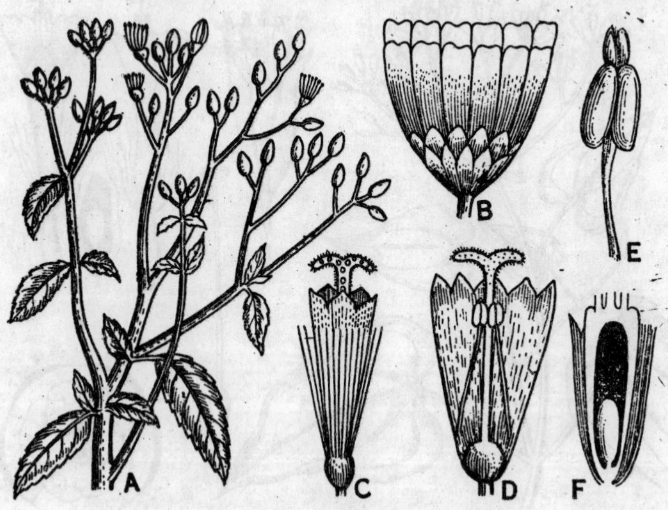

Fig. 710. Asteraceae (*Ageratum conyzoides*).
A, Portion of a flowering shoot; B, Capitulum; C, Floret; D, The same split open; E, Stamen; F, V.s. of ovary.

cockle-bur (*Xanthium strumarium* L.) occurs everywhere. (25) *Synedrella nodiflora* Gaertn., occurs in cultivated fields and waste places. (26) *Spilanthes acmella* Murr. occasionally found. (27) *Silybum marianum* Gaertn., occurs in gardens. (28) *Launaea asplenifolia* DC., and *L. pinnatifida* Cass. =*L. cermentora* Alston., very common weeds in grassy glades and open fields. (29) *Ethulia conyzoides* L., an erect annual herb. (30) *Erigeron asteroides* Roxb., another common weed. (31) Sagebrush (*Artemisia caruifolia* Ham.), a soft-stemmed plant, 2–4 ft. high. (32) *Echinops echinatus* Roxb., a branched annual, 1–2 ft. high, not common. (33) *Cichorium intybus* L., an erect herb. (34) *Centrotherum anthelmenticum* O. Kuntze., a common tall robust annual. (35) *Sigesbeckia orientalis* L., a very common weed on the hills.

Affinity

Compositae has been regarded as the highest evolved family of dicotyledons by many taxonomists. Its similarity with the members of Rubiales, such as, Dipsaceae and Valerianaceae, is very remarkable. The notable features of similarity between Rubiaceae and Compositae are the aggregation of flowers into head or head-like structure and in the reduction of calyx-lobes. If the polyphyletic origin is taken into consideration, then it may be assumed that the origin of Rubiales and Compositae commenced from Umbelliferae,

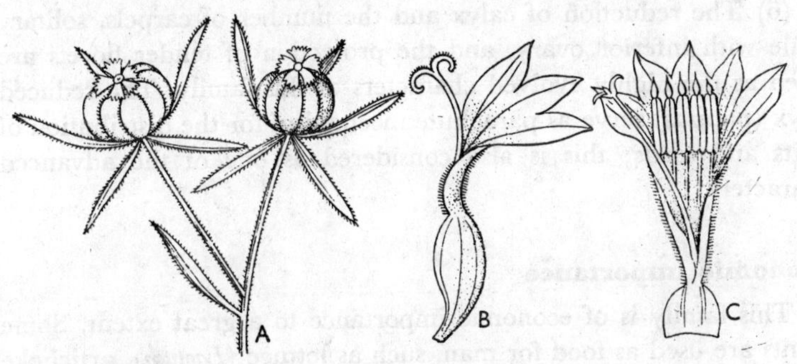

Fig. 711. Asteraceae (*Sigesbeckia orientalis*). A, Portion of a flowering shoot; B, Ray floret; C, Disc floret partially split open.

which exhibits a tendency towards aggregation of small flowers in crowded umbels. Compositae, however, can be readily recognized by capitulum inflorescence with an involucre, presence of pappus, gamopetalous corolla (tubular or ligulate or both), syngenesious stamens, 1-celled inferior ovary with a single basal ovule, and cypsella fruit.

The reasons for treating Compositae as the highest evolved family are given below:

(1) The dominance of herbaceous habit.

(2) Presence of large number of species and their cosmopolitan distribution.

(3) The remarkable adaptation for cross-pollination by insects in the following:

(*a*) Easily accessible nectar and its protection from mechanical injury, such as, rain, cold, etc.

(*b*) Crowding of florets in capitula with ligulate marginal florets which act as flag for the attraction of insects.

(*c*) All the disc florets can be pollinated by a single insect within a very short time.

(4) The presence of syngenesious protandrous stamens along with epigyny are considered as one of the advanced characters.

(5) The capacity of the florets to avoid self-pollination by brushing system (piston mechanism) along with the mechanism in the stigmas for the same purpose is undoubtedly the most advanced character of this family.

(6) The reduction of calyx and the number of carpels, solitary ovule with inferior ovary, and the protection of tender florets are taken as the highly evolved characters of this family. The reduced calyx (pappus) serve as parachute mechanism for the distribution of fruits and seeds; this is also considered as one of the advanced characters.

Economic importance

This family is of economic importance to a great extent. Some plants are used as food for man, such as lettuce (*Lactuca*), artichoke (*Helianthus tuberosus*), endive (*Cichorium*), salisfy (*Tragopogon*), etc. A kind of orange dye is obtained from safflower (*Carthamus tinctorius*); the dried petals are adulterated with saffron. *Eupatorium*, *Calendula*, *Wedelia*, *Vernonia*, *Eclipta* and *Sausseria lappa* are used in medicine. Oil is extracted from *Guizotia* and *Carthamus*. Several species of the genus *Artemisia* (*A. cina*, *A. vulgaris*, *A. maritima* var. *stechmaniana*) yield 'santonin' of medicine. Pyrethrum is obtained from *Chrysanthemum*, *cinerariefolium*. Some plants are ornamentals, such as Asters, *Chrysanthemum*, *Cosmos*, *Dahlia*, *Calendula*, *Gallardia*, Sunflower (*Helianthus*), *Tagetes*, *Zinnia*, *Senecio*, *Echinops*, etc.

Comparison between Compositae and Orchidaceae

The Compositae and the Orchidaceae are regarded as the most highly developed families of the Dicotyledons and the

Monocotyledons respectively, and as such a comparison of them is given below:

Compositae	*Orchidaceae*
(1) Plants—usually erect, terrestrial and autophytic annual herbs.	(1) usually trailing, epiphytic, parasitic or saprophytic perennial herbs.
(2) Roots—mostly true and normal; bundles tetrarch.	(2) mostly adventitious and epiphytic; bundles generally polyarch.
(3) Stems—vascular bundles conjoint collateral, open and arranged in a ring.	(3) vascular bundles conjoint, collateral, closed and scattered.
(4) Leaves—usually simple with reticulate venation.	(4) simple with parallel venation.
(5) Inflorescence—capitulum.	(5) usually raceme or spike.
(6) Flowers—individually minute, regular or zygomorphic, neuter or unisexual or bisexual, pentamerous, epigynous, with reduced carpels.	(6) large, showy, zygomorphic, bisexual, trimerous, epigynous, with reduced stamens.
(7) Calyx—absent or highly reduced.	(7) well-developed, sometimes brightly coloured.
(8) Corolla—gamopetalous.	(8) polypetalous.
(9) Androecium—stamens usually five in number, syngenesious; pollen grains distinct and powdery.	(9) stamens originally six in number, finally reduced to three, of which one or two become sterile forming staminodes; gynandrous, producing pollinia.
(10) Gynoecium—carpels (2), unilocular; ovary with basal placentation and a single anatropous ovule.	(10) carpels (3), tricarpellate, unilocular; ovary with parietal placentation and numerous anatropous ovules.
(11) Fruit—cypsella.	(11) capsule.
(12) Embryo—straight.	(12) undifferentiated.

GLOSSARY OF PLANT NAMES

The following abbreviations have been used:—

E.=English; *S.*=Sanskrit; *B.*=Bengali; *H.*=Hindi; *U.*=Urdu; *A.*=Assamese; *O.*=Oriya; *P.*=Punjabi; *G.*=Gujrati; *Bom.*=Bombay; *Mar.*=Marhati; *M.*=Malayalam; *T.*=Tamil; *Te.*=Telugu; *C.*=Canarese; *Sin.*=Sinhalese; *Bur.*=Burmese.

Abroma augusta L.
E. Devil's cotton; *B & H.* Ulatkambal; *A.* Bon-kopashi; *O.* Pishachogonjai; *G.* Gumchi; *Bom. & Mar.* Olatkambol; T. Sivaputtutti; *C.* Melpundigida.

Abrus precatorius L.
E. Indian liquorice, Crab's eye; *S.* Gunja; B. Kunch; *H.* Rati; *U.* Ghunja; *A.* Latummoni; *O.* Roti; *P.* Ratak; *G.* Chanoti; *Bom.* Ghungchi, Gunja; *Mar.* Gunj; *M.* Kunni; *T.* Kundomani; *Te.* Guruginja *C.* Galaganji, Guruganji; *Sin.* Olinda-wel; *Bur.* Ywegne.

Abutilon indicum G. Don.
E. Indian mallow; *S.* Kankatika; *B.* Potari; *H.* Kanghi; Jhampi; *U.* Kanghi; *O.* Nakochons; *P.* Pilibuti; *G.* Dabali; *Bom.* Kangoi, Pamadni; *Mar.* Mudra; *M.* Tutti; *T.* Nallatutti, Tuthal; *Te.* Thutiribenda; *C.* Hettuti; *Sin.* Anode; *Bur.* Bonkhoe.

Acacia arabica Willd.
E. Babul, Gum tree; *S.* Babula; *B.* Babla; *H. & P.* Kikar, Babul; *U.* Babul; *A.* Torua-kadam; *O.* Baburi; *P.* Kikar; *G.* Babulia, Baval; *Bom.* Babhula; *Mar.* Babhul; *M. & T.* Karuvelam; *Te.* Nallatumma; *C.* Jali; *Bur.* Naloakyine, Huanlongkyain.

Acacia catechu Willd.
E. Cutch; *S.* Khadira; *B.* Khayer; *H. & P.* Katha, Khair; *A.* Khair; *O.* Khaira; *G.* Kher, Kherio; *Bom.* Khaderi, Khaira; *Mar.* Khair; *M.* Kadaram; *T.* Kadiram; *Te.* Khadiramu; *C.* Kungli; *Sin.* Ratkhiri; *Bur.* Sha.

Acalypha indica L.
S. Arithamunjariye; *B.* Muktajhuri; *H.* Kuppi, Khokli; *O.* Indramaris; *P.* Kokali kuppamani; *G.* Vanchhikanto; *Bom.* Khokli; *Mar.* Khajoti, Kupi; *M. & T.* Kuppamani; *Te.* Kuppintaku; *C.* Kuppi; *Sin.* Kuppamaniya.

Acanthus ilicifolius L.
S. Harikusa; *B.* Hargoza; *H.* Harkuchkanta; *O.* Kilichiri; *Bom.* Nivagur; *Mar.* Marandi; *M.* Payinachhulli; *T.* Kaludaimulli; *Te.* Alchi; *C.* Holeculli; *Sin.* Ikiti; *Bur.* Khaya.

Achras sapota L.
E. Sapota, Sapodilla plum; *B.* Safeda; *H. & M.* Sapota; *A.* Sapheda; *O.* Sapeta; *Bom.* Chikali; *T.* Simaiyiluppai; *Te.* Simaippa; *Bur.* Twottapat.

Achyranthes aspera L. = *Aerva aspera* Spreng.
E. Prickly chaff-flower; *S.* Apamarga; *B.* Apang; *H.* Laljiri, Chirchiri; *A.* Ubtisath; *O.* Apamaranga; *P.* Kutri; *G.* Aghedo; *Bom.* Aghada; *Mar.* Aghara; *M.* Katalati; *T.* Nayurivi; *Te.* Uttareni; *C.* Utranigida; *Sin.* Karalsebo; *Bur.* Kivalamon.

Aconitum napellus L.
E. Monk's hood; *S.* Kalkuta, Visha; *B.* Katbish; *H.* Mitha-zahar; *A.* Bish; *G.* Shangadio, Vachnag; *Mar.* Bachneg, Vashanav; *M.* Vatsanbhi; *T.* Vasanabhi; *Te.* Ativasa, Nabhi; *C.* Vasnabhi; *Sin.* Vachanabhi.

Acorus calamus L.
E. Sweet flag; *S.* Vacha; *B. & A.*

Bach; *H.* Gorbach; *U.* Bacha; *P.* Warch; *G.* Godavaj; *Mar.* Wekhand; *M.* Vayambu; *T.* Vasambu; *Te.* Vadaja, Basa; *G.* Baje; *Sin.* Wadakaha; *Bur.* Linhe.

Acronychia laurifolia Bl.=*A. pedunculata* Miq.

E. Clawflowered laurel; *O.* Madhugodiyamado; *M.* Muttanari; *Te.* Muttainari; *C.* Bhutali; *Sin.* Ankenda.

Adansonia digitata L.

E. Baobab; *H.* Gorakamali; *G.* Bukha; *Bom.* Gorokchincha; *Mar.* Gorakhchinch; *T.* Anaippuli; *Te.* Brahmamlika; *C.* Brahmomlika.

Adenanthera pavonina L.

E. Red wood; *S.* Ranjaka; *B.* Ranjan; *H.* Barigumchi; *A.* Chandan; *O.* Sokakainjo; *G.* Badigumchi; *Mar.* Thorligunj; *M.* Manjati; *T.* Monjadi; *Te.* Gurivenda; *C.* Munjuti; *Sin.* Madateya; *Bur.* Ywegyi.

Adenostema viscosum DC.

B. Boro-keshurti.

Adhatoda vasica Nees.

E. Malabar nut; *S.* Atarusha, Vasika; *B.* Basak; *H.* Adalsa; *U.* Arusa; *A.* Banhaka; *O.* Basanga; *P.* Basuti; *G.* Adulso; *Bom.* Adulasa; *Mar.* Adulsi, Baksa; *M.* Adalodakam; *T.* Adatodi; *Te.* Atarushamu; *C.* Adsele; *Sin.* Agaladara; *Bur.* Ba-wa-net.

Adina cordifolia Hook f.

S. Dhara-kadamba; *B. & A.* Kelikadam; *H.* Haldu, Hardu; *O.* Keli kodombo, Holondo; *G.* Aldavan; *Mar.* Hedu; *M.* Katampa; *T.* Kadambai; *Te.* Kamba; *C.* Kadambe; *Sin.* Kolong; *Bur.* Hnaubeng.

Aegle marmelos Corr.

E. Wood apple, Bael tree; *S.* Sriphal, Vilva; *B & A.* Bel; *H.* Bili, Sriphal; *U.* Bel; *O.* Bela, Bilwa; *P.* Bil; *G.* Billy; *Bom.* Bela; *Mar.* Bel; *M.* Vilvam; *T.* Vilvamaram; *Te.* Bilambu, Sriphalamu; *C.* Bilva; *Sin.* Belli; *Bur.* Okshit.

Aerua lanata Juss.=*Aerva lanata* Juss.

S. Astmabayda; *B.* Chaya; *H.* Kapurijadi; *P.* Buikallan; *G.* Kapurimadhuri; *Mar.* Kapurmadhura; *T.* Sirupulai; *Te.* Pindikumda; *Sin.* Polkudupala.

Aerua scandens Wall.=*Aerva sanguinolenta* Bl.

B. Nuriya; *T.* Perumbulai; *Te.* Pindikonda.

Aeschynomene aspera L.

E. Indian cork-plant; *B.* Shola; *H.* Sola; *A.* Kunhila; *O.* Sholo; *M.* Kadesuattukedcsu; *T.* Attunettee; *Te.* Jiluga.

Aganosma caryophyllata G. Don.=*A. dichotoma* K. Schum.

S. Sumana, Malati; *B. & H.* Malati; *O.* Maloti; *G. & Mar.* Malati; *M.* Cherupaval; *Te.* Palamalle; *C.* Malatilata.

Agave americana Roxb.

E. Century plant, American Aloe; *S.* Kantala; *B.* Bilati anarash; *H.* Kantala; *O.* Kolakantalo; *P.* Wilayati kantala; *G.* Jangli-kanvar; *Bom.* Parkanda; *Mar.* Ghaypat; *M.* Nattukaita; *T.* Anakuttilai; *Te.* Bontharakasi; *C.* Anekatalle, Bhutale.

Ageratum conyzoides L.

B. Dochunty; *G.* Ajgandha; *Bom.* Osari; *Mar.* Ghaneraosadi; *M.* Appa; *Sin.* Hulantala.

Aglaia roxburghiana Miq.

S. Anganapriya, Gauro; *B. & H.* Priyangu; *O.* Priyongo; *M.* Punyeva, Sempuli; *T.* Kannikkombu; *Te.* Ettanduga; *C.* Tottila.

Albizzia lebbeck Benth.

E. Silk flower, Parrot tree; *S.* Kapitana, Shukapuspa; *B & A.* Sirish; *H.* Garso, Seris; *U.* Darash; *O.* Sirisa; *G.* Pitosarshio; *Bom.* Harreri, Siris; *Mar.* Kalashiris, Shirish; *M.* Vaga; *T.* Vagai; *Te.* Dirisana; *C.* Bage, Sirisa; *Sin.* Mara; *Bur.* Kokko.

Allamanda cathartica L.

Bom. Jaharisontakka; *C.* Arasinhu.

Allium cepa L.

E. Onion; *S.* Palandu; *B.* Pianj; *H.* & *U.* Piyaz; *A.* Ponoru; *O.* Piaja; *P.* Peyaz; *G.* Dungari; *Bom.* Puyaj; *Mar.* Kanda; *M.* Ulli; *T.* Irulli; *Te.* & *C.* Nirulli; *Sin.* Lunu; *Bur.* Kesunni.

Allium sativum L.

E. Garlic; *S.* Lashuna; *B.* Rasun; *H.* Lashun; *U.* Lehsun; *A.* Naharu; *O.* Rasuna; *G.* Lasan; *Bom.* Lusoon; *Mar.* Lasun; *M.* Veluthulli; *T.* Vellaipundu; *Te.* Tellagadda; *C.* Belluli; *Sin.* Sudulunu; *Bur.* Kesumphiu.

Allophylus cobbe Bl.=*A. serratus* Radlk. *B.* Rakhalphul; *O.* Khondokoli; *Mar.* Tipani; *M.* Mukkanamperu; *T.* Amalai; *Te.* Eravalu, Juthika; *C.* Sisidale; *Bur.* Thankjot.

Alocasia indica Schott.

S. Manaka; *B.* & *A.* Mankachu; *H.* Mankanda; *O.* Manasaru; *P.* Arvi; *G.* Alavu; *Mar.* Alu; *C.* Manaka.

Aloe indica Willd.

E. Indian aloe; *S.* Adala; *B.* Ghritakumari; *H.* Ghikavar; *A.* Chalkunwari; *U.* Ghiqwara; *O.* Ghritokumari; *P.* Ghikuar; *G.* Kunvar; *Mar.* Korphad; *M.* Kattarvazha; *T.* Kuttilai; *Te.* Kalabanda; *C.* Kuttilai.

Alpinia galanga L.

S. Kulanja; *B.* Kulinjan; *H.* Punnagchampa, Kulinjan; *U.* Kulanjan; *G.* Kolinjan; *Bom.* Baripankijar; *Mar.* Koshtkulinjan; *M.* Aratta; *T.* Arattai; *Te.* Kachoramu; *C.* Rasmi; *Bur.* Padagoji.

Alstonia scholaris R. Br.

E. Devil tree; *S.* Saptaparni; *B.* Chatim; *H.* Chatium; *A.* Chatian; *P.* Satona; *O.* Chhatiana; *Mar.* Satvin; *M.* Ezhilampala; *T.* Elilaipillai; *Te.* Edakulapala; *C.* Hale, Madala; *Bur.* Lettop.

Alternanthera sessiles R Br.

B. Chanchi; *O.* Madaranga; *P.* Chura; *G.* Jalajambo; *Bom.* & *Mar.* Kanchari; *M.* Kozhuppa; *T.* Ponnankanni; *Te.* Ponagantikura; *C.* Honaganne; *Sin.* Mokunuwanna.

Amaranthus gangeticus L.

S. Marisha; *B.* Dengo, Lal-shak; *H.* Lalnatiya, Rajkiri; *U.* Lalsag; *G.* Adbondambho; *Bom.* Matichulai; *Mar.* Ranmat; *Sin.* Sudutampala.

Amaranthus spinosus L.

E. Prickly amaranth, Foxtail; *S.* Tandula; *B.* Katanotey; *H.* Kantamiris; *A.* Katakhutura; *O.* Kantaneutia; *P.* Chulai; *G.* Tanjalio; *Mar.* Katemath; *M.* Mullancheera; *T.* Mullukkerai; *Te.* Nalladoggali; *C.* Mulladantu; *Sin.* Katutampala; *Bur.* Hinnoesuba.

Amaranthus viridis L.

E. Amaranth; *S.* Tanduliya; *B.* Notey; *H.* Chaulai, Janglichurai; *G.* Dhimdo; *Mar.* Lhanamat; *T.* Kuppaikiral; *Te.* Mundlathotakura; *Sin.* Kuratampala.

Ammania baccifera L.

E. Blistering ammania; *S.* Kuranli; *B.* Dadmari; *H.* Kuranda; *U.* Agya; *P.* Dederbuti; *G.* Jalaagiyo; *Bom.* Agiya; *Mar.* Bharajambhula; *M.* Kallarvanchi; *T.* Kallarivi; *Te.* Agnivendapaku.

Amomum subulatum Roxb.

E. Cardamon; *S.* Upakunchika; *B.* Boro alach; *H.* Elachi; *Mar.* Veldode.

Amoora cocculata Roxb.

B. Amurlatmi; *Bur.* Thitni.

Amoora rohituka W. & A. = *Aphanamixis polystachya* Blatter.

S. Rohitaka; *B.* Tiktaraj; *H.* Harinhara; *G.* Ragtarohido; *Mar.* Raktarohida; *M.* Sim; *T.* Vangul; Sem; *Te.* Rohitaka; *C.* Mullumuttaga; *Sin.* Hingalgass; *Bur.* Chayankayou.

Amorphophallus campanulatus Bl.

E. Teliga potato; *S.* Arsaghna; *B.* & *A.* Ol-kachu, Ol; *H.* & *P.* Zaminkand; *O.* Olua; *Bom.* Jangli-suran; *G.* & *Mar.* Suran; *M.* Chaena; *T.* Karunakilangu; *Te.* Thiya kandha; *Sin.* Kidaran; *Bur.* Wa.

Anacardium occidentale L.

E. Cashewnuts; *S.* Kajutaka; *B.* Hijlibadam, Kaju; *H.* Kaju; *A.* Kajubadam; *O.* Lanka badam; *G.* & *Bom.* Kaju; *Mar.* Kajucha; *M.* Kashumavu; *T.* Mundiri; *Te.* Jidimamidi; *C.* Geru; *Sin.* Kaju; *Bur.* Thayet.

Andrographis paniculata Nees.

E. Creat; *S.* Bhuinimba, Kirata; B. Kalmegh; *H.* Kirayat; *A.* Kalpatita; *O.* Bhuinimba; *P.* Charaita; *G.* Kiryato; *Mar.* Palekiraiet; *M.* Kiriyaththu; *T.* Nelavembu; *Te.* Nelavema; *C.* Kreata; *Sin.* Ninbinkohomba.

Andropogon aciculatus Retz.

E. Love thorn; *B.* Chorkanta, Nilaji; *H.* Bhatui, Chirchira; *A.* Bon-guti; *O.* Guguchia; *P.* Chorkanda; *T.* Thutiri; *Te.* Gaddi; *Sin.* Tuttiri.

Andropogon sorghum Brot.=*Sorghum vulgare* Pers.

E. Indian millet; *S.* Yavanala; *B.* Juar; *H.* Jowar; *A.* Joudhan; *O.* Bajra; *P.* Chotijuar; *G.* & *Bom.* Juar, Jowar; *Mar.* Juari; *M.* Chavela; *T.* Cholam; *Te.* Janu, Jonna; *C.* Jolah; *Sin.* Karaliringu; *Bur.* Pyoung.

Andropogon squarossus Cooke=*Vetiveria zizanioides* Stapf.

E. Khuskhus; *S.* Ushira; *B.* Khaskhas, Bena; *H.* Khas, Panni; *U.* Khas; *O.* Khas; *P.* Panni; *G.* Valo; *Bom.* Khasakkasa; *Mar.* Vata; *M.* & *T.* Vettiver; *Te.* Vattiveru; *C.* Lavancha; *Sin.* Saivandera; *Bur.* Miyamoe.

Aneilema nudiflora R. Br.

B. Kenduli, Kureli; *H.* Siyahmusli; *G.* Sismulia; *M.* Nelampulla; *C.* Nelacalu, Hullu.

Anisomeles ovata R.Br.=*A. indica* O. Kuntze.

B. Gobura; *O.* Bhuta-airi; *Bom.* & *Mar.* Gopali; *M.* Poothachetayan; *T.* Peyameratti; *Sin.* Yokwanasa.

Anogeissus latifolia Wall.

E. Button tree; *S.* Dhavala; *B.* Dhaoya; *H.* Bakli, Dhau; *U.* Bakla; *O.* Dhou; *C.* Dhavdo; *Bom.* Dhavada; *Mar.* Dhavda; *M.* Vellanava; *T.* Namai, Vekkali; *Te.* Vellama; *C.* Dinduga; *Sin.* Daawa.

Anona reticulata L.

E. Bullock's heart; *S.* Krishnabija; *B.* Nona; *H.* Ramphal; *A.* Atlas; *O.* Neua; *G.*, *Bom.* & *Mar.* Ramphal; *M.* Atha; *T.* Ramasita; *Te.* Ramapandu; *C.* Ramaphala; *Sin.* Anoda; *Bur.* Awza.

Anona squamosa L.

E. Custard apple; *S.* Sitaphala; *B.* Ata; *A.* Atlas; *H.* Sarifa; *O.* Ato, Sitapholo; *G.* Anan; *Mar.* Sitaphal; *M.* Seema-atha, Sitaphalam; *T.* Atta, Sitaphalam; *Te.* Sitapandu; *C.* Sitaphala; *Sin.* Atta; *Bur.* Auza.

Anthocephalus cadamba Miq.=*A. indicus* A. Reich.

S. Kadamba; *B.* & *H.* Kadam; *A.* Roghu; *O.* Kadamba; *G.* & *Bom.* Kadamba; *Mar.* Kadamb; *M.* & *T.* Kadambu; *Te.* Kadambe; *C.* Bale; *Sin.* Kadamba; *Bur.* Ma-doo.

Antedesma ghaesembila Gaertn.

E. Black currant; *B.* Khudijam; *H.* Umtoa; *Mar.* Amati; *M.* Nulittali; *T.* Nolaidali; *Te.* Anepu; *C.* Nayikute; *Bur.* Kywepyisin.

Antigonon leptopus Endl.

E. Virginian creeper; *B.* Ananta lata.

Antirrhinum majus L.

E. Snapdragon; *H.* Sanipat.

Aphania danura Radlk.

B. Danura

Apium graveolens L.

E. Celery; *S.* Ajmoda; *B.* Chiluri; *H.* Ajmud, Bariajmud; *U.* Ajmod; *G.* Bodiajamoda; *Bom.* Ajmud; *Mar.* Ajmoda.

Arachis hypogaea L.

E. Groundnut, Peanut; *B.* & *A.* Chinabadam, *H.* & *P.* Mungphali; *G.* Maffali; *Bom.* Bhuiseng; *Mar.* Bhuimug; *M.* Nelakkatala; *T.* Nilakkadalai; *Te.* Veru sanaga; *C.* Kadale; *Sin.* Ratakaju; *Bur.* Myepe.

Areca catechu L.

E. Betel-nut; *S.* Gubaka; *B.* Supari, Gua; *H.* Kasaili; *U.* Supari; *A.* Tambul; *O.* Gua; *G.* Sopari; *Mar.* Supari, Pung; *M.* Adakka; *T.* Pakku; *Te.* Poka; *C.* Adike, Bette; *Sin.* Puwak; *Bur.* Kunse.

Argemone mexicana L.

E. Mexican poppy, Prickly poppy; *S.* Srigalkanta; *B.* Shialkanta; *H.* Katola, Pila katari; *A.* Kuhumkata; *O.* Kantakusham; *P.* Kandiari; *G.* Darudi; *Mar.* Piwala dhotra; *M.* Brahmadanti; *T.* Brahmadandu; *Te.* Brahamadandi, Datturi; *C.* Datture; *Sin.* Balurakksia.

Arisaema speciosum Mart.

E. Snake plant; *H.* Sanpbuti; *P.* Samp-ki-khumb; *Sin.* Walkidaran.

Argyreia speciosa Sw.=*A. nervosa* Boj.
E. Elephant creeper; *S.* Hastiballi; *B.* Guguli; *H.* Samandarkapat; *U.* Samandarsotha; *O.* Monda; *G.* Samudrasosh; *Bom.* & *Mar.* Samudrashoka; *M.* Samudrapala; *T.* Samuthrappalai; *Te.* Samudrapachcha; *Sin.* Mahadumudu.

Artabotrys odoratissimus R. Br.=*A. uncinatus* Merr.

B. Kantali-champa; *H.* & *P.* Champa; *A.* Kothalichampa; *O.* Chinichampa; *Bom.* Vilayati-champa; *Mar.* Hirwachapha; *M.* & *T.* Manoranjini; *Te.* Manoranjitham; *C.* Manoranjanballi.

Artemisia caruifolia Ham.

E. Sage brush; *H.* Vilayti afsanten.

Artiplex hortensis L.

E. Salt brush.

Artocarpus incisa L.f.

E. Bread fruit; *T.* Erpillakai; *Sin.* Rata-del.

Artocarpus integrifolia L.=*A. heterophylla* Lamk.

E. Jack; *S.* Panasa; *B.* Kantal; H. Katahar; *U.* Katahal; *A.* Kothal; *O.* Panasa; *P.* Katar; *G.* Manphanasa; *Bom.* & *Mar.* Phanas; *M.* & *T.* Pila; *Te.* Panasa; *C.* Halasu; *Sin.* Cos; *Bur.* Peinne.

Artocarpus lakoocha Roxb.

E. Monkey jack; *S.* Dahu; *B.* Deophal; *H.* Barhal, Lakuch; *A.* Chama, Dewa; *O.* Jeuta; *P.* Deheo; *G.* Lakucha; *Bom.* Lahu, Lovi; *Mar.* & *M.* Lakuch; *T.* Irappala; *Te.* Lakuchamu; *C.* Lakucha; *Sin.* Kaunagona; *Bur.* Mianktot.

Asclepias acida Roxb. = *Sarcostemma acidum* Voigt.

B. & *H.* Somelata; *Bom.* Soma; *Mar.* Ransher; *Te.* Tigatshumoodoo.

Asclepias curassavica L.

E. Milk weed, Silk weed; *P.* Kaktundi; *Bom.* Kuraki.

Asparagus racemosus Willd.

E. Asparagus; *S.* Shatavari; *B.* Satamuli; *H.* Satwar; *U.* Satavara; *A.* Shatmul; *O.* Chhatuari; *P.* Satwar; *G.* & *Bom.* Satavari; *Mar.* Satmuli; *M.* Satavali; *T.* Sathavari; *Te.* Sadavari; *C.* Satamulike; *Sin.* Hatavari; *Bur.* Kanyomi.

Asphodelus tenuifolius Cav.

E. Asphodel; *H.* Bokat; *P.* Piyazi; *G.* Dungru.

Asystasia gangetica T. And.

T. Peyppatchotti; *Sin.* Puruk.

Atalantia monophylla Corr.

S. Atavijambira; *O.* Narguni; *M.* Malanarakam; *T.* Perungurundu; *Te.* Adavinimma; *C.* Adavimimbi.

Atropa belladonna L.

E. Deadly nightshade; *B.* Yebruj; *H.* Luckmuna; *P.* Suchi; *Bom.* Girbutita.

Avena sativa L.

E. Oat; *B.* Jai; *H.* Ganer, Jai; *P.* Ganerji; *C.* Togekoddi.

Averrhoa bilimbi L.

E. Bilimbi, Cucumber tree; *B.* Bilimbi; *H.* Belambu; *G.* Blimbu; *Mar.* Bilambi; *M.* Vilimbo; *T.* Pilimbi, Pulima; *Te.* Bilumbi, Bilibiti.

Averrhoa carambola L.

E. Carambola; *S.* Karmaranga; *B.* Kamranga; *H.* Khamrak, Karmal; *U.* Kamarakha; *A.* Kordoitenga; *O.* Karmanga; *G.* Kamrakha; *Bom.* Karamara; *Mar.* Kamranga; *M.* Irimpanpuli; *T.* Kamarankai; *Te.* Tamarta; *C. & Sin.* Kamaranga; *Bur.* Zoun-ya-si.

Avicennia officinalis L.

E. White mangrove; *S.* Tuvama; *B. & H.* Bina, Tuvar; *G.* Tavariyan; *Mar.* Tiwar; *M.* Urppam; *T.* Kandal; *Te.* Madda; *C.* Upatti; *Bur.* Thamenet.

Baccaurea sapida Muell—Arg.

B. Latkan; *H.* Lutko; *A.* Leteku; *P.* Kala bogati.

Bambusa arundinacea Willd.

E. Bamboo; *S.* Vansha, Kichaka; *B.* Bans; *H.* Bans, Kattang; *A.* Buah; *U.* Banse; *O.* Baunsa; *P.* Magac; *G.* Kapura; *Bom.* Dougi, Mandgay; *Mar.* Kallak; *M.* Illi, Venu; *T.* Mulai, Kambul; *Te.* Veduru; *C.* Bidaru; *Sin.* Kattuna; *Bur.* Kyakatwa.

Barleria cristata L.

S. Jhinti; *B.* Janti; *H.* Jhinte; *A.* Jhinli; *O.* Koilekha; *P.* Tadrelu; *T.* Udamulli; *Te.* Nirugoranta; *C.* Kuruvaka.

Barleria prionitis L.

S. Karuntaka; *B.* Kanta-janti; *H.* Vajradanti; *A.* Nilbagi; *O.* Daskaranta; *G.* Kantasherio; *P.* Gat sariya; *Bom.* Vajradanti; *Mar.* Koranti; *M.* Kanakambaram; *T.* Chemmulli; *Te.* Mundlagobbi; *C.* Kairantaka; *Sin.* Katakarardu; *Bur.* Leithaywa.

Basella rubra L.

E. Indian spinach; *S.* Putika; *B.* Pui-shak; *H. & O.* Poi; *U.* Poh; *A.* Purai; *G.* Pothi; *Bom.* Mayakbhaji, Velgond; *Mar.* Velbondi; *M.* Samparcheera; *T.* Sambarkeerai; *Te.* Karubachchali; *C.* Kempabasale; *Sin.* Niviti.

Bassia latifolia Roxb. = *Madhuca indica* Gemel.

E. Mohwa tree, Butter tree; *S.* Madhuka; *B. & H.* Mahua, Maul; *U.* Mahuava; *O.* Mahula; *P.* Mohwa; *G.* Mahuda; *Bom.* Moha; *Mar.* Moha; *M.* Irippa; *T.* Illuppai; *Te.* Ippa.

Bauhinia acuminata L.

E. Mountain ebony; *S.* Juggapatra; *B. & A.* Kanchan; *H.* Kachnar; *O.* Kanchona; *P.* Kairal.

Bauhinia purpurea L.

E. Mountain ebony; *S.* Vanaraja; *B.* Devakanchan; *H.* Kaliar; *O.* Debkanjoro; *P.* Koralli; *Bom.* Atmatti; *Mar.* Debakanchana; *M.* Suvannamandaram; *T.* Mandarai; *Te.* Devakanjan; *C.* Utipe; *Sin.* Petan, Koblila; *Bur.* Mahahlegani.

Bauhinia variegata L.

E. Camel's foot; *S.* Raktakanchana; *B.* Raktokanchan; *H. & P.* Kachnar; *U.* Kachnal; *O.* Kanchana; *G. & Bom.* Kanaraj, Kovidara; *Mar.* Raktakanchan; *M.* Mandarum; *T.* Tiruvatti; *Te.* Adavimandara; *C.* Kanjivala; *Bur.* Bwechin.

Benincasa cerifera Savi = *B. hispida* Cong.

E. Ash gourd; *S.* Kushmanda; *B.* Chalkumra; *H. & P.* Petha; *A.* Komora; *U.* Petha; *O.* Panikakharu; *G.* Kohwla; *Bom. & Mar.* Kohala; *M.* Kumpalam;

T. Kumpaly; *Te.* Pulla gummudi; *C.* Budekumbalakayi; *Sin.* Alupuhul; *Bur.* Kyaukpayon.

Beta vulgaris L.

E. Sugar beet; *B.* Palangshak; *H.* Chukandar, Polak; *U.* Chakundar; *A.* Beet-palang; *O.* Palanga saga; *G.* & *Mar.* Beet; *T.* Chakunda.

Biophytum sensitivum DC.

E. Sensitive wood-sorrel; *S.* Jalapuspa; *B.* & *A.* Bon-naranga; *H.* Lajalu; *G.* Jaharera; *Mar.* Lajari; *M.* Mukkutti, Thindanazhi; *Sin.* Gas-nidikumba.

Bischofia javanica Bl.

E. West Indian cedar, Java cedar; *H.* Bhillar, Kain; *A.* Uriana; *O.* Dingiri; *Bom.* Bok; *M.* Nira, Tirippu; *T.* Tondi; *Te.* Nalupumushti; *Bur.* Yepadauk.

Blumea lacera DC.

S. Kukuradru; *B.* Barokukshima, Kukursunga, Shealmotra; *H.* Kukkurbanda, Kokronda; *A.* Kukurshuta; *O.* Pokasunga; *G.* Kalarunda; *Bom.* Nimurdi; *Mar.* Burando; *T.* Katumullangi; *Te.* Karupogaku; *Bur.* Maiyagan.

Blyxa octandra L.

B. Seyala; *Sin.* Diya-hawariya.

Boehmeria nivea Hook. & Arn.

E. Rhea, Rami grass; *B.* & *H.* Kankhura; *A.* Rhea; *O.* Bryddhingi; *M.* Battischoriagenam.

Boerhaavia repens L.

E. Pigweed; *S.* Punarnava, Sathagni; *B.* Punarnaba; *H.* Thikri, Ghadapurva; *U.* Bashkira; *A.* Ponomua; *O.* Ghodapuruni; *P.* Itsit; *G.* Vakhakaparo; *Bom.* Khapara, Punarnava; *Mar.* Kharaparya, Vasu; *M.* Thazuthama; *T.* Mukkaratai; *Te.* Punarnaba; *C.* Kommegida; *Sin.* Petasudupala.

Bombax malabaricum D.C.=*Salmalia malabarica* Schott.

E. Silk-cotton tree; *S.* Shalmali; *B.* Shimool; *H.* & *P.* Simar, Simbal; *A.* Simalu; *O.* Simuli; *G.* Ratoshemalo; *Bom.* Semul, Shembal; *Mar.* Kate savar; *M.* Mullilavu; *T.* Elavu; *Te.* Salmali; *C.* Hatti, Kempuburaga; *Sin.* Kattu-imbul.

Bonnaya brachiata Link & Otto.= *Lindernia ciliata* Pennel.

B. Bhui-nim; *Sin.* Wila.

Borassus flabellifer L.

E. Palmyra-palm; *S.* Taruraja, Tali; *B.* & *A.* Tal; *H.* Tar; *U.* Tad; *O.* Tala; *G.* Tad; *Mar.* Tad, Tamar; *M.* Karimpana; *T.* Panai; *Te.* Thadi; *C.* Tali; *Sin.* Tal; *Bur.* Tan.

Bougainvillaea spectabilis L.

E. Glory of garden; *B.* Baganbilas.

Brassica campestris L.

E. Turnip; *B.* Shalgom; *H.* Chukandar.

Brassica juncea Hook. f. & Thom.

E. Mustard; *B.* Raisarisha; *H.* Rai.

Brassica napus L.

E. Rape; *S.* Sarsopa; *B.* Sarisha; *H.* & *P.* Sarson; *A.* Sariah; *O.* Sorosha; *G.* Rai; *Bom.* Raisarson; *Mar.* Mohori; *M.* Katuku; *T.* Karuppukadugu; *Te.* Avelu; *C.* Sasiva.

Broussonetia papyrifera Vent.

E. Paper Mulberry.

Brownlowia lanceolata Benth.

B. Bolasundri, Kedarpundri.

Bruguiera gymnorhiza Lamk.

B. Kankra; *M.* Kantal; *T.* Ugappukakhandal; *Te.* Dudduponna.

Bryophyllum calycinum Salisb.

E. Sprout-leaf plant; *S.* Parnabija; *B.* Patharkuchi, Koppata; *H.* Zakhm-i-hayat; *A.* Petegaza; *O.* Amarpoi; *U.* Chubehayat; *P.* Pathurchat; *Bom.* Ahiravana; *Mar.* Panphuti; *T.* Ranakalli; *Te.* Simajamudu; *C.* Lonnahalakanagida.

Buchanania latifolia Roxb. = *B. lanzan* Spreng.

S. Piyalaka, Priyala; *B.* Piyal; *H.* Chironji, Piyar; *U.* Chironji; *O.* Priyalo; *P.* Chiroli; *Bom.* Charoli; *Mar.* Chirauli; *M.* Niruvi; *T.* Kattuma, Sarai; *Te.* Moralli, Sara; *C.* Charpoppu, Morale; *Bur.* Lambo.

Buettneria herbacea Roxb.

B. Kambraj.

Butea frondosa Roxb. = *B. monosperma* Taub.

E. Flame of the forest, Parrot tree; *S.* Palasha; *B. & A.* Palas; *H. & P.* Dhak; *U.* Palashpapra; *O.* Palasa; *G.* Khakara; *Bom.* Khakara, Palasa; *Mar.* Palash; *M.* Chamatha; *T.* Palasam; *Te.* Moduga; *C.* Muttuga; *Sin.* Kalukeale; *Bur.* Poukpex.

Butomus umbellatus L.

H. Briktshee.

Caesalpinia bonducella Flem. = *C. crista* L.

E. Fever nut; *S.* Kuberakshi; *B.* Nata; *H. & P.* Katkaranj; *A.* Letaguti; *O.* Gila; *G.* Kakachia; *Bom.* Gaja; *Mar.* Sagargota; *M.* Kazhanchikkuroo; *T.* Kalakkodi; *Te.* Gacha; *C.* Gajjiga; *Sin.* Kumburuwel; *Bur.* Kaliendza.

Caesalpinia pulcherrima Sw.

E. Peacock flower; *S.* Krishnachuda; *B.* Krishnachura; *H.* Guletura; *A.* Swarnakanti; *O.* Krushnachuda; *G.* Sandesharo; *Mar.* Shankasur; *M.* Rajmalli; *T.* Mayuram; *Te.* Turayi; *C.* Kenjige, Ratnagandhi; *Sin.* Monaramal; *Bur.* Ts-an-pan-pin, Daungsop.

Cajanus indicus Spreng. = *C. cajan* Mill.

E. Pigeon pea; *S.* Adhaki, Tuvarika; *B.* Arhar; *H.* Rahar; *A.* Rahar-mah; *O.* Harada; *P.* Tohar, Dingeri; *G.* Tuvare; *Bom.* Tura; *Mar.* Tur; *M.* Thuvara; *T.* Thovaray; *Te.* Kandulu; *C.* Togari; *Sin.* Ratatora; *Bur.* Pai-si-song.

Calamus tenuis Roxb.

E. Cane palm; *S.* Vetasi; *B.* Bet; *O.* Beta; *Mar.* Vet; *M.* Choorai; *T.* Sural.

Calamus rotang L.

E. Rattan; *S.* Vetra; *B.* Chanchibet; *M.* Purampu; *T.* Pirambu, Vettirom; *Te.* Bettamu; *C.* Betta; *Sin.* We-wel.

Callicarpa arborea Roxb.

B. Bormala, Kojo; *H.* Ghiwala; *A.* Khoja; *O.* Bornopatri; *Bur.* Daungsatpya.

Callicarpa macrophylla Vahl.

B. Mathara; *H.* Daya; *M.* Chimpompil.

Calophyllum inophyllum L.

E. Alexandrian laurel; *S.* Nagachampa, Punnag; *B.* Punnag, Sultan-champa; *H.* Surpan; *O.* Polanga; *Bom.* Undi; *Mar.* Nagchampa, Undi; *M. & P.* Punna; *T.* Punnagam; *Te.* Punnaga; *C.* Honne; *Sin.* Dumba; *Bur.* Pengnyet.

Calotropis gigantea R. Br.

E. Madar, Swallow-wort; *S.* Arka; *B.* Akanda; *H.* Akond, Madar; *U.* Ak; *A.* Akon; *O.* Arka; *G.* Akado; *Bom. & Mar.* Rui; *M.* Erukku; *T.* Arkkam, Erukku; *Te.* Jilledu; *C.* Arka, Ekke; *Sin.* Wara; *Bur.* Maioh.

Calotropis procera R. Br.

S. Alarka, Shveta; *B.* Shet-akanda; *H.* Safed-ak; *O.* Arka; *P.* Ak; *Mar.* Mandara; *T.* Vellerukku; *Te.* Jilledu; *Bur.* Mayopin.

Canavalia ensiformis DC. = *C. gladiata* DC.

E. Sword bean; *S.* Mahashimbi; *B.* Makhan-shim; *H.* Bara-sem; *A.* Kantal-urahi; *O.* Badasimba; *P.* Sem; *G.* Gavria; *Bom.* Gaivara; *Mar.* Abai; *M.* Kanavala; *T.* Valavarakkai; *Te.* Tumbattan kaya; *C.* Kadavare, Sambe; *Sin.* Walawara; *Bur.* Paikalag.

Canna indica L.
E. Indian shot; *S.* Sarvajaya; *B.* Sarbajaya, Kalabati; *H.* Kiawra; *A.* Parijat-phul; *O.* Sarbajaya; *P.* Hakik; *G.* Kardali; *Mar.* Kardal; *M.* Kattuvazha; *T.* Kalvalai; *Te.* Krishnatamara; *C.* Kalahu; *Sin.* Butsarana; *Bur.* Buddatharana.

Cannabis sativa L.
E. Hemp; *S.* Ganjika; *B.* Ganja, Bhang, Sidhi; *H.* Bhang, Charas; *O.* Bhanga, Ganji; *P.* Bhangi; *G.* Bhang, Ganja; *Mar.* Bhang; *M.* Kanchavu; *T.* Ganja, Bangi; *Te.* Ganja chettu; *C.* Bhangi; *Sin.* Ganjagaha; *Bur.* Ben.

Canscora decussata Roem. & Schult.
S. Mahatikta, Sankhapuspi; *B.* Dankuni; *H.* Sankhahuli; *Mar.* Titavi; *M.* Cansjancora.

Canthium angustifolium Roxb.
E. Ceylon box-wood; *B.* Kottamalli; *T.* Yorkoli, Nakkani; *Te.* Balasu; *C.* Hetteranike; *Sin.* Galkarinda.

Capparis horrida L.f.
B. Bagnai; *H.* Jhiri, Kalis.

Capparis sepiaria L.
S. Gridhranakhi; *B.* Bagashra, Kanta-gurkamai; *H.* Hiun; *O.* Kantikapali; *P.* Hius; *G.* Kantharo; *Mar.* Kakadani; *M.* Thoratti; *T.* Karindu; *Te.* Nalluppi; *C.* Kadukattari.

Capparis spinosa L.
E. Caper plant; *B.* Kabra; *H.* Kiari, Kobra; *U.* Kabar; *P.* Kabarra; *Bom.* Kabar; *Te.* Kokilakshmu; *C.* Mullukattari.

Capparis zeylanica L.
S. Kantakalata, Govindi; *B.* Keleykora, Ashareylata; *O.* & *Mar.* Govindi; *P.* Karvila; *T.* Kattotti, Tondai; *Te.* Doddi, Palaki; *C.* Totte, Tottulla.

Capsella bursa-pastoris Moench.
E. Shepherd's purse.

Capsicum frutescens L.
E. Chilli, Red pepper; *S.* Marichiphala, Ujjvala; *B.* Lanka. Morich; *H.* & *P.* Lal-mircha; *U.* Lalmarach; *A.* Jolokia; *O.* Lankamaricha; *G.* & *Mar.* Mirchi; *Bom.* Lalmirchi; *M.* & *T.* Mulagu; *Te.* Mirapakaya; *C.* Menashinakayi; *Sin.* Gasmiris.

Carapa obovata Bl.
B. Dhundul; *O.* Susambar; *Bur.* Penglayoang.

Cardiospermum helicacabum L.
E. Balloon vine; *S.* Karnasphota, Jyotishmati; *B.* Lataphatki, Shibjhul; *H.* Kanphuti; *A.* Kopalphota; *O.* Phutphutkia; *P.* Hab-ul-kulkul; *G.* Karodio; *Bom.* Kanphuti; *Mar.* Kapalphodi; *M.* Valliyuzhinja; *T.* Modakathan; *Te.* Buddakakkira; *C.* Erumballi; *Sin.* Penelvel; *B* Malamai.

Carissa carandus L.
E. Currant; *S.* Karamandaka; *B.* Karamcha, Karja; *H.* Karonda, Karaunda; *U.* Karwanch; *A.* Korjatenga; *O.* Korondo, Khirakoli; *G.* Karamarda; *Bom.* Karwand; *Mar.* Karvanda; *M.* Elimullu; *T.* Kalakkai; *Te.* Kalivi; *C.* Heggarichige; *Sin.* Mahakaramba.

Carthamus tinctorius L.
E. Safflower; *S.* Kusumbha; *B.* & *A.* Kusumphul; *H.* & *P.* Kusam; *O.* Kusuma; *G.* Kusumbo; *Bom.* Kusumba, Kardai; *Mar.* Kardai; *M.* Shinduram; *T.* Kusumba; *Te.* Agnisikha; *C.* Kusumbe.

Carum carui L.
E. Caraway; *S.* Krishnajiraka; *B.* Jira; *H.* Shiajira; *U.* Shahjirah; *P.* Zirasiyah; *G.* Shajiru; *Bom.* Vilayatizirah; *Mar.* Sahajire; *T.* Simaishembu; *Te.* Shimaisapu.

Carum copticum Benth. = *Trachyspermum amni* Spreng.
E. Ajowan; *S.* Yamanika, Yavani; *B.* Jowan; *H.* & *P.* Ajowan; *A.* Joni-guti; *O.* Juani; *G.* Ajamo; *Bom.* Ajwan, Owa; *Mar.* Owa; *M.* Ayamodakam; *T.* Omam; *Te.* Omamu; *C.* Oma, Omu; *Sin.* Assamodum.

Carum roxburghiana Benth. = *Trachyspermum roxburghianum* Craib.
B. Radhuni; *H.* Ajmot; *U.* Karafas; *G.* Ajmod; *Mar.* Koranza, Ajmodàvoma; *T.* Ashamtavomam; *Te.* Ajumodavoma.

Caryota urens L.
E. Indian sago-palm, Fishtail palm; *S.* Madadruma; *B.* Golsabu; *H.* Mari; *A.* Baraflawar; *O.* Solopo; *G.* Shankarjata; *Bom.* Birhimhad; *Mar.* Berli, Bherawa; *M.* Anappana; *T.* Tippilippanai, Irambanai; *Te.* Jivalaggu; *C.* Baini; *Sin.* Kittul; *Bur.* Minbo.

Cassia auriculata L.
H. Tarwar; *M.* Ponnaviram; *T.* Avari, Avaram; *Te.* Tangedu; *C.* Tangedi; *Sin.* Rana-wara.

Cassia fistula L.
E. Indian laburnum; *S.* Suvarnaka; *B.* Shondal, Sonali, Bandar lathi; *H. & U.* Amaltash; *A.* Sonaru; *O.* Sunari; *P.* Alash; *G.* Garmala; *Mar.* Bahawa; *M.* Konnai; *T.* Irali, Konnai; *Te.* Rela, Kolaponna; *C.* Konde; *Sin.* Ehela; *Bur.* Gnoo-kye.

Cassia occidentalis L.
E. Western senna; *S.* Kasamarda; *B.* Kalkashunda; *H.* Kasunda; *U.* Kasonji; *O.* Kasundri; *G.* Kasundari; *Bom.* Hikal; *Mar.* Kasoda; *M.* Karintakara; *T.* Peyavirai; *Te.* Kasinda; *C.* Kolutagase; *Sin.* Penitora; *Bur.* Maizali.

Cassia sophera L.
S. Talapota; *B.* Kalkashunda; *H. & P.* Kasunda; *U.* Kalakasonji; *A.* Medelua; *O.* Kolokasunda; *G.* Kasundari; *Mar.* Kala-kasbinda; *M.* Ponnamthakara; *T.* Ponnaviran; *Te.* Tagara; *C.* Kasamarda; *Sin.* Urutora.

Cassia tora L.
E. Foetid cassia; *S.* Chakramarda; *B. & H.* Chakunda; *O.* Chakundo; *P.* Pawar, Chakunda; *G.* Kovariya; *Bom.* Kowaria; *Mar.* Takala; *M.* Takara; *T.* Tagarai; *Te.* Tagirise; *C.* Chogache; *Sin.* Petitora; *Bur.* Dangywe.

Cassytha filiformis L.
S. Akashavalli; *B.* Akasbel; *H. & P.* Amarbeli; *O.* Akasha bela; *Bom.* Akaswel; *Mar.* Amarvela; *M.* Akasavalli; *T.* Indiravalli; *Te.* Nubutga; *C.* Akashaballi; *Bur.* Shwaynwaypin.

Casuarina equisetifolia Forst.
E. Beef-wood tree, She-oak; *B. & A.* Jhau; *H.* Janglisaru; *O.* Jhaun; *G.* Vilayati saru; *Bom.* Sarokajhar; *Mar.* Khadsherani; *M.* Choolamarum; *T.* Savukku; *Te.* Saravu; *C.* Chabaku; *Sin.* Kasa; *Bur.* Tinyu.

Cedrela toona Roxb.
E. Moulmein cedar, Toon; *S.* Tooni, Nandivriksha; *B. & A.* Toon; *H.* Tun; *U.* Tun; *O.* Mahalimbo; *Bom.* Tuni, Tunna; *Mar.* Mahanim; *M.* Chuvannagil; *T.* Malavembu; *Te.* Galimanu; *C.* Devadari, Garige; *Bur.* Tawtama.

Celosia argentea L.
E. White cock's comb; *S.* Vitunna; *B.* Sadamoragphul; *H.* Debkoti; Safaidmurga; *U. & P.* Sarwali; *G.* Lapadi; *Bom.* Khudu, Kurdu; *Mar.* Kurada; *T.* Pannai; *Te.* Guruga; *Sin.* Kirihenda.

Celosia cristata L.
E. Cock's comb; *S.* Mayurasikha; *B.* Morag-phul; *H.* Lalmurga, Jatadhari; *U.* Asnana; *A.* Kukura-joa-phul; *O.* Ganjachulia; *P.* Kukur-phul; *G.* Lalpadi; *Mar.* Mayursikha; *M.* Kozhipullu; *Te.* Kodijuttutotakura; *Bur.* Kyetmonk.

Celsia coromandeliana Vahl. = *Verbascum coromandeliana*
S. Bhutakeshi; *B.* Kokshima; *H.* Gadartambaku; *O.* Kuntze; *G.* Kulahala; *Bom.* Kolhal; *Mar.* Kolhala, Kutki.

Centratherum anthelminticum O. Ktze.
S. Somraji; *B.* Babchi, Somraj; *H.* Bakshi, Somraj; *U.* Janglijiri; *O.* Somraj; *G. & Bom.* Kaligiri; *Mar.* Kalajira; *M.* Kalajirakam; *T.* Kattuchiragam; *Te.* Nelavavili; *C.* Kalajirige; *Sin.* Nironchi.

Cephalandra indica Naud. = *Coccinia cordifolia* Cng.
E. Scarlet gourd; *S.* Bimba, Tundika; *B.* Telakucha; *H.* Bhimba;

U. Kundaru; *A.* Belipoka; *O.* Kunduri; *P.* Kundru; *G.* Ghol; *Bom.* Bhimb, Tenduli; *Mar.* Tondale; *M.* Kovel; *T.* Kovarai; *Te.* Kakidonda; *Sin.* Kovaka; *Bur.* Kenbung.

Ceriops roxburghiana Arn.
B. Goran; *M.* Ankantal; *T.* Pendikutti; *Te.* Gedera.

Cestrum nocturnum L.
E. Queen of the night, Mexican Jasmine; *B.* Hasnahana; *H.* Rat-ki-rani.

Chenopodium album L.
E. Goosefoot, Lamb's quaters; *B.* Bethoshak; *H.* Bethua; *A.* Jilmil-sak; *O.* Bathu saga; *P.* Bathu; *G.* Cheel; *Bom.* Chakwit; *Mar.* Chakavat; *T.* Parupukkirai; *Te.* Pappukura; *C.* Chakravati.

Chenopodium ambrosoides L.
E. Sweet pigweed; *M.* Katuaya-modakam; *C.* Kadavoma.

Chrozophora plicata A. Juss.
S. Suryavarta; *B.* Khudi-okra; *H.* Sonaballi, Subali; *P.* Nilakrai; *G.* Okharada; *Te.* Guruguchettu.

Chrysanthemum coronarium L.
E. Chrysanthemum; *S.* Chandramallika; *B. & A.* Chandramallika; *H. & G.* Guldaudi; *O.* Sebati; *U.* Gulechini; *P.* Guldaud; *Bom.* Seoti; *Mar.* Gulesevati; *M.* Shevanti; *T.* Shamantippu; *Te.* Chamanti; *Sin.* Lavulugas.

Cicer arietenum L.
E. Gram, Chick pea; *S.* Balabhojya; *B.* Chola; *H.* But, Chana; *A.* Bootmah; *O.* Buta; *P.* Channa; *G. & Bom.* Chana; *Mar.* Harabhara; *M.* Kadala; *T.* Kadalai; *Te.* Sanikalu; *Sin.* Kondakadala; *Bur.* Kalapai.

Cichorium intybus L.
E. Chicory; *H.* Kasni; *U. & G.* Kasani; *P.* Gul; *T.* Kashini; *Te.* Kasini.

Cinnamomum camphora Nees.
E. Camphor; *S.* Karpura; *B. & A.* Karpur; *O.* Karpura; *H. & G.* Kapur; *P.* Kafur; *Mar.* Kapur; *M.* Karpuravriksham; *T.* Karuppuram; *Te.* Kappuramu; *Sin.* Kaparugala.

Cinnamomum tamala Nees.
E. Bay leaf; *S.* Tejapatra; *B.* Tejpata, Tamal; *H.* Tezpat; *A.* Tejpat, Mahpat; *O. & P.* Tejpatra; *Bom.* Tamala; *G.* Tamalpatra; *Mar.* Tamal; *T.* Talishappattiri; *Te.* Talisha; *C.* Patraka; *Bur.* Thitchabo.

Cinnamomum zeylanica Breyn.
E. Cinnamon; *S.* Durusita; *B. & A.* Dalchini; *H.* Darchini; *O.* Dalochini; *Mar.* Darachini; *M.* Erikkolam; *T.* Illavangam; *Te.* Lavangamu; *C.* Lavangapatta; *Sin.* Kurundu; *Bur.* Hmanthin.

Citrullus colocynthis Schrad.
E. Colocynth, Bitter cucumber; *S.* Chitrala; *B.* Makal; *H. & U.* Indrayan; *A.* Koabhaturi; *O.* Indrayana; *P.* Tumma; *G.* Indranan; *Bom. & Mar.* Indrayan; *M. & T.* Peykummatty; *Te.* Patsakaya; *C.* Tumtikayi; *Sin.* Yakkomadu.

Citrullus vulgaris Schrad.
E. Water melon; *S.* Tarambuja; *B.* Tarmuj; *H. & P.* Tarbuza; *U.* Tarbuj; *A.* Khormuja; *O.* Tarabhuja; *G.* Karigu; *Bom.* Kalinga, Turbuj; *Mar.* Kalingad; *M.* Vattaka; *T.* Kummattikkai; *Sin.* Penikomadu; *Bur.* Paye.

Citrus aurantium L. = *C. reticulatus* Blanco.
E. Orange; *S.* Naranga; *B.* Kamala; *H. & U.* Narangi; *A.* Kamala-tenga; *O.* Naranga; *P.* Sangtra; *G. & Bom.* Naringi; *Mar.* Santra; *M.* Narakam; *T.* Narangam; *Te.* Naranji; *C.* Naranga, Kittile; *Sin.* Dodan; *Bur.* Thanbaya, Shonsi.

Citrus decumana L. = *C. maxima* Merr.
E. Shaddock, Pummelo; *S.* Madhukarkati; *B.* Batabi-nebu, Jambura; *H. & P.* Chakotra; *U.* Chokutrah; *A.* Rebab-tenga; *O.* Batapi; *G.* Obakotru; *Bom.* Papnas; *Mar.* Papanas; *M.* Bamblinarakam; *T.* Bambalmas; *Te.* Pampalamasam; *C.* Sakkota; *Sin.* Jambula; *Bur.* Shanktones.

Citrus medica L.
E. Lime, Lemon; *S*. Ruchaka, Vijapura; *B*. Nebu; *H*. Limbu, Bijaura; *O*. Lembu; *P*. Galgal, Bijauri; *G*. Limbu; *Bom*. Limu, Bijori; *Mar*. Limbu; *M*. Gilam, Cherunarakam; *T*. Elimichcham, Sidalai; *Te*. Nimmapandu; *Sin*. Sedaran; *Bur*. Shauktakera.

Clausena heptaphylla W. & A.
B. Karanphul; *H*. Ratanjot.

Clematis gouriana Roxb.
E. Traveller's joy, Virgin's bower; *B*. Chagalbati; *H*. Belkangu; *O*. Boromojhanti; *Bom*. Moriel, Ranjai; *C*. Telejadari.

Cleome viscosa L.=*Polanisia viscosa* DC.
S. Arkakanta, Adityabhakta; *B*. Holdey hurhure; *H*. Hulhul; *P*. Gandhuli; *O*. Anasarilia; *G*. Tilvan; *Bom*. Pivalatilavana; *Mar*. Kanphodi; *M*. Katkudugu; *T*. Naikkadugu; *Te*. Kukka vavinta; *C*. Nayibela; *Sin*. Wal-aba.

Clerodendron inerme Gaertn.
S. Kundali, Vanajai; *B*. Bonjui, Batraj; *H*. Sangkupi; *U*. Cholora; *Bom*. & *Mar*. Vanajai; *M*. Nirnochi; *T*. Sanganguppi, Pinari; *Te*. Erupuchcha; *C*. Vishmadhar; *Sin*. Walguranola.

Clerodendron infortunatum Gaertn. = *C. viscosum* Vent.
S. Bhantaka; *B*. Ghetu; *H*. Bhant; *A*. Bhettita; *O*. Kunti; *P*. Karu; *Bom*. & *Mar*. Kari; *M*. Peru-vallem; *T*. Karukanni; *Te*. Basavanapadu; *C*. Ittevu, Parele; *Sin*. Gaspinna; *Bur*. Bujiphyu.

Clerodendron siphonanthus R. Br.
S. Bhargi; *B*. Bamanhati; *H*. Barangi; *P*. Arni; *Bom*. Bharangi; *T*. Kavalai; *Te*. Bharangi, Brahmi; *Bur*. Naijamphati.

Clinogyne dichotoma Salisb.
B. Sithalpati.

Clitoria ternatea L.
E. Butterfly pea; *S*. Gokarnika; *B*. & *A*. Aparajita; *H*. Aparajit, Vishnukranti; *O*. Oporajita; *P*. Aparajit; *G*. Garani; *Bom*. Kajali, Gokaran; *Mar*. Gokarna; *M*. Sankupushpam; *T*. Kakkatan; *Te*. Sangapushpam; *C*. Sankapuspaballi; *Sin*. Kattarodu; *Bur*. Bukiyu.

Cocos nucifera L.
E. Coconut-palm; *S*. Narikela; *B*. Narikel; *H*. & *P*. Narial; *U*. Nariyel; *A*. Narikol; *O*. Nadia; *G*. Nariel; *Bom*. Mar, Naril; *Mar*. Naral; *M*. Nalikeram; *T*. Thengu; *Te*. Kobbera, Tenkaya; *C*. Kobari, Narikela; *Sin*. Polgaha; *Bur*. Ungbin.

Codiaeum variegatum L.
E. Garden croton; *B*. Patabahar; *M*. Cera; *T*. & *Sin*. Croton.

Coffea arabica L.
E. Coffe; *B*. Kafi; *H*. Kahwa; *M*. Kappi, Bunnu; *T*. Kaddumallikal, Kapi; *Te*. & *C*. Kapi; *Sin*. Kopee.

Coix lachryma-jobi L.
E. Job's tears; *S*. Gojivha; *B*. Kalo-kunch; *H*. Sankru; *A*. Kaurmoni; *O*. Garagada; *P*. Kala-kunch; G. Kasai; *Bom*. Kassaibija; *Mar*. Ranjon dhala; *M*. Catri, Conda; *T*. Kattu kundumani; *Sin*. Karibu; *Bur*. Kycikphun.

Colchicum luteum Baker.
E. Autumn crocus, Meadow saffron; *S*. Hiranyatutha; *H*. Hirantutiya; *U*. Suranjanetalkh.

Coldenia procumbens L.
S. Tripakshi; *B*. & *H*. Tirupunkhi; *G*. Basriookharad; *Bom*. Tripakshi; *Mar*. Tripunkhi; *T*. Sirupadi; *Te*. Hamapadi.

Colebrookea oppositifolia Sm.
H. Binda, Bindu; *O*. Bosiki; *Bom*. Bahmani, Dasari; *P*. Basuti.

Coleus aromaticus Benth.
S. Pashanabhedi; *B*. Patharchur; *H*. Pathorchur; *Bom*. Owa, Pathorchur; *Mar*. Pathurchur.

Colocasia antiquorum Schott. = *C. esculenta* Schott.
E. Arum, Taro; *S*. Kachchi; *B*. & *A*. Kochu; *H*. Kachalu; *O*. Saru; *P*. Alu, Kachalu; *Bom*. Kachualu, Terem; *Mar*. Kasalu; *M*. Chempu; *T*. Samakilangu; *Te*. Chema; *Sin*. Gahala; *Bur*. Mahuyapein.

Commelina benghalensis L.
E. Day flower; *S.* Kanchata; *B.* Kanshira, Dholapata; *H.* Kankauoa, Kanchara; *A.* Konasimolu; *O.* Kansiri; *P.* Kanna; *G.* Mhotunshushmuliyun; *Mar.* Kena. *T.* Kanangakarai; *Te.* Nirukassuvu; *C.* Hittagani.

Commelina obliqua Ham.
B. Jatakanshira; *H.* Kanjuna, Kana.

Convolvulus arvensis L.
E. Bindweed; *S.* Prosarani; *B.* Gandal; *H.* Beri, Harinpadi; *G.* Veladi; *Mar.* Chandvel; *T.* Hiranpaddi.

Corchorus capsularis L.
E. Jute; *S.* Kalasaka; *B.* Desi-pat; *H.* Narcha; *Bom.* Chouchen; *Mar.* Chaunchan.

Corchorus olitorius L.
E. Jute; *S.* Nadika, Singgika; *B.* Pat; *H.* Koshta, Pata; *O.* Joto; *P.* Banphal; *Bom.* & *Mar.* Motichunch; *T.* Peratti; *Te.* Parinta.

Cordia myxa L.=*C. dichotoma* Forst. f.
E. Indian cherry; *S.* Bhutadruma; *B.* Bohari; *H.* Lasora, Bhairala; *U.* Lasora; *O.* Gondi; *G.* Gundomoto; *Bom.* & *Mar.* Bhokara, Bargund; *M.* Karati, Viri; *T.* Naruvili; *Te.* Nakkera, Virigi; *C.* Challe; *Sin.* Lotu; *Bur.* Thanat.

Cordia sebestena L.
E. Sebesten plum; *H.* Bhokar.

Coriandrum sativum L.
E. Coriander; *S.* Dhaniyaka; *B.* Dhoney; *H.* Dhania; *U.* Dhania; *G.* Dhane; *Bom.* Dhanya, Kothamira; *Mar.* Dhanya, Kothimbir; *M.* & *T.* Kottamalli; *Te.* Dhaniyalu, Kotimiri; *C.* Havija, Kotambari; *Sin.* Kotthamallie; *Bur.* Naunau.

Corypha umbraculifera L.
E. Talipot palm, Fan palm; *S.* Sritala, Tali; *B.* Tali; *Mar.* Bajarbattu, Tali; *M.* Talippana; *T.* Talipanai; *Te.* Sritalamu; *C.* Sritali, Baini; *Sin.* Tala; *Bur.* Pebin.

Costus speceosus Smith
S. Kustha; *B.* & *H.* Keu, Kust; *O.* Khudo; *G.* Pokaramula; *Bom.* Kemuka; *Mar.* Pushkarmula, Pinnga; *M.* Anappu, Pushkaramulam; *T.* Kuttam; *Te.* Kushthamu; *C.* Chikke, Pushkaramula; *Sin.* Tebu; *Bur.* Patangtoungwae.

Crataeva religiosa Forst. = *C. nurvala* Buch.—Ham.
E. Caper tree; *S.* Ajapa; *B.* & *A.* Barun; *H.* & *U.* Barna; *O.* Baruna; *P.* Barna; *G.* Varno; *Bom.* Vayavarna, Kumla; *Mar.* Wayawarna; *M.* Nirmathalam; *T.* Mavalingam; *Te.* Vulemeri; *C.* Mavilinga; *Sin.* Lunuwarana; *Bur.* Kadat.

Cressa cratica L.
S. Rudantika, Sanjivani; *H.* Lana; *U.* Rudanti; *Bom.* Khardi; *Mar.* Rudanti, Kharvi; *Te.* Uppusanga.

Crescentia cujete L.
E. Calabash tree; *T.* Tiruvottukkay; *C.* Sokeburde.

Crinum asiaticum L.
S. Srikhanda, Vishari; *B.* Barokanur; *H.* Chindar, Kanwal; *U.* Nagadauna; *O.* Arisa; *G.* Nagdamani; *Bom.* Nagdown; *Mar.* Nagdauna; *M.* Polathali; *T.* Vishamungi; *Te.* & *C.* Vishamungali; *Sin.* Tolabo; *Bur.* Koyangi.

Crinum latifolium L.
S. Chakrangi, Vrishakarni; *B.* Sukhadarsan; *H.* Sukhdarsan; *Bom.* Gadambikanda; *T.* Vishamungil; *Sin.* Godamanil.

Crocus sativus L.
E. Saffron; *B.* & *A.* Jafran; *H.* Zafran; *G.* & *Mar.* Keshar; *T.* Kungumapu; *Te.* Kunkumapave.

Crossandra undulaefolia Salisb.
M. Mannakhurinni; *Te.* Gobbi; *C.* Abboliga.

Crotalaria juncea L.
E. Sunn hemp; *S.* Shana; *B.* Shone; *H.* San; *A.* Shon; *O.* Chhanapata; *G.* San, Suna; *Bom.* Santag; *Mar.* Khulkhula; *M.* Thanthalakotti; *T.* Sanappai; *Te.* Jannamu; *C.* Sanabu; *Sin.* Hauna; *Bur.* Paikpiven.

Crotalaria retusa L.
E. Rattlewort; *S.* Shanarghandika; *B.* Atasi; *H.* Jhunjhunia; *A.* Ghantakarna; *O.* Junka; *P.* Jhanjhanian; *G.* Ghughra; *Bom.* & *Mar.* Ghagri; *M.* Thanthalakotti; *Te.* Pottigilligichcha; *Sin.* Kaha-andana-hiriya.

Croton sperciflorum Merr. = *C. bonplandianum* Baill.
B. Ban-tulasi.

Croton tiglium L.
E. Croton-oil plant, Purging croton; *S.* Jayapala, Nepala; *B.* & *A.* Joypal; *H.* Jamalgota; *O.* Joyopalo, Baksa; *G.* Jamal goet; *Bom.* Jaipa; *Mar.* Jepal, Jeyapal; *M.* & *T.* Nirvalam; *Te.* Nepalamu; *C.* Japala, Nepala; *Sin.* Jayapala; *Bur.* Kanako.

Cryptocoryne ciliata Fisch.
B. Kerali; *T.* Nattativadayam; *Te.* Nattativasa.

Cryptolepis buchanamia Roem. & Schult.
H Karanta; *O.* Gopikonirio; *M.* Kalipalvalli; *Te.* Gurugupalatege.

Cryptostegia grandiflora R. Br.
Mar. Vilayativakhandi; *M.* Pala; *T.* Palai.

Cucumis melo L.
E. Melon; *S.* Kharbuja; *B.* Kharmuj; *H.* Kakri, Kharbuza; *U.* Kharbuzah; *A.* Bangi; *O.* Kharbuja; *G.* Tarbuch; *Mar.* Kharbuj; *M.* Thannimathai; *T.* Mulam, Vellarikai; *Te.* Peddakai; *C.* Kekkarikeballi, Ibbudtu.

Cucumis sativus L.
E. Cucumber; *S.* Trapusha, Sushitala; *B.* Sasha; *H.* Khira; *A.* Tianh; *O.* Kakudi; *G.* Kakri; *Mar.* & *P.* Khira; *M.* Mullenvellarai; *T.* Mulluvellari; *Te.* Dozakaya; *C.* Santekayi; *Sin.* Pipina; *Bur.* Thakwa.

Cucurbita maxima Duchesne.
E. Sweet gourd; *S.* Kushmanda; *B.* Mitha-kumra; *H.* Komara, Mitha-kaddu; *A.* Rongalau; *O.* Mitha-kokharu; *P.* Halwa-kaddu; *Bom.* Laldudiya; *Mar.* Kala bhopala; *M.* Mathangai; *T.* Pushanikai; *Te.* Gummadi; *C.* & *Sin.* Kumbala; *Bur.* Shwepayon.

Cucurbita pepo DC.
E. Pumpkin; *S.* Karkaru; *B.* Kumra; *H.* Safed kumra; *U.* Luki; *G.* Dudia; *Bom.* Kaula; *Mar.* Kohala; *Te.* Pottigummadi; *C.* Kumbala.

Cuminum cyminum L.
E. Point caraway; *S.* Jiraka; *B.* Jira; *H.* Safed zira; *U.* Jirah; *G.* Jiru; *Mar.* Jiregire; *M.* Jirakam; *T.* Shiragam; *Te.* Jiraka; *Sin.* Duru; *Bur.* Ziya.

Curculigo orchioides Gaertn.
S. Musali; *B.* Talamuli; *H.* Mushali; *U.* Musali; *O.* Talomuli; *Bom.* Mushali; *Mar.* Kalimusali; *M.* Nelappanakizhanna; *T.* Nilapanni; *Te.* Nelatatigaddalu; *C.* Nelatatigadde; *Sin.* Heen-bin-tal.

Curcuma amada Roxb.
E. Mango ginger; *S.* Amragandha; *B.* & *A.* Amada; *H.* Am-haldi; *U.* Ambahaladi; *O.* Amba kassia ada; *G.* Amba-haldar; *Bom.* Kajuragauri; *Mar.* Ambe-halad; *Te.* Mamidiallam; *C.* Ambaholdi.

Curcuma longa L.
E. Turmeric; *S.* Haridra; *B.* Halud; *H.* & *P.* Haldi; *U.* Haladi; *A.* Halodhi; *G.* Halad; *Mar.* Halede; *M.* Kuva; *T.* Manjal; *Te.* Pasupu; *C.* Arishina; *Sin.* Kaha; *Bur.* Hsanwen, Sanae.

Curcuma zedoaria Roscoe.
E. Indian arrowroot; *S.* Kachura; *B.* Sathi, Ekangi; *H.* & *U.* Kachura; *G.* Kachuri; *Bom.* Kachura; *Mar.* Kachari; *M.* Kachcholam; *T.* Pulankilhangu; *Te.* Kachoram; *C.* Kachora; *Sin.* Harankaha; *Bur.* Thanuwen.

Cuscuta reflexa Roxb.
E. Dodder; *S.* Amaravela; *B.* Swarnalata, Alokelata; *H.* Akashbel; *U.* Imalbel; *A.* Akashilota; *O.* Nirmuli; *P.* Amarbel; *G.* Akaswel; *Mar.* Amarvel; *T.* Kodiyagundal; *Te.* Lanjasavaramu; *Sin.* Agamulaneti-wel.

Cyanotis axillaris Schult. f.
H. Baganulla, Soltraj; *Bom.* Itsaka; *T.* Niriopalti; *Te.* Golagandhi.

Cycas circinalis Roxb.
E. Cycas; *B.* Biletikhejur; *M.* Toddamaram; *T.* Kama, Payindu; *Te.* Ranaguvva; *Sin.* Mahamadu.

Cynodon dactylon Pers.
E. Doob grass, Bermuda grass; *S.* Durva; *B.* Durba; *H. & P.* Doob; *U.* Dub; *A.* Duboribon; *O.* Dubaghasa; *G.* Durva; *Mar.* Harali; *M. & T.* Arugampullu; *Te.* Gericha gaddi; *C.* Garikehulla

Cynoglossum lanceolatum Forsk.
Sin. Bu-katu-henda.

Cyperus rotundus L.
E. Common sedge; *S.* Mustaka, Gundra; *B. & H.* Mutha; *A.* Motha; *O.* Mutha ghasa; *G.* Barik-motha; *Bom.* Barikmoth; *Mar. & P.* Nagar-motha; *M.* Kora; *T.* Korai; *Te.* Pura gaddi; *C.* Tungegadde; *Sin.* Kalanduru.

Cyperus tegetum L.
E. Mat grass; *B.* Madurkati.

Daemia extensa R. Br. = *Pergularia daemia* Chois.
S. Uttarvaruni; *B.* Dudhilata; *H.* Sadowani, Utran; *O.* Utturuti; *G.* Amaradudheli; *Bom.* Utarni; *Mar.* Utarana; *M.* Veliparutti; *T.* Uttamani; *Te.* Guruti, Juttupaku; *C.* Belihatti.

Dalbergia latifolia Roxb.
E. Indian rosewood; *S.* Shishapa; *B.* Sitsal; *H.* Vilayati shisham, Sitsal; *O.* Pahadi sisu; *P. & G.* Shisham; *Bom.* Shisar, Tivas; *Mar.* Sissu; *M.* Karithi; *T.* Itti; *Te.* Jittegi; *C.* Todagatti.

Dalbergia sissoo Roxb.
E. Sisso; *S.* Aguru, Pichhila; *B.* Sisu; *H. & P.* Shisham; *A.* Shishoo; *O.* Sisu; *G.* Sissam; *Bom.* Sissu; *Mar.* Sisavi; *M.* Veeti; *T.* Nukku, Pichai; *Te.* Sissu; *C.* Birade.

Datura fastuosa L. = *D. metel* L.
E. Thorn-apple; *S.* Dhutura, Unmattaka; *B.* Dhutura; *H. & U.* Dhutura; *A.* Dhotura; *O.* Dudura; *P.* Dattura; *G.* Dhatoora; *Mar.* Dhotra; *M.* Ummam; *T.* Umathai; *Te.* Ummatha; *C.* Dattura, Ummatta.

Datura stramonium L.
E. Black datura; *S.* Krishnadhustura, Unmattavriksha; *B.* Kalo-dhutura; *H. & G.* Kaladhatura; *A.* Dhotura; *O.* Jambunodo; *Mar.* Kaladhotra; *M.* Ummata; *T.* Umattai; *Te.* Ummetta; *C.* Ummatta; *Sin.* Kaluattana; *Bur.* Pa-dain-game.

Daucus carota L.
E. Carrot; *S.* Gajara; *B.* Gajar; *H. & U.* Gazar; *G. & Bom.* Gajar; *Mar.* Gazara; *T.* Gajjarak kilangu; *Te.* Gajjaragedda Pitakanda; *C.* Gajjari.

Deeringia celosioides R. Br. = *D. amaranthoides* Merr.
B. Gholemouni; *H.* Latman.

Dendrocalamus strictus Nees.
E. Solid bamboo; *S.* Venu; *B.* Karail; *H.* Bans, Kopar; *O.* Sanc baunso; *G.* Nakorvans; *Mar.* Ban Velu; *M.* Arinkantam, Karinkana *T.* Karanai, Mungil; *Te.* Veduru *C.* Kiribidiru; *Bur.* Myinwa.

Dentella repens Forst.
B. Bhuipat.

Derris scandens Benth.
E. Hog creeper; *B.* Noalata; *H.* Gonj; *O.* Kamocho; *P.* Gun *M.* Nulavalli; *T.* Anaikkat Tirani; *Te.* Chiratalabodi, Surul *Sin.* Kalawel; *Bur.* Mukyoungnway

Desmodium gangeticum DC.
S. Shaliparni; *B.* Shalpani; *H.* Salpan; *U.* Shalwan; *O.* Kurs pani; *P.* Shalpurhi; *G.* Salva *Bom. & Mar.* Salparni; *M.* Pulla *T.* Pulladi; *Te.* Gitanaram; Murelehonne.

Desmodium gyrans DC. = *D. motori* Merr.
E. Telegraph plant; *B. & A.* Gor chand, Boncharal; *H.* Ban-chal; Gora chanda; *P.* Pauda tar; *S* Chanchala.

Dianthus barbatum L.
E. Sweet-William.

Dianthus caryophyllus L.
E. Carnation.

Dianthus chinensis L.
E. Pink.

Dicliptera roxburghiana Nees.
P. Kirch, Semni.

Digera arvensis Forsk. = *D. muricata* Mart.
S. Manjarika; *B*. Latamouri; *H*. Latmahuria; *P*. Tartara; *G*. Kanajaro; *Bom*. Getan; *Mar*. Titana; *Te*. Chanchalikura.

Digitalis purpurea L.
E. Purple foxglove.

Dipterocarpus turbinatus Gaertn. f.
E. Gurjan balsam; *B*. Garjan; *A*. Kuralsal; *G*. Gurjun; *C*. Guge; *Sin*. Hora; *Bur*. Inbo.

Dischidia rafflesiana R. Br.
H. Bandikuri.

Dodonaea viscosa Jacq.
H. Aliar, Sonatta; *P*. Banmendu; *Bom*. Bandari; *Mar*. Luchmi; *M*. Virali; *T*. Verali; *Te*. Bandaru; *C*. Bandare; *Sin*. Etaverella.

Dolichandrone spathacea Schum.
M. Nirpoonalyam; *T*. Attukombudi, Kanabillai; *Sin*. Deyadanga; *Bur*. Thakutma.

Dolichos lablab L.
E. Country bean; *S*. Shimbi; *B*. Shim; *H*. Sem; *A*. Urohi; *O*. Sima; *P*. Katjang; *G*. Avri; *Bom*. Pauli, Valpapri; *Mar*. Pavata; *M*. Simbapayaru; *T*. Avarai; *Te*. Chikkudi; *C*. Avre; *Sin*. Irivija; *Bur*. Pai.

Dopatrium junceum Ham.
Bur. Bin-sawan.

Dracaena spicata Roxb.
H. Hiradukhi; *T*. Kandamiruga, Ratham; *Te*. Khadgarviru; *C*. Khadgarmurga, Netturu.

Dregea volubilis Benth. = *Marsdenia volubilis* Cooke.
S. Hemavalli; *B*. Titakunga; *H*. Nakchhikni; *O*. Madhumaloti; *G*. Dodi; *Bom*. Dodhi; *Mar*. Ambri; *M*. Vattakkakkakkoti; *T*. Sivandi; *Te*. Palakura, Dudipala; *C*. Dugdhike; *Sin*. Kirianguna; *Bur*. Gwaytankpin.

Duabanga sonneratioides Ham.
B. Bandormulla.

Duranta plumieri Jacq.
B. Belatimehedi, Duranta; *H*. & *P*. Nilkanta; *A*. Jeora-goch; *O*. Benjuati; *Mar*. Duranta.

Dysophylla verticillata Benth.
B. Panikula; *Sin*. Hemanilla.

Ecbotium linneanum Kurz. = *E. viridis* Alston.
B. Nilkanta; *H*. & *P*. Udajati; *O*. Nilakantha; *Mar*. Ranaboli; *M*. Kuranta; *T*. Nilambari; *Te*. Nakkatoka.

Echinops echinatus Roxb.
S. Utkantaka; *H*. Gokhru, Utakanta; *U*. Untkatara; *G*. Utkanto; *Mar*. Utanti, Utkantara.

Eclipta alba Hessk. = *E. prostrata* L.
S. Bhringaraja, Kesharaja; *B*. Kesutti, Kesaraj; *H*. Safed bhangra; *U*. Bhangra; *A*. Kehoraji; *O*. Keshdura; *G*. Bhangra; *Mar*. Maka; *M*. Kaithonni; *T*. Kaikeshi, Kayyanyam; *Te*. Guntagalijeru, Galagara; *C*. Garaga; *Sin*. Kikirindi.

Ehretia acuminata R. Br. = *E. serrata* Roxb.
E. Heliotrope tree; *B*. Kulaja; *H*. Panyan, Chamror.

Eicchornia crassipes Solms.
E. Water hyacinth; *B*. Kachuripana, Kachuri.

Elaeocarpus ganitrus Roxb. = *E. sphaericus* K. Schum.
E. Bead tree; *S*. Sivapriya, Rudraksha; *B*. Rudraksha; *H*. Rudrak; *O*. Rudrakhyo; *Mar*. Rudraksh; *M*. Rudraksham; *T*. Akkam; *Te*. Rudrachallu; *C*. Rudraksha.

Elephantopus scaber L.
E. Elephant's foot; *S*. Gojivha; *B*. Hostipada; *H*. Gobhi; *O*. Gobi; *P*. Gaozban; *G*. Bhopa thari;

Bom. Hastipata; *Mar.* Hastipad; *M.* & *T.* Anachuvadi; *Te.* Hastikasaka; *Sin.* Et-adi; *Bur.* Katoopin.

Eleusine coracana Gaértn.
E. Ragi, African millet; *S.* Rajika; *B.* Marua; *H.* Makra; *O.* Mandia; *P.* Kodra; *G.* Navto; *Bom.* & *Mar.* Nachani; *M.* Panjappullu; *T.* Kolvaraku; *Te.* & *C.* Ragi; *Sin.* Kurakkan.

Eletaria cardamomum Maton.
E. Cardamon; *B.* Choto alach; *H.* Chota elachi.

Emilia sonchifolia DC.
B. Sadimodi; *H.* Sudhimude; *Bom.* Sadhimandhi; *M.* Mulshevi; *C.* Ihikivi; *Sin.* Kadupara.

Enhydra fluctuans Lour.
E. Water cress, Marsh herb; *S.* Hilamochika; *B.* Hingcha, Halencha; *H.* Haruch; *A.* Helachisak; *O.* Hidimichi, Pani-saga; *Mar.* Harkuch.

Entada scandens Benth. = *E. phaseoloidus* Merr.
E. Mackay bean; *B.* Gila; *H.* Garbi; *A.* Ghila; *O.* Giridi; *P.* Kastorikaman; *G.* Suvali-amli; *Bom.* Garambi, Garbi; *Mar.* Garbi; *M.* Kakkuvally; *T.* Chillu; *Te.* Gillatigai; *C.* Hallekavi; *Sin.* Puswel; *Bur.* Gonnyin.

Enterolobium saman Prain. = *Samanea saman* Merr.
E. Rain tree; *B.* Belati-sirish; *A.* Sirishgoch; *O.* Bona sirisha; *Mar.* Saman; *M* Urakkam-thoongimaram.

Eragrostis cynosuroides Beauv.
S. Kusha; *B.* Kush; *H.* Duv; *P.* Kusha; *Mar.* Darbha; *Te.* Kusha darbha, Durpa.

Eriobotrya japonica Lindl.
E. Loquat; *B.* Loket; *H.* Lokat; *U.* Lakhota; *T.* Ilakotta, Nakotta; *C.* Lakote.

Eriodendron anfructuosum DC. = *Ceiba pentandra* Gaertn.
E. White cotton tree; *B.* Shetsimul; *H.* Kapok, Hattian; *U.* Sambal; *Mar.* Pandhari, Shamicula; *M.* Illavi, Pula; *T.* Ilavam, Ilaku; *Te.* Burga; *C.* Apurani, Bilibu-raga; *Sin.* Imbul; *Bur.* Thinbawle.

Erythrina indica Lamk. = *E. variegata* L.
E. Coral tree; *S.* Parijata, Mandara; *B.* Palitamadar; *H.* Panjira; *A.* Modar; *O.* Paldhua; *P.* Pangra; *G.* Panarawas; *Mar.* Pangara; *M.* Kulumurikku; *T.* Murukku; *Te.* Baridamu, Baditachettu; *C.* Halivana, Hongara; *Sin.* Erabadu; *Bur.* Pinle-kattit.

Eucalyptus globosus Labil.
E. Eucalyptus tree; *T.* Karpuram; *Te.* Karpuramu; *C.* Karpura.

Eugenia caryophyllaea Wight. = *Syzygium aromaticum* Merr. & Perry.
E. Clove; *B.* Lavanga; *H.* & *A.* Laung; *O.* Labanga; *G.* Lavang; *Mar.* Lawang; *M.* Grampu.

Eugenia jambolana Lamk. = *Syzygium cumini* Skeels.
E. Jambu, Black plum; *S.* Jambu; *B.* Kalo-jam; *H.* & *P.* Jamun; *U.* Jaman; *A.* Jamu; *O.* Jamukoli; *G.* & *Bom.* Jamdudo; *Mar.* Jambul; *M.* Naval; *T.* Arugadam, Naval; *Te.* Jambuvu, Neredu; *C.* Neralu; *Sin.* Mahadan; *Bur.* Thabyebyu.

Eugenia jambos L. = *Syzygium jambos* Alston.
E. Rose apple; *S.* Jambu; *B.* Golap-jam; *H.* & *Bom.* Gulab jamun; *U.* Gulabjaman; *A.* Golapijamu; *O.* Golap jamu; *Mar.* Gulab jamb; *M.* Paninirchampa; *T.* Naval; *Te.* Neredu; *C.* Jamba; *Sin.* Jambu.

Eugenia malaccense L. = *Syzygium malacense* Merr. & Perry
E. Malay apple; *B.* Jamrool; *H.* Malaya-jaman; *A.* Pani-jamu; *P.* Malay ka seb; *Mar.* Safed jamb.

Eupatorium ayapana Vent.
B. & *H.* Ayapan; *G.* Alleppa; *Mar.* Ayapana; *T.* & *Te.* Ayapani.

Euphorbia antiquorum L.
E. Cactus; *S.* Vajrakantaka; *B.* Tesiramonsa, Bajbaran; *H.* & *P.* Tidhara-sehud; *U.* Zakum; *O.* Dokanasiju; *G.* Tandhari;

Mar. Chaudhari niwdung; *M.* Chathirakkalli; *T.* Shadraikalli; *Te.* Bonthakali; *C.* Bontekalli; *Sin.* Daluk; *Bur.* Pyathal.

Euphorbia microphylla Heyne.
B. Choto-karni; *G.* & *Mar.* Dudhi.

Euphorbia neriifolia L.
S. Snuhi; *B.* Monshasij, Monsa; *H.* Sij; *A.* Siju; *O.* Patara siju; *P.* Gangiehu; *G.* Thor; *Bom.* Minguta, Thor; *Mar.* Nevagunda; *M.* & *T.* Illakkalli; *Te.* Akujemudu; *C.* Yalekalli; *Bur.* Shasoung.

Euphorbia pilulifera L. = *E. hirta* L.
S. Pushitoa; *B.* Baro-karni; *H.* Dudhia; *Bom.* Nayetti; *Mar.* Dudnali; *M.* Nelapalai; *T.* Pallavi; *Te.* Nanabala; *Sin.* Bu-dada-kiriya.

Euphorbia pulcherrima Willd. = *Poinsettia pulcherrima* R. Grah.
E. Poinsettia; *B.* Lalpata; *A.* Lalpat; *O.* Panchutia; *P.* Lal-patti; *T.* Mayilkunni.

Euphorbia thymifolia Burm.
S. Laghudugdhika; *B.* Shet-karni; *H.* Chhoti-dudhia; *P.* Baradodak; *G.* Nahanidudheli; *Bom.* Nayata; *Mar.* Lahandudhi; *T.* Sittrapaladi; *Te.* Reddivarimanubala; *Sin.* Bindadakuriya.

Euphorbia tirucalli L.
E. Milk hedge; *S.* Trikuntaka; *B.* Lanka-sij; *H.* Sehund, Konpal; *U.* Zakum; *O.* Lonka siju; *G.* Dandaliothora; *Bom.* Thora; *Mar.* Nevli; *M.* Kolkalli; *T.* Tirukkalli, Kombukalli; *Te.* Chemudu; *C.* Kodukalli; *Sin.* Navahandi; *Bur.* Shashoungleknyo.

Euryale ferox Salisb.
E. Foxnut; *S.* Kakhana; *B.* Makhna, Kanta-padma; *H.* & *U.* Makhana; *A.* Nikori; *O.* Kanta padma; *P.* Jewar; *Mar.* Padma kant; *Te.* Mellunipadmanu.

Evolvulus alsinoides Wall.
S. Vishnukranta; *H.* Shyamakranta; *O.* Bichamalia; *P.* Shankholi; *G.* Jhinkiphudardi; *Bom.* Shankhavalli; *Mar.* Vishnukrant; *M.* Vishnukanthi; *T.* Vishnukirandi; *Te.* Vishnukranthi; *Sin.* Vishnukranta.

Evolvulus nummularius L.
B. Bhui ankra.

Exacum tetragonum Roxb.
B. Kuchuri; *H.* Titakhana.

Excoecaria agallocha L.
E. Blinding tree, River poison; *S.* Agaru; *B.* Geo; *H.* Gwa; *O.* Ghona; *Bom.* Geva; *Mar.* Surund; *M.* Katappala; *T.* Agadil, Tillai; *Te.* Chilla, Tellachettu; *Sin.* Telakiniya; *Bur.* Kayan.

Feronia elephantum Corr. = *F. limonia* Swingle
E. Elephant apple; *S.* Kavittha; *B.* & *A.* Kathbel; *H.* & *U.* Kaitha; *O.* Kaintha; *P.* Kait; *G.* Kotha; *Bom.* Kavit; *Mar.* Kawath; *M.* Blanka; *T.* Velamarum; *Te.* Velanga; *Sin.* Diwul; *Bur.* Thibin.

Ferula asafoetida Boiss.
E. Asafoetida; *S.* Hingu; *B.* & *H.* Hing; *U.* Anjadana; *O.* Hengu; *G.* Hing; *Bom.* Hingra; *M.* Kayam; *T.* Perungayam; *Te.* Inguva.

Ficus benghalensis L.
E. Banyan; *S.* Vitapi, Vata; *B.* Bot; *H.* & *P.* Barh; *U.* Bargoda; *A.* Borgoch; *O.* Bara; *G.* & *Mar.* Wad; *M.* Vatam; *T.* Vadam, Ala; *Te.* Vitapi; *C.* Ala, Vata; *Sin.* Mahanuga; *Bur.* Pyinyoung.

Ficus cunea Ham.
E. Fig; *S.* Kharapatra; *B.* Dumur; *H.* Khenan; *O.* Godima; *Mar.* Porodumer; *M.* Perina; *T.* Taragadi; *Te.* Bommamatti; *Bur.* Thadut.

Ficus glomerata Roxb.
E. Fig; *S.* Udumbara; *B.* Jagyadumur; *H.* & *U.* Gular; *A.* Dimoru; *O.* Dimuri; *P.* Anjir, Kathgular; *G.* Umbaro; *Bom.* Umbar; *Mar.* Umbar; *M.* Andumbaram; *T.* Anjimaram; *Te.* Bodda; *C.* Rumadi; *Sin.* Atteeka; *Bur.* Thapan.

Ficus hispida L. f.
S. Kakodumbarika; *B.* Kak-dumur; *H.* Kagsha, Gobla; *O.* Bhaidimiri; *P.* Daduri, Degar; *G.* Janglianjir;

Bom. Dumbar; *Mar.* Bhokada, Kharoti; *M.* Peyatti; *T.* Ottannalam; *Te.* Kukkabodda; *C.* Kadatti; *Sin.* Kotadimbula; *Bur.* Kadot.

Ficus infectoria Roxb.
S. Parkati; *B.* Pakur; *H.* Pakar; *U.* Pakharia; *O.* Pakodo; *P.* Pakhar; *G.* Pepri; *Bom.* Pakri; *Mar.* Pakari; *M.* Bakri; *T.* Jovi, Kallal; *Te.* Jovvi; *C.* Basari; *Sin.* Kiripella; *Bur.* Nyoungchin.

Ficus religiosa L.
E. Peepal, Bo-tree; *S.* Asvatha, Bodhidruma; *B.* Aswatha; *H.* & *U.* Pipal; *A.* Anhot; *O.* Ashwatha; *P.* Pipal, Bhor; *G.* Pipul; *Bom.* Pipal, Jari; *Mar.* Pimpal; *M.* Arayalu; *T.* Arasu; *Te.* Aswatham; *C.* Aswatha, Aralimara; *Sin.* Bo-gaha; *Bur.* Nyoungbaude.

Fimbristylis junciformis Kunth.
B. Bindi-muthi.

Finlaysonia obovata Wall. = *F. maritima* Backer
B. Dudhi-lata.

Fleurya interrupta Gaud.
E. Nettle; *B.* Lal-bichuti; *H.* Surat; *A.* Sharuchorat, Sirnat; *O.* Bichati; *M.* Anachoriyanam; *T.* Ottapilavu, Ottarbata; *Sin.* Mausa; *Bur.* Pheytakyee.

Foeniculum vulgare Gaertn.
E. Fennel, Anise; *S.* Madhurika; *B.* Mouri; *H.* & *P.* Saunf; *U.* Sonf; *A.* Guamoori; *O.* Pan mohuri; *G.* Wariari; *Bom.* Barishopa; *Mar.* Badisep; *T.* Sohikirai; *Te.* Peddajilakaramu; *C.* Badisopu.

Fragaria nilgherrensis Schldl.
E. Strawberry.

Gangrea maderaspatana Poir.
B. Namuti; *H.* Mustaru; *U.* Afsantin; *G.* Jhinkimundi; *Mar.* & *T.* Mashipatri; *M.* Nelampala; *Te.* Save; *C.* Dovana; *Sin.* Velkolondu.

Garcinia cowa Roxb.
E. Cowa tree; *B.* Kaglichu, Kau; *H.* Cowa; *Bur.* Madow.

Garcinia mangostana L.
E. Mangosteen; *B.* & *H.* Mangustan; *O.* Sitambu; *G.* Mangosteen; *Mar.* Mangustan; *M.* Sulampuli; *T.* Sulambuli; *Sin.* Mangus; *Bur.* Mengkop.

Gardenia florida L. = *G. jasminoides* Ellis.
E. Cape jasmine; *S.* Gandharaja; *B.* Gandharaj; *H.* Papra; *A.* Togor; *O.* Sugandharaj; *G.* Dikamali; *Mar.* Gandhraj; *T.* Kambil; *Te.* & *C.* Adavibkki; *Sin.* Galis.

Gelonium multiflorum A. Juss.
B. Bon-naranga; *H.* Bannaringa; *Te.* Karujuggilam.

Geranium nepalense Sw.
E. Crane's bill; *H.* & *P.* Bhand, Bhanda.

Geranium ocellatum Camb.
H. Bhanda.

Globba bulbifera Roxb.
B. Kandha-puspa; *Te.* Kondapasupu.

Gloriosa superba L.
E. Glory lily; *S.* Agnisikha, Langulika; *B.* & *A.* Ulatchandal, Bisalanguli; *H.* Kaliari; *U.* Kulhar; *O.* Panchangulia; *P.* Kulhari; *G.* Khadyanag; *Bom.* & *Mar.* Karianag; *M.* Manthonni; *T.* Kalapaikilangu; *Te.* Agnishika; *C.* Agnisikhe; *Sin.* Niyangalla; *Bur.* Hseemee-touk.

Glycyrrhiza glabra L.
E. Liquorice; *S.* Madhuka; *B.* Jastimodhu; *H.* Jethimadh, Mulhatti; *P.* Muleti; *G.* Jethimadha; *Bom.* Jashtimadhu; *Mar.* Jesthamadha; *M.* Yashtimadhukam; *T.* & *Sin.* Atimaduram; *Te.* Atimadhuramu; *C.* Yasthimadhuka; *Bur.* Noekhiyu.

Glycosmis pentaphylla Corr.
E. Toothbrush plant; *S.* Ashvashakota; *B.* Ash-shaora; *H.* Bannimbu; *A.* Chauldhoa; *O.* Chauladhua; *Bom.* Kirmira; *M.* Panal; *T.* Kattukkonji, Anam; *Te.* Golugu; *C.* Guruvede; *Sin.* Dodampana; *Bur.* Obok, Tanshouk.

Gmelina arborea Roxb.
E. White teak; *S.* Gambhar; *B.* Gamari; *H.* Gam[illegible] Sewan; *A.* Gomari; *O.* Gombhari; *G.* Savan; *Bom.* Kashmari, Shewun; *Mar.* Gamar, Shiwan; *M.* Kumbili; *T.* [illegible]mil, Kumba[illegible] *Te.* Gumudu, [illegible]mari[illegible] [illegible]ashmiri, Kumule; *Sin.* Atdemmata; *Bur.* Ya-ma-nai.

Gnetum scandens Roxb.
O. Lolori; *Bom.* Kumbal, Umbli; *M.* Ula; *C.* Kodkamballi; *Bur.* Gyutnwa.

Gomphrena globosa L.
E. Globe amaranth, Bachelor's buttonhole; *B.* Gulmakamal; *H.* Gul-i-makhmal.

Gossypium herbaceum L.
E. Cotton; *S.* Karpasi; *B.* Kapas, Tula; *H.* Kapas; *A.* Kopah; *O.* Kapa; *P.* & *G.* Rui; *Bom.* Rui, Kapas; *Mar.* Kapus; *M.* Kuruparathy; *T.* Parathy; *Te.* Patti; *C.* Hatti, Arabi; *Bur.* Wah.

Gouania leptostachya DC.
U. Khanta; *C.* Shingarballi; *Bur.* Thayawnyonway.

Grewia asiatica L. = *G. subinaequalis* DC.
S. Purusha; *B.* Phalsa; *H.* Sukri; *U.* Phalasah; *O.* Pharosaholi; *P.* Phalsah, Pharnu; *G.* Phalsa; *Bom.* Phalasi; *Mar.* Phalsi; *M.* Chadicha; *T.* Tadachi; *Te.* Phutiki; *C.* Tadasala; *Sin,* Dowaniya.

Guazuma tomentosa Kunth.
E. Bastard cedar; *B.* Nepal-tunth; *O.* Debodaru; *M.* Rudraksham; *T.* Tengai, Tenbachai; *Te.* Udrikpatta; *C.* Rudrakshi, Bucha.

Guizotia abyssinica Cass.
E. Niger; *B.* Sarguja; *H.* Surguja, Kalatil; *G.* Kalatel; *Bom.* Kerani, Ramatila; *Mar.* Kalitil; *Te.* Valesulu, Vulisi.

Gynandropsis pentaphylla DC. = *G. gynandra* Briq.
E. Spider flower; *S.* Surjyavarta, Arkapuspika; *B.* Sada hurhure; *H.* Safaid hurhur; *A.* Bhutmula; *O.* Anasorisia; *P.* Hul-hul; *G.* Adiya-kharam; *Bom.* Mabli; *Mar.* Tilvan; *M.* Kathukatuku; *T.* Naikadugu; *Te.* Vaminta; *Sin.* We-la.

Gyrocarpus americana Jacq.
B. Zaitan.

Hamiltonia suaveolens Roxb.
P. Kantalu, Pudari; *Bom.* Didesa, Gidasawa.

Hardwickia pinnata Roxb.
B. Anjan; *Mar.* Anjana; *M.* Kiyavu; *T.* Acha; *Te.* Yepi; *C.* Enne.

Hedychium coronarium Koenig
B. Dulal champa.

Helianthus annuus L.
E. Sunflower; *S.* Adityabhakta; *B.* Surjyamukhi; *H.* & *P.* Surajmukhi; *U.* Surajamakkhi; *A.* Beliphul; *G.* Suryamukhi; *Bom.* Surajmaki; *Mar.* Suryaphul; *M.* & *T.* Suriyakanti; *Te.* Suriyakanta; *C.* Hottutirugana: *Sin.* Siriyakanthiya.

Helianthus tuberosus L.
E. Artichoke; *B.* Hatichoke; *H.* Atipich, Hathichak.

Helicteres isora L.
S. Mrigasingha; *B.* Antmora; *H.* Bhendu, Marosi; *U.* & *P.* Marophali; *O.* Orola; *G.* Murdasing; *Bom.* Kawun; *Mar.* Kewan, Muradsing; *M.* Valampiri; *T.* Valambui; *Te.* Gubalada, Kavanchi; *C.* Edamuri, Murudi; *Sin.* Zimiagaha; *Bur.* Thungeche.

Heliotropium indicum L.
E. Heliotrope; *S.* Hatisunada; *B.* Hatisura; *H.* Hattasura; *A.* Hatisur; *O.* Hatisunda; *P.* Unth-chara; *G.* Hathisundhana; *Bom.* Burundi; *Mar.* Bhurundi; *M.* Tekkada; *T.* Telkodduki; *Te.* Telumani; *Sin.* Dimibiya.

Heliotropium ovalifolium Forsk.
B. Nag-phuli; *Te.* Nagadanti.

Hemerocallis fulva L.
B. Gulnargis.

Hemidesmus indicus R. Br.
E. Indian sarsaparilla; *S.* Anantamula, Sugandhi; *B.* & *A.* Anantamul; *H.* Salsa; *O.*

Anantamula; *P.* Desi sarva; *G.* & *Mar.* Upalasari; *Bom.* Upasara; *Mar.* Anantmul; *M.* Narunari; *T.* Nannari; *Te.* & *C.* Sugandipala; *Sin.* Irimusu.

Heritiera minor Roxb.
E. Looking-glass tree; *B.* Sundri; *H.* Sundari; *M.* Mukuram; *T.* Chemuntiri, Conmundiri; *Te.* Adavibademu; *Sin.* Etuna.

Herpestis monnieria H. B. & K.
S. Brahmacharini; *B.* Brahmi; *H.* Barambhi, Safed chamni; *U.* Jalanim; *O.* Krishnaparni; *Bom.* Bama; *T.* Brame, Hirbrami; *Te.* Sambranichattu; *Sin.* Lumuvila.

Heterophragma adenophyllum Seems.
Bom. Pullung, Warras; *Mar.* Panlag, Waras; *Te.* Bondugu; *C.* Adwinuggi, Bechadi.

Hevea braziliensis Muell-Arg.
E. Para rubber.

Hewittia bicolor W. & A. = *H. sublobata* O. Kuntze.
H. Jarad kalmi; *Sin.* Waltrastavalu.

Hibiscus cannabinus L.
E. Madras hemp, Deccan hemp; *B.* Mestapat; *H.* Pātwa, Ambari; *O.* Kaunria; *P.* San-kukra; *Mar.* Ambadi; *M.* Kanjaru; *T.* Kachurai; *Te.* Gogu, Gonkura.

Hibiscus esculentus L. = *Abelmoschus esculentus* Moench.
E. Lady's-finger, Ram's horn; *S.* Gandhamula; *B.* Dhenras; *H.* Bhindi, Ramturai; *U.* Bhendi; *A.* & *O.* Bhendi; *G.* Bhinda; *Bom.* Bhenda; *M.* Vanta, Vendakka; *T.* Vendi, Vendikai; *Te.* Benda; *C.* Bende; *Sin.* Bandakka.

Hibiscus mutabilis L.
E. Changeable rose; *B.* & *A.* Sthalpadma; *H.* & *U.* Guliajaib; *O.* Thalapadma; *G.* Upalsari; *P.* Gul-i-ajaib; *Mar.* Gulabi bhendi; *M.* Chinapparatti; *T.* Sembarattai; *C.* Suryakanti.

Hibiscus rosa-sinensis L.
E. China-rose, Shoe flower; *S.* Padmacharini; *B.* Jaba; *H.* Gurhal, Jasum; *A.* Joba; *O.* Mandara; *P.* Gurhal; *G.* Jasunt; *Bom.* Jasavanda; *Mar.* Jaswand; *M.* Chemparathy; *T.* Sambathochedi; *Te.* Dasani; *C.* Dasavala, Nadeya; *Sin.* Sapatthumal; *Bur.* Koungyan.

Hibiscus sabdariffa L.
E. Rozelle; *B.* Mesta; *H.* Kudrum, Lal-patwa; *A.* Meseka-tenga; *O.* Khata kaunria; *Bom.* & *Mar.* Lal-ambadi; *M.* Pulichi; *T.* Simaikkasuru; *Te.* Shimagonguru; *Sin.* Ratabilincha; *Bur.* Chinbaung.

Hibiscus tiliaceus L.
E. Tree mallow; *B.* Bhola; *H.* Bola; *O.* Bariya; *M.* & *T.* Nirparutti; *Sin.* Belipatta; *Bur.* Thengben.

Hibiscus vitifolius L.
B. Bonkapas.

Hodgsonia heteroclita Hook. f.
B. Gulur; *H.* Til-lau.

Holarrhena antidysenterica Wall.
E. Easter tree; *S.* Girimallika, Kutaja; *B.* Kurchi; *H.* Karchi; *A.* Dudkhori; *O.* Pita korua; *P.* Kawar; *G.* Indrajavanu; *Bom.* Dolakura; *Mar.* Kuda; *M.* Kodakappala; *T.* Kulappalai, Veppalai; *Te.* Amkudu, Kodaga; *C.* Kudsalu, Korchu; *Bur.* Let-top-gyee.

Holmskioldia sanguinea Retz.
H. Kapni.

Holoptelea integrifolia Planch.
H. Papri, Chilmil; *O.* Dharango; *P.* Kacham; *G.* Kanjho; *Mar.* Papara, Vavli; *M.* Aval; *T.* Avali, Kanji; *Te.* Nemali, Tapasi; *C.* Kaladri; *Sin.* Dadahirilla; *Bur.* Myaukseik.

Hordeum vulgare L.
E. Barley; *S.* Yava; *B.* & *A.* Job; *H.* Jawa; *U.* Jav; *O.* Jaba; *P.* Jau; *G.* Bajri; *Bom.* Jav, Satu; *Mar.* Satu; *T.* Barliyarisi; *Te.* Yavaka; *C.* Javegodhi; *Bur.* Muyau.

Hoya parasitica Wall.
E. Wax flower; *B.* Paragacha.

Hydrilla verticillata Casp.
B. Jhanji.

Hydrocera triflora W. & A.
B. Domuti.

Hydrocotyle asiatica L. = *Centella asiatica* Urban.
E. Indian pennywort; *S.* Mandu-Kaparni, Brahmamanduki; *B.* Thankuni, Thulkuri; *H.* Brahmi-booti; *U.* Brahmi; *A.* Manimuni; *O.* Thalkudi; *G.* Karbrahmi; *Bom.* Karinga; *Mar.* Brahmi; *M.* Kodangal; *T.* Vullarai; *Te.* Babassa; *C.* Vondelaga; *Sin.* Hingotukola; *Bur.* Minkuabin.

Hygrophila spinosa T. And. = *Asteracantha longifolia* Nees.
S. Kokilaksha; *B.* Kuleykhara; *H.* Gokula-kanta; *U.* Talimkhana; *O.* Kantakalia; *P.* Talmakhana; *G.* Ekharo; *Bom.* Kolsunda, Talima-khana; *Mar.* Kolshinda; *M.* Vayal-chulli; *T.* Nirmulli; *Te.* Nirguvivera; *C.* Kalavankabija; *Sin.* Katreiriki.

Hyoscyamus niger L.
E. Henbane; *S.* Madakarini; *B.* Khorasaniajowan; *H.* Khuro-saniyayamani; *U.* Khorasaniajwar; *P.* Bangidewana; *G.* Khora-saniajmo; *Bom.* Khorasaniowa; *Mar.* Khorasanivova; *T.* Kura-saniyoman; *Te.* Kurashaniva-mam; *C.* Khurasanivoma.

Hyptis suaveolens Poit.
O. Gangatulsi.

Iberis amara L.
E. Candytuft.

Ichnocarpus frutescens R. Br.
S. Shyama; *B.* Shyama-lata; *H.* Kalidudhi; *O.* Syamolota; *Mar.* Kantebhouri; *M.* Palvalli; *T.* Udargodi; *Te.* Nallatige; *C.* Gorwiballi; *Sin.* Kirivel; *Bur.* Tansapai.

Impatiens balsamina L.
E. Balsam; *S.* Swipatra; *B.* Dopati, Hajraphul; *H.* Gulmendi; *U.* Gulemendi; *A.* Damdeuka; *O.* Haragoura; *P.* Bantil; *G.* Pantam-bol; *Mar.* Terada; *M.* & *T.* Balsam; *Te.* Kasithumbai; *C.* Gaurihu; *Sin.* Kudalikola; *Bur.* Dandalet.

Imperata arundinacea Cyrill.
B. Ulu; *H.* Dirghugas.

Indigofera linifolia Retz.
B. Bhangra; *H.* Torki; *G.* Jhinki-gali; *Bom.* Burbura; *Mar.* Bhangra.

Indigofera tinctoria L.
E. Indigo; *S.* Nili; *B.*, *H.* & *A.* Nil; *U.* & *O.* Nila; *G.* Gali; *Bom.* Nilaguli; *Mar.* Neel; *M.* Amary; *T.* Avary, Nilam; *Te.* Aviri; *C.* Ajara; *Sin.* Nilaiwara; *Bur.* Mai-nai.

Ionidium suffruticosum Ging. = *Hybanthus enneaspermus* F. V. Muell.
S. Charati; *B.* Nunbora; *H.* Ratan-purus; *Bom.* Ratanpuras; *M.* Orelatamara; *T.* Orilaitamarai; *Te.* Suriyakanti.

Ipomoea batatas Lamk. = *Batatas edulis* Choisy.
E. Sweet potato; *S.* Kandagranthi; *B.* Ranga-alu, Misti-alu; *H.* Shakarkand; *U.* & *P* Shakar-kanda; *A.* Mitha-alu; *O.* Chini-alu, Kandamula; *G.* Shakkaria; *Bom.* Ratalu; *Mar.* Ratala; *M.* Madhura-ki zhangu; *T.* Vallikilangu; *Te.* Genusu; *C.* Genasu; *Sin.* Batala; *Bur.* Kazwan.

Ipomoea biloba Forsk.
E. Goat's foot creeper; *S.* Maryada; *B.* Chagal karui; *H.* Dopatilata; *O.* Kansarinata; *G.* Mariadavela; *Bom.* & *Mar.* Marjadvel; *M.* Atampa; *T.* Adambu, Adappangode; *Te.* Bedatige; *C.* Adumbaballi; *Sin.* Mudu-bin-tamburu; *Bur.* Pinlai-kazum.

Ipomoea bona-nox L. = *I. alba* L.
E. Moon flower; *S.* Chandrakanti; *B.* Kalmi-lata, Halkalmi; *H.* Dudhikalmi, Chandrakant; *Bom.* Gulchandni; *M.* Mandavalli; *T.* Alangi, Nagamukkori; *Te.* Nagara-mukkatte; *C.* Chandrakanti; *Sin.* Alanga; *Bur.* Nwekazumbyi.

Ipomoea hederacea Jacq.
E. Indian jalap; *S.* Krishnabija; *B.* Nil-kalmi; *H.* Kaladana; *U.* & *Bom.* Kaladanah; *O.* Kanik-hondo; *P.* Bildi; *Mar.* Nilpushpi; *T.* Kodikakkatan; *Te.* Kolli; *C.* Tali.

Ipomoea pes-tigridis L.
E. Tiger's foot; *B.* Languli-lata; *O.* Kansarinata; *P.* Ishopechan; *M.*

Vellatampu; *T.* Punaikkirai; *Te.* Purtikada; *Sin.* Diviadiya.

Ipomoea pulchella Roth. = *I. purpurea* Sw.
E. Morning glory, Railway Creeper; *B.* Rel-lata.

Ipomoea reptans Poir. = *I. aquatica* Forsk.
E. Water bindweed; *S.* Kalambi; *B.* Kalmi-shak; *H.* Karmi, Patua-saga; *U.* Narikakal; *A.* Kalmau; *O.* Kalamasaga; *P.* Nali; *G.* Nalinibhaji; *Bom.* Nalichibaji; *Mar.* Kalambi; *T.* Koilangu; *Te.* Tutikura; *Sin.* Kankun.

Ischaemum angustifolium Hack.
E. Sabai grass.

Ixora corcinea L.
E. Flame of the woods; *S.* Raktaka, Bandhuka; *B.* & *A.* Rangan; *H.* Gotagandhal; *O.* Rangani; *P.* Rungan; *Bom.* Bakoral, Abuli; *Mar.* Makadi; *M.* Chetti; *T.* Setti, Vedji; *Te.* Bandhukamu, Korani; *C.* Kepala, Kisukare; *Sin.* Ratambala; *Bur.* Pansayeik.

Ixora parviflora Vahl. = *I. arborea* Roxb.
E. Torch tree; *S.* Nevali; *B.* Shet rangan; *H.* Makrichijhar, Nevari; *O.* Telokrya; *G.* Nevari; *Bom.* Kurat, Raikuri; *Mar.* Khura, Raikora; *T.* Koran, Sulundu; *Te.* Kori, Puttupala; *C.* Gorvi, Suragi; *Sin.* Maharatambala; *Bur.* Pansayeip.

Jasminum auriculatum Vahl.
E. Jasmine; *S.* Yuthika; *B.* Jui, Janti; *O.* Bonomollika; *T.* Vana-malligai; *Te.* Magadhi, Sudimalle; *C.* Hurinaballi.

Jasminum grandiflorum L.
E. Spanish jasmine; *S.* Jati; *B.* Jati; *H.* Chameli; *U.* & *P.* Chambeli; *O.* Chombeli, Jati; *G.* & *Bom.* Chambeli; *M.* Malati, Pichakam; *T.* Kodimalligai, Pichi; *Te.* Jaji; *C.* Ajjige, Jati; *Bur.* Myatloe.

Jasminum pubescens Willd.
E. Downy jasmine; *S.* Kunda; *B.* Kunda, Kundphul; *H.* Kunda; *O.* Kontabelo; *Mar.* Mogra; *M.* Kundam, Gujari; *T.* Malligai; *Te.* Kundamu, Molla; *C.* Kunda, Molle; *Bur.* Sabe.

Jasminum sambac L.
E. Arabian jasmine; *S.* Mallika, Vanachandrika; *B.* Ban-mallika, Belphul; *H.* Bel, Motia; *U.* Raibel; *A.* Jutiphul; *O.* Malli; *P.* Mugra; *G.* Batmogri; *Bom.* Mogri; *Mar.* Mogara; *M.* Mulla; *T.* Malli; *Te.* Malle; *C.* Mallige; *Sin.* Pich-chimal; *Bur.* Mali, Sabay.

Jatropha curcas L.
E. Physic nut, Purging nut; *S.* Parvateranda; *B.* Bag-bharenda; *H.* Jangli-arandi; *A.* Bongali-ara; *O.* Baigaba; *P.* Jamalgota; *G.* Jepal; *Bom.* Irundi, Jepal; *Mar.* Mogali erand; *M.* Katalavanakku; *T.* Adalai, Kattukkottai; *Te.* Ada-viyamudamu, Pepalemu; *C.* Ada-lubaralu; *Sin.* Erandu; *Bur.* Thin-bankyekku.

Jatropha glandulifera Roxb.
S. Nikumbha; *B.* Lal-bharenda; *H.* Jangli-erandi; *O.* Simanora-kokalo; *Bom.* Janglierandi, Undar-bibi; *Mar.* Jangli-arandi; *M.* Nakadanti; *T.* Kattamanaku; *Te.* Dundigamu; *C.* Tottagida.

Jatropha gossypifolia L.
S. Sayambara; *B.* Lal-bharenda; *H.* Lal-eranda; *A.* Bhotera; *O.* Verenda; *Mar.* Vilayati erand; *M.* Simayavanakku; *T.* Adalai; *Te.* Nepalemu; *C.* Kariturukaharalu.

Juncella inundatus C. B. Clarke.
B. & *H.* Pati.

Jussiaea repens L.
B. Keshardam; *H.* Kessara; *A.* Taljuria; *Mar.* Pan lawang; *M.* Nirgrampu; *T.* Nirkirampu; *Te.* Niruyagnivendramu; *Sin.* Beru-diyanilla.

Jussieua suffructicosa L.
S. Bhulavanga; *B.* Lal-bonlabanga; *O.* Bilolobongo; *Mar.* Panalavanga; *M.* Karyampu; *T.* Nirkkrambu; *Te.* Niruyagnivendramu; *C.* Kava-kula; *Sin.* Haemarago.

Justicia betonica L.
Sin. Sudupuruk.

Justicia gendarussa L. f.
S. Nilanirgundi; *B.* Jagatmadan; *H.* Nilinargandi; *O.* Kukurodonti; *Bom.* & *Mar.* Kalaadulsa, Tao; *M.* Karinochil; *T.* Karunochi; *Te.* Nallanochili; *C.* Nachukaddi; *Sin.* Kaluvarania; *Bur.* Bawanet.

Kaempferia rotunda L.
S. Bhuchampaka; *B.* & *H.* Bhuichampa; *G.* Bhuichampo; *Mar.* Bhuichampa; *T.* & *Te.* Kondakalava; *C.* Nalasampige; *Sin.* Lukenda.

Kalanchoe spathulata DC.
S. Hemasagara; *B.* Himsagar; *H.* & *P.* Haiza, Rungru; *Bom.* Parnathij; *T.* Malakalli.

Kandelia rheedei W. & A. = *K. candel* Druce.
B. Koria; *O.* Rasunia; *M.* Kantal; *T.* Kandal; *Te.* Kandigala; *C.* Kandale.

Kleinhovia hospita L.
E. Tree antigonon; *B.* Bola.

Kydia colycina Roxb.
H. Potari, Pula; *O.* Bharimo; *P.* Pola, Puli; *G.* Mothinirwani; *Bom.* Motipotari; *Mar.* Potari; *M.* Velukku; *T.* Vendai; *Te.* Kondapatari; *C.* Belagu; *Bur.* Bokemaiza.

Kyllinga brevifolia Rottb.
S. Nirvisha; *B.* Bindi-muthi; *H.* Nirbisi; *Mar.* Mostu; *M.* Kolpullu.

Lactuca sativa L.
E. Garden lettuce; *B.* Letush; *H.* Salad; *U.* Kahu; *T.* Sabattu; *Te.* Kavu; *Sin.* Salada.

Lagenaria vulgaris Ser.
E. Bottle gourd; *S.* Alabu; *B.* & *O.* Lau; *H.* Kaddu, Lauki; *U.* Tumbari; *A.* Jati-lau; *P.* Ghiya; *G.* Dudhi; *Bom.* Karwabopla; *Mar.* Dudhya bhopala; *M.* Bellashora; *T.* Chorakkai; *Te.* Alaburu; *C.* Kahesore; *Sin.* Diyalabu; *Bur.* Businswai.

Lagerstroemia flos-reginae Retz. = *L. speciosa* Pers.
E. Crape myrtle, Indian Lilac; *B.* Jarool; *H.* & *P.* Jarul; *A.* Ajar; *O.* Patoli; *Bom.* & *Mar.* Taman; *M.* Nirventekku; *T.* Pumaruthu; *Te.* Varagogu; *C.* Maruvachalla, Hobdachalla; *Sin.* Murute; *Bur.* Pyinma.

Lagerostroemia thorellii Gagnep.
B. Bilati jarool; *Bom.* Dhayti; *T.* Sinappu; *Te.* Chinagoranta.

Lantana camara L.
B. Chotra; *H.* Aripple; *O.* Nagaairi; *P.* Desi lantana; *G.* Ghanidalia; *Mar.* Ghaneri; *M.* Puchedi; *T.* Arippu; *Te.* Lantana; *C.* Joli, Parale; *Sin.* Gandapana, Tonkinna.

Lathyrus aphaca L.
E. Wild pea; *B.* & *A.* Ban-matar; *H.* Jangli-matar; *O.* Jangali matar; *P.* Rawari; *Mar.* Vanmatar.

Lathyrus sativus L.
B. & *H.* Khesari; *A.* Kola-mah; *P.* Kisari dal; *G.* Mater; *Mar.* Lakh.

Launea asplenifolia Hook. f.
B. & *H.* Tikchana.

Launea pinnatifida Cass.
H. Bankau; *G.* Bhoupatri; *Bom.* Pathri; *Mar.* Pathradi, Paththa.

Lamsonia alba Lam. = *L. inermis* L.
E. Henna plant, Indian privet; *S.* Mendhika, Raktagarbha; *B.* Mehedi; *H.* Mehndi; *U.* Mehendi; *O.* Rangota; *P.* Hinna; *G.* Medi; *Bom.* & *Mar.* Mendi; *M.* Mayilanji; *T.* Marudondri, Aivanam; *Te.* Goranta; *C.* Gorante; *Sin.* Maritondo; *Bur.* Danbin.

Lawsonia indica L.
B. Purush.

Leea acquata L.
S. Dasi, Kakangsika; *B.* & *H.* Kak-jangha; *G.* Aghedi; *Mar.* Kanga; *M.* Kakanasika; *Te.* Surapadi; *C.* Jirichilecha; *Bur.* Nagamauk.

Leea macrophylla Hornem.
S. Samudraka; *B.* Dhol samudra; *H.* Hatikan; *Bom.* & *Mar.* Dinda.

Lemna trisulea L
E. Duckweed; *B.* Khudi-pana; *A.* Sorupuni; *O.* Chunidala; *P.* Bur; *Mar.* Tikliche shewale.

Lens esculenta Moench. = *L. culinaris* Medic.
E. Lentil; *S.* Masurika; *B.* Musuri; *H. & U.* Masur; *A.* Musurmah; *O.* Masura; *G.* Masuridal; *Mar.* Masur; *T.* Misurpurpur; *Te.* Misurpappu; *C.* Massur.

Leonotis nepetifolia R. Br.
B. & H. Hejurchei; *G. & Bom.* Matijer, Matisul; *Mar.* Dipmal; *Te.* Ranabheri; *Sin.* Mahayak-wanassa.

Leonurus sibiricus L.
E. Motherwort; *B.* Raktodrone; *H.* Halkusha, Guma; *A.* Ronga-doron; *O.* Koilekhia, Bhuta-airi; *Mar.* Kamba; *Te.* Enugutummi.

Lepidium sativum L.
E. Garden cress; *S.* Chandrika, Raktabija; *B. & A.* Halim-shak; *H. & U.* Halim; *O.* Hidamba saga; *P.* Halon, Tezak; *G.* Asaliya; *Bom.* Asalia; *Mar.* Aliv; *T.* Ativerai; *Te.* Adiyalu, Adeli; *C.* Allibija; *Bur.* Mongnyin.

Leucas aspera Spreng.
S. Dandakalash; *B.* Shetadrone, Ghalghase; *H.* Bara-halkusa; *A.* Doron, Durumphul; *O.* Gaisa; *Bom.* Tamba; *M.* Thumpa; *T.* Tumbai; *Te.* Tummachettu. Tummikura.

Leucas linifolia Spreng. = *L. lavendulaefolia* Rees.
S. Dronopushpi. Kumbhi; *B.* Halkasa; *H.* Chota-halkusa; *U.* Guma; *A.* Doron; *O.* Gaisa; *Mar.* Guma; *M.* Thumpa; *T.* Thumbai; *Te.* Tamma chettu; *C.* Jhinanpan-nikubo.

Ligustrum robustum Bl.
E. Privet.

Limnanthemum cristatum Griseb.
B. Panseuli; *Sin.* Hinamtala.

Limnophila gratioloides R. Br.
S. Ambuja; *B.* Karpur; *H.* Kuttra; *Mar.* Ambuli; *M.* Manganari.

Linaria ramosissima Wall.
E. Toad-flask; *G.* Bhintgalodi, Kanodi.

Lindenbergia urticaefolia Link. & Otto.
B. Basanti; *G.* Bhintachati; *Bom.* Gazdar; *Mar.* Dhol, Gajhdra.

Linum usitatissimum L.
E. Linseed, Flax; *S.* Masina; *B.* Tishi; *H.* Alsi; *U.* Alesi; *A.* Tichi; *O.* Pesi; *P.* Alish, Alsi; *G.* Alshi; *Mar.* Jawas; *M.* Cheruchanaviltintevilta; *T.* Alivirai; *Te.* Alasi; *C.* Alashi

Lippia nodiflora Rich. = *Phyla nodiflora* Green
S. Chitrapatri; *B. & H.* Bhui-okra; *O.* Bukkan; *P.* Bakkan, Jalnim; *G.* Ratoliya; *Bom.* Ratolia; *Mar.* Jala-pimpali; *M.* Kattuttippali; *T.* Podutalei; *Te.* Bokenaku, Bokkena.

Litsea sebifera Pers. = *L. chinensis* Lam.
E. Tallow laurel; *S.* Adhavara, Meda; *B.* Kukur-chita, Gorur; *H.* Garbi-jaur; *O.* Jadamo; *Bom.* Chickana; *Mar.* Miri; *T.* Ama; *Te.* Meda; *Sin.* Bombi.

Lodoicea seychellarum Labill.
E. Double coconut palm; *H.* Daryakanaryal; *G.* Daryanu-nariyal; *Bom.* Jaharinaral; *M.* Kataltenna; *T.* Kadattengai; *Te.* Samudraputenkaya; *Sin.* Mudupol; *Bur.* Penle-on-si.

Loranthus longiflorus L.
B. Manda; *H.* Banda; *A.* Roghumala; *O.* Madanga; *G.* Vando; *P.* Pand; *Mar.* Bandgul; *M.* Iththil; *T.* Pulluruvi; *Te.* Badanika.

Luffa acutangula Roxb.
E. Ribbed gourd; *S.* Jhingaka; *B.* Jhinga; *H. & P.* Kalitori; *U.* Torai; *A.* Jika; *O.* Jahni; *G.* Gonsali; *Bom.* Jinga, Turai; *Mar.* Dodaka; *M.* Peechil; *T.* Peechanka; *Te.* Burkai; *C.* Hirekayi; *Sin.* Vetakola; *Bur.* Thapwot.

Luffa aegyptiaca Mill. = *L. cylindrica* M. V. Roem.
E. Sponge gourd; *S.* Ghoshaka; *B.* Dhundul; *H. & P.* Ghiya-tori; *U.* Turi; *A.* Bhol; *O.* Pita tarada; *G.* Turia; *Bom.* Ghosali; *Mar.* Ghosale; *T.* Pikku; *Te.* Guttibira; *Sin.* Neyangnattakolu; *Bur.* Thabwot.

Lycopersicum esculentum Mill.
E. Tomato; *B.* Bilati-begun; *H.* & *P.* Tamatar; *A.* Belahi-bengena; *O.* Bilati baigana; *G.* Tameta; *Mar.* Tambeta. *M.* & *T.* Thakkalikkai; *Te.* Thakkali.

Machilus villosa Hook. f.
C. Chittutanti; *M.* Puravu; *T.* Anaikkuru; *Sin.* Ululu.

Magnolia grandiflora L.
E. Lily tree; *B.* Udaypadma; *H.* Himchampa.

Magnolia pterocarpa Roxb.
B. & *H.* Dulee champa.

Mallotus philippinensis Muell.-Arg.
E. Monkeyface tree; *S.* Kapila, Ranjaka; *B.* Kamila; *H.* Kamela; *U.* Kalileh; *A.* Gangai; *O.* Kopilogundi; *G.* Kapilo; *Bom.* Kapila; *Mar.* Shindur; *M.* Ponni; *T.* Kopilapodi; *Te.* Sinduri; *C.* Kunkuma; *Sin.* Hamparila; *Bur.* Tanthieden.

Malva viscus L.
B. Lanka-jaba.

Mangifera indica L.
E. Mango; *S.* Ambrah; *B.* & *H.* Am; *U.* & *O.* Amba; *A.* Ghariam; *P.* Amb, Mawashi; *G.* Ambo, Amri; *Bom.* Amba, Ambo; *Mar.* Amba; *M.* Amram; *T.* Ambiram, Mamagam; *Te.* Amramu, Mamidi; *C.* Mavu; *Sin.* Etamba; *Bur.* Thayet.

Manihot utilissima Pohl.
E. Cassava, Tapioca; *C.* Maragenosu; *Sin.* Manyokka; *Bur.* Pooloopinanmyouk.

Maranta arundinacea L.
E. Arrowroot; *B.* Araroot; *H.* Tikhor; *T.* Araruttukkilangu; *Te.* Palagunda; *Sin.* Hulankiriya; *Bur.* Pen-bwa.

Marsdenia tenacissima W. & A.
B. Jitti; *H.* Tongus.

Marsilea quadrifolia L.
B. Sushni-shak; *A.* Pani-tengechi; *O.* Sunsunia; *P.* Chaupati; *M.* Nalilakkotakan; *T.* Arakkodai; *Te.* Chiktitakura.

Martynia diandra Glox.
E. Tiger's nail; *B.* Baghnokh; *H.* Shernui; *U.* Hattajori; *A.* Baghnakhi; *O.* Bagha nakhi; *P.* Hathajori; *G.* Vichchida; *Mar.* Winchauri; *M.* Pulinagam; *T.* Ṇagathali; *Te.* Garudamukku; *Sin.* Ṅagadarana.

Medicago denticulata Willd.
B. & *H.* Maina.

Melaleuca leucadendron L.
E. Cajeput oil tree; *B.* Cajuputte; *H.* Kayaputi; *Mar.* Cajuputa; *Te.* Kaiyapuddai; *Sin.* Lothsumbul.

Melastoma malabathricum L.
E. Indian rhododendron; *A.* Futki; *O.* Koroti; *Mar.* Palore; *M.* Katali; *T.* Kadalai; *Te.* Pattudu; *C.* Kenkarike; *Sin.* Katakaluwa; *Bur.* Myetype.

Melia azadirachta L. = *Azadirachta indica* A. Juss.
E. Neem, Margosa; *S.* Nimba; *B.* & *H.* Nim; *U.* Neem; *A.* Moha-nim; *O.* Nimba; *P.* Bakam, Nim; *G.* Limba; *Bom.* Bakayan, Nim; *Mar.* Kadu ḷimb; *M.* Veppu; *T.* Vembu; *Te.* Veppai; *C.* Nimba; *Sin.* Kohumba; *Bur.* Tha-ma-ka.

Melia azedarach L.
E. Persian lilac; *S.* Mahanimba; *B.* Ghoranim; *H.* Mahanimb, Bakayan; *U.* Bakayana; *A.* Thamaga; *O.* Mahanimbo; *P.* Bakain; *G.* Bakanlimbodo; *Bom.* Mahalimbo; *Mar.* Bakananimb; *M.* Malaveppu; *T.* Malaivembu, Tittam; *Te.* Vettiveppa; *C.* Bevu; *Sin.* Mahanimba; *Bur.* Tha-makha.

Melilotus alba Lamk.
E. White melilot; *S.* Methika; *B.* Sadamethi; *H.* Safed methi.

Malachra capitata L.
B. Bon-dhenros; *H.* Ban-bhindi; *Bom.* Bonbhendi; *Mar.* Ranbhendi.

Melilotus indica All.
E. Small melilot; *S.* Vanamethika; *B.* & *H.* Ban-methi; *P.* Sinjee.

Melochia corchorifolia L.
B. Tikiokra; *O.* Nolita; *M.* Seruvuram; *T.* Punnakkukhirai; *Te.* Sittantakura; *Sin.* Galkura.

Memecylon edule Roxb.
E. Ironwood; *S.* Anjani; *O.* Bonohorono; *Bom.* Anguni; *Mar.* Anjani, Kurpa; *M.* Kayavu; *T.* Anjani, Pungali; *Te.* Midalli; *C.* Alle; *Sin.* Dedikaha; *Bur.* Myenphaetenyet.

Mentha viridis L.
E. Mint; *B.* & *P.* Pudina; *H.* & *A.* Podina; *G.* Phudino; *Bom.* Pudinah; *Mar.* & *Te.* Pudina; *M.* Putiyina; *T.* Jech-chak-kirai; *C.* Chetnimaragu; *Sin.* Meenchi.

Meriandra benghalensis Benth.
E. Bengal sage; *H.* Kafurka-pat; *Bom.* Kafurkapatha, Sesti; *T.* Sayayitai; *Te.* Simakarpuramu.

Merremia emarginata Hook. f.
S. Mushakarni; *B.* Indur-kani-pana; *H.* Musakani; *U.* Chukakani; *G.* Undarakani; *Bom.* Undirkani; *T.* Perettaikkiray; *Te.* Toinnuatali.

Mesua ferrea L.
E. Ironwood; *S.* Nagakesara; *B.* Nageswar; *H.* Nagkesar; *U.* Narmiskha; *A.* Nahor; *O.* Nageswara; *P.* Nagar kesar; *Bom.* & *Mar.* Nagchampaka; *M.* Nagachempakam; *T.* Nagesuram; *Te.* Nagakesiara; *C.* Nagakessara; *Sin.* Deyana; *Bur.* Kengau.

Michelia champaca L.
E. Golden champa; *S.* Champaka; *B.* Swarnachampa; *H.* & *P.* Champak; *A.* Champa-phul; *O.* Champa; *G.* Rae-champac; *Bom.* Champa; *Mar.* Sonchapha; *M.* Chempakam; *T.* Senbagam; *Te.* Sampaka; *C.* Champaka; *Sin.* Champak; *Bur.* Changal, Saga.

Mikania scandens Willd.
E. Climbing hempweed; *B.* Taralata; *Sin.* Gampalu.

Millingtonia hortensis L.
E. Indian cork tree; *B.* & *H.* Akasnim; *O.* Riali.

Mimosa pudica L.
E. Sensitive plant; *S.* Anjalikarika; *B.* Lajjabati; *H.* Lajwanti; *A.* Lajukilota; *O.* Lajakuli; *P.* Arlu; *G.* Lajjawanti; *Mar.* Lajalu; *M.* Thottalvadi; *T.* Thottasinigi; *Te.* Nidrakhanta; *C.* Lajja; *Sin.* Nidikumba; *Bur.* Ntikha-yone-bin.

Mimusops elengii L.
E. Elengi, Indian medlar; *S.* Vakula; *B.* Bakul; *H.* Mulsari; *U.* Molsari; *O.* Bokulo; *G.* Bolsari; *Bom.* Borsali; *Mar.* Ovalli; *M.* Bakulam, Elengi; *T.* Vagulam, Lanji; *Te.* Pogade, Vakalamu; *C.* Vakula; *Sin.* Munemal; *Bur.* Kaya.

Mirabilis jalapa L.
E. Marvel of Peru, Four o'clock plant; *S.* Sandhyakoli; *B.* Krishnakoli, Sandhyamoni; *H.* Gulabbas; *U.* & *P.* Gul-e-abbasi; *A.* Godhuligopal; *O.* Rangani; *Bom.* Gubhaji; *Mar.* Gulbaksh; *M.* Nalumanichedi; *T.* Andimandarai; *Te.* Chandrakanta; *C.* Chandramallige; *Sin.* Sendrikka; *Bur.* Mizubin.

Modecca palmata Lamk.
M. Mutakku; *Te.* Modikka; *Sin.* Hondala.

Momordica charantia L.
E. Bitter gourd; *S.* Karavella; *B.* Karala; *H.* Kareli; *U.* Karella; *A.* Tita-kerala; *O.* Kalara; *G.* Karelu; *Bom.* Karla; *Mar.* Karle; *M.* & *T.* Paval; *Te.* Kakara; *C.* Hagola; *Sin.* Kirilla; *Bur.* Kyethenka.

Momordica cochinchinensis Spreng.
S. Karkata; *B.* Kankrol; *H.* Gulkakra; *U.* Kakrol; *G.* Karapata; *Mar.* Kakana; *Te.* Adavikakara; *Bur.* Samongnway.

Morinda citrifolia L.
E. Indian mulberry; *S.* Achchhuka; *B.* Auch; *H.* Ach; *O.* Achu; *G.* Alsaraoji; *Bom.* Aal, Nagakuda; *Mar.* Bartondi, Nagakunda; *M.* Mannanatti; *T.* Manjanatti, Nuna; *Te.* Mulugu, Togaru; *C.* Maddi, Tagase; *Sin.* Ahugaha; *Bur.* Nyahgyi.

Morus indica L.
E. Mulberry; *S.* Tuta; *B.* Toont; *H.* Toot, Tutri; *U.* Sahetuta; *A.* Nooni; *O.* Tutakoli; *P.* Tut; *G.* Tutri; *Bom.* Tutri, Ambor; *Mar.* Ambat, Tuti; *M.* Tulam; *T.* Kambali, Musukattai; *Te.* Putikainerale; *Bur.* Posa.

Mucuna pruriens Bak.
E. Cowage plant; *S.* Atmagupta; *B.* Alkushi; *H.* & *P.* Kawanch;

U. Kavancha; *A*. Bandarkekoa; *O*. Alokushi; *G*. Kivanch; *Bom*. Kuhili; *Mar*. Khaj kuira; *M*. Naikoruna; *T*.. Amudari, Punaikkali; *Te*. Dubagoudi; *C*. Kadavare; *Sin*. Achariyapalle; *Bur*. Khuele.

Mukia scabrella Arn.
B. Billari; *H*. Agumaki; *M*. Mukkalpiran; *T*. Musumusukkai; *Te*. Kutarubudama; *Bur* Sathakhiva.

Murraya exotica L. = *M. paniculata* Jack.
E. Chinese box; *B*. & *O*. Kamini; *H*. Marchula; *A*. Kaminiphul; *P*. Marua; *Bom*. & *Mar*. Pandharikunti; *M*. Maramulla; *T*. Kattukaruveppilai; *Te*. Nagagolugi; *C*. Nagadala; *Sin*. Etteriya; *Bur*. Thanatkha.

Murraya koenigii Spreng.
E. Curryleaf plant; *S*. Girinimba, Suravi; *B*. Barsunga; *H*. Katnim, Bursunga; *O*. Basango; *P*. Bowala; *Bom*. Karriapat; *Mar*. Karipat; *M*. Kareapela; *T*. Karuvippilai; *Te*. Karepeku; *C*. Karibevu; *Sin*. Karapincha; *Bur*. Pindosin.

Musa balbisiana Colla.
E. Banana; *S*. Rambha, Kadali; *B*. Kala; *H*. & *U*. Kela; *A*. Kol; *O*. Kodoli; *G*. & *Bom*. Kela; *Mar*. Kadali, Kel; *M*. Vazha; *T*. Vazhai; *Te*. Kadali, Rambha; *C*. Budibale; *Sin*. Kehel; *Bur*. Yathilan.

Musa paradisiaca L.
E. Plantain; *B*. Kanch-kala; *H*. Kacha-kela; *M*. Kadalam, Vala; *T*. Valai; *Te*. Arati; *C*. Bale; *Sin*. Kehel.

Mussaenda frondosa L.
S. Nagaballi; *H*. Bedina; *Bom*. Bebana; *Mar*. Shivardole; *M*. Vellila; *T*. Vellimadandai; *C*. Bellotti; *Sin*. Maasenda; *Bur*. Ywethla.

Myrtus communis L. = *Acmena communis* Merr. & Perry.
E. Myrtle; *B*. Bilati-mehedi; *H*. & *P*. Vilayatimehndi, Murad; *U*. Habulas; *T*. Kulinavak.

Naravelia zeylanica DC.
E. Traveller's joy; *B*. Chagalbati; *H*. Chagoolbatee; *Te*. Mukkupinatatega.

Nasturtium indicum DC. = *Rorippa montana* Small.
E. Water cress; *B*. Bilrai; *Sin*. Kakutupala.

Nelumbium speciosum Willd. = *Nelumbo montana* Small.
E. Lotus; *S*. Kamala, Padma; *B*. & *O*. Padma; *H*. & *P*. Kanwal; *U*. Nilofer; *A*. Podum; *G*. Suriyakamal; *Mar*. Kamal; *M*. Thamara; *T*. Thamarai; *Te*. Damara; *C*. Tavarigadde; *Sin*. Nelum; *Bur*. Padungma.

Nephelium litchi Camb. = *Litchi chinensis* Sonner.
E. Litchi; *B*. Lichu; *H*. Litchi; *U*. Lichur; *O*. Lishi; *Bom*. Lichi; *T*. Illichi, Tarain; *Bur*. Kiak-mauk.

Nephelium longana Camb. = *Euphoria longana* Lamk.
E. Longan; *B*. Ansphal; *Bom*. Wumb; *Mar*. Vomb; *T*. Kattupuvam; *C*. Malehakuta; *Sin*. Mora, Murale; *Bur*. Tawthayet.

Neptunia oleracea Lour.
B. Panilajuk; *H*. Lajalu; *Bom*. Panilajak; *M*. Nittitoddavaddi; *T*. Sundaikkirai; *Te*. Nidrayam; *Sin*. Diyanidikumba.

Nerium odorum Soland. = *N. indicum* Mill.
E. Oleander; *S*. Karavira; *B*. Karabi; *H*. & *P*. Kaner; *U*. Kanir; *A*. Korbiphul; *O*. Konero; *G*. Kanher; *Bom*. Kanhera; *Mar*. Kanheri; *M*. Araly; *T*. Alari; *Te*. Ganneru; *C*. Kanagile; *Sin*. Araliya.

Nicotiana plumbaginifolia Viv.
B. Bon-tamak; *H*. Ban-tamaku.

Nicotiana tabacum L.
E. Tobacco; *S*. Tamrakutta; *B*. Tamak; *H*. Tamaku; *U*. Tambaku; *A*. Dhopat; *O*. Dhuanpatra; *G*. & *Mar*. Tambaku; *Bom*. Tambakhu; *M*. Pukayila; *T*. Pugailai; *Te*. Pogaku; *C*. Hogesappu; *Sin*. Dhumkola; *Bur*. Se, Ts-ay-bin.

Nigella sativa L.
E. Black cumin, Fennel flower; *S.* Krishnajiraka; *B.* Kalojira; *H.* Kalounji; *O.* Kala-jira; *P.* Kalongi; *G.* Kadujeroo; *Bom.* Kalonji; *Mar.* Kala jire; *T.* & *M.* Karun-jiragam; *Te.* Nellajilakaira; *C.* Karijirigi; *Sin.* Kaluduru.

Nipa fruticans Wurmb.
E. Water coconut; *B.* Golpata; *H.* Gulga; *G.* Pardeshitadio; *Te.* Nipamu; *Sin.* Gimpol.

Nyctanthes arbor-tristis L. = *Jasminum multiflorum* Andr.
E. Night jasmine, Sad tree; *S.* Sephalika, Parijataka; *B.* Sheuli; *H.* Harishingar; *U.* Gulejafari; *A.* Sewali; *O.* Singadhara; *P.* Harsanghar; *G.* Ratrane; *Bom.* Parijataka; *Mar.* Parijatak; *M.* Pavizhamulla; *T.* Pavelam; *Te.* Parijatham; *C.* Harisringi; *Sin.* Sepalika.

Nymphaea lotus L.
E. Water lily, Pond lily; *S.* Kambal; *B.* Shalook, Shapla; *H.* & *P.* Nilofar; *A.* Bhet; *O.* Kumuda; *G.* Nilopal; *Mar.* Kamal; *M.* Ampal; *T.* Alli, Valjambal; *Te.* Allikada, Kaluva; *C.* Tavare; *Sin.* Olu; *Bur.* Kya-pin.

Nymphaea rubra Roxb.
E. Red wate rlily; *S.* Raktotpala, Indivara; *B.* Rakto-kamal; *G.* Kanval, Nilophar; *Mar.* Lalkamal; *M.* Ampala; *T.* Allitamarai, Ambal; *Te.* Allitamara, Koteka; *C.* Bilitavarai; *Sin.* Otu; *Bur.* Kiyani.

Nymphaea stellata Willd.
E. Blue water lily; *S.* Nilotpala; *B.* Nil-padma; *H.* Nilkamal, Nilpadma; *G.* Nilkamal; *Bom.* Upliakamal; *Mar.* Krishnakamal; *M.* Sitambel; *Te.* Nitikulava; *Sin.* Manel; *Bur.* Kyanyu.

Ocimum basilicum L.
E. Common basil; *S.* Manjariki; *B.* Babui-tulsi; *H.* Barbar; *U.* Janglitulshi; *O.* Dhalatulasi; *G.* Sabje; *Bom.* Sabja; *Mar.* Sabza; *M.* Pachcha; *T.* - Tirunitru; *Te.* Rudrajada; *C.* Ramkasturi; *Sin.* Suwandutala; *Bur.* Pinzainpinzin.

Ocimum gratissimum L.
S. Ramatulasi; *B.* Ram-tulsi; *H.* Bantulsi, Ramtulsi; *U.* Ramtulasi; *O.* Ramotulsi; *P.* Banjere; *Bom.* Ramatulasa; *G.* & *Mar.* Ramtulasi; *M.* Kattutrittavu; *T.* Elimuchantulasi; *Te.* Nimmatulasi; *C.* Ramkasturi; *Sin.* Otala.

Ocimum sanctum L.
E. Sacred basil; *S.* Krishnamula; *B.* Kalo-tulsi; *H.* Tulsi; *A.* Tulashi; *O.* Tulasi; *P.* Bantulsi; *G.* Talasi; *Bom.* & *Mar.* Tulasa; *M.* Sivatulasi; *T.* Thulasi; *Te.* Oddhi; *C.* Tulasigidda; *Sin.* Madurutala; *Bur.* Lun.

Odina woodier Roxb. = *Lannea coromondelica* Merr.
E. Indian ash tree; *S.* Jivala; *B.* Jiyal, Jeuli; *H.* Jingan, Kaimil; *O.* Jiyolo; *P.* Kamlai; *G.* Mavedi; *Bom.* Gajel; *Mar.* Shimti; *M.* Oti; *T.* Odi; *Te.* Oddi; *C.* Godde, Udi; *Sin.* Hik; *Bur.* Hnanbai.

Oenanthe stolonifera Wall. = *O. javanica* DC.
B. Panturasi.

Olea europaea L.
E. Olive; *T.* Saidun; *Te.* Jaitun; *C.* Julipe.

Oldenlandia corymbosa L.
S. Parpata; *B.* Khet-papra; *H.* Damanpappar; *O.* Gharpodia; *G.* Parpat; *Mar.* Pitpapada; *T.* Parpadagaru; *Te.* Verinellavamu; *Sin.* Val-pat-paadagam.

Oldenlandia crystallina Roxb.
B. Panki.

Oldenlandia umbellata L.
B. & *O.* Surbuli; *H.* Chirval; *M.* Chayaver; *T.* Chiruver; *Te.* Cherivelu; *Sin.* Saya.

Opuntia dillenii Haw.
E. Prickly pear; *S.* Nagaphana; *B.* Phanimansha; *H.* Nagphani; *U.* Nagaphani; *A.* Sagorphena; *O.* Nagapheni; *P.* Chitarthor; *G.* Nag-neval; *Mar.* Phadya niwdung; *M.* Elakkalli; *T.* Sappaththikkalli; *Te.* & *C.* Nagadali; *Sin.* Kodugaha; *Bur.* Kalazaw.

Oroxylon indicum Vent.
E. Indian trumpet flower; *S.* Shona; *B.* Sona; *H.* & *U.* Arlu; *A.* Bhatghila; *O.* Phapani; *P.* Sanna; *G.* Podval; *Bom.* Tetu, Ulu; *Mar.* Tetu; *M.* Pathiri; *T.* Payyalantha; *Te.* Pampini; *C.* Sonpatte; *Sin.* Totila; *Bur.* Kyaungya.

Oryza sativa L.
E. Paddy; *S.* Dhanya; *B.* & *A.* Dhan; *H.* Chaul, Chaval; *O.* Dhana; *P.* Chawal; *G.* Chokha; *Bom.* Bhatta, Dangar; *Mar.* Bhat; *M.* Ari; *T.* Arishi; *Te.* Urlu; *C.* Akki; *Sin.* Uruwi; *Bur.* Sa-ba-bin.

Ottelia alismoides Pers.
B. Parmilkala; *H.* Panikela.

Ougeinia dalbergioides Benth.
E. Chariot tree; *S.* Tinashaka, Vanjula; *B.* Tinis; *H.* Sandan, Tinnas; *O.* Bandhono; *P.* Sannan; *G.* Tanasse; *Bom.* Tinsa, Tunnus; *Mar.* Tivas; *M.* Malavenna, Nemi; *T.* Narivengai; *Te.* Nemmi, Vanjubamu.

Oxalis corniculata L.
E. Wood-sorrel; *S.* Amlalonika; *B.* Amrul-shak, Amboli; *H.* Chukatripati; *A.* Sengaitenga; *O.* Ambiliti; *P.* Khattibuti; *Bom.* & *Mar.* Amboshi; *M.* Puliyarila; *T.* Puliyarai; *Te.* Ambotikura, Pulichinta; *C.* Pullampurachisappu; *Sin.* Hinambulembiliya.

Oxystelma esculentum R. Br.
S. Dugdhika; *B.* Dudhi, Dudhialata; *H.* Dudhi, Dudlutta; *U.* Dudhi; *O.* Dudhai; *P.* Gani; *G.* Jaldudhi; *Bom.* Dudhika; *Mar.* Dudhari; *T.* Usippalai; *Te.* Dudipala; *C.* Dugdhike.

Paederia foetida L.
S. Prosarini, Gandhabhadra, Gandhali; *B.* Gandhal; *H.* Gandhali; *U.* Gandha; *A.* Bhedailota; *O.* Pasaruni; *P.* Gundali; *G.* Gandhana; *Bom.* Prasaram; *Mar.* Prasarum; *M.* Talanili; *Te.* Savirela; *C.* Hesarane.

Pancratium verecundum Ait.
B. Kumur; *M.* Cattulipola; *Te.* Tellagata.

Pandanus fascicularis Lamk.
E. Screw-pine; *S.* Ketaka; *B.* Keya, Ketaky; *H.* & *P.* Keora; *U.* Keora; *A.* Keteki; *O.* Kia; *G.* Kewoda; *Bom.* Kenda, Keura; *Mar.* Kewada; *M.* Kaitha; *T.* Thazhai; *Te.* Mogil; *C.* Kedige; *Sin.* Mudukeyiya; *Bur.* Tsatthapu.

Panicum miliaceum L.
E. Common millet; *S.* China, Varaka; *B.*, *H.* & *P.* Cheena; *G.* Samli; *Bom.* Chenah, Sama; *Mar.* Warai; *M.* Thena; *T.* Varagu; *Te.* Varagi; *C.* Baragu, Save; *Sin.* Mainairi.

Panicum miliare Lamk.
E. Little millet; *B.* Gondula; *H.* Kungu; *P.* Kutki; *Bom.* Warai; *T.* Shamai; *Te.* Nellashamalu; *Sin.* Meneri.

Papaver somniferum L.
E. Opium poppy; *S.* Ahiphena; *B.* Afing-gach, Posto; *H.* & *P.* Post; *U.* Khaskhassufaid; *A.* Afugoch; *O.* Aphima; *G.* Aphim; *Bom.* Khaskhas, Post; *Mar.* Aphu; *M.* Kashakasha; *T.* Postaka; *Te.* Abhini; *C.* Khasakhasi; *Sin.* Abin; *Bur.* Bhainzi.

Paramignya citrifolia Hook. f. = *Merope angulata* Swingle.
B. Bon-nebu; *Bom.* Karivageti; *Mar.* Kariwageti; *C.* Kadukanji; *Sin.* Wellangiriya.

Parkinsonia aculeata L.
E. Jerusalem thorn; *B.* Bilatibabla; *H.* Vilayati kikar.

Passiflora foetida L.
E. Passion-flower; *B.* & *H.* Jhumkalata; *A.* Junuka; *O.* Jhumuka-lata; *Mar.* Krishna kamal; *M.* Kristhupazham; *T.* Siruppunaikkali; *Te.* Tellajumiki.

Pastinacea vera L.
E. Parsnip.

Pavetta indica L.
S. Papata; *B.* Kukurchura; *H.* Papari; *O.* Bonki; *Bom.* Papat; *Mar.* Papadi; *M.* Pavatta; *T.* Pavattai; *Te.* Papidi; *C.* Pavati; *Sin.* Pawatta; *Bur.* Hmitgyin.

Pavonia odorata Willd.
S. Vala; *B.* Bala; *H.* Sugandhabala; *G.* Kalowalo; *Bom.* & *Mar.* Kalavala; *M.* Karuntotti; *T.* Peramutti; *Te.* Chittibenda; *C.* Mudivala.

Pedilanthus tithymaloides Poit.
E. Jew's slipper; *B.* Rangchita, Berachita; *H.* Nag daman; *O.* Bilatisiju; *P.* Nag daun; *Mar.* Vilayati sher; *M.* Verakkodi.

Peltophorum ferrugineum Benth. = *P. pterocarpum* Backer.
E. Caper pod; *T.* Iyavakai.

Pennisetum typhoideum Rich.
E. Pearl millet; *S.* Varjarika; *B.*, *H.* & *O.* Bajra; *P.* Bajza; *Bom.* Bajri; *Mar.* Bajari; *M.* Mathari, Bajra; *T.* Kampu; *Te.* Sajja.

Pentapetes phoenicia L.
E. Noon flower; *S.* Suryabhakta; *B.* Surjyamoni, Dupurey chandi; *H.* & *P.* Guldupaharia; *O.* Dipaharia; *G.* Duporio; *Bom.* Doopahuria; *Mar.* Dupari; *T.* Nagappu.

Pentatropis microphylla W. & A.
S. Suryavalli, Shringariti; *H.* Kanathodi, Ambarvel; *G.* Singroti, Suryavel; *Mar.* Shingrota; *T.* Uppili; *Te.* Pulapala.

Peperomia pellucida Kunth.
B. Luchi-pata.

Pergularia minor Andr. = *Telosma minor* Craib.
E. Cowslip creeper; *B.* Kunja-lata.

Peristrophe bicalyculata Nees.
B. Nasabhanga; *H.* Itrelal, Nasbhanga; *G.* Kaliadhedi; *Bom.* Pitpatra; *Mar.* Rankireyat; *Te.* Chebira; *Sin.* Mahanelu.

Petunga roxburghii DC.
B. Pitanga.

Peucedanum sowa Kurz. = *Anethum sowa* L.
E. Anet; *S.* Satapuspika, Shipha; *B.* Sulpa; *H.* Sowa; *U.* & *P.* Soya; *G.* Surva; *Bom.* & *Mar.* Shepu, Shupa; *T.* Satakkuppi; *Te.* Sompa; *Sin.* Sathakuppai; *Bur.* Samyeit.

Phaseolus aureus L.
E. Golden gram; *B.* Sonamoog; *H.* Sonamung; *A.* Mogu-mah; *O.* Jhain-muga; *P.* Mung; *Mar.* Hirave mug; *M.* Cherupayaru; *T.* Pachapayaru; *Te.* Pesalu.

Phaseolus mungo L.
E. Black gram; *S.* Mudga; *B.* Mashkalai; *H.* Urid; *U.* Mung; *A.* Mati-mah; *O.* Muga; *P.* Mash; *G.* Udad; *Bom.* Mung; *Mar.* Udid; *T.* Ulunnu; *Te.* Uddulu; *Bur.* Pai.

Phaseolus radiatus L.
S. Masha; *B.* Mashkalai; *H.* Thikiri, Urid; *U.* Mash; *G.* Arad; *Mar.* Maga, Udid; *M.* Cherupoyara; *T.* Patchaippayarai; *Te.* Patchapesalu; *C.* Uddu; *Sin.* Ulundumae.

Phaseolus roxburghii L.
B. Mash-kalai.

Phoenix dactylifera L.
E. Arabian date palm; *S.* Pindukharjura; *B.* Khejur; *H.* Khaji, Khajur; *U.* Khurma; *O.* Khorjuri; *P.* Khaji; *G.* & *Bom.* Khajur; *Mar.* Kharjur; *M.* Itta; *T.* Inju; *Te.* Kharjuramu, Ita; *C.* Kajura; *Sin.* Indi; *Bur.* Sunbalun.

Phoenix paludosa Roxb.
B. Hintal; *Te.* Hintalamu.

Phoenix sylvestris Roxb.
E. Date-palm; *S.* Kharjuri; *B.* & *A.* Khejur; *H.* & *G.* Khajur; *O.* Khajuri; *P.* Khajur, Khaji; *G.* Kajuri; *Bom.* Khajur; *Mar.* Kharik; *M.* Itta; *T.* Ichcham; *Te.* Itha; *C.* Ichala; *Sin.* Indi.

Phragmites karka Trin.
E. Nodding reed; *S.* Nala; *B.* Nalkhagra; *H.* Nuda-nar; *A.* Khagra; *O.* Jankai; *G.* Nali; *Mar.* Nala; *M.* Nalam; *T.* Perunanal; *Te.* Kikkasagaddi; *C.* Hulugalagu; *Bur.* Kaing.

Phyllanthus distichus Muell-Arg. = *Cicca acida* Merr.
E. Country gooseberry; *S.* Lavali; *B.* Nohr; *H.* Chalmeri; *U.* Harpharuri; *A.* Holpholi; *O.* Narakoli; *Bom.* Harparawri; *Mar.* Ray awali; *M.* Arinelli; *T.* Arunelli;

Te. Ratsavusiriki; *C.* Aranelli; *Sin.* Ratanelli; *Bur.* Thinbawnibyu.

Phyllanthus emblica L. = *Emblica officinalis* Gaertn.
E. Emblic myrobalan; *S.* Amlika; *B.* & *A.* Amloki; *H.* Amla; *U.* Anwala; *O.* Anla; *P.* Amla; *G.* Ambala; *Bom.* Avala; *Mar.* Awala; *M.* Amalakam; *T.* Amalagam, Nelli; *Te.* Usiri; *C.* Amalaka; *Sin.* Awusadanelli; *Bur.* Hziphyu.

Phyllanthus niruri L.
S. Bahupatra; *B.* & *U.* Bhuiamla; *H.* Bhonyaabgli, Jaramla; *O.* Bhuiaola; *G.* Bhonyaanmati; *Bom.* Bhuiavala; *Mar.* Bhuiavali; *M.* Kirganelli; *T.* Kilanelli; *Te.* Nelausirika; *C.* Kiranelligida; *Sin.* Pittawaka; *Bur.* Miziphiyu.

Phyllanthus urinaria L.
S. Shiva; *B.* & *H.* Hazarmani; *G.* Kharsadabonyaanmali; *Mar.* Lal-mundajanvali; *M.* Chirukizhukanelli; *T.* Shivappunelli; *Te.* Ettausirika; *C.* Kempukiranelli; *Sin.* Ratpittawaka; *Bur.* Miziphivuani.

Physalis minima L.
S. Tankari; *B.* Bon-tepari; *H.* Chirpoti, Tulatipati; *P.* Kaknaj; *G.* Parpoti; *Bom.* Thanmori; *Mar.* Chirboti, Dhanmori; *Te.* Kupanti; *Sin.* Hinmottu.

Physalis peruviana L.
E. Cape gooseberry, Ground cherry; *S.* Tankasi; *B.* Tepari; *H.* Tipari, Macao; *P.* Rasbhari; *Mar.* Phopti; *T.* Siruthakkali; *Te.* Busarakaya, Buddabusara; *C.* Bondulla; *Bur.* Pongpin.

Pilea microphylla Liebm.
E. Gunpowder plant.

Pinus longifolia Roxb.
E. Pine; *S.* Dhupavrikshaka; *B.* Saralgach; *H.* & *P.* Chil, Chir; *O.* Sorolokatho; *G.* & *Mar.* Saraladeodara; *M.* Saralam; *Te.* Devadaru; *T.* Suruldevadari; *C.* Saraladevadaru.

Piper betle L.
E. Betel leaf plant; *S.* Tambula; *B.* & *Bom.* Pan; *H.* Tambuli, Pan; *U.* & *O.* Pan, Pana; *Mar.* Nagweli; *M.* & *T.* Vethila; *Te.* Tamalapaku; *Sin.* Balat; *Bur.* Kwan; *T.* Vethilai.

Piper cubeba L.
E. Cubeb; *B.* & *H.* Kabab-chini; *G.* Tadamiri; *Mar.* Kankol; *M.* & *T.* Thippli; *Te.* Tokamiriyalu.

Piper chaba Hunter
S. Chavana; *B.* Choi; *H.* Chab; *G.* Chavaka; *Mar.* Chavala; *C.* Chavya; *T.* Chaikama.

Piper longum L.
E. Long pepper; *S.* Pippali, Chanchala; *B.* Pipool; *H.* Pipli; *U.* Pipul; *A.* Pipoli; *O.* Pipali; *P.* Maghan; *Bom.* & *G.* Pipara; *Mar.* Pimpali; *M.* Thippali; *T.* Tippili; *Te.* Pippali; *C.* Hippali, Tippali; *Sin.* Tippli.

Piper nigrum L.
E. Black pepper; *S.* Maricha, Krishna; *B.* Golmarich, Kalomarich; *H.* Golmirch, Gulki; *A.* Jaluk; *O.* Gola maricha; *P.* Kali marich; *Bom.* & *G.* Kalomirich; *Mar.* Kali miri; *M.* Kuru-mulagu; *T.* Milagoo; *Te.* Savyamu; *C.* Menasu; *Sin.* Miris; *Bur.* Nayukon.

Pisonia aculeata L.
B. Baganchra; *O.* Hationkuso; *T.* Karindu, Udappu; *Te.* Konki, Pisangi; *C.* Etharumullinaballi.

Pistacia vera L.
E. Green almond, *B.* Pesta; *H.* Pista.

Pistia stratiotes L.
E. Water lettuce; *S.* Kumbhika; *B.* Toka-pana; *H.* & *P.* Jalkhumbi; *A.* Borpuni; *O.* Boro jhanji; *G.* Jalakumbhi; *Bom.* Gondala, Prashni; *Mar.* Gangabati; *M.* Muttappayal; *T.* Agasatamarai; *Te.* Akasatamara; *C.* Antaragange; *Sin.* Deyaparandella.

Pisum sativum L.
E. Pea; *S.* Satila; *B.* & *O.* Matar; *H.* Mattar; *A.* Motor; *P.* Khanda, Mattar; *G.* & *Bom.* Vatana; *Mar.* Watane; *M.* Payaru; *T.* Pattani; *Te.* Patanlu; *C.* gundusanighelu; *Sin.* Ratagoradiya; *Bur.* Pai.

Pithecolobium dulce Benth. = *Inga dulcis* Willd.
E. Manilla tamarind; *B.* Dekani

tentul; *H.* Vilayatiimli; *O.* Simakoina; *G.* Vilayatiambli, Ekadati; *Bom.* Vilayatiyamli, Chinch; *Mar.* Vilayatichinch; *T.* Kodukkappuli; *Te.* Simachinta; *Bur.* Kywetanyin.

Plumeria acutifolia Poir. = *P. rubra* L.
E. Temple tree, Pagoda tree; *S.* Devaganangalu; *B.* Gorurchampa, Gulancha; *H.* Golainchi; *U.* Achin; *A.* Gulanchi; *O.* Katha champa; *P.* Gulchin; *G.* Radh-champo; *Bom.* Khurchampa; *Mar.* Sonchampa; *M.* Ezava-chempakam; *T.* Ilattalari, Perungalli; *Te.* Arhataganneru, Nuruvarahalu; *C.* Devaganagile, Ganagala; *Sin.* Alariya; *Bur.* Ta-yop-sagah.

Pogostemon plectranthoides Desf.
B. Pachouli, Juilata; *H.* Pangla, Lujra; *O.* Gondripulu; *Bom.* Pangla; *Te.* Kussurijang.

Poinciana regia Boj. = *Delonix regia* Raf.
E. Goldmohur; *B.* & *A.* Radhachura; *H.* Gulmohor; *O.* Radhachuda; *Bom.* Vayni; *Mar.* Sankasura; *M.* Maramandaram; *T.* Mayilkonnai; *Te.* Sunkevaramu, Maramandaram; *C.* Sunkesari, Kattikayi.

Polianthes tuberosa L.
E. Tuberose; *S.* & *B.* Rajanigandha; *H.* & *P.* Gulshabo; *Bom.* Gulcheri; *Mar.* Gulchhadi; *T.* Nilasampangi; *Te.* Sukandharaji; *Bur.* Hnenben.

Polyalthia cerasoides Hook. f.
H. Kudumi.

Polyalthia longifolia Benth. & Hook. f.
E. Mast tree; *S.* Devadaru, Putrajiva; *B.* Debdaru; *H.* Ashok; *A.* & *O.* Dabadaru; *P.* Devidari; *G.* Ashopalo; *Bom.* & *Mar.* Asoka, Asupala; *M.* Aranamaram; *T.* Nettilingam; *Te.* Asokamu, Devadaru; *C.* Putrajivi.

Polycarpon loeflinge Benth. & Hook. = *P. indicum* Merr.
S. Bhisatta; *B.* Gima-shak; *H.* Sureta; *T.* Nilaisedachi; *Te.* Bommasari, Rajuma.

Polygonum barbatum L.
B. Bekhunjubaz; *P.* Narri; *Mar.* Dhaktasheral; *M.* Vellutamodelamukku; *T.* Atalari; *Te.* Kondamalle, Niruganneru; *Sin.* Ratukimbulwenna.

Polygonum hydropiper L.
E. Water pepper; *B.* Pakurmul.

Polygonum orientale L.
E. Oriental pepper; *B.* Pani-marich, Bishkatali; *H.* Machoti; *A.* Bihlongoni; *O.* Muthi saga; *P.* Narri; *M.* Mothala-mooka; *T.* Atalarie; *Te.* Kondamalle; *Sin.* Sudu-kumbulwenna.

Polygonum plebejum R. Br.
E. Alpine knotweed; *U* Anjabar; *P.* Bilauri, Maslun.

Pongamia glabra Vent. = *P. pinnata* Pierre.
E. Indian beech; *S.* Karanja, Rochana; *B.* Karanja; *H.* Karanj, Kiramal; *U.* Karanjwah; *O.* Koronjo; *P.* Karanj; *G.* Kanaji; *Bom.* Kiramal; *Mar.* Karanja; *M.* Minnari; *T.* Kanjanam, Ponga; *Te.* Kranuga; *C.* Batti; *Sin.* Magulkaranda; *Bur.* Thawen.

Pontederia vaginalis Roxb.
B. Nanku; *Te.* Nirokanob.

Populus alba L.
E. Poplar.

Porana paniculata Roxb.
E. Bridal creeper; *H.* Safedbel.

Portulaca oleracea L.
E. Purslane; *B.* Choto-lunia; *H.* Kulfa-sag; *U.* Khurfah; *A.* Hanhthengia; *O.* Balbalua; *P.* Lunia, Lunak; *G.* Loni; *Bom.* Gol, Kurfah; *Mar.* Ghol; *M.* Karicheera; *T.* Karikeerai; *Te.* Pavilikura; *C.* Dudagorai; *Sin.* Gendakola; *Bur.* Mayabyit.

Portulaca quadrifida L.
S. Upadyhi; *B.* Baro-lunia; *H.* Loniya; *G.* Jhiniluni; *P.* Haksha; *Bom.* Barikaghola, Kota; *Mar.* Ranghol; *T.* Passelikkirai; *Te.* Kura, Pavili; *C.* Halibachcheli; *Sin.* Hingendakola.

Portulaca tuberosa Roxb.
B. Nunia; *Mar.* Jangligajar; *Te.* Boddakura; *Sin.* Uragenda.

Pothos scandens L.
B. Gajpipul; *A.* Hatilota; *O.* Gaja pipali; *P.* Gazpipal; *G.* Moto pipar; *Mar.* Aanjan vel; *M.* Anapparuva; *C.* Adikabiluballi; *Sin.* Potawel.

Pouzolzia indica Gaud.
H. Piparisari; *Te.* Eddumutteedumpa.

Premna integrifolia L.
S. Arani; *B.* Gambari; *H.* Agetha, Arni; *U.* Arani; *O.* Ogobothu; *G.* Arni; *Bom.* Arni, Marvel; *Mar.* Aran; *M.* Munna; *T.* Munnai; *Te.* Nagura, Tukkadu; *C.* Ichu; *Sin.* Karnika; *Bur.* Toungthangyee.

Prosopis spicigera L.
S. Shami; *B.* & *O.* Shomi; *H.* Chhokara, Sami; *A.* Somidh; *P.* Jand; *G.* Kando; *Bom.* Shemi, Shemri; *Mar.* Shemi; *M.* Parampu; *T.* Perumbai; *Te.* Jambi; *C.* Banni.

Prunus amygdalus L.
E. Almond; *S.* Badama; *B.* Bilati badam; *H.* & *P.* Badam; *U.* Badamshirin; *O.* Badamo; *Mar.* & *M.* Badam; *T.* Vadumai; *Te.* Badamu; *C.* Badami.

Prunus cerasoides L. = *P. puddum* Roxb.
E. Cherry; *S.* Charu, Padmaka; *H.* Padam; *P.* Paddam; *G.* Padmak; *Bom.* Padmakasta; *Mar.* Padmaka.

Prunus communis Hudson.
E. Plum; *H.* Alubukhara, Alucha; *C.* Alubokara.

Prunus domestica L.
E. Prunce.

Prunus persica Benth. & Hook. f.
E. Peach; *H.* Aru; *U.* Adud; *O.* Pishu; *P.* Aru, Arui; *C.* Pichesu.

Psidium guyava L.
E. Guava; *S.* Perala; *B.* Peyara; *H.* & *U.* Amrud; *A.* Modhuri-am; *O.* Pijuli; *P.* Anjirzard, Amrud; *G.* Jamphal; *Bom.* Jam, Peru; *Mar.* Peru; *M.* Perakka; *T.* Koyya; *Te.* Jama; *C.* Perala; *Sin.* Peragadi; *Bur.* Malakaben.

Psoralea corylifolia L.
S. Bakuchi, Kushthahantri; *B.* Latakasturi; *H.* & *P.* Babchi; *U.* Babechi; *O.* Bakuchi; *G.* Bavacha; *Bom.* Bawachi; *Mar.* Babachi; *T.* Karpuvarishi; *Te.* Bhavanji.

Psychotria ipecacuanha Stocks. = ***Uragoga*** *ipecacuanha* Baill.
E. Ipecac; *H.* Kakatund; *Mar.* Kurki.

Pterocarpus marsupium Roxb.
E. Indian kino; *S.* Pitasalaka; *B.* Pitsal; *H.* Bijasal; *U.* Damulakhvain; *O.* Piyasalo; *G.* Bibla; *Bom.* Asan, Bibala; *Mar.* Asana. Bibla; *M.* Venna; *T.* Asanam, Vengai; *Te.* Pedegu, Vengisa; *C* Benga; *Sin.* Gummalu.

Pterocarpus santalinus L.
E. Red sandal wood; *S.* Raktachandana; *B.* Lalchandan; *H.* Rukhtochandan, Undum; *G* & *Bom.* Ratanjali; *Mar.* Raktachandan; *T.* Sandanam; *Te.* Raktachandanamu, Ettachandanamu; *C.* Raktashandana; *Sin.* Ructhandun; *Bur.* Sandaku.

Pterospermum acerifolium Willd.
S. Karnikara, Mushukunda; *B.* Kanakchampa, Moochkunda; *H.* Kathachampa, Kaniar; *A.* Konokchampa; *O.* Moochkunda; *Bom.* Kanakchampa, Karnikara; *Mar.* Much kund; *T.* Vennangu; *Te.* Matsakanda; *C.* Kanakchampaka; *Bur.* Toung-pet-wun.

Pueraria tuberosa DC.
S. Ikshugandha; *B.* Shimiabatraji; *H.* & *P.* Badar, Siali; *G.* Karwinai; *Bom.* Dari, Darni; *Mar.* Badra, Pithana; *Te.* Darigummadi.

Punica granatum L.
E. Pomegranate; *S.* Darimba; *B.* & *A.* Dalim; *H.* & *P.* Anar; *O.* Dalimba; *G.* Dadam; *Mar.* Dalimb; *M.* Matalam; *T.* Madulam.

Putranjiva roxburghii Wall.
E. Wild olive; *S.* Apatyajiva; *B.* Putranjib; *H.* Jiaputa; *O.* Bholokoli;

P. Jiyaputra; *Bom.* & *Mar.* Putajan; *M.* Pongalam; *T.* Karupalli; *Te.* Putrajivika; *C.* Amani; *Bur.* Tankyat.

Pyrus communis L.
E. Pear; *B.* Nashpati; *H.* Nukh; *P.* Batang; *T.* Perikkay; *Te.* Berikaya, Beripandu.

Pyrus malus L.
E. Apple; *S.* Savane; *B.* Apel; *H.* Seb; *C.* Sevu.

Quamoclit pinnata Boj. = *Ipomoea quamoclit* L.
E. Needle creeper; *S.* Kamalata; *B.* Tarulata, Kunjalata; *H.* & *P* Kamlata; *A.* Kunjalota; *O.* Kunjalata; *Bom.* Ganeshvel; *Mar.* Ganesh puspa; *M.* Suriyakanti; *T.* Kembumalligai; *Te.* Kasiratnamu; *C.* Kamalate; *Bur.* Myatlaeni.

Quisqualis indica L.
E. Rangoon creeper; *B.* Brahmolata; *H.* & *P.* Lal-malti; *A.* Madhabilota; *O.* Modhumalati; *G.* Barma sinivel; *Bom.* Vilayatichambeli; *Mar.* Lal chameli; *T.* Rangoon malli; *Te.* Rangonimalle; *Bur.* Dawchmaing.

Randia dumetorum Lamk.
E. Emetic nut; *S.* Madana; *B.* Madan; *H.* Main; *U.* Mainphal; *A.* Gurol; *O.* Potua; *P.* Mindla; *G.* Mindhal; *Bom.* Ghela; *Mar.* Peralu, Gelaphala; *M.* Karalikkaya; *T.* Karai, Kadudam; *Te.* Madanamu, Mangara; *C.* Kare; *Sin.* Kukuruman; *Bur.* Thaminsa.

Randia uliginosa DC.
E. Grey emetic nut; *S.* Pindalu; *B.* Piralo; *H.* Pendua, Pindar; *U.* Pindalu; *O.* Pendovoha; *G.* Gangeda; *Bom.* Pendari; *Mar.* Pendru; *M.* Punankara; *T.* Valikkarai; *Te.* Peddamranga; *C.* Kare, Pandri; *Sin.* Wadiga; *Bur.* Nyangyee.

Ranunculus sceleratus L.
E. Indian buttercup; *B.* Palik; *H.* Bondhoniya, Shim.

Raphanus sativus L.
E. Radish; *S.* Mulaka; *B.* & *A.* Mula; *H.* Muli, Muroi; *P.* Muli; *G.* Mula, Mura; *Bom.* Mul Muro; *Mar.* Mula, Muri; *M.* Mullanki; *T.* & *Te.* Mullangi *C.* Bili; *Sin.* Rabu; *Bur.* Moula.

Rauwolfia serpentina Benth.
S. Chandrika; *B.* Sarpagandha, Chandra; *H.* Sarpgandh, Chotachand; *A.* Chando; *O.* Patala garuda; *Bom.* Amelpodi, Chandra; *Mar.* Harki, Sarpasanda; *M.* Amalporiyan; *T.* Sovannamilbori; *Te.* Dumparasana; *C.* Chandrike; *Sin.* Ratekaweriya; *Bur.* Bongamaiza.

Ravenala madagascariensis Sonn.
E. Traveller's tree; *B.* Pantha padap.

Rheum emodi Wall.
E. Rhubarb; *S.* Revatchini; *B.* Revanchini; *H.* Dolu; *U.* Rewanchini; *G.* Gamnirevanchini; *P.* Atsu, Rewandchini; *Bom.* Ladakirevandachini; *Mar.* Revachini; *T.* Nattirevalchini; *Te.* Nattureval-chini; *C.* Natrivalchini.

Rhinacanthus communis Nees.
B. Juipana; *H.* & *U.* Palakjuhi; *Bom.* Nagamalli; *Mar.* Gajakarni; *T.* Kaligai; *Te.* Nagamalle; *C.* Nagamallige; *Sin.* Anilta; *Bur.* Anitia.

Rhizophora conjugata L.
B. Khamo, Bora.

Rhizophora mucronata Lamk.
E. Mangrove; *B.* Khamo, Bhura; *O.* Rohi, Rai; *Bom.* Kandel, Hariya; *Mar.* & *T.* Kandal; *M.* Kantal; *Te.* Ponna; *C.* Kandale.

Rhus succedanea L.
E. Crab's claw; *B.* Kakrasringi; *H.* Kakrasing; *P.* Arkhol, Titri; *T.* Karkhadagachingi; *Te.* Karkkarasringi; *C.* Karkatakashringi.

Ricinus communis L.
E. Castor; *S.* Eranda; *B.* Rehri; *H.* Arand, Rendi; *U.* Erenda; *A.* Erigoch; *O.* Jada; *P.* Rendi; *G.* & *Bom.* Erandi; *Mar.* Erand; *M.* & *T.* Avanakku; *Te.* Amidamu; *C.* Avudalu, Haralu; *Sin.* Eudaru; *Bur.* Kyeksu.

Rivea hypocrateriformis Choisy.
B. Kalmilata.

Rosa centifolia L.
E. Cabbage rose; *S.* Vrittapuspa; *B.* Golap; *H. & U.* Gulab; *O.* Golabo; *P.* Gulisurkh, Gulab; *Mar.* Gulapha; *T.* Irosā, Gulā; *Te.* Roja; *C.* Gulabi; *Bur.* Nhin-su-bin, Hninsi.

Rosa damascena Mill.
E. Bussora rose; *S.* Shatadali; *H.* Gulab, Sudburg; *U.* Gulab; *O.* Bosora golabo; *Bom.* Sudburg; *M.* Penimirpushpam; *T.* Irosa; *Te.* Gulābi; *C.* Panniru, Tarana.

Rubia tinctoria L.
E. Indian madder; *S. & B.* Manjistha; *H. & P.* Manjit; *A.* Majothi; *Bom.* Madar; *Mar. & C.* Manjeshta; *M.* Manjetti; *T.* Manjitti, Shevelli; *Te.* Tamravalli.

Rubus hexagynus Roxb.
E. Bramble; *B.* Hirachura.

Ruellia prostrata Lamk.
G. Kalighavani; *M.* Upudali; *Sin.* Nilparuk.

Ruellia tuberosa L. = *Dipterocanthus tuberosus* Nees.
B. Chotpotey.

Rumex maritima L.
B. Bonpalang; *H.* Julpalam; *U.* Bijaband; *P.* Junglipalak.

Rumex vesicorius L.
E. Dock, Sorrel; *S.* Shatavedhi; *B.* Tak palang; *H.* Khatta-palak; *U. & A.* Chuka-sak; *O.* Palanga; *P.* Khatta-mitha; *Bom. & Mar.* Chuka; *T.* Shakkankirai; *Te.* Chukkakura; *Sin.* Suri; *Bur.* Kalak-henboun.

Rungia parviflora Nees.
S. & H. Pindi; *G.* Mothokadsalio; *T.* Tavashumurungi, Punaka-pundu; *Te.* Pindikunda.

Ruta graveolens L.
E. Common rue; *S.* Sadapaha; *B.* Ermul; *H.* Satari; *U.* Sudah; *O.* Maruya;. *G. & Mar.* Satapa; *Bom.* Satap; *T.* Arvada; *Te.* Aruda, Sadapa; *C.* Sadabu; *Sin.* Aruda.

Saccharum munja Roxb.
S. Munja; *B.* Sar; *H.* Munja, Sarkanda; *P.* Kharkara; *Te.* Gundra, Ponika.

Saccharum officinarum L.
E. Sugarcane; *S.* Ikshu; *B.* Akh; *H.* Ganna, Tetari; *U.* Gana; *A.* Kunhiar; *O.* Akhu; *P.* Kamand, Gunna; *G. & Bom.* Sherde; *Mar.* Usa; *M.* Ikshu; *T.* Karimpu; *Te.* Cheruku; *C.* Ikshu; *Sin.* Uk; *Bur.* Keyan.

Saccharum spontaneum L.
E. Thatch grass; *S.* Kasha; *B.* Khagra, Kash; *H. & G.* Kans; *O.* Kashatandi; *A.* Kanibon; *P.* Kahi; *G.* Kansado; *Mar.* Bagberi; *M.* Nainkana; *T.* Eruvai, Nanal; *Te.* Billugaddi, Koregadi; *C.* Darbhe; *Bur.* Thetkiakyn.

Sagittaria sagittifolia L.
E. Arrowhead; *B.* Chotokut.

Salix tetrasperma Roxb.
E. Willow; *B.* Panijoma; *H.* Baishi; *A.* Bhi; *O.* Panijamo; *P.* Bakshel; *Bom.* Bacha, Baishi; *Mar.* Bitasa; *M.* Nirunji; *T.* Niruvanji; *Te.* Etipala; *C.* Bayise; *Bur.* Momaka.

Salsola kali L.
E. Saltwort; *H.* Shora; *P.* Sajjibuti.

Salvia plebeja R. Br.
E. Sage; *B.* Bhui-tulsi; *P.* Sathi; *Bom.* Kammarkas.

Santalum album L.
E. Sandalwood; *S.* Chandana; *B. & A.* Chandan; *H.* Sufed chandan; *O. & P.* Chandana; *G.* Sukhada; *Bom.* Chandan, Sandal; *Mar.* Chandan; *M.* Chandanam; *T.* Channanamaram; *Te.* Chandanamu; *C.* Chandala; *Sin.* Rathiri; *Bur.* Santaku.

Sapindus mukorossi Gaertn.
E. Soap-nut; *S.* Aristha: *B.* Ritha; *H. & P.* Dodan; *A.* Haitaguti; *O.* Ita; *Bom.* Kannar.

Sapindus trifoliatus L. = *S. emarginatus* Wall.
E. Soap-nut; *S.* Aristha, Phenila; *B.* Baro-ritha; *H. & U.* Ritha; *O.*

Ritha; *G.* Aritha; *Bom.* Rhita; *Mar.* Ritha; *M.* Urvanji; *T.* Ponnankottai; *Te.* Kunkudu; *C.* Arishta; *Sin.* Antavala; *Bur.* Meav-me-suekhati.

Sapium sebiferum Roxb.
E. Chinese tallow tree; *S.* Agaru; *B.* Momchina; *H.* Lendwa; *O.* Ronojita; *Bom.* Pipalyank; *M.* Bengieri; *Te.* Badike.

Saponaria vaccaria L.
E. Soapwort, Cow herb; *B.* Sabuni; *H.* Musna.

Saraca indica L.
E. Asoka; *S.* Vanjula; *B.* Asoke; *H.* & *P.* Asok; *O.* Asoka; *G.* Ashupala; *Bom.* Ashok; *Mar.* Sitecha-ashoke; *M.* Hemapushpam; *T.* Asokam; *Te.* Asokamu; *C.* Ashoka; *Sin.* Diyaratmal; *Bur.* Thawka.

Sarcolobus globosus Wall.
B. Badlilata.

Sarcostemma brevistigma Wight.
S. Somavalli; *B.* & *H.* Somlata; *O.* Somolota; *G.* Somvel; *Bom.* Soma; *Mar.* Somyel; *M.* & *T.* Somam; *Te.* Somalata; *C.* Somaballi; *Sin.* Muwakiriya.

Saussurea lappa Clarke
E. Costus; *S.* Kushtha: *B.* Kur; *H.* Kust; *U.* Kut; *G.* Kut, Upaleta; *Bom.* Ouplate; *M.* Seppudy; *T.* Kostum; *Te.* Kustam; *Sin.* Godamahanel.

Schleichera trijuga Willd. = *S. oleosa* Oken.
E. Ceylon oak; *S.* Koshamra; *H.* Gausam, Kosum; *O.* Kusumo; *P.* Jamoa; *G.* Kossame; *Bom.* Kosam; *Mar.* Kosimb; *M.* Puvam; *T.* Konji, Puvam; *Te.* Paparti, Pullakaya; *C.* Kakuta; *Sin.* Kong; *Bur.* Kyet-mouk.

Scindopsus officinalis Schott.
S. & *U.* Gajapippali; *B.* Gajpipul; *H.* Baripipli, Gajapipli; *O.* Gojopippoli; *G.* Mottoper; *Mar.* Thorapimpli; *M.* Attittippali; *T.* Anaittippili; *Te.* Enugatippali; *C.* Gajahippali.

Scirpus articulatus L.
B. Patpati.

Scirpus grossus L. f.
S. Kaseruka; *B.* Kesur; *H.* Kasuru; *U.* Kaseru; *P.* Kaseru, Dila; *Bom.* Kachera; *Mar.* Kasara: *Te.* Gundatengagaddi.

Scirpus littoralis Schrad.
E. Clubrush.

Scoparia dulcis L.
E. Sweet broom weed; *B.* Bon dhoney.

Semecarpus anacardium L.
E. Marking nut; *S.* Bhallataka; *B.* Bhela; *H.* Bhilawa; *U.* Bhitanvana; *O.* Bhollia; *G.* Bhilamu; *Bom.* Bhiba; *Mar.* Bibwa; *M.* Chera; *T.* Serangottai; *Te.* Bhallataki, Jidi; *C.* Bhallataka; *Sin.* Kiribadulla; *Bur.* Claybeng.

Sesamum indicum DC.
E. Sesame, Gingelly; *S.* Tila, Jatila; *B.* Til; *H.* Gingli; *U.* & *P.* Til; *A.* Tisi; *O.* Rashi; *G.* Mithho-tel; *Bom.* Ashadital, Bariktil; *Mar.* Tila; *M.* Chitelu; *T.* Ellu; *Te.* Nuvvulu; *C.* Yallu; *Sin.* Talla; *Bur.* Hnan.

Sesbania grandiflora Pers.
E. Swamp tree, Sesban; *S.* Agasti, Vaka; *B.* & *A.* Bakphul; *L.* Agast; *U.* Agast; *O.* Agasti; *G.* Agathio; *Bom.* & *Mar.* Agasta; *M.* Agathi; *T.* Agathykkeerai; *Te.* Avisi; *C.* Agase; *Sin.* Katuru murunga; *Bur.* Pankpan.

Seseli indicum W. & A.
S. Vanayamani; *B.* Bonjowan; *Mar.* Kiriminjiajwan.

Setaria glauca Beauv.
S. Italian millet; *S.* Kanguni; *B.* Kakni, Kauni; *H.* Cheena, Kakni; *A.* Konidhan; *O.* Tangun; *P.* Kangni; *G.* Kang; *Bom.* Kangi; *Mar.* Kangu; *M.* Navana, Tauna; *T.* Tennai; *Te.* Korra; *C.* Naoni; *Sin.* Tanahal; *Bur.* Puki.

Shorea robusta Gaertn.
E. Sal; *S.* Ashvakarna, Sala: *B.* Sal; *H.* & *P.* Sal; *U.* Ral: *O.*

Sala; *P.* Seral, Sal; *G.* Ral; *Bom.* Sal; *Mar.* Shala; *M.* Maramaram; *T.* Shalam; *Te.* Gugal, Saluva; *C.* Guggala; *Sin.* Dammala; *Bur.* Enkhyen.

Sida acuta Burm.
S. Bala; *B.* Kureta; *H.* Kareta, Kharenti; *O.* Siobola; *G. & Bom.* Bala, Janglimenthi; *Mar.* Chikana; *M.* Malatanni; *T.* Malaidangi; *Te.* Nelabenda; *C.* Vishakaddi; *Sin.* Gasbevila; *Bur.* Katsaynai.

Sida cordifolia L.
S. Svetbarila, Batyalaka; *B.* Berela; *H.* Bariara; *A.* Bariala; *O.* Bisiripi; *P.* Kharenti; *G.* Kharati; *Bom. & Mar.* Chikana; *M.* Kuruthotti; *T.* Karumthotti; *Te.* Chirubenda; *C.* Hettutti; *Sin.* Walbevila.

Sida rhombifolia L.
S. Lalbarila, Atibala; *B.* Lalbarela; *H.* Bariara; *O.* Nalobadianala; *G.* Baladana; *Mar.* Sadeda; *M.* Totti, Anakkuruntotti; *T.* Anaikurundotti; *Te.* Atibala; *C.* Bennagaragu; *Sin.* Kotikanbevila.

Siegesbeckia orientalis L.
H. Katampam.

Smilax macrophylla Roxb. = *S. zeylanica* L.
E. Indian sarsaparilla; *B.* Kumarilata, Kumarika; *H.* Chobchini; *A.* Hastikarna-lota; *O.* Kumbhatua; *P.* Ushba; *Mar.* Ghot vel; *M.* Kaltamara; *T.* Ayadi; *Te.* Kondatamara; *Sin.* Kabarasa; *Bur.* Kuku.

Smithia sensitiva Ait.
B. Nalakashina; *H.* Odabirni.

Solanum ferox L.
S. Sitakanta; *B.* Rambegun; *A.* Bon-bengena; *O.* Bheji baigana; *Mar.* Bajiche wange; *M.* Anachchunta; *T.* Anaichundai; *Te.* Mulaka; *C.* Biligulla; *Sin.* Mallakattu; *Bur.* Sinkayan.

Solanum indicum L.
S. Kantakini; *B.* Byakur; *H.* Birhatta, Barhanta; *U.* Janglibringan; *A.* Tit-bhekuri; *O.* Kantara; *P.* Kandiari; *G.* Ubhiringani; *Bom.* Motiringi, Ringani; *Mar.* Dorli; *M.* Kattuchunda; *T.* Karimulli; *Te.* Nellamulaka; *C.* Badane, Gulla; *Sin.* Tibbatu.

Solanum melongena L.
E. Brinjal; *S.* Bartaku, Brihati; *B.* Begun; *H.* Baigon; *U.* Baingan; *A.* Bengena; *O.* Baigana; *P.* Bengan; *G.* Baigana, Ringni; *Bom.* Baigana, Venge; *Mar.* Wange; *M.* Vazhuthana; *T.* Kaththiri; *Te.* Vanga; *C.* Bhantaki; *Sin.* Wambatu; *Bur.* Ka-yan.

Solanum nigrum L.
E. Black nightshade; *S.* Kakamachi, Jaghenephala; *B.* Kakmachi; *H.* Gurkamai; *U.* Makoya; *A.* Pokmou; *O.* Nunnunia; *P.* Mako; *G.* Piludu; *Bom.* Kamuni, Mako; *Mar.* Kangani; *M.* Mulaguthakkali; *T.* Manathakkali; *Te.* Kamanchi; *C.* Kanchi, Ganike; *Sin.* Kalukanweriya.

Solanun torvum Swartz.
B. Titabegun; *A.* Hathibhekuri; *M.* Kattuchunta; *T.* Sundai, Kottukkattari; *Te.* Kondavusta; *C.* Sonde; *Bur.* Kayangyin.

Solanum tuberosum L.
E. Potato; *B.*, *A.*, *H.* & *O.* Alu; *G.* Papeta; *Mar.* Batata; *M.* & *T.* Urulakkizhangu; *Te.* Urulagadda.

Solanum verbascifolium L.
E. Potato tree; *S.* Vidari; *B.* Arasa, Urusa; *U.* Ola; *P.* Kalamewa; *Mar.* Kutri; *M.* Erichunta; *T.* Anaichundai; *Te.* Budama; *C.* Kadusonde; *Sin.* Hekarilla.

Solanum xanthocarpum Schrad.
S. Kantakari; *B.* Kantikari; *H.* Kateli; *U.* Katilla; *A.* Kantakari; *O.* Ankaranti; *P.* Kandiali; *G.* Bhoyaringani; *Bom.* Bhuringni; *Mar.* Kateringani; *M.* Kandankarychunda; *T.* Kandankaththiri; *Te.* Nelavakudu; *C.* Kantakari; *Sin.* Ellabattu.

Sonchus arvensis L.
E. Sow thistle; *B.* Bonpalang; *H.* Sadhi; *U.* Sahadevi; *P.* Bhangra; *Te.* Nallatapata.

Sorghum vulgare L.
E. Great millet; *B.* Juar; *H.* & *P.* Jowar; *A.* Joudhan; *O.* Bajara; *Mar.* Jawar; *M.* & *T.* Cholam.

Spatholobus roxburghii Benth.
H. Maula.

Spermacoce hispida L. = *Borreria hispida* K. Schum.
S. & *H*. Madanaghanti; *Bom*. Dhoti, Ghantachibaji; *T*. Nattaichuri; *Te*. Madana, Modina.

Sphaeranthus indicus L.
S. Mundirika; *B*. Chagalnadi, Gorakhamundi; *H*. Mundi, Gorakmundi; *U*. Mundi; *P*. Gurukmundi; *G*. & *Mar*. Gorakhamundi; *Bom*. Gorakhmundi; *M*. Attakkamanni; *T*. Kottakkarandai; *Te*. Bondatarapu; *C*. Karande; *Sin*. Mudumahana.

Spilanthes acmella Merr.
B. Marhati-tiga; *H*. Akarkaru; *A*. Pirazha; *P*. Akarkarha, Pokormul; *Bom*. Akarkara; *Te*. Maratitige, Maratimogga; *Sin*. Akmalla; *Bur*. Henkala.

Spinacea oleracea L.
E. Spinach; *S*. Chhurika; *B*. Palang; *H*. Chirvapalak, Pinnis; *U*. Palak; *P*. Isfanak; *Bom*. Isfanaj, Palang, *T*. Vasaiyilaikkirai; *Te*. Dumpabachchali.

Spinifex squarrosus L.
E. Seashore grass; *M*. Edimula; *T*. Iravananbul; *Te*. Rananasurunimisalu; *Sin*. Maharawanarequala.

Spondias dulcis Willd.
E. Hogplum; *B*. Amrah; *H*. Amarat.

Spondias mangifera Willd. = *S. pinnata* Kurz.
E. Indian hogplum; *S*. Amrataka; *B*. Desi-amrah; *H*. Ambara; *A*. Amara; *O*. Ambula; *P*. Bahamb, Ambara; *Bom*. Amra, Jangliam; *Mar* Ambada, Ranamba; *M*. Ampalam; *T*. Ambalam, Marima; *Te*. Ambalamu, Kondamamidi; *C*. Amate, Pundi; *Sin*. Ambarella; *Bur*. Kywae.

Stachytarpheta indica Vahl.
E. Aronis' rod; *H*. Kariyuttarani; *M*. Katapunuttu; *T*. Simainaivirungi; *Sin*. Balanakutta.

Stellaria media L.
E. Chickweed, Starwort.

Stephegyne parvifolia Korth. = *Mitragyne parvifolia* Korth.
B. Kelikadam; *H*. Kaddam; Kangi; *P*. Kalam, Keim; *Bom*. Kadamb, Kangi; *Mar*. Kadamb, Karamb; *M*. Vimpu; *T*. Kadambai; *Te*. Pulakadimi; *C*. Kadambe; *Sin*. Helembe; *Bur*. Hteinthay.

Sterculia alata Roxb. = *Pterygota alata* R. Br.
E. Buddha's coconut; *B*. Buddhanarikel; *A*. Tula; *M*. Anattonti; *T*. Anaittondi; *Bur*. Letkope.

Sterculia foetida L.
B. & *H*. Jangli-badam; *A*. Ban-badam; *O*. Jangali badam; *G*. Narkya-uda; *Bom*. Pun; *Mar*. Goldaru; *M*. Anaththondi; *T*. Paemar..n; *Te*. Guttapubadamu; *C*. Bhatala; *Sin*. Kaditeni; *Bur*. Letkok.

Stereospermum chelonoides Clarke.
S. Patoli; *B*. Atkapali; *H*. Padri, Parral; *A*. Parolli; *O*. Patoli; *G*. Padeli; *Bom*. & *Mar*. Kirsel, Padal; *M*. Patiri; *T*. Padali, Padiri; *Te*. Kaligottu, Tagada; *C*. Hadari, Kaludi; *Sin*. Elapatol; *Bur*. Thakhwotthpo.

Stereospermum suaveolens DC.
S. Ambuvasani; *B*. Parul; *H*. Paral; *O*. Poridi; *Bom*. Paddal, Paral; *Mar*. Kalagori, Parul; *M*. Patiri; *T*. Ambu, Padiri; *Te*. Ambuvasini, Patali; *C*. Hadari; *Bur*. Kywemagyolein.

Streblus asper Lour.
E. Siamese rough bush; *S*. Bhutavriksha; *B*. Shaorah; *H*. Siora, Sahora; *O*. Sahada; *P*. Jindi; *Bom*. Karvati; *Mar*. Kharota; *M*. Paruva; *T*. Parayan; *Te*. Barinika, Paki; *C*. Mitli, Punje; *Sin*. Getanetul.

Striga densiflora Benth.
S. Kurandika; *G*. Agiyo; *Mar*. Laghukurandika.

Strobilanthes auriculatus Nees.
Bom. Kara, Karvi; *T*. Kurinji.

Swertia chirata Ham.
S. Bhunimba, Chiratika; *B.* Chireta; *H.* Charayatha; *U.* Chiarayata; *G.* Chirayata; *Bom.* Chiraita, Kiraita; *Mar.* Chirayita; *M.* Nilaveppu; *T.* & *Te.* Nilavembu; *Bur.* Sekhagi.

Swietenia mahogoni L.
E. Mahogony; *B.* Mehagoni; *H.* Abnus.

Tabernaemontana coronaria Willd. = *Ervatamia divaricata* Burhill.
E. Wax flower; *S.* Nandibriksha, Tagara; *B.* Tagar; *H.* & *P.* Chandni; *A.* Kothonaphul; *O.* Tagara; *G.* Sagar, Tagar; *Bom.* Tagar; *Mar.* Ananta, Tagar; *M.* Tagaram; *T.* Nanthiarvattam; *Te.* Nandivardhanamu; *C.* Kottuhale; *Bur.* Zalat.

Tagetes patula L.
E. Marigold; *B.* & *H.* Genda; *U.* Genda; *A.* Narjiphul; *O.* Gendu; *P.* Gutta; *G.* Guljharo; *Bom.* Makhmal, Guljari; *Mar.* Gulja-phiri; *M.* Rojiachaphul; *Te.* Banti.

Tamarindus indica L.
E. Tamarind; *S.* Tintiri; *B.* Tentul; *H.* & *P.* Imbli; *A.* Teteli; *O.* Tentuli; *G.* Amli; *Bom.* Amli, Chintz; *Mar.* Chinch; *M.* Amlam; *T.* Puli; *Te.* Chintha; *C.* Amla, Huli; *Sin.* Siyambula; *Bur.* Magyi.

Taxus baccata L.
E. Yew; *P.* Barmi, Tung.

Tecoma stans Juss.
T. Sonnapatti; *Te.* Pachagotla; *C.* Koranekelar.

Tectona grandis L.f.
E. Teak; *S.* Sakha; *B.* & *A.* Shegun; *H.* & *P.* Sagun, Shagwan; *U.* Sagun; *O.* Saguan; *P.* Sagwan; *G.* Saga; *Bom.* Sagwan, Tegu; *Mar.* Sag; *M.* Thekku; *T.* Tekku; *Te.* Teku; *C.* Saguvani, Tega; *Sin.* Tekka; *Bur.* Kywon.

Tephrosia purpurea Pers.
E. Wild indigo, Hoary pea; *S.* Sharapunkha, Plihari; *B.* & *A.* Bon-nil; *H.* Jangli-nil; *U.* Sarabhika; *O.* Bana nila; *P.* Jhana; *G.* Jhila; *Bom.* Janglikulthi, Sarpunkha; *Mar.* Sharapunkha; *M.* Kozhingil; *T.* Kolingi; *Te.* Vempali; *Sin.* Pila.

Teramnus labialis Spreng.
S. Mashaparnia; *B.* Mashani; *H.* Mashoni; *G.* Valiyovelo.

Terminalia arjuna W. & A.
E. White murdah; *S.* Arjuna; *B.* & *H.* Arjun; *A.* Arjun-goch; *O.* Arjuna; *P.* Arjan; *G.* Sajadan; *Bom.* Arjun, Jamla; *Mar.* Arjuna; *M.* Velli-lavu; *T.* Maruthu; *Te.* Tella madoi; *C.* Arjuna; *Sin.* Kumbuk; *Bur.* Toukhyan.

Terminalia belerica Roxb.
E. Beleric myrobalan; *S.* Beheduka, Vibhitaka; *B.* Bahera; *H.* Bhairah; *U.* Behera; *A.* Bhomra-guti; *O.* Bahada; *P.* Bayrah; *G.* Berang; *Bom.* Beheda; *Mar.* Behada; *M.* Thanni; *T.* Tanri, Vibidagam; *Te.* Tandra, Vibhitakamu; *C.* Vibhita, Tari; *Sin.* Bulu; *Bur.* Thitsein.

Terminalia catappa L.
E. Country almond; *S.* Desa-badama, Ingudi; *B.* Deshi-badam; *H.* Badami, Jangli-badam; *A.* Badam-goch; *O.* Badam; *G.* Bada-malili; *Bom.* Badam; *Mar.* Jangli-badam, Natbadam; *M.* Adamaram; *T.* Nattuvadumai; *Te.* Ingudi, Badami; *C.* Badami; *Sin.* Kotamba.

Terminalia chebula Retz.
E. Black myrobalan; *S.* Himaja, Haritaki; *B.* Haritaki; *H.* Harara; *U.* Haejarad; *A.* Shilikha; *O.* Harida; *P.* Harrar; *G.* Pilo-harde; *Bom.* Harada; *Mar.* Hirda; *M.* & *T.* Kadukkai; *Te.* Karaka; *C.* Harade; *Sin.* Aralu; *Bur.* Pungah.

Terminalia tomentosa W. & A.
E. Black murdah; *S.* Sajada; *B.* Asan; *H.* Asna; *A.* Amari; *O.* Sahajo; *P.* Aisan; *G.* Sadada; *Bom.* Asna, Sadri; *Mar.* Madat, Sadada; *M.* Marutu; *T.* Maru-dam; *Te.* Maddi; *C.* Matti; *Sin.* Kumuk; *Bur.* Toukhyan.

Thalictrum javanicum Bl.
E. Meadow rue; *B.* Gurbiani; *H.* Mamira; *P.* Chireta.

Theobroma cacao L.
E. Cocoa tree.

Thespesia populnea Corr. = *Hibiscus populneus* L.
E. Portia tree, Tulip tree; *S.* Parisa, Gardabhanda; *B.* Paresh-pipul; *H.* Paras-pipal; *O.* Habali; *P.* Bendi; *G.* Purusa-pipalo; *Bom.* Bhendi, Gunjausto; *Mar.* Bhendicha jhar; *M.* Pupparutti; *T.* Puvarasu; *Te.* Gangaravi; *C.* Bugari Huvarasi.

Thevetia neriifolia Juss. = *T. peruviana* K. Schum.
E. Yellow oleander; *S.* Karavira; *B.* Kolkey-phul, Holdey-karabi; *H.* & *P.* Pila-kaner; *A.* Karabi; *G.* Kaniara; *Bom.* & *Mar.* Pilwala-kanher; *M.* Sivanarali; *T.* Tiruvachippu; *Te.* Pachchaganperu.

Thunbergia grandiflora Roxb.
B. & *H.* Nil-lata.

Thymus serphyllum L.
E. Thyme.

Toddalia aculeata Pers. = *T. asiatica* Lamk.
E. Forest pepper; *S.* Dahana; *B.* Kada-todali; *H.* Kanj; *O.* Tundopoda; *Bom.* Janglikalimirchi; *Mar.* Limri, Manger; *M.* Tutali; *T.* Kattumilagu; *Te.* Kondakasinda; *C.* Kadumenasu; *Sin.* Kudumirish; *Bur.* Kyanzah.

Tragia involucrata L.
E. Nettle; *S.* Vrischikali; *B.* Bichuti; *H.* & *P.* Barhanta; *A.* Chorat; *O.* Bichhuati; *Bom.* Kanchkuri, Khajkotti; *Mar.* Khajakolti; *M.* Choriyanam; *T.* Kanjuri; *Te.* Dulagondi, Telumani; *C.* Dulagondi; *Sin.* Welkahambiliya.

Trapa bispinosa L.
E. Water chestnut; *B.* Pani-phal; *H.* & *P.* Singarha; *A.* Shingori; *O.* Singada; *G.* Shengoda; *Mar.* Singada; *M.* Karimpola; *T.* Singarakottai; *Te.* Kubyakam.

Trema orientalis Bl.
E. Charcoal tree; *S.* Jivani; *B.* Jibon; *Bom.* Gol, Khargul; *Mar.* Gol; *M.* Omi, Ratti; *T.* Munnai, Oman; *Te.* Morali, Priyalu; *C.* Gorklu; *Sin.* Gedumba; *Bur.* Sapchapen.

Trewia nudiflora L.
S. Pindara; *B.* Pituli; *H.* Bhillaura; *A.* Bhelkora; *O.* Jandakhai; *G.* Tumari; *Bom.* Petari, Tumri; *Mar.* Pitari; *M.* Thavala; *T.* Attarasu; *Te.* Eruponaku; *Bur.* Thitmyoke.

Trichodesma indicum R. Br.
S. Andhapuspi; *B.* Chotakulpa; *H.* Andhahuli, Chhotakulpha; *P.* Ratmandu; *G.* Undhaphuli; *T.* Kalhudaitambai; *Te.* Guvvagutti.

Trichosanthes anguina L.
E. Snake gourd; *S.* Chichinda; *B.* Chichinga; *H.* & *U.* Chachinda; *A.* Dhunduli; *O.* Chachindra; *P.* Parol; *G.* Padavali; *Bom.* Padavala, Pandolu; *Mar.* Padval; *M.* Padavalam; *T.* Podivilangu, Pudalai; *Te.* Potla; *C.* Padavala; *Sin.* Patola; *Bur.* Pai-lenmwae.

Trichosanthes dioica Roxb.
E. Palwal; *S.* Patola; *B.* Patol; *H.* Parwal; *U.* Parawal; *A.* Patal; *O.* Patala; *P.* Palwal; *G.* Potala; *Mar.* Parwar; *M.* Patolam; *T.* Kombuppudalai; *Te.* Kommupotla.

Trichosanthes palmata Roxb. = *T. bracteata* Voigt.
S. Mahakala; *B.* Makal; *H.* & *U.* Indrayan; *G.* Rataindravanan; *Bom.* Kaundal; *Mar.* Mukal; *M.* Kakatonti; *T.* Korattai; *Te.* Donda; *C.* Avagudehannu.

Tridax procumbens L.
B. Tridaksha.

Trigonella corniculata L.
S. Malya; *B.* Piring, Bon-methi; *H.* Mathi; *U.* Pirang; *Mar.* Tirapa.

Trigonella foenum-graecum L.
S. Methika; *B.* & *H.* Methi; *U.* Methi; *A.* Mithiguti; *P.* Methri; *G.* Methro, Methini; *Mar.* Methi; *M.* Venthiam; *T.* Vendayam; *Te.* Mentikura, Mentula; *C.* Mente; *Sin.* Uluhal; *Bur.* Penantazi.

Triticum sativum Lamk. = *T. vulgare* Vill.
E. Wheat; *S.* Godhuma; *B.* Gom; *H.* & *P.* Gehun; *A.* Ghenhu; *O.*

Gahama; *G.* Gahun; *Bom.* Gahu, Gohum; *Mar.* Gahu; *M.* Kothampu; *T.* Ghodumai; *Te.* Godumulu; *C.* Godhi; *Sin.* Tiringu; *Bur.* Giyonsaba.

Triumfetta rhomboidea Jacq. = *T. bartramia* L.
E. Spiny cockle-bur; *S.* Jhinjharita; *B.* Bon-okra; *H.* Chikti; *O.* Bojoromuli, Jotojoti; *G.* Jhiapato; *Bom.* Nichardi; *Mar.* Jhinjudi; *T.* Ottuppulu; *Te.* Tutturubenda; *Sin.* Epala.

Tylophora asthmatica W. & A. = *T. indica* Merr.
B. Anantomool; *H.* Antamul; *O.* Mendi, Mulini; *Bom.* Anthamul, Pitmari; *Mar.* Pitakari; *M.* Vallippala; *T.* Kodagam, Kagittam; *Te.* Kakapala; *C.* Nepala; *Sin.* Binnuga.

Typha angustata Chaub. & Bory.
Te. Jambu, Jammu.

Typha elephantina Roxb.
E. Bulrush, Elephant grass; *S.* Eraka, Shari; *B.* Hogla; *H.* Pater; *O.* Hogola; *P.* Patira; *G.* Ghabajarin; *Bom.* Ramban; *Mar.* Pankanis; *T.* Chambu; *Te.* Kandra; *C.* Apu, Jambuhullu.

Typhonium trilobatum Schott.
B. Ghetkachu, Ghetkol; *H.* Khain; *A.* Samakachu; *M.* Chena; *T.* Karunkarunai; *Te.* Jammugaddi; *Sin.* Pankala.

Uraria picta Desv.
B. Sankarjata; *H.* Prishniparri.

Urena lobata L.
S. Vanabhenda; *B.* Ban-okra; *H.* & *P.* Bachata; *A.* Bon-agara; *O.* Jatjatia; *Mar.* Van-bhendi; *M.* Orpum; *T.* Ottatti; *Te.* Peddabenda; *C.* Otte; *Sin.* Vabtaepala; *Bur.* Katsenai.

Urena sinuata L.
B. Kunjia; *H.* Lotloti; *Mar.* Ramkopasi; *M.* Uram; *T.* Ottatti; *Te.* Nallabenda; *Sin.* Hin-appele.

Urtica urens L.
E. Common stinging nettle; *B.* Bichuti; *H.* Bichubuti.

Utricularia stellaris L.
E. Bladderwort; *B.* Jhanji; *O.* Bhatudia dala; *Mar.* Gelyachi vanaspati; *M.* Mullanpayal, Kalakkannan; *Sin.* Nilmonaressa.

Uvaria macrophylla Roxb. = *Fissistigma macrophylla* Merr.
B. Baghranga.

Vallisneria spiralis L.
E. Tape grass, Eel grass; *B.* Pata-jhanji, Baicha; *H.* Sawala, Syala; *G.* Jalasarpolian; *T.* Velampasi; *Te.* Punatsu.

Vanda roxburghii R. Br.
E. Common orchid; *S.* Vandaka, Nakuli; *B.* Rasna; *H.* Banda, Nai; *U.* Banda; *A.* Kopouphul; *O.* Madanga; *G.* Rasna-nai; *Bom.* Rasna; *Mar.* Bande; *M.* Maravazha; *Te.* Mardaru; *C.* Bandanike.

Vangueria spinosa Roxb. = *Meyna laxiflora* Robyns.
S. Pindu; *B.* Moyna; *H.* Moina; *A.* Moyentenga; *O.* Gurbeli; *Bom.* Alu, Atu; *Mar.* Alu; *T.* Manakkarai; *Te.* Segagadda; *C.* Gundkare, Mullakare; *Bur.* Hsaymakyi.

Vanilla planifolia Andr.
E. Vanilla; *T.* Vanikkodo.

Vatica scaphula Dyer.
B. Bollshura.

Ventilago maderaspatana Gaertn.
S. Raktoballi; *B.* Raktopit; *H.* Pitti; *O.* Ruktupita; *G.* Ragatarohado; *Bom.* Kanvel; *T.* Vembadam; *Te.* Ettashirattalativva.

Verbena officinalis L.
E. Vervain; *U.* Faristariun.

Vernonia anthelmintica Willd.
S. Somraji; *B.* Somraj; *H.* Somraj, Kali-ziri; *Mar.* Karalye; *T.* Kattushiragam; *Te.* Advijilakara.

Vernonia cineria Less.
E. Ironwood; *S.* Sahadevi; *B.* Kukshim, Shealmotra; *H.* Sahadevi; *O.* Jhurjhuri; *P.* Kukshim; *G.* Sadori; *Bom.* Motisadori; *Mar.* Sahadevi, Sadodi; *M.* Poovankurunthila; *T.* Puvamkurundal; *Te.*

Garitikamma; *C.* Sahadevi; *Sin.* Monarakudimbiya.

Vicia faba L.
E. Broad bean, Windsor bean; *B.* Shim; *H.* Bakla; *T.* Vempadam.

Vigna catjang Endl.
E. Cow pea, Asparagus bean; *S.* Rajamasha; *B.* Barboti, Lalsha; *H.* Bora; *A.* Nesera-mah; *O.* Bargada; *P.* Raung; *G.* Chola; *Bom.* Lobeh; *Mar.* Chabli; *M.* Nisendi; *T.* Thattapayeru; *Te.* Alachandalu; *C.* Alasandi; *Sin.* Mekaral.

Vinca rosea L. = *Lochnera rosea* Reichb.
E. Periwinkle. *B.* & *A.* Nayantara; *H.* Sadabahar; *O.* Sadabihari; *P.* Rattan jot; *Mar.* Sadaphuli; *M.* Kasithumpa; *T.* Pottipu; *Te.* Billaganneru; *C.* Sadamallikai, Kempukasiganegilu; *Sin.* Sohanmal, Mini-mal; *Bur.* Thembanmahnyoban.

Viola odorota L.
E. Sweet violet; *S.* Nilapuspa, Vanapsa; *B.* Banosa; *H.* Banafsha; *G.* Banaphsa; *Mar.* Bagabanesa.

Viola tricolor L.
E. Pansy.

Viscum album L.
E. Mistletoe; *B.* Banda; *H.* & *P.* Bhangra; *U.* Maizakeasli; *A.* Roghumala; *O.* Malanga; *Mar.* Jalundar; *M.* Iththil; *T.* Ottu.

Vitex negundo L.
E. Chaste tree; *S.* Indrani, Nirgundi; *B.* Nishinda; *H.* Shamalu, Sambhalu; *O.* Begudia; *P.* Banna; *G.* Nigari; *Bom.* Katri; *Mar.* Nirgundi, Vanai; *M.* Indrani; *T.* Vellainochi, Nirkundi; *Te.* Nallavavili; *C.* Bilenekki; *Sin.* Nikka.

Vitis quadrangularis Wall. = *Cissus quadrangularis* L.
E. Large granadilla; *S.* Vajraballi, Asthisanhari; *B.* Harjora, Harbhanga; *H.* Nallor, Kharbi; *A.* Harhjora; *O.* Hadavanga; *P.* Drukri; *G.* Chordari; *Bom.* Harsankar; *Mar.* Kandawel; *M.* Piranta; *T.* Pirandai; *Te.* Nalleru; *Sin.* Hiressa; *Bur.* Shazanlese.

Vitis pedata Vahl. = *Cayratia pedata* Gagnep.
S. & *H.* Godhapadi; *B.* Goalilata; *Mar.* Gorpadvel; *M.* Tripadi; *T.* Naralai; *Te.* Edakula; *Sin.* Mediya-wel.

Vitis setosa Wall. = *Cissus setosa* Roxb.
E. Hairy wild vine; *B.* Chotogoalilata; *H.* Harmal; *O.* Ambilidonkonio; *Mar.* Khajgotichavel; *T.* Kauri; *Te.* Pallatachali; *C.* Talavaranaballi.

Vitis trifolia Clarke
B. Amal-lata; *H.* & *P.* Amalbel; *O.* Amarlata; *G.* Khat-khatumbo; *Bom.* Odi; *Mar.* Ambatvel; *M.* Sorivalli; *C.* Heggoli; *Te.* Kadepatige; *Sin.* Valratdiyalbau.

Vitis vinifera L.
E. Grape vine; *S.* Draksha; *B.* & *H.* Angur; *O.* Angura; *P.* Dakh, Dakki; *G.* Mudraka; *Bom.* Abai; *Mar.* Draksha-vel; *M.* Muntirika; *T.* Munthiryvally; *Te.* Draksha; *C.* Drakshe; *Sin.* Muddrap; *Bur.* Sabyit.

Waltheria indica L.
B. & *H.* Khardudhi.

Webera campaniflora Hook. f.
B. Kankra.

Wedelia calendulacea Less.
S. Bhringaraj; *B.* Bhringaraj, Kesaraj; *H.* Bhangra; *A.* Bhimraj; *O.* Bhuranga-raja; *G.* Bhangaro; *Bom.* Pivala-bhangra; *Mar.* Pivalamaka; *M.* Pee-kayyannyam; *T.* Tatalaikaintagerai; *Sin.* Ranyan, Kikirindi.

Wendlandia exserta DC.
H. Chattlai, Tilai; *M.* Puvu; *T.* Kadambaram; *Te.* Tellapukku; *C.* Koyire; *Sin.* Navanidala.

Willughbeia edulis Roxb.
B. Lata-am.

Withania somnifera Dun.
S. & *B.* Aswagandha; *H.* & *P.* Asgandh; *A.* Lakhana; *O.* Ajagandha; *G.* Asundha; *Bom.* Asgund; *Mar.* Askandh; *M.* Pevetti; *T.* Amukkiram; *Te.* Asvagandi; *Sin.* Amukkara.

Woodfordia floribunda Salisb. = *W. fruticosa* Kurz.
S. Dhataki; *B.* Dhatriphul, Daiphul; *H.* Dhai, Dhawi; *O.* Jatiko; *P.* Dahai, Dawi; *G.* Dhawani; *Bom.* Dhatuko; *Mar.* Dhaiti; *T.* Velakkai; *Te.* Sirinji; *C.* Are, Bela; *Sin.* Malitta; *Bur.* Pattagyi.

Wrightia coccinea Sims.
B. & *H.* Pallam.

Wrightia tomentosa Roem & Schult.
B. Indrajab; *H.* Dudhi, Darauli; *A.* Dhudkhoroi; *O.* Phaokurni; *P.* & *G.* Dudhi; *Bom.* Daira; *Mar.* Katainderjaw; *M.* Nilam-pala; *T.* Palsi; *Te.* Pala; *C.* Kadunagalu; *Bur.* Lettopthein.

Xanthium strumarium L.
E. Cockle-bur; *S.* Shankapuspi; *B.* Gagra, Bichaphal; *H.* Okra; *A.* Agara; *O.* Chota goghuru; *P.* Gokhru kalan; *G.* Gadiyan; *Bom.* & *Mar.* Shankeshvar; *T.* Marlumutta; *Te.* Marulamathangi; *Bur.* Koukpin.

Xylia dolabiformis Benth.
S. Kanakakuli; *H.* Jambu; *O.* Boja, Kongora; *Bom.* Jamba, Surai; *Mar.* Jambha; *M.* Irimpullam; *T.* Iruvul; *Te.* Boja; *C.* Jambe.

Yucca gloriosa L.
E. Adam's needle.

Zanthoxylum trifoliatum L. = *Acanthopanax trifoliatum* Merr.
E. Prickly ash; *S.* Laghubalkala; *B.* Bazinali; *A.* Brojonali; *G.* Gejabala; *Bom.* Chirphal, Triphal; *Mar.* Chiphal; *M.* Kattumurikku; *T.* Iratchai; *Te.* Rachamam; *Sin.* Kattukina.

Zea mays L.
E. Maize, Indian corn; *S.* Makaya; *B.* Bhutta; *H.* Bhutta, Makka; *U.* Makai; *A.* Makoi-joha; *O.* Maka; *P.* Makki; *G.* Makkari; *Bom.* Buta, Makai; *Mar.* Maka; *M.* Cholam; *T.* Makksholam; *Te.* Mohka-jonna; *C.* Mekkejola; *Sin.* Bada-irangu; *Bur.* Py-on-eg-boon bin.

Zehneria umbellata Thw.
B. Rakhal-sasha, Kudari; *H.* Tarali; *Bom.* Gometta; *Te.* Tiddanda.

Zeuxine sulcata Lindl.
B. Shet huli.

Zingiber officinale Roscoe.
E. Ginger; *S.* Adraka, Sringavera; *B.* & *A.* Ada; *H.* Adrak, Adi; *U.* Adraka; *O.* Adraka, Ada; *G.* Adhu; *Bom.* Ale, Adu; *Mar.* Ale; *M.* Inchi; *T.* Inji; *Te.* Allam; *C.* Sunti, Alla; *Sin.* Inguru; *Bur.* Khyen-seing.

Ziziphus jujuba Lamk.
E. Jujube, Indian plum; *S.* Badari; *B.* Kul, Borui; *H.* Ber, Baer; *U.* Ber; *A.* Bagari; *O.* Barkoli; *P.* Ber, Beri; *G.* Boradi; *Bom.* & *Mar.* Bor; *M.* Elanthai; *T.* Illandai, Kulvali; *Te.* Regu; *Sin.* Mahadebara; *Bur.* Zi, Ziben.

Ziziphus oenoplia Mill.
E. Indian buck-thorn; *S.* Srigalkoli; *B.* Shiakul; *H.* Mahkoa; *A.* Ban-bagari; *O.* Bhuinkoli; *P.* Makoh; *Mar.* Burgi; *M.* Thodali; *T.* Surai; *Te.* Banka; *C.* Barige, Challi; *Sin.* Uk, Erraminyavel.

Zornia diphylla Pers.
M. Nelammari.

INDEX

(Generic names of angiospermic plants only are given in Italics)

A

C

H

K

L

N

O

T

U

V